AFRICANA

THE ENCYCLOPEDIA OF THE AFRICAN AND AFRICAN AMERICAN EXPERIENCE

SECOND EDITION

AFRICANA

THE ENCYCLOPEDIA OF THE AFRICAN AND AFRICAN AMERICAN EXPERIENCE

SECOND EDITION

EDITORS

Kwame Anthony Appiah

*Laurance S. Rockefeller University Professor of Philosophy
and the University Center for Human Values,
Princeton University*

Henry Louis Gates, Jr.

*W. E. B. Du Bois Professor of the Humanities
Chair of the Department of African and
African American Studies,
Harvard University*

VOLUME 5

Soca–Zydeco

Index

OXFORD

UNIVERSITY PRESS

2005

OXFORD
UNIVERSITY PRESS

Oxford University Press, Inc., publishes works that further
Oxford University's objective of excellence
in research, scholarship, and education.

Oxford   New York
Auckland   Cape Town   Dar es Salaam   Hong Kong   Karachi
Kuala Lumpur   Madrid   Melbourne   Mexico City   Nairobi
New Delhi   Shanghai   Taipei   Toronto

With offices in
Argentina   Austria   Brazil   Chile   Czech Republic   France   Greece
Guatemala   Hungary   Italy   Japan Poland   Portugal   Singapore
South Korea   Switzerland   Thailand   Turkey   Ukraine   Vietnam

Published by Oxford University Press, Inc.
198 Madison Avenue, New York, New York, 10016
http://www.oup.com/us

Oxford is a registered trademark of Oxford University Press

Library of Congress Cataloging-in-Publication Data

Africana : the encyclopedia of the African and African American experience / editors,
Kwame Anthony Appiah, Henry Louis Gates, Jr.—2nd ed.
v. cm.
Includes bibliographical references and index.

ISBN-13: 978-0-19-517055-9 (set)   ISBN-10: 0-19-517055-5 (set)
ISBN-13: 978-0-19-522325-5 (v. 1 : alk. paper)   ISBN-10: 0-19-522325-X (v. 1 : alk. paper)
ISBN-13: 978-0-19-522326-2 (v. 2 : alk. paper)   ISBN-10: 0-19-522326-8 (v. 2 : alk. paper)
ISBN-13: 978-0-19-522327-9 (v. 3 : alk. paper)   ISBN-10: 0-19-522327-6 (v. 3 : alk. paper)
ISBN-13: 978-0-19-522328-6 (v. 4 : alk. paper)   ISBN-10: 0-19-522328-4 (v. 4 : alk. paper)
ISBN-13: 978-0-19-522329-3 (v. 5 : alk. paper)   ISBN-10: 0-19-522329-2 (v. 5 : alk. paper)
1. Africa—Civilization—Encyclopedias. 2. Blacks—Encyclopedias. 3. African diaspora—Encyclopedias.
4. African Americans—Encyclopedias. I. Title: Encyclopedia of the African and African American experience.
II. Appiah, Anthony. III. Gates, Henry Louis.
DT14.A37435 2005
960'.03—dc22
2004020222

Printed in China

S

(*continued*)

Soca

Dance-oriented variety of calypso music that first appeared in Trinidad in 1977 and predominated in the country's local music since that time.

During the 1970s TRINIDAD'S CALYPSO music appeared to be in decline; trapped by its own narrow stylistic conventions, it faced stiff competition from rock and roll and REGGAE music. Moreover, during the 1960s and 1970s the island experienced transforming political and economic changes. A significant Black Power movement became a political force to be reckoned with, inspired by the unfolding CIVIL RIGHTS MOVEMENT in the United States and nationalistic movements in AFRICA and LATIN AMERICA. Trinidad's economic prospects improved markedly due to its membership in the Organization of Petroleum Exporting Countries (OPEC), which vastly increased the value of the island's petroleum resources. An increase in the price of SUGAR made that export crop more valuable as well.

As the people of Trinidad experienced new forms of empowerment, calypso music seemed increasingly out of touch. The calypso musician Lord Shorty—who is about 2 m (6 ft 4 in) tall—took the lead in making calypso music more compelling. In 1977 Lord Shorty and arranger Ed Watson developed a new and danceable rhythm that they termed *soca*. It features a steady bass drum beat set against intricate syncopated patterns played on the cymbals and snare drum. Besides employing a new rhythm, soca makes use of a wider range of instruments, including electric bass, electric guitar, and synthesizers.

The term *soca* is often used to refer to all calypso music performed since the late 1970s, but there is a difference between calypso, in which the lyrics are of primary importance, and soca, which is mainly dance music. The lyrics of soca are slight; most soca tunes are invocations to "jam and wine," Trinidadian Creole terms for "dance and drink." Although such socially oriented calypso singers as Chalkdust (Hollis Liverpool) lament soca as "mindless" music, it has regained some of the audience that calypso had lost. Given the current interest in WORLD MUSIC, some observers regard it as the style most likely to win Trinidad an international music audience.

See also Black Power Movement in the Caribbean; Dance in Latin America and the Caribbean.

James Sellman

Soccer

A worldwide sport that is enormously popular in Africa.

Soccer is a game in which opposing teams kick, dribble, and pass a ball across a field toward the opponent's netted goal. Each team's goal is defended by a single player called the goalkeeper; only the goalkeeper may touch the ball with the hands.

In 2000 CAMEROON won the AFRICAN CUP OF NATIONS title. After winning the competition again in 2002, Cameroon became the first team in nearly forty years to successfully defend its African Cup of Nations title.

See also Burkina Faso; Cameroon Lions; Garrincha, Mané; Lima Barreto, Afonso Henriques de; Nemours, Jean Baptiste and Sicot, Wéber; Nigerian Super Eagles; Olympics, Africans and the; P'Bitek, Okot; Pelé; Soccer in Latin America and the Caribbean; Weah, George.

Soccer in Latin America and the Caribbean

A British export at first played only by local elites, the sport was appropriated by blacks who through it achieved prominence and participated in the construction of national identities.

Although a number of ancient societies practiced games that involved moving a ball to a goal, the game of soccer in its modern form arose from an agreement between British gentlemen in 1863, when the sport was effectively unified. The sport was soon exported by the British along with other products, so that in turn-of-the-century LATIN AMERICA, for instance, soccer as well as a variety of industries were dominated by British companies. The introduction of soccer in different Latin American countries thus followed similar patterns, with Englishmen founding the first clubs in ARGENTINA (Buenos Aires F.C.), CHILE (Valparaíso F.C.), and URUGUAY (Albion F.C.) in the last decades of the nineteenth century. Charles Miller, the man credited with introducing soccer to BRAZIL, was Brazilian-born, of British parents.

Although at first the practice of soccer was limited to privileged European expatriates, gradually local elites joined the Europeans in the restricted spaces where soccer was played, and the sport became a ritual uniting national and foreign elites. Tradition claims that non-elite locals began to imitate the game upon seeing British sailors playing at docks, but it is certain that soccer was seized rapidly by the lower classes and that soon many working-class players attracted the attention of elite soccer clubs. This process was aided by the nature of soccer itself, a game that has been described as ideally suited for the poor: the space in which it is practiced can be easily improvised on practically any surface, with two objects of any kind playing the role of goal posts; the only equipment necessary is a ball, and this too has often been improvised; furthermore, the game does not excessively privilege particular physical characteristics.

The spread of soccer to the popular classes allowed for the participation of disenfranchised blacks, yet the history of their inclusion in the formal settings where the sport was practiced is filled with conflicts. According to historian Eduardo Galeano, Uruguay was the first country in the world to include black players on its national team. When Uruguay beat Chile in the first South American championship in 1916 with a team that included two black players, Isabelino Gradín and Juan Delgado, Chile asked that the game be annulled, claiming its opponent had used "two Africans." Both men were, of course, Uruguayan, great-grandchildren of slaves.

Early soccer in Brazil was also contaminated by the racism of the society at large. It is believed that early idol ARTHUR FRIEDENREICH straightened his hair, while Carlos Alberto, the only mulatto (of African and European descent) playing for Fluminense, whitened his face with rice powder. When a black player was signed by the América team in Rio de Janeiro, nine members left in protest. Most disturbing, however, was governmental racism: in 1921 Brazilian president Epitácio Pessoa prohibited blacks from playing on the team that was to represent Brazil in the South American championship in Buenos Aires.

The competitive pressure that followed professionalization in the 1930s made it increasingly difficult to limit the choice of players to elite whites. Soon many of the most admired players in Brazil, like Leonidas da Silva and Domingos da Guia, were black and played in the World Cup of 1938. National and international admiration of black Brazilian players, however, was not enough to dispel the racist ideology that claimed that Brazil would never be successful when facing European teams or "whiter" South American teams such as Uruguay. After Brazilian defeats in the World Cups of 1950 and 1954 (to Uruguay and Hungary, respectively), racist explanations were quickly given for Brazil's ineptness and old theories condemning MISCEGENATION as degeneration were recycled.

The manner in which ethnic and class conflicts were played out symbolically on soccer fields can be demonstrated with the example of a team from PERU. Alianza Lima was founded in 1901 by working-class players and soon developed a fierce rivalry with the upper-class Universitario de Deportes. As early as the 1920s, Alianza's teams had a significant presence of nonwhite players while Universitario fielded mostly light-skinned players. Alejandro Villanueva and José María Lavalle, both black, played for Alianza Lima and were among the earliest sports idols in Peru. Games between Alianza and Universitario played out the ethnic and class conflicts present in the larger Peruvian society. Many players from Alianza were finally chosen to play in the national selection, yet later resigned in protest over preferential treatment given to the team's nonblack players in 1929. Alianza Lima has continued to be tied to the historically working-class Rímac neighborhood, even as, to the dismay of Peruvian elites, it won numerous national championships.

Throughout much of Latin America soccer became a privileged milieu for the construction of a positive national identity. The unique ways in which soccer developed allowed for the imagination of a larger community of which people could be proud and made it impossible to ignore the physical presence of blacks or black cultural practices. The process through which soccer was localized may be compared with similar tendencies in Latin American Carnivals, where an elite diversion with European traditions was gradually appropriated by the lower classes and then profoundly transformed. As José Sergio Leite Lopes has argued, "The Brazilian style of football is associated with bodily techniques . . . which resemble those physical activities which have ethnic Afro-Brazilian origins. One can look, for instance, to those occasioning features of Afro-Brazilian dances of different kinds (like SAMBA) or of those manifest in Afro-religions, or in martial arts such as CAPOEIRA. These footballing bodily techniques, largely subconscious as most bodily hexis and bodily habitus appear to be, were probably developed after the massive influx of blacks and mulattoes into the first division."

Of the countless black, mulatto, and *mestizo* (of indigenous and European descent) soccer players in Latin America who have enchanted the world with their skill, a few may be highlighted: Obdulio Varela from Uruguay; Alejandro Villanueva and José María Lavalle from the 1920s and Teofilo Cubillas from 1970s Peru; Arthur Friedenreich, Domingos da Guia, Leonidas da Silva, MANÉ GARRINCHA, Didi, and PELÉ from Brazil; and Faustino Asprilla, Carlos Valderrama, and Freddy Rincón, the Colombian trio that delighted the world in the 1990s. In 2002 Ronaldo led Brazil to the World Cup championship, the nation's fifth title.

See also Carnivals in Latin America and the Caribbean; Latin America and the Caribbean, Blacks in; Soccer.

Bibliography

Galeano, Eduardo. *El futbol a sol y sombra.* Tercer Mundo, 1995.

Lopes, José Sergio Leite. "Successes and Contradictions in 'Multiracial' Brazilian Football." In *Entering the Field: New Perspectives on World Football.* Edited by Gary Armstrong and Richard Giulianotti. Berg, 1997.

Mason, Tony. *Passion of the People? Football in South America.* Verso, 1995.

Stein, Steve J. "Visual Images of the Lower Classes in Early Twentieth-Century Peru: Soccer as a Window to Social Reality." In *Windows on Latin America.* Edited by Robert M. Levine. University of Miami, 1987.

Marcos Natalí

Social Gospel

Social movement with roots in eighteenth-century African American communities and churches that attempts to use Christian principles to remedy the social problems associated with industrialization, capitalism, and urbanization.

Social Gospel is often identified solely with a reform movement by white Protestant groups in the late nineteenth and early twentieth centuries. However, its earliest manifestations developed in African American communities and churches in the late eighteenth century, when educated, freed African Americans in the North formed societies to provide services to and

improve conditions for newly-freed African Americans. Societies such as the Free African Union Society in Newport, Rhode Island; the FREE AFRICAN SOCIETY in PHILADELPHIA, PENNSYLVANIA; and the African Society in BOSTON, MASSACHUSETTS, combined social reform with missionary zeal. These groups attempted to improve economic opportunities, promote freedom and social justice, and provide education for freed African Americans. At the same time they spread a Christian message of brotherly love and the fatherhood of God. After the AMERICAN CIVIL WAR ended in 1865, many of these societies sent missionary groups to the South to aid and educate former slaves.

During RECONSTRUCTION the groups joined with African American clergy to improve economic and social conditions in the rural South and to build "social institutions of redemption," such as churches, schools, and social settlements. These groups taught freedpeople that the way to succeed and prove their faith to God was through self-help and education. They also encouraged the freedpeople to maintain family ties, acquire property, and avoid alcohol. Their efforts peaked between 1889 and 1908 when these organizations focused on ways to help the large numbers of African Americans migrating to urban centers to find work. During this period many churchwomen created settlement houses to ease the burdens of urbanization and the demands of factory work by providing a Christian environment. Janie Porter Barrett founded the Locust Street Settlement in Hampton, Virginia; MARGARET MURRAY WASHINGTON established the Elizabeth Russell Settlement in Tuskegee, Alabama; and VICTORIA EARLE MATTHEWS founded the White Rose Mission in NEW YORK CITY.

At the same time, the clergy extended the role of their churches to provide services and guidance for migrants from the rural South. Churches such as Saint Philip's Episcopal Church in New York City, led by Hutchens C. Bishop; the First Congregational Church in ATLANTA, GEORGIA, led by HENRY H. PROCTOR; and Bright Hope Baptist Church in Philadelphia, led by WILLIAM H. GRAY, soon became locations of religious, social, and political power in urban areas. Such churches have been instrumental in mobilizing the African American community against social inequality.

Elizabeth Heath

Socialism

Economic and social doctrine that critiques capitalist production and advocates state control over vital industries, income distribution, and private property.

The roots of American socialism can be found in antebellum communitarian settlements, such as those of the Shakers and other utopian experiments that sought to establish cooperative societies within the emerging nation. Although some of these settlements were officially abolitionist, few offered refuge to African Americans. With the industrial boom that followed the AMERICAN CIVIL WAR (1861–1865), however, immigrant socialists lay the groundwork for a well-defined socialist doctrine and political party that, at least in theory, represented working people of all races against the growing might of capitalism in the United States.

German immigrants brought Marxist socialist ideals to American organizations and in 1877 helped form the Socialist Labor Party. Meanwhile, American utopian reformers such as Edward Bellamy and Laurence Gronlund sought to achieve a classless society through peaceful means. From these two strands emerged a socialist doctrine reflecting the labor conditions particular to post-Civil War industrialization in the United States.

Prior to WORLD WAR I (1914–1918), the socialist movement in the United States devoted little attention to racial inequality. Formed in 1901 from Socialist parties in several states, the Socialist Party of America urged African Americans to join the party and participate in the "world movement for economic emancipation." The party did not, however, establish a policy on race issues. As a result, positions on race differed from member to member and reflected their particular attitudes and beliefs.

Socialist leader and presidential candidate Eugene V. Debs, for example, refused to address racial inequality as an issue separate from the issue of class. Instead, he maintained that there was "no Negro question outside the labor question" and believed that the overthrow of the capitalist system would free both whites and blacks. Debs claimed that African Americans, as a group that suffered keenly from capitalism and the wage labor system, would reap great benefits from the work of the Socialist Party and the eventual overthrow of capitalism. As a result, Debs recruited African Americans and refused to address segregated audiences.

Other members of the Socialist Party of America took a more active position on race. William English Walling and Mary White Ovington, for example, worked against racial inequality and helped found the NATIONAL ASSOCIATION FOR THE ADVANCEMENT OF COLORED PEOPLE (NAACP) in 1909. On the other hand, some members, such as Victor L. Berger and William Noyes, refused to address black audiences due to their belief that "negroes and mulattos constitute a lower race."

As a result of these divergent attitudes, state Socialist parties varied greatly in the extent to which they challenged the economic, social, and political inequalities faced by blacks. Socialists in Louisiana actively recruited African Americans but insisted on segregated chapters of the state party. Socialists from Oklahoma promoted black voting rights and economic equality but, like other Socialist parties in the South and Southwest, refused to support social equality for blacks for fear that it would promote MISCEGENATION. In contrast, some Northern Socialist parties advocated complete equality for blacks and made concerted efforts toward those goals. The New York party, for example, nominated African American candidates such as A. PHILIP RANDOLPH for municipal and state public offices. Regardless of state policies, however, the national Socialist Party of America remained conspicuously silent on the issue of race and did little to recruit black members at the national level.

Some African Americans did nevertheless join the Socialist Party. GEORGE WASHINGTON WOODBEY, a Baptist minister, was the first black to join and later actively recruited other African Americans. Like Debs, Woodbey did not consider the issue of racial inequality to be separate from that of class. Other African American Socialists criticized those in the party who marginalized the issue of race, however. HUBERT H. HARRISON, for example, chastised the Socialist Party of America for its failure to understand that blacks suffered the indignities of capitalism more acutely than did white workers. Harrison argued against the party's ineffectual efforts to counter African American political disfranchisement and eventually formed his own party, the Liberty League of Negro-Americans.

Two of the most notable African American Socialists were Randolph and CHANDLER OWEN. Randolph and Owen worked together to transgress racial boundaries in the labor force and in unions. Beginning in 1917 they published THE MESSENGER, a radical magazine promoting desegregated labor unions. In the 1920s Randolph used The Messenger to denounce the Pullman company and its union and to issue support for the nascent BROTHERHOOD OF SLEEPING CAR PORTERS, an independent black union.

By this time, however, the Socialist Party of America had splintered into fractions and lost political credibility, partly because of the party's split during World War I. Ironically, the party had just started to establish a consistent policy on race and had begun working to eradicate racial inequality. Apart from a short resurgence prior to WORLD WAR II (1939–1945), socialism all but disappeared in the United States after World War II and the McCarthy era, when Cold War politics prompted government intimidation and discrimination against socialism. The socialist organizations that exist today tend to be closely involved with antiracist and anti-imperialist politics.

See also Abolitionism in the United States; Labor Unions in the United States.

Elizabeth Heath

Sociedad Abolicionista Española

Abolitionist organization in Cuba and Puerto Rico in the late nineteenth century.

The Sociedad Abolicionista Española (Spanish Abolitionist Society, or SAE) was founded in 1865 with the objective of abolishing slavery in the Spanish colonies of Cuba and Puerto Rico. The SAE and Spanish abolitionism, while sharing characteristics of abolitionism elsewhere, were also specific to the history of Spain and its colonies. Indeed, Spanish abolitionism—the last European abolitionist movement—stands as one of the most remarkable and original of its type.

The slave trade was nominally abolished in SPAIN in 1817; but subsequently the Cuban and Puerto Rican slave economies boomed, fed by an illegal slave trade largely based in the United States. British diplomatic pressure to end the trade had limited effect in CUBA, though Puerto Rican slave imports virtually ended in the 1850s. During the AMERICAN CIVIL WAR (1861–

1865), however, the Union Navy joined GREAT BRITAIN in blockading the slave trade to Cuba, which soon became extinct. However, slavery itself could have endured in the Spanish colonies far longer. Slavery had powerful defenders in Spain, including dynamic (and protectionist) bourgeois groups, such as the Catalan textile industrialists.

The SAE sprang from the free-trade Sociedad Libre de Economía Política (Free Society of Political Economy). Julio Vizcarrondo, a Puerto Rican, was the driving force and perennial secretary of the SAE, which attracted rising liberals and radicals and Cuban and Puerto Rican reformers. All four of the future presidents of the Spanish Republic belonged to the Sociedad, as did leading figures in the Spanish Cortes (the national parliament) after 1868. Colonial slavery was the strategic nexus between economic protectionism, military government in the colonies, and oligarchic rule in Spain, and presented Spanish liberals and radicals with a powerful and concrete metaphor for limited freedom in Spain. Secret abolitionist societies were formed in Cuba and PUERTO RICO, and their impetus made itself felt in the SAE through Vizcarrondo and the other Antillian members.

The SAE was banned from public activity in 1866, but returned with the September Revolution which overthrew Queen Isabella II of Spain in 1868 and the start of Cuba's TEN YEARS' WAR, an unsuccessful war for independence from Spain, that same year. It engaged in petitioning, lobbying, poetry contests, parades, and public meetings that featured members of Madrid's small black community. The SAE also published a newspaper, *El Abolicionista* (thrice-monthly in 1872–1873). These activities combined with strategies akin to British abolitionism. In general the SAE appealed to humanitarian sentiment.

After 1868 abolition became a commonplace theme. Several SAE members were catapulted to the Cortes and the ministries. The SAE became very active in parliamentary politics, as well as in the press and among republican groupings throughout Spain. A special parliamentary commission was created to address slave emancipation. With SAE concourse, projects for immediate abolition were presented, but only emancipation for newborn children and slaves over age sixty was enacted.

Proslavery groups, too, were quick to mobilize. Beginning in 1871 they created Centros Hispano-Ultramarinos in Madrid and major port cities. In 1872 these forces launched the broader Liga Nacional contra las Reformas (National League against Reforms) throughout Spain. Like the SAE, the Liga was active on the extraparliamentary front, especially through the press and in meetings.

Unlike those in the Southern United States, Spanish proslavery forces offered no moral defense of slavery but claimed instead that abolition entailed economic and political catastrophe. The religiosity, disciplinarian bent, and dourness of British abolitionism also contrasted with the libertarian and expressive strains of Spanish abolitionism and its numerous anticlerical republicans (while Vizcarrondo was a devout Protestant). Faced by an impervious Catholic Church, Spanish abolitionism relied on poetry in theaters rather than on lectures in churches.

From 1868 to 1872 the contending forces on both sides of the slavery issue attained an unprecedented breadth and cohesion. Their major confrontation was over a proposal for immediate abolition in Puerto Rico, presented in December 1872. In Puerto Rico slavery had never been as important as in Cuba and the slave population was down to 7 percent: around 29,000 slaves, as compared with Cuba's 350,000 (or 40 percent of the population). However, Puerto Rican emancipation was perceived on all sides as the threshold of Cuban emancipation. The controversy over Puerto Rican emancipation was perhaps the most representative episode of the abolition controversy in Spain; the political context allowed the SAE a margin of expression it would not have during the Restoration, which brought back the Spanish monarchy in 1876.

In mid-December 1872 the Liga provoked an unsuccessful military mutiny in Madrid, and a small riot in a working-class neighborhood. They also forced the resignation of the colonial minister and demanded the abdication of Amadeus of Savoy, the invited monarch (who eventually did abdicate in February 1873). Immediately after the project for Puerto Rican abolition was filed, 300 of the most powerful rightist figures in Spain (including virtually all the Grandes de España) held an emergency meeting and agreed to support the Liga's opposition to the project.

In response, in December 1872 and January 1873 the SAE held public meetings in theaters and in the streets of Madrid, Barcelona, and Seville. Republican societies throughout Spain held parades, poured petitions on Madrid, and printed abolitionist manifestos, making slave abolition their paramount issue for the first time. In Madrid the SAE and its republican allies organized a street demonstration in January 1873 with over 15,000 participants.

The Puerto Rican abolition law was finally enacted in March 1873, though with full compensation to the slaveholders and a three-year "apprenticeship" that continued to tie slaves to their masters—both of which the SAE had originally opposed. The Republic faltered through 1873 and collapsed in 1874; the SAE was again banned between 1875 and 1879. In the midst of the Restoration and the Cuban war, there was little discussion of further abolition. When Cuban emancipation was finally broached (1879), the SAE renewed its efforts. Abolition was decreed on the island in 1880, though an eight-year apprenticeship period was also introduced. The SAE criticized the law's harsh regulations and lobbied successfully for ending the apprenticeship period in 1886.

The SAE developed in a context in which the overseas slave trade was ending but where a vigorous plantation system fueled by slave labor was enmeshed in relatively advanced capitalist relations and sheltered by protectionist walls. From the start the SAE contended with slavery and the wider Spanish polity. Perhaps for this reason Spanish abolitionism sparked a relatively broad-based movement.

Anarchists and Marxists, as well as separatists in Puerto Rico and (especially) Cuba, viewed SAE efforts as a distraction from larger struggles. The SAE, however, weakened proslavery forces in the metropolis and deepened Spanish republicanism. The strength of the Spanish proslavery forces suggests that the demise of Spanish colonial slavery may have been "inevitable" only in the long run.

Spain demonstrates forcefully the interplay between colonial antislavery and metropolitan radicalism that C. L. R. James sketched for Saint-Domingue (present-day HAITI) and FRANCE in *The Black Jacobins* (1963). In Madrid in 1872–1873 as in Paris in 1791, the "aristocrats of the skin" suddenly condensed all that was contemptuous about the metropolitan state.

See also Transatlantic Slave Trade.

Juan Giusti Cordero

Société des Amis des Noirs

French antislavery organization founded in 1788.

The Société des Amis des Noirs (Society of Friends of the Blacks), founded during the French revolutionary era, condemned the institution of slavery. It reflected, however, contradictions in Enlightenment thinking on FRANCE's plantation colonies and the status of Africans and people of African descent.

A branch of the English Society for the Abolition of the Slave Trade, the French Société was founded by the publicist Jacques-Pierre Brissot in Paris in 1788. He became engaged in the antislavery movement following a trip to London, where he met some of England's leading abolitionists. The Société, which attracted more than one hundred members, consisted mainly of aristocrats and professionals with moderate political views, including such notables as the Marquis de Lafayette, the Comte de Mirabeau, and Charles-Maurice de Talleyrand. The abolitionists depicted in vivid detail the devastating effects of the slave trade on African societies and sought to counter the negative images of Africans perpetuated by the slave traders. Some abolitionists, however, retained the belief that Europeans were superior to Africans. One Société member, the academician Marquis de Condorcet, even argued that blacks, because of their longtime enslavement, could achieve equality with whites only through intermarriage.

The Société arose at a time when onerous racial policies aimed at blacks prevailed not only in the colonies but also in France. The French authorities feared that France's growing number of black slaves and freedpeople, inspired by egalitarian ideas, would return to the colonies and incite revolt. According to scholar William B. Cohen, "racist fears of being 'contaminated' by blacks also played a role. For it was not just the entry of slaves but of any person of color that the metropolitan authorities opposed." Thus in 1738 the French government established laws aimed at eradicating interracial marriage in France. By the late 1770s slaves and free blacks were forbidden entry into France, and authorities deported many resident slaves back to the colonies. Indeed, in 1789 even the Revolutionary Assemblies refused to grant equal rights, such as full citizenship, to people of color.

The Société's title reflects Enlightenment thinking on the subject of people of color. During the seventeenth and early eighteenth centuries, the French usually equated the term *nègre* with black slaves in the colonies. After Enlightenment thinkers such as the Baron de Montesquieu began to attack slavery and defend the slaves' humanity, *nègre* acquired a pejorative meaning and writers began to use the word *noir* to refer to blacks. Many French Enlightenment thinkers, however, such as Denis Diderot and Voltaire, had contradictory and ambiguous views on the institution of slavery; while they openly condemned it, they also recognized the importance of the plantation colonies to the French economy and their own personal and economic interests. As Cohen notes, "the abolitionists were usually practical men who were not willing to sacrifice national advantage to humanity." Instead of building a large and socially diverse membership, the Société focused on attracting members of the French elite, many of whom had a vested interest in maintaining slavery for economic reasons, despite their condemnation of human bondage and their appeals to "the rights of man."

Moreover, some abolitionists believed that blacks had become too degraded and morally desensitized by slavery to be emancipated immediately. They thought that sudden emancipation would result in collective chaos and violence against the slave masters. Thus they promoted a gradual program of emancipation and compensation of the slave masters for their losses—an approach that reflected their lingering conception of slaves as "property." Indeed, Société member Abbé Grégoire considered the Revolutionary Assembly's 1794 decision to emancipate the slaves "a disastrous measure." Abolitionists also espoused the idea of supplanting the slave colonies with plantations based on free labor in West Africa. In this way, they believed, France would fulfill both its economic needs and human rights ideals—a viewpoint that helped to pave the way for European expansion into Africa.

The fact that the Société was a branch of an English organization raised questions in the minds of many about its loyalty to France. The Société called for an international agreement to abolish slavery, which French authorities reckoned would give the English a commercial and political advantage, since, it was thought, England was less dependent on slavery than France. Thus the Société hesitated to wage a full-scale attack on slavery and, as Cohen asserts, "was but a pale imitation of its British counterpart." Meanwhile, the slave trade reached a record high in the French colonies during the period 1783–1791.

In 1791 a large-scale slave rebellion broke out in the French colony Saint-Domingue (present-day HAITI)—a development that French authorities blamed on the abolitionist movement. As the revolution became more repressive, many Société members were forced to flee France. Abolitionism lost favor among French intellectuals, who, stunned by the events in Saint-Domingue, began to reassess their views of people of African descent. Although Grégoire founded a new abolitionist society in 1796, abolitionism as a concerted movement did not resurface in France for more than three decades.

See also Haitian Revolution; Transatlantic Slave Trade.

Bibliography

Cohen, William B. *The French Encounter with Africans: White Response to Blacks, 1530–1880.* Indiana University Press, 1980.

Manceron, Claude. *Blood of the Bastille, 1787–1789.* Simon and Schuster, 1989.

Roanne Edwards

Society of Friends of the Blacks

See Société des Amis des Noirs.

Sodré, Muniz

1942–

Prominent Afro-Brazilian writer and academic.

Muniz Sodré was born Muniz Sodré de Araújo Cabral in Salvador, BAHIA, BRAZIL. Sodré's grandmother was a member of the Tupinambá indigenous tribe that lived in the *recôncavo* region of the state of Bahia. His grandfather was a NAGÔ (or YORUBA) African who came from what the Portuguese called the Mina Coast (at that time the Kingdom of DAHOMEY, now BENIN) in West Africa. Sodré graduated from the city of Salvador's Universidade Federal da Bahia in 1964. While studying law there, he also worked as a journalist for the *Jornal da Bahia* newspaper.

Sodré moved to RIO DE JANEIRO to develop his career as a journalist but in 1964 a military dictatorship was established in Brazil, so he left for FRANCE. At Sorbonne University in Paris, he studied sociology of information until 1968. Returning to Brazil, Sodré wrote for several newspapers and magazines, such as *Jornal do Brasil, Visão, Manchet,* and *Fatos e Fotos.* He also taught at the Universidade Federal do Rio de Janeiro and at the Universidade Federal Fluminense. He worked as a translator of many languages, such as English, French, German, Russian, Italian, and Yoruba. From 1980 to 1982 Sodré was the vice director of an educational television channel in Brazil.

Sodré has published more than twenty books of nonfiction and fiction, including *Samba, o dono do corpo* (1979; Samba, Owner of the Body), *A verdade seduzida: por um conceito de cultura no Brasil* (1983; The Truth Seduced: Toward a Concept of Culture in Brazil), *Santugri: histórias de mandinga e capoeiragem* (1988; Santugri: Stories of Magic and Capoeira), and *O Terreiro e a cidade: a forma social negro Brasileira* (1988; The Temple and the City: The Social Form of Black Brazilians). His recent works include *Mestre Bimba, corpo de mandinga* (2002) and *O império do grotesco* (2002). Sodré is a full professor of mass media and culture theory at the Universidade Federal do Rio de Janeiro and a practitioner of the Afro-Brazilian religion Candomblé.

See also Afro-Brazilian Culture; Literature, Black, in Brazil.

Soga

Ethnic group of Uganda; also known as Basoga and Lusoga.

The Soga primarily inhabit southeastern UGANDA, just north of LAKE VICTORIA. They speak a Bantu language. About 1.5 million people consider themselves Soga.

See also Bantu: Dispersion and Settlement.

Soglo, Nicéphore

1934?–

President of Benin from 1991 to 1996.

Born in TOGO, Nicéphore Soglo received degrees in public and private law and in economics from the University of Paris and the École Nationale d'Administration in Paris. After returning from FRANCE, he served as inspector of finance (1965–1967) in BENIN (then called DAHOMEY) until he received an appointment as minister of finance and economic affairs by his cousin, Colonel Christophe Soglo, following the latter's overthrow of President Sourou Apithy. In 1972, in the wake of the coup by MATHIEU KÉRÉKOU, Nicéphore Soglo left Benin, serving first as a governor at the International Monetary Fund (IMF), and then as director for Africa at the International Bank for Reconstruction and Development (1979–1986).

In February 1990 Soglo was appointed interim prime minister by delegates at a national conference responsible for implementing Benin's transition to civilian rule. In March 1991 Soglo defeated Kérékou in Benin's first multiparty elections in twenty years, drawing sixty-seven percent of the runoff vote. Following a period of ill health, and widespread rumors that exaggerated the extent of his illness and attributed it to witchcraft, Soglo began efforts to refurbish Benin's devastated economy. Harsh economic measures, including currency devaluation and the failure to pay overdue salaries, inspired civil unrest and undermined Soglo's popular support. Soglo had entered office with the backing of a parliamentary alliance that constituted a majority, but by 1995 his opponents in parliament occupied fifty of eighty-three seats. In March 1996 presidential elections, Soglo was defeated by former dictator Kérékou. In 2001 Soglo sought to regain the presidency, receiving 27 percent of the vote in the first-round elections. He withdrew, however, prior to the second round of balloting, alleging electoral fraud. Kérékou, virtually unopposed, easily won reelection, while Soglo remains head of the Benin Resistance Party (PRB).

See also Political Movements in Africa.

Sojo, Juan Pablo

1908–1948

Afro-Venezuelan novelist, poet, journalist, scholar, dramatist, and musician.

Juan Pablo Sojo was one of the first intellectuals to study the African influences on contemporary Venezuelan culture and society. His father, Juan Pablo B. Sojo *el Viejo* (the Elder) (1865–1929), a prestigious musician, composer, dramatist, professor, and folklorist, was the first to teach him about African heritage in VENEZUELA and the Caribbean region. As a result of this early exposure, Sojo's interest was manifested in a wealth of scholarly articles about the diverse cultural manifestations of African people in Venezuela during colonial times as well as in a number of important literary texts.

Sojo's work ranges from the collection of his early articles in *Tierras del Estado de Miranda, sobre la ruta de los cacahuales* (Lands of the State of Miranda, on the path of the cacao plantations, 1938) to his critically acclaimed 1943 novel *Nochebuena Negra* (Black St. John's Eve), and the collection of interpretive essays on the role of Afro-Venezuelans in mestizaje (the cultural mixing characteristic of Latin America) entitled *Temas y apuntes afro-venezolanos* (Afro-Venezuelan Themes and Notes, 1943). His unpublished work includes poetry, *Cantos Negros* (Black Songs), the short stories collected in *Zambo* (short stories), essays *Los abuelos de color* (The Colored Grandparents), and the three novels *La historia de un novelista* (The Story of a Novelist, finished in 1938), *La luz misteriosa* (The Mysterious Light), and *La tía Benedicta* (Aunt Benedicta). A more complete reading of his entire work is still necessary in order to make a definite assessment of Sojo's contribution to BLACK LITERATURE IN SPANISH AMERICA.

His anthropological, historical, and literary works attempted to rewrite the social history of Venezuela, especially in reference to the participation of the diverse ethnic groups, and within this context, the protagonist role of the African. Sojo was strongly influenced by the legacies of the 1930s NÉGRITUDE and AFROCUBANISMO movements. The ideas of transculturation (which, unlike acculturation, implies a substantial retention of culture despite the pressure to assimilate) elaborated by the Cuban ethnographer and cultural historian FERNANDO ORTIZ (1880–1869), and that of *cultural mulatez* (mulatto culture) espoused by the Cuban poet NICOLÁS GUILLÉN (1902–1989), played a central role in Sojo's intellectual perspective. He applied these concepts and methodologies to the analysis of Venezuelan history and culture in his book *Temas y apuntes afro-venezolanos*.

Sojo's novel *Nochebuena Negra* (1943) was, together with *Juyungo* (1943), the novel by the Ecuadorian ADALBERTO ORTIZ (b. 1914), one of the first published black novels in Spanish America. It has been praised because it perfectly combines the author's understanding of the problems faced by Afro-Venezuelans, his extraordinary linguistic knowledge of Venezuelan Spanish (strongly influenced by the diaspora's oral culture), and the presence of popular myths and legends. All of these elements constitute a work which the literary critic Marvin Lewis said "demonstrates clearly an attempt to escape intolerable social and economical circumstances through the creation of Afro-Venezuelan spiritual and psychological alternatives."

Carlos L. Orihuela

Sokoto Caliphate

Islamic empire that united much of Hausaland from 1804 to 1903.

The Sokoto caliphate conquered and united for the first time the HAUSA STATES of present-day northern NIGERIA, under the leadership of a mostly FULANI aristocracy. It also incorporated neighboring non-HAUSA territories. The caliphate was the largest independent state in Africa during the nineteenth century.

Muslim Fulani pastoralists migrated into Hausaland as early as the twelfth century. They played an important part in spreading Islam to the Hausa, and over the centuries many Fulani took up settled life in the rich Hausa city-states as Islamic scholars. One such scholar, USUMAN DAN FODIO of the Qadiriyya Sufi order, initiated a reform movement in Hausaland during the late eighteenth century. This movement promoted an ascetic and purist version of Islam and advocated a society based on the *Shari'a* (Islamic Law). It united Hausa and Fulani communities of devout Muslims in a populist campaign to reform the wealthy Hausa states, which Usuman's followers considered corrupt.

Usuman's movement posed a growing threat to the existing Hausa elites. When the rulers of Gobir, Usuman's home state, repressed the reform movement, Usuman, following the model of the prophet Mohammed, fled Gobir and launched a jihad (holy war) in 1804 to overthrow the Hausa states. Usuman made conquered territories emirates and placed them under the control of leaders acknowledging his authority. In 1808 Usuman defeated the rulers of Gobir, renamed the city Sokoto, and made it the capital of an Islamic caliphate ruling over the subject emirates.

A ruling class composed chiefly of Fulani clan chiefs ruled over the emirates. They enjoyed a degree of autonomy but acknowledged the leadership of the caliph, or sheikh, in Sokoto, to whom they paid tribute. Sokoto engaged in periodic warfare against neighboring non-Muslim peoples, taking many captives to use as slaves, as well as against other Muslim kingdoms, such as Kanem-Bornu to the east. The Damagaram kingdom, based at ZINDER to the north, successfully resisted conquest by Sokoto until it fell to the French.

Under the rule of Sokoto, Hausaland prospered. The austere style of Sokoto's Islamic aristocrats enabled them to reduce the tax burden that supported conspicuous consumption by the preceding rulers of the Hausa states. At the same time the caliphate economically unified a vast and rich area, stretching from the NIGER RIVER nearly to LAKE CHAD. The creation of a large and secure economic unit facilitated a boom in trade and artisanal production. Hausa traders assumed a dominant position in much of West Africa, and Sokoto's cowrie shell currency was widely accepted beyond its boundaries. Around Sokoto and other cities, slave villages produced much of the urban food supply; large numbers of slaves also worked as soldiers, porters, domestics, and concubines.

Unity under Sokoto also promoted a sense of Hausa nationhood among the caliphate's rich and powerful merchant

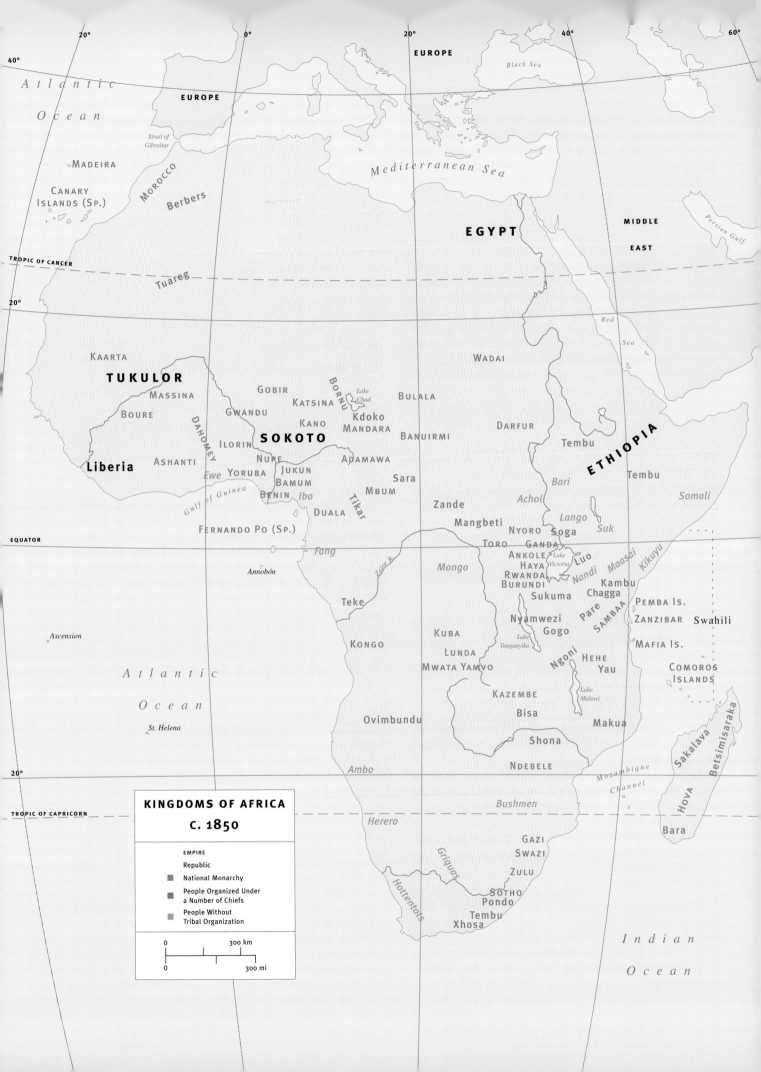

EUROPE

Atlantic Ocean

EUROPE

Black Sea

Strait of Gibraltar

Mediterranean Sea

MADEIRA

CANARY
ISLANDS (SP.)

MOROCCO
Berbers

EGYPT

MIDDLE

EAST

Persian Gulf

TROPIC OF CANCER

Tuareg

Red Sea

KAARTA

WADAI

TUKULOR

GOBIR
Massina
KATSINA
BORNU
Lake Chad
BULALA

BOURE
GWANDU
KANO
KDOKO
MANDARA
BANUIRMI

DARFUR

Tembu

ETHIOPIA

DAHOMEY
ILORIN
SOKOTO
ADAMAWA

Tembu

Liberia
ASHANTI
NUPE
Bari

Ewe
YORUBA
JUKUN
Sara
MBUM
Somali

BAMUM
Gulf of Guinea
BENIN
Ibo
Tikar

Achol

DUALA
Zande
Lango

FERNANDO PO (SP.)
Mangbeti
NYORO
Soga
Suk

EQUATOR

Fang
TORO
GANDA

Annobón
ANKOLE
Lake Victoria
Luo

Mongo
HAYA
Nandi
Maasai
Kikuyu

RWANDA
Kambu

BURUNDI
Pare

Teke
SUKUMA
Chagga

Ascension
PEMBA IS.

Nyamwezi
SAMBAA
ZANZIBAR
Swahili

KUBA
Gogo

KONGO
Lake Tanganyika
MAFIA IS.

LUNDA
Ngoni
HEHE

St. Helena
MWATA YAMVO
Yau
COMOROS
ISLANDS

Atlantic Ocean
KAZEMBE
Lake Malawi

Bisa

Ovimbundu
Makua

Shona
Sakalava
Betsimisaraka

Ambo
NDEBELE
Mozambique Channel

20°

HOVA

TROPIC OF CAPRICORN

Bushmen
Bara

Herero

**KINGDOMS OF AFRICA
C. 1850**

Gazi
Swazi

Zulu

EMPIRE

Republic

National Monarchy

People Organized Under
a Number of Chiefs

People Without
Tribal Organization

Griquas
Hottentots
SOTHO
Pondo
Tembu
Xhosa

Indian Ocean

0   300 km

0   300 mi

class. Together with the Hausa merchants, a largely Fulani class of Islamic scholars enjoyed an authority that tempered the power of the emirate chiefs. The prominence of Islamic scholarship also encouraged an increase in literacy.

However, the caliphate's loose federal structure eventually undermined its strength. Sokoto experienced civil wars in the 1840s and 1850s and again in the 1890s. This disunity reduced the ability of the caliphate to withstand British imperialism at the turn of the twentieth century. Until 1900 the relationship between Europeans and the caliphate was tense but peaceful. Europeans were allowed to trade in the region but had no political power in the caliphate. In 1900, however, F.D. LUGARD, a British colonial official, declared Northern Nigeria a British protectorate. His campaign of military conquest put an end to peaceful British attempts to establish informal political control over the caliphate. The British finally occupied Sokoto in 1903. The caliph attempted to flee but lost his life in a battle the same year that ended military resistance to British colonial rule.

Lugard inaugurated the classic British policy of indirect rule in the conquered caliphate when he appointed a new caliph, Attahiru II, in 1903. British rule retained the administrative organization of the caliphate and tolerated the practice of Islam throughout the colonial period. This helped to preserve many administrative elements of the caliphate that remain an important part of Nigeria's political structure down to the present day.

See also Islam in Africa; Pastoralism; Sufism.

Esperanza Brizvela-Garcia

Solomon, Job ben

1702?–?

Aristocratic Fulani, captured and sold into slavery in America and later sent to England, where he became a celebrity and was freed to return to Africa.

Job ben Solomon was born around 1702 to an aristocratic TUKULOR or FULANI family in Bundu, formerly a Muslim state in present-day SENEGAL. His father was an imam, or Muslim prayer leader, and Job became an Islamic scholar, able to recite the Qur'an (Koran) from memory. He married twice and had four children.

In 1731 MANDINKAS captured Solomon as he himself attempted to sell slaves. They sold him as a slave, and a plantation owner in Maryland eventually purchased him. In desperation Solomon sent a letter in Arabic to his father in AFRICA by way of GREAT BRITAIN, where the philanthropist and founder of Georgia, General James Oglethorpe, intercepted and translated it. Impressed by Solomon's literacy and story, Oglethorpe paid the Maryland planter for Job's release and transport to Great Britain. On the voyage Solomon met English traveler and writer Thomas Bluet, who introduced Solomon to intellectual circles in London.

Solomon became very popular among the educated class as a source of information on Africa and ISLAM. British aristocrats admired his manners and lineage. Solomon's intelligence and stories of Africa helped to disprove accounts of Africa as a land of uncivilized savages and heathens.

After spending a year in Great Britain, Solomon returned to his family in 1734. Little is known of the remainder of his life in Bundu. Solomon is a rare example of an African forced into slavery who was fortunate enough to regain his freedom and return to his home.

Leyla Keough

Somali

Major ethnic group in the Horn of Africa.

The Somali are one of the largest ethnic groups in AFRICA, over eight million living in a territory that stretches north from Northern KENYA to DJIBOUTI, and west from the Indian Ocean to the OGADEN in ETHIOPIA. They are often cited as one of the few ethnic groups that define a nation, though the country of SOMALIA contains some small pockets of other groups. They share the language of Somali and the Sunni Muslim religion.

Genealogy is of great importance among the Somali. Some histories based on early Arab sources and northern oral traditions trace the origins of the Somali to the region of the Red Sea. According to this history the Somali migrated during the tenth century into the OROMO-populated region and later moved further south, into the BANTU-speaking area. Somali oral history traces descent from a single family, with the father Aquil Abuu Ta'alib begetting the two major lines of descent through his sons Sab and Samaale. Other historians have challenged the idea of the migration of a southern Arab people, arguing that Islamic identification has prompted a revision of ethnic history. These historians cite early documents that link contemporary Somali clans to earlier inhabitants. The six clans of present-day Somalia carry these family lines: the Dir, Issaq, Darod, and Hawiye of the Samaale family, and the Digil and Rahanweyne (Digil-Mirifle) of the Sab family. Some of these clans claim relation to the Arab elite who settled along the coast, though such claims are also debated.

Kinship formed the basis of traditional political units. The unit closest to the individual is the *diya*-paying group, a group within a clan that is responsible for paying and receiving diya, or blood compensation, for infractions of one group against another. The traditional Somali legal system integrated Islamic law with a type of verbal social contract known as *Xeer* that set out obligations and rights. Councils of elders negotiate these contracts, which delineate such important economic considerations as rights to water and pasture. This political system continued in the rural areas through the colonial period and even into the 1980s in the military regime of President MOHAMED SIAD BARRE, who attempted to use tribal leadership to secure his control of the rural areas. Following the onset of drought and civil war in the early 1990s, many of the organized political structures have disintegrated.

Poetry plays an unusually important role in Somali society, serving as both a form of artistic expression and a political tool. Its highly stylized forms have been compared to western legal rhetoric, and it is used in diplomatic situations to promote animosities as well as counsel peace.

Most rural Somali, such as the Samaale clans, practice nomadic PASTORALISM and migrate seasonally with their herds to grazing fields. The Digil and Rahanweyne clans, who live in the fertile region between the Juba and Shabelle rivers, combine livestock raising with agriculture. Others, such as the Hawiye in MOGADISHU, historically have lived in coastal towns where they have been influenced by the language and culture of SWAHILI traders. In the late twentieth century many rural Somali have migrated to Mogadishu and other cities, partly to search for wage labor and partly to escape drought.

Bibliography

Bradbury, Mark. *Somaliland: Country Report.* Catholic Institute for International Relations, 1997.

Lewis, I. M. *A Modern History of Somalia: Nation and State in the Horn of Africa.* Westview Press, 1988.

Marian Aguiar

Somalia

Country on the northeastern Horn of Africa, along the Red Sea coast.

On the surface, Somalia is perhaps the most homogenous country in Africa—most of its citizens share the same language, ethnic identity, religion, and culture. Yet it has never achieved lasting stability as a nation; since the early 1990s its civil war has been one of the most devastating in modern African history. Some scholars attribute this political instability to the Somali clan system, in which retaliation for offenses committed by members of rival clans can easily escalate into warfare. Others argue that Somalia's recent turmoil reflects efforts by the powerful elite to manipulate clan loyalties in the hope of increasing their own wealth. Still others contend that Somalia's homogeneity is in fact a myth that obscures long-standing tensions between nomadic groups and the descendants of Bantu-speaking slaves. Finally, some trace the roots of conflict to the colonial period, when access to power and pastoral resources—long regulated by Somalia's many widely dispersed clan leaders—came under the control of the centralized colonial (and then postcolonial) state.

Whatever the precise reasons for violence during and since the military dictatorship of Major General MOHAMED SIAD BARRE, it has clearly taken its toll. The collapse of the state in the early 1990s not only undermined Somalia's ability to cope with the immediate crisis of famine, it also left the country without the government structures needed to provide educa-

Two boys study the Qur'an from a printed text. Behind them are Qur'an boards, on which verses of the Qur'an are written and used for teaching purposes. *CORBIS/Kevin Fleming*

tion, health care, and other basic social services for the general population.

Early History

Linguists trace Somali to the Cushitic language group. According to Arab historical sources, the ancestors of the Somali people migrated south from the shores of the Red Sea into the Cushitic-speaking Oromo regions beginning around the tenth century, with the Oromos later displacing Bantu speakers further south. According to another source, based in northern oral history, the Somali are a hybrid group originating in the marriages of two Arab patriarchs and local Dir women, the descendants of whom migrated from the Gulf of Aden toward northern KENYA in the tenth century. Some contemporary scholars, however, argue that the ancestors of the Somali came not from Arabia but from an area between southern ETHIOPIA and northern Kenya. The uncertainty stems in part from the late use of the term *Somali*, the first known written appearance of which is in a fifteenth-century Ethiopian song.

It is known, however, that coastal settlements of non-Somali people existed well before the tenth century. The coastal culture was a hybrid one, incorporating the influences of the

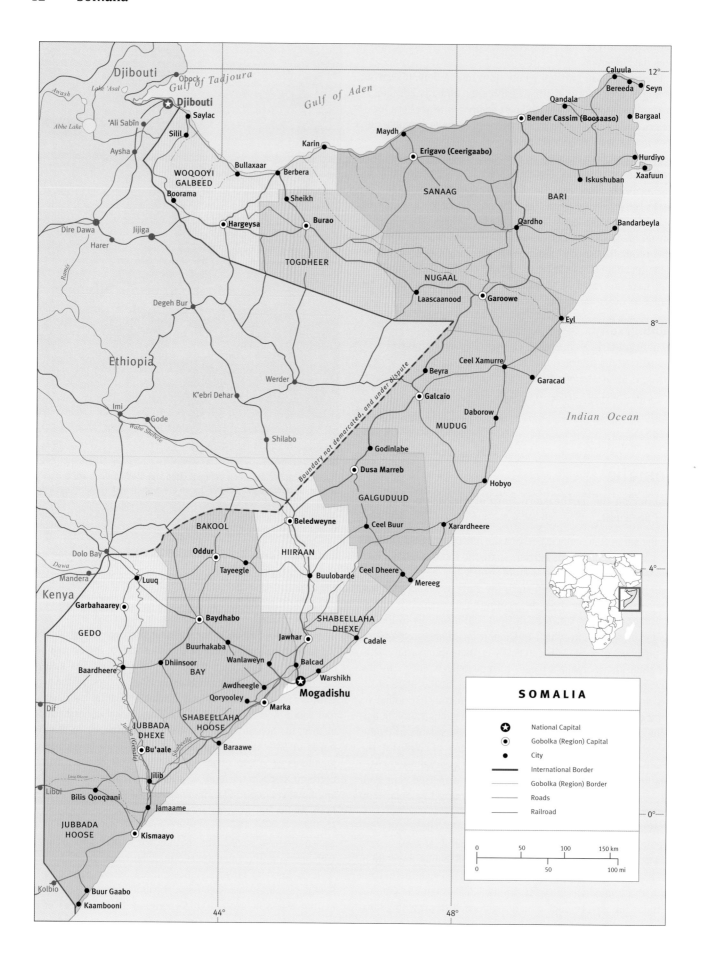

SOMALIA

- ★ National Capital
- ◉ Gobolka (Region) Capital
- ● City
- ▬ International Border
- ─ Gobolka (Region) Border
- ─ Roads
- ─ Railroad

Egyptians, Phoenicians, Persians, Greeks, and Romans who came to trade and to tap frankincense and myrrh along the Gulf of Aden, and sometimes to settle. The market town of Zelia, or Seylac, on the coast of northern Somalia, dates back to the sixth century C.E. Merchants there traded goods from the African interior, such as hides, leopard and giraffe skins, ostrich feathers, ivory, rhinoceros horns, and slaves. Coffee was also brought from the Abyssinian highlands to supply the large local market. Zelia would later become the northern region's center of Islamic culture.

On the whole, however, both urban commerce and Islamic institutions were more highly developed in the south, where coastal towns came in contact with SWAHILI PEOPLE who traded with the Indian subcontinent, China, and Southwest Asia. By the ninth century, MOGADISHU was the most prosperous of these towns, due in part to exports of gold transported from Central Africa.

Between the eleventh and thirteenth centuries, many Somali converted to Islam. Along the coast, generations of intermarriage created communities of Islamic Arab-Somali elite, who dominated trade and local politics in cities such as Mogadishu and Merka. During this period, trade in livestock, leather, ivory, and slaves also strengthened ties between the south's coastal towns and its inland nomadic pastoralists. Such commercial linkages were relatively weak in the north. By the late thirteenth century the Arab-influenced Hawiye Somali clan, which had expanded from the Shebelle region toward the coast, assumed political leadership in the coastal region between Itala and Merka. A related clan, the Ajuran, established a sultanate in the fertile Shebelle basin, trading with the coastal cities.

The political unit that developed in the interior from the thirteenth century onward—and that forms a prototype for contemporary political structures—was the *diya*-paying group. In this system, groups belonging to the same clan have a contractual alliance that joins them together in the payment to and receipt of damages from another group. These groups were governed by the *Xeer*, a type of social contract that incorporated elements of the *Sharia*, or Islamic law, and common laws determined by consensus among the males of the community. In addition, Somali songs and poetry took on the social and political importance they retain today, preserving oral histories of the clan as well as expressing political ideas and military ambitions.

Beginning in the thirteenth century, rulers of emirates based in Zelia and other coastal towns sought to extend their control over the interior's nomads, partly as an effort to strengthen their defenses against the powerful Christian Abyssinia (later ETHIOPIA) to the west. In the early fourteenth century, skirmishes gave way to a large holy war as Haq al-Din, sultan of Ifat, seized the Christian territory that the Dynasty held until his successor Sad al-Din was defeated in 1415. A century later, the legendary Ahmed ibn Ibrahim al-Ghazi, "Ahmed the Left-Handed," solicited the help of the Ottomans to fight alongside his Somali troops and conquered a large portion of Abyssinia, establishing his capital at Harer. The Abyssinians, allied with the Portuguese—who had captured Zelia in 1516—overthrew

and killed Ahmed. Fighting between the Abyssinians and the Somali was interrupted in the 1570s, at least temporarily, by Oromo migration into the contested territory. The Turkish presence along the coast of the Horn, however, continued long after Ahmed's death. The Ottomans occupied Massawa and Arkikio in present-day Eritrea in 1557 and maintained claims along the coast well into the nineteenth century.

From the late fifteenth century until the early seventeenth century a series of migrations brought clans more or less into the regions they now occupy. The Rahanweyn, for example, migrated south to the Juba and Shebelle river basins, where they displaced the ruling Ajuran confederation. By the mid-seventeenth century the Rahanweyn clan had settled in the rich agricultural region and established its own confederations.

From the sixteenth century through the eighteenth century trade between the interior and the coast increased and clans struggled to establish control over caravan routes to the Benadir Coast. Eventually, the Somali clans were able to dislodge the Arab-dominated merchant oligarchies in the coastal towns, though in the early nineteenth century these towns fell under the nominal control of the Omani Sultanate, then based in ZANZIBAR.

One of the most important trades during this period was in slaves. The INDIAN OCEAN SLAVE TRADE was booming at this time, and many captives passed through port towns such as Bimal, Merka, Mogadishu, and Baraawe. Land-holding Somali had long used slaves, since farming was considered a lowly occupation. Bantu-speaking slaves captured from the interior in modern-day TANZANIA and MALAWI harvested grain and cotton along the Shabelle and Juba rivers for the Digil and Rahanweyn clans. Oromo women and children were also captured for use as domestic slaves and concubines. During the nineteenth century some 50,000 agricultural slaves escaped into the wooded areas of the Shabelle valley, where they established permanent settlements; others settled in the Juba valley. After abolition in 1900, both these areas would become destinations for freed slaves.

Colonization

As the European powers' SCRAMBLE FOR AFRICA gained momentum during the latter half of the nineteenth century, the strategic Somali coastal region became a site of imperial contest. In 1855 the explorer SIR RICHARD BURTON led an expedition into the Ogaden region of Ethiopia. After the opening of the Suez Canal in 1869, the British negotiated treaties with coastal clans to establish a protectorate over the coast in return for payments from the British Crown. Great Britain was particularly interested in securing a meat supply for its base at Aden, which was in turn important to the defense of British-ruled India. To this end, they encouraged livestock production, as they would during the later period of colonial occupation.

EGYPT also asserted a claim to the northern coast, taking the towns of Zelia, Bulhar, and Berbera by 1874. France negotiated claims to the port of Obock, near the French colony of DJIBOUTI, in 1859. It became the home base for the Franco-

Somalia (At a Glance)

OFFICIAL NAME: Somalia

AREA: 637,657 sq km (246,200 sq mi)

LOCATION: Eastern Africa; borders the Gulf of Aden, the Indian Ocean, Kenya, Ethiopa, and Djibouti

CAPITAL: Mogadishu (population 1,208,800; 2003 estimate)

OTHER MAJOR CITIES: Hargeysa, Kismayu, and Marka

POPULATION: 8,025,190 (2003 estimate)

POPULATION DENSITY: 12.5 persons per sq km (32.5 persons per sq mi)

POPULATION BELOW AGE 15: 44.8 percent (male 1,802,154; female 1,792,749; 2003 estimate)

POPULATION GROWTH RATE: 3.43 percent (2003 estimate)

TOTAL FERTILITY RATE: 6.98 children born per woman (2003 estimate)

LIFE EXPECTANCY AT BIRTH: Total population: 47.34 years (male 45.67 years; female 49.05 years; 2003 estimate)

INFANT MORTALITY RATE: 120.34 deaths per 1,000 live births (2003 estimate)

LITERACY RATE (AGE 15 AND OVER WHO CAN READ AND WRITE): Total population: 37.8 percent (male 49.7 percent; female 25.8 percent; 2001 estimate)

EDUCATION: Before Somalia's government collapsed in 1991, education was free and compulsory for children between ages six and fourteen. As a result of Somalia's civil war, most schools have closed, including the Somali National University (1954–1991) in Mogadishu. In 1993 a primary school opened in Mogadishu; the only other primary schools are being operated by fundamentalist Islamic groups.

LANGUAGES: Somali is the official language. Arabic, Italian, and English are also spoken.

ETHNIC GROUPS: Most of the population consists of Somali, a Cushitic people. A small minority of Bantu-speaking people live in the southern part of the country. Other minority groups include Arabs, Indians, Italians, and Pakistanis.

RELIGION: Sunni Muslim

CLIMATE: The climate of Somalia ranges from tropical to subtropical and from arid to semi-arid. Temperatures usually average 28° C (82° F), but may be as low as 0° C (32° F) in the mountain areas and as high as 47° C (116° F) along the coast. The monsoon winds bring a dry season from September to December and a rainy season from March to May. The average annual rainfall is only about 280 mm (11 in).

LAND, PLANTS, AND ANIMALS: Somalia has a long coastline, but it has few natural harbors. A sandy coastal plain borders on the Gulf of Aden in the north, and a series of mountain ranges dominates the northern part of the country. To the south the interior consists of a rugged plateau. In the south a wide coastal plain, which has many sand dunes, borders on the Indian Ocean. The country's two major rivers are found on the southern plateau, the Genale (Jubba) in the southern part and the Shabeelle in the south central section. Vegetation in Somalia consists chiefly of coarse grass and stunted thorn and acacia trees, but flora producing frankincense and myrrh are indigenous to the mountain slopes. In the south eucalyptus, euphorbia, and mahogany trees are found. Wildlife includes crocodiles, elephants, giraffes, leopards, lions, zebras, and many poisonous snakes.

NATURAL RESOURCES: Livestock, agricultural crops, petroleum, copper, manganese, iron, gypsum, marble, salt, tin, and uranium

CURRENCY: The Somali shilling

GROSS DOMESTIC PRODUCT (GDP): $4.1 billion (2001 estimate)

GDP PER CAPITA: $550 (2001 estimate)

GDP REAL GROWTH RATE: 3 percent (2001 estimate)

PRIMARY ECONOMIC ACTIVITIES: Until the civil war intensified, the economy of Somalia was based primarily on livestock raising and small-scale commerce. Crop farming was of importance only in the south.

PRIMARY CROPS: Maize, sorghum, bananas, sugar cane, cassava, and mangoes

INDUSTRIES: Some small industries, including sugar refining, textiles, and petroleum refining

PRIMARY EXPORTS: Livestock, bananas, fish, hides, charcoal, scrap metal

PRIMARY IMPORTS: Petroleum products, foodstuffs, and construction materials

PRIMARY TRADE PARTNERS: Saudi Arabia, United Arab Emirates, Djibouti, Yemen, Kenya, India, Brazil, Thailand, Bahrain

GOVERNMENT: Somalia has been in a state of civil war with no clear central governmental authority since the January 1991 ouster of President Muhammad Siad Barre. In 2000 a National Assembly appointed Abdikassim Salad Hassan president of an interim government; the head of state since December 2003 is Prime Minister Muhammad Abdi Yusuf The authority of this transitional government, however, is tenuous and insurgencies continue to threaten political stability, especially in the south.

Marian Aguiar

Ethiopia trading company in 1881 and later served as a coal-fueling station for French ships traveling to Indochina. Italy, meanwhile, scrambled for the Horn of Africa's leftovers. In 1870 an Italian shipping company bought the port of Assab in present-day Eritrea from the local Afar ethnic group, and by 1885 Italy held most of present-day Eritrea. In 1889 they acquired lease rights to the southern Benadir Coast, including Mogadishu, as a result of treaties with the sultan of Zanzibar and the British East Africa Company. By the 1890s Italian claims in both the north and south had expanded to parts of the interior, leading to war with the kingdom of Ethiopia, which after 1889 was ruled by Menelik II. Ethiopia also had imperial claims to territory in present-day Somalia and ERITREA, but an 1898 treaty between Ethiopia and Italy secured the border, at least temporarily.

By the end of the nineteenth century years of treaty-making had partitioned the Somali homeland into the British Somaliland Protectorate, French Somaliland, Italian Somalia, northern Kenya, and the Ogaden in Ethiopia. These divisions traversed traditional clan boundaries and disrupted centuries-old seasonal migrations.

Early Somali resistance crossed the boundaries drawn by colonizers. Beginning in 1899, Sayyid Muhammad A. Hasan, the leader of an Islamic brotherhood, commanded thousands of followers, known as dervishes, in a sustained battle against British, Italian, and Ethiopian occupation. Heavy retaliation by imperial forces—including several thousand British regulars, Indian units, King's African Rifles, Afrikaner mounted troops, and Somali irregulars—brought heavy casualties. In 1920 the British defeated Sayyid Muhammad with a series of air raids.

Both the British and the Italian colonial governments relied on Somali regional leaders to collect taxes and Somali judges to administer customary and Islamic law. In Italian Somalia, the colonial economy centered on plantation agriculture, producing export crops such as bananas, sugar, and cotton. Faced with a labor shortage—relatively few Italian farmers settled in the colony, and Somali nomads had no interest in agriculture—the colonial administration used forced labor from settlements of former slaves. The British colonial government, meanwhile, encouraged the commercialization of livestock production. It was a policy that, according to Mark Bradbury, "affected the entire social, economic and political culture of pastoralists, their livelihood, security of food supplies and their relationship with the environment."

In the 1930s Italy, then ruled by Mussolini, recruited more than 40,000 Somali to pursue its claims in Ethiopia, particularly the Ogaden region. The Ethiopian emperor HAILE SELASSIE I also recruited Somali nomads, but in smaller numbers. Hostilities between the two imperial powers continued after Italy took the Ogaden, and were still ongoing when Italy entered World War II in 1940. That year Somali troops helped Italy take the British Somaliland Protectorate, but seven months later the Allied army retook both Somalia and the Ogaden. For the next ten years, Great Britain held all Somali areas except French Somaliland. This period of unity, in a region that had originally been under the control of separate groups and then divided under different imperial rulers, helped create a pan-Somali identity that would become stronger during the independence struggle.

Independence

By the end of World War II (1939–1945), the rapidly growing Somali coastal cities had become centers of labor organizing as well as an emerging anticolonial movement. War veterans were prominent in early political organizations, as were Somali civil servants. The Somali Youth League (SYL), founded in 1943 in Mogadishu, called for the unification of all Somali territories and opposed the return of any form of Italian rule in Somalia. In 1950 the United Nations did, in fact, grant Italy trusteeship over Somalia, but only under close supervision and on the condition—first proposed by the SYL and other Somali political organizations—that Somalia achieve independence within ten years.

Britain, meanwhile, had begun withdrawing from some of its Horn territories. It ceded the Ogaden region to Ethiopia in 1948, and after a gradual withdrawal culminating in a 1954 treaty, it relinquished the adjacent Haud region. Both areas were home to grazing lands frequented annually by more than 300,000 nomadic Somali pastoralists, who strongly opposed the transfer. Although they were still allowed some seasonal access, the nomads viewed the treaty as a betrayal; it became a rallying point for anti-British sentiment and a pan-Somali movement that lasted well after independence.

In a negotiated settlement in 1960, the British Somaliland Protectorate and Italian Somalia were united to form the independent Somali Republic. The southern-based SYL dominated the parliament and its leader, Abdirashid Ali Sharmarke, became the first prime minister; Aadan Abdulle Osmaan Daar, of the northern Somali National League (SNL), was elected president. Both leaders served until 1964. Afterward the SYL controlled the parliament entirely, creating some tensions between political parties in the north and south, both of which had fought for independence.

During the 1960s and 1970s the SYL-dominated government expanded and grew increasingly centralized. Government economic policy focused on developing the country's fisheries and its manufacturing, mining, and oil-refining industries, but most Somali remained in rural areas, and more than half the population continued to practice nomadic pastoralism.

Somalia's economic growth during the 1960s and 1970s was undermined by heavy spending in an ongoing campaign to reunite the Somali homeland. The five points of the Somali flag symbolized the territory's colonial-era division into five parts; the Somali republic sought to retrieve the missing pieces—Ethiopia's Ogaden, and a portion of northern Kenya. As Kenya neared independence, the Somali government provided support for Somali guerrilla campaigns in Kenya's Northern Frontier District (NFD) as well as in the Ogaden, and fought a brief, inconclusive war against Ethiopia in 1964.

Hopes of greater unity between the north and south were raised when Sharmarke, a southerner, became president in 1967 and appointed as his prime minister Mohamed Ibrahim Egal, a northerner. Egal attempted to move the country away from the movement to reclaim Somali-occupied territories. Some saw this as a betrayal of the pan-Somali dream that had propelled the nationalist struggle; others, particularly outside the country, saw his regime as one that would bring peace to the Horn. But these hopes were dashed with the military-sponsored assassination of Sharmarke in October 1969. Six days later the army seized power, disbanded the National Assembly, and suspended the constitution. It placed Major General Mohamed Siad Barre at the head of the Supreme Revolutionary Council (SRC). Siad Barre's main support outside of the military came from urban intellectuals and technocrats who wished to diminish the power of clan identification and establish Somalia as a modern nation.

A proponent of scientific socialism, Siad Barre nationalized manufacturing and agricultural trade, accelerated infrastructure development, and built an oil refinery in Mogadishu. The government went deeply into debt as a result of this spending, which coincided with a decline in agricultural production. When a 1974–1975 drought destroyed approximately 30 percent of Somalia's livestock, many Somali were faced with famine. In 1984 the Somali economy went into a tailspin after Saudi Arabia, Somalia's major trade partner, banned the importation of meat because of an alleged outbreak of rinderpest.

Yet even as Somalia became increasingly dependent on international food aid, the Siad Barre regime stepped up military spending, which by the early 1980s consumed approximately three-quarters of the national budget. Although the government granted the Union of Soviet Socialist Republics (USSR) rights to naval and air installments in return for military aid, it also acquired weapons from China, the Middle East, and the United States and other Western powers. These military resources were used in 1977 in another war against Ethiopia, which resulted in Somalia taking the Ogaden. A year later, the USSR switched sides, transferring more than $2 billion worth of arms to Ethiopia. Although the United States under President Jimmy Carter initially offered aid, it soon withdrew the offer, and Somalia lost the territory.

Siad Barre continued to receive international aid, however, claiming the burden of 1.5 million refugees fleeing the Ethiopian-ruled Ogaden. Western relief organizations provided large amounts of food aid, which some claim were consistently stolen to be used or resold by Siad Barre's military. The camps, which disrupted the traditional economy by attracting nomads who historically had sought sustenance from the land, were filled with both disease and bureaucratic corruption. Italy and the United States continued other types of aid to Siad Barre. Italy poured more than $1 billion into large infrastructure development projects in its former colony and showed support of Siad Barre by publicly congratulating the dictator on his victory in a 1987 reelection in which he was the only legal candidate. Later, under U.S. Presidents Ronald Reagan and George Bush, Siad Barre received more than $100 million a year in military and economic aid, becoming the third-largest recipient of U.S. foreign aid at the time.

Increasingly, Siad Barre used this money and his military to quash real or suspected internal dissent. Although Siad Barre came to power with the avowed mission to stamp out tribalism, he in fact manipulated clan loyalties and antagonisms to secure his own power. He also targeted whole clans in reprisals for the actions of clan members against his regime. In 1978, after an attempted coup organized by members of the Majeerteen clan, Siad Barre sent soldiers on a scorched-earth mission aimed at the clan's grazing land and reservoirs, which were crucial to both human and livestock survival. Between May and June of 1979 more than 2,000 people died of thirst and sun exposure; many livestock were lost as well. Siad Barre also sponsored an urban terrorist militia, commonly called the Victory Pioneers, which systematically raped women associated with the clan.

Later challenges to Siad Barre's power met with similarly severe reprisals. The Somali National Movement (SNM) was organized in London in 1980 by intellectuals, businessmen, and religious leaders, most of whom belonged to the Isaaq clan. This clan, which had constituted a majority in the north under Great Britain and later held key political positions in the post-independence civilian governments, also played an important part in the lucrative livestock and qaat trades. By the 1980s they faced trade restrictions and feared genocide by the military government. After the SNM soldiers took the northern cities of Burco and Hargeisa in 1988, Siad Barre's soldiers retaliated against the Isaaq population, killing more than 5,000 Isaaqs in eight months. Other rebel militias formed in Ethiopia, as well as in the northern and southern regions of Somalia. Several clandestine militias operated from different regions: the SNM, in the northwest; the Somali Salvation Democratic Front (SSDF), operating out of Ethiopia; and the United Somali Congress (USC), in the south. The latter group, organized in 1988 by Rome-based exiles of the large southern-based Hawiye clan, would ultimately overthrow Siad Barre. The price, however, was high: bodies of executed Hawiye lay in Somalia's riverbeds and in half-covered mass graves.

In Mogadishu, demonstrators protested the government's use of censorship and other repressive measures, as well as its mismanagement of the economy. In 1989, following the assassination of a Catholic bishop and the subsequent arrest of religious leaders, riots broke out and mass arrests followed. The Manifesto Group, comprised of more than one hundred prominent citizens, published an open letter of condemnation that called for the government to begin discussion with opposition groups. The arrest of forty-five of those who signed the letter led to internal riots and international criticism. Under pressure, Siad Barre agreed to their release and later to a multiparty system and a new constitution. But these reforms came too late. Forces of the USC, backed by other organizations, drove the dictator out of Mogadishu in January 1991.

As faction leaders played on clan rivalries, the resulting power vacuum gave way to civil war. The USC's interim president, Ali Mahdi Mohamed, was opposed first by other factions and then by the USC's own General Mohamed Farah Aidid; the resulting war in Mogadishu left more than 30,000 dead and effectively destroyed the central state. That same year the northern-based SNM, led by the Isaaq clan, declared an independent Republic of Somaliland in the former British protectorate and set up a new government, disbanding all existing militias and beginning negotiations among clans. This state has yet to be recognized by the United Nations.

The war's disruption of farming and food marketing, combined with ongoing drought, plunged southern Somalia into severe famine. Battles over the allocation of relief aid led, after considerable debate, to the United Nations' Operation Restore Hope. For the intervention the United States authorized 30,000 troops, the first of whom arrived in 1992. Although the mission's stated purpose was to support humanitarian relief operations, it was widely criticized for coming too late and for legitimating the "warlords" by negotiating with them. The UN expanded its operations in 1993, bringing in peacekeeping forces from twenty-seven countries. Violence continued in Mogadishu, however, and clashes between UN troops and various Somali factions led to the deaths of an estimated 6,000 Somali and eighty-three UN soldiers. After media coverage of dead U.S. soldiers being dragged through the streets of Mogadishu outraged the American public, the United States withdrew in March 1994. Pakistani forces took over the leadership of the UN mission, which finally retreated in March 1995.

In 1996 General Aidid was killed and replaced by his son Hussein Mohammed—a former U.S. marine—whose clan controls one section of Mogadishu. In 1996 the flooding of the Juba River destroyed the crops of more than 20,000 families and ushered in another wave of famine; the shortages hit particularly hard because few international aid organizations were operating out of Somalia. Ironically, the private sector has flourished amid the chaos, offering formerly government-provided services such as health care, telephone connections, and education at premium prices. But drug and arms smuggling have also allegedly taken hold, creating conditions that some believe are favorable to international terrorists.

In August 2000 a conference of clan leaders and politicians elected a transitional legislative body and a president. The new Transitional National Government (TNG) faced numerous challenges as it attempted to establish control over Somalia by ending sporadic clan warfare, rebuilding the country's infrastructure, writing a new constitution, and reintegrating Somaliland and another northern breakaway republic called Puntland. Economic recovery also remains a critical issue, complicated by Somalia's alleged support of terrorist groups. The United States government, citing links with al Qaeda, froze the assets of Somalia's largest financial company in 2001.

See also Islam in Africa.

Marian Aguiar

Somali Songs and Poetry

Art form with traditional social and political importance to the Somali people.

The art of poetry occupies a particularly important place in SOMALIA, a land known as "a nation of poets." As an aesthetic, social, and political form, Somali poetry has reflected the continuity and transformation of Somali society as it passed through colonialism into independence and then through years of bloody civil war. More importantly, the poets and poetry have played an active role in shaping this history.

Somali verse has historically been oral, although since the 1950s some has been transcribed. Somali poems recorded the history, lineage, and major events of a clan and were meant to be enjoyed communally. Poets, both male and female, enjoyed high status within the clan, and prior to European colonization they wielded considerable influence over political affairs within and between clans. In fact, according to B. W. Andrzejewski, before colonization poets took the role of spokespeople for clans, territorial groups, or confederacies, using praise or censure to incite war or counsel peace. Classical poetry often took as its metaphor the valued objects of Somali nomadic culture, including camels and horses. In a place where Islamic scholars had spread Islam through the use of Islamic poetry, Somali classical poetry sometimes integrated Islamic beliefs as well. In southern Somalia the agricultural communities that lived in the area between Somalia's two main rivers developed a distinct form of poetic praise-song.

Somali verse is highly stylized and uses both alliteration and strict scansion (metrical patterns). This structure facilitated memorization, allowing nomadic, nonliterate poets to perform and pass on their verses without alteration.

In the early twentieth century Somali poetry served as an expression of anticolonial resistance. The "Dervish Movement," a twenty-year guerrilla war against British, Italian, and Ethiopian COLONIAL RULE, used poetry to incite rebellion as well as to record the movement's history. The leader of the movement, Sayyid Muhammad A. Hasan, was himself a well-known poet and composed the famous poem "Koofilow!" in response to a British campaign to defeat the Dervishes.

Technological and demographic changes during the late colonial period both affected Somali poetic traditions. For example, the spread of radios, first in the cities and towns and then in the countryside, brought the poetry of a select group of composers to a much wider audience. Even on the radio, however, poetry remained a source of community entertainment and learning, with groups gathering to hear evening broadcasts. Rapid urbanization in the 1940s and 1950s also affected the content of Somali verse. Unlike more classical forms, poetry by urban poets sometimes focused on romantic love, as well as on more traditional subjects such as politics. But urban poetry still made references to Somalia's rural nomadic culture even as it undertook contemporary themes that spanned urban and rural realities, such as the continuing dispossession of people under the postindependent government. Unlike earlier poets, the most famous of these innovative poets, such as Cali Xuseen, Cabdullaahi Qarshe, and Cali Sugulle, were recorded on audio.

Even after Somali was officially transcribed in the early 1970s, poetry remained most powerful as a form of oral performance, at least until the civil war in the 1990s. Poets spoke out against the military dictatorship of Mohamed Siad Barre during his reign from 1969 to 1991. Although Siad Barre censored or detained poets such as Mohamed H. "Gaariye" and Mohamed Ibrahim Warsame "Hadrawi," oral poetry evaded the type of censorship that successfully shut down broadcasting corporations or newspapers. Thus, poetry remained an important method for transmitting news. Since the beginning of the civil war in the early 1990s, the displacement caused by violence and the threat of famine has undermined the custom of community poetry performances. Somali poets, however, both inside and outside the country, have continued to speak out against the devastating war. For example, in "O Kinsman, Stop the War," Salaan Arrabay calls for peace between rival factions in northern Somalia.

Marian Aguiar

Somba

Ethnic group of West Africa; also known as Bataba and Temberma.

The Somba primarily inhabit northwestern Benin and northern Togo. They speak a Niger-Congo language. About 300,000 people consider themselves Somba.

See also Languages, African: An Overview.

Son

Afro-Cuban dance music that became a defining element in the Cuban national consciousness and served as the foundation for much twentieth-century Latin American popular music, including mambo and salsa music.

The *son* is a strongly syncopated style of Cuban dance music that coalesced in the early twentieth century. The term *son* refers both to the dance and to the music that accompanies it. A distinctly Afro-Cuban musical style, son is closely tied to the creation of a Cuban cultural and national identity during a period in which the island was economically and politically dominated by the United States.

The first *sones* (plural of *son*) appear at the end of the nineteenth century, not long after the 1886 abolition of slavery in Cuba. The new music first emerged in the rural province of Oriente, located in eastern Cuba, where the African influence was particularly strong. Son is a product of the musical heritages of Cuba's black and white forebears, but it was mainly developed by poor and working class Cubans who were either black or of mixed racial backgrounds. Son combined African percussion and rhythmic patterns (especially of Bantu origins) with Spanish stringed instruments and lyrical styles.

As musicologist John Storm Roberts pointed out, scholars regard the *clave* beat, the basic rhythm of son (and other forms of Cuban music), as "the first rhythm *invented* by Cubans."

The clave beat is named for the claves, two hand-held hardwood cylinders approximately 12 to 18 cm (5 to 7 in) long. The musician plays the claves by cupping one in one hand and striking it with the other, producing a high-pitched, resonant sound. Typically the claves player sets the clave beat. It is played in common time, with four beats to the measure, and involves a two-measure repeating rhythm. In the first measure the musician strikes the claves on the first downbeat, on the second upbeat, and on the fourth downbeat. In the second measure the rhythm is played on the second and third downbeats. The result is a loping, off-balance beat that defies American rhythmic conventions, which emphasizes the downbeats, accenting either one and three, or two and four, in a four-beat measure.

The son with its three-two clave—which in some songs is reversed to produce a two-three clave—eventually became the key musical form, not only in Cuba, but also throughout the Spanish-speaking Caribbean and beyond. Indeed, its musical descendants—popularized as the modern RUMBA, the MAMBO, and SALSA music—also shaped the musical culture of the United States and Europe.

Son began as vocal music, with lyrics that addressed a wide range of topics. The most influential lyrical traditions were the *décima* and *punto guajiro,* two popular Spanish poetic forms in which improvisation plays a major role. Ethnomusicologist Peter Manuel observed that often *soneros'* "song texts were rooted in Afro-Cuban street life." For example, the lyrics of perhaps the most famous son, Moises Simons's *"El manisero,"* (The Peanut Vendor) evokes the flavor of the streets of Havana by invoking the cries of a peanut seller:

Peanuts, peanuts, peanuts, peanuts,
Little maid, don't go to sleep,
Without eating a little bunch of my peanuts.

Other popular topics for sones are love, nostalgia for past times, patriotic themes, or social and political issues.

At first *soneros* were individual musicians, mostly from the rural eastern portion of the country. They were in some ways analogous to rural blues musicians of the southern United States, singing to the accompaniment of their own guitar playing. Apart from the guitar, soneros often played two other Spanish-derived stringed instruments, the *tres,* a six-stringed instrument with three sets of doubled strings, and the *laúd.*

In the early twentieth century, Cuban musicians began to organize son groups—larger ensembles that included a *marímbula* (derived from the African thumb piano)—later replaced by the double bass—and percussion, in particular, the *güiro* or gourd, bongos, maracas, and claves. From the outset soneros emphasized improvisation in their playing, and when urban musical styles such as the popular late nineteenth-century *danzón* made their appearance in rural areas, soneros incorporated them into their repertoire.

The rise of son groups, particularly those with multiple vocalists, permitted greater complexity in the montuno call-and-response patterns. During the early 1920s, when the style appeared in Havana, son groups added one or two trumpets to create the ensemble styles known as *septeto* and *conjunto*, exemplified by the legendary Ignacio Piñeiro's Septeto Nacional, the Conjunto Casino, and, above all, Arsenio Rodríguez's path-breaking conjunto. These styles of trumpet playing can still be heard in the performances of Afro-Cuban trumpeter Alfredo "Chocolate" Armenteros.

As Manuel noted, son helped create a sense of Cuban national identity, in particular, by serving to "unite the entire population—white, black, and mulatto." Son, which Cuban musicologist Ordilio Urfé considered the most perfect synthesis of the Caribbean's Afro-Hispanic heritage, provided a poetic meter for many Cuban poets. During the early 1930s Nicolás Guillén used the son's syncopated rhythms in his poetry, for example, in his collections *Motivos de Son* (1930) and *Sóngoro Cosongo* (1931). The son was more than Cuba's leading dance music; it came to be seen as an intrinsic part of what it was to be Cuban.

For many years, however, Cubans of the middle and upper classes remained aloof from the music—in particular because of its association with lower-class black life. Despite its lower-class origins, *son* nevertheless grew increasingly popular. As middle-class Cubans embraced *son* as a distinctive national music, it became less spontaneous and more formalized. It also began to attract the attention of well-established composers of popular and classical music, such as Ernesto Lecuona, Amadeo Roldán, and Moises Simons, whose "El Manisero" ("The Peanut Vendor") became a huge hit in the United States.

Son retained its musical significance through the subsequent decades. Beyond Cuba and Latin America, it had a direct impact on American popular music. In the United States the popularity of Latin music coincided with a series of dance crazes—the rumba in the 1930s, the mambo in the 1940s, and the chachachá in the 1950s. In *The Latin Tinge*, Roberts noted that most of the songs that Americans labeled rumbas during the rumba craze were actually sones. Mambos were also generally based on up-tempo versions of the son—or the *guaracha*, another Cuban dance genre. Likewise, since the 1960s, a majority of the pieces identified as salsa music have been sones in form.

American music also effected changes in the son. Prior to the Cuban Revolution the political dominance of the United States in the Caribbean basin encouraged this process of cross-fertilization. When son—and its descendants rumba and mambo—intersected with American jazz, one result was the appearance of large Latin music bands—including those of Xavier Cugat, Dámaso Pérez Prado, Machito, and Tito Puente—which combined the trumpet, trombone, and saxophone sections of American swing-era big bands with Afro-Cuban rhythms and repertoire. More significant, the U.S.-Cuban-American musical synthesis produced a new style or genre, Afro-Latin jazz.

Bandleaders such as Beny Moré of Cuba; Puente of Puerto Rico; Pérez Prado, a Cuban who settled in Mexico City; and the Cuban expatriate Machito in New York City—helped popularize the new genre. From the 1930s to the 1990s Cuban jazz musicians—including Mario Bauzá, Chico O'Farrill, Israel "Cachao" López, Chocolate Armenteros, Rubén González, and

Chucho Valdés—have repeatedly turned to the traditional son as the foundation for further musical innovations.

See also Afro-Latino Cultures in the United States; Creolized Musical Instruments of the Caribbean; Décima; Percussion Instruments of the Caribbean.

James Sellman

Songhai

Ethnic group of West Africa; also known as Songhay, Songhoi, Songrai, Sonhrai, and Sonhray.

The Songhai primarily inhabit southeastern Mali, along the bend of the Niger River, and western Niger. Others live in Benin, Burkina Faso, and Nigeria. Some have migrated to Togo and Côte d'Ivoire, and to Ghana, where they are known as the Zabrama or Gao. They speak a unique Nilo-Saharan language, also called Songhai. The ancestors of the Songhai established a kingdom on the Niger bend as early as the seventh century C.E.. Its ruling dynasty would last until 1491. The Songhai trace descent patrilineally, or along the father's line. Traditionally they inherited a distinct social position as noble, commoner, griot (professional bard), or slave.

Today the Songhai are mostly subsistence farmers. They grow rice along riverbanks, as well as millet, sorghum, peanuts, black-eyed peas, sorrel, and other crops. Many Songhai also live in cities such as Tombouctou (or Timbuktu), Niamey, and Bamako, where they engage in a wide range of trades and professions. Paramount chiefs from noble lines hold office and continue to exert at least symbolic authority in rural regions. The Songhai include a number of regional subgroups, including the Fono, the Gabibi, the Gow, the Kado, the Kortey, the Sorko, and the Zerma (also known as Djerma or Zaberma). Over 2 million people consider themselves Songhai.

See also Languages, African: An Overview; Music, African; Songhai Empire.

Ari Nave

Songhai Empire

Former West African empire.

As early as the seventh century C.E., a polity known as Songhai existed in the area of the great northward bend of the Niger River. In the thirteenth century it was part of the empire of ancient Mali, but in 1335 the Songhai people broke away from Mali and began to conquer the surrounding area with a well-trained army and cavalry. Like the empires before it, the wealth of Songhai came largely from the Saharan trade in salt and gold, mostly through the great trading cities of Gao, Djenné, and Tombouctou.

In the late fifteenth century the empire was led by Sunni Ali (1462–1492), a military commander, who defeated armies of the Mossi to the south and the Tuareg to the north. Soon after the death of Sunni Ali, control of the empire was taken by Askia Muhammad, who was from a Mande-speaking family. The new rulers, whose ancestors had governed ancient Mali, were Muslims who opposed the pagan Songhai rulers. Under Askia Muhammad the Songhai empire reached its greatest expanse. It stretched from the borders of Kanembornu and the Hausa States in the east to the upper Senegal River in the west and included the salt-mining area of Teghaza in the desert to the north. The capital was Gao, a town in modern Mali that still contains part of the mosque where Askia Muhammad was buried in 1538.

Late in the sixteenth century the empire began to decline because its area was too large to control effectively. Other states began to compete for the rich Saharan trade. Around 1585 Songhai was attacked by an army from Morocco, which captured the salt-mining areas of Teghaza and Taodeni and defeated the Songhai at the battle of Tondibi. The Songhai rulers retreated southward to the region of Dendi on the Niger, to the northwest of the present border of Nigeria. There they continued to rule over their own people although their economic and military power in the Sudan was broken.

Meanwhile, the Moroccans could not control the many different peoples of the Sudan and the desert, and in the seventeenth century a number of smaller states took the place of the empire. But none of them was powerful enough to bring peace and prosperity to the Sudan region.

Today there are still several hundreds of thousands of Songhai who claim descent from the people of the historic empire. They are mainly farmers and fishermen who live along the great north bend of the Niger in Mali.

Songye

Ethnic group of the Democratic Republic of the Congo; also known as the Songe.

The Songye primarily inhabit the Kasai-Oriental region of south-central Congo-Kinshasa. They speak a Bantu language and are closely related to the Luba people. Approximately 1 million people consider themselves Songye.

See also Bantu: Dispersion and Settlement.

Soninké

Ethnic group originating in Mali, Senegal, and Mauritania that has dispersed to other West African countries and is known by a variety of names, including Sarakole, Diankanke, and Wangarawa.

Soninké oral history traces their descent from Berbers, but both their traditional Mande language and archaeological evidence suggest that their ancestors have lived in present-day Mali and

Mauritania for thousands of years. They were the founders and rulers of ancient Ghana, centered in Koumbi Saleh. Straddling the desert and the Sahel, Ghana developed into a center of trans-Saharan exchange, and the Soninké became famous merchants. In 1076 Almoravid Berbers briefly conquered ancient Ghana and forcibly converted some Soninké to Islam. Although the kingdom regained independence for more than a century, Muslim Berbers remained influential, and increasing numbers of Soninké adopted Islam. Some of the most prominent and devoted Muslim scholars in West Africa since have been Soninké. Today approximately half of all Soninké are Muslims; the majority of these follow a form of Sufi Islamic mysticism known as Tijaniyya. However, except for the members of clerical clans, most Soninké Muslims also retain many traditional religious beliefs.

The Mali empire absorbed the remnants of ancient Ghana, including most of the Soninké homeland. Some Soninké were absorbed into the Dyula ethnic group, which was also known for its trading activities. Still others dispersed from their homeland and settled throughout West Africa, where they maintained a distinct identity. The Marka of Mali and Burkina Faso claim Soninké ancestry, as do the Yarsé of Burkina Faso and the Dyankanké of The Gambia and Senegal. Each of these groups is known for its mercantile traditions and adherence to Islam.

Traditional Soninké society is highly stratified, with status determined by an individual's patrilineal descent group. Wealthy Islamic clerical lineages are distinguished from secular ruling families; together these groups form the Soninké elite. However, most Soninké lineages belong to the class of commoners, the caste-defined artisan groups, or a poor and disenfranchised underclass largely descended from slaves. During precolonial times, one-third to one-half of the Soninké population was composed of chattel slaves, who labored at farming, and crown slaves, who collected taxes. Many Soninké villages continue to have distinct quarters that segregate slaves' descendants, known as "serfs," whose status has changed little since slavery.

Today the majority of Soninké proper continue to live in the Kayes, Yelimane, Nioro, and Nara districts of northwestern Mali, and adjacent parts of Senegal and Mauritania. However, Burkina Faso, Côte d'Ivoire, Guinea-Bissau, The Gambia, and Guinea all have significant Soninké populations. Today the Soninké number more than 2.6 million people. Except in Mauritania and Senegal, most Soninké have abandoned their native tongue, Azer, for the languages of surrounding peoples. Many adult males travel to France, where they work as laborers and send home remittances.

The Soninké continue to have a reputation throughout West Africa as itinerant traders of diamonds and other goods. Those living in coastal communities have become skilled sailors, and some have even enlisted in the French merchant marines. In the Soninké homeland, however, most are small-scale farmers who cultivate millet, sorghum, fonio (a crabgrass cereal), maize, and other grain crops.

Ari Nave

Sophiatown

South African township that was a center for artistic and political activity in the 1940s and 1950s.

Sophiatown, located on the outskirts of JOHANNESBURG, was founded in 1897 by Herman Tobiansky, a white developer who named the settlement after his wife. His grand plans for a white suburb were thwarted by the construction of a sewage disposal facility nearby. By WORLD WAR I (1914–1918), however, booming industrialization had created a huge demand for workers' housing near Johannesburg, so Tobiansky began selling plots of land to blacks, "coloureds," and Indians, as well as whites. As the township expanded it earned a reputation as a place where gangsters with nicknames like "King Kong" reigned, and where informal pubs and wild parties drew white bohemians like the young NADINE GORDIMER. Writers, artists, and journalists of different races came to share both creative and political ideas, and later the township became an early stronghold for opposition to APARTHEID.

Considered one of the most intellectually and creatively vibrant communities in the history of SOUTH AFRICA, Sophiatown in the 1940s and early 1950s has been compared to HARLEM during the 1920s HARLEM RENAISSANCE. Writers such as Can Themba, Lewis Nkosi, ES'KIA MPHAHLELE, Bloke Modisane, Nat Nakasa, and Arthur Maimane had their creative beginnings in the cultural milieu of Sophiatown. The prominent South African magazine *Drum*, founded in 1951 by Jim Bailey and later under the editorship of Anthony Sampson, brought these writers' works to the larger nation and to interested readers abroad. The magazine served an important historical role in South Africa, spreading and legitimating the work of black authors, poets, and journalists. Anglican Father TREVOR HUDDLESTON, who operated a school and ministry out of the township, became a key figure in the community and later led a fight against the early apartheid Bantu Education Act.

As one of the few areas near Johannesburg where blacks could own property alongside whites, coloureds, and Asians, Sophiatown became a target for the forced relocation campaigns undertaken by the NATIONAL PARTY's apartheid government, which came to power in 1948. By 1953 the government had drawn up a plan to evict all of Sophiatown's residents and relocate blacks to the newly built Meadowlands housing project, 24 km (15 mi) outside Johannesburg. The threat of relocation turned Sophiatown into a center for antiapartheid resistance. Residents met in the large Odin Cinema to discuss tactics for opposing the relocation. National organizations such as the AFRICAN NATIONAL CONGRESS (ANC) and the Indian Congress also drew many members from Sophiatown. Leaders of the antiapartheid struggle such as NELSON MANDELA and Lillian Ngoyi addressed giant protest rallies in Sophiatown during the early 1950s.

The government scheduled the Sophiatown relocation for February 10, 1955. The ANC planned a nonviolent demonstration in Sophiatown for that day, but the minister of justice, wishing to justify the use of force against the protesters, told Parliament the ANC was planning armed resistance. Police arrived two days early, in the middle of the night. Many black residents were moved immediately to the Meadowlands; those who remained faced the immediate bulldozing of their property. Over the next few years Sophiatown was demolished entirely, and an all-white suburb, named Triomf, replaced it.

See also Antiapartheid Movement.

Marian Aguiar

Soriano, Florinda Muñoz

1914?–1974

Afro-Dominican peasant organizer who fought and died defending peasant lands and fighting for social justice.

Florinda Muñoz Soriano was born in the DOMINICAN REPUBLIC. An illiterate, hardworking farmer, she gained recognition for advocating the causes of poor landowners and tenant farmers in Hato Viejo, Yamasá, in the Dominican province of Monte Plata. In the 1930s Soriano married Felipe, who inherited from his father a parcel of land in Hato Viejo. There Soriano reared her ten children. With her husband she raised cattle, pigs, and harvested vegetables and fruit to provide for their family. Several years after the death of her first husband she married Jesús María de Paula, also a poor farmer from Hato Viejo.

Because of her strong will and tenacity she became known throughout her region and later throughout the country as Mamá Tingó, or Doña Tingó. *Tingó* is a Dominican expression referring to someone or something that brings happiness. Constantly concerned with the rights of poor landowners, Mamá Tingó became a local leader on behalf of FEDELAC (Federación de las Ligas Agrarias Cristianas/Federation of the Christian Agrarian Leagues). The ruthless and powerful landowner Pedro Díaz Hernández claimed that he had bought the land of her fellow farmers in the region. To protect their rights as landowners, she helped launch a legal defense against him. In retaliation Díaz enclosed the farmers' land with wire and posted armed guards around it. Subsequently he plowed up their crops to demonstrate his alleged ownership of the land.

According to accounts, Mamá Tingó was shot to death on November 1, 1974, at age sixty, on her way home from a court hearing on Díaz's claim. She had been informed that one of Díaz's employees had released her hogs. While she was searching for them she was ambushed and shot in the head by the same man who had released them.

Silvio Torres-Saillant summed up the importance of Florinda Muñoz Soriano's legacy for social justice, and for the role of blacks in Dominican cultural history, in this way: "The social indignation caused by the brutal murder of Mamá Tingó led the Balaguer government, if not to side with peasants against the landowning class, at least to declare the disputed lands state property with the declared purpose of employing them in the implementation of land reforms." Mamá Tingó became a martyr for her people because of a tenacity she shared with the Dominican peasantry.

At least two published works have been dedicated to the life of Mamá Tingó. Ramon Alberto Ferrarras, in *Negros,* offered a revealing and suitable dedication: "To Florinda Soriano (Mamá Tingó) and to other black women who have known throughout our history how to defend—even with their lives—the sacred land on which they were born and the land which gave them a means of survival." Celsa Albert Batista, in *Mujer y esclavitud en Santo Domingo* (Women and Slavery in Santo Domingo), lauded her martyrdom thus: "To the Dominican woman in the person of Florinda Soriano 'Mamá Tingó,' a woman who struggled and sacrificed for the right to work and for social justice." Finally, Dominican poet Blas Jiménez immortalized her in his poem "Mamá Tingó." The final verses read: "How black you were/Mamá Tingó/ with your machete/ and with your pride/how brave and beautiful/Mamá Tingó/ Mamá Tingó."

Sosa, Domingo

1788–1866

Afro-Argentine military figure, founding member of the Artisans Club (an Afro-Argentine social club), and national representative to the legislature of the province of Buenos Aires from 1856 to1862.

Domingo Sosa, born in Buenos Aires, joined ARGENTINA's military in 1808 and remained in the service for his entire career. After returning from service in the sixth Infantry, he was assigned to duty as a drill instructor in the Argentine Auxiliaries, an all-black regiment. In 1828 Sosa was called up for service in the all-black fourth Militia Battalion, where he would remain for seventeen years, fighting in both the Indian wars of the 1820s and civil wars of the 1830s.

The next stage in Sosa's career came in 1845, when Juan Manuel Rosas, Argentine dictator in the 1830s and 1840s, named him colonel and granted him command of the Provisional Battalion. After the demise of Rosas's federalist regime, Sosa remained in Argentina's succeeding Unitarian government, maintaining both his rank and command of his troops. Sosa was later appointed national representative to the legislature for the province of Buenos Aires and remained in this post from 1856 to 1862. By the end of his career, Domingo Sosa had served Buenos Aires for more than forty years. The provincial army was renamed the Sosa Battalion in his honor.

See also Struggles for Independence in Latin America, Racial Questions during.

Joy Elizondo

Sosa, Sammy

1968–

Dominican baseball player, and one of the leading home run hitters in major league baseball history.

The home run duel between Chicago Cubs outfielder Sammy Sosa and St. Louis Cardinals first baseman Mark McGwire was the highlight of the 1998 major league baseball season. Although at the end of the season Sosa trailed McGwire by four home runs, both had surpassed Roger Maris's longstanding single-season record of sixty-one, and Sosa had captured the hearts of baseball fans with his easy smile and enthusiasm for the game. The year represented a breakthrough for Sammy Sosa. Aside from hitting sixty-six home runs (including a record twenty in June alone), Sosa led the Cubs to the team's first playoff appearance in nine years, hit for a season average of .308, drove in 158 runs (at the time the fourth-highest total in National League history), and won the National League Most Valuable Player award in a landslide, capturing thirty of the thirty-two first-place votes.

Born in San Pedro de Macoris in the DOMINICAN REPUBLIC, Sosa was five when his father died, leaving Sosa and his mother, four brothers, and two sisters. The family shared two bedrooms in a converted public hospital, and Sosa shined shoes to contribute money to the household. He began playing baseball with other neighborhood children at the age of ten, using a crushed milk carton to field a ball made of a tightly wound sock. Signed to play in the Texas Rangers organization at sixteen, Sosa broke into the majors in 1989. Later that season he was traded to the Chicago White Sox, who then dealt him to the Cubs in 1992. He developed into an all-around player, combining power and speed to twice produce thirty home runs and thirty stolen bases in the same season.

Deeply involved in charitable causes, Sosa has donated both money and time to community projects in CHICAGO, ILLINOIS and the Dominican Republic, where he has purchased ambulances to improve medical care and constructed a retail complex and a fountain. Coins dropped in the fountain are donated to shoeshine boys in San Pedro de Macoris. Sosa spent much of the 1998 off-season helping his nation to recover from the damage inflicted by Hurricane George, which struck in September. In recognition of his charitable pursuits, Sosa received the ROBERTO CLEMENTE Award in 1998, baseball's highest honor for community service, named for Sosa's hero, the late Pittsburgh Pirate outfielder from PUERTO RICO.

Sosa followed up his remarkable 1998 season by hitting sixty-three home runs in 1999, earning him the Hank Aaron Award, which is given to the best hitter in each league. In 2000 he led the major leagues with fifty home runs. The following season was even better as he batted .328, belted sixty-four homeruns, and drove in 160 runs. Sosa had a roller-coaster year in 2003. In April he hit his 500th career homerun. Soon after, however, he was beaned, fell into a slump, and spent twenty days on the disabled list after foot surgery. In June he was suspended for seven games for using a corked bat. Sosa rebounded to hit forty homeruns and help lead Chicago to its first division title in fourteen years. But his season ended in heartbreaking fashion as the Cubs fell to the Florida Marlins in seven games in the National League Championship Series. Sosa remains one of baseball's highest paid (his 2003 salary exceeded $16 million) and most beloved sluggers.

See also Baseball in Latin America and the Caribbean; Baseball in the United States.

Soso

Coastal West African ethnic group living primarily in Guinea; also called Susu, Sosso, or Sousou.

Among Guinea's major ethnic groups—including the MANDINKA, FULANI, and various forest peoples of southeast Guinea—the Soso are the third largest. Some Soso also live in SENEGAL and SIERRA LEONE. The most recent estimates place the total Soso population at more than one million. Guinean Soso mostly inhabit the coastal regions known as Lower Guinea. On the coast itself, many Soso earn their livelihood from fishing or salt production; other Soso are traders or farmers, cultivating a mix of subsistence and cash crops such as rice, MILLET, coconuts, pineapples, bananas, and palm kernels.

Although the exact history of the Soso people is unclear, most anthropologists now believe that they arrived in Guinea around 900 C.E. However, they carry the name of a powerful kingdom that dominated parts of present-day MALI and MAURITANIA from the early twelfth century until its defeat by the MALI EMPIRE in the thirteenth century. Refugees from the defeated kingdom may have settled among the people who then became known as the Soso. One theory argues that, because the two groups speak similar MANDE languages, the Soso later split off from the YALUNKA (or Djallonka) people who once inhabited the Middle Guinea empire of FOUTA DJALLON. According to this theory, the Soso migrated to the coast when the Muslim Fulani took over that region, probably around the eighteenth century, joining the Konangi, Baga, and Nalou peoples.

The majority of the Soso are now Muslims, but some still observe traditional religious practices. Soso society is organized into patrilineal clans; polygamy and marriage between cousins are common. The Soso are also known for their crafts, such as basketry, cabinetry, and leatherwork.

See also Marriage, African Customs of.

Kate Tuttle

Sotho

Southern African ethnic groups that speak the seSotho language; also known as Suthu or Suto.

Over seven million people who inhabit southern Africa speak seSotho, a BANTU language. These people are known collectively as the Sotho. Scholars believe that the ancestors of the present-day Sotho migrated around a millennium ago into the region near the Caledon River, where they cultivated sorghum and raised cattle. The large number of KHOISAN loan words found in seSotho suggests that Sotho farmers traded their agricultural produce for game that was hunted by the neighboring foraging communities. The Sotho themselves lived in densely populated villages; archaeological remains indicate that as many as 1,500 people clustered together in a single settlement, perhaps as a defense against neighboring cattle-raiding groups. Hereditary chiefs are believed to have ruled over these large villages.

The Sotho are commonly seen as three distinct groups—the Basotho (also known as the baSotho or Basuto) of LESOTHO, the TSWANA of Botswana, and the Sotho of TRANSVAAL. The Basotho recognized no collective identity or centralized state until the 1820s, when the ZULU campaign of conquest and expansion known as the *MFECANE* provoked a wave of NGUNI migrations into areas inhabited by Sotho clans. In the face of Nguni invasions, the young chief of the Sotho Kwena clan, MOSHOESHOE, led his people onto the Thaba Bosiu plateau, where they were later joined by other seSotho-speaking clans. Moshoeshoe united these clans into the Basotho kingdom (also known as Basutoland). He established a royal hierarchy that was maintained during British COLONIAL RULE—a hierarchy that is still recognized by the constitution of contemporary Lesotho.

The Tswana are thought to have migrated from southwestern Transvaal along the edge of the KALAHARI DESERT, where they intermingled with Khoikhoi pastoralists. They are believed to have settled in their current location in Botswana after 1700. The groups known as Transvaal Sotho, including the PEDI, are believed to have migrated from the area around PRETORIA to their present location in northern Transvaal and SWAZILAND during the seventeenth century.

CHRISTIANITY is widespread, particularly among the Basotho, in part because of Moshoeshoe's friendly relations with European missionaries. Polygamy is still widely practiced, however. Virtually all Sotho groups trace descent and inheritance through the male line. These patrilineal lineages are divided into age grades. Members of each age grade undergo initiation rites around the age of puberty.

Farming remains an important source of livelihood for rural Sotho communities. Many rural Sotho keep goats and cattle, the latter being an important currency of bride wealth. Horses are also raised on the highlands of Lesotho. In addition, large numbers of men from Lesotho and Botswana migrate to jobs in the gold and diamond mines of SOUTH AFRICA, leaving women to tend the farms. In recent years, however, fewer and fewer migrant Sotho laborers have been able to find employment in South African mines, as a drop in gold prices has forced mining companies to cut production.

See also Marriage, African Customs of.

Soukous

Contemporary dance music, related to the rumba, with strong roots in the traditional music of the Democratic Republic of the Congo and the Republic of the Congo.

Soukous features extremely intricate, high-pitched improvised electric guitar playing and sometimes incorporates large brass and percussion sections. The word *soukous* is derived from the French word *secouer*, meaning "to shake." It was originally used in reference to a specific dance style popular in ZAIRE during the late 1960s. Soukous is usually sung in Lingala—a language spoken by several ethnic groups in the Democratic Republic of the Congo—or in French.

Beginning in the 1940s Afro-Cuban rumba groups such as Septeto Habanero and Trio Matamoros gained widespread popularity in the Congo region as a result of airplay over Radio Congo Belge, a powerful radio station based in Léopoldville (now Kinshasa, DRC). A proliferation of music clubs, recording studios, and concert appearances of Cuban bands in Léopoldville spurred on the Cuban music trend during the late 1940s and 1950s. At the same time, *maringa,* a type of dance music that was popular in Léopoldville and other urban areas across West Africa, was being played in clubs by ensembles using instruments such as the *likembe,* a Congolese lamellaphone similar to the *mbira* of southern Africa, and/or the *madimba,* a local xylophone. The dance and rhythm associated with the maringa were similar to those of Cuban RUMBA. As a result of this similarity and the growing Cuban music craze, local musicians began adapting maringa to the modern instruments used by Cuban bands and made available by the Léopoldville recording studios, such as guitars, flutes, saxophones, clarinets, and Latin percussion instruments. Maringa then evolved into a type of rumba peculiar to the Congo region, thus becoming a precursor to soukous.

Large Congolese rumba dance bands soon became common in the 1950s. These early bands included the seminal orchestra, African Jazz, under the direction of band leader Joseph Kabasele, considered the father of Congolese rumba. Another major Congolese rumba band was O.K. Jazz, led by the highly influential and prolific bandleader Franco Luambo Makiadi. Other artists who contributed to the development of the rumba style were Papa Noel, Edo Ganga, Nino Malapet, and Jean-Serge Essous. After stints in both African Jazz and O.K. Jazz and a Belgian tour in 1960, Essous formed Les Bantous de le Capitale with popular singers Tchico Tchicaya and Pamelo Mounka.

Congolese rumba took the form of the Cuban import, performed in two sections. Typically a composition would open with a relatively slow theme followed by a much faster, energetic, improvisational section. This improvisational section, known as *seben,* consisted of a repeated chorus around which horns, percussion and, most significantly, the guitarist would improvise. In the late 1960s the term *soukous* was given to a specific dance associated with the contemporary form of Congolese rumba.

The soukous sound continued to evolve. Musicians began minimizing or dispensing with the slower section, focusing instead on the stylistically distinct, virtuosic playing of the guitarist, often characterized by high-pitched, fast-paced lines. A third guitar line was sometimes added in addition to the rhythm and lead guitar parts and various instrumental configurations and ensemble sizes were used.

Congolese soukous music achieved popularity in the late 1960s and early 1970s with bands such as Negro Success, Conga Success, Orchestra Cobantou, Veve, Los Nickelos, Josky Kiambukuta, Vox Africa, and numerous others. In the 1970s the

influential band Zaiko Langa Langa was formed with vocalist Nyoka Longo and percussionist D. V. Moanda. The group dropped the horn section, focused more heavily on guitars, and stressed the high-energy seben. Other more recent and influential performers of soukous include Papa Wemba, Viva La Musica, Kanda Bongo Man, Pepe Kalle, Quatre Étoiles with Wuta Mayi, Nyboma, Bopol Mansiamina, and Syran M'benza.

The lyrics usually sung with soukous cross ethnic boundaries, making them accessible to French and Lingala-speaking audiences in Africa. Early soukous lyrics dealt with everyday issues of urban life. In contrast, Franco Makiadi's songs changed the focus of soukous by introducing important social and political issues into the lyrics and making the music a vehicle for social consciousness.

With the growing international popularity of soukous in the 1980s, lyrics began to deal with a broader range of topics not limited to life in the DRC and the Republic of the Congo. The popularity of soukous spread across Africa, probably because of its widely understood lyrics, the appeal of highly skilled guitarists, and the existence of a distribution network that brought recordings to remote regions of Africa and to other parts of the world. This global popularity of soukous also led the way for other forms of African music to enter the global music market.

In the 1980s Paris, FRANCE, became a magnet for soukous musicians, serving as a musical crossroads where other African and European music styles, synthesizers, and production values could feed into the soukous sound. As a result, in the 1990s soukous attracted an international audience. It remains one of the most influential and recognizable African popular music styles.

Soul Music

Style of African American popular music, heavily influenced by gospel music, that emerged in the 1960s from rhythm and blues and had a powerful impact on American vernacular culture.

During the soul music era of the 1960s, African American music—for the first time in American history—gained popularity in an undiluted and culturally black form. Black music has long exerted a significant influence on American popular culture. Turn-of-the-century RAGTIME, classic JAZZ in the 1920s, 1930s big-band swing, and 1950s doo-wop vocal groups each served to shape the musical tastes of mainstream America. In the 1960s, however, white Americans heard a genre of black music performed almost exclusively by African American artists, rather than watered-down versions by white performers: it became known as soul music.

The soul music style was rooted in earlier forms of African American popular music. It was a direct extension of RHYTHM AND BLUES (R&B) but drew its primary influences from GOSPEL MUSIC rather than from the BLUES. Important precursors to the soul style appeared during the 1950s, including RAY CHARLES's sanctified sound introduced on "I've Got a Woman" (1955);

James Brown's "Please, Please, Please" (1956); Sam Cooke's "You Send Me" (1957); and the rich gospel sonorities heard in Arlene Smith and the Chantels' "Maybe" (1957) and Jerry Butler and The Impressions' "For Your Precious Love" (1958).

The soul aesthetic crystallized in the 1960s. Many elements of the new style are evident in Gladys Knight and the Pips' recording of "Every Beat of My Heart" (1960), especially in Knight's emotional lead singing, the prominent church-like organ, and the emphasis on the back beats, two and four—in this case by percussive guitar chords. There were a number of distinct styles or approaches to soul. Most significant was the harder-edged "Memphis sound" associated with Stax Records (1960–1975) of Memphis, Tennessee, and the slicker, more pop-oriented "Motown sound" represented by Berry Gordy's Detroit-based Motown Records (founded in 1959). In addition, James Brown had a rhythmic and danceable style all his own.

The hard soul of Stax—and of New York City's Atlantic Records—featured stripped-down production values and gritty small ensembles, such as Stax's Booker T. and the MG's or the Bar-Kays, that provided a powerful rhythmic drive and tightly riffing horns behind the gospel- and blues-tinged vocals of such singers as Otis Redding, Sam and Dave (Sam Moore and David Prater), Carla Thomas, the Staple Singers, Wilson Pickett, and Aretha Franklin. Gordy's Motown recordings employed more lavish production values, including the use of string sections, and achieved a sweeter sound that appealed to whites as well as blacks. Among Motown's most influential artists were Diana Ross and the Supremes, Smokey Robinson and the Miracles, Stevie Wonder, the Jackson Five, and the Temptations.

In the 1960s, during the height of the Civil Rights Movement, a historic process of racial integration began in the previously segregated realm of American popular music. Black artists achieved significant crossover success, producing hit records that sold in significant numbers to both whites and blacks. During the 1950s the popularity of black performers such as Nat "King" Cole, Dinah Washington, Chuck Berry, and the Platters revealed the beginnings of integration in American pop music. But prior to the soul music era, black musicians had gained success primarily by appealing to the musical tastes of white listeners. During the 1960s an unparalleled number of black artists scored hits that made few concessions to white tastes, including Booker T. and the MG's "Green Onions" (1962), James Brown's "Papa's Got a Brand New Bag" (1965) and "I Got You (I Feel Good)" (1966), Pickett's "In the Midnight Hour" (1965), Sam and Dave's "Hold on! I'm Comin'" (1966), Percy Sledge's "When a Man Loves a Woman" (1966), and Franklin's "Respect" (1967). Soul music also inspired a "white soul" counterpart, exemplified in the early 1970s by such white pop singers as Carole King and Van Morrison.

Unlike R&B artists of the 1940s and 1950s who emphasized good-time music and made little effort to confront social issues, soul musicians engaged in cultural politics. Soul music—like R&B—concentrated mainly on themes of love and its discontents. But in the hands of a soul singer like Aretha Franklin, the frustrated lover's complaint in "Respect" became a sweeping anthem to freedom and empowerment. By the late 1960s a number of soul musicians gained popularity with songs that addressed a wide range of contemporary social issues and expressed black pride, exemplified by James Brown's Top Ten hit "Say It Loud, I'm Black and I'm Proud" (1969). At the height of the Vietnam conflict, Edwin Starr's "War" (1970) delivered an impassioned antiwar message. Marvin Gaye's "Mercy Mercy Me" (1971) was a gentler but no less earnest form of protest music, informed by ecological concerns.

Curtis Mayfield and Stevie Wonder in particular invested their music with a strong social conscience. As part of the Impressions in the 1960s and as a solo artist in the 1970s, Mayfield wrote many examples of soul music with a message, including "If There's a Hell Below We're All Going to Go" (1970) and "We People Who Are Darker Than Blue" (1970). Wonder proved equally adept at addressing issues of social injustice or spiritual uplift in songs such as "Living for the City" and "Higher Ground," from his album *Innervisions* (1973). Along with Isaac Hayes and Marvin Gaye, Mayfield and Wonder experimented with ambitious musical forms, for example the artistically unified "concept album," including Wonder's *Music of My Mind* (1972) and Mayfield's *There's No Place Like America Today* (1975).

Soul music retained an undiminished vigor into the 1970s and remained popular with black listeners. But by the late 1960s the larger white public had become less receptive. This change in musical tastes was part of a larger shift in white attitudes that was reflected in the waning of white support for the Civil Rights Movement, in the nation's growing political conservatism, and in a general heightening of racial tensions. In popular culture, white and black musical styles seemed once more to retreat from each other. White pop music returned to the spotlight through the "British invasion" of such hit-making rock 'n' roll bands as the Beatles and the Rolling Stones, and black musicians found fewer opportunities. Although some African American artists, such as Donna Summer and the Commodores, had hits during the 1970s disco craze, black listeners preferred the contemporaneous but harder-edged funk style. As soul music became increasingly marginal and record sales dropped, Stax Records folded in the mid-1970s.

Both Motown and Atlantic have continued to be major forces in American popular music, as have Aretha Franklin, Curtis Mayfield, and Stevie Wonder. But the distinctive sound and aesthetic of soul music appears to have been lost. Subsequent developments in black popular music—most notably rap—reflect a general distancing from the gospel overtones and broad, quasi-religious themes of affirmation that lay at the heart of soul music.

Bibliography

Gordy, Berry. *To Be Loved: The Music, The Magic, The Memories of Motown: An Autobiography.* Warner Books, 1994.

Guralnick, Peter. *Sweet Soul Music: Rhythm and Blues and the Southern Dream of Freedom.* Harper & Row, 1986.

Pruter, Robert. *Chicago Soul.* University of Illinois Press, 1991.

Taraborrelli, J. Randy. *Motown: Hot Wax, City Cool, and Solid Gold.* Doubleday, 1986.

James Sellman

Soulouque, Faustin Elie

1788–1873

President of Haiti from 1847 to 1849; self-proclaimed emperor of Haiti from 1849 to 1859.

Faustin Elie Soulouque was elected president of HAITI by the National Assembly, under the belief that he could be easily manipulated. On the contrary, Soulouque established a strong and repressive regime. In 1849 he unsuccessfully attempted an invasion of the neighboring DOMINICAN REPUBLIC, which had won its independence from Haiti five years earlier. Later that year he declared himself Emperor Faustin I. He was forced into exile in 1859, defeated by the forces of General Fabre-Nicolas Geffrard.

Soul Stirrers

Creators of the modern male gospel quartet.

Founded in Trinity, Texas, by Roy Crain in 1926, the Soul Stirrers were the first GOSPEL QUARTET to add a second lead to solo over the usual four-part harmony. Further innovations by this group include the use of guitar accompaniment and the performance of concerts consisting solely of gospel compositions. Alan Lomax recorded the Soul Stirrers for the Library of Congress because it was "the most polyrhythmic music you ever heard." According to scholar Tony Heilbut, their lead singer, Rebert H. Harris, "created the entire gospel quartet tradition."

Harris's style of singing is often said to have influenced every male vocalist in gospel, SOUL, pop, and rock 'n' roll. Some of his methods that have become standard are solo improvisation over the background repetition of key phrases, rising into falsetto at climactic moments, and singing off-time to create polyrhythms with the backup singers. Harris himself claims that "I was the first to sing delayed time. I'd be in and out, front and behind, all across there." Harris and the Soul Stirrers' rendition of C.A. Tindley's hymn "By and By" is considered a gospel classic.

In 1950 Harris quit the group, tired of touring. SAM COOKE replaced Harris and developed a smoother, more modern pop sound. With the addition of instrumental accompaniment and Cooke's stylistic changes, the group attracted a younger audience. While Cooke was with the Soul Stirrers their most well-known recordings were "Wonderful" and "Jesus Wash Away My Troubles." Cooke left the ensemble in 1957 and became an internationally popular soul singer until his death in 1964. Other members of the group, including Jesse Farley, James Medlock, Leroy Taylor, Paul Foster, Willie Rogers, and Jimmy Outler, continued to perform as two groups, the Original Soul Stirrers and the Soul Stirrers.

Soul Train

One of the first nationally successful television shows conceived and produced by African Americans.

Soul Train creator Don Cornelius envisioned the show as a black analog to *American Bandstand,* a popular dance and music show. After gaining popularity in the early 1970s on a local channel in CHICAGO, ILLINOIS, *Soul Train* was adopted by stations nationwide. The show appealed to a far broader audience than the black teenagers for whom Cornelius had designed it. *Soul Train* returned season after season during the 1980s and 1990s, charting the evolving trends of pop music by showcasing RHYTHM AND BLUES, SOUL MUSIC, and eventually RAP.

Soul Train was among the few major television programs of the 1970s that did not portray blacks by drawing on formulas and RACIAL STEREOTYPES. After the major civil rights victories of the 1960s—which redressed overt legal injustices—African Americans faced the equally formidable obstacle of ingrained cultural discrimination expressed both on and off screen. The National Black Media Coalition, an organization that protested such racism, criticized the larger broadcasting networks, while some African Americans fought racial prejudice on the local level. *Soul Train* was the most successful among regional programs whose content was engineered by African Americans for African Americans.

Bibliography

MacDonald, J. Fred. *Blacks and White TV: African Americans in Television since 1948.* 2nd ed. Nelson-Hall Publishers, 1992.

Eric Bennett

Sousa, Dona Anna de

See Njinga Mbandi.

Sousa, Noémia de

1926–

Leading Mozambican poet known for her social consciousness and affirmation of African culture, Sousa was the first woman of color to publish poetry in her home country, and possibly the first published woman of color poet in southern Africa.

Noémia de Sousa was born in Catembe, MOZAMBIQUE, the youngest of six children born of mixed-race parents. She was given the name Carolina Noémia Abranches de Sousa Soares, but she is better known as Noémia de Sousa. By the time Sousa was sixteen and living in Lourenço Marques (now MAPUTO), the repressive racial hierarchies of the Portuguese colonial government had begun to awaken her social consciousness.

In 1945, at the urging of a friend, she published her first poem, titled "O Irmão Negro" (The Black Brother), in a minor school newspaper. At nineteen years old the young poet was too shy to reveal her identity, so she signed that poem and some later poems with the initials N.S.E., or used the pseudonym Vera Micaia. With the encouragement of José Craveirinha, one of the greatest poets in Lusophone Africa (Portugal's former African colonies), Sousa went on to submit poems to such publications as O Brado Africano (The African Roar), an important black- and mixed-race-owned newspaper.

Sousa wrote all of her poems between 1945 and 1951. The only exception is a poem she composed in 1986 for the funeral of SAMORA MACHEL, the first president of independent Mozambique who perished that year in an airplane accident. This poem was written to be recited by a chorus of women.

In 1951 Sousa left Mozambique to escape harassment by the colonial secret police, who objected to her anticolonial political views. She emigrated to PORTUGAL, where she lived and worked as a journalist for an international news agency. In 1962 Sousa married Mozambican poet and journalist Guálter Soares. From 1964 until their separation in 1970, the couple lived in Paris along with their daughter. After the breakup of her marriage, Sousa remained in Paris until 1972, when she returned to Lisbon, Portugal.

Despite her truncated career as a publishing poet, Sousa is unquestionably a significant, if somewhat controversial, figure in Mozambican letters. Some critics have questioned the aesthetic value of her politically and socially motivated poems. Many others have celebrated Sousa as an innovator and the founder of Mozambican NÉGRITUDE, the assertive cultural and political movement that swept through black intellectual circles beginning in the mid-twentieth century. Sousa herself denies any direct influence of Négritude on her poetry, noting that only after emigrating to Lisbon in the 1950s did she even encounter the word.

The early international influences that she does acknowledge come from the literature and music of black America. While in Mozambique she read, in English, the poems of such HARLEM RENAISSANCE writers as LANGSTON HUGHES. She also listened to radio broadcasts, transmitted from neighboring SOUTH AFRICA, of AFRICAN AMERICAN SPIRITUALS. In 1950 she wrote one of her best-known poems, "Deixa Passar o Meu Povo" (Let My People Go), which describes how she was captivated by the singing of MARIAN ANDERSON and PAUL ROBESON.

Other of Sousa's poems that have become minor classics are "Negra" (Black Woman, 1951), "Sangue Negro" (Black Blood, 1951), and "Se Me Quiseres Conhecer . . ." (If You Want to Know Who I Am . . . 1958). The passionate cultural affirmation that characterizes these few pieces turned the poem into something akin to anthems for the first generation of black, mixed-race, and some white writers and intellectuals in their quest for an elusive Mozambican Africanness, or national character.

Despite her relatively short publishing career, Noémia de Sousa's reputation is secure. She stands as one of Lusophone Africa's premier poets. Though her poems were often published in poetry anthologies in Portuguese and in translation in several other languages, Sousa resisted collecting her verse into a single volume. In 2001 she finally relented to the wishes of her friends and admirers. Sangue Negro, her first published book of poetry, was launched at a ceremony in Maputo on Sousa's seventy-fifth birthday. She currently lives in Lisbon.

See also Colonial Rule; Poetry, African.

South Africa

Southernmost country of Africa, bordered on the north by Namibia, Botswana, Zimbabwe, Mozambique, and Swaziland; on the east and south by the Indian Ocean; and on the west by the Atlantic Ocean.

On May 9, 1994, longtime antiapartheid activist NELSON ROLIHLAHLA MANDELA marked his election as president of South Africa with a speech from the balcony of CAPE TOWN's city hall, overlooking the Cape of Good Hope. Originally named by Europeans, the Cape was the site of one of the earliest European colonies in sub-Saharan Africa. The small colony grew and prospered, and eventually became the continent's wealthiest country. This prosperity was possible primarily because South Africa's extraordinary racial oppression created a large pool of low-wage labor. Mandela's speech, however, reclaimed the Cape as a symbol of hope for a new South Africa, marking the conclusion of decades of struggle against the apartheid regime. In his speech Mandela challenged South Africa's citizens to "heal the wounds of the past," a goal that later became the defining project of the TRUTH AND RECONCILIATION COMMISSION (TRC).

Upon taking office Mandela faced enormous challenges, among them high unemployment, escalating rates of crime and HIV infection, and continuing political violence. Staunch resistance from some conservative white South Africans also threatened South Africa's stability. Since 1994 the government has made some progress in its efforts to alleviate poverty while also luring back foreign investment after decades of sanctions and economic turmoil. But these modest gains have hardly been enough to satisfy the country's highly politicized citizenry. At the same time, the end of APARTHEID has transformed South Africa from a pariah state into an influential economic and political power, both on the African continent and beyond.

Indigenous Communities in Southern Africa

The earliest known human societies in southern Africa were groups of hunter-gatherers, often referred to today as the SAN. These small communities generally relied on the region's rich natural resources for subsistence, hunting game in the grasslands and collecting fish and shellfish along the coast. Around 2,000 years ago, the San were joined by the KHOIKHOI, pastoralists who migrated south from the middle ZAMBEZI RIVER valley in what is today ZAMBIA and ZIMBABWE.

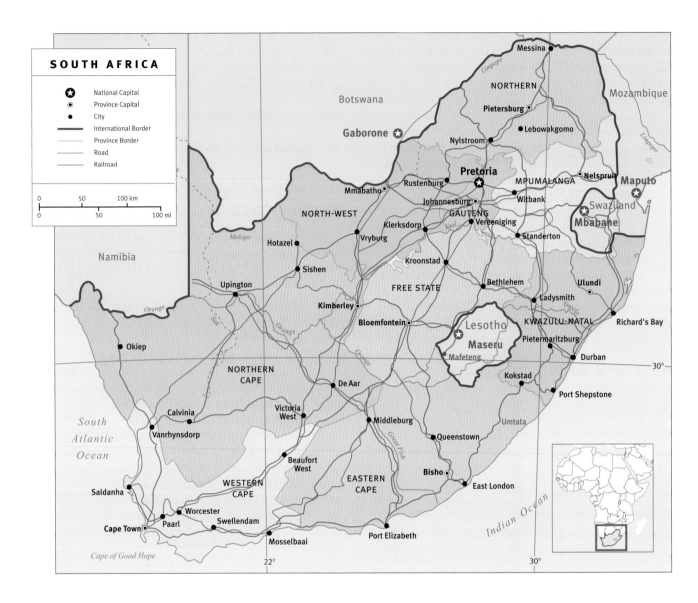

SOUTH AFRICA

- ★ National Capital
- ◉ Province Capital
- • City
- ━━ International Border
- ─── Province Border
- ─── Road
- ─── Railroad

In the first few centuries C.E., ethnic groups of the Bantu language family migrated to the region. The new settlers brought livestock and, more importantly, introduced iron tools, weapons, and agriculture to the region. The number of Bantu peoples grew rapidly, and they established southern Africa's first large settled communities. Ancestors of the SOTHO people, for example, lived in towns of up to 20,000 people. Some San and Khoikhoi were incorporated into these communities, while others were pushed onto more marginal lands. Although cattle raiding between Bantu peoples was common, little concentrated political power was built on the basis of this wealth. Political power in the region of present-day South Africa remained relatively decentralized. This form of political organization contrasted sharply with the kingdoms established by the SHONA to the north.

Cape Colony

The first Europeans to come ashore in southern Africa were Portuguese explorers looking for a sea route to Asia. In Feb-

ruary 1488 Bartolomeu Dias landed at what is now known as Mossel Bay. In 1497 VASCO DA GAMA sailed around the Cape of Good Hope and went on to become the first European explorer to reach India by sea. For the next 150 years, European sailors stopped periodically along the Cape, which was about halfway between India and ports in Europe, to collect food and fresh water and to repair their battered ships. In 1647 the crew of the grounded Dutch ship *Haarlem* were left at Table Bay to salvage the cargo and await the arrival of the following year's trading fleet. Upon their return to Amsterdam, they recommended the area around Cape Peninsula as a suitable site for a provisioning post. Three years later the Dutch East India Company sent JAN VAN RIEBEECK and more than 100 others to establish a supply station. They arrived at Table Bay on April 6, 1652, and established the settlement of Cape Town.

The settlement soon became the administrative center of an expanding Dutch colony. Its primary purpose was to provide services and provisions, such as wheat, vegetables, and livestock, for passing ships. From the earliest days of white settlement, the settlers supplemented their own production by trading metal goods, tobacco, and alcohol for livestock from local Khoikhoi groups. Although the settlers arrived on the Dutch East India Company payroll, a small number of them were released from their contracts in 1657 and were granted land to cultivate independently. These farmers gradually moved northward, out of the company's direct control.

Both the original settlement of Cape Town and the outlying farms depended on a low-cost labor force. Beginning in 1658 the company began to import slaves from throughout the Dutch East Indian empire, as well as Madagascar, Angola, and Mozambique. Slavery lasted nearly 180 years in South Africa, during which time racial distinctions became more complicated. The descendants of Asian slaves, for example, were eventually officially classified as Coloured, a category for people of mixed descent. As racial distinctions became more complex, the racial hierarchy became more deeply entrenched, and slave ownership became a mark of social status and wealth within the white population.

Peaceful relations between the settlers and the Khoikhoi did not last long. The settlers began encroaching on Khoikhoi-occupied land, and the company curbed its use of Khoikhoi intermediaries by trading directly with African groups in the interior. Open conflict between the Khoikhoi and the settlers first broke out in 1659, and again in 1673. The second conflict lasted four years and led to the death or imprisonment of thousands of Khoikhoi. Colonial records show that the settlers also confiscated more than 14,000 cattle and 32,000 sheep from the Khoikhoi between 1660 and 1675. By 1677 the Khoikhoi population had been reduced to several thousand. Slavery further reduced their number, and a smallpox epidemic in 1713 left the Khoikhoi virtually extinct.

A steady stream of European immigrants continued to swell the colony's population during the eighteenth century. The white population increased from about 2,000 people in 1717 to more than 10,000 by 1780. The area under white control expanded with the arrival of the new settlers—mostly Dutch, Germans, and French Huguenots fleeing religious persecution. Those who moved into and around the northern reaches of the colony became known as *trekboers,* due to their livelihoods as seminomadic farmers and ranchers. The name was later shorted to *Boer,* the Dutch word for "farmer." The settlers were also known as *Afrikaners,* the Dutch word for "African." Encouraged by the Dutch East India Company to settle new lands, they eventually pushed into territories occupied by Bantu ethnic groups such as the Xhosa. Competition for pasture and water in these territories led to increasingly hostile relations.

By the middle of the eighteenth century the Afrikaners had erected a series of military forts to enforce their control of the region. But the threat of war with an unknown number of Africans frightened officials in the Cape. They reacted to Afrikaner expansion and its destabilizing effects by establishing a colonial border at the Great Fish River, about 800 km (500 mi) east of the original settlement at Table Bay. The 1780 border was initially designed to separate the Xhosa people from the Afrikaner settlers, but it was established without the consent of the several Xhosa clans who already occupied the land.

In addition, colonial officials forcibly removed Xhosa who lived west of the Great Fish River, destroying villages, seizing livestock, and killing Xhosa elders in the process. Sporadic fighting between colonial militias and outgunned Xhosa fighters stretched into the last decade of the eighteenth century.

Nineteenth Century

The nineteenth century brought three major developments to southern Africa. First came the consolidation of the Zulu kingdom under Shaka. This period, known as the mfecane (Nguni for "the crushing"), led to the complete destruction of some African ethnic groups and spurred other groups to migrate as far north as what is now Zambia. Second was a sustained conflict between Afrikaners and Africans over control of parts of what are now the Eastern Cape, KwaZulu-Natal, and Free State provinces. Third was the discovery of gold and diamonds in the region. This development led white authorities to force Africans to labor in the mines and spurred the British to wrest control of the colony from the Afrikaners.

Mfecane

Shaka became leader of the Zulu people in about 1816 and immediately set out to improve Zulu military capability. With improved weapons and tactics, Shaka was able to extend Zulu control well beyond his base in what is now KwaZulu-Natal. The number of Zulus swelled as many groups opted to join Shaka rather than fight his formidable armies. Shaka's military campaign also caused some ethnic groups to disintegrate as communities scattered to avoid the military conflict. This increase in refugees, in turn, disrupted scores of communities throughout the region. But the effects of the mfecane were not purely destructive. In some instances the pressure of Shaka's military expansion led ethnic groups to form strategic alliances, leading to the formation of new states. In this way the Sotho leader Moshoeshoe built a strong and independent nation, creating what would eventually become Lesotho. Historians still dispute the overall legacy of the mfecane. But most agree that through the mfecane Shaka created the strongest military and political state in the region, and that this had a significant, if not decisive impact on southern Africa. The Zulu kingdom became one of the most formidable barriers to white settlement in southern Africa. In addition, the location of some ethnic groups in southern Africa today can be traced to the mfecane.

Cooperation and Conflict on the Frontier

Britain took control of the Cape Colony during the Napoleonic Wars (1799–1815), initially to protect British maritime trade with Asia. But the establishment of British rule in the Cape Colony in 1806 quickly brought dramatic political, economic, and cultural changes within the colony itself. A wave of immigration from Europe boosted the colony's white population from about 4,500 in 1750 to nearly 43,000 in 1820, narrowing what the British administration had viewed as a disturbingly

South Africa (At a Glance)

OFFICIAL NAME: The Republic of South Africa

AREA: 1,223,201 sq km (about 472,281 sq mi)

LOCATION: Southern Africa, at the southern tip of the continent of Africa. Includes the Prince Edward Islands (Marion Island and Prince Edward Island). South Africa borders Botswana, Namibia, Zimbabwe, and Mozambique. Lesotho and Swaziland lie within its borders.

CAPITALS: Pretoria (administrative; population 1,249,700); Cape Town (legislative; population 2,733,000); and Bloemfontein (judicial; population 378,000) (2003 estimates)

OTHER MAJOR CITIES: Johannesburg (1,675,200), Port Elizabeth (848,400), Soweto (1,242,500, some estimate the number is closer to 2 million), and Durban (2,396,100) (2003 estimates)

POPULATION: 42,768,678 (2003 estimate)

POPULATION DENSITY: 35 persons per sq km (about 90 persons per sq mi)

POPULATION BELOW AGE 15: Total population: 30 percent (male 6,460,273; female 6,377,090; 2003 estimate)

POPULATION GROWTH RATE: 0.01 percent (2003 estimate)

TOTAL FERTILITY RATE: 2.24 children born per woman (2003 estimate)

LIFE EXPECTANCY AT BIRTH: Total population: 46.56 years (male 46.57 years; female 46.54 years; 2003 estimate)

INFANT MORTALITY RATE: 60.84 deaths per 1,000 live births (2003 estimate)

LITERACY RATE (AGE 15 AND OVER WHO CAN READ AND WRITE): Total population: 86.4 percent (male 87 percent; female 85.7 percen; 2003 estimate)

EDUCATION: The legacy of apartheid in South Africa has continued to pose challenges in education. Although government spending on black education has increased significantly since the mid-1980s, at the end of the apartheid era expenditures for white pupils were about four times higher than those for black pupils. The teacher-to-student ratio for blacks was 1 to 60 in urban areas and 1 to 90 in rural areas. By comparison, the teacher-to-student ratio for whites averaged 1 to 30 or even lower. By the early 2000s efforts to boost attendance for black students led to a net primary school enrolment of 95 percent. South Africa's twenty-one major universities are publicly funded and open to students of all races. In addition, the country has fifteen technical schools, 128 technical colleges, and seventy teacher-training colleges.

LANGUAGES: South Africa has eleven official languages: Afrikaans, English, Ndebele, Sesotho sa Leboa, Sesotho, siSwati, Tsonga, Tswana, Venda, Xhosa, and Zulu. Afrikaans, a variant of the Dutch language, is the first language of almost all Afrikaners and many Coloured people. English is used as the primary language by many whites and is also spoken by some Asians and blacks. Most blacks, however, primarily use one of the Bantu languages such as Xhosa, Sesotho, or Zulu.

ETHNIC GROUPS: South Africa has a multiracial and multiethnic population. Blacks constitute 75.2 percent of the population, whites make up 13.6 percent of the population, and Coloreds and Asians compose 8.6 and 2.6 percent of the population respectively. Blacks belong to nine ethnic groups: Zulu, Xhosa, Pedi, Sotho, Tswana, Tsonga, Swazi, Ndebele, and Venda. The Zulu are the largest of these groups, making up about 22 percent of the total black population. Whites are descended primarily from British, Dutch, German, and French Huguenot (Protestant) settlers. South Africans of Dutch ancestry, who often have German and French heritage as well, are known as Afrikaners or Boers and form about three-fifths of the white population. Those of mixed racial origin, mainly black and Afrikaner and known as Coloured in South Africa, live chiefly in the Cape provinces. The Asians are mainly of Indian ancestry and are most numerous in the province of KwaZulu-Natal. A small number of people of Malay origin are also included in the Asian population. They reside mostly in the Cape provinces.

RELIGIONS: Christianity (followed by most whites and Coloreds and about 60 percent of blacks), Hindu (embraced by 60 percent of Indians), and Muslim (2 percent)

CLIMATE: Nearly all of South Africa enjoys a mild, temperate climate. The High Veld receives about 380 to 760 mm (15 to 30 in) of precipitation annually, the amount diminishing rapidly toward the west, where rainfall is often as low as 50 mm (2 in) annually. Rainfall is deposited by the trade winds mainly between October and April. In the drier regions of the plateaus the amount of rainfall and the beginning of the rainy season vary greatly from year to year. The extreme south-west receives about 560 mm (22 in) of rainfall, mostly between June and September.

The average January temperature range in Durban is 21° to 27° C (69° to 81° F). The corresponding temperature range in Johannesburg is 14° to 26° C (58° to 78° F); in Cape Town it is 16° to 26° C (60° to 78° F); the winter temperature ranges follow the same regional pattern. The average July temperature range is 11° to 22° C (52° to 72° F) in Durban, 4° to 17° C (39° to 63° F) in Johannesburg, and 7° to 17° C (45° to 63° F) in Cape Town. Snow is rare in South Africa, although winter frosts occur in the higher areas of the plateau.

LAND, PLANTS, AND ANIMALS: The topography of South Africa consists primarily of a great plateau region, which occupies about two-thirds of the country, bordered by the Drakensberg Mountains. The chief rivers of South Africa are the Orange, Limpopo, and Vaal. Numerous large mammals, including lions, elephants, zebras, leopards, monkeys, baboons, hippopotamuses, and antelope are indigenous to South Africa. For the most part such animals are found only on game reserves. One of the most notable national game reserves is Kruger National Park in the northeast along the border with Mozambique.

NATURAL RESOURCES: Gold, chromium, antimony, coal, iron ore, manganese, nickel, phosphates, tin, uranium, gem diamonds, platinum, copper, vanadium, salt, and natural gas

CURRENCY: The rand

GROSS DOMESTIC PRODUCT (GDP): $432 billion (2002 estimate)

GDP PER CAPITA: $10,000 (2002 estimate)

GDP REAL GROWTH RATE: 3 percent (2002 estimate)

PRIMARY ECONOMIC ACTIVITIES: Gold, platinum, chromium, diamonds, agriculture, timber, and fishing

PRIMARY CROPS: Corn, wheat, sugar cane, fruits, and vegetables; dairy and beef cattle, poultry, and sheep

INDUSTRIES: Mining, automobile assembly, metalworking, machinery, textile, iron, steel, chemical, fertilizer, and foodstuffs

PRIMARY EXPORTS: Gold, other minerals and metals, foodstuffs, and chemicals

PRIMARY IMPORTS: Machinery, transport equipment, chemicals, oil, textiles, and scientific instruments

PRIMARY TRADE PARTNERS: European Union, the United States, Japan, and Switzerland

GOVERNMENT: South Africa is a republic. It is divided into nine provinces or administrative divisions: Eastern Cape, Free State, Gauteng, KwaZulu-Natal, Mpumalanga, North-West, Northern Cape, Northern Province, and Western Cape. President Thabo Mbeki presides over a bicameral legislature that comprises the National Assembly (400 seats) and the Senate (90 seats). Currently, any political party that wins 20 percent or more of the National Assembly votes in a general election is enti-

tled to name a deputy executive president, and to become a member of the governing coalition, currently made up of the African National Congress, the Inkatha Freedom Party, and the National Party. Together they constitute a Government of National Unity.

The legislature adopted a constitution on April 27, 1994 (this interim constitution replaced the constitution of September 3, 1984). On May 8, 1996, the Constitutional Assembly voted 421 to 2 to pass a new constitution that, after certification by the Constitutional Court, gradually went into effect over a three-year period and came into full force with the national elections in May 1999. South Africa has universal suffrage for those age eighteen and over.

Alonford James Robinson, Jr.

---

high black-to-white ratio. Although more than 80 percent of the colony's settlers were of Dutch origin, British lawmakers replaced the Dutch legislature in Cape Town. A British-style educational system replaced Dutch traditions of schooling, and English became the official language.

Slavery soon became a contentious issue between the Afrikaner settlers and the British administration. By 1800 the Cape Colony was deeply marked by the institution of slavery. Town-dwellers had gradually reduced their reliance on slave labor by the late eighteenth century, often selling their slaves to farmers in need of laborers. Slave ownership thus came to be a defining feature of Afrikaner society in rural areas. Slave-owning farmers in the outlying areas, many of them poor and illiterate, came to see themselves as a separate community. They spoke a variant of Dutch known as Afrikaans and gradually grew to resent their generally better-educated and wealthier town-dwelling counterparts. Over time the schism between the two white communities widened, even though white settlers as a group represented a small fraction of the colony's population.

Many Afrikaners resented the increasing influence of British laws and culture, particularly the new limits on the physical punishment of African slaves and servants. British influence soon permeated town life, becoming visible in traditional English activities such as cricket, tea drinking, and debating so-

cieties. But from the Afrikaners' perspective, perhaps the most crippling blow to the Afrikaner way of life came in 1833 when the British abolished slavery in the Cape Colony. This eliminated the primary source of labor for white farmers, which in turn threatened the financial viability of Afrikaner agriculture.

The Afrikaners chafed under British rule, and in 1835 they began abandoning their farms in the Cape Colony and migrating east into what is now KwaZulu-Natal. This gradual migration lasted into the 1840s and became known to the Afrikaners as the Great Trek. During the migration, several thousand Afrikaner *voortrekkers* (Afrikaans for "pioneers") traveled east by ox-drawn wagons into the interior, often into areas that had recently been abandoned because of the turmoil of the mfecane. The voortrekkers viewed the lack of settlement in the area as a sign that God had created the land specifically for the Afrikaner people. The social disruption of the mfecane also led some African groups to seek alliances with groups of voortrekkers, and cooperation became relatively common.

In other instances, however, white encroachment onto African land led to violent conflicts. The well-armed voortrekkers defeated NDEBELE and, later, Zulu resistance as the Afrikaners pushed east. One early group of voortrekkers suffered a serious setback when their leader, Piet Retief, was killed in February 1838 during a meeting with the Zulu leader, DINGANE. The exact circumstances surrounding his death are disputed, but there is no doubt that the voortrekkers waged brutal revenge later that year in what became known as the Battle of Blood River. Although vastly outnumbered, they defeated the Zulu army through superior firepower. Many Afrikaners later interpreted Piet Retief's death as proof of the treachery of Africans, and viewed the voortrekkers' victory at the Battle of Blood River as further evidence of divine approval of their dominance in South Africa. Both events became touchstones in the Afrikaners' understanding of their history.

Mineral Wealth, British Imperialism, and War

The voortrekkers created the Republic of Natal in what is now the KwaZulu-Natal province, but it lasted only five years as an independent country before it was seized by the British in 1843. The Afrikaners continued to try to establish independent republics, forming the Orange Free State in 1854, and in 1860 merging three smaller states into the South African Republic (in the area of what later became TRANSVAAL).

The Cape Colony administration's tolerant attitude toward Afrikaner statehood changed dramatically with the discovery of diamonds in Kimberley in 1867 and then gold to the east in Witwatersrand in 1886. Both discoveries were in Afrikaner-populated areas. Britain viewed control of the region's abundant mineral resources as imperative, even if it took military action to claim them. By 1899 tensions between the British authorities and the Afrikaners had reached the point at which war appeared inevitable.

In October 1899 the Afrikaner republics invaded British-held Natal and the Cape Colony. The South African War (often called the Boer War) took the lives of approximately 22,000 British and over 7,000 Afrikaner soldiers, as well as 20,000 to 25,000 Afrikaner civilians. But the war between whites also took a huge toll on black Africans. Both sides relied on black soldiers and laborers, and some 100,000 blacks were interned in British concentration camps, leaving over 10,000 dead. The British emerged victorious from the bitter conflict. The Treaty of Vereeniging, signed in 1902 after the Afrikaners conceded defeat, formally established British rule over the Transvaal and Orange Free State and promised eventual self-government. In 1907 the Transvaal and the Orange Free States became self-governing British colonies.

In 1910 the British government created the Union of South Africa, a largely autonomous dominion of Britain. Under the 1910 constitution the four colonies—now reconstituted as provinces—surrendered their autonomy to a new national government, but the British granted the national government broad discretion over internal matters. The new government moved quickly to mend differences between English-speakers and Afrikaners, primarily by guaranteeing white privilege and domination of blacks. The government provided generous loans and capital to Afrikaner farmers and British miners and granted white women the right to vote. It made both Afrikaans and English the country's official languages and allowed for the formation of the Afrikaner-dominated NATIONAL PARTY. Blacks were excluded from voting in three of the four provinces and granted

only limited franchise in the Cape. But as the province's mineral wealth fueled an industrial revolution, the government experienced increasing difficulty addressing demands for African labor for farms owned by Afrikaners while ensuring necessary labor for mines and other businesses owned by English-speakers.

By 1904 more than one million people, most of them black, had migrated to urban areas, making JOHANNESBURG and Kimberley two of southern Africa's largest cities. Most of the blacks sought employment in the gold and diamond mines. The government's answer to urbanization, and the increased social contact between whites and Africans that it inevitably brought, was to formalize existing practices of segregation into strict laws. Africans, Coloureds, and Asians were confined to nonwhite slums, including SOPHIATOWN, Alexandria, and Orlando (in what is now SOWETO).

Resistance in the Early Twentieth Century

Africans resisted white domination from the earliest days of Dutch settlement in the seventeenth century, but urbanization and industrialization led to new tactics in the early twentieth century. In 1902 Coloured activists formed the African Political Organization (APO), led by Abdullah Abdurahman. Originally focused on advancing the interests of Coloureds, the APO increasingly forged ties with African groups and by 1910 boasted more than 100 local branches and nearly 20,000 members. Within the Indian community, Mohandas Gandhi led a passive resistance campaign against the discrimination targeted at Indians. Gandhi's tactic of passive resistance, which he termed *Satyagraha* (Sanskrit for "truth and firmness"), later propelled Gandhi to international fame when he led India to independence from the British in 1947.

Black political groups, however, mobilized the largest protests against the white government. The South African Native Congress (SANC) was the first black political organization, founded in 1898 in what is now Eastern Cape province by members of the first generation of Africans educated in mission schools. In 1912 more than 100 black activists assembled in Bloemfontein to create an even larger civil rights organization, the South African Native National Congress (SANNC), which became the AFRICAN NATIONAL CONGRESS (ANC) in 1923. Pixley ka Izaka Seme, John Tengo Jabavu, Walter Rubusana, SOLOMON TSHEKISHO PLAATJE, and JOHN LANGALIBALELE DUBE were among the movement's most notable leaders. The initial motivation for forming the SANNC was the erosion of African political rights following the creation of the Union of South Africa in 1910, which led to such repressive laws as the 1913 Natives Land Act, which restricted black ownership of land to only 7 percent of the country. (A 1936 law increased the land reserved for blacks to 13 percent of the country.) Restrictions on land ownership destroyed African agriculture, forcing thousands of Africans to take low-wage jobs on white-owned farms and in the mining industry.

As SANNC pushed to defend rights for Africans, African labor unions multiplied and grew increasingly vocal. The unions organized workers to demand better wages and an end to the color bar—the practice of reserving skilled positions for whites while forcing Africans to take dangerous, low-paying jobs. By 1918 black railway workers, municipal sanitary workers, and gold and diamond miners had begun waging a series of strikes. These strikes set a precedent for labor protests that spread to rural areas in the 1920s. By the late 1920s the Communist Party of South Africa (later renamed the SOUTH AFRICAN COMMUNIST PARTY), founded in 1921 as a mostly white organization, also offered support to the black labor movements.

Increasing industrialization in the 1940s spurred a new wave of migration to urban areas, and with it a new round of political protest. Blacks repeatedly protested against the PASS LAWS, which required blacks to carry pass books, or identity papers. The pass laws restricted movement between rural areas and cities. In addition, the ANC and community groups organized boycotts of government-run beer halls and bus lines, and thousands squatted on vacant land to protest urban housing shortages. By the end of the 1940s, uncontrollable urbanization and militant black resistance became the major themes in white electoral politics.

Apartheid Era

In 1948 the election of the Afrikaner-led National Party heralded a much more extreme policy known as apartheid. Under apartheid the government recognized three distinct racial groups: white, Bantu or black African, and Coloured. Asians were later recognized as a distinct racial group as well. Apartheid sought to control and divide South African society through an elaborate set of race-based laws. These laws restricted not only where people could live or work but also with whom they could marry—or even associate.

In addition to racial categories, apartheid recognized ten black African "tribes" or "Bantu nations," each of which was assigned a rural *bantustan,* or Bantu homeland. Although the National Party claimed that these homelands allowed blacks to maintain their "tribal" customs and political structures, the primary objective of the homelands was to prevent black workers from forming class-based resistance movements. In fact, intense poverty in rural areas forced blacks to continue to migrate to urban areas in search of work, which in turn led to growing tensions in the cities. In response, the government passed increasingly restrictive policies, such as the effective outlawing of trade unions in 1953.

Apartheid provided an ideological justification for systematically destroying racially mixed communities to create government-controlled segregated housing areas. As black townships located on the outskirts of major white cities grew to accommodate black workers, the government tore them down and moved the residents further from white areas. The township of Sophiatown, for years the home of a thriving community of writers and artists, was torn down beginning in 1955. The destruction of nonwhite communities continued for four decades, during which more than three million Africans, 300,000 Coloureds, and 150,000 Asians were forcibly relocated.

Mass Resistance in the 1950s

In 1952 the ANC united with several Coloured political groups to wage a nonviolent campaign of boycotts, strikes, and marches. These activities quickly revitalized ANC membership, which by 1953 numbered nearly 100,000. The ANTIAPARTHEID MOVEMENT gained momentum on June 26, 1955, when several organizations, including the ANC, the South African Indian Congress, and the South African Coloured People's Organization, gathered at Kliptown outside Johannesburg at a meeting known as the Congress of the People. At Kliptown delegates from all over the country adopted the FREEDOM CHARTER, which outlined demands for a free, nonracial South Africa.

Although the ANC protests were peaceful, the South African police often arrested demonstrators and subjected them to beatings and torture, which sometimes resulted in deaths. The government's brutal tactics led the ANC and its allies to back only carefully controlled protests through much of the 1950s. But many segments of the African, Indian, and Coloured populations were determined to protest at any cost. Trade union members and African women were particularly militant in the 1950s, often prodding the reluctant ANC leadership to act. In 1958, when it was clear that nonviolent protest would be met consistently with government-sanctioned violence, some members of the youth wing of the ANC broke away and formed the more militant PAN-AFRICANIST CONGRESS (PAC).

Further evidence of the government's brutality came in 1960, when police shot and killed sixty-nine unarmed demonstrators at a PAC-sponsored anti-pass protest in the township of SHARPEVILLE. Shortly afterward the government banned the ANC and other antiapartheid organizations. Over the next several years the government continued to rely on pass laws, relocations, and other apartheid mechanisms to suppress resistance efforts. In response, the banned ANC and the South African Communist Party, then led by JOE SLOVO, together formed the guerrilla army Umkhonto we Sizwe (MK). The National Party government responded by jailing many black political leaders and embarking on a campaign of severe repression that squelched most organized resistance during the 1960s. Consequently, the ANC was forced to move its operations out of South Africa. Throughout the 1960s and 1970s it struggled to build an effective political and military organization in neighboring countries, such as Botswana, Mozambique, and Tanzania. Meanwhile, the South African economy enjoyed unparalleled growth, contributing to the already vast disparity in wealth between whites and blacks.

In the 1970s organized political protest again intensified, largely due to the militancy of high school and college-age students. Student activists, among them the popular STEPHEN BIKO, promoted Black Consciousness, a philosophy of black pride and unity influenced by the ideas of black American leaders such as MALCOLM X and by African NÉGRITUDE thinkers. In June 1976 elementary and secondary school students marched in Soweto in protest of apartheid educational policies. At this demonstration, police fired into the crowd, killing several children and injuring many more. The uprising then spread through Soweto,

Police walk among the bodies of those killed when police opened fire on demonstraters in Sharpville in 1960. Out of an estimated 2,000 people who had gathered to protest pass laws, at least 69 were killed and another 200 injured during the demonstration. *CORBIS/Bettman*

and within days it hit townships throughout the country. The massacre of students provoked international condemnation and economic boycotts against South Africa and fueled the spread of the antiapartheid movement within South Africa. In 1977 the death of Steve Biko—who died after being severely beaten while in police custody—further galvanized the protest movement.

The government banned Black Consciousness organizations in an effort to squelch the resurgence of mass resistance. Fearing complete collapse, Prime Minister PIETER WILLEM BOTHA and his government adopted a "Total Strategy" to maintain the economic and political viability of apartheid. Total strategy amounted to a wide-ranging but tightly coordinated plan of repression and reform. Elements of the strategy included tighter limits on protests, modest social and political reforms to divide nonwhite groups along class lines, and military attacks on countries in southern Africa that supported the ANC.

UDF and Insurrection in the 1980s

In 1981, aiming to win support abroad and to divide the antiapartheid movement within South Africa, the government approved a new constitution granting Asians and Coloureds—but not Africans—seats in the country's new tricameral (three-house) parliament. But this and other reform efforts failed to curb opposition to minority rule. Instead, the constitutional reform gave resistance groups a rallying point, and in 1983 they formed a massive coalition dubbed the United Democratic Front (UDF). The UDF embraced hundreds of organizations representing virtually all segments of South African society, including churches, student groups, civic organizations, women's groups, sporting teams, and trade unions.

The UDF helped build mass opposition on a scale not seen in South Africa since the 1950s. UDF affiliates relied on a wide range of resistance tactics, including rent boycotts to protest poor conditions in government-owned housing, consumer boycotts against white businesses to protest police violence in black areas, and increased international pressure against the apartheid regime. At the same time the ANC stepped up its campaign of sabotage, which was generally limited to non-civilian sites such as military bases, power plants, and police stations. By the mid-1980s the government had lost control of many parts of the country to the UDF. As the UDF and the ANC intensified their resistance, government military and intelligence agencies initiated a covert program to identify and assassinate opposition activists. Generally using black collaborators for assistance, these government-organized hit squads killed thousands of pro-UDF South Africans. At the same time, the violence allowed the government to claim that "black-on-black" violence showed that blacks could not be trusted to run the country.

But even the systematic assassinations failed to dampen resistance, so in 1986 the government declared a state of emergency. This declaration allowed the police and the military to detain thousands of people without trial, censor the press, and clamp down on virtually all expressions of resistance. But the sheer cost of maintaining order, combined with international sanctions, took a serious toll on the South African economy, and some members of the government began to realize that change was inevitable. The pressure for change increased in 1988 as the South African military suffered costly setbacks in its efforts to control Angola and Namibia. In 1989 the National Party signaled its desire for a new approach when it replaced President Botha with the more moderate FREDERIK WILLEM DE

In April 1994 black residents of Katishong, a township east of Johannesburg, lined up to vote in the first South African elections open to members of all races. Lines like this one were seen throughout the country. *CORBIS/Juda Ngwenya*

KLERK. Although de Klerk initially reaffirmed his party's commitment to apartheid, late in 1989 he began freeing ANC political prisoners and lifting some controls on protest. Among the freed prisoners was Nelson Mandela, a hero of the anti-apartheid struggle who had been in jail since the 1960s. The UDF, reborn as the Mass Democratic Movement, responded by launching a new series of highly publicized demonstrations that made it impossible for de Klerk to turn back from his tentative steps toward dismantling apartheid.

Negotiations to end apartheid took nearly four years and proceeded against a backdrop of increasing violence. Thousands died, primarily in conflicts between the ANC and the INKATHA FREEDOM PARTY (IFP), led by MANGOSUTHU GATSHA BUTHELEZI. In the 1980s Buthelezi's IFP had collaborated with the National Party against the UDF and the ANC, but by the early 1990s it was clear that the ANC would soundly defeat the IFP if elections were held. Rather than face such a certain loss, the IFP stepped up its attacks on the ANC in an effort to gain leverage that it could use to obtain a guaranteed share of political power. In late 1993 the ANC, the National Party, and the numerous other parties involved in the negotiations completed an interim constitution, providing for a postapartheid state based on multiparty elections, a two-house legislature, provincial assemblies, and a bill of rights. The new constitution also

abolished the bantustans and created nine new provinces. The IFP and the far-right Afrikaners both initially threatened to boycott elections planned for April 1994, but at the last minute Buthelezi joined the National Party and the ANC in the race.

In the election Nelson Mandela led the African National Congress to an overwhelming victory. The National Party won only in Western Cape province, and despite election irregularities, the IFP was credited with a majority of the votes in KwaZulu-Natal, which gave the party control of that province. After the elections the country came under the Government of National Unity, which was dominated by the ANC but included members of the National Party, the IFP, and the Freedom Front, a coalition of white extremist groups. Under the interim constitution, every party that won at least 5 percent of the vote was guaranteed a cabinet seat.

New South Africa

The results of the 1994 elections did not complete the transition to democratic rule in South Africa. For the next two years negotiators representing all the members of the Government of National Unity worked to craft a new, permanent constitution. Largely attributed to ANC leader Cyril Ramaphosa and trade unionist Jay Naidoo, the 1996 constitution provides for shared rights and responsibilities among the central government, nine provinces, and local governments. Traditional authorities were recognized in limited areas, but their decisions were subject to review by courts. On balance, the ANC succeeded in its effort to keep much power in the hands of the central government.

The first rupture of the Government of National Unity came in 1996, when de Klerk and the National Party pulled out of the Government of National Unity. The move came after Mandela and de Klerk were unable to agree over the mandate of the Truth and Reconciliation Commission (TRC), established in 1995 to investigate apartheid-era crimes. Headed by former archbishop DESMOND MPILO TUTU, the TRC ultimately had to determine which of its more than 7,000 applicants would receive amnesty for their crimes. De Klerk, under whose presidency some acts of kidnapping, torture, and murder of antiapartheid activists had taken place, continued to defend his police force as "good and honorable men"—an assertion Mandela called "a joke." For its part, the ANC reported its own apartheid-era crimes, including the execution of suspected spies.

Not surprisingly, the TRC's work generated considerable controversy. Although most black South Africans supported the TRC's efforts to document apartheid atrocities, some victims' families felt that it was unjust to grant amnesty to the perpetrators of apartheid's crimes. For many white South Africans, however, the TRC's highly publicized hearings represented an opening up of old wounds that should simply be forgotten.

Race relations in the new South Africa remain complicated. Although the school system is officially unified and open to all, white families have boycotted some recently integrated schools, claiming that educational standards have declined since integration. Black and white families have faced harassment and even violence from some of the boycotters. Despite their still-dominant role in corporate culture, some whites have opposed affirmative-action laws and have labeled the hiring of black government officials as "cronyism" or even "reverse apartheid."

Pressing Issues

The demise of apartheid did not end all of South Africa's social problems. By the late 1990s, South Africa's high crime rate had become a major political issue, although the government claimed that some types of crime had become less common since the 1994 elections. Concerns of whites about violent crime led to a dramatic rise in white emigration from South Africa in the first few years after the 1994 elections, but poor and predominantly black urban neighborhoods remain some of the hardest hit areas. White farmers report that they face a rising trend in attacks and robberies in remote areas.

Along with crime, the new government has had to grapple with a somewhat unstable and sluggish economy. Although the end of minority rule improved South Africa's economic performance, growth remains less than many had hoped. In 1998 the value of the South African currency (the rand) fell to a record low, raising fears of a long-term economic crisis.

Other developments in 1998 threatened South Africa's role as a regional leader. South Africa sent 800 troops into nearby Lesotho in September 1998 at the invitation of Lesotho's government. The troops were part of an SADC action to quell public unrest and to prevent a possible military coup in Lesotho. The South African troops met unexpectedly stiff resistance, however, and the botched military intervention drew sharp criticism in both South Africa and Lesotho. South Africa has also proved unwilling to send its military to halt regional military conflicts, dashing hopes that South Africa could stabilize the region.

Two years before the scheduled 1999 elections, Nelson Mandela handed over the ANC leadership to the deputy president, THABO MBEKI. Most observers believed that Mbeki, who is considered less conciliatory toward whites than Mandela, would face his biggest challenge from other black South Africans. In particular, Mbeki was likely to face sharp criticism from within the ANC over the party's free-market economic policies.

In addition, the ANC has faced continuing opposition from outside the party. Violence in the late 1990s in KwaZulu-Natal was caused by rivalry between the ANC and the United Democratic Movement, a new party drawing from former members of the ANC and National Party. The violence prompted some to speak again of a "third force," a term used in the late 1970s and 1980s to refer to clandestine destabilization efforts directed against the ANC. Another important party vying for power in the late 1990s was the white-dominated Democratic Party. This party has attracted many voters from the dwindling ranks of the National Party, which was reconstituted as the New National Party. Smaller numbers of voters supported the extreme right-wing Conservative Party and the Freedom Front.

In the June 1999 national elections the ANC won an even larger share of votes than it did in 1994, and Mbeki was chosen by parliament as president. The ANC fell just short of winning enough votes to garner the two-thirds majority necessary to amend the constitution, which the party set as its goal during the campaign. Some observers, however, saw this as a positive development for both the ANC and the country. For the ANC it meant that the party would face less internal division over which constitutional amendments to try to implement. For the country it meant that no single party could change the constitution at will. The 1999 elections also saw another historic shift when the Democratic Party won more votes than the New National Party. This marked a major defeat for the New National Party, which had hoped to gain ground against the ANC. Instead, the New National Party lost support compared to 1994, and the Democratic Party became the official opposition party in parliament.

South Africa's most pressing crisis, however, is the prevalence of acquired immunodeficiency syndrome (AIDS). South Africa has more HIV-infected people than any other country in the world—some five million, or more than 11 percent of its total population, by 2003. Yet steps to treat AIDS patients and stop the spread of the disease came late; indeed, leaders scarcely acknowledged the extent of the problem until late in the 1990s, and Mbeki refused to authorize antiretroviral drugs for needy patients even after pharmaceutical companies agreed to provide medications at reduced cost. In 2003 Mbeki, who has repeatedly stressed that combating poverty is crucial to battling AIDS, agreed to provide the drugs through the country's public health system. By 2003 the epidemic had created more than 600,000 orphans in South Africa and led demographers to estimate a 44 percent decline in the country's population by 2050.

Despite its problems, South Africa's economy remains the largest in sub-Saharan Africa. This relative prosperity has allowed the government to improve living conditions for many of its citizens. Although the country still faces an acute housing shortage, the government has been able to provide millions of homes with water and electrical service. In 1997 alone it appropriated $500 million for new housing loans. In addition, there are hopes that South African industry and capital will help drive economic growth across the continent, or at least within the SOUTHERN AFRICAN DEVELOPMENT COMMUNITY (SADC), a regional economic bloc. By the late 1990s South African firms were investing in West and Central African mining operations, as well as in hotels and other tourist facilities across eastern and southern Africa.

See also Bantu: Dispersion and Settlement; Black Consciousness in Africa; Great Zimbabwe.

Alonford James Robinson

South African Communist Party

Political party important in the overthrow of apartheid

An influential force in the ANTIAPARTHEID MOVEMENT, the South African Communist Party (SACP) has long cooperated with other organizations, especially the AFRICAN NATIONAL CONGRESS (ANC). Although its ultimate goal remains the creation of a socialist society in SOUTH AFRICA, during the APARTHEID era the SACP worked for another goal as well. Calling for an end to the white supremacist state, the party sought the formation of a democratic government in which all South Africans would be equally represented.

Founded in 1921 as the Communist Party of South Africa (CPSA), the party was initially concerned more with overthrowing capitalism than with achieving racial justice and an independent African nation. Its early membership was overwhelmingly white, but within a decade the majority of its 1,750 members were black. Debate over the direction of the party led to a 1928 proclamation that the CPSA was a "nationalist revolutionary organization" dedicated to fighting "the white bourgeoisie and British imperialists."

At the time, the ANC was the leading anti-segregationist group in South Africa, but after it fell under conservative leadership in 1930 it spurned cooperation with the CPSA. A combination of internal conflict and a weakened labor movement during the Great Depression led to a dramatic decline in the CPSA's membership during the 1930s. During World War II (1939–1945), however, the revival of the organized labor movement in turn helped revive the party. Together the ANC and the CPSA organized the African Mine Workers' Union, and the 1946 strike of 100,000 mineworkers brought the party new energy, attention, and members.

In 1948 South Africa's conservative NATIONAL PARTY was voted into power and began implementing apartheid policies. Two years it later passed the Suppression of Communism Act, effectively banning the CPSA. But the party's renewed mission—which emphasized "the unity of interests that exist between workers of all races"—was not crushed. In 1953 the party re-formed as an underground movement, renamed the South African Communist Party (SACP). Operating illegally but relatively openly, SACP members such as JOE SLOVO worked with the ANC on the 1952 Defiance of Unjust Laws campaign. SACP members also participated in the 1955 Congress of the People (the meeting that drafted the FREEDOM CHARTER, a document adopted by both the ANC and the SACP).

The party's participation in the antiapartheid campaign, however, made its members targets for government harassment. Many SAPC members, for example, were among the 156 activists charged with treason in 1956. Slovo, a defendant in the trial, also acted as defense attorney; no convictions resulted. After the government banned the ANC in 1960, Slovo, NELSON MANDELA, and others formed *Umkhonto we Sizwe* (Spear of the Nation, also known as MK), an armed resistance body that carried out acts of sabotage. A raid on Umkhonto's headquarters at Rivonia in 1963 led to the arrest and conviction of many in the party, along with ANC leaders such as Mandela and WALTER SISULU. Slovo, out of the country at the time, was forced into exile for the next twenty-seven years.

Operating mostly out of London and MOZAMBIQUE, the SACP contributed to the antiapartheid movement mostly by its role as a conduit for foreign aid, particularly from the Soviet Union and other communist countries, to support Umkhonto. Since its unbanning in 1990, the SACP has played an important role in South African political life. Joe Slovo, its secretary general, helped negotiate the peaceful transition that led to multiracial, democratic elections in 1994. Although Slovo died in 1995, the SACP remained influential. It is currently part of the governing coalition in South Africa.

See also African Socialism.

Kate Tuttle

South America

Fourth largest continent, consisting of twelve nations and an overseas department of France. The destination for millions of African slaves from the sixteenth to the nineteenth century, South America has vibrant cultures that still display aspects of African life. Music, dance, and religions of South America show the strength of African traditions. South America is home to about 348 million people, or less than 5 percent of the world population. The continent accounts for 12 percent of Earth's land area.

For information on
Countries and a French department on the northern coast of
    South America: *See* French Guiana; Guyana; Suriname;
    Venezuela.
Countries on the east coast of South America: *See* Argentina;
    Brazil; Uruguay.
Countries on the west coast of South America: *See* Bolivia;
    Chile; Colombia; Ecuador; Peru.
Landlocked country in South America: *See* Paraguay.

South America, Blacks and Indians in

See Latin America, Blacks and Indians in: An Interpretation.

South America, Blacks in

See Andes, Blacks During Colonial Times in the; Latin
America and the Caribbean, Blacks in.

South Asia, Africans in

**People of African descent who live in South Asia, mainly
in India.**

For centuries African slaves were part of an African-Asian trade,
and today many of their descendants remain in South Asia. In
a few areas African Asians actively maintain aspects of their
cultural heritage, some living in separate communities. Many
African Asians, however, have completely assimilated into the
local cultures. Anthropologists and historians have conducted
few studies of African slaves and their descendants in South
Asia, so much of the history of African Asians remains poorly
known. Some African traders may have settled voluntarily in
South Asia, but historians know even less about them.

African-South Asian Slave Trade

Archaeological evidence of contact between South Asia and
AFRICA dates as far back as the second millennium B.C.E., but
it seems the slave trade did not begin until the sixth century
C.E. The trade remained relatively small until the eighteenth
century, when, according to estimates, the number of slaves
brought to South Asia reached more than 3,000 per year. GREAT
BRITAIN—the colonial ruler of much of South Asia—abolished
the slave trade in India in 1811 and outlawed slavery itself in
1843. These laws, however, were not fully enforced until
decades later.

The INDIAN OCEAN SLAVE TRADE resembled that of the TRANSAT-
LANTIC SLAVE TRADE, except that it was smaller. Most slaves were
captured in raids inland and marched to the coast bound in
chains. In the early years Indian bankers usually financed the
raids, and Arabs conducted them, supported by the African
rulers. On arriving at the coast, the raiders sold their captives

in open slave markets. Those chosen for Asia were packed into
the holds of ships, lying side by side, several platforms deep,
with only a few centimeters between platforms. Food and water were scarce on the ships, if even provided, and many slaves
died before they arrived in South Asia. If a slave died there
was no way to remove him or her until the voyage was over.
During the height of the trade, Portuguese, Dutch, French, and
British shippers all participated.

Africans in South Asian History

Most of the slaves, known as Siddis or Habshis, served as soldiers, though some became plantation and domestic workers.
Most slaves converted to ISLAM. Sometimes they became free
under various circumstances, and a few became military and
social leaders. The earliest well-known Siddi, Jalaluddin Yakut,
was the favorite slave of thirteenth-century Sultana Raziya of
Delhi (present-day India). She appointed Yakut the royal stable master; however, her father and the kingdom's nobles disapproved and eventually killed Yakut.

Other notables of the early period included Siddi Maula, a
religious figure who attracted many followers, and Malik Sar-
var, who in 1389 became deputy of the sultan Muhammad of
Delhi. He was later appointed governor of the eastern province
of Jaunpur. Later another Siddi, Ibrahim, ruled Jaunpur during
a time of great prosperity and learning. In fifteenth-century Ben-
gal, King Rukn-ud-din Barbak promoted many African slaves
to high posts. Barbak had about 8,000 slave soldiers and in
1486, after Barbak's death, Sultan Shahzada led the Siddis in
a takeover of the kingdom. They ruled until 1493. In 1573 Sheik
Sayeed al-Habshi Sultani, a well-known Siddi ruler of Ahmad-
abad, constructed a mosque still noted for its superior floral
tracery. In the province of Sind, currently in Pakistan, Hosh
Muhammad became famous as a leader of eighteenth-century
battles against the British. Also in Sindh, Zahur Shah Hasmi,
Murad Sahir, and Muhammad Siddiq Mussafar gained fame as
writers, while Muhammad Jharak excelled as a singer.

Malik Ambar

The best-known Siddi leader of South Asia was Malik Ambar,
born about 1550 in ETHIOPIA. Ambar was brought to what is
now central India as a slave. He became a Muslim and received
some education from various owners. Ambar was promoted to
the position of military commander of a group of Arab troops
in central India. He later built a mercenary army of over 1,500
and was invited by the king of Ahmadnagar to join him in a
fight against the powerful Mughal invaders of the time. Following his success in this endeavor, Ambar founded his own
capital at Kirkee and again kept the Mughals at bay. He maintained a 60,000-horse cavalry, obtained artillery from the
British, and received naval support from the Siddis who controlled the island of Janjira. By the 1620s, however, after twenty
years of war, strife beset Ambar's community. Upon his death
in 1626, his son could not keep the kingdom together. Ambar's
civic achievements were many: a postal service, educational

support for all ethnic groups, communal ownership of land for the poor, graduated taxes, and support of the courtly arts. He also built many public buildings, some using black stone, which, it is said, was a reference to his heritage.

Janjira

The island of Janjira, a critical trading locale about 70 km (about 45 mi) southwest of Bombay (now Mumbai), was under Siddi control for a long period. According to some accounts Malik Ahmad Siddi, founder of a dynasty at Ahmadnagar, installed Abyssinians as the captains of the island fort of Janjira in about 1500. By 1636 the Mughal armies had conquered Ahmadnagar and were conquering everyone in the area, yet they maintained an alliance with the Siddis of Janjira. These Siddis were also a powerful force in the later struggles between the Dutch, English, and Portuguese as those colonial powers vied for control. In 1759 the British finally overpowered the Siddis in Janjira.

Siddi Risala

Once Britain outlawed the slave trade, British forces confiscated and freed many slaves en route to South Asia. The British attempted to find employment for the freed slaves or to return them to Africa. During this period, the trade was especially large in the province of Hyderabad, which soon became home to many freed African captives from other parts of India. In addition, many freed slaves migrated there. The local king organized many of them as the African Cavalry Guard in 1863. Siddi Risala, meaning "African regiment," refers, after the guard, to the area in Hyderabad, still in existence, in which they lived.

In Siddi Risala, the Siddis built their own mosque and established a community for their families. But there were few Siddi women, so many Siddi men had to marry outside the group. Maintaining African culture was difficult because the Siddis themselves were from many different African regions and spoke many different languages. But some musical instruments and ceremonial dances were kept alive, and some can be seen today. In 1882 the British restricted movements in Hyderabad, fearing that the sizeable Siddi population would organize against them. The Siddis of Hyderabad today number about 2,000. They are aware of their ancestry but identify largely with the Muslim community. They occasionally perform African-style dances and songs for the public.

Other Siddis Today

Because they are still associated with the disadvantages of slavery, many Siddis face discrimination in South Asia. Indians have a long history, perhaps dating back several thousand years, of associating light skin with high castes. Many South Asian societies, moreover, were most likely influenced by British derogatory attitudes toward the Africans during the colonial period. As most Siddis today are Muslims, they also sometimes confront the difficulties of being a religious minority in India, which is mostly Hindu. Many Siddis, of course, have intermarried and moved away from their communities, although distinct Siddi communities exist in Mumbai, north Karnataka, Junagarh, and Amod (formerly Broach), in India; and Sind and Baluchistan in Pakistan, as well as in other places in South Asia. Perhaps due to the small size or lack of financial power of these communities, Africans in other countries have largely ignored them. For their part, the Siddis have shown little interest in PAN-AFRICANISM.

See also Indian Communities in Asia; Indian Ocean Slave Trade.

Bibliography
Harris, Joseph E. *The African Presence in Asia.* Northwestern University Press, 1971.

South Asians in Africa

See Indian Communities in Africa.

Southern African Development Community

Group of southern African nations promoting economic growth and development and economic interdependence.

During the 1960s a sense of common purpose developed among the countries in southern Africa that were involved in struggles for political independence from colonial and white-minority governments. After years of informally coordinating resources and strategies, several nations agreed to meet with donor governments and development organizations in GABORONE, BOTSWANA, in May 1979 and again in July in ARUSHA, TANZANIA. The purpose was to discuss the possibility of forming an organized coalition. In 1980 nine countries, including ANGOLA, Botswana, LESOTHO, MALAWI, MOZAMBIQUE, SWAZILAND, TANZANIA, ZAMBIA, and ZIMBABWE met in LUSAKA, ZAMBIA, to form the Southern African Development Coordination Conference (SADCC). (NAMIBIA, SOUTH AFRICA, and MAURITIUS joined in the early 1990s.) In their mission statement, known as the Lusaka Declaration, SADCC members pledged to "pursue policies aimed at economic liberation and integrated development of our national economies."

SADCC members initially focused on coordinating and pooling resources around communications, energy issues, and agricultural research. The end of the Cold War followed by the end of APARTHEID in South Africa, however, brought the necessity and the possibility for closer ties among these nations. In 1992 SADCC changed its name to the Southern African Development Community (SADC), and expanded its mission. In addition to aiming for regional economic integration, SADC had goals that included the evolution of common political values and institutions, environmental protection, and the preservation of the social and cultural affinities in the region. Most recently SADC developed a defense and security branch for the purpose of peacefully resolving both civil and cross-border conflicts.

SADC has sponsored projects ranging in scope from environmental protection to tourism in conjunction with regional and foreign non-governmental organizations, but the group has been criticized by the regional press for failing to address HUMAN RIGHTS concerns, such as police brutality. Additionally, SADC has not effectively tackled the massive debts that plague most southern African nations. Despite these shortcomings SADC continues to attract new members beyond the region; SEYCHELLES and the DEMOCRATIC REPUBLIC OF THE CONGO were the most recent to join.

Jessica Hochman

Southern African Large Telescope

An array of hexagonal mirrors eleven meters across, the Southern African Large Telescope (SALT), located near the Karoo town of Sutherland, South Africa, will be the largest single optical telescope in the southern hemisphere when it becomes fully operational in 2005.

The racist policies of the APARTHEID regime in South Africa inhibited international scientific cooperation and technology transfer with the country before the 1990s. Scientists at the South African Astronomical Observatory (SAAO) were concerned that their instrumentation was becoming obsolete. The largest SAAO telescope, the 1.9 meter Radcliffe telescope, had been erected in the 1940s. Half a century later, South African astronomers found it increasingly challenging to do cutting-edge research; in order to remain scientifically productive they contemplated a new large, technologically advanced telescope.

After the first non-racial elections in 1994 the new democratic South African government ordered a reassessment of national science and technology policy. A 1996 government White Paper identified astronomy as a focus for competence in basic science. In 1998 the cabinet, led by President Nelson Mandela, announced support for the Southern African Large Telescope with an appropriation of 50 million Rands (roughly U.S. $10 million).

Institutional partners from Britain, Germany, New Zealand, Poland, and the United States joined a scientific consortium with the National Research Foundation of South Africa to plan, finance and utilize the giant instrument. The optical design of SALT was based on the innovative Hobby-Ebberly Telescope at the McDonald Observatory of the University of Texas. Although SALT will be capable of optical/infrared imagining, its chief mission will be that of a spectrographic survey instrument, enabling scientists to study the early history of the universe, probe quasars and active galaxies, and search for planets orbiting other stars.

SALT represents a major interface between Africa and developed countries with regard to cooperation in pure scientific research. African scientists as well as astronomers from partner institutions will have access to the facility. The SALT program also includes a collateral benefits plan for the development of South African technology and engineering expertise, science education and popularization, and local economic advancement. SALT will ensure South Africa's status as a vital player in the international astronomical community well into the twenty-first century.

Keith Snedegar

Southern Christian Leadership Conference

Civil rights group led by Martin Luther King, Jr., and a coalition of other Southern black ministers, which organized protests in the 1950s and 1960s against segregation and barriers to voting.

The civil rights activist BAYARD RUSTIN once described the Southern Christian Leadership Conference (SCLC) as the "dynamic center" of the cluster of organizations that made up the CIVIL RIGHTS MOVEMENT. It differed from such organizations as the STUDENT NONVIOLENT COORDINATING COMMITTEE (SNCC) and the NATIONAL ASSOCIATION FOR THE ADVANCEMENT OF COLORED PEOPLE (NAACP), which functioned nationwide and sought to recruit individual members. SCLC served as an umbrella group for affiliates, and initially concentrated its energies on America's segregated South. With prominent black ministers on its executive board and the Reverend MARTIN LUTHER KING, JR., at its helm, SCLC proved to be the guiding force and inspiration to the organizations and protesters engaged in the exhausting struggle for civil rights. In the words of one activist, "Southern Christian Leadership Conference is not an organization—it's a church."

In January 1957, sixty activists responded to a call for an Atlanta conference on nonviolent integration. Among the leaders were Northern activists Bayard Rustin, ELLA BAKER, and Stanley Levison, and Southern civil rights veterans Martin Luther King, Jr., FRED SHUTTLESWORTH, RALPH ABERNATHY, C. K. Steele, JOSEPH LOWERY, and WILLIAM HOLMES BORDERS. Shortly after this meeting, the group established a permanent organization, the Southern Christian Leadership Conference, and elected King as its president. The goal was to "to redeem the soul of America" through nonviolent resistance, based on the teachings of Mohandas Gandhi. The organization drew its strength from the black churches of the South, whose ministers were said to mirror the spirit of the community.

John Tilley and, later, Ella J. Baker took the job of running the Atlanta headquarters. Despite the increasingly contentious climate in the South, where black students conducted SIT-INS and Freedom Rides to protest segregation, SCLC's early activities were fairly mild, focusing on education programs and on bringing rural blacks to the voting booth.

A SNCC-led protest against segregation in Albany, Georgia, was already under way in late November 1961, when King and executive director WYATT TEE WALKER brought the SCLC into its first major nonviolent campaign. In some ways it failed;

demonstrations and arrests provoked few changes and little national attention. The federal courts, unlike their actions in earlier desegregation disputes, refused to back up the protesters. After an unsuccessful attempt to raise national support by calling attention to the imprisonment of King and Abernathy, SCLC retreated from Albany.

SCLC's 1963 campaign in Birmingham, Alabama, succeeded in every way the Albany campaign had not. In a city where white supremacist Eugene "Bull" Connor controlled the police, SCLC launched Project C (C for confrontation). The movement drew criticism from white liberals, such as Robert Kennedy, as well as from some blacks, who suggested that the protesters wait for the reforms promised by the recently elected mayor. But as the Reverend King pointed out: "Justice too long delayed is justice denied." Without its usual supporters, the demonstration limped on, and black protesters who sat-in at white-only counters soon filled the city jails.

A brilliant strategic move turned the tide of the faltering demonstration. On May 2, 1963, more than 700 black children marched from the Sixteenth Street Baptist Church through town. After police wagons were filled, the children were carted to jail in school buses. When 2,500 more young protesters marched the next day, the police turned fire hoses on them and the international press turned their cameras on Birmingham's police. The world saw horrifying pictures of black children knocked down by a force of water powerful enough to remove the bark from nearby trees. Now under international pressure and the growing threat of a riot, Birmingham's officials returned to the bargaining table more willing to deal with SCLC.

As a result of the Birmingham protest, SCLC won a desegregation settlement. More important, the protest laid the groundwork for the Civil Rights Act of 1964. After its Birmingham triumph, SCLC organized other desegregation campaigns in Savannah, Georgia, and St. Augustine, Florida, and played a pivotal role in the March on Washington in 1963. During Freedom Summer of 1964, SCLC joined the Congress of Racial Equality (CORE) for a massive voter registration campaign.

In its 1965 campaign in Selma, Alabama, SCLC took aim at unjust registration tests designed to keep blacks from voting. In some Southern counties, less than 5 percent of eligible black voters were registered; in other counties, no blacks could vote. When 400 prospective black voters, led by King and John Lewis, staged a "stand-in" at the Dallas County Courthouse, they were harassed and arrested. King wrote in *The New York Times* that more blacks were in Selma jails than were registered to vote.

Galvanized by a surge of police brutality in neighboring Perry County, SCLC organized a 50-mile march from Selma to Montgomery. As 600 marchers began the walk, state troopers, under orders from Governor George Wallace, attacked them with clubs and tear gas. The day was dubbed Bloody Sunday.

More protesters came to Selma to undertake the march again, but tension between the two organizing groups, SCLC and SNCC, delayed the protest. King led a second march just over the Pettus Bridge. SNCC members accused King of lead-

ing this much shorter march after negotiating a compromise with Wallace, and the rift between the organizations widened. By the time the full march occurred, led by both organizations, the landmark Voting Rights Act of 1965, which banned unfair voting tests, had already been passed. The march took place anyway as a symbolic gesture of the solidarity that existed for the long struggle still ahead.

Some observers criticized the SCLC for being too dependent on white liberal support and, at a time of the rising Black Power movement, too moderate. SCLC responded to the criticism by expanding its operations north to Chicago, Illinois where, according to one historian, "SCLC discovered . . . that discrimination was a far more insidious and tenacious enemy than segregation." The organization shifted its attention to economic inequality.

Operation Breadbasket, organized in July 1967 as a national program to put "bread, money, and income into the baskets of black and poor people," became the economic arm of SCLC, organizing black consumers to press for jobs and to encourage black-owned businesses. Seeing poverty as the root of inner-city violence, SCLC began to plan the Poor People's Campaign to push for federal legislation to guarantee employment, income, and housing for the nation's economically disadvantaged blacks.

The assassination of Martin Luther King, Jr., on April 4, 1968, interrupted plans for the Poor People's Campaign. The organization, which had sometimes been overshadowed by its leader's brilliance, resumed planning the Washington demonstration. Under its newly elected leader, Ralph Abernathy, the SCLC brought between 50,000 and 100,000 people to Washington to rally support for economic justice for African Americans.

After King's death, the organization went into a tailspin, beset by declining contributions and internal dissension over Abernathy's leadership. Joseph Lowery revived SCLC in the late 1970s by expanding the organization's operations beyond traditional civil rights programs, but the organization never regained its former stature.

See also Integration: An Interpretation.

Bibliography

Fairclough, Adam. *To Redeem the Soul of America: The Southern Christian Leadership Conference and Martin Luther King, Jr.* University of Georgia Press, 1987.

Marian Aguiar

Southern Negro Youth Congress

Organization established in Richmond, Virginia, in February 1937; until its demise in 1949, the Southern Negro Youth Congress (SNYC) played a critical role in the struggle of black Americans for full citizenship and for social, political, and economic justice.

In the spring of 1937 black tobacco stemmers spontaneously walked out of Richmond-area tobacco plants protesting poor wages and hazardous working conditions. With the American Federation of Labor refusing assistance, C. Columbus Alston, Francis Grandison, and James E. Jackson, Jr., helped the stemmers organize a Congress of Industrial Organizations (CIO)-affiliated union, which successfully struck Richmond's Export Leaf Tobacco Company. The victory had the effect of raising wages throughout the tobacco industry and it inaugurated the SNYC's work in the South. By 1939 the organization had established a headquarters in Birmingham, Alabama, from which it coordinated organizing efforts across the South.

The SNYC's initial membership drew from the 1930s student movement, the Communist Party, and the CIO. Early leaders included Edward Strong, William Richardson, Louis Burnham, and James E. Jackson, Jr. These men worked to connect the ongoing black struggle for civil rights to the industrial union movement of the late 1930s. But from its inception women played key roles in the organization, and by the early 1940s they assumed formal leadership positions. Esther Cooper Jackson served as SNYC's executive secretary during the 1940s. Jackson, Dorothy Burnham, Sallye Davis, and Augusta Jackson Strong agitated for gender equity within the organization. At the same time they worked to establish ties between the SNYC and preexisting networks of protest and resistance within Southern black communities.

The SNYC's connection with the Communist Party provided important links to an international arena of struggle and to a cadre of aggressive grassroots organizers. The SNYC was, however, firmly rooted in the institutional and intellectual life of black communities across the South. Its members and constituencies came to the organization from the black Baptist church, the National Association for the Advancement of Colored People (NAACP), women's clubs, and fraternal and benevolent associations. Members of the SNYC worked hard to build coalitions, drawing on organizations, institutions, and individuals across lines of class, gender, and generation. They also attempted to reach out to white Southerners interested in economic and political transformation.

During its twelve-year existence the SNYC organized eight youth legislatures in cities like Richmond; Birmingham; Chattanooga, Tennessee; and Columbia, South Carolina. The youth legislatures were living laboratories of the SNYC's vision of life and struggle. The meetings brought together various individuals and organizations active in struggles for justice in the South and the nation. Local advisory boards were formed and older leaders from respective host cities filled positions in them. Federal government officials, national labor leaders, and icons of the black struggle for freedom, like W. E. B. Du Bois and Paul Robeson, attended and addressed meetings of the youth legislature. Through small working groups, legislature participants developed plans of action and drew up resolutions for federal government legislation. The legislatures invigorated local struggles and helped garner support for the SNYC's agenda of political and economic transformation. They also provided important venues for connecting local struggles to broader international ones. At the 1946 Columbia, South Carolina, meeting Du Bois explained, "This is the firing line not simply for the emancipation of the American Negro but for the emancipation of the African Negro and the Negroes of the West Indies . . . and for the emancipation of the white slaves of modern capitalist monopoly."

In 1940 the House Un-American Activities Committee listed the SNYC as a Communist Party front and agent of foreign powers. The Federal Bureau of Investigation placed the organization and its leaders under surveillance over the next twelve years. Although the SNYC's affiliation with the Communist Party did little to hamper its support in black communities through the years of World War II (1939–1945), by 1947 and the advent of the Cold War the organization encountered increased opposition along many fronts. In 1948 the Internal Revenue Service withdrew its tax-exempt status. Liberal organizations stopped providing financial and public support. Its final youth legislature, held in Birmingham, was smashed by local vigilantes and the city's chief of police, Eugene "Bull" Connor. By 1949 the organization ceased operations and its members were forced to pursue new avenues of struggle. The SNYC, however, anticipated the student movement of the 1960s and left a lasting imprint on the black struggle for freedom.

See also American Federation of Labor and Congress of Industrial Organizations.

Peter Lau

Southern Rhodesia

Former name of Zimbabwe.

See also Zimbabwe.

South-West Africa

Former name of Namibia.

See also Namibia.

South West Africa People's Organization

Nationalist organization that became the governing party of independent Namibia; also known as SWAPO.

In the late 1950s Andimba Toivo ja Toivo and other nationalists formed the Ovambo People's Congress, later named the Ovambo People's Organization, or OPO, to protest South Africa's occupation and its discriminatory labor and land policies. In April 1960, seeking to broaden its appeal and thwart rival nationalist groups, it changed its name to the South West Africa People's Organization (SWAPO), and redefined its goal as "the liberation of the Namibian people from colonial oppression and exploitation." The organization described its struggle in terms of class warfare and colonial racial discrimination. Supported by workers and educated youth, SWAPO was dominated by ethnic Ovambos, including its president SAMUEL NUJOMA. The other major nationalist group at the time, dominated by the ethnic HERERO, was the South-West African National Union (SWANU), which sought support among the rural youth. By 1961 SWAPO claimed about 50,000 members, although much of its leadership was either in prison or exile.

Around 1962 SWAPO began sending members overseas for military training, and in 1966 it launched a guerrilla war for independence that lasted twenty-three years. In addition to its armed wing, the People's Liberation Army of Namibia, the party expanded its support base, forming a Women's Council as well as a radical Youth League. It also publicized its campaign internationally through the party paper, the *Namibian News,* and nine overseas offices. In 1973 SWAPO won international recognition as the sole representative of the Namibian people. But in 1976 disagreement about how the party should approach South Africa's offers for an "internal settlement" led to a serious rift in the party, as did the killing and torture of many dissident members throughout the struggle. Still, SWAPO emerged from this crisis the unchallenged leader of the nationalist cause. From the late 1970s onward, Nujoma led SWAPO in both the war effort and international negotiations for Namibian independence, which was achieved in 1990. Its majority position in the country's first parliament increased to 72 percent in 1994 elections. Since independence, SWAPO has opted for a mixed economy, and has done little to challenge the white minority population's hold over much of the country's land and industry.

Eric Young

Souza, Ruth de

1928–

Afro-Brazilian actress who pioneered the participation of Afro-Brazilians in theater, popular films, and television.

Ruth de Souza was born in RIO DE JANEIRO and was popular during the 1940s and 1950s. She was among the first members of the TEATRO EXPERIMENTAL DO NEGRO (Black Experimental Theater), founded by ABDIAS DO NASCIMENTO in 1944. She debuted in Eugene O'Neill's *The Emperor Jones* at Rio's Teatro Municipal and was the first Afro-Brazilian actress to perform there on Brazil's main stage. In 1950 she was awarded a Rockefeller Fellowship to study at the KARAMU HOUSE, a cultural center in Cleveland, Ohio.

De Souza began appearing in Brazilian films in 1947 and became known as one of the greatest actresses in the history of Brazilian film. She was nominated as best actress for her role in *Sinhá Moça* at the Venice Film Festival in 1954, the first Brazilian actress nominated for an international prize. The other nominees included Katherine Hepburn, Michele Morgan, and Lili Palmer, to whom she lost by two points. Starting in 1952, de Souza was one of the pioneers of Brazilian television, act-

ing in the television dramas that were the precursors to Brazil's popular *telenovelas* (soap operas). She was also part of the initial team of actors at Rede Globo, which became one of South America's leading television networks. De Souza had starring roles on television at a time when important roles were extremely rare for Afro-Brazilian actors. In April 1998 the government of Brazil honored de Souza for her lifelong contribution to Brazilian arts and culture.

See also Grande Otelo.

Sowande, Fela

1905–1987

Nigerian composer and jazz musician, an innovator in West African classical or art music.

During the 1950s Fela Sowande gained international recognition as an organist and composer of contemporary art music. He was the first African composer to combine African traditional music with Western classical styles and forms—a development exemplified in his *African Suite* for strings (1952) and *Nigerian Folk Symphony* (1960). According to Nigerian literary scholar Abiola Irele, Sowande's musical style "harks back to the nationalist music of nineteenth-century Europe in its use of Nigerian melodies and rhythms within a work that is conceived essentially along the lines of Western orchestral writing before the contemporary period." In 1986 Sowande's *African Suite* was performed at WOLE SOYINKA's Nobel Prize ceremony in Stockholm, and his work continues to attract a following in both African and Western art music circles.

Born in Oyo, NIGERIA, Sowande spent his youth in LAGOS, NIGERIA. His father, Emmanuel Sowande, was among the early twentieth-century musicians who based church hymns on traditional African music and thus laid the foundation for modern Nigerian art music. After beginning his musical studies in Lagos, Fela Sowande went to England, where he performed as a JAZZ musician to support himself. Music historian Eileen Southern wrote that during the late 1930s he "established himself as one of the leading jazzmen in London and introduced jazz organ to the city, using the Hammond organ." He played in London nightclubs, toured on the vaudeville circuit, and socialized with a number of African American musicians, including jazz pianist THOMAS "FATS" WALLER and cabaret singer Adelaide Hall.

Although Sowande focused his early performing career on jazz, he composed in various genres. During the 1940s he began performing his art compositions publicly at West London's Mission of the Methodist Church, where he served as choirmaster until 1950. In 1944 his orchestral work *Africana* was performed by the BBC Symphony Orchestra. He also pursued studies at Trinity College of Music and London University, where in 1956 he obtained a bachelor's degree in music.

In 1953 Sowande returned to Nigeria. He became musical director of the Nigerian Broadcasting Service and in 1962 founded the Sowande School of Music at Nsukka. He also taught at Nigeria's Ibadan University. He toured widely in the United States and Europe as a lecturer, organist, guest conductor, and composer. His musical nationalism inspired the works of several later Nigerian composers, including AKIN EUBA and AYO BANKOLE.

See also Great Britain.

Roanne Edwards

Soweto, South Africa

South African township near Johannesburg.

Situated 24 km (about 15 mi) to the southwest of JOHANNESBURG in GAUTENG Province, Soweto is one of the largest urban areas in SOUTH AFRICA, with an estimated population of about 1.2 million people. It has also become one of SOUTH AFRICA's most famous townships, mostly due to a massive uprising there in 1976, in which police killed hundreds of protesters. Once a squatter's camp, Soweto became not only a center of the fight against APARTHEID, but also one of the most visible symbols of its brutality.

During the time between World War I (1914–1918) and World War II (1939–1945), rapid industrialization in South Africa sparked a massive migration of rural Africans to Johannesburg, which was the center of the country's mining industry. Many of the migrant workers lived in camps outside of town. In part due to white fears of black self-rule in the squatters' camps, the South African government in 1948 set aside 65 sq km (25 sq mi) of land to accommodate the workers. They built thousands of two-room houses and named the new township Soweto, an abbreviation of the words "South-Western Townships." Its population grew quickly as the result of continued voluntary migration and the new policies of the AFRIKANER-dominated NATIONAL PARTY government, which forcibly resettled blacks into townships.

Poverty, overcrowding, and oppression characterized life in Soweto under apartheid. The former Archbishop DESMOND MPILO TUTU, who lived there in the mid-1970s, recalled that at the time more than one million residents shared a single swimming pool. The schools were ill equipped and underfunded—and increasingly staffed by teachers who had not completed university degrees. The typical house, a home for twelve to fifteen people, lacked both internal plumbing and, until the 1980s, electricity.

By 1976, the year of the uprising, political protest had become an established part of township life, and students were among the most active participants. That year the government's ruling that half the classes in the nation's secondary schools were to be taught in Afrikaans—which many Africans considered the language of the oppressor—led student groups to organize a protest march on June 16, 1976. An estimated 15,000 schoolchildren attended. Most observers now agree that the demonstration was peaceful until police fired a tear gas canister into the crowd, and the children retaliated by throwing rocks. The police opened fire, killing and wounding hundreds of Soweto residents, including many children. The incident set off rioting throughout the country, leading to more than 575 deaths.

Soweto, home to Desmond Tutu, WINNIE MANDIKAZELA-MANDELA, and—after his release—NELSON ROLIHLAHLA MANDELA, continued to be the epicenter of the ANTIAPARTHEID MOVEMENT. Protests continued even after PIETER WILLEM BOTHA cracked down on opposition groups in the 1980s. The political atmosphere became so tense that some Soweto residents suspected of working as informants for the South African government were assaulted or killed, a situation decried by Mandela and others. Since the end of apartheid and Mandela's election as South Africa's first black president in 1994, conditions in Soweto improved somewhat, although poverty, unemployment, and crime remained pressing problems. One of the most dramatic signs of change is that Soweto is now a popular tourist destination, with several local entrepreneurs guiding visitors through a postapartheid Soweto where growing numbers of educated middle class blacks reside.

See also Black Consciousness in Africa.

Kate Tuttle

Soyinka, Wole

1934–

Nigerian playwright, poet, novelist, essayist, and critic who in 1986 became the first African writer and the first black writer to win the Nobel Prize for literature.

When awarding the prize, the Nobel committee described Wole Soyinka, the creator of over twenty major works at that time, as "one of the finest poetical playwrights that have written in English," and also remarked that his writing was "full of life and urgency." Soyinka (pronounced Sho-yin-ka) is the recipient of numerous other prestigious awards, including several honorary doctorates from universities throughout the world. Apart from his stature as a pioneer in African drama written in English, Soyinka has produced a vast body of work—as poet, dramatist, theater director, novelist, essayist, autobiographer, political commentator, critic, and theorist of art and culture. Above all, he has remained a responsible citizen committed to the values of human freedom, truth, and justice. "Social commitment," he remarks, "is a citizen's commitment and embraces equally the carpenter, the mason, the banker, the farmer, the customs officer, etc., not forgetting the critic. I accept a general citizen's commitment which only happens to express itself through art and words." From his earliest work to the present, spanning over forty years, Soyinka has retained a remarkable consistency of vision in his dedication as an artist and as a socially responsible citizen.

Wole Soyinka's vast creative talent is expressed in some sixteen published plays—comedies, tragedies, and satires. His

Portrait of Nobel Prize for Literature winner Wole Soyinka during the ceremony at UNESCO. *Langevin Jacques/Corbis Sygma*

early play, *A Dance of the Forests* (1960), was written on the occasion of Nigeria's independence and includes his characteristic watchful irony and a warning to avoid romanticizing the past, as the Nigerian people and leaders forge a future for the new nation. *Death and the King's Horseman* (1975) typifies his imaginative engagement with tradition. *Priority Projects* (1982) are satirical agitprop (literary propaganda) sketches, written and performed with the University of Ife Guerrilla Theatre Unit. His play *The Beatification of Area Boy: A Lagosian Kaleidoscope* (1996) is about the survival of the underclass in a deteriorating urban landscape around LAGOS. Soyinka has created dramatic and memorable characters including Elesin Oba, Iyaloja, Eman, Kongi, Sidi, Sadiku, as well as the autobiographically inspired figures of his mother ("The Wild Christian") and his father ("Essay") in *Ake: The Years of Childhood* (1981). He has published four volumes of poetry, the most recent entitled *Mandela's Earth and Other Poems* (1988) with the striking opening lines, "Your logic frightens me, Mandela . . . Your bounty . . . that taut/Drumskin on your heart on which our millions/dance." His three collections of essays include *Myth, Literature and the African World* (1976); *Art, Dialogue*

and Outrage: Essays on Literature and Culture (1988); and most recently, *The Open Sore of a Continent: A Personal Narrative of the Nigerian Crisis* (1996). Soyinka has also written lyrics and musical compositions for a record album, *Unlimited Liability Company*, with songs such as "Ethike Revolution" and "I Love My Country" that are, like his newspaper articles, topical, hard-hitting, and responsive to particular situations.

An artist to the core—indeed, a cultural worker in the best tradition—Soyinka is deeply rooted in the African tradition of an artist who functions as the voice of vision of his times. He is not afraid to take action when necessary; he is never merely a commentator from the sidelines, and never untrue to the demands of his craft, whether his work is in the form of a poem, an essay, or a play. Indeed, in Soyinka one discovers the remarkable fusing of the creative and the political. He invents new ways (often misunderstood by his critics) of linking the mythic and political, and of forging imaginative links between harsh political realities and cosmological, spiritual realms.

Soyinka is a member of the YORUBA, one of the largest ethnic groups in Nigeria, and he has strong roots in the Yoruba culture and worldview. Although his parents, Ayo and Eniola, had converted to CHRISTIANITY, Soyinka himself never embraced the Christian religion, feeling more at home with traditional Yoruba religion; he is a personal devotee of the Yoruba god Ogun, who also figures prominently in his writings. Soyinka describes Ogun as "god of creativity, guardian of the road, god of metallic lore and artistry. Explorer, hunter, god of war . . . custodian of the sacred oath." Changing historical times enable creative redefinitions of roles played by anthropomorphized deities like Ogun. Today, Ogun, as god of iron and the forge, is worshiped not only by blacksmiths, but also by truck drivers and airline pilots—all workers in metal.

In addition to his Yoruba-Christian upbringing, Soyinka received a Western academic education. Born Akinwande Oluwole Soyinka near ABEOKUTA, NIGERIA, Soyinka began his Western schooling in the Nigeria of the 1930s and 1940s, when it was still ruled by British colonists. He spent two years (1952–1954) at the newly established University College of Ibadan (now the University of Ibadan), where his classmates included CHINUA ACHEBE, CHRISTOPHER OKIGBO, and JOHN PEPPER CLARK, all of whom later made their mark in Nigerian literature. He then earned a B.A. degree from the University of Leeds (1954–1957) in GREAT BRITAIN. He spent a year as a play reader at the Royal Court Theatre in London (1958–1959) and returned to Nigeria in 1960 on a Rockefeller Fellowship for the study of Nigerian traditions and culture.

Through his education, Soyinka absorbed the Western intellectual tradition, but in his writing he comes across first and foremost as a Yoruba, and it is from a base in Yoruba culture—his inspiration—that he responds to other literary and cultural traditions. His art is eclectic, a successful blend of African themes with Western forms and techniques. In his hands, African traditions assume meanings that are much wider than the ones accepted within their geographical location. "We must not think that traditionalism means raffia skirts," Soyinka has remarked. "It's no longer possible for a purist literature for the simple reason that even our most traditional literature has never been purist."

Just as Soyinka confronts African "traditionalism" in the narrow sense, he also recognizes the irony of using the English language—a lingering legacy of colonialism. However, he is never apologetic about this matter; rather, he proudly accepts the challenge of making the English language "carry the weight," as Achebe puts it, "of [his] African experience. But it will have to be a new English, still in full communion with its ancestral home, but altered to suit its new African surroundings . . . The price a world language must be prepared to pay is submission to many different kinds of use." The role of English as a link language among people with various indigenous languages is certainly a historical reality in postcolonial societies. Language itself becomes a weapon for writers like Achebe, Soyinka, and others from the developing world to confront the disruptive remnants of colonialism and the negative continuities of neocolonialism in contemporary times.

Along with adapting the English language to his African experience, Soyinka optimally uses his education to transform literary forms from their European origins—often problematically considered universal—to suit his own cultural reality. In such dramas as *The Road* (1965) and *Death and the King's Horseman,* Soyinka presents a new form: Yoruba tragedy that departs in significant ways from Western dramatic forms, such as Greek or Shakespearean tragedy. In this form, ritual, masquerade, dance, music, and mythopoeic language all work toward the very purpose of Yoruba tragedy, which is communal benefit.

Soyinka's contribution to Nigerian drama has gone beyond his considerable achievement as a playwright to his key role in professionalizing the English-language theater in Nigeria, forming companies such as the 1960 Masks and the Orisun Theatre. The history of English-language professional theater in Nigeria is related integrally to Soyinka's dramatic career. There is a clear correspondence between the timing of his plays and the prevalent political climate. Biting satirical plays such as *The Trials of Brother Jero* (1963), *Opera Wonyosi* (1981), *Kongi's Harvest* (1965), and *A Play of Giants: A Fantasia on the Aminian Theme* (1984) indict African presidents-for-life (such as IDI AMIN) as a "parade of monsters." Most recently, *The Beatification of Area Boy: A Lagosian Kaleidoscope* (1996), theatrically enacts the survival of the urban underclass under SANI ABACHA's military regime.

Soyinka has the unique capacity not simply to write about social injustice in his creative work, but to meet the challenge and be an activist whenever necessary. There is no contradiction between Soyinka the artist, imaginatively exploring metaphysical matters in his creative work, and Soyinka the engaged citizen, commenting on Nigerian sociopolitical issues. He is concerned with the quality of public life and speaks openly as the conscience of his nation. (An example of Soyinka's civic activism and his attempt to improve the safety of road travel in Nigeria was his establishment of the Oyo Road Safety Corps in 1980.) His incarceration for nearly two years (although he was never formally charged or tried) during the Nigerian civil war

(1967–1970) was a painful manifestation of his attempt to redress "the colossal moral failure" in the nation. "The man dies in all who keep silent in the face of tyranny," he remarks in his prison notes, entitled *The Man Died* (1972). Soyinka considers "justice . . . the first condition of humanity" and recognizes that "books and all forms of writing have always been objects of terror to those who seek to suppress truth."

Soyinka's deep and energetic concern for his country has remained unflagging over the past forty years of his literary career. He has always been a stern and uncompromising critic of social injustice, whoever the perpetrators might be. He roundly criticized YAKUBU GOWON's military government in *The Man Died,* just as he criticized Shehu Shagari's "civilian" government in *Priority Projects* (1982) and Sani Abacha's military rule in *The Open Sore of a Continent.*

Soyinka's artistic vision, even as it engages with Nigeria, encompasses a universal scope. "A historic vision is of necessity universal," he remarked in "The Writer in an African State," a 1967 essay. In *The Open Sore of a Continent,* even as he explores the troubled notion of the nation in Nigeria, he makes links to similar crises of nationhood in Yugoslavia and the Soviet Union. He asks directly and poignantly, "what price a nation?" especially when atrocities are committed in the name of "national protection, sovereignty, [and] development." His personal voice—bitter, angry, anguished—recognizes the traps of nationhood when the state acts as a repressive force crushing those who dissent. Soyinka's criticism of Abacha's brutal regime in the mid-1990s led to a close government scrutiny of all his activities. The government's repression forced him into exile from 1994 until 1998, when democratic reforms began in Nigeria under General Abdulsalam Abubakar.

Like Ogun, god of the forge, Soyinka's creativity and courage blaze paths toward democratic ideals and social justice in Nigeria. "I have one abiding religion, human liberty," he has remarked. With his passion for freedom, with his deep concern for the quality of human life, Soyinka's work has profound significance in contemporary world literature. Wole Soyinka has held teaching positions at several universities, including Harvard, Yale, and Cornell. In 1996 he was the Robert W. Woodruff Professor of the Arts at Emory University in ATLANTA, GEORGIA. He currently teaches and collaborates in artistic productions, creative writing, and other programs at the university.

See also Decolonialization in Africa: An Interpretation.

Ketu Katrak

Spain

Country in southwestern Europe where blacks have had a presence for centuries.

Black Africans have inhabited the Iberian Peninsula since the beginnings of recorded history. Blacks accompanied the Carthaginians when they colonized the Iberian Peninsula in the fifth century B.C.E. and blacks, both free and enslaved, were present in the social life of the Roman province of Spain.

Throughout the Middle Ages, both Christian and Muslim states on the peninsula enslaved black Africans. Moors, a people from northern Africa, provided most of the troops for the Muslim conquest of the Iberian Peninsula (711–718). Although the Arab ruling minority claimed political power under the caliphate of Cordoba (850–1033), the Moorish majority pushed for most of the changes in the emerging new society. The cultural life of al-Andalus, as Muslim Spain was known, helped shape modern Spanish society. Black African slaves, as well as gold transported across the SAHARA, contributed to the wealth of Muslim Spain. Records indicate that Christian bishops in Catalonia purchased black slaves as early as the tenth century. In the eleventh century King Alfonso VI of Castile and León sponsored the arrival of the French clergy of Cluny to his kingdom with donations of gold from West Africa.

In Muslim Spain, after the fall of the Córdoba caliphate, a series of invasions and immigrations from northwestern Africa—led by the ALMORAVIDS and ALMOHADS—brought significant numbers of blacks to Iberian soil. Black troops in the Almoravid army of Yusuf helped deal a serious defeat to Alfonso VI in the battle of Sagrejas. The Moorish political ascendancy in the Iberian Peninsula lasted until the final defeat in 1492 of the kingdom of Granada by the Catholic monarchs Isabella and Ferdinand.

The Atlantic expansion of the kingdom of Castile in the fifteenth century dramatically affected the business of slavery. PORTUGAL and Spain established modern slavery in the West through the forced importation of an almost exclusively black African work force first to the Iberian Peninsula, then to the CAPE VERDE ISLANDS, and finally to the Americas after 1492. The diaries of Christopher Columbus reveal an early connection between the enslavement of Africans and the possible enslavement of the indigenous inhabitants of the New World.

The forced relocation of black Africans to Renaissance Spain provoked changes in Spanish society. Discriminatory policies alternated with measures for the Africans' welfare. In 1478 Ferdinand and Isabella appointed Juan de Valladolid, "black of high birth in his nation," as judge of blacks in Seville—a position similar to the ones existing in Portugal to police the increasing urban black population. Black religious guilds and confraternities (cofradías de negros) also appeared in the major cities such as Valencia, Barcelona, Seville, and Jaén. These confraternities followed the model of the trade guilds that then existed throughout Europe. Confraternities were among the most popular forms of civil association in Spanish society. For the black population they were the only means of acquiring social recognition for the group and for its members. These groups provided mutual help and religious association like other confraternities of the day, but because of the nature of slavery as an institution, black confraternities were always under suspicion and faced staunch opposition and rejection from their white counterparts.

In Seville, the city with the largest black population in Spain during the Renaissance, blacks were frequently denied proper burial. Recent archaeological discoveries have unearthed literal dumping grounds outside the old city walls for people who were of African descent. The *Cofradía de los negritos* fought for space in churches allotted to their members for proper religious burial. The religious education of enslaved blacks was the responsibility of their owners, who often favored or discriminated against slaves according to their show of religious devotion. The Inquisition also persecuted black slaves; most were accused of blasphemy. In many cases, abused black slaves resorted to blasphemy because they believed that Inquisition authorities would treat them more mercifully than their masters.

The discovery and conquest of America by the Spaniards propelled the demographic revolution of modern slavery. Portugal, through its African colonies and *feitorias* (trading posts), provided slaves to private individuals to whom the king of Spain granted special licenses—*licencias* and later *asientos*—to import slaves to America and the Spanish mainland. SUGAR plantations in the Canary Islands were the forerunners of the Caribbean system of labor, which relied on contingents of African slaves. Seville, as the center of commerce in the new American colonies, became one of Europe's foremost slave ports, second only to Lisbon. Muslim prisoners and victims of slaving raids from North Africa—present-day ALGERIA and TUNISIA—were also living in captivity on Spanish soil during the sixteenth and seventeenth centuries.

The West African slave trade, however, soon became the main source of a captive labor force in Spanish society, to the extent that the Spanish word *negro* (meaning "black") became synonymous with "slave." Slave owners belonged to all sectors of society, from the aristocracy to the clergy, artisans, businessmen, and wealthy peasants. At the end of the sixteenth century in Seville and its surrounding area, more than 14,000 slaves were counted out of a total population of 150,000. Estimates for that period suggest that 100,000 slaves lived in Spain, of whom the majority were black. African slaves were generally employed to perform unsafe and difficult tasks. Women, for instance, were hired out by their owners to make soap or to sell produce in the streets. Their masters forced many into prostitution, although it was illegal. Male slaves typically worked in taverns and gambling houses, where violence erupted frequently. Black slaves were on the staff of the printing houses in Seville that sent the first books to the Americas. But most slaves, male and female, were employed both as agricultural workers and domestic servants.

Life for black Africans was harder than for any other group in Spanish society. Malnutrition, physical exhaustion, and punishment was their common lot. In larger cities special quarters existed for blacks, both free and in bondage, since some masters did not allow slaves to live with them, and officials sought to keep blacks separate from the white population. Escape was very difficult in a hostile society, and punishment for it very harsh, in the form of lashes, branding, and amputations.

Free blacks had little opportunity to advance in society because they were excluded from almost every trade and profession. Laws and local ordinances limited the access of blacks to professional ranks, the church hierarchy, convents for women, universities, and practically all legitimate trade guilds. Various cities enacted laws limiting the movement of blacks, both free

Portrait of painter Juan de Pareja by Diego Rodriquez de Silva y Velázquez. *The Metropolitan Museum of Art, Fletcher Fund, Rogers Fund, and Bequest of Miss Adelaide Milton de Groot (1876–1967), by exchange, supplemented by gifts from friends of the Museum, 1971. Photograph © 1981 The Metropolitan Museum of Art*

ebrations. The influence of African music and dance in Spain during the Renaissance was formidable, and it crossed the Atlantic to Mexico, PERU, the Caribbean, and elsewhere. The *zarabanda* (saraband) was blamed for the decay in morals, and the *chacona* (chaconne), *mozambique, guineo, zamba,* and dozens of other dancing rhythms influenced popular music on both sides of the ocean.

Most importation of African slaves to Spain ended in the early seventeenth century, when Portugal lost its control of the coast of Guinea to the Dutch and the Spanish economy began to decline. Seville's commercial monopoly in the colonies eroded, and it lost its position as a slave trade center. The price of black slaves became too expensive in relation to free labor. The remaining population of African descent ceased to be a distinct group within a few generations. The Spanish Crown tried to establish diplomatic ties with the kingdom of Allada (in present-day BENIN), and Capuchin missionaries were sent there in the 1660s. The mission failed when the king of Allada realized that he would not obtain commercial benefits in the short term.

By the eighteenth century the West African slave trade had shifted almost exclusively to the Americas. The only regular supply of slaves to Spain during the eighteenth century came from North Africa—MOROCCO, ALGERIA, and TUNISIA—in the course of the continuous wars between Spain and North African states. Combatants on both sides of the Mediterranean enslaved prisoners of war well into the late eighteenth century, when warfare began to give way to diplomatic missions between King Carlos III of Spain and the Sultan of Morocco.

Intermarriage after manumission and merger within a few generations with the nonblack population led to the disappearance of a significant black population in Spain by the mid-eighteenth century. The absence of large plantations for the cultivation of sugar, cotton, coffee, and tobacco, or even extensive mining limited the demand for slave labor in Spain. The local supply of free labor also competed successfully with slaves (whose purchase and maintenance could be expensive). In cities like Seville, Madrid, Jaen, or Valladolid, religious confraternities of blacks—both free and enslaved—saw the numbers of their brothers dwindle. As among the descendants of Spanish Jews, there was little incentive among the descendants of black Spaniards to preserve the memory of their African origins. Black African ancestry had been a severe social handicap in Spain for centuries.

The only new group of Africans to arrive to Spain in the eighteenth century were escapees from the southern Portuguese region of Alentejo. They crossed the Spanish border and established themselves in the towns of Gibraleón and Niebla, in western Andalusia. As in the American colonies, the govern-

and enslaved. Laws prohibited blacks in most cases from carrying weapons either in cities or in the countryside at a time when violent crime was rampant, especially in cities like Madrid or Seville. Laws of *limpieza de sangre,* or "purity of blood" permitted legal discrimination against anyone of black African descent.

Many free blacks decided to emigrate to America soon after the conquest. One of them, Juan Garrido, introduced wheat to MEXICO when Hernán Cortés conquered the country (1519–1521). Other blacks who achieved fame in their time were the sixteenth-century scholar and humanist Juan Latino, author of the *Austriad,* an epic poem written in Latin, and the seventeenth-century painter, Juan de Pareja.

Blacks made a major impact on Spanish culture during the Golden Age (c. 1500–1681). Contemporary writers portrayed the presence of blacks in a variety of ways. The playwright Lope de Vega created the first full dramatic roles for black men and women, both as comic-relief characters and as protagonists. Imported from Portugal, black speech—*lengua de negro*—was used as a typical form of characterization. Blacks were also hired as dancers and entertainers in religious pageants and cel-

In the *Chessbook* of Alfonso X of Castile, dating from 1283, a Muslim nobleman plays chess with a black servant. *Image of the Black Project, Harvard University*

ment established special military companies comprised entirely of black soldiers employed in defending and patrolling the border with Portugal along the Guadiana River. The descendants of these eighteenth-century blacks who fled slavery in Portugal still constitute the only group of established Spaniards who trace their ancestry back to sub-Saharan Africa.

Spain never officially abolished slavery. Although the government signed treaties with Great Britain to abolish the slave trade, Spain did not free slaves when they entered the European part of the empire, a practice followed in other European countries. Thus slave owners from CUBA and PUERTO RICO who traveled back to Spain with black slaves did not lose them when they touched Spanish soil. The 1870 Moret Law, which proclaimed the gradual abolition of slavery in the Caribbean colonies, was the first document to suppress the institution legally. Restrictions imposed by the Spanish government successfully blocked any massive immigration of black colonial subjects to Spain. After the loss of Cuba and Puerto Rico in 1898, this possibility became even more remote.

During the Spanish Civil War (1936–1939), General Francisco Franco's Nationalists employed Moroccan troops. These soldiers, however, were purposely isolated from the rest of society and were seen as a sort of occupying force—ironically, from one of Spain's few remaining colonies. Spain's other remaining colony in Africa was the territory known as Spanish Guinea. After 1959 the black population of Spanish Guinea gained equal legal standing with whites. This facilitated the migration of many to Spain seeking work and higher education. The Catholic Church aided many Guineans in obtaining grants to study in Spain. Profound political and economic instability followed the independence of the new republic of EQUATORIAL GUINEA in 1968, partly caused by the actions of different factions in the Spanish government of General Franco. Large num-

bers of Equatorial Guineans chose exile in Spain, many as dual citizens. They still compose the largest single national group of African descent in Spain today. Their acceptance by Spanish society is lukewarm at best, even though they share language, religion, and culture with the Spanish white majority.

Spanish society underwent a remarkable transformation during the 1970s. After General Franco's death in 1975 and the installation of a democratic regime in 1977, the Spanish economy, once so weak that its surplus work force had to emigrate to northern Europe, now needed immigrants to fill low-wage jobs. The agricultural sectors of eastern Andalusia and Catalonia employed thousands of undocumented African immigrants, mostly from the Maghreb countries—Morocco, Algeria, Tunisia, and MAURITANIA—and from the West African states of SENEGAL, GHANA, SIERRA LEONE, and NIGERIA. These workers face severe housing shortages and discrimination from the majority population. The 1984 Spanish film *Las cartas de Alou* (Letters from Alou), by Montxo Armendáriz, was one of the first attempts by a Spanish artist to address the new issues of African immigration to Spain.

In addition to African immigrants, Dominican citizens of African descent, mostly women, have traveled to Spain seeking domestic employment in the houses of the Spanish urban middle class. They form a growing group of workers, together with Equatorial Guinean women, who are employed in domestic work because of their Spanish-language ability. Their lack of legal rights and vulnerability to deportation, as in many more affluent countries, make them victims of physical and sexual abuse as well as economic exploitation.

The substantial presence of black African and Maghrebi citizens has challenged certain monolithic cultural and religious traditions. There are more practicing Muslims in Spain today than at any time since 1492. With Spain's integration into the

European Union in 1986, which was followed by rising unemployment, the government adopted measures to stop the arrival of undocumented workers. Attacks against Africans and people of African descent have occurred, and non-governmental organizations and immigrant associations continually challenge discriminatory practices and forced repatriations of so-called illegal workers, mostly African.

A new generation of Afro-Spaniards is growing in numbers: the Spanish Constitution of 1978 confers automatic citizenship to all born on Spanish soil. The present population of African descent in Spain was estimated in 1998 at over half a million—as a proportion of the Spanish population, the highest since the Middle Ages.

See also Transatlantic Slave Trade; Trans-Saharan and Red Sea Slave Trade.

Bibliography

Cornelius, Wayne A. "Spain: The Uneasy Transition from Labor Exporter to Labor Importer." In *Controlling Immigration: A Global Perspective.* Edited by Wayne A. Cornelius, Philip L. Martin, and James F. Hollifield. Stanford University Press, 1994.

Cortés López, José Luis. *La esclavitud negra en la España peninsular del siglo XVI.* Ediciones Universidad de Salamanca, 1989.

Domínguez Ortiz, Antonio. "La esclavitud en Castilla durante la Edad Moderna." In *Estudios de historia social de España.* 2 vols. Edited by Carmelo Viñas y Mey. C.S.I.C., 1952.

Baltasar Fra-Molinero

Spanish-American War, African Americans in the

War between the United States and Spain in 1898 in which the United States Army's four black regiments played a prominent role.

The Spanish-American War began in April 1898 when the United States intervened in the CUBAN WAR OF INDEPENDENCE (1895–1898; also known as the Spanish-Cuban-American War), and actual hostilities lasted until the surrender of Spanish forces in August. The Paris Treaty, signed on December 10 of that year, formally brought the war to a close and an end to Spain's colonial empire.

In the Spanish-American War, as in the AMERICAN CIVIL WAR (1861–1865), WORLD WAR I (1914–1918), and WORLD WAR II (1939–1945), black involvement served to challenge the American racial status quo because African Americans were involved from the very start. When the battleship USS *Maine* exploded in the harbor of HAVANA, CUBA, on February 15, 1898, there were twenty-two blacks among the 266 fatalities. Although a 1976 United States Navy inquiry headed by Admiral Hyman

Rickover concluded that the sinking of the *Maine* was most likely due to the sparking of coal dust in one of the ship's holds, Americans in 1898 viewed it as an act of Spanish sabotage. As the U.S. Army mobilized, its four black regiments—the 9th Cavalry, 10th Cavalry, 24th Infantry, and 25th Infantry—stood at the forefront.

In March the army transferred the 25th Infantry from Montana to Dry Tortugas Island, located between Key West, Florida, and CUBA. On April 14 the 9th Cavalry, 10th Cavalry, and 24th Infantry left their stations in the west for southern staging areas. Their leading role was a product of the widely held but ill-grounded belief that African Americans were immune to tropical diseases. Aware of the health hazards that its men would face in Cuba, the army turned to its black regiments. There was, in any case, no shortage of manpower, black or white. The war was popular and hundreds of thousands volunteered.

Since African Americans were generally barred from existing state militias, several states—among them Alabama, Illinois, Indiana, Kansas, North Carolina, Ohio, and Virginia—hastily organized all-black regiments. In addition, the Congress of the United States authorized the army to raise ten new regiments, four of which were for black recruits. The volunteers, however, never completed their training in time to see action in the ten-week war. The regular army bore the brunt of the fighting, with the nation's four black regiments playing a key role.

Many blacks hoped that loyal service might win their race better treatment. As the *Boston Evening Transcript* reported, they thought that "willingness to die on an equality with white men [gave] them the claim to live on something like an equality with them." Some black soldiers took the opportunity to act on such principles. In Macon, Georgia, black soldiers cut down a tree well known as a site for lynchings and destroyed a sign that declared "No Dogs and Niggers Allowed." In Tampa, Florida, members of the 24th and 25th regiments attacked soldiers from an Ohio unit who were using a two-year-old black boy for target practice by competing to see who could come closest without harming the child.

In Cuba black soldiers distinguished themselves in combat. The 24th Infantry played a key role in the charge up San Juan Hill on July 1, 1898. The 10th Cavalry and 25th Infantry fought well in the Battle of El Caney, which took place that same day. Most significantly, in the war's first battle, on June 23, 1898, at Las Guâsimas, the 10th Cavalry was conspicuous in relieving the First Volunteer Cavalry Regiment, better known as the Rough Riders, when it was pinned down by enemy fire. Future American president Theodore Roosevelt, one of the beleaguered Rough Riders, later declared, "I don't think any Rough Rider will ever forget the tie that binds us to the . . . 10th Cavalry." The 10th Cavalry's regimental quartermaster, Captain John J. Pershing, acquired the nickname "Black Jack" through his service with African American troops; he later served as the American commander in World War I.

Ironically, one by-product of victory in the war was the gradual exclusion of African Americans from the U.S. Navy. Blacks had accounted for 10 to 15 percent of naval manpower throughout the nineteenth century. Even though they had increasingly been relegated to menial roles in galleys and boiler rooms since the 1870s, blacks served on racially integrated ships. After the Spanish-American War, however, the U.S. Navy began recruiting its messmen in the newly acquired Philippines, and by the early twentieth century blacks accounted for only about 5 percent of naval manpower.

James Sellman

Spanish Abolitionist Society

See Sociedad Abolicionista Española.

Spanish Black Codes

See Black Codes in Latin America.

Spanish Guinea

Former name of Equatorial Guinea.

See also Equatorial Guinea.

Spanish Sahara

Former name of Western Sahara.

See also Western Sahara.

Spasm Bands

Ensembles of black children who improvised music on the streets of New Orleans, Louisiana.

At the turn of the twentieth century, spasm bands roamed the Storyville district of NEW ORLEANS, adding to the hodgepodge of musical styles that filled the city's air. Adolescent boys brandished kitchen utensils, fiddles, whistles, harmonicas, cowbells, brass, gourds, kazoos, ukuleles, guitars, drums, and crude, jerry-built instruments. Some musicians punctuated their performances with yells of "hi-de-ho, ho-de-ho," while others danced and did headstands as part of the act.

Often spasm bands played in front of brothels and gambling joints, mischievously drowning out the music from within. Although the sound of these spontaneous groups reflected more novelty than skill, spasm bands contributed to the creative, synthetic milieu of New Orleans from which JAZZ emerged.

Bibliography
Barker, D. *A Life in Jazz*. Edited by A. Shipton. Macmillan, 1986.

Eric Bennett

Spaulding, Charles Clinton

1874–1952

American entrepreneur, leader of the North Carolina Mutual Life Insurance Company.

In 1923 C. C. Spaulding became president of NORTH CAROLINA MUTUAL LIFE INSURANCE COMPANY, which became the largest insurer of African Americans in the United States. His reorganization plan for the company enabled it to survive the GREAT DEPRESSION, during which Spaulding served on state and federal relief committees, attempting to ensure equitable distribution of relief services for African Americans. In his home city of Durham he worked to register African American voters and convinced the city to hire African American police officers. Spaulding also served as a trustee for HOWARD UNIVERSITY, Shaw University, and North Carolina College.

Bibliography
Franklin, John Hope, and August Meier, eds. *Black Leaders of the Twentieth Century*. University of Illinois Press, 1982.

Robert Fay

Speke, John Hanning

1827–1864

British explorer who was the first European to discover the correct source of the Nile River.

Born in Bideford, Devon, England, John Hanning Speke began serving in the British Indian Army at age seventeen. After serving in Punjab, he explored the Himalayas and then took a leave from the army to hunt in AFRICA.

In 1855 Speke accompanied explorer RICHARD BURTON to Somaliland (present-day SOMALIA). When their party was attacked by Somalis, Burton was wounded and Speke was captured and stabbed eleven times, bringing the expedition to an abrupt end. In 1856 the two men met again in ZANZIBAR and headed for the Great Lakes region of East Africa, determined to find the source of the NILE RIVER.

By the time they reached LAKE TANGANYIKA in February 1858, Burton was too ill to continue so Speke, although also sick, went on alone. He arrived in July on the shores of Ukerewe, a vast body of water that he renamed LAKE VICTORIA. When local inhabitants told him that the waters of the lake flowed out rather than in, Speke concluded it was the source of the Nile.

Lacking significant evidence, Speke's claim was disputed by Burton and others. Speke returned in 1860 to map portions of the lake, accompanied by his longtime army friend James Grant. Traveling alone through the region in 1862, Speke came to the court of MUTESA I, the king of BUGANDA. Three months later, Speke claimed to have discovered the actual outlet to the Nile, which he named Ripon Falls. Local warfare prevented him, however, from tracing the river north.

In 1864 Speke and Burton, now estranged, were invited to debate Speke's claims at a highly publicized meeting of the Royal Geographical Society. The morning of the debate, however, Speke shot himself dead while hunting, apparently by accident. Burton wrote his friend Frank Wilson, "The charitable say that he shot himself, the uncharitable that I shot him."

Ari Nave

Spelman College

Prestigious historically black college located in Atlanta, Georgia; the oldest black women's college in the United States.

Spelman College asserts that "since 1881, Spelman has sought to develop the total woman; to help our students discover their own power—and to prepare them to wield that power in a positive way." Spelman was founded by two white New England missionaries, Sophia Packard and Harriet Giles, who were concerned about the lack of educational opportunities for Southern black women. In 1881 they raised enough money from a Massachusetts church and the Women's American Baptist Home Missionary Society to open their new school, and the first classes of the Atlanta Baptist Female Seminary, as it was originally called, met in a church basement with eleven students. Three months later the enrollment had grown to eighty, and within a year, 200 women ranging in age from fifteen to fifty-two attended the school.

On an 1882 fund-raising trip Giles and Packard received a donation from American industrialist John D. Rockefeller that helped finance the school's move into a building of its own. Two years later Rockefeller made another contribution that helped stop a proposed merger with a nearby men's institution, the Atlanta Baptist Seminary (later MOREHOUSE COLLEGE). The school was renamed Spelman Seminary after Rockefeller's wife, Laura Spelman Rockefeller. By this time the school included normal, industrial, and college preparatory departments. A nurse training department opened in 1886, a missionary training department in 1891, and a college department in 1897. In 1901 Spelman granted its first two college degrees.

In 1924 the school officially changed its name to Spelman College. In the mid-1920s enough college-level courses were offered and enough students were enrolled in the college program that Spelman began phasing out other departments. By 1930 its focus was solely on liberal arts education. In 1929 Spelman chose to affiliate its financial and administrative sources with Morehouse College and Atlanta University, making those three schools the founding members of what became Atlanta University Center, the consortium of ATLANTA's black colleges and universities.

Spelman's first four presidents were all white women, as were the majority of its instructors for its first four decades. Beginning in the 1920s, larger numbers of black women—including many Spelman graduates—were hired as faculty; by 1937 they outnumbered white teachers two to one, and even-tually the faculty became predominantly African American, including both women and men. The college's first black president, Alfred E. Manley, took office in 1953.

During the CIVIL RIGHTS MOVEMENT of the 1950s and 1960s, Spelman students were among the cofounders of the STUDENT NONVIOLENT COORDINATING COMMITTEE (SNCC), and many others participated in Atlanta-area SIT-INS and boycotts. In 1976 students locked Spelman's board of trustees in their boardroom for twenty hours to protest the appointment of Donald Steward as the college's next president, arguing that it was time for Spelman to be led by a black woman. Eleven years later that hope finally came to pass when Johnnetta Betsch Cole, the popular "Sister President," became the college's seventh president.

In 1988 African American entertainer BILL COSBY and his wife Camille gave Spelman a widely publicized $20 million gift. In the 1990s Spelman received national attention for its role as a site of the 1996 Olympic Games in Atlanta and for its recognition, by a leading poll of American colleges and universities, as the best liberal arts college in the South. Spelman alumnae include Pulitzer Prize–winning author ALICE WALKER, attorney and children's rights advocate MARIAN WRIGHT EDELMAN, former Acting Surgeon General Audrey Manley, and many physicians, attorneys, educators, and other professionals. In 2000, 1,899 women were enrolled at Spelman.

See also Colleges and Universities, Historically Black, in the United States.

Bibliography

Guy-Sheftall, Beverly, and Jo Moore Stewart. *Spelman: A Centennial Celebration.* Delmar, 1981.

Manley, Albert E. *A Legacy Continues: The Manley Years at Spelman College, 1953–1976.* University Press of America, 1995.

Read, Florence. *The Story of Spelman College.* Atlanta, 1961.

Lisa Clayton Robinson

Spencer, Anne

1882–1975

American writer and Harlem Renaissance poet whose work combined nineteenth-century and modernist literary traditions.

Annie Bethel Bannister was born in Henry County, Virginia. She spent her early years with a foster family while her mother, Sarah Scales, separated from her husband Joel Bannister, worked nearby as a cook. At age eleven she began formal schooling in the Virginia Seminary in Lynchburg under the name Annie Scales. With her first poem "The Skeptic" (1896), Scales revealed the independent thinking that would characterize her life and work. She graduated in 1899, taught for two years in West Virginia, and then returned to Lynchburg to marry Edward Spencer and raise their children Bethel Calloway, Alroy Sarah, and Chauncey Edward.

During this time Spencer cultivated her poetry as well as her famous garden. When NATIONAL ASSOCIATION FOR THE ADVANCEMENT OF COLORED PEOPLE (NAACP) activist JAMES WELDON JOHNSON visited her in 1917, he convinced her that she ought to publish, and "Before the Feast of Shushan" appeared in the February 1920 issue of THE CRISIS. For the next twenty years her voice was heard in every collection of African American poetry.

Spencer's poetry invokes biblical and mythological allusions to speak of beauty in a decaying world. Her writing has been described as depicting a private vision, and she often employed images of the natural world. Despite the apparent influences of literary romanticism, Spencer has often been characterized as modernist, both for her complex style and her contemporary feminist concerns. She worked powerfully with detailed, focused images: a woman's hand, "Twisted, awry, like crumpled roots,/ bleached poor white in a sudsy tub," portrays the condition of women in "Lady, Lady."

Spencer's political activism in Lynchburg attested to her commitment to African American equality. She agitated for the hiring of African American teachers at the local segregated high school, she refused to ride segregated public transportation, and she initiated an African American library, where she worked from 1923 to 1945. Her garden home became a Southern locus for prominent African Americans, visited regularly by such guests as W. E. B. DU BOIS, PAUL ROBESON, and LANGSTON HUGHES. In the mid-1930s Spencer moved out of public life and lived as a recluse until her death in 1975.

Marian Aguiar

Spingarn Family

Two white brothers, Joel E. and Arthur B., and Joel's wife, Amy, all of whom were important participants in the National Association for the Advancement of Colored People (NAACP) during the first half of the twentieth century.

For information on
Activities of Joel E. Spingarn: *See* Amenia Conference of 1916; Amenia Conference of 1933; Pickens, William.
Book dedicated to the two brothers: *See* Downing, Henry F(rancis).
Collection of books by Arthur B. Spingarn: *See* Collectors of African American Books; Howard University; French, William P.; Moorland-Spingarn Research Collection.
Establishment of prizes for accomplishments in the arts funded by Amy Spingarn: *See* Harlem Renaissance: The Vogue of the New Negro.

Spinks, Leon

1953–

American boxer and heavyweight gold medal winner in the 1976 Summer Olympic Games.

Leon Spinks was born in St. Louis, Missouri. He served in the Marines before winning a spot on the Olympic BOXING team. He won the heavyweight gold medal in the 1976 Summer Olympic Games in Montréal, an accomplishment matched by his younger brother, Michael, in the middleweight division.

After turning professional in 1977, Spinks was unbeaten in his first eight bouts. In February 1978 he stunned the boxing world by taking the world heavyweight title from MUHAMMAD ALI in a fifteen-round decision. After losing to Ali in a rematch in September of 1978, Spinks was not able to duplicate his earlier success. By 1986 Spinks was forced to file for bankruptcy, after which he worked at a bar in DETROIT, MICHIGAN.

Spinks continued to box in the late 1980s and early 1990s, with mediocre results. He finally retired from the ring in 1995. In the late 1990s he signed with Tri Star Sports Promotions to join its year-round touring autographs shows. His son Cory Spinks is currently a successful boxer in the welterweight division.

See also Olympics, African Americans and the; Sports and African Americans.

Aaron Myers

Spirituals, African American

Over the years immigrant groups from across the world have brought their national music to America, but aside from Native Americans, African Americans were the first to create an indigenous American music. The African experience was unique: stolen from their homes, transported involuntarily in chains, and sentenced to lifetimes of SLAVERY, Africans were cut off from their various ethnic cultures and their languages. Their first challenge in America, therefore, was to transcend their different traditions and come together as a single people. During that process an astonishing and still little-recognized cultural interchange and transformation took place.

Cultural Synthesis

As Africans were themselves uniting, they were at the same time thrown into constant contact with Europeans. The first Africans were brought to British North America at Jamestown, Virginia, in early August 1619. Before the Pilgrims landed at Plymouth Rock the cultures of the two continents and the two races had begun the process of interaction and synthesis. It was a long time before white Americans believed that African American history was fundamental to an understanding of American history. Now, however, as we come to understand just how intermingled African and European cultures really were, we can see that American history is actually African American history as well.

This melding is the basis and background for the emergence of spirituals as a new and distinct musical form. As BENJAMIN MAYS, longtime president of MOREHOUSE COLLEGE, explained,

"The creation of the spirituals was no accident. It was a creation born of necessity, so that the slave might more adequately adjust himself to the conditions of the new world."

Music and dance were vital dimensions of daily African life, and if slaves could not carry physical cultural artifacts with them to North America, they could, and did, bring their extensive and complex expressive cultures. It has been suggested that the earliest synthesis of Europe and AFRICA and the first manifestation of African American culture took place on the slave ships during the horrendous MIDDLE PASSAGE between Africa and America. On the upper decks slaves were forced under the lash to dance for exercise. The rhythms, patterns, music, and lyrics have been lost, but it was here that Africa and Europe met, that the process of creative interaction began, and that a vital new people and culture suffered the pains of birth.

The emergence of the spirituals is rooted in the encounter between African traditional life and the evangelical Protestant CHRISTIANITY of the white American South. In that encounter the African village became the slave quarters and the slave congregation; the root doctor and GRIOT—or storyteller—became the preacher-healer-song leader; spirit possession became the ecstasy of emotional revivalism; the circle dance became the ring shout; community participation became call-and-response; and the history of the ancestors became the narratives of the King James Bible. The theologian JAMES CONE writes: "Through song they built new structures for existence in an alien land. The spirituals enabled blacks to retain a measure of African identity while living in the midst of American slavery, providing both the substance and the rhythm to cope with human servitude."

Music of the People

The Library of Congress identifies more than 6,000 spirituals, but some exist only in fragments. Many spirituals have been lost forever—especially, we can assume, the earliest ones, as well as earlier versions of spirituals that have survived. The creation of the spirituals was organic, coming up from below, coming up from the people. Spirituals constituted a living folk art—with no authors, no composers, no dates, no lyricists, nothing written down, no fixed or authoritative texts—belonging to the community. The same phrases might appear in different songs, the same words might be sung to different tunes, and every set of lyrics had its variants across the plantation South.

Like the BLUES and JAZZ, for which they are the foundation, spirituals are improvisational. Usually a lead singer, although it could be anyone, would sing one line, and the others present would repeat it or reply with a familiar chorus in a call-and-response antiphony. Anyone could add new verses, and the best of these survived through a kind of natural selection. In singing the spirituals there was no separation between artist and audience, no distinction between creator and performer, and this style continued in later AFRICAN AMERICAN MUSIC. "The singer is found by the song," the writer JAMES BALDWIN once commented. Spirituals were never meant to be performed on a concert stage. As folklorist ZORA NEALE HURSTON points out,

these songs are authentic only when they are sung by and for the people themselves, expressing feelings of the moment and of the situation. They are spontaneous songs, Hurston says, whose "truth dies under training like flowers under hot water."

With some exceptions African American slaves were a nonliterate people with a strong and sophisticated oral tradition of songs, stories, historical accounts, proverbs, and tales. Facility with speech, cleverness with words, verbal wit, and dramatic oratory were—and remain—highly admired qualities within the African American community. The spirituals are poems, expressing emotions and full of symbols, tropes, and metaphors, often containing layers of meaning. Their use of vernacular language is sometimes striking. Deceptively simple, spirituals can rise to piercing directness and immediacy. Many have lines of poetic power and a provocative turn of phrase:

I sweep my house with the gospel broom
I'm a-rolling in Jesus' arms
I'm going to sit down at the welcome table
Fix me, Jesus, fix me right
If anybody asks you what's the matter with me /just tell
   him I say/
I'm running for my life
Mary set her table /'Spite of all her foes

Sometimes entire lyrics are startlingly innovative in their use of words:

When the preacher, the preacher done give me over,
King Jesus is my only friend,
When my house, my house become a public hall,
King Jesus is my only friend. When my face, my face
   become a looking glass,
King Jesus is my, only friend.

Religious Songs

The spirituals are essentially religious songs. Early white American Protestants sang the psalms in meter along with the traditional stately hymns of the church. But on the rural frontier religion was more informal, more individualistic and personal, more emotional, and a new kind of vernacular music emerged to reflect the new religious democracy. Called "spiritual songs," the new music was religious in nature but lacked the dignity of conventional hymns. The African American slave songs influenced spiritual songs, so it is not surprising that the name spirituals was given to these religious slave songs when, following the AMERICAN CIVIL WAR (1861–1865), they were first recognized as a discrete African American creation.

The earliest known mention of a distinctive black religious music, according to scholar Dena J. Epstein, was published in 1819 by John F. Watson, a white man who was criticizing black "excesses" at Methodist camp meeting revivals. Watson's words are revealing:

We have, too, a growing evil in the practice of singing in our places of public and societal worship, merry airs, adapted from old songs, to hymns . . . most frequently composed and first sung by the illiterate blacks of the society . . . [At camp meetings] in the blacks' quarter, the colored people get together, and sing for hours together, short scraps of disjointed affirmations, pledges, or prayers, lengthened out with long repetitive choruses. These are all sung in the merry-chorus manner of the southern harvest field, or husking frolic method of the slave blacks; and also very like the Indian dances. With every word so sung, they have a sinking on one or other leg of the body alternately, producing an audible sound of the feet at every step and as manifest as the steps of actual Negro dancing in Virginia, etc. If some in the meantime sit, they strike the sounds alternately on each thigh.

Despite its critical stance Watson's description is full of relevant and important information. African Americans may have been segregated at camp meetings but they were present and participating. We can see the process of cultural interaction and blending taking place: as Watson's words "first sung by" suggest, whites picked up both songs and styles from blacks. Whatever the meldings, however, spirituals remained distinctly different from white spiritual songs, and the African retentions and influences are clear: the "long repetitive choruses," the "merry airs," and, most clearly, the elements of African dance in the rhythmic body movements.

Watson's comparison of the religious music to harvest and husking songs shows the relationship of spirituals to other slave musical creations such as work songs, love songs, shouts, songs for dancing, and railroad songs. And the reference to "actual Negro dancing" reveals that black dance, with its strong African character, was perceived as distinct from European forms of dance. In a fascinating aside, Watson even touches on the possibility of Native American influences. Overall, Watson's account tells us that spirituals were well formed by 1819. Of course, we do not know what the black community sang by and for itself when it was not in the presence of whites, but we can assume it was less, rather than more, European.

Experiencing the Bible

What was the content of these slave songs? "The clue to the meaning of the spirituals," writes the theologian HOWARD THURMAN, "is to be found in religious experience and spiritual discernment." As religious songs the spirituals reflect many of the characteristics of evangelical Protestantism of the day: the centrality of the Bible, the sovereignty of a God of justice, personal accountability for one's life on earth, trust in Jesus, and hope for eternal life in heaven. Spirituality accompanied theology, and the spirituals reveal the slaves' deep personal and collective faith. Tied to this was a surprisingly hopeful optimism, which transcended the wretchedness of the slave experience. The anguished cry of despair in one version of "Nobody Knows the Trouble I See" ends with an affirmation as positive as it is unexpected:

Nobody knows the trouble I see,
Nobody knows my sorrow.
Nobody knows the trouble I see.
Glory, Hallelujah!

Some slave owners permitted white ministers and missionaries to preach to their slaves. The ministers' usual text was Colossians 3:22, "Servants, obey in all things your masters." But as they accepted the Protestant principle of scriptural authority, African Americans would hear or read the rest of the Bible, and they would encounter there another message altogether. In the words of James Cone they discovered that "faith, as trust in God's Word of liberation stands at the heart of biblical revelation" and that "God's liberation is at work in the world."

The biblical narrative that resonated most strongly with the slaves' bitter experiences, while at the same time promising hope for deliverance, was the story of the Israelites' bondage in Egypt. Moses is one of the most often mentioned persons in the spirituals. African Americans also identified with Noah, Daniel, Jonah, and others of God's faithful people who were rescued by a just God from a sinful world of unfaithfulness and oppression. The nonliterate slaves told the biblical stories by turning them into songs, which, when stitched together, recount the Scriptures from beginning to end—from Adam in the garden to John the revelator. The Bible is whole: personalities from both Testaments are indiscriminately lumped together. Jesus appears in several forms: as the innocent child, the victim of whipping, the king on a milk-white horse who protects his subjects. In James Cone's potent words Jesus is even "God's black slave who has come to put an end to human bondage."

"Go Down, Moses" is perhaps the best-known spiritual. The song's direct and powerful appeal for human liberation exemplifies the theme and thread of freedom that runs through all spirituals. "Go Down, Moses" has even been associated with NAT TURNER—the leader of a slave revolt in Southampton County, Virginia, in 1831, the bloodiest of the 250 North American slave revolts. Turner is thought to have been either the author or subject of the song. The message of "Go Down, Moses" was so clear that some slaveholders forbade its singing on their plantations. The song's great popularity and widespread use not only demonstrate the inspiration the slaves got from the Bible and their identification with the chosen Israelites but show that freedom for the slaves was a physical reality in this world and not merely an otherworldly aspiration.

Hidden Messages

The metaphorical nature of the spirituals has been greatly debated and disputed. Most white critics have thought that the spirituals are essentially concerned with life in heaven, undoubtedly because they believed black slaves were docile folks, content with their lives of servitude. But African Americans have always known that the spirituals are full of coded words and secret signals, messages between and among only themselves, communications that could be concealed from the white master class. The testimonies of FREDERICK DOUGLASS—and other self-liberated slaves who recounted their experiences—confirm that the spirituals were full of symbolic language. The slaves themselves were God's people: Israel. Moses was a leader and deliverer. Egypt or Babylon represented the South, and hell the Deep South. Pharaoh was a slave owner. The River Jordan was the Ohio River or a similar body of water between the North and the South. The Red Sea was the Atlantic Ocean. Home, Canaan, camp meeting, or the Promised Land were Africa, the free states, CANADA, or LIBERIA. Any agency of travel or movement—trains, shoes, chariots, wheels—spoke of escape.

This political aspect of the spirituals is perhaps their most important legacy, both historically and now; it cannot be overemphasized. A few lyrics obviously convey political statements: "Master going to sell us tomorrow," or "No more hundred lash for me /Many thousand gone." Numerous verses mention family members, remembering those sold away in slave owners' cruel disregard for human relationships. Other songs are subtler. Frederick Douglass said that the words "Run to Jesus /Shun the danger" first gave him the idea of escaping from bondage. Still other songs are also about running away, the UNDERGROUND RAILROAD, and God's promised destruction of a sinful social order: "I don't intend to die in Egypt land"; "When the train comes along /I'll meet you at the station"; "God's going to set the world on fire." There are songs of the liberation that is to come: "You can hinder me here, but you can't hinder me there" are lines from "Free at Last," the spiritual MARTIN LUTHER KING, JR., quoted in his "I Have a Dream" speech in WASHINGTON, D.C., in 1963. A profoundly radical, even revolutionary, thrust to these songs came as the slaves expanded their struggle for freedom to encompass all the disinherited: "Didn't my Lord deliver Daniel/And why not every man?"

New Poetics

The anonymous slave poets, those "black and unknown bards," as the poet JAMES WELDON JOHNSON called them, were the progenitors of a great new Afropoetics. The first African American to publish a book was PHILLIS WHEATLEY, a slave whose book of poetry was published in London in 1773. Despite making unappreciated references to Africa and liberty, Wheatley nonetheless followed the European and classical literary tradition. It is the vibrant vernacular language of the spirituals, their marriage of Africa and Europe, and their grand obsession with freedom that makes them unique. Antonin Dvorak, the Czech composer, recognized this early on and incorporated African American themes into his *New World Symphony* of 1893. He writes, "The so-called plantation songs are among the most striking and appealing melodies that have been found this side of the water."

African American spirituals have not been particularly well documented, either historically or musically. AFRICAN MUSIC, especially its complex polyrhythms, is not easily comprehended by Western-trained ears, and whites of the slavocracy did not take the slaves' music seriously or treat it with respect. There are surprisingly few references to spirituals in antebellum di-

aries and letters. The first sympathetic interest on the part of whites came during the Civil War from abolitionists in and out of the United States Army who heard the singing of so-called contrabands, self-liberated slaves who had escaped the protection of Union lines.

One of the earliest white reports of spirituals came from the Reverend Lewis Lockwood, an agent of the American Missionary Association sent to do educational and relief work among contrabands at Fortress Monroe on Chesapeake Bay. Lockwood first heard black singing on September 3, 1861, and soon provided the *New York Tribune* with the text of "Go Down, Moses," facilitating the song's first appearance in print. The discussion over the accurate representation of both African American words and music began then and has not yet been resolved. Curiously, little attention has been paid to the use of spirituals in the writing of African Americans. MARTIN DELANY's novel *Blake, or The Huts of America,* issued serially in 1881 and 1882, includes what the scholar Allen Austin calls "the largest compendium of black-created or black-adapted verses and songs in the antebellum period." PAULINE E. HOPKINS also utilizes spirituals significantly in her novel *Of One Blood, or The Hidden Self,* serialized in the *Colored American Magazine* in 1902 and 1903.

One achievement of the spirituals was to offer the nation its first compendium of authentic African American music and lyrics. White America had been so fascinated with black life that throughout the nineteenth century the country's most popular entertainment came in the form of minstrel shows. MINSTRELSY was a grotesque white parody of black singing, dancing, humor, and style, even though it was based, as blues composer W. C. HANDY and others have pointed out, on real African American expressive culture. A less demeaning form of white imitation of blacks can be recognized in the sentimental ballads of Stephen Foster. Foster had heard black songs and adapted them for white audiences, combining theft with homogenization—a practice that continued with RAGTIME and jazz.

Saving the Spirituals

Despite the fact that the spirituals were, in the scholar W. E. B. Du BOIS's words, "the slaves' one articulate message to the world," the truth is that they were nearly lost. Beyond the flutter of abolitionist interest during the Civil War there were few white people who had heard spirituals, and the freedpeople were eager to forget the songs as a relic of the slavery they were trying to put behind them. In particular, members of the small but influential African American middle class were anxious to embrace European culture in order to prove that they were as capable and deserving as white people were. A similar attitude would develop later in response to blues, jazz, RAP, and Ebonics—all expressions that have bubbled up from the underclass to challenge and even subvert the dominant cultural establishment.

The spirituals were actually saved for posterity by a small group of African American men and women at FISK UNIVERSITY, a school for freedpeople established just after the Civil War in Nashville, Tennessee, by the American Missionary Association. The school was so overcrowded and so poor that students and faculty sold the iron from Nashville's former slave pens to buy spelling books. George White, Fisk's music teacher, organized a small choir called the Jubilee Singers and then hit upon the idea of taking the group on a concert tour to raise money for the floundering college. Leaving Nashville in 1871 on borrowed money, the choir was markedly unsuccessful until they began singing spirituals to white church groups in the North, which included former abolitionists sympathetic to African Americans, their struggle for freedom, and their culture. Suddenly the singers became a smashing success—they sang in Henry Ward Beecher's Brooklyn church, for President Ulysses Grant, and for Queen Victoria in England. (At the request of the British prime minister's wife, the Fisk Jubilee Singers sang "John Brown's Body" for the Grand Duchess Maria Fyodorovna, whose father-in-law, Tsar Alexander II, had just liberated the Russian serfs.) The Fisk Jubilee Singers rescued the spirituals and made it respectable to sing them. As the music scholar Mary Jo Sanna points out, "Negro spirituals" became commonplace in American popular culture, marking "the only way whites knowingly and willingly participated in the contributions of blacks to American culture."

The lasting power of the spirituals lies in their message. Calling the spirituals "sorrow songs," W. E. B. Du Bois wrote, "They are the music of an unhappy people, of the children of disappointment; they tell of death and suffering and unvoiced longing toward a truer world." There is a little-noted parallel between the spirituals and their secular offspring, the blues—a body of music that also deals with the sadness and melancholy of men and women struggling with the "blue devils" of despair. The contemporary writer RALPH ELLISON describes the redemptive function of blues: "The blues is an impulse to keep the painful details and episodes of a brutal experience alive in one's aching consciousness, to finger its jagged edge, and to transcend it, not by the consolation of philosophy, but by squeezing from it a near-tragic, near-comic lyricism." The same holds true for the spirituals. These songs reflect the slaves' sorrows, but the pain is transformed by the act of expression, by fingering the "jagged edge." They are metamorphosed, like the blues, into songs of resilience and overcoming, and even into affirmations of divine redemption and human triumph.

See also Slave Narratives; Slave Rebellions in the United States.

Richard Newman

Spivey, Victoria Regina

1906–1976

American urban blues singer who was one of the first African American women to found a record label.

Known to many as "Queen Victoria," Victoria Regina Spivey was born in HOUSTON, TEXAS. She learned the piano while singing with her father's band in Dallas. After her father died she performed wherever she could find work. In 1926 Spivey moved to St. Louis, Missouri, where she wrote and recorded songs, including her best-known "T.B. Blues", for the St. Louis Music Company and for Okeh Records. Leaving Okeh but continuing to record between 1929 and 1952, she also appeared in several stage shows including *Hellzapoppin'* and in an all-black movie, *Hallelujah*. Her signature vocal sound was a nasal type of evocative moan, which she termed her "tiger squall."

After a brief retirement Spivey returned to music with the revival of the BLUES in the 1960s. In 1961 she formed Queen Vee Records, changing the name to Spivey Records the following year. She died in 1976, the same year she released her last album, *The Blues Is Life*.

Sports and African Americans

Field in which African Americans have achieved notable success and which has been the stage for important racial dramas in American history.

Sports have played a major role in the lives of African Americans dating from their African roots to the present. From the earliest civilizations of Africa, common sporting activities included wrestling and BOXING, foot racing, jumping contests, stick fighting, hunting and fishing, and a variety of games of skill and chance, such as stones (marbles) and gambling. Thus Africans who were later enslaved and transported to the New World nevertheless brought with them a rich culture of sport.

Rise of Popular Sports among Blacks

Africans in America, from slavery to freedom, found sport a necessity for their physical and psychological survival. Enslaved Africans supplemented their diets through hunting and fishing. Treeing opossums and raccoons, snaring rabbits, and catching fish were art forms among blacks and the source of bragging rights and fuller bellies for one's self and family. Physical contests of wrestling and boxing were popular as well. Some blacks gained recognition as able prizefighters even during the days of slavery, winning great sums for their masters, and in rare cases, slaves such as TOM MOLINEAUX even earned their freedom through boxing. Cockfighting was also a popular activity, and blacks were widely known for their skills at training and handling the fighting birds. Horse racing was popular among the white gentry, but the art of jockeying the horse was a role that the owners typically relegated to others, and by the mid-nineteenth century black jockeys dominated the profession. In the first twenty-eight years of the Kentucky Derby, from 1875 to 1902, black jockeys won the race fifteen times, including three victories by ISAAC MURPHY, the most celebrated jockey of the age. Blacks engaged in baseball as early as the 1860s, and numerous black teams flourished in local leagues and barnstorming tours by the turn of the century. From the 1920s through the early 1940s, black organized baseball reached its peak with the success of the NEGRO LEAGUES. Football burst onto the national scene in the 1890s at colleges and universities in the East and rapidly gained in popularity among African Americans as black athletes, such as WILLIAM H. LEWIS and William Tecumseh Sherman Jackson, won early national acclaim in the sport.

First Golden Era in African American Sports

The 1920s were in many respects the first golden era of sports in the United States. Virtually all sports grew and prospered during this period. Already well established, boxing, baseball, and football now rose to even greater stature. As a result of the efforts of organizations in the early twentieth century, including the Colored (later the Central) Intercollegiate Athletic Association, TRACK AND FIELD emerged as a popular organized athletic activity among African Americans of all ages. The successes of the first African American professional BASKETBALL team of note, the NEW YORK RENAISSANCE, helped immensely to popularize the sport among all races. Tennis and golf were able to make modest inroads into the African American world of sports in the 1920s owing to the work in particular of two black athletic organizations: the American Tennis Association, founded in 1916, and the United Golfers Association, established in 1926.

Sports as a Racial Barometer

Sports, like the arts, literature, and politics, have been a mirror of American society. And in sports the contradictions between democratic principles and racial discrimination have been particularly glaring, because athletics have been considered a sanctum of sportsmanship and fair play. Despite those ideals, in every avenue of sport African Americans faced restrictions or were barred outright from participation because of the color of their skin. Blacks first made their marks in individualized sports such as boxing, but not without overcoming tremendous racial obstacles. In team sports, the overwhelming majority of African American athletes who competed prior to WORLD WAR II (1939–1945) did so on all-black teams. Only a small number of white colleges and universities in the North allowed blacks to participate in their athletic programs. Even then, a so-called gentlemen's agreement was typically adhered to, under which those teams with black athletes on the roster would agree to leave them at home when they went to play an all-white team. Integrated teams and interracial sporting competitions were against the law in many Southern states until as late as the 1950s.

Black Athletes and the Struggle for Equality

Two black athletes dominated American sports in the years immediately prior to World War II—JESSE OWENS in track and field and JOE LOUIS in boxing. Owens's four gold medals in the 1936 Olympic Games in Berlin, Germany, were seen as a triumph for American democracy over Nazism, as was Louis's defeat of German boxer Max Schmeling in their second heavyweight fight in 1938. Owens and Louis made their statements for racial equality by proving themselves as athletes, but others turned to more direct forms of protest. Boxing great Henry Armstrong hammered away at discrimination in the 1930s and 1940s by refusing to fight in segregated arenas. Students at New York University launched a protest in 1940 against racial discrimination in collegiate athletics that gained national recognition and support for the eradication of the color line in intercollegiate sports.

America's entry into World War II, in December 1941, had a tremendous impact on the color line in sports as the diversion of American manpower to the war effort left a vacuum in professional and amateur athletics that African Americans helped to fill. During this period, SATCHEL PAIGE and his Negro Baseball All-Star Team were given the opportunity to play the major league champions of baseball, and the Negro Collegiate All-Stars of Football played successive games against the champions of the National Football League. The number of African American athletes in predominantly white collegiate conferences also increased.

The integration of sports continued after the war ended in 1945. In 1947 JACKIE ROBINSON broke the color line to become the first black player in major league baseball. In professional basketball, Chuck Cooper and Sweetwater Clifton came into the National Basketball Association in 1950. That year also marked an important first in tennis when ALTHEA GIBSON became the first African American woman to compete in the National Championships (later the United States Open) at Forest Hills in Queens, New York, an event she would later win in 1957 and 1958. In the 1960s WILMA RUDOLPH and WYOMIA TYUS won international acclaim for African American women in track. The brash boxing champion MUHAMMAD ALI and his defiant stand against military induction during the VIETNAM WAR defined the mood of the 1960s. Baseball outfielder Curt Flood's battle against the reserve clause, which bound individual players to their teams even after the end of their contracts, helped to define sports in the 1970s.

Athletic Success and the African American Dream

Despite its many barriers, sports stood as one of the early venues where blacks gained a foothold, and it remains one of the best publicized routes to success for African Americans. The high visibility of black athletes with multimillion-dollar contracts, however, feeds into the limited and unrealistic dreams of millions of young African Americans who pin their hopes for the future on becoming a professional athlete, usually at the expense of academic excellence and intellectual pursuits.

Race and Athletic Ability

Black success in athletics has created racial problems as it has helped to overcome others. Superior performances by black athletes over whites have been met with pseudoscientific speculation that people of African descent are more physically gifted and possess natural anatomical advantages (and corresponding mental deficiencies) relative to whites. Long-held racist views about the inborn attributes of blacks surfaced anew after Jesse Owens's spectacular performance in the 1936 Olympics. The speculation so outraged WILLIAM MONTAGUE COBB, an African American physician and physical anthropologist, that he devoted careful study to the subject. Cobb personally examined Owens and conducted numerous scientific tests and measurements on him, and he found the track star no different from other men. Despite the research and publications of Cobb and others, some continue to postulate about the physiognomy of African Americans as an explanation for their success in sports. The stereotype of black athletes as gifted in body but not in mind has contributed to the belated acceptance of blacks as coaches and managers and in on-field leadership positions, such as football quarterback. Only in the recent years have the successes of such coaches and managers as Dennis Green in football, LENNY WILKENS in basketball, and Cito Gaston and Dusty Baker in baseball, as well as those of star football quarterbacks Doug Williams, Warren Moon, and Randall Cunningham, begun to break that stubborn barrier.

See also African Americans and the Olympics; Baseball in the United States; Collegiate Football.

Bibliography

Ashe, Arthur R., Jr. *A Hard Road to Glory: A History of the African-American Athlete.* 3 vols. Amistad, 1993.

Henderson, Edwin B. *The Negro in Sports.* Rev. ed. Associated Publishers, 1949.

Spivey, Donald, ed. *Sport in America: New Historical Perspectives.* Greenwood, 1985.

Squatter Settlements in Brazil

See Favelas.

Stanley, Sir Henry Morton

1841–1904

Anglo-American journalist and explorer, the first European to map the Congo Basin.

Sir Henry Morton Stanley was born John Rowlands in Denbigh, Wales. Beginning his career as a journalist, Stanley first traveled to AFRICA in 1869 on assignment for the *New York Herald.* The newspaper dispatched Stanley to find DAVID LIVINGSTONE, a Scottish missionary who had gone to explore Africa and subsequently disappeared from the public eye. Traveling from ZANZIBAR into the interior of east Africa, Stanley finally met the ailing Livingstone at Ujiji, a town on LAKE TANGANYIKA, on November 10, 1871. Stanley is said to have greeted Livingstone

with the famous remark, "Dr. Livingstone, I presume?" After Livingstone was nursed back to health, they explored the northern end of Lake Tanganyika. Stanley returned to Europe in 1872 but was sent back to West Africa the following year to report on the British campaign against the ASANTE.

In 1874 the *New York Herald* and *London Daily Telegraph* sent Stanley back to Africa to continue Livingstone's work. Stanley first visited King MUTESA I of BUGANDA and then circumnavigated LAKE VICTORIA and Lake Tanganyika. Finally, he traveled down the Lualaba and Congo rivers. Amazed by the enormous navigability of the CONGO RIVER, Stanley returned to Europe in 1878 to share his "discoveries."

The following year, under the sponsorship of King LEOPOLD II of Belgium, Stanley returned to the Congo for yet another expedition. Taking with him hundreds of laborers, he laid the foundations for the CONGO FREE STATE by constructing a road from the lower Congo to Pool Malebo and making contracts with local African peoples. This expedition helped Leopold II establish control over the Congo basin.

Stanley returned to Africa briefly in 1887 and 1897. After his 1897 trip, he retired to London, England, where he served in the British Parliament.

Bibliography

Hall, Richard Seymour. *Stanley: An Adventurer Explored.* Collins, 1974.

Stanley, H. M. *In Darkest Africa.* Charles Scribner's Sons, 1890.

Stanley, H. M. *Through the Dark Continent.* Harper & Brothers, 1878.

Elizabeth Heath

Staple Singers

Well-known African American family music group that has performed and recorded gospel, folk, and soul music since the early 1950s.

The Staple Singers, composed of various members of the Staples family of CHICAGO, ILLINOIS, made significant contributions to GOSPEL and SOUL MUSIC as well as to the folk music revival. Even after leaving the realm of religious music the group has continued to perform songs with an inspirational or uplifting message. At the heart of the four-person group was Roebuck "Pop" Staples, whose lead vocals and Delta blues-influenced guitar playing helped give the Staple Singers their distinctive sound. His youngest daughter, Mavis Staples, added an exhilarating contralto. Over time, as various family members joined or left the group, the Staple Singers gradually altered its style. For the first decade the Staples performed gospel music but in the early 1960s the group took its increasingly secular repertoire on the folk music circuit. In 1968 the Staple Singers signed with STAX RECORDS, perhaps the most important soul music record company, and soon emerged as one of the country's top soul groups.

Pop Staples was born in 1915 in Winona, Mississippi, where he came under the influence of the guitar style of such legendary Delta bluesmen as ROBERT JOHNSON, Bukka White, and BIG BILL BROONZY. In 1935 Staples moved to Chicago with his wife Oceola and two children, Pervis and Cleotha. In Chicago the family grew with the additions of Yvonne and Mavis. The elder Staples sang in gospel quartets during the 1930s and began teaching his children music when they were quite young in the hope of forming a group. In the early 1950s Pervis, Cleotha, and Mavis joined him in performances at local churches.

Although the Staple Singers first recorded in 1953, they did not gain recognition until moving to Chicago's black-owned Vee Jay Records in 1955, which released five notable gospel albums by the group over the next five years. The Staples, however, achieved their greatest popularity with a series of more elaborately produced recordings for Stax, which featured fuller instrumentation, including horn sections and synthesizers, exemplified by the hits "Respect Yourself" (1971), "I'll Take You There" (1972), and "If You're Ready (Come Go with Me)" (1973), as well as by their 1975 album for CURTIS MAYFIELD's Custom label, *Let's Do It Again,* the group's all-time best-seller. The Staple Singers became less visible as soul music lost its popular appeal in the late 1970s, although the group briefly returned to prominence in the mid-1980s when it backed actor Bruce Willis's cover of "Respect Yourself," which gained considerable airplay on MTV.

James Sellman

Starvation in Africa

See Hunger and Famine.

Stax Records

American recording studio based in Memphis, Tennessee, that played a key role in defining soul music and in popularizing the horn-driven "Memphis sound" during the 1960s.

Stax Record Company of MEMPHIS, TENNESSEE, helped define the SOUL MUSIC era of the mid-1960s with what came to be known as its Memphis sound, which combined GOSPEL and BLUES-tinged vocals, tightly riffing horn sections, and a powerful rhythmic drive. Important Stax performers included OTIS REDDING, Booker T. and the MG's, Carla and Rufus Thomas, Sam and Dave (Sam Moore and David Prater), and the STAPLE SINGERS. Stax recordings also benefited from talented songwriters, especially the team of Isaac Hayes and David Porter, who were responsible for such hits as Sam and Dave's "Hold On, I'm Comin'" and Carla Thomas's "B-A-B-Y."

White siblings Jim Stewart and Estelle Axton opened the recording studio that would become Stax in 1960. They named their company Satellite Records, but in order to avoid confusion with another record company of the same name, they changed their label to Stax, derived from the first two letters of their last names. The Stax studio was located in a former movie theater, the marquee of which soon proclaimed: "SOULSVILLE USA." After a regional RHYTHM AND BLUES (R&B) hit in 1960, a Rufus and Carla Thomas duet titled "'Cause I Love You," the fledgling company reached a long-term agreement with Atlantic Records to distribute that and future Stax recordings.

In search of the Memphis magic, Atlantic executive Jerry Wexler also began to bring his own artists to Stax, most notably WILSON PICKETT. After several unsuccessful Atlantic recordings with large orchestras and elaborate arrangements, Pickett found his key to success in the leaner Stax approach, utilizing a small R&B band and simple riff-based accompaniments. His career-making Stax sessions of May and December 1965 yielded the hits "In the Midnight Hour," "634-5789," and "Ninety-Nine and One-Half Won't Do," and introduced what would be Pickett's signature sound.

One of the keys to Stax's success was the hiring in 1965 of Al Bell, a black disc jockey who had previously founded his own record label, to manage national promotion and sales. Bell was the first African American in the otherwise all-white Stax management. In 1968 he bought out Axton's share of the company and became a co-owner. The combination of Bell's vision and energy and the company's compelling music propelled Stax into a period of rapid growth and expansion. The management and musicians at Stax began to view their studio as an alternative to DETROIT's far larger MOTOWN Records.

In contrast to Motown, which took a sweeter and slicker approach, often using lush string sections and producing music that seemed to emulate white pop songs, Stax brought an earthier, more hard-driving sound to American popular music. Al Jackson, Jr., drummer for Booker T. and the MG's as well as for many other Stax recording sessions, dismissed Motown recordings as being "made from the switchboard." Daily operations at Stax were marked by a closeness and informality that cut across racial barriers and seemed to draw everyone— musicians, engineers, and principal partners—together. Regular Stax session players included blacks, such as Jackson, keyboard player Booker T. Jones, and sax player Andrew Love, and whites, including guitarist Steve Cropper, bass player Donald "Duck" Dunn, and trumpeter Wayne Jackson.

Despite numerous hits in the 1960s and early 1970s, the company's success was short-lived. A combination of economic and political factors, including the consequences of the company's own sudden success and a deteriorating racial climate, particularly following the assassination of African American civil rights leader MARTIN LUTHER KING, JR., in 1968, resulted in growing internal frictions that contributed to the bankruptcy that put Stax out of business in 1975.

Bibliography
Guralnick, Peter. *Sweet Soul Music: Rhythm and Blues and the Southern Dream of Freedom.* Harper & Row, 1986.

James Sellman

Stevens, Siaka

1905–1988

Prime minister and president of Sierra Leone from 1971 to 1985, and a major force in Sierra Leone politics for almost forty years.

Siaka Stevens was educated at Albert Academy at FREETOWN and went on to study trade-union operation and industrial relations at Ruskin College, Oxford, England (1947–1948). He first gained national recognition through his work in trade-union organization. In 1943 he cofounded the United Mine Workers' Union, after becoming a mine worker at the Marampa Mines with the Sierra Leone Development Company (DELCO). His energetic prominence in the labor movement resulted in his appointment to the Sierra Leone Protectorate Assembly in 1946.

In 1951 Stevens, Milton Margai, and several others formed the Sierra Leone People's Party (SLPP). The SLPP became a powerful force in national politics. In the same year Stevens was also elected to the Legislative Council and in 1952 went on to become minister of Lands, Mines, and Labour.

Stevens's growing disillusionment with the SLPP culminated in him leaving it in 1958, and he then cofounded, with Albert Margai, the People's National Party (PNP). From 1958 to 1960 Stevens was a deputy leader of PNP. In 1960 all the national parties, including the PNP, formed a united front to negotiate independence from GREAT BRITAIN, and Stevens was chosen as a member of the delegation to be sent to the Constitutional Conference in London. He objected to the decisions taken there and argued that the SLPP government was unrepresentative, demanding new elections before independence. His agitation in the Elections Before Independence Movement, which was later to become the All People's Congress (APC), resulted in him being imprisoned on independence day, April 27, 1961, although his sentence of conspiracy and libel was soon quashed.

Stevens became the major opposition leader. He was also mayor of Freetown (1964–1965). In elections on March 17, 1967, the APC won a majority and Stevens became prime minister, although not for long because the commander of the Sierra Leone Military Force, Brigadier Lansana, intervened and military officers seized power. This coup government only lasted until April 1968, when an inquiry into the elections showed that Stevens and the APC had fairly won the election and Stevens was reinstated as prime minister. After another unsuccessful coup attempt in 1971 Stevens's government introduced a republican constitution, and on April 21, 1971, Stevens was sworn in as the country's first executive president. Stevens became increasingly concerned with consolidating his authority, and in 1978 Sierra Leone became a one-party state under the APC and Stevens's presidency. Despite unease at Stevens's authoritarianism, his rule never degenerated into total repression and he preferred a policy of coopting his opponents; he enjoyed a sound level of popular support, which earned him the affectionate nickname of "Pa" among large numbers of the population.

In October 1985 Stevens retired and was succeeded by Brigadier Joseph Momoh. He died in May 1988 and was given a state funeral, accompanied by a great expression of public grief.

Bibliography

Sierra Leone. *Twelve Years of Economic Achievement and Political Consolidation under the APC and Siaka Stevens, 1968–1980.* Office of the President, 1980.
Stevens, Siaka. *What Life Has Taught Me.* Kensal Press, 1984.

Chloe Campbell

Stevenson, Teófilo

1952–

Afro-Cuban boxer who was the first fighter to win three consecutive Olympic gold medals in the same weight class.

Teófilo Stevenson, along with champions Roberto Balado and Félix Savón, received training from Cuban national coach Alcides Sagarra. Stevenson fought in the heavyweight class (known as super heavyweight since 1981) and was undefeated in twelve career matches at three consecutive Summer Olympic Games. At his first Olympics, the 1972 games in Munich, West Germany, Stevenson dominated the heavyweight field, winning three matches before gaining the Olympic gold medal when his opponent, United States fighter Duane Bobick, defaulted in the final round because of injury. Stevenson received several lucrative offers to turn professional after his 1972 success, but he chose to remain in CUBA to box as an amateur and to represent his country in international competition. Because of his skills he was widely compared to American boxers MUHAMMAD ALI, JOE FRAZIER, and GEORGE FOREMAN. Stevenson almost had the opportunity to fight Ali in the 1970s, but the match was canceled and he never again had the chance to enter in the ring against him.

Stevenson won his second Olympic gold medal at the 1976 games in Montréal, Québec, Canada, easily defeating another American, John Tate, with the first blow of the first round. At his third Olympics, the 1980 games in Moscow (then the capital of the Soviet Union), Stevenson again won the heavyweight gold medal by scoring a 4-1 decision over the Soviet Union's Pyotr Zaev. This was the only game of his twelve Olympic matches in which his opponent lasted long enough to lose by decision instead of by knockout. Stevenson was the first boxer to win three consecutive Olympic gold medals in the same weight division. He did not have the opportunity to try for a fourth gold medal, however, because Cuba joined the Soviet Union in a boycott of the 1984 Olympics in LOS ANGELES, CALIFORNIA.

During his career, Stevenson won 309 of 321 events. In addition to his Olympic gold medals, Stevenson won three amateur heavyweight world titles, ten national BOXING championships, one gold medal in the Pan American Games, eight Central American Championships, and 72 international tournaments. He retired in 1988 and became Cuba's national boxing coach. In 2002 Cuban leader FIDEL CASTRO honored him as one of the top one hundred Cuban athletes of the twentieth century. Stevenson is currently the vice-president of the Cuban Boxing Federation and remains a national hero in Cuba.

Bibliography

Mullan, Harry. *The Ultimate Encyclopedia of Boxing: The Definitive Guide to World Boxing.* Hodder & Stoughton, 1996.

Page, James A. *Black Olympian Medalists.* Libraries Unlimited, 1991.

Pettavino, Paula J., and Geralyn Pye. *Sport in Cuba: The Diamond in the Rough.* University of Pittsburgh Press, 1994.

Steward, Frank Rudolph

1872–1931

African American lawyer and army officer.

Frank Rudolph Steward was born in Wilmington, Delaware, one of eight children of THEOPHILUS GOULD STEWARD and Elizabeth (Gadsden) Steward. His father was a prominent clergyman, chaplain, author, and educator. Steward prepared for college at Phillips Exeter Academy in Exeter, New Hampshire, and received his B.A. degree from Harvard College in 1896. He graduated from Harvard Law School in 1899. In the same year he was appointed captain, Forty-ninth Infantry, U.S. Volunteers, and served from 1899 to 1901 with the regiment in the Philippines, where his father also served as government superintendent of schools for the province of Luzon. According to an article in the *Colored American Magazine* (1901), Steward was provost judge in San Pablo, a city near Manila.

Steward was admitted to the bar in PITTSBURGH, PENNSYLVANIA, and practiced law there until his death. A general practitioner, he believed that he had tried more than the average number of homicide cases. He took a relatively active interest in politics and was a member of the Electoral College of Pennsylvania, casting his vote for presidents Warren G. Harding and Calvin Coolidge. On October 27, 1910, he married Adah M. Captain; there is no record of children. A year later he received the LL.D. degree from WILBERFORCE UNIVERSITY, where his father after 1907 had served as vice president, chaplain, and teacher.

At Harvard, Steward was a contemporary of noted black activists WILLIAM MONROE TROTTER, W. E. B. DU BOIS, and WILLIAM H. LEWIS. Although Steward appears not to have received honors upon graduating from Harvard College, he had some of the same professors as Du Bois and Trotter, notably George Herbert Palmer and George Santayana (philosophy), Francis Peabody (social ethics), and Albert Bushnell Hart (history). He did not have courses with Josiah Royce and William James, who greatly influenced Du Bois and Trotter. The records fur-

nished by the Harvard University Archives do not list the courses he pursued in law school. The requirements for graduation, however, were rigorous.

From *Dictionary of American Negro Biography* by Rayford W. Logan and Michael R. Winston, editors. Copyright © 1982 by Rayford W. Logan and Michael R. Winston. Reprinted by permission of W. W. Norton & Company, Inc.

Rayford W. Logan

Steward, Susan Maria Smith McKinney

1847–1918

African American physician.

Susan Maria Smith McKinney Steward was born in Brooklyn, New York, the daughter of Sylvanus Smith, a pork merchant, and Ann Springstead. She grew up in a farming community with her large, prosperous family. As a teenager she learned to play the organ, studying under two prominent NEW YORK CITY organists, John Zundel and Henry Eyre Brown. She became an accomplished organist, but she had other goals. The deaths of two of her brothers during the CIVIL WAR and the high death rates from a cholera epidemic in Brooklyn in 1866 may have influenced her choice of a medical career. Her versatile mind and disciplined approach earned her an M.D. in 1870 from the New York Medical College for Women. She was the first African American woman to graduate from a medical school in the state of New York and only the third in the United States.

In 1874 Susan Smith married the Reverend William G. McKinney and then practiced under the name of Dr. Susan Smith McKinney. Two children were born of this marriage before her husband died in 1892. Dr. McKinney conducted a private general practice at 205 DeKalb Avenue in Brooklyn from 1870 to 1895. Serving both white and black patients, she had another office in Manhattan. During the period of her medical practice in Brooklyn, she also served as the organist and choir director at the Bridge Street AFRICAN METHODIST EPISCOPAL CHURCH (AME) near her office.

In 1881 McKinney cofounded the Brooklyn Women's Homeopathic Hospital and Dispensary (later renamed Memorial Hospital for Women and Children), a hospital for African Americans, where she served as a staff physician until 1896. During 1887 and 1888 she was engaged in postgraduate study at the Long Island Medical College Hospital in Brooklyn. She was also on the staff of the New York Medical College and Hospital for Women in Manhattan from 1892 to 1896. From 1892 to 1895 she was one of two female physicians at the Brooklyn Home for Aged Colored People and served as a member of its board of directors. McKinney was an active member of the Kings County Medical Society and the New York State Homeopathic Medical Society.

In 1896 the widowed McKinney married the Reverend Theophilus G. Steward, a U.S. Army chaplain with the 25th

U.S. Colored Infantry. She accompanied him for two years on tours of duty in Montana and Wyoming, where she gained medical licenses and practiced. In 1898, shortly before her husband's retirement from the army, she became a faculty member, teaching health and nutrition, and a resident physician at WILBERFORCE UNIVERSITY, Wilberforce, Ohio, a school supported by the African Methodist Episcopal Church. She held both positions for twenty-two years until her death. Rev. Steward joined his wife at Wilberforce and became a member of the history faculty.

In 1911 Steward and her husband participated as delegates of the AME church at the First Universal Races Congress at the University of London. She addressed the interracial group of delegates with a presentation entitled "Colored Women in America." In 1914 she presented a paper, "Women in Medicine," before the National Association of Colored Women's Clubs in Wilberforce, Ohio; it included a nearly complete list of African American women who had completed medical school and practiced in America up until that time.

With forty-eight years in the medical profession, Steward was a leading woman physician as well as a musician, public speaker, and devoted churchwoman. The Susan Smith McKinney Steward Medical Society, the first organization of African American female physicians, founded in 1976 in the greater New York area, took the name of this pioneer. Steward died at her home on the campus of Wilberforce University.

Bibliography

Alexander, Leslie L. "Early Medical Heroes: Susan Smith McKinney-Steward, M.D. 1847–1918." *The Crisis* (January 1980): 21–23.

———. "Susan Smith McKinney, M.D. 1847–1918." *Journal of the National Medical Association* (March 1975): 173–175.

Brown, Hallie Q. *Homespun Heroines and Other Women of Distinction*. 1988.

Seraile, William. "Susan McKinney Steward: New York State's First African American Woman Physician." *Afro-Americans in New York Life and History*, July 1985.

From *American National Biography*. John A. Garraty and Mark C. Carnes, eds. Oxford University Press, 1999. Reprinted by permission of the American Council of Learned Societies.

Robert C. Hayden

Steward, Theophilus Gould

1843–1924

American preacher and author.

Although Theophilus Steward had only a grammar school education, his interest in history and literature was nurtured by his family's home instruction. His mother, Rebecca Steward, encouraged him to question ideas commonly accepted as the truth. With this background he began preaching in 1862 and

the following year received a license from the AFRICAN METHODIST EPISCOPAL CHURCH (AME). Steward was one of the three people who accompanied Bishop DANIEL PAYNE to South Carolina in 1865 to reestablish the AME church that had been banned there in 1822 as a result of the DENMARK VESEY CONSPIRACY.

Steward continued to build churches and schools in South Carolina and Georgia through 1870, although his outspoken criticism of all-white juries in 1870 made him a controversial figure among his peers in the clergy. From 1870 to 1891 Steward served as the pastor of several churches along the east coast. He joined the Twenty-fifth U.S. Colored Infantry as a chaplain at the end of this period of church service. Finally, in 1907 Steward became a faculty member at the AME's WILBERFORCE UNIVERSITY, where he taught for the last seventeen years of his life.

In 1873 he made a brief missionary trip to HAITI, during which he produced two books on theology: *Genesis Re-reread* (1885) and *The End of the World* (1888). Steward revisited Haiti and its history in his 1914 book *The Haitian Revolution*. He was a prolific author, even while serving in the military, where he wrote a novel, *Charleston Love Story* (1899) and a highly acclaimed nonfiction book entitled *The Colored Regulars*.

Bibliography

Seraile, William. *Voice of Dissent: Theophilus Gould Steward (1843–1924) and Black America*. Carlson, 1991.

Aaron Myers

Stewart, Maria Miller

1803?–1879

American women's rights activist, orator, writer, educator, first U.S.-born woman to speak publicly on political issues before a mixed-gender audience.

Born to a free family but orphaned at the age of five, Maria Stewart lived with the family of a clergyman until the age of fifteen. She acquired literacy and a religious education at Sabbath schools. Stewart married James Stewart on August 10, 1826, in BOSTON, MASSACHUSETTS. After her husband's death in 1829, Stewart worked through the 1860s as a teacher in the public school systems of NEW YORK CITY, BALTIMORE, MARYLAND and WASHINGTON, D.C. In Washington she established a Sunday school for children in 1871 and worked and lived at the HOWARD UNIVERSITY–affiliated Freedmen's Hospital for the last nine years of her life.

Stewart's two-year speaking career began in 1832 and included four lectures, all published in WILLIAM LLOYD GARRISON's abolitionist newspaper, the *Liberator*. Her lecture to the New England Anti-Slavery Society on September 21, 1832, was the first public lecture by an American-born woman before an audience of men and women. Stewart's speeches and subsequent writings emphasized women's ability and activism: "Daughters of Africa, awake! arise! distinguish yourselves." Her words were imbued with religious significance and delivered with a militancy also inherent in the writings of her contemporary DAVID WALKER. Stewart criticized racism and sexism in an era in which it was deemed inappropriate for women to participate publicly in political debates. She is the author of *Religion and the Pure Principles of Morality, the Sure Foundation on Which We Must Build* (1831), *Productions of Mrs. Maria W. Stewart* (1835), and *Meditations From the Pen of Mrs. Maria W. Stewart* (1879).

Aaron Myers

Stewart, Sylvester

See Sly and the Family Stone.

Stewart, T. McCants

1854–1923

African American lawyer, pastor, author, editor, and educator.

Born free in CHARLESTON, SOUTH CAROLINA, the son of George Gilchrist and Anna (Morris) Stewart, McCants Stewart attended school in that city. He entered the academy at HOWARD UNIVERSITY in WASHINGTON, D.C., in 1869, remaining there until 1873. He then entered the University of South Carolina and received his B.A. degree in 1875 as valedictorian and his LL.B. (bachelor of laws) degree in the same year. In that year he became a partner with ROBERT BROWN ELLIOTT and DAVID AUGUSTUS STRAKER in their Charleston law firm. At the same time, he was professor of mathematics in the State Agricultural College, Orangeburg. According to his own account, he then studied theology and philosophy at Princeton Theological Seminary in New Jersey.

Ordained a minister in the AFRICAN METHODIST EPISCOPAL CHURCH (AME) on October 13, 1877, he was pastor of Bethel AME Church in NEW YORK CITY, where at the same time he practiced law. In 1883 he and his wife, in the company of educator HUGH M. BROWNE, went to LIBERIA as Charles Sumner Professor of Belles Lettres, History and Law at the College of Liberia. En route they visited Scotland, England, FRANCE, and GERMANY. He wrote a series of letters, published in the *New York Globe* in 1884, some describing West Africa. Somewhat disillusioned by the prospects for liberal arts education in Liberia, he returned to the United States to observe vocational education at Hampton Institute (now HAMPTON UNIVERSITY). In 1886 he resumed the practice of law in NEW YORK CITY. He gained widespread attention in 1890 as counsel for fiery editor T. THOMAS FORTUNE. Fortune was awarded $1,016.23 from the proprietor of a saloon who refused to serve him because of his race and used force to have him ejected. Stewart wrote editorials for Fortune's newspaper, the *New York Freeman*. He and Fortune lobbied in 1891 to get New York State to adopt a law prohibiting insurance companies from "making any distinction between white and colored persons . . . as to the premium or rates charged for policies."

When a group of destitute blacks from Oklahoma arrived in New York City in 1892, Stewart and Fortune sought to provide relief for them so that they could return to Oklahoma rather than continue to Liberia. From 1891 to 1895 Stewart was a member of the Brooklyn Board of Education. In 1898 Stewart moved to Honolulu, Hawaii, and his glowing reports stimulated Fortune to go there. In 1903 Stewart established the weekly *Portland Advocate* in Oregon, then returned to Liberia in 1906 and became associate justice of its Supreme Court. In an *Address to the Executive Committee of the Liberia Bar Association* (1909) he sharply criticized the administration of justice. He was removed from his position in 1915.

Stewart lived in England from 1915 to 1921, respectfully known as Judge McCants Stewart, and continued his interest in AFRICA, particularly Liberia. In October 1918 he founded the African Progress Union to promote the solidarity of African Americans and Africans. Active from 1918 to 1931, the union became a key organization for PAN-AFRICANISM in GREAT BRITAIN when, after Stewart's death in 1923, the League of Colored Peoples was formed. The cold and damp winters of England forced the Stewarts in 1921 to move to SAINT THOMAS, Virgin Islands, where he practiced law and became a prominent citizen. He was a member of a delegation from the VIRGIN ISLANDS to the United States in 1922. Becoming ill, he returned to Saint Thomas, died on January 7, 1923, and was buried there. He was survived by his second wife, Alice. His first wife, Charlotte, the mother of their three children, had died some years earlier.

Stewart's son Gilchrist Stewart, an attorney whose report on the Brownsville riot in August 1906 helped spur the Senate investigation, was active in the Constitution League. The league provided a bridge between the Niagara Movement—organized in 1905 by sociologist W. E. B. DU BOIS and others to oppose the conservative policies of political leader BOOKER T. WASHINGTON—and the NATIONAL ASSOCIATION FOR THE ADVANCEMENT OF COLORED PEOPLE (NAACP).

McCants Stewart generally placed greater emphasis on economic improvement than on political action. Along with Straker, Fortune, and members of the Colored Farmers' Alliance, Stewart was somewhat influenced in the 1880s by economist Henry George's single-tax views and the exploitation of the poor by the rich. This economic approach led him to encourage the development of commercial relations with Liberia rather than large-scale colonization. In addition he advocated a stay-at-home policy for African Americans as a distinct ethnic group who would help "build up a new Christian Negro Nationality in the 'Fatherland.'" He urged industrial education in 1889 so that blacks could win recognition in organized labor and in racial business cooperation. It is not known whether the exclusionist policies of trade unions or his life in Hawaii led him to modify his views about colonization. When he returned to Liberia with his family, in 1906 he was quoted as saying: "I watch with great interest the fight which you are making in the United States for equality of opportunity. But I regard it as a hopeless struggle, and am not surprised that many Afro-Americans turn their faces toward Liberia." Encouraging African Americans to migrate to Africa was a continuing issue during the rest of Stewart's life. It is probable that his removal from office as a justice of the Supreme Court of Liberia in 1915 made him less enthusiastic about this part of the "Fatherland."

As a member of the Brooklyn Board of Education he is said to have won the fight to have the word "colored" removed from the school system and to have black teachers teach classes of white and black students. A one-time Democrat, he became a Republican in 1895 partly because of disillusionment with the policies of U.S. president Grover Cleveland, but also because Stewart, like some other prominent blacks, was being "frozen out of a job" by objections from Democrats.

See also Brownsville, Texas, Affair.

From *Dictionary of American Negro Biography* by Rayford W. Logan and Michael R. Winston, editors. Copyright © 1982 by Rayford W. Logan and Michael R. Winston. Reprinted by permission of W. W. Norton & Company, Inc.

Clarence G. Contee, Sr.

Still, William

1821–1902

American abolitionist and author who documented the experience of fugitive slaves in the book *The Underground Railroad*.

The last of eighteen children born to former slaves Levin and Charity Still, William Still spent the majority of his life in PHILADELPHIA, PENNSYLVANIA, where he had moved in 1844. By 1847 Still began his involvement in the antislavery movement while working for the Pennsylvania Society for the Abolition of Slavery. Until the CIVIL WAR he headed the Society's Philadelphia Vigilance Committee, harboring FUGITIVE SLAVES and directing them to Canada. Still would later compile the first detailed account of the UNDERGROUND RAILROAD, as told by its participants. Published in 1872, *The Underground Railroad* remains a ground breaking text.

Leaving the organization in 1861, Still advocated for the economic development of Philadelphia's African American community, exemplified by the founding of his own coal business during the Civil War. Still remained attached to civil rights groups as a researcher, writer, and activist until his death in 1902.

Still, William Grant

1895–1978

American composer whose musical works included African American themes and spanned jazz, popular, opera, and classical genres.

Born in Woodville, Mississippi, William Grant Still grew up in Little Rock, Arkansas, where as a boy he played the violin. He dropped out of WILBERFORCE UNIVERSITY where he had been studying to become a medical doctor in order to pursue music. He studied music for two years at Oberlin Conservatory, and in 1921 he became a student of George Chadwick at the New England Conservatory in BOSTON. Still received a scholarship to study composition with Edgar Varese in NEW YORK CITY, as well as a Guggenheim and a Rosenwald fellowship.

Early in his career, Still gained experience playing the oboe, violin, and cello for dance and theater orchestras. He toured the South with W. C. HANDY's band then went to New York where he worked as a songwriter, arranger, and director of the black-owned recording company Black Swan Records. In 1921 Still performed in NOBLE SISSLE and EUBIE BLAKE's path-breaking show *Shuffle Along*, playing oboe in the pit orchestra. In the late 1920s Still turned to composing classical music. He created over 150 musical works including a series of five symphonies, four ballets, and nine operas. Two of his best-known compositions are *Afro-American Symphony* (1930) and *A Bayou Legend* (1941).

After studying the works of European masters, Still developed his own compositional style that incorporated African American folk and Native American songs. He was the first black composer to have a work performed by a major orchestra, to have an opera performed by a major company, and to conduct a major orchestra.

Bibliography

Still, Judith Anne. *William Grant Still*. Greenwood Press, 1996.

Aaron Myers

Stokes, Carl Burton

1927–1996

American politician, the first black mayor of a major American city.

Carl Stokes began his political career in 1958 as an assistant city prosecutor in Cleveland. In 1967, after serving three terms in the Ohio House of Representatives, he was elected mayor of Cleveland, Ohio, the eighth largest city in the United States. Stokes thus became the first black person elected mayor of such a large American city.

Initially successful at negotiating between conservative white interests and urban black concerns, Stokes faced a decline in popularity after an armed conflict between black nationalists and Cleveland police officers sparked rioting in an African American neighborhood. Stokes served two terms as mayor of Cleveland, until 1971, but decided not to run for a third term when this conflict overshadowed the improvements his administration had made in city streets, welfare, and water purification. He later worked as a reporter, a labor lawyer, and a municipal court judge.

See also Black Nationalism in the United States.

Bibliography

Weinberg, Kenneth G. *Black Victory: Carl Stokes and the Winning of Cleveland.* Quadrangle Books, 1968.

Stokes, Louis

1925–

Democratic member of the United States House of Representatives from Ohio from 1969 to 1999; Stokes's 1968 election made him the first black member of Congress from Ohio.

Louis Stokes was born in Cleveland, Ohio. He served in the United States Army from 1943 to 1946 and then attended Case-Western Reserve University from 1946 to 1948. Stokes received a law degree from the Cleveland-Marshall Law School in 1953 and worked as a lawyer before becoming the U.S. Representative from Ohio's Eleventh Congressional District. He was re-elected every two years beginning in 1970 and defeated his Republican opponent by nearly 125,000 votes in 1996.

A predominantly black, Democratic area, the Eleventh District covers eastern Cleveland and its suburbs, including Cleveland Heights, Shaker Heights, and University Heights. Redistricting during the 1990s has added more white and middle-class voters to the district. Case Western Reserve University and many of Cleveland's prominent cultural institutions are located here.

In 1993, as a member of the Appropriations Committee, Stokes became the chair of the Veterans Affairs, Housing and Urban Development, and Independent Agencies Subcommittee. After the REPUBLICAN PARTY gained control of Congress in 1995, Stokes lost his chairmanship and became ranking member. In the 105th Congress (1997–1999), he also served on the Labor, Health and Human Services, and Education Subcommittee of the Appropriations Committee. He was also a member of the CONGRESSIONAL BLACK CAUCUS. He retired from Congress at the end of his term in 1999. Stokes is currently a visiting scholar at Case-Western Reserve University and is senior counsel at the WASHINGTON, D.C.–based Squire, Sanders, and Dempsey LLP law firm.

See also Democratic Party; United States House of Representatives, African Americans in.

Stono Rebellion

One of the most significant slave uprisings in an American colony before the American Revolution.

On the morning of Sunday, September 9, 1739, about one hundred slaves gathered along the banks of South Carolina's Stono River to fight for their freedom. The rhythmic cadence of African drumbeats, combined with cries of "Liberty!" followed a small army of slaves as they marched along the river, freeing fellow slaves, killing their masters, and torching plantations. The uprising, which occurred near CHARLESTON, SOUTH CAROLINA, began while whites were attending church services and lasted until nightfall, when it was crushed by state militias. At least sixty people were killed in the fighting, roughly two-thirds of whom were slaves.

There are 250 documented cases of violent slave disturbances on the American mainland and 250 more at sea. While subtle forms of slave resistance were daily features of life, such as working slowly or pretending to misunderstand orders, the potential for overt and violent disturbances terrified whites. Whites in colonial South Carolina had special cause for fear because by the beginning of the eighteenth century South Carolina had become the first and only British colony to have a black majority. A Swiss visitor once wrote that the colony "looks more like a Negro country than like a country settled by white people."

Colonial officials tried desperately to deal with the growing number of slaves. Armed militias patrolled the colony and were allowed to detain "suspicious" blacks at will. Slaves traveling beyond the boundaries of their plantations were required to carry identification passes, and all slaves were forced to observe a nightly curfew. Those who violated colonial laws were whipped in public. Captured runaways were routinely convicted of insurrection and publicly executed.

By the summer of 1739, South Carolina's black majority had begun to organize a massive rebellion. A black slave named Jemmy emerged as the leader of the uprising. Little is known about Jemmy. His age, slave occupation, and education are a mystery, but historians believe that he was captured in AFRICA and forced into SLAVERY IN THE UNITED STATES. In fact, the vast majority of South Carolina's 32,000 slaves came from the same region of Africa, ANGOLA, and their kinship and linguistic ties made secrecy and communication about plans for the insurrection easier. Although it is not known how the uprising was planned, eyewitness accounts provide vivid details of its execution.

Early on the morning of September 9, about twenty slaves assembled in Saint Paul's Parish, located near the western edge of the Stono River. At daybreak the group marched to Stono Bridge, broke into a white-owned firearms store, and seized boxes of guns and ammunition. The white storeowners stumbled upon the burglary and were killed in a brief struggle. Their severed heads were placed on the front porch of the store.

As the slaves traveled along the plantations lining the Stono River, they murdered twenty-five whites, including women and children. They set fire to Charleston's most valuable estates and knocked white-owned stores to the ground. By midday more than fifty slaves had gathered on a site 16 km (10 mi) outside town. The rhythmic cadence of drumming and chants of "Liberty!" drew more slaves to the battlefield. Scholar HENRY LOUIS GATES, JR., identified the beating of African drums as a form of literacy, arguing that "both forms of literacy—of English letters and of the black vernacular—had been pivotal to the slave's capacity to rebel."

Late that evening an army of twenty to one hundred white soldiers arrived upstream of the celebrating slaves. A battle followed, but the slaves were badly outgunned. Many slaves who attempted to fight were shot and killed. Some tried to return to their plantations, hoping they could avoid being implicated in the uprising. But most of them were captured, convicted, and executed. The heads of those executed were posted on fences throughout the Charleston area. A small group of slaves managed to escape and hide for several weeks but an armed white militia eventually caught up with them and killed them all after a brief gunfight.

In response to the Stono Uprising, South Carolina officials tried to reduce the provocation for insurrection, imposing penalties on masters who overworked their slaves or beat them excessively. Colonial officials established a Negro school in Charleston, largely to teach slaves selected Christian values such as obedience and submissiveness. But the benevolence of colonial officials was overshadowed by the severe, legal attacks on the mobility and limited personal liberties of South Carolina slaves.

One of the most definitive measures of the Negro Act of 1740 led to the abolition of the "talking drum," the beating of African drums during slave gatherings. According to historian Peter H. Wood, "freedom of movement and freedom of assembly, freedom to raise food, to earn money, to learn to read English" were also restricted in some cases and abolished in most. Strict laws were passed that closely monitored the ratio of blacks to whites.

The Stono Rebellion did not succeed, but it persuaded many whites to leave South Carolina. Hundreds fled to neighboring colonies. Armed white patrols increased in and around Charleston and after the uprising slaves were routinely beaten and harassed. But despite the consequences, as Wood explains, "the troubled waters of resistance did not subside any more abruptly than they had risen." The GABRIEL PROSSER CONSPIRACY in 1800 and the DENMARK VESEY CONSPIRACY in 1822 are two noteworthy examples of later acts of resistance.

See also Slave Rebellions in the United States.

Bibliography

Wood, Peter. *Black Majority: Negroes in Colonial South Carolina from 1670 Through the Stono Rebellion.* Knopf, 1974.

Alonford James Robinson

Straker, David Augustus

1842–1908

Caribbean-born African American lawyer, political activist, educator, and author.

David Straker was the son of John and Margaret Straker of BRIDGETOWN, BARBADOS, in the WEST INDIES. After graduating from Codrington, the island's college, he taught school and became principal of one of the island's high schools, Saint Mary's Public School. In 1868 he came to the United States to assist in educating former slaves. From 1868 to 1869 he taught school in LOUISVILLE, KENTUCKY. In 1869 he entered the Law Department of HOWARD UNIVERSITY in WASHINGTON, D.C., and received his law degree in 1871. In the same year he married Annie M. Carey and obtained employment as a clerk in the United States Post Office. He left this post in 1875 and moved to South Carolina, where he became a member of the law firm of ROBERT BROWN ELLIOTT and T. McCANTS STEWART.

In 1876 Straker began his political career. He made speeches in support of the REPUBLICAN PARTY ticket headed by the gubernatorial candidate Daniel H. Chamberlain. Straker won a seat representing Orangeburg County in the state's House of Representatives on November 28, 1876. Because the state election results were disputed, the DEMOCRATS and Republicans of South Carolina formed separate Houses, each contending that it was the legal body. After the Compromise of 1877 deciding the presidential victory of Rutherford B. Hayes over Samuel Tilden, U.S. president Hayes recognized Wade Hampton, the Democratic claimant, as governor of the state. When Hampton took office the state House excluded those members who had sat with the Republican House after the election of 1876 and had refused to purge themselves of contempt as required by the representatives. Straker, a rock-ribbed Republican, refused to purge himself and was unseated in favor of his Democratic opponent. Orangeburg County was just as steadfast as Straker, however, for it reelected him for two more consecutive terms, although he was rejected by the House each time. In a letter to the secretary of the treasury in 1880, Robert Brown Elliott urged that his partner be appointed inspector of customs. He asked this because Straker's "professional prospects" had been "ruined and his business destroyed by the proscription of the Democrats on account of his steadfast devotion to his party and its principles." Appointed in July 1880, Straker was stationed in Charleston. He held this post until March 1882, when he was appointed dean and professor of the new law school at Allen University in Columbia, where he also taught French. Under Straker's guidance the first class from the law school graduated in May 1884. The class consisted of four young men who, according to the *South Carolina Daily Register* on June 12, 1885, when they were examined by the Supreme Court of the state, were "highly complimented for their fitness, and admitted to practice."

While dean of the law school, Straker continued to practice law and received wide recognition for his work as the defense counsel in a murder case, *Coleman v. State* (1884). James Coleman, a black man in his mid-20s, had confessed to murdering his sister-in-law, Sarah Willis, with an axe. When Coleman was brought to trial in April 1883 Straker relied on the defense of transitory insanity, which was a relatively new defense in criminal cases. Lawyers and doctors debated the insanity defense at the end of the nineteenth century. In spite of Straker's novel and untiring efforts, Coleman was found guilty. Straker then appealed the case to the state supreme court, which refused to overturn the judgment of the circuit court. As a last resort

Straker petitioned the governor to commute Coleman's sentence to imprisonment for life on the ground of his "impulsive insanity." His plea was in vain, and Coleman was hanged on May 9, 1884. Straker had built a strong case in support of Coleman's "temporary insanity," and he believed that if Coleman had been white he would not have been hanged. Straker later wrote "this inequality in the administration of justice lies deep in the social condition of the South." He was further disheartened because his political ambitions were thwarted by the growing strength of the Democrats in the state. Increasing political impotence, racial discrimination, and personal intimidation convinced Straker that he should leave South Carolina.

In 1887 Straker moved to DETROIT, MICHIGAN. After he was admitted to the bar of the state he opened a law office. He became popular among both races as a lawyer and lecturer on the New South. Many commendatory references were made to his court work by the daily papers. He reportedly enjoyed a "lucrative" mixed practice which increased after his handling of *Ferguson v. Gies,* a civil rights case that he appealed to the Michigan Supreme Court. The case served as a precedent for civil rights cases from the turn of the twentieth century. The case was initiated by William W. Ferguson, a black man from Detroit who was the publisher of Straker's own work *The New South Investigated* (1888). Ferguson later became a realtor, lawyer, and state legislator. On August 15, 1889, Ferguson took a friend to George H. Gies's restaurant for dinner. Although whites could sit anywhere in the restaurant, blacks were permitted to sit on one side only. After Ferguson and his friend sat on the side reserved for whites, a waiter informed them that they could not be served until they moved to the other side. Irate, Ferguson questioned Gies, the owner, who confirmed the statement made by the waiter. Ferguson insisted that he be served where he sat, but the equally obstinate owner refused. After some words were passed between the men, Ferguson and his friend left the restaurant without being served. Shortly after the incident, Ferguson retained Straker to represent him in a suit against Gies.

Straker argued that Gies had violated a Michigan statute of 1885 that made it illegal to discriminate in public places on account of race. In addition he contended that the Thirteenth, Fourteenth, and Fifteenth Amendments had been enacted to prohibit discrimination in legal rights among citizens. Therefore Gies had no right, in law, to discriminate between patrons on account of color and could not justify racial discrimination by saying that it was a regulation of business. Although Straker's arguments were well founded in law, the "separate but equal" concept was gaining strength throughout the country during the post-RECONSTRUCTION period. When the jury trial ended in defeat Ferguson and Straker appealed to the Michigan Supreme Court. The *Detroit Plaindealer* reported of Straker's appellate argument that "it was the prevailing opinion of those who were present that the Supreme Court of the state of Michigan has not heard for many years a stronger or more forcible plea that justice should be meted out." This time Straker and Ferguson won by a unanimous decision. Judge J. Morse, in writing the decision for the court, declared that "the

man who goes either by himself or with his family to a public place must expect to meet and mingle with all classes of people. He cannot ask, to suit his caprice or prejudice or social views, that this or that man shall be excluded because he does not wish to associate with them. He may draw his social line as closely as he chooses at home, or in other private places, but he cannot in public places carry the privacy of his home with him."

Despite this decision racial discrimination in public places began to increase notably after 1896, when the United States Supreme Court sanctioned the "separate but equal" doctrine in the *Plessy v. Ferguson* decision. JIM CROW practices of segregation, however, were continually challenged, and *Ferguson v. Gies* served as a precedent for some of these attacks.

The *Ferguson v. Gies* case increased Straker's popularity, and in 1893 he became the first black elected a circuit court commissioner for Wayne County. He compiled *The Circuit Court Commissioner's Guide, Law and Practice* after a brief trip to BARBADOS. He was elected for a second term in 1895 but his militant support of equal rights for blacks virtually ensured defeat for a third term.

As a political activist Straker was associated with some of the most eminent men of his time, including Oliver O. Howard, Charles Sumner, FREDERICK DOUGLASS, BOOKER T. WASHINGTON, and W. E. B. DU BOIS. Straker shared some of Washington's views but he did not adhere to Washington's public philosophy of accommodation. Straker argued eloquently for the right of every citizen to vote, as well as to hold public office if he so desired and was qualified. He also argued for the right of every citizen to obtain an education in keeping with his abilities, to live wherever he pleased, to work at whatever job suited his talents, and to have equal access to all public facilities. Straker agreed with Washington, however, that racial discrimination would ultimately cease as blacks became more educated and their economic status improved. Like Washington he also promoted industrial education. He thought that it would provide the average black youth with some marketable skills but he insisted that training in the professions was equally important, for he believed with Du Bois that the progress of the black race depended on the leadership of talented black professionals.

Straker supported black unity, in America and elsewhere. He was one of the organizers and the first president of the National Federation of Colored Men, a forerunner of the NATIONAL ASSOCIATION FOR THE ADVANCEMENT OF COLORED PEOPLE (NAACP). Founded in Detroit in December 1895, the federation divided the United States into districts where subordinate branches would be established. It sought remedies against lynching, fraudulent elections, and disfranchisement. In addition, it pledged to work for equal employment opportunities, to fight discrimination in public facilities, and to seek equal enforcement of the law for all citizens. Nonpartisan, it proposed to achieve its objectives through political pressure and agitation. One of the political achievements of the federation was the adoption by the National Republican Executive Committee in 1896 of an anti-lynching plank in the Republican platform.

Henry Sylvester Williams, who organized the Pan-African Conference in London in 1900, consulted with Straker prior to the conference.

Straker expounded his philosophy in numerous books and articles and in his newspaper, the *Detroit Advocate* (1901–1908). Straker died of pneumonia on February 14, 1908, at his home, 230 Bagg Street, Detroit. His wife of thirty-six years had died also in 1908. His funeral was held on February 17 at St. Matthew's Church and he was buried in Woodmere Cemetery. An adopted daughter, Anna Glover, survived him.

Straker's books include *Reflection on the Life and Times of Toussaint L'Overture* (1885); *The New South Investigated* (1888); *A Trip to the Windward Islands* (1896); *Circuit Court Commissioner's Guide: Law and Practice* (1897); and *Compendium of Evidence* (1899).

At the turn of the twentieth century, Straker exercised a great deal of political influence and enjoyed wide public recognition. Shortly before he died he had been nominated as a delegate to the State Constitutional Convention of 1908. "The passing of Augustus Straker," commented Du Bois in the *Horizon,* "calls for some tribute of respect. He represented the rapidly dwindling number of Reconstruction actors, and one, too, who never gave up his ideas and never crawled and kow-towed to the 'New South'."

From *Dictionary of American Negro Biography* by Rayford W. Logan and Michael R. Winston, editors. Copyright © 1982 by Rayford W. Logan and Michael R. Winston. Reprinted by permission of W. W. Norton & Company, Inc.

Dorothy Drinkard-Hawkshawe

Strayhorn, Billy

1915–1967

American jazz composer, arranger, and pianist; associate of the Duke Ellington orchestra from 1939 to 1967.

Billy Strayhorn was born into a family that relocated from his birthplace in Dayton, Ohio, to Hillsborough, North Carolina, and finally to PITTSBURGH, PENNSYLVANIA. In Pittsburgh Strayhorn received private piano instruction in the classics. A technically accomplished student, he coupled his classical music training with an inventive approach, working out his own chromatic harmonies.

In December 1938 Strayhorn showed some of his own compositions to DUKE ELLINGTON, hoping to impress him enough to be taken on as a lyricist. Three months later Ellington recorded Strayhorn's "Something to Live For." As Ellington later recounted in his memoir, "Billy Strayhorn successfully married melody, words, and harmony, equating the fitting with happiness." "Something to Live For" was followed by four more recordings with Ellington's orchestra in 1939.

For the next thirty years Strayhorn worked with Ellington as an associate arranger and second pianist. The two collaborated so closely that it is difficult to assess the contribution of each on an arrangement such as the popular "Satin Doll." Stray-

horn's musical language and basic approach to composition were very similar to Ellington's, and the bandleader recalled that he and Strayhorn were so like-minded that once, when composing separately on a given mood, they chose the same first and last notes.

Strayhorn produced an album in his own name, the 1950 *Billy Strayhorn Trio,* and also participated in small group recordings with Ellington sidemen. His main work continued to be collaborative, creating such compositions as "Such Sweet Thunder," "Suite Thursday," and "Far East Suite" for Ellington's orchestra before his death in 1967.

See also Jazz.

Marian Aguiar

Street Children in Brazil

Children under the age of eighteen, often of African descent, who spend most of their time on the streets of the urban centers of Brazil.

It is difficult to characterize BRAZIL's street children in a simple manner, as children of many different circumstances might be considered "street children." In general they are children who work, beg, and sometimes steal in order to supplement their family's income and/or ensure their own survival. They spend varying amounts of time on the street and have different reasons for being there: some work on the street part-time, others go there to find friendship and sometimes protection from dangerous home situations; and others live on the street full-time. Most of the children are of African descent.

The exact number of street children in Brazil is not known. According to unofficial estimates, the number ranges from 200,000 to one million. A 1990 UNICEF report estimated that 7.5 million children between the ages of ten and eighteen work on Brazil's streets. But this number does not necessarily correspond to the number of children who *live* on the street. These children do what they can to survive, from selling candy on street corners, shining shoes, and watching parked cars, to drug dealing, petty theft, and prostitution.

The presence of street children in Brazilian cities is not a new phenomenon; it has been documented extensively since the end of the nineteenth century, when slavery was abolished. Traditionally, however, this phenomenon was not seen as a consequence of abolition. Ever since the abolition of slavery in 1888 race has not been taken into account, and in studies these children are often simply identified as male minors who, because of their lack of resources and frequent state of addiction, commit crimes. They are widely considered dangerous, immoral, and a threat to the public order.

Scholars such as Irma Rizzini, Irene Rizzini, and Gilberto Dimenstein have shown, though, that these children are often the descendants of emancipated slaves. The factors after abolition that helped create this population were industrialization, the promotion of immigration from Europe, and the lack of official programs for the adjustment of emancipated slaves. As a result, families of former slaves often had two choices: remaining in rural poverty or emigrating to the cities, where they faced severe obstacles to regular, formal employment. With few means of supporting themselves, they often sought employment in urban centers. Extremely limited access to education, because of discrimination, also led children to the streets. At that time, education was reserved for a few aristocrats and wealthy families. It was still seen as a privilege of the upper classes.

In the twentieth century the phenomenon of street children in Brazil has been addressed mainly through policies of social control, with little attention to structural causes. Street children have been regarded as minors who were abandoned by their families and who thus deviated from the norm. The state typically responded by placing the children in institutions. State shelters became places where these minors were lodged in order to be "rehabilitated." In effect, the state further excluded and marginalized this population.

During the 1980s, as a consequence of Brazil's economic recession, the number of children living and working in the streets of Brazilian cities increased significantly. In a groundbreaking investigation conducted in 1984, Irene Rizzini interviewed a total of 300 children between the ages of five and eighteen years on the streets of RIO DE JANEIRO and found that 87 percent were male, and 72 percent were of African descent.

The gradual process of democratization that took place in Brazil in the 1980s saw the expansion of social movements. One such movement that took up the cause of street children was the Movimento Nacional de Meninos e Meninas de Rua (MNMMR, National Movement of Street Children), established in 1985. The MNMMR strongly influenced the Constituent Assembly, which was drafting Brazil's constitution, and pushed for the incorporation of a new legal definition of children's rights. The constitutional draft proposed by the MNMMR was endorsed by 200,000 voters and ultimately became the chapter on the rights of children and adolescents in the 1988 constitution, which finalized Brazil's return to full democracy after twenty-one years of military dictatorship.

This legislation set the stage for the Estatuto da Criança e Adolescente (ECA, Children's Statute), which was enacted in 1990. The ECA inaugurated a new era in children's rights in Brazil, closely following the provisions laid out in two United Nations international legal documents that Brazil has ratified: the Universal Declaration on the Rights of the Child, and the Convention on the Rights of the Child. Unlike previous children's legislation, the Código de Menores (Minors Code), which was discriminatory and aimed at minors in what were seen as "irregular" situations, the ECA has a broader orientation, recognizing the rights of all children and adolescents.

By the end of the 1990s the problem of street children as well as the violence committed against them had drawn increased attention. The federal police estimated that between 1988 and 1990 some 4,611 children were victims of murder. According to the nongovernmental organization CEAP, the Centre for the Mobilization of Marginalized Populations, in 1990 in Rio de Janeiro alone 1,770 children were killed. More recently the Rio de Janeiro courts estimated that 1,221 children in the state of Rio were violently killed in 1994; of these, 570 were victims of gunshots and 334 were under eleven years of age. Children who live on the streets or in urban FAVELAS (squatter communities) represent the great majority of victims. The killings are often committed by "death squads," armed groups comprised of retired and off-duty policemen. Such death squads are organized with the goal of killing children or young adults whom they believe are or will become thieves as a result of poor education and lack of material resources. Children are also sometimes killed by on-duty police, most commonly by the military police.

Despite Brazil's legal progress on this subject, street children are still considered dangerous and a threat to public order by a number of people who financially or ideologically support the activities of death squads. At the state level, impunity guarantees that these groups persist. Police inquiries into the killing of street children are often inadequate and, when undertaken, few are completed and referred to the courts. In addition the military policemen who are often accused of these killings are tried in a separate military justice system, where they are judged by other members of the military police force and rarely face conviction for violent crimes against civilians.

Despite increased attention to the issue of violence against street children—and against Brazil's poor and dark-skinned adolescents in general—there are no official data about the racial identity of these children. The first study of the relationship between race and the systematic killing of street children and children of low-income families in Rio de Janeiro was conducted by CEAP in 1991. The organization found that of the murder victims below the age of eighteen described in newspaper reports between June and August of 1990, 75 percent were of African descent and 13 percent were female.

CEAP concluded that most of the victims of violence are Afro-Brazilian boys who live on the streets or in the city's peripheral neighborhoods and who have no significant criminal records. Violence against children attracted particular attention in July 1993 when eight street children who were sleeping in front of downtown Rio de Janeiro's Candelária Church were killed by a group of off-duty policemen. Almost all of the victims were black boys.

See also Human Rights in Latin America and the Caribbean.

Michelle Gueraldi

Structural Adjustment in Africa

National economic reform programs undertaken by countries in return for assistance from the World Bank and other international donor institutions.

Numerous countries in AFRICA began to experience difficulty meeting their financial obligations during the 1970s. By the early 1980s most African countries were receiving loans from international financial institutions that were subject to conditions on borrowers' national economic policies. The conditions that accompanied these loans were known collectively as structural adjustment policies (SAPs). The lending agencies responsible for devising SAPs included the World Bank, the International Monetary Fund (IMF), and bilateral agencies such as the United States Agency for International Development and European aid agencies.

The history of SAPs is controversial in Africa, possibly more so than elsewhere. The results have been disappointing. Critics portray SAPs as a failure, foisted on Africa by heartless outsiders. Other critics have complained that theorists unfamiliar with African problems designed policies that are poorly suited to African realities. Defenders claim that incomplete and incoherent implementation of SAPs often accounted for their disappointing results. They emphasize the benefits of these policies, rather than the failings.

Background

The mid-1970s increase in oil prices caused problems for African oil importers in their balance of payments (in a given country, total money received in export earnings and financial assistance, less total money spent on imports and external debt). When oil prices increased many countries found that the money they received (in export earnings and aid funding) failed to cover the cost of oil imports. Many countries met their increased need for foreign exchange by borrowing funds rather than by curtailing other imports or increasing exports. Thus, they failed to adjust to the new scarcity of foreign exchange.

Meanwhile they increased their foreign debts and only worsened their long-term balance of payments problems, because in the future they would have to pay not only for oil imports but also for debt service. There were a number of commodity booms in the mid-1970s that temporarily generated increased foreign exchange earnings for some African countries. Prices of coffee, cocoa, tea, and phosphates were all high, and the boom encouraged even more borrowing. Banks were willing to loan to African countries because of the countries' high export earnings at the time and because of the banks' need to find ways to invest the petrodollars on deposit from the oil exporters. The recession in the early 1980s, however, caused commodity prices to collapse as global demand dropped. High interest rates imposed by the Federal Reserve Bank to fight inflation in the United States caused real interest rates to rise to highs that were unforeseen when African countries negotiated their external loans. By the early 1980s many African countries, facing potential bankruptcy, turned to the World Bank, IMF, and bilateral agencies for assistance.

Structural Adjustment Programs

Assistance included additional lending, some grants, and some debt forgiveness. Lenders required acceptance of conditions intended to promote short-term stabilization, generally combining devaluation of the local currency with government financial austerity. They also required policy changes aimed to increase growth over the medium to long term. Currency devaluation was expected to improve the balance of payments because it would make imports more expensive and hence reduce demand for them, while it would make exports more attractive on the global market and hence increase the supply of foreign exchange. Financial austerity required governments to reduce expenditures or increase taxes, or both. This was supposed to reduce monetary growth and, therefore, inflation. Inflation contributed to currency overvaluation by making domestic prices rise faster than international prices, so inflation increased demand for imports and reduced supply of exports. Reducing inflation was essential to regaining balance of payments equilibrium. Because devaluation itself spurred inflation by increasing the prices of imported goods, it needed to be combined with austerity to keep overvaluation from recurring.

SAPs also compelled countries to implement longer-term policy reforms, among them the privatization of public enterprises, the deregulation of prices and interest rates, and financial liberalization, encompassing free trade in all sorts of commodities and financial instruments, including foreign exchange. Foreign trade was also supposed to be liberalized and trade barriers of all types reduced. These things were expected to attract foreign investment and improve the efficiency of resource use.

The World Bank published a major study of structural adjustment in Africa in 1994. They found evidence that countries that adhered to SAPs improved their economic performance and that they had better performance than countries that flouted SAP requirements. They cited increased growth in gross domestic product (GDP, a measure of the volume of economic activity), industrial output, and exports in countries that followed SAPs. The improvements, however, were extremely modest and would be considered poor in other developing regions. Economic growth rates remain too low to expect much reduction in poverty in the next twenty or thirty years. SAPs, which included additional loans, have left the adjusting countries still deeply indebted and vulnerable to economic downturns in the future.

Assessment

Why has the record of structural adjustment been so disappointing in Africa? There has been little political support from within Africa for SAPs, which has made their implementation difficult. Policymakers are especially sensitive to the interests of urban populations because of the danger of rioting in countries' capitals. Devaluation makes locally produced goods relatively less expensive, and imports more expensive. The income of many urban residents comes from selling services locally while they consume many imported goods. Hence devaluation hurts the standard of living of many urban residents. Likewise, government austerity hurts many urban dwellers via higher taxes or lower expenditures, especially if there are layoffs of public employees. Thus governments have often implemented SAPs reluctantly, partially, and only under duress.

The logic behind SAPs includes many assumptions about the ways in which markets allocate resources. In Africa markets have often not worked according to the assumptions of neoclassical models. African governments have often had a much bigger economic role than is presumed in such models. Also, much of the economy may still be focused on subsistence production, which does not pass through markets and may not respond to market incentives, especially if farmers lack the physical or institutional infrastructure that would permit marketing. For example, government bodies, rather than market forces, have often set commodity prices in Africa. Partial implementation of SAPs in such an environment can have perverse consequences. In one such example, when government bodies set prices, devaluation does not automatically translate into higher producer prices for exported goods. Paying producers higher prices—in line with the increased export earnings that result from devaluation—would mean higher costs for government marketing boards. Thus higher producer prices contradicted the logic of austerity, and governments sometimes failed to implement them fully. The result of devaluation without passing through price increases to producers was to increase farmers' costs (for imported inputs) and to make it less rather than more profitable to produce export crops. Thus, partial implementation of SAPs can be ineffective or even harmful.

Critics of SAPs have often claimed that SAPs harm the welfare of the poor because they result in higher prices for basic goods and cutbacks in government services. Supporters of SAPS counter that countries needing balance of payments support are already experiencing economic problems; for example, per capita gross domestic product (GDP) in Ghana had declined for nearly a decade before Ghana began structural adjustment. There is no doubt that the poor in Ghana suffered mightily during structural adjustment, but supporters claim that structural adjustment stopped the shrinkage of the economy and helped most people, including the poor. Ghana is often cited as the country with the best adjustment record in Africa. In theory, those employed in exporting sectors should gain from SAPs, and to the extent that this includes large numbers of peasant farmers, SAPs in Africa may raise incomes and improve the welfare of the poor.

The countries of West Africa that share the CFA franc as their currency (comprising most of the countries of former French West Africa) have had the most difficult time with structural adjustment. Because they could not devalue their currency without a unanimous vote of all of the countries using it, they had to adjust without devaluation. This left austerity as the only real tool to achieve adjustment: they needed to slow their own price increases below those of trading partners to achieve real devaluation, in order to improve their balance of payments. The degree of austerity necessary to achieve such deflation proved politically unacceptable, so that these countries floundered with less austerity than necessary to be effective, but enough to ensure prolonged recession. Finally, they devalued their currency in 1994 for the first time since the 1940s.

Western donors compounded the controversy over SAPs in the 1990s by adding a whole new set of political conditions.

Following the end of the COLD WAR and the collapse of communist regimes in the former Soviet bloc, Western donors had less need to secure third-world allies and a simultaneous desire to distribute aid to the former Soviet-bloc countries. In this context, donors became less willing to offer support to African regimes that they viewed as corrupt and undemocratic. They added conditions requiring less corruption and greater democracy to the long list of conditions already required under SAP lending. Some believe that these requirements helped the emerging democratic opposition, but incumbent rulers deeply resented the intrusive nature of these conditions. The effectiveness of these political conditions is questionable. They probably worked best in KENYA, where President DANIEL ARAP MOI responded to a moratorium on balance of payments assistance by restoring multiparty elections. The case of the former ZAIRE (today the DEMOCRATIC REPUBLIC OF THE CONGO) is more troubling: there President MOBUTU SESE SEKO refused to accept a democratic transition, clinging to office as the state decayed and collapsed.

Barbara Grosh

Struggles for Independence in Latin America, Racial Questions during the

As early as the seventeenth century, blacks formed part of the Spanish colonial armed forces throughout the Americas. Many men of African descent commanded or comprised military units whose actions in combat often turned the tide in military conflicts. This trend continued throughout the nineteenth century, a period (1808–1843) characterized by the prevalence of revolutionary and independence movements throughout the continent.

Traditionally the history of the wars of independence in LATIN AMERICA has been presented as the struggle of CREOLES (American born colonists) to liberate themselves from Spanish rule. The lesser-known dimension of racial tensions between whites (Spanish and Creoles) and people of African descent, however, has been overlooked despite its significant impact on the development and outcome of the independence wars. Not only were the Creole rebels and the Spanish colonizers' armies composed, and in some cases led, by many blacks and mulattos but the future status of people of color became one of the leading incentives for supporting or opposing independence from the Spanish Crown. The participation of American-born blacks in the pro-Spanish rule as well as the pro-independence armies made the armed confrontations, in terms of popular participation, into civil wars. American-born blacks and mulattos found themselves on both sides of the battlefield, having to choose armies based on who they thought would carry out promises of a better future for people of color.

On one side, at the beginning of the nineteenth century, the idea of revolutionary independence sparked hope for broad social changes. Throughout Spanish America black and mulatto leaders interpreted the possibility of forming new and independent nations as an opportunity to change the social order and to abolish slavery. Optimists saw independence as an occasion for bringing about new regimes under the government of the *castas* (or castes, a term used for socioracial stratification for racially "mixed" peoples), which they called a *pardocracia*. This hope, or illusion, and the fear that it generated might have been a factor in determining the later development of Spanish America's nations.

On the other hand, many blacks and mulattoes thought that it was safer for them to continue under Spanish rule. Despite occupying the lowest strata in the colonizers' society, people of color felt they had more guarantees under the Spanish laws that ordered some restrictions on Creole abuse than under the future rule of those who had enslaved and exploited them.

Both the Spanish and the Creole commanders, therefore, took advantage of the uncertain future for blacks and encouraged racial animosities as a weapon in the battlefield. For example, in 1815 SIMÓN BOLÍVAR (1783–1830), the greatest figure in the rebellions for independence in Spanish America, complained that "the Spanish commanders of Venezuela . . . following the example of Saint Domingue, though ignoring the real causes of that revolution, strove to subvert all people of color, even slaves against white Creoles, in order to establish a wasteland under the flags of [Spanish king] Fernando VII."

Venezuela is a case in point. Radical divisions among Indians, Spaniards, mestizos, blacks, and *pardos* made it hard to choose which side to be on during the era of independence fervor (1808–1821). For many blacks, slave and free, Spanish Commander José Tomás Boves's promise of freedom and the reluctance to fight with their Creole masters convinced them to join the Spanish army voluntarily in 1813 and 1814. According to Mr. Robinson, a British tradesman of La Guayra, in 1814 "under Boves'[s] command there were at least seven or eight thousand men, among whom there were no more than 50 whites or European Spaniards and 1,000 free pardos; the rest were slaves, blacks and *zambos*." The black and mulatto officers reached the highest ranks in the Spanish army and carried on a "war until death" against the white patriots. This turned the confrontation into a civil war in which most Creoles hesitated between siding with the Spanish Crown or against it, dreading a later government of the castas.

Despite the strong fear of a racial revolution, Bolívar needed to recruit soldiers. To do so, he had to follow the strategy of the Spanish commanders: promising freedom for slaves and promoting some mulattos and mestizos to positions of command. At one point a few colored leaders gathered enough power to threaten to control the patriot army and were sentenced to death by the white Creoles for allegedly promoting a "race war." The most notorious executions were those of General MANUEL PIAR in 1817, before the total independence from Spain was achieved; Colonel Leonardo Infante in 1825; and Admiral José Prudencio Padilla in 1829, when the wars were over and the former *caudillos* (military leaders) were internally defining the allocation of power among them.

Another example of the role that blacks played in the wars of independence is that of ARGENTINA. Slaves were recruited into defensive forces as early as 1806, when the white Creoles repelled the English invasion and finally defeated the British army of General Whitelocke. Seventy of the Afro-Argentine combatants were emancipated in recognition of their deeds. A decade later, during the struggles for independence, forcibly conscripted slaves composed at least 25 percent of the army. Creoles resorted to using pardo and mestizo regiments, often commanded by mulatto captains. Some captains were even honored with the title of "Don" (Sir) from 1811 on, but none of them ever rose above this rank.

Despite the fact that during the struggles for independence the black or mulatto population in Buenos Aires was between 25 and 30 percent of the total population, white supremacy in Argentina was never questioned. The same could be said for other countries of the Southern Cone where no attempts were made to establish a government of the castes. However, in 1814 Chilean rebel leaders established that male slaves able to carry arms would be granted their freedom upon enlisting. When General José de San Martín led his army across the Andes into CHILE to liberate the country from Spanish rule, half of his forces were comprised of ex-slaves from Buenos Aires and the provinces of western Argentina. These units were organized into the all-black Seventh and Eighth Infantry Battalion and the integrated Eleventh Infantry. In PERU, by virtue of a decree issued by the Argentine liberator San Martín, slave soldiers were declared free in 1821.

In the Spanish Caribbean the Batallón de los Morenos (Battalion of Mixed/Black Persons) of Santo Domingo is yet another example of the crucial presence of enlisted blacks in the wars for independence. The battalion was active in two critical independence movements that took place in what is now the DOMINICAN REPUBLIC. The first occurred in 1821 when José Núñez de Cáceres led elite white Creole insurgents against Spanish rule. In order to garner military strength, Núñez de Cáceres promised freedom to enslaved blacks if they fought on the side of the insurgents. He managed to enlist blacks and gained the support of Dominican commander PABLO ALÍ, who led the Batallón de los Morenos. Haitian general JEAN-PIERRE BOYER subsequently gained control of the entire island (today's Haiti and Dominican Republic) in 1822.

Blacks became increasingly disgruntled as land promised to them by the new Haitian government remained in the hands of white landowners reluctant to release their properties. Eager to escape the conditions on the plantations, Afro-Dominicans enlisted in Batallón 32. Batallón 32 became the primary military unit to protect the eastern section of the island and was an essential part of the independence movement in April 1843. The black battalion opted to side with the revolutionaries led by La Trinitaria, an underground insurgent group that advocated for the creation of the eastern part of the island into an independent state free from Haitian rule.

In Mexico, Father Miguel Hidalgo y Costilla led the Batallón de los Morenos, in which mestizo (mixed European and indigenous) and indigenous individuals also participated in an attempt to abolish Spanish rule in September 1810. The revolt was halted and the insurgents were executed on July 30, 1811.

Besides the obvious participation of men of color in the white-led wars mentioned above, it is still uncertain to what extent the general population of blacks and mulattos was in fact aware of the possibility of a radical sociopolitical change. British pressure for abolition of slavery was publicly known, and it is conceivable that many blacks knew of it. The ideas of the French Revolution also reached blacks, free and slave alike. At the same time, president ALEXANDRE PÉTION's rise to power in Haiti was widely known. Venezuelan black and mulatto leaders were well informed that the economic and military support he had given to Bolívar for the cause of independence in 1816 was conditioned to the abolition of slavery. In fact, Manuel Piar was accused, tried, and condemned in part for allegedly intending to follow Haiti's political experience in GUYANA.

One historian claims that the revolutionary ideals did promote a separatist character in Venezuela and the area east of the Rio de la Plata. In other areas, however, it is not clear if these outbreaks were isolated and spontaneous or had similar political intentions. For example, racial struggle became a mass mobilizing phenomenon in Peru during the 1780 and 1781 Indian rebellions headed by the mestizo José Gabriel Condorcarqui, known as Tupac Amarú II. Even though it was an Indian revolt, many blacks joined the fight against the Creoles and Condorcarqui's brother, Diego, issued a decree abolishing slavery in 1781. In Venezuela the bloody riot of the Coro Peninsula was clearly a black insurrection against slavery, rather than an independence movement. In COLOMBIA, the comunero revolt against new taxes also had a racial element. There the castas were not revolting against the Spanish Crown but against the white Creoles controlling the local government. Three decades later this claim acquired a definite shape in Venezuela, where the clamor, "Kill the whites! Long live the King!" spread in 1813. Such claims threatened the stability of the new regime even after the Spaniards had been defeated, as in the popular riot in the town of Petaré in 1824.

On the other hand, accounts tell us that in several other places of South America the racial question reached the status of a social revolution. When the rebels fled from Caracas before the arrival of the Spanish commander Boves and the "Mulato" Machado, a foreigner merchant witnessed that "only a few people could embark [in the port of La Guayra]. Those who remained were relentlessly massacred. The African Race carried on every kind of excess, and in La Guayra black people started the massacre [even] before the arrival of the troops."

In sum, backing the Spanish flag for blacks (free and slave) was more of a pretext to wage war against their masters. Blacks feared further oppression under the Creoles in power, who would certainly wipe out the few legal protections they had under the Spanish Crown. On the other side, most of the black or mulatto leaders struggling for independence had little or no education, and the few who did were killed during the internal struggles that followed the wars. This made it extremely difficult for the colored masses to conceive an alternative social order through a strong and vocal leadership. The revolts never went any further than a temporary havoc, and the few

attempts to set up a government controlled by the castas were severely repressed by the white Creole commanders.

The third aspect of the racial question during this period is to what extent the white Creoles, influenced by the French Revolution's ideas of liberty, equality, and fraternity, as well as by the North American concept of democracy, were willing to accept the sociopolitical ascent of black and mulatto people. For example, the Argentine liberator San Martín (1778–1850) introduced several protections in favor of slaves, such as the free womb laws and the ban to slave trade, but at the same time he questioned the mental capabilities of the blacks and precluded the ascent of any black or mulatto to the highest military ranks. General Manuel Belgrano, another Argentine leader, shared this view. He said "the blacks and mulattos are a rabble that is as cowardly as it is bloodthirsty." Creole leaders used blacks and mulattos when they needed them, but they were by no means committed to promoting racial equality.

The same is true for other South American leaders. As the war in those countries became bloodier they had to accept a greater participation of the black population in order to defeat the Spaniards, but again, the supremacy of the whites was never questioned. Bolívar, for example, admired republican institutions but considered that too many individual rights, especially those concerning representation and equality, were unsuited for nations in which whites were a minority. In Argentina historians attribute the "disappearance" of two-thirds of the black population in the region to the significant number who died, deserted, or whose presence simply was unaccounted for while in the army.

At the end of the period of independence struggles in Spanish America (1808–1843), the vows of general freedom were forgotten and only some of the slaves who fought against Spain as soldiers were freed. The so-called "revolutions" were not such for indigenous people and blacks, whose social and economic situation of the castas remained almost unaltered and in many cases deteriorated under the new governments of the white Creoles. Abolition, and a slight improvement in black sociopolitical status, was to come only thirty years later.

See also Complexities of Ethnic and Racial Terminology in Latin America and the Caribbean; Latin America, Blacks and Indians in: An Interpretation.

Juan Botero

Student Nonviolent Coordinating Committee

Civil rights organization that played a major role in the 1960s campaign to end segregation in the Southern United States.

On February 1, 1960, four black college students attracted national attention when they refused to leave a whites-only lunch counter in an F. W. Woolworth store in Greensboro, North Carolina. The SIT-IN continued for several weeks and inspired dozens of similar actions across the South. Although not the first time students had taken part in civil rights protests, the sit-in movement was one of the largest and most spontaneous. Reacting to the protests, ELLA BAKER, executive director of the SOUTHERN CHRISTIAN LEADERSHIP CONFERENCE (SCLC), held a conference for student activists in April at Shaw University in Raleigh, North Carolina. Baker believed that larger, more cautious civil rights groups, such as the SCLC, might have failed to serve students who were impatient for racial equality. She urged the 200 attendees to establish a new student group that would harness its energy and frustration to challenge white racism as well as the larger and more conventional civil rights groups.

Other civil rights leaders, such as SCLC's MARTIN LUTHER KING, JR., argued that a united movement would be stronger than a divided one and invited the students to create a wing within SCLC. Representatives of the NATIONAL ASSOCIATION FOR THE ADVANCEMENT OF COLORED PEOPLE (NAACP) and the NATIONAL URBAN LEAGUE made similar invitations. The students created a temporary coordinating committee to debate the issue; in May the committee embraced the mainstream's practice of nonviolence but created an independent group, the Temporary Student Nonviolent Coordinating Committee. ("Temporary" was dropped from the name in October.) Consisting of both black and white members, the group elected MARION BARRY—a student at FISK UNIVERSITY in Nashville, Tennessee, who would later become mayor of WASHINGTON, D.C.—SNCC's first chairman and set up its headquarters in ATLANTA, GEORGIA. When Barry returned to his graduate studies a few months later, Charles McDew, a student at South Carolina State College, replaced him.

In its first months SNCC served mostly as a channel for student groups to communicate and coordinate the sit-in campaign. The images on national television of well-groomed, peaceful protesters being refused a cup of coffee and, in some instances, being hauled off to jail generated sympathy among many whites across the country. Several SNCC and other protesters capitalized on the publicity with a "jail-no-bail" campaign. Refusing to pay fines or bail, the students served jail sentences, thereby filling Southern jails and continuing media coverage. By the end of 1960 several chain stores in the upper South and Texas responded to the movement by ending segregation at their lunch counters. Several cities also agreed to desegregate public restaurants.

Freedom Rides

From the end of 1960 through the fall of 1961, SNCC underwent a critical internal debate that it never completely resolved. One faction wanted to continue generating white sympathy through sit-ins and demonstrations, while another faction wanted to give Southern blacks power more directly by helping them register to vote. SNCC's JAMES FORMAN, a schoolteacher-turned-coordinator, urged the group to pursue both goals. Forman reasoned that helping blacks register to vote was a form of nonviolent protest that would stir up Southern hos-

tility, generate white sympathy, and give blacks more power. SNCC's membership agreed.

As the debate over SNCC's direction was taking place, the CONGRESS OF RACIAL EQUALITY (CORE) was undertaking the FREEDOM RIDE of 1961. On May 4 seven blacks and six whites left Washington, D.C., on two public buses bound for the Deep South. They intended to test the Supreme Court's ruling in *Boynton v. Virginia* (1960), which declared segregation in interstate bus and rail stations unconstitutional. In the first few days the riders encountered only minor hostility, but in the second week the riders were severely beaten. Outside Anniston, Alabama, one of the buses was burned, and in Birmingham several dozen whites attacked the riders only two blocks from the sheriff's office. With the intervention of the United States Department of Justice, most of CORE's Freedom Riders were evacuated from BIRMINGHAM, ALABAMA, to NEW ORLEANS, LOUISIANA. JOHN LEWIS, a former seminary student who would later lead SNCC and become a U.S. congressman, stayed in Birmingham, as did another rider.

SNCC leaders hurriedly decided that letting violence end the trip would send the wrong signal to the country. They reinforced the pair of remaining riders with volunteers, and under SNCC leadership the trip continued. The group traveled from Birmingham to Montgomery without incident, but on their arrival in Montgomery, they were savagely attacked by a mob of more than 1,000 whites. The extreme violence and the indifference of local police prompted a national outcry of support for the riders, putting pressure on President John F. Kennedy to end the violence. The riders continued to Mississippi, where they endured further brutality and jail terms but generated more publicity and inspired dozens more Freedom Rides. By the end of the summer the protests had spread to train stations and airports across the South, and in November the Interstate Commerce Commission issued rules prohibiting segregated transportation facilities.

Gaining the Vote

Following the sit-in and Freedom Ride victories, SNCC joined with CORE, the NAACP, SCLC, and the Urban League in the Voter Education Project (VEP). Funded by large private grants, VEP sought to increase the number of Southern blacks registered to vote. SNCC had failed at a similar voter-registration effort in rural Georgia in 1961 and 1962. When VEP funds became available in 1962, SNCC shifted its focus to Mississippi and Louisiana, where it also met stern resistance and succeeded in registering only a few blacks.

In 1963, however, several highly publicized conflicts changed the course of the movement. In May police in Birmingham brutally beat black and white protesters, prompting another wave of public sympathy. The next month Kennedy introduced a strong civil rights bill to the Congress of the United States that was passed during the administration of Lyndon Johnson as the Civil Rights Act of 1964. (The act prohibited segregation in several types of public facilities.) Liberal contributors responded to the violence by pouring large donations into virtually all of the civil rights groups, whose staffs and programs grew accordingly. In late 1963, when VEP decided to abandon Mississippi for lack of progress, SNCC, now led by Lewis, could afford to stay.

Many SNCC activists were critical of the way larger civil rights groups "invaded" towns for a protest, then left after the protest ended. SNCC's field workers in Mississippi believed they could best help blacks by living in their communities and working with them over the long term. In late 1963, with help from CORE and, nominally, other civil rights groups, SNCC revitalized the COUNCIL OF FEDERATED ORGANIZATIONS (COFO); COFO had been created in 1961 to help free jailed Freedom Riders. It would now oversee voter registration in Mississippi. BOB MOSES, a Harvard graduate student, veteran SNCC field worker, and leading advocate of commitment to communities, was placed in charge of COFO. COFO functioned largely as an arm of SNCC.

Despite COFO's efforts, whites effectively used intimidation and discriminatory tactics to keep blacks from registering in Mississippi. To Northern reporters, Mississippi officials argued that the state's blacks did not vote because they were too apathetic. COFO countered the claim by holding a Freedom Vote at the same time as the November 1963 elections. In mock elections 80,000 blacks cast ballots in their own communities, where they did not have to face hostile whites.

Amid the success, many of COFO's black workers were angered by the role whites were playing in the organization. White students often came to the South for a few months (typically a summer), assumed high-profile leadership positions while there, then returned to safe campuses in the North leaving the blacks to continue the hard work. Many black activists were also tired of the beatings and jail sentences they endured in order to win sympathy from white federal officials, white liberal donors, and the public in general. They were weary as well of having to tone down their militancy and rhetoric at the request of white people in power. SNCC's Lewis voiced many of these frustrations during a speech in the MARCH ON WASHINGTON of August 1963; that Lewis was made to tone down his remarks by mainstream civil rights groups and white officials only further angered blacks in SNCC. For these reasons many COFO activists argued it was important for blacks to succeed on their own, without the help of white volunteers. Some even wondered if it would be possible to continue working with mainstream civil rights groups.

Moses was forced to address this debate when he proposed the FREEDOM SUMMER of 1964, a registration and education project that would build on the Freedom Vote. Moses argued forcefully that if COFO excluded whites, blacks had no moral standing to demand integration. Moreover, the movement would not receive as much publicity since national news groups would pay more attention to violence against whites than blacks. Moses's words were borne out when COFO's Michael Schwerner, JAMES CHANEY, and Andrew Goodman were murdered in June (Schwerner and Goodman were white) and the press and public responded with shock and outrage.

For years murders of blacks by whites in the South had gone unnoticed in the national media. President Johnson ordered a large Federal Bureau of Investigation (FBI) presence in Mississippi, and many whites became aware of the obstacles blacks faced when trying to vote in the Deep South. Still, COFO's 1,000 volunteers managed to register only 1,200 blacks statewide. Within COFO many student workers were convinced after the Schwerner, Chaney, and Goodman murders that nonviolence would not win blacks the vote. By the end of the summer SNCC officially defended the right of its Mississippi field secretaries to carry weapons.

Moses was able to exploit COFO's failure to register voters by creating a new party, the MISSISSIPPI FREEDOM DEMOCRATIC PARTY (MFDP). Some 60,000 blacks joined the MFDP, which served as an alternative to Mississippi's all-white Democratic Party. With the presidential election of 1964 approaching, the MFDP sent forty-four delegates to the national Democratic convention in Atlantic City, New Jersey. The delegation demanded to be seated at the convention in place of the regular Mississippi delegation. They were pledged to Johnson, while the white Democratic delegates were not. Although several Northern states supported seating the MFDP, Southern states threatened to walk out of the convention if the MFDP were seated. Johnson, wary of losing the conservative South in the general election that fall, offered the MFDP a compromise: two of its black delegates would be seated along with the white delegates. The MFDP rejected the offer and, in a move largely coordinated by SNCC, walked out of the convention. In the aftermath many whites across the country saw SNCC as an extremist group unwilling to bend, while many blacks became even more convinced that they could not work with whites.

Selma and Beyond

In early 1965 King and the SCLC attempted to register voters in Selma, Alabama. Learning from past mistakes, state and local officials denied the SCLC the brutal attacks that had created sympathy for blacks elsewhere. Instead, officials simply jailed blacks who tried to register. In March, King called for a march from Selma to the capitol in Montgomery to protest black exclusion from the polls; however, he abruptly called off the protest on the eve of the march, probably to avoid antagonizing Johnson. After King left Selma, SNCC field workers and other activists urged local SCLC leaders to go ahead with the march. On March 7, 500 protesters headed by the SCLC's Hosea Williams and SNCC's Lewis began the march. In a matter of minutes a large deputized posse and dozens of state troopers attacked the marchers. The gruesome reports and photographs prompted one of the nation's largest outcries in support of the CIVIL RIGHTS MOVEMENT. Largely as a result, Congress passed the VOTING RIGHTS ACT OF 1965, which provided federal protections and guarantees for black voters.

Although many SNCC members were pleased that the events in Selma had generated white sympathy, many others were again weary of taking abuse. They were also angered that a second Selma march, led by King a week later, was cut short after federal officials cautioned against it. When riots broke out in the black Watts neighborhood of LOS ANGELES, CALIFORNIA, in the summer of 1965, many SNCC members argued that the time had come for blacks to seize power rather than seek accommodation with whites. In May 1966 SNCC formalized its shift in this direction by electing STOKELY CARMICHAEL (later Kwame Ture), a recent graduate of HOWARD UNIVERSITY in Washington, D.C., to the chairmanship over Lewis. Rejecting nonviolence, Carmichael argued at first that violence should be used in self-defense; later he called for offensive violence to overthrow oppression. Carmichael also denounced Johnson's civil rights bills, which were supported by the SCLC and the NAACP.

In June 1966 in Greenwood, Mississippi, Carmichael advocated BLACK POWER in a well-publicized speech. Although "Black Power" had been used before as shorthand for black pride and political equality, Carmichael popularized the term through repeated speeches. Many whites were offended by Carmichael's views, which they saw as separatist or racist, and most of the mainstream civil rights groups severed their few remaining ties with SNCC. SNCC's white staff and volunteers, who had already begun to drift away from the group, soon left. Eventually Carmichael expelled the remaining white staff and denounced SNCC's white donors. By early 1967 SNCC was near bankruptcy and both its staff and membership had dwindled.

In June 1967, when Carmichael left SNCC to help lead the BLACK PANTHER PARTY, he was replaced by twenty-three-year-old H. RAP BROWN. In his first months Brown removed the word "nonviolent" from SNCC (renaming the group the Student National Coordinating Committee) and made urgent calls for violence. When DETROIT, MICHIGAN, rioted in the summer of 1967, Brown urged an audience in Cambridge, Massachusetts, to do the same. When a Cambridge school was set aflame hours later Brown was charged with inciting a riot, one of several charges he would face in the following years. In May 1968 his legal problems forced him to resign SNCC's chairmanship. SNCC continued to operate into the early 1970s, but its impact on politics was minimal.

See also Jim Crow; Watts Riot of 1965.

Suárez y Romero, Anselmo

1818–1878

Novelist, university professor, and journalist.

Anselmo Suárez y Romero was an important member of a literary coterie that gathered at the home of Domingo del Monte (1804–1853), a white CREOLE intellectual and patron to the principal antislavery writers of the period.

Although Suárez y Romero was born into the ruling plantation class—his father, José Ildefonso Suárez, was the legal adviser to the despotic Captain General Miguel Tacón, the Spanish Crown's principal administrator in Cuba—his life was marked by periods of economic impoverishment. Suárez y Romero's father died in SPAIN in 1843, leaving the family in economic ruin. In 1842 Suárez y Romero began a sporadic

career in teaching as a substitute for a friend, José Zacarías González del Valle. The writer received a law degree in 1866 but he never practiced as an attorney.

Suárez y Romero is recognized today primarily in connection with two events: the copying and correction between 1835 and 1839 of the slave and poet JUAN FRANCISCO MANZANO's *Autobiografía de un esclavo* (Autobiography of a Slave, only published in Spanish a century later in 1937) and the 1839 writing of one of the earliest antislavery novels, *Francisco* (published in New York in 1880). The latter was, in fact, commissioned by Domingo del Monte as part of a portfolio of writings about slavery for the Irish abolitionist Richard Robert Madden. Madden, who translated Manzano's autobiography into English in 1840, was eager to collect texts that highlighted the abuses of slavery. Del Monte, in order to heighten the sense of what was peculiarly Cuban in the text, added the subtitle *El ingenio, o las delicias del campo* (The Sugar Mill, or the Delights of the Countryside). The book describes the tragic love between two slaves, Francisco and Dorotea, which ends with the suicide of the latter. Although the novel has been criticized for presenting a highly sentimental and idealized portrait of Afro-Cubans, its value in registering the tensions of the time is beyond question.

See also Abolitionist Novels in Cuba: An Interpretation; Giral, Sergio.

Bibliography

Barreda-Tomás, Pedro M. *The Black Protagonist in the Cuban Novel.* University of Massachusetts Press, 1979.
Williams, Lorna. *The Representation of Slavery in Cuban Fiction.* University of Missouri Press, 1994.

Edward Mullen

Suburbanization and African Americans

Relationship between African Americans and the creation and settlement of communities, usually separate municipalities, in the outlying areas of cities.

Throughout American history very few African Americans have lived in suburbs. In colonial and early nineteenth-century America, suburbs were sparsely settled, marginal areas on the periphery of densely populated cities. In NEW YORK CITY, for example, shantytowns, junkyards, and cemeteries occupied land on the outskirts of the densely populated city. African Americans occasionally lived in such places, but suburban populations were heterogeneous and highly mobile and did not develop lasting communities. By the late 1700s, some wealthy white urbanites began to build summer homes and estates just outside of the cities. During the first half of the nineteenth century, an increasing number of wealthy urbanites built homes in the suburbs. Few African Americans lived in these exclusive communities. Most of those who did were household servants.

With the advent of the streetcar and railway in the mid-nineteenth century, many middle- and upper-class urbanites moved to the suburbs, which had become accessible, and hired African Americans to do household work. As the suburban white populations increased in the late nineteenth century, a few small African American suburban enclaves developed. For example, African American domestics, gardeners, cooks, and chauffeurs lived in modest homes in Ardmore, Pennsylvania, on PHILADELPHIA's Main Line (west of the city along the main line of the Pennsylvania Railroad).

Migration and White Flight

By the late nineteenth century, as public transportation became more affordable, suburbanization increased. As cities attracted immigrants from Europe and Asia and black migrants from the South, a growing number of whites fled to suburban communities away from neighborhoods with sizeable immigrant and African American populations. By the 1920s most suburban communities protected their exclusive status by implementing zoning laws that prevented blacks and other minorities from building affordable houses or apartments. In addition, many suburbs preserved their racial homogeneity through the use of restrictive covenants that banned the sale or occupancy of a house by nonwhites. During and after the GREAT MIGRATION, the mass movement of blacks to Northern cities in the early twentieth century, however, some African Americans who sought the independence of home ownership built small suburban communities such as Inkster, Michigan (near DETROIT), Lincoln Heights, Illinois (near CHICAGO), and Chagrin Falls Park, Ohio (near Cleveland).

The nature of suburbanization changed dramatically during the 1930s. Three federal programs encouraged widespread home ownership and made home loans and mortgages affordable for working class and middle class Americans. The Home Owners' Loan Corporation, created in 1933, and the Federal Housing Administration, created in 1934, underwrote large-scale suburban development. After WORLD WAR II (1939–1945) the Veterans Administration also made available affordable home loans to returning veterans. But these government programs disproportionately benefited whites. Neighborhoods that were mixed-race or predominantly African American were deemed to be high credit risks by federal loan officers and bankers, and therefore homebuyers in those neighborhoods were refused mortgages. The Home Owners' Loan Corporation prepared "Home Security Maps" that rated neighborhoods on a scale of A (most worthy of loans) to D (least worthy of loans). (The use of red to mark the D neighborhoods led to the term *redlining,* which refers to the practice of refusing to grant mortgages or insurance within entire neighborhoods.) African American neighborhoods were always ranked lowest on this scale. In addition, loan guidelines prohibited the sale of a home to African Americans in predominantly white communities. The result of these federal programs was a dramatic expansion of white suburbanization and a virtual bar on black suburbanization.

The period following World War II witnessed a massive white migration to the suburbs, often called "white flight." Most suburban communities remained overwhelmingly white, despite antidiscrimination rulings and legislation. The decision of the U.S. Supreme Court in *Shelley v. Kraemer* (1948) ruled that courts could not enforce racially restrictive covenants, and the federal Fair Housing Act of 1968 forbade discrimination against minorities by real estate brokers, property owners, and landlords. In some suburban areas white homeowners created a hostile environment for black newcomers. In 1957 white residents in the planned suburban community of Levittown, Pennsylvania, attacked the home of a black family that had moved there. In addition, real estate agents developed furtive tactics to preserve the racial homogeneity of neighborhoods. The most significant was "steering," that is, the practice of directing white homebuyers to all-white communities and black homebuyers to predominantly black or racially transitional neighborhoods. In the 1980s and 1990s the Department of Housing and Urban Development and local housing and nonprofit agencies studied housing discrimination by sending matched pairs of black and white "testers" to randomly selected real estate offices. The studies consistently showed the persistence of discriminatory treatment of black home buyers and renters.

Since the 1960s

The effects of white suburbanization and black concentration in urban areas have exacerbated city-suburban political conflict since the 1950s. In the United States most municipal services, such as education, road construction, zoning, and recreation have been funded and controlled locally. Suburbanites, mostly white, have frequently rejected programs to distribute tax dollars, social expenditures, and resources equitably across municipal boundaries. During the 1960s and 1970s suburbanites resisted cross-district school desegregation. Many suburban communities around the country used zoning laws to prevent the construction of affordable housing. In its famous *Mount Laurel* decisions in 1975 and 1983, the New Jersey Supreme Court countered such local laws by requiring the construction of affordable housing in predominantly white suburbs. The decisions were met with over two decades of litigation and delays by town officials. Proposals to construct public housing for racial minorities in suburbs also came under attack in the suburbs of many cities including Norwalk, Connecticut; Detroit, Michigan; and Oakland, California.

Since 1970 there has been a significant migration of African Americans away from city centers to suburbs. Suburban areas, such as Prince George's County, Maryland (near WASHINGTON, D.C.), Mount Vernon, New York (adjacent to the Bronx), and Southfield, Michigan (outside of Detroit), have gained attention for their growing African American populations. Some observers have suggested that black suburbanization is a sign of significant change in American race relations, a move toward a more racially integrated society. But such optimistic views are not borne out by evidence; patterns of residential segregation have persisted as blacks move to suburbia. It is a fallacy to equate suburbanization with racial integration. In most places black suburbanites have been greeted with white flight and white abandonment of public schools. The movement of blacks to formerly all-white communities was a noteworthy development in the late twentieth century, but patterns of black-white separation remained deeply rooted.

See also Integration: An Interpretation; School Desegregation in the United States; Segregation in the United States.

Eric Bennett

Sudan

Country in northeastern Africa, with a coastline along the Red Sea, and bordering Eritrea, Ethiopia, Kenya, Uganda, the Democratic Republic of the Congo, the Central African Republic, Chad, Libya, and Egypt.

Covering a territory of close to a million square miles, the Republic of the Sudan is the largest nation in Africa. Stretching from the NUBIAN and Libyan deserts along the Egyptian border to the rainforests of the Nile-Congo divide, Sudan is a bridge between the Arabic-speaking peoples of northern Africa and the peoples of sub-Saharan Africa. The NILE RIVER flows the length of the country, providing a common focus for the diverse peoples of Sudan. Its waters have transformed a narrow stretch of desert along the banks of the lower Nile into a fertile valley capable of supporting large urban centers.

With the exception of a narrow strip of arable land along the Nile, the area north of KHARTOUM is desert, sparsely populated by nomadic Arab or Nubian communities. Cultivation is possible only with the aid of irrigation. At Wadi Halfa, a riverine community along the Egyptian border, rainfall averages less than 7 cm (3 in) per year. Rainfall is heavier in the south, averaging 90 cm (35 in) per annum at Malakal and over 127 cm (50 in) along the Congo border. With the exception of the western portion, southern Sudan has been isolated from the north by a variety of natural obstacles. A 800-km (500-mi) stretch of floating masses of vegetation, known as the Sudd (Arabic for "barrier"), clogged the White Nile and its tributaries over an area of roughly 100,000 sq km (40,000 sq mi), thereby preventing all significant water transportation until the 1840s.

Early History

Archaeological evidence indicates that people have inhabited the area known today as Sudan for at least 30,000 years. By about 3000 B.C.E., the descendants of these early hunter-gatherers had domesticated animals and begun to practice agriculture.

The inhabitants of the region known as NUBIA, located along the Nile in the northern part of present-day Sudan, had extensive contact with EGYPT just to the north and with the more agrarian cultures to the south and west. Early Egyptian chronicles report numerous military expeditions up the Nile and periodic conquests of Nubia before 2000 B.C.E. During times of peace, the Nubians and neighboring pastoral peoples, such as the Blemmyes (BEJA) of the Red Sea Hills, traded gold, cattle, ivory, and slaves to Egypt. They also served as intermediaries in the Egyptian trade with PUNT, a kingdom in present-day SOMALIA.

By about 2000 B.C.E., a Kushitic culture, drawing on African traditions of the upper Nile and the eastern savannas as well as those of Egypt, became the dominant culture of Nubia. In the sixteenth century B.C.E., Ahmose, an Egyptian pharaoh, conquered Nubia and increased slave-trading activities. Kush regained its independence under the Kingdom of Napata, which in the eighth century B.C.E. conquered and ruled most of Egypt for more than fifty years. By the fourth century B.C.E., Meroe had replaced Napata as the capital of the Kushitic kingdom, while Napata remained as a religious center. Kush successfully resisted conquest by Egypt, but its power gradually declined. The Ethiopian kingdom of AKSUM invaded Meroe in about 350 C.E.

Beginning in the sixth century, missionaries from Egypt converted the ruling classes of the small Nubian states to Coptic Christianity, which gradually spread to the rest of the population, reaching as far as the present-day region of DARFUR to the southwest. Two kingdoms, Makuria and Alwa, emerged as the most powerful states in Nubia. Twelve years after the Arab conquest of Egypt in 639, Arab armies tried unsuccessfully to conquer Nubia. Instead, Egypt and Makuria signed a treaty pledging to respect each other's political and cultural integrity. The king of Makuria agreed to permit the construction of a mosque at his capital, Dunqulah, to return runaway slaves who entered his territory, and to pay an annual tribute of 360 slaves to the governor of Aswan in Egypt. Outside the terms of the treaty, Makuria received goods that often exceeded the strictly commercial value of the exported slaves. The treaty governed Egyptian-Nubian relations for almost 600 years.

In subsequent years, Egyptian Arabs, seeking greater freedom and opportunity, settled in Nubia. Arab men married into matrilineal families of the Nubians and the Beja and attained powerful positions in Nubian society. While they received Nubian inheritances from their mothers, they bestowed their inheritances patrilineally, thus bringing these newly acquired properties and titles under Arab control. Arab settlers also brought Islam to Nubia, where it gradually spread. In time, an Arabized Nubian society emerged as the dominant cultural form in the region. Beginning in the thirteenth century, the MAMLUK STATE in Egypt carried out a series of devastating military campaigns that weakened the Christian kingdom of Makuria. By the fifteenth century, Makuria could no longer resist conquest by a powerful confederacy of Arab nomads allied with Egypt. By the end of the fifteenth century, Alwa, the last Christian kingdom of Nubia, had fallen to the Arab confederacy.

Era of Muslim Hegemony

While the Egyptian Mamluk state occupied Nubia, Amara Dunqas founded the Funj kingdom in the area just to the south,

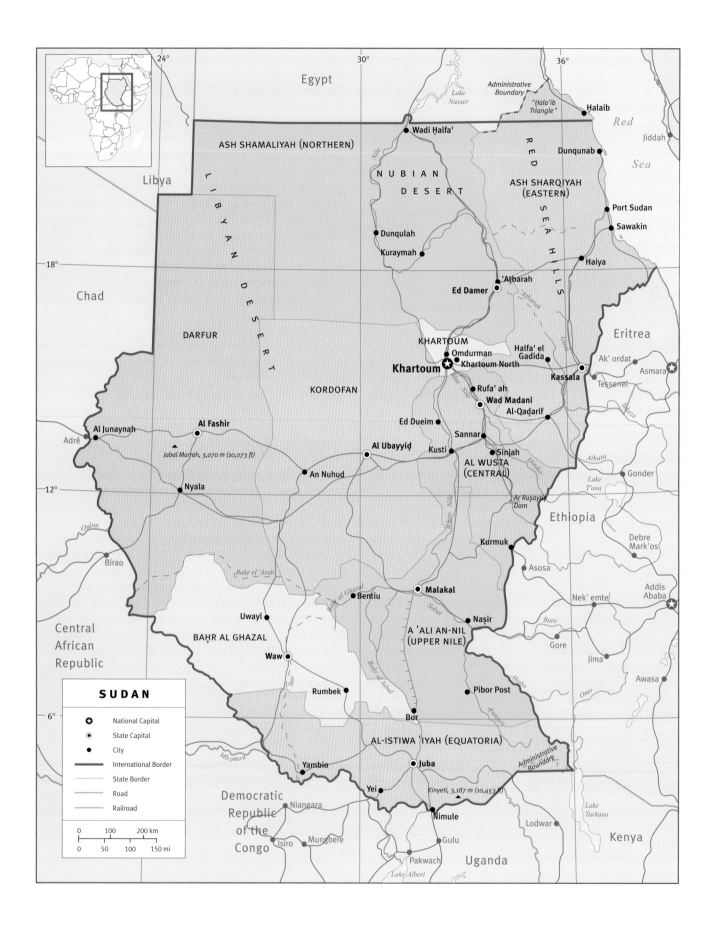

Egypt

24°   30°   36°

Lake Nasser

Administrative Boundary

"Ḥala'ib Triangle"

Ḥalaib

Jiddah

Wadi Ḥalfa'

ASH SHAMALIYAH (NORTHERN)

Dunqunab

Red Sea

RED SEA HILLS

ASH SHARQIYAH (EASTERN)

Libya

N U B I A N   D E S E R T

Port Sudan

Sawakin

Dunqulah

Kuraymah

18°

Haiya

L I B Y A N   D E S E R T

Chad

'Atbarah

Ed Damer

Eritrea

DARFUR

KHARTOUM

Omdurman

Khartoum North

Halfa' el Gadida

Ak' ordat

Asmara

Khartoum

Kassala

Tessenei

Rufa' ah

Wad Madani

Al-Qaḍarif

KORDOFAN

Al Fashir

Ed Dueim

Sannar

Al Junaynah

Adré

Jabal Marrah, 3,070 m (10,073 ft)

Al Ubayyiḍ

Kusti

Sinjah

AL WUSTA (CENTRAL)

Gonder

Lake T'ana

An Nuhud

Ar Ruṣayriṣ Dam

12°

Nyala

Ethiopia

Debre Mark'os

Oulou

Birao

Bahr el 'Arab

Kurmuk

Asosa

Bahr al Ghazal

Bentiu

Malakal

Nek' emte

Addis Ababa

Uwayl

Sobat

Naṣir

Baro

Central African Republic

BAḤR AL GHAZAL

A 'ALI AN-NIL (UPPER NILE)

Gore

Jima

Waw

Bahr al Jabal

Pibor Post

Awasa

Rumbek

Sue

Bor

6°

SUDAN

⊙ National Capital
◉ State Capital
• City
━━ International Border
── State Border
── Road
── Railroad

0   100   200 km
0   50   100   150 mi

AL-ISTIWA 'IYAH (EQUATORIA)

Yambio

Juba

Administrative Boundary

Lake Turkana

Democratic Republic of the Congo

Niangara

Yei

Kinyeti, 3,187 m (10,453 ft)

Lodwar

Isiro

Mungbere

Nimule

Gulu

Kenya

Mbomou

Pakwach

Uganda

Lake Albert

the Gezira, between the White and Blue Niles, where he ruled from 1504 until 1534. Dunqas converted to Islam during his reign and promoted Islam throughout present-day central Sudan. At its peak in the seventeenth century, the Funj kingdom, with its capital at Sennar, incorporated most of Nubia and extended to the Ethiopian border in the southeast and the semi-arid steppes of Kordofan in the west. The Funj kingdom's control of important trade routes from West Africa and Ethiopia to Egypt assured it prosperity into the eighteenth century. By the seventeenth century an independent Islamic sultanate, Darfur, was able to exert control over trade routes to Kanem-Bornu, thereby becoming the major state in the western portion of present-day Sudan.

In the early nineteenth century two Turkish-Egyptian armies, sent by Muhammad Ali, moved to conquer the Funj kingdom and Darfur. Muhammad Ali valued the area because of its high potential for slave raiding and saw little risk in attacking either kingdom. As Muhammad Ali wrote to his son-in-law, in command of one of the armies: "You are aware that the end of all our efforts and this expense is to procure Negroes." Many of these captives were conscripted into a modernized, standing Egyptian army. The technological superiority of the Turkish-Egyptian forces, called the Turkiyya in Sudan, allowed the small army to conquer the Nile Valley without major difficulties. During the 1820s the Turkiyya established a colonial administration in northern and central Sudan and encouraged the production of cotton and indigo for market. Northern Sudanese increasingly raided southern Sudan for slaves.

However, the Sudd, the vast swamp to the south of the Shilluk kingdom, hindered northerners from asserting control over the peoples of the far south, such as the DINKA. Moreover, the Shilluk army was able to repel external threats. In 1831 the Shilluk kingdom defeated a Turkiyya slaving expedition of more than 2,000 troops. The transhumant Dinka retreated into the swamps, where their greater mobility protected them from northern slave raiders. Thus the main supply of ivory and slaves came from the present-day Bahr al Ghazal province to the west, which was subject to raids by the BAGGARA and FUR peoples of the Darfur region. In the south, in the eighteenth century, the Azande and the Dinka slowly expanded their control over neighboring peoples. The expansion of the Azande and Dinka propelled a NUER expansion into areas surrounding the Sudd and an Anuak expansion into the foothills of the Ethiopian escarpment.

Meanwhile, the Turkiyya aimed to extend its control south of the Sudd. In 1841 a Turkiyya-sponsored expedition found a river channel through the Sudd to the present-day Equatoria province. Once a route to the upper Nile was opened, the Turkiyya government promoted the ivory, gold, and slave trades. Northern Sudanese came to control the slave trade by organizing private armies of up to 2,500 men, supported by as many as 500 porters. Some slave traders became virtual rulers of vast tracts of southern Sudan. In exchange for exclusive territorial concessions, traders paid substantial sums to the Turkiyya treasury. The most powerful of these slave traders was al-Zubayr Rahman, who exported approximately 1,800 slaves a year in the 1850s and 1860s. The infamous slave trader and empire builder RABIH AL-ZUBAYR started his career as an aide to al-Zubayr Rahman.

While the slave trade and interethnic warfare had existed before the opening of the river route to southern Sudan, the level of violence escalated in the last half of the nineteenth century. What had previously been intermittent warfare and raiding became nearly constant, with heavy casualties and widespread seizures of slaves. Preferring a subservient position in a traditional antagonist's community to slavery in a raider's army or a foreign land, many of the smaller ethnic groups of southern Sudan sought refuge among the Dinka or Azande.

Although the Turkiyya administration in Egypt signed various agreements with European powers abolishing the slave trade, it made little effort to enforce them. After issuing several edicts outlawing the slave trade, in 1872 Khedive Ismail appointed Zubayr governor of the Bahr al Ghazal, an area where Zubayr had recently dominated the slave trade. In the late 1870s the khedive appointed an Englishman, Gen. Charles Gordon, as governor of Equatoria. Gordon banished Zubayr and attempted to eliminate the slave trade. His abolitionist campaign, however, disrupted the Sudanese economy and alienated traders and northern Sudanese alike.

The lavishness of the Egyptian court, its neglect of Islamic obligations, government corruption, and heavy taxation all contributed to the growing discontent. In 1879 the British deposed Khedive Ismail and replaced him with a puppet ruler, Muhammad Tawfiq. Armed resistance to this new government erupted in Egypt and Sudan. In 1881 a man named Muhammad Ahmad announced that he was the Mahdi, "the guided one," who had been sent by Allah to cleanse the Islamic community of corruption and to establish a truly Islamic state. From his base in the Kordofan region he called for a *jihad* (holy war) against the Turkiyya, which had surrendered to a foe of Islam, the British. The initial followers of the Mahdi were Baggara pastoralists, but he quickly expanded his support among ascetic religious communities, traders who resented government interference, and nomadic Arabs. By 1885 his followers had defeated the Turkiyya and established a Muslim state controlling most of present-day Sudan. But the Mahdi died shortly thereafter, and his successors failed to eliminate the corruption that had plagued the Turkiyya administration.

Anglo-Egyptian Condominium

Determined to prevent French expansion into the Nile Valley, the British organized an Anglo-Egyptian force that reoccupied Sudan and overthrew the Madhdist state in 1898. In 1899 the British and Egyptian governments signed what became known as the Condominium Agreement, providing for joint rule over Sudan. While the agreement dictated joint and equal rule by the two partners, during the early stages of Condominium rule Egypt was a virtual British protectorate and could not act autonomously. The Condominium government sought to appease Muslims and discourage the nationalistic Islam of the Mahdists by confining Christian missionaries to southern Sudan, where

Sudan (At a Glance)

OFFICIAL NAME: The Republic of the Sudan

FORMER NAME: Anglo-Egyptian Sudan

AREA: 2,505,813 sq km (about 967,495 sq mi)

LOCATION: North Africa, on the Red Sea, bordered by Ethiopia, Kenya, Uganda, Democratic Republic of the Congo, Central African Republic, Chad, Libya, and Egypt

CAPITAL: Khartoum (population 1,397,900; 2003 estimate)

OTHER MAJOR CITIES: Omdurman (population 2,103,900; 2003 estimate), Khartoum North, and Port Sudan (450,400; 2003 estimate)

POPULATION: 38,114,160 (2003 estimate)

POPULATION DENSITY: 8 persons per sq km (about 21 persons per sq mi)

POPULATION BELOW AGE 15: 44 percent (male 8,562,412; female 8,195,201; 2003 estimate)

POPULATION GROWTH RATE: 2.71 percent (2003 estimate)

TOTAL FERTILITY RATE: 5.1 children born per woman (2003 estimate)

LIFE EXPECTANCY AT BIRTH: Total population: 57.73 years (male 56.59 years; female 58.93 years; 2003 estimate)

INFANT MORTALITY: 65.59 deaths per 1,000 live births (2003 estimate)

LITERACY RATE (AGE 15 AND OVER WHO CAN READ AND WRITE): Total population: 61.1 percent (male 71.8 percent; female 50.5 percent; 2003 estimate)

EDUCATION: Between 1992 and 2001, 54 percent of eligible boys and 52 percent of eligible girls attended primary school. Between 1995 and 1999, about 22 percent of all boys and 36 percent of all girls attended secondary school. Some 3,600 students attended vocational and teacher-training institutions, and more than 60,000 attended institutions of higher education, including the University of Khartoum, Omdurman Islamic University, the University of Juba, and the College of Fine and Applied Art.

LANGUAGES: Arabic is the official language. English is widely spoken, and African languages, used mainly in the south, include Nubian, Ta Bedawie, and numerous dialects of Nilotic, Nilo-Hamitic, and Sudanic languages.

ETHNIC GROUPS: 39 percent of the Sudanese population is Arab, inhabiting the north of the country. Also in the north are the Beja, Jamala, and Nubian peoples. The Azande, Dinka, Nuer, and Shilluk inhabit the south.

RELIGIONS: The majority (70 percent) of Sudan's citizens are Sunni Muslim; indigenous beliefs account for about 20 percent of the population, and 5 percent of the Sudanese are Christian.

CLIMATE: Arid desert in north, tropical in south. In the desert temperatures vary from 4.4° C (about 40° F) in the winter to 43.3° C (about 110° F) in the summer. Around Khartoum the average annual temperature is about 26.7° C (80° F); and annual rainfall, most of which occurs between mid-June and September, is about 254 mm (10 in). In southern Sudan the average annual temperature is about 29.4° C (85° F), and annual rainfall is more than 1,015 mm (40 in).

LAND, PLANTS, AND ANIMALS: The northern third of Sudan is desert; central Sudan is characterized by steppes and low mountains; and the south has vast swamps and rain forests. Numerous species of acacia tree can be found along the Nile valley in the north, and central Sudan has forests that include hashab, talh, heglig, and acacia. Ebony, silag, and baobab trees are common in the Blue Nile valley, and ebony and mahogany trees grow in the White Nile basin. Other species of indigenous vegetation include cotton, papyrus, castor-oil plants, and rubber plants. Animal life includes elephants, crocodiles, hippopotamuses, giraffes, leopards, lions, monkeys, tropical birds, and snakes.

NATURAL RESOURCES: Petroleum, iron ore, copper, chromium ore, zinc, tungsten, mica, silver, and gold

CURRENCY: The Sudanese pound

GROSS DOMESTIC PRODUCT (GDP): $52.9 billion (2002 estimate)

GDP PER CAPITA: $1,420 (2002 estimate)

GDP REAL GROWTH RATE: 5.1 percent (2002 estimate)

PRIMARY ECONOMIC ACTIVITIES: Agriculture, industry, and services

PRIMARY CROPS: Cotton, groundnuts, sorghum, millet, wheat, gum arabic, sugarcane, cassava, mangos, papayas, bananas, sweet potatoes, sesame, and sheep

INDUSTRIES: Cotton ginning, textiles, cement, edible oils, sugar, soap distilling, shoes, and petroleum refining

PRIMARY EXPORTS: Oil and petroleum products, cotton, sesame, livestock, groundnuts, gum arabic, sugar

PRIMARY IMPORTS: Foodstuffs, manufactured goods, refinery and transportation equipment, medicines, chemicals, textiles, wheat

PRIMARY TRADE PARTNERS: China, Japan, Saudi Arabia, European Union, South Korea

GOVERNMENT: A military junta led by Lt. Gen. Umar Hasan Ahmad al-Bashir took power in 1989 and retained control through a series of interim governments. Al-Bashir was popularly elected as president in 1996 and reelected in 2000 in voting that was widely viewed as rigged. The cabinet, consisting of twenty federal ministers, is appointed by the president. The legislative branch is the National Assembly, which consists of 360 seats, 270 of which are popularly elected. The president, however, dismissed this body in 1999 after an internal power struggle with National Assembly speaker Hassan al-Turabi, who was jailed in 2001. The president has also partially suspended Sudan's new constitution, implemented in 1998.

Barbara Worley

there were few Muslims. The Condominium government did establish secular schools in the north, however, primarily in order to train indigenous Sudanese civil servants.

In southern Sudan, the British reopened the Nile channel and began to consolidate their control of the region. Freed from all but sporadic interference during the Mahdist era, southerners sought to retain their independence from the British. The British faced armed resistance from the Azande, Nuer, and Dinka. The Nuer and Dinka, led by prophets claiming direct revelation from powerful spirits of the sky, resisted British rule into the 1930s. Hoping to create a Christian and "civilized" region in the south, the Condominium decided to separate the two regions of Sudan. The 1906 Closed Districts Ordinance and subsequent legislation required northern Sudanese and non-Sudanese to have visas in order to enter southern Sudan. Expatriates replaced northern administrators, and the British introduced indirect rule, in which "traditional" rulers, appointed by British provincial governors for their loyalty, exercised local government. Among the Nuer and Dinka, who lacked a tradition of community rulers, the government arbitrarily endowed members of the priestly class with civil powers, including the power to adjudicate minor offenses and to impose punishments. The government left the educational development of the south to Christian missionaries. It specifically prohibited instruction in Arabic and encouraged the use of English.

During the first half of the twentieth century, the Condominium developed the economy and infrastructure of Sudan, including a railroad connecting most northern Sudanese cities. The Condominium absorbed many former slaves into its military and police forces. Their children were some of the first students at the new government schools and eventually found their way into the civil service. In 1925 workers completed the Sennar dam, which provided the essential water for the Gezira Scheme, a vast cotton-farming project that began a year later. The Gezira Scheme involved an unusual partnership among the Condominium government, the private Sudan Plantations Syndicate, and tenant farmers who actually grew the cotton. Profits were divided among the three parties. Other agricultural schemes in Kassala and Gash also centered on cotton. Apart from a limited trade in ivory and tropical foodstuffs, southern Sudan saw little economic development under the Condominium. The GREAT DEPRESSION of the 1930s, however, devastated Sudan's economy and revealed the dangers of overreliance on the single cash crop of cotton.

Meanwhile, anticolonial organizations began to emerge in Sudan. In 1921 Ali Abd al-Latif, a Dinka Muslim, founded the Sudanese United Tribes Society. Drawing on support in both regions of Sudan, he demanded complete independence for Sudan and a federal government that would provide autonomy for the various Sudanese peoples. His arrest generated a wave of nationalist sentiment, not only in Sudan but in Egypt as well. In 1938 alumni of Sudan's Gordon College established the Graduates General Congress. Under Ismail al-Azhari's leadership in the 1940s, the congress broadened its membership and demanded the right to self-determination through a representative legislature as well as the abolition of the Closed Districts Ordinance, which separated the northern and southern parts

of the country. In 1944 two political parties organized to contest the first elections to the Advisory Council for northern Sudan. The Shaqqa party, led by Azhari, advocated independence with close ties to Egypt, while the Umma party favored complete independence.

During the 1940s, administrators of southern Sudan debated whether to integrate the region into a unified Sudan, join it to a possible East African federation, or allow it to progress toward independence on its own. However, British East African states showed little interest in integrating their poorer neighbor into a federation. An independent south would lack an economic base, a transportation and communications infrastructure, and a basis for regional unity. Integration with the north seemed to be the only viable alternative, yet considerable expenditures would be required to raise the south's education, its infrastructure, and its political institutions to levels comparable to the north's. In order to accomplish this, the government implemented the Zande Scheme in 1948 to encourage cotton and other cash crops in southern Sudan; increased government expenditures for schools; and reintegrated the two halves of the country.

In 1949 Sudanese, Egyptian, and British representatives drafted a new constitution providing limited self-rule for an integrated Sudan. Southern Sudanese preferred to postpone unification with the north until, through economic and educational development, they could enter into an equal partnership; however, the new constitution took effect in a unified Sudan in 1950. Sudanization of the civil service replaced British expatriates with northern Sudanese; southerners occupied less than 1 percent of administrative posts. In 1955 southern politicians called for a new constitutional assembly to consider a federal system for Sudan. Despite this request, in 1956 a unitary Sudan became a sovereign nation.

Independent Sudan

As Sudanese independence approached, however, rumors began to circulate that the new government was going to disarm the Equatoria Corps, the southern regiments in the Sudanese army. Rather than leave the south defenseless, the Equatoria Corps refused orders to leave for the capital at Khartoum. Southerners looted northern Sudanese shops and killed many northerners. The Sudanese government responded with a reign of terror, including mass arrests and summary executions. Thousands of refugees fled to the bush or to neighboring countries. Remnants of the Equatoria Corps continued a guerrilla war.

Ismail al-Azhari was the first prime minister of an independent Sudan. In the 1956 elections, however, the Umma Party and the Peoples Democratic Party, which opposed formal ties with Egypt, defeated Azhari's pro-Egyptian Union Party. When the new Southern Bloc began to forge an alliance with northern groups like the Beja and ethnic minorities in Kordofan and Darfur in support of a federal structure, the military decided to seize power. It dissolved the legislature and banned all political parties. In the south, the military regime encouraged the spread of Islam and the Arabic language and suppressed both armed and peaceful forms of resistance. South-

A Sudanese women walks among the bags of food that the World Food Program air dropped on the village of Mayiendit in southern Sudan in January 2004. The food was distributed to help refugees returning after a cease fire in the civil war that has rocked the nation for over twenty years. *Pool/Reuters NewMedia Inc./Corbis*

ern exile organizations estimate that the military government arrested around 5,000 political prisoners in the south. Several hundred thousand refugees fled to neighboring countries.

In 1963 southern Sudanese refugees formed the nonviolent Sudan African National Union (SANU) to advocate an independent Southern Sudan. They charged the government of Sudan with genocide and petitioned the United Nations to intervene. Sudan's military government rejected offers by the ORGANIZATION OF AFRICAN UNITY (OAU) to mediate the dispute. During the same period, remnants of the Equatoria Corps and other military groups formed a coalition called Anya-Nya (meaning, literally, "snake poison") in Dinka to fight for independence.

Northerners also lost patience with the conflict in the south and the continued ban on political activity throughout the country. In 1964 student riots and labor strikes in the Khartoum region toppled the military regime. Sir al-Khatim al-Khalifa, the new prime minister, granted a general amnesty and assured all Sudanese of the right to free political expression and freedom of religion. He held a conference on the future of the south at Khartoum and included representatives from the OAU as outside observers. Opposing the government of Khalifa, conference-appointed mediators called for a federal system of government, with strong regional governments.

Despite rising tensions, Khalifa held parliamentary elections. The elections brought to office a new prime minister, Muhammad Ahmad Mahjub, who promptly rejected the mediators' recommendations. Mahjub opted for a military solution. In 1965 Sudanese soldiers targeted southern leaders for execution and killed many other southerners. Refugees fled the cities and Anya-Nya regained a central role in southern resistance. In 1967 Anya-Nya proclaimed the independence of the Southern Sudan and set up a shadow government. Warfare intensified and the Sudanese economy collapsed.

Once again, the government's inability to resolve problems in the south provoked a military coup. In 1969 Colonel GAAFAR MUHAMMAD AL-NIMEIRY and a group of junior officers overthrew the government of Prime Minister Mahjub, and in 1971 Nimeiry assumed the presidency. The Nimeiry government na-

tionalized foreign businesses and private banks and implemented land reform in the north. Nimeiry invited southern leaders to the conference table and declared his acceptance of cultural pluralism in Sudan. He blamed the civil war on the legacy of British colonialism and stressed that neocolonialism, which was "oppressing and exploiting the African and Arab peoples," was the common enemy of both north and south. He appointed a minister for southern affairs and supported a general amnesty for all civil war activity. Despite his offer, the civil war continued.

In 1972, however, negotiations between the Sudan government and the Anya-Nya resulted in a cease-fire and peace agreement. A southern regional government assumed full control of economic development and the preservation of public order. A governor, appointed by the president, held executive power within the south. Arabic remained the official language of Sudan, but the government permitted the use of English and southern Sudanese languages. An amnesty protected participants in the civil war. The accords also provided for the reabsorption of refugees and the integration of Anya-Nya soldiers into the military.

Islamic groups and the urban poor, however, opposed Nimeiry's regime. A coup attempt by Islamic groups associated with Sadiq al-Mahdi led Nimeiry to forge an alliance with the Muslim Brotherhood. In 1983, attempting to accommodate Muslim opposition, Nimeiry imposed *Shari'ah* (Islamic law) in Sudan. This provoked widespread opposition in the south, where there were few Muslims. The government decided to divide the three southern provinces and to transfer former Anya-Nya soldiers to the north. Southern troops mutinied in 1983, and southern politicians created the Sudan People's Liberation Movement, led by Colonel JOHN GARANG DE MABIOR. The civil war resumed. Meanwhile, Nimeiry's accommodation failed to appease Islamic groups. In 1985 military officers supported by the National Islamic Front overthrew the Nimeiry government and established an Islamic state under the leadership of Nimeiry's former chief of staff, General 'Abd ar-Rahman Siwar ad-Dahab.

Elections in 1986 brought Nimeiry's longtime foe, Sadiq al-Mahdi, to office, but he was unable to gain effective control of the government. In 1989 the Revolutionary Command Council for National Salvation (RCCNS), led by Lieutenant General Omar Hassan al-Bashir, overthrew Mahdi. The RCCNS followed the agenda of the National Islamic Front and sought the arrest of its opponents, including politicians, trade unionists, and student leaders. The RCCNS escalated the military conflict in the south and established an Islamic police force in the north. The imposition of Islamic law, support for Iraq in the first PERSIAN GULF WAR, and accusations that the Bashir regime supported terrorism brought increasing isolation for Sudan.

The intensification of the civil war and the loss of investments and international credits from the imposition of economic sanctions crippled the Sudanese economy. A drought-related famine from 1984 to 1986 and a war-related famine from 1988 to 1992 cost several million lives, mostly in the south, and devastated the national economy. As warfare escalated, it became increasingly difficult to grow food or to transport famine relief. Observers charged that the Sudanese government and the Sudan People's Liberation Army were impeding food shipments for short-term political gains. The politicization of famine relief left thousands of southern Sudanese dead of hunger and disease, while refugees poured into neighboring countries and to the more secure areas of northern Sudan. Colonel Garang expanded the nature of the conflict by seeking the support of northern ethnic minorities for a genuine federal system. By 1997 the forces of Garang, aided by new access to tanks and other sophisticated weaponry, were able to threaten the major cities of the south. By 2003 the civil war had taken at least two million lives and displaced more than four million people.

The war, occurring largely in the poor and inaccessible regions of Darfur, has been termed a "genocide" by human rights groups. Backed by the Sudanese government, Arab Janjaweed militias have massacred civilians, burned towns and villages, and forcibly depopulated great stretches of land long inhabited by the FUR, Masalit, and Zaghawa peoples. As refugees flee to camps and settlements, the conflict threatens to affect neighboring countries. Militia members have already raided refugee camps in Chad, where the government declared that its army would fight back against marauders. In the summer of 2004, both Kofi Annan (secretary general of the United Nations) and Colin Powell (U.S. secretary of state) traveled to Sudan to call attention to the dire humanitarian condition in Darfur.

See also Ancient African Civilizations; Islam in Africa; Mahdist State.

Robert Baum

Suez Canal

Constructed waterway across the Isthmus of Suez in northeastern Egypt that connects the Mediterranean and Red seas.

The Suez Canal is 195 km long (121 mi), and at least 60 m (200 ft) wide for its entire length, and permits direct passage from Europe and the Mediterranean Sea to the Indian Ocean, instead of the long voyage around the Cape of Good Hope in SOUTH AFRICA. The canal links the Mediterranean Sea at Port Said to the Red Sea at Suez by connecting a series of lakes: Lake Manzilah, Lake Timsah, and the Bitter Lakes. It has no locks, because these lakes lie nearly at sea level. In most places the canal has only one shipping lane; however, passing lanes exist at several points.

The canal was constructed by the French- and Egyptian-owned Compagnie Universelle du Canal Maritime de Suez (Universal Company of the Suez Ocean Canal), which had obtained a ninety-nine-year lease from the Egyptian viceroy, Said Pasha. After the expiration of the lease, control would revert to EGYPT. Construction was begun in 1859, performed mostly by Egyptian workers under poor conditions, and completed in 1867. The canal opened to sea traffic on November 17, 1869.

In 1875 the British government bought Egypt's shares in the company. In 1936 GREAT BRITAIN negotiated an agreement with the Egyptian government that granted Great Britain the right to defend the Suez Canal Zone, including the canal's approaches. The canal became a symbol of Third World emergence from colonialism when Egypt contested British control in the years after WORLD WAR II (1939–1945). Egyptian nationalism compelled the British in 1955 to agree to withdraw its troops by 1962.

In July 1956, however, after the United States withdrew monetary support for construction of the ASWAN HIGH DAM, Egyptian president GAMAL ABDEL NASSER seized the canal, despite the claims of British and French shareholders. He earmarked its revenues for dam construction costs. Nasser did promise, however, to reimburse shareholders and to keep the canal open to ships from all nations.

The British and French governments, citing the strategic importance of the canal, demanded that Nasser relinquish control. On October 29, 1956, Israeli forces, under an agreement with Great Britain and FRANCE, invaded Egypt across the Sinai peninsula. They took control of most of the peninsula in less than a week, and advanced to within a few miles of the Suez Canal. On October 30 the British and French, with the public intent of maintaining free passage through the canal, issued an ultimatum demanding that both Israeli and Egyptian forces evacuate the canal zone. After Nasser's refusal the following day, combined British and French forces conducted an air strike that crippled the Egyptian air force before it could leave the ground. In response Nasser ordered the sinking of forty vessels, rendering the canal impassable.

The United States, the Union of Soviet Socialist Republics, and the United Nations then intervened, demanding a withdrawal of British, French, and Israeli forces. The withdrawal was completed by the end of 1956. Control of the canal, as well as the Sinai, returned to Egypt and the canal reopened in March 1957.

Robert Fay

Sufism

Mystical form of Islam that has existed in Africa since the twelfth century.

Derived from the Arabic *suf*, meaning wool, the term *sufi* was originally used to describe a type of ascetic Muslim who wore coarse woolen garb. Unlike Islamic law and theology, which emphasize the severity of God and the strict codes of conduct described in the Qur'an (Koran) and Hadiths, Sufism—often referred to as Islamic mysticism—emphasizes the beneficence of God and the spirit of faith and submission. Sufism developed in the seventh century alongside the emergence of formal Islam in the MIDDLE EAST and spread to Africa in the twelfth century C.E. Beginning in the nineteenth century, Sufi orders proliferated in Africa, and in the twentieth century they became a venue for political and economic organization.

Sufis emphasize a personal and direct experience of God, which they believe is possible through disciplined renunciation, humility and love toward God, and a yearning for paradise. Scholars claim that the Qur'an's call for *ihsan*, or "doing what is beautiful," is ritually translated for Sufis into *dhikr*, honoring God through the methodical repetition of phrases from the Qur'an and through various ways of saying God's name. Ibn al-Arabi, the great theoretician of Sufism, asserted that the ultimate goal of these rituals is "assuming the character traits of God." By imagining the face of God, a Sufi attempts to "unveil" this image and perceive God's unifying presence in the world and within the self. In this state a Sufi can mediate between the divine and material worlds, allowing Sufi *shaykhs* (masters) to perform magic and miracles.

Sufic knowledge is passed down through masters, and initiation rites promote disciples from one "station" of knowledge to another. Thus the lineage of a Sufi is important and determines the order (in Arabic, *tariqah*, meaning "path" or "way") to which he or she belongs. The Qadiriya and Shadhiliya orders are the two most widespread Sufi lineages in Africa.

The loosely structured Qadiriya order, inspired by the teachings of the Baghdad scholar 'Abd al-Qadir al-Jilani, proved easily adaptable to existing religious beliefs and local authority structures in the SUDAN, allowing it to spread quickly to other parts of Africa. The Qadiriya order and its suborders are now present throughout West Africa and the Nile Valley.

Like the Qadiriya, the Shadhiliya order is a large and inclusive tradition based on a core devotional literature and organized around one influential master. The Shadhiliya order was established by Abu al-Hasan al-Shadhili in EGYPT and, influenced by the teachings of Abu 'Abdallah Muhammad ibn Sulaiman al-Jazuli and other Sufi masters, extended throughout North Africa in the fifteenth century. As frequently happened with Sufi orders, this order branched into suborders, such as the Hamidiya Shadhiliya, founded in 1867 by Salama al-Radi in CAIRO. This order's members celebrated its founder at his shrine every year, a ritual called the *mawlid*. Such Sufi shrines have often become places of pilgrimage.

Like the Hamidiya Shadhiliya, other Sufi orders in the nineteenth century branched into new orders that sought to replace mysticism with a more structured and "pure" form of Sufism. The best-known leader of such a revivalist movement was the FULANI scholar and Qadiriya USUMAN DAN FODIO. Beginning in 1804 he led a *jihad* (holy war) against the emirs of Hausaland, eventually forging the SOKOTO CALIPHATE, the largest state in nineteenth-century West Africa.

Another example of the Sufi mission for a purist Islam was the Tijanya, founded by the North African Ahmad Tijani. UMAR TAL extended this order's influence to the far reaches of West Africa, where he led a holy war against impending French colonization. The Tijanya remained a political force in West Africa well into the twentieth century.

These new Sufi orders often helped African Muslims respond to the tumultuous changes brought by COLONIAL RULE. While the West African Tijanya resisted European conquest, other orders willingly collaborated with colonial authorities who in turn appreciated the Sufi leaders' capacity to discipline and recruit labor from among their followers. In colonial SENEGAL, for example, the French came to depend on the spiritual authority of Amadou Bamba, the founder of the highly popular Mourides (or Muridiyah) order. The Mourides recruited tens of thousands of peasants and young male "apprentices" to clear land and cultivate export crops such as peanuts, providing the colony with valuable revenue.

In North Africa, Sufi orders' relations with foreign powers also varied considerably. The order best known for its resistance to colonial rule was the Sanusi, or Sanusiya, founded by Muhammad ibn Ali al-Sanusi in LIBYA. This order drew followers from among the BEDOUIN of the Cyrenaica region of Libya, where lodges provided shelter and meeting places for trans-Saharan trade caravans. Sanusi resistance began when the Italians invaded Cyrenaica in 1911, and continued intermittently for decades. The order was granted considerable autonomy as the colony moved toward independence, and the Sanusi leader, IDRIS I, eventually became the king of independent Libya.

In Sudan in the 1880s the Sammaniya order, led by Ahmad al-Mahdi, launched the MAHDIST revolt against Egyptian rule and helped to oppose British intervention. Another order in Sudan, the Khatmiya, founded upon the teachings of Muhammad 'Uthman al-Mirghani, opposed the Mahdist state and cooperated with the British in this conflict. Eventually the Khatmiya order became the basis for the nationalist Union Party of the early twentieth century. Sufism was also an important discipline for Hasan al-Banna, who organized the Muslim Brotherhood in Egypt.

Some secular governments claimed that Sufism could not coexist with twentieth-century modernity, rationality, and science. But in fact Sufism has found a place in contemporary Africa, where it serves as a popular alternative to formal Islamic traditions of religious expression as well as a basis for modern political and economic organization.

See also Islam and Tradition: An Interpretation; Islam in Africa.

Leyla Keough

Sugar

In that place the people sucked little honeyed reeds, found in plenty throughout the plains, which they called 'zucra'; they enjoyed this reed's wholesome sap, and because of its sweetness once they had tasted it they could scarcely get enough of it. This kind of grass is cultivated every year by extremely hard work on the part of the farmers. Then at harvest time the natives crush the ripe crop in little mortars, putting the filtered sap into their utensils until it curdles and hardens with the appearance of snow or white salt. They shave pieces off and it seems to those who taste it sweeter and more wholesome even than a comb of honey. Some say that it is a sort of that honey which Jonathan, son of King Saul, found on the face of the earth and disobediently dared to taste. The people, who were troubled by a dreadful hunger, were greatly refreshed by these little honey-flavored reeds during the sieges of Albara, Ma'arra and Arga.

These words, written by an obscure German monk named Albert of Aachen almost a thousand years ago, explain how the Crusaders discovered the use of sugar in the Holy Land during the Middle Ages, and indicate the reasons that sugar would later fuel the rise of the TRANSATLANTIC SLAVE TRADE.

Slavery in Europe was over by the year 1000, except in a few areas around the Mediterranean; but slaves were used in sugar production, and as the consumption of sugar spread around the world, so did slavery. Along with precious metals, the sugar-slave trade provided the first enduring economic links between the Old World and the New. The Atlantic trade based on slave-grown sugar was key to the economic development of Europe, North and SOUTH AMERICA, the Caribbean, and (perversely) AFRICA.

Spread of Sugar and Slavery

The Venetian Crusaders introduced sugar to Europe after they found Muslims cultivating it in the Holy Land—Palestine and Syria—in the late Middle Ages, as Albert of Aachen described. The Muslims finally expelled the Europeans from the Holy Land at the end of the thirteenth century. To sustain the lucrative sugar industry the Venetians transplanted it to islands in the eastern Mediterranean: first Cyprus, then Crete and Sicily. Islamic conquest introduced sugar plantations to SPAIN and PORTUGAL, but soon this production was overshadowed by the output on the islands off Africa's Atlantic coast.

The uninhabited island of Madeira was rediscovered by Portuguese in the service of Prince Henry the Navigator in 1425. To make their new colony profitable the Portuguese introduced sugar production. By 1500 Madeira was the world's largest sugar producer. The Spanish conquered the Canary Islands, off the coast of Africa, in the middle of the fifteenth century. They easily overcame the islands' inhabitants, the Guanches, and initiated sugar cultivation in parts of the islands where growing conditions were favorable. Eventually the Canaries came to rival Madeira as Europe's primary source of sugar.

From the Canaries sugar production moved down the African coast to the island of SÃO TOMÉ, colonized by the Portuguese. Sugar production methods were transported from there across the Atlantic to BRAZIL, from Brazil to the Caribbean, and from the Caribbean to the British North American colonies. Modern slavery followed this path.

From the start of the sugar industry, slaves were an essential part of the labor force. As sugar production moved west slavery became increasingly important. Some scholars believe that slaves were already in use for sugar production in Mesopotamia in the late Sassanid period and in Palestine before the Crusades. The Venetians had slave markets on Crete and used slaves there for sugar production. Venetians and Genoese had slave markets on Cyprus, where slaves from Arabia and Syria worked alongside indigenous serfs and immigrants from Palestine. Slaves were apparently not used for Sicilian sugar production.

The slave labor force for sugar production on Madeira and the Canaries included BERBERS, Arabs, Spanish Moors, and Africans, working alongside nonslave labor. After the discovery of São Tomé, the Portuguese used Jews kidnapped in Portugal and black slaves from Africa to convert the island into an important exporter of sugar to Europe.

Brazil was not planned as a sugar colony but became one. Portugal sought gold in Brazil but in the meantime it needed an economic base to pay for the colony and fend off rivals. Among the ten early Portuguese settlements established, only those associated with sugar survived. Native Americans provided the first labor force, but as the sugar industry expanded they were supplanted by African slaves.

The first European settlers in the WEST INDIES struggled to survive by growing tobacco, indigo, and cotton, using white indentured labor as well as slaves. They did not succeed. Once sugar was introduced to the West Indies the small-scale farms were transformed into large sugar plantations, worked by African slaves.

In both Europe and the Americas, besides working on plantations slaves labored in workshops as craftsmen and as servants. But these slave occupations either dwindled away or were overwhelmed by the number of slaves in plantation agriculture.

Why Slavery Is Associated with Sugar

Why is it that sugar (and to a lesser extent cotton, rice, indigo, and tobacco) used slave labor? Albert of Aachen understood why in the year 1100. Wherever the work was difficult, and free laborers would shrink from performing it unless offered very high wages, slavery was a likely outcome. Slaves would presumably dislike the work as well, and be motivated to do it badly, commit sabotage, or in extreme cases run away. So a crop that required onerous labor—and was thus a likely candidate for slave labor—would have to be produced under conditions conducive to the supervision and control of the labor force. Moreover, the crop would have to be important enough

Many field hands are needed for the grueling work of cultivating sugarcane. *CORBIS*

skill and judgment. The liquid mass is then ladled into a series of copper pans, skimmed of impurities, and finally poured into containers with holes in the bottom. The syrup eventually crystallizes and the molasses drips through.

Consider this production system. First, the fieldwork requires tremendous strength; death rates on sugar plantations exceed those for other crops. Second, harvesting must be done rapidly; thus the demand for labor peaks at certain times. Third, there are economies of scale in milling; it costs as much to build a mill for 100 hogsheads of sugar as for 300, so small-scale mills cannot compete. The optimal plantation size in the Caribbean in the eighteenth century was about a hundred acres. This required the labor of a hundred slaves who worked in unison as gangs holing, planting, cultivating, and cutting cane.

Free labor would avoid this difficult and dangerous work, with its concomitant regimentation and discipline. Workers were reluctant to submit to the rigors of factory work in the early days of the Industrial Revolution; in the sugar-producing colonies the rigidities of the industrialized world had yet to be introduced into economic life. Using slaves to mobilize for peak labor requirements was much easier than depending on hired free labor.

At the same time the cost of monitoring slave labor was low. One overseer with a whip could control a large gang of field hands, especially for the strenuous but uncomplicated work of sugar production. On a small mixed farm where the work involved a variety of tasks requiring skill and judgment, slaves could easily have expressed their resentment, and it would have been very costly to monitor them; in the extreme case, it might have taken one overseer to watch one slave. This is one of the chief reasons that most agriculture is poorly suited to collectivization. The sugar plantation, however, is well suited. It has rightly been called a factory in a field.

Of all agricultural crops, sugar offers the greatest cost advantages in the use of slave labor rather than free labor. Gang labor is also economical in the production of cotton, rice, and indigo. Slave labor is not necessarily cheaper than free labor for the production of tobacco and coffee.

No insignificant crop could have justified the reintroduction of slavery. Albert of Aachen thought that sugar was addictive: "because of its sweetness once [people] tasted it they could scarcely get enough of it." Since its introduction in Europe, sugar has played a major role in international trade. It was England's dominant import from the middle of the eighteenth century until the middle of the nineteenth. The combination of sugar and its complements, tea and coffee, captured a large proportion of international trade before 1850.

in the world economy to induce European countries to adopt slavery and the attendant legal, social, and political ideas—ideas with which they had had little familiarity for half a millennium.

Albert of Aachen saw in sugar the characteristics that made it a likely candidate for slave labor: (1) the difficulty of growing it and (2) the great demand it was likely to engender. From the time he wrote about sugar until the emancipations of the nineteenth century, sugar and slavery were inextricably bound together. Sugar was grown with slave or coerced labor in North and South America, the Caribbean, Britain's Natal Colony (part of present-day SOUTH AFRICA), Australia (Queensland), and the South Seas (Fiji).

Sugar production indeed requires hard labor. The plantation fields must first be cleared. The next task, also physically demanding, is to plant the sugar by burying sections of old cane in deep holes. As the plants grow they must be weeded and cultivated. Unwanted shoots must be cut back, and sometimes fertilizer must be applied. When the growing season is over the cane must be cut—an extremely difficult job in tropical climates. After it is cut the cane must be rushed to the mill immediately to prevent the sucrose in the cane from turning to starch.

The cane is ground in a mill by three vertical rollers, powered at one time by animals or wind and later by steam. The juice is pressed out and the crushed cane is removed for fuel. Then the juice is transferred to a large copper receptacle where it is boiled to just the right temperature, a task that requires

Atlantic System before Columbus

Just as the methods of sugar production explain why sugar was the vehicle for the rise of modern slavery, so does the organization of the sugar industry as a whole explain why sugar and slavery were so important in the development of the Atlantic world. When most of Europe was slowly emerging from feudalism, the slave-based sugar industry was organized along capitalistic lines. It required large investments, capital and credit markets, imported labor, disciplined production, and a marketing system involving shipping and insurance. It was a long-distance trade, requiring facilities for ships and harbors.

Even before Columbus sailed for America the slave-based sugar economy was established on the Atlantic islands. Genoa, GERMANY, and Portugal sent capital to the islands; Africa and the Iberian peninsula sent labor; England and THE NETHERLANDS sent textiles and other supplies; and the sugar was sent to northern Europe to be marketed. The slave-based sugar industry of the Atlantic islands drew together ITALY, Germany, Portugal, Spain, the Netherlands, and Africa in an interdependent economic network that could not have emerged without the labor of slaves on sugar plantations.

New World before Sugar and Slavery

For two centuries after Columbus discovered America, the economic impact of the New World on the Old was barely felt, aside from Spain's trade in precious metals. Only Virginia, BARBADOS, and Brazil were built on a firm economic foundation, and further economic growth would require slaves.

All new colonies require an export crop to pay for what they cannot yet produce and to sustain themselves while they build up their societies. The Spanish found nothing to develop in the Caribbean islands. Long before the end of the sixteenth century the Spanish abandoned the West Indies. The indigenous peoples had been killed off by disease and social dislocation, and the islands themselves, inhabited by a small number of mostly transient Spaniards and some slaves, served as nothing more than a support area for the mining interests of mainland South America. When mining declined, the Spanish Empire fell into a state of stagnation and decay.

The British and French occupied the islands the Spanish abandoned but they too were initially unable to build viable economies. The white population of the British West Indies peaked in the 1640s. It consisted of small farmers trying to make a living from tobacco and other crops with the labor of white indentured servants and a few slaves. The early history of the British West Indies is one of corruption, famine, disease, and failure, with the greatest concentration of poverty-stricken free people in any part of Britain's colonial dominions.

The French fared no better. Their earliest colonists also tried tobacco; when it failed to yield the necessary profits, they tried cotton, indigo, and other, lesser crops. Like the early English colonies in the West Indies, the French colonies remained outposts of impoverished farmers. The future greatness of British North America—the United States and CANADA—was nowhere apparent in the early colonial period, and Europe's links with the New World were frail and unimportant.

After the Introduction of Sugar and Slavery

Portugal's transfer of the slave-based sugar plantation economy across the Atlantic to Brazil was one of the most momentous events of modern times. It initiated the forced removal of some 11 million slaves from Africa to the Western Hemisphere and the inclusion of the Western Hemisphere in the world economy. With an assured labor supply and a dependable staple crop, Europe began to send capital to the New World and organize production there. The introduction of the sugar plantation with slave labor solved the problem of economic development in the colonies and turned them into valuable assets.

With sugar production twenty times higher in Brazil than in the Atlantic islands at the close of the seventeenth century, the per capita income of white settlers in Brazil far exceeded the prevailing per capita income in Europe. In the late seventeenth and early eighteenth centuries the sugar industry spread from Brazil to the British and French islands of the Lesser Antilles: Barbados, SAINT KITTS AND NEVIS, MONTSERRAT, GUADELOUPE and MARTINIQUE. By the middle of the eighteenth century sugar production had reached its peak in JAMAICA and Saint-Domingue (now HAITI) in the Greater Antilles, making the latter the most successful colony in the New World. By this time also the Atlantic was crisscrossed by ships laden with human and economic cargoes to support the sugar industry: slaves, the products of slave labor, supplies and capital bound for slave colonies, and European goods purchased with the profits of the slave colonies. Not much else of human origin moved in the Atlantic at this time.

In 1650 the British mainland colonies in North America were 97 percent white and the British West Indies were 80 percent white. By 1750 the mainland was 80 percent white and the islands only 16 percent white. Nineteen out of twenty slaves shipped to the mainland colonies were sent below the Mason-Dixon Line to work in crops suited to slave labor.

By the third quarter of the eighteenth century, the exports of the Upper and Lower South attributable to slave labor amounted to 50 and 75 percent of their total exports, respectively. Forty-two percent of the exports of the Middle Colonies went to slave colonies, and 78 percent of New England's exports went there. The colonies with the greatest wealth per (white) person were those with the closest links to slavery. The West Indies and the American South were the wealthiest colonies, the Middle States and New England the least wealthy. The transformation of these latter colonies from simple agricultural economies into mercantile societies was due in large measure to trade with the West Indies slave colonies. To a great extent the development of the United States in the colonial era depended on the sugar of the West Indies, and on the slavery there and in the American South.

Once the Atlantic system was in place European trade shifted accordingly. Europe realized great economic benefits by combining European investment, technology, and organizational skills with labor stolen from Africa and land stolen from Native Americans. Saving and investment increased, commercial services—banking, shipping, and insurance—developed, and above all, industrialization accelerated. The most dynamic sectors in Europe at the end of the eighteenth century were exporting simple manufactures and other industrial products to the Americas.

In particular the notable increase in the growth of the British economy in the last quarter of the eighteenth century was fueled in large part by American demand for goods. Without this demand, ultimately generated by slave production, England would have been less commercial, less industrial, and poorer, and it would have grown more slowly.

Conclusion

The Renaissance marked the start of the modern era. Until then the civilizations of classical Greece and Rome were considered unsurpassed in the Western world. As long as this view persisted the idea of progress could not take hold. With the Renaissance it became apparent that the ancients had lacked many important inventions. A famous series of prints made at the end of the sixteenth century portrays, among others, these discoveries: printing, gunpowder, the mariner's compass, windmills—and sugar.

See also Mining in Latin America and the Caribbean; Slavery in Latin America and the Caribbean.

Barbara L. Solow

Sugarhill Gang

African American musical group whose "Rapper's Delight" was the first rap song to achieve commercial success

With the phenomenal success of their 1979 single "Rapper's Delight," the Sugarhill Gang became the first RAP group to break out of the dance clubs of NEW YORK and LOS ANGELES and achieve international fame. Ironically, the group did not originate in the post-disco DJ scene of other rap innovators, like Grandmaster Flash and Afrika Bambaataa. Instead, the Sugarhill Gang was the creation of Sugar Hill Records, a black-owned label that was the first to bring rap to a commercial audience.

The Sugarhill Gang consisted of three relatively unknown rappers—Big Bank Hank (Henry Jackson), Master Gee (Guy O'Brien), and Wonder Mike (Michael Wright)—whom Sylvia Robinson of Sugar Hill Records approached in early 1979. Backed by a track sampled from the disco group Chic's hit song "Good Times," the group's hit single exemplified the playful, positive, dance-oriented feel of early rap (which later fans have dubbed "old school"). Accused by veteran rappers of appropriating their trademark lyrics, the Sugarhill Gang popularized, rather than created, the sound for which they became famous. Despite the issues surrounding the group's authenticity, their work spawned a host of imitators and brought rap music into the American mainstream.

After the success of "Rapper's Delight," which was the first rap record to break into Top Forty radio play, the group dropped out of the public eye, though they continue to play (with manager Joey Robinson, Jr., replacing Master Gee). In 1997 Rhino Records re-released the Sugarhill Gang's first record, now considered a classic of old school rap. In 2001 the group won a three million dollar settlement from Snapple Beverage Corporation and Turner Broadcasting for wrongful use of its image in nationally televised commercials.

See also Grandmaster Flash, Melle Mel, and the Furious Five; Music, African American.

Kate Tuttle

Sukuma

Ethnic group of northwestern Tanzania.

Ancestors of the Sukuma are believed to have first settled near LAKE VICTORIA in the Mwanza region of present-day TANZANIA during the period of Bantu expansion. They were long thought to be a subgroup of the NYAMWEZI, who speak a similar language and share many customs; the Sukuma derive their name, which means "people from the north," from their geographical relation to the larger ethnic group. But although the Sukuma may originally have been a group that broke off from Nyamwezi, the Sukuma have since developed a distinctive culture based on farming and raising livestock (or PASTORALISM).

Prior to European COLONIAL RULE the Sukuma lived in farming villages scattered throughout the Mwanza region and organized into loosely affiliated chiefdoms. They cultivated grain crops such as sorghum, MILLET, and maize and also kept cattle, which continue to be an important symbol of wealth. Unlike the Nyamwezi, who participated actively in the East African IVORY TRADE and the INDIAN OCEAN SLAVE TRADE and thus interacted with coastal Arab and SWAHILI traders and Europeans, the Sukuma sought to isolate themselves from such influences. They avoided missionaries and other Europeans until the German East African Company took control of the area in 1891. At that time the Germans relocated the Sukuma onto commercial farms where they were expected to grow export crops such as tea and coffee. At first resentful, the Sukuma later excelled at commercial farming under British colonial rule and grew prosperous from sales of cotton, tobacco, and grain crops. Today Sukumaland, which covers over 52,000 sq km (20,000 sq mi), continues to be one of the most important farming areas in Tanzania.

See also Bantu: Dispersion and Settlement.

Bibliography

Brandström, Per. "Who is Sukuma and Who is a Nyamwezi?: Ethnic Identity in West-Central Tanzania." In *Working Papers in African Studies*, no. 27 (1986).

Cory, H. H. *Sukuma Law and Custom.* Eagle Press, 1953.

Elizabeth Heath

Sullivan, Leon Howard

1922–2001

American minister and author of the "Sullivan Principles," guidelines for American companies doing business in South Africa.

Leon Howard Sullivan was born in Charleston, West Virginia, and raised by his grandmother who encouraged him to help the disadvantaged. He pursued this goal by entering the ministry. He was pastor of PHILADELPHIA's Zion Baptist Church from 1950 to 1988. In 1964 he founded the Opportunities Industrialization Centers of America (OIC), which provided educational and vocational training for unskilled African American workers. For this work Sullivan was awarded the prestigious Spingarn Medal by the NATIONAL ASSOCIATION FOR THE ADVANCEMENT OF COLORED PEOPLE in 1971. By 1980 the OIC had grown into a national force, and by 1993 despite funding cuts, the OIC's programs had been instituted in several sub-Saharan African countries.

In 1977 Sullivan enumerated six principles that were guidelines for American corporations doing business in SOUTH AFRICA. Known as the Sullivan Principles, these guidelines were designed to use American corporate power to promote fair treatment for black workers. The principles concerned equal pay, equal working conditions, integration of blacks and whites in work facilities, training programs, supervisory positions for nonwhites, and improvements in living conditions outside the workplace. Sullivan himself declared the principles a failure in 1987 because APARTHEID continued. In 1991 Sullivan received two honors for his work with the American and African poor: the Presidential Medal of Freedom in the United States, and the Distinguished Service Award, the highest honor awarded in the CÔTE D'IVOIRE. In 1998 Sullivan published an autobiography, *Moving Mountains.* He died in 2001. That same year the African-African American Summit was renamed the Leon Howard Sullivan Summit.

See also Economic Development in Africa.

Bibliography
Smith, William E. "Commandments Without Moses: Abandoning His Principles, Sullivan Wants U.S. Firms to Pull Out." *Time,* Jun. 15, 1987.

Sumbwa

Ethnic group of Tanzania.

The Sumbwa primarily inhabit the region south of LAKE VICTORIA in northwestern TANZANIA. They speak a Bantu language and are closely related to the NYAMWEZI and SUKUMA peoples. Approximately 200,000 people consider themselves Sumbwa.

See also Bantu: Dispersion and Settlement.

Sundi

Ethnic group of west Central Africa; also known as the Basundi and the Kongo-Sundi.

The Sundi primarily inhabit ANGOLA, the REPUBLIC OF THE CONGO (Congo-Brazzaville), and the DEMOCRATIC REPUBLIC OF THE CONGO (Congo-Kinshasa). They speak a Bantu language and are one of the KONGO peoples. Approximately 200,000 people consider themselves Sundi.

See also Bantu: Dispersion and Settlement.

Sundiata Keita

1210?–1260?

Founder and ruler of the Mali empire in West Africa.

Sundiata Keita was the son of Nare Maghan, the ruler of Kangaba, a small state located on a tributary of the upper NIGER RIVER. Sundiata left Kangaba, but the reason is unknown: he may have gone into voluntary exile to avoid a jealous half-brother, or he may have been exiled by Sumanguru Kante, king of the SOSO, who killed Sundiata's father and took over his kingdom. Sundiata responded to the requests of his people to return to Kangaba to help them regain independence. He assembled a coalition of Malinke chiefdoms and in 1235 led them to victory in the Battle of Kirina. According to popular tradition, Sundiata triumphed because he was a stronger magician than his opponent. This victory marked the beginning of the MALI EMPIRE.

After defeating the Soso, Sundiata consolidated his authority among the Malinke people and established a strong centralized monarchy. According to IBN KHALDUN, a fourteenth century North African historian, Sundiata ruled MALI for twenty-five years. He expanded the state by incorporating the GHANA empire and the West African gold fields. Sundiata built his capital at Niani, which was in his home region. Mali gained economic strength by controlling the region's trade routes and gold fields. Although he was Muslim, Sundiata allowed the people to practice their own religions. When Sundiata died his son Uli became the *mansa,* or king, of Mali. The Malinke people of West Africa continue to regard Sundiata as a national hero.

Sunnah

See Islam and Tradition: An Interpretation.

Sunni Ali

?–1492

Founder of the Songhai empire; also known as Sunni Ali Ber and Si.

At a time when the collapse of the once powerful Mali empire left a power vacuum in western and central Sudan, Sunni Ali undertook a series of military campaigns that united the area under a new power—the Songhai empire. Through military acumen and skillful leadership he amassed an empire that, by the time of his death in 1492, spanned most of present-day Mali and parts of present-day Niger, Nigeria, and Benin. He conquered important trading centers such as Djenné and Tombouctou. Sunni Ali's empire continued to control the area until the late sixteenth century, when it was destroyed by Moroccan invaders.

A Songhai state had existed since the seventh century, and in 1335 it declared independence from the enfeebled Mali empire. Its rulers, however, had done little to strengthen and expand the state before Sunni Ali ascended the throne in 1464. He immediately launched a campaign against Tuareg raiders, who had seized the important trading center of Tombouctou and were attacking the valuable trans-Saharan trade caravans that traveled through the area. In 1468 he wrested Tombouctou from the Tuareg. Sunni Ali immediately set out to defeat other neighboring groups such as the Mossi, Dogon, and Fulbe. These campaigns earned Sunni Ali a reputation as a shrewd military ruler and brilliant strategist. Relying on the strength of his Niger River navy, Sunni Ali was able to push the Mossi and other groups out of the rich river ports. Sunni Ali was also a skilled ruler who established a centralized structure to ensure control over the cities and outlying regions of his empire.

Highly skilled at warfare, Sunni Ali is also reputed to have used sorcery to undermine his enemies and guarantee victory. Legend tells that he not only transformed himself and his horse into vultures before battle, but gave his troops amulets that enabled them to become invisible and fly. His failure to renounce sorcery eventually led to conflicts with Islamic leaders and scholars. Although Sunni Ali claimed to be a Muslim, his decision to restrict religious practices in the empire and to continue practicing magic earned him a reputation as a heathen. His status among Muslims declined further after he ordered the massacre of the Tombouctou scribes. Although his motives were political, not religious, many believe that this act united some of his Muslim subjects behind his nephew, Askia Muhammad. According to legend Askia Muhammad, a devout Muslim, murdered his uncle and seized the throne to avenge the death of the scribes. According to another legend, however, Sunni Ali drowned in a flash flood after a military expedition. Some believe that Sunni Ali's head is buried in Wanzerbe, purportedly the center of Songhai magical power.

See also Magic, Sorcery, and Witchcraft in Africa.

Elizabeth Heath

Sun Ra

1914–1993

American jazz bandleader, arranger, and pianist, pioneer of collective improvisation and electric instruments who mounted multimedia, futuristic concerts from the 1950s through the early 1990s.

Sun Ra was born Herman P. "Sonny" Blount and grew up in Birmingham, Alabama, before moving to Chicago, Illinois during his teenage years. He played the piano as a boy, led his own band while in high school, and studied music education at Alabama A&M (now University). After touring with John "Fess" Whatley's band during the mid-1930s, Blount played piano and arranged songs for Fletcher Henderson in Chicago.

In the late 1940s Blount adopted the name Sun Ra, began calling Saturn his birthplace, and sported the motto "Space is the Place." His characteristic flowing Egyptian clothes reflected his new spiritual outlook. In 1953 Ra formed a musical ensemble called the Arkestra, which fused Afro-Cuban, avant-garde jazz, big-band, and hard bop styles. At the same time, Ra founded Saturn Records, which released the Arkestra's albums during the following four decades. In the late 1970s the group moved its base from New York City to Philadelphia. Over the course of the Arkestra's forty years they recorded numerous albums, toured the United States, Europe, and Asia, and won international acclaim.

Sun Ra's music is characterized by a cosmic consciousness and outer space overtones. His performances incorporated dance, film, lighting effects, and music, and featured many notable soloists, including John Coltrane's mentor, tenor saxophone player John Gilmore. Three documentaries were produced about Sun Ra: *The Cry of Jazz* (1959), *Space is the Place* (1971) and *Sun Ra: A Joyful Noise* (1980).

Aaron Myers

Supremes, The

American female Motown popular music group that achieved commercial success in the 1960s by bringing African American singing style to a national audience.

From their first number one hit, "Where Did Our Love Go?" (1964), to later chart-toppers such as "Reflections" (1967) and "Someday We'll Be Together" (1969), the Supremes stand as the most commercially successful female group in 1960s popular music. They emerged as the top "model" in Berry Gordy, Jr.'s "fleet" of acts at the Motown Record Company in Detroit, Michigan. Gordy, who worked briefly at Ford Motor Company, sought to produce and market his artists with an assembly-line technique. He wanted Motown music to appeal to audiences across racial boundaries. The Supremes achieved this goal and transformed American popular music.

The group's original members, Diana Ross, Florence Ballard, and Mary Wilson first began singing together in the late 1950s.

The Supremes (left to right)—Florence Ballard, Diana Ross, and Mary Wilson—were the most commercially successful female group in pop music in the 1960s. *The Everett Collection*

They called themselves the Primettes, singing as the sister group to the Primes, who eventually became known as the TEMPTATIONS. After they won a local talent show the women secured an audition at Motown Records. They earned a contract with the label and changed their name to the Supremes. Their first few recordings—"I Want A Guy" (1960) and "Buttered Popcorn" (1961)—were only modest successes and by 1963 the group had earned the nickname No-Hit Supremes. In 1964, however, the group's fate changed dramatically when "Where Did Our Love Go?" raced to the top of the charts. "Baby Love" and "Come See About Me" quickly followed that same year, and the Supremes were a national sensation.

The Supremes' success exemplified Motown's ability to market African American music to the teenagers of the 1960s. The skillful songwriting team of Eddie Holland, Lamont Dozier, and Brian Holland—also known as Holland-Dozier-Holland—was responsible for the group's unique sound. The company's in-house charm school groomed the young women for the public spotlight. They learned manners, choreography, and fashion tips from entertainment veterans. As the group's fame grew the women became regulars on top television shows and toured around the world. For many the Supremes epitomized elegance and glamour—a refreshingly new public image of black womanhood.

By the late 1960s the Supremes faced several professional and political challenges. In 1967 Cindy Birdsong replaced Florence Ballard, who struggled with the pressures of celebrity life, and Motown changed the group's name to Diana Ross and the Supremes. The group's music began to reflect the social turmoil of the times. Songs such as "Love Child" (1968) and "I'm Living in Shame" (1969) spoke of the trials of life in an urban ghetto.

In January 1970 Diana Ross performed her last show as a Supreme at the Frontier Hotel in Las Vegas. She went on to pursue a solo singing and motion picture career and received an Academy Award nomination for her portrayal of jazz singer BILLIE HOLIDAY in *Lady Sings the Blues* (1972). Jean Terrell replaced Ross, and the new Supremes were successful with songs such as "Stoned Love" (1970). The group never regained the popularity it attained throughout the 1960s, however, and it disbanded in 1977. The musical *Dreamgirls*, which was largely based on the Supremes' story, became a hit on Broadway in 1981.

Bibliography

George, Nelson. *Where Did Our Love Go: The Rise and Fall of the Motown Sound.* St. Martin's Press, 1985.

Wilson, Mary. *Dreamgirl: My Life as a Supreme.* St. Martin's Press, 1986.

Leyla Keough

Suriname

Country located on the northeastern coast of South America, bordered on the west by Guyana, on the east by French Guiana, and on the south by Brazil.

Suriname is a former Dutch colony located on the northeast corner of South America. Although Dutch is the official language, English, Hindi, Javanese, Sranana and Papiamento (both Creole languages), and numerous Amerindian languages are spoken widely. Suriname's 435,449 inhabitants come from diverse backgrounds, giving the country a unique mix of ethnicities: its population includes people of Javanese, so-called Hindustani (or East Indian), and Chinese origin, in addition to the region's original indigenous inhabitants. But Suriname is perhaps best known for its communities of CREOLES and maroons (sometimes also called *bosnegers,* or Bush Negroes by outsiders) communities. Creoles are Afro-Surinames, the descendants of former slaves, freed blacks, and people of mixed African and European ancestry. Maroons are descendants of runaway slaves who are now organized into six distinct groups and live in semiautonomous villages. The maroon population in Suriname was the largest community of escaped slaves in South America, and (with the notable exception of HAITI) long constituted one of the most highly-developed and autonomous communities of African descendants in the Americas. Both the maroon and Creole communities retain elements of African culture, including traditional African languages, oral histories, and religious ceremonies. In 1998 Creoles and maroons composed nearly 41 percent of Suriname's total population.

Early History

The earliest inhabitants of Suriname were Amerindian migrants from South America and the Caribbean, who arrived in waves

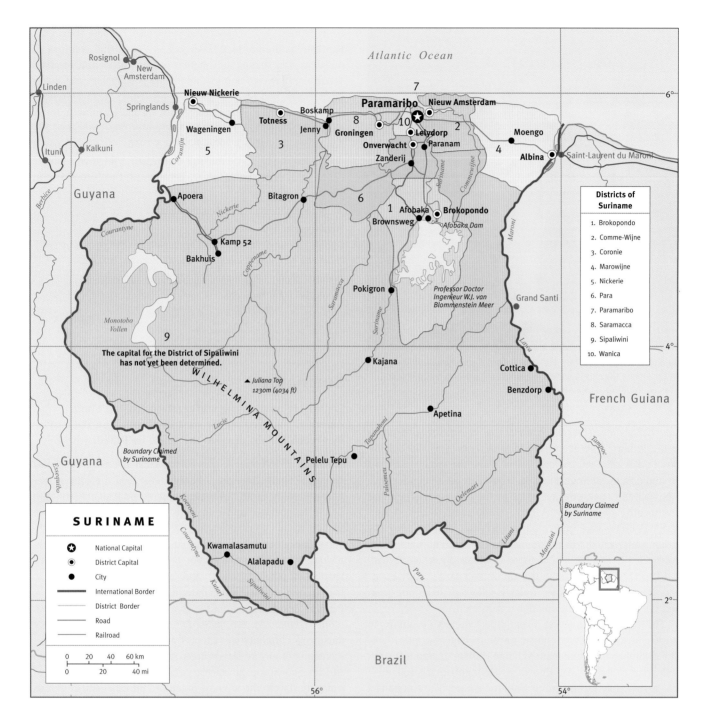

beginning in the fifteenth century. They are often referred to as Arawak, Carib, and Warrau, and lived primarily in small subsistence communities. They cultivated crops such as cassava and separated into residential communities often based on linguistic patterns. Those who spoke the Arawakan language tended to reside along the coast, while those who spoke Cariban lived in the area's hilly interior.

European explorers from England, France, and Holland began investigating the coastline of Suriname in the sixteenth century. Most were looking for gold, but some were following tales of a wealthy indigenous community located in the region's in-

terior called El Dorado. Although El Dorado was never discovered, European explorers established trading posts all along the coastline to provide supplies for European vessels traveling between the Caribbean and South America.

In 1650 England established the first permanent settlement on Suriname—a plantation colony on the Suriname River. However, in 1667 England traded the territory of Suriname to Holland in exchange for the Dutch colony of New Amsterdam (now NEW YORK, NEW YORK). The Dutch West India Company controlled Suriname until 1794, when it became an official Dutch colony.

A Ndjuka man paints a canoe paddle in the traditional style that dates from the founding of one of Suriname's largest maroon communities. *CORBIS/Adam Woolfitt*

Slavery

Like BRAZIL, Suriname's colonial economy was driven by slavery. SUGAR, coffee, cotton, and cocoa plantations were supported by more than 325,000 African slaves transported to Suriname between 1667 and 1863, the year that Holland abolished slavery. Scholars believe that by 1800 there were more than 600 plantations in Suriname, operated by Dutch, German, French, and English landowners. Indeed, Suriname was so well known at this period that in the mid-1700s the French philosopher Voltaire cited it in his novel *Candide* as an example of the cruelty of slavery. During the seventeenth and eighteenth centuries almost one-third of these plantation owners were Jews, many of whom had originally fled Europe for Dutch-controlled northeastern Brazil during the Inquisition, and later left Brazil for Suriname. Overall, these plantation owners occupied the highest social strata in colonial Suriname, and reserved many of the most powerful government positions for themselves.

Chattel slavery allowed Suriname's wealthy European elite to earn enormous profits from agricultural plantations through-

out the seventeenth, eighteenth, and nineteenth centuries. The African provenance of the slaves who were brought to Suriname is not entirely clear, and varied over time and according to the arrangements made by the DUTCH WEST INDIA COMPANY, responsible for bringing the vast majority of African slaves to Suriname in the TRANSATLANTIC SLAVE TRADE. Nonetheless, the Dutch planters in Suriname—as with the English, Spanish, and Portuguese elsewhere in the New World—were often highly interested in what they thought were the national characteristics of slaves from different ethnic groups, and did compile some records on the origins of slaves.

In broad terms, according to statistics compiled by anthropologist Richard Price, from the 1640s to 1725, the majority of slaves were brought from the Slave Coast (present-day BIGHT OF BENIN) with significant numbers also coming from the Angola region in southwestern Africa. In the second and third decades of the eighteenth century slaves were also imported, in equal proportions, from the Gold Coast (the area of modern GHANA). By the late eighteenth century almost half of the slaves sold in Suriname came from the Windward Coast (coastal area of West Africa stretching approximately from modern-day SENEGAL to CÔTE D'IVOIRE) and the ANGOLA REGION, and fewer from the Slave Coast. In Suriname these groups of slaves were called Gangu, Kormantines, and Loangu respectively, though their precise ethnic origins are unclear. Overall, studies have argued that Bantu-speaking Africans from the Loango/Angola region of southwestern Africa composed perhaps the single largest group of Africans sent to Suriname.

The rapid expansion of slavery, with its high mortality rates, meant that Suriname's black population included an unusually high proportion of African- to American-born slaves, and a high ratio of recently arrived slaves to ones who had been in the colonies for longer periods of time. Indeed, according to Price, during the first one hundred years of Suriname's colonial history, over 90 percent of the slave population was African-born, and well into the eighteenth century over one-third of Suriname's blacks had left Africa within the previous five years (in comparison, in North America as early as 1680, native-born blacks already outnumbered Africans, who after then never came to constitute a majority). The linguistic and cultural ties of these displaced Africans meant that Suriname was deeply marked by African cultures and languages, and also allowed Suriname's slaves to secretly organize numerous acts of resistance, both overt and hidden.

Although violent slave insurrections were a common feature of slave resistance in the Caribbean and South America, the most common form of slave resistance in Suriname was self-emancipation—running away. Beginning in the 1690s, groups of Africans, the descendants of today's maroon communities, began to engage in large-scale flight from the plantations where they were held captive. This did not imply a peaceful situation, though, as deserting slaves often set fire to plantations and, by the mid-eighteenth century, wars between organized bands of maroons and settlers led one traveler at that time to call Suriname a "theater of perpetual war."

Suriname (At a Glance)

OFFICIAL NAME: Republic of Suriname

FORMER NAME: Netherlands Guiana, Dutch Guiana

AREA: 163,270 sq km (63,039 sq mi)

LOCATION: Northern South America between French Guiana and Guyana, bordered by the North Atlantic Ocean

CAPITAL: Paramaribo (population 240,000; 2004 estimate)

POPULATION: 436,000 (2004 estimate)

POPULATION DENSITY: 2.6 persons per sq km (7 per sq mi)

POPULATION BELOW AGE 15: 30.7 percent (male 68,536; female 65,165; 2003 estimate)

POPULATION GROWTH RATE: 0.37 percent (2003 estimate)

TOTAL FERTILITY RATE: 2.4 children born per woman (2003 estimate)

LIFE EXPECTANCY AT BIRTH: Total population: 69.23 years (male 66.79 years; female 71.78 years; 2003 estimate)

INFANT MORTALITY RATE: 24.74 deaths per 1,000 live births (2003 estimate)

LITERACY RATE (AGE 15 AND OVER WHO CAN READ AND WRITE): Total population: 93 percent (male 95 percent; female 91 percent; 2003 estimate)

EDUCATION: Education is compulsory to age twelve, and free at all levels. The educational system is based on that of the Netherlands, with instruction in Dutch. The Anton de Kom University (formerly the University of Suriname) is located in Paramaribo.

LANGUAGES: Dutch is the official language of Suriname. English is widely spoken, as is Sranang Tongo (Surinamese, sometimes called Taki-Taki, the native language of Creoles and much of the younger population). Also spoken are Hindustani (a dialect of Hindi) and Javanese.

ETHNIC GROUPS: 37 percent Hindustani (also known locally as East Indians), 31 percent Creole (mixed white and black), 15 percent Javanese, 10 percent are descendants of African slaves who escaped to the interior, or maroons, 2 percent Amerindian, 2 percent Chinese, 1 percent white, and 2 percent other ethnicities

RELIGIONS: 27.4 percent of the population is Hindu, 19.6 percent is Muslim, 22.8 percent is Roman Catholic, 25.2 percent is Protestant (predominantly Moravian), and 5 percent practice indigenous religions.

CLIMATE: Tropical, with an average annual temperature in Paramaribo of 81° F (27° C). Daily temperature extremes may vary by as much as 18° F (11° C) in the interior. The rainy season is late April to mid-August, with the highest rainfall in the southeastern and central parts of the country.

LAND, PLANTS, AND ANIMALS: Suriname's 226-mile coastal zone and the adjacent New Coastal Plain consist of sand and mud deposited at the mouth of the Amazon River. The New Coastal Plain is essentially 6,600 square miles of clay and peat swampland; diking and drainage provide tracts of very fertile soil. The Old Coastal Plain, south of the New Coastal Plain, is 1,550 square miles of clay flats, swamps, and old ridges. There are also occasional grassy savannas, but the majority of the country is covered with tropical rainforest. Vegetation includes 4,000 species of ferns and more than 1,000 species of trees, including the kapok, which grows to more than 150 feet. Animals include manatees, monkeys, jaguars, iguanas, marine turtles, parrots, vultures, and hummingbirds.

NATURAL RESOURCES: Timber, hydropower, fish, kaolin, shrimp, bauxite, gold, and small amounts of nickel, copper, platinum, and iron ore

CURRENCY: Surinamese guilder (SRG)

GROSS DOMESTIC PRODUCT (GDP): $1.469 billion (2002 estimate)

GDP PER CAPITA: $3,400 (2002 estimate)

GDP REAL GROWTH RATE: 1.2 percent (2002 estimate)

PRIMARY ECONOMIC ACTIVITIES: Agriculture, industry, and services; beef, chickens, forest products, and shrimp

INDUSTRIES: Bauxite and gold mining, alumina production, oil, lumbering, food processing, and fishing

PRIMARY EXPORTS: Alumina, crude oil, lumber, shrimp and fish, rice, and bananas

PRIMARY IMPORTS: Capital equipment, petroleum, foodstuffs, cotton, and consumer goods

PRIMARY TRADE PARTNERS: United States, Norway, France, Trinidad and Tobago, Iceland, Canada, Netherlands, China, Netherlands Antilles, and Japan

GOVERNMENT: Suriname is a constitutional democracy. The chief of state and head of government is President Runaldo Ronald Venetiaan (since August 2000; elected by the National Assembly to a five-year term). The legislative branch is the unicameral fifty-one member National Assembly (members popularly elected to serve five-year terms). The judicial branch is the Court of Justice, whose judges are nominated for lifelong service.

Shelle Sumners

Maroons

The escape of slaves from plantations plagued Suriname since the early days of slavery. Runaway slaves, called maroons or sometimes Bush Negroes, from the Dutch word *bosneger,* were a major problem for European slave owners throughout the region. But the intense heat and hilly interior made it much more difficult for slave owners in Suriname to recapture runaways, and after large-scale escapes in the late seventeenth century, major maroon communities were established along the Marowijne and Saramacca rivers. Some of the most famous maroon villages were located along major rivers, such as the Claes and Pedro villages in the area surrounding the Saramacca River. Although legend and the fears of the colonists has inflated the number of maroons, scholars believe that there may have been nearly 1,500 runaway slaves living in hidden villages throughout Suriname by the mid-eighteenth century. Most lived autonomously, finding their own food and establishing their own communities.

Stories about their history and origins are treated with great respect by Suriname's maroons, and are seen as spiritually powerful. Some of these stories, collected by Richard Price, reveal the origins of some of the oldest maroon communities. For example, the Matjáu subgroup of the Saramaka trace their origins to a small core group of Africans who escaped from slavery sometime around 1685. They lived for a time along a small creek just beyond the area colonized and settled by plantation owners. Around 1690 they returned to conduct a large raid on a plantation (which historical records indicate was owned by Imanuel Machado), freeing slaves who came to constitute the core of their communty.

Maroon Wars

The existence of communities of self-emancipated former slaves was seen by colonial officials as a serious threat. They feared maroon-inspired insurrections, although few actually formed, and they created colonial militias with the sole purpose of recapturing maroons. Those who were recaptured were often publicly tortured and executed, to serve as an example to other slaves—a practice that continued into the late eighteenth century. Several of the larger maroon groups also fought intermittent wars with colonial militias.

Between 1760 and 1762, two of the largest maroon communities, the Ndyuka and Saramaka, ended a century-long war with the colonists and won their independence by signing peace treaties with the Dutch colonial government. But the desire to escape continued, and new maroon communities were formed in the nineteenth century as more slaves escaped. This led to further wars between the colonists and other maroon communities, especially the Aluku (or Boni) during the eighteenth century.

The peace treaties signed between the Ndyuka, Saramaka, and Matawai maroons and the Dutch gave these maroon communities wide freedom in regulating their internal affairs. In return, they pledged to turn over to the colonists any newly-escaped slaves or other maroons that they might encounter.

The Dutch authorities, on their part, pledged to provide the maroon communities with periodic tribute and allowed them to conduct trading trips from their homes in the rain forest to the coastal cities. Other maroon tribes probably developed from new escapes and from groups that split off of the older communities. After the peace treaties with the Ndyuka, Saramaka, and Matawai, the main leaders of warfare against the colonists were the Aluku (or Boni). During the late 1700s warfare was so intense that the colonists established a 60-meter-wide protective cordon, manned by soldiers posted at short intervals all along the outer edges of the forested southern plantation region. Overall, the combination of treaties between the maroons and the colonial authorities and stiff maroon resistance meant that, unlike many other maroon communities in Latin America and the Caribbean, Suriname's maroons were not defeated by colonial armies nor gradually assimilated into the general population, but have constituted flourishing, semiautonomous societies.

The maroon communities have survived over the years and in the mid-1980s the maroon population was about 45,000. There are six maroon groups in Suriname: the two largest maroon communities are the Ndyuka and the Saramaka, and others are the Paramaka, Aluki, Kwinti, and Matawai. Many of these communities have managed to retain traditional African-derived customs, including a matrilinial kinship structure, local political leadership forms, spiritual practices such as Obeah and the Winti religion, and agricultural techniques such as shifting cultivation or slash and burn.

Today maroons also engage heavily in logging, and the men often work as wage laborers on the coast, away from their home communities. Though the communities retain their pride in their own culture—for example, the Saramaka keep memories of the dark days of war alive in oral history known as first time stories—they also face a series of threats to their survival. Nevertheless, they face both strong pressure to assimilate, as well as discrimination and harassment. In addition, during the 1960s almost half of the Saramaka's territory was flooded when a dam was built on the Saramacca river to provide electricity to a massive bauxite smelter. Periodic development plans have also called for the consolidation of scattered maroon villages into large, new planned towns as a precondition to their integration into the nation. Finally, a war between the military government of Dési Bouterse, and a guerrilla group known as the Surinamese Liberation Army (SLA), also known as the Jungle Commando (led by Ronnie Brunswijk, and composed largely of Ndyuka maroons) has also had a devastating impact on Suriname's maroons. In the 1980s, some 10,000 fled to French Guiana to escape bombings, massacres, and other attacks on their communities by the Surinamese military.

Emancipation

The maroons were not the only ones who resisted slavery. In perhaps the most dramatic act of resistance, rebellious slaves burned much of the capital in 1832, and as late as 1860 the entire slave population of a plantation escaped to the forest.

Responding to these and other pressures, in 1863 Holland abolished slavery in all of its colonial territories, freeing close to 33,000 slaves. Even before this period, the collapse of the plantation economy in the late 1700s had significantly altered Surinamese society—many of the Dutch plantation owners and overseers left the colony to return to Europe. Jewish plantation owners remained, though, and intermarriage between white plantation owners and slave women became increasingly legitimate during this period. Some scholars argue that the offspring of these semi-accepted unions were manumitted and received better education and a higher social status. It also seems to be true that the majority of free blacks and coloreds (people of mixed race) in the cities of colonial Suriname were female.

Abolition, however, brought even more challenges, as free blacks and Creoles struggled to make a living in the new wage-based economy. A large number of Creoles emerged as the non-white elite, securing coveted positions as miners, industrial workers, and merchants. Those blacks that were not Creoles found few opportunities outside the plantation. Many migrated to the country's capital, PARAMARIBO, in search of employment.

Throughout the latter half of the nineteenth century black workers routinely searched for employment in urban areas. In an effort to replace these workers, colonial officials began importing indentured servants from Asia in 1873. More than 60,000 Javanese, Indian, and Chinese indentured servants emigrated to Suriname between 1873 and 1939. In 1916 large bauxite deposits were discovered, and mines were established by the Alcoa mining company. Most of the workers who came to Suriname at this time thus worked on colonial plantations, and some joined black and Creole workers in the country's bauxite and gold mines. This has given Suriname an ethnically diverse population: by the early 2000s, the population was 37 percent East Indian, 31 percent Creole, 15 percent Javanese, 10 percent maroon, 2 percent Amerindian, 2 percent Chinese, and 2 percent European, Lebanese, and others.

Independence

In 1954 Suriname became an autonomous state within the kingdom of the Netherlands. This allowed all of the residents of Suriname to elect a Parliament which formed the government, along with a governor appointed by colonial officials. Between 1954 and 1972 several political parties were established in Suriname, and most represented the interests of a specific ethnic group. In 1973 a Creole-Javanese political coalition won a majority of the parliamentary seats and exercised their constitutional right to appoint Creole politician Henck Arron as prime minister. Arron initiated the negotiations with the Dutch government that culminated two years later on November 25, 1975, in independence for Suriname. Victory was bittersweet when in the months preceding independence more than 40,000 Asians immigrated to the Netherlands, citing concerns over the stability of the new nation.

In 1977 Arron was reelected as prime minister of Suriname, but was overthrown three years later by a coup led by then-sergeant Bouterse. Army officers under Bouterse's command dissolved the parliament, suspended the constitution, declared a state of emergency, and violently repressed all opposition. Bouterse's government ruled through force, stifling opposition. In the notorious December 8, 1982, murders the security forces arrested, tortured, and summarily executed fifteen prominent Surinamese, including former government ministers, a professor, a prominent trade unionist, and others. Distrusted by the urban population, Bouterse came to surround himself with young military officers from maroon communities. The Bouterse regime was also unable to manage the country's economy, and the economic stagnation that hit the country in the early 1980s left military dictators vulnerable to challengers.

In 1986 Bouterse's reliance upon maroon supporters backfired. A small guerrilla group, drawn mainly from the Ndyuka group of maroons, joined former presidential bodyguard Ronnie Brunswijk, himself a Ndyuka maroon, to form the Surinamese Liberation Army (SLA). The SLA waged a guerrilla war against the Bouterse regime, demanding a full restoration of the country's constitution. During the war, maroon communities were often singled out for harsh reprisals for their alleged support of the SLA. Following massacres carried out against maroon civilians by the military in 1986, as many as 10,000 maroons became refugees in French Guiana. The country endured civil war and political instability until 1992, when the SLA signed a peace treaty with former education minister Ronald Venetiaan, who was chosen president of Suriname by the national assembly. The following year Bouterse was removed as commander-in-chief of the military.

Current Situation

The deteriorating economic situation, international and local pressures, and raids by the Jungle Commando led Bouterse and the military to relinquish control of the government, and in 1985 a national assembly was formed. After a new constitution was drafted in 1987, elections were held in November of that year, and the military's political wing was defeated. Though many observers doubted the independence of the new civilian government, it opened peace talks with Brunswijk's Jungle Commando in 1989. But on December 24, 1990, the military once again seized control of the government in a coup engineered by Bouterse.

In response to pressure from the United States, the Netherlands, France, and the Organization of American States, new elections were held in May 1991. The New Front for Democracy and Development, a group which combined several pre-coup political parties, won a majority of seats in the assembly. Despite its position of power, the New Front was not able to control the requisite two-thirds of parliament needed to select a president until September 1991, when Ronald Venetiaan was chosen. The New Front government eventually officially deprived the military of much of its prior power, opened peace negotiations with the Jungle Commando and dissident Amerindian groups, and continued negotiations on the repatriation of maroon refugees in French Guiana. In new elections held in 1996, which proved to be the closest in Suriname's independent history, Jules Wijdenbosch, a former chief member of the military government, defeated Venetiaan and began a five-year term. Wijdenbosch's administration was criticized for its inability to control increasing inflation and high rates of unemployment, and in 2000 Venetiaan reclaimed the presidency. The country continues to rely on its bauxite industry, leaving it susceptible to international fluctuations in price.

The economic and political challenges have posed particular difficulties for Suriname's maroon communities. Most continue to live in the country's hilly interior and struggle to keep pace with the country's transition from a military dictatorship to an open democracy. More than half of Suriname's population live in rural areas, and 90 percent of those who live in urban areas are concentrated along the country's narrow coastal plain. In 2002 an estimated 70 percent of Surinamese lived in poverty. Although these political and economic challenges pose formidable obstacles, Suriname is working to provide a stable environment for the future.

See also African Ethnic Groups in Latin America and the Caribbean; Maroonage in the Americas; Slavery in Latin America and the Caribbean.

Alonford James Robinson

Suriname and French Guiana, Maroon Communities in

Communities of runaway slaves that have survived and prospered since the 1600s in the interior regions of Suriname and French Guiana.

For nearly 500 years, maroon societies have dotted the peripheries of plantation America. Ranging from tiny bands that survived for less than a year to powerful states encompassing thousands of members and surviving for generations or even centuries, these communities still form semi-independent enclaves in several parts of the hemisphere. They remain fiercely proud of their maroon origins and, in some cases, continue to carry forward unique cultural traditions that were forged during the earliest days of the arrival of Africans to the Americas.

Historical Background

Over the past three centuries, maroon communities have existed in the forested interior of Suriname, which until 1975 was a Dutch colony also known as Dutch Guiana, in northeastern South America. The Suriname maroons (formerly also known as Bush Negroes) have long been the largest maroon population in the Americas, representing one extreme in the range of cultural adaptations that persons of African descent have made in the hemisphere.

From the mid-seventeenth century to the late eighteenth century, the ancestors of present-day maroons escaped from the coastal plantations on which they were enslaved, in many cases soon after their arrival from Africa, and fled into the forested interior where they regrouped into small bands. Their hardships in forging an existence in a new and inhospitable environment were compounded by the persistent and massive efforts of the colonial government to eliminate the threat that the maroons posed to the plantation colony.

The colonists reserved special punishments for recaptured slaves: hamstringing (crippling by cutting leg tendons), amputation of limbs, and a variety of deaths by torture. The organized pursuit of Suriname maroons and expeditions to destroy their settlements date at least from the 1670s, but these efforts rarely succeeded because the maroons established and protected their settlements with great ingenuity and had become expert at all aspects of guerrilla warfare.

By the middle of the eighteenth century when, in the words of a prominent planter, "the colony had become the theater of a perpetual war," the colonists finally sought to make peace with the maroons. In 1760 and 1762 peace treaties were successfully concluded with the two largest maroon peoples, the Ndyukas and the Saramakas, and in 1767 with the much smaller Matawai, guaranteeing maroons their freedom and territory (even though slavery persisted for another century in coastal Suriname). In return, the maroons pledged nonaggression and agreed not to harbor runaway slaves. New slave revolts and the large-scale war of subsequent decades, for which an army of mercenaries was imported from Europe, eventually led to the formation of the Aluku (Boni), Paramaka, and Kwinti groups.

Culture and Way of Life

Today these six maroon peoples, each a distinct group, continue to live in Suriname and French Guiana. The Ndyuka and Saramaka each have a population of about 24,000; the Matawai, Aluku, and Paramaka of about 2,000 each; and the Kwinti number fewer than 500. Large numbers of maroons also live outside of their traditional territories, mainly in Paramaribo (the capital of Suriname) and the coastal towns of French Guiana.

Although formed under broadly similar historical and ecological conditions, these maroon societies display significant variation in everything from language, diet, and dress, to patterns of marriage, residence, and migratory wage labor. From a cultural point of view, the greatest differences are between the maroons of central Suriname (Saramaka, Matawai, and Kwinti) on the one hand, and those of eastern Suriname and western French Guiana (Ndyuka, Aluku, and Paramaka) on the other. For example, Saramakas, Matawais, and Kwintis speak a creole language called Saramaccan, whose vocabulary has many words derived from Portuguese and English as well as from a variety of African languages. Ndyukas, Alukus, and Paramakas speak Ndyuka, which has more English-derived words and is closer to Sranan-tongo, the creole language of coastal Suriname.

In politics, a loose framework of indirect rule has prevailed in each society. Except for the Kwinti, each group has a paramount chief (who from an internal perspective might better be described as a "king"), as well as a series of headmen and other village-based officials. Traditionally, social and political leaders govern with the guidance of oracles, spirit possession, and other forms of divination. Ancestors play an active role in community affairs and many problems of daily life are dealt with in a ritual context. The justly renowned artistic production of maroons ranges from spectacular woodcarvings made by men to decorative textiles and carved calabashes (the gourd-like fruit of a tree) made by women. Arts of performance include a variety of song, dance, and drumming styles as well as tale telling and other verbal genres.

Until the mid-twentieth century, almost all maroons lived by a combination of forest horticulture, hunting, and fishing, on the one hand, and men doing wage labor on the coast to buy and bring back Western-manufactured goods, on the other. This way of life began to change rapidly in the 1960s, as the widespread use of outboard motors and the development of air service to interior areas encouraged increased traffic of people and goods between maroon villages and the coast. At the same time, Alcoa, an American aluminum company, and the Suriname government jointly constructed a giant hydroelectric project on the Suriname River, bringing a dramatic migration toward the coast. Some 6,000 Saramaka maroons were forced to abandon their homes as the artificial lake gradually flooded almost half their territory. In French Guiana in the 1970s, the Aluku were subjected to intense pressures from Paris to abandon their traditional culture and adapt to French ways of life. This has caused wrenching economic, cultural, and political transformations.

Suriname's independence from Dutch control in 1975 had less consequence for most maroons than for coastal populations. From 1986 to 1992, however, a civil war pitted the national army of Suriname against a rebel group known as the Jungle Commandos, which was largely made up of Ndyukas but also a significant number of Saramakas. The Jungle Commandos waged a guerrilla war, which they likened to their ancestors' eighteenth-century liberation struggles against the military government of Dési Bouterse. Ndyuka villages along the Cottica River were annihilated, and some 10,000 maroons fled across the eastern border to French Guiana. Continuing battles over control of the valuable mining and timber rights in the interior affect every aspect of contemporary maroon life in Suriname. The national government claims sovereignty over the territories the maroons' ancestors died for. Many outside observers fear the government has embarked on a policy of ethnic genocide against the maroons.

See also Human Rights in Latin America and the Caribbean; Maroonage in the Americas; Punishment of Slaves in Colonial Latin America and the Caribbean.

Bibliography

Price, Richard. *Alabi's World*. Johns Hopkins University Press, 1990.

Price, Richard. *First-Time: The Historical Vision of an Afro-American People*. Johns Hopkins University Press, 1983.

Price, Richard, and Sally Price. *Enigma Variations*. Harvard University Press, 1995.

Price, Richard, and Sally Price. *Maroon Arts: Cultural Vitality in the African Diaspora*. Beacon, 1999.

Price, Richard, and Sally Price, eds. *Stedman's Surinam: Life in an Eighteenth-Century Slave Society*. Johns Hopkins University Press, 1992.

Price, Sally. *Co-Wives and Calabashes*. 2nd ed. University of Michigan Press, 1993.

Thoden van Velzen, H. U. E., and W. van Wetering. *The Great Father and the Danger: Religious Cults, Material Forces, and Collective Fantasies in the World of the Surinamese Maroons*. Foris, 1988.

Sutton, Percy Ellis

1920–

American attorney, politician, and media businessman

Percy Ellis Sutton was born in San Antonio, Texas. In the 1950s, after completing his education under the G.I. Bill, he opened a law firm in HARLEM that specialized in civil rights cases. Sutton's political career began when he was elected to the New York State Assembly in 1964. He became president of the Manhattan Borough in 1966, a position he held through 1977. After an unsuccessful mayoral bid he retired from public office, but continued to be a prominent adviser to New York politicians, including United States Representative CHARLES RANGEL and Mayor DAVID DINKINS.

In 1971 Sutton began purchasing black-owned media businesses, becoming the owner and chairman of the Inner-City Broadcasting Company in 1977. Through this corporation he purchased and restored the APOLLO THEATER, a Harlem landmark. Sutton was awarded the Spingarn Medal for his work by the NATIONAL ASSOCIATION FOR THE ADVANCEMENT OF COLORED PEOPLE in 1987. Ten years later, along with Dinkins, Sutton served as the attorney for Malcolm Shabazz, the twelve-year-old grandson of MALCOLM X who admitted to setting a fire that led to the death of Betty Shabazz, Malcolm X's widow. In November 2002 Sutton welcomed the first Marketing Opportunities in Business and Entertainment (MOBE) Business Building Clinic in Harlem. He continues to serve the Harlem community with his expertise in politics, business, and communication.

Suzman, Helen

1917–

South African politician and outspoken opponent of apartheid.

Born Helen Gavronsky in Germiston, in what is now Gauteng province, northeastern SOUTH AFRICA, of Jewish immigrant parents, Helen Suzman was educated at the Parktown Convent until 1933 and then attended the University of the Witwatersrand in JOHANNESBURG. In 1937 she married Moses Meyer Suzman, and they settled in Johannesburg. During World War II (1939–1945) she worked for the War Supplies Board. She joined the United Party (UP) in 1949 and became a well-known speaker as honorary information officer, before being elected as the party's member of parliament (MP) for the Johannesburg suburb of Houghton in April 1953.

In 1959 the party was split between conservatives and progressives following the party's decision to oppose further land allocations for blacks. Eleven of its progressive members resigned, including Suzman. In August 1959 they formed the new Progressive Party (PP), but in the general election of 1961 only Suzman was returned to Parliament to be the sole PP representative there for the next thirteen years. She was a staunch opponent of the Nationalist Party government's racially biased policies, sometimes being the only voice in Parliament raised against new oppressive legislation. She retained her seat in the elections of 1966 and 1970, and only in 1974 was she joined by seven more Progressive Party MPs. The PP continued to increase its strength in Parliament, and the new members took much of the burden of opposition from Suzman. During the 1970s, with the terminal decline of the UP, the PP and the Reform Party merged in 1977 to become the Progressive Federal Party (PFP). As the party with the second-largest representation in Parliament, the PFP was the official opposition party.

Suzman traveled extensively in the United States and Europe, and in 1971, with PP leader Colin Eglin, she visited SENEGAL, THE GAMBIA, SIERRA LEONE, and TANZANIA, an almost unheard of event for a white South African MP. She has received many awards from universities in GREAT BRITAIN, the United States, and South Africa. In 1985 and 1986 she lost considerable support inside and outside South Africa for opposing international sanctions against South Africa on the grounds that these would encourage a siege mentality; she argued instead for internal black boycotts. Suzman retired from Parliament in 1989, just before the dismantling of APARTHEID began. She was one of eleven veteran South African figures of all races chosen to sit on the Independent Electoral Commission, which was appointed by the Transitional Executive Council that was set up in December 1993 to oversee the transition to majority rule. That same year she published her autobiography, *In No Uncertain Terms: A South African Memoir*. In 2002 she received the Liberal International Prize for Freedom in recognition of her lifelong support of human rights in South Africa. Suzman, who continues to speak publicly on political issues, was made an honorary member of the South Africa's Democratic Alliance in 2003.

See also Antiapartheid Movement; Verwoerd, Hendrik Frensch; Vorster, Balthazar Johannes.

Swahili Civilization

The people known as Swahili live in a string of permanent settlements along the coastline of eastern AFRICA from southern SOMALIA to central MOZAMBIQUE and on the offshore islands of ZANZIBAR, Pemba, Mafia, and the COMOROS. Throughout their history they have been traders, middlemen in the intercontinental commerce between the interior of Africa, Arabia, Persia, and India, as well as fishing people and sailors. Accounts as far back as the first century C.E. tell of Arab traders on this coast, and excavations have shown towns built in the eighth century that were very similar to those of today. Unlike the case with most African peoples, the archaeological and written historical record here is long, and the Swahili, a Muslim and literate people, know of their past and are proud to tell of it.

Multiethnic and Diverse

The name *Swahili* (properly the plural form is WaSwahili) was given to them in the eighteenth century by the first rulers of the sultanate of Zanzibar. It is from the Arabic and means "the people of the coast," often considered a pejorative term. The Swahili rarely use it for themselves, preferring names based on their towns: the people of Mombasa, the people of Pate, and so on. Their language, KiSwahili (often referred to simply as Swahili), has many dialects, each town having its own (the standard form used today is that of Zanzibar). It is closely related to languages spoken by many non-Swahili peoples. However, the name Swahili has been used for so long and so widely that it is generally accepted in writings about the people as a whole.

The KiSwahili language is frequently taught in the United States as a sign of pride in African American slave origins. In historical fact, however, virtually no Swahili people ever came to the Americas as slaves, and indeed the Swahili merchants were themselves owners of and traders in slaves to Arabia and to the East but not across the Atlantic Ocean.

Swahili society is multiethnic in composition, with many internal differences in social stratification, occupation, and religious conformity. Its boundaries are ill-defined, as Swahili towns are built along the coastline only and do not extend for more than about 1.5 to 3 km (about 1 to 2 mi) inland, where they become intermingled with the settlements of other neighboring peoples. There are a few Swahili towns in the far interior but these are recent, built as part of the nineteenth-century trading networks controlled by the coastal towns. Today some formerly distinct Swahili towns have become merely parts of modern conurbations, such as MOMBASA in KENYA and Zanzibar City and DAR ES SALAAM in TANZANIA.

It is generally reckoned that the Swahili number in all somewhere between 300,000 and 500,000, but their preference to be called by names other than Swahili has led to continual confusion in censuses, and this figure is little more than an estimate.

Swahili "identity" has always been uncertain and difficult to define in any clear-cut manner. Many of them claim to have come from Arabia or Persia rather than from Africa. This view was also held in the past by European observers but has by now been discarded in favor of an African origin, even though their civilization has certainly been strongly influenced by Asian population and trade contacts. The same is true of the KiSwahili language, which is grammatically firmly Bantu (that is, African) but with much admixture with words of Arabic origin. In brief, the Swahili are an African people and not a form of Asian Creole society, although many of their upper-ranking members persistently claim Arabian origins.

One of the basic criteria for Swahili is the adherence to ISLAM, which reached this area in the ninth or tenth century; before that time there were no Swahili as such. And since Bantu-speaking peoples did not reach this region until about the fifth century, it is assumed that the earlier peoples were Cushitic speakers, akin to those still living in southern ETHIOPIA. It is clear that this potentially wealthy coast has attracted immigrants from both Asia and Africa for many centuries, all adding to the rich civilization that is uniquely Swahili, not only in language and religion but also in architecture, cuisine, dress, and other cultural forms. To ask about clearly definable origins is to ask a narrow and ethnocentric question that cannot be answered in simple racial or ethnic terms in the case of a complex and subtly organized society such as this. But the Swahili themselves remain perfectly clear as to their own unique sense of single identity and culture.

Swahili society has never formed a single polity with clear boundaries and a centralized form of government. It has comprised clusters of towns, some mercantile and others not, and has almost always been subject to outside colonial rule. Until the end of the fifteenth century the Swahili people appear to have been subject to some form of mercantile control from Yemen. From 1498 until 1729 they were subject to Portuguese overrule from Goa. The Portuguese did little except take over the rich GOLD TRADE of ZIMBABWE from Swahili traders in the south, build several immense forts (the greatest being Fort Jesus in Mombasa), attempt (without success) to convert Swahili to CHRISTIANITY, and make much personal profit by what can only be called forms of theft and corruption. The Portuguese were finally removed, to the relief of the local people, by the Arab rulers of Oman, in southeastern Arabia, who established the sultanate of Zanzibar. The Arab rulers took over political control and commerce from the Swahili, and over time these rulers and later immigrants from southern Arabia became "Swahili-ized" themselves. Zanzibar became wealthy and notorious from the slave and ivory trades and spread its domination far inland during the nineteenth century. In the later part of the century, Zanzibar's dominions were taken over by British and German colonial powers, the latter taking TANGANYIKA and the former the remainder, ruling Zanzibar and the sultan's possessions in coastal Kenya in the form of a protectorate. The British had slavery and the slave trade abolished in Zanzibar and Tanganyika in 1897 and in Kenya in 1907, destroying much of the former economy. Independence of Tanganyika took place in 1961 and that of Kenya in 1963; and in 1964 the revolution in Zanzibar brought the sultanate to an end.

During the twentieth century the coast became seriously impoverished as the centers of production and wealth moved inland, especially in Kenya. The centuries-old intercontinental commerce was taken from the Swahili by central governments and international companies, and the Swahili became largely marginal citizens in their own countries. Their adherence to Islam and the memory of the days of slavery set them apart from most of the peoples of the new countries of which they unwillingly became citizens.

Yet in the face of these events the Swahili people themselves have retained their pride, their notable abilities as merchants and entrepreneurs, and their religion. Despite the decline of commerce, wealth, and power, and in many towns the insulting subjection to the demands of the tourist industry, they regard their own unique mercantile civilization as persisting and setting them apart from the surrounding world, giving sense to their world, which they view as being at one stage, and not the final one, in their long history.

Lifestyle Variations

The Swahili use two words for their own way of life: *ustaarabu*, usually translated as "civilization" and literally "long residence in a single place," and *utamaduni*, literally "urbanity." They are both urban and urbane people.

There are between 300 and 400 towns of various sizes along the coast as well as many sites of long-forsaken and ruined places. These settlements have many detailed variations in size, composition, occupation, and style, yet all may be seen as having a single theme. The Swahili word for a town is *miji*, and all settlements are properly *miji*: the defining feature is the possession of a central or congregational mosque, the "Friday" mosque that must be attended by all men five times on Fridays and, if possible, also on the other days. Women are not allowed to enter mosques but may sit outside to hear the prayers and sermons. A settlement without a mosque is not a "town" and is not even said to have been "founded" (*kubuni*). There are two categories of towns: both are miji, but they may be distinguished as "stone-towns" and "country-towns." These may be set along a continuum, and many towns have features of both, but they are essentially distinct.

Stone-towns are built of houses made of "stone"—that is, blocks of coral—sometimes two or three stories high and set in narrow streets. These houses can last for as long as two or three centuries if looked after. Most stone-towns were once walled. Almost all are ports, typically set on the banks of estuaries and saltwater creeks or on the leeward sides of small islands and so protected from the force of the Indian Ocean. These towns are densely built-up places and appear truly urban in any sense. Country-towns appear more like rural villages, their houses built of palm-leaf matting, mud, and wattle. However, all are miji, a term with a social rather than a physical reference.

The stone-towns have been and remain occupied by Swahili merchants, have been the entrepôts for commercial exchanges, and are the centers of traditional Swahili civilization. The country-towns are rather fishing and gardening settlements, without merchants. Merchants kept slaves, whereas country-towns had none. Today perhaps a third to half of the population of any stone-town is composed of people of slave ancestry as well as of people of free merchant descent: all are Swahili. There are also in the stone-towns many citizens of different ancestries: the descendants of nineteenth-century immigrants from Arabia, today generally counted as Swahili, Muslim Indians, and in the case of the larger places, recent immigrants from inland African groups who work as laborers and who are never considered Swahili. The country-towns are far less mixed, and in some, such as in those of Zanzibar Island, people originally non-Swahili are not accepted as residents. Stone-towns were and are owned by the *waungwana,* the "patricians," merchants who own plantations, sailing vessels, and the stone-built houses. They themselves, however, have produced little other than grains and mangrove poles for export to Arabia, which has neither. The country-towns were and are the homes of the producers of food, especially the staples rice and fish, for the stone-towns and have also supplied labor for them since the abolition of slavery. Despite these differences, which are still widely found throughout the coast, although they are not as rigidly marked as these words might imply, these many towns together form a single society of interdependent local communities.

Stone-towns and some of the constituent groups, such as the country-town dwellers of Zanzibar and Pemba islands, formerly had kings and queens. Not a great deal is known about them, and some queens might be personages of myth. They had elaborate regalia (mainly thrones of ebony and ivory, immense side-blown horns of ivory and brass, and several kinds of drums) and acted as representatives of their city-states toward outsiders more than as holders of internal authority. The last of them, the indigenous ruler of Zanzibar Island, died in 1865.

All towns are divided into two moieties. Opposition between the moieties of any particular town is typically expressed in fighting at the New Year and in competition in dancing and football; they were formerly important as organs of local government, moieties providing ruling councils for alternate periods. The last function fell into desuetude under British rule, but the others persist. Moieties are divided into territorial wards that are corporate landholding groups in the country-towns but not in the stone-towns, where they are mainly mere places of residential address.

Descent, Rank, and Marriage

Swahili ways of reckoning descent, kinship, rank, and marriage are complex and vary considerably from one area to another. The patricians organize themselves into ranked patrilineal subclans claimed generally to be constituent units of clans in southern Arabia; subclans are divided into corporate patrilineal lineages that also act as commercial business houses. Patrilineal descent is also found among immigrant Hadhrami and Omani Arab families. The members of country-towns and those of slave ancestry reckon cognatic descent and kinship only (except occasionally, when they acquire property such as clove trees, as in parts of Pemba Island, they may assume patrilineal descent). Families linked by patrilineal descent are exclusive units in terms of possession and inheritance of rights in

land and other property, which are thus theirs alone. The patricians of the stone-towns practice the purchase and sale of private property and use the Islamic institution of *waqf.* This is a form of entail by which property may not be sold or disposed of by future generations and must be passed down by Islamic rules of inheritance. It also ensures that descent groups own their property in perpetuity and without taxation. Without waqf the patrician groups of this society could not function as they have. On the other hand, families linked only by cognatic descent are broadly inclusive in terms of rights in land and property, which are shared and dispersed over wide circles of cognatically linked families. The former pattern is linked to commerce and wealth from trade, the latter is not: rights in property provide the key to chosen mode of descent and inheritance.

Closely related are differences of rank. The populations of stone-towns are strictly divided by rank, with the patricians at the top; those of country-towns make no such distinctions. Lineages of the MaSharifu, the direct descendants of the Prophet, stand apart; of high religious standing, their ranking position is a socially ambiguous one.

Differences of descent and rank are reflected and perpetuated by the several forms of marriage, an institution that is part of a group's long-term strategies involving the inheritance of rights in property and wealth. All patrician marriages are arranged, clan endogamous, and must be between partners of exactly the same rank. Those of first-born patrician daughters are uxorilocal, monogamous, and in them divorce is formally prohibited. Those of other patrician daughters, usually to clan members living in other towns, are virilocal, frequently polygynous, and perhaps usually end in divorce. Formal betrothal is mainly a feature of first patrician marriages, and any later marriages after divorce are decided by the marital pair concerned. Marriages of members of country-towns are exogamous, polygynous, often neolocal, and with very high divorce rates; these marriages are part of strategies to bestow wide inclusive rights in land over wide areas, in contrast to the exclusive marriages of patricians. Marriages between Swahili of slave ancestry are rarely arranged and are perhaps typically short-lived.

All these forms of marriage include marriage payments of several kinds. The transfer of a relatively small bridewealth, *mahari,* from the groom's to the bride's side is always made; this is obligatory under Muslim law, although the actual transfer may be delayed until long after the wedding. A donation known as the *kitu* (literally, "thing") is also made by the groom to the bride's father. This payment may be very high, as young men may earn large amounts by working in the Gulf. The bride's father gives a dowry to his daughter, and there are also many small payments from groom to bride during the actual wedding itself. Finally, mainly among patricians, the bride's father gives her right of residence in either a new house built for her or in part of his own house: the house belongs to the lineage and not to her, as no right of disposal is given, only that of residence.

Marriages are virtually always between cousins (except for maternal parallel cousins). The marriage of a patrician firstborn daughter should certainly be with her paternal parallel cousin, because both she and he are of the same lineage, which is thereby strengthened and perpetuated.

So-called "secret marriages," secondary marriages between people who are typically unrelated, also take place. In these marriages there are no transfers of wealth or property; the marriages are, however, legal and children from them are legitimate offspring of the husband. In the past concubinage with slave women was frequent; the children of these relationships were also legitimate, and the mother was usually freed. The status of concubine, *suria*, was a formally recognized one and quite distinct from casual unions.

Swahili Mercantilism

The context of these forms of local organization, kinship, and marriage has been until very recently the intercontinental commerce controlled by the Swahili patricians. Although this commerce is now slight, it still provides the people themselves with the historical memory of the ways in which their society and culture have been shaped as they are today and is the basic element in the formation of Swahili civilization.

The Swahili have for centuries been at the hub, as commercial and cultural brokers between widely separated societies, of a single immense exchange system stretching from the African Great Lakes to China. Until the mid-nineteenth century they were at the fringes of the Arabian, Persian, and above all Indian pre- or proto-capitalist systems, and since then on the periphery of European-American capitalism. Africa has exported its raw materials in exchange for manufactured commodities, whose makers have taken the profits. From East Africa for many centuries went IVORY, slaves, gold, timber, grain, hides and skins, iron, gums, fragrances, and many more items. Into Africa from Asia came textiles, beads, Chinese and Japanese porcelain, metal wire, paper, arms and ammunition, bullion, and many other commodities, including religious teaching. All this commerce passed through the ports of the Swahili coast. Carriage between the African interior and the coast was by caravans; that to and from Asia was by sailing ships, mostly owned and crewed by Arabs and, until steamships came into use, dependent on the regular monsoons.

The Swahili towns have never been isolated but all are interdependent, both among themselves and with neighboring peoples. Their trading partners have been far in the interior or far overseas, and all are of different ethnicities, languages, and cultures from those of the Swahili. The Swahili merchants organized the indirect exchanges between their partners, who did not themselves meet each other but dealt directly with only the Swahili middlemen. These provided facilities for harboring and careening ships, watering and victualling; provided financial, legal, recreational, and religious services; ensured protection of crews and storage of cargoes; and carried out the tasks of having both caravan and ship cargoes ready at the proper times. The commerce was complex and difficult.

Until the late nineteenth century, Swahili merchants did not venture far inland. Along the coastline the patricians of each town built up wide networks of exchange between themselves as patrons and others, their clients. These networks each comprised at the center the patricians and their slaves; beyond were other Swahili-speaking groups, and inland, non-Swahili groups. The patron-client networks have covered vast distances, as far as the eastern Congo, Arabia, and India. They exist today and are concerned with matters such as political representation, Islamic education, religious activities, especially those of the Sufi brotherhoods, and local urban employment under the aegis of Swahili patron-entrepreneurs.

The Swahili towns had no markets other than for local foodstuffs until the Zanzibar sultans established a slave market in Zanzibar City in the nineteenth century. Neither does it seem that they used money, at least not until the mid-nineteenth century or so, when the British at Zanzibar introduced Indian coinage. A few of the greater towns had their own mints making gold, silver, and copper coins from the thirteenth to the seventeenth century, but their coins were ceremonial rather than commercial, used as wedding payments and of no immediate commercial use in the interior or overseas. To the indigenous objects of exchange in the interior (iron, salt, and copper), the Swahili very early added cotton and silk cloth as well as beads. Cloth in particular was imported from India in enormous quantities and was used as a medium of exchange.

Until the late nineteenth century exchanges typically took the form of personal barter and gifts between kin and fictive kin. Exchange with partners in the interior was by patronage and clientship, "joking" relationships, blood-brotherhood, and concubinage between merchants and the daughters of their trading partners. Sons of concubines were legitimate and took the subclan membership of their fathers, so that there were many Swahili born and living in the interior who acted as agents of their paternal kin, the coastal merchants. Links with Asian trading partners were typically by marriage between a visiting trader and a younger daughter of the particular patrician with whom he traded regularly and in whose house he stayed as a son-in-law when in Africa.

Patricians made profit not in money but by the exchange of luxury items from Asia among themselves as a self-contained elite; they still do so. The items were decommoditized "treasures" such as the locally minted coins and Chinese and Japanese porcelain and silk. With slave labor they could run plantations and build their elaborate houses and mosques, and they gained prestige by religious devotion and learning, charity, and commercial reputation.

Religion, Knowledge, and Purity

The Swahili inhabitants of the coastal towns have faced certain areas of contradiction and ambiguity. They have formed a Janus-society, facing toward both the African interior and Asia. The patricians have needed for commercial reasons to claim affinity with their Asian trading partners and also to show differences from their slaves and those of slave ancestry. They have done this by being Muslims, knowing Arabic, and claiming non-African origins. Virtually all Swahili patrician subclans claim origins in southern Arabia and so close ties with Mecca and Islam. Some certainly came in small groups from Arabia (although only recently). There is no evidence for others, except that under Islamic rules of succession a single Arab ancestor enables all his patrilineal descendants to claim Arabian origins. In fact it is evident that most Swahili subclans originated in the "traditional" northern homeland known as Shungwaya, almost certainly in the region of Manda Bay and the mouth of the Tana River. The claim to Arabian origins is still commonly made, even though it goes against archaeological and linguistic findings and many oral traditions that imply local African origins.

A key defining factor of Swahili identity has always been Islam. Status and rank are determined not only by claimed origins but also by the possession of knowledge that is bestowed on the living by God. Mere belief in God is not enough to define one as a proper Muslim: one must have "knowledge," *elimu*, about God and His works and laws that is acquired by studying the writings and life of the Prophet and for men by participating in mosque activities. Knowledge may also be acquired by the performance of ecstatic dance, as with the Sufi brotherhoods, and through possession by spirits.

In Swahili religion usually two strands are distinguished, referred to as *dini* and *mila*. The essential distinction is that dini comprises matters discussed in the Qur'an (Koran), the Hadith of the Prophet, and the writings of Islamic scholars, many of whom have been Swahili. These are written in Arabic, the sacred language of Islam that is taught to Swahili children. Mila is concerned mainly with links to the many forms of local spirits. Among the Swahili, dini and mila are closely linked and complementary, and any rigid distinction is facile and misleading.

There have been continual changes and reforms in Swahili religious practice, especially in the period of radical economic and political change in the late nineteenth century, when influential reformers came from Arabia and took over religious leadership from the patricians. Since then religious leaders have typically been the more important and learned men of Omani and Hadhrami origin, many of who have received higher religious education in Arabia and Egypt. In addition, women have played an increasingly important role as theologians and religious poets. Such women whom I have met—including the women scholars who are descended from the late-nineteenth-century reformers—have high prestige, and it is doubtful whether women other than those who became poets or saints played this role before. There has also been a rise in the importance of Sufi orders or brotherhoods on the coast and inland in areas where non-Swahili Muslims are numerous. The most important in this region are the Qadiriyya, Shadiliyya, and Alawiyya, most members being nonelite and poorly educated men.

Almost all Swahili other than the most devout religious leaders recognize the existence of spirits, more widely associated with the mila than with dini. There are two main categories of spirits: the *mizimu,* who are linked with places where ancestors have dwelt and act as protectors of land and locality, and the *majini.* Majini are more directly linked to God, who cre-ated them from fire; they lived in Paradise with their leader, Iblis, were driven out because Iblis refused to obey God, and since then have roamed the earth among the living. Those majini who have learned Arabic and accepted Islam are good, and others who have not done so are evil. The former are associated in popular thought with Arabia, the latter more with Africa, but too rigid a distinction should not be made.

They are said to cohabit with and marry humans and have children with them, so long as proper rules of ranking are followed. The principal majini comprise those known as *pepo* ("wind"), who are, in general, good, and *shaitani,* who are evil. They are said to possess the living, especially women of nonpatrician ancestry whose status has become increasingly insecure since the abolition of slavery. They do so by sitting on their heads or riding them; they may then be exorcised by a "teacher" or "doctor" or accepted by their victims, who typically join associations devoted to obedience of a particular spirit that is controlled for them by a male "teacher" or "doctor." Associations are usually led by patrician women, and ordinary members are of other and slave ancestries. These associations, which are many and short-lived, are the feminine equivalent to the Sufi brotherhoods and orthodox mosque associations of men. All are devoted in the eyes of their members to the acquisition of knowledge and give them a degree of certain identity and security in the poverty of most modern coastal towns.

Knowledge is closely linked to purity. Purity, *usafi,* is acquired or brought out by women at marriage but to differing degrees. It is closely linked to a woman's inner "beauty," which is publicly displayed at the highly ritualized weddings of the Swahili. The most pure must be a firstborn patrician daughter, who, as it were, represents her lineage. Her beauty, a sign of inner purity, is brought out by her complex ritual purification before her wedding, when she must be shown to be a virgin, and her house must continually undergo ritual purification from the pollution of the town outside its door. After marriage she should live a life of seclusion and piety: her life will then endow her husband with *heshima,* meaning "reputation" or "honor." Firstborn daughters marry their father's brother's sons, who are of the same lineage, which is thereby also given honor. Such women are highly regarded as possessing moral purity and skills in commerce, poetry, and theology. A woman who is not a virgin at marriage or fails to observe formal seclusion after it can bring disgrace to her husband and lineage, and she may even be accused of being a witch and so an outcast from proper society.

Swahili "civilization" is ideally one of wealth and elegance, and even today, when there is little of the former remaining, the visitor can soon see the difference in this respect from most other African societies. Sumptuary conventions are a means of asserting societal rank and identity and of denying isolation by recognizing cultural links with the outside world. Subtleties of food and clothing; ritual use of fumigants, fragrances, and flowers; respect for physical and moral beauty; courtesy in speech and gesture; elegance in furnishing and decorating houses; and skill in woodcarving, in music, and in the formidably intricate forms of Swahili poetry are all highly important and are continual subjects of rivalry between and within subclans and lineages. The rules change continually with the introduction of new forms of elegant behavior from the "global" world beyond the coast; they define the elite and deny Swahili elite identity to non-Swahili nouveaux riches. Today radio, television (although limited to only a few coastal areas), videos imported from India, Japan, and the United States, and the several newspapers published in English and Swahili are all means of widening the local horizon. Also the widespread tourism on the East African coast is strongly influential—and destructive of tradition—in bringing global culture to the Swahili towns. All these factors lead to increased intergenerational conflict as to the aims of education and occupation by which younger people, at least, can better cope with the outside world, which appears to most Swahili as hostile and unwilling to accept legitimate Swahili political and cultural aspirations.

See also Sufism.

John Middleton

Swahili Coast

Stretch of East African coastline between southern Somalia in the north and northern Mozambique in the south that is home to more than 400 settlements.

The Swahili coast (3,000 km, or about 1,865 mi) has been the site of cultural and commercial exchanges between East Africa and the outside world—particularly the Middle East, Asia, and Europe—since at least the second century C.E. The earliest coastal communities practiced ironworking and were mainly subsistence farmers and riverine fishers, who supplemented their economy with hunting, keeping livestock fishing in the ocean, and trading with outsiders. Between 500 and 800 C.E. they shifted to a sea-based trading economy and began to migrate south by ship. In the following centuries, trade in goods from the African interior such as GOLD, IVORY, and slaves stimulated the development of market towns such as MOGADISHU, Shanga, Kilwa, and MOMBASA. By around the ninth century C.E., Africans, Arabs, and Persians who lived and traded on the coast had developed a lingua franca, Kiswahili, a language based on the Bantu language Sabaki that uses Arab and Persian loan words. They had also developed the distinctive Swahili culture, characterized by the almost universal practice of ISLAM, as well as by Arabic and Asian-influenced art and architectural styles.

The arrival of the Portuguese explorer VASCO DA GAMA in 1498 signaled a new era of foreign rule on the Swahili Coast. By this time Mombasa was the dominant Swahili power, so control over this city meant control over the coastal region. Portugal, seeking to monopolize trade throughout the Indian Ocean trade, built Fort Jesus in Mombasa and also set up a customs house on PATE ISLAND. The Portuguese were finally pushed out of power on the Swahili Coast in 1698 by combined forces from Oman and Pate, though the Portuguese remained in Mozambique until the late twentieth century.

The imam (religious leader) of Oman then sought control of the coast, but matters closer to home drew his attention. It was instead the Mazrui clan of Mombasa (whose ancestors came from Omani long before) who gained predominance in the region. They were in turn driven out of the city in 1837 by Omani forces. The sultan of Oman then moved his capital to ZANZIBAR and established a commercial empire, bringing renewed prosperity to the coast.

The sultan then expanded his trading empire, sending caravans into the African interior to trade firearms for gold, ivory, and slaves. The slave trade on the East African coast had persisted for centuries but it intensified during the early nineteenth century in order to meet the labor demands on French plantations on RÉUNION and MAURITIUS, as well as on the sultan's plantations on Zanzibar. By the late nineteenth century, pressure from the British had forced an end to the trade and the Swahili Coast was exporting a variety of spices and other tropical crops.

Following the SCRAMBLE FOR AFRICA of the late nineteenth century, during which the European powers divided East Africa among themselves, the hegemony of the sultan in Zanzibar gave way to European overrule. The colonial powers began to control trade in the interior, bypassing the Swahili middlemen. Today DAR ES SALAAM and Mombasa are the biggest port cities on the Swahili Coast; both have been significantly transformed by industrial development as well as by the migration of upcountry Africans. Smaller Swahili towns, however, such as Pate in KENYA, retain much of their traditional culture. For these towns beachfront TOURISM has become an important economic component.

See also Indian Ocean Slave Trade; Slavery in Africa; Swahili Civilization; Swahili Language; Swahili People.

Robert Fay

Swahili Language

Bantu language and one of the most widely-spoken African languages.

Swahili is the official language of TANZANIA and KENYA and is spoken as a *lingua franca* throughout most of East Africa, as well as parts of Central Africa. The language is heavily influenced by Arabic—a result of the long-standing trading relationships in the region—while many contemporary words are adapted from English. The main dialects of Swahili, or Kiswahili, as it is also called, are Kiunguja, Kimvita, and Kiamu.

Swahili has a long tradition of literary production, and poetry has been written in Swahili since at least the middle of the seventeenth century. It draws on Arabic, Persian, and Urdu literary sources. Though Swahili was originally only written in Arabic script, Latin script became more popular in the mid-nineteenth century and has since become standard. The oldest survivng Swahili epic is the *Hamziya*, which was written by Sayyid Aidarusi in Arabic script in the old Kingozi dialect in 1749. Bwana Muku II, the ruler of the island of PATE, off the coast of present-day Kenya, commissioned the poem. Mwana Kupona binti Msham was a well-known poet of the nineteenth century who wrote *tenzi*, didactic poems that were traditionally concerned with Islamic religious subjects and public commentary. This form is still used by contemporary poets such as Abdilatif Abdalla. Muyaka bin Haji al-Ghassaniy (1776–1840) wrote poetic commentaries of urban life in the form of mashairi. Perhaps the most famous contemporary Swahili author is Shaaban Robert, a Tanzanian known for his poetry, children's literature, essays and novels. Many works of Western authors have been translated into Swahili, such as the well-known renderings of William Shakespeare's plays by JULIUS NYERERE.

See also Languages, African: An Overview.

Swahili People

Ethnic group occupying coastal areas in parts of Somalia, Kenya, and Tanzania.

The Swahili people number approximately half a million, inhabiting a string of small settlements along the East African coast from MOGADISHU in the north to MOZAMBIQUE in the south, spanning approximately 1,800 km (about 1,118 mi). They are believed to have descended from Bantu speaking agriculturalists who lived in an area reaching roughly from KENYA's Tana River in modern Kenya to the Webi Shebelle region of SOMALIA. Although they had long supplemented their farming with fishing, it is believed that around 500 C.E. these people began to trade and migrate along the coast. Over the next three centuries migrant groups moved south by ship, establishing settlements both on the coast and on adjacent islands. These independent polities were linked by trade as well as by a common culture and language, SWAHILI. From an early date merchants from the Arab peninsula, Persia, and India settled among and intermarried with the Swahili towns' African founders.

By the twelfth century Swahili culture exhibited Arab and Asian cultural influences. A distinctive Swahili architecture had emerged that reflected these influences. Houses made of coral rag and coral stone had replaced the circular mud-and-wattle buildings found in parts of inland East Africa. The ruins at the GEDI in Kenya provide one example of early Swahili architecture. ISLAM was also well established along the SWAHILI COAST by the twelfth century, though elements of indigenous African religions remained.

For centuries Swahili merchants served as middlemen, exporting products from the East African interior in exchange for goods purchased from Indian Ocean merchant ships. Especially during the nineteenth century, Swahili caravans traveled far into the interior in search of slaves and IVORY, and some of these traders established inland trading posts. One of the most renowned nineteenth-century Swahili traders was the Zanzibari TIPPU TIP, whose trading empire stretched from the East African coast to the western bank of the Lualaba River in the modern DEMOCRATIC REPUBLIC OF THE CONGO (formerly ZAIRE).

The Swahili were never unified politically and their towns and states varied considerably in size and structure. Royal dynasties ruled some Swahili polities such as those on PATE ISLAND, while local oligarchies, known as *waungwana*, ruled others. Most Swahili towns were divided into wards, each dominated by a few families. In addition, Swahili towns were divided into northern and southern halves, with the wealthier and older families occupying the northern half, and the less well off, including Swahili migrants and foreigners, occupying the southern half.

In smaller and less prosperous Swahili towns most of the townspeople engaged in agriculture and supplemented their own production with trade. The most powerful families in the larger and more prosperous Swahili towns typically oversaw agricultural production in the surrounding countryside, where slaves or hired labor tended crops. In the larger towns Swahili society became highly hierarchical. The waungwana attempted to consolidate their power through family alliances forged through marriage. Women were prohibited from marrying people who were considered below their social level in this hierarchy. Married women were to retain ritual purity and remain indoors during daylight hours. When traveling outside, married women were veiled. They often traveled in a tent-like cover called a *shirra*, until the British outlawed the practice. In addition, wives were to be observant Muslims; they were to pray and read sacred texts in the home, as well as to practice works of charity. The less wealthy, the poor women, and the women in smaller towns had fewer restrictions, out of economic necessity.

The arrival of the Portuguese in the late fifteenth century began a long era of foreign rule on the Swahili Coast but not all foreign powers left equally lasting influences. The Portuguese, for example, established only a limited presence on the Swahili Coast compared to the size of their colonies in southern Africa. They left behind few traces beside the ruin of Fort Jesus on Mombasa.

The imam (religious leader) of Oman drove the Portuguese from the coast in 1698 and gradually established his hegemony over the coast. Omani influences on Swahili culture proved much more significant. In addition to introducing many Arabic loan words into the Swahili language, the Omani cultivated the belief that the way they practiced Islam and their social status was superior to that of the Swahili. Arab ancestry thus became a marker of status.

Beginning in the late nineteenth century European COLONIAL RULE brought further changes to Swahili society. Although parts of the Swahili Coast remained under Omani control, European colonialism eventually brought an end to slave trading and more generally undermined the Swahili's traditional role as East African middlemen. Modern shipping has taken over the long-distance ocean trade routes once traveled by *dhows*, the Swahili's wooden sailing vessels. Cities such as Mogadishu and MOMBASA, now major industrial ports, have attracted many migrants from the East African interior. Kiswahili now contains many loan words from English and has become the lingua franca (a means of communication among peoples of different languages) of much of East Africa, spoken by more than 130 million people.

See also African Religions: An Interpretation; Indian Communities in Africa; Languages, African: An Overview; Marriage, African Customs of; Portugal; Zanzibar.

Bibliography

Middleton, John. *The World of the Swahili: An African Mercantile Civilization.* Yale University Press, 1992.

Nurse, Derek, and Thomas Spear. *The Swahili: Reconstructing the History and Language of an African Society, 800–1500.* University of Pennsylvania Press, 1985.

Robert Fay

Swazi

Founding ethnic group of the kingdom of Swaziland.

The name Swazi derives from that of a nineteenth-century ruler, Mswati II, under whom Swaziland expanded into an empire that incorporated numerous peoples and covered an area roughly twice its present-day size. Prior to the reign of Mswati, the Swazi people were a group of Nguni clans known either as the Dlamini, after their ruling clan, or collectively as the Ngwane. The Ngwane arrived in southern AFRICA as part of the great Bantu migrations and by the fifteenth century had established small, pastoral communities along the coast of Delagoa Bay in southern MOZAMBIQUE. The heavily forested terrain proved unsuitable for agriculture, and the Ngwane clans eventually migrated further into southern Africa.

In the early nineteenth century the military conquests of the ZULU king SHAKA pushed the Ngwani clans, under the leadership of Sobhuza I, into the grasslands that comprise modern-day Swaziland's "middleveld" region. There Sobhuza I and later his son Mswati II conquered and incorporated the NGUNI, SOTHO, and TSONGA clans, by the 1840s forging one of southern Africa's largest kingdoms.

Although the Ngwane had probably encountered Portuguese explorers and traders as early as the sixteenth century, Swazi-European relationships did not begin in earnest until the 1840s. At that time Boer settlers began trading cloth, beads, and guns in exchange for cattle-grazing privileges in Swazi territory, and English missionaries began converting the Swazi to Methodism (nearly 60 percent of Swazi today profess Christianity). When gold was discovered in the Lembombo Mountains in 1882, European mining concessions began pouring into Swaziland, and in 1894 the kingdom was officially annexed by the South African Boer Republic. Following the Boer War (1899–1902), Swaziland reverted to British rule and its boundaries were redrawn, leaving many Swazi involuntary residents of SOUTH AFRICA.

Today more than 1 million Swazi live in Swaziland and an additional 700,000 reside in South Africa, where until 1990 they were confined to Swazi homelands called the KaNgwane. King Sobhuza II launched a diplomatic campaign to annex the KaNgwane homelands after Swaziland gained independence in 1968, but the South African government refused. Even in the postapartheid era most South African Swazi have chosen to remain in South Africa, where many work in the mining industry.

Swaziland survived colonial rule with much of its political structure and many of its customs intact. The nation is still ruled by a king, known as the Ngwenyama (lion), and a queen mother, called the Ndlovuzaki (female elephant), both of whom trace their ancestry back to the Nkosi Dlamini, the royal line of the ruling Dlamini clan. Despite the prominent presence of Christian churches in Swaziland, ancestor worship and other elements of traditional Swazi religion remain part of everyday life for many Swazi.

See also Bantu: Dispersion and Settlement.

Andrew Hermann

Swaziland

A small landlocked southern African kingdom bordering South Africa to the north, west, and south, and Mozambique to the east.

Swaziland's beautiful, mountainous topography and unusually peaceful transition from COLONIAL RULE to independence have earned it the nickname "the Switzerland of Africa." Swaziland is a kingdom, ruled jointly by a king and a queen mother, who trace their royal lineage back to the fifteenth century, making Swaziland one of only a handful of African nations to have survived the colonial period with most of its traditional political system intact. This is due largely to the efforts of one man, King SOBHUZA II, who managed to maintain his position and popularity under nearly half a century of British control. Since Swaziland became independent in 1968, however, and particularly since Sobhuza's death in 1983, the nation's urban intellectuals and businesspeople have become increasingly dissatisfied with the old system of hereditary, autocratic rule. As mounting foreign debt and natural resource depletion have weakened Swaziland's once relatively prosperous economy, general strikes and civil unrest have jeopardized the fragile political stability that the current ruler, MSWATI III, inherited from his revered predecessor. Bowing to domestic and international pressure, Mswati declared his support for democratic reforms and a new constitution in 1996, but so far he has failed to deliver on his promises.

Precolonial History

Swaziland's earliest inhabitants were KHOISAN-speaking hunter-gatherers who lived in small, scattered nomadic communities throughout southern Africa. Many lived solely from foraging

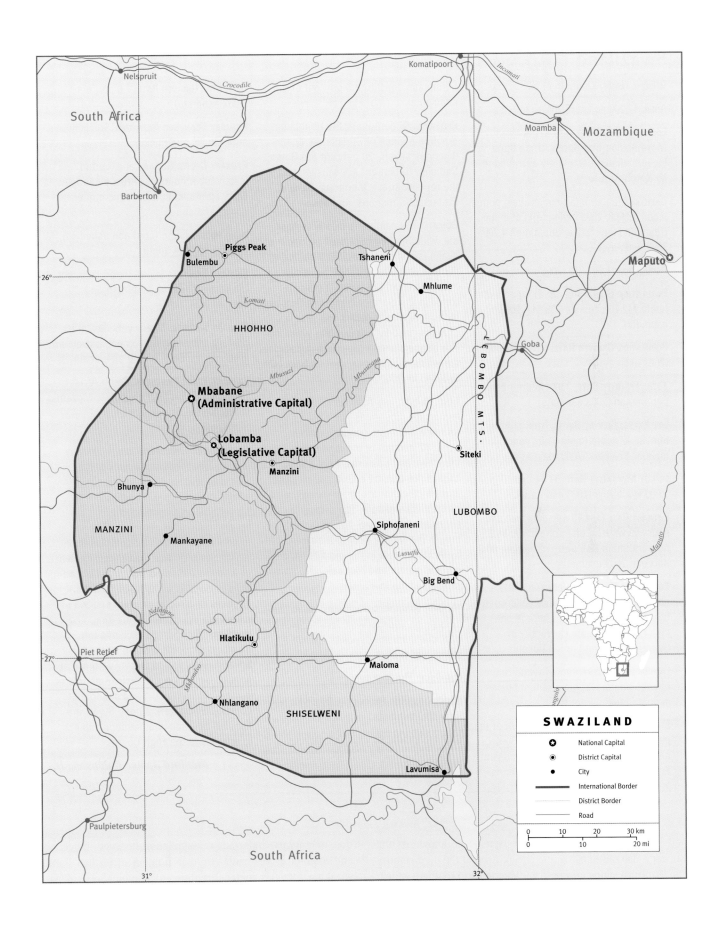

Swaziland (At a Glance)

Official Name: Kingdom of Swaziland

Area: 17,360 sq km (6,704 sq mi)

Location: Southern Africa, between Mozambique and South Africa (land-locked; almost completely surrounded by South Africa)

Capital: Mbabane (administrative; population 69,000; 2003 estimate); Lobamba (royal and legislative; population 4,200; 2003 estimate)

Population: 1,161,219 (2003 estimate)

Population Below Age 15: 41.4 percent (male 242,762; female 238,141; 2003 estimate)

Population Growth Rate: 0.83 percent (2003 estimate)

Total Fertility Rate: 3.92 children born per woman (2003 estimate)

Life Expectancy at Birth: Total population: 39.47 years (male 41.02 years; female 37.87 years; 2003 estimate)

Infant Mortality Rate: 67.44 deaths per 1,000 live births (2003 estimate)

Literacy Rate (age 15 and over who can read and write): Total population: 81.6 percent (male 82.6 percent; female 80.8 percent; 2003 estimate)

Education: Between 1995 and 2001, about 71 percent of eligible children attended primary school. There is one major university, the University of Swaziland, located in Kwaluseni.

Languages: English and siSwati are the official languages; government business is conducted in English.

Ethnic Groups: Roughly 97 percent of the people in Swaziland are ethnic Swazi, although there are small populations of Zulu, Tsonga, Asians, and Europeans. Europeans constitute 3 percent of the population.

Religions: 40 percent of the population practice a blend of Christianity and indigenous beliefs, 20 percent are Roman Catholic, 10 percent are Muslim, and the remainder are Mormons, Baha'is, Protestant Christians, and Jews.

Climate: The climate is mostly temperate, with cool temperatures at higher elevations and more tropical weather in the low veld. Precipitation, which is heavier toward the west, is concentrated in the warmer months of October through April; the rest of the year is characterized by sunny, clear weather. The temperature in Mbabane, located in the western highlands, ranges from (42° to 67° F) in July.

Land, Plants, and Animals: Swaziland has mostly mountains and hills, as well as some moderately sloping plains. Some 62 percent of the land comprises meadows and pastures. About 57 percent of the country's land has been set aside by the monarchy for exclusive use by the Swazi people. The principal rivers are the Komati, Lusutfu, and Umbuluzi. The steady flow of the rivers, fed by abundant rain in the mountains, supports irrigation and hydroelectric power projects in the lowlands.

Natural Resources: Asbestos, coal, clay, cassiterite, hydropower, forests, small gold and diamond deposits, quarry stone, and talc

Currency: The lilangeni

Gross Domestic Product (GDP): $4.8 billion (2002 estimate)

GDP per Capita: $4,400 (2002 estimate)

GDP Real Growth Rate: 1.6 percent (2002 estimate)

Primary Economic Activities: Subsistence agriculture, and mining

Primary Crops: Sugar cane, cotton, maize, tobacco, rice, citrus, pineapples, corn, sorghum, and peanuts; cattle, goats, and sheep

Industries: Mining (coal and asbestos), wood pulp, and sugar

Primary Exports: Sugar, wood pulp, cotton yarn, asbestos, and fresh and canned fruit

Primary Imports: Motor vehicles, machinery, transport equipment, petroleum products, foodstuffs, and chemicals

Primary Trade Partners: South Africa, European Union (EU) countries, Mozambique, United States, Japan, and Singapore

Government: Swaziland is a monarchy and an independent member of the Common-wealth. National executive power in Swaziland is vested in a king, Mswati III, who appoints a prime minister and council of ministers. One house of parliament is the National Assembly, which has sixty-five members, fifty-five of whom are elected from a list of candidates nominated by traditional local councils or directly elected, and ten of whom are appointed by the king. The thirty-member Senate includes ten members who are elected by the National Assembly and twenty who are appointed by the king. Judicial authority is vested in a high court and subordinate courts. Civil matters among Swazi are handled by traditional leaders, subject to appeals to the High Court.

Alonford James Robinson, Jr.

and hunting, but the people who came to be known as the KHOIKHOI also raised cattle and sheep. Around the third century C.E., Bantu-speaking groups began migrating to southern Africa, bringing with them iron tools to clear and cultivate the land as well as more livestock. Centuries of population growth, periodic migrations, and gradual assimilation between indigenous and migrant groups gave rise to a number of distinct Bantu-speaking societies, practicing different combinations of agriculture and PASTORALISM. One of these societies, the Dlamini, are believed to be the ancestors of modern-day Swazis.

A worker shapes blown glass in a factory in Swaziland. *CORBIS/Lindsay Hebberd*

According to Swazi oral traditions, the Dlamini chief Ngwane III founded the kingdom around 1750, when he led his people out of the mountains of southern MOZAMBIQUE and founded a permanent settlement at Lobamba, which remains the royal capital of modern Swaziland. The fertile, temperate valleys of this region, which had long served as an important migratory route for many Bantu-speaking groups, were conducive to agriculture and cattle grazing, and the Dlamini quickly grew from a small nomadic clan into one of the region's most prosperous kingdoms.

The early nineteenth century was a period of increased militarization for all southern African kingdoms, as they resisted the encroachment of both AFRIKANER (or Boer) settlers from the Cape and African groups fleeing the Portuguese colonies to the north. The Swazi kingdom expanded dramatically during this violent period, led by two aggressive kings, Sobhuza I (1816–1836) and Mswati II (1839–1865). By mid-century the kingdom was roughly twice its present-day size, stretching from the coastline of what is now MOZAMBIQUE into the interior bushlands as far north as ZIMBABWE. The victims of this expansion, mostly NGUNI, SOTHO, and TONGA clans, were allowed to maintain their traditional leaders and customs if they submitted peacefully to Swazi rule, and were brutally assimilated if they did not. The resulting polyglot kingdom came to be known, after Mswati, as Swaziland, although to this day Swazi citizens who can trace their clan name back to the original Lobamba settlement refer to themselves as "true Swazi."

In 1846 the Swazis had their first direct contact with Europeans, in the form of Boer settlers and English missionaries. (Present-day Swaziland is about half Christian, but many incorporate traditional beliefs into their religious practice.) Early Swazi-European relations were cordial, and the Boers and Swazis even aided one another in skirmishes against rival king-

doms, particularly the powerful ZULU peoples to the west. In 1860 Mswati signed the first of several concessions allowing for Boer and English settlements in Swazi territory. Although these agreements did nothing to contravene Swazi independence, they laid the groundwork for the coming period of colonial rule.

Period Of Concessions

Swazi laws of royal succession are complex and often involve a protracted period of infighting and bloodshed before a new king and queen mother can assume control. Such a period ensued following the death of Mswati II in 1865, and the Boers seized the opportunity to gain further influence in the region. By providing military backing to Mbandzeni, one of several potential monarchs, the Boers won the young king's favor and were rewarded with further territorial concessions.

In the 1880s, conventions between GREAT BRITAIN and the Boers over the disputed TRANSVAAL territory reaffirmed Swazi sovereignty, but the discovery of gold in the Lembombo Range in 1882 spoke louder than any treaty. Soon hundreds of European prospectors from around southern Africa were making the trek to Lobamba to buy Mbandzeni's permission to mine the Lembombo Range. Called concessionaires, these Boer and English fortuneseekers had soon overrun the western half of Swaziland and had virtually taken control of the kingdom's economy.

Confused and overwhelmed, Mbandzeni turned to an English ally, a former colonial administrator named Theophilus Shepstone, whose past diplomatic dealings with Swaziland had earned him the king's trust. On Shepstone's advice, Mbandzeni appointed Shepstone's son Offy to the position of Resident Advisor and Agent. It was the king's last and greatest mistake. Over the next three years Offy Shepstone accelerated the concessions process and used his office to dismantle most of the political power still held by the king and his advisers. Mbandzeni, realizing too late what he had done, declared on his deathbed in 1889, "Swazi kingship ends with me." When Great Britain and the South African Boer Republics together declared Swaziland a political dependency of Transvaal in 1894, it appeared that Mbandzeni had been right.

Boer Swaziland

Swaziland remained a dependency of Transvaal only until 1899, when the Anglo-Boer War broke out. But it was an incredibly turbulent five-year period. Swaziland's economy and national pride was ravaged by livestock disease, a hut tax that drove thousands of Swazis off their farms to seek wage labor in the mines and on white-owned ranches, and the absconding of Mbandzeni's successor, Bhunu, who decided in 1898 to flee to Zululand rather than stand trial in a Boer court for the murder of a political rival.

Ironically, the Anglo-Boer War brought to Swaziland a brief period of peace, as the Boer government fell into disarray and the kingdom reverted to semiautonomous rule. Bhunu died that

A member of a Swaziland labor union demonstrates on the South African side of the Oshoek border between the two countries in 2000, calling for democracy in Swaziland. Heavy deployment of police and army troops made protesting inside Swaziland impossible. *AFP*

tion disrupted Swazi clan life and severely depleted the country's work force.

Sobhuza II, who enjoyed an unusual degree of sovereignty throughout the colonial period, went to court in Great Britain to attempt to reclaim the Swazi's appropriated land, but without success. So instead he created a royal land trust, funded by taxes paid by his subjects, which he then used to buy back the appropriated areas. He then redistributed most of this land to Swazis—a tactical show of patronage which simultaneously eased the land shortage crisis, reaffirmed his own royal authority, and paved the way for a new period of prosperity. Following the war, foreign firms, impressed by the colony's rich natural resources and apparent economic stability, invested extensively in Swaziland's manufacturing, mining, and commercial farming and forestry sectors, transforming it over the next decade from "the least reputable and most neglected of the British dependencies" into a small regional powerhouse, exporting sugar, citrus, and forestry products.

Rapid economic growth was followed in the early 1960s by the proliferation of Swazi nationalist and labor movements. The most influential of the early political parties was the Ngwane National Liberatory Congress (NNLC), which called for universal adult suffrage and complete independence, leaving the monarch relatively few powers. The NNLC organized a series of industrial strikes in 1962 and 1963, followed by a general strike in the capital city, Mbabane, which was put down by British troops. Sobhuza sided with the British, taking advantage of the crisis to improve his standing in the eyes of the increasingly disillusioned colonial government.

Independent Swaziland

Britain had intended to phase out dependency in Swaziland and cede the kingdom to SOUTH AFRICA, but that nation's maverick government and policies of APARTHEID precluded such a route. Britain therefore switched to a strategy of decolonization which would preserve the royal status of the pro-British Sobhuza while providing for a British-style constitution and bicameral parliament. Sobhuza's supporters formed the royalist party, the Imbokodvo National Movement, in preparation for elections, while the constitution allowed the king to nominate half the senate. But when Swaziland was finally awarded independence in 1968, Sobhuza acted quickly to consolidate his power even further. Within five years he had abolished the constitution, banned all political parties, and effectively marginalized the role of the parliament.

Despite his autocratic style, Sobhuza was revered by the people. He was seen as their deliverer from colonial subjugation, and he took much credit for restoring traditional Swazi culture and sustaining the kingdom's prosperity, which was largely fed by foreign investment in manufacturing and agroprocessing, and close economic ties to South Africa. Although the king was sharply critical of the latter country's regime under apartheid, postcolonial Swaziland drew not only trade, investment capital and labor remittances from South Africa, but also increasing numbers of tourists, who came to enjoy the kingdom's wildlife, scenery, and gaming halls.

same year and the Queen Mother, Gwamile Mdluli, who took over as regent, maintained Swaziland's neutrality throughout the conflict.

British Swaziland

With the end of the Boer War in 1902, Britain assumed control of Swaziland. At about the same time, the Swazi royal family, in an effort to reestablish the legitimacy and stability of the Dlamini line, chose the son of Bhunu's highest-ranking wife as heir to the throne. That son, Sobhuza II, was then only three years old, but the intent was that Gwamile and Sobhuza's uncle Malunge would serve as regents until the boy came of age.

When Sobhuza was finally installed on the throne in 1921, he inherited a kingdom splintered by colonial land and labor policies. Britain's 1907 Partition Proclamation had used an elaborate tally of Mbandzeni's and Mswati II's concessions as a pretext for awarding roughly two-thirds of their protectorate's lands to white settlers. The remaining "Native Areas" were largely unsuitable for agriculture or cattle-grazing, and so many Swazis stayed on their former lands—now owned by Boer and English ranchers and farmers—to work as cattle herders, or to harvest cotton and tobacco. Others, mostly men between the ages of eighteen and forty, migrated across the border into South Africa to find work in the diamond mines. Such reloca-

Sobhuza's death in 1982 left the country devoid of strong leadership and led to a period of political turmoil that continues to the present day. Sobhuza's successor, Mswati III, did not assume the throne until 1986, and in the intervening years pro-democratic forces in Swaziland, particularly trade unions, did much to undermine the royal power base. Mswati III's extreme youth (he was eighteen at the start of his reign) has further goaded on reformists, who see their king as too inexperienced to contend with the many challenges posed by the dramatic political, economic and social changes sweeping southern Africa.

The end of apartheid in South Africa, for example has already proved a mixed blessing. During the 1980s Swaziland became a refuge for South African as well as Western firms—including Coca-Cola—seeking to avoid the international sanctions and boycotts imposed on the regime of apartheid. To this day Swaziland maintains one of Africa's largest per capita manufacturing sectors, and boasts an extensive modern infrastructure. Unlike almost every other country on the continent, Swaziland has never confronted an economic crisis so severe that it had to undertake the difficult austerity measures required as part of World Bank structural adjustment loan programs. But with sanctions now lifted from its nearest neighbor, Swaziland's ability to compete for foreign capital and tourists has suffered.

Natural resource depletion and growing foreign debt have also hurt the national economy. Swaziland's once-profitable mining industry is now almost completely nonexistent. The country relies on agriculture (mainly sugar and citrus products) and forestry for its exports, while subsistence farming and cattle ranching account for most of its domestic economic base. Swaziland's other major, hidden export continues to be labor—it is estimated that remittance from Swazi mineworkers in South Africa adds as much as 20 percent to Swaziland's GDP. The spread of acquired immunodeficiency syndrome (AIDS) represents another major domestic crisis, with some rural areas reporting an infection rate as high as 50 percent.

In 1993 Mswati III called for Swaziland's first general election in twenty years, and fifty-five of the sixty-five seats in the general assembly were included in the voting. The king, however, retained power to appoint the prime minister, cabinet, and a majority in the senate; prodemocratic forces viewed the elections as inadequate. More recently Swaziland has been rocked by waves of general strikes, most of them organized by the Swazi Federation of Trade Unions (SFTU). The last major strike, in early 1996, led to the formation of a Constitutional Review Commission, which Mswati promised would deliver several democratic reforms. But Mswati has restricted membership on the commission to his own appointees, prompting the SFTU and its allies to reject the commission and call for further strikes. So far Mswati has refused to recognize the SFTU or any of the nation's many democratic and socialist political parties, but international pressure—particularly South Africa, upon which Swaziland depends for 90 percent of its imports—may ultimately force him to relinquish Swaziland's monarchic system of government.

Andrew Hermann

Sweatt v. Painter

Landmark case in which the Supreme Court of the United States outlawed segregation in graduate education (1950), providing a legal basis for Brown v. Board of Education **(1954).**

In 1946, after decades of challenging state-imposed segregation, the NATIONAL ASSOCIATION FOR THE ADVANCEMENT OF COLORED PEOPLE (NAACP) joined in a lawsuit that paved the way for its eventual victory in BROWN V. BOARD OF EDUCATION. The case, *Sweatt v. Painter,* originated several years earlier when Heman Sweatt, an African American letter carrier, was rejected on racial grounds for admission to law school at the University of Texas. Following his protest a district court ordered Texas to provide a law school for black students. Rather than accept the state's attempts at compliance by creating separate facilities, Sweatt chose to pursue his case.

Sweatt was represented by THURGOOD MARSHALL of the NAACP LEGAL DEFENSE AND EDUCATION FUND. The NAACP's long-standing strategy—paradoxically based on PLESSY V. FERGUSON (1896), an earlier case that defended segregation—was to force states into choosing between providing expensive "equal" graduate schools and admitting black students to existing all-white schools. In *Sweatt* and a related case, *McLaurin v. Oklahoma* (1950), Marshall went further. He argued that a segregated education, however comparable the physical facilities, was inherently unequal in that it denied black students interaction with classmates, access to extracurricular activities, and the status and alumni network of established white schools.

In a sign of the case's significance, several groups filed *amicus curiae* (Latin for "friend of the court") briefs when it reached the Supreme Court. Eleven southern states argued in support of Texas's segregation, while nearly 200 law professors signed a brief backing the NAACP. Perhaps the most influential amicus brief was presented by the U.S. Justice Department. For the first time, the U.S. government said it was time to overturn *Plessy.*

The justices, however, were not prepared to go that far. Writing for a unanimous court, Chief Justice Fred Vinson declared that Heman Sweatt was denied an equal legal education in the segregated school. But the cautious opinion declined to overturn *Plessy*'s doctrine of "separate but equal." Despite this shortcoming, *Sweatt* and its companion case helped prepare the Court for its most significant civil rights case of the twentieth century, *Brown v. Board of Education.*

Kate Tuttle

Sweet Honey in the Rock

African American female a cappella group formed in 1973, which addresses global issues of social injustice through its music.

Sweet Honey in the Rock draws upon a wide range of styles, including the BLUES, spirituals, gospel, JAZZ, RAP, and African traditional songs. Though an a cappella group, hand clapping, foot stomping, and light percussive African instruments such as *shekeres* sometimes accompany the group's harmonious vocal arrangements.

Struggle is a major theme in the music of Sweet Honey in the Rock, and the group's songs have consistently aimed to raise social consciousness. The group's founder and vocal director, Bernice Johnson Reagon, was a civil rights activist during the 1960s with the STUDENT NONVIOLENT COORDINATING COMMITTEE (SNCC) and was a member of the SNCC Freedom Singers. Reagon has preserved a socially and politically responsible vision in her ongoing work with Sweet Honey in the Rock. Some of the issues addressed by the group are racism, acquired immunodeficiency syndrome (AIDS), and worker and environmental exploitation.

Sweet Honey in the Rock refers to a land described in a religious parable that is so rich that if a person cracks a rock, honey will flow. Bernice Johnson Reagon also relates the name to the legacy of African American women in the United States: "So, too, we black women, have had to have the standing power of rocks and of mountains—cold and hard, strong and stationary. That quality has often obscured the fact that inside the strength, partnering the sturdiness, we are as honey." The group has witnessed about twenty personnel changes during the past twenty-five years and currently includes Reagon, Ysaye Maria Barnwell, Nitanju Bolade Casel, Shirley Childress Johnson (a sign language interpreter), Aisha Kahlil, and Carol Maillard. Sweet Honey in the Rock has recorded eighteen albums, toured extensively within and beyond the United States, and won a Grammy Award in 1988 for the album *A Vision Shared: A Tribute to Woody Guthrie and Leadbelly*. The group's recent recordings include *Still the Same Me* (2000) and *The Women Gather* (2003).

See also Acquired Immunodeficiency Syndrome in the United States; Gospel Music; Music, African American; Spirituals, African American.

Aaron Myers

Swing

Musical term that refers to the rhythmic feeling intrinsic to jazz music in general, as well as to the style of jazz and jazz-based popular music that dominated the American scene between 1930 and 1945, a period commonly called the swing era.

In the most general sense, *swing* refers to the feeling of rhythmic momentum or forward motion that is an important element in JAZZ, regardless of style. More specifically, swing refers to the style of jazz that was played primarily for dancing during the 1930s and early 1940s. This was the only period in American history in which a form of jazz was the most popular music of the time. Big bands were the predominant vehicle for swing, and dancing to swing bands was the principal form of popular entertainment.

New Approach to Jazz

The advent of swing was an evolutionary development in jazz rhythm. Swing was characterized by a more buoyant and flexible approach to rhythm than was used in the NEW ORLEANS style that preceded it. Drummers in the New Orleans style kept a heavy beat on the bass drum, playing most of their accompaniment to the melody or solo on the snare drum. Swing drummers aimed for a smooth, flowing quality by shifting the rhythmic emphasis to the hi-hat, a pair of cymbals operated by a foot pedal. The heavy bass line of the New Orleans style, played either on the tuba or the string bass, was replaced by a supple "walking" bass line that was played exclusively on the string bass.

Swing rhythm sections were four-piece units consisting of piano, guitar, bass, and drums. The rhythm section of each of the most influential swing-era big bands had its own identifiable sound and feel. In addition to the rhythm section, a typical big band contained a brass section composed of three or four trumpets and two or three trombones, as well as a four- or five-piece saxophone section. Big-band saxophone sections were also referred to as reed sections, because in every band at least one and often all of the saxophonists also played clarinet and occasionally other woodwind instruments. Although the swing era produced many notable small-group performances, it is chiefly remembered as a period dominated by big bands.

Major Swing Figures

The most popular stars of the swing era were white virtuoso bandleaders such as Benny Goodman, Artie Shaw, Harry James, and Tommy Dorsey. Most of the important innovators, however, were African American instrumentalists and arrangers. The history of the swing era is full of stories of unsung black heroes whose work was widely influential but whose names are largely unfamiliar to the general public. Among the most notable of these were arrangers FLETCHER HENDERSON and Don Redman. Both originated many of the big-band arranging techniques that survive to this day. The most important black bands of the period were those of Henderson, JIMMIE LUNCEFORD, Andy Kirk, CAB CALLOWAY, Chick Webb, DUKE ELLINGTON, and COUNT BASIE.

The Basie band boasted the quintessential swing rhythm section, with guitarist Freddie Green, bassist Walter Page, drummer Jo Jones, and Basie himself at the piano. Basie's band included many notable soloists, the most influential being tenor saxophonist LESTER YOUNG.

Ellington, whose career predated and outlasted the swing era, justified his reputation during the period as the greatest composer and bandleader of jazz. Many admirers and scholars of Ellington's music consider the 1940 and 1941 edition of the Ellington band to be his finest.

Notwithstanding the importance of rhythm sections and soloists, it was that unseen force, the arranger, who was most responsible for shaping the sound of every big band. The most prominent of the swing era, besides Henderson, Redman, and

Ellington, were black arrangers Sy Oliver, MARY LOU WILLIAMS, Edgar Sampson, and Jimmy Mundy, as well as white arrangers Eddie Sauter and Glenn Miller.

Other important soloists of the period were tenor saxophonists COLEMAN HAWKINS and BEN WEBSTER, guitarist CHARLIE CHRISTIAN, vocalist BILLIE HOLIDAY, and trumpeter ROY ELDRIDGE.

Black and White Swing

Though dancing to swing bands was the most widespread form of popular entertainment for both black and white Americans, social and economic conditions for black bands and audiences reflected the difficulties encountered by African Americans in all walks of life. White bands and performers reaped the lion's share of the financial rewards generated by the swing craze.

Audiences were mostly segregated. Some venues featured black entertainers but maintained a whites-only policy for the clientele. Black bands played before segregated audiences of both races. Travel to the Deep South was often part of their itineraries; finding food and lodging there presented huge obstacles for band members. The constant threat of racial violence led some musicians to pack firearms on Southern tours.

Despite these conditions black and white musicians collaborated more frequently in the 1930s. At first most of this collaboration took place behind the scenes as top white bandleaders employed some of the leading black arrangers. Henderson, Sampson, and Mundy were responsible for writing most of Goodman's best arrangements. One of the biggest commercial hits of the era was Miller's recording of "In the Mood" (1939), written by black saxophonist and arranger Joe Garland.

In 1935 and 1936 Goodman led the first interracial groups in public performance when he presented his trio and quartet with pianist Teddy Wilson and vibraphonist LIONEL HAMPTON. Holiday became the first black female vocalist to be featured with a white group when she joined Artie Shaw's band in 1938.

Legacy of Swing

The end of the swing era coincided roughly with the end of WORLD WAR II (1939–1945). Modern jazz, or BEBOP, began to take shape in the early 1940s as young African American musicians experimented with new ideas in rhythm, harmony, and melody. Bebop is often referred to as a revolt against the confines of the swing style. The originators of bebop, however, had roots in swing, having served apprenticeships in big bands. Most of the established stars of swing refused to change with the times, with the notable exception of Hawkins, who encouraged the experiments of the younger musicians and even appeared on some of the earliest bebop recordings. The influence of swing today exists mostly in the form of nostalgic recreations of swing music, dances, and clothing styles.

See also Segregation in the United States.

Bibliography

DeVeaux, Scott. *The Birth of Bebop: A Social and Musical History.* University of California Press, 1997.

Porter, Lewis, Michael Ullman, and Ed Hazell. *Jazz: From Its Origins to the Present.* Prentice Hall, 1992.

Schuller, Gunther. *The Swing Era: The Development of Jazz, 1930–1945.* Oxford University Press, 1989.

Swoopes, Sheryl

1971–

American basketball player known for her speed and shooting ability, Swoopes is one of the top stars of the Women's National Basketball Association (WNBA).

Sheryl Denise Swoopes was born in Brownfield, Texas. She was a leading scorer for her high school BASKETBALL team and earned the Texas high school player of the year award in 1988. During her career at Texas Tech University in Lubbock, Texas, Swoopes averaged 25.1 points and ten rebounds per game. In 1993 she led Texas Tech to the National Collegiate Athletic Association (NCAA) championship, averaging 28.1 points per game in the postseason tournament. She scored forty-seven points in the final, breaking the NCAA title game record of forty-four points set by Bill Walton in 1973. For her performance that year, Swoopes won the Naismith Award as the nation's outstanding female college basketball player.

Swoopes played for a professional team in Italy during the 1994 season but returned to the United States to train for the 1996 Olympic Games in ATLANTA, GEORGIA. During Olympic play she was the third-leading scorer on the U.S. team (averaging thirteen points per game) and helped the U.S. win the gold medal. Swoopes signed with the Houston Comets of the WNBA for the league's inaugural season in 1997.

Swoopes quickly became one of the leaders for the Comets, helping the club to four consecutive WNBA championships (1997, 1998, 1999, 2000). She led the league in scoring during the 2000 season (20.7 points per game) and was named the WNBA's most valuable player (MVP). Swoopes also won a second gold medal at the 2000 Summer Olympics in Sydney, Australia, recording the second-highest scoring average (13.4 points) on the U.S. team. In 2001 Swoopes suffered a knee injury that caused her to miss the entire WNBA season. She returned in 2002 to win the league MVP and Defensive Player of the Year honors. The following season she led the WNBA in steals and repeated as Defensive Player of the Year. In 1996 Swoopes published an autobiography for children titled *Bounce Back*.

See also Olympics, African Americans and the; Sports and African Americans.

Sylvain, Georges

1866–1925

Haitian politician, writer, staunch promoter of literature, arts, and education in Haiti, best remembered as a symbol of Haitian resistance to the United States military occupation from 1915 to 1934.

Trained as a lawyer in Paris, Georges Sylvain founded a law school in HAITI in 1888 and worked in the Department of Public Education in 1894. As a great defender of culture he originated several writing and theatrical venues, including the influential L'Oeuvre des écrivains haïtiens (an organization for Haitian writers), and participated in the cultural events that celebrated the hundredth anniversary of the HAITIAN REVOLUTION in 1904. Among his literary incursions, his collection of poems *Confidences et mélancolies* (Confidences and Melancholia) and his fables in Créole, *Cric?Crac!,* stand out for their beauty and passion.

He received the distinguished title of "Chevalier de la légion d'honneur" by the French government after he opened a branch of the "Alliance Française" in Haiti—an organization that sought to expand the influence of FRANCE abroad through the propagation of the French language and culture. From 1909 to 1912 he held several posts in France as a Haitian official.

After the American occupation in 1915 he fought fiercely for his country's independence. He founded the newspaper *La Patrie* (Homeland) and a political organization, *L'Union Patriotique* (The Patriotic Union), that served to restore patriotism and educate the Haitian population. When he died in 1925 the whole of PORT-AU-PRINCE mourned him, and a magnificent funeral was organized to pay a last tribute to his courage and patriotism.

Martine Fernandes

Syncretism

See Creolization: An Interpretation; Magic, Sorcery, and Witchcraft in the Americas; Transculturation, Mestizaje, and the Cosmic Race: An Interpretation.

T

Tabwa

Ethnic group of South-Central Africa.

The Tabwa primarily inhabit the Marungu highlands of the southeastern DEMOCRATIC REPUBLIC OF THE CONGO. Others live in southwestern TANZANIA and northernmost ZAMBIA. They speak a dialect of Bemba, a Bantu language, and are closely related to the BEMBA people. Over 300,000 people consider themselves Tabwa.

See also Bantu: Dispersion and Settlement; Ethnicity and Identity in Africa: An Interpretation; Languages, African: An Overview.

Tacky

?–1760

West African–born Akan slave leader who in 1760 led the most widespread slave revolt in Jamaica's history.

Tacky's rebellion began in northeastern JAMAICA and soon engulfed much of the island. The rebellion lasted for six months before British colonial forces were finally able to suppress it, with help from the maroons (escaped slaves who formed their own settlements), who were required by treaty to aid the colonial government. Tacky was shot dead by a maroon, and nearly 400 slaves were executed in the aftermath.

See also Akan; Maroonage in the Americas; Slave Rebellions in Latin America and the Caribbean.

Taita

Ethnic group of Kenya; also known as the Teita.

The Taita primarily inhabit the Taita Hills in the Coast Province of southern KENYA. They speak a Bantu language. Approximately 300,000 people consider themselves Taita.

See also Bantu: Dispersion and Settlement; Ethnicity and Identity in Africa: An Interpretation; Languages, African: An Overview.

Talbert, Mary Burnett

1866–1923

African American educator and civil rights advocate.

Born in Oberlin, Ohio, Mary Burnett Talbert graduated from Oberlin High School and went on to graduate from Oberlin College at the age of nineteen in 1886. After serving as assistant principal of Bethel University in Little Rock, Arkansas, she resigned to become principal of the Union High School there. She married William A. Talbert and moved to Buffalo, New York, where she remained the rest of her life. The statement that she earned a Ph.D. degree from the University of Buffalo at an unspecified date cannot be substantiated.

She served as treasurer of the Michigan Avenue Baptist Church and founded the Christian Culture Congress, of which she was president for twenty years. A charter member of the Empire State Federation of Colored Women, she was president of the NATIONAL ASSOCIATION OF COLORED WOMEN (NACW) from 1916 to 1921 and a director of the NATIONAL ASSOCIATION FOR THE ADVANCEMENT OF COLORED PEOPLE (NAACP). During World War I (1914–1918) she sold thousands of dollars of Liberty bonds and served as a Red Cross nurse in FRANCE. Talbert started the crusade for the passage of the DYER BILL, which would have made lynching a federal crime. She traveled thousands of miles, spoke to mixed audiences, and raised $12,000 in a vain effort to obtain the bill's passage. Talbert represented the NACW at the sixth quinquennial meeting of the International Council of Women in Christiana, Norway (1920), and lectured on race relations and women's rights in many European countries. She was largely responsible for the restoration of the FREDERICK DOUGLASS home in Anacostia, D.C., in 1922. In that year she became the first black woman to win the NAACP Spingarn Medal for notable achievement.

There is a brief sketch in Sylvia G. Dannett's *Profiles of Negro Womanhood* (1964). Several notices were published in *THE CRISIS* (February 1917, pp. 174–176; August 1917, pp. 167–168;

July 1921, p. 130; July 1922, p. 125; August 1922, p. 171; December 1923, pp. 56–57).

From *Dictionary of American Negro Biography* by Rayford W. Logan and Michael R. Winston, ed. Copyright © 1982 by Rayford W. Logan and Michael R. Winston. Reprinted by permission of W. W. Norton & Company, Inc.

See also Women's Organizations, Early African American.

Rayford W. Logan

Talensi

Ethnic group of Ghana; also known as Tale, Talen, and Tallensi.

The Talensi primarily inhabit northeastern GHANA. Others live across the border in southern BURKINA FASO. They speak a Niger-Congo language. Approximately 300,000 people consider themselves Talensi.

See also Ethnicity and Identity in Africa: An Interpretation; Languages, African: An Overview.

Talented Tenth, The

W. E. B. DuBois's label for a small group of African Americans charged with elevating the entire race.

Articulating the principles of one of his best-known concepts, Du Bois published the essay "The Talented Tenth" in the anthology *The Negro Problem* in 1903, the same year *The Souls of Black Folk* appeared. Du Bois contended that no nation was ever civilized by its uneducated masses and concluded that "the Negro race, like all other races, is going to be saved by its exceptional men." Including such contemporaries as KELLY MILLER, ARCHIBALD GRIMKÉ, FRANCIS J. GRIMKÉ, HENRY O. TANNER, PAUL LAURENCE DUNBAR, and CHARLES WADDELL CHESNUTT, the talented tenth profile encompassed mostly male college-educated urban northerners descended from relative privilege or affluence. Including artists, doctors, lawyers, undertakers, preachers, teachers, businessmen, and politicians, the talented tenth advocated a controversial class-based dynamic of racial progress, which regarded the uplifting of the African American lower classes as its burden and duty. The theory behind Du Bois's recognition of the need to perform this service may in part be traced to his Harvard teacher William James's contention that a culture's greatness is measured in the way it takes care of its least empowered individuals. Du Bois's paternal system of racial elevation met strong resistance from BOOKER T. WASHINGTON and the "Tuskegee Machine." The talented tenth's high regard for "classical" education and its lack of faith in the African American masses to help themselves opposed Washington's strategy of accommodation and economic self-determination through technical and industrial education.

Bibliography

Lewis, David Levering. *W. E. B. Du Bois: Biography of a Race, 1868–1919,* 1993.
Rampersad, Arnold. *The Art and Imagination of W. E. B. Du Bois,* 1976.

Lawrence R. Rodgers

Tama

Ethnic group of north-Central Africa.

The Tama primarily inhabit eastern CHAD and western SUDAN. They speak a Nilo-Saharan language. Approximately 200,000 people consider themselves Tama.

See also Ethnicity and Identity in Africa: An Interpretation; Languages, African: An Overview.

Tambo, Oliver

1917–1993

Former president of the African National Congress, law partner of Nelson Mandela, and important South African antiapartheid leader.

Oliver Tambo was eulogized at his funeral by longtime friend and partner NELSON MANDELA as the man who had made the AFRICAN NATIONAL CONGRESS (ANC) "the strongest political force in the country." Born into a devout Anglican farming family in Bizana, in the Transkei region of SOUTH AFRICA, he described his childhood as politically sheltered. While a student at the University of Fort Hare, however, Tambo led protests against the administration, resulting in his expulsion in 1942. At Fort Hare Tambo also met Mandela, then a fellow student.

Tambo was teaching science and mathematics at Saint Peter's University (he had received a bachelor's degree in science before his expulsion) when he and Mandela helped form the ANC's Youth League in 1944. The Youth League energized the historically conservative ANC and facilitated the elections of Tambo and Mandela to the ANC's executive body in 1949. In the 1950s Tambo, Mandela, and other ANC leaders led a bold new protest effort, which included mass demonstrations, strikes, boycotts, and acts of civil disobedience. In 1952 Tambo and Mandela combined their experiences as apprentices at a JOHANNESBURG law firm (both positions were arranged by fellow Youth League member WALTER SISULU) and formed South Africa's first black law practice.

In 1956 they and 154 other antiapartheid activists were charged with treason. They were acquitted in 1960, but the government banned the ANC later that year. While Mandela went underground and founded the ANC paramilitary wing *Umkhonto we Sizwe* (Spear of the Nation), Tambo left the country, partly to escape increasingly frequent threats on his life but mostly to recruit international support in the fight against apartheid. After Mandela was captured in 1962 and sentenced to life in prison, it was Tambo who held the ANC together. He was elected ANC president in 1967.

Leading the banned organization from Lusaka, Zambia, Tambo oversaw growing resistance to apartheid, both within and beyond South Africa's borders. By 1981 *Umkhonto we Sizwe* was carrying out frequent sabotage attacks on police and military bases, government records offices, and other strategic sites. By the mid-1980s international economic sanctions and internal violence had placed enormous strain on the South African government, and Tambo's meetings with leaders in the West helped convince the regime that, in order to avert full-scale civil war, negotiations with the ANC were needed. Tambo suffered a disabling stroke in 1989 but continued as ANC president. In 1990 Mandela was released from prison, and a year later took over the ANC presidency. Tambo's 1993 death came just a year before Mandela was elected president of a newly democratic South Africa.

See also Antiapartheid Movement.

Kate Tuttle

Tambor de Mina

African-derived religion of Brazil, practiced mainly in the northeastern state of Maranhão; also called Casa de Mina.

See also Religions, African, in Brazil.

Tampa Red

1900–1981

American blues guitarist and singer who helped define the urban blues sound in Chicago.

Hudson Whittaker, born Hudson Woodbridge in Smithville, Georgia, took the last name of the grandmother who raised him. He adopted the stage name Tampa Red after moving to Chicago in the 1920s. Initially, he played bottleneck slide guitar on recordings for Ma Rainey and Memphis Minnie. Whittaker wrote and performed his first hit, "It's Tight Like That" (1928), with gospel composer and impresario Thomas Dorsey. He formed a quintet in 1932 and continued to perform and record until 1953 when his wife died. In the early 1960s, he made an unsuccessful comeback attempt.

See also Blues; Gospel Music; Music, African American.

Aaron Myers

Tanala

Ethnic group of Madagascar.

The Tanala primarily inhabit the highlands of southeastern Madagascar. They speak Malagasy, a Malayo-Polynesian language. More than 600,000 people consider themselves Tanala.

See also Ethnicity and Identity in Africa: An Interpretation; Languages, African: An Overview; Madagascar, Ethnicity in.

Tangale

Ethnic group of Nigeria; also known as Biliri and Tangle.

The Tangale inhabit primarily eastern Bauchi State in northeastern Nigeria. They speak an Afro-Asiatic language in the Chadic group. Approximately 200,000 people consider themselves Tangale.

See also Ethnicity and Identity in Africa: An Interpretation; Languages, African: An Overview.

Tanganyika

Former name for the mainland of present-day United Republic of Tanzania.

See also Tanzania.

Tanganyika, Lake

Lake in east Central Africa, in the Great Rift Valley, bordered on the north by Burundi, on the east by Tanzania, on the south by Zambia, and on the west by the Democratic Republic of the Congo.

The first Europeans to see the lake were British explorers John Speke and Sir Richard Burton, when they arrived in the region in 1858. The lake is 680 km (420 mi) long, about 72 km (about 45 mi) wide at the widest point, and covers 32,900 sq km (12,700 sq mi). The greatest depth is 1,436 m (4,710 ft), making it the second deepest freshwater lake in the world. The only outlet is the Lukuga River, which flows into the Congo River. The lake is noted for its many varieties of fish; crocodiles and hippopotamuses are found on the shores, and the surrounding area is very fertile. Climate changes in the last thirty years, however, have caused a drop in the fish population—a decrease of as much as 40 percent in certain species. Scientists have linked the problem to rising temperatures and falling wind speeds in the region, and predict "potentially dire" consequences for the four countries bordering the lake.

Tangier, Morocco

Northern coastal city in Morocco.

According to Greek myth, Tangier stands above the final resting place of the mythic giant Antaeus, who was undefeated until he met the brute strength and wiles of the hero Hercules.

Prior to 500 B.C.E., Phoenician sailors are said to have erected a trading post at this site, perched on a chalky limestone hill between the Mediterranean Sea and the Atlantic Ocean. Later travel documents record the visits of Carthaginians. When the surrounding region came under Roman dominion by the first century C.E., a semiautonomous BERBER kingdom made its capital in what became known as the city of Tingis.

Beginning in 429, a series of four dynasties seized control of the city in approximately 200 years: the Vandals, the Byzantines, the Visigoths, and in 682, the Arabs. The Arabs set up a garrison in Tangier as early as 707, and two Arab dynastic powers, the Umayyads and Idrisids, wrestled for control of the city.

Under the successive Berber dynasties of the ALMORAVIDS, the ALMOHADS, and the Merinids, Tangier prospered as a port of trade exporting leatherwork, wool, carpets, cereals, and sugar to EUROPE. The Spanish and Portuguese vied for control of the lucrative port until 1471, when the Portuguese conquered and occupied the city. When Portuguese princess Catherine of Braganza married Charles II of England, she brought control of Tangier to England as part of her dowry. Moulay Ismail built the Casbah and palace, enclosing the city in ramparts.

After a successful blockade staged by the Moroccan sultan Moulay Ismail, the English returned Tangier to Moroccan control in 1684. Although the English destroyed much of the city—as well as the port—on their way out, Tangier soon recovered its international appeal.

In the mid-nineteenth century, investors and wanderers alike arrived in the diplomatic capital of MOROCCO from England, FRANCE, SPAIN, GERMANY, and, eventually, the United States. Writer Mark Twain described the old quarter, filled with square, stone, whitewashed houses, as "a crowded city of snowy tombs." French painter Henri Matisse was inspired by the city's lush gardens and Islamic architecture.

When France declared Morocco a protectorate in 1912, Tangier was granted special status as an international zone, governed by representatives of GREAT BRITAIN, Spain, France, PORTUGAL, ITALY, Belgium, THE NETHERLANDS, Sweden, and later, the United States. During World War II (1939–1945), Spain held Tangier. After the war, artists and investors again flocked to the city, as the international zone gained the reputation for free enterprise and "free-living." Writers such as Tennessee Williams, Paul Bowles, Jean Genet, and William S. Burroughs praised the absence of stifling Western prohibitions, particularly those proscribing homosexuality. They described a decadent city where aimless bohemians puffed hashish from clay pipes and wealthy expatriates imitated the lifestyles of pashas of old. Despite the city's image as a den of iniquity, however, most of the local population were Muslim merchants and artisans who shared neither the attitudes nor the leisure activities of the Europeans and Americans crowding the city's cafés.

Following Moroccan independence in 1956, many of the city's European residents left. Tangier has maintained its status as a shipping center, exporting textiles, carpets, fish, and building materials. Tourists drawn by legends of Tangier visit the crowded bazaars of the Grand Socco and the Petit Socco, walk beneath 800-year-old trees in the Mendoubia gardens, and

explore the passageways of the fifteenth-century Casbah. In 2003 Tangier had a population of more than 600,000.

See also Homosexuality in Africa; Islam in Africa; North Africa, Roman Rule of; Tourism in Africa.

Bibliography
Finlayson, Iain. *Tangier: City of the Dream.* HarperCollins Publishers, 1992.

Serels, M. Mitchell. *A History of the Jews of Tangier in the Nineteenth and Twentieth Centuries.* Sepher-Hermon Press, 1991.

Woolman, David S. *Stars in the Firmament: Tangier Characters, 1660–1960s.* Three Continents Press, 1997.

Marian Aguiar

Tango

Argentine dance and musical genre, rooted in a combination of African, European, and native Argentine music and dance traditions.

Often referred to by Argentines as "a sad feeling that can be danced," the tango has become one of the most popular dance and musical forms worldwide. As a dance, the tango requires a couple to be chest-to-chest, in a tight embrace. "As the couple sways and pauses, bodies locked, feet twining in intricate *ochos* (figure eights) and *cortes* (short, rapid steps), it's as if they're carrying on an intensely intimate exchange," writes Chiori Santiago in *Smithsonian* magazine. As a musical form, tango has evolved from improvised dance pieces of the mid- to late nineteenth century—often performed by black and mulatto instrumentalists—to the modern *nuevo tango* compositions of the late Argentine musician Astor Piazzolla.

The black community of Buenos Aires played an indirect but significant role in the creation of the tango. By the mid-nineteenth century, nearly a quarter of Buenos Aires's inhabitants were black, owing to the city's role as a port of entry for the slave trade in the previous century. Argentine blacks, who resided in poor neighborhoods, succeeded in preserving their culture through community events such as dance and music festivals. The most popular Afro-Argentine dance was the *candombe,* which fused syncopated rhythms and improvised steps from various African traditions. According to the early Argentine scholar of tango, José Gobello, the candombe was the precursor of the tango.

Gobello suggests that contact between Afro-Argentines and the *compadritos*—poor urban street roughs, who recalled in their behavior and dress the nineteenth-century gaucho, or Argentine cowboy—gave rise to the tango at a late 1870s dance venue. In an article published in 1913, Gobello wrote that the Afro-Argentines of Mondongo improvised a dance they called tango, based on the candombe. Some compadritos from Corrales Viejos, the slaughterhouse district of Buenos Aires, saw the dance, and soon after introduced it into their own community. Here the style and movements of the Afro-Argentine tango became fused with the *milonga*—a popular Argentine dance inspired by the European polka and the Cuban *habanera*. As scholar Simon Collier confirms, "The distinctive features of the new dance-form came entirely from the *compadritos* parodistic borrowings from the African-Argentine tradition . . . [yet in the new dance] partners danced *together*, not, as in the African-Argentine 'tango', apart." Many of the early tango musicians were Afro-Argentine: the noted pianist Rosendo Mendizábal played a central role in the development of tango music, while Sebastián Ramos Mejía became the first notable player of the bandoneon—an accordion-like instrument of German origin that later became fundamental to tango music.

The Argentine historian Ricardo Rodríguez Molas contends that the word "tango," which in certain African languages means "closed place" or "reserved ground," is likely to be of African origin. Other scholars have traced the word back to the Latin verb *tangere*, meaning to touch; they believe that African slaves might have picked up the word "tango" from their European captors. In many parts of LATIN AMERICA, "tango" came to connote a place where blacks, both free and enslaved, gathered together to dance; while in Argentina, "tango" came to be associated with black dances in general. "It was in this sense," notes Collier, "that the word eventually reached SPAIN, as a name for African-American or African-influenced dances of transatlantic provenance."

Before World War II, the tango was developed in dance halls, cafés, and brothels in the working-class *barrios* (districts) of ARGENTINA's major cities. By 1913 the tango had become popular among the Argentine middle classes, who contributed to the development of a tango craze in EUROPE and Russia. By the 1920s Argentina had become one of the world's wealthiest nations. As the focal point of economic and demographic growth, Buenos Aires attracted a massive influx of predominantly Italian and Spanish immigrants. These immigrants introduced new instruments, such as the accordion and mandolin, and contributed to the development of *tango liso,* a style of tango that toned down some of the rougher movements. As Collier affirms, "This early division of dancing styles was fraught with significance for the future: the 'smooth' tango was undoubtedly the forerunner of the ballroom tango of the twentieth century, while the fierce, lubricious aggressiveness favoured in the outer barrios eventually faded away." Since the golden age of tango in the 1920s, tango music and dance have continued to gain popularity worldwide.

See also Dance in Latin America and the Caribbean.

Roanne Edwards

Tanner, Benjamin Tucker

1835–1923

American bishop of the African Methodist Episcopal Church, editor, and writer.

Benjamin Tucker Tanner studied at Avery College from 1852 to 1857 and at Western Theological Seminary from 1857 to 1860. In 1858 he married Sarah Miller. One of their seven children was the painter HENRY OSSAWA TANNER.

Tanner edited the *Christian Recorder,* an AFRICAN METHODIST EPISCOPAL CHURCH (AME) publication, from 1868 to 1884, and founded the *A.M.E. Church Review,* a journal devoted to African American concerns, in 1884. After serving as a deacon and then an elder in the AME church, he was consecrated a bishop in 1888 and retired in 1908. He is the author *An Apology for African Methodism* (1867).

Aaron Myers

Tanner, Henry Ossawa

1859–1937

American painter who was called "the first genius among Negro artists" by art historian James A. Porter.

The son of a bishop of the AFRICAN METHODIST EPISCOPAL CHURCH, Henry Ossawa Tanner was born in PITTSBURGH, PENNSYLVANIA. He was named after Osawatomie, the site of John Brown's antislavery raid in Kansas. Tanner began painting at the age of thirteen, and beginning in 1880 was a student at the Pennsylvania Academy of the Fine Arts, where he studied with Thomas Eakins, among others. Tanner taught at Clark College in ATLANTA, GEORGIA, from 1889 to 1891, when he relocated to Paris, largely to escape racial prejudice in America. In Paris, Tanner took courses at the Académie Julien and, with the exception of two brief visits home in 1893 and 1896, continued to live and paint there until his death in 1937.

While at the Pennsylvania Academy of the Fine Arts and through 1890, Tanner painted traditional European subjects such as landscapes and animals. In the 1890s, however, Tanner began painting genre scenes of African American life, including his well-known work, *The Banjo Lesson* (1893), and *The Thankful Poor* (1894). He is best known, though, for his painting of biblical subjects that he began in the mid-1890s. From 1894 to 1914, Tanner regularly exhibited his work at the Salon de la Société des Artistes Français in Paris, and after 1900 he also exhibited widely in the United States as well.

Tanner's work is grounded in the techniques of romantic realism and impressionism. His somber rendering of scenes from the Old and New Testaments won awards at the Paris Salon in 1896 and 1897. *The Raising of Lazarus* (1896) was purchased by the French government, which named Tanner a chevalier of the French Legion of Honor in 1923.

See also Art, African American; Tanner, Benjamin.

Bibliography

Matthews, Marcia M. *Henry Ossawa Tanner, American Artist.* University of Chicago Press, 1969.

Mosby, Dewey F., Darrell Sewell, and Rae Alexander-Minter. *Henry Ossawa Tanner.* Rizzoli International Publications, 1991.

Aaron Myers

Tansi, Sony Labou

1947–1995

Renowned Central African novelist, playwright, and poet.

Born Marcel Sony, Tansi moved from his home in what was then the BELGIAN CONGO to independent Congo (now Congo-Brazzaville) in 1959 to attend French schools. Starting in 1971 he worked as a schoolteacher in BRAZZAVILLE, and in 1979 he was appointed both to a position with the ministry of culture and to the directorship of the Rocado Zulu Theatre. That same year, Tansi published his first novel, *La Vie et Demie* (Life and a Half), as well as his first play, *Conscience de Tracteur* (Tractor Awareness). In the latter, Tansi used some of the conventions of science fiction to tell a political parable; the play won second place in a theatre competition sponsored by Radio France.

Tansi wrote three more novels in the 1980s—*L'Etat Honteux* (1981), *L'Anté-Peuple* (1983), and *Les Yeux du Volcan* (1988)—and four plays, becoming well known not only throughout Francophone Africa but also in FRANCE and elsewhere. Critics hailed his work for its social conscience and rich verbal playfulness. Tansi's fiction is liberally infused with puns, literary allusions, and allegory; he said that he wanted his writing "to contain madness, humor, and tragedy, mixing everything up in the same way life does." Deeply committed to a literature of and for AFRICA, Tansi wrote about colonialism's "rape" of Africa and the resulting obsession with power in the postcolonial era. Especially in his plays, Tansi explored both the brutality and the dramatic absurdity of dictatorships and dictators.

In 1992 and 1993 Tansi was elected to the national assembly, but never attended. He published his first works of poetry in the 1990s, along with two novels and two plays. He told friends he wanted to write nonfiction, and planned a manifesto arguing for an African Marshall Plan, saying that "Africa is the only continent left that has not found its way." He never finished that work, but his last novel, *The Seven Solitudes of Lorsa Lopez,* was published posthumously in the fall of 1995.

Tansi and his wife, Pierrette, both suffering from acquired immunodeficiency syndrome (AIDS), were hospitalized in Paris in the spring of 1995. Returning to REPUBLIC OF THE CONGO, they secluded themselves in a small village not far from Brazzaville, where they placed their faith in traditional healing and Christian mysticism. Although he told newspaper reporters that he felt he was getting better under this regimen, Tansi and his wife died in June, only four days apart.

See also Francophone Writing; Literature, French-Language, in Africa; Traditional Healing in Africa.

Bibliography

Harrow, Kenneth W. *Thresholds of Change in African Literature: The Emergence of a Tradition.* Heinemann, 1994.

Kate Tuttle

Tanzania

Country located on the southeastern coast of Africa, comprising former Tanganyika and the island of Zanzibar.

Tanzania defies most perceptions of poor, nonindustrialized nations. The first East African country to achieve independence, Tanzania immediately developed a stable, popularly supported, and democratically elected government that has successfully weathered both its political unification with the historically separate island of ZANZIBAR and the turmoil of neighbors afflicted with civil conflict, ethnic stratification, and autocratic regimes. Tanzania's economic path has also been different than most. Under the guidance of the country's first president, JULIUS K. NYERERE, Tanzania attempted to avoid the traps of neocolonialism and foreign dependency, instead embarking on a socialist experiment that sought to achieve local as well as national self-sufficiency. Although the experiment proved an economic disaster—not helped by the fact that much of rural Tanzania is resource-poor—it did raise Tanzania's standards of social welfare above those of most of its wealthier neighbors. Today Tanzania continues to struggle with widespread poverty, but progressive leaders have enabled the nation to seize new economic opportunities, and some observers note promising signs of recovery.

Precolonial History

Early human history in Tanzania centers on the Great Rift Valley, which served as home and highway for the region's first inhabitants. Among them were two of the world's oldest known hominids—*Zinjanthropus boisei* and *Homo habilis*—whose remains were discovered by archaeologist MARY LEAKEY at Olduvai Gorge in the 1960s. Although evidence is inconclusive, it appears that many of the early stages of human evolution may have occurred in Tanzanian sections of the Rift Valley several million years ago. It was not until ten thousand years ago, however, that human societies began to settle in Tanzania. The first were KHOISAN-speaking foragers who established residence in small villages throughout the eastern Rift Valley. Around the first millennium B.C.E. they were joined by Chushitic-speaking people who migrated along the Rift Valley from ETHIOPIA. Finally, BANTU speakers emigrated to Tanzania and settled in the western mountainous region around the first millennium C.E.

For several hundred years, these groups lived in small communities with relatively little interaction. In the tenth century, however, semi-nomadic Nilotic-speaking groups that had been gradually migrating from the north and northwest settled in

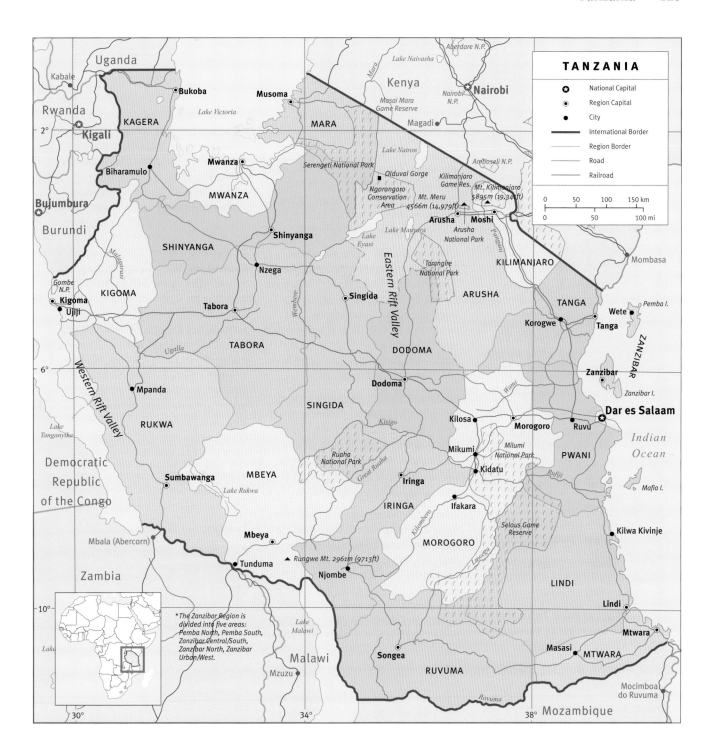

East Africa. Although some, such as the MAASAI, retained their semi-nomadic lifestyle, most Nilotics settled in permanent villages, and in some cases assimilated with Bantu speakers.

Even after centuries of migration, human settlements in the East African interior remained small, scattered, and self-governing. Consequently few foreign travelers or traders ventured through the interior's thick bush until the eighteenth century, when traders employed by the sultan of Zanzibar and financed by Indian merchants began leading caravans inland,

seeking slaves and ivory. Although a few interior groups—such as the NYAMWEZI—began participating in the trade around 1800, their control over routes was limited by the well-armed and well-organized coastal traders. By 1830 Arab/Swahili traders had established routes from the coast to LAKE TANGANYIKA and the kingdom of BUGANDA and built trading posts in Tabora and Ujiji. Despite these advances, the sultan's power remained weak in the interior, a fact that would later facilitate German colonialism in East Africa.

Tanzania (At a Glance)

OFFICIAL NAME: United Republic of Tanzania

FORMER NAMES: United Republic of Tanganyika and Zanzibar

AREA: 945,087 sq km (364,898 sq mi)

LOCATION: Eastern Africa, on the Indian Ocean, bordered by Burundi, Kenya, Malawi, Mozambique, Rwanda, Uganda, the Democratic Republic of the Congo, Zambia

CAPITAL: Dar es Salaam (population 2,336,055); 2002 estimate

OTHER MAJOR CITIES: Arusha (population 270,485); Mbeya (population 230,318); Mwanza (population 209,806); Morogoro (population 206,868); Zanzibar (205,870); 2002 estimates

POPULATION: 35,922,454 (2003 estimate)

POPULATION DENSITY: 38 persons per sq km (about 98.4 persons per sq mi); 2003 estimate

POPULATION BELOW AGE 15: 44.3 percent (male 7,988,898; female 7,938,979); 2003 estimate

POPULATION GROWTH RATE: 1.72 percent (2003 estimate)

TOTAL FERTILITY RATE: 5.24 children born per woman (1998 estimate)

LIFE EXPECTANCY AT BIRTH: Total population: 44.56 years (male 43.33 years; female 45.83 years); 2003 estimate

INFANT MORTALITY RATE: 103.68 deaths per 1,000 live births (2003 estimate)

LITERACY RATE (AGE 15 AND OVER WHO CAN READ AND WRITE): Total population: 78.2 percent (male 85.9 percent; female 70.7 percent); 2003 estimate

EDUCATION: Primary education in Tanzania is compulsory, but only 50 percent of eligible children are enrolled because not enough schools are available. Adult education campaigns have contributed to relatively high literacy rates. In the early 1990s government schools were attended annually by some 3.5 million elementary pupils and about 167,000 secondary students. In addition, many children attended private schools, which were mostly run by religious groups.

LANGUAGES: Tanzania's official languages are English and Swahili, and the latter is almost universally understood. Many people, however, continue to use the language of their ethnic group.

ETHNIC GROUPS: The Sukuma and the Nyamwezi represent about one-fifth of the population. Other significant groups include the Haya, Ngonde, Chagga, Gogo, Ha, Hehe, Nyakyusa, Nyika, Ngoni, Yao, and Maasai. The population also includes people of Indian, Pakistani, and Goan origin, and small Arab and European communities.

RELIGIONS: About 35 percent the population follow traditional religions and another 35 percent practice Islam. Christians make up about 30 percent of the population. Catholicism is the largest Christian denomination of Tanzania, with some 6 million adherents.

CLIMATE: On the mainland coastal strip along the Indian Ocean the climate is warm and tropical, with temperatures averaging 27° C (80° F) and annual rainfall varying from 750 to 1,400 mm (30 to 55 in). The inland plateau is hot and dry, with annual rainfall averaging as little as 500 mm (20 in). The climate on the islands is generally tropical, but the heat is tempered by a sea breeze throughout the year. The annual mean temperature for the city of Zanzibar is 29° C (85° F) maximum, and 25° C (77° F) minimum; for Wete in Pemba, 30° C (86° F) maximum and 24° C (76° F) minimum.

LAND, PLANTS, AND ANIMALS: Mainland Tanzania is generally flat and low along the coast, but a plateau at an average altitude of about 1,200 m (about 4,000 ft) constitutes the greater part of the country. Isolated mountain groups rise in the northeast and southwest. The volcanic Kilimanjaro (5,895 m/19,340 ft), the highest mountain in Africa, is located near the northeastern border. Three of the great lakes of Africa lie on the borders of the country and partially within it. Lake Tanganyika is located on the western border, Lake Victoria on the northwest, and Lake Malawi (Nyasa) on the southwest. Lakes Nyasa and Tanganyika lie in the Great Rift Valley, a tremendous geological fault system extending from the Middle East to Mozambique. Zanzibar, separated from the mainland by a 40-km (25-mi) channel, is about 90 km (55 mi) long and covers an area of 1,658 sq km (640 sq mi). It is the largest coral island off the coast of Africa. Pemba, some 40 km (25 mi) northwest of Zanzibar, is about 68 km (42 mi) long and has an area of approximately 984 sq km (380 sq mi). Wildlife includes antelope, zebra, elephant, hippopotamus, rhinoceros, giraffe, lion, leopard, cheetah, and monkey. Tanzania's national parks, among them Serengeti National Park, are home to many of these species.

NATURAL RESOURCES: Hydropower, tin, phosphates, diamonds, gemstones, gold, coal, iron ore, nickel, and natural gas.

CURRENCY: The Tanzanian shilling

GROSS NATIONAL PRODUCT (GDP): $22.5 billion (2002 estimate)

GDP PER CAPITA: $630 (2002 estimate)

GDP REAL GROWTH RATE: 5.2 percent (2002 estimate)

PRIMARY ECONOMIC ACTIVITIES: Agriculture, industry, services, and mining

PRIMARY CROPS: Coffee, sisal, tea, cotton, pyrethrum (insecticide made from chrysanthemums), cashews, tobacco, cloves (Zanzibar), corn, wheat, cassava (tapioca), bananas, fruits, vegetables, cattle, sheep, and goats

INDUSTRIES: Agricultural processing (sugar, beer, cigarettes, sisal twine), diamond and gold mining, oil refining, shoes, cement, textiles, wood products, and fertilizer

PRIMARY EXPORTS: Gold, doffee, cotton, cashew nuts, and sisal.

Primary Imports: Manufactured goods, machinery and transportation equipment, cotton piece goods, crude oil, and foodstuffs

Primary Trade Partners: Germany, United Kingdom, United States, Japan, Italy, Denmark, Netherlands, Kenya, and China

Government: Tanzania is governed under a constitution of 1977, as amended. The internal affairs of Zanzibar are administered under a constitution of 1985. Tanzania's chief executive is a popularly elected president, who serves a five-year term. The president (Benjamin Mkapa since November 22, 1995) appoints a vice president, prime minister (Ali Mohammed Shein since July 5, 2001), and cabinet. Zanzibar also elects a president (Amani Abeid Karume) since October 29, 2000) who oversees internal government affairs on the island. Tanzania's legislature is the multiparty unicameral National Assembly. Of its 274 members, 232 are popularly elected to terms of up to five years. Most of the rest of the members are either elected by the National Assembly, appointed by the president, or sit by virtue of being commissioners of the country's regions.

Scramble for Africa

By the mid-nineteenth century, the sultan of Zanzibar had established amicable relations with most European powers, who saw the island as an ideal launching point for European forays into mainland Africa. On the understanding that land was easily attainable on the East African coast, the Society for German Colonization sent Dr. Carl Peters on an exploratory mission in November 1884. Within two months, Peters acquired roughly 6,500 square kilometers (2,500 square miles) through treaties with mainland chiefs. Peters subsequently used these treaties to persuade the ambivalent German government that African colonization was an easy way to acquire land and to divert the attention of their European rivals away from Europe. In February 1885 German Emperor Wilhelm I and Chancellor Otto von Bismarck acquiesced and granted a government charter to Peters's German East Africa Company.

The company immediately tried to consolidate power in the region. Feeling threatened by BARGHASH IBN SA'ID, the sultan of Zanzibar, the Germans met secretly with the British in 1886 and created a German protectorate north of the Ruvuma River and south of the present-day border between KENYA and Tanzania. Although the Europeans permitted the sultanate to maintain control over the coastal islands and a small strip of coast, two years later the Germans forced the sultan to cede the mainland strip. All of these actions were facilitated by the British, who exercised tremendous influence on Barghash ibn Sa'id.

German East Africa

The German East Africa Company's attempts to establish colonial rule in East Africa met immediate resistance. The sultan is widely believed to have encouraged revolt among the Swahili peoples on the coast who resented the Germans' tax policies and considered Germans to be unpleasant drunkards with little respect for ISLAM. In the interior, resistance came from both Arab merchants who feared losing their trading routes and village chiefs who resented the German requisition of their village labor. United by their discontent, people throughout the region formed small military bands in the coastal towns from which they initiated attacks on the Germans in August 1888.

After two years of fighting, the German colonialists appeared to be near defeat. In March 1891, however, the Germans brought in mercenaries from MOZAMBIQUE and SUDAN, and their sheer firepower quickly overwhelmed resistance forces.

Once the company established control, it began building a colonial economy based on the production of export crops, especially coffee and tea. The administration seized land for plantations, conscripted African laborers, and forced Africans to grow export crops on their own land. It also confiscated land to give to newly arrived German settlers.

In 1902 German Governor Count Adolf von Götzen added cotton to the list of obligatory crops, despite the fact that it was difficult to cultivate and hard on the soil. Already strained by colonial taxes and labor policies, Africans soon rebelled against the mandate. On July 31, 1905, the Matumbi people, led by Abdullah Mapanda, initiated an attack—later called the MAJI-MAJI REVOLT—that forced German colonists in the southern coastal area out of their homes. The Germans retaliated with a scorched earth campaign that killed between 75,000 and 120,000 Africans (out of a population of 2 million) and provoked international outrage.

Shortly thereafter, the German government took control of the colony, instituted reforms, and began providing basic services, such as public education for Africans. Only a few years later, however, World War I began and GREAT BRITAIN soon occupied most of GERMAN EAST AFRICA. After the defeat of the Axis powers, the League of Nations gave Great Britain control of the territory, and it was renamed TANGANYIKA.

Administering Tanganyika

Although Tanganyika was technically an internationally mandated territory, Great Britain treated it as a new colony. In 1925 Sir Donald Cameron was appointed governor and created a government based on indirect rule, a British colonial policy that attempted to use "native authority" as the foundation for colonial administration. Although this policy worked relatively well in areas historically governed by hierarchical states, most ethnic groups in Tanganyika had no tradition of centralized political authority. Consequently the British imposed an invented

This lateen-rigged vessel, called a dhow, differs little from the boats used by by early Swahili traders in their role as East Africa's middlemen in the Indian Ocean ecomony.
M & E Bernheim

hierarchy on many ethnic groups and nominated chiefs to collect taxes, recruit labor, and enforce other colonial mandates. Thus, many appointed chiefs commanded little respect among their "subjects," and often proved either unable or unwilling to carry out their duties.

Like the Germans, the British based the colonial economy on export crops that were produced both on plantations and peasant farms. To ensure an adequate supply of plantation labor, the British encouraged village families to move to the plantations by building educational and health facilities nearby, and by offering technical support and price incentives for crops grown on the family's land. Although the plant-more-crops campaign did increase cash crop production considerably, it also led to the dangerous neglect of food crops. With the majority of fertile land devoted exclusively to export crops, Tanganyika was affected by several serious food shortages during the interwar years.

Although plantation communities may have disrupted precolonial social systems, they did foster the formation of African associations and community collectives that would later provide the foundation for political organizing. Some groups, including Bahaya Union, the HAYA civic association, began in agricultural communities such as Bukoba. Others, such as the Tanganyika African Association, a multiethnic welfare agency and social club formed in 1927, originated in DAR ES SALAAM and then spread to the rural communities, where it ultimately

merged with the extremely popular Tanganyika African National Union (TANU). These groups were among the first to contest British post–World War II agricultural policies and political reforms and initiate the independence movement.

After World War II, two competing requirements were imposed on Tanganyika: first, increased agricultural export production, in order to help rebuild Great Britain's postwar economy, and second, demonstrable progress toward self-government, as mandated by new UNITED NATIONS regulations. To comply with the latter, the colonial administration made "native" authorities responsible for devising and implementing development plans with funds available from government agencies. In addition, Governor Sir Edward Twining tried to implement self-rule by creating local councils. Twining required equal representation for the unequal populations of Europeans, Asians, and Africans, even in areas with small or nonexistent European or Asian populations. These plans were at best ineffective, but more often they provoked serious and even violent opposition, which soon found a collective voice in one organization: TANU.

Created in 1954, TANU was led by a dynamic schoolteacher, Julius Kambarage Nyerere, who immediately announced the organization's goal to be nothing less than self-governance without ethnic or racial divisions. Nyerere launched a massive recruitment campaign, and within a year TANU had become the largest political organization in Tanganyika. Emboldened by popular support, it entered candidates in the 1958–1959 elections for the Tanganyika Legislative Council, an advisory group that had always been dominated by non-Africans. Governor Twining managed to keep TANU members largely out of the Council by reserving two-thirds of the seats for Europeans and Asians, and by restricting voter registration.

With tensions clearly mounting in the colony, the British government replaced Twining with a new governor, Sir Richard Turnbull, who was instructed to guide Tanganyika toward gradual decolonization. In subsequent elections for the Legislative Council and for a new government of internal affairs, TANU candidates easily triumphed and Nyerere was named chief minister. In this position, Nyerere guided Tanganyika towards self-rule and on December 9, 1961, became prime minister of an independent Tanganyika.

United Republic of Tanzania

After independence, Nyerere immediately instituted a number of major changes to complete the process of decolonization. Casting off the British model, he hired Tanganyikan citizens to fill civil servant positions and restructured the government into a one-party republic of which he was elected president. Soon afterward he offered assistance to the troubled island of Zan-

Of the two goals, however, Nyerere had greater success with the first. Within months of his reelection Nyerere began asserting his views on international affairs, particularly the events of southern Africa. In December 1965 Tanzania broke diplomatic relations with Great Britain over its support for the white-ruled government of colonial RHODESIA (now ZIMBABWE). Shortly afterwards, Nyerere launched an ANTIAPARTHEID campaign and urged neighboring nations to boycott South African goods and divest from South African companies. In subsequent years, Nyerere supported independence causes in the Portuguese colonies of ANGOLA and Mozambique and denounced South Africa's occupation of NAMIBIA. In addition, he ordered the 1978 Tanzanian military invasion of Uganda in opposition to its dictator, IDI AMIN. By the time he stepped down from office in 1985, Nyerere's statesmanship had won international respect and he has continued to play an active diplomatic role in African affairs.

Nyerere's attempt to build a debt-free and self-sufficient national economy, however, was less successful. In the 1967 Arusha Declaration Nyerere described his vision of African SoCIALISM, which drew on Maoist principles of rural mobilization but incorporated what he called "traditional" African values and social organization. He also outlined the specific measures needed to realize this vision. The engine of economic and social development would be large, collectivized villages; the driving ideology would be *ujamaa,* "familyhood." The government ordered millions of peasants into the communal villages and by 1977 more than thirteen million people (about 80 percent of the population) had been resettled into more than eight thousand *ujamaa* villages.

Although rural collectivization did improve access to clean water, health care, and schools—helping Tanzanians become one of the most literate populations in sub-Saharan Africa—it failed to increase agricultural productivity and in fact did the opposite. The villages tended to be overcrowded and the surrounding lands were usually incapable of supporting dense populations. Many people continued to depend on farmland they had left behind for food, and women, in particular, commonly worked daily both on communal fields and on their family's farms several kilometers away. By the late 1970s it was evident that *ujamaa* had failed to create a sustainable economy and Tanzania was forced to take out loans from donor countries and the International Monetary Fund (IMF).

As Tanzania sank further into debt, international donors threatened to stop assistance until the government undertook major economic reforms, including liberalization and privatization. Unwilling to enact these reforms himself, Nyerere offered to step down from office, although he remained president of the Tanzanian socialist party, Charma Cha Mapinduzi (CCM, formerly TANU). In 1985 ALI HASSAN MWINYI was elected president. During the next ten years Mwinyi attempted to revive the national economy. Despite Nyerere's protests of his successor's willingness to "starve the children to pay the debts," Mwinyi accepted and implemented stiff IMF austerity measures. In addition, Mwinyi privatized businesses, authorized the country's first private bank, and led a campaign against government

Only ruins remain of the mosque at what was Kilwa Kisiwani, an Islamic city-state that flourished from the eleventh to the fifteenth century. *M & E Bernheim*

zibar, and on April 26, 1964, the two formed a union later called the United Republic of Tanzania. In this new arrangement, Nyerere was named president and Zanzibari president Sheikh Abeid Amani Karume became one of two vice presidents, but the mainland and the island retained mostly autonomous control of their own internal affairs.

In addition to building a government, Nyerere sought to forge a sense of national identity. His first step was to facilitate dialogue among Tanzania's 120 different ethnic groups, such as the HA, SUKUMA, CHAGGA, MAKONDE, and IRAQW. He achieved this goal in part by making Swahili the official national language and mandating that it be universally taught. Soon Swahili became the *lingua franca* even in areas where it had not been widely used before. Upon election to a second term in 1965, Nyerere articulated the goals that would guide his policies for the next twenty years: to bring a moral order to international affairs, and to build Tanzania into a self-sufficient nation free of neocolonial dependencies. Both goals quickly defined Tanzania as one of the "radical" postcolonial African states and distinguished it from its pro-Western neighbor, Kenya.

corruption. Although he failed to eradicate either debt or corruption, Mwinyi did initiate the transition to a multiparty state and promoted free speech. He completed his term in 1995 after the election of CCM member BENJAMIN MKAPA.

As president, Mkapa has been forced to address a number of difficult problems, of which the most visible is the country's lagging and debt-saddled economy. In an effort to balance the budget and increase government revenue, he has downsized the civil service and enacted stringent new laws against tax evasion. He has also cracked down on gold and gemstone smuggling in Dar es Salaam and Magauzo that, like other black markets, has long diverted a significant amount of potential government revenue. Much more than his predecessors, Mkapa has tried to attract international investment and revive trade relations in the EAST AFRICAN COMMUNITY (which includes Uganda and Kenya). Finally, Mkapa has taken steps to promote the country's tourist industry, particularly along Zanzibar, and the mainland coast, and in the many national parks around ARUSHA, including the SERENGETI, Taragnire, Arusha national parks, MOUNT KILIMANJARO, and Olduvai Gorge.

The Tanzanian government's scarce resources have limited its capacity to confront a number of noneconomic problems. One of the most difficult is an ACQUIRED IMMUNODEFICIENCY SYNDROME (AIDS) epidemic—estimated to affect over one million people in Tanzania—for which adequate care and medication are not available. In addition, Mkapa has had to address environmental concerns, such as urban pollution and wildlife and forest conservation, on a budget that makes it difficult to catch and punish industrial polluters and poachers. Finally, Mkapa has played a relatively active role in regional affairs, particularly in the civil conflicts with neighboring RWANDA and BURUNDI. He has recently come under attack for his decision to close the border with Burundi in order to prevent the entrance of new refugees, whom the Tanzanian government is financially unable to support.

In October 2000 Mkapa was reelected as Tanzania's president, and Abeid Amani Karume was elected president of Zanzibar. The Zanzibar election, however, was plagued by irregularities leading to political violence that cost more than twenty lives. Afterwards, sixteen legislators from the losing CUF party boycotted the Union Parliament to protest the elections results. The protesting legislators were subsequently expelled from parliament. The following year the CCM and CUF signed an agreement to reconcile their differences, investigate the deaths that occurred following the election, and implement electoral reforms. As of late 2003, both parties were still honoring the agreement.

Mkapa has also continued the economic reforms begun under his predecessor, Mwinyi. To attract foreign investment, Mkapa has revised the country's tax code, licensed foreign banks, and privatized even more state-run industries. As of 2002, the government has privatized more than three-quarters of the formerly state-owned enterprises such as railroads, waterworks, and sewage companies. In addition, Mkapa is considering changes to Tanzania's land laws, a move promoted by the World Bank as a way for the country to encourage foreign investment. These policies are unpopular with many Tanzanians—especially rural dwellers and the poor—who fear that the most attractive and profitable parts of their country will be sold to foreigners.

See also Colonial Rule; Germany; Indian Communities in Africa; Rift Valleys; South Africa; Swahili Language; Swahili People; Tourism in Africa.

Bibliography

Ayany, S. G. *A History of Zanzibar.* East African Literature Bureau, 1970.

Clayton, Anthony. *The Zanzibar Revolution and Its Aftermath.* Archon Books, 1981.

Duggan, William. *Tanzania and Nyerere: A Study of Ujamaa and Nationhood.* Orbis Books, 1976.

Iliffe, John. *A Modern History of Tanganyika.* Cambridge University Press, 1979.

Kimambo, I. N., and A. J. Temu, eds. *A History of Tanzania.* East African Publishing House, 1969.

Yeager, Rodger. *Tanzania: An African Experiment.* Westview Press, 1989.

Elizabeth Heath

Tap Dance

Art form, indigenous to the United States, that combines African and European dance with a complicated jazz-based percussive sensibility created by elaborate footwork.

Tap dance originated in the cross-fertilization of African and Anglo-European cultures in the Americas. During the 1600s the social dances of Irish and Scottish indentured laborers were fused with African juba and ring dances. Slaves in the southern United States imitated the rapid toe and heel action of the Irish jig and the percussive sensibility of the Lancashire clog, danced in wooden shoes. Combined with West African body movements and rhythms, these new dances were the forerunners of the buck-and-wing dancing and clogging of the southern United States and of modern-day tap dancing.

The names of the innovators from the early slave community went unrecorded. When the slave dances were adapted theatrically for minstrel shows in the late 1820s, individual artists began to be recognized. However, the first of these performers were black-faced white minstrels. William Henry Lane was the first African American to rise to prominence on the minstrel stage. Described by music historian Eileen Southern as "a link between the white world and authentic black source materials; [whose] dancing contributed to the preservation of artistic integrity in the performance of black dances on the minstrel stage," Lane is a legendary figure in the history of tap. Known as Master Juba, Lane was born free in Rhode Island in the 1820s and began his career in the dance halls of Manhattan's notorious Five Points district. Mastering the moves of the slave dances and the routines of white minstrels, Lane's agility and grace made him the only African American to perform on the whites-only minstrel stages of the antebellum era.

When the ban on black performers on the minstrel stage was lifted after the CIVIL WAR (1861–1865), these venues became the sites of numerous innovations in steps and choreography. Alongside the increasingly popular vaudeville performance of the late 1800s, the exposure on the minstrel stage helped launch the Broadway careers of performers such as Williams and Walker (BERT WILLIAMS and George Walker), Ulysses "Slow Kid" Thompson, and Bill Bailey. At the same time, their performances forged the aesthetics of Broadway jazz dance and the Broadway musical. Behind these performers were many master tap dancers, including King Rastus Brown, who were born too soon to be accepted on the white stages.

Broadway ushered in a golden age for tap. The combination of sharply choreographed chorus lines performing to RAGTIME and early JAZZ with tap and other vernacular dances proved a hit with audiences and critics. During this period the marquee performers popularly associated with the genre, such as BILL "BOJANGLES" ROBINSON, rose to prominence. By combining an irresistible onstage persona with his impeccably timed routines, Robinson became the best-known hoofer of his generation.

John "Bubbles" Sublett is widely acknowledged as the most innovative dancer of the era. Part of the popular duo BUCK AND BUBBLES (with Ford Lee "Buck" Washington), Sublett played the original Sportin' Life in PORGY AND BESS. He also invented rhythm tap. When most tap dancers performed on their toes before launching into a flashy routine of kicks and splits, Sublett reemphasized the percussive aspect of tap and reintroduced it to a jazz idiom. He switched its accenting and dropped his heel to give his performances a more syncopated sound. By slowing his tempo, he was able to add more steps. In addition, Sublett extended his combinations over a previously unheard-of number of bars, aligning himself with the polyrhythmic movements of jazz.

If Broadway, and, later, Hollywood cinema, gave tap its greatest exposure, the Hoofer's Club provided its unofficial academy. Both rookies and veterans gathered at this small venue next to Lafayette Theatre in HARLEM, NEW YORK. The fiercely competitive atmosphere of the Hoofer's Club produced a stunning array of fresh routines. Dancers would watch, imitate, and steal each other's moves in an effort to gain prominence among their peers.

By the 1930s tap had become an integral part of Hollywood musicals. Prominent African American dancers, including Robinson, Sublett, the NICHOLAS BROTHERS, and the Berry Brothers, were often featured, but Hollywood best served the careers of whites such as Shirley Temple and Fred Astaire. Their success further popularized tap, making it the premier form of theatrical dance in the United States. Yet some critics have suggested that as whites became more closely aligned with tap, its integrity was compromised: its meter became regimented, and its percussive and improvisational aspects were deemphasized.

By the 1950s tap dance had fallen out of vogue with American audiences, and many preeminent dancers were unable to find work. Many dancers link tap's decline to a number of phenomena, including Agnes de Mille's ballet-influenced choreography for the 1943 production of *Oklahoma!* and the rise of modern jazz dance, both of which created new paradigms for popular dance. In addition, dancers note the demise of the big-bands, nightclubs, and theaters that provided the performance culture in which tap was embedded.

In the 1970s tap underwent a resurgence. Buoyed by a series of documentaries, films, television specials, and live performances—and the emergence of ambassadors such as Gregory and Rupert Hines—tap began a popular revival. By the 1990s, as the long run of the young, dreadlocked virtuoso Savion Glover's highly acclaimed Broadway show *Bring in da Noise, Bring in da Funk* attests, tap had regained its place as one of the most important American dance forms.

See also Dance, African American; Hines, Gregory; Minstrelsy.

Bibliography

Stearns, Marshall, and Jean Stearns. *Jazz Dance: The Story of American Vernacular Dance.* Macmillan, 1968.

Peter Hudson

Tarrant, Caesar

c. 1740–1797

African American patriot.

Caesar Tarrant was born into slavery, probably at Hampton, Virginia. The identity of his parents is unknown. In his early adulthood, Caesar was sold to Carter Tarrant upon the death of his master Robert Hundley. His purchase price exceeded the normal price for male slaves because Tarrant had a particular skill, that of a river pilot. Just how Tarrant acquired the skill is unclear. Typically, the Tidewater area river pilot was white and passed the skill on to his son. In any case, Tarrant would eventually use this skill to parlay his freedom.

Sometime prior to the AMERICAN REVOLUTION, Tarrant married Lucy, the slave of neighbor John Rogers. This so-called "broad" marriage of slaves who resided apart from one another produced three children. Throughout his life, Tarrant longed for his family's freedom.

The American Revolution provided Tarrant with the opportunity to secure his own freedom. As a pilot, his knowledge of the waterways could have been valuable to either side. John Murray, Lord Dunmore, the last royal governor of Virginia, promised in his 1775 Proclamation freedom to all runaway slaves who would join his "Ethiopian Regiment." Many African Americans decided to do just that. Indeed, many more African Americans actively supported the British than the patriots. Tarrant, however, for reasons that are not known, chose to support the patriot cause. This was fortunate for the patriots, as Tarrant quickly demonstrated his abilities. His skill induced the Virginia Navy Board to appoint him a pilot in the Virginia State Navy, one of seven such appointments. For three years Tarrant successfully piloted a number of vessels, enhancing his reputation as a skilled and valiant pilot.

Among the several ships Tarrant piloted was the tender *Patriot*. In 1777 a group of ships commanded by Commodore Richard Taylor encountered the British naval vessel *Lord Howe*. When it appeared that the British privateer would escape, Taylor personally took command of the *Patriot*, piloted by Tarrant. Tarrant skillfully maneuvered the faster ship, which succeeded in ramming the larger and better-armed British vessel. Fierce fighting resulted in numerous deaths and injuries on both sides, including Taylor, who was shot. Nevertheless, Tarrant's skill and bravery in the face of enemy fire earned him praise from his captain, who stated he had "behaved gallantly."

In addition to this engagement, Tarrant piloted the vessel when the Americans captured the British ship *Fanny*, which was attempting to bring supplies to British troops in Boston. Although the *Patriot* was later itself captured, no record indicates that Tarrant was on board at the time.

Following the Revolution, Tarrant returned to the status of slave despite the heroism he had displayed. His master Carter Tarrant continued to make money from his slave's important skills. When Carter Tarrant died in 1784, Caesar Tarrant was willed to Mary Tarrant, Carter Tarrant's wife. The will stipulated that Caesar Tarrant was to remain her slave for her natural life and, further, he was to be given to Francis Tarrant, their son, upon the death of Mary. If it had not been for the intervention of the Virginia General Assembly, Caesar Tarrant might not have seen freedom for himself.

In 1789 the Virginia General Assembly moved to secure Tarrant's freedom. The reason for this action is not clear, though numerous possibilities exist. Other pilots who were his friends may have petitioned in his behalf, the navy board may have taken some action, or Tarrant may have petitioned. What is clear, however, is that Tarrant was finally free by 1789.

By the act of the assembly, "in consideration of which meritorious services it is judged expedient to purchase the freedom" of Tarrant, a representative contacted Mary Tarrant and expressed the assembly's intention to manumit Caesar Tarrant. After the purchase price was agreed upon, a certificate manumitting Caesar Tarrant was issued to Mary Tarrant. Having become a free man, Caesar Tarrant, infected with what BENJAMIN QUARLES termed blacks' "contagion of liberty," then worked to secure the freedom of his family.

At the time of Tarrant's manumission, John Rogers held his wife and children in bondage. In 1793 Rogers manumitted Lucy and their fifteen-month-old daughter Nancy. The other children, Sampson and Lydia, remained enslaved, presumably because of their high value. What prompted the manumissions is not clear. It is not known if Caesar Tarrant worked for Rogers, Tarrant raised the money through his own efforts, or Rogers felt some need to liberate the mother and young child. The "Reason for Manumission" expressed in the records of Elizabeth City County simply state that Lucy was the "wife of Caesar Tarrant" and Nancy was the "daughter of Caesar Tarrant." Payment of some specified amount or "faithful service" as indicated for others manumitted were not listed as reasons for Lucy or Nancy's freedom.

With part of his family free, Tarrant purchased a lot in Hampton in a section where white river pilots lived. This further indicated how highly regarded Tarrant was among this closed brotherhood of river pilots. Indeed, these white river pilots petitioned the legislature in 1791 to include skilled blacks among those granted licenses. They more than likely thought of Tarrant as they fashioned this request.

Yet freedom proved ephemeral. Although Tarrant had the respect of his peers, was now a property holder, and apparently continued to navigate the rivers, he, like other free African Americans, could not fully enjoy the benefits of liberty. As an African American he could not vote or hold public office, neither could he testify against any white person nor serve on a jury. Full citizenship was reserved for others; "freedom" for African Americans was limited. Robert Francis Engs has argued that Hampton may have been something of an anomaly among southern communities as there appeared to be a strong "cordiality between" the races. Yet even there Tarrant's dream for his family went unrealized.

Tarrant died in Hampton, Virginia, only eight years after gaining his freedom, while his two older children remained in bondage. The thirst for freedom—Tarrant's legacy—did not end with his death. Tarrant had specified in his will that all his property be given to his wife and at her death, the proceeds from the sale of that property be used to purchase his eldest daughter's freedom. Whatever remained was to be given to Tarrant's son, Sampson. In a concluding comment, Tarrant asked the county court to "see justice done my children."

After another twenty-five years, Lydia obtained her freedom. Prior to that, she was sold to a Norfolk resident for the sum of $250. When in 1822 her mother was able to purchase her freedom, Lydia herself left a child in bondage. The fate of Sampson is unclear because his name disappears from the records. It is possible that he died still enslaved. What is clear, however, is that despite Tarrant's contributions to American freedom, he, like so many antebellum African Americans, was unable to secure justice for his children.

Bibliography

A few scattered references, such as manumission records, a deed to a lot purchased in Hampton, and Tarrant's will, are in the Elizabeth City County court records in the Virginia State Library in Richmond. In addition, several unpublished papers on Tarrant are in the office of the city of Hampton's archivist/historian among the Hampton Historical Records, including Sandidge Evans, "Caesar Tarrant, The Resurrection of a Black Hero of the Revolutionary War" and "To See Justice Done My Children."

Engs, Robert Francis. *Freedom's First Generation: Black Hampton, Virginia, 1861–1890.* 1979.

From *American National Biography*. John A. Garraty and Mark C. Carnes, eds. Oxford University Press, 1999. Reprinted by permission of the American Council of Learned Societies.

Michael E. Hucles

Tatum, Art

1909–1956

American jazz pianist whose harmonic and technical innovations set new standards in jazz music during the 1930s, 1940s, and 1950s.

Art Tatum was born in Toledo, Ohio. He was partially blind from birth, his vision impaired by cataracts in both eyes. Tatum began playing the piano as a child, using his keen ear to imitate songs he heard on the radio. Encouraged by his musically inclined parents, Tatum also learned to play accordion, guitar, and violin at a young age. He further developed himself as a musician at the Cousino School for the Blind in Columbus, Ohio, and at the Toledo School of Music.

Tatum's career took off in 1929 when he began to play regularly for a Toledo radio station. After being hired by singer Adelaide Hall in 1932, Tatum went to NEW YORK CITY, where he performed at 52nd Street nightclubs. Over the course of the following decade, he toured the United States and England, electrifying audiences with his virtuosity. He enjoyed continued success from 1944 until his death in 1956 as a member of a JAZZ trio featuring guitarist Tiny Grimes and bassist Slam Stewart. Tatum's bold exploration of extended harmonies deeply influenced the birth of BEBOP.

Tatum first recorded in 1933 after his arrival in New York City. While he intermittently collaborated with other jazz musicians on recordings, he is best known for his solo performances, of which he recorded more than 100 between 1953 and 1955. Two of his outstanding renditions of popular songs are "Tea for Two" (1933) and "Rosetta" (1944). Tatum's dexterity was so refined that he could play the piano just as effectively with the backs of his fingers, palms up, as with the tips of his fingers, palms down.

See also Music, African American.

Aaron Myers

Taya, Maaouya Ould Sidi Ahmed

1943–

President of Mauritania since 1984.

Born in Atar, in western MAURITANIA, Maaouya Ould Sidi Ahmed Taya received advanced military training after joining the Mauritanian army. He served as aide-de-camp (military assistant) to MOKTAR OULD DADDAH, Mauritania's first president and deputy chief of operations and commander in the northern region during the war against the POLISARIO FRONT, the nationalist movement in adjacent WESTERN SAHARA. Taya was appointed deputy chief of staff in 1978 and, after Daddah was deposed later that year, minister of defense. In July 1980, after another coup, he became army chief of staff and in April 1981 prime minister, but was demoted back to army chief of staff in early 1984 by President Mohamed Ould Haidalla, who considered Taya a

threatening political rival. Taya responded, in December 1984, by leading a bloodless coup.

In one of his first acts as president, Taya formally recognized the independence of Polisario's SAHRAWI Arab Democratic Republic in Western Sahara, initially heightening tensions with neighboring MOROCCO (which occupies Western Sahara); diplomatic relations with Morocco were restored in April 1985. Domestically, he appointed civilians to government posts and drafted a new constitution in 1991, which both consolidated his power and allowed for the registration of opposition parties. In January 1992 Taya, backed by the newly formed Democratic and Social Republican Party, was elected to a six-year term as president amid protests of fraudulent election practices. Taya included an opposition member in his new, civilian-dominated, cabinet. Taya's economic reforms, including currency devaluation and other austerity measures, provoked violent protests. Ethnic clashes, between those of sub-Saharan descent and those of North African descent, have also produced tension both within Mauritania—with government purges of dark-skinned army officers and violent repression of protests against the institution of Islam as the state religion—and with neighboring SENEGAL, where nearly 200,000 Mauritanian refugees reside.

In December 1997, Taya was virtually uncontested as he won another six-year term as president. However, ethnic and religious tensions remained high. In June 2003 he briefly lost control of the county before his troops put down a coup attempt. Taya's opponents are now concentrating on using the ballot box to remove him.

See also Islam in Africa; Nationalism in Africa.

Taylor, Alrutheus A(mbush)

1893–1954

African American historian and educator.

Alrutheus Ambush Taylor was born in WASHINGTON, D.C., the son of Lewis Taylor and Lucy Johnson (occupations unknown). Educated in the Washington, D.C., public schools, Taylor entered the University of Michigan and received a B.A. in mathematics in 1916. He taught English for one year at TUSKEGEE INSTITUTE and then worked with black migrants at both the national and the New York branch of the Urban League as a social worker from 1917 to 1918. In 1919 he accepted a position at West Virginia Collegiate Institute, where he taught mathematics, history, economics, and logic and began his long association with African American historian CARTER G. WOODSON. That year he married Harriet Wilson; they had no children.

Taylor had been brought to the institute by John W. Davis, its enterprising young black president, who was determined to improve the quality of the faculty and staff. In 1920 Davis hired Woodson, who soon befriended Taylor and encouraged his interest in history. Woodson published Taylor's first investigation, on Negro congressmen during RECONSTRUCTION, in the *Journal of Negro History* in 1922. At Woodson's suggestion, and under the auspices of the Association for the Study of Negro Life and History, which Woodson had founded in 1915, Taylor enrolled in the graduate degree program in history at Harvard University. Woodson had also received his doctorate from Harvard and studied under the same eminent historians, Edward Channing and Albert Bushnell Hart. Taylor also worked with social historian Arthur M. Schlesinger, Sr., who further stimulated Taylor's interest in African American history. Woodson not only guided but also financed Taylor's studies for an M.A. and Ph.D. in American history, which were received from Harvard in 1923 and 1935, respectively.

In 1922 Taylor became the first young black scholar to join Woodson's research staff at the Association for the Study of Negro Life and History, where he served as a full-time investigator. His research on blacks in the Reconstruction of South Carolina after the Civil War was published in Woodson's journal in 1924 and brought out in book form the same year. Taylor continued his studies of southern Reconstruction, focusing on Virginia, and published an essay and monograph in 1926. In these works Taylor began to overturn the prevailing view of black ineptitude during Reconstruction by demonstrating that white racism, violence, and greed were largely responsible for the failure of political reform. He pointed to the many accomplishments and achievements of black politicians. Taylor's interpretation were largely echoed in W. E. B. Du Bois's masterly interpretation, *Black Reconstruction* (1935), as well as in subsequent studies of the period. In 1938 Taylor published a historiographical essay in the *Journal of Negro History* on historians and their interpretations of Reconstruction that praised the work of Du Bois but acknowledged that the work of black scholars had largely gone unnoticed.

In 1926 Taylor joined the faculty at Fisk University, where he served as professor of history and chairman of the department. A gifted and popular teacher, Taylor also was known for his administrative skills. He assumed additional administrative responsibilities as dean of the College of Arts and Sciences from 1930 to 1951. Among his accomplishments was the admission of Fisk as a fully accredited institution in the Southern Association of American Universities; it was the first black school to obtain accreditation.

In the 1920s Taylor assisted Woodson with research and revisions for the textbook *The Negro in Our History* (1922) by providing surveys on former slaves, black Baptists, and the status of free blacks in the antebellum South. Using the manuscript census, Taylor assisted Woodson in the compilation of lists of free blacks who owned property, including slaves. In the 1940s he published a study of blacks in Tennessee (*The Negro in Tennessee 1865–1880* [1941]) and coauthored a study of community activities among black youth (*A Study of the Community Life of the Negro Youth* [1941]). Taylor retired from Fisk in 1951, but remained active in Nashville. He was a member of several local community organizations and served on the board of trustees of Nashville Kent College of Law. At his death, he left unfinished a history of Fisk University.

After his first wife's death in 1941, Taylor founded a scholarship at Fisk in her honor. He married Catherine Buchanan in 1943; they had no children. Taylor died in Nashville, Tennessee.

Bibliography

Taylor's papers are in the Fisk University Archives. Other correspondence can be found in the papers of his black contemporaries, especially Luther Porter Jackson, whose papers are housed at Virginia State University in Petersburg.

Goggin, Jacqueline. *Carter G. Woodson: A Life in Black History*. 1993.

Meier, August, and Elliott Rudwick. *Black History and the Historical Profession, 1915–1980*. 1986.

From *American National Biography*. John A. Garraty and Mark C. Carnes, eds. Oxford University Press, 1999. Reprinted by permission of the American Council of Learned Societies.

Jacqueline Goggin

Taylor, Cecil

1929–

African American pianist and one of the most influential figures in avant-garde jazz.

Cecil Taylor was born in New York City. At age five he began piano lessons on Long Island. He later studied percussion, and in 1952 he enrolled for four years at the New England Conservatory of Music. Studying piano and music theory, he explored the work of Jazz innovators such as Dave Brubeck and classical modernists such as Igor Stravinsky. He became particularly interested in great black jazz innovators such as Duke Ellington, Bud Powell, Horace Silver, and Thelonius Monk.

Taylor's renown began with his 1956 recording *Jazz Advance* with soprano saxophonist Steve Lacy, bassist Buell Neidlinger, and drummer Dennis Charles; his six-week run the same year at the New York club the Five Spot; and his expansive performance at the 1957 Newport Jazz Festival. He had moved from strikingly original renditions of jazz standards to performances featuring his trademark abstract, percussive style in which he used any and all parts of his hands and arms to play hammered or running clusters of notes.

In 1962 *Down Beat* magazine named Taylor the year's "new star" on piano, but he had difficulty finding work, in part because innovative saxophonist Ornette Coleman had stolen the limelight in experimental jazz. At the same time, Taylor continued to profoundly impress the most knowledgeable critics.

Taylor's groups occasionally played at venues such as the Five Spot and in Europe, where he began a collaboration with revolutionary saxophonist Albert Ayler. To promote jazz innovation, Taylor in 1964 helped form the Jazz Composers' Guild. His reputation growing, he worked during the late 1960s and early 1970s with other progressive jazz players such as saxophonists Sam Rivers and Jimmy Lyons, and drummer Andrew Cyrille. He led his own Cecil Taylor Unit while also playing solo concerts notable for his prolonged, dazzling attack and exquisite abstract gestures. To explain his percussive approach, he has referred both to dance and to a distinctly black rather than European or European-American aesthetic.

By the 1970s Taylor's renown had brought him more work and touring success in both solo and group settings. A 1979 collaboration with veteran drum innovator MAX ROACH led to a rush of bookings and to a new phase of his career in which he worked with many of the most advanced American and European improvisers. Now in his seventies, Taylor continues to record and tour. At his multimedia concerts he sings, chants, reads poetry, and dances, all of which complement his masterful work at the piano.

See also Music, African American.

Taylor, Charles Ghankay

1948–

President of Liberia from 1997 to 2003.

By the time Charles Ghankay Taylor won elections held in July 1997, he had already considered himself LIBERIA's president for nearly seven years. Little is known about the former rebel leader's early life. The son of an American father and an AMERICO-LIBERIAN mother, Taylor was born in Liberia but left for the United States in the early 1970s and attended Bentley College in Massachusetts, from which he graduated in 1977.

Although a member of Liberia's elite, in the United States Taylor joined with fellow Liberian expatriates in denouncing the Americo-Liberian domination of his country's government, then headed by President WILLIAM TOLBERT. Soon after SAMUEL K. DOE led a military overthrow of Tolbert in 1980, Taylor returned to Liberia and became one of Doe's advisers, as well as the director of the government's General Services Agency. Three years later he was accused of embezzling $900,000. Taylor fled to BOSTON, MASSACHUSETTS, where he was soon arrested on the Liberian warrant. Rather than return to face charges, Taylor escaped from prison and made his way back to Africa, where he spent the next several years traveling and building support for an anti-Doe movement.

Along with other exiled Liberians, Taylor became involved in the National Patriotic Front of Liberia (NPFL), and by the late 1980s had become its leader. On Christmas Day, 1989, he led NPFL forces in an attack on Liberia's northern Nimba County. Within months Taylor's rebels had taken control of most of the countryside, and Doe was effectively trapped in MONROVIA, the capital. Prince Yormie Johnson, leader of a rival rebel group, assassinated Doe in September 1990, leading to a transitional government headed by Dr. Amos Sawyer, a moderate professor.

Over the next seven years Taylor, who had declared himself president in October 1990, consolidated his power over the Liberian population. The NPFL controlled the interior's transportation, commerce, and banking systems, and won over supporters from the ethnic groups historically at odds with the Krahn, who had dominated the Doe government. But Taylor's bid to elicit U.S. support faltered as he was charged with repeated human rights abuses, including the military conscription of children and the assassination of rivals. His increasing use of foreign soldiers also put him in conflict with neighboring governments, which feared the NPFL would set off a broader regional conflict.

After years of fighting among the NPFL, other dissident factions, and ECOMOG (the monitoring group of the Economic Union of West African States, a multinational peacekeeping force whose proclaimed neutrality Taylor repeatedly attacked), Liberia held elections in July 1997. Unlike the previous election in 1985, which Doe was widely believed to have won through fraud, most international observers believe the 1997 voting was legitimate. Taylor, representing the newly formed National Patriotic Party, won about 75 percent of the vote. In the months following the election, questions remained about Taylor's pledge to lead Liberia as a modern, progressive president. The silencing of independent media and the unsolved murder of a former rival generated fears that Taylor had returned to his warlord past, but Taylor also brought in respected financial advisers and made efforts to fight corruption.

Only three years after his election, Taylor's grip on power began to weaken. In 2000 insurgents within Liberia launched a military campaign to oust him. In 2001 the United Nations placed sanctions on Liberia for supporting rebel forces and diamond trafficking in neighboring SIERRA LEONE. In March 2003 a UN-backed Special Court in Sierra Leone indicted Taylor for war crimes committed in Sierra Leone's civil war. By this time, the anti-Taylor forces in Liberia controlled 60 percent of the county. In August Taylor went into exile in NIGERIA. Though he vowed to return to Liberia, Nigeria faces international pressure to turn him over to the Special Court. Meanwhile, much of Liberia's population suffers from starvation and homelessness after more than a decade of almost constant civil war.

See also Human Rights in Africa; Political Movements in Africa; United Nations in Africa.

Kate Tuttle

Taylor, Gardner Calvin

1918–

American Baptist minister known as the "Dean of Black Preachers" who led church support for the civil rights struggle.

Gardner Calvin Taylor was born in Baton Rouge, Louisiana, and graduated with a bachelor's degree from Leland College. He began his theological training at Oberlin Theological Seminary in 1937. He was ordained a Baptist minister in 1939, and he followed his theological degree (1940) with pastorates in NEW ORLEANS and Baton Rouge.

In 1948, Taylor moved to NEW YORK CITY to preach at the Concord Baptist Church of Christ in the Bedford-Stuyvesant section of Brooklyn. He was a dynamic leader, establishing social service programs such as a nursing home and clothing exchange. In 1962, with 12,000 members, the church became the largest Protestant congregation in the United States. Taylor was known internationally for the brilliance of his preaching, and was called the best preacher in America.

An active proponent of educational reform, Taylor risked his position on the New York City Board of Education in 1958 to support the demand for better school conditions for African American children. He served on the Citywide Committee for Integrated Schools, and in 1961, he and his wife Laura founded the Concord Elementary Day School.

During the 1960s, Taylor rose to prominence as a civil rights leader through his involvement in the CONGRESS ON RACIAL EQUALITY (CORE). During this time, he worked closely with a group of Baptist ministers that included the Reverend MARTIN LUTHER KING, JR. In 1961, dissatisfied with the leadership of Joseph H. Jackson, the group split from the National Baptist Convention, USA, Inc. The newly formed Progressive National Baptist Convention (PNBC) publicly supported the civil rights struggles of CORE and the SOUTHERN CHRISTIAN LEADERSHIP CONFERENCE (SCLC).

Taylor retired from full-time preaching in 1990, and is currently senior pastor emeritus at Concord Baptist Church of Christ. In 2000 President Bill Clinton awarded him the Presidential Medal of Freedom, the nation's highest civilian honor. Renowned for his mastery of the spoken word, Taylor remains a highly sought-after guest preacher.

See also Civil Rights Movement.

Marian Aguiar

Taylor, Koko

1935–

African American blues singer and a master of the electric Chicago blues style, known as the "Queen of the Blues."

The youngest of six children, Koko Taylor—whose name was originally Cora Walton—was born in MEMPHIS, TENNESSEE. Her sharecropper father brought the children up after their mother's death in 1939. Taylor's father raised cotton, and she and her siblings worked in the fields. Taylor began singing GOSPEL MUSIC in church, but she listened to the BLUES and RHYTHM AND BLUES (R&B) broadcasts of B.B. KING and Rufus Thomas on Memphis's black radio station, WDIA. "The first blues record I ever heard," she recalled, "was 'Me and My Memphis Blues,' by Memphis Minnie [Douglas]. I was twelve or thirteen, and just loved it."

At eighteen, Taylor met truck driver Robert "Pops" Taylor. When he decided to leave Tennessee to work in a CHICAGO slaughterhouse, Taylor married him and moved north. In 1953, Taylor arrived in Chicago, part of a vast migration of African Americans leaving the South for greater opportunities in the urban North and West. She arrived in Chicago at the height of the new Chicago blues style, which featured electric guitars in small combos and used heavier, more driving rhythms than traditional rural blues. During the week, she worked cleaning suburban homes, but she spent her weekends in Chicago's South Side blues bars.

During the mid-1950s, Chicago's South Side nightspots featured such blues musicians as guitarist and singer MUDDY WATERS, the person most responsible for creating the Chicago blues style; harmonica player and vocalist HOWLIN' WOLF; guitarist and vocalist Buddy Guy; and guitarist, harmonica player, and vocalist Jimmy Reed. Taylor began sitting in with various performers, joining them on the stand to sing. Her powerful and rough-edged singing—in particular, her use of growling, raspy effects—quickly attracted attention. Taylor's singing reflected the influence not only of female blues singers BIG MAMA THORNTON and BESSIE SMITH, but also bluesmen Muddy Waters and Howlin' Wolf, but she quickly forged her own distinctive style.

One evening in 1962, bass player and composer WILLIE DIXON, a prominent figure in the Chicago blues community, heard Taylor perform. Dixon took Taylor under his wing, and her career took off. In 1963 she made her recording debut, recording her own "Honky Tonky" for the small record label USA, but she soon signed a contract with CHESS RECORDS, Chicago's leading blues recording company. Taylor's 1966 rendition of Dixon's "Wang Dang Doodle" became a million-selling recording and gave Chess Records its last Top Ten R&B hit.

During the early 1970s, however, interest in blues music waned, and Taylor dropped from sight until signing with Alligator Records in 1974. The first of her six albums for Alligator, *I Got What It Takes* (1975), was nominated for a Grammy Award. There were many more Grammy nominations in the following years. During the 1980s Taylor gained widespread recognition, including a Grammy Award for the album *Blues Explosion* (1984) and, between 1983 and 1992, a total of ten Handy Awards, the blues music equivalent of the Grammy, which is named for blues composer W.C. HANDY.

While on tour in 1988, however, Taylor experienced a profound personal tragedy when her tour van was involved in an accident. Two band members and her husband Pops Taylor were seriously injured; six months later Pops Taylor died of his injuries. Koko Taylor suffered a fractured shoulder, collarbone and ribs, which kept her from performing for several months. But she resolved to return to music, and soon resumed an active touring schedule, including appearances at many blues and folk music festivals. In 1993 she recorded *Forces of Nature* and followed with *Royal Blue* (2000). Taylor continues a steady schedule of live performances.

See also Music, African American.

James Sellman

Taylor, Susie Baker King

1848–1912

American teacher, nurse, and writer; the only known black woman to write of her experiences during the Civil War.

Born a Georgia slave, Susie Baker King Taylor was quite young when an arrangement was made sending her to live with her grandmother in Savannah. She learned to read and write from two white children, even though doing so was illegal prior to the AMERICAN CIVIL WAR. When war broke out Taylor moved with her uncle's family to the Sea Islands of South Carolina. The Union Army, fighting for these islands, pressed her into service as a teacher of freed slave children and adults. Soon after, the men in her family joined the Union's First South Carolina Infantry, and she traveled with them as a nurse and laundress. In 1862 she married one of the regiment's sergeants, Edward King. In her memoir, *A Black Woman's Civil War Memoirs,* she recounted the events of her life in camp with the regiment. She is the only black woman known to have written of her life during the war.

After the war she remained in Georgia. At different times she began and ran schools for black children and adults. In 1879 she married Russell Taylor and moved to BOSTON, MASSACHUSETTS. She returned south in 1898 to care for her dying son in Louisiana, riding in a segregated rail car and witnessing a LYNCHING. Her memoir, published in 1902, not only spoke of the war, but of life after the war, ending with hopeful memories of the "wonderful revolution" which had taken place in 1861.

See also Women Writers, Black, in the United States.

Tayyib, Salih al-

1929–

Contemporary Sudanese writer.

Al-Tayyib Salih was born in al-Dabba, a large village in the northern province of the SUDAN, where as a young man he received an Islamic schooling and worked on the family's farm. Salih continued his education at KHARTOUM University and then left the Sudan to study in England. After completing degrees at the University of London and the University of Exeter, he returned to his home country to teach. Salih joined the British Broadcasting Corporation, working his way up from scriptwriter to head of the Arabic language service. He has since continued working in the fields of broadcast and print journalism. Salih, who considers himself a socialist, has also occupied various advisory government positions.

Salih started writing stories in the 1950s, but did not publish until 1964, when his friend the poet Tawfiq Sayigh began printing Salih's work in the Beirut journal *Hiwar*. His stories, based on his childhood village life, were infused with the mystical vision of Sufi Islam. In these stories his writing style, often compared to magical realism, shows the influence of traditional Arabic storytelling. He depicts a troubled marriage between a European woman and a Sudanese man. (Salih himself had married a British woman.) Many critics interpret his portrayal of personal relations as representing the fraught relations between the first and third world. In 1966, he published

the stories as *Urs al-Zayn: Riwaya wa-sab qusas* (*The Wedding of Zein and Other Stories*; 1966). The title novella *Urs al-Zayn* was made into a play in LIBYA, and in 1976 it was made into an award-winning Kuwaiti film.

Mawsim al-hijrah ila al-shamal (1966; *Season of Migration to the North*, 1969) is Salih's best known novel; it is credited with transforming modern Arabic writing. Taking up what would become a common theme in postcolonial writing, the novel represented the alienation of an Islamic African man returning from the West. It went beyond the issue of exile to consider what it means to belong to a community, and traversed conventional norms in its use of graphic sex and violence as metaphors for the penetrating, often brutal, ways that cultures intersect. According to critic Kamal Abu-Deeb, the novel also breaks with regional traditions of writing, "[focusing on] African rather than Arab identity, social, cultural, and artistic issues rather than political and ideological ones, the community rather than the State, ordinary people rather than intellectuals, popular culture rather than official culture, religious and mystical belief rather than secularism, the Sudanese dialect rather than Standard Arabic, and the small village rather than the great metropolis."

In 1971 Salih published *Bandar Shah, Daw al-bayt,* which explores the nature of leadership in a contemporary village. He continued the story in *Bandar Shah, Maryud* (1977). In 1976 he published "Al-Rajul al-qubrusi" (translated as "The Cypriot Man;" 1980). In this story, Salih took on one of the most difficult subjects: the meaning of death. "Al-Rajul al-qubrusi" was his last story before an extended literary silence, which continues to the present.

See also Socialism; Sufism.

Bibliography
Salih, al-Tayyib. *Season of Migration to the North.* Heinemann Educational, 1969.

Marian Aguiar

Teatro Experimental do Negro

Company of actors, actresses, artists, and playwrights in Rio de Janeiro, created to redefine the roles of Afro-Brazilians in Brazilian theater.

In 1941 black Brazilian activist ABDIAS DO NASCIMENTO saw a performance of Eugene O'Neill's *The Emperor Jones* in Lima, PERU. He was disturbed to see the black hero of this drama being played by a white actor in blackface. Nascimento could find no justification for this, since there was a sizable Afro-Peruvian population in Lima. He then contemplated the fact that people of African descent were constituting the majority in his homeland, BRAZIL, yet they had been almost completely excluded from the stage. As a result, he created the *Teatro Experimental do Negro* (TEN; also known as Black Experimental Theater) in 1944.

Until then, Afro-Brazilians were allowed on stage only in the roles of servants and folklore figures—or, after the show, as janitors. TEN's principal objectives were to affirm the values of African culture, to eliminate the use of white actors in blackface and the use of black actors in debased roles, and to act out Afro-Brazilian problems in a white racist society. TEN's first production was the play that had inspired its creation, *The Emperor Jones*. The play opened on May 8, 1945, in RIO DE JANEIRO's Municipal Theater with Afro-Brazilian actor Aguinaldo Camargo in the lead role of Brutus Jones. The play was lauded in reviews.

In spite of TEN's successful debut, in subsequent years the group repeatedly clashed with the government's Censorship Bureau. For example, the police prevented Nascimento's *Sortilégio* (*Black Mystery*) from being performed on the grounds that it contained pornographic language. Nascimento argued that the show was banned because of its subject matter, which depicts the transformation of an assimilated black character, Emanuel, into an Afro-Brazilian who asserts his African heritage. When the play was finally presented in 1957, it was labeled a racist play that had been designed to foment Afro-Brazilians' hate for whites.

TEN launched the careers of the first generation of Afro-Brazilian actors and actresses, including José Maria Monteiro, Arinda Serafim, and Marina Gonçalves. In order to train the hundreds of men and women eager to join the company, TEN set up a literacy course, a "general culture" course, and a course in the fundamentals of acting. TEN also generated numerous Afro-Brazilian playwrights, including Joaquim Ribeiro (author of *Aruanda*), José de Morais Pinto (author of *Filhos de Santo*, or Children of the Saint), and, of course, Abdias do Nascimento (author of *Sortilégio* and *Rapsódia Negra*, or Black Rhapsody). Their scripts were among the first exploring Afro-Brazilian themes without reducing them to folklore. Instead, Afro-Brazilians were portrayed as complex human beings and as heroes, transcending the traditional stereotypes.

TEN made unique use of drama to redeem African identity and aesthetics, and to defend the human rights of Afro-Brazilians. After TEN's emergence, one-dimensional caricatures of Afro-Brazilians could no longer be easily accepted. Although the group was dissolved with Nascimento's exile to the United States in 1968, TEN inspired many other similar theatrical companies that preserved its legacy, including the *Teatro Negro Experimental* of São Paulo, the *Grupo dos Novos* in Rio de Janeiro, and the Brazilian Popular Theater.

See also Afro-Brazilian Culture.

Bibliography

Nascimento, Abdias do. *Drama para Negros e Prólogo para Brancos*. TEN, 1961.

Nascimento, Abdias do. *Sortilege (Black Mystery)*. Third World Press, 1967.

Nascimento, Abdias do. *Teatro Experimental do Negro-Testemunhos*. Editora GRD, 1966.

Aaron Myers

Teixeira e Souza, Antonio Gonçalves

1812–1861

Afro-Brazilian poet and novelist; one of Brazil's most popular authors of fiction in the nineteenth century.

Antônio Gonçalves Teixeira e Souza was born of humble parents and orphaned at a young age. He worked as a carpenter during his early years of study. Teixeira e Souza moved to the city of RIO DE JANEIRO and worked in the printing office of the well known intellectual Paula Brito, and it was there that he met the literary figures of his time and began to write his first poetry and prose.

Teixeira e Souza later taught and worked as a registrar, and these jobs allowed time for his writing. In 1843 he wrote *O filho do pescador* (The Fisherman's Son). This work was marked by Brazilian nationalistic tendencies of the sort that would later be taken up by José de Alencar, the late-nineteenth-century Brazilian nationalist novelist, and others. Teixeira e Souza is considered one of the first Romantics to espouse the historical novel, a genre that allowed him to explore issues of racial and national identity. The epic narrative *A independência do Brasil* (Brazil's Independence) is an example of one work that explores these themes. Other important novels by Teixeira e Souza are *O três dias de um noivado* (The Three Days of a Betrothal), *Contos lyricos* (Lyric Stories), and *O Cavaleiro teutônico* (The Teutonic Knight, 1855).

See also Literature, Black, in Brazil.

Nicola Cooney

Téké

Ethnic group in central Republic of the Congo.

Since Congolese independence in 1960, the Téké of central Congo have often acted as a swing group between the politically dominant northern MBOCHI and the more numerous southern KONGO. However, few Téké have held senior government, military, or economic positions, although they comprise 17 percent of the population.

The Téké's political marginalization was a gradual process. Historians believe that the Téké probably migrated to the central plateau in the late fifteenth century and became part of the decentralized Kongo kingdom. With the disintegration of the Kongo kingdom in the seventeenth century, the vice-royalty of the Anzika, by which name the Téké are also known, established his own decentralized kingdom, known as Tio. The Makoko, or king, ruled from his capital at Mbé through appointed subchiefs. But the kingdom's commercial hub developed in the Pool region farther south, where the Téké exchanged slaves captured in the interior for goods brought by European merchant ships. The Mbochis and other northern groups' efforts to circumvent the Téké control of trade contributed to the slow disintegration of the kingdom. In 1880, the Téké Makoko signed a treaty with Pierre de Brazza to gain protection from FRANCE. This agreement effectively gave up the northern bank of the Congo to France. By the time the last Makoko died in 1918, the kingdom had been in serious decline for several decades. Under French COLONIAL RULE many Téké migrated south to the capital, BRAZZAVILLE, for employment. Today they make up a large proportion of the city's population; many are engaged in mask making and fetish carving.

See also Ethnicity and Identity in Africa: An Interpretation; Republic of the Congo; Slavery in Africa.

Eric Young

Television and African Americans

The history of African American depiction on and involvement in the medium of television.

From the negative stereotypes in *BEULAH* and *AMOS 'N' ANDY* to the "white Negroes" in *Julia* and *I Spy* to the arguably too-perfect Huxtable family on *The Cosby Show*, the majority of portrayals of African Americans on television have been one-dimensional, distorted, insulting, or sugarcoated. For many viewers, though, even unsatisfactory images seem preferable to the general absence of black television characters during television's early days. The history of the depiction of blacks on television has evolved from near invisibility broken by a parade of stereotypes to greater diversity and realism, but most critics agree that the medium has far to go.

Early Years

Commercial television was born in 1948 as each of the three major networks, ABC, CBS, and NBC, began broadcasting. The year 1948 was also a significant one in African American history, with the desegregation of the United States armed forces and an endorsement of civil rights in the presidential platform of the DEMOCRATIC PARTY, headed by President Harry S. Truman.

But black presence in the early years of television followed the pattern earlier set by radio. In fact, the first two series starring African Americans both came to television after decades of popularity on radio—and each replaced white radio actors with black actors. *Beulah,* which showcased a supporting character on the popular *Fibber McGee and Molly* show, debuted in 1950. As played by ETHEL WATERS, HATTIE MCDANIEL, and LOUISE BEAVERS on television, Beulah was cast in the stereotypical mold of the happy, overweight, black female "mammy." Cheerfully caring for the white family who employed her as housekeeper, Beulah had little discernible life of her own (although the cultural critic Donald Bogle points out that the interaction between Beulah and her long-time boyfriend provided some of the show's best moments). Beulah ran until 1953, when protests by the NATIONAL ASSOCIATION FOR THE ADVANCEMENT OF COLORED

A veteran of both silent and talking films, Louise Beavers potrayed family maid Beulah in the 1950s television show of the same name. *The Everett Collection*

PEOPLE (NAACP) and other groups forced the network to cancel the series.

Amos 'n' Andy, which ran from 1951 to 1953, was based on the most listened-to radio show of the 1930s and 1940s. Unlike *Beulah, Amos 'n' Andy* portrayed an all-black world in which the shiftless, joking Andy (played by SPENCER WILLIAMS) and the passive, long-suffering Amos (Alvin Childress) interacted with characters depicting the entire range of stereotypical black images. Its roots in the tradition of MINSTRELSY caused the NAACP to launch lawsuits and boycott threats that were instrumental in causing the show's cancellation. Speaking in the documentary *Color Adjustment,* written and directed by MARLON RIGGS, the actress DIAHANN CARROLL remembers being forbidden to watch *Amos 'n' Andy,* which her parents felt was demeaning to blacks. But some modern critics have praised the show's intricate and sophisticated comedy and lauded the actors, many of whom came from the black vaudeville tradition. After the series was cancelled, it continued to appear in syndication until 1966.

Other black images in 1950s television included variety shows, which occasionally featured African American entertainers. DUKE ELLINGTON, CAB CALLOWAY, PAUL ROBESON, ELLA FITZGERALD, SARAH VAUGHAN, and others appeared on shows hosted by veteran white entertainers such as Ed Sullivan, Milton Berle, and Steve Allen. But no African American had his

African American Emmy Award Winners

Year	Performer	Category	Performance
1959	Harry Belafonte	Outstanding Performer in a Variety or Musical Program	"Tonight with Belafonte," Revlon Revue
1966	Bill Cosby	Outstanding Continued Performance by an Actor in a Leading Role of a Dramatic Series	I Spy
1967	Bill Cosby	Outstanding Continued Performance by an Actor in a Leading Role of a Dramatic Series	I Spy
1968	Bill Cosby	Outstanding Variety or Musical Program	The Bill Cosby Special
1970	Flip Wilson	Outstanding Writing Achievement in a Variety or Musical Series	The Flip Wilson Show
1971	Ray Charles	Outstanding Achievement in Music Composition	The First Nine Months are the Hardest
1972	Ray Charles	Outstanding Achievement in Music Composition	The Funny Side of Marriage
1973	Cicely Tyson	Best Lead Actress in a Drama—Special Program	The Autobiography of Miss Jane Pittman
	Cicely Tyson	Actress of the Year—Special Program	The Autobiography of Miss Jane Pittman
1976	Olivia Cole	Outstanding Single Performance by a Supporting Actress in a Drama or Comedy Series	Roots Part 8
	Louis Gossett, Jr.	Outstanding Lead Actor for a Single Appearance in a Drama or Comedy Series	Roots Part 1
	Quincy Jones	Outstanding Music Series Composition	Roots Part 1
1978	Robert Guillaume	Outstanding Supporting Actor in a Comedy Series or Music Series	Soap
	Esther Rolle	Outstanding Supporting Actress in a Limited Series	Summer of My German Soldier
1980	Isabel Sanford	Outstanding Lead Actress in a Comedy Series	The Jeffersons
1981	Debbie Allen	Outstanding Choreography	"Come One, Come All," Fame
	Nell Carter	Outstanding Individual Achievement—Special Class	"Ain't Misbehavin'"
1982	Debbie Allen	Outstanding Choreography	"Class Act," Fame
	Leontyne Price	Outstanding Individual Performance in a Variety or Music Program	From Lincoln Center
	Leslie Uggams	Outstanding Host/Hostess in a Variety Series	Fantasy
1983	Suzanne de Passe	Outstanding Producing	Motown 25: Yesterday, Today and Forever
1984	Robert Guillaume	Outstanding Lead Actor in a Comedy Series	Benson
1985	Alfre Woodard	Outstanding Supporting Actress in a Drama Series	"Doris in Wonderland," Hill Street Blues
	George Stanford Brown	Outstanding Direction in a Drama Series	"Parting Shots," Cagney & Lacey
	Roscoe Lee Brown	Outstanding Guest Performer in a Comedy Series	The Cosby Show
	Suzanne de Passe	Outstanding Producing	Motown at the Apollo
	Whitney Houston	Outstanding Individual Performance in a Variety or Music Series	The 28th Annual Grammy Awards
1986	Alfre Woodard	Outstanding Guest Performer in a Drama Series	L.A. Law
1987	Jackée (Harry)	Outstanding Supporting Actress in a Comedy Series	227
1988	Beah Richards	Outstanding Guest Performer in a Comedy Series	Frank's Place
1989	Suzanne de Passe	Outstanding Producing	Lonesome Dove

African American Emmy Award Winners (*Continued*)

1990	Thomas Carter	Outstanding Directing in a Drama Series	"Promises to Keep," Equal Justice
1991	Debbie Allen	Outstanding Choreography	Motown 30: What's Goin' On!
	Ruby Dee	Outstanding Supporting Actress in a Miniseries or Special	"Decoration Day," Hallmark Hall of Fame
	James Earl Jones	Outstanding Lead Actor in a Drama Series	Gabriel's Fire
	James Earl Jones	Outstanding Supporting Actor in a Miniseries or Special	Heat Wave
	Madge Sinclair	Outstanding Supporting Actress in a Drama Series	Gabriel's Fire
	Lynn Whitfield	Outstanding Lead Actress in a Miniseries or Special	The Josephine Baker Story
	Thomas Carter	Outstanding Directing in a Drama Series	"In Confidence," Equal Justice
1992	Eric Laneuville	Outstanding Individual Achievement in Directing in a Drama Series	"All God's Children"
1993	Mary Alice	Outstanding Supporting Actress in a Drama Series	I'll Fly Away
	Laurence Fishburne	Outstanding Guest Actor in a Drama Series	"The Box," Tribeca
1998	Andre Braugher	Outstanding Lead Actor in a Drama Series	Homicide: Life on the Street
1999	Paris Barclay	Outstanding Directing in a Drama Series	"Hearts and Souls," N.Y.P.D. Blue
	Judith Jamison	Outstanding Choreography	Dance in America: A Hymn for Alvin Ailey
2000	Halle Berry	Outstanding Lead Actress in a Miniseries or Special	Introducing Dorothy Dandridge

Source: The African American Almanac, 9th Edition. 2003. Gale/Thompson Group

own national variety show until 1956, when *The Nat "King" Cole Show* premiered. Cole, who had hosted a radio program in the 1940s, was urbane, elegant, and considered nonthreatening by white viewers. His show featured both white and black entertainers, including Pearl Bailey, Count Basie, and Mahalia Jackson, and was a great source of pride for black viewers starved for positive African American television images. But with the deepening racial tensions of the 1950s, Cole had difficulty attracting corporate sponsors, especially after some white viewers became outraged when Cole touched the arm of a white female guest. The show was cancelled after one season.

Civil Rights and the "White Negro"

One arena in which African Americans appeared on television beginning in the 1950s—and reaching a peak in the 1960s—was in the serious documentaries about rural poverty, segregation, and the growing Civil Rights Movement. In addition, as the white segregationist backlash exploded into violence throughout the American South, "images of black people dominated the news," according to the writer and scholar Henry Louis Gates, Jr. Seen as a noble, almost saintly figure, the Reverend Martin Luther King, Jr., whose marches in Selma, Birmingham, and Montgomery, Alabama, heightened white America's awareness of the Civil Rights Movement, became black America's spokesperson on television in the eyes of many newly sympathetic white viewers. By contrast, some black leaders were treated harshly on television. Malcolm X was the subject of a documentary titled *The Hate that Hate Produced* (1959), which did little to dispel white fears of the Nation of Islam leader.

At the same time, as television news shows began to report seriously on racism and the fight for civil rights, television's entertainment programs became even more overwhelmingly white. Since its birth, the medium had avoided controversy, possibly offensive to viewers (and advertisers). During the 1960s, as protests rose against both racism and the Vietnam War, programming became less and less realistic. (For example, some of the most popular shows on television at that time featured witches, genies, and other escapist fantasy). As the cultural critic J. Fred McDonald pointed out, comedies such as *Petticoat Junction* and *The Andy Griffith Show*, both set in the South, portrayed all-white worlds in which prejudice seemingly did not exist.

When black characters did appear, network executives crafted the most inoffensive, blandly perfect images possible. *I Spy* (1965–1968), which starred Bill Cosby and Robert Culp as an interracial team of secret agents, presented Cosby's character, Alexander Scott, as a Rhodes scholar, an elegant sophisticate whose education was superior not only to the vast majority of African Americans but also to nearly all whites. *Julia* (1968–1971) featured Diahann Carroll as a widowed nurse and single mother. Carroll's character was bland, bleached of all evidence of black culture. Derided as a "white Negro" by critics—and suspected of being played by a white actress in darkening makeup—Carroll's Julia never encountered poverty or racism. Still, Julia was, according to African American actress Esther Rolle, "a step above the grinning domestic."

Designed to overcome negative stereotypes, such series presented "fully assimilable black people," according to Gates. In an era that featured so few black representations in the mass media, even positive images were heavily scrutinized by African Americans and usually found wanting. Shows like *I Spy, Julia,* and the action series *Mod Squad* and *Mission Impossible* (each of which featured black costars) clashed with the reality of most African Americans' lives. But attempts to present a more balanced picture, such as the short-lived dramatic series *East Side, West Side* (1963–1964), usually failed quickly. Starring JAMES EARL JONES and CICELY TYSON, *East Side, West Side* featured sophisticated writing and provocative situations depicting both ghetto life and the pain of integration. The show lasted only one season.

Relevance and Roots

By the late 1960s television began to emerge from its fantasy world to present programming more in touch with the reality of the tumultuous times. The first comedy series to deal with race was *All in the Family* (1971–1979), a show with a mostly white cast. At its head was Archie Bunker (played by Carroll O'Connor), an unrepentant racist, bigot, and homophobe. While some felt that Archie's use of racial slurs amounted to condoning prejudice, most saw the series as an important move toward realism, particularly in terms of race relations, on television (the Bunkers' next door neighbors were a black family whose characters were later featured in a popular spinoff series, *The Jeffersons,* which aired from 1975 to 1985).

One of the most dramatic changes came in children's television, which had been a wasteland in terms of black images. Starting in 1969 the public television series *Sesame Street* showed children and adults of a variety of racial and ethnic backgrounds interacting and learning. *Fat Albert and the Cosby Kids* (1972–1989) was an animated version of children and events from producer Bill Cosby's own Philadelphia childhood. More shows followed, including cartoons based on the adventures of the Jackson Five and the HARLEM GLOBETROTTERS.

Produced by the *All in the Family* team, *Good Times* (1974–1979) was the first television comedy to focus on a poor black family—one including both father and mother—living in the midst of a vibrant, diverse black community. But social relevance gave way to echoes of the minstrel character STEPIN FETCHIT, as the show increasingly revolved around the buffoonish character of JJ, the elder son. According to Esther Rolle, the actress who played JJ's mother, "negative images have been quietly slipped in on us" through the clowning, wide-eyed JJ.

Although the 1970s saw a dramatic rise in the number of television shows built around black characters, most made no pretense of seriousness or realism. *Sanford and Son* (1972–1977) starred the veteran comedian REDD FOXX as an irascible junk dealer and Demond Wilson as his long-suffering son. Despite the implied social relevance of its ghetto setting, the show was vintage 1970s escapism. Its wide popularity derived in part from its self-aware use of stereotypical aspects of black humor—elaborate insults, shrill women, scheming men—and it inspired a succession of inferior shows, including *Grady* (1975–1976), *Baby I'm Back* (1978), and *What's Happenin'* (1976–1979), which critics dubbed "the new minstrelsy."

No dramatic series starring a black actor aired until the 1980s. But it was in drama—made-for-television movies and miniseries—that some of the most significant television images of African Americans emerged in the 1970s. *The Autobiography of Miss Jane Pittman* (1974), starring Cicely Tyson, was hailed as "possibly the finest movie ever made for television." The movie, a series of flashbacks, is set in 1962 and traces Pittman's life from her childhood in slavery to the civil rights era she lived to see (the character is 110 years old). Its climactic scene features Pittman bending to take a sip from a whites-only water fountain.

Roots, which aired over eight nights in 1977, was a television event not only for African Americans but for all Americans. The highest-rated miniseries ever, *Roots,* based on ALEX HALEY's book about his family's history from freedom in Africa to slavery in the American South, attracted an estimated 130 million viewers. According to the cultural critic Marlon Riggs, *Roots* was presented as an immigrant tale that white audiences could relate to, "transforming a national disgrace into an epic triumph of the family and the American dream." Although carefully crafted to appeal to the white audience (it was reported that the actor LeVar Burton, who played Kunta Kinte, was nearly dropped from the project because producers thought his lips were too large), *Roots* was nonetheless a stirring and powerful drama. It was also a showcase for many black actors, including Burton, LOUIS GOSSETT JR., and Cicely Tyson.

Material Success

By the late 1970s no obvious color line remained in television. Black actors appeared in soap operas, as costars in dramatic series, and as the focus of comedies. In the wake of *Roots,* several television movies, including *King* (1978), *Roots: The Next Generations* (1979), and *Attica* (1980), featured African American historical themes. But most depictions of blacks in television continued to follow the pattern of either high-minded history lesson or low-rent stereotypic comedy. Rarely allowed to exist as fully realized human beings, some of the most popular black characters of the early 1980s were wisecracking black children adopted into white families—the situation in both *Different Strokes* (1978–1986) and *Webster* (1983–1987)—or, as in earlier television history, loyal sidekicks to white heroes.

When *The Cosby Show* debuted in 1984, it won enthusiastic reviews and a loyal audience, both black and white. Fo-

Beginning with his co-starring role on the television series *I Spy* in the 1960s, Bill Cosby has been one of television's most popular performers. With *The Cosby Show,* which ran from 1984 to 1992, the actor countered what he saw as negative racial sterotyping in the entertainment media. In addition to his work in television, Bill Cosby holds a doctorate in education and is a producer, writer, and philanthropist. *The Everett Collection*

cusing on a loving, intact, successful African American family, *The Cosby Show* starred Bill Cosby and Phylicia Rashad as the upper-middle-class parents of five children. Like the white families in 1950s television, theirs was a caring, supportive unit that blended humor with wisdom. Cosby, who had long criticized the negative portrayals of African Americans in television, consulted psychiatrist Dr. ALVIN POUSSAINT in writing and producing the program, resulting in a positive, almost educational tone. The top-rated series for many of its nine seasons, *Cosby,* according to critic Patricia Turner, reinforced "the notion that the Civil Rights Movement took care of all the racial inequities of society."

One series that attempted a more balanced depiction was the short-lived *Frank's Place* (1987–1988), about a black professor who inherits a NEW ORLEANS restaurant. Tim Reid, who had previously costarred in *WKRP in Cincinnati,* produced and starred in *Frank's Place,* which he said reflected his desire to see blacks portrayed not monolithically but with the full range of humanity. Although the well-written show won an Emmy Award, it was cancelled after one season.

Like Cosby and Reid, a rising number of African Americans began working behind the television camera in the late 1980s,

resulting in a flowering of black-themed shows. *A Different World,* which spun off from *Cosby* and was produced by Debbie Allen, depicted life at a historically black university. Others included QUINCY JONES's *Fresh Prince of Bel Air,* starring WILL SMITH, and *In Living Color,* produced by Keenan Ivory Wayans. *In Living Color,* one of the then-new Fox network's first hits, brought freshness and irreverence to its humor, much of which was based on racial stereotypes (the show's outrageousness reminded some critics of *The Flip Wilson Show,* which ran from 1970 to 1974).

Fox, which also produced *Living Single, Martin,* and *South Central,* was the first network to focus so much energy on attracting black audiences with shows featuring African American actors. Some critics, among them Frank Reid, charged that the Fox shows merely perpetuated the old, negative stereotypes, this time in the lingo of the HIP-HOP generation. (One Fox series, *Roc,* with a brilliant ensemble cast culled mostly from AUGUST WILSON's stage play *Fences,* escaped this criticism.) But with the increasing fragmentation of the television audience—caused in part by the growth of cable television—black viewers responded eagerly to the new black shows. Another venue for television geared exclusively to the African American community came of age in the early 1990s. BLACK ENTERTAINMENT TELEVISION (BET) capitalized on music videos, sports, and reruns of black-focused series to attract a nationwide audience.

Black programming was lucrative because it appealed not only to the black audience but also to whites, especially white youth, increasingly enamored of black culture. MICHAEL JORDAN and other basketball stars became some of corporate America's favorite spokespersons, and white teenagers took their fashion and language cues from rap musicians. The success of African Americans ARSENIO HALL and OPRAH WINFREY in late-night and daytime talk shows led to dozens of imitators, both black and white. In addition, Winfrey produced and acted in *The Women of Brewster Place,* a 1988 miniseries based on GLORIA NAYLOR's novel, and in 1998 produced the television adaptation of DOROTHY WEST's *The Wedding,* among other made-for-television projects. A cultural phenomenon and one of the richest people in America, Winfrey's naturalness, warmth, and pride in her African American culture have found favor with both blacks and whites.

By the late 1990s more African Americans than ever were involved in the television industry, some in executive and production roles. Taboos against interracial sex and other forms of social equality had eroded. But there were still no prime-time dramatic series devoted to telling the stories of black Americans, and many of the images seen by black children (who are estimated to watch television at a higher rate than the national average) continued to perpetuate limited stereotypes. In 1999 NAACP President KWEISI MFUME issued a highly publicized statement criticizing the television industry for excluding African Americans. The big four networks (NBC, CBS, ABC, and Fox) responded by pledging to employ more minority actors, directors, and writers. By 2002 racial minorities accounted for nearly one quarter of all theatrical and television roles, the highest level ever. Black actors comprised 15.5 percent of all

As co-anchor of NBC's popular *Today* show from 1981 to 1997, Bryant Gumbel became one of America's most recognizable black journalists. *Reuters/NewMedia Inc./CORBIS*

such roles. Kweisi Mfume praised the recent progress, but pointed out in 2003 that minorities were still underrepresented in positions behind the camera.

See also Desegregation in the United States; Film, Blacks in American; Jackson, Michael, and the Jackson Family; Racial Stereotypes; Radio and African Americans; Segregation in the United States.

Kate Tuttle

Temne

Ethnic group of Sierra Leone and Guinea; also known as Timne or Timmanee.

The Temne, who speak a Niger-Congo language, trace their origins to the FOUTA DJALLON (Futa Jallon) region of GUINEA. Some Temne remain in Guinea, but the majority migrated southward into what is now northern SIERRA LEONE, probably as a result of FULANI invasion into the Fouta Djallon in the fifteenth century. In Sierra Leone the Temne encountered Muslim traders, and as a result, many converted to Islam in the following centuries. Historically most Temne have been farmers, raising rice, cassava, and MILLET and growing peanuts, tobacco, and KOLA for sale.

Temne political structure is decentralized. Each village is overseen by a leader, who in turn reports to a higher-level leader of several villages. Historically such leaders were selected on the basis of their ancestry, but the British colonized Sierra Leone, and they instituted a system of electoral politics in the late 1700s. Alongside their administrative and judicial roles, the village leaders also belong to one of the brotherhood organizations, known as *poro*, which play an important part in Temne life. Poro are part religious order, part social and historical brotherhood. Poro members, all male, consider themselves guardians of traditional Temne values. A corresponding women's movement, known as *bundu*, serves similar functions in the lives of Temne girls and women.

See also Ethnicity and Identity in Africa: An Interpretation; Islam in Africa; Languages, African: An Overview.

Temple, Lewis

1800–1854

African American blacksmith, abolitionist, and inventor.

Lewis Temple was born in RICHMOND, VIRGINIA. Nothing is known about his parents or about any formal education he might have had. According to one biographer, he was unable to sign his name. Sometime during the 1820s, Temple migrated to the whaling town of New Bedford, Massachusetts, where he married Mary Clark, a native of Maryland, in 1829. Their first child, Lewis Jr., was born in 1830, followed by a daughter, Nancy, in 1832. Several years later, a third child, Mary, was born, but she died at the age of six.

What little is known about Temple suggests that he was a resourceful and principled individual. Whether he escaped Virginia as a slave or left as a freeman is uncertain, but in any case he had a better life in Massachusetts than the one he would have led in Richmond, apparently finding work in New Bedford soon after his arrival. Town records indicate that by 1836 Temple had established his own whalecraft shop on one of the wharfs that serviced ships. An active participant in local affairs, he paid the annual poll tax and was elected vice president of an antislavery organization, the New Bedford-Union Society, established in 1833. In 1847 the middle-aged Temple was arrested and charged with "rioting," after he and three other black men were accused of disrupting a pro-slavery lecture. New Bedford was, in fact, home to a large African American community. As a prominent resident of the town, he almost certainly aided a number of runaway slaves, including FREDER-ICK DOUGLASS.

In 1848 Temple invented the so-called Temple toggle, which historians of maritime technology have proclaimed as the most important innovation in whaling since the twelfth century. Whalers harvested their prey by first piercing the animal's body with a fluted (barbed) harpoon that was tied to a boat or floating drag. After a period of struggle, the hunters finished off the exhausted whale with a lance. Unfortunately for whalers, however, many whales dislodged traditional harpoons, which were forged from a single piece of iron. Temple's solution was a two-piece harpoon—once the Temple harpoon entered the whale, the animal's movements caused the fluted part to pivot on an axle by ninety degrees (i.e., "toggle"), thereby making its removal through the surface wound all but impossible. This simple idea dramatically increased the efficiency of whaling, and in a few years virtually all American harpoonists used the Temple toggle, continuing to do so into the 1950s.

Temple's role in the invention of the toggle harpoon was far more complex than this story suggests, however. European whale hunters had used similar harpoons centuries earlier, although they abandoned the device during the Middle Ages. The toggle subsequently survived in various forms among the Eskimos of Greenland. Curiously, European and American whalers knew of the Eskimo harpoons as early as 1654 but continued to use single-piece irons. Two centuries later many, if not most, of the half dozen or more blacksmiths in New Bedford probably had heard of the Greenland technology, but Temple took the initiative of translating that knowledge into American form. The Temple toggle also owes its origins to the unique ethnic diversity of the whaling industry. During the early nineteenth century American owners of whaling ships, largely because of the difficulty of recruiting local sailors, began signing on men who came from virtually every corner of the world. Although the proportion of African American sailors declined after 1830, it is nevertheless possible that Temple learned of Eskimo harpoons from an Eskimo seaman.

After inventing the toggle, Temple continued to live and work in New Bedford for six more years. Doubtless still active in an abolitionist movement energized by the Fugitive Slave Act of 1850, he also signed a temperance petition addressed to the town's mayor in 1853. Regrettably, he never attempted to patent his invention, although he lived long enough to witness the whaling industry begin to adopt it almost universally. Nevertheless, he began to achieve a measure of prosperity, partly because he obtained a maintenance contract with the city government. In 1854 he hired a contractor to build a large whale-craft shop.

Temple died under tragic circumstances. On an autumn evening in 1853 he tripped over a plank of wood that city workers had carelessly left behind at a sewer construction site. The injuries ruined him for physical labor and weakened his health. Although Temple petitioned the city for $2,000 in compensation, a favorable decision eluded him until ten days after his death, on May 18, 1854. Although the Common Council ordered the sum to be paid to his estate, for unknown reasons his heirs collected none of it.

Bibliography

Grover, Kathryn. *The Fugitive's Gibraltar: Escaping Slaves and Abolitionism in New Bedford, Massachusetts.* 2001.

Haber, Louis. *Black Pioneers of Science and Invention,* 1970.

Hayden, Robert C. *Eight Black American Inventors.* 1972.

James, Portia P. *The Real McCoy: African-American Invention and Innovation, 1619–1930.* 1989.

Kaplan, Sidney. "Louis Temple and the Hunting of the Whale," *Negro History Bulletin.* Oct. 1953.

Gary L. Frost

Temptations, The

An African American vocal group that enjoyed its greatest successes during the 1960s and 1970s with a repertoire encompassing romantic ballads and hard-edged soul music.

The Temptations was one of the most successful groups in the history of black music. Over the course of twenty-five years, the group had forty-three Top Ten singles and by the early 1980s had sold more than twenty million records. The vocal quintet, initially called the Elgins, was founded in DETROIT in 1961 by members of two local RHYTHM AND BLUES (R&B) groups: Eddie Kendricks and Paul Williams sang with the Primes; Melvin Franklin, Eldridge Bryant, and Otis Williams came from the Distants. In that year Berry Gordy signed them to his Detroit-based MOTOWN RECORDS and renamed them the Temptations. The group attained its classic lineup in 1963, when Bryant was replaced by David Ruffin. Many of the group's hits featured the contrasting leads of Ruffin's gritty baritone and Kendricks's crystalline high tenor and falsetto.

In conjunction with two gifted Motown producers—SMOKEY ROBINSON, 1962–1966, and Norman Whitfield, 1966–1975—the Temptations created memorable pop music. Robinson, a songwriter as well as a record producer, provided the group with several hits during 1965–1966. He cowrote the group's first number-one pop hit, "My Girl" (1965), an irresistible confection that set the Temptations' shimmering harmonies against a pungent electric-guitar line, with lush orchestral accompaniment that suggested classical music.

Whitfield continued the Temptations' success, encouraging performances of raw urgency that made it the only Motown group to match the harder SOUL MUSIC produced by STAX and Atlantic Records. The group also recorded "psychedelic soul music"—such as "Cloud Nine" (1968)—that reflected the influence of SLY AND THE FAMILY STONE. On occasion, the Temptations even performed protest music such as "Stop the War Now" (1970). The group's most significant hit with Whitfield was the soulful and funky "Papa Was a Rolling Stone" (1972), which won Motown its first Grammy Award.

By the mid-1970s, however, the Temptations had fallen from prominence. During 1976–1980, the group left Motown for an unsuccessful stint with Atlantic Records before returning to Berry Gordy's label. Personnel changes undermined the group's identity. Ruffin left in 1968; Kendricks and Paul Williams followed three years later. Although Otis Williams and Franklin continued with the group for more than thirty years, the Temptations became less a band and more a brand name.

By the late 1990s, all of the original, hit-making Temptations had died, except for Otis Williams. Paul Williams shot himself in 1973. Ruffin died of a 1991 drug overdose. In the following year Kendricks succumbed to lung cancer. Franklin died in 1995 of a heart attack. Following Franklin's death, Otis Williams told the *Chicago Tribune*, "I almost see us like a football franchise or a baseball franchise. People come and go, but [the group] still goes on."

In 1998 the Temptations line-up included Otis Williams, Ron Tyson, Harry McGillberry, Terry Weeks, and Barrington Henderson. This quintet sparked a renewed popularity with the album *Phoenix Rising* (1998), which went Platinum. They followed with *Ear Resistible* (2000), a Grammy winner, and *Awesome* (2001). In June 2003 the group fired Henderson and replaced him with G.C. Cameron. Henderson responded by suing the group for millions of dollars in royalties. Notwithstanding, the Temptations "franchise" is still going strong after more than four decades.

See also Music, African American.

James Sellman

Tennis

Game played by two or four players with rackets and ball on a court divided by a net; one of the most popular sports around the world, tennis has attracted black players since the 1920s.

For information on
Tennis players: *See* Ashe, Arthur Robert, Jr.; Gibson, Althea; Slowe, Lucy Diggs.
Olympic gold medal winner: *See* Olympics, African Americans and the.
Popularity of tennis among African Americans in the 1920s: *See* Sports and African Americans.

Ten Years' War

War waged from 1868 to 1878 to gain Cuba's independence from Spain; ended unsuccessfully.

In 1865, when efforts by a reform commission to the Spanish Cortes (National Parliament) concerning greater autonomy for CUBA and PUERTO RICO failed, the groundwork was laid for the first major war for Cuban independence in the nineteenth century. Then in 1867, without consulting the colonies, the Spanish Crown increased taxes on real estate, incomes, and all types of businesses. Coupled with an economic downturn, this furthered the already widespread discontent.

On October 10, 1868, Carlos Manuel de Céspedes, a wealthy landowner from Oriente province, freed his thirty slaves and issued a call for an uprising to overthrow Spanish colonialism, known as El Grito de Yara. Céspedes began fighting with a group of 147 men, but by the end of the month the insurrectionists had a force of 12,000. Ignacio Agramonte and his rebels took Puerto Príncipe. Soon Perucho Figueredo wrote the verses "La Bayamesa," later to become Cuba's national anthem. The Spanish had an army of 7,000 regular soldiers and 30,000 volunteers, a kind of civilian paramilitary force known for its brutality and anti-Cuban sentiments. By 1869 Spain had sent about 35,000 more troops as reinforcements.

The Cuban insurrectionists, despite popular support, soon faced two major political obstacles: the question of abolition and the disunity of forces fighting for independence. To obtain the backing of wealthy landowners in the western provinces (some of whom were living in New York), Céspedes, despite his freeing his own slaves, did not immediately put forth abolition as a demand. This, of course, cost the rebels popular support. Nonetheless, some of the revolutionary generals, like MÁXIMO GÓMEZ and ANTONIO MACEO Y GRAJALES, despite their overall loyalty to the government-in-arms, would on their own initiative free slaves in territory they captured from the Spanish. The crisis led to the Constitutional Convention of Guaimaro in April 1869. Article Twenty-Four of the document that emerged states, "All citizens of the Republic are completely free." Conservative elements of the movement, however, remained entrenched on this issue. The convention also favored U.S. annexation, but the United States continued to favor Spanish control over the island.

The tension between conservatives and radicals cost the revolution dearly. The radicals reasoned, for example, that if the war did not extend to all of Cuba, the landed elite in the western provinces would continue to back antirebel forces financially. The conservatives, themselves constituted in part by members of the elite, claimed that Maceo, an Afro-Cuban, favored blacks in his ranks and ultimately wanted to set up a black republic. The Spanish often used this argument to discredit and divide the revolutionary forces. Agramonte was killed in 1873; in the same year, Céspedes was thrown out as president of the rebel forces, and was killed the following year in an ambush by the Spanish. Gómez and Maceo eventually attempted an invasion of the western provinces. They waged a successful but costly campaign in Camagüey which would ultimately force them to turn back. The conservative factions kept the western provinces free from combat for the duration of the war.

More internal strife between conservatives and radicals in 1875 and 1876 weakened the rebel cause, as did the hope, ultimately dashed, that the United States would recognize the Cubans as a legitimate political force. Dissension within the ranks, along with Spanish counterattacks, further weakened rebel efforts. Spanish offers of amnesty followed, which encouraged defection and the laying down of arms. Ultimately, in February 1878, the war ended with the signing of the Pact of Zanjón. Some leaders, particularly Maceo, rejected the terms of the pact, since abolition and independence were both denied, and instead issued the Protest of Baraguā in March 1878. A year later, on August 26, 1879, Maceo, Calixto García Iñiguez, and others attempted to revive the insurrection with what became known as La Guerra Chiquita (the Little War), which lasted only a year. As with its predecessor, lack of unity and equipment, racism, indifference and even hostility to the cause of independence on the part of the landowners, and confusion among the popular classes brought defeat.

Despite its immediate outcome, however, the Ten Years' War marked an important chapter in Cuba's struggle for independence. It made crucial political inroads in the consciousness of the nation. Slavery would be abolished six years later. The costs of the war were huge: 208,000 Spanish and 50,000 Cuban dead, and an economic damage of $300 million.

See also Afro-Cubans, Revolts, and Wars for Independence; Anti-Slavery Movement in Latin America; Nationalism in Latin America and the Caribbean.

Alan West

Terrell, Mary Eliza Church

1863–1954

African American educator, prominent advocate for African American civil rights, women's rights, and nineteenth-century black women's club organizations.

Mary Eliza Church Terrell was born in MEMPHIS, TENNESSEE, to Louisa and Robert Church, who had emerged from slavery to become prosperous business owners. Although her parents separated, Robert Church financially supported her as she completed a classical education at Oberlin College. When she received her bachelor's degree in 1884, her father wanted her to assume the role of hostess, a refined position he felt appropriate for the daughter of the wealthiest black man in the South. She refused the conventional role, however, and entered the professional world of education instead.

Mary Church put her energy and training to work as a teacher at Ohio's black Wilberforce College in 1885. Two years later, she moved to the M Street High School in WASHINGTON D.C., where she met her future husband, ROBERT HEBERTON TERRELL. She completed a master's degree at Oberlin, followed, in 1888, by a two-year European tour. For an African American woman, this American rite of passage, usually reserved for the white elite, provided more than the opportunity to see diverse cultures; it was a chance for her to experience a different racial environment than that of the United States. Church also used the trip to develop the language skills she would later use in EUROPE to promote the cause of African American equality.

When Church returned to the United States in 1890, she married Terrell, retired from teaching, and focused on managing her household. That quiet life ended in 1892, when a life-

long friend, Tom Moss, was lynched in Memphis. Mary Church Terrell, along with her friend FREDERICK DOUGLASS, demanded a meeting with President Benjamin Harrison. Although they did receive a hearing, Harrison made no public statement opposing the violence. The event galvanized Terrell into activism, a vocation that lasted for over sixty years.

Terrell became an active participant in the BLACK WOMEN'S CLUB MOVEMENT, leading the Colored Women's League in 1892. When this group merged with several others to form the NATIONAL ASSOCIATION OF COLORED WOMEN (NACW) in 1896, she became the president. Under Terrell's leadership, the NACW organized around issues of health, housing, employment, and child care, as these matters specifically applied to the lives of African American women.

As a member of the National American Woman Suffrage Association, Terrell took the podium for the cause of women's voting rights, often speaking before all-white audiences. She was striking in her learning and political savvy: at the 1904 International Council of Women conference in Berlin, for instance, she delivered her speech in German, and then translated into French and English.

Terrell worked alongside many prominent African American activists of the era on issues of racial equity. She supported the work of BOOKER T. WASHINGTON, despite others' criticism of his vocational educational programs. In 1909, she joined W. E. B. DU BOIS as a founding member of the NATIONAL ASSOCIATION FOR THE ADVANCEMENT OF COLORED PEOPLE (NAACP).

An active supporter of the REPUBLICAN PARTY until 1952 and the wife of a federal judge, Terrell used her political clout in the upper echelons of American politics to fight for social justice for African Americans. Yet she often risked this position to speak what she saw to be the truth. In 1906, when three companies of black soldiers were dismissed from the U.S. Army without a hearing after a racial incident in Brownsville, Texas, Terrell publicly attacked President Theodore Roosevelt's decision. After her meeting with Secretary of War William Howard Taft, the soldiers were granted a hearing, although the dismissal ultimately remained in place.

During the two world wars, Terrell positioned herself as an advocate for the black women and girls who were entering the employment arena. Following World War II (1939–1945), she became even more militant in her activism, seeing the discrimination and economic hardship that continued in the nation after black soldiers had given their lives abroad.

Despite the privileges afforded her by her social status and fair skin, Terrell encountered the same discrimination faced by other African Americans. In her autobiography, *A Colored Woman in a White World* (1940), she wrote of the difficulty of being black and female: "A White woman has only one handicap to overcome—that of sex. I have two—both sex and race."

In 1950 Terrell entered a segregated Washington, D.C., restaurant with an interracial group. After the blacks were refused service, they filed affidavits against the restaurant. Three years of protest and legal battles ended in the protesters' favor, in *District of Columbia v. John Thompson*. At ninety years of age,

Terrell saw the desegregation of eating facilities in Washington, D.C.

See also Brownsville, Texas, Affair; Desegregation in the United States; Women's Organizations, Early African American.

Marian Aguiar

Terrell, Robert Herberton

1857–1925

African American municipal court judge.

Robert Herberton Terrell was born in Charlottesville, Virginia, on November 27, 1857, the son of Harris and Louisa Ann Terrell. He received his early education in the public schools of the District of Columbia and at Groton Academy in Groton, Massachusetts. He worked to help finance his college education at Harvard College, from which he graduated as one of seven magna cum laude scholars in June 1884. He later studied at HOWARD UNIVERSITY Law School, receiving an LL.B. (bachelor of laws) degree in 1889 and an LL.M. (master of laws) degree in 1893. Terrell taught for five years in the District of Columbia public schools from September 1, 1884, to August 30, 1889. He resigned to work as a chief clerk in the office of the auditor of the United States Treasury.

On October 28, 1891, Terrell married Mary Eliza Church of MEMPHIS, TENNESSEE, an Oberlin College graduate. From 1892 until 1898 he practiced law in WASHINGTON, D.C. He left his practice to become a teacher, and later, the principal of the M Street High School in Washington, D.C. In the 1890s he was elected to the Board of Trade.

Terrell's later career revealed the ambivalence of many other black leaders, including his wife, who were torn between their belief in civil rights and the conservative views of BOOKER T. WASHINGTON. Terrell owed to Washington his appointment as a justice of the peace in the District of Columbia in December 1901. Nevertheless, he criticized Washington for condoning U.S. president Theodore Roosevelt's summary discharge without honor of black soldiers of the Twenty-fifth Infantry after the BROWNSVILLE, TEXAS, AFFAIR in August 1906. This criticism led another Bookerite, Charles W. Anderson, to comment that "Judge Terrell had better take a stitch in his tongue." Regarding officeholders who, like Terrell and Anderson, owed their appointments to Washington, newspaper editor WILLIAM MONROE TROTTER charged: "The Colored people understand they are talking for pay and not for truth, and so pay little heed to their orations." Through Washington's influence, U.S. president William Howard Taft nominated Terrell for the position of judge of the Municipal Court of the District of Columbia on January 15, 1910. Taft signed the appointment, despite bitter protests on racial grounds in the Senate. Terrell continued to serve under Republican presidents throughout his career.

As early as 1896 Terrell regretted that blacks were generally unfamiliar with their own history. In 1903 he delivered an address, *A Glance at the Past and Present of the Negro,* in (Robert R.) Church's Auditorium before the Citizen's Industrial League of Memphis in Tennessee on September 22, 1903.

During his tenure as judge, Terrell also served on the faculty of the Howard University Law School from 1910 to 1925. He was for many years grand master of the Grand United Order of Odd Fellows of the District of Columbia. In February 1911 he was one of the charter members of Epsilon Boulé. In Washington he was a charter member of Sigma Pi Phi fraternity, which included some of the most distinguished blacks in the nation. The Robert H. Terrell Law School existed in the District of Columbia from August 12, 1931, to 1950, and an elementary school, at First and Pierce Streets NW, Washington, D.C., was named for him. He and his wife were among the most prominent members of Washington's black elite.

Terrell suffered a stroke about four years before his death. A year later, a second stroke left him paralyzed on one side. By early December 1925, asthma had aggravated his condition. He died at his home, 1615 S Street NW, on December 20, 1925. Funeral services were held in Metropolitan Baptist Church, and he was buried in Harmony Cemetery, Washington, D.C. He was survived by his wife; an adopted daughter Mary Terrell Tancil of CHICAGO, ILLINOIS; a natural daughter, Phyllis Terrell Goines (Langston) of Washington; a half-brother, William H. H. Terrell of Washington; and a half-sister, Laura Terrell Jones of Tuskegee, Alabama.

A good source of information is MARY CHURCH TERRELL's work *A Colored Woman in a White World* (1940). Information about the law school is available in the *Catalogue of the Robert H. Terrell Law School, 1949–1950* (vertical file, Moorland-Spingarn Research Center, Howard University). See the obituary, probably written by CARTER G. WOODSON, in THE JOURNAL OF NEGRO HISTORY (January 1926, pp. 223–225). For Terrell's obituary see the *Washington Tribune,* December 26, 1925, p. 1.

From *Dictionary of American Negro Biography* by Rayford W. Logan and Michael R. Winston, eds. Copyright © 1982 by Rayford W. Logan and Michael R. Winston. Reprinted by permission of W. W. Norton & Company, Inc.

Aubrey Robinson, Jr.

Tetela

Ethnic group of the Democratic Republic of the Congo.

The Tetela primarily inhabit east-central Congo-Kinshasa. They speak a Bantu language. Approximately 800,000 people consider themselves Tetela.

See also Bantu: Dispersion and Settlement; Congo, Democratic Republic of the; Ethnicity and Identity in Africa: An Interpretation; Languages, African: An Overview.

Tharaka

Ethnic group of Kenya.

The Tharaka primarily inhabit the highlands of central Kenya. They speak a Bantu language and are closely related to the Meru people. Over 100,000 people consider themselves Tharaka.

See also Bantu: Dispersion and Settlement; Ethnicity and Identity in Africa: An Interpretation; Languages, African: An Overview.

Tharpe, "Sister" Rosetta

1915–1973

Gospel singer who paved the way for gospel's golden age in the 1940s and 1950s.

Sister Rosetta Tharpe was born Rosetta Nubin to Katie (Bell) Nubin, a singing and mandolin-playing evangelist for the Church of God in Christ (COGIC), the leading Pentecostal denomination. Tharpe made her gospel debut at the age of five, singing "I Looked Down the Line and I Wondered," in front of an audience of 1,000 people. She became known as "Little Sister" as she traveled with her mother between 1923 and 1934, and she gained a reputation among Pentecostal Holiness people as a singer and guitar player. Tharpe's style was influenced by the sanctified blind pianist, Arizona Dranes, also a member of COGIC. Both Tharpe and Dranes traveled with the Reverend F. W. McGee on the tent-meeting revival circuit.

In 1938 Thorne made national headlines, including a feature in *Life* magazine, when she performed her sacred music with Cab Calloway at the Cotton Club in New York City. That same year Tharpe became the first gospel performer to sign with a major record label when Decca Records offered her a recording contract. Her subsequent recording of Thomas A. Dorsey's composition "Hide Me in Thy Bosom" under the title "Rock Me," became a hit. Also in 1938 Tharpe performed in John Hammond's legendary Carnegie Hall concert, "Spirituals to Swing."

By 1940, Tharpe had become very popular and toured America and Europe, performing in nightclubs, concert halls and jazz festivals. Her success in these secular spaces created a controversy among the Holiness Churches. In spite of the controversy, Tharpe teamed with Marie Knight and the two made the Billboard charts with their song "Up Above My Head." She and Knight later recorded and performed the blues. This action caused a rift between Tharpe and the Holiness people that never completely healed. Tharpe continued to perform in secular venues throughout the 1940s, 1950s and 1960s. She toured with secular performers such as Roy Acuff, Mary Lou Williams, and Lucky Millender, as well as with gospel groups like the James Cleveland Singers, the Golden Gate Quartet, and the Dixie Hummingbirds.

Tharpe generally sang solo while accompanying herself on the guitar. Her style of playing placed her in a category with bluesmen Big Bill Broonzy and Lonnie Johnson. She used the guitar to respond to her vocal melodies, playing single note lines that were improvised variations of the vocal melody. Her biggest hits came from her upbeat and syncopated renditions of songs like "I Looked Down the Line," "That's All," and "This Train."

By the late 1960s, Tharpe's popularity had waned but she continued to tour the country on the "chitlin circuit," playing in backwoods bars and small-town theaters. She suffered a stroke in 1973 and died in Philadelphia, Pennsylvania, one day before an anticipated recording session.

See also Gospel Music; Music, African American; Pentecostalism.

Bibliography

Heilbut, Tony. *The Gospel Sound: Good News and Bad Times.* Simon and Schuster, 1971.

Theater, African

Overview of theatrical traditions in Africa.

Africa is home to several traditions of theater. Some of these traditions are of ancient origin, while others emerged with formal European colonization of the continent in the nineteenth century and the subsequent imposition of Western education, religion, and culture.

The older traditions are mostly nonscripted, improvisatory, and performed in indigenous African languages. Their conceptions of theater space and stage-audience relations are fluid and informal: any space can be turned into a performance stage, while the audience is free to interact with the performance in a variety of ways and even move in and out of the theater space during performance. This type of performance is often public and the audience does not pay a fee, although performers could be rewarded in cash or kind for their artistry.

Many of the newer theater traditions are text-based, written in European languages or indigenous African languages with Latin script. The plays are designed to be performed in more or less formal theater buildings with fixed relations between performers and audience. The audience usually pays a fee, although the theater may not be expressly commercial.

In all cases, as indeed in all societies, the functions of the theater traditions are broadly similar in their mixing of the pleasing and the pedagogical: their representations provide the audience with pleasurable entertainment while simultaneously channeling passions and sentiments in certain directions.

Theater in Africa could be categorized into four distinct traditions: festival theater, popular theater, development theater, and art theater.

Festival Theater

In many African communities, the foremost indigenous cultural and artistic institution is the festival. These might be organized around certain deities or spirits, to celebrate rites of passage, or to mark the passage of seasons. Festivals incorporate diverse forms, such as singing, chanting, drama, drumming, masking, miming, costuming, and puppetry. The accompanying theatrical enactments—from the sacred and secretive to the secular and public—can last from a few hours to several days, weeks, or months. Each festival dramatizes a story or myth (or sometimes related sets of stories or myths) connecting the particular subject of the festival, for example a deity or a season, to the life of the community. Artistically, the performances also serve to showcase the community's new artistic forms as well as changes in existing ones.

Festival theater is performed in an open space in the town square or a similarly appointed location. The audience members sit or stand in layers of circles around the performers, and are able to drift in and out of the performance. They close in or fan out depending on perceptions of the volume of space needed by the performers at particular moments of the action. There is a close relationship between the performers and the audience, with the latter sometimes even serving as chorus, but there are also distinctions, and it is treasured cultural knowledge to know when to and when not to interject in the performance. Aesthetically, the performance may take a full range of styles, from realism to surrealism and spirit possession. This is partly why an empty space, with little prop or theatrical pretensions, is all that is needed for the communion between performer and audience on one hand, and the performance and society on the other.

There are two ways in which scholars have tried to understand African festivals. Some scholars label the festival as "pre-drama" or "traditional ritual" or "ritual drama," because of its expansive multimedia format, its firm integration of the dramatic amid the other arts, and the presence of both religious and secular reenactments. The assumption of these scholars, whether acknowledged or not, is that contemporary Western theater, with its packaged three hours, strict compartmentalization of the arts, and the virtual absence of the sacred, constitutes the norm of "theater."

Other scholars have argued that the festival is in fact the fully-fledged theater and that contemporary Western theater could in fact be seen as nothing more than severely abbreviated festival. The argument of WOLE SOYINKA, Africa's leading dramatist and winner of the Nobel Prize in Literature, best exemplifies this view. He insists that festivals be seen as constituting "in themselves pure theater at its most prodigal and resourceful . . . the most stirring expressions of man's instinct and need for drama at its most comprehensive and community-involving." In one sweeping move, he turns a colonialist interpretation of the festival on its head: "instead of considering festivals from one point of view only—that of providing, in a primitive form, the ingredients of drama—we may even begin examining the opposite point of view: that contemporary drama, as we experience it today, is a contraction of drama, necessitated by the productive order of society in other directions."

Popular Theater

Theater forms that have large followings at the point of reception—popular theater—cut across class or status boundaries. Early forms have their roots in sacred ceremonies and involve elaborate masking, such as the Alarinjo and Apidan theaters of NIGERIA.

Today, the recurring themes in African popular theater are those with broad appeal, and are intimately linked with genre. Particularly common in comedies and melodramas are themes such as unrequited love; marital infidelity; unemployment; pretensions to wealth, status, or sophistication; the conundrums of modern city life; dreams of travel abroad, and so on. Satires have targeted egotistical chiefs, the rich but miserly, the strange manners of Europeans (explorers, missionaries, or colonial administrators and their spouses), corrupt politicians, overly Westernized African men and women, prostitutes, the rural village teacher, and so on. Matters of fate and predestination, and the mythological lives of deities, legends, and powerful historical figures have been explored in tragedies and other serious dramas.

One reason for such wide appeal of popular theater is that it is most often performed in the indigenous language, or hybrids of them designed to be understood across linguistic borders. Increasingly, many subtraditions are being produced in forms of the European languages that came with colonization, or in "pidgin"—a distinctive mixture of one such foreign language and an indigenous language.

Early forms, and even more recent forms such as the Ghanaian Concert Party, have traditionally been composed only of male performers. Generally, more recent forms such as the YORUBA Popular Travelling Theater, the Chikwakwa Theater of Zambia, and the South African Township Theater, are comprised of both male and female performers. The performers are in most cases organized as traveling troupes, performing in a variety of available spaces: open squares, enclosed courtyards of kings and chiefs, school classrooms, concert or cinema halls, bars or nightclubs, and well-equipped theaters. Most popular theater forms are not scripted but based on improvisations, giving the performers much leeway but also demanding an unusual dexterity in speech, movement, and gesture.

Development Theater

In certain radical or leftist traditions of African theater scholarship, development theater is also known as popular theater, but the conception of the "popular" in this case is vastly different from that mentioned above. While in popular theater the "popular" is marked at the point of consumption or reception, in development theater, the "popular" is read at the point of production. In other words, "popular" here means produced by an alliance of intellectuals, workers, and peasants and expressly constructed to advance the interests of the oppressed classes in society. This conception of the popular is inspired by the radical Marxist German dramatist Bertolt Brecht.

This form of theater is geared to raising the consciousness of the exploited classes so they can struggle for their liberation. To liberate themselves, in the Marxist understanding, is also to liberate the productive forces of the society from private appropriation and so ensure genuine development. It is in this sense that this tradition of theater is called "development theater." In addition to Brecht, other significant conceptual supports for development theater come from Augusto Boal and PAULO FREIRE.

However, not all forms of development theater are obviously or tendentiously ideologically charged. Many are designed as adult education programs to teach literacy or explain the political process so people can better know their rights and responsibilities. Others communicate better agricultural techniques, teach ways of treating or preventing certain diseases, or encourage community mobilization for self-help projects and general rural development. Workshops are held regularly to teach the people how to organize themselves to use the theater both as an expression of culture and as a tool for fostering social, political, and economic development.

Development theater practitioners are mostly professional intellectuals, often affiliated with a university, working with a variety of groups in mostly rural areas—areas that are in much of Africa the least recipients of the benefits of "modernity" and therefore the target of development schemes.

Given the direct, instrumentalist goal of the theater, the performances are often didactic and exhortatory, though the more skilled adult educators go to great lengths to emphasize aesthetics and even incorporate popular forms from the people's indigenous performance traditions. A minor form of development theater practice is the "guerrilla theater," in which committed groups emerge unannounced at carefully chosen public locations and stage provocative performances, usually against particular government policies, and disappear before the agents of law and order appear.

An important example of development theater practice includes the Laedza Batanani of BOTSWANA in the mid-1970s, which subsequently served as a model and inspiration for similar experiments in LESOTHO, ZAMBIA, MALAWI, SIERRA LEONE, and Nigeria. Perhaps the most oppositional of the experiments was the Kamiriithu Education and Cultural Center, led by NGUGI WA THIONG'O, the leading Kenyan writer. The center was so successful in mobilizing the community to explore their history and culture and contemporary situation critically through theater that Ngugi was imprisoned for a year without trial in 1977. By 1982 the Kenyan government had razed the center and banned all theater activities in the area.

African Theater in the Outside World

Art theater is the tradition of African theater most familiar to the outside world through the published works of the continent's notable playwrights such as Wole Soyinka, ATHOL FUGARD, Femi Osofisan, AMA ATA AIDOO, Zulu Sofola, Efua Sutherland, Ola Rotimi, J. P. Clark-Bekederemo, SONY LABOU TANSI,

Guillaume Oyono-Mbia, Werewere Liking, and Tess Onwueme, among others. Art theater in Africa is of colonial origin; it emerged with the training of Africans in European languages and literatures and dramatic traditions, and it is most often written in the colonial languages. The label "art theater" signifies the tradition's relationship to, and investment in, notions of "high art" or "great works" characteristic of Western bourgeois cultural discourse since the nineteenth century.

The practitioners of art theater are usually professional intellectuals affiliated with universities or other institutions of higher education. Although the best dramas of this tradition borrow richly from indigenous performance forms, the overall "mold" of drama into which those borrowings are poured into, as well as the languages in which they are written and performed, are European and greatly circumscribe their popularity with the majority of Africans who are not schooled in those aesthetics or languages. The Nigerian dramatist J. P. Clark-Bekederemo, comparing the Yoruba Popular Travelling Theater with the art theater, once observed that "[s]ome would say that the latter has its head deep in the wings of American and European theater!" It was for this reason that Ngugi wa Thiong'o, after a distinguished career of several novels and plays in English, switched to producing plays in his KIKUYU language.

Some have questioned whether art theater could really be original and authentically African as long as it borrows aesthetic structures from and speaks the language of EUROPE. Such a charge and its purist conceptions of transcultural relations have never been much handicap for the truly creative minds of African art theater. They continue to confront the colonial inheritance and revise it from a variety of perspectives, without any surrender of initiative. For them, the centuries of African unequal contact with Europe are undeniable, and cultural purism, absolutism, or insularity are not necessarily worthy coordinates of "originality." The Mexican writer Octavio Paz speaks for the writers of the ex-colonial world when he argues that the literatures they write "did not passively accept the changing fortunes of their transplanted languages: they participated in the process and even accelerated it. Soon they ceased to be mere transatlantic reflections. At times they have been the negation of the literatures of Europe; more often, they have been a reply."

The hub of art theater activity in Africa is mostly the urban areas—cities and universities. This is also where most of the audience, those schooled in Western languages, is located. Performance takes place in formal theater buildings, frequently with the proscenium stage, which is hegemonic in Europe and America. Art theater is primarily state-subsidized and rarely self-sustaining as a commercial enterprise. Indeed, art theater is consumed more as dramatic literature—read widely in schools and colleges—than as theater.

Many practitioners of art theater have attempted to ameliorate the obvious elitism of the tradition by establishing community theaters or traveling theaters run by university resident professionals or drama students. These projects designed to take the art theater to the masses of the people are often very expensive and have existed only intermittently. Some of the famous examples are the University of Ibadan traveling theater (Nigeria, in the 1960s), the Makerere Free Travelling Theater (Uganda, 1960s and 1970s), the University of Malawi Travelling Theater (1970s), and the University of Zambia Chikwakwa Theater (1970s and 1980s). There is the particularly unique case of the South African Athol Fugard, who broke for some time from his normal routine of formal playwriting in the 1970s to collaborate with the actors Winston Ntshona and John Kani. Their improvisations led to many well-received plays against the apartheid state and inaugurated a genre of popular theater labeled South African protest theater. The most performed of such plays is *Sizwe Bansi Is Dead* (1973). These efforts, in less formal surroundings, make art theater performances—sometimes of plays in translations or in pidgin, or of text-based improvisations—available to audiences that would otherwise not have access to them.

See also Development in Africa: An Interpretation; Forestry, Participation, and Representation in Africa: An Interpretation; Music, African; Religions, African; Rites of Passage and Transition.

Tejumola Olaniyan

Theater in the Caribbean

The history of theater in the Spanish-, French-, and English-speaking Caribbean, particularly as it pertains to people of African descent.

Contemporary theater in the Caribbean has been shaped by the different cultures—NATIVE AMERICAN, European, African, East Indian, Madeiran, and Chinese—that have brought forms of performance from around the world to the Caribbean basin. Throughout the nineteenth and twentieth centuries in the Caribbean, the elements of stage and street performance, including written plays, storytelling, festivals, music, and dance, combined to create new types of theater. During colonial times stage performance was often sponsored by the wealthy and evolved separately from African culture. More recently, however, performers and directors have begun to explore the African roots of a Caribbean theater through the incorporation of Afro-Caribbean religious practices and social rituals (such as dance, storytelling, and singing) which date to the period of slavery or before their arrival.

Early Influences

Performance was a critical part of the early colonial history of the islands, mediating the contacts between natives and European missionaries. The native Carib and Arawak peoples of the ANTILLES enacted *areítos* which, according to scholar Sandra Cypess, were "complex theatre-dance forms that incorporated music with full-dress costume to recount the historical, religious, and cultural repertoire of the society." When missionaries arrived, they appropriated the *areítos* dramatic form to teach the tenets of CHRISTIANITY.

Later, European colonizers, as well as elite mulattos (people of African and European descent) in the French and Spanish territories such as the present-day CUBA, PUERTO RICO, DOMINICAN REPUBLIC, and HAITI, enjoyed imported theatrical performances on stage. From the seventeenth century onward and during the course of the TRANSATLANTIC SLAVE TRADE, landholders and the small commercial elite watched professional companies from EUROPE, and later North America, perform plays written abroad. The audience of mostly white CREOLE (offspring of Europeans born in the Americas) plantation owners and wealthy merchants attended performances in newly built playhouses and public halls. By 1800, strolling players from North America were entertaining those who could not afford the expensive theater tickets.

On the plantations, slaves kept alive African performance traditions, developing these into new forms that were both modes of resistance and expressions of celebration. Gifted storytellers integrated tale and performance, often incorporating music and dance. ASANTI slaves from the African GOLD COAST (now GHANA) brought one narrative tradition, the ANANCY STORY, that developed as a form throughout the Afro-Caribbean. Originally centered on the trickster character of a spider who was a master of wit and cunning, the Anancy (Anansi) stories evolved to include African beast fables and sometimes even European fairy tales, but maintained the element of song. Frequently these stories centered on survival strategies to maintain the spirit in the face of slavery. Festivals such as the Christmas celebration *jonkonnu* in JAMAICA incorporated the sounds of drums, horns, flutes, rattles, and fiddles—instruments that later made their way into the music of contemporary Caribbean theater. Some of these festivals also brought elements of closed stage to the streets: often a performer reproduced stage drama scenes and costumes for audiences outside the theater.

Starting in the mid-nineteenth century, another group added their dramatic traditions to the mix. Indentured laborers came from India, bringing their own festivals to the islands of Trinidad, GUYANA, SURINAME, and Jamaica. The Caribbean transformed these performances: for example, the Muslim celebration of *Muharram,* a reenactment of a mythical story staged the first month of the Muslim year, came to incorporate influences from Hindus and Afro-Caribbean participants as well.

Over the years, Afro-Caribbean performance grew from an art form barely tolerated by plantation owners, to an underground movement after abolition, and finally to an expression of national culture in the twentieth century. Yet even as traditions of storytelling, music, dance, and festival maintained their presence in their homes and on the streets, Afro-Caribbeans themselves also sought to enter the world of stage theater. It was not until well into the twentieth century, however, that plays by Afro-Caribbeans began to be produced in considerable numbers. The same was true in BRAZIL, where the Teatro Experimental do Negro (Black Experimental Theater) brought Afro-Brazilian plays to the stage beginning in 1944. When blacks finally made their way onto the stage, they transformed the Caribbean theater world by incorporating their performance traditions and by emphasizing community building through theater.

Theater in the Hispanic Caribbean

In 1588, the first white *criollo* (American born of Spanish descent) playwright, Cristóbal de Llerena de Rueda from HISPANIOLA (now the Dominican Republic), began the Caribbean theatrical traditions of parody and social commentary that would continue to characterize Spanish-speaking Caribbean theater well into the twentieth century. Although it was some time before Afro-Caribbeans themselves made it into the exclusive ranks of art theater, their presence was felt on the stage long before that. In PUERTO RICO, Alejandro Tapia y Rivera, for example, wrote plays such as "La cuarterona" (*The Quadroon,* 1867), that underscored the racially mixed milieu of the colony. Sometimes the awareness of an African presence took the form of anxious ridicule: Francisco Covarrubias, considered the "father of Cuban national theater," used the trope of 'el negrito,' or blackface. This *teatro bufo,* as it came to be known, became increasingly popular in mid-to-late nineteenth century Cuba, demonstrating the centrality of the African presence in Cuba. Performed by white actors who parodied the looks and manners of blacks, *el negrito* revealed more about the racism of white society than it presented an accurate portrayal of Afro-Cubans. As scholar Jill Lane points out, *teatro bufo* used stereotypical portrayals of Africans to define a distinct white *criollo* identity: "blackface performance catered to the anxieties of a white social class deeply concerned with their own racial definition in an unstable matrix of race, class, and power." In other words, in a racial milieu that was increasingly mixed, the Caribbean-born whites forged their own identity in uneasy opposition to the Afro-Caribbeans.

By the 1930s theater in Puerto Rico became an important vehicle to represent and define national identity. In 1938, playwright and director Emilio Belaval developed the short-lived national theater in SAN JUAN, producing plays with national themes such as the need for social reform. The theater used drama to advocate the cause of the *jíbaro* (peasant), a figure that was increasingly becoming a rallying point for national identity. Belaval's theater also explored such politicized issues as the immigrant experience in the United States. Between 1944 and 1956—the politically tense period prior to and following the adoption of commonwealth status in 1952—the presentation of Puerto Rican plays at the University of Puerto Rico was banned, possibly because of the genre's potential for political commentary. After 1956, Puerto Rican theater found its renewal under the direction of Francisco Arriví, Manuel Méndez Ballester, and René Marqués. They dominated the theater scene, producing plays that explored a range of social, political, philosophical and psychological quandaries. These directors were responding to the political and economic situation after the U.S.-sponsored plan for accelerated development known as Operation Bootstrap. Like many Puerto Rican writers and intellectuals of the time, they reacted to U.S. imperialism by de-

fending the Hispanic culture: Marqués' *La carreta* (1952; The Ox-Cart), for example, underscored the economic difficulties faced by Puerto Ricans in the island and focused on the need to preserve Hispanic culture. As a result, within nationalist narratives of Puerto Rico, the history of Hispanic culture was frequently emphasized over that of Africans.

Early-twentieth-century theater in Cuba, particularly Luis A. Baralt's *Teatro la Cueva* (Cave Theatre, 1928), drew on avant-garde movements of Latin American and European theater more closely than other places. Since the 1959 Cuban revolution theater has enjoyed a privileged position in the island. Seeing theater as a critical tool of education to reach working classes, the Cuban leader FIDEL CASTRO encouraged the movement of the theater into public spaces, and the development of community-based theater. This was the theater of collective creation, according to scholar Martin Banham: Community based, this movement adopts the method of research into problems of a given geographic area in which the theater is located with attempts to solve these problems in a dramatic presentation with community involvement. For example, *Grupo Teatro Escambray,* founded in 1968, used regional interviews to create local performances incorporating the concerns of a particular community. Cuban theater has explored Cuba's vibrant African traditions. For example, Eugenio Hernāndez Espinosa, with his plays *María Antonia* (1976), *Oba y Shangó* (1980; King and Shangó) and *Odebí el cazador* (1980; Obedí the Hunter), has focused on issues of ethnic marginality and African mythic traditions. However, given the administration's official position that class conflict is the main factor underlying racial tensions, plays that emphasize class issues have frequently been supported over those that accentuate the African racial and cultural heritage of Cuba.

Theater in Haiti and
the Francophone Caribbean

Early Haitian theater can be divided into two linguistic groups: French-speaking and Creole-speaking. The first type was the most popular within elite classes, even after the HAITIAN REVOLUTION (1791–1804). Early Francophone stage theater in Haiti was mostly confined to imported performances, or theater focused on the themes dominant in FRANCE. The second theatrical form developed around Creole, the everyday language of most Haitians. The *Indigéniste* (Autochthonous) Movement was an early Haitian movement that asserted folk culture in response to the 1915–1934 United States occupation. It has only been recently, however, as Creole gains official recognition within Haiti, that art theater has expanded to include Creole performances.

In French-speaking MARTINIQUE and GUADELOUPE, theater underwent a transformation during the 1930s, shifting from themes that emphasized French cultural heritage to a celebration of African identity. The NÉGRITUDE movement that shaped Francophone theater in the twentieth century was initiated by AIMÉ CÉSAIRE from Martinique, LÉON-GONTRAN DAMAS from

FRENCH GUIANA, and Léopold Senghor from Senegal. According to scholar Juris Silenieks, the 1960–1975 period of the Négritude movement and its followers "feature a spirit of confrontational combativeness and a commitment to intervene in the burning sociopolitical issues of the day." Those issues were most often colonization and African identity. Three of Césaire's plays from that period, *La Tragédie du Roi Christophe* (1963; *The Tragedy of King Christophe*), *Une saison au Congo* (1966; *A Season in Congo*) and *Une tempête* (1969; *A Tempest,* an adaptation of Shakespeare's *The Tempest*), focus on the impact of colonialism and the need for a decolonization that is cultural as well as political. In both historical and contemporary plays, Césaire integrated African, Caribbean, and French themes to engage with the black liberation movements of the 1960s.

Despite their Afrocentric outlooks, for the most part Négritude playwrights chose French as their mode of expression over the Creole spoken by many of African descent. They also looked more toward a pure African identity rather than the hybrid culture of the Caribbean. Haitians Félix Morisseau-Leroy and Gérard Chenet, despite their dissimilar politics and styles, continued to turn to Africa as a source of inspiration for their work.

As interest in Afro-Caribbean identity widened, more writers became interested in theatrical works incorporating Creole language. As early as 1954, Morriseau-Leroy had published the play *Antigone en creole,* in part as a response to elite notions that French was the only language for intellectual works in Haitian theater. EDOUARD GLISSANT, a student of Césaire, began using Creole words and phrases as well as syntax in his work. More recent playwrights, such as Martiniquan writers Ina Césaire and PATRICK CHAMOISEAU, have integrated Creole as well as other elements of oral culture and folklore into their theatrical works.

Many contemporary playwrights have concerned themselves with exploring the many cultural, as well as linguistic, influences in the French-speaking Caribbean. MARYSE CONDÉ's plays *Dieu nous l'a donné* (1972; *God Gave it to Us*) and *Mort d'Oluwémi d'Ajumako* (1973; *The Death of Oluwémi of Ajumako*), examined the impact of new values upon tradition communities in the Caribbean. Franck Fouché integrated elements from Catholic and VODOU rituals to produce *Général Baron-la-Croix ou le silence masqué* (1971; *General Baron of the Cross or Masked Silence*), a play performed in Creole.

Theater in the Anglophone Caribbean

The 1930s were a turning point in Anglophone Caribbean theater, as cultural leaders, spurred by the Négritude movement, turned to DRAMA with the end goal of validating African identity and retelling Caribbean history. This was accompanied by a movement to take art theater outside the confines of the stage, begun as early as 1869, when Henry G. Murray toured Jamaica with oral performances representing Jamaican society. In 1931, Guyanese writer Norman Cameron, for example, wrote plays based on African history and performed them in Guyanese schools. By integrating political drama with the vibrant cultural forms of storytelling and festival, producers and playwrights

sought to promote political causes such as decolonization and nationalism. In Jamaica, the Pan-Africanist MARCUS GARVEY created a "theater for the masses" in 1930 on an open air stage in KINGSTON. Along with three of his own productions, the stage hosted the popular comedy work of Ranny Williams. In 1939, as labor unrest increased in Jamaica, Frank Hill produced *Upheaval,* using the stage to promote social revolution.

In London, Trinidadian C. L. R. JAMES brought the experience and aftermath of the Haitian revolution to the world with his production of *Toussaint L'Overture* (1936). The play was groundbreaking, not only because it represented the little-known history of the Haitian Revolution, but also because it turned the attention of the Caribbean theater as a whole toward the relatively unexplored subject of Caribbean history. Others, such as Una Marson, considered by some to be the most successful playwright in 1930s Jamaica, explored the social milieu of the Caribbean with plays such as *Pocomania* (1938).

The expansion of national theater in the Anglophone Caribbean during the 1930s was followed by an increased interest in both folk tradition and the production of local plays. The opening of the University of the West Indies in 1947 was a critical factor in the increase in writing and publication of plays by Anglophone West Indians. The production of local plays expanded exponentially during the 1950s: writers included Cicely Waite-Smith, Barry Reckord, Samuel Hillary in Jamaica; Douglas Archibald, Errol Hill, and Errol John in Trinidad; DEREK WALCOTT and twin brother Roddy Walcott in SAINT LUCIA; Frank Pilgrim and Sheik Sadeek in Guyana. The most internationally successful of this group was NOBEL PRIZE winner Derek Walcott, whose early plays such as *Dream on Monkey Mountain* (1967) and *Pantomime* (1980) merged the language of poetry with a condemnation of colonialism and racism. Walcott also founded the Trinidad Theatre Workshop in 1959, a group that was instrumental in bringing to the stage *patois*—a dialect mixing European and African languages that was, for many, the everyday language in this part of the Caribbean.

Also during the 1950s LOUISE BENNETT of Jamaica was fundamental in the development of a style that came to be known as "speech theater." Integrating storytelling techniques with stage theater, she helped validate traditional Afro-Caribbean cultural forms such as the already mentioned Anancy story. Later dramatists such as Paul Keens-Douglas were influenced by her groundbreaking work.

Bennett combined drama with social organizing by working with villages to help identify their needs and solve them. This kind of work was taken up by the Sistren Collective, founded in 1977. Led by director Honor Ford-Smith, the theater's first major production was "Bellywoman Bangarang" in 1978, which used experiences drawn from working-class women's lives, as well as games, songs, and dances. Sistren Collective has been instrumental in recuperating the history of women's contribution to Afro-Caribbean struggles: the play Nana Yah was about the seventeenth-century slave maroon leader Nanny. The Sistren Collective, which published *Lionheart Gal: Life Stories* of *Jamaican Women* in 1986, has been an important role model in a Caribbean theater world that remains dominated by male playwrights. It continues to promote grassroots cultural expression, social change, and awareness of gender issues in Jamaica.

See also Afro-Brazilian Culture; Afro-Latin American and Afro-Carribean Identity: An Interpretation; Afro-Latino Cultures in the United States; Catholic Church in Latin America and the Caribbean; Colonial Latin America and the Caribbean; East Indian Communities in the Caribbean; Latin America and the Caribbean, Blacks in; Theater, African; Trinidad and Tobago.

Marian Aguiar

Thebes, Egypt

Capital city and ceremonial center of the ancient Egyptian empire.

The ancient city of Thebes was situated on both sides of the Nile in upper Egypt. It comprised a residential town on the eastern bank, whose ruins extend into present-day Luxor and Karnak, and a more famous western side, which contained the pharaonic cemetery and the Valley of the Kings. It is in this location that the graves of the New Kingdom pharaohs lie (also called the Theban necropolis and the "city of the dead").

The history of the city of Thebes can be traced back approximately 4,500 years, to the twenty-fifth century B.C.E. The city began as an obscure village called *Waset,* named after *Wast,* the village's local goddess. During a period of political instability in Egypt referred to as the first intermediate period (2134–2040 B.C.E.), however, powerful Theban *nomarchs* (governors) emerged, and the city grew in importance with them. Eventually, these nomarchs successfully challenged the Heracleopolitan pharaohs of the north. Mentuhotep II of Thebes, who reigned 2008–1957 B.C.E., reunited Egypt. He established Thebes as his capital as well as the center of worship of the national god, Amon, which was brought to the city at that time. Though during the Twelfth Dynasty (1991–1783 B.C.E.) the descendants of Mentuhotep moved their capital to Memphis to the north, they continued to bestow riches on the temples and tombs of the city of Amon.

Hyksos invaders took control of Egypt during the second intermediate period (1640–1550 B.C.E.). However, powerful ruling families from Thebes succeeded in driving the Hyksos out of Egypt in about 1540 B.C.E. They reunited the kingdom and made Thebes the center of Egyptian political and religious life. As Egypt expanded to encompass an empire that spanned from Syria to Nubia, vast wealth from every corner of the empire funneled into Thebes. During the early fourteenth century B.C.E. Thebes reached the height of its power and prosperity.

After a brief eclipse when Akhenaton, who ruled from 1353–1335 B.C.E., moved the capital to Memphis, Thebes enjoyed renewed prosperity. Pharaohs such as Ramses II, who ruled from 1290–1224 B.C.E. resided in Thebes only for part of each year but generously funded the maintenance and expansion of the temple complex. From the twelfth century B.C.E. onward, however, Thebes began a slow and irreversible decline. The Assyrians sacked the city in 663 B.C.E., and the Romans destroyed it in the first century B.C.E.

Under Roman rule, a provincial center rose among the southernmost ruins of Thebes. This town, the forerunner of modern Luxor, was home to a substantial community of Coptic Christians, who built churches among the ruins. Today, many of Luxor's inhabitants are Christian.

Modern visitors can explore the town of Karnak, located among the northern ruins of Thebes. Situated in Karnak are the ruins of the precinct of Amon, a complex of buildings commissioned by a succession of pharaohs. In addition, Karnak features ruins of the precinct of Amon's wife Mut, the war god Montu, and an avenue of sphinxes. In Luxor to the south, one can visit the ruins of the old and new winter palaces, and the Luxor temple.

Robert Fay

Theiler, Max

1899–1972

South African virologist and Nobel Prize winner who made major contributions to research on the viral disease known as yellow fever.

During the 1930s Max Theiler developed vaccines that protected millions of people from the incurable tropical affliction known as yellow fever. For his contributions, he was awarded the 1951 Nobel Prize in physiology or medicine.

Born in Pretoria, Theiler studied medicine at the University of Cape Town, leaving for England in 1919 for Saint Thomas's Hospital Medical School, London, where he completed his medical training in 1922. That year, he moved to the United States, joining the Department of Tropical Medicine at the Harvard Medical School. In 1930 he accepted a post with the Rockefeller Foundation in New York City. He remained with the foundation until 1964, when he became professor of epidemiology at Yale University, New Haven, Connecticut.

At Harvard, Theiler's early research interest was in amoebic dysentery, but he soon switched his efforts to yellow fever. An important finding during the 1920s was that monkeys could be infected with the virus and then used for experimentation. Theiler, in a major advance, demonstrated that mice could serve as a much more convenient and inexpensive experimental model.

Using mice, he developed highly efficient methods for breeding the yellow fever virus as he pursued various strategies for vaccines. In 1934 Theiler developed a vaccine based on an "attenuated," or weakened, form of the virus cultivated in mice. Scratched into the skin, the virus would not cause yellow fever, but would provoke the body's immune system to protect against any subsequent infections. Because this vaccine sometimes caused encephalitis, an inflammation of the brain, Theiler continued to refine his vaccine experiments. In 1937 he introduced another vaccine, designated 17D, based on another strain of the virus that was grown in chicken embryos. Between 1940 and 1947 the 17D vaccine was used to protect more than twenty-eight million people in AFRICA and the Americas. Today, although still a problem in remote areas, yellow fever has been vastly reduced as a health threat.

In addition to his Nobel Prize, Theiler received the Albert Lasher Award in 1945. Theiler remained in the United States for the rest of his life; however, he never became a U.S. citizen.

See also Disease and African History; Diseases, Infectious, in Africa; South Africa.

Barbara Worley

Thierry, Camille

1814–1875

African American poet.

Camille Thierry was born in NEW ORLEANS, LOUISIANA, the son of a Frenchman from Bordeaux and his mistress, an octoroon. Little more is known about Thierry's birth and parentage. Although an American, Thierry spent most of his life in FRANCE, which he considered more enlightened and cultured than his native land; he also believed he could escape prejudice against his African American heritage in Europe.

Thierry was well educated; he was initially tutored at home but later went to day school as an adolescent. However, as he prepared to sail to attend college in Paris, his father died, and Thierry was left with a healthy patrimony. Subsequently Thierry scrapped his plans for college and went into business in New Orleans. Although he accumulated a small fortune, was considered one of the wealthiest African Americans in antebellum Louisiana, and was a member of the New Orleans Freedmen's Aid Association, he soon discovered that he was not cut out for the uninspiring daily grind of the financial world. Thierry then spent several months ferrying between the United States and France, until 1855, when he decided to make France his permanent home, and he left his substantial holdings in America in the care of the agents Lafitte, Dufilho & Company. Although he spent several months frequenting salons and literary events and writing poetry in vibrant Paris, Thierry soon tired of the socialite's life and retreated to Bordeaux, where he lived quietly and in solitude. No longer burdened by financial cares or drudgery, Thierry was free to give himself entirely to his aesthetic interests.

Thierry became especially interested in poetry as a young man and began to write large amounts of verse in French. In 1843 his poem "Idees" was published in *L'Album Littéraire* of New Orleans. Thierry was one of the earliest and most prolific African American poets of Louisiana; his style was described by Rodolphe Desdunes as "elegant and graceful, with a natural mode of expression and a felicitous use of symbols." In 1845

Armand Lanusse selected fourteen of Thierry's poems for inclusion in his anthology titled *Les Cenelles,* a collection of French poetry written by African American men; Lanusse chose for publication twice as many poems by Thierry as any other poet represented in the volume. Thierry went on to publish a few more poems in 1850 in the *Orléanais.* Thierry's popularity and reputation are also evidenced in the words of Paul Trevigne, a critic for the New Orleans *Louisianian* who wrote in the December 25, 1875, edition, "His poems are composed with peculiar care, and comprise all the various rhythms of French prosody. Some of them are to be classed among the finest poetical efforts of Louisiana's most gifted writers." However, Thierry never felt completely free in the hierarchical CREOLE society, despite his wealth and fame. Not until his move to Bordeaux did he feel unfettered enough to write poems not only about love and nature, but of racial discrimination and prejudice as well.

Thierry suffered a major financial loss in 1873, when his agents went bankrupt and the poet lost both his rental income and his investment capital in their firm. Although he left Bordeaux to untangle the confusion of his business holdings, he was persuaded to transfer the titles of all his real estate (including six houses) to his brokers, who had reincorporated. In exchange for a perpetual annuity of $50 per month, Thierry agreed to place his net worth of approximately $43,000 into their hands. Thierry soon returned to Bordeaux, getting back to his true love, poetry, and he soon collected his scattered poems (some of which had already been printed in Louisiana). They were published at his own expense in 1874 in *Les Vagabondes.* Although this small volume was highly acclaimed in Europe in Thierry's day, it was virtually unknown in the United States for several years and is now a very rare book. These poems showed the influence of Lamartine and Charles-Hubert Millevoye; they are carefully structured and graceful. The book centers on the lives of three Creole beggars whom Thierry remembered from his boyhood in New Orleans, and one of the most famous of the verses was "Mariquita La Calentura," which details the trials of one Spanish family.

Shortly after the publication of *Les Vagabondes,* Thierry lost his annuity and was left destitute when Lafitte, Dufilho & Company failed again. The shock of the financial loss was immense, and Thierry died soon thereafter in Bordeaux. He never married.

In the years after Thierry's death, his verse remained popular in France and was frequently reprinted in the Creole press of Louisiana. Today, most Americans know very little about Thierry, for his poems were primarily published in Louisiana periodicals, his verse is entirely written in French, and the few books containing his verse are rare and out of print. Few translators, critics, or biographers have focused on Thierry and his work beyond passing references. However, despite his self-imposed exile and use of French language verse, Thierry discussed clearly American issues. As Desdunes notes, Thierry "understood the apathetic disposition of his people. He realized that a man such as he could count only upon himself in the battles of life." Thierry represented the tragedy of a divided nation; though wealthy, talented, and sophisticated, Thierry could never achieve the promises of the American Dream, and some of his most scathing stanzas depicted this angst. In one short poem, he wrote,

I heard no voice speak to me,
Not even the voice of a mother.
I fought alone when the thunder roared . . .
I comforted myself!

In the antebellum South and during RECONSTRUCTION, Thierry voiced his pain and his disapproval of American racism through his verse, exhibiting courage and a subtle appeal for change in the face of racial hostility.

Bibliography

Thierry's poems and papers, including *Les Vagabondes,* are in the New Orleans City Hall Archives and the Howard Memorial Library. Information about Thierry's life can be found in the *Comptes Rendues de l'Athénée Louisianais,* Jan. 1878, pp. 134–135; the complete files of this source are also in the Howard Library.

Blassingame, John W. *Black New Orleans, 1860–1880.* 1973.
Caulfield, Ruby Van Allen. *The French Literature of Louisiana.* 1929.
Coleman, Edward Maceo. *Creole Voices: Poems in French by Free Men of Color.* 1945.
Desdunes, Rodolphe Lucien. *Nos Hommes et Notre Histoire.* 1911.
Herrin, M. H. *The Creole Aristocracy: A Study of the Creole of Southern Louisiana.* 1952.
Rousseve, Charles B. *The Negro in Louisiana: Aspects of His History and His Literature.* 1937.

From *American National Biography.* John A. Garraty and Mark C. Carnes, eds. Oxford University Press, 1999. Reprinted by permission of the American Council of Learned Societies.

Anne M. Turner

Third Cinema

Type of film and film theory prevalent in Africa, Latin America, and Asia that aims to transform society by educating and radicalizing the film audience through "subversive" cinema; also called Third World cinema.

In the early 1960s a series of events paved the way for a new and distinctive type of Third World film. In AFRICA, decolonization freed film directors such as OUSMANE SEMBÈNE, MED HONDO, and HAILE GERIMA to make films for and about Africans. In LATIN AMERICA and Asia, revolutionary movements, combined with the development of Marxist film theory and Italian neorealism, inspired film directors such as Bolivian Jorge Sanjines and Indian Satyajit Ray to make politically charged films. Guided by the assumption that all film is ideological, they experimented with film as a weapon against the cultural imperialism of Hollywood.

During the next decade, film directors from Africa, Asia, and Latin America met and discussed their work at meetings and international film festivals. They called their cinema "Third Cinema" to identify it with the Third World and to differentiate it from the "first," or traditional, cinema (characterized by commercial films produced by Hollywood) and the "second," or counter, cinema (characterized by art film movements such as French New Wave). By the late 1960s, Third Cinema had established itself as an influential theory, especially in Africa.

Inspired by Marxist film criticism and by the writings of FRANTZ FANON, Third Cinema theory radically reinterprets the relationship between film, audience, and film director. It characterizes traditional film directors as agents of capitalism who "sell" to their passive audiences movies that promote colonial stereotypes and consumer society values. According to African American filmmaker Charles Taylor, traditional Hollywood cinema "concocts an artificial mental landscape harmonious with [capitalism's] need to depersonalize its audiences into zombies of its economy and addicts of its industrial culture, and to trash, trivialize, and erase the human culture that supply its victims."

By contrast Third Cinema must, in the words of Latin American directors Fernando Solanas and Octavio Gettino, produce "films that directly and explicitly set out to fight the System." Director Jorges Sanjines said, "The work of revolutionary cinema must not limit itself to denouncing, or to the appeal for reflection; it must be a summons for action." In fact, films such as *La Hora De Los Hornos* (The Hour of the Furnaces, 1968) and *Me Gustan Los Estudiantes* (I Like Students, 1968) provoked student riots in URUGUAY and VENEZUELA during the late 1960s. Since the mid-1970s, however, the goal of most Third Cinema directors has been to inspire political and social change rather than complete revolution.

In sub-Saharan Africa, most filmmakers subscribe to the ideas of Third Cinema and make films that are often quite critical of the postcolonial bourgeoisie. The films of Ousmane Sembène, Med Hondo, and SOULEYMANE CISSÉ fuse documentary and fiction, and use ambiguous and unresolved endings to invite discussion from the audience. In Latin America and Asia, Third Cinema filmmakers now constitute only a small minority, but they continue to denounce capitalism and cultural imperialism as well as the persistent problem of racism.

See also Cinema, African.

Bibliography
Gabriel, Teshome. *Third Cinema in the Third World.* UMI Research Press, 1982.

Elizabeth Heath

Thomas, Clarence

1948–

Associate justice of the Supreme Court of the United States known for his conservative views and judicial record.

Clarence Thomas was born in Pin Point, Georgia, and raised by his grandparents in Savannah, Georgia. He attended Roman Catholic schools, and in 1967 enrolled in Immaculate Conception Seminary in Conception, Missouri, to study to become a priest. Subjected to overt racism at the school, however, he transferred to Holy Cross College in Worcester, Massachusetts, where he became active in the Black Power Movement.

After graduating cum laude with an A.B. degree in English literature in 1971, Thomas entered Yale University Law School later that year. At Yale, Thomas developed the view that the Democratic Party had failed and was continuing to fail African Americans. By the time of his graduation in 1974, Thomas had become staunchly conservative and decided to work for John Danforth, Missouri's Republican attorney general, whom he followed to Washington, D.C., when Danforth became a U.S. senator.

Known within the Republican Party as a consistently conservative critic of governmental civil rights activity and affirmative action, Thomas was appointed assistant secretary for civil rights in the Department of Education. In 1982 President Ronald Reagan named Thomas chair of the Equal Employment Opportunity Commission (EEOC), a post to which he was reappointed in 1986, passing both confirmation processes with little difficulty despite opposition from civil rights groups.

In 1989 President George Bush nominated Thomas for the U.S. Circuit Court of Appeals for the District of Columbia and he was easily confirmed by the Senate on March 6, 1990, despite the concerns of some Democrats about his record at the EEOC. When Thurgood Marshall announced his retirement from the Supreme Court in July 1991, Bush nominated Thomas for the opening, despite his brief judicial record. The Senate Judiciary Committee reached an impasse regarding Thomas's nomination and sent his nomination to the full Senate without recommendation

Soon after, Anita Hill, a law professor at the University of Oklahoma, went public with allegations that Thomas had sexually harassed her when she worked with him as an EEOC staff attorney. Hearings held in October to examine Hill's claims were given extraordinary popular media coverage. Despite heated sentiment against Thomas from many groups, the Senate voted fifty-two to forty-eight to confirm Thomas by the second closest margin ever for a Supreme Court nominee.

Thomas was sworn in on October 19, 1991. Since that time he has amassed one of the Court's most conservative records and has also continued to attract public criticism from many prominent African Americans. In his early years on the Court, Thomas kept a low profile, writing few opinions and saying little during oral arguments. In the late 1990s, however, he took a more vocal and independent role, and in a number of opinions he took an even more conservative position than that of Justice Antonin Scalia, the strongest conservative voice on the Court. Like Scalia, Thomas has argued for a narrow role for both the federal government and the judiciary. He also favors a doctrine of *original intent,* which claims that the Constitution of the United States should be interpreted according to the intentions of the men who wrote it. These principles have led

him to vote to limit federal control in areas such as education, welfare, and voting rights and to limit individual claims to constitutional rights. In *Saenz v. Roe* (1999), for instance, the Court ruled that limitations on welfare for new residents of California interfered with the right to travel implied in the Privileges and Immunities Clause of the Fourteenth Amendment. Thomas, in his dissent, claimed that such a decision went against the intentions of the amendment's original framers and that the decision threatened to make the clause "yet another convenient tool for inventing new rights." An opponent of affirmative action, Thomas cast a dissenting vote in the Court's decision (in 2003) to uphold a program at the University of Michigan law school to boost minority enrollment.

See also Black Power in the United States; Hill-Thomas Hearings.

Bibliography
Morrison, Toni, ed. *Race-ing Justice, Engendering Power.* Pantheon Books, 1992.

Thomas, Franklin Augustine

1934–

American lawyer, community developer, and the first African American president of the Ford Foundation.

Franklin Thomas grew up in Brooklyn, New York's Bedford-Stuyvesant community and graduated with a B.A. in 1956 and a law degree in 1963, both from Columbia University. He worked stints as an attorney with the Federal Housing and Home Finance Agency, with the District Attorney's Office, and with the Police Department. From 1967 to 1977 he was President of the Bedford-Stuyvesant Restoration Corporation, working on business, job, and housing development in his home neighborhood. He was named the President of the Ford Foundation in 1979, the first African American to hold this position, and he remained in this post until 1996. Thomas later became head of the TFF Study Group, which assists development in southern Africa. In 2001 he chaired the board that directed the activities of the September 11th Fund and the September 11th Telethon Fund. Thomas is an advisor to the Secretary General of the United Nations and serves on several corporate and nonprofit boards.

See also Economic Development in Africa.

Thomas, Isiah

1961–

American professional basketball player who was one of the top point guards in the National Basketball Association during the 1980s and early 1990s.

Isiah Thomas, adept at dribbling, passing, and shooting, was a quick and dazzling player. At only six foot one inch—small when compared to most National Basketball Association (NBA) players—he was one of only a few players of his size who could dominate a professional BASKETBALL game.

Born Isiah Lord Thomas in CHICAGO, he attended Indiana University. After his first college season (1979–1980) he won a place on the 1980 United States Olympic basketball team, although the United States boycotted the Olympic Games, held in Moscow that year, for political reasons. As a sophomore Thomas led the Indiana University team to the 1981 National Collegiate Athletic Association (NCAA) basketball championship. He left Indiana University after two seasons and was selected by the Detroit Pistons as the second pick (after Mark Aguirre) in the 1981 NBA draft.

The Pistons earned the nickname Bad Boys in the 1980s for their physical style of play, but Thomas, who often used a variety of fancy moves, was a popular and charismatic player, emerging as the leader of the team. Beginning in his rookie season (1981–1982), he was named to the NBA All-Star team twelve consecutive times. He led the league in assists in the 1984–1985 season, averaging 13.9 per game, and over his thirteen-season career he recorded averages of 19.2 points per game and 9.3 assists per game. Thomas led the Pistons to the NBA Finals three consecutive times (1988–1990). In 1988 the Pistons lost in the finals to the Los Angeles Lakers, but they won the championship in 1989 and 1990. In 1990 Thomas was named most valuable player of the championship finals. After his retirement in 1994, he became an executive with the Toronto Raptors, an NBA expansion team that began playing in the 1995–1996 season. In 1997 Thomas left his position in the Raptors franchise to work as a basketball analyst for the National Broadcasting Company (NBC).

In 1999 Thomas became the owner and chief executive officer of the Continental Basketball Association (CBA), a professional basketball minor league affiliated with the NBA. A year later he left that position to become head coach of the Indiana Pacers; the CBA subsequently folded. In 2000 Thomas was elected to the Naismith Memorial Basketball Hall of Fame. In 2003, after the Pacers lost in the first round of the playoffs for the third consecutive year, Thomas was fired from his job as head coach. Then in December, Thomas was named president of basketball operations for the New York Knicks.

See also Olympics, African Americans and the; Sports and African Americans.

Thomas, James P.

1827–1913

African American barber and businessman.

James P. Thomas was born in Nashville, Davidson County, Tennessee. He was the son of Judge John Catron, one of the justices in DRED SCOTT V. SANDFORD case involving the constitutional rights of slaves, and a black slave named Sally. While Catron neglected his son, Sally earned enough money as a cleaning woman to purchase Thomas's freedom in 1834. Under Tennessee law, however, he was a slave as long as he remained in the state. He performed chores for his mother, mastered the basics of reading, writing, and arithmetic in a drafty one-room school, and became an apprentice in 1841 in the barbershop of another slave, Frank Parrish. In 1846 he opened his own shop in the house where he was born, while his mother still operated a laundry. Located at 10 Deaderick Street, within a few blocks of several banking houses, the courthouse, and the Capitol, Thomas's shop attracted many well-known customers and was advertised in the city's first business directory in 1853.

Thomas accompanied Tennessee plantation owner Andrew Jackson Polk through LOUISVILLE, KENTUCKY; CINCINNATI, OHIO; and Buffalo and Albany, New York, to NEW YORK CITY in 1848. They stayed at the Hotel Astor, but Thomas was denied a seat on a bus and rudely ejected from a theater. After a second trip to the North in 1851, Thomas's master, Ephraim Foster, petitioned the Davidson County Court for his freedom. Foster praised Thomas's "exemplary character," and the court ordered him to be emancipated. Thomas petitioned the court to grant him immunity from the law that required free blacks to leave the state. The court granted his petition, and Thomas became the first black man in the county—and perhaps in the state—to gain both freedom and residency.

Learning that William Walker, a boyhood playmate, was organizing a confederation of states in Central America and that a quadroon (person of one quarter black ancestry) had been appointed secretary of state, Thomas and his nephew John H. Rapier, Jr., joined Walker in Granada, NICARAGUA. When they learned that Walker was planning to establish a dictatorship and restore slavery, they returned to Nashville by way of several Midwestern states. Despite requests that he reopen his barbershop, Thomas left Nashville for the last time in 1856. After another trip through the Midwest, he settled in St. Louis, Missouri, and found employment on the Mississippi steamer *William Morrison*. He courted the beautiful, wealthy, free mulatto (of African and European descent) Antoinette Rutger, whose grandfather had been one of the first slaves brought to Missouri. Rutger's mother opposed her marriage to an ex-slave, but Thomas's persistent courtship won him acceptance among upper-class blacks and recognition in the directory *The Colored Aristocracy of St. Louis* in 1857.

During the CIVIL WAR (1861–1865), Thomas opened a barbershop in the city, began speculating in real estate, and like some other affluent free blacks, supported the Confederacy. Late in his life, however, he severely criticized the racial attitudes of white Southerners. In 1868, after a ten-year courtship, he finally married Antoinette Rutger. "It was a most imposing affair. The elite of the city were present," noted the conservative *St. Louis Dispatch*. "The bride has property and money to the value of $400,000. The husband is worth nearly the same amount. The bridal veil [alone] cost $750. The Reverend Mr.

Thomas Berk performed the ceremony at Saint Vincent's [Catholic] Church."

Although the *Dispatch* overestimated his wealth, Thomas became one of the richest men, white or black, in St. Louis during the next quarter century. He bought and sold real estate, built and improved a number of rental apartments (mostly on Rutger Street, between Sixth and Seventh Streets), oversaw a ten-chair barbering business in the central business district, and speculated in the stock market, mostly on railroad and insurance company stock. He accumulated an estate worth at least $250,000. At the height of his financial career, he rented forty-eight apartments (thirty-eight on Rutger Street and ten on Jefferson Avenue) and controlled real estate in various sections of the city. He also owned two mansions: one in the city and one in Alton, Illinois, across the Mississippi River and thirty-two kilometers (twenty miles) north of St. Louis. In a single city block, as conservatively estimated by city tax officials, Thomas owned property valued at $98,430. One business transaction, typical of many others, illustrated his business acumen. In 1870 he purchased five hectares (thirteen acres) of city property for $7,000. Only three years later, he sold the same real estate for $28,000.

Late in 1873, seemingly unaffected by the worst depression the United States had known, Thomas set out for EUROPE. Traveling to England, FRANCE, ITALY, Austria, GERMANY, and the Low Countries, he was greatly impressed with the style of life on the continent. "In Paris, I saw people who could pass for colored in America without trying, but [judging] from their general demeanor and bearing, [they] had never worn the yoke" and Rome was "a most interesting place, where visitors of all colors, from all clims [sic] visit." In Berlin, with its "patient, plodding, hard working set of people," he enjoyed extended stays. Upon his return, Thomas said bitterly: "Every colored man ought to know, although he has been treated as a companion [in Europe], on American soil, all that comes to an end. [Blacks] are supposed to take [their] regular place. Custome [sic] has so ordered it."

During the depression of 1893–1896, Thomas was forced to mortgage much of his property, and he never really recovered from the economic downturn, which caught many businessmen by surprise. He devoted the last years of his life to his family. Although Antoinette died in 1897, his children James, Pelagie, John, Joseph, Anthony, and Thomas were a continual source of satisfaction. He also spent his last years writing some autobiographical reminiscences, unpublished, about life in the antebellum South. In a collage of memories about slaves and free blacks, "poor whites" and planters, and some of the excitement in the decade before the Civil War, Thomas recalled that "slaves had no fair conception of time nor money." They belonged to no unions but simply did what they were told to do, "whether it required one or fifteen hours." Significantly, he placed poor whites at the bottom of the social ladder, below free blacks. They had neither land nor slaves and were something of an anomaly in the South.

After a lingering illness, Thomas died on December 17, 1913. Although he had still owned a few apartments, he had lost most of his wealth. His personal estate, which had once included items such as a $2,000 piano, had almost no value. Despite having so little at the end of his life, Thomas had achieved a great deal, and at a time when blacks were relegated to the lowest caste in the society of the United States, his accomplishments were remarkable.

A copy of his manuscript autobiography is in the Moorland-Spingarn Research Center, Howard University.

From *Dictionary of American Negro Biography* by Rayford W. Logan and Michael R. Winston, eds. Copyright © 1982 by Rayford W. Logan and Michael R. Winston. Reprinted by permission of W. W. Norton & Company, Inc.

See also Free Blacks in the United States; Slavery in the United States.

Loren Schweninger

Thomas, Piri

1928–

Afro–Puerto Rican writer, known for his innovative autobiographical works.

Piri Thomas was raised in the *barrios* (ghettos) of Spanish Harlem in NEW YORK CITY. His parents had immigrated to the United States from PUERTO RICO. He attended public schools, where he was first introduced to institutionalized assimilation and racism. In 1952 he was incarcerated on charges of attempted armed robbery, and in prison he began writing his first book, the autobiography *Down These Mean Streets* (1967).

Down These Mean Streets gained critical acclaim for its portrayal of Spanish Harlem and its bold new literary style, which mixed Spanish Harlem dialect with slang Thomas had learned in prison. Thomas is known for his use of authentic Afro–Puerto Rican settings and dialect. Thomas went on to publish two more autobiographical works, *Saviour, Saviour, Hold My Hand* (1972) and *Seven Long Times* (1974). He also established himself as a playwright, authoring *Las calles de oro* (The Golden Streets; 1970), and published a young-adult book, *Stories of El Barrio* (1978). Thomas's works are included in the anthology *Boricuas: Influential Puerto Rican Work* (1995).

In addition to his writing, Thomas has also been a community activist since his release from prison. He has volunteered in prison and drug rehabilitation programs in New York City since 1956, and received the Louis M. Rabinowitz Foundation Grant in 1962. In 1964 Time-Life Associates produced a documentary on his work with youth in street gangs titled *Petey and Johnny*. He was awarded a Lever Brothers Community Service Award in 1967, and since that year has been a staff associate for the Center for Urban Education in New York.

Thomas moved to San Francisco in 1983, where he has expanded his work to explore musical mediums of expression, continuing to channel a voice from marginalized populations in the United States into the larger public consciousness. His albums include *Sounds of the Street* (1994) and *No Mo' Barrio*

Blues (1996), which combine his poetry with Afro-Latin jazz. Thomas is the subject of the film *Every Child is Born a Poet: The Life and Work of Piri Thomas* (2003).

See also Poetry, Black, in English.

Thompson, Bennie

1948–

Democratic member of the United States House of Representatives from Mississippi since 1993.

Born in Bolton, Mississippi, Bennie Gordon Thompson earned a bachelor's degree from Tougaloo College in 1968 and a master's degree from Jackson State University in 1972. He ran for alderman of Bolton when he was twenty. Although victorious at the polls, Thompson was initially denied the seat by white officials. A court order secured his position, and he served from 1969 to 1973. He was mayor of Bolton from 1973 to 1979 and a member of the Hinds County Board of Supervisors from 1980 to 1993.

When Congressman Mike Espy was selected by President Bill Clinton to serve as secretary of agriculture in 1993, Thompson moved to fill Espy's vacant seat in Mississippi's Second Congressional District. Thompson placed second in an open primary and won the runoff election in April 1993. He was returned to office in subsequent elections. He is a member of the Congressional Black Caucus and currently serves on the Committee on Agriculture and the Select Committee on Homeland Security.

See also Democratic Party; United States House of Representatives, African Americans in.

Thompson, Casildo

1856–1928

Afro-Argentine poet, musician, and composer.

Casildo Thompson grew up in a family that was active in the vibrant and creative Afro-Argentine community of nineteenth-century Buenos Aires. His father, Capitán Casildo Thompson, a veteran of the Paraguayan war (among others), founded the most successful and the longest lasting Afro-Argentine mutual aid society of his time, *La Sociedad Fraternal* (The Fraternal Society). According to historian George Reid Andrews, Capitán Thompson was also a respected vocalist and composer who enjoyed a large following and wrote some of the most popular songs of his era. These included "La Locomotiva" (The Locomotive) and "Recuerdo del Campamento" (Memory of the Encampment), commemorating the anniversary of Argentina's first railroads and memorializing the Paraguayan campaign, respectively.

Thus Casildo Thompson had a powerful family legacy to live up to. Andrews highlights the tendency "of some Afro-Ar-

gentine families to produce two or more generations of musicians. . . ." Thompson was no exception. Following his father's example, he, too became an accomplished musician and composer, attending the conservatory in Buenos Aires and winning a series of national awards for his religious compositions. Like his father, he also rose to the rank of captain by participating in a series of wars between 1870 and 1890.

A talented pianist and composer, Thompson also played guitar. Ezequiel Martínez Estrada, a biographer of nineteenth-century Afro-Argentines, even contends that Thompson's "inseparable friend," Gabino Ezeiza, the most famous Afro-Argentine *payador,* learned a lot from him. (Payadores were guitar-playing singers who swapped witty digs in a kind of poetic competition.) Thompson's works ranged from popular music to literature and included poetry published in local black newspapers like *La Juventud,* where his most famous poem, *Canto al África* (Song to Africa) first appeared in 1877. Ironically, it is one of few Afro-Argentine poems to invoke black pride thematically by constructing mythical images of precolonial Africa in an indictment of slavery and colonialism.

Argentine blacks, considered by many other Argentines as social pariahs at the time, have until recently been consistently written out of national history. Indeed Thompson's poetry, whether because of its quality, quantity, or Thompson's lack of a wide audience, was never published in book form. Still, this poem, like some by his contemporary Horacio Mendizábal, stands as a testament to the existence of a bustling black community in nineteenth-century Buenos Aires.

See also Argentina; Colonial Latin America and the Caribbean; Music, Classical, in Latin America and the Caribbean.

Joy Elizondo

Thoms, Adah Belle Samuels

1870?–1943

African American nurse and nurse administrator.

Adah Belle Samuels Thoms was born in Richmond, Virginia, the daughter of Harry Samuels and Melvina (maiden name unknown). She attended public school in Richmond and taught there before deciding to pursue a career in nursing. In 1893 she moved to Harlem in New York City to study elocution and public speaking at the Cooper Union. After attending the Woman's Infirmary and School of Therapeutic Massage in New York City, Samuels received a diploma in 1900. She worked initially as a private duty nurse in New York City before returning south in 1902 to Raleigh, North Carolina, where she joined the nursing staff of St. Agnes Hospital. At some point she married a physician, Dr. Thoms, about whom very little is known. The couple had no children, and her husband died shortly after they returned to New York in 1903.

After resettling in New York, Adah Thoms entered the newly organized school of nursing at Lincoln Hospital and Home.

White women founded the hospital in 1893 to provide health care to black New Yorkers, and the nursing school was opened in 1898. Thoms, in her second year at Lincoln, secured the position of head nurse on a surgical ward. She graduated in 1905, and Lincoln immediately hired her as a full-time operating room nurse and as the supervisor of the surgical division.

Possessed of keen social skills and a healthy regard for work, Thoms had a long and eventful career at Lincoln Hospital. In 1906 she became assistant superintendent of nurses, a position she held until her retirement eighteen years later. As assistant superintendent she improved nursing training by launching, in 1913, a six-month postgraduate course for registered nurses. In 1917, just five years after the establishment of the National Organization for Public Health Nursing, she inaugurated a course in public health nursing.

Although Thoms was admired for her pioneering administrative work at Lincoln Hospital—few black women were accorded such opportunities—she left an even more important legacy as a result of her involvement in the successful struggle to professionalize black women nurses. In 1906 Martha Minerva Franklin, an 1897 graduate of the Woman's Hospital Training School for Nurses in Philadelphia, launched a bold initiative. She mailed more than 1,500 letters to black graduate nurses, hospitals, and nursing schools to gauge interest in forming a professional association of black nurses. She envisioned an organization that would challenge the exclusion of black nurses from membership in the American Nurses' Association while providing a space for them to meet and address their own need for employment registries, better jobs, advanced training, and greater access to supervisory positions within hospital hierarchies.

Adah Thoms, as president of the Lincoln Hospital School of Nursing Alumnae Association, responded to Franklin by inviting her and interested nurses to meet in New York City as guests of the association. Thoms and the Lincoln association sponsored the August 1908 meeting of fifty-two nurses. Out of their deliberations emerged, in 1908, the National Association of Colored Graduate Nurses (NACGN), with twenty-six charter members. Franklin was elected president and was reelected to the same office in 1909. Thoms was named the treasurer. In 1916 she was elected president of the NACGN, and she occupied that position until her retirement from Lincoln Hospital in 1923.

As one of the most prominent black nurses, Thoms became a staunch advocate for stronger educational programs in the black hospital nursing schools, and she advocated greater use of black nurses in public health work sponsored by public and private agencies. Indeed, throughout the last decade of her career, she became the model for black nurse involvement in a variety of community organizations and projects. In 1916 she collaborated with both the National Urban League and the National Association for the Advancement of Colored People (NAACP) in an attempt to improve conditions for black patients at local hospitals and for nursing students enrolled in the training schools.

America's entry into World War I created a great demand for nurses, and Thoms worked on many fronts to ensure that black nurses become a part of the war effort. When Congress declared war on Germany in April 1917, she rallied black nurses to enroll in the American Red Cross Nursing Service, which was the only way for them to enter the U.S. Army Nurse Corps. However, the black nurses who applied to the American Red Cross were rejected. Thoms, along with a number of African American leaders, protested the racial practices of the Red Cross and of the U.S. military. She met with policymakers and wrote letters to Jane A. Delano, head of the American National Red Cross Nursing Service, protesting the exclusion of black nurses. Thoms was told in December 1917 that a limited number of black nurses would be allowed to enroll. The Red Cross accepted its first black nurse in July 1918. However, appointment to the Army Nurse Corps, with full rank and pay, did not come for black nurses until December 1918, too late for the war but just in time to help with the massive influenza epidemic.

Not content to sit and wait for the Red Cross and the U.S. military to recognize and accept black nurses, Thoms helped to establish a new order of black war nurses, the Blue Circle Nurses. The Circle for Negro War Relief hired black nurses to work in poor or rural black communities, teaching residents the importance of sanitation, a healthy diet, and appropriate clothing. In 1921 the assistant surgeon general of the army appointed Thoms to serve on the Woman's Advisory Council of Venereal Diseases of the U.S. Public Health Service.

After her retirement in 1923 Thoms married Henry Smith who died months later. During the next few years Thoms concentrated her considerable energies on compiling statistical information about, and writing the history of, black nursing schools and their graduates. In 1929 she published the first book on black nursing, *Pathfinders: A History of the Progress of Colored Graduate Nurses*. Throughout the next decade she remained committed to the advancement of black women in the nursing profession and to the integration of the American Nurses' Association. She had a number of close professional relationships with white nurses. She objected to suggestions that nurses merge with black doctors in their National Medical Association. Ultimately, Thoms was a racial pragmatist. She believed that until integration was accomplished, black nurses had to support and strengthen their own organizations and institutions. In other words, they had to create their own paths to equality.

To celebrate her record of outstanding service to black nursing and her relentless efforts to improve conditions within a still-segregated health care delivery system, the NACGN in 1936 named Thoms the first recipient of the Mary Mahoney Medal, named in honor of the first black graduate nurse. Thoms's active involvement in the St. Mark's Methodist Episcopal Church and her work with the Hope Day Nursery, a unique day-care center for the black children of working mothers, was limited only by failing health because of heart disease and diabetes. During these later years her niece, Nannie Samuels, lived with her. Even after her death in New York City, Thoms received recognition for her many contributions to her chosen profession. In 1976 she was inducted into the prestigious Nursing

Hall of Fame. She was buried in Woodlawn Cemetery in New York under the surname Smith.

Bibliography

Cannon-Huffman, Linda. "Adah Thoms." In *African American Women: A Biographical Dictionary,* edited by Dorothy C. Salem. 1993.

Davis, Althea T. "Adah Belle Samuels Thoms, 1870–1943." In *American Nursing: A Biographical Dictionary,* edited by Vern L. Bullough, et al. 1988.

Hine, Darlene Clark. *Black Women in White: Racial Conflict and Cooperation in the Nursing Profession, 1890–1950.* 1989.

Logan, Rayford W. "Adah B. Samuels Thoms." In the *Dictionary of American Negro Biography,* edited by Rayford W. Logan and Michael R. Winston. 1982.

From *American National Biography.* John A. Garraty and Mark C. Carnes, eds. Oxford University Press, 1999. Reprinted by permission of the American Council of Learned Societies.

Darlene Clark Hine

Thornton, Willie Mae ("Big Mama")

1926–1984

American blues singer, songwriter, and musician known for boisterous stage performances, shouting vocals, outspoken lyrics, and an eccentric lifestyle that influenced a later generation of popular musicians.

Born in Montgomery, Alabama, Willie Mae Thornton sang GOSPEL MUSIC as a child in her minister father's church. Shortly after her mother's death, when she was fourteen, Thornton joined Sammy Green's *Hot Harlem Revue*, traveling throughout the South's "chitlin circuit," singing and teaching herself the harmonica, guitar, and drums.

In 1948, Thornton moved to HOUSTON, TEXAS, and signed an exclusive contract with Peacock Records. Thornton's six-foot tall and 250-pound frame earned her the nickname Big Mama, which she celebrated in "They Call Me Big Mama." Her recording sessions with the Johnny Otis RHYTHM AND BLUES Caravan yielded "Hound Dog," which reached number one on the rhythm and blues charts and was made famous in the 1950s by Elvis Presley, and "Ball and Chain," which became Janis Joplin's signature song in the late 1960s. Though both songs earned Thornton enough fame to tour nationally, she had signed away her royalty rights, and saw little of the money that Presley and Joplin later did.

In the early 1960s, her popularity fading, Thornton moved to San Francisco in an attempt to revitalize her career. Because of the BLUES revival occurring in the late 1960s, Thornton's career rebounded. Through the 1960s and 1970s, she played JAZZ and blues festivals in the U.S. and Europe, and recorded several albums.

Thornton entertained audiences with her rugged blues style and with her unconventionality. She was a heavy drinker, and she preferred to dress in men's clothing. Often she wore a dress over jeans and boots.

Thornton suffered from alcohol-related problems and she died of a heart attack, poor and little known. A benefit concert was given to raise burial money. Though popular acclaim eluded Thornton, she influenced many later musicians, including Joplin, ARETHA FRANKLIN, Grace Slick, Stevie Nicks, and Angela Strehli. Thornton was inducted into the Blues Foundation's Hall of Fame in 1984.

See also Music, African American.

Robert Fay

Thrash, Dox

1893–1965

American artist and printer; also coinventor of the carborundum print-process.

Dox Thrash was born in Griffin, Georgia. After studying for several years at the Art Institute of Chicago, Thrash settled in PHILADELPHIA, PENNSYLVANIA. Once there he painted signs and worked on the Federal Arts Project (FAP) to earn a living. Working with the FAP, in the Graphic Division, he helped invent a new lithographic process, called the carborundum print-process. This created prints with more expressive tones and variation. His carbographs explored the portraits of African Americans, landscapes, and scenes of slum life. *My Neighbor* (1937) and the landscape *Deserted Cabin* (1939) are examples of Thrash's carbographs. In the late 1930s and through the 1940s Thrash's work was shown in many prominent places, including a 1942 solo exhibition at the Philadelphia Museum of Art.

See also Artists, African American.

Bibliography

Brigham, David R. "Bridging Identities (The Works of Dox Thrash, Afro-American Artist)." *Smithsonian Studies in American Art*, spring 1990.

Thuku, Harry

1895–1970

Kenyan nationalist and first president of the East African Association.

Harry Thuku was among KENYA's first nationalists, known for his opposition to British colonial land and labor policies. Born in Mbari ya-Gathirimu in northern Kenya, he attended a Gospel Mission Society school, and at the age of sixteen moved to NAIROBI. He held several jobs and even served a prison term for fraud before he began working as a typesetter at the publication *Leader of British East Africa*, a job that awakened his political consciousness.

In 1921 Thuku became president of the newly founded Young Kikuyu Association, later named the East African Association (EAA), a group devoted to fighting colonial policies that forced Africans off Kenya's most fertile farmland and into menial employment. The EAA's early demands were moderate, asking only for an end to the appropriation of Kikuyu lands, not for a return of what had been taken. Their methods of protest included writing letters to the colonial secretary in London and organizing protest meetings. But colonial officials considered Thuku a radical, and arrested him in 1922. When the EAA demonstrated to protest Thuku's arrest, the British responded with force, killing twenty Africans. The colonial government subsequently sent Thuku away from Nairobi, and he spent almost nine years in detention in coastal and northern Kenya. During this time other Kenyan nationalists, including future president Jomo Kenyatta, stepped up the EAA's activities.

Thuku was released in 1930 and spent the rest of his life working on his farm, which earned him considerable wealth. He published *Harry Thuku: An Autobiography* in 1970, the same year he died.

See also Nationalism in Africa.

Bibliography

Roelker, Jack R. *The Genesis of African Protest: Harry Thuku and the British Administration in Kenya, 1920–1922.* Maxwell Graduate School of Citizenship and Public Affairs, 1968.

Thuku, Harry. *Harry Thuku: An Autobiography.* Oxford University Press, 1970.

Kate Tuttle

Thurman, Howard

1900–1981

African American pastor, poet, theologian, and educator, widely regarded as the spiritual leader of the nascent Civil Rights Movement in the 1920s, 1930s, and 1940s.

Howard Thurman was born among the working poor in Daytona, Florida, and reared principally by his grandmother, a former slave. Raised and ordained in the Baptist church, he was educated at Florida Baptist Academy and received a B.A. degree from Morehouse College in 1923 and a B.D. (bachelor of divinity) degree from Rochester Theological Seminary in 1926. By the time he was a young man, he had integrated into his religious inheritance from the black church elements of various mystical traditions, the pragmatism of American philosopher John Dewey, and the ideals of the Social Gospel movement to form the basis of a distinctive, intercultural, interracial ministry.

While still a student, Thurman began his public career as a youth movement leader, mainly through the Young Men's Christian Association (YMCA) in the 1920s. His first pastorate, at Mount Zion Baptist Church in Oberlin, Ohio, from 1926 to 1928, was followed by a joint appointment as professor of religion and director of religious life at Morehouse and Spelman colleges in Atlanta, Georgia. Thurman spent the spring semester of 1929 studying at Haverford College with Rufus Jones, a Quaker mystic and leader of the pacifist, interracial Fellowship of Reconciliation. His first wife, Kate Kelly Thurman, whom he had married in 1926, died in 1930 of tuberculosis.

After marrying his second wife, musician, historian, and international secretary of the Young Women's Christian Association (YWCA), Sue Bailey Thurman, Thurman went on to serve at Howard University in Washington, D.C., as professor of Christian theology and dean of Rankin Chapel from 1932 to 1944. From 1935 to 1936 Thurman also led the first black Delegation of Friendship to India, Burma (now Myanmar), and Ceylon (now Sri Lanka). On this trip he and two others became the first African Americans to meet Indian colonial independence leader Mohandas Gandhi. Thurman's conversations with Gandhi broadened his international political vision and strengthened his Christian commitment promoting intercultural understanding.

Thurman was the author of twenty books of ethical and cultural criticism. The most famous of his works, *Jesus and the Disinherited* (1949), deeply influenced Martin Luther King, Jr., and other leaders of the modern Civil Rights Movement. In 1944 Thurman left his prestigious tenured position at Howard to help the Fellowship of Reconciliation establish the first racially integrated, intercultural church in the United States, the Church for the Fellowship of All Peoples in San Francisco, California. From 1953 to 1965 he served as professor of spiritual resources and dean of Marsh Chapel at Boston University—the first black man to occupy the post of dean at a traditionally white university. He continued his ministry as director of the Howard Thurman Educational Trust in San Francisco from its founding in 1965 until his death.

See also Baptists; Spelman College.

Bibliography

Thurman, Howard. *With Head and Heart: the Autobiography of Howard Thurman.* Harcourt Brace Jovanovich, 1979.

Thurman, Wallace

1902–1934

American writer of the Harlem Renaissance who espoused a frank and sometimes stark assessment of African American life in America.

Wallace Thurman was born in Salt Lake City, Utah. In 1925, Thurman began his writing career at the University of Southern California, where he started and edited the short-lived *Outlet*, a literary magazine which discussed many ideas of the HARLEM RENAISSANCE. Leaving school for HARLEM that same year, Thurman became a part of the Harlem Renaissance, which he had been observing. He began working in NEW YORK as an editorial assistant at a small magazine called *Looking Glass* followed by other publications, such the white magazine *The World Tomorrow*. At the left-wing MESSENGER, where he was temporary editor, Thurman became associated with other writers in Harlem such as LANGSTON HUGHES and ZORA NEALE HURSTON.

In 1926, Thurman helped found *Fire!!*, a journal intended to expose the new thinking of the Harlem Renaissance and publish writing about African Americans who broke free from mainstream American culture. Unfortunately, the journal, which Thurman edited, was plagued with financial problems, and an actual fire in a basement where many issues of *Fire!!* were stored secured the downfall of the publication after only one issue. Thurman started a similar magazine in 1928, *Harlem, a Forum of Negro Life*, which failed after one issue.

Despite his failures as a publisher, Thurman wrote three books, a play, and several articles and editorials for numerous magazines. His writing often satirized African American life and the Harlem Renaissance, depicting the contradictions within black thought of the time, especially in his novels *The Blacker the Berry* (1929) and *Infants of the Spring* (1932). His play *Harlem* was originally produced at the APOLLO THEATER in 1929 and may have been his largest success. His final novel, *The Interne* (1932), exposed the injustices at City Hospital on Welfare Island (now Roosevelt Island). He died at that hospital in 1934, of tuberculosis and consumption, related to chronic alcoholism.

See also Literature, African American.

Bibliography
Notten, Eleonore Van. *Wallace Thurman's Harlem Renaissance*. Rodopi, 1994.

Tia Ciata

1854–1924

One of several legendary black Brazilian women, known as *tias* (aunts), who hosted social gatherings where Afro-Brazilian culture was celebrated and samba music was developed.

At the end of the nineteenth century, just at the time of the abolition of slavery in BRAZIL, RIO DE JANEIRO's Praça Onze was the center of a neighborhood composed largely of Afro-Brazilians. Many of these people were recent migrants from the state of BAHIA, and the Praça Onze neighborhood became known as "*Pequena África*" (or small Africa). Tia Ciata moved to Rio from Bahia at the age of twenty-two, and during the day worked selling home-cooked food at a food stall. Tia Ciata was also deeply involved in the Afro-Brazilian religion of CANDOMBLÉ.

At night and on the weekends she hosted gatherings at her home in Praça Onze that united some of the most famous black Brazilian musicians and composers, probably serving as one of the birthplaces of SAMBA music.

See also Afro-Brazilian Culture.

Ben Penglase

Tigre

Ethnic group of the Horn of Africa who live in Eritrea and neighboring parts of Sudan; sometimes erroneously known as Tigray.

The Tigre are a loose grouping of predominantly Muslim people who speak a Semitic language of the Afro-Asiatic linguistic family. The Tigre language is closely related to TIGRINYA, a main language of ERITREA, and AMHARA, the leading language of ETHIOPIA. The Tigre should not be confused with the predominantly Christian Tigrinya people of Eritrea and Ethiopia's Tigray Province. Europeans have repeatedly confused the two related but distinct groups.

The Tigre and Tigrinya probably share a common ancestry dating back to the arrival of Semitic-speaking peoples in the region more than 2,000 years ago. Coptic Christianity spread from EGYPT throughout the Horn of Africa during the fourth and fifth centuries C.E. The ancient sacred language of the Ethiopian church is Ge'ez, a language from which both Tigre and Tigrinya later evolved. However, Islam, which Arabian traders brought to the Dahlak Islands around the year 700, gradually spread along the coast and across the western plains. The pastoral nomads of these dry plains, who migrated periodically in search of water and pastures for livestock, were organized into clans based on extended family ties. Gradually these nomads, the ancestors of the Tigre, converted to Islam. By the nineteenth century, the Tigre were solidly Muslim. Arabic was the language of scholarship. This worked to prevent the growth of literature in the Tigrean language. Ironically, it was Christian missionaries and European scholars who began compiling Tigre's rich tradition of oral stories and poetry in the 1970s and who spurred a Tigre literary flowering.

The Tigre were long subject to the control of neighboring peoples. Many Tigre are serfs owing obligations to aristocratic clans, especially the BENI AMER people. In fact, the word "Tigre" is sometimes taken to mean "serf." The Tigre have also clashed periodically with the dominant Christian Tigrinya farmers of the highlands. Religious and cultural differences have heightened the inevitable competition for scarce water and desirable land. Following World War II, bloody clashes broke out between Muslim Tigre, who overwhelmingly favored an independent nation of Eritrea, and Christians, supporting union with Ethiopia. Fearing domination by a primarily Christian Ethiopia, Tigreans helped found the Eritrean Liberation Front (ELF) and got early support from Muslim states.

In an effort to counter Tigrean independence sympathies, the Ethiopian government began Tigre-language radio broadcasts in the 1960s. This did little to rally the Tigre to Ethiopia's cause, but it promoted a widespread awareness of Tigre music and culture. The Eritrean People's Liberation Front (EPLF) also promoted the use of Tigre for political purposes and employed it as a language of instruction in areas it controlled. The rival ELF generally favored Arabic as the language of instruction.

Today, Eritrea has one of the most nomadic populations in the world. But the Tigre also farm when possible and raise an indigenous cereal called *teff* as well as corn, wheat, barley, sorghum, and MILLET. Numbering close to two million, the Tigre compose about 40 percent of Eritrea's population.

See also Christianity: Missionaries in Africa; Ethiopian Orthodox Church; Ethiopic Script and Language; Ethnicity and Identity in Africa: An Interpretation; Islam and Tradition: An Interpretation; Languages, African: An Overview.

David P. Johnson, Jr.

Tigrinya

Major language and ethnic group in the Horn of Africa.

The Tigrinya language belongs to the Semitic family of the Afro-Asiatic linguistic grouping. It is closely related to AMHARA, the main language of ETHIOPIA, and to TIGRE, the second most common language in ERITREA. Tigrinya speakers live primarily in the central highlands of Eritrea and in northern Ethiopia. Their ancestors—descendants of indigenous Cushitic peoples and Semitic peoples from the Arabian Peninsula—probably settled this region more than 2,000 years ago. The Tigrinya language most likely evolved from Ge'ez, the language spoken in the ancient kingdom of AKSUM. Unlike Ge'ez, however, early Tigrinya appears to have been primarily a spoken language. The oldest existing document in Tigrinya is a law code from the nineteenth century.

The Tigrinya people have long been settled agriculturalists, though many also keep livestock. Their staple crops include the indigenous grain *teff*, wheat, barley, MILLET, sorghum, and pulses. Along with the Amhara, the Tigrinya consider themselves descendants of the people of Aksum, and until the twentieth century they historically accepted as legitimate the rule of Ethiopia's Amharic emperors. Both Tigrinya and Amhara speakers are adherents of Coptic Christianity, which became the religion of Aksum in the mid-fourth century C.E. Relatively few Tigrinya speakers converted to Islam, which was brought by Arab traders beginning in the eighth century C.E.

When the Italians began their colonial conquest of the Horn in the 1880s, the highland regions were suffering through a period of poor harvests and food shortages and the Tigrinya people initially put up relatively little resistance. Shortly after ITALY declared rule over Eritrea in 1890, however, the colonial administration began a massive land expropriation campaign in the highlands, intending to create an Italian settler colony. An 1894 uprising in Tigrinya-speaking areas forced the administration to scale back these plans, but many Tigrinya remained landless and became laborers either on Italian settler farms or in the industrializing cities of ASMARA and MASSAWA. Tigrinya peasants participated in the colonial economy as producers of export crops such as coffee.

After World War II, the Tigrinya, along with other Christians, fought bloody street battles with Muslims over Eritrea's proposed unification with Ethiopia. Generally, Christians supported unification and Muslims opposed it. However, the Tigrinya became increasingly disenchanted with Emperor HAILE SELASSIE's autocratic rule and with the imposition of Amharic language and culture. The Tigrinya also had economic reasons for joining their Muslim neighbors in the battle for independence. The Ethiopian government discriminated against non-Amharic when hiring for civil service positions, and it relocated much of the industry from Asmara, the main city in the Tigrinya highlands, to ADDIS ABABA, the Ethiopian capital.

By the late 1960s many Tigrinya, including the future Eritrean president ISAIAS AFWERKI, had joined the Eritrean Liberation Front (ELF). Afwerki and a number of other Christians later split from the ELF and formed the Eritrean People's Liberation Front (EPLF), which subsequently became the larger of the two rebel forces and increasingly multiethnic. By the late 1980s the EPLF was cooperating with rebel groups within Ethiopia, such as the Ethiopian People's Revolutionary Democratic Front, led by MELES ZENAWI, a Tigrinya.

Since Eritrea attained independence in 1991, Eritrea and Ethiopia have been led by Afwerki and Zenawi, respectively—both Tigrinya heads of state. Afwerki has his critics but remains overwhelmingly popular with the Eritrean people. Zenawi, on the other hand, has been accused of favoring Tigrinya-speaking regions in Ethiopia at the expense of the once-dominant Amhara. About two million Tigrinya speakers live in Eritrea and four million in Ethiopia.

See also Christianity, African: An Overview; Ethiopian Orthodox Church; Ethiopic Script and Language; Ethnicity and Identity in Africa: An Interpretation; Languages, African: An Overview.

David P. Johnson, Jr.

Tikar

Ethnic group of Cameroon.

The Tikar inhabit primarily the North-West Province of CAMEROON. They speak a Niger-Congo language and are closely related to the BAMILÉKÉ people. Approximately 100,000 people consider themselves Tikar.

See also Ethnicity and Identity in Africa: An Interpretation; Languages, African: An Overview.

Tilapia

Genus of African tropical fishes that serve as an important food source in Africa.

Tilapias make up the genus *Tilapia*, which belongs to the family Cichlidae, and is thought to have existed for about twenty-four million years. All fourteen African species are native to tropical fresh waters of Africa; the smallest, *Tilapia guinasana*, is considered an endangered species.

Tilapias adapt fairly easily to a wide range of habitats. Some species can survive in waters with oxygen concentrations as low as 0.1 parts per million, and one species inhabits hot springs with water temperatures as high as 40° C (104° F). Because of their adaptability, Tilapias are farmed in East Africa, where they are sold locally and exported. Tilapias are now also farmed abroad especially in Israel, Indonesia, and Malaysia. Fresh and smoked tilapia are readily available all over the world. Tilapias also play an important part in the diet of subsistence fisheries because they are a rich protein source, especially the larger species. In addition, several species are popular aquarium fishes because of their interesting behavior and attractive coloring.

Tilapias have laterally flattened bodies that range from about ten to thirty centimeters (about four to twelve inches) long. They feed on a wide variety of food, including insect larvae, crustaceans, juvenile fish, worms, various plants, and detritus. Most tilapias are highly territorial and engage in intense aggressive behavior toward males of the same species and toward members of other species. All species of tilapia, however show remarkable care for their offspring.

See also Fisheries, African; Food in Africa.

Robert Fay

Till, Emmett Louis

1941–1955

African American teenager who was an early victim of civil rights–era violence.

Emmett Till was born and raised in CHICAGO, ILLINOIS. When he was fourteen years old, he was sent to Mississippi to spend the summer with his uncle, Moses Wright. Because of his upbringing in the North, Till was unaccustomed to the racial taboos of the segregated South. He bragged to his Southern black friends that in Chicago he even had a white girlfriend. One afternoon Till saw a twenty-one-year-old white woman, Carol Bryant, and whistled at her. According to some accounts, he also spoke to her. His friends, aware of the danger that Till's flirting might cause, rushed him away to his uncle's tenant farmhouse.

On August 28, 1955, Carol Bryant's husband, Roy, and his half-brother, J. W. Milam, abducted Till from his uncle's home. Three days later, Till's naked, beaten, and decaying body was found in the Tallahatchie River. He had been shot in the head.

The two white men were tried by an all-white jury a month later, and despite the fact that they admitted abducting Till, they were acquitted. The foreman of the jury credited the acquittal to doubts about the positive identification of the body, which had been beaten beyond recognition.

Till's murder and the acquittal of his killers, who later confessed to the murder in an article in *Look* magazine, became a rallying point for the CIVIL RIGHTS MOVEMENT. Photographs of his open casket were reprinted across the country, and protests were organized by the NATIONAL ASSOCIATION FOR THE ADVANCEMENT OF COLORED PEOPLE (NAACP), the BROTHERHOOD OF SLEEPING CAR PORTERS, and leaders such as W. E. B. DU BOIS. The public outrage over the injustice of the trial helped ensure that Congress included a provision for federal investigations of civil rights violations in the Civil Rights Act of 1957.

In 2004 the Justice Department reopened the investigation into the death of Emmett Till because of "renewed interest in the case." For years the Till family had maintained that more than two people were likely involved in the murder. At a news conference in May 2004, R. Alexander Acosta, assistant attorney general for civil rights, noted that "if others are implicated and can be identified, they can still be prosecuted." Although the federal statute of limitations has expired, prosecution can still be brought in state court.

Bibliography

Whitfield, Stephen J. *A Death in the Delta: The Story of Emmett Till.* Free Press, 1988.

Lisa Clayton Robinson

Tillman, Nathaniel Patrick, Sr.

1898–1965

African American educator and philologist; he was an eminently successful debating coach and won acclaim as a director of theater productions of the works of English playwright William Shakespeare.

The only son of Nathan and Catherine Tillman, Nathaniel Patrick Tillman, Sr. was born on January 17, 1898, in BIRMINGHAM, ALABAMA. Tillman's parents died when he was still a boy, and he was reared by his grandmother. He received his B.A. degree in 1920 from MOREHOUSE COLLEGE in ATLANTA, GEORGIA. On September 13, 1920, Tillman married Mattie V. Reynolds. Two children were born from that union: Nathaniel P., Jr., who later became a well-known educator, and Virginia, later Mrs. Whatley. After spending two years as a teacher at Alcorn College in Mississippi, Tillman returned to Atlanta in 1924 and spent the remainder of his academic career there.

Tillman earned both his M.A. and Ph.D. degrees from the University of Wisconsin, in 1927 and 1940, respectively. He also studied at the University of Oxford in England in the summer of 1934 and at the University of Chicago in Illinois. The recipient of numerous fellowships, he was a University Scholar (1926–1927) and a General Education Board Fellow (1931–

1932), and he held a Rosenwald Travel Fellowship in 1934. Tillman was coeditor with Hugh M. Gloster of *My Life, My Country, My World: College Readings for Modern Living*, a reader-composition text for college freshmen published in 1952. This publication was adopted widely enough to warrant a second edition. Tillman's most important scholarly work was done on medieval English poet John Lydgate and was entitled *Lydgate's Rhyme as Evidence of His Pronunciation*. The handbook that governed the format and style of theses produced at Atlanta University in the 1940s and 1950s was coauthored by G. Lewis Chandler and Tillman. Tillman also contributed scholarly articles to journals such as *American Speech, Phylon: The Atlanta University Review of Race and Culture*, and the *Quarterly Journal of Higher Education Among Negroes*.

From 1924 to 1932 Tillman worked as the Morehouse College registrar. He also served as professor of English and chairman of the college's English Department after 1927. He was acting academic dean of the school from 1932 to 1934, and he continued to serve as chairman and teacher until 1957. During these years he taught courses at Atlanta University (now Atlanta University Center), and in 1942 he became professor and chairman of the English Department of that university. Between 1955 and 1961 Tillman was first acting and later dean of the School of Arts and Sciences of Atlanta University. He combined the duties and responsibilities of chairman and dean with those of a stimulating classroom teacher until physical disabilities forced his resignation as department chairman and dean in 1961. From then until his death he was professor of English.

Active in the national councils and associations in his academic field, Tillman was in demand as a speaker and consultant for national groups such as the National Council of Teachers of English and the College Language Association, which awarded him its Distinguished Contributor's Award. It was as a teacher, however, that he had his greatest and most lasting impact and made his most significant contribution. Admired for his scholarship, wit, and compassion by generations of students, as early as the 1930s he was regarded by Arthur D. Wright, president of the John F. Slater Fund, as "one of the best teachers of English in the South." A tribute paid to him in 1963 by former students for his "sincere interest in guiding and teaching" and for the "high standards" he exemplified in his profession reflects his ability to both teach and inspire youth. He was regarded by his colleagues as "a great teacher, an excellent scholar, a skilled administrator, a wise counselor and a true friend," who represented "a rare combination of talents, skills, and capacities in a single individual."

A diabetic who had lost both his legs, Tillman died on October 17, 1965, a few hours after he had been presented, in absentia, a plaque by the trustees of Atlanta University in appreciation of twenty-five years of devoted service to the university. Funeral services were held in the Dean Sage Auditorium on the Atlanta University campus, with interment in Atlanta's South View Cemetery. He was survived by his widow and two children.

This sketch is based on the records of Morehouse College, Atlanta University, interviews, personal reminiscences, and

Clarence A. Bacote's *Story of Atlanta University: A Century of Service, 1865–1965* (1969).

From the *Dictionary of American Negro Biography* by Rayford W. Logan and Michael R. Winston, editors. Copyright © 1982 by Rayford W. Logan and Michael R. Winston. Reprinted by permission of W. W. Norton & Company, Inc.

See also Educational Organizations in the United States.

Edward F. Sweat

Tindley, Charles Albert

1851–1933

American minister and gospel musician whose hymns became a basis of twentieth-century African American church music.

In 1916 Charles Albert Tindley published *New Songs of Paradise*, a collection of thirty-seven gospel songs. By 1941 the collection had run to its seventh edition. Among his best known songs are "A Better Home," "Stand by Me," "What Are They Doing in Heaven Tonight?," "We'll Understand It By and By," and "I'll Overcome Some Day." Many of them and other of his works are now standards in African American churches. His work inspired the gospel songs of THOMAS A. DORSEY and Reverend Herbert Brewster.

See also Gospel Music.

Robert Fay

Tinné, Alexandrine Pieternella Françoise

1835–1869

Dutch explorer of the Nile River and North Africa.

Alexandrine Tinné was born in The Hague, Netherlands, to a wealthy family. An unhappy love affair may have prompted her to leave home and embark on a voyage in search of the Nile River's source. In 1862 Tinné hired a small fleet of boats in CAIRO, EGYPT, and left on her first expedition up the Nile. Accompanying her were her mother, her aunt, several scientists, and a number of assistants and servants. Tinné ascended the Nile as far as Gondokoro, in present-day southern SUDAN, above which the river became unnavigable. She planned to meet British explorer JOHN HANNING SPEKE, who was exploring the upper reaches of the Nile to the south. When Speke's expedition failed to arrive when expected, Tinné set off on her own to determine the source of the Nile. Traveling overland, she ventured into the watershed region between the Congo and Nile rivers, in the northeastern part of present-day DEMOCRATIC REPUBLIC OF THE CONGO. Tinné's explorations took her into regions of Central Africa that were not yet mapped and seldom visited by Europeans. She returned to Gondokoro in September 1862, and after again failing to meet up with Speke, she headed downriver and back to Cairo. Both her mother and aunt, as well as two of the scientists, died of fever during the trip.

Tinné lived in Cairo until moving to ALGIERS, ALGERIA, in 1867. She resumed her African explorations in 1869, intending to become the first European woman to cross the SAHARA. From TRIPOLI, on the Mediterranean Sea coast of LIBYA, she headed south to the oasis city of Murzuk. While waiting there for an Arab caravan with which she planned to continue her journey southward, Tinné took a side trip to visit the nomadic TUAREG peoples. On the way to a Tuareg encampment, Tinné was robbed and murdered by her guides.

Tippu Tip

1837–1905

One of the most powerful traders in Central and East Africa in the late nineteenth century.

Born Hamed bin Muhammed el-Murjebi in ZANZIBAR, Tippu Tip began his career at the age of twelve, when he began to accompany his father on short trading trips. In 1850 he set out on his own. Within fifteen years he built one of the most extensive trade empires in Central Africa.

Trading slaves and ivory for firearms, Tippu Tip's large caravans also served as his personal armies and hunting bands. He accumulated incredible wealth and power, expanding his territorial control through raids as well as deals with regional chiefs and other traders. By the early 1880s he was the most powerful trader in Central and East Africa.

Tippu Tip's caravans carried goods between Zanzibar on the east coast of Africa and Kasongo on the west coast of the Lualaba river. His bands of followers hunted elephants and raided villages for slaves in Central African forests. Many of the captives were put to work cultivating sugarcane, rice, and maize on plantations near the towns of Kasongo and Nyangwe. Tippu Tip's power, however, was short-lived. In 1885 LEOPOLD II of Belgium claimed control over the CONGO FREE STATE, which included Tippu Tip's empire. Tippu Tip resisted the European presence at first, but after negotiations with HENRY MORTON STANLEY, Leopold's agent in the Congo, Tippu Tip forfeited his empire in return for the governorship of what is now the eastern DEMOCRATIC REPUBLIC OF THE CONGO. Although this deal kept Tippu Tip in power, it angered his traders, who resented the ban on the slave trade. After numerous revolts, Tippu Tip stepped down and retired to Zanzibar, where he wrote his biography in the SWAHILI LANGUAGE.

See also Ivory Trade; Slavery in Africa.

Bibliography

Tip, Tippu. *Maisha ya Hamed bin Muhammed el Tippu Tip.* Translated by W.H Whitely. East African Literature Bureau, 1966.

Elizabeth Heath

Tiv

Ethnic group of more than two million people who live mostly in the Benue Valley of central Nigeria.

One of the largest ethnic groups in NIGERIA, the Tiv are concentrated on both sides of the Benue River in the central part of the country. The Tiv probably came to that area from the southeast, migrating from the Cameroon Mountains. Traditionally the Tiv have been subsistence farmers, raising chickens and growing yams, MILLET, sorghum, cassava, and sweet potatoes. Women perform most of the farming duties. In the past, Tiv men assumed the role of hunters, but their territory contains little game today.

Before the advent of European influence in the area—which did not come until the mid-nineteenth century—the Tiv amassed some regional power, encroaching on neighboring ethnic groups. But the British, who went on to colonize the entire region that later become Nigeria, soon stopped Tiv expansion. Colonial intervention brought other changes to Tiv life as well. Communities of up to 600 people, who lived in fortified towns near communal farmland, shrank to much smaller communities and farms. Before British rule there had been no central Tiv authority; however, in 1948, the British named a paramount chief of the Tiv. The traditional Tiv marriage arrangement, in which two family groups would exchange brides, was replaced by a system of marriage based on bridewealth, or dowry.

The Tiv place great importance on patrilineal kinship, in which ancestry is traced through the male line. The father's family line is paramount, and their social structure reflects this. A typical Tiv village comprises several households, each headed by a man related to the other men through the father's side. Dwellings are arranged in a circle, with separate sleeping buildings behind the main "reception" dwellings. Multiple marriage is permitted, and in some cases a man's reception dwelling will have two or more sleeping buildings behind it, one for each wife and her children.

Although waves of missionaries from SOUTH AFRICA, GREAT BRITAIN, and the United States brought CHRISTIANITY to the Tiv in the twentieth century, many Tiv adhere to traditional beliefs, and some are Muslim. Tiv religion revolves around unseen spirits and forces, called *akombo*, some of which cause death and disease and must be appeased or defeated through ritual.

See also Christianity: Missionaries in Africa; Ethnicity and Identity in Africa: An Interpretation; Religions, African.

Tlali, Miriam

1933–

South African writer, many of whose works were banned under apartheid.

Born to educated parents in JOHANNESBURG, SOUTH AFRICA, as a child Miriam Tlali was encouraged to study and write. But as a black South African she found her educational opportunities limited. After attending local elementary schools and studying art in high school, she won a scholarship to the University of Witwatersrand, but her hopes of studying medicine were dashed by the university's quotas for black students, which would allow her to study only administration. Tlali later pursued pre-medical training at Roma University in LESOTHO but ran out of money after a year and never finished her medical training.

Back in Johannesburg, Tlali drew on her experiences working as a bookkeeper in a furniture store to write her autobiographical first novel, *Muriel at Metropolitan*. Written in 1969, the book was not published in SOUTH AFRICA until 1975, partly because of its subtle but scathing portrayal of white insensitivity and everyday cruelty toward black people. In the 1970s, Tlali also began writing articles and stories that appeared in South African magazines such as the *Rand Daily Mail* and *Staffrider*.

Leaving Africa for the first time, Tlali attended the International Writers Program at the University of Iowa in 1978–1979. Her second novel, *Amandla* (1980), told the story of a black family living in SOWETO during the 1976 uprising and was, like Tlali's first novel, banned in South Africa. (Tlali herself was banned from political activity for many years.) In the 1980s Tlali, by then a wife and mother, wrote an interview series for *Staffrider* called *Soweto Speaking*. She also published three books in 1989 alone: *Mihloti* and *Soweto Stories*, both collections of Tlali's journalism, and *Footprints in the Quag: Stories and Dialogues from Soweto*. Declining to describe herself as a feminist in "the narrow, Western" sense, Tlali has become an important proponent of WOMANISM, the theory that black women living in a racially oppressive society must empower their community's men while at the same time supporting their sisters. As one of Tlali's female characters says to another in one of her short stories, "We're all alike; we're women. We need each other when things are difficult." Tlali lives in Soweto and continues to write.

See also Apartheid; Fiction, English-Language, in Africa.

Kate Tuttle

Tlemcen, Algeria

City in western Algeria; also called Tilimsen.

Even before the Romans came to the region, BERBERS had created small villages near the mountain-fed springs of the city known today as Tlemcen. The Romans built a fort called Pomaria early in the fourth century C.E., and a Berber settlement grew around the perimeter. Christians arrived in the region by the fifth century, even as Roman power in North Africa waned. Historians believe that the settlement was under the rule of a Berber chieftain by the sixth century.

In the eighth century, the Arab Abu al-Muhajir led the wave of conquerors and settlers who brought Islam to Tlemcen. The Islamic settlement took shape as a military garrison for the Karijites, a sect of Islam that included many Berbers. Although migrants from the east developed Arab Tlemcen, Tlemcen's proximity to FÈS to the west historically linked Tlemcen to what would later be MOROCCO. In the year 790, the sultan of Fès, Idris ibn 'Abd Allah, claimed the garrison and its environs. Over the centuries, the burgeoning city would pass back and forth between competing dynasties of the east, the west, and the regional Berber confederacy, the Zenata.

The great Almoravid and Almohad dynasties made Tlemcen a center of empires stretching across North Africa and into Andalusia, or Southern SPAIN, during the eleventh and twelfth centuries. The Moorish (or Andalusian) style of this period shaped art and architecture in the city for the next several centuries. The ALMORAVIDS created another city, Tagrart, nearby, which the ALMOHADS later joined with the original settlement. Tlemcen, from a Berber word that means "springs," became an entrepôt, or trading center, for goods passing from the sub-Saharan territories through the port city of Oran, and then on to EUROPE and the MIDDLE EAST.

Starting in 1236, Tlemcen blossomed under the reign of the 'Abd al-Wâdid (or Zayyanid) Dynasty, founded by Zenata Berbers. The great historian IBN KHALDUN wrote of the city during this period, "Tlemcen is the capital of the central Maghreb. . . . The city has acquired the appearance of a true Muslim capital, the government center of a Sultanate."

The prosperity attracted the Merinid Dynasty. In 1299 the Merinids began an eight-year siege against Tlemcen, as well as the construction of a wall around the city in order to block the entrance of supplies. Remarkably, the Merinids built an entire city, Mansourah, nearby, complete with a mosque and a palace for royal family members, as well as a garrison for soldiers. They diverted the trade caravans and established competing artisan industries. Although that initial siege was not successful, the Merinids ultimately won possession of Tlemcen nearly thirty years later.

Tlemcen never regained its former glory, although it did moderately well as a center of craftsmanship and learning. In the early sixteenth century, rival powers again fought over Tlemcen; Spain, the Turkish corsair KHAYR AD-DIN, and the Moroccan Sa'dians all vied for control of the city. As part of the Ottoman empire from the mid-sixteenth century to 1830, Tlemcen was a commercial center where traders exchanged sub-Saharan luxury goods—dates, ostrich feathers, wool, ivory, and gold—for wheat, barley, and European manufactured goods. Kouloughlis, people of mixed Turkish and Arab descent, made up the majority of the city's population by the eighteenth century.

When the French began to occupy ALGERIA in 1830, Tlemcen attempted to join Morocco. In a treaty, France promised Tlemcen to resistance leader ABD AL-QADIR, but after twelve years the French retook the city. The French used Tlemcen as a military base and administrative center for western Algeria, an area that remained vulnerable until most of Morocco fell under a French protectorate. Despite or perhaps because of its role as a French stronghold, Tlemcen became a hotbed for anticolonialist ferment: Ahmad Messali Hadj founded Algeria's first contemporary independence organization there in 1924. In 1962 the city served as headquarters for nationalist leader and future president AHMED BEN BELLA. Following independence the same year, Ben Bella shifted his headquarters to the capital city of ALGIERS. Tlemcen is a small bustling city of 141,600 (2004 estimate). Agriculture supplements an economy based on the artisan trades of textiles, leatherwork, and metalwork.

See also Gold Trade; Islam in Africa; Ivory Trade; North Africa, Roman Rule of.

Marian Aguiar

Tobias, Channing Heggie

1882–1961

American public official, Young Men's Christian Association and National Association for the Advancement of Colored People leader, domestic and international emissary for improved race relations.

Channing Heggie Tobias received bachelors' degrees from Paine College (then Paine Institute) and Drew University. In 1911, he became secretary of the National Council of the Young Men's Christian Association (YMCA) in WASHINGTON, D.C. Tobias remained with the YMCA for the next three decades, and was a strong advocate for the organization's desegregation.

In 1946, he left the YMCA to become the first black director of the Phelps-Stokes fund, which supported black education. Tobias won the NATIONAL ASSOCIATION FOR THE ADVANCEMENT OF COLORED PEOPLE's (NAACP) Spingarn Medal in 1948, and was chairman of the board of the NAACP from 1953 to 1959.

See also Desegregation in the United States.

Lisa Clayton Robinson

Togo

West African country situated on the Atlantic Ocean, bordering Benin, Ghana, and Burkina Faso.

Despite its small size, Togo's considerable geographic, ethnic, and economic diversity has haunted the country's political development. The German and French colonial administrations concentrated economic development in the mostly EWE coastal region south of the Togo Mountains, while the more ethnically diverse north remained impoverished. Since independence, Ewe prosperity and separatism have aroused northern resentment and fear. Togo has been called "the Jurassic Park of

Africa," because of the persistence of its military dictatorship, led by a northerner, General GNASSINGBÉ EYADÉMA, since 1967. Eyadéma's patronage has solidified his base of support in the north and among the powerful market women of the capital but alienated many in the more urbanized, mostly Ewe south. Eyadéma has been promising a transition to more democratic rule since 1989, but his government and military have repeatedly harassed opposition figures, disrupted elections, and blocked the formation of an independent electoral commission. Eyadéma's military regime seems determined to deflect the winds of democratic change.

Precolonial History

Archaeological finds demonstrate a human presence in the area extending back at least 50,000 years. A gradual shift from hunting and gathering to agriculture began about 5,000 years ago with the cultivation of yams in the forest zone surrounding the Togo Mountains and MILLET in the savanna to the north and south. On the country's northern plateaus, livestock herding has supplemented agriculture since prehistoric times, as has fishing along the Atlantic coast.

The area of present-day Togo never developed the strong state structures characteristic of ASANTE to the west or DAHOMEY to the east. Although some of its peoples repeatedly fell under the domination of neighboring kingdoms, the southern Ewe region as well as the territories of the Gurma, KABIYÉ, and other groups in the north remained divided among numerous small chiefdoms. While the neighboring kingdoms participated in the export of GOLD and slaves, the Togolese peoples retained a subsistence economy.

The Portuguese first visited the Togo coast during the late fifteenth century. Other Europeans, including the Dutch, English, French, and Danish, arrived by the seventeenth century, when the demand for slaves in the Americas began to dominate commercial relations. Local rulers exchanged slaves for firearms, which they used to maintain power and conduct more raids. Soon, the southern and central parts of Togo fell prey to slave raiders from the neighboring Asante and Dahomey states, and northern regions fell under the domination of the kingdoms of Mamprusi and DAGOMBA, centered in what is today northern Ghana. Much of the trade in Ewe slaves operated through ports just outside present-day Togo, such as Whydah to the east and Keta to the west, but some of the trade flowed through Petit Popo, now known as Aného—the only significant port on the Togolese coast until the colonial period. By the eighteenth century, Denmark dominated the trade along the Togolese coast. The Danes prohibited the slave trade in 1802 and withdrew from the area in 1850.

Meanwhile, the region attracted missionaries. From the eighteenth century onward, Danes sponsored Protestant missionaries in the region, many of them German-speaking. During the 1850s the North German Mission Society, based in Bremen, became the dominant Christian organization in Togolese territory, and during the 1860s a number of German merchants, also based in Bremen, set up operations on the Togolese coast.

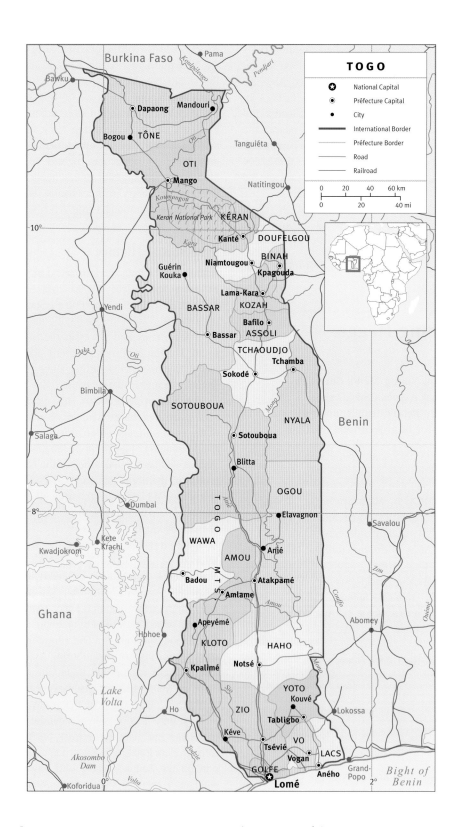

German Togoland

By the 1880s, the SCRAMBLE FOR AFRICA was in full swing, and the neighboring French and British colonial establishments' efforts, supported by some local elites, to secure a dominant position on the Togolese coast alarmed the German merchants of Aného. They appealed to the imperial government in Berlin to

intervene, and in 1884 GUSTAV NACHTIGAL, one of Germany's foremost African strategists, concluded a treaty with the chief of a small coastal village called Togo. The treaty granted Germany an exclusive protectorate over the entire coast of Togoland, which derived its name from this tiny chiefdom. The Germans quickly assumed control of the mostly Ewe region near the coast, but began their conquest of the interior only af-

In the capital city of Lomé, a woman operates a stall selling cloth dyed using a traditional batik process. The Lomé market women have been called the "principal socioeconomic force" in Togo. *Betty Press/Woodfin Camp*

ter 1893. They successfully subdued the north by 1897, although they confronted minor rebellions during the next few years. In 1897 they chose LOMÉ, until then a small fishing village, as the colonial capital.

Exports of Ewe-produced palm oil, along with a harsh system of taxation, resulted in a positive financial balance for the colony by 1907. For this reason, the Germans referred to Togo as their *Musterkolonie*, or "showcase colony." The Germans required twelve days of forced labor yearly from every able-bodied male in the colony, or a cash payment calculated on the basis of an individual's (often non-cash) income. Forced labor was deployed primarily on public works projects—such as the pier at Lomé, completed in 1904—and a series of railroads radiating out from the capital to the major cash-crop production zones in the south.

The possibility of substituting a cash payment for forced labor encouraged many Togolese to cultivate cash crops or accept wage labor. Germans enlisted researchers, including several from the TUSKEGEE INSTITUTE of Alabama, in finding a variety of cotton suited to the climate, and cotton became one of the colony's major exports. Though a few German settlers managed plantations, the colonial administration left production of both subsistence and cash crops mostly in the hands of Togolese, while German firms on the coast handled processing and export. Ownership of COCOA plantations in the mountainous interior provided the basis for an indigenous, mostly Ewe, bourgeoisie. Together, these developments yielded steadily increasing export earnings as well as the growth of a class of wage laborers, particularly in the south, no longer tied to subsistence agriculture. The Germans also recruited Togolese, especially Ewe educated in mission schools, to positions in the local administration.

When World War I broke out in 1914, FRANCE and GREAT BRITAIN invaded Togo from neighboring Dahomey and the GOLD COAST, and within a month had seized the entire colony. In 1919 the two countries agreed to partition German Togoland into two League of Nations mandates. France received the eastern two-thirds, including Lomé and the entire coastline and rail network, and Britain received a strip of land bordering its Gold Coast colony (modern-day GHANA).

French Togo

Although the two parts of Togoland were to be held in "trust" with the implicit goal of future reunification, the French and British incorporated the mandates into their respective colonial spheres. The French administered Togo jointly with Dahomey from 1934 to 1936 and as a subunit of French West Africa from 1936 to 1946. In 1946 Togo became a UNITED NATIONS trust territory, separate from the rest of FRENCH WEST AFRICA, with representation in the French parliament and an eventual goal of independence.

The French built on foundations laid by the Germans. They introduced coffee cultivation in the Togo Mountains, extended the railway network, and improved the Lomé port. They also replaced the German requirement of forced labor with a system of taxation that more effectively compelled cultivation of cash crops or wage labor. Like the Germans, the French focused most of their investments on the country's more developed south. An international consortium to exploit Togo's rich phosphate deposits formed in 1954 but would not begin extensive production until the country had achieved independence.

Beginning in 1947, the All-Ewe Conference, based in the Gold Coast, and the Comité de l'Unité Togolaise (CUT) argued before the United Nations Trusteeship Council for reunification of the French and British portions of Togoland, or alternatively for the unification of all Ewe territories, including those in the Gold Coast. The French viewed this Ewe unification movement

Togo (At a Glance)

OFFICIAL NAME: Togolese Republic

FORMER NAME: French Togoland

AREA: 56,785 sq km (21,925 sq mi)

LOCATION: Western Africa, bordered by Burkina Faso, Benin, Ghana, and the Atlantic Ocean

CAPITAL: Lomé (population 900,000); 2000 estimate

OTHER MAJOR CITIES: Sokodé (population 55,000) and Kpalimé (population 31,000); 1987 estimates

POPULATION: 5,429,299 (2003 estimate)

POPULATION DENSITY: 95.6 persons per sq km (about 247.6 persons per sq mi); 2003 estimate

POPULATION BELOW AGE 15: 44.5 percent (male 1,211,252; female 1,203,564); 2003 estimate

POPULATION GROWTH RATE: 2.37 percent (2003 estimate)

TOTAL FERTILITY RATE: 4.97 children born per woman (2003 estimate)

LIFE EXPECTANCY AT BIRTH: Total population: 53.43 years (male 51.47 years; female 55.45 years); 2003 estimate

INFANT MORTALITY RATE: 68.73 deaths per 1,000 live births (2003 estimate)

LITERACY RATE (AGE 15 AND OVER WHO CAN READ AND WRITE): Total population: 60.9 percent (male 75.4 percent; female 46.9 percent); 2003 estimate

EDUCATION: In the early 1970s the Togolese government undertook a campaign to provide free education to all children between ages two and fifteen. By the early 1990s nearly 76 percent of all school-age children attended school. Missionary schools are also important and educate roughly half of all students.

LANGUAGES: French is the official language; it is used for administration, commerce, and in schools. Ewe, Mina, Dagomba, and Kabye (sometimes spelled Kabiye) are the four major African languages spoken in Togo.

ETHNIC GROUPS: There are 37 different ethnic groups in Togo. The largest of these are the Ewe in the south, the Mina and the Kabré in the north.

RELIGIONS: About half of the population adhere to indigenous beliefs. About 29 percent are Christian; 20 percent are Muslim.

CLIMATE: Tropical in the south and semi-arid in the north. Average annual temperatures range from 27° C (about 80° F) at the coast to 30° C (86° F) in the north. The south has two rainy seasons, from March to July and October to November. The annual rainfall in the south averages 875 mm (35 in) and doubles in the mountains, a few kilometers in from the coast. In the north, where there is one rainy season between April and July, the average rainfall is 1,145 mm (45 in).

LAND, PLANTS, AND ANIMALS: Togo's geography varies from tropical forest at the coast to savanna in the rest of the country. There are buffalo, antelopes, lions, and deer in the northern regions. In the forests there are snakes and monkeys. Hippopotamuses and crocodiles live in the rivers.

NATURAL RESOURCES: Phosphates, limestone, and marble

CURRENCY: The CFA franc

GROSS DOMESTIC PRODUCT (GDP): $8 billion (2002 estimate)

GDP PER CAPITA: $1,500 (2002 estimate)

GDP REAL GROWTH RATE: 3 percent (2002 estimate)

PRIMARY ECONOMIC ACTIVITIES: Agriculture, industry, and services

PRIMARY CROPS: Coffee, cocoa, cotton, yams, cassava (tapioca), corn, beans, rice, millet, sorghum, meat, and fish

INDUSTRIES: Phosphate mining, agricultural processing, cement, handicrafts, textiles, and beverages

PRIMARY EXPORTS: Phosphates, cotton, cocoa, and coffee

PRIMARY IMPORTS: Machinery and equipment, consumer goods, food, and chemical products

PRIMARY TRADE PARTNERS: European Union, Africa, United States, and Japan

GOVERNMENT: Togo is a republic under transition to multiparty democratic rule. The executive branch is led by President Gen. Gnassingbé Eyadéma and Prime Minister Koffi Sama. The legislative branch is the elected 81-member National Assembly.

---

with alarm because it played into the hands of Kwame Nkrumah's campaign to unify Togo with Ghana, which would eliminate French influence in the region. Meanwhile, in 1956 a plebiscite in British Togoland approved a merger with the Gold Coast, although a majority in the southern Ewe districts opposed the merger. British Togoland merged with the Gold Coast and in 1957 gained independence under NKRUMAH as Ghana.

The French held a referendum in 1956 approving the creation of an autonomous republic of French Togo, despite Ewe opposition. Nicolas Grunitzky, a northerner, was appointed premier. After a protest by the mostly Ewe CUT to the United Nations, an election held in 1958 approved complete independence for Togo and replaced Grunitzky with a government led by CUT's Sylvanus Olympio. Togo proclaimed full independence on April 27, 1960.

Independent Togo

Olympio's Ewe-based government maintained economic and political ties with France and Francophone Africa. But Olympio moved ruthlessly to suppress opposition, and his program of austerity alienated not only northerners but much of his Ewe constituency. He resisted Nkrumah's desire for integration of Togo with Ghana, and the subsequent border closings alienated Lomé's market women, who have been called the "principal socioeconomic force in the country." Meanwhile, the end of French colonialism meant layoffs for Togolese soldiers (mostly Kabiyé from the impoverished north) who had served in the French military. In 1963, when the widely unpopular Olympio refused to offer a group of unemployed Kabiyé soldiers positions in the country's army, they staged West Africa's first military coup. Though little blood was actually shed, Étienne Gnassingbé (later Gnassingbé Eyadéma) murdered Olympio as he sought refuge at the gates of the United States embassy.

During a four-year interlude, Nicolas Grunitzky served as "provisional president" with the backing of the expanded, mostly Kabiyé military. But Grunitzky's indecisive leadership alienated a number of constituencies, including the crucial market women, and his subjection to the military made him unable to appease Ewe leaders, who demanded that Eyadéma and other participants in the 1963 coup be brought to justice. When Ewe unrest threatened the survival of Grunitzky's regime, Eyadéma and his military colleagues acted to ward off their certain doom at the hands of Olympio's political heirs. In 1967 the military demanded Grunitzky's resignation, and Eyadéma declared himself president and banned all political parties.

Togo Under Eyadéma

Eyadéma's ascent to power coincided with the onset of unprecedented prosperity in Togo, which helped him win popular support. Togo's growing phosphate-export earnings bankrolled a lavish program of patronage, and civil servants and other employees received generous pay increases. Eyadéma's government, freed from reliance on customs duties, enacted a free trade policy that opened up a profitable smuggling trade with neighboring Ghana. This ingratiated him with Togo's market women, as did his construction of a network of regional markets across the country. Meanwhile, Eyadéma carried out an extensive building program in Lomé and development projects benefiting the hitherto neglected north, including the completion of a paved road linking Lomé to Burkina Faso.

Eyadéma followed the pattern of his idol, General Mobutu Sese Seko of the Democratic Republic of the Congo (later Zaire), in institutionalizing his military rule. In 1969 he created the Rassemblement du Peuple Togolais (RPT) as the country's sole legal party. Legislative elections in 1979 and 1985 confirmed a single slate of candidates prepared by the RPT. In response to his call for "authenticity," the government abandoned colonial place-names and required civil servants to follow his example

in dropping his European name (Étienne) for an indigenous one (Gnassingbé). With the assistance of North Korean advisers, he built a personality cult around himself. Massive photographs and statues of the general, referred to as "The Savior of the Common Man" or simply "Le Guide," were installed throughout Togo.

When phosphate prices soared briefly in the mid-1970s, Togo nationalized the phosphate sector and based an "industrialization drive" on the construction of massive state enterprises with international borrowing. By the late 1970s, however, phosphate prices had plummeted, and when newly built facilities such as a petroleum refinery and a steel mill began operation, they proved economically nonviable. Meanwhile, Togo had accumulated a massive external debt that it could not repay.

During the 1980s, the government, under pressure from the French government and the International Monetary Fund (IMF) was forced to privatize state enterprises, eliminate widespread mismanagement and cronyism, and implement an austerity plan. This put an end to Eyadéma's patronage system and precipitated a severe economic decline, which in turn led to growing popular dissatisfaction with the regime, particularly in the more commercial south. Eyadéma responded by staging elections in 1986 that showed virtually unanimous support for his continued leadership, while the military, led by Eyadéma's relatives and neighbors, mounted a campaign of imprisonment, torture, and murder in an attempt to suppress dissent. But the regime's rigorous adherence to the IMF austerity plan earned it international support, and in 1986 French troops helped repress an attempted coup, reportedly organized by the exiled sons of Olympio.

Revelations of the regime's HUMAN RIGHTS abuses, however, put Eyadéma under international pressure to allow a more open political process. After demonstrations calling for Eyadéma's resignation met with bloody military responses in 1990 and 1991, Eyadéma agreed to the formation of political parties and a National Conference on political reforms. Opposition leaders attempted to use the National Conference as a vehicle to replace Eyadéma's government, but ongoing military harassment and attempted assassinations of opposition leaders confirmed the general's hold on power. The pattern of harassment and the government's delay in scheduling national elections sparked a wave of general strikes in 1992 and 1993 that crippled Togo's ailing economy.

When elections finally took place in 1993, government-sponsored violence and electoral manipulation led to the withdrawal of an international monitoring team and a boycott by opposition leaders. With a turnout of about 36 percent, Eyadéma was reelected to a five-year term. Despite continued military harassment, legislative elections in 1994 yielded a slim majority for the opposition. However, government manipulation led to the disqualification of several opposition legislators and the formation of a government favorable to General Eyadéma.

Since 1994 the Togolese economy has seen a partial recovery, based on strong export earnings, from the preceding fifteen-year decline. Funding has been approved for an improvement of the port of Lomé and the highway to Burkina Faso. But the current political scene is less encouraging: in 1997 Eyadéma's government blocked the creation of an independent electoral commission, and military harassment of opposition leaders marred the 1998 presidential campaign, in which Eyadéma was proclaimed the victor. The election results sparked opposition protests and rioting in the streets of the capital. The president's political opponents boycotted the next year's legislative elections, which also were marked by fraud and misrepresentation of voter turnout.

In 1999 the RPT met with opposition leaders in Paris and crafted the Lomé Framework Agreement, under which Eyadéma agreed not to seek a new term as president when his current one expired in 2003. The agreement also outlined the rights and responsibilities of political parties and the media, and called for the safe return of political refugees and compensation for those affected by political violence. Eyadéma agreed to hold new legislative elections in 2000, but never honored that part of the agreement. In 2003 he also reneged on his promise to not stand for re-election, winning a third term in June of that year. In 2004 Eyadéma—the longest-serving head of state in Africa—celebrated thirty-seven years in power by presiding over a lavish parade in Lomé.

See also Christianity: Missionaries in Africa; Colonial Rule; Germany; Transatlantic Slave Trade.

Mark O'Malley

Toivo ja Toivo, Andimba

1924–

Leading Namibian nationalist and senior government minister.

The founding father of Namibian nationalism, Andimba Toivo ja Toivo remains one of Namibia's most venerated public figures. Toivo ja Toivo was born in Umungundu, South-West Africa (now NAMIBIA). He received a mission school education in SOUTH-WEST AFRICA, then occupied by SOUTH AFRICA, and served as a corporal in the Native Military Corps during World War II. After the war he worked in South Africa, first in a mine on the Witwatersrand and then in a CAPE TOWN grocery. In a Cape Town barbershop Toivo ja Toivo organized South-West Africa contract laborers into what became the Ovambo People's Organization, or OPO, in 1958. When he returned home in 1961 to help organize the successor to the OPO, the SOUTH WEST AFRICA PEOPLE'S ORGANIZATION (SWAPO), the South African government placed him under house arrest.

Despite the arrest, Toivo ja Toivo continued his organizing activities, and consequently was tried and convicted at the Terrorism Trial in 1966. Sentenced to twenty years of imprisonment on ROBBEN ISLAND, Toivo ja Toivo became a close associate of NELSON MANDELA. In 1984 he was released from prison

early in what some considered an attempt by South Africa to divide the SWAPO leadership. Instead Toivo ja Toivo, then sixty-nine years old, returned to WINDHOEK a hero, and became secretary general of the party. In the 1989 elections Toivo ja Toivo was elected to the National Assembly, and a year later became Minister of Mines and Energy in independent Namibia. In 1991 he stepped down from his party post to devote more time to his ministerial position. He later served as Minister of Labor and since 2003 has been the Minister of Prisons and Correctional Services in Namibia. Toivo ja Toivo has repeatedly demanded an investigation into torture and disappearances at SWAPO camps during the war for independence.

See also Nationalism in Africa; Political Movements in Africa.

Eric Young

Tolbert, William Richard, Jr.

1913–1980

President of Liberia from 1971 until his assassination in 1980.

When William Richard Tolbert Jr. took office as LIBERIA's twentieth president in 1971, he seemed poised to continue the dominance of the True Whig Party (TWP), which had ruled Liberian politics for more than a century. Instead, Tolbert's administration was plagued by indecision and confusion, and his 1980 assassination marked the beginning of two decades of political, economic, and social chaos.

A member of the Americo-Liberian elite, William Tolbert attended a private Episcopal high school and the University of Liberia, from which he graduated in 1934. He worked in various government jobs before his 1943 election to the House of Representatives. In 1951 Tolbert became WILLIAM V. S. TUBMAN's vice president, a position he maintained through five elections until Tubman's death in 1971, when he became president.

Long under Tubman's shadow, Tolbert took immediate steps to distinguish himself from his predecessor. Wearing casual dress to his inauguration, the KPELLE-speaking president promised greater openness to opposition groups as well as economic growth that would aid the country's poor. But while Tolbert's vague pronouncements were intended to appeal to both populist Liberians and the more conservative business community, his actual policies pleased few on either side. In 1979 the deregulation of food prices sparked protests and, after Tolbert sent in the army to break them up, widespread rioting. On April 12, 1980, an army master sergeant, SAMUEL K. DOE, led a small group of soldiers into Tolbert's presidential palace and assassinated him. Doe subsequently proclaimed himself Liberia's new head of state.

See also Americo-Liberians.

Kate Tuttle

Tolson, Melvin Beaunorus

1898–1966

American poet, chronicler of Harlem cultural scene.

Melvin Beaunorus Tolson attended FISK UNIVERSITY before transferring to Lincoln University, where he received his bachelor's degree in 1922. He took positions teaching English literature and coaching the debate team at Wiley College in Marshall, Texas, but was inspired to develop his talent for poetry after attending Columbia University on a Rockefeller Foundation scholarship from 1931 to 1932. Tolson's year at Columbia put him in HARLEM at the end of the HARLEM RENAISSANCE, and he became friendly with many writers associated with it, most notably LANGSTON HUGHES. In several poems over the next two decades, Tolson would revisit the atmosphere of 1930s Harlem.

Tolson's first major work, *Rendezvous with America*, was published in 1944. Throughout the 1940s, his poems, characterized by their allusive, complex, modernist style and their long poetic sequences, were published in such magazines and journals as the *Atlantic Monthly*, the *Modern Quarterly*, the *Arts Quarterly*, and *Poetry*. In 1947, the government of LIBERIA named Tolson its poet laureate and commissioned him to write a piece for the country's centennial; the result was *Libretto for the Republic of Liberia* (1953). Tolson's best known piece, the poetic sequence *Harlem Gallery*, was published in 1965. In 1966, he won the Arts and Letters Award in literature from the American Academy and Institute of Arts and Letters. *A Gallery of Harlem Portraits*, an extended work Tolson had begun with a single sonnet in 1932, was published posthumously in 1979.

See also Poetry, Black, in English.

Bibliography

Farnsworth, Robert M. *Melvin B. Tolson, 1898–1966: Plain Talk and Poetic Prophecy.* University of Missouri Press, 1984.

Flasch, Joy. *Melvin B. Tolson.* Twayne Publishers, 1972.

Lisa Clayton Robinson

Tolton, Augustus

1854?–1897

First African American Catholic priest in the United States.

Augustus Tolton was raised in Quincy, Illinois. He began studying for the priesthood in 1873, and though initially refused admission at local seminaries, was eventually able to attend Quincy College and complete his studies in Rome, ITALY.

Tolton was ordained in Rome in 1886, and returned to the United States to serve as one of the first African American Catholic priests. His first congregation was in a racially mixed parish in Quincy, but after pressure from local priests, he took

over a black congregation in CHICAGO, ILLINOIS. Tolton was a leader in the black Catholic congresses between 1889 and 1894.

Lisa Clayton Robinson

Tombalbaye, François

1918–1975

Prime minister of French-governed Chad and first president of independent Chad.

Raised in southern CHAD, François Tombalbaye was educated in BRAZZAVILLE, Congo, and was one of the few Chadians to have obtained a secondary education by the end of World War II (1939–1945). While working as a teacher in 1947, Tombalbaye helped organize the Parti Progressiste Tchadien (PPT or Chadian Progressive Party), the Chadian branch of the African Democratic Rally, an interterritorial political party across FRENCH WEST AFRICA. Tombalbaye's political career prospered after 1952. He was elected to the regional legislature and also began to climb the ranks of the PPT leadership. Tombalbaye represented Chad in the 1957 General Council for FRENCH EQUATORIAL AFRICA and in 1959 he became leader of the PPT and Chad's prime minister. Tombalbaye led Chad to independence in 1960 and became its first president. In his first years in power he worked to isolate and eliminate all political rivals, and in 1962 banned all opposition parties. Tombalbaye ruled in authoritarian fashion, surviving uprisings in southern and eastern Chad, a full-scale rebellion in northern Chad in 1965, border conflicts with LIBYA, and coup attempts in 1971 and 1972. Tombalbaye's presidency was associated with turning opposition groups against each other, an attempt to promote African cultural practices, and overambitious development projects that achieved less than promised. In a 1975 military coup he was killed in the cross fire between rebels and palace guards.

See also Nationalism in Africa.

Tombouctou, Mali

Principal southern terminus of trans-Saharan trade and former center of Islamic studies, famous for its university in medieval times.

Founded by TUAREGS nine miles from the northwest bend of the NIGER RIVER in MALI, Tombouctou's fame goes back to its prominence as a commercial, religious, and educational center in the Middle Ages, especially during the 1500s. At present, Tombouctou, with an estimated population of 35,900, is a town of mostly adobe buildings, with a prominent cone-shaped great mosque on its western skirts. Two other mosques, Sidi Yahia, at the town's center, and Sankoré, located northeast of the town, punctuate its skyline. The majority of the town's inhabitants are SONGHAI. Tombouctou is connected with the Niger River by canals, and the town of Kabara serves as its port. Between March and June, caravan traders and nomadic herders camp out around town to sell their goods at the market, increasing the population significantly. Tombouctou has a variety of resident artisans, including weavers, potters, leatherworkers, and smiths. Most of the town's permanent residents are merchants and traders. Salt brought by camel caravan from salt mines at Taodeni 375 miles to the north and livestock from Tuareg herders inhabiting sparse pasture lands in the southern Saharan regions of Mali are two of the major commodities sold at the market, along with dates from oasis gardens.

In ancient times the region around Tombouctou is said to have been populated by the Songhai, who reputedly migrated to the bend of the Niger from the valley of the Nile in EGYPT. Rock inscriptions showing horse-drawn chariots west of Tombouctou place it along the pre-Roman trade routes of the SAHARA, linking it with MOROCCO. Early Songhai settlers first established Gao along the northeastern bend of the Niger, directly east of Tombouctou, and DJENNÉ-JENO to the south, both commercial centers along the trans-Saharan caravan routes. In the eleventh century, a market center was founded at Tombouctou by Tuareg pastoralists. From the twelfth century onward, caravans carrying West African gold passed through Tombouctou en route to the Barbary Coast.

When the Moroccan Berber historian IBN BATTUTAH visited Tombouctou in 1353, he noted that most of its inhabitants were "wearers of the face-veil," a style used by Tuareg men to wind their turbans so that they drape across the face creating a mask or "veil." Battutah describes a fourteenth-century "turbaning ritual" at Tombouctou very similar to those performed among some Tuareg groups today, in which the ruling governor presents an ascending Tuareg confederation chief with a new robe, a turban, and trousers of indigo dyed cloth. In the ceremony, the governor wrapped the new turban around the Tuareg ruler's head and face, "bade him sit upon a shield, and the chiefs of his tribe raised him on their heads."

The Songhai captured Tombouctou in 1468. Between 1494 and 1529 Tombouctou reached what was perhaps its greatest height under ASKIA MUHAMMAD's rule. During this period a center of higher learning, the "university" of Tombouctou, was established at the mosque of Sankoré. It became a renowned center of Islamic studies, with scholars educated in leading Islamic academies of the MIDDLE EAST. Tombouctou is still the repository of a number of valuable manuscripts in Arabic, including the *Tarik es-Sudan*, a history of the SUDAN written by the religious scholar Abderrahman Sadi in the 1600s.

In 1591 the Sultan of Morocco sent an army to Tombouctou to capture the city and take control of the GOLD TRADE. This brought the SONGHAI EMPIRE to an end. The Moorish invaders from Morocco who controlled the city began feuding among themselves, however, and the town was almost in ruins by the time the Tuaregs took over again in 1800. The city was subsequently captured by FULANI tribesmen in 1813 and by the TUKULOR in 1840.

By the time British and French explorers began arriving at Tombouctou in the 1800s, Tombouctou had fallen into decay. Major Gordon Laing traveled across the Sahara from TRIPOLI, arriving at Tombouctou in 1826, but he was murdered by the Fulanis. RENÉ CAILLIÉ visited Tombouctou for two weeks, traveling from the coast in 1828; he noted that, although its commercial significance had diminished, many Tombouctou merchants were still receiving commodities from North Africa, and certain European goods—in particular, double-barreled French guns—were much sought. The marketplace also sold gold and slaves from the West Africa savanna and forest regions.

The explorer HEINRICH BARTH spent six months in Tombouctou from 1853 to 1854, traveling across the Sahara to represent the British government and establish British influence there. He noted the decreasing trade in slaves and the volume of trade in Moroccan tobacco, cloth from EUROPE, and Saharan oasis-grown dates, as well as sword blades from GERMANY. Explorer Oskar Lenz traveled to Tombouctou from Morocco in 1880. The following year French troops began the conquest of the regions along the Niger bend, arriving at Tombouctou in 1893 just after Tuaregs had again taken control of the town, and capturing the city in 1894.

Tombouctou remains a crossroads of Saharan and Sahelian peoples, including Tuareg camel nomads and caravaneers, Fulani cattle herders, Hassaniya-speaking Arabized Berber nomads, Songhai traders and gardeners, and Mandingo and BAMBARA farmers and traders. It can be reached by boat from Bamako and Gao on the Niger River.

See also Islam in Africa; Salt Trade; Trans-Saharan and Red Sea Slave Trade.

Barbara Worley

Tonga

Linguistic and ethnic group of the Zambezi basin; also known as Batonga.

The Tonga include approximately 12 percent of ZAMBIA's ten million inhabitants. While the majority live in southern Zambia along Lake Kariba and the ZAMBEZI RIVER, some Tonga also live in northern ZIMBABWE, BOTSWANA, MALAWI, and MOZAMBIQUE. Other ethnic groups also speak the Tonga language, including the Lenje, Soli, Ila, Toka, Leya, Sala, and Gowa. Altogether, about one-fifth of Zambians speak Tonga. Archaeological evidence (namely, stylistic continuity in pottery) shows that the Tonga have occupied Sebanzi Hill in Zambia since about 1100 C.E. Some sources suggest that the Tonga migrated from an area south of the Zambezi River, though their Bantu language suggests an ancient migration from the north.

The Tonga fall into two broad groups: the Plateau Tonga and the Valley (or Gwembe) Tonga. Traditionally, each group inhabited a distinct ecological niche. Since the soils are not particularly fertile, the Plateau Tonga raise cattle, although they also cultivate maize and peanuts. The Plateau Tonga are also known for their iron working. The Valley Tonga traditionally practiced floodplain cultivation, primarily of maize, MILLET, and sorghum. During the dry season, the Valley Tonga lived near the river to protect their crop against invading pests. However, after the crops were harvested and the water levels rose, they abandoned these garden settlements for higher ground until the following year.

The Tonga traditionally lacked chiefs and political hierarchies. They remained divided into numerous matrilineages. These lineages traditionally provided the basic structure for the Tonga's small, widely dispersed, permanent hamlets, consisting of related women and their husbands and sons. Daily politics, such as land-tenure disputes, fell under the purview of the lineage. The loosely organized Tonga suffered heavily from the actions of more hierarchical neighboring groups such as the Lozi, who periodically raided for slaves.

When the British took control of the region, they identified native authorities to administer local government under their policy of indirect rule. Among groups such as the Tonga who lacked such political leaders, the British appointed them. Thus, over the course of the twentieth century, Tonga political organization has become more centralized and hierarchical. In 1913 many Tonga were forced off their lands, particularly those adjacent to the railroad, to make way for European settlers. Deprived of land and forced to pay taxes, some young men traveled to the mines of Southern Rhodesia (today Zimbabwe) in search of employment. The majority of the Tonga remained, and shifted from the cultivation of finger millet to maize, which they sold for consumption in the burgeoning mining towns. Thus the Tonga have remained less urban than other ethnic groups.

The Tonga have faced a number of setbacks in recent years. Relatively affluent Tonga farmers helped found the nationalist movement after World War II, and supported the (Zambian) African National Congress (ANC), led by the Tonga-speaking Harry Nkumbula. In the late 1950s, however, the colonial government dammed the Zambezi River causing Lake Kariba to submerge the farms of many of the Valley Tonga. Some 60,000 farmers, forcibly relocated around the lake, continued to depend upon agriculture on the sandier soils of the lakeshore. Some took up fishing. However, the lifestyle of the Valley Tonga, previously revolving around the seasonal floods, had radically changed. The group became increasingly marginalized after its forcible relocation to more marginal areas. In the early 1960s the United National Independence Party, dominated by Bemba-speakers, eclipsed the Tonga-led ANC. Recent constitutional amendments have barred traditional chiefs, including the Tonga leader Chief Munyumbwe, from politics in a ploy to further disenfranchise already marginal groups.

See also Bantu: Dispersion and Settlement; Ethnicity and Identity in Africa: An Interpretation; Languages, African: An Overview.

Ari Nave

Tontons Macoute

Also known as Tonton Makout, a fearsome paramilitary group established in Haiti under the dictatorship of François Duvalier.

The name Tonton Macoute was originally attached to a haunting character in Haitian folk literature. Translating roughly as "bogeyman with a basket," the name referred to an old bearded man who carried a bag of woven straw (a *macoute* in Creole) and appeared at night to carry away naughty children. Haitian mothers invoked the image of Tonton Macoute to encourage obedience among their children, saying: "If you do not behave, I'll call Tonton Macoute and he will drag you away."

When François Duvalier took power in Haiti on October 22, 1957, he soon inaugurated a regime of terror against his opponents. He desired a source of power parallel to, but independent from, the armed forces; in order to serve Duvalier's needs, the new group would have to attach its loyalty exclusively to the Haitian leader. By July 1958 Duvalier had established his personal militia, the Tontons Macoute. Duvalier's henchmen attacked, beat, raped, and harassed the opponents of his regime, initially wearing hoods to mask their features. (As a hood is called a *cagoule* in French, these forces were initially called *Cagoulards*; eventually the more popular Tontons Macoute took hold.) Early in Duvalier's rule this force targeted academics and other intellectuals who might oppose Duvalier, provoking one of many waves of migration from Haiti to the United States and elsewhere. Though there are no solid estimates, it is believed that during the early Duvalier years the Tontons Macoute killed tens of thousands of people. The militia's abuses were generally documented in urban Haiti, but less is known about the actions of the Tontons Macoute in rural areas, where their presence was stronger and where the vast majority of the Haitian population resides.

The Tontons Macoute, which was not officially acknowledged by the Haitian government, soon evolved into a pervasive secret police force in Haiti. In 1962 the Duvalier regime created a militia called the Volontaires de la Sécurité Naitonale (VSN), whose connection to the Tontons Macoute was suspected if not explicit. The true status of the VSN is unclear: some believe it served as a virtual cover for the Tontons Macoute, but others hold that it was a second official military force designed to neutralize the army. Supporters of the latter belief point out that the VSN was created shortly after a coup attempt against Duvalier.

Regardless of its official affiliation, the Tontons Macoute was an ominous presence, particularly in rural Haiti. Notorious for their blue uniforms, straw hats, and red sashes—made to appear like the traditional dress of the Haitian peasantry—the Macoutes not only carried out violence but exercised overwhelming power in government administration; most rural section chiefs and other local officials were Macoutes. As the militia's power increased, so did its numbers: the Tontons Macoute eventually became twice as large as the army (estimates of the militia's full membership range from 9,000 to as high as 300,000). This led not only to serious rivalry between the Tontons Macoute and other political and military forces, but also to rivalry within the Macoutes ranks.

When François Duvalier's rule passed on to his son, Jean-Claude Duvalier, the links between the police, the army, and the VSN/Tontons Macoute became stronger, and many feel that the head of the Macoutes, Minister of the Interior Roger La-fontant, became the real power behind Jean-Claude Duvalier's rule. But some observers also argue that the Tontons Macoute came to be increasingly critical of "Baby Doc" Duvalier, whom they saw as betraying the "ideals" of his father. These divisions within the VSN/Tontons Macoute were partially responsible for the collapse of Jean-Claude Duvalier's spectacularly corrupt regime, which finally fell on February 7, 1986. Nevertheless, at the end of his rule, "Baby Doc" Duvalier declared a state of siege and called the Tontons Macoute and the army into the streets, where they killed hundreds. The end of Duvalier's sovereignty thus provoked Carnivals and street celebrations. It also incited the *dechoukaj*, or "uprooting," a strong backlash against the Tontons Macoute in which citizens killed scores of the organization's more visible members.

Though the Tontons Macoute was not the first or the last paramilitary organization in Haiti, their use by Duvalier established a legacy of fear and violence that poses powerful dilemmas. Particularly urgent in a post-Duvalier and incipiently democratic Haiti is the issue of how to deal with past abuses: whether or not to bring past abusers to justice while seeking to create a unified, just, and democratic Haiti.

Paulette Poujol-Oriol

Toomer, Jean

1894–1967

American writer whose experimental novel of Southern life, *Cane*, profoundly influenced twentieth-century black writers.

Jean Toomer's position in the canon of African American literature rests on his haunting narrative of Southern life, *Cane*. Despite Toomer's later ambivalence toward his racial identity, the novel has been rediscovered by successive generations of black writers since its original publication in 1923. Toomer, who was racially mixed but able to pass for white, sought a unifying thesis that would resolve the conflicts of his identity. He spent his life trying to evade the categories of American racial and ethnic identification, which he believed constricted the complexity of a lineage like his.

As a writer, Toomer was nurtured by Greenwich Village progressive aesthetes of the 1910s and 1920s, such as Waldo Frank and Hart Crane. His inspiration for *Cane*, however, came from his two-month stint as a substitute principal at the black Sparta Agricultural and Industrial Institute in Georgia in 1921. Entranced by Georgia's rural geography and its black folk traditions, he saw in Southern life the harmony that escaped him, although he believed the rich black culture was disappearing through migration to the North and its encounter with modernity.

Cane is a series of vignettes; its narrative structure moves from the South to the North and back to the South, forming a troubled synthesis of the two regions. The book was a commercial failure when first published, but critics lauded it, initi-

Admired for its sensitive treatment of black life, Jean Toomer's novel *Cane* (1923) influenced generations of African American writers, including Toni Morrison and Alice Walker. *CORBIS/Bettmann*

ating a chorus of praise that has spanned generations. Members of the HARLEM RENAISSANCE and the BLACK ARTS MOVEMENT, as well as later African American women writers such as TONI MORRISON and ALICE WALKER, have cited its influence and acclaimed the author's sensitive treatment of black folk life, his formal elegance, and his progressive, uninhibited approach to sexuality and gender.

Cane was Toomer's only work that explicitly treated the lives of African Americans, and the author disappeared from literary circles after its publication. In 1924 the restless Toomer made the first of several pilgrimages to Fontainebleau, FRANCE, to study with mystic and psychologist Georges Ivanovich Gurdjieff at the Institute for the Harmonious Development of Man. Gurdjieff believed that a transcendent essence, obscured by a socially determined personality, could be recovered through his teachings. Through Gurdjieff, Toomer found a way to express his attempts at defining a holistic identity. He taught Gurdjieff's philosophy in HARLEM in New York and in CHICAGO, ILLINOIS, until his break with the mystic in the mid-1930s.

Toomer wrote voluminously until his death. Although much of his writing received occasional praise for its experimentation, it was largely dismissed by African American critics, who saw it not only as propaganda for Gurdjieff's teachings but also as being white-identified. Indeed, in 1930 Toomer declined to be included in JAMES WELDON JOHNSON's *Book of American Negro Poetry*, on the grounds that he was not a Negro. Toomer continued to strive for a sense of wholeness, however, and for a definition of what HENRY LOUIS GATES, JR., has described as a "remarkably fluid notion of race." He found this in the potential of an "American" race, described in the 1936 long poem *Blue Meridian* as a hybrid "blue," comprising the black, the white, and the red races. *Blue Meridian* was Toomer's last work to be published while he was alive.

See also Literature, African American; Poetry, Black, in English.

Peter Hudson

Toposa

Ethnic group of Sudan; also known as Topotha.

The Toposa primarily inhabit far southern SUDAN. They speak a Nilo-Saharan language. Approximately 180,000 people consider themselves Toposa.

See also Ethnicity and Identity in Africa: An Interpretation; Languages, African: An Overview.

Toro

Ethnic group of Uganda; also known as Rutoro.

The Toro primarily inhabit western UGANDA. They speak a Bantu language and are closely related to the NYANKORE people. Over 700,000 people consider themselves Toro.

See also Bantu: Dispersion and Settlement; Ethnicity and Identity in Africa: An Interpretation; Languages, African: An Overview.

Tosh, Peter

1944–1987

Jamaican singer and songwriter, and an internationally popular solo artist with an emphatic political and prophetic bent; best known as an original member of The Wailers, the singing trio that also included Bob Marley and Bunny Wailer (Neville O'Riley Livingston).

Born Peter McIntosh, Tosh's entrance into music began during his teenage years in the Trenchtown ghetto of KINGSTON, where he and his friends BOB MARLEY and Bunny Wailer imitated the vocal harmonies of CURTIS MAYFIELD. Tosh's early recordings as part of a SKA/REGGAE trio with Marley and Wailer (who became known as "The Wailers") made clear that his singing and song-writing talents were strongly flavored by rage against hypo-critical individuals and institutions. Songs like "400 Years" and "Downpressor" are prime examples of his mastery of political protest songwriting. His first recordings as a solo artist in the early 1960s include a wry commentary on sexual mores

("Shame and Scandal") and a boastful declaration of Rastafarian identity ("Rasta Shook Them Up").

After quitting The Wailers in 1972, Tosh pursued a performing and recording career as a solo artist, marked by the cultivation of a persona of supreme toughness and righteous wrath, sentiments encapsulated in the song that became his anthem, "I'm the Toughest." This stance was reinforced during a Jamaican concert when Tosh lectured JAMAICA's prime minister, sitting in the audience, about the errors of the minister's ways. An overview of his recording career is available on CD as *Peter Tosh: Honorary Citizen* (Columbia). His murder silenced reggae's most politically inspired artist.

See also Rastafarians.

Norman Weinstein

Totó la Momposina

1946–

Afro-Colombian singer, dancer, and performer of traditional rhythms from Colombia's Atlantic and Pacific coasts.

Totó la Momposina, as she is known, was born Sonia Bazanta in the town of Talaigua, COLOMBIA, on the river island of Mompós, from which she took her stage name. The small towns on the Magdalena River (on Mompós and in surrounding areas, including Soplaviento, PALENQUE DE SAN BASILIO, Botón de Leyva, and Altos del Rosario) are heirs to a rich Afro-Indian musical tradition. Originally inhabited by indigenous peoples, during the colonial period these areas became a safe haven for fugitive slaves, who built fortified villages known as *palenques*.

Totó is a fourth-generation musician—her grandfather was an accordionist, her father is a traditional drummer (*tambolero*), and her mother was a traditional singer (*cantadora*). Totó's parents and family sought to preserve secular and sacred musical forms played at religious festivals, funerals, ritual ceremonies, and local Carnivals. From an early age, Totó learned the Afro-Colombian rhythms of *chandé, mapalé, fandango, currulao, porro, puya,* and CUMBIA. Totó was also raised in the tradition of the cantadoras, female singers who improvise verses (*coplas*). She learned about music from the many musicians and cantadoras who visited the family home, and by taking part in fiestas and ceremonies in neighboring villages.

In the late 1960s Totó traveled to Paris to study dance history at the Sorbonne. In FRANCE, she began her musical career by singing in train stations and on street corners. She was "discovered" in Europe and it was there that she released her first two albums, *Totó la Momposina* and *Colombia: Musique de la Cité Atlantique.* She later traveled to CUBA to learn more about BOLERO, SON, *guaracha,* RUMBA, and other Afro-Cuban rhythms, and went on to include these sounds in her repertoire.

In 1982 Totó and her group—Totó la Momposina y Sus Tambores—accompanied Colombian writer Gabriel García Márquez to receive the Nobel Prize for literature in Stockholm.

In the 1990s British singer and producer Peter Gabriel invited the group to record for his Real World label and to be part of the annual World of Music, Arts, and Dance (WOMAD) tour.

Totó has since gained much popularity in Europe performing the traditional rhythms she began learning in childhood. Her success is attributable not only to her music but to her lively performances, which feature traditional dress and authentic Afro-Colombian instruments.

In one interview Totó stated that she disliked having the term "folklore" applied to her music, because it connotes a "stiff and archaic form of expression." Totó prefers to describe these Afro-Colombian rhythms as vibrant, living "traditional music." "At home," she says, "the rural people have always composed music based on nature, and when music comes from the land, its language knows no frontiers. When I listen to drummers from Senegal or Congo, I can hear affinities with Cuban, Brazilian and Colombian drummers."

Totó continues to tour and record. Her recent albums include *Carmelina* (1996) and *Pacanto* (2000).

See also Music, Afro-Cuban.

Liliana Obregón

Toubou

Ethnic group of Chad, Niger, and Libya, in the southern Sahara.

A nomadic group numbering about 250,000 people, the Toubou were once the dominant pastoralists of the central SUDAN. Their early origins are unknown; they are believed to be related to the BERBERS, but their Nilo-Saharan language is closely related to that of the KANEMBU to the south.

According to legend, the Toubou originally migrated to their present location from the Nile Valley during the seventh century. Upon their arrival, they joined with the Kanembu to help form the Kanem Kingdom and took control of the valuable salt mines of Bilma, in present-day NIGER. After a series of succession disputes in the thirteenth century, however, the group lost the protection of the Kanem Kingdom, and came into conflict with such neighboring groups as the MOBEUR and the TUAREG. During subsequent centuries, the Toubou practiced pastoralism and oasis agriculture, though some smaller groups broke off and settled in sedentary agricultural communities. Many supplemented their incomes with the tariffs imposed on trade caravans. By the nineteenth century the Toubou had split into two main subgroups—the Teda and the Daza—each comprised of smaller clans, and dispersed throughout northern CHAD and NIGER and southern LIBYA.

Both Toubou groups fiercely resisted French colonialism until 1920, when they were defeated and forced to accept COLONIAL RULE. The brutal French conquest devastated the fragile economy of these desert people, and taxes imposed by the colonial administration thwarted the trans-Saharan trade that had once underlain their prosperity. Their resistance to external rule reemerged after Chadian independence in 1960, and they were integral to the defeat of the southern N'DJAMENA government.

Since the 1970s, droughts and famines have impoverished the Toubou, especially the Teda. Some have joined with Nigerian Tuareg rebel groups in advocating a secessionist state, and in Niger the Teda have formed their own liberation front.

See also Drought and Desertification; Ethnicity and Identity in Africa: An Interpretation; Languages, African: An Overview.

Elizabeth Heath

Touré, Ali Farka

1939–

African blues musician.

With a Grammy award to his name and years of worldwide touring, Ali Farka Touré is one of the best-known African musicians outside of Africa. As Touré, who is particularly popular in America, told the *New York Times*, "Where you are, you may call it the blues." But he says that his guitar style, which reminds listeners of JOHN LEE HOOKER, LIGHTNIN' HOPKINS, and other legends of BLUES, is really in the "African tradition."

Growing up amid poverty in MALI, Touré was his parents' tenth child, but the first to reach adolescence. Nicknamed "the donkey" (Farka) by his family because of his stubbornness, Touré made music despite his parents' objections. By age seventeen he had learned the traditional Malian instruments, including the single-stringed *njarka* and the harp-like *ngoni*. During the 1960s he directed a group specializing in traditional music. They toured Europe, where he acquired his first guitar and began to learn about Western music.

In 1970 Touré joined the house band of Mali's national radio station as its guitarist, and spent the next ten years recording six albums, which were released in FRANCE and West Africa. By the 1980s Touré began to build a reputation outside Mali, which culminated in worldwide fame after the 1988 release of his self-titled album, *Ali Farka Touré*. Collaborations with Western artists such as Ry Cooder, Clarence "Gatemouth" Brown, the Chieftains, and Taj Mahal have expanded Touré's popularity as a guitarist and singer. His 1994 album *Talking Timbuktu* won a Grammy for best world music album. Despite that record's success, Touré had to cancel concert plans, in part to help defend his family's farming community during Mali's war with the TUAREGS. In 1999 he released *Niafunké*, an album named after the Malian village where it was recorded.

See also Music, African.

Kate Tuttle

Touré, Sékou

1922–1984

Guinea's first president and a well-known political figure throughout Africa.

Many in the former French colonies of West Africa consider Sékou Touré an independence movement hero. In his own country, however, where his twenty-six-year-long presidency was characterized by increasing violence and suppression of civil liberties, his legacy is more complex.

Raised in a poor Muslim farming household, Touré claimed to be descended from the renowned nineteenth-century military leader SAMORY TOURÉ. His parents sent Touré to the Georges Poiret technical school in CONAKRY when he was fourteen. Expelled for unruly behavior one year later, he nevertheless continued to read and to educate himself, particularly in the works of Karl Marx. After holding several different jobs, Touré went to work for the Post and Telecommunications Service in 1941; he became the secretary general of PTT Workers' Union in 1945. As a union leader, Touré organized labor strikes in the late 1940s, and, according to some historians, began to use the strong-arm tactics that characterized his presidency. In 1946 Touré joined with nationalist leaders such as FÉLIX HOUPHOUËT-BOIGNY of the CÔTE D'IVOIRE to found the RASSEMBLEMENT DÉMOCRATIQUE AFRICAIN (RDA), which became a powerful engine of opposition to French colonialism.

For Touré, membership in RDA meant that, although he was elected twice to the French National Assembly (in 1951 and 1954), he was kept from taking his seat until 1956, when he was elected mayor of Conakry. In the meantime he became secretary general of the Parti Démocratique de Guinée, the national wing of the RDA. He went on to become vice president of the Executive Council of GUINEA, and founder of the Union Générale des Travailleurs d'Afrique Noire (UGTAN), a French West African labor union. An eloquent speaker who reached out not only to Guinea's workers but to peasants and women, Touré became one of Africa's strongest voices for independence.

In 1958 FRANCE offered the colonies internal self-government within a new international "French Community." Declaring "We prefer poverty in freedom to opulence in slavery," Touré and other Guineans rejected the offer, voting overwhelmingly instead for total independence in the September 28, 1958, referendum. Guinea was the only French colony to choose autonomy, and France responded by repatriating most of its skilled workers as well as all the infrastructural equipment it could transport. Touré, who was elected Guinea's first president shortly after the independence vote, sought help for his stripped-bare country from both the West and the Eastern bloc.

Touré soon steered Guinea down a socialist path, and into a closer alliance with the Eastern bloc. But as agricultural collectivization and state-run industries failed to alleviate poverty, the president resorted to increasingly authoritarian means of suppressing dissent. Although at least initially he remained sensitive to the appeals of certain groups—Guinea's politically active market women, in particular—it is estimated that as many as one million Guineans fled Touré's police state, and many thousand others were killed under his leadership. Still, he was considered an influential diplomat, especially within the Islamic world. Like his friend Ghanaian president KWAME NKRUMAH, he was also an outspoken proponent of Pan-African unity, and published dozens of books and pamphlets (including one book of poetry) calling for an "African Africa." Touré, who had visited the United States many times, died in a hospital in Cleveland, Ohio, in 1984.

See also Islam in Africa; Labor Leaders; Nationalism in Africa; Pan-Africanism; Socialism.

Bibliography

Rivière, Claude. *Guinea: The Mobilization of a People.* Cornell University Press, 1977.

Kate Tuttle

Tourism in Africa

Recreational travel in Africa.

In 2002, twenty-nine million tourists traveled to AFRICA's game parks, natural wonders, historic sites, markets, and beaches. Tourism accounted for approximately one-eighth of the average gross domestic product for African countries and employed thirteen million people. The World Tourism Organization predicted that tourism in Africa would grow by 5 percent each year in the coming decade. Africa's share in the global tourism market is low, however. In 2002 only about 4.1 percent of the 703 million tourists worldwide chose Africa as a destination. The continent claimed only about 2 percent of the $474 billion that tourists spent worldwide that year.

In many African countries, tourism is a major source of jobs and foreign currency. Tourism gives African governments an incentive to protect endangered species and historic monuments, and it can provide foreign visitors with a deeper appreciation of Africa's history and cultures than they could ever obtain from movies and textbooks.

Still, how much Africa's economies, ecosystems, and citizens really benefit from tourism remains open to debate. Tourism is typically a low-wage and often highly seasonal industry, and the popularity of a particular region or site can shift according to the promotional campaigns of foreign travel agencies. In addition, much of the revenue generated by tourism does not remain in the host country. The amount that goes to foreign airlines, hotel chains, and tour operators, known as "leakage," is very high in countries where many visitors come as part of organized package tours. For example, in KENYA, leakage has been estimated to consume about 70 percent of tourism revenue; in THE GAMBIA, the figure is 60 percent.

Also, the development of the infrastructure necessary to house, transport, and entertain tourists can harm the environment, even where the tourist attractions themselves—be they animals, beaches, or monuments—are carefully protected. The creation of wildlife parks and other tourist facilities has displaced some African peoples, such as the MAASAI of East Africa, from their pastures and farmlands. Finally, some African countries have found that tourism has generated negative side industries, such as prostitution and the smuggling of art objects. Regardless of its drawbacks, however, many African countries look to tourism as a source of future economic growth.

Early Tourism

Some of the activities associated with tourism in Africa date back centuries. As far back as the Roman occupation of EGYPT beginning around 30 B.C.E., Romans explored the ruins of THEBES and tombs in the VALLEY OF THE KINGS. For centuries, Arab, Asian, and later European explorers trekked across portions of the continent, often keeping records of the sites and peoples they encountered.

It was not until the early colonial period, however, that modern tourism emerged in Africa. Inspired by the published accounts of nineteenth-century European explorers, well-to-do Europeans and Americans began to travel to Africa, to glimpse first the wonders of Egypt and the NILE, then other scenic wonders, such as MOUNT KENYA and KILIMANJARO. By the turn of the century, wealthy sportsmen were traveling to East and southern Africa to hunt big game, eager to return with trophies of LIONS, elephants, or RHINOCEROS.

But even though the numbers of foreign travelers in Africa increased during the colonial period, the tourism infrastructure—transportation systems, hotels, guide services—remained minimal. After World War II, this changed: the development of fast, easy, and relatively inexpensive transoceanic travel and the construction of luxury accommodations around Africa's prime attractions set the stage for mass tourism. By the late twentieth century, tourism in Africa took many forms.

Cultural Tourism

Cultural tourism has been popular for many years in Africa. Egypt, which boasts some of the continent's most ancient and spectacular monuments and artifacts, has for decades received a steady stream of tourists, most of whom come to see the Valley of the Kings, Thebes, the Nile, and the museums in CAIRO. Together with cities such as CASABLANCA, MARRAKECH, and FÈS, Egypt has helped make North Africa the continent's most visited region. For European tourists, North Africa's proximity makes it a viable destination even for short trips.

Since the late 1970s, cultural tourism has expanded to encompass a broader range of activities. West African countries, for example, are now attracting African Americans and other tourists interested in learning more about the TRANSATLANTIC SLAVE TRADE. Such tourists typically visit GORÉE ISLAND, a major slave port off the coast of SENEGAL, as well as sites in BENIN and GHANA. Three former slave forts in Ghana were declared World Heritage sites by the United Nations: Cape Coast Castle, Elmina Castle, and Fort Saint Jago. In The Gambia, the village of Jufurre became a pilgrimage site for many African Americans after the television series based on ALEX HALEY's 1977 book *Roots* made it famous. Now The Gambia holds an annual Roots Homecoming Festival, which highlights the cultural ties between diasporic Africans and Africa. In addition to historic sites related to the slave trade, visitors can attend demonstrations of dance and wrestling, purchase traditional African crafts, and arrange to stay with local families.

Cultural tourism is also a growing business in southern Africa. Visitors to SOUTH AFRICA, for example, can spend a night in the dwelling of a XHOSA, SOTHO, PEDI, or ZULU family in the

Lesedi Cultural Village outside JOHANNESBURG. Residents of the village wear the traditional dress of their own people—cotton wraps for the Xhosa, fur loincloths for the Zulu—and perform dances and storytelling for the visitors. In ZIMBABWE, members of the SHANGAAN ethnic group began construction on a similar model village, where small numbers of visitors will be able to stay overnight and participate in village activities. Its organizers estimated that the venture had the capacity to generate $1 million annually, helping fund such social services as schools and hospitals for Shangaan communities. Proponents of this kind of cultural tourism maintain that it helps keep traditional cultural practices alive. Critics insist that tourists witness nothing more than "staged authenticity" in model villages, and in the process intrude on the privacy of village residents.

Wildlife Tourism

Africa's wildlife has long fascinated foreigners. Wildlife safaris remain one of the most popular forms of tourism in Africa and an important source of revenue for countries such as Kenya, TANZANIA, UGANDA, NAMIBIA, BOTSWANA, Zimbabwe, ZAMBIA, MALAWI, and South Africa. In these countries, private companies drive visitors through wildlife parks or game reserves and provide lodging in lodges or luxury tent camps nearby. Tours in game reserves are aimed at hunters, who pay for the trophies they take, but most safari tourists visit national parks and take only photographs. Many companies in South Africa guarantee a sighting of the Big Five, that is, lions, elephants, rhinoceros, LEOPARDS, and buffalo.

The revenue generated from safari tourism has made the survival of endangered species a high priority for African governments. In Kenya, for example, a single lion is worth an estimated $7,000 per year in tourist income, while an elephant herd is worth $610,000 annually. Hunting of both species in Kenya is legal only with a permit. On the other hand, citizens of wildlife-rich countries—some of whom have been displaced from their traditional lands to make way for wildlife parks, and many of whom face the chronic threat of crop destruction and even attack by wild animals—have often claimed that their governments protect animals at the expense of people.

Some wildlife management programs, however, are trying to win local communities' support for conservation by giving them a voice in the planning processes and awarding them a share of the profits from safari tourism. In Zimbabwe, for example, the Communal Areas Management Programme for Indigenous Resources (CAMPFIRE) gives farming communities in elephant-hunting areas a portion of the trophy fees paid by foreign hunters (each area sets an annual limit on the number of animals that can be legally killed). Among other things, the communities can use the money to fence their fields, thus protecting them from elephant damage. In return, the communities look out for the local elephant populations by maintaining watering holes during the dry season and discouraging poaching.

Coastal Resort Tourism

Sunbathing, snorkeling, and sailing on Africa's balmy coastlines are favorite pastimes for European and South African tourists. The beaches of Kenya, TOGO, MAURITIUS, the SEYCHELLES, and The Gambia are all popular winter vacation spots for Europeans. Like other tourist destinations in Africa, coastal resorts have generated problems along with profits. In The Gambia, for example, resorts have created strong local markets for crafts and fresh produce, but the behavior and skimpy clothing of the tourists themselves offend many of The Gambia's conservative Muslims. Both female and male prostitution is widespread in coastal areas, as is drug addiction among the Gambian youth.

Ecotourism and Beyond

In response to the many criticisms leveled at conventional forms of tourism, many national and local governments and private companies are now promoting ecotourism. In principle, ecotourism is environmentally and culturally sensitive, educational, and locally controlled—or at least locally beneficial. Thus, host communities would see the economic value of preserving resources and biodiversity.

Some ecotourism organizations focus on the preservation of a particular culture or historic site. In TUNISIA, for example, an ancient, abandoned agricultural community in the Matmata Mountains, Doiret, has been undergoing restoration since 1986. The nongovernmental organization behind the project sought to rebuild the economy as well as the physical structure of the town, but erratic rainfall makes agriculture alone an insufficient source of revenue. So now the restoration effort is focused on developing educational, "low-impact" tourist facilities in and around Doiret: an old primary school has become a youth hostel; the town's distinctive troglodyte (cave) houses will be turned into additional tourist lodging; and volunteers are building a museum and a model Roman theater.

Another variation on the ecotourism theme is the research holiday. The nonprofit organization Earthwatch funds its scientific research projects partly with the fees paid by the projects' volunteer participants. In Africa, Earthwatch volunteers in recent years have taken part in archaeological digs in Namibia; gathered data on ecological change around Kenya's Lake Naivasha; and investigated the feasibility of wind and solar power in Kenya.

Since 1990, more and more tourist enterprises have adopted the prefix "eco" to appeal to tourists seeking environmentally friendly recreation. In some cases, these enterprises bear little resemblance to ecotourism as it is normally understood. For example, the South African–based Conservation Corporation (Conscorp) has been building an international chain of luxury "eco-tourist" resorts since 1990. By the end of the decade the corporation had completed more than fifty lodges in South Africa, Kenya, Zimbabwe, and Tanzania. Room costs average $350 per night. Conscorp claims that its lodges benefit local people by providing not only jobs but also tax revenues that have paid for schools and health clinics. Conscorp also claims that its resorts stimulate local entrepreneurialism. For example, much of the food served at the resort restaurants is grown locally, and at the South African resorts, Zulu people own the safari vehicles.

On the other hand, resorts like Conscorp's do not allow local communities much if any say over how local resources are used. Nor are their facilities remotely affordable for most Africans. But for some of Africa's poorest countries, high-end tourism ("eco" or otherwise) appears to offer the quickest possible source of much-needed foreign investment and jobs.

See also Commodification of African Art: An Interpretation; Explorers in Africa Since 1800; Hunting in Africa; Safari Hunting; United Nations in Africa; Wildlife Management in Africa.

Robert Fay

Toussaint, Pierre

1766–1853

Haitian American businessman and philanthropist whose support for nineteenth-century orphans is recognized in his candidacy for sainthood a century and a half later.

Born in HAITI, Pierre Toussaint was a slave until 1809. After his owners moved from Haiti to NEW YORK CITY in 1787, he was apprenticed to a New York hairdresser. Toussaint eventually developed his own thriving career, and supported his widowed mistress and her daughter with his earnings.

Toussaint and his wife Juliette, both devout Catholics, also used their money to raise African American orphans, support the Catholic Orphan Asylum in New York City, and help fund the building of Saint Vincent de Paul's. In recognition of his piety and charity, John Cardinal O'Connor of New York and other Catholics began seeking Toussaint's canonization in the 1990s.

Bibliography

Césaire, Aimé. *Toussaint Louverture: La Révolution française et le problème colonial.* Présence Africaine, 1981.

James, C. L. R. *The Black Jacobins: Toussaint Louverture and the San Domingo Revolution.* Allison & Busby, 1980.

Korngold, Ralph. *Citizen Toussaint.* Hill and Wang, 1965.

Lisa Clayton Robinson

Toussaint Louverture, François Dominique

1743?–1803

Leader of the slave revolution that brought Haiti independence from France in 1804; a man who, in the words of Aimé Césaire, took "a population and turned it into a people."

There is little documentation regarding the life of François Dominique Toussaint Louverture before the first slave uprising in 1791 in SAINT-DOMINGUE (as HAITI was known before independence). According to contemporary oral accounts, his parents

Toussaint Louverture as shown in Marcus Rainford's *An Historical Account of the Black Empire of Hayti*, published in 1805. *Image of the Black Project, Harvard University*

the only literate officer in the revolt, was named secretary of the movement. As Toussaint and others noted, those who rose up were reacting to a chasm between the ideals, on the one hand, of liberty, equality, and fraternity for all—which French political and intellectual leaders had been spreading throughout the world during and after the French Revolution of 1789—and their lived experience, on the other hand, as blacks, mulattos, and free men of color on Saint-Domingue. If all men were created equal, they asked, how could slavery exist? The French responded to these questions and to the revolts they inspired by abolishing slavery in all the colonies on September 4, 1793. The first slave revolt had been successful. (Slavery, however, would be reinstated a few years later in all the French colonies and would remain in place until 1848.)

With the abolition of slavery by the French and with the western part of the island under siege by the British and the Spanish in 1794, Toussaint offered his services to the French army. His valor and shrewdness in repelling the invaders allowed him to rise quickly through the ranks and become lieutenant governor of Saint-Domingue. But Toussaint was not satisfied with being second in command of the colony. As commander in chief of the military, he did not hide his ambition to become the sole leader of Saint-Domingue. His considerable influence over the black population worried the French so much that in 1798, the French general Hédouville was sent to the colony with the secret mission of undermining Toussaint's authority. But Toussaint outmaneuvered Hédouville and others sent to diplomatically unseat him. Having gained control of the entire island of HISPANIOLA (present-day Haiti and the DOMINICAN REPUBLIC), Toussaint formed a commission of ten called the Central Assembly, which drafted a constitution in 1801. While affirming that Saint-Domingue was still a French colony, the constitution rendered it administratively independent and named Toussaint governor general of Saint-Domingue for life. Thereafter relations with FRANCE disintegrated completely. Napoleon Bonaparte, now first consul of France, sent forces led by his brother-in-law General Charles Leclerc to reclaim control of the colony. Leclerc and his 22,000 troops surrounded Toussaint in his stronghold in Crête-à-Pierrot, and on May 5, 1802, forced him to surrender. Toussaint was shipped to the Fort de Joux prison in France, where he died on April 6, 1803, from malnutrition and tuberculosis. Though the Haitian Revolution had lost its mastermind and leader, those who had served under him continued to fight for what he had envisioned and nearly achieved. On January 1, 1804, JEAN-JACQUES DESSALINES, a protégé of Toussaint, was able to declare that the French colony of Saint-Domingue was now the independent republic of Haiti.

Toussaint's heroism and martyrdom have been memorialized by some of the Caribbean's most significant writers, including Martinican authors EDOUARD GLISSANT (*Monsieur Toussaint*, 1961) and AIMÉ CÉSAIRE (*Toussaint Louverture*, 1961) and C. L. R. JAMES (*The Black Jacobins*, 1938) of TRINIDAD AND TOBAGO. While not discounting the complexities and paradoxes that shaped his character, these writers and others have pointed to Toussaint's singular importance in the formation of modern

were from DAHOMEY (present-day BENIN), and his father was a powerful chief in that country before his enslavement. Toussaint was the first of eight children born on the Bréda plantation, near the northern coast of Saint-Domingue. Born in the French colony, and familiar with its culture, Toussaint was considered a Creole rather than an African, which—according to the logic of European colonialism—guaranteed him a more elevated social status. This status, and the plantation owner's affection for him, freed Toussaint from ever having to toil in the sugarcane fields. Instead, he worked as a domestic servant in the plantation house. Toussaint was emancipated in 1776 at the young age of thirty-three. In 1779 he rented a plot of land with thirteen slaves attached to it and enjoyed the prerogatives of a colonizer, which included the amassing of a small fortune. From 1791, when he became politically active, until his death in 1803, he never publicly referred to this part of his life, choosing for political reasons to focus on his once having been a slave. Yet, in keeping with his complex history, his status as slave owner allowed him to gain the confidence of the French after the first slave revolts, though he had actively participated in them. This confidence would prove decisive in his drive to bring independence to Saint-Domingue.

On the evening of August 22, 1791, the first slave revolt began under the leadership of the Jamaican BOUKMAN. Toussaint,

Caribbean identity and to the inspiration he continues to provide in the struggles of the Caribbean people for cultural and political independence.

See also Haitian Revolution; Nationalism in Latin America and the Caribbean; Slave Rebellions in Latin America and the Caribbean; Slavery in Latin America and the Caribbean.

Richard Watts

Towns, Edolphus

1934–

Democratic member of the United States House of Representatives from New York since 1983.

Edolphus Towns was born in Chadbourn, North Carolina. He received a bachelor's degree from North Carolina Agricultural and Technical State University in 1956 and entered the U.S. Army the same year. He served until 1958 and then moved to New York, where he worked as a hospital administrator, and a professor at Medgar Evers College. In 1973 he earned a master's degree in social work from Adelphi University. In 1976 Towns began his political career, serving eight years until 1982 as Brooklyn borough deputy president. In 1982 Towns was elected to the U.S. House from New York's 11th Congressional District. Following redistricting in 1992, Towns won election from the new Tenth District, which included much of his old district. He was reelected in subsequent elections, sometimes receiving close to 90 percent of the vote. He is currently a member of the Congressional Black Caucus and the Energy and Commerce Committee.

See also Democratic Party; United States House of Representatives, African Americans in.

Townsend, Willard Saxby, Jr.

1895–1957

African American labor leader.

Willard Saxby Townsend, Jr., was born in Cincinnati, Ohio, the son of Willard Townsend, a contractor, and Cora Beatrice Townsend. (His parents had the same last name because they were cousins.) After graduating from the local high school in 1912, Townsend worked for two years as a redcap at the Cincinnati railroad station. He joined the army in 1916, served in France during World War I, and later helped to organize the Cincinnati company of the Ohio National Guard. He studied chiropody at the Illinois School of Chiropody, practiced briefly, and then moved to Canada. After two years in the University of Toronto's pre-medicine program, he transferred to the Royal College of Science in Toronto, where he graduated in 1924 with a degree in chemistry. Meanwhile, he supported himself working as a redcap and dining car waiter on the Canadian National Railways.

After teaching school in Texas for several years, Townsend moved to Chicago in 1929 and the following year married Consuelo Mann. They had one son. Some years after Townsend's death, singer Alberta Hunter said that she had been married briefly to Townsend (presumably before he married Consuelo Mann), but little more is known about that union.

The Great Depression hit blacks with particular ferocity, and in 1932 Townsend went back to working as a redcap. Men in this occupation (predominantly African Americans) were paid hardly any wages; they were expected to survive on customers' tips. Determined to improve matters, Townsend began to explore the possibility of forming a union. He faced formidable odds because redcaps had so few other work options in a racially segregated job market and because their experience with discrimination in unions had made them distrustful of organized labor. But he had the advantage of working in Chicago, a transportation hub, and he could profit from the example of another pioneering black union, the Brotherhood of Sleeping Car Porters (BSCP). After organizing redcaps in five Chicago train stations, Townsend convened a meeting in 1936 to talk about forming an international union. Within the year the men founded the Labor Auxiliary of Redcaps, which was affiliated with the American Federation of Labor (AFL); it became the International Brotherhood of Red Caps in 1938. Townsend was elected as the first president, and after beating down an insurgency the following year he held the office the rest of his life.

Like the sleeping-car porters before them, the redcaps faced intense opposition from the white railroad workers, who sought to exclude them from bargaining rights by claiming that, since redcaps worked mainly for tips, they were independent contractors rather than railroad employees. Learning from the BSCP's example, Townsend persuaded the Interstate Commerce Commission to rule in 1938 that the redcaps were employees, which enabled him to negotiate contracts for better pay and working conditions. He also began organizing train porters and Pullman laundry workers, and in 1940 the union was renamed the United Transport Service Employees (UTSE). Meanwhile, Townsend fought another battle to make the railroads obey the minimum wage rules of the 1938 Fair Labor Standards Act.

In 1942 the UTSE affiliated with the Congress of Industrial Organizations (CIO). Townsend joined its executive council and was made a vice president, thus becoming the first African American to hold office in the national labor movement. He joined the CIO's Committee to Abolish Racial Discrimination and the following year served as its secretary. He also threw himself into a successful battle to have his members classified as "essential workers" during the war and continuously resisted efforts by the Railway Clerks Union to absorb his union.

During his career, Townsend experienced frequent conflicts with other black activists. He competed with A. Philip Randolph's BSCP for members. In addition, many critics maintained that the Committee to Abolish Racial Discrimination made little progress under his leadership. Black outworkers were enraged when he appeared before the 1949 United Automobile Workers convention to endorse President Walter Reuther's decision not to name a black vice president; Townsend argued that to do so would represent "racism in reverse."

Despite these controversies, Townsend was active and influential in African American public affairs, earning a Race Relations Leadership Award from the ARTHUR SCHOMBURG Collection of the New York Public Library in 1942 and serving as an officer or trustee of organizations such as the NATIONAL ASSOCIATION FOR THE ADVANCEMENT OF COLORED PEOPLE (NAACP), Hampton Institute, the NATIONAL URBAN LEAGUE, and the American Council on Race Relations. After the race riots in DETROIT during WORLD WAR II, he stated, "This violence flows from basic economic ills," and he called for improved opportunities in voting, education, housing, and jobs for African Americans. He played a significant role in Chicago politics, and he consulted frequently on race relations with Chicago's Urban League.

Townsend was a director of the American Labor Education Service, he lectured on industrial relations at Seabury Western Theological Seminary in Evanston, Illinois, and he represented the CIO at many international conferences. In 1947 he served on a World Federation of Trade Unions committee that studied working conditions in Japan, China, Korea, the Philippines, and the Malayan states. He strongly opposed Communist influence in the labor movement. Also in 1947 he went so far as to undermine an organizing drive among North Carolina tobacco workers by bringing a weak union into the field and denouncing the competing (and much stronger) union as a Communist front; frightened by Townsend's allegations but unwilling to join the union he supported, the workers voted to have no union at all.

Late in his life Townsend began studying law through correspondence courses and night school; he received an LL.B. from Blackstone Law School in 1951. Four years later, when the AFL and CIO were reunited, he became a vice president of the new AFL-CIO. By this time his union had entered a period of decline, largely because of the railroad industry's own hard times. At the time of Townsend's death, the membership was 3,000—down from 12,000 in 1944. He died of stomach and kidney problems in Chicago, and some years later his union was absorbed by his old rival, the Railway Clerks Union.

Townsend often failed to act with the militance that his critics thought necessary, yet many of his contemporaries saw him as a realist, working for what he believed was achievable in the context of his time. It is the tension between these two perspectives, as much as Townsend's actual accomplishments, that make the story of his life an illuminating chapter in the history of African American labor.

Bibliography

Foner, Philip S. *Organized Labor and the Black Worker, 1619–1973.* 1974.

Foner, Philip S., and Ronald L. Lewis, eds. *Black Workers: A Documentary History from Colonial Times to the Present.* 1989

Townsend, Willard Saxby, Jr., and Raymond Logan. *What the Negro Wants.* 1944.

Townsend, Willard Saxby, Jr. *Full Employment and the Negro Workers.* 1945.

Obituaries: *American Federationist*, March 1957; *AFL-CIO News*, February 9, 1957; and *New York Times*, February 5, 1957.

From *American National Biography*. John A. Garraty and Mark C. Carnes, eds. Oxford University Press, 1999. Reprinted by permission of the American Council of Learned Societies.

Sandra Opdycke

Toxi

German film released in 1952 about a black girl who was adopted by a German family.

In the early 1950s, just as the postwar children of African American GIs and German women were entering West German schools in large numbers, the movie *Toxi* was released. The film, about a black girl adopted briefly by a wealthy German family, starred five-year-old Elfie Fiegert (the daughter of an American soldier and a German woman). The story depicted Toxi's ability to charm her foster family until her father came to take her back to the United States. Though it presented an unrealistically positive picture of the black experience in GERMANY, *Toxi* raised awareness of and sympathy for black children in West Germany, and also provided them with a point of identification.

Belinda Cooper

Track and Field in the United States

One of the oldest sports in the world, track and field, or athletics as it is called in many countries, consists of more than two dozen events that usually include running, jumping, walking, and throwing.

Early American Society

Foot racing was a common feature of early American slave society. In the narratives of former slaves foot racing is recounted as a popular sport on southern plantations. In one such narrative, former slave FREDERICK DOUGLASS described the popularity of sports such as BOXING, wrestling, and foot racing in his autobiography, *The Life and Times of Frederick Douglass* (1881; revised 1892).

Since most sporting competitions during slavery were segregated, the opportunities for blacks to compete against whites in foot races were limited. However, in the 1830s the Highland Games—organized by Scottish American civic groups—and col-

African Americans in the Track and Field Hall of Fame

Year of Induction	Member	Born/Died	Year of Induction	Member	Born/Died
1974	Ralph Boston	1939	1984	Joseph Yancey	1910–1991
1974	Lee Calhoun	1993–1989	1985	John Thomas	1941
1974	Harrison Dillard	1923	1986	Barney Ewell	1918–1996
1974	Rafer Johnson	1935	1987	Eulace Peacock	1914–1996
1974	Jesse Owens	1913–1980	1987	Martha Watson	1946
1974	Wilma Rudolph	1940–1994	1988	Greg Bell	1928
1974	Mal Whitfield	1924	1988	Barbara Ferrell (Edmonson)	1947
1975	Alice Coachman (David)	1932	1989	Milt Campbell	1933
1975	Edward Hunt	1900–1989	1989	Nell Jackson	1929–1988
1975	Ralph Metcalf	1910–1978	1989	Ed Temple	1927
1976	Mae Faggs (Starrs)	1932–2000	1990	Charles Dumas	1937–2004
1976	Bob Hayes	1942–2002	1992	Charles Greene	1944
1976	Hayes Jones	1938	1992	Charlie Jenkins	1934
1977	Bob Beamon	1946	1992	Archie Williams	1915–1993
1977	Andy Stanfield	1927–1985	1995	Florence Griffith-Joyner	1959–1998
1978	Tommie Smith	1944	1993	Rod Milburn	1950–1997
1978	John Woodruff	1915	1994	Cornelius Johnson	1913–1946
1979	Jim Hines	1946	1994	Edwin Moses	1955
1979	Dehart Hubbard	1903–1976	1995	Valerie Brisco	1960
1979	Edith McGuire (DuVall)	1944	1996	Cleve Abbott	1894–1955
1980	Dave Albritton	1913–1994	1997	Henry Carr	1942
1980	Wyomia Tyus Tillman	1945	1997	Renaldo Nehemiah	1959
1981	Willye White	1939	1998	Greg Foster	1958
1982	Willie Davenport	1943–2002	1999	Willie Banks	1956
1982	Eddie Tolan	1908–1967	2000	Arnie Robinson	1948
1983	Lee Evans	1947	2001	Carl Lewis	1961
1983	Mildred McDaniel (Singleton)	1933	2001	Larry Myricks	1956
1983	Leroy Walker	1918	2003	John Carlos	1945
1984	Madeline Manning (Mims)	1948	2003	Larry James	1947

ored branches of the Young Men's Christian Association (YMCA) featured inter-racial and inter-ethnic competition. Foot racing and fast walking (pedestrianism) were among the events in which African American athletes excelled.

In the latter half of the nineteenth century the performance of African American short and long distance runners were celebrated moments. Francis Smith and Frank Hart were among the most notable. Both were legendary walkers who dominated the sport in the 1830s and 1870s, respectively. But the High-

land Games and the YMCA races were unique in their willingness to allow inter-racial competition.

Racial Segregation

In 1868 the all-white New York Athletic Club held what some scholars believe to be the first formally organized track-and-field meet in the United States. In 1876 the club sponsored the first U.S. national championship. African Americans were not allowed to participate in either meet. In 1888 white athletic clubs united to form the Amateur Athletic Union (AAU), an organizing body responsible for promoting athletic competition throughout the country. However, like the New York Athletic Club, it too excluded blacks from participating.

Nineteenth Century Black Stars

Despite these obstacles a small number of black athletes did participate and did excel in track and field during the late nineteenth century. Most were students at predominantly white colleges and universities in the north. One of the earliest such stars was William Tecumseh Sherman Jackson who attended Amherst College in Massachusetts (1890–1892). In addition to Jackson, Napoleon Bonaparte Marshall (Harvard College, 1895–1897), Spencer Dickerson (University of Chicago, 1896–1897), G. C. H. Burleigh (University of Illinois), and John Baxter "Doc" Taylor (University of Pennsylvania, 1904, 1907–1908) were also major stars at predominantly white schools.

Contrary to contemporary stereotypes, most of these early black stars were long-distance runners. Long-distance events were the most prestigious and those who excelled at longer distances were held in great esteem by other athletes. It was not until the first half of the twentieth century that speed and power in the shorter distances became a celebrated talent.

Early Black Track and Field Organizations

In the face of racial segregation and discrimination, African Americans established their own athletic organizations and programs. In 1893 Tuskegee Institute (now Tuskegee University) in Alabama held the first major black track and field meet in the country. The meet consisted of events such as running, jumping, tug-of-war, and a new event called the relay race. The relay race was one of the most popular events at black track and field meets and soon became a regular feature at white track and field meets.

In 1906 the Interscholastic Athletic Association (ISAA) held the first inter-city track and field meet for African American boys in Washington, D.C. Schools throughout the city sent athletes to the meet, including Howard University, "M" Street High School (now Dunbar High School), and the Colored Young Men's Christian Association. One year later African American runner Matthew Bullock created the first black intercollegiate track and field meet for Southeastern colleges.

Early Black Olympians

After making a mark at the collegiate level, several black stars went on to enjoy successful careers. At the turn of the twentieth century the most important postcollegiate event in the career of a track and field athlete was undoubtedly the Olympic Games. Held every four years, the Olympic Games showcased some of the best athletes in the world.

Since women were not allowed to participate in the Olympics until 1928, black men represented the country and their race as they competed against white athletes from around the world. At the 1904 Olympic Games George Poage captured a bronze medal in the 400-meter hurdles. Four years later, at the Olympic competition in London, England, black sprinters "Doc" Taylor and J. C. Carpenter both competed in the 400-meter race. Taylor became the first African American in Olympic history to earn a gold medal after running the third leg on the 4-by-400-meter relay team.

Early Twentieth Century

The first African American to emerge victorious in a field event was Theodore "Ted" Cable, an athlete at Harvard in Cambridge, Massachusetts. Cable won the broad jump (22 feet $10^1/4$ inches) and hammer throw (154 feet and $11^1/4$ inches) at the 1912 Harvard-Yale meet. Later that year, at the Intercollegiate Track & Field Meet, Cable became the first African American in the meet's history to win the hammer throw competition. Although Cable proved that African American athletes could win at field events, it was still in the sprinting events that African Americans captured international attention.

African American sprinters were so dominant in the period immediately preceding World War I that some states barred them from competing in more than two events. One of the most successful was Howard Porter Drew, a sprinter from Springfield, Massachusetts. Drew held world records in the 100-yard dash (1913, 9.6 seconds), 220-yard dash (1914, 21.2 seconds), and the 100-meter dash (1912, 10.2 seconds). World War I prevented him from participating in the 1916 Olympic Games, and he failed to qualify for the Games in 1920. Despite these setbacks Drew ended his career as one of the most talented sprinters in American history.

Interwar Period

Participation in track and field declined briefly in the years between World War I and II. Black club and college programs suffered from a lack of financial support as track and field was forced to compete with other sports, such as football and baseball. Track and field coaches at black colleges and universities in the 1920s had a difficult time convincing young athletes to pursue a sport that had few professional organizations or leagues.

The Colored Intercollegiate Athletic Association (CIAA), founded in 1924, was the exception. For nearly twenty years the CIAA was the only major collegiate conference to hold regular track and field meets for athletes at predominantly black colleges and universities. During this period Hampton Institute in Virginia (now Hampton University) dominated black track and field. Between 1924 and 1931 Morgan State University and Lincoln University (Philadelphia, Pennsylvania) were the only schools to defeat Hampton.

The only other major track and field meet open to blacks at the time was the Tuskegee Relay Carnival, created in 1927.

Modeled after the Penn Relays—the only major white track and field meet open to black athletes in the 1920s—the Tuskegee Relay Carnival sponsored competition between some of the best black sprinters, long jumpers, and distance runners in the country.

Black collegiate track and field received a boost in 1933 when the Midwest Athletic Association (MWAA) was formed. Six years later the Southwestern Athletic Association (SWAC) joined the list of black collegiate athletic conferences. All three conferences—the CIAA, MWAA, and SWAC—made great strides in the development of track and field programs at predominantly black schools. However, most of these strides benefited black men, expanding their opportunities to participate on a competitive level.

Black Women in Track and Field

In the 1920s and early 1930s black women were excluded by almost every major track and field program in the country. The New York Mercury Club, the Illinois Women's Athletic Club, and Tennessee State University were among the exceptions. However, the institution most committed to developing black female track and field athletes was Tuskegee Institute. Under the leadership of Athletic Director Cleveland Abbott, the Tuskegee female track and field team became one of the leading programs of its kind.

In 1936 the team finished second in the Amateur Athletic Union (AAU) national competition. At the time it was the highest finish ever by a black team competing at the AAU. Tuskegee captured the AAU title the following year and remained champions from 1938 to 1942 and again between 1944 and 1948. Tuskegee's success was due to a long list of exceptional athletes and coaches, such as Amelia C. Roberts, Christine Evans Petty, and Jessie Abbott. Other black female standouts include three-time AAU 80-meter hurdles champion Lillie Purifoy and Hattie Turner, the first African American crowned champion in the discus and baseball throw.

Black men also excelled in the interwar years. Two of the best sprinters at the 1932 Olympic Games were black Americans Ralph Metcalfe and Thomas "Eddie" Tolan, Jr. Tolan became the first African American to win two gold medals when he defeated Metcalfe in the 100- and 200-meter races. The growing success of black American track and field superstars set the stage for an international drama at the 1936 Olympic Games in Berlin, GERMANY.

Jesse Owens

German leader Adolf Hitler planned to use the 1936 Olympic Games to showcase what he thought was German athletic superiority. Hitler believed that if German athletes could dominate the games, particularly those events in track and field, they would convince the world of the superiority of the Aryan race. But JESSE OWENS, a black sprinter from Oakville, Alabama, disrupted Hitler's plans.

Owens won an unprecedented four gold medals at the 1936 Olympic Games and was reportedly snubbed by Hitler during the award ceremonies. His success was a symbolic victory for America and it was a proud moment for black America. In a matter of days Jesse Owens challenged every notion of black inferiority.

But in victory he inspired a whole new set of equally disturbing racial stereotypes. Previous explanations concluded that blacks were successful in athletics because they lacked the mental aptitude for other endeavors. White athletes now suggested that blacks somehow had an unfair advantage because they were genetically predisposed to athletic competition. After the performance by Jesse Owens critics attributed black success in athletics to the size of their thighs and length of their feet. Athletic accomplishment was a genetic gift, and not the result of hard work and unwavering commitment.

Postwar Era

Track and field experienced dramatic changes after the war ended. The success of black sprinters such as Jesse Owens, Ralph Metcalfe, and Thomas Tolan, Jr., opened doors for other young black athletes. The competition for coveted athletic scholarships to predominantly white colleges and universities was fierce. Those blacks who did not earn scholarships were forced to pursue track and field with black club teams.

But the Olympic Games continued to occupy center stage. Athletes did not need to attend a wealthy school or wear the newest shoes to earn a spot on the national Olympic team. Track and field was considered the great equalizer because it gave black athletes from some of the most impoverished backgrounds the opportunity to shine. One of the most famous success stories is that of WILMA RUDOLPH, a black female sprinter from St. Bethlehem, Tennessee.

Rudolph overcame a physical disability to her leg that she suffered at birth to become one of the most dominant athletes at the 1960 Olympic Games. She brought home gold medals in the 100-, 200- and 400-meter dashes. Rudolph was the first African American woman to win three gold medals during a single Olympic competition.

Civil Rights and Black Power

By the mid-1960s black athletes were regular participants at track and field events around the world. However, their celebrity status did not make them immune to the political and economic challenges facing African Americans at home. The Civil Rights and Black Power Movements of the 1960s had a tremendous impact on black track and field stars. With the help of organizations such as the black-led Olympic Project for Human Rights, African American athletes used their status as stars to call attention to the pernicious effects of American racism.

One of the most famous examples of the political activism of black athletes came during the 1968 Olympic Games in Mexico City, MEXICO. Wearing black socks and no shoes, African

American sprinters Tommie Smith and John Carlos placed a single black glove on their fists and stepped up to the victory podium. During the playing of the American anthem, Smith and Carlos gave a salute to the black power movement by raising their fists defiantly in the air.

In an interview given to sports commentator Howard Cosell (and quoted in the comprehensive volume, *A Hard Road to Glory*), Tommie Smith explained his actions. "I wore a black right-hand glove and Carlos wore the left-hand glove of the same pair. My raised right hand stood for the power in black America. Carlos' raised left hand stood for the unity of black America. Together, they formed an arch of unity and power. The black scarf around my neck stood for black pride. The black sock with no shoes stood for black poverty in racist America." The totality of our effort was the regaining of black dignity." Both athletes were ejected from the Olympic village by the International Olympic Committee (IOC).

Black sprinters continued to dominate track and field throughout the 1970s and 1980s. Between 1972 and 1980 blacks won more than seventy-five Olympic medals in track and field events. New superstars emerged, including hurdler Edwin Moses and sprinters CARL LEWIS, EVELYN ASHFORD, MICHAEL JOHNSON, FLORENCE GRIFFITH JOYNER ("Flo-Jo"), and JACKIE JOYNER-KERSEE. Carl Lewis holds nine gold medals, the most by any American track and field athlete.

New Competition

In the late 1980s black runners from AFRICA, GREAT BRITAIN, and the Caribbean began to challenge the reign of African American speedsters. Sprinters from England, JAMAICA, TRINIDAD AND TOBAGO, CUBA, and Canada have set or tied world records once held by American men and women. Donovan Bailey (Canada), Merlene Ottey (Jamaica), Daniel Komen (KENYA), Noureddine Morceli (ALGERIA), and Haile Gebrselassie (ETHIOPIA) are just a few of the blacks outside of America who have dominated track and field. African runners from Kenya, SOUTH AFRICA, and Ethiopia routinely win major long distance events, including many of the most prominent competitions in the world, such as the Boston Marathon.

Despite the increased competition, African American athletes have still excelled in track competitions in the twenty-first century. At the 2000 Olympic Games, Maurice Green won two gold medals (100-meter dash and 4x100-meter relay). The following year he won his third consecutive world title in the 100-meter race. In 2000 Marion Jones become the first woman to win five track medals at one Olympiad. That same year Michael Johnson became the first man to win gold in the 400-meter race at consecutive Olympic Games.

Black athletes from around the world have made a lasting impression on the sport of track and field. They have pushed the limits of human ability, shattering old records and setting new ones that were unimaginable just a few years ago. In the process, black athletes have defied racial stereotypes, and with hard work and dedication, have set new standards of excellence for athletes around the world.

See also Baseball in the United States; Black Power in the United States; Civil Rights Movement; Football, Collegiate; Olympics, African Americans and the; Segregation in the United States; Slavery in the United States; Sports and African Americans.

Alonford James Robinson

Traditional Healing in Africa

Numerous techniques in Africa used to cure illnesses, maintain health, and solve human physical and emotional problems.

In most African countries, some healing techniques are known by almost everyone. People in many parts of AFRICA, for example, know which herbs relieve upset stomachs. Ordinary people pick these herbs themselves and use them the way people use medications that they purchase in pharmacies without a prescription.

For more complicated problems, people can consult healers who have been specially trained. Some of these traditional healers work only on a small scale, providing services for people who live nearby. Other healers become quite famous and are consulted over a large area. Some famous healers travel widely or build clinics or city offices. The famous healers treat people drawn from a broad region.

No one knows how many traditional healers there are in Africa. Most African countries do not have laws requiring traditional healers to sign up on an official registry, so there is rarely a single, comprehensive list of healers. African countries usually have many more traditional healers than there are Western-style physicians or nurses, however. In 1980, for example, a village of 700 people in northern TANZANIA was served by more than twenty healers. Some of these healers practiced part-time, others full-time. The people in the village also went to consult Western-style physicians, but just a few physicians were available to treat people in a great many villages. On the whole, in this part of Tanzania, there were hundreds of traditional healers for each physician. The relative balance between traditional healers and physicians varies from place to place in Africa, but there is almost always a large majority of traditional healers.

Principles and Techniques

In many of Africa's healing traditions, people make a distinction between illnesses that just happen and those with some kind of human cause. The ones that just happen are often described as "illnesses of God." When people say this, they do not mean that God intends for people to be sick. They are thinking of the illness as something that would happen to anyone in the same way in the natural course of events. Illnesses of God are seen as different from illnesses with human causes. Illnesses with human causes may be a result of errors of judgment, violations of the basic rules of behavior, or anger or aggression.

Many African healing techniques are based on empirical techniques—careful observation of how the body works or diligent use of trial and error. Some kinds of empirical healing involve manipulating the body, as in the case of healers who set broken bones or midwives who help women deliver babies. People have found effective drugs and other natural sources. These have been used successfully to treat fever, intestinal disorders, worms and other parasites, asthma, arthritis, earaches, and headaches, as well as to help wounds heal and to help mothers begin producing milk so they can breast-feed their babies.

Drugs used in traditional healing are mostly drawn from plants but can also be animal or mineral substances. Healers are often experts on the environment, since they must know about the growing patterns and surroundings of the healing plants they use. Over the years laboratories in different parts of the continent have tested many different herbal drugs. They have found that hundreds of them (but not all) have demonstrable scientific reasons for their effectiveness. MADAGASCAR periwinkle, for example, contains the raw material for making vinca alkaloids, a type of anticancer drug.

Another way of healing is through the reordering of human relationships, aiming to resolve the personal and emotional causes of illnesses. Sometimes a whole extended family is drawn together for a kind of kinship therapy. This heals the body by changing the way it is located in a set of people. Sometimes therapy draws a more diverse set of people together. These may be neighbors or even people who start out as strangers. People then join together in a healing association. The treatment involves many different actions, all done in connection with healing ceremonies. It involves taking the appropriate foods and herbal medicines and also experiencing the healing effects of music and dance.

In the parts of Africa where Bantu languages are spoken—all through eastern, central, and southern Africa—healing associations are often called *ngoma*, meaning "the drum." Some scholars have called these associations "drums of affliction." Examples are the drum of the Chihamba ritual of the Ndembu people in northwestern ZAMBIA, the drum of the Majini ritual of Swahili speakers on the East African coast, the historic Lemba drum in eastern DEMOCRATIC REPUBLIC OF THE CONGO (DRC), and a great many others. People who are sick, or women who are having difficulty getting pregnant, often join the healing associations (the "drums of affliction") to be treated, so that they will get better. By participating in the healing process, they learn about healing techniques. Often patients, after a long period of being treated, learn to become healers themselves. They then treat the patients who come after them.

In most parts of tropical Africa, friends and relatives of the sick person help with the process of diagnosis. In eastern DRC, urban ZIMBABWE, and many other places, relatives and neighbors accompany the patient from one healer to another in an attempt to determine what is wrong and how to treat it. The people organizing the care can also get the help of a diviner.

A diviner uses special means to understand the cause of an illness so that the patient can get the correct treatment. The diviner's means include learning details about the patient's situation, consulting spirits of various kinds, or using special divinatory objects.

From Ancient Beginnings

Africa's healing traditions have histories that date back thousands of years, yet some of the traditions remain strong today. Early evidence shows traditional healing techniques as long ago as ancient Egypt. A small group of medical manuscripts from Egypt's early royal dynasties show that healing techniques were used. Farther south, in the Bantu-speaking regions of Africa, linguists specializing in the origins of African languages have identified words that show that some healing ideas are thousands of years old. There are ancient words for "healer," for "drum" (related to healing associations), for "ancestor," and for defining the kinds of environments in which healing herbs are found. The languages and cultures of these regions are closely related to one another even today, and so their healing traditions resemble one another.

Still other healing traditions are found in West Africa, with its heritage extending across the Atlantic Ocean. As a result of the TRANSATLANTIC SLAVE TRADE, healing techniques of the YORUBA ethnic group spread from present-day NIGERIA to BRAZIL and the Caribbean. For example, in Africa, LATIN AMERICA, and the Caribbean, one kind of healer in the Yoruba tradition is known by the Yoruba word *babalawo*. Not only have African societies sent their healing practices abroad, but they have also taken in healing traditions from outside their societies. Islamic styles of healing, for example, were incorporated into traditional practices in western and eastern Africa as Islamic religion became more influential over roughly the last thousand years.

Before European conquest, the most effective techniques for promoting health were public disease prevention and control programs, rather than treatment. Several examples illustrate this. In KUMASI, the capital of the ASANTE kingdom in West Africa, a special public official took charge of urban sanitation. He made sure that streets and latrines were clean to prevent the spread of typhoid and other diseases. In northern Tanzania people put smallpox victims in quarantine. They also took care to live at higher elevations to avoid the mosquitoes that transmit MALARIA. In one NGONI kingdom, in MOZAMBIQUE, people used ecological control measures to limit the spread of trypanosomiasis, or sleeping sickness, a deadly disease transmitted by the TSETSE FLY. They battled the disease by clearing brush that harbored tsetse flies and by hunting down wild animals that were infected with the disease.

The major wars of European conquest, in the late nineteenth and early twentieth century, led to the founding of colonies and to attacks on African healing. There were several reasons for this. In some cases, as in the MAJI MAJI REVOLT in Tanzania from 1905 to 1907, healers were among the resistance leaders. The same was true in the war against the white conquerors in SOUTHERN RHODESIA (now ZIMBABWE) in 1896 and 1897. Because the healers resisted, the European rulers made African healing illegal. In many cases the Europeans defined any kind of traditional healing as witchcraft.

Christian missionaries also attacked African healing in many places. They sometimes chopped down sacred groves of forest—small parts of forest in which people kept ritual healing objects. The missionaries did this to show that they could attack the most powerful African medicines without being harmed. Sometimes they said that people could only come for treatment in mission hospitals if they promised not to use traditional medicines. The attacks on traditional healing did not stop people from using it or from combining it with Western-style medicine. Often, however, people took care to practice traditional healing privately. Traditional healers in the colonial period could not be publicly visible political leaders. This was tragic because their skills were of the greatest use in ecological techniques of disease control, which could only be done through public, collective efforts. In some places this led to an increase in the spread of diseases.

From the 1960s onward, after most European powers left, some African governments took measures to recognize the great contribution that traditional healers had made. Associations of traditional healers negotiated with governments in the hope of achieving public recognition. This movement went the furthest in Zimbabwe, where healers had played a role in mobilizing support for the guerrilla army that defeated the white government. But in the end, African physicians in ministries of health usually felt that giving a formal role to traditional healers would undermine the kind of medicine they knew best. The result is that in most African countries traditional healing is enormously important in daily life, but government doctors do not give it.

See also Christianity: Missionaries in Africa; Disease and African History; Disease, Medicine, and Health; Diseases, Infectious, in Africa; Egypt, Ancient Kingdom of; Traditional Healing in Latin America and the Caribbean.

Traditional Healing in Latin America and the Caribbean

Practices and techniques used to cure physical illnesses, spiritual afflictions, and social ills.

Illness is a constant part of the life of any community, and communities develop ways of responding to illness: through prevention, avoidance of disease, and ultimately the treatment and healing of illness when it attacks. African peoples in LATIN AMERICA and the Caribbean brought with them complex beliefs about illness and its healing, and adapted these to the new and often brutal circumstances of the New World. In the new lands to which they were brought against their will, unknown diseases killed thousands and malnutrition claimed the lives of many children. The partial immunity to West African diseases developed over thousands of years of adaptation was of little

benefit in protecting Africans from the new assaults to their health.

African peoples arriving in the Caribbean and Latin America encountered infectious diseases such as leprosy, yellow fever, smallpox, and measles. Some of these were familiar; West Africans had developed partial immunity to some, such as MALARIA. Others were new and deadly, including diseases native to the New World as well as those introduced by Europeans. The conditions of slavery exacerbated the effects of infectious disease, producing high rates of illness and frequent resort to healing ritual and the use of curative substances.

Healing practices derive from beliefs about the nature of persons as well as about illness. For Africans arriving in Latin America and the Caribbean, persons were composed of bodies and spirits, and thus illness was thought to afflict either or both of these components. Illnesses caused or affected by supernatural forces were the domain of religious practitioners. In some parts of SOUTH AMERICA for example, Obeah men and other ritual practitioners interacted with the supernatural forces that controlled human fortune, whether in the form of luck, fertility, crop success, or health. As in major West African religious systems, common diseases such as smallpox were believed to be controlled by specific gods, who could be addressed in ritual. In the sixteenth and seventeenth centuries the Roman Catholicism of Latin America's European conquerors also incorporated beliefs in a variety of supernatural beings active in human affairs, from angels and saints to demonic spirits. The religious healing practices of Africans (and New World Indians) were thus highly valued by whites and blacks alike, and flourished in the "enchanted" cosmological world of the time.

In contemporary South America, African-based religious systems retain many of these healing functions. In modern BRAZIL, especially, Afro-Brazilian religions such as CANDOMBLÉ and Macumba have been adapted to the treatment of a wide variety of health problems, from psychiatric illness to acquired immunodeficiency syndrome (AIDS). Indigenous religious beliefs have also been incorporated into Amazonian Afro-Brazilian religious movements such as Santo Daime, which uses the hallucinogenic drug *ayahuasca* to contact the spirit world, often for healing purposes. Similarly, Afro-Caribbean religions such as SANTERÍA have adapted themselves to contemporary social and medical conditions, and have emerged as important features of contemporary folk healing practices.

For the illnesses of bodies, the tropical and semitropical environments of Latin America and the Caribbean provided numerous plant medications—more than 5,000 have been identified in MEXICO alone. Many of these plants were familiar from related West African plants; others were borrowed from local Indians. Still others were discovered through experimentation or from presumed similarities to African curative plants. Phytotherapy is the technical term for the use of curative plants; phytotherapies are among the most ancient forms of illness treatment, and have a long history among the African peoples in the Caribbean and throughout Latin America.

The traditional use of plant medications in Latin America has not been widely studied, but recent interest in the curative potential of disappearing rain-forest plants has stimulated new research into the subject. A recent comprehensive study of folk medical practices in VENEZUELA, for instance, found that the descendants of African slaves retain numerous beliefs and practices regarding medicinal plants. In each case, the plants used in Venezuela were identical, or closely related, to plants used for similar medical purposes in West Africa. In some cases the associations are very specific: for example, the use of tobacco juice in the treatment of snakebites. In other cases, broad curative powers are attributed to the same plants: heliotrope, for example, is used to make an infusion in the treatment of dysentery, fever, and convulsions; *Annonia senegalensis* is used on both sides of the Atlantic to treat arthritis, leprosy, and indigestion and is used as a laxative and during pregnancy. African phytotherapy was so popular in the history of Venezuela that slave curers were often able to purchase their freedom with the proceeds of their medical practices.

The distinction between spiritual practitioners and phytotherapists was not always rigid. A recent study of FOLK MEDICINE in GUYANA, for instance, notes that Obeah men were not only priest-healers who could contact the spirit world; they also had extensive knowledge of both poisonous and curative plants. In an era before scientific medicine their influence was considerable, even among plantation owners.

Among African peoples enslaved in Latin America and the Caribbean, the power of traditional healers was not only important in curing illness; it was a unifying force for the preservation of culture and even a form of resistance to oppression. As in West African cultures, healing was often directed at curing social ills—the illness of an individual might be only the symptom of tensions and disruption in a community. The effectiveness of this power has to be measured not only in the rates of curing disease, but in the persistence and even spread of such belief systems throughout Latin America and the Caribbean. In their modern forms, such as Candomblé and Santería, and the renewed interest in research into the possible pharmacological effects of traditional plant medications, this deep legacy continues to affect us.

See also Catholic Church in Latin America and the Caribbean; Disease, Medicine, and Health; Religions, African, in Brazil; Religions, African, in Latin America and the Caribbean; Slavery in Latin America and the Caribbean; Traditional Healing in Africa.

Donald Pollock

Trans-Saharan and Red Sea Slave Trade

Traffic in African slaves across the Sahara and the Red Sea for export, mainly to Arabia and South Asia.

The trans-Saharan and Red Sea slave trades both date back several millennia. Ancient Egyptians, as well as Romans, Arabs, Turks, and Europeans, all drew slaves from the Nile Valley, particularly NUBIA. But little is known about slave trades in and from AFRICA prior to the spread of Islam across North Africa beginning in the eighth century.

Because many of the Arab, and later BERBER, slave traffickers in North Africa were Muslim, and because they were supplying slaves primarily to Islamic societies in Arabia and South Asia, scholars often refer to the trans-Saharan and Red Sea commerce as the "Islamic Slave Trade." This is a misnomer, however, because the demand for slave labor and the role of slaves in the host societies predate the rise of Islam.

Compared to the TRANSATLANTIC SLAVE TRADE, slaving in the SAHARA and North Africa was always far less institutionalized, and most of the traders operated on a relatively small scale. The lack of written records combined with the huge time span of the commerce make it extremely difficult to estimate how many slaves were exported from the continent via these trade networks or how many died en route. Some scholars suggest that, since about 1500 C.E., approximately four million slaves traveled along trans-Saharan routes while another two million people were sold into slavery by way of the Red Sea.

The trans-Saharan and Red Sea slave trades were also distinctive because approximately two-thirds of the slaves exported on these routes were female, destined to serve as concubines and domestic servants in Arabia and South Asia. In contrast, demand for cheap plantation labor in the Americas created the need for the high proportion of male slaves who were shipped across the Atlantic.

Along with items such as salt, gold, and ivory, slaves were among the few commodities considered valuable enough to merit risky long-distance journeys by CAMEL caravan across the Sahara, or on foot in the Horn of Africa. Trans-Saharan traders procured slaves taken primarily from the savanna and forest zones of West Africa, while slaves bound for the Red Sea came mostly from the Nile Valley, the Horn of Africa, and, to a lesser extent, the East African coast. Traders exchanged luxury items such as Indian cotton, perfumes, spices, and horses for slaves sold either by other merchants, based in market towns such as TOMBOUCTOU (also known as Timbuktu, in present-day MALI) or DARFUR (in present-day SUDAN), or by local rulers, who acquired slaves through raids, warfare, or tribute.

Once purchased, slaves typically traveled on foot, and many had to assist with daily chores en route. The routes they took shifted over time, partly due to the rise and fall of medieval savanna empires such as ancient Mali and SONGHAI. From Darfur, one of the main routes was the Darb al-Arbain "Forty Day Road" to Asyut in EGYPT. Mortality rates, not surprisingly, were high.

Upon their arrival in the Mediterranean port cities such as TUNIS and TRIPOLI, or Red Sea towns such as Sawakan, slaves were sold in marketplaces where overseers monitored exchanges between brokers and buyers. After the eighth century, Islamic principles defined many of the rules of commerce: children under the age of seven could not be separated from their mothers, for example, and Muslim slaves could not be sold to non-Muslims. Buyers were also allowed a three-day trial period to inspect the constitution and health of the slave they had purchased. Women sold as concubines or into harems were often held in escrow by a third party until menstruation proved they were not pregnant.

Although many slaves stayed on the African continent—especially men used in the armies of North Africa and Egypt—most boarded ships bound for the eastern Mediterranean, the Arabian Peninsula, the Persian Gulf, or India. Africa became an increasingly important source for slaves in Arabia and South Asia as more traditional sources from northern and central EUROPE were depleted during the twelfth century. Beginning in about the fourteenth century, slaves were also shipped to ITALY and other European destinations. In addition to using female slaves for concubinage or domestic service, these buyers used male slaves for low-ranking soldiers or manual laborers on plantations or in cities. A relatively small number of male slaves were castrated; they served as eunuchs, often rising to positions of wealth and power because they were entrusted with important financial and political transactions.

Many scholars have noted the absence of a distinct African population in contemporary southwest Asia, suggesting that the majority of slaves, particularly women who served as concubines, became integrated into the host societies, most often under Muslim law. Male slaves were also circumcised and given Muslim names. Upon bearing a son to their owner, concubines could not be sold or given away. Furthermore concubines were liberated upon their owner's death and the child was considered a free individual. Many other slaves were probably manumitted after working a nine-year period, after which many pious Muslims felt that the slaves had worked sufficiently to have earned their freedom.

The trans-Saharan and Red Sea slave trades began to taper off as the abolitionist movement, particularly in England, gained momentum. The abolitionists imposed their political will on slavers through the administrations of newly established European colonies in North and West Africa, beginning with French-controlled ALGERIA in 1830. As late as 1910, however, slaves were secretly being moved from Tibesti (northern CHAD) to the Libyan port city of Benghazi. Demand for African slaves in the MIDDLE EAST has still not disappeared, particularly as the region has grown wealthy from its oil resources. Although Middle Eastern countries abolished slavery when they entered the League of Nations in the 1920s, a minor underground trade in slaves probably still exists.

See also Egypt, Ancient Kingdom of; Indian Ocean Slave Trade; Islam in Africa; Slavery in Africa.

Bibliography

Gordon, Murray. *Slavery in the Arab World.* New Amsterdam, 1989.

Lovejoy, Paul E., ed. *Transformations in Slavery: A History of Slavery in Africa.* Cambridge University Press, 1983.

Manning, Patrick. *Slavery and African Life: Occidental, Oriental, and African Slave Trades.* Cambridge University Press, 1990.

Savage, Elizabeth. *The Human Condition: Perspectives on the Trans-Saharan Slave Trade.* Frank Cass, 1992.

Ari Nave

TransAfrica

An African American lobby that focuses on U.S. policy toward Africa and the Caribbean.

TransAfrica was created in 1977, after a Black Leadership Conference convened by the CONGRESSIONAL BLACK CAUCUS declared that "the conspicuous absence of African Americans in high-level international affairs positions and the general subordination, if not neglect, of African and Caribbean priorities could only be corrected by the establishment of a private advocacy organization." According to its executive director, Randall Robinson, "TransAfrica is a foreign-policy education advocacy organization . . . interested in all aspects of American policy that have consequences for Africa and the Caribbean."

TransAfrica lobbies Congress and the national administration with funding from various corporations, corporate grants, and individual donations. In 1981, Robinson created the TransAfrica Forum to collect, analyze, and disseminate information about U.S. foreign policy concerning AFRICA and the Caribbean. The Forum publishes two quarterly journals (*TransAfrica Forum* and *TransAfrica News*), hosts an annual foreign policy conference, and helps prepare black students for the Foreign Service exam. TransAfrica and its educational affiliate, TransAfrica Forum, are based in WASHINGTON, D.C.

One of TransAfrica's principal concerns has been to ensure that countries in Africa and the Caribbean that are shifting toward democracy receive an equal amount of financial aid from the U.S. government as democracy-bound countries in EUROPE and Asia. It has also concerned itself with human rights issues, refugee questions, and the drug war. TransAfrica has successfully lobbied the U.S. government in foreign policies concerning SOUTH AFRICA and HAITI, and is currently working to influence U.S. foreign policy toward NIGERIA.

From its inception in 1977, TransAfrica worked to end APARTHEID in South Africa, the policy of racial segregation intended to promote and maintain white supremacy. The organization's demonstrations against apartheid at the South African Embassy in 1985 led to the 1986 Anti-Apartheid Act by the U.S. Congress that imposed sanctions over President Ronald Reagan's veto. As a result, the United States placed a political and economic embargo against South Africa that contributed to the demise of apartheid.

On April 11, 1994, Robinson began a hunger strike to protest the U.S. policy that denied entrance to the country by Haitian refugees. After twenty-seven days, the United States agreed to ease its admission policy. Later in the year, TransAfrica lobbyists persuaded the government to help restore Haitian president JEAN-BERTAND ARISTIDE to power.

In 1995, TransAfrica launched a campaign to force Nigeria's eleven-year-old military government to return to civilian rule.

In a March 1995 letter endorsed by a host of black politicians, educators, and celebrities, Robinson accused General SANI ABACHA, the military leader who took control of Nigeria's government in 1993 following a military coup, of killing political opponents and shutting down the press. Robinson urged him "to expedite the restoration of democracy" to Nigeria's people or face "incalculable damage" and "eventual economic and political isolation of your regime." Robinson has followed up with advertisements, speeches, and protests meant to direct negative attention to Nigeria's military rule.

Robinson contends that, "African Americans ought to care about Africa and the Caribbean because we are much stronger together than separate. Our potential as black people is to harness our power globally. Then our [African American] business communities will trade with those [African and Caribbean] communities, invest in those communities, and we will all be healthier for it."

In 2001 Bill Fletcher replaced Robinson as TransAfrica's president. The organization remains active in its efforts to influence U.S. foreign policy in Africa and the Caribbean.

See also Human Rights in Africa; Human Rights in Latin America and the Caribbean.

Aaron Myers

Transatlantic Slave Trade

Transport of millions of enslaved Africans to the Americas in the sixteenth through nineteenth centuries.

From the 1520s to the 1860s an estimated eleven to twelve million African men, women, and children were forcibly embarked on European vessels for a life of slavery in the Western Hemisphere. Many more Africans were captured or purchased in the interior of the continent but a large number died before reaching the coast. About nine to ten million Africans survived the Atlantic crossing to be purchased by planters and traders in the New World, where they worked principally as slave laborers in plantation economies requiring a large work force. African peoples were transported from numerous coastal outlets from the SENEGAL RIVER in West Africa and hundreds of trading sites along the coast as far south as Benguela (ANGOLA), and from ports in MOZAMBIQUE in southeast Africa. In the New World slaves were sold in markets as far north as New England and as far south as present-day ARGENTINA.

Early European Trade with Africa

The marketing of people in the interior of AFRICA predates European contact with West Africa. A TRANS-SAHARAN AND RED SEA SLAVE TRADE developed from the tenth to fourteenth centuries that featured the buying and selling of African captives in Islamic markets, such as the area around present-day SUDAN. A majority of those enslaved were females, who were purchased to work as servants, agricultural laborers, or concubines. Some captives were also shipped north across the deserts of northwest Africa to the Mediterranean coast. There, in slave markets such as Ceuta (MOROCCO), Africans were purchased to work as servants or laborers in SPAIN, PORTUGAL, and other countries.

By the mid-1400s, Portuguese ship captains had learned how to navigate the waters along the west coast of Africa and began to trade directly with slave suppliers who built small trading posts, or "factories," on the coast. European shippers were thus able to circumvent the trans-Saharan caravan slave trade. The slave trade to EUROPE began to decrease in the late 1400s with the development of SUGAR plantations in the Atlantic islands of Madeira and São Tomé. These two islands, located off West Africa and in the Gulf of Guinea, became leading centers of world sugar production and plantation slavery from the mid-1400s to the mid-1500s. Portuguese merchants dominated this early trade.

Much of the earliest European trade with West Africa, however, was in gold, not people. Europeans did not have the power to overcome African states before the late nineteenth century, and gold production, centered in AKAN gold fields in the backcountry of present-day GHANA, remained in African hands. Europeans called this region the GOLD COAST. Agreements between African and European elites and rivalries for the African GOLD TRADE resulted in the construction of dozens of trading forts, or stone castles, along a 161-kilometer (100-mile) coastal stretch of Ghana. Several of these forts survive, have been repaired by the government of Ghana, and are tourist attractions today. It was not until the late seventeenth century that the value of European goods traded for African people surpassed the value of goods exchanged for gold. Over time, these gold forts became slave forts, where hundreds of Africans were confined in prisons awaiting sale and shipment.

Slave Trade and Plantations in the Americas

Christopher Columbus's "discovery" of the New World in 1492 marked the beginning of a transatlantic trading system. Via the slave trade, Africans played a leading role in the creation and evolution of this large and long-lasting "Atlantic system." Spanish adventurers arrived in the Americas hoping to trade for riches but soon enslaved the Native American peoples in their search for gold and silver. Disease, malnutrition, and Spanish atrocities led to the deaths of millions of the Indians of the Americas. By the 1520s the depopulation of the region prompted the Spanish government to look for alternative sources of labor. Officials contracted with Portuguese merchants to deliver Africans to Spanish territories in the New World. The first transatlantic slave voyages from Africa to the Americas occurred in the early 1520s on Portuguese vessels sailing from West Africa to the large Caribbean island of HISPANIOLA, the earliest European name for present-day HAITI and the DOMINICAN REPUBLIC.

The transatlantic slave trade increased in the mid-1500s, when the Spanish began to use African slave labor alongside Native Americans to mine silver in PERU. Slave ships sailed from Africa to COLOMBIA and PANAMA, and African captives then were

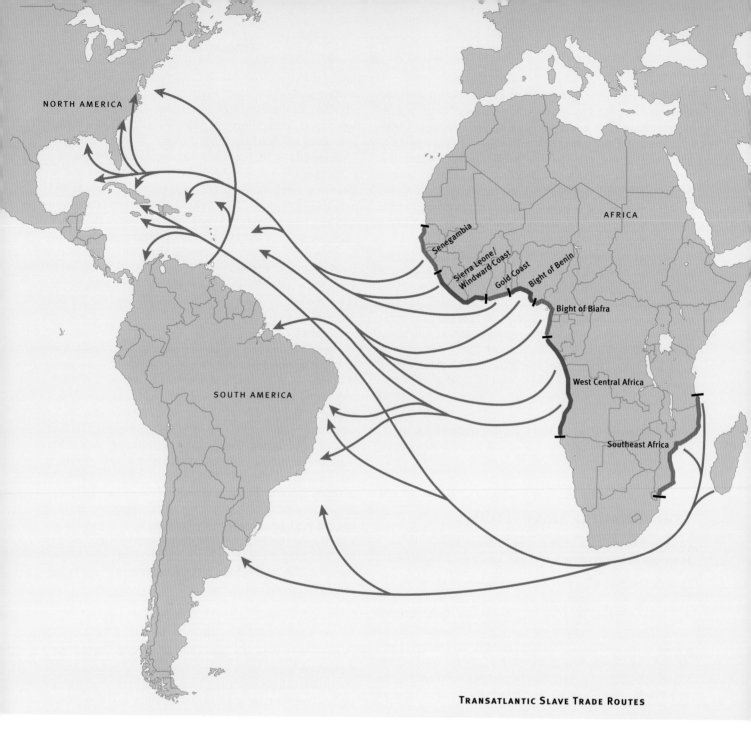

NORTH AMERICA

AFRICA

Senegambia

Sierra Leone/
Windward Coast

Gold Coast

Bight of Benin

Bight of Biafra

West Central Africa

SOUTH AMERICA

Southeast Africa

TRANSATLANTIC SLAVE TRADE ROUTES

transported overland to the Pacific coast of SOUTH AMERICA. Until the early 1600s, most Africans enslaved in the Americas worked in Peruvian or Mexican mines. The 1570s marked the development of sugar plantations in BRAZIL, a Portuguese colony, where merchants adopted production techniques pioneered in Madeira and São Tomé. By the 1620s African labor had replaced Indian labor on Brazilian sugar plantations.

The development of an export-based plantation complex in North America and the Caribbean, areas neglected by the Spanish and Portuguese, awaited the arrival of the British, French, and Dutch in the early 1600s. In the initial development of the British colonies Virginia and BARBADOS (1630s–1640s), JAMAICA (1660s), and South Carolina (1690s) and the French colonies SAINT-DOMINGUE (present-day Haiti), MARTINIQUE, and GUADELOPE (1660s–1680s), most laborers on the plantations were young

European males who agreed to work for three to five years in return for free oceanic passage and food and housing in the Americas. These workers were called indentured laborers. By the later seventeenth and early eighteenth centuries, tobacco, sugar, indigo (used to make blue dye), and rice plantations switched from European indentured labor to African slave labor. By the mid-1700s, Brazil, Saint-Domingue, and Jamaica were the three largest slave colonies in the Americas. By the 1830s, CUBA emerged as the principal Caribbean plantation colony. Throughout the history of the transatlantic slave trade, however, more Africans arrived as slaves in Brazil than in any other colony.

Dutch merchants did not develop extensive plantation colonies in the New World but they became large slave traders in the mid-seventeenth century. The small Dutch Republic was

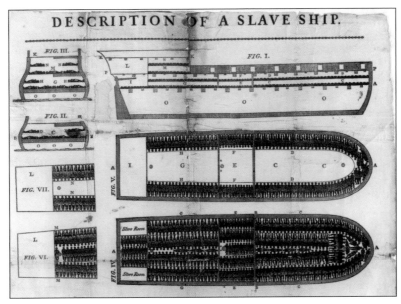

Published in 1789, this engraving shows a cross section of the slave ship *Brookes,* based in Liverpool. British parliamentarian William Wilberforce used this diagram in arguments for the abolition of the slave trade that he presented on the floor. *Hickey & Robertson, Houston/Image of the Black Project, Harvard University*

among the first European nations to develop modern commerce, and merchants there had access to shipping, port facilities, and banking credit. Dutch traders occupied several trading castles on the African coast, the most important of which was Elmina (in Ghana), a fort they captured from the Portuguese and rebuilt. The Dutch wrested control of the transatlantic slave trade from the Portuguese in the 1630s, but by the 1640s they faced increasing competition from French and British traders. By the 1680s, a variety of nations, private trading companies, and merchant-adventurers sent slave ships to Africa: merchants from Denmark, Sweden, and the German states also organized slave voyages. Throughout the eighteenth century—the height of the transatlantic slave trade—the largest traders were the British, Portuguese, and French.

Organization of Slave Voyages

Transatlantic slave voyages were complex commercial endeavors. Voyages based in Europe sailed a route linking Europe, Africa, and the Americas. Contemporaries saw this as a profitable "triangular trade." European goods were exchanged for slaves in Africa; slaves were sold in the Americas for plantation produce, such as sugar, which was transported back to Europe in the holds of slave vessels. Trade cargoes organized in Europe cost several millions of dollars in today's money, and the average value of outward cargoes was greater than most overseas trades. Cargoes typically included India cotton textiles, cowrie shells from the Indian Ocean, Brazilian tobacco, glassware from ITALY, brandies and spirits from FRANCE, Spain, and Portugal, Irish linen and beef, and a range of British and European manufactures. At one time, historians argued that cheap trinkets were sold for African slaves, but recent research

shows that African traders demanded a large variety of goods—in particular, textiles—and that over time more and more European goods were exchanged for African captives as slave prices increased.

Slave vessels sailed from Europe with large crews, including surgeons, carpenters, coopers (barrel-workers), cooks (some of whom were of African descent), sailors (who apprenticed to sea at a young age), and others hired to guard slaves on the African coast and on THE MIDDLE PASSAGE, where threats of rebellion and insurrection were constant. Slave vessels ranged in size from small sloops and schooners to larger ships measuring hundreds of tons. Some of these larger three-masted ships had three decks and were more than thirty meters (100 feet) in length and twelve meters (forty feet) in breadth. Few slave vessels were constructed specifically for the trade. By the mid-1800s, some slave vessels were built of wood and iron and powered by steam; these vessels sailed up rivers such as the Congo and sometimes purchased over 1,000 African slaves. Smaller, shallower-built slave vessels traded in the Gambia, Senegal, and Sierra Leone rivers in West Africa and along the Windward Coast (coastal area in West Africa stretching approximately from modern-day SENEGAL to CÔTE D'IVOIRE). Because the Gold Coast lacks large river outlets or safe anchorages, slave vessels anchored several miles offshore, where they were met by large trading canoes. In the major slaving-trading sites of Whydah (in modern-day Republic of BENIN), Bonny, and Old Calabar (in present-day NIGERIA), slave vessels anchored in lagoons or bays close to African villages and small towns. Large slave ships also traded in rivers and bays on the Angolan coast and in Mozambique in southeast Africa. In comparison with other Atlantic traders, however, most slave vessels were small, relatively inexpensive vessels, and were rigged

Volume of the Transatlantic Slave Departures by African Region and Period of Years, 1519–1867 (number of people, in thousands)

	Senegambia	Sierra Leone	Windward Coast	Gold Coast	Bight of Benin	Bight of Biafra	West-central Africa	South-east Africa	All Regions
1519–1600	10.7	2	0	10.7	10.7	10.7	221.2	0	266.1
1601–1650	6.4	0	0	5.2	2.4	25.5	461.9	2.0	503.5
1651–1675	17.7	0.4	0.1	35.4	21.9	58.6	104.3	1.2	239.8
1676–1700	36.5	3.5	0.7	50.3	223.5	51.5	132.6	10.9	509.5
1701–1725	39.9	7.1	4.2	181.7	408.3	45.8	257.2	14.4	958.6
1726–1750	69.9	10.5	14.3	186.3	306.5	166	552.8	5.4	1311.3
1751–1775	130.4	96.9	105.1	264.0	250.5	340.1	715	3.3	1905.2
1776–1800	72.4	106.0	19.5	240.7	264.6	360.4	816.2	41.2	1921.1
1801–1825	91.7	69.7	24.0	69	263.3	260.3	700.8	131.8	1610.6
1826–1850	22.8	100.4	14.4	0	257.3	191.5	770.6	247.5	1604.5
1851–1867	0	16.1	0.6	0	25.9	7.3	155.0	26.8	231.7
All Years	498.5	412.7	182.0	1043.2	2034.6	1517.9	4887.5	484.5	11062
% of Trade	4.5	3.7	1.6	9.4	18.4	13.7	44.2	4.4	100

Source: David Eltis, "The Volume and Direction of the Transatlantic Slave Trade: A Reassessment," *William and Mary Quarterly* 60 (2001): 17–46.

for speed. Most slave vessels made only a few voyages to Africa and transported between 250 and 300 slaves.

When a slave vessel arrived on the African coast, trade was "broken" by a variety of customs payments to local African rulers or merchants. Captains also paid fees to African sailors who piloted slave vessels across sandbars to anchorages. The captains' first tasks included purchasing (or gathering) wood, water, and other provisions from shore. The wood was brought on board for fuel and for the carpenter to build a large box-shaped barricade placed above the upper deck. Slaves were led through a small door on the barricade to the hatches and decks below. The barricade was a security precaution and it kept Africans from seeing their homeland, according to the testimony of some slave traders. In many parts of Africa a "trust trade" developed as European captains advanced trading goods to African slave dealers with the promise of future slave deliveries. These dealers often were small-scale traders who built factories with connecting warehouses to store goods and outdoor, fenced pens or enclosed "barracoons" to confine slaves. Sometimes sons or daughters of the local chiefs were given temporarily to the slave-ship captains as a form of credit known as pawnship. When a captain kidnapped "pawns" (which occurred infrequently), the local African ruler would cut off all slave trading from the region. Often the captain and crew of the next vessel from that port would be killed or taken hostage as retribution.

There was a complex system of exchange between European, Afro-European, and African agents. Bundles, or assort-

ments, of European trading goods were traded for a specified number of African units of exchange which then were exchanged for a specified number of slaves. The units of exchange varied regionally in Africa and included European iron bars, cowrie shells from the Indian Ocean, Italian beads, blue-dyed Indian textiles, or Brazilian gold. In the late eighteenth century, an assortment of European textiles, firearms, and alcohol would, for example, be equivalent to twelve ounces of gold along the Gold Coast; twelve ounces of gold would be the "price" of an adult male African slave. The profitability of a slave voyage often depended upon the ability of a merchant or captain to "assort" his trading goods to meet short-term African demand. There were many coastal agents who traded with slave-ship captains who did not have a properly "assorted" cargo. Many of these agents, particularly those who lived on the coast from present-day GUINEA-BISSAU southeast to LIBERIA, were of Afro-European descent.

Slave vessels remained on the coast of Africa usually from four to six months, depending on the trading location, availability of slaves and provisions, and the health of slaves and crew. Some provisions for the coastal stay and Middle Passage were loaded in Europe, but often captains purchased rice, beans, fish, and yams on the coast of Africa. Some small vessels loaded slave cargoes in a few weeks from small wooden factories or the larger stone trading forts. At some trading sites, such as late eighteenth-century Bonny (in Nigeria), African merchants created sophisticated slave-trading road and river networks from the interior to the coast. Slave supplies were reg-

Volume of Transatlantic Slave Departures by Region of Arrival in the Americas and Period of Years, 1519–1867 (number of people, in thousands)

	British mainland N. America	British Leewards	British Windwards + Trinidad	Jamaica	Barbados	Guianas	French Windwards	St. Domingue
1519–1600	0	0	0	0	0	0	0	0
1601–1650	0.8	1	0.2	0	22.4	0	1	0
1651–1675	0.9	5.6	0	22.3	63.2	8.2	6.5	0
1676–1700	9.8	26.6	0	73.5	82.3	27.4	16.6	4.8
1701–1725	37.4	35.4	0.6	139.1	91.8	24.4	30.1	44.5
1726–1750	96.8	81.7	0.3	186.5	73.6	83.6	66.8	144.9
1751–1775	116.9	123.9	120	270.4	120.9	111.9	63.7	247.5
1776–1800	24.4	25.3	197.5	312.6	28.5	71.2	41.2	345.8
1801–1825	73.1	5.3	43	70.2	7.6	71.8	58.8	0
1826–1850	0	0	0.5	2.1	0.9	4.8	19.5	0
1851–1867	0.3	0	0	0.4	0	0	0	0
All years	360.4	304.2	362	1077.1	491.2	403.7	304.2	787.4
% of Trade	3.7	3.2	3.8	11.2	5.1	4.2	3.1	8.2

	Spanish N. and S. America	Spanish Caribbean	Dutch Caribbean	N.E. Brazil	Bahia	S.E. Brazil	Other Americas	Africa	All Regions
1519–1600	151.6	0	0	35	15	0			201.6
1601–1650	187.7	0	1	86.3	60	30	0	0	390.4
1651–1675	0	0	38.8	15.6	15.6	15.6	0.6	0	192.8
1676–1700	7	0	26	56.1	104	54.5	11	0	500
1701–1725	30	2.1	30.5	24.3	199.6	122	14.2	0	825.8
1726–1750	12.7	1.6	10.2	51.4	104.6	213.9	8.3	0	1136.9
1751–1775	5	13	15.3	126.9	94.4	210.4	13.8	0	1653.9
1776–1800	10.2	56.9	6.9	210.8	112.5	247.2	44.1	0.4	1735.4
1801–1825	17.4	268.7	0	212.5	182	408.7	14.1	22.7	1455.9
1826–1850	5.8	297	0	78.5	146.5	736.4	3.9	91.3	1387.2
1851–1867	0	152.6	0	1.4	1.9	3.6	0.4	16.8	177.3
All Years	427.2	791.9	128.7	8986.8	1036.1	2042.3	110.4	131.2	9657
% of Trade	4.4	8.2	1.3	9.3	10.7	21.1	1.1	1.4	100

Source: David Eltis, "The Volume and Direction of the Transatlantic Slave Trade: A Reassessment, *William and Mary Quarterly* 60 (2001): 17–46.

ular, and sometimes ten to twenty slaves would be purchased and loaded on board ship per day. The supply of slaves from the interior depended largely on political warfare (since many male slaves were war prisoners) and ecological conditions. During times of drought or famine, slave supplies increased as people who could not be supported by villages were sold for money or provisions. Slave raiding also occurred, though it is likely that a smaller percentage of Africans entered slavery through village raids. Often, however, the distinction between wars and slave raids was blurred. Within a few weeks of departure from the coast, captains purchased final supplies of food, water, and wood for the Middle Passage.

Notorious Middle Passage

From a European geographic perspective, the Middle Passage was the second, or middle, leg of the triangular voyage between Europe, Africa, and the Americas. This was the notorious cross-Atlantic journey where hundreds of slaves were confined in irons below deck in crowded, hot, unsanitary, and inhumane conditions. The chance of insurrection was greatest during the first few weeks of the Middle Passage. During this time, most slaves were kept below deck, naked or only partially clothed with a loincloth, shackled in pairs, right leg to left leg. Nonetheless, slaves sometimes broke free of their chains and attacked the crew with a variety of tools and small weapons. Slave vessels were equipped with guns and cannons, which were placed on the raised quarterdeck to fire down on slaves trying to escape through the hatches. Occasionally, Africans in war canoes attacked slave vessels from shore. Researchers have documented more than 450 slave insurrections or shore-based attacks, and there were undoubtedly many more that went unrecorded. Occasionally, some captives would regain the shores of Africa. More often the crew regained control of the ship or Africans were re-enslaved upon reaching shore. Uprisings were extremely violent, and sometimes many slaves and most crew were killed. When African captives gained control of the ship, they kept a few crewmembers alive to navigate the vessel.

Ships' officers confined the men, women, boys, and girls in separate compartments. Slave vessels were fitted with numerous wooden platforms between decks to allow captains to pack in greater numbers of captives. As the between-deck space was generally from 1.2 meters (four feet) to 1.8 meters (six feet), platforms reduced the headroom for captives to only a few feet. All slaves suffered from numerous scrapes and bruises from lying on these bare planks. Captains claimed that when safely away from shore, slaves were given greater freedom of movement. Women and children, some claimed, were never shackled and were allowed to roam above deck with minimal supervision. Recently, however, archaeologists discovered many small-sized leg irons from the wreck of the slave ship *Henrietta Marie* (c. 1700) off Florida. Women may have been separated from male slaves and given greater freedom of movement to increase the crews' sexual exploitation of them.

Cooks prepared meals of fish, beans, or yams in large copper vats below deck. Surgeons sometimes assisted in the preparation and distribution of food. Slaves were given food at mid-morning and late afternoon in small bowls (or pannikins). Weather permitting, groups of African captives were exercised above deck (in their leg irons) in an attempt to offset the debilitating effects of the Middle Passage. Officers, usually boatswains, mates, and surgeons, were armed with whips such as the cat-o'-nine-tails and forced the African captives to dance. The crew's power was enforced through such torture devices as thumbscrews and iron collars. There were several tubs in each compartment below deck in which slaves could relieve themselves, though hindered by being shackled in pairs. Mates generally had the job of cleaning the slave compartments below deck, which each day would be covered with excrement, blood, and filth. Some captains frequently ordered the rooms washed and dried with fire pans, though sometimes the filth was simply scraped off the decks. To counteract the stench, which was thought to promote sickness, slave vessels were fumigated with vinegars, berries, limes, tars, and turpentines.

By any measurement, mortality rates of both slaves and crew were extraordinarily high on the Atlantic crossing. The crowded, unsanitary conditions below deck were an ideal disease environment for outbreaks of dysentery, the disease from which many slaves died. In addition to gastrointestinal diseases, Africans also died from dehydration, smallpox, or measles. Slaves who resisted captivity sometimes died from flogging or other forms of punishment. Some slaves committed suicide by jumping overboard or by starving or hanging themselves. The resistance to eating was so common that vessels carried metal devices to force-feed slaves. Sailors died mostly from malarial and yellow fevers, to which African-born peoples had some acquired immunities. Early in transatlantic slave trade about 15 to 20 percent of African captives died on the Passage. By the later eighteenth century, about 5 to 10 percent died, a reduction perhaps caused by improvements in hygiene and sanitation. Slave mortality rose in the nineteenth century during years when the British navy tried to enforce an international ban on the slave trade. About 15 to 20 percent of the crew died on the triangular voyage and sailors died at rates often greater than for all other overseas trades combined. Slave mortality usually increased during the last stages of a particularly long passage when there were shortages of food and water.

The Atlantic crossing lasted three to five weeks from West African trading sites such as the Gambia, Senegal, and Sierra Leone rivers. Near the equator, in regions such as the BIGHT OF BENIN and Bight of Biafra (near present-day Nigeria), the voyage to the Americas took several months. A few French ships transported slaves from Mozambique or MADAGASCAR to the Mascarene Islands in the Indian Ocean and then returned to France via Saint-Domingue in the WEST INDIES, where additional cargoes of captives from southeast Africa were disembarked. These voyages—via the Indian Ocean—were the most complex in the transatlantic slave trade and took several years to complete. In the nineteenth century, passage time in the trade fell dramatically due to advances in shipbuilding and speed.

Marketing of Enslaved Africans

Following their arrival in the Americas, African captives who survived the Atlantic crossing were "refreshed" with water and colonial provisions (such as citrus fruit), shaved, and cleaned. Ointments (to hide scars from diseases, such as yaws) and oils were applied on their skin in preparation for sale. Agents placed advertisements in colonial gazettes and in taverns for the sale of African labor, which usually began a few weeks after arrival. Many sales occurred on ship deck; other sales took place on wharves or in agents' houses or slave pens. Some planters contracted with merchants to purchase a preset number of slaves. Many slaves were sold by "scramble" or by auction.

During the scramble, planters or their representatives placed ropes or handkerchiefs around groups of slaves whom they wanted to purchase. During auctions, the highest-valued slaves, often adult men, were sold first; then, over several weeks or even months, less-valued slaves were sold. The last slaves sold were often old, sick, or debilitated Africans. Termed "refuse slaves," they usually were purchased by doctors or poor colonists. In some sales "prime" slaves were sold by scramble and "refuse" slaves were sold at public auction. Occasionally slave cargoes included family members or relatives, but separation during sale was almost inevitable. Cargoes also usually comprised Africans from different ethnic groups, as can be noted through ethnic scarification. Some planters purchased slaves from a variety of ethnic backgrounds as part of labor control; other planters purchased Africans from the same areas of Africa to maintain work force unity.

Ship captains and colonial agents sold slave cargoes to planters for bills of exchange, which often were resold for return cargoes of plantation produce. Slave vessels were not specialist "West Indiamen" (large produce vessels built for storage capacity), however, and transported only a fraction of the produce of the Americas back to Europe. By the mid-eighteenth century, many slave vessels began returning to Europe with the planters' bills of exchange and only small cargoes of plantation produce. Thus, though many slave vessels sailed on triangular voyages over the course of about a year, some did not carry on a triangular trade. An important exception to the concept of a triangular trade was the large Brazil-to-Angola shuttle trade, which dates from the 1680s. By the nineteenth century, small Brazilian vessels, built for speed, sometimes made three or four slave voyages per year in this direct trade.

Abolition of the Transatlantic Slave Trade

After centuries of broad acceptance, in the mid-eighteenth century some religious leaders began to question the morality of enslaving and owning humans. They began a campaign, termed the abolition movement, to end slavery. Faced with overwhelming opposition of colonial and business groups, the "abolitionists" realized that the first step toward ending slavery would be to end the transatlantic slave trade. Attacking the British slave trade was vital: the British were the largest slave traders by the mid-1700s. The abolition of the British trade was a twenty-year process: Parliament first regulated the trade, limiting the number of slaves British vessels could carry from Africa, then closed a number of colonies to slave imports, and then in 1807 abolished the trade itself. The size of the British trade highlights the important abolitionist triumph: during the previous decade, 150 British slave vessels had sailed per year for the African coast to purchase more than 40,000 African men, women, and children.

Four years earlier, in 1803, the small Danish slave trade ended by a government order enacted in 1792. The United States slave trade—centered in Rhode Island—became illegal in 1808, the first year Congress could address the question of abolition, as agreed to by the compromise between Northern and Southern states writing the Constitution in 1787. The French slave trade ended temporarily in the early 1790s after the slave revolution in the largest French colony, Saint-Domingue, removed the principal French slave market, and then the French government abolished slavery throughout French colonies in 1793–1794. With the ending of the Napoleonic Wars in 1814–1815, British diplomats attempted to end the international slave trade. The Dutch trade, which largely ended during the late-eighteenth-century warfare with France, was abolished by decree in 1814. The restored, conservative French monarchy, however, did not agree to end French participation in the slave trade. French vessels continued to ship slaves to Martinique, GUADELOUPE, and CAYENNE (in modern-day FRENCH GUIANA), and the French government did not abolish slavery in French colonies until 1848. The French trade, however, had effectively ended by 1831 after a political revolution in the country.

After 1815 the transatlantic slave trade centered on the expanding sugar and coffee colonies of Brazil and Cuba. British diplomats continued to negotiate for a total ban on the slave trade, and British naval ships cruised the African coast to capture illegal slave ships. By the 1820s most slave voyages originated from the West Indies or Brazil. To avoid British confiscation, "flags of convenience" were carried on board. Many European or American-owned slave vessels sailed under Spanish-Cuban registration. British naval pressure and changing Brazilian attitudes about the slave trade led to government measures that effectively ended the trade by the early 1850s. The remaining market of Cuba experienced a short-term increase in slave imports from 1853 to 1860 as slave and sugar prices rose. Prices fell in the 1860s, and by 1867 British, Spanish, and U.S. authorities were able to end the direct slave trade from Africa to Cuba.

Long-term Effects of the Slave Trade

The Transatlantic Slave Trade first centered on West Africa, the Gold Coast, Hispaniola, MEXICO, and Peru. Most of the slaves shipped from Africa during the period of 1520 to 1570 were male and worked in Spanish American mines. Over time, an increasing number of Africans transported across the Atlantic left from outlets in Nigeria or Angola, and more and more would work in Brazil and the British and French Caribbean colonies. Two of every five Africans arrived in Brazil; in the nineteenth century, perhaps four of five African slaves were destined for Brazilian plantations. The British and French Caribbean colonies each accounted for about one-fifth of the total trade. In the eighteenth century, Saint-Domingue and Jamaica were the largest plantation economies in the West Indies and the principal destinations for most African captives on French and British slave vessels. Slave imports, sometimes numbering 20,000 men, women, and children per year, replaced populations that did not increase by natural rates. The slave trade to what is now the United States constituted only about 7 percent of the total trade. This number may seem surprising, given the fact that the U.S. South developed one of the largest slave societies in the nineteenth century. But the development of a cotton plantation economy in the first half of the 1800s occurred after the abolition of the slave trade. In contrast to many plantation regimes, slave populations increased markedly within the United States. Most African captives arrived in British North America and the United States from the Congo River area, Senegambia, the Bight of Biafra, the Gold Coast, and the SIERRA LEONE region. In the four years prior to abolition, 5,000 to 7,000 slaves landed annually in CHARLESTON. This was the height of the transatlantic slave trade to the United States.

During the history of the transatlantic slave trade, conditions of slave supply in Africa, the demand of planters for slaves of certain gender, ages, or broadly understood African ethnicities, and European commercial rivalries shaped the movement of slaves from African to American markets. Brazil received perhaps two-thirds of African captives from Angola (with principal ports of LUANDA and Benguela under Portuguese control), one-quarter from the Bight of Benin, called also the Slave Coast (near present-day Benin), and smaller numbers from Mozambique and the region around the Bijagós Islands off West Africa. French slave vessels delivered African labor to Saint-Domingue mostly from Angola, the Bight of Benin, the Senegal River area, Calabar, and GABON. French merchants had few slaving contacts on the Windward Coast (near Liberia) or the Gold Coast. Most African captives arrived in British North America and the United States from the Congo River area, Senegambia, the Bight of Biafra, the Gold Coast, and the Sierra Leone region. The British Caribbean drew laborers from a wide range of African coastal outlets, though by the later eighteenth century the Bight of Biafra (Nigeria) and Angola began to predominate. Jamaica had particularly close commercial links with the Bight of Biafra and the Gold Coast. The Cuban plantation economy developed from the 1760s to 1860s with the most "diversified" African slave labor force. Cuba contracted slave shipments from various European merchants, each with their own African trading contacts. By the late eighteenth century, the Spanish government opened the HAVANA market to flags of all nations. No single African region supplied more than one-third of Cuban slave imports.

Over time there were changes in the stream of men, women, and children who entered transatlantic slaving networks. Throughout most years of the trade, the Bight of Biafra supplied the most women captives to coastal traders. Disproportionate numbers of adult male slaves were shipped from the Gambia and Senegal rivers. Often more than one in five Africans transported from the Windward Coast were children. By the nineteenth century greater numbers of children were forced into the trade from almost all regions in Africa. The proportion of men also increased. Scholars have yet to explain fully these age and gender variations between African regions and over time.

Why was African labor forcibly transported thousands of miles to the Americas to work in the economies of the New World? In the past, historians have argued that Africans were a low-cost labor alternative to scarce Indian labor (scarce, because most Indian populations were destroyed by disease) or

expensive European labor. African skin color also identified plantation slaves from other colonial workers, which facilitated planter control. Further, there were declining numbers of European men who were willing to work as plantation laborers because job opportunities increased in Europe; there was greater competition among European slave shippers, which increased the regularity and lowered the price of Africans in the Americas; and there were entrenched racist attitudes that justified European dominance over peoples from Africa. Others have argued that African peoples had a biological advantage over European laborers in the Americas. With some acquired immunities to tropical diseases such as yellow fever and MALARIA, Africans proved better able to survive the disease environments of the South Atlantic and Caribbean. Recent scholarship has pointed out that the organization of the European slave trade to Africa was a costly endeavor and that it would in fact have been less expensive to ship European convicts to work the plantations of the Americas. In this view, the organization of a European slave trade to the African coast has less to do with economics and more to do with developing European imperial ambitions to enslave and dominate those people defined as outsiders.

Scholars have also disagreed over the size of this forced Atlantic migration. To many, the size of the transatlantic slave trade represents the scale of European destructive impact on Africa. We may never know the extent of the slave trade in the interior of Africa, or the numbers of slaves who died en route to the coastal barracoons. As an Atlantic maritime enterprise, however, the transatlantic slave trade is well documented: European governments taxed vessels clearing and entering customs, and many newspapers and colonial gazettes survive, as do general shipping documents such as muster rolls and ship registers. Moreover, slave vessels often were at sea for more than a year and were on the coast of Africa and harbors in the Americas for several months. These vessels were noticed. The large British trade is particularly well-documented, and British navy officials kept extensive records of the illegal slave trade of the nineteenth century. Studies based on these numerous shipping and government documents, including Harvard University's W. E. B. Du Bois Institute's database of 27,500 slave voyages, compiled in 1993–1997, have supported an estimate of about eleven to twelve million slave exports and nine to ten million slave imports into the Americas. Importantly, these totals represent more than 60 percent of all Atlantic migrants before the nineteenth century. By the 1820s, after the abolition of the British, U.S., and Dutch slave trades, African migrants crossing the Atlantic still outnumbered all other European migrant groups. Also, African women outnumbered European female migrants by a ratio of more than five to one. Only by the 1840s would the number of migrants voluntarily leaving Europe for the Americas exceed the number of enslaved migrants from Africa.

What was the impact of this massive population shift? Scholars have argued that the transatlantic slave trade was an extremely profitable business that created pools of investment capital linked to industrialization in areas of Europe and North

In 1855 belgian sculptor Victor van Hove dramatized the horrors of slavery in two plaster statues, *Negro after a Flogging* and *Revenge* (shown here). *Hickey & Robertson, Houston/Image of the Black Project, Harvard University*

America. Extraordinary profits were achieved, however, on only a handful of voyages per year. Slave trading was extremely competitive and risky. In a broader view, the transatlantic slave trade provided African labor necessary to develop the plantation economies of the Americas. Most colonies specialized in single crops, such as sugar, and were dependent largely on Europe or North America for supplies and provisions. Thus within the Atlantic system regional, specialized economies, linked through maritime trade, developed. Such trade specialization likely stimulated economic growth and increased prosperity for those living in Europe and the Americas.

By the eighteenth century, standards of living had increased among many of the middle and lower classes in Europe and British North America. This in turn increased consumer demand for plantation luxuries such as sugar, tobacco, coffee, and spices. In response to this increased demand, planters in the Americas enlarged their estates, purchasing more labor from Africa to increase production. This expansion of the transatlantic slave trade in the eighteenth century, therefore, is a function of the income of European consumers and their demand for plantation goods. Without the forced labor of peoples of African descent, European consumers would have paid much higher prices for a wide range of subtropical produce. Economic growth in the North Atlantic thus stimulated the slave trade and the latter in turn encouraged economic growth.

The demand for African labor on plantations transformed a few African societies into slave-export economies. Slave-distribution networks developed in the interior to ensure a regular flow of African captives to coastal outlets, which in turn became slave-export centers with facilities to provision and confine Africans for several months. As prices rose over time, African traders gained a greater share of slaving profits. Some argue that the increasing influx of European goods limited African social and economic development. Access to inexpen-

sive Indian- or European-produced textiles, for example, retarded the growth of African textile industries. Also, guns and alcohol are viewed as "socially disruptive" trading goods, and there was a "slave-gun cycle" whereby Africans sold slaves to acquire more firearms for slave raiding. It is likely, however, that the strength of indigenous African domestic economies meant that the major African impact of the slave trade was social rather than economic. Foreign trade constituted a small percentage of African gross domestic product, and ordinary African peoples would have never seen goods produced outside Africa.

The slave trade undoubtedly increased the incidence of warfare and slave raiding among many African societies. Moreover, as about two-thirds of the captive Africans were men between the ages of eighteen and thirty, the slave trade likely removed essential workers and soldiers. In response to renewed external threats, villages may have been abandoned as they consolidated with other communities for protection. In certain areas the slave trade altered the ratio of men to women and adults to children, thus prompting further social changes, particularly in kinship structure and marriage patterns. The incidence of slavery increased in Africa during the slave trade era and increased again in the immediate aftermath of abolition, when external demand for slaves ended rather suddenly.

In the Americas the slave trade ensured that, for three centuries, the subtropical areas remained the focal point of New World economic activity. It also ensured a much more complex social milieu and cultural environment than would have been possible without contacts with Africa. With all of its horrors and inhumanity, the transatlantic slave trade was critical in the formation of the modern world.

See also Indian Ocean Slave Trade; Slavery in Africa; Slavery in Latin America and the Caribbean; Slavery in the United States; Transatlantic Slave Trade Database.

Bibliography

Rawley, James A. *The Transatlantic Slave Trade: A History.* Norton, 1981.

Tibbles, Anthony, ed. *Transatlantic Slavery: Against Human Dignity.* HMSO, 1994.

Stephen Behrendt

Transatlantic Slave Trade Database

Collection and analysis of data pertaining to transatlantic slave trading voyages.

Slaves constituted the most important reason for contact between Europeans and Africans for nearly two centuries. The shipment of slaves from Africa was related to the demographic disaster consequent to Europeans meeting Amerindians, which greatly reduced the numbers of Amerindian laborers and raised the demand for labor drawn from elsewhere, particularly Africa. As Europeans colonized the Americas, it is not surprising that a steady stream of European peoples migrated to the Americas between 1492 and the early nineteenth century. But what is often overlooked is that before 1820, perhaps three times as many enslaved Africans crossed the Atlantic as Europeans. This was the largest transoceanic migration of a people up to 1820, and it provided the Americas with a crucial labor force for its own economic development. The slave trade is thus a vital part of the history of some millions of Africans and their descendants who helped shape the modern Americas culturally, as well as in the material sense. In many ways it is now possible to find out more about the African stream of peoples to the New World than about their European counterparts. Coerced African migrants were property and better records were kept of their movements than of the movement of their free or indentured counterparts.

Collecting and Organizing the Data

While scholars had long known about some of these records, such abundant records could not be fully exploited until the computer revolution of the second half of the twentieth century. From the late 1960s, Herbert S. Klein and other scholars began to collect archival data on slave trading voyages from unpublished sources and code them into a machine readable format. In the 1970s and 1980s, scholars created a number of slave ship data sets, while others had published in hard copy form several catalogs of slave voyages. The most notable of these were three volumes of voyages from French ports published by Jean Mettas and Serge and Michéle Daget, and two volumes of Bristol voyages (expanded to four by 1996) collected by David Richardson. The basis for each set was usually the records of a specific European nation or the particular port where slaving voyages originated, with the information available reflecting the nature of the records that had survived

rather than the structure of the voyage itself. Scholars of the slave trade spent the first quarter century of the computer era working largely in isolation of each other, each using one source only as well as a separate format. Voyage records combining data from several national or port archives were unusual.

The accumulation of individual data sets and catalogs made it seem feasible to integrate the records for the very large British slave trade with the Dutch, French and Portuguese data, and to thereby create a single set for the trade as a whole. The W. E. B. Du Bois Institute for Afro-American Research at Harvard University provided a launching pad for successful grant applications to the National Endowment for the Humanities and the Mellon Foundation. With this preliminary funding, the project undertook three major tasks between 1993 and 1999. The first was standardizing the existing data. Pioneers in the field had collected their data using different definitions of variables, sometimes of apparently similar items of information, as well as a range of organizational formats (for example, using ship- rather than voyage-based data). The second was collating voyages that appeared in several different sets, converting single-source data sets into multisource equivalents and even checking on the validity of old compilations. The third, which became increasingly important as the project progressed, was adding new information. New voyages—new in the sense that they have not appeared in any other published compilation—accounted for about half of the 27,233 voyages that were published on a CD-ROM by Cambridge University Press in 1999. The data set provided for 227 separate pieces of information on each voyage. These were arranged according to the voyage pattern spanning the date of departure from the vessels' home port to the date of return, and included geographic and temporal information, as well as details of those on board (names of owners and captains are provided, but no names of slaves), mortality experienced on, and duration of, the various stages of the voyage, the age categories and sex of the slaves, whether or not a rebellion occurred, and some characteristics of the ship itself. Finally, a full presentation of the sources was supplied for every voyage so that the "transparency" of the researchers work is readily apparent, and in addition a separate file was supplied with a few hundred voyages that may or may not have been slavers. The implicit assumption here was that future research would be able to resolve the doubts.

With publication of the CD-ROM, funding for the project came to an end, and the base of the project moved from the W. E. B Du Bois Institute to the University of Hull in England. In 2001, major additional funding from the British Arts and Humanities Research Board made possible a new research assault on Portuguese, Brazilian, Spanish, Dutch and British archives. In the course of the three years, 2001–2004, researchers have added approximately 7,000 voyages to the 1999 data set, and have been able to add new information for about 10,000 voyages that were already included on the Cambridge CD-ROM. They have removed about 90 voyages that were originally thought to have been slaving voyages, but in fact returned to their home ports direct from Africa carrying African produce rather than slaves. It has also been possible to add additional facts on each voyage, including the prices that nearly 1,000 slaving expeditions received for their slaves when they sold them in the Americas. There are further plans to establish a framework that would allow additions to be made to the data on an ongoing basis. The database would thus take on similar status to an electronic journal. An editor would vet new data that users discovered and correct and amend the set as appropriate. However, instead of the data being published at regular intervals, the database would be maintained on a Web site and be subject to continuous updating. The physical location of the editorial office would move between institutions over time. A new and more user-friendly interface will be incorporated into this new method of distributing the data.

What is the outcome of this collaboration? It is probable that after twelve years of work, the slave voyages data set now includes over 95 percent of all slave voyages that left French ports and perhaps two-thirds of those leaving Portuguese and Brazilian ports, with the proportion covered by the remaining national groups of slave trading nations falling somewhere between these two marks. Over 90 percent of all British slave ship voyages are included, and after the Portuguese, the British accounted for the largest number of slaving voyages of any national group. There are, of course, numerous slave voyages that are not included in the set. The largest gaps that remain are for the Portuguese trade (based largely in BRAZIL). Nevertheless, it should be noted that this is a multisource database, with less than 10 percent of the voyages it contains relying on a single source, and some voyages drawing on no less than eighteen separate sources located in various parts of the Atlantic world. Overall, it is likely that some record of 85 percent of all transatlantic slaving voyages can be found in the new database. How is it possible to derive an indication of completeness? One method that any reader can perform for his or her own satisfaction arises from the two-volume published catalog of French voyages compiled by Jean Mettas and Serge and Michelle Daget. Each French slaving captain had to report to port authorities when he returned home and among other information had to provide an account of all vessels he had met—the vast majority of these being slave ships. Ninety-five percent of the vessels identified in the captains' reports themselves have a separate entry in the Mettas-Daget catalogs as slave ships. One may conclude therefore that the French trade is very well represented indeed in the CD-ROM. Similar tests can be carried out for other national branches of the trade. At the very least, the data set is sufficiently complete that it can be used to analyze and represent the major trends over time in the history of the transatlantic slave trade.

One other test of the representativeness of the data may be derived from estimates of the volume of the slave trade prepared prior to the appearance of the 1999 CD-ROM. Two widely cited essay-length surveys of the size and direction of the trade, reviewing work published since Curtin's 1969 *Census*, appeared in 1982 and 1989. These have become the scholarly consensus figures of the last two decades. Broadly, these suggested modest increases in Curtin's global estimate of the volume of the trade to 12 million departures from Africa and 10.5 million arrivals in the various reception zones. It should be noted that these estimates include trade to some areas, particularly the Mascarene Islands, that the Cambridge data set does not purport to cover. If we exclude these areas then the scholarly consensus figures would be 11.8 million departures and 10.3 million arrivals. If we further exclude voyages setting out prior to the seventeenth century—on the basis that the Cambridge CD-ROM contains only a handful of ships setting out before 1600—then the consensus figures would be 11.4 million departing and 10 million arriving. In the present set, the average number of slaves on board a slave ship as it left Africa was 331, and 281 when it arrived in the Americas. Simple division of these averages into the aforementioned "consensus" aggregates suggests a total of between 34,482 voyages based on numbers leaving Africa, and 35,561 based on numbers disembarking slaves. From this perspective, the 33,000 voyages in the new data set constitute a very large proportion of all slaving voyages. Of course, other estimates of the trade exist. If we take a higher estimate of say 14.5 million departures, then the ratio falls, but not below two-thirds. However, it should be noted that higher estimates are based on what might be termed a "top-down approach," or the opinions and impressions of well-placed officials and other observers. None of the estimates in excess of 12 million departures have engaged the voyage-based data that comprise the transatlantic slave ship database. The most recent estimate of the magnitude of the slave trade suggests a small downward revision, and this implies a small proportionate increase in the sample size of the new data set. Given the commoditization imposed on the human beings carried from Africa, and the profit-maximizing nature of the traffic, records of the movement of slaves are necessarily superior to those for free migrants, indentured servants, and convicts where the financial stakes and potential returns for owners and merchants were considerably lower. It may not be too rash to suggest that some written record of every transatlantic slave voyage ever undertaken has survived somewhere.

Interpreting the Data

What do we know about the slave trade that we did not know prior to the publication of the consolidated data set? The work of interpreting the data is just beginning. Nevertheless, some major new patterns are now apparent that are more important than the new light shed on the volume of the trade discussed above. The Cambridge set provides a good basis for estimating deaths during the middle passage. It contains no less than 5,300 voyages with data on the number of Africans who died on board. For reasons that are as yet poorly understood, deaths as a proportion of those embarked differed markedly by African region of embarkation. One in eight of those taken on board a slave vessel on the African coast died before reaching the Americas and many more died before embarkation and after disembarkation without any such deaths entering the historical record. But the shipboard mortality among those leaving the Bight of Biafra was between two and three times greater than among those leaving West Central Africa (19.1 percent versus

8.4 percent). Such differences are far greater than those among slaves arriving in different regions in the Americas. Further, mortality declined markedly between the mid-seventeenth century and the early nineteenth century, before increasing once more in the illegal phase of the slave trade (mainly after 1830).

It is also now apparent that in sending ships to the African coast, merchants selected cargoes for specific markets because Africans had regionally distinct preferences for the merchandise that they expected to receive in return for the slaves. Ninety-five percent of the cowries carried to the coast went to BIGHT OF BENIN ports. Almost all the metal shipped from Europe to Africa went to Senegambia or the Bight of Biafra, and manillas (wristlets) would sell only in the latter region. Almost all New England rum sold on the Windward and Gold Coasts, and all roll tobacco from BAHIA went to the Slave Coast. Textiles were welcomed in many places, but a pattern and texture that would sell in one place would often sell nowhere else. The point is that ships leaving on a slave voyage would normally trade in only one region, though often at several ports in that region. It was unusual for ships trading in southeast Africa to buy slaves anywhere else, and the same is true for ANGOLA, the Bight of Biafra, and, to a slightly lesser extent, Senegambia. Generally, then, if we know the region in which a ship traded, we can be reasonably certain that it did not trade in any other region, though it may have traded at more than one port. This is particularly the case if that region lay east of the Bight of Benin, which part of Africa, it might be noted, supplied more than 60 percent of all the slaves entering the trade. For those few ships that did trade in more than one region, nearly half began buying slaves on the Senegambian, SIERRA LEONE, and Windward coasts before making the balance of their purchases—usually by far the larger share at that—at either the Gold Coast or the Bight of Benin. Some further cross-regional purchasing occurred between the Gold Coasts and Bight of Benin exclusively, and a little more on the adjacent Senegambian, Sierra Leone, and Windward Coasts exclusively. Even with these cases, however, a vessel tended to get the majority of its slaves from just one region.

On the American side there were also broadly systematic patterns of trading. Slavers in the large Brazilian trade typically sailed direct to the final port, but further north, the eastern Caribbean acted as a filter for all ships heading for the Caribbean, and Central and North America. Many more ships called at BARBADOS, for example, than sold slaves on the island, as captains sought the information on markets elsewhere in North America. The data set, it should be noted, makes no attempt to track slaves who were landed and then re-shipped, however quickly, to other parts of the Americas. Asiento slaves destined for Spanish America and disembarked temporarily at Barbados, CURAÇAO, and JAMAICA are thus counted as arrivals in these temporary staging areas. Some vessels did make short trips to adjacent markets. Barbados and then one of the Leewards was one combination, Cap Français and Saint Marc another, Virginian ports and Maryland yet another. Others split their slaves between eastern and western Caribbean or the eastern Caribbean and North American mainland markets. As might

be expected, vessels trading first in a major western Caribbean or mainland Americas market before moving on to another major market distributed their slaves fairly equally between the two trading regions. As in Africa, however, slave ships typically disembarked their slaves at a single major market. Less than one in a hundred vessels disembarked at three or more different ports.

Patterns Emerge

For Europe and the Atlantic Americas, one of the major patterns to emerge from the data is the pervasiveness of the slave trade. Every Atlantic port in Western Europe and the Americas as well as a host of minor shipbuilding centers were heavily involved in the business at one point or another. Within these ports, ownership was widely based. The old picture of a small dominant elite organizing and benefiting from the traffic is in need of revision. Particularly in England, slave ships would have a dozen or more owners, ownership concentration ratios were very low, and small investors numerous. Despite, indeed, because of the fact that the commodities traded were human, it is also possible to track long-run productivity trends in this trade more easily than in any other business. Small secular improvements may be discerned, but there were also differences in productivity between the major national carriers, and, indeed, between ports within national areas. Analysis of tonnages, crew, slaves carried, and voyage lengths indicate that British eighteenth-century dominance of the trade was rooted in an efficiency advantage. Specifically, the British carried more slaves per crew member and per ton, and their voyages were faster than those of other West European slave traders.

The other side of productivity trends, of course, are the conditions under which people—both crew and slaves—traveled. On the first of these, the data establishes with more clarity than ever before that slaves and crew were far worse off than their counterparts on board ships in the contemporary transatlantic indentured servant traffic, or on convict ships heading to both the Americas and Australia, as well as galleys operating in Mediterranean and Atlantic coastal waters. On the issue of the mortality of slaves and crew on board ship, it is now possible to get a more definitive picture. The business was deadly for both slaves and crew—although the basis of the mortality and morbidity of the two groups was different. Slave mortality has been discussed above, but here we should note that mortality rates (taking into account time at risk) were more severe for slaves, and crew as well as slave mortality rates differed by African region of trade. These systematic variations are not easy to explain on the basis of influences controlled by Europeans alone.

But the major contribution of the new data is that it raises the profile of Africa on the shaping of the trade, and beyond that, on the Atlantic world as a whole. The coastal distribution of slaving activity in Africa, for example, has attracted much recent attention since it relates, inter alia, to some central questions for historians, notably the impact of the slave trade on Africa as well as its legacy for the cultural history of the Atlantic world. The Cambridge data set suggests that West Africa's share of slaves shipped to the Americas was rather larger than previously assumed, accounting for nearly half of the total between 1595 and 1867. Moreover, among the West Africa provenance zones, the Gold Coast and Bight of Benin seem to have been more important than was earlier thought. But while the Cambridge data set has helped to redraw regional patterns of slave shipments from Africa, perhaps its main contribution to discussion of the origins of slaves lies in its disaggregation of regional patterns and its identification of specific ports of call of ships at the coast. This enables scholars to begin to reconstruct histories of slave shipments from subregions or even single ports in Africa. In fact, there was a high level of concentration of slave shipments through a small group of ports in Africa, with trade in most regions being heavily centered at no more than two or three principal outlets.

Further, regions and ports appear to have been very important in shaping the gender structure of slaves shipped by African region between 1663 and 1864, with, for example, proportionally more females leaving from the Bight of Biafra than from other regions. The proportions of males and children among shiploads of slaves carried from all the major slave supply regions in Africa increased during the final two centuries of the transatlantic traffic. As one might anticipate, the scale of the change varied somewhat between regions, but in each region the rise in proportions of children entering the trade was steep, notably in the nineteenth century. The causes of these shifts in the composition of the slave trade include the role of female labor in agriculture in Africa, American planters' preferences for male labor, and the demographic histories of societies on the two sides of the Atlantic, but what is emerging is that Africa is at least as important as the Americas in explaining these patterns.

Effects of Rebellion

A further sign of the importance of seeing Africans as agents as well as victims, is demonstrated by analysis of shipboard slave revolts and attacks on ships from the shore. It is likely that at least one in ten slave vessels experienced a slave revolt. But more important than the incidence of rebellions is the remarkable differences in the distribution of violent endings of slaving voyages along the African coast. Specifically, the costs of doing business were simply greater in some areas than others because of the nature of African resistance. Ships leaving the Upper Guinea coast—from Senegambia to the Windward Coast inclusive—accounted for over 40 percent of the shipboard revolts recorded in the data set but less than 10 percent of all the slaves carried to the Americas from Africa. Explanations for such variation in regional distribution still have to be uncovered, but it is striking that Upper Guinea is closer to both Europe and the Americas in terms of both distance and voyage times and has some major rivers that act as transportation routes from the interior to the coast. Such a region should have been in the forefront of slave provenance zones for any activity that was preoccupied with intercontinental transportation

costs—and such costs, it should be noted, accounted for 50 percent of the selling price of the newly arrived slave in the Americas. Yet Europeans simply avoided this part of the coast in the sense that it supplied a very small part of slave departures from all Africa in most of the slave trade era. Indeed, most of the slave trading in the Upper Guinea regions was confined to the half-century, 1750–1800, when, as is well known, slave prices climbed steeply and the time taken to load slaving vessels on the coast increased. Tightening supplies of slaves perhaps forced Europeans to temporarily overcome their aversion to the heightened risks of violence associated with slaving in Upper Guinea (and the higher costs that always attended such violence). Indeed, it has been argued that slave resistance generally raised the costs of carrying slaves to the Americas. Extra crew and extra weapons were reflected in the prices that plantation owners paid. Thus while most slave rebellions were unsuccessful, the very threat of their occurrence increased the costs (and therefore the price of slaves in the Americas) to the point that many fewer slaves entered the traffic than would have been the case, if lower (or no) threat of resistance had existed. Thus violence on the part of slaves was partially effective. The vast majority of Africans involved in the slave trade may not have been willing participants, but it is now time to recognize that their ability to shape the trade was no less than that of the Europeans.

Distribution of Africans

But perhaps the major findings yielded by the data relate to transatlantic connections. The Cambridge data make available unprecedented detail on which parts of Africa supplied the different parts of the slaveholding Americas. The distribution of Africans in the New World was no more randomized than it was for Europeans. Broadly, with the exception of the *recôncavo* of Bahia, and probably the province of Minas Gerais for which Bahia was a major conduit, the African part in the repeopling of South and Central America was as dominated by West-Central Africa, as was its European counterpart by Iberians. Peoples from the Congo basin and Angola formed by far the greater share of arrivals in south-central Brazil—the largest single slave reception area in the Americas—as well as in northeastern Brazil, Central America, and, to a lesser extent, Rio de la Plata. West-Central Africa formed the second largest provenance zone for all other South American regions. Bahia—one of the two most important points of entrance into the New World for Africans—was a major exception. In Bahia, the dominance of peoples from the hinterland of the Bight of Benin was almost complete. A large West African presence is also apparent in Spanish Central America, and the less important region of Rio de la Plata. The latter, in fact, is the only region on the continent of South America where Africans from the Bight of Biafra—overwhelmingly Igbo and Ibibio peoples—were to be found in large numbers. West Africa is also well represented in the Guyanas and Surinam, but as in Central America, it was the Gold Coast, rather than the Bight of Biafra and the Slave Coast, which supplied almost half of those arriving. This is the only region in the whole of South America where peoples from the Gold Coast have a major presence.

In the Caribbean, West Africa was as dominant as was West-Central Africa in South America, though generally the mix of African peoples was much greater here than it was further south. Only in SAINT DOMINGUE did Africa south of the equator provide half of all arrivals. And only in the French Leewards and CUBA did that ratio approximate one-third. Generally, a single West African region was a clear leader in supplying each specific American region. Barbados, the Danish islands, and Spanish Central America—utilizing mainly the Dutch entrepot of Curaçao—drew disproportionately on the Gold Coast. The Bight of Benin played a similar role for the French Leewards. In JAMAICA and the British Leewards, the Bight of Biafra was easily the single most important provenance zone, though in none of these cases did a single region, unlike the situation in all Brazilian regions, provide as many as half of all arrivals. In the Caribbean, "West Africa" effectively meant the Gold Coast, the Slave Coast (Bight of Benin), and the Bight of Biafra. Senegambia was of some importance in the French Caribbean, and the long Windward Coast stretching south from Sierra Leone was responsible for almost one-fifth of disembarkations in the British Leewards; but generally, as noted, these regions played a minor role in the slave trade to the major American regions. Also as noted, the relative proximity of Senegambia and the Windward Coasts to the Americas—passages from Senegambia to the Caribbean are typically half as long as their more southerly transatlantic counterparts—suggests some factor other than geography was at work.

The data set shows that of all the receiving areas in the Americas, Cuba and Barbados received the greatest mix of African peoples, although the United States was not far from this pattern. No single part of Africa supplied more than 28 percent of arrivals in either island and the only major regions not well represented were southeast Africa in Barbados and the Gold Coast in Cuba. In addition, the region that supplied the greatest number of slaves—west-central Africa—covered by the nineteenth century a wider range of coastline than in earlier centuries and drew on a vast slaving hinterland, suggesting a further mixing of peoples. Moreover, there was no regional segregation within Cuba. Almost all the arrivals moved through HAVANA and ports in the west of the island and for the rest of their lives worked in the sugar heartland which formed the hinterland of these ports. Large numbers of YAO from the southeast, of YORUBA from West Africa, and of LUNDA from the Kasai valley in the Angolan interior intermingled on the plantation labor forces. They arrived, moreover, within a relatively short space of time in the first half of the nineteenth century, a pattern that clearly separates Cuba from Barbados and the United States; Cuba, then was an exception. An examination of shifts over time in these transatlantic links suggests that some American regions, such as Bahia and south-central Brazil, drew on the same region of Africa throughout the slave trade era, and others, such as the British and French areas, may have drawn on a mix of regions, but tended to do so in sequence—a sequence moreover that in the British case was played out very

slowly. Perhaps the picture of a confusing mix of African cultures with all the attendant barriers to establishing African influence on the New World needs revising.

Geography and patterns of winds and ocean currents help to explain some of these transatlantic linkages, particular within the so-called South Atlantic System. But other patterns, including the Bight of Benin–Bahia and the Bight of Biafra–West Indies connections, are less easily explained by reference to geography or transport economics. European influences were also important. With the exception of the Spanish colonies, the great majority of the slaves arriving in the Americas did so in ships belonging to subjects of the colonial powers governing the territories in question. It follows, therefore, that linkages between African and American regions reflected in part the patterns of influence by national groups of carriers over trade of specific African regions or ports. But it is the African role that requires more attention. Why should Europeans as a group focus first on the Bights, and later, on West-Central Africa, when regions in Upper Guinea were both closer to the Americas and provided larger ratios of the males, which we are told planters in the Americas wanted? Why should loading (or slaving) times on the African coast lengthen well prior to the peak period of departures and then fall in the last quarter of the eighteenth century when the transatlantic slave trade was at its height? Why should some African peoples (for example, the Yoruba) have left more easily identifiable legacies in the Americas than others (for example, the Igbo) even when the latter outnumbered the former among forced migrants? It is not likely that answers to these and many other key questions will come from the European side of the slave trade. Of more immediate importance, such questions could not even be framed without these new data.

Overall, perhaps the single most important preliminary conclusion to emerge from these new data is a large role for Africans in the Atlantic world. Decisions on who entered the trade, where slaves embarked and where they disembarked, and where the trade first began and first ended emerged from an exchange between Africans—both elite, and, via resistance, enslaved—and Europeans. The data set contributes to the recent trend in the study of Africa and Africans that sees Africans as more than just victims. The data also allows a much clearer view of transatlantic connections between Africa and the Americas, and promotes a fresh evaluation of the role of the slave trade in European and African societies, value systems, and economic development.

David Eltis

Transculturation, Mestizaje, and the Cosmic Race: An Interpretation

In 1940 Cuban scholar FERNANDO ORTIZ (1881–1969) coined the term *transculturation* (*transculturación* in Spanish) to replace the concept of "acculturation" (the modification of one culture that adopts traits from another, dominant culture). Ortiz offered the term in order to acknowledge the ongoing history of conflict and difference in which cultural adaptation was above all a process of creative resistance—not just assimilation. Ortiz came to this acknowledgement after having pathologized African culture in CUBA. During his career as a lawyer, Ortiz studied the late-nineteenth-century theories of Cesare Lombroso, the Italian criminologist who claimed that delinquents were born with certain identifiable physical traits. Like other Latin Americans of this period, Ortiz adapted this theory to a local setting, and concluded that blacks were congenitally nonconformist. But the attention he was paying to black nonconformism soon made Ortiz take stock of Cuba's cultural debts to AFRICA. It became clearer to him that the process by which Hispanics and Africans were first uprooted from their soil and later orphaned in the Americas was so complex that it could not have melded in the harmony evident in such friendly words as SYNCRETISM, hybridism, or even *mestizaje*, all of which were widely used to describe the mixing of cultures that have taken place in the Caribbean continent since the late fifteenth century. These existing words described the results but ignored the 500-year long tortuous process.

Whereas acculturation seems to indicate a smooth transition of a subcultural group into the mainstream of national culture, the most promising feature of transculturation is its admission of conflict. Though crediting it with the power to recognize violence may almost appear to be a perverse thing to say about a word that describes creativity in a national culture, to Ortiz it was more perverse to deny the conflict. It is true that transculturated practices—such as Caribbean dances, for instance—can be used to create the sense of a happy resolution to the antagonisms at the origins of Latin American history. National governments, for example, often celebrate musical, culinary, religious, visual, and other forms of transculturation as signs of an existing racial democracy that accepts a country's mixed heritage, as if to say that more democratic change and tolerance for difference were superfluous or anachronistic. Two such prominent and recent cases are the showcasing of SANTERÍA religious practices as official tourist attractions in Cuba and the use of the slogan "PUERTO RICO is Salsa" as the island's official theme for its participation in the 1992 quincentennial celebration of the Spanish in America held in Seville, SPAIN. In both cases, transcultured forms (Santería and SALSA MUSIC) have gained emblematic status of everything that is national (Cuban or Puerto Rican). But it would be a mistake to dismiss transculturation as merely a mechanism for social control that would miss its measure of novelty and resistance. Before nation-states co-opt its results, transculturation is the exhilarating moment of creating new cultural forms from parent cultures in collision. Before the results are stable and usable for state policies, transculturation plays with dangerous mixes in unpredictable ways.

Ortiz appreciated the dangers, and the tragic necessity of compensating for losses in the Americas. What joins Caribbean peoples, he wrote in his classic study of the Caribbean *Con-*

trapunteo cubano del tabaco y el azúcar (1940; *Cuban Counterpoint of Tobacco and Sugar*, 1995) is the fact that none of us really belongs there. Nevertheless, Africans suffered far more losses than did Europeans: "Men, economies, cultures, ambitions were all foreigners here, provisional, changing, "birds of passage" over the country, at its cost, against its wishes, and without its approval . . . All those above and those below, living together in the same atmosphere of terror and oppression, the oppressed in terror of punishment, the oppressor in terror of reprisals, all beside justice, beside themselves. And all in the painful process of transculturation."

Ortiz's significant improvement over the existing concepts (mestizaje, syncretism) was to make pain and loss the background for a heightened pleasure of cultural coherence. In such case, the value of a national culture derived, in part, from the enormous cost of forging the nation.

Taken as a process that produces cultural harmony, transculturation may be as heavy with conservative assumptions as the words that it hoped to replace (mestizaje). The problem is precisely the univocalism it shares with competing concepts, the presumption that a single word should describe heterogeneous patterns, as if they boiled down to a process of simplification. Therefore, debate over political implications of the word leads to predictable and justified objections. Critics of programs to homogenize national cultures are surely right to object to the depuration of difference in the processes of transculturation, along with the more benign names for the reduction of antagonisms that it would dislodge, names like *mestizaje*, syncretism, hybridity, or "the cosmic race."

JOSÉ VASCONCELOS (1882–1959), the Mexican philosopher and politician, wrote a book with that title (*The Cosmic Race*) in 1925, when he was MEXICO's minister of education, right after the Mexican Revolution (1910–1920). Vasconcelos's utopian vision of Mexico, where the existing four races in the world would meld into one "cosmic," postracialized race, was meant to counter the hypocrisy of Latin American "democracies" that excluded their populations of color from active citizenry. Though his "Cosmic Race" is a shorthand for white, black, indigenous, and Asian characteristics, it shows familiar elitist biases such as the emphasis on the need for black and indigenous communities to assimilate into a white dominated culture. Nevertheless, Vasconcelos was imagining a future in which that hierarchy would no longer exist, and the transformative project that he advocated gives his own prejudices an obsolescent quality. As Vasconcelos imagined it Mexico, at the vanguard of truly democratic change, would lead a global movement into a racially harmonious future. This is evident from the book's full title, *The Cosmic Race: The Mission of the Ibero American Race*. In that book "*Mestizaje*" is the first and most important chapter. In English, the translation is "MISCEGENATION," and the clumsy word is a sign of the bad fit between the Anglo-American and the Latin American linguistic and social codes. Miscegenation has often been pronounced with mistrusts or revulsion by North American white intellectuals, while Latin American racial mixing has often been an official slogan in Spanish and Portuguese. Even GONZALO AGUIRRE BELTRÁN, Mexico's foremost student of black culture, perceived mestizaje as the necessary entryway by Afro-Mexicans into their modern nation.

Mestizaje endorses the particularity of New World peoples through a rhetoric of national brotherhood that is meant to ease racial tensions, not necessarily to address material equity. Vasconcelos's manifesto for merging already had a long tradition, and had become a conventional banner of cultural pride. It was, for example, the standard of the independence movement throughout the continent (1810–1830), when white CREOLES such as SIMÓN BOLÍVAR (1783–1830) proclaimed that Spanish Americans have many fathers, but only one mother, that they are neither Spanish, nor Indian, nor black, but all of these. Bolívar's pronouncement, however, did not resolve racial tensions; it merely acknowledged them.

A century later, after many variations on the theme, Vasconcelos proposed mestizaje as the way in which Mexico reaffirmed itself as a modern country with a mission to the world. For a hundred years, the republic had been torn between indigenist liberals like President Benito Juárez (1806–1872), and the Europeanizing monarchists who replaced him with Maximilian (1832–1867). Both sides would contribute, said the minister of education during the Mexican Revolution, to making "the new man" (a goal that FIDEL CASTRO would take up much later in the 1959 Cuban Revolution). Whites and Indians would be joined by blacks and Asians in the unprecedented culmination of one "cosmic race." This would happen in Mexico, José Vasconcelos wrote in 1925, because no other country was as free from the racial prejudice that obstructs human progress. The United States had been claiming leadership in the march of freedom, but Vasconcelos disputed this lead. U.S. writers and politicians were celebrating more than ideals, they also celebrated their Anglo-Saxon selves in racial terms. And they seemed to prosper by divine will, but, Vasconcelos underlined, "they committed the sin of destroying those races, while we assimilated them, and this gives us new rights and hopes for admission without precedent in History."

Fernando Ortiz's innovation was to admit to the violence in that self-congratulatory process of assimilation. His *Cuban Counterpoint of Tobacco and Sugar* replaced the emphasis on racial inheritance implied in mestizaje, for one on cultural process active in his concept of transculturation. The new concept took account of the pain and the costs (mostly of blacks) of amalgamation, even though the end product was the admirable and fascinating Cuban culture. In the case of assimilationists in the United States, a word like "acculturation" missed the novelty altogether by reducing New World clashes of culture into—as Ortiz wrote—a one-way "process of transition from one culture to another, and its manifold social repercussions."

Ortiz was a cultural anthropologist not an ideologue. Unlike institution-builder Vasconcelos, Ortiz was describing an already existing cosmic culture. Cubans were not all equally flattered by the black-and-white boldness of the picture, to be sure. An indigenous culture that owed as much to Africa as to Europe could not have appealed to the white elitism that official Cuba had cultivated since the conquest. To the extent that *Cuban Counterpoint* affirms a more complicated culture, the book is political. It requires acknowledgment of the difference within, the admission for example, that the religion of the ORISHAS plays in counterpoint to the cult of Catholic saints. That is, one cult comes to depend on the other for its sacred and social power. To the extent that this counterpoint and mutuality are now publicly recognized, transculturation has apparently provided state governments with "resolutions" to racial and cultural conflicts, so that any politics of change seems superfluous and distracting. The only sensible response is to celebrate a complex (rather than a simply coherent) New World self. Understandably, transculturation (along with mestizaje and the cosmic race) came under criticism during the 1990s as an ideology of social affirmation that amounts to control. If difference is already part of the self, neutralized and melted down to merge with its agonist, how—critics ask—can transculturation promote political vitality? How can it focus on the unequal histories of participants?

Nevertheless, for the purpose of appreciating cultural performances that might otherwise remain incomprehensible, Ortiz's neologism offers a decided advantage: it admits conflict, pain, loss as constitutive of American cultures. To stretch his point, transculturation can even admit the enduring melancholia of banished cultural forms that haunt new national constitutions. For example, the poem *Sóngoro Cosongo* (1931), by the Cuban NICOLÁS GUILLÉN, can recreate an African ritual to the point of including some non-Spanish words, but the mostly Spanish poem is a record of having displaced the original language of the ritual. In other words, a contemporary reading of transculturation that insists on respecting difference should hesitate at the point before differences would merge and make, for example, a seamless poem; it lingers on the tension between ill-fitting partners. Displaced people will defend their freedom of speech and continue to live in normally double (or multiple) codes, sometimes for generations.

This slightly willful reading of transculturation follows from Ortiz's historically inflected improvement on effortlessly friendly words. But it also departs from Ortiz, along the very fault line that he described between cultural partners trapped in a forced marriage, an apt image for transculturation as creativity demanded by unbearable antagonism. But before the coerced marriage, and perhaps surviving it, there is an implied scorn for the requirement to relinquish one's identity, to "bleach one's soul," in the words of W. E. B. DU BOIS, for the sake of amalgamation. That scorn is an expression of pride in one's difference, and the energy that keeps one's cultural particularity in productive tension with others. Thanks to this tension, to the fact that the pieces of history and culture fit badly and that the bad fits produce internal differences in "national cultures," there are troubled or unsettled spaces that demand the continued creativity of transculturation. This should be our contemporary response to the eagerness of modernization that insists on privileging assimilation over difference: to appreciate the emphasis on movement that doesn't necessarily lead to rational improvements, and also to value cultural variety (that demands tolerance and flexibility) over modernity's taste for normalization. Does the Ortiz who would modernize through merging convince contemporary readers? Perhaps, one would want to hope, we no longer believe in an incrementally truer and more coherent national consciousness, along with the eugenic arguments for mestizaje as an improvement over dark races by melding them with whites in a single cosmic race.

See also Blackness in Latin America and the Caribbean: An Interpretation; Colonial Latin America and the Caribbean; Creolization: An Interpretation; Latin America and the Caribbean, Blacks in; Myth of Racial Democracy in Latin America and the Caribbean; Race: An Interpretation; Whitening.

Doris Sommer

Transition

Literary and political magazine.

Founded in 1961 by Rajat Neogy, a Ugandan of Indian descent, *Transition* was inspired by the famed European modernist literary magazine of the same name, as well as by BLACK ORPHEUS, the Nigerian literary magazine. But Neogy was interested in more than literature: *Transition,* an early editorial declared, would champion and nurture "the perpetual change which is the nature of live bodies" with a lively mix of voices and opinions on such questions as freedom of the press, democracy in one-party states, AFRICAN SOCIALISM, and neocolonialism.

Operating on a shoestring budget, the early *Transition* published up-and-coming East African writers and artists, including NGUGI WA THIONG'O (then James Ngugi), ALI A. MAZRUI, and John Nagenda, as well as American expatriates like Paul Theroux and JAMES BALDWIN. Neogy also published Africans from across the continent, in the interest of stimulating the East African literary scene. In 1963 *Transition* cosponsored an African writers conference in KAMPALA, UGANDA, attended by CHINUA ACHEBE, WOLE SOYINKA, CHRISTOPHER OKIGBO, JOHN PEPPER CLARK, and Gabriel Okara from NIGERIA; KOFI AWOONOR from GHANA; and Bloke Modisane, Arthur Maimane, and ES'KIA MPHAHLELE from SOUTH AFRICA, among others.

Transition never shied from controversy. It published essays criticizing African writers for using European languages, as well as passionate rebuttals. It became well known as a home for serious critiques of the philosophy of NÉGRITUDE and attacks on the personality cults surrounding such African independence leaders as KWAME NKRUMAH and JULIUS NYERERE, as well as harsh portrayals of racism among European expatriates and of anti-Asian bigotry among black Africans. The magazine had earned a reputation for energy, irreverence, unpredictability, and intellectual toughness.

At the height of its cultural and commercial success, however, *Transition* suffered two serious setbacks. First, the 1967 revelation that the American Central Intelligence Agency (CIA) had secretly funded the magazine (through the Congress for Cultural Freedom, an international organization that had supported intellectual magazines throughout the world, including *Encounter* in the United Kingdom and *Black Orpheus* in Nigeria) eroded some of the magazine's credibility, although Neogy had been unaware of the CIA's involvement. Second, the 1968 imprisonment of Rajat Neogy by the government of Ugandan President MILTON OBOTE nearly shut the journal down for good.

Neogy's detention—in part, for publishing an essay critical of UGANDA's new constitution for instituting "preventive detention"—was protested in Kampala and around the world; Amnesty International declared him a "prisoner of conscience." Held in solitary confinement for six months, Neogy was eventually acquitted of sedition charges; the following year he revived *Transition* in ACCRA, GHANA. But ideological tensions and personal difficulties frustrated Neogy, and in 1974 he resigned in favor of Wole Soyinka, the Nigerian writer, who had himself only recently been jailed by the Nigerian government for his efforts to end the Biafran War.

Soyinka's *Transition* was less interested in "establishment democracy" than the "African revolution" and the black diaspora; it covered the sixth Pan-African Congress, the successful armed struggle in GUINEA-BISSAU, the Black Power Movement in the United States, and the cultural production of Afro-Brazilians. It remained controversial, publishing withering attacks on HAILE SELASSI of ETHIOPIA and especially IDI AMIN of Uganda; the cover of one issue featured a cartoon of Amin's face with a caption in Swahili and English that read, "FINISH HIM."

Desperate for funding, *Transition* folded in 1976. Fifteen years later, it was reborn as "an international journal with Africa at its center," edited by the writers and professors HENRY LOUIS GATES, JR., and KWAME ANTHONY APPIAH. Now based in Cambridge, Massachusetts, the new *Transition* has won several major awards, publishing an eclectic mix of writers, artists, and political figures, including NADINE GORDIMER, KRS-ONE, ANGELA DAVIS, JERRY RAWLINGS, JAMAICA KINCAID, SPIKE LEE, and Caetano Veloso.

Kate Tuttle

Transkei

Former *bantustan,* or black homeland, in South Africa, one of ten territories assigned to the black majority population in the 1950s as part of the South African government's policy of apartheid, or racial segregation.

Transkei consisted of three fragments of land that covered a total of 41,001 square kilometers (15,831 square miles). The largest fragment was located on the Indian Ocean coast between the Kei and Mzimvubu rivers and the two smaller fragments were located inland, one bordering LESOTHO. Umtata was Transkei's capital. Other towns included in the territory were Butterworth, Engcobo, Idutywa, Lusikisiki, Port St. Johns, Qumbu, and Tsolo. In 1994, when SOUTH AFRICA was divided into nine new provinces, Transkei was incorporated into the province of EASTERN CAPE.

The Transkei was part of a larger area inhabited primarily by Xhosa-speaking groups (such as the Gcaleka, Mpondo, Tembu, Mpondomise, and Bomvana) who settled in the area in at least the sixteenth century. In the nineteenth century British colonizers conquered Xhosa land, and British officials used the name *Transkei* to refer to lands "across the Kei river," which were still occupied by African groups. Shortly after the Union of South Africa (later the Republic of South Africa) was formed in 1910, the white leaders of South Africa began to implement national policies of racial segregation. These policies culminated in the 1950s when the government divided the black majority according to ethnic identity and defined them as citizens of separate ethnic homelands, or bantustans. Along with the bantustan of Ciskei to the south, Transkei was designated as one of the so-called homelands for Xhosa-speaking people. The majority of people living in Transkei were Xhosa, but Basotho made up a significant minority.

Transkei was the first bantustan to begin to press for self-government in 1961. The South African government had already indicated that independence, in some form, was the goal for the bantustans, but the details of such self-rule were yet to be established. The government finally granted Transkei self-governing status in 1963, under the Transkei Constitution Act. The new administrative body of Transkei included the Transkei Legislative Assembly and an executive cabinet. The assembly was partially elected, but the majority of the seats were reserved for chiefs, most of whom had cooperated with the white South African government during the earlier administration of the bantustan. The Bantu Homelands Constitution Act of 1971 subsequently gave the South African president the power to establish constitutions and legislative assemblies for any of the bantustans. Once a bantustan was considered to be self-governing, its legislators could collect taxes and pass laws relating to certain areas, such as schools, hospitals, and transportation, but all of these laws still required the approval of the South African president. The South African government also retained final control over the bantustan's finances.

Transkei received so-called independence in 1976. In theory, independent bantustans were given complete control over their internal affairs and foreign relations. Some did repeal racially discriminatory laws, but the independence of these bantustans was limited by the fact that the South African government still supplied most of the funding for their budgets and contributed many key civil servants and army officers to the bantustan administrations. Besides South Africa, no other country recognized Transkei's independence, because recognition would have implied acceptance of South Africa's policy of APARTHEID.

More than three million people were defined as citizens of Transkei, but about half of those lived outside its borders. The lack of economic opportunities within the bantustans forced many blacks to live outside the bantustans as migrant laborers or to commute from border towns within the bantustans to work in white-run industries in other parts of South Africa. Few black people supported the bantustan system because it meant they were considered primarily citizens of the bantustans in-

stead of citizens of South Africa, even if they had never lived within the bantustans. When a bantustan chose to become independent, its citizens lost their South African citizenship completely. In spite of popular opposition, some black politicians accepted the bantustan system, and the South African government gradually transferred political power to those individuals.

Transkei held periodic elections from the time it attained supposed self-government, but until the late 1980s effective power rested with two brothers, Kaiser Matanzima and George Matanzima, and their Transkei National Independence Party. Kaiser Matanzima became prime minister in 1976, and George Matanzima became minister of justice. In 1979 Kaiser Matanzima became president and made his brother prime minister. Kaiser Matanzima retired from the presidency in 1986, and in September 1987 George Matanzima resigned as prime minister after an investigation revealed that he was involved in government corruption. Stella Sigcau then became prime minister, but she was overthrown in December 1987 by Transkei soldiers led by Bantu Holomisa, a general of the Transkei Defense Force. Tutor Ndamase was made prime minister, and Holomisa remained in power as commander of the Transkei Defense Force. At the time of South Africa's first multiracial elections in April 1994, Transkei was reintegrated into a unified South Africa.

Transvaal

Former province in northeastern South Africa.

Europeans named the region Transvaal, meaning "across the Vaal River," because the region was located north of the river. In April 1994, at the time of South Africa's first free elections, Transvaal was divided into four provinces: Northern Province, Mpumalanga, North-West Province, and Gauteng.

Remains of *Australopithecus africanus,* an ancestor of *Homo sapiens* (humans), have been discovered in the territory north of the Vaal River. These remains are 2.5 million to three million years old. Bantu-speaking people first arrived in the region around 500 C.E., and evidence of Sotho-Tswana peoples, a branch of Bantu-speakers, in the Transvaal area dates to around the thirteenth century.

In the eighteenth century a group of Sotho formed the Pedi kingdom. At the beginning of the nineteenth century southern African peoples experienced a period of forced migrations called the Mfecane, caused largely by the expanding Zulu empire in the Natal region. A group of Ndebele people broke off from the Zulu empire under the leadership of Mzilikazi and invaded the Transvaal, attacking the Tswana, the Pedi, and other Ndebele groups already occupying the region. Many Tswana fled west toward the Kalahari Desert. Beginning in 1835, Afrikaners, or Boers (people of Dutch and French Huguenot descent), left the Cape Colony on the Great Trek to escape British rule, and many of them traveled north to the Transvaal. The arrival of these Afrikaners, along with the continued pressure of the Zulu empire, pushed Mzilikazi's Ndebele across the Limpopo River, leaving large expanses of land open for the Afrikaners.

For a time the British extended their rule to the Transvaal, but in 1852 they permitted the Afrikaners in the territory to manage their own affairs. In the late 1850s the Afrikaners established the Transvaal as the South African Republic. The neighboring Orange Free State was granted independence as an Afrikaner republic in 1854. By the mid-nineteenth century the Pedi kingdom in the eastern Transvaal had gained strength and engaged in several confrontations with Afrikaners who were interested in Pedi land. The South African Republic became politically unstable, and the British annexed it in 1877. Two years later, British regiments conquered the Pedi (now also known as Northern Sotho), who subsequently lost most of their land and were forced to work for the Afrikaners. The Afrikaners—led by Paul Kruger, their commandant general—fought the British at Majuba in 1881. They defeated the British, and the South African Republic was then recognized as autonomous, although under British authority. In 1883 Kruger was elected president.

The beginning of gold mining in the Witwatersrand area in 1886 brought a sudden influx of immigrants, mostly British, who soon outnumbered the Afikaners. To maintain their supremacy, the Afrikaners did not permit the foreigners (*Uitlanders* in Afrikaans) to share in the government of the South African Republic. Eventually, the immigrants plotted a rebellion, backed by CECIL RHODES, prime minister of the Cape Colony. In 1895 the rebels were joined by an armed force from the Cape Colony, led by Sir Leander Starr Jameson, but their uprising failed. The Uitlanders continued to agitate for political freedom and petitioned Queen Victoria for aid in 1899. The British government intervened on their behalf, but the negotiations that followed resulted in the Afrikaners rejecting British control altogether. The South African Republic and the Orange Free State mobilized their troops, beginning the Boer War, which the British won. The Transvaal and the Orange Free State became British crown colonies in 1902 and remained so until 1907, when both states were granted self-government. In 1910 the Transvaal joined the Cape Colony, the Orange Free State, and Natal to form the Union of South Africa (the Republic of South Africa since 1961).

From 1948 until 1994 South Africa was racially segregated under a system known as APARTHEID (Afrikaans for "separateness"). In the 1950s the white South African government divided all black South Africans according to ethnicity and assigned them to certain territories called bantustans, or black homelands. Most of these bantustans comprised many fragmented pieces of land. The bantustans of Gazankulu, KaNgwane, KwaNdebele, Lebowa, and Venda, as well as parts of the bantustan of BOPHUTHATSWANA, were established in Transvaal. (The other parts of Bophuthatswana were within the boundaries of Cape Province and the Orange Free State.) In 1994 all of the bantustans were dissolved and incorporated into the new provinces.

Today four diverse provinces comprise the Transvaal region. The Northern Province is primarily agricultural and has more than five million residents. The province encompasses the northern portion of Kruger National Park. The North-West Province, with more than 3.5 million residents, is one of South Africa's poorest provinces. It has among the lowest life expectancy and adult literacy rates and the highest unemployment rates in the country. The province of Mpumalanga has more than three million residents and includes the southern portion of Kruger National Park. After tourism, its primary industries include manufacturing and electricity. Gauteng, with nine million residents crowded into 1.4 percent of the nation's land area, is South Africa's most densely populated province. It is highly urbanized, derives much of its income from mining, and has the highest per-capita income in the country.

See also Bantu: Dispersion and Settlement.

Bibliography

Delius, Peter. *A Lion Amongst the Cattle: Reconstruction and Resistance in the Northern Transvaal.* Heinemann, 1996.

Alonford James Robinson

Traoré, Moussa

1936–

President of Mali from 1969 to 1991.

The son of peasant farmers, Moussa Traoré was born in the Kayes region of the French Sudan (present-day MALI). He joined the French army in his early twenties and attended Fréjus Military College in FRANCE. When MALI became independent in 1960, Traoré returned to the country and joined the Malian army. In 1967 Mali's first president, MODIBO KEITA, established a militant youth organization, the Popular Militia, which began to threaten the power of the military.

Traoré led a military coup that ousted Keita in 1968 and established the Comité Militaire pour la Libération Nationale (CMLN). Traoré assumed the presidency in early 1969 and promised to return the country to civilian rule as soon as his transitional government had improved the Malian economy. Although Traoré fulfilled this promise in 1979, he maintained political control by establishing a one-party state under his Union Démocratique du Peuple Malien, which assured him successive wins at the ballot box—and millions of dollars in his secret bank accounts.

As president, Traoré did not immediately reverse the popular Keita's socialist policies for fear of alienating Keita's supporters. Instead, Traoré supplemented existing programs with renewed financial aid from France and other Western donors. Throughout the 1970s Traoré devoted most of his effort toward consolidating his political power. In the early 1970s and again in the mid-1980s, however, Mali suffered from debilitating droughts that increased economic hardship throughout the country.

In order to acquire new aid during the 1980s, Traoré was forced to comply with the economic programs of the International Monetary Fund (IMF) and World Bank. Under structural adjustment policies, Traoré cut government spending, liberalized the economy, and privatized state businesses throughout the 1980s. The reforms caused rampant unemployment, and prompted massive protests by students, workers, and civil servants. At first, Traoré attempted to deflect public unrest by making minor economic concessions and dismissing officials accused of corruption. However, public discontent continued to mount, and by 1990 a pro-democracy movement had mobilized. When Traoré sent troops to quell pro-democracy demonstrations in BAMAKO in 1991, his troops killed at least 106 people and injured hundreds more.

Lieutenant Colonel Amadou Toumani Touré led a military coup to remove Traoré and arrested him for corruption and murder. A court sentenced Traoré to death in 1993, but President ALPHA OUMAR KONARÉ later commuted his sentence to life in prison. In 1999 Traoré was sentenced to death, along with his wife Mariam, for economic crimes. Once again, however, the sentences were later commuted to life imprisonment. In May 2002 President Konaré, one month before leaving office, pardoned Traoré and his wife for humanitarian reasons.

See also African Socialism; Drought and Desertification; Political Movements in Africa; Structural Adjustment in Africa.

Bibliography

Imperato, Pascal James. *Historical Dictionary of Mali.* Scarecrow Press, 1996.

Elizabeth Heath

Trévigne, Paul

1825–1908

African American editor and historian.

A mulatto born in NEW ORLEANS, LOUISIANA, Paul Trévigne was the son of a veteran of the Battle of New Orleans in 1815. For about forty years he taught in his native city at the Catholic Indigent Orphan School. Later he served as editor of the militant Republican journal *L'Union* (1862–1864) and then of its successor *La Tribune de la Nouvelle-Orléans* (1864–1868 and 1869), owned and published by New Orleans physician and editor LOUIS CHARLES ROUDANEZ. These papers aroused the animosity of white Southerners so much that there were threats to kill Trévigne and burn *La Tribune.* The editor then chose to use a more easygoing style, laughing as he chastised and using satire to make his points. This style probably spared him reprisals and rebuttals, particularly at a time when white people were little accustomed to accepting the opinions of a man of color. Trévigne's newspapers, published in French and English, reflected prose and poetry written in the florid style of correspondents well versed in the works of French writers and philosophers Blaise Pascal, François Marie Arouet Voltaire, Jean Jacques Rousseau, Charles Montesquieu, Abbé Grégoire, and the Greek philosopher Plato. Since the articles were not signed, it is virtually impossible to determine those written by Trévigne. Even the fact that Roudanez was the senior editor does not provide a satisfactory answer.

The closing of *La Tribune* severely hampered the efforts of the CRÉOLES to continue the enrichment of their already highly advanced ethnic society in New Orleans. *L'Union,* from its inception in 1862, revealed perhaps the first true attempt of Louisiana blacks to mold their energies into a political force. Blacks, chiefly brokers, realtors, and planters, claimed ownership of some fifteen million dollars of taxable property in New Orleans and exercised a decided influence there. They reiterated the fact that they were educated, refined, and cultured, and they pleaded for an end to hypocritical democracy and asked for rank as human beings with full civil and economic equality.

Trévigne's "Centennial History of the Louisiana Negro," serialized in 1875 and 1876 in the *Louisianian,* a newspaper of former governor P. B. S. PINCHBACK, is still a valuable source. In this tribute, which was part of the commemoration of the 100th anniversary of American Independence, Trévigne dealt with the literary, artistic, and scientific contributions of blacks in Louisiana. Apparently RODOLPHE L. DESDUNES, then a young man, received inspiration and some material for his *Nos Hommes et Notre Histoire* (1911) from the pioneering venture of Trévigne.

Trévigne died at the age of eighty-three in his native city. He had been a valuable observer of his era, manifesting courage and daring even at risk to his life. He helped bring about a closer bond and a degree of appreciation between his constituents and their white neighbors. He prepared the way for such writers as Desdunes, ALICE DUNBAR-NELSON, and later, Charles B. Rousséve and Marcus Christian.

The career and evaluation of Trévigne are based on Desdunes's *Nos Hommes et Notre Histoire* (1911), translated and edited as *Our People and Our History* (1973) by Dorothea Olga McCants. See Charles B. Rousséve's work *The Negro in Louisiana; Aspects of His History and His Literature* (1937); Finnian Patrick Leaven's "*L'Union* and the *New Orleans Tribune* and Louisiana Reconstruction" (master's thesis, Louisiana State University, 1966); and Charles Vincent's "Negro Leadership in Louisiana" (master's thesis, Louisiana State University, 1968).

From *Dictionary of American Negro Biography* by Rayford W. Logan and Michael R. Winston, eds. Copyright © 1982 by Rayford W. Logan and Michael R. Winston. Reprinted by permission of W. W. Norton & Company, Inc.

See also Historians, African American; Press, Black, in the United States.

Dorothea Olga McCants

Tribe

See also Ethnicity and Identity in Africa: An Interpretation.

Tribe Called Quest, A

African American rap group whose innovative sound helped stretch the sonic parameters of hip-hop.

The members of A Tribe Called Quest—DJ Ali Shaheed Muhammad, and MCs Phife (or Malik Taylor) and Q-Tip (or Jonathan Davis)—were friends from high school in NEW YORK CITY. The group came together in 1988 and released their debut album, *People's Instinctive Travels and the Paths of Rhythm*, in 1990. It was a wild critical success, a playfully Afrocentric album full of wit ("I Left My Wallet in El Segundo") and verve ("Bonita Applebum"), and it garnered a rare five-microphone review from the HIP-HOP magazine of record, *The Source*. *People's Instinctive Travels and the Paths of Rhythm* also helped define the "Native Tongues" posse, an informal group of like-minded RAP bands that also included DE LA SOUL, Jungle Brothers, and Black Sheep.

On their second album, *The Low End Theory* (1991), A Tribe Called Quest further pared down their already sparse sound. Tribe set their casual rhymes against deceptively simple JAZZ samples on tracks ranging from the thumping, kinetic "Scenario," with future rap star Busta Rhymes, to the more contemplative "Verses from the Abstract," featuring an original groove by renowned jazz bassist Ron Carter. Perhaps more importantly, *The Low End Theory* marked the creative peak of the jazz-rap movement that also included Guru's *Jazzmatazz* (1993) and Digable Planets' *Reachin' (A New Refutation of Time and Space)* (1993).

Midnight Marauders (1993) confirmed A Tribe Called Quest's reputation as consistently original performers, although after *Beats, Rhymes, and Life* (1996) some critics complained that the band was running low on inspiration. Q-Tip, the highest-profile member of the group, has made memorable guest appearances on Deee-Lite's "Groove is in the Heart," the Beastie Boys' "Get it Together," and Janet Jackson's "Got 'Til It's Gone." The group recorded *The Love Movement* in 1998, but then broke-up after touring to support the album. Five years later A Tribe Called Quest released *Hits, Rarities & Remixes* (2003).

See also Afrocentricity; Jackson, Michael, and the Jackson Family; Music, African American.

Andrew Du Bois

Trindade, Solano

1908–1974

Afro-Brazilian poet, filmmaker, stage director, and folklorist known especially for his contribution to and preservation of black popular arts in Brazil.

Solano Trindade was born in 1908 in Recife, a town in northeastern BRAZIL, the son of a mulatto cobbler and a mestizo (of indigenous and European descent) woman. His interest in folklore and popular arts was instilled at an early age, as he would routinely accompany his father to local folk dances and read aloud to his illiterate mother.

After some advanced schooling, Trindade became a Presbyterian deacon and began to write poetry. His early works were mystical writings, and his black poetry would evolve soon thereafter. In 1936 Trindade published his first book, *Poemas Negros,* and founded the Frente Negra Pernambucana (Black Front of Pernambuco) and the Centro Cultural Afro-Brasileiro (Afro-Brazilian Cultural Center). These groups united a group of contemporary black writers with a view to collecting and disseminating the work of fellow Afro-Brazilian poets and painters. In 1959 Trindade founded the Teatro Popular Brasileiro (Brazilian Popular Theater), which he would later take to EUROPE with its eclectic cast of business people, laborers, and students.

In his poetry Trindade cultivated Afro-Brazilian rhythms with extraordinary musicality, exalting the uniqueness of black culture while promoting social awareness of the black experience. A proponent of Marxist ideology, Trindade identified in his work with all oppressed peoples, be they black or white, and condemned all forms of social injustice.

In his time Trindade mingled with both black militants and the literary and artistic elite. He published four books of poetry including *Poemas de uma Vida Simples* (*Poems of a Simple Life,* 1944) and *Cantares ao meu Povo* (*Songs to my People,* 1962). In addition to being a poet, painter, and stage director, Trindade was also an accomplished filmmaker and folklorist.

See also Afro-Brazilian Culture; Literature, Black, in Brazil.

Nicola Cooney

Trinidad and Tobago

Country consisting of the two southernmost Windward Caribbean islands, which lie just northeast of Venezuela.

Trinidad and Tobago is often celebrated as the birthplace of CALYPSO, the famous Caribbean musical form that has spread across the world. The words to one popular calypso song praise another of the country's distinctive legacies—its ethnic diversity:

It is fantastic yes it is
The way how we live as one.
The integration of the nation
Is second to none.
Where the negro, the whiteman, the Chinee, the Indian
We all live together in this land.
In this wonderful land of calypso
In this wonderful land of steelpan.

While these lyrics may idealize the country's racial harmony, the fact remains that Trinidad and Tobago is one of the most diverse Caribbean nations. Some of this diversity can be traced to the country's colonial origins. Tobago changed hands twenty-

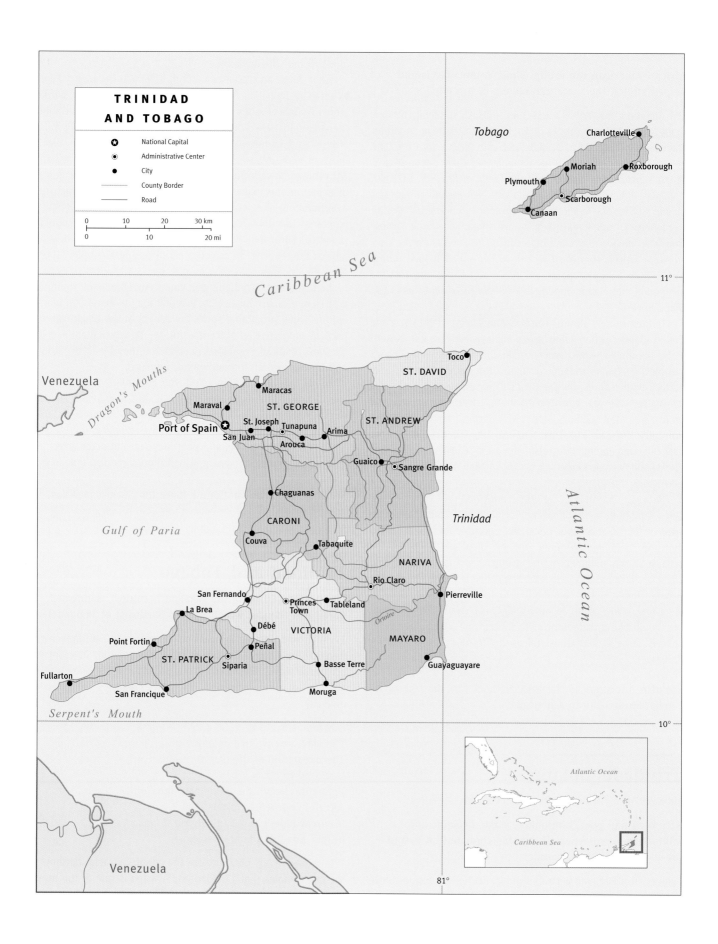

TRINIDAD AND TOBAGO

National Capital
Administrative Center
City
County Border
Road

0   10   20   30 km
0   10   20 mi

Tobago

Charlotteville
Moriah
Roxborough
Plymouth
Scarborough
Canaan

Caribbean Sea

11°

Toco
ST. DAVID

Venezuela

Dragon's Mouths

Maracas
Maraval
ST. GEORGE
St. Joseph   Tunapuna
Port of Spain
San Juan   Arouca   Arima
ST. ANDREW

Guaico   Sangre Grande

Chaguanas

CARONI

Trinidad

Gulf of Paria

Couva
Tabaquite

NARIVA

Rio Claro

San Fernando   Princes   Tableland
                            Town   Pierreville
La Brea
Débé
Point Fortin   VICTORIA   MAYARO
Peñal
Fullarton   ST. PATRICK   Siparia   Basse Terre   Guayaguayare
San Francique   Moruga

Ortoire

Atlantic Ocean

Serpent's Mouth

10°

Atlantic Ocean

Caribbean Sea

Venezuela

81°

two times between 1626 and 1814. Trinidad place names in English, Spanish, French, Hindi, and native Carib Indian reflect the shifts in the island's population. Today over 80 percent of Trinidadians and Tobagians are the descendants of either African slaves or East Indian indentured servants; this large segment of the population comprises nearly equal numbers of blacks and East Indians. While the two groups share a common history of colonial oppression, the country's greatest challenge for the next century is uniting them in a common vision for a shared future.

Early History

Trinidad and Tobago are the southernmost islands in the LESSER ANTILLES chain and are only 10 miles off the northern coast of South America. Trinidad lies within sight of the Venezuelan coast; because the island was originally part of the South American subcontinent, its flora, fauna, and natural resources resemble those of South America much more than they do those of other Caribbean islands. As a result of the country's affinity to South America, settlement patterns, agriculture, and industry all developed differently in Trinidad and Tobago than they did in many other Caribbean countries. Like those of most other Caribbean islands, however, Trinidad and Tobago's earliest populations were South American indigenous groups gradually migrating north from the South American continent.

Trinidad and Tobago's first inhabitants were Ienian Arawaks. Like the Tainan Arawaks who flourished on other Caribbean islands, the Ienian Arawaks were primarily fishers and farmers. They named Trinidad Lere, or "land of the hummingbirds." The next arrivals on Trinidad and Tobago were the Carib, who quickly outnumbered the Arawaks on Tobago. On Trinidad the Arawaks and the Caribs were able to coexist for a longer period of time. These groups occupied the islands when Christopher Columbus first sighted the islands on his third voyage to the New World in 1498.

European Settlement and Colonization

In his journal Columbus renamed Lere La Trinidad, or "the Holy Trinity," for the three mountain summits that surrounded the southern bay where he landed. While Columbus almost certainly passed by Tobago on the same trip, he did not mention the smaller island in his log. Its name came from the indigenous word *tabaco*, referring to one of its earliest crops. Although Columbus claimed Trinidad for Spain in 1498, over the next 300 years Spanish colonists generally only returned to the island long enough to capture many of the indigenous Arawaks and Caribs and sell them into slavery in other Spanish Caribbean colonies. As European powers throughout the region focused on islands with richer mineral resources, Trinidad was largely ignored.

In 1702 a small number of black slaves who had been taken from their homes in West Africa were imported to Trinidad to work on cacao plantations. This trend would become more important by the end of the century, but for most of the 1700s the numbers of blacks and whites on Trinidad remained relatively small. Tobago, on the other hand, was identified early in the sixteenth century as a valuable strategic harbor and a source of unusually fertile soil. As a result, it was hotly contested by the British, Spanish, French, and Dutch. As each group established or reestablished itself on the island, it brought new white colonists who soon brought African slaves. By 1791, 94 percent of Tobago's 15,102 residents were African slaves, most of whom worked on the many SUGAR plantations that had sprung up on the island.

In an attempt to replicate Tobago's agricultural success, in 1776 the Spanish government relaxed immigration restrictions and allowed any Roman Catholic, regardless of nationality, to establish a plantation on Trinidad. As French Catholic planters began creating new sugar, coffee, and cotton plantations on the island, there was a new demand for African slaves to perform the plantations' labor. While there were only 310 Trinidadian slaves in 1783, by 1797 there were nearly 10,000. That same year there were also 4,476 free nonwhites in Trinidad, mostly the mixed-race offspring of white planters and slaves or immigrants from other Caribbean islands. Trinidad had the largest free Afro-Creole population in the Caribbean. Many of these free blacks were landowners, and some were even slaveholders. Under Spanish government and French influence, free blacks enjoyed a legal status almost equivalent to that of whites.

However, the year 1797 brought political change to the island. British colonial forces had begun to covet Trinidad's growing wealth. After attacking the harbor at Port of Spain in February 1797, the British were granted control of the island. After several more attacks they also won control of Tobago in 1814. The free black population on Tobago was not significant, and so the British did not interfere with its legal status. On Trinidad, however, the British government quickly began stripping away the rights held by free blacks. In the 1820s a coalition of Trinidadian free blacks, led by wealthy doctors and lawyers who had been educated in Europe, began organizing to protest the changes. By that time free blacks made up nearly one-third of Trinidad's population. In 1823 Dr. John Baptiste Philip led a delegation to England to air the community's grievances. The delegation was successful in reinstating civil and political rights for free black Trinidadians, but it did not even attempt to address the injustices faced by the island's enslaved black majority.

The abolition of the British slave trade in 1807, and growing British support for the abolition of slavery in all British possessions, soon brought some positive change for all slaves in Trinidad and Tobago and other British islands. On August 1, 1834, slavery was legally abolished throughout the British WEST INDIES. Official abolition was to be followed by a six-year period of legal APPRENTICESHIP, in which all slaves were to remain on their owners' estates and continue to work there in return for small salaries. But when apprenticeship proved too difficult to administer, it was ended two years before the designated period had elapsed. By 1838 Trinidad and Tobago, like the rest of the British Caribbean, suddenly had substantial newly freed black majorities.

Trinidad and Tobago (At a Glance)

OFFICIAL NAME: Republic of Trinidad and Tobago

AREA: 5,128 sq km (1,980 sq mi)

LOCATION: Islands between the Caribbean Sea and the North Atlantic Ocean, northeast of Venezuela

CAPITAL: Port-of-Spain (population 54,000; 2004 estimate)

POPULATION: 1,303,000 (2003 estimate)

POPULATION DENSITY: 253 persons per sq km (658 per sq mi)

POPULATION BELOW AGE 15: 22.2 percent (male 125,470; female 119,270; 2003 estimate)

POPULATION GROWTH RATE: −0.68 percent (2003 estimate)

TOTAL FERTILITY RATE: 1.78 children born per woman (2003 estimate)

LIFE EXPECTANCY AT BIRTH: Total population: 69.59 years (male 67.07 years; female 72.23 years; 2003 estimate)

INFANT MORTALITY RATE: 24.97 deaths per 1,000 live births (2003 estimate)

LITERACY RATE (AGE 15 AND OVER WHO CAN READ AND WRITE): Total population: 98.6 percent (male 99.1 percent; female 98 percent; 2003 estimate)

EDUCATION: Primary and secondary education is free and compulsory for ages six to twelve. The University of the West Indies is located at St. Augustine.

LANGUAGES: English is the official language of Trinidad and Tobago. Hindi, French, Spanish, and Chinese are also spoken.

ETHNIC GROUPS: 39.5 percent black, 40.3 percent East Indian (mostly immigrants from northern India), 18.4 percent mixed race, 0.6 percent white, and 1.2 percent Chinese and other ethnicities

RELIGIONS: 29.4 percent of Trinidad and Tobago's inhabitants are Roman Catholic, 23.8 percent are Hindu, 10.9 percent are Anglican, 5.8 percent are Muslim, 3.4 percent are Presbyterian, and 26.7 percent are other religions

CLIMATE: Tropical and humid. Average temperatures range from 77° F (25° C) to 85° F (29° C). The dry season is January to May. Although Trinidad and Tobago are not in the hurricane zone, hurricanes do occasionally strike the island.

LAND, PLANTS, AND ANIMALS: Trinidad and Tobago are islands north of Venezuela; Trinidad's Northern Range of mountains continues the Venezuelan Andes coastal ranges. There are several spectacular waterfalls, among them the Blue Basin and the Maracas Falls, each 298 feet high. The mountains of the Central Range, and the Southern Range, mostly low hills, help to vary the primarily flat landscape of Trinidad. The topography of Tobago, with its mountainous Main Ridge, continues the Northern Range of Trinidad. There are a number of coral reefs that are popular with scuba divers and snorkelers. The highest elevations of the islands have lush tropical rainforest vegetation, among which is the mountain immortelle, a tree with orange flowers that grows eighty feet high. A bird sanctuary known as the Caroni Swamp is home to white flamingos and scarlet ibis (the national bird). Other wildlife includes the agouti (a rabbit-like rodent), wild hogs, porcupines, and iguana.

NATURAL RESOURCES: Petroleum, natural gas, and asphalt

CURRENCY: Trinidad and Tobago dollar (TTD)

GROSS DOMESTIC PRODUCT (GDP): $11.07 billion (2002 estimate)

GDP PER CAPITA: $10,000 (2002 estimate)

GDP REAL GROWTH RATE: 3.2 percent (2002 estimate)

PRIMARY ECONOMIC ACTIVITIES: Services, manufacturing, mining and quarrying, construction and utilities, and agriculture

PRIMARY CROPS: Cocoa, sugarcane, rice, citrus, coffee, vegetables, and poultry

INDUSTRIES: Petroleum, chemicals, tourism, food processing, cement, beverages, and cotton textiles

PRIMARY EXPORTS: Petroleum and petroleum products, chemicals, steel products, fertilizer, sugar, cocoa, coffee, citrus, and flowers

PRIMARY IMPORTS: Machinery, transportation equipment, manufactured goods, food, and live animals

PRIMARY TRADE PARTNERS: United States, United Kingdom, Jamaica, France, Côte d'Ivoire, Japan, and Brazil

GOVERNMENT: The government of Trinidad and Tobago is a parliamentary democracy. The chief of state is President George Maxwell Richards (since March 2003; elected for a five-year term by an electoral college comprised of the members of the Senate and House of Representatives). The head of government is Prime Minister Patrick Manning (since December 2001; the leader of the majority party in the House of Representatives is appointed prime minister by the president). The legislative branch is the bicameral Parliament, consisting of the thirty-one-member Senate (appointed by the president to maximum five-year terms) and the thirty-six-member House of Representatives (elected by popular vote to five-year terms). The judicial branch includes the Supreme Court of Judicature, the High Court of Justice, and the Court of Appeals (the Privy Council in London being the highest court of appeal).

Shelle Sumners

Trinidad and Tobago After Abolition

When the slaves were emancipated, fertile Tobago ranked as one of the Caribbean's most important sugar producers. The sugar plantations continued to require a large labor force, and since they represented the island's dominant industry, many black Tobagians were forced to accept low-paying jobs on the same estates where they had been slaves in order to make a living. But on Trinidad, where there was considerably more land for squatting and cultivation, larger numbers of ex-slaves were able to leave their estates and establish their own small farms. By 1840 only 4,000 ex-slaves still worked on Trinidadian plantations, and this left the plantations with the same tremendous demand for labor that had first led them to imprison African slaves. This time Trinidadian planters turned to indentured workers from India as a new solution.

In 1846 the first shipment of 226 Indians arrived, most of them Hindu workers from Calcutta (now Kolkata). Two years later the number of Trinidadian East Indians (as distinguished from West Indians) had risen to 5,000. Over the next 20 years nearly 45,000 more were brought to the island to work on the sugar plantations for a minimum of five years each. Portuguese and Chinese laborers were also imported, but in smaller numbers. Employers often made it difficult for the indentured workers to leave when the five-year period had ended, and of the first 45,000 East Indian immigrants only 4,000 returned to India. The numbers of new East Indian immigrants and their descendants continued to grow over the next several decades. As they did, East Indian and black Trinidadians found themselves fighting against one another to wrest political and financial gains from the white minority that continued to control the island's power and wealth.

The competition between blacks and East Indians was made even worse toward the end of the nineteenth century by the decline of the sugar industry, which instigated a recession in the working-class economy of Trinidad and Tobago. In 1888 the British government made the official decision to administer the two islands as a single political unit in an effort to secure more financial stability for Tobago. But one of the main complaints of residents of Trinidad and Tobago concerned precisely their British colonial rule. Trinidad and Tobago's local government consisted of an all-white legislative council whose members were appointed by British representatives in the colony. There was no universal suffrage for the black and East Indian majority, and as Trinidad and Tobago approached the twentieth century it was clear that change was needed.

The first push for this change came from Trinidad's Afro-Creoles. As Afro-Creoles began to secure even more education and many professional civil service positions, the class division between them and the black working class grew larger, and middle-class Afro-Creoles sometimes emphasized that division. For example, Afro-Creoles were initially hesitant to celebrate Carnival, the African-derived black cultural festival that has since become one of Trinidad and Tobago's trademarks, because they saw the event as too unrefined. They were also opposed to state-sponsored East Indian immigration and had no desire to form a coalition with East Indians. But at the same time Afro-Creoles were vocal opponents of white supremacy and segregation and strong supporters of equal rights for blacks—these causes did unify them with the black working class.

The emergence of the Pan-African Movement in 1897 further cemented this solidarity along color lines. Suddenly, Trinidadian intellectuals such as H. S. Williams and George Padmore were among the black scholars across the diaspora who were celebrating the culture and accomplishments of sub-Saharan Africa and emphasizing the common experience shared by people of African descent in Africa, South America, and the Caribbean. That year the Trinidadian Workingmen's Association (TWA) became the first organization in the country to attempt to unify the black middle and working classes. The TWA's goal was to push for better working and living conditions and for constitutional reform.

Twentieth-Century Developments

In the midst of this political activity major economic changes came to the country with the rise of the oil industry after 1909. Trinidad is the only Caribbean island to have substantial petroleum reserves, and in a period when the agricultural economies of many other islands were in decline Trinidad beckoned workers from Tobago and across the Caribbean to work in its oil fields. But the arrival of the oil industry only underscored the fact that Trinidad and Tobago's economy continued to be based on the hard labor of the majority of its population.

After several internal disputes the TWA had almost disappeared as a strong force by the outbreak of World War I, but in the postwar period it returned to prominence. The TWA's new leader after the war was Captain Andrew Arthur Cipriani, a Corsican Trinidadian who had served as commander of the West India regiment during World War I. As a white Trinidadian, Cipriani was the first leader able to unify the black and East Indian factions in the working class, since he belonged to neither group. When limited elections for the legislative council were allowed for the first time in 1925, Cipriani became one of the body's first elected members. By 1934 the TWA was renamed the Trinidad Labour Party (TLP), signifying the organization's goal of becoming more involved in the larger political process. But as the Great Depression of the 1930s worsened living conditions in the islands, workers wanted more radical leadership than Cipriani provided.

One of the new leaders to emerge was Tubal Uriah Butler, a black Grenadian who worked in Trinidad's oil fields. Butler led oil workers in several island-wide strikes during the 1930s. In 1937 several of these strikes turned violent, leading to twelve deaths and over fifty injuries, and the British commission that investigated the causes of those strikes eventually recommended more representative government. The 1946 election in Trinidad and Tobago was the first held under universal adult suffrage, but there was no cohesive workers' vote. Instead, in the months leading up to the election labor unions split their support along the old black/East Indian racial divides, and for

Trinidad and Tobago have the most diverse populations of all the Caribbean islands, including people of African, East Indian, British, Spanish, French, and native Carib Indian descent. *Hutchinson Library*

the next ten years Portuguese trade unionist Albert Gomes presided over a fragmented legislative council.

The rise of ERIC WILLIAMS and the People's National Movement (PNM) in 1956 marked a new era in Trinidadian and Tobagian government. Williams, the son of a Trinidadian postal official, had received a Ph.D. in history from Oxford University in 1938. Over the next ten years he rose to prominence as a well-respected scholar and a professor of social and political science at HOWARD UNIVERSITY in Washington, D.C. Williams returned to Trinidad in 1948 as deputy chairman of the Caribbean Research Council of the Caribbean Commission, but he disliked the organization's conservative politics and in 1955 left the commission to found the PNM.

Although the PNM declared itself a multiracial party, its supporters were primarily black. Adherents did include members of both the middle and working classes, however, for while Williams was clearly an educated, articulate member of the middle-class elite, he was also a proponent of Trinidadian and Tobagian nationalism and self-government for the islands' people. The PNM won the national elections in 1956, making Williams chief minister of Trinidad and Tobago. He remained in charge of the country's government until his death in 1981.

Independence and Beyond

Williams's views on self-government were being echoed across the British Caribbean, and British leaders realized that that change was probably inevitable. On August 31, 1962, Trinidad and Tobago achieved independence from GREAT BRITAIN, be-

coming an independent country within the British Commonwealth. Trinidad and Tobago was only the second British Caribbean colony to become an independent state—JAMAICA had become the first just weeks earlier—but the transition in national status was handled with relative ease. Even white citizens felt a grudging respect for Williams, and this helped to unify the new country. At independence Williams's title changed to prime minister, making him the first in the country to hold that title. He was often called the "Father of the Nation" and had become one of the most popular leaders in the Caribbean.

But Williams eventually came under criticism. His standing as a member of the educated, middle-class elite was a particular liability during the BLACK POWER movement that flourished in Trinidad starting in 1970. Students and activists accused Williams of having Anglo-Saxon values and being complicit in oppressing "black" African and East Indian workers. Williams responded to these and other criticisms during the 1970s by moving farther to the right and taking more power into his own hands, and this led to even more dissatisfaction with his government. A poll taken a month before his March 1981 death showed that 50 percent of voters felt he should resign.

The two decades since Williams's death brought even more political challenges, as racial animosities again divided the country in the 1980s and 1990s. More East Indians were able to rise into the highest ranks of government in these years, but their leadership was met with resistance from some black Trinidadians. After the multiracial National Alliance for Reconstruction Party was elected in 1986 under the campaign slogan "One Love," a radical black Muslim sect staged a brief government coup in 1990. Tensions arose again after Basdeo Panday became the country's first East Indian prime minister in 1995. Panday's United National Congress (UNC) won the legislative elections in December 2000, but three of its members of parliament defected in October 2001, causing the government to collapse. New elections held the following month produced an eighteen-to-eighteen stalemate in parliament. After nearly a year of divided government, the PNM returned to power in October 2002 and Panday announced his retirement from politics. Since that time the PNM has strengthened its control over government, winning nine of fourteen regional elections in 2003. In that election the PNM appeared to perform well in areas that traditionally have supported the UNC.

Despite the apparent broadening of the PNC's appeal to non-black Trinidadians, tensions between blacks and East Indians still run high. In 2003, some members of the UNC accused the government of giving black males preference in enrollment in Trinidad's top technical colleges. Trinidad and Tobago is also becoming one of the most overpopulated countries in the region, and there is suspicion among some that the unusually high birthrates among both blacks and East Indians represent a subtle form of competition, one that has prevented either group from gaining a clear majority in the population.

However, the country does have sources of strength. Trinidadians and Tobagians are fortunate that the oil industry has afforded them the highest standard of living in the Caribbean, and while that industry is not immune to recessions and downswings it still promises to be a reliable backbone for the country for years to come. Like many commonwealth Caribbean nations, Trinidad and Tobago has a national passion for cricket, and Trinidad and Tobago's contributions to literature, drama, and music are a crucial part of the country's cultural heritage.

Many of the Caribbean's most celebrated writers, such as C. L. R. JAMES, V. S. NAIPAUL, and SAMUEL SELVON, are from Trinidad. Nobel Laureate DEREK WALCOTT lived in Trinidad for years, and while there he founded the Trinidad Theatre Workshop. The country is also well known for its popular music and cultural celebrations. Calypso and steelpan both originated in Trinidad, and the annual Carnival festival is one of the largest Carnival celebrations in the world and attracts thousands of visitors from outside the country each year. These cultural resources help unify all Trinidadians and Tobagians; common celebrations and traditions in the "land of steelpan" strengthen the cherished brotherhood and sisterhood that are idealized in the calypso song.

See also Colonial Latin America and the Caribbean; Colonial Rule; East Indian Communities in the Caribbean; Pan-Africanism; Political Movements in Latin America and the Caribbean; Political Parties and Black Social Movements in Latin America and the Caribbean; Slavery in Latin America and the Caribbean; Transatlantic Slave Trade.

Lisa Clayton Robinson

Tripoli, Libya

Capital of the North African nation of Libya.

Located on the coast of the Mediterranean Sea, Tripoli is the capital and largest city of LIBYA, with an urban population estimated at 1,269,700 in 2003. Until the twentieth century, Tripoli seemed destined to share the fate of whatever empire held it. Alternately built up, captured, bombarded, and leveled, it rose and fell with these empires. BERBER-speaking people were the original inhabitants of the North African peninsula where the city of Tripoli stands, but Phoenician traders from the eastern Mediterranean created the settlement. Later Rome ruled the region for more than 500 years. Three cities grew up under the Roman name Tripolitanos: Ouia (the site of the present-day city), Sabrata, and Libtes. When an invading Germanic tribe called the Vandals took the three cities in the fifth century C.E., they broke down the walls between them, and the single city Tripoli grew over the old boundaries.

The Arab conquest of Tripoli in the seventh century brought Islam and an Arab elite to the city. The new rulers rebuilt the city's crumbling infrastructure, and Tripoli became a busy port. Sicilian Normans held it briefly in the twelfth century, but Arabic culture was dominant in Tripoli and the surrounding region. Then, in the sixteenth century, the Christian-Islamic rivalry that had dominated the Mediterranean region for centuries came to Tripoli. SPAIN captured the port and built a castle that still dominates the modern city. But in 1551 the Ottomans, rulers of an Islamic empire based in modern Turkey, took the city they called Tarablus al-Gharb (Tripoli West) to distinguish it from another Tripoli in Lebanon. The Ottoman presence would be long and influential. The city's rulers came from the ranks of the *janissaries,* men who arrived in the region as members of the Ottoman military but later adopted a distinct North African identity and claimed power for themselves. Other inhabitants included Berber speakers, *cologhlis* (descendants of Turkish men and local women), Jews, and Greeks.

Under Ottoman rule, Tripoli was connected to several important trans-Saharan trade routes as well as the to east-west pilgrimage path to Mecca. Most of the city's wealth, however, came from CORSAIRS who forced passing ships to pay for safe passage. European travel narratives of the corsair era record the presence of Christian slaves and the European representatives who negotiated for their freedom. The corsairs' financial backers, as well as the captains and sailors, had great influence over Tripoli's economic and political affairs. From 1801 to 1805, however, the United States bombarded Tripoli to end the corsairs' attacks on American ships. In the following years, corsair profits declined and local power weakened.

In 1835, the Ottoman empire reclaimed direct control of Tripoli. It undertook modernization projects, installing water lines and sewers and improving the port. Yet when Italy became ambitious for a North African territory, Tripoli had little protection—the city fell to the Italians in 1911. Italian colonization brought the mass emigration to Libya of unemployed Italians, many of whom settled in Tripoli. During World War

II (1939–1945), the city suffered from its association with Italy's fascist government; Allied forces bombed it ten times in one year.

Although most organized resistance to the Italian occupiers took place outside Tripoli, the city was the site of eventual negotiations for Libyan independence, which was gained in 1952. Tripoli became one of the new nation's two royal capitals (the other was Bangazi). In 1970, when Libya became a republic, Tripoli was made the national capital. The discovery of oil in 1959 had sparked a wave of industrialization in Tripoli, luring job-seeking migrants from the Libyan countryside as well as from neighboring countries. During the late 1970s, the city was the site of large political demonstrations, including student protests against Muammar al-Qaddafi, who had taken control of Libya after a coup ended the monarchy, and an anti-American demonstration during which the U.S. embassy was burned. In the early years of the twenty-first century, Tripoli flourished as an oil depot and a center for the trade of regional products such as olives, tobacco, fish, grains, fresh vegetables, and citrus fruits.

Marian Aguiar

Tropicália

Extraordinary flourish of cultural production in Brazil during the late 1960s that coalesced as a controversial movement in popular music.

The tropicalist movement helped to open Brazilian music to international influences, including music of Africa and the diaspora. In the 1970s, the leaders of the tropicalist movement, Gilberto Gil and Caetano Veloso, encouraged and defended the emergence of Afro-Brazilian musical movements, particularly in Salvador, Bahia.

Participants in the Tropicália movement included composer-performers Caetano Veloso, Gilberto Gil, Gal Costa, and Tom Zé; poets José Carlos Capinam and Torquato Neto; and intellectual provocateur Rogério Duarte. Except for Torquato Neto, the group hailed from Bahia, the northeastern state noted for its vibrant Afro-Brazilian culture. After migrating to São Paulo, the industrial capital of Brazil, the so-called "Bahian group" hooked up with vanguard composer-arranger Rogério Duprat, and the psychedelic rock group Os Mutantes. Concrete poet and cultural critic Augusto de Campos provided theoretical orientation and defended the group's activities in São Paulo's local press. Journalists Luiz Carlos Maciel and Nelson Motta also helped to define and disseminate the group's project in Rio de Janeiro.

The tropicalist movement emerged at the height of political tensions between an increasingly repressive military regime, which took power in 1964, and the left-wing opposition, led primarily by students, artists, and labor activists. At that time, the field of urban popular music was divided between cultural nationalists, who defended "authentic" Brazilian popular music (known as *Música Popular Brasileira,* or MPB) and the mas-

sively popular *Jovem Guarda* (Young Guard), a homegrown rock movement led by Roberto Carlos. Key proponents of cultural nationalism, such as Geraldo Vandré, Sérgio Ricardo, and Carlos Lyra, were engaged in creating protest music based on northeastern folk themes and styles. Much of this music promised future redemption for the "people," who were oppressed by a right-wing regime allied with multinational capital interests. The populist left regarded the Jovem Guarda as culturally and politically alienated for singing about everyday desires and using electric instruments.

The most visible sites of cultural struggle in popular music were the immensely popular televised music festivals of São Paulo and Rio de Janeiro. While the Jovem Guarda and international pop dominated the Brazilian music market, defenders of MPB, like Elis Regina, Chico Buarque, Edu Lobo, and Geraldo Vandré, dominated the festivals. The Bahian group identified with MPB but was also fascinated with the pop appeal of Roberto Carlos and globally famous pop luminaries such as the Beatles, Janis Joplin, Jimi Hendrix, and James Brown. In an interview, Veloso explained the group's eclectic vision: "We took the example of *antropofagia,* or cultural cannibalism, a notion put forward by the modernist movement in the 1920s, especially by the poet Oswald de Andrade. You take in anything and everything, coming from anywhere and everywhere, and then you do whatever you like with it, you digest it as you wish. You eat everything there is and then produce something new."

In September 1967, Gil and Veloso introduced their "universal sound" at the Third Festival of Brazilian Popular Music aired by TV Record in São Paulo. The live audience was initially hostile to their experiments, which combined electric instrumentation with Brazilian rhythms and themes. By the end of the festival, Gil and Veloso had won second and fourth prizes, respectively, for "Domingo no Parque" and "Alegria, Alegria." By early 1968, their "universal sound" was dubbed *tropicalismo* by the local press and located within a broad range of artistic production.

Key influences on the tropicalists included Glauber Rocha's film *Terra em Transe* (Land in Anguish), a bitter allegory of the collapse of populist politics and the ascension of authoritarianism in Brazil. The play *O rei da vela* (The Candle King), written by Oswald de Andrade in 1933 and staged by the Oficina Theater Group in 1967, under the direction of José Celso Martinez Corrêa, was another famed "happening" of the period. This expressionist farce reveled in the aesthetics of kitsch while cruelly exposing economic dependency, foreign imperialism, and the cynical preservation of class interests. The tropicalist musicians also found allies in two currents of visual arts, *Neorealismo Carioca,* a Brazilian variation of pop art, and *Nova Objetividade,* led by Hélio Oiticica, a radical conceptual artist. His 1967 installation, *Tropicália,* provided the namesake for a song by Caetano Veloso and for the movement.

Each of the tropicalist musicians released solo albums in 1968 and 1969 and the entire group released an acclaimed concept album, *Tropicália: Panis et Circensis,* which was hailed as Brazil's response to the Beatles' *Sgt. Pepper's Lonely Hearts Club*

Band. Veloso and Gil did not perform in the televised festivals of 1968, yet staged important alternative "happenings" in nightclubs and on television. At one event, the emerging REGGAE star, JIMMY CLIFF, who was representing JAMAICA at Rio's International Song Festival, joined Gilberto Gil on stage while he performed "Batmacumba." The tropicalists also had a short-lived television program, "Divino Maravilhoso," named after a hit recorded by Gal Costa. The tropicalists' irreverent activities attracted the scrutiny of military authorities. In late 1968, Gil and Veloso were arrested, jailed for several months, and then exiled to London for two years. The tropicalist movement came to a close, but its impact continued to reverberate in Brazilian popular music.

Tropicália was arguably the most important cultural movement in Brazil since *modernismo* of the 1920s. The 1990s saw a new wave of artistic and critical interest in the movement in Brazil and abroad. In 1993 Veloso and Gil commemorated the twenty-fifth anniversary with the album *Tropicália II,* which updates many of their original concerns. In 1997 Veloso published a highly acclaimed memoir, *A Verdade Tropical* (Tropical Truth), which relates his personal experience in the tropicalist movement and its painful aftermath. The city of Salvador, Bahia, where the original Bahian group converged in the early 1960s, chose Tropicália as its Carnival theme in 1998. During the Carnival, contemporary pop bands and percussion troupes performed updated versions of tropicalist classics, and Caetano Veloso was publicly awarded an honorary doctorate degree from the local university.

See also Afro-Brazilian Culture; Carnivals in Latin America and the Caribbean.

Christopher Dunn

Tropiques

Literary journal published in Martinique from 1941 to 1945, edited by Aimé Césaire, his wife Suzanne Césaire, and René Ménil.

Tropiques represents one of the first attempts to identify and promote Afro-Caribbean culture in the French overseas departments. The editors of *Tropiques,* who at the time of its inception in 1941 were all teachers at the Lycée Schoelcher in FORT-DE-FRANCE, MARTINIQUE, conceived of the journal as a way of filling what AIMÉ CÉSAIRE saw as the "cultural void" that existed on their island. In the view of Césaire and his collaborators, Martinicans of African descent were essentially consumers of culture—notably, of culture imposed on them by the French colonizer—rather than producers of it. *Tropiques* would address this problem by showcasing the poetry, prose fiction, and essays of the three editors (one of whom, Césaire, was on his way to becoming one of the best-known poets, playwrights, and essayists writing in French during the mid-twentieth century) as well as the work of other Martinicans.

The journal has often been identified with NÉGRITUDE, a movement that sought to put colonized Africans and people of African descent in touch with the rich cultural heritage that French colonialism had attempted to replace with French culture. For the editors at *Tropiques,* black Martinicans were the descendants of African slaves, but those Africans had not always been slaves. As Suzanne Césaire wrote in the first issue, it was essential that black West Indians reconnect with the glorious precolonial past of AFRICA. The process of rediscovering their African personality would allow Martinicans to produce authentic works of art, as opposed to the bland imitations of European models the island produced at the time. It was precisely Césaire's poetry that the journal offered as an example of the successful integration of a forgotten African heritage. *Tropiques* also looked beyond the horizons of MARTINIQUE for writers who shared a similar set of concerns. Cuban writers such as ALEJO CARPENTIER and LYDIA CABRERA contributed essays and works of fiction, and several essays were devoted to the Afro-Cuban painter WIFREDO LAM. With these contributions, the editors at *Tropiques* sought to present African diasporic culture as it existed not just in Martinique but throughout the Caribbean. In so doing, they anticipated CRÉOLITÉ, a recent literary and cultural movement that emphasizes a multifaceted Caribbean identity, drawing on African, Asian, and European influences. But the Césaires and Ménil also acknowledged the particular status of the Caribbean as cultural nexus and warned that the focus on African heritage should not obscure the importance of other cultural influences. As they wrote, "We stand at the crossroads. The meeting point of races and cultures." This implied the acknowledgment of European influences; the editors paid homage to André Breton and the surrealists in essays as well as in poems written in a style inspired by surrealism.

The dense and sometimes obscure style of writing in the journal was also partly a response to the context in which it was published. When the first issue of *Tropiques* appeared in April 1941, Martinique was under the control of the Vichy government in FRANCE, which was collaborating with the Nazis. Paper was hard to come by, and all writing on the island was subjected to vigorous censorship by the Vichy authorities in Martinique. *Tropiques* was allowed to appear only because its editors had presented it as a nonpolitical journal that concerned itself with Martinican folklore. The allusive style of the essays and poems in *Tropiques* allowed it to pass unnoticed initially, but the journal was eventually deemed subversive and forced to cease operations from May 1943 until the end of Vichy control of Martinique in October 1943. Given these difficult conditions, that the journal ever appeared is a testament to the commitment of the Césaires and Ménil to subverting the Vichy regime and, more significantly, to presenting Afro-Caribbean culture in a positive light.

See also Literature, French-Language, in the Caribbean; Poetry, Caribbean.

Richard Watts

Trotter, James Monroe

1842–1892

African American army officer, politician, black music historian, and author.

James Monroe Trotter was born on February 7, 1842, in Grand Gulf, Mississippi, the son of a white man, Richard S. Trotter, and his slave Letitia. When Richard Trotter was married in 1854, Letitia, her son, and two younger daughters from the union were sent to live in the free city of CINCINNATI. Here Trotter attended the Gilmore school for freed slaves and worked as a hotel bellboy and as cabin boy on a riverboat. Later he briefly attended academies in Hamilton and Athens, Ohio, but according to his son he was largely self-educated. When the CIVIL WAR came, he was a schoolteacher in Pike County, southwestern Ohio.

In 1863 Trotter was recruited by black lawyer and activist John Mercer Langston and traveled to BOSTON to join the Fifty-fifth Massachusetts Regiment, a black unit with mostly white officers. Trotter rose through the ranks to become a second lieutenant and one of the regiment's four black commissioned officers. He was slightly wounded leading his men in battle near Honey Hill, South Carolina, in November 1864. In camp he held classes in reading and writing, and he helped organize a regimental band that, he later wrote, gave "a certain refinement to what would have been without it but a life of much coarseness."

On racial issues Trotter displayed the genteel militancy that marked his entire life. His commission as a second lieutenant was delayed for several months, to the satisfaction of some of the regiment's white officers. "O how discouraging!" Trotter wrote, "How maddening, almost! . . . An officer told me that it was 'too soon,' that time should be granted white officers to *get rid of their prejudices* so that a white lieutenant would not refuse to sleep in a tent with a colored one. Of course he *supposed* that an objection of this kind would be made always by the white lieut., and that an educated decent colored officer would never object to sleeping with the former whatever might be his character."

When black troops received a laborer's wage of ten dollars a month instead of the soldier's pay of thirteen dollars, Trotter took a leading role in persuading his regiment to decline remuneration until the scale was equalized by Congress. For over a year, then, the regiment served without pay. At one point the Massachusetts legislature voted to make up the difference in pay, and sent two men with the funds to the regiment's encampment in South Carolina. But Trotter made a stirring speech arguing that the principle of equality was more important than the money in question. As he later wrote to one of the men from Massachusetts, it was "a great Principle, that for the attainment of which we gladly peril our lives—Manhood and Equality." The soldier's wage was finally granted to the black troops, and Trotter finished his military service with the Commission on Labor in South Carolina. "The duties are quite arduous," he noted, "but I am very glad to be here, as I have ample opportunity to be of service to the freedmen."

In August 1865 Trotter was mustered out, or discharged, in Boston and decided to settle there, as he and several other black officers were rewarded with appointments in the Boston Post Office. He was married in 1868 to Virginia Isaacs of Chillicothe, Ohio, whom he had known since his school teaching days. According to family tradition, she was a great-granddaughter of Thomas Jefferson, descended from the liaison between Jefferson and his slave SALLY HEMINGS. In any case, the family of James and Virginia Trotter was a model of Victorian rectitude. "In the home is *safety*," wrote Trotter; "over its members are extended the protecting wings of guardian angels; while without are often snares and danger, either in palpable forms, or in those hidden by the glittering, the alluring disguises which are so often thrown over vice." Three children were born: William Monroe in 1872, Maude in 1874, and Bessie in 1883.

Trotter's racial pride and lifelong interest in music combined in 1878 to produce a book, *Music and Some Highly Musical People,* published by Lee and Shepard in Boston and by the firm of Charles W. Dillingham in New York. It was racially ambivalent, proud of black achievements but leaning toward the "higher" forms of white culture. The preface disavowed "all motives of a distinctively clannish nature," yet declared that the book, a record of black musicians in the United States, was "a much-needed service" to some of music's "noblest devotees and the race to which the latter belong." Sharpening the point, Trotter hoped his book would inspire "the people most concerned (if that be necessary) with a greater pride in their own achievements, and confidence in their own resources."

The volume included a general, nonracial discussion of music, with quotations from English poets such as John Dryden, John Milton, Alexander Pope, William Wordsworth, and Lord Byron. But there was also a firm indictment of "the hateful, terrible spirit of *color-prejudice."* Blind pianist THOMAS GREENE BETHUNE, "Blind Tom," was praised without reservation: "unquestionably and conspicuously the most wonderful musician the world has ever known." The slave spirituals, as performed by the FISK JUBILEE SINGERS, were described as "our only distinctively *American* music; all other kinds in use being merely the echo, more or less perfect, of music that originated in the Old World." Trotter was still the Victorian gentleman, however, and hoped that the Jubilee Singers would reach "a higher aim" in their music while keeping "the heartiness, the soulfulness, of their style of rendition." Similarly, he liked the music played by the Georgia Minstrels but "was not pleased, of course, with that portion of the performance [a part of which he was compelled to witness] devoted to burlesque," a practice common in MINSTRELSY.

Trotter resigned his post office job in 1882 as a protest when a white man was promoted over him. With the federal bureaucracy controlled by Republicans, he extended his protest by switching allegiance to the Democrats, thus joining a small group of black mugwumps, or political independents, in the North. In 1883 he worked for Benjamin F. Butler's campaign to be governor of Massachusetts, and after Butler's victory, he called on blacks to stop selling their votes for money: "Our race is yet so far 'in the woods' that it cannot afford to imitate these Caucasian vices. Let us not contaminate our holy cause by baseness of any kind." Three years later Trotter served as chairman of a meeting, held in Boston, of black "Independents" from the New England states.

Ultimately his prominence among black Democrats brought Trotter nomination by President Grover Cleveland to be recorder of deeds in WASHINGTON, D.C., at the time the highest federal job held by blacks of the majority political party. Democrats opposed him because of his color and Republicans because of his politics. Trotter owed his confirmation by the Senate (32-10, March 3, 1887) to endorsement by the two Republican Massachusetts senators and votes of other Republicans who constituted two-thirds of the majority. The position—previously held by FREDERICK DOUGLASS, who later became minister to HAITI—was highly lucrative during Trotter's tenure from 1887 to 1889 because a real estate boom in Washington increased his salary, which was based on a percentage of the transactions. While in office he refused to participate in any protest activities.

Trotter returned to Boston after the Republicans won the election of 1889, and he started a real estate business. He died of tuberculosis on February 26, 1892, and was survived by his widow, his son, and two daughters.

Trotter's *Music and Some Highly Musical People* (1878) contains valuable biographical information and is a major source for the subject. See especially Stephen R. Fox's *Guardian of Boston: William Monroe Trotter* (1970) and Jack Abramowitz's "A Civil War Letter: James M. Trotter to Francis J. Garrison" (*Midwest Journal*, 1952, pp. 113–122). Trotter's Civil War letters are in the Edward W. Kingsley Papers, Duke University, and a manuscript sketch of Trotter is in the George W. Forbes Papers, Boston Public Library.

From *Dictionary of American Negro Biography* by Rayford W. Logan and Michael R. Winston, eds. Copyright © 1982 by Rayford W. Logan and Michael R. Winston. Reprinted by permission of W. W. Norton & Company, Inc.

See also Democratic Party; Historians, African American; Military, Blacks in the American.

Stephen R. Fox

Trotter, William Monroe

1872–1934

African American newspaper publisher and civil rights activist.

William Monroe Trotter was born in Chillicothe, Ohio, the son of JAMES MONROE TROTTER, a politician who served as recorder of deeds under President Grover Cleveland, and former slave Virginia Isaacs. Raised among BOSTON's black elite and steeped in the abolitionist tradition, Trotter entered Harvard University

and made history as the institution's first African American elected to Phi Beta Kappa. After graduating magna cum laude and earning his master's degree from Harvard, Trotter returned to Boston to learn the real estate business. He founded his own firm in 1899, the same year that he married Boston aristocrat Geraldine Pindell.

A turning point in Trotter's life occurred in 1901 when discrimination in his real estate business and worsening racial conditions throughout the country, and especially in the South, led to his increased militancy. In response to his frustration with segregation, disfranchisement, and violence against blacks, Trotter founded the *Boston Guardian*, a crusading weekly newspaper. Cofounder George Forbes soon left the paper in Trotter's able hands. The *Guardian* was an overnight success that boasted a circulation of 2,500 by its first birthday. As editor and publisher, Trotter was articulate, fearless, and defiant. The *Guardian* reestablished the black press as a force in the struggle for CIVIL RIGHTS.

Trotter's great crusade in the pages of his newspaper was a vendetta against BOOKER T. WASHINGTON. Trotter opposed Washington's complacent optimism in the face of increasingly intolerable racial conditions. He also disagreed with Washington's emphasis on manual and industrial training for blacks, with its accompanying denigration of the classical education. Trotter's opposition to Washington forced white America to acknowledge that all of black America did not adhere to Washington's conciliatory and accommodationist views. Trotter's frustration with Washington reached its boiling point in July 1903. When Washington came to Boston for a public appearance, Trotter and some thirty associates heckled the orator and asked him several embarrassing questions. A free-for-all erupted into what became known as the Boston Riot. Washington supporters then pursued the case to its conclusion, resulting in Trotter being fined $50 and imprisoned for a month. Trotter thereafter assumed the mantle of martyr.

Trotter has been credited with leading a resurgence of the protest tradition among African Americans of the early twentieth century. In 1905 he joined W. E. B. DU BOIS in founding the NIAGARA MOVEMENT, an early civil rights organization and precursor of the NATIONAL ASSOCIATION FOR THE ADVANCEMENT OF COLORED PEOPLE (NAACP). Trotter helped to push Du Bois away from research and into defiance as the avenue down which African Americans would secure equal rights. The tenacity and independence that served Trotter well as a journalist, however, hampered his work as a political leader. Personal quarrels with Du Bois created an estrangement between the two leaders. Chief among their disagreements was Trotter's insistence that a national civil rights organization had to be led and financed exclusively by African Americans. In 1908 Trotter founded the National Equal Rights League, an all-black organization that advocated militant efforts to secure racial equality. Although Trotter participated in the founding of the NAACP a year later, he would not accept the white leadership and financial support underpinning the association. As the NAACP's influence swelled, the uncompromising Trotter became isolated on the left wing of black leadership.

One of Trotter's most fiery interchanges occurred at the White House. Trotter, a political independent, supported Woodrow Wilson for president in 1912. When Wilson approved increased segregation in federal office buildings, however, the new president lost Trotter's support. The radical black leader took a delegation to the White House in 1914 and engaged Wilson in a jaw-to-jaw argument. After nearly an hour, the president ordered the vitriolic Trotter out of his office.

Trotter moved the struggle for racial equality in the direction of mass mobilization. In 1915 he experimented with picket lines and demonstrations by orchestrating a nonviolent effort to ban D. W. Griffith's epic motion picture BIRTH OF A NATION. Trotter's arrest did not prevent him from leading some 1,000 marchers to the State House two days later, thereby creating one of the earliest protest marches by Americans of African descent.

In 1919 Trotter announced plans to attend the Versailles Peace Conference in an attempt to have a racial equality clause adopted in the treaty. When the U.S. government denied his request for a passport, the defiant Trotter secured a job as a ship's cook and sailed to France. Although his efforts at Versailles ultimately failed, they garnered worldwide publicity—and Wilson's wrath. Trotter continued to raise his voice through the *Guardian,* doing so only by sacrificing both his own and his wife's personal wealth to finance the newspaper.

After Geraldine Trotter died in the influenza epidemic of 1918, her husband grew ever more isolated. The economic downturn of the GREAT DEPRESSION proved too overwhelming for Trotter, and he lost his newspaper early in 1934. Trotter died later that year, apparently of suicide, when he plunged from the roof of a three-story building in Boston on his sixty-second birthday.

Bibliography

A small collection of Trotter papers is at Boston University, and some Trotter correspondence is in the papers of W. E. B. Du Bois at the University of Massachusetts, Amherst.

Fox, Stephen R. *The Guardian of Boston: William Monroe Trotter.* 1970.

Rodger Streitmatter

Trujillo, Rafael

1891–1961

Military dictator of the Dominican Republic.

Rafael Leónidas Trujillo Molina was born in the town of San Cristóbal, located some eighteen miles from the capital, SANTO DOMINGO, DOMINICAN REPUBLIC, on October 24, 1891. The period from 1930 to 1961 has been called the Era of Trujillo. During this time, Trujillo exercised power as an absolute dictator, though he occupied the presidency only from 1930 to 1938 and from 1942 to 1952. In the intervening years, he ruled through puppet presidents and maintained his position as commander of the armed forces. From 1953 until his death in 1961, he occupied the position of foreign minister.

In 1918, during the U.S. occupation of the DOMINICAN REPUBLIC (1916–1924), Trujillo joined the National Guard established by the United States and quickly rose in its ranks. In 1927, after the Guard was renamed the National Army, he became commander in chief and brigadier general. Trujillo used strong-arm tactics, intimidating and imprisoning many of his opponents, to win the presidential election of 1930. For the next three decades, he would dominate political life in the country.

Trujillo is remembered as one of the most brutal dictators of the Dominican Republic and perhaps in all of LATIN AMERICA. His reign was characterized by state terror, censorship, the omnipresence of the secret police and military corruption, and nepotism. Immediately following the 1930 election he organized a terrorist group known as *La 42,* whose job was to assassinate and persecute his political opposition. Trujillo used his power to amass wealth for himself, his family, and his political cronies, establishing monopolies on salt, meat, and other basic goods. According to historian Frank Moya Pons, by 1961 Trujillo controlled approximately 80 percent of the nation's industrial production. According to Robert Alexander, "A 'cult of personality' was established according to which the dictator had to be credited as the ultimate authority in all fields of human knowledge, and numerous things and places, including the capital city, were renamed in his honor."

Among the atrocities that occurred during the Trujillo dictatorship is the massacre of approximately 20,000 Haitians and Dominican-Haitians in 1937. Haitian peasants had long settled in the Dominican Republic, along the border, a fact that Dominican elites had seen as threatening to Dominican territorial integrity and culture (despite a treaty that finally settled the border dispute between the two countries in 1935). Beyond the cultural, political, and economic reasons for the 1937 massacre was Trujillo's personal conflict with race and ethnicity. While Trujillo cannot be credited with developing anti-Haitianism and antiblackness in the Dominican Republic, his actions demonstrated that he was one of the greatest proponents of what Silvio Torres-Saillant called "the negrophobia of the elite." Trujillo's disdain for blacks and Haitians is perplexing, for he was a mulatto himself who had Haitian blood through his maternal grandmother. This fact was consistently omitted in biographies sanctioned by Trujillo and his family.

After the 1937 massacre Trujillo continued his efforts to Dominicanize and "whiten" (*blanquear* in Spanish) a country that he saw as too phenotypically black. He initiated a plan to "import" persons of European, Asian, and Middle Eastern lineage. Trujillo's attitude and policy regarding the new immigration are reflected in his statement: "A great quantity of immigrants of the White race is needed. The immigrants should be Spanish, Italian, and also of French origin. Immigrants of Caucasian stock shall pay a fee of six pesos for the residency permit and those not of such origin shall pay 500 pesos." In addition, Trujillo built a number of towns and military installations along the border with HAITI to ensure that this territory would become Dominicanized and to prevent renewed Haitian penetration.

In the late 1950s economic crisis shook the regime; the situation worsened after the Organization of American States imposed economic sanctions on the country following Trujillo's attempt to assassinate Venezuelan President Rómulo Betancourt in 1959. The Venezuelan leader's car was bombed in an act of retaliation for his support of a Dominican exile group which attempted to topple the Dominican dictator earlier that year. In the context of economic and political instability, Trujillo was shot to death by opposing military leaders on May 30, 1961, on a highway between his native San Cristóbal and Santo Domingo. His death by no means meant the death of *Trujillismo,* for he left an indelible imprint in the psyche of the Dominican nation.

See also Dominican-Haitian Relations; Whitening.

James Davis

Truque, Carlos Arturo

1927–1970

Afro-Colombian playwright and master of the short story form.

Carlos Arturo Truque is best known for his collection of stories, *Granizada y otros cuentos* (1953; Hailstorm and Other Stories), and the posthumous *El día que terminó el verano y otros cuentos* (1973; The Day Summer Ended and Other Stories).

See also Literature, Black, in Spanish America.

Truth, Sojourner

1797?–1883

African American abolitionist, women's rights advocate, and religious visionary.

Sojourner Truth was one of the best-known black women of her time, rivaled only by African American abolitionist HARRIET TUBMAN, yet her life remains surrounded by mystery. Truth, who was illiterate, left no written record apart from her autobiographical *Narrative of Sojourner Truth,* dictated to white abolitionist Olive Gilbert in the late 1840s. Much of what we know about her was reported or perhaps invented by others. More so than FREDERICK DOUGLASS, her prolifically autobiographical contemporary, Truth has been transformed into myth. Feminists emphasize her challenge to restrictive Victorian codes of femininity; Marxist historians proclaim her solidarity with the working class. Her spirit has been invoked on college campuses in the United States in struggles to create African American and Women's Studies programs. Yet most interpretations of Truth fail to understand the centrality of her evangelical religious faith.

In their writings, both Harriet Beecher Stowe and Douglass recount a central illustration of Truth's faith that occurred at a

I Sell the Shadow to Support the Substance.

SOJOURNER TRUTH.

During the 1840s and 1850s, Sojourner Truth was a prominent abolitionist speaker and an outspoken advocate of women's rights. This photograph, dating from between 1864 and 1870, shows Truth in the Quaker plain dress she preferred. *National Portrait Gallery, Smithsonian Institution/Art Resource*

protest gathering at Faneuil Hall in BOSTON, MASSACHUSETTS, after the passage of the Fugitive Slave Act of 1850. Truth sat in the front row, listening to Douglass speak. Events had led him to abandon the nonviolent approach of moral suasion, and he exhorted Southern slaves to take arms and free themselves. Truth accepted his frustration but not his loss of faith in God's justice. In a voice that carried throughout the hall, she asked a single question: "Frederick, is God dead?"

By Truth's own account, this empowering faith came to her in a moment of divine inspiration after long and traumatic experiences under slavery, which included beatings by her master John Dumont and, according to Truth's biographer Nell Irvin Painter, sexual abuse by his wife. Religion lay at the heart of Truth's transformation from victimized slave to powerful and charismatic leader. Her decision to take the name Sojourner

Truth was, in fact, the culmination of a long process of self-remaking.

Born around 1797 in Ulster County, New York, 130 kilometers (eighty miles) north of NEW YORK CITY, she was the next to youngest of ten or twelve children. Her parents, James and Elizabeth Bomefree, named her Isabella. Her slave parents were Dutch speaking, and Isabella first spoke Dutch. Isabella belonged to a series of slave owners, including, from 1810 to 1827, Dumont. When Isabella was about fourteen, she married Thomas, an older slave owned by Dumont. Between about 1815 and 1826, they had four children, Diana, Peter, Elizabeth, and Sophia, and perhaps a fifth who died.

During 1826 and 1827, Isabella had a series of life-changing experiences. In 1826 she ran away from her master. After her son Peter was illegally sold into slavery (he was an indentured servant) and taken to Alabama, she successfully sued in 1827 for his return with the help of local QUAKERS. She also joined the Methodist Church after a profound conversion experience recounted in her *Narrative*: "God revealed himself . . ." with all the suddenness of a flash of lightning, showing her that he pervaded the universe—"and that there was no place where God was not." Her conversion led her to a lifelong involvement in predominantly white communes and fringe religions as well as to the reform activism for which she is better known. When New York abolished slavery in 1827, Isabella gained her freedom and traveled to New York City, taking Peter and leaving her daughters with their father.

In the city, Isabella did housework for a living and attended both the AFRICAN METHODIST EPISCOPAL ZION CHURCH and a white Methodist church. She also began preaching at camp meetings, honing her oratorical skills and learning how to hold an audience. She became a follower of self-proclaimed white prophet Matthias (Robert Matthews), joining his messianic commune from 1832 until its dissolution in scandal three years later. Little is known of the next several years of her life, although she evidently came under the influence of the Millerites, followers of William Miller, who calculated from biblical prophecies that the world would end in 1843.

In that year, Isabella made a complete break with her past, took the name she believed that God had given her—Sojourner Truth—and preached at Millerite gatherings in New York, Connecticut, and Massachusetts. By December, however, with the Millerite prophecy unfulfilled, she joined the Northampton Association, a white utopian community in Florence, Massachusetts. This community, embracing the most advanced ideas of social reform, opened new vistas for Truth. There she first met Douglass and white abolitionist WILLIAM LLOYD GARRISON and began speaking on social reform as well as religious salvation. Although the Northampton Association broke up in 1846, Truth remained in Florence until ten years later, when she moved to live among spiritualist Progressive Friends in Battle Creek, Michigan, a Seventh-day Adventist community.

Truth insisted on the need to include black and working women in any vision of social reform, grounding her speeches in her own experience as a black woman and former slave. She earned a reputation for oratorical power and a ready wit, as seen in the best-known speech of her career, delivered at an 1851 women's rights convention in Akron, Ohio. As reported at the time by Marius Robinson, editor of the Salem, Ohio, *Anti-Slavery Bugle*, Truth spoke proudly of her own strength and accomplishments, and by implication those of all women: "I have plowed and reaped and husked and chopped and mowed, and can any man do more than that? . . . And how came Jesus into the world? Through God who created him and woman who bore him. Man, where is your part?" However, Robinson's contemporary report of this speech is far less widely known than a later account by white reformer Frances Dana Gage.

In Gage's memorable retelling, Truth punctuated her speech again and again with the emphatic question, "And ain't I a woman?" Scholars have come to doubt the accuracy of Gage's account, which was published twelve years after the event in question. Gage portrayed Truth facing down a hostile crowd dominated by male skeptics of women's rights and female advocates of sharply distinct gender roles, which Painter argues was Gage's own dramatic invention. In rendering Truth's words, Gage employed a nearly unreadable dialect that reflected contemporary literary conventions about black speech far more than it did Truth's own voice. And Painter believes that Truth probably never uttered the line that has become central to her historical image.

Although her subsequent career is less widely known, Truth continued her reform activism. During the CIVIL WAR (1861–1865), she journeyed to WASHINGTON, D.C., and met President ABRAHAM LINCOLN. From 1864 to 1868, she worked with the private National Freedmen's Relief Association and the federal Freedman's Bureau, assisting freed slaves. In the 1870s, Truth participated in the American Woman Suffrage Association. She also championed a proposal to allot Kansas lands to destitute former slaves, making her last major speaking tour in a fruitless effort to rally support. When thousands of Southern blacks, known as the EXODUSTERS, actually moved to Kansas in 1879, Truth applauded them and offered her assistance. She returned from Kansas in 1880 and lived with her daughters in Battle Creek until her death.

See also Bureau of Refugees, Freedmen, and Abandoned Lands; Fugitive Slave Laws; Slavery in the United States.

Bibliography

Painter, Nell Irvin. *Sojourner Truth: A Life, A Symbol.* W. W. Norton, 1996.

Truth, Sojourner, and Olive Gilbert. *Narrative of Sojourner Truth.* Privately printed, 1850.

James Sellman

Truth and Reconciliation Commission

The body charged with investigating crimes committed during the apartheid era in South Africa.

On April 15, 1996, SOUTH AFRICA's Truth and Reconciliation Commission (TRC) began its hearings. The TRC was a compromise solution to the problem of dealing with the thousands of assaults, kidnappings, and murders that were carried out during the era of APARTHEID. The commission received amnesty applications from more than 7,000 people who participated in apartheid-era crimes, which were defined as those having taken place between 1960 and 1994. More than 10,000 witnesses gave testimony, either written or verbal. Despite persistent doubts about both its impartiality and its effectiveness, most observers agreed that the TRC—which continued to work past its original eighteen-month deadline—has helped reconcile the new South Africa with its past. It concluded most of its work in late 1998, but continued to consider amnesty requests during 1999.

Led by Archbishop DESMOND TUTU, the TRC had a multiracial staff of more than sixty, and consists of three committees. Each committee was charged with one of the TRC's three separate mandates: to gather evidence, to make decisions regarding amnesty, and to determine what, if any, reparations were granted to victims. The TRC grew out of negotiations between NELSON MANDELA, the AFRICAN NATIONAL CONGRESS leader elected president of South Africa in 1994, and the AFRIKANER-dominated NATIONAL PARTY government. It was modeled after truth commissions in other countries where citizens had suffered years of violent injustices, such as ARGENTINA, CHILE, and GUATEMALA.

These tribunals operated on the assumption that the only way to discover the truth about large-scale, politically motivated crimes is to offer amnesty to those who committed them. In exchange for their truthful testimony, perpetrators were shielded from criminal prosecution and civil lawsuits—unless the commission determined that their crimes were either nonpolitical or disproportionately brutal. For victims and their families, the TRC hearings provided previously unavailable information about the torture and death of relatives, often including the location of bodies which families can then re-bury according to their religious traditions. Perhaps the most important goal, however, comes from the belief that only by acknowledging the crimes of the past can South Africans begin to heal from them.

Before it even convened, the TRC faced criticism from suspected perpetrators as well as victims' groups. Survivors and the families of victims brought two separate lawsuits in hopes of retaining the right to bring criminal or civil charges against those who had tortured or murdered their relatives. Another legal challenge came from police and security officials fearful of being named in the proceedings. In addition, many white South Africans believed that the TRC would be biased toward the ANC and its supporters, and would end up a "witch hunt," seeking only to humiliate and destroy the reputations of those who had served in the former government.

In fact, Tutu and his associates questioned both former police officers and former ANC officials, although many have questioned the controversial blanket amnesty that the TRC granted to thirty-seven ANC leaders. The TRC heard testimony that at last confirmed the details of the torture and murder of STEPHEN BIKO, an antiapartheid leader and important figure in the Black Consciousness movement. It also called on WIN-NIE MADIKIZELA-MANDELA, the president's former wife, to explain her role in the deaths of SOWETO youths accused of being government informants. Beyond such high-profile cases, the TRC heard from thousands of ordinary South Africans. Their tales of beatings, torture, rape, murder, and burial in unmarked graves have left many, including Tutu—who often broke down and cried from the bench—stunned at the extent of apartheid's brutality.

The degree of cooperation by former government officials varied. Dirk Coetzee, a white police officer who was sheltered by the ANC after threatening to expose high-level orders to murder antiapartheid activists, was among the first to testify. Coetzee said that he did not expect forgiveness for his crimes. Others, such as former president F. W. DE KLERK, denied that torture and murder were the result of official government orders. Tutu later apologized to de Klerk for implying, during de Klerk's appearance before him, that this was a lie. De Klerk's predecessor, P. W. BOTHA, faced contempt of court charges in 1998 for refusing to appear before the TRC, which he characterized as "a circus."

Despite pressure from many sides, the TRC showed independence in its pursuit of the truth. When reports came that witnesses were prepared to offer testimony about secret weapons' research and development, President Mandela, fearing international publicity, asked Tutu to hold private hearings on the matter. Tutu ruled that, while the government was entitled to legal representation, such hearings would go forward in public.

In October 1998 the TRC issued its final report, despite objections from the ANC that the party deserved time to preview the report and to issue a rebuttal. Little in the report was surprising, but it documented for the historical record many allegations that had surfaced during the apartheid era. Botha was held responsible for a wide array of abuses, and Madikizela-Mandela was closely tied to abductions, torture, and killings by township youths under her direction. The report also documented the existence of a "third force"—covert intelligence units that acted in concert with right-wing whites and the INKATHA FREEDOM PARTY to violently suppress antiapartheid organizations, and later to destabilize the country prior to the 1994 elections. The report also implicated senior members of the apartheid government in the torture and assassination of antiapartheid activists, and concluded that the ANC had committed serious human rights abuses during the resistance struggle. After the final report was issued, the TRC closed most of its operations, but continued to assess the large backlog of amnesty applications.

In November 2003 South African government started issuing payments to the 22,000 victims who testified before the TRC. However, the one-time payment of 33,000 Rand ($5,200) to each person is well short of the amount recommended by the Commission.

See also Antiapartheid Movement; Black Consciousness in Africa.

Kate Tuttle

Tsetse Fly

Any of several species of bloodsucking fly that feeds on humans and animals and causes sleeping sickness in humans and nagana in cattle; the organism has influenced population distribution and farming practices in Africa.

Tsetse flies make up the family Muscidae in the order Diptera. The South African tsetse fly is classified as *Glossina palpalis*. The tsetse fly that transmits Rhodesian sleeping sickness and nagana is classified as *Glossina morsitans*. Tsetses are found abundantly in forests and along the edges of lakes and rivers in central and coastal West AFRICA. The adult flies, which are about 2.5 centimeters (about one inch) long, are brown above and brown with yellow stripes or spots below. The female periodically produces one full-size larva and buries it in the ground or among decayed leaves, where it metamorphoses into an adult fly.

Tsetse flies transmit the parasitic protozoan known to produce the often fatal disease trypanosomiasis, or sleeping sickness. The parasites are drawn into the body of the fly with the blood sucked from an infected person and, after a period of development, can be conveyed to the bloodstream of healthy victims. African sleeping sickness gradually attacks the nervous system, starting with an accelerated heartbeat, enlarged spleen, and fever, followed during the next several months by mood changes, lack of appetite, sleepiness, coma, and often death. Sleeping sickness has had a profound effect on population distribution in Africa. Between 1902 and 1930, sleeping sickness struck an area of UGANDA near LAKE VICTORIA, killing 30,000 people and leaving the area sparsely settled.

The tsetse fly also shaped the history of African agriculture and PASTORALISM. Because cattle and horses are both vulnerable to sleeping sickness (known as nagana in animals), agrarian societies in vast areas of the continent have been unable to depend on the use of livestock for draught power or fertilizer, and have had to rely instead on labor-intensive hoe cultivation. The range of nomadic pastoral societies has also been circumscribed by tsetse fly prevalence. Not surprisingly, the elimination of nagana is a high priority for veterinary researchers in Africa.

See also Disease and African History; Diseases, Infectious, in Africa.

Robert Fay

Tshombe, Moise-Kapenda

1919–1969

Congolese politician, president of the secessionist state of Katanga, and prime minister of the Democratic Republic of the Congo.

Born in Musumba, the son of a wealthy businessman and descendant of Lunda rulers, Moise-Kapenda Tshombe was trained as an accountant under Belgian rule. When the Congo attained independence in 1960, he turned to politics, emerging as a spokesman for decentralization. In July 1960, supported by Belgian mining interests, he declared Katanga independent. The secession was crushed by early 1963, and Tshombe went into exile, having previously displayed to the world his formidable political shrewdness. Recalled by President JOSEPH KASAVUBU in 1964, Tshombe served as prime minister until exiled following a military coup in November 1965. The victim of a plane hijacking in 1967, he landed in ALGERIA, where he was held under arrest until his death.

See also Democratic Republic of the Congo.

Tsimihety

Ethnic group of Madagascar.

The Tsimihety primarily inhabit northern MADAGASCAR. They speak MALAGASY, a Malayo-Polynesian language. Over 1,200,000 people consider themselves Tsimihety.

See also Ethnicity and Identity in Africa: An Interpretation; Languages, African: An Overview; Madagascar, Ethnicity in.

Tsiranana, Philibert

1910–1978

President of the First Republic of Madagascar.

While attending the University of Montpellier in FRANCE, Tsiranana, an ethnic TSIMIHETY, formed the Union des Etudiants Malgaches in reaction to the MERINA-dominated Association des Etudiants d'Origine Malgache. The Merina had historically dominated precolonial MADAGASCAR, and the non-Merina population, also known collectively as côtiers or déshérités, feared continued subjugation at the hands of Merina rulers. These ethnic and political divisions would shape Tsiranana's political career.

When Tsiranana returned to Madagascar in 1950, he became a schoolteacher in Majuna and took up local politics, joining the Parti des Déshérités de Madagascar. In 1956 he returned to France to represent his district in the French National Assembly, where he also joined the French Socialist Party. Later that year, Tsiranana returned to Madagascar and formed the Parti Social Démocrate (PSD), an anti-Merina political party favoring close ties to France over immediate independence. In 1957 he was elected vice president of the Loi-Carde Government Council, created to provide French colonies in Africa greater autonomy.

Tsiranana was elected president of a semiautonomous Madagascar within the French Union in May 1959. Full independence was granted in 1960. For the ten years that followed, Tsiranana embraced market economic principles and took a staunch anti-Communist stance. Although his political rivals labeled him a puppet of French interests, he was credited with an ability to compromise and a sensitivity to ethnic concerns. At first, Tsiranana's administration generally abided by democratic principles, allowing a free press, permitting political opposition, and maintaining an autonomous judicial system. While Madagascar remained one of the poorest nations in the world, from 1960 to 1965 the MALAGASY economy performed relatively well: unemployment fell, inflation stabilized at reasonable levels, and budget deficits were tolerable. A popular vote confirmed Tsiranana's position as president in 1965.

By the late 1960s, however, the economy had deteriorated significantly, and Tsiranana faced opposition on several fronts. In 1970 Tsiranana suffered from a stroke and subsequently spent several months hospitalized in Paris. Following rebellions in the south, Tsiranana attempted to reestablish control by holding elections with him as the only candidate. Despite receiving 99 percent of the vote, his political legitimacy was undermined. Civil unrest continued to intensify, culminating in the May 1972 Revolution, when student strikes escalated into a full civil revolt. Lacking popular or military support, Tsiranana was forced to relinquish power to General Gabriel Ramanantsoa. Although he remained involved in Malagasy politics, Tsiranana never again held office.

See also Madagascar, Ethnicity in.

Bibliography

Allen, Philip. M. *Madagascar: Conflicts of Authority in the Great Island.* Westview Press, 1995.

Rajoelina, Patrick. *Quarante Années de la Vie Politique de Madagascar, 1947–1987.* l'Harmattan, 1988.

Ari Nave

Tsonga

Name for peoples of southern Mozambique and the Northern Province of South Africa; also known as Thonga and Tonga.

The people now known as Tsonga descend from a group of small communities that did not conceive of themselves as one people, although they were culturally and linguistically related. These people live north of the area populated by the ZULUS and are thought to have arrived there before the sixteenth century. The name *Tsonga* derives from a word meaning "east" or "people from the east" and was first used by Christian missionaries. Experts disagree about the process by which the Tsonga came to be seen, and to see themselves, as a distinct ethnic group. Some argue that the persistent cultural pressures applied by the neighboring Zulu in the nineteenth century forced smaller groups to band together. Others claim that the people began reflecting the theories proposed by missionaries, chief among them the Swiss minister Henri Junod, who studied one clan in the early twentieth century.

Whatever the source, the various clans that came together under the name Tsonga now feel a strong group identity. Over three million people consider themselves Tsonga. Traditionally most of these people have raised crops—such as cassava, MILLET, sorghum, and corn—and livestock, such as cattle. However, in the late eighteenth century many Tsonga men began working as migrant laborers, a practice they continue to this day.

Village life is arranged according to patrilineal kinship groups, families related through the male line. Polygyny is permitted, and each bride's family pays a dowry to the husband or his family. Many Tsonga are Christian, but some traditional religious practices are still followed. The Tsonga are known for their rituals of initiation into adulthood and other life events. Such rituals involve music—especially drumming—dance, and theater in addition to the use of hallucinogenic plants.

See also Christianity: Missionaries in Africa; Ethnicity and Identity in Africa: An Interpretation; Languages, African: An Overview; Mozambique; Northern Province; South Africa.

Tswana

Ethnic group of Botswana, Namibia, and South Africa numbering around five million people.

During the eleventh or twelfth century, the ancestors of the Tswana settled on the rolling plains around the Vaal River in what is now the South African province of TRANSVAAL. They tended livestock, mostly cattle, and grew crops such as MILLET and sorghum. They were seminomadic and did not privately own land, but measured wealth in terms of cattle. Clan chiefs maintained their wealth and authority by collecting tribute, and in turn loaned parts of their vast royal herds to peasant farmers for milk and breeding purposes.

By 1800 Tswana territory extended into parts of present-day eastern BOTSWANA but still lay mostly to the south. That changed in the 1820s, during the time of warfare known as the MFECANE, when the NDEBELE, fleeing ZULU aggression, invaded the Transvaal region and began raiding Tswana and SOTHO settlements. Many Tswana fled into the KALAHARI DESERT, where the inhospitable climate of sparse rainfall and extreme temperature changes deterred the Ndebele from pursuing them further. By the mid-1830s the Ndebele had continued northward into what is now ZIMBABWE, and the refugee Tswana clans resettled in the more arable lands near the Limpopo, one of the region's only perennial rivers. Nineteenth-century European explorers and missionaries were surprised to encounter the Tswana's large settlements, where up to 20,000 people lived in villages composed primarily of cylindrical mud dwellings with conical thatched roofs.

Although the Tswana language is closely related to other Sotho languages, most Tswana do not identify themselves as Sotho. Today the Tswana are the largest ethnic group in Botswana and dominate that country politically. The Tswana of Botswana are divided into more than fifty subgroups, defined by membership in a lineage traced through the male line. The Tswana are also divided into numerous animal-totem groups that crosscut subgroup lines. Particularly in Botswana, Tswana groups may include members of non-Tswana ethnic origin. SOUTH AFRICA's APARTHEID regime created a separate "homeland," called BOPHUTHATSWANA, for that country's Tswana. However, this state never achieved international recognition. During the 1990s South Africa's majority government dissolved the homeland, and its Tswana residents are now South African citizens.

Traditionally, Tswana women farm maize, sorghum, and millet for subsistence, and men spend much of their time herding livestock. Many men now also migrate to industrial areas, where they are often employed as wage laborers in mines. As the cash economies of Botswana and South Africa have grown, increasing numbers of Tswana have given up traditional rural life for wage labor in towns. Likewise, most Tswana have abandoned traditional religious beliefs for CHRISTIANITY, though some elements of ancestral worship remain.

See also Christianity: Missionaries in Africa; Ethnicity and Identity in Africa: An Interpretation; Languages, African: An Overview.

Ari Nave

Tuareg

Ethnic group of Niger, Mali, Burkina Faso, Algeria, and Libya.

Often called "the blue people" because of the color that the indigo dye of their clothing leaves on their skin, the Tuareg are a seminomadic people who live in the western and southwestern regions of the SAHARA as well as in the SAHEL. Known to Greek and Roman scholars as the "veiled Sanhadja," the Tuareg claim descent from the BERBERS of North Africa and are believed to have migrated southward during Arab invasions of North Africa in the seventh century C.E. These migrants eventually developed several political confederations, called *kels,* all of them affected by caste hierarchies and clan membership, but sharing an adherence to Islam and the use of the Tamacheq language.

Some Tuareg confederations, particularly the Kel Eway and Kel Gress, migrated into the savanna zones of the Sahel. There they combined their traditional pastoralist livelihoods with trans-Saharan trade and sedentary agriculture, allowing them to guard against drought. Beginning around the eleventh century, to assure an adequate agricultural labor supply while the Tuareg nobles traveled on long-distance trade journeys, these confederations conducted raids on communities to the south, acquiring slaves, serfs, and tribute states, which made payments in crops such as MILLET.

By the fifteenth century, Tuareg society recognized numerous categories of status and caste. These included *iklan*

(slaves), the *irewelen* (descendants of iklan), and the *imrad* (tribute-paying clients), as well as the Tuareg nobles—fair-skinned nomads who called themselves the *imageren* (Arabic for "the proud and free"). Most slaves, once captured, were traded to another federation to reduce the chances of escape. The slaves were then assimilated into Tuareg society, cultivating palms, vegetables, and grains on their owner's land and sometimes accompanying trade caravans. Although subordinate to the nobles, the iklan were generally considered part of the family, and both loyalty and marriage offered opportunities for social mobility.

At this time, Tuareg confederations had established control over several important trans-Saharan trade routes. In the face of increasing external pressure from the HAUSA, FULANI, and SOKOTO CALIPHATE, Tuareg nobles attempted to forge a more centralized kingdom. The leaders of several kels established a sultanate based in AGADEZ, a city in present-day NIGER. Although the Tuareg were then able to dominate much of the southern Sahara, acquiring control of important trade-centers such as Gao and TOMBOUCTOU, they never established the kind of enduring centralized authority structures that were forged by neighboring groups such as the Kanuri-Bornu and Hausa. This was in part due to their preference for nomadic rather than sedentary living—a preference that later put the Tuareg in direct opposition to both colonial and postcolonial governments.

Beginning in 1900, the colonial governments of FRENCH WEST AFRICA began a relentless campaign to relocate the Tuareg and other nomads into agricultural villages. They also imposed taxes on the trans-Saharan trade caravans, and confiscated camels from the Tuareg to use for their own desert military campaigns. In addition, the prohibition of slavery deprived many Tuareg communities of vital sources of labor and food. The resulting economic decline, coupled with a series of devastating droughts in the 1910s, rallied the Tuareg into rebellion. Throughout the next twelve years the French and Tuareg attempted to undermine each other by filling in wells, destroying crops, and stealing animals and supplies from sedentary farmers, actions that ultimately destroyed much of Tuareg farmland. By 1922 many Tuareg groups sought refuge in non-French colonies, such as NIGERIA and LIBYA, though most returned home after the French West African colonies became independent in the early 1960s.

In recent years the Tuareg have been involved in a series of conflicts with national governments. Beginning in the 1970s, Niger and MALI both started mining for uranium in territory that had traditionally been claimed by the Tuareg. Displaced and suffering from ongoing drought, Tuareg groups began attacking towns for supplies. In Mali, these attacks were met with violent military repression. Many groups attempted to flee the area, but were turned back from Niger, and forced to settle in refugee camps until the drought subsided.

In the early 1990s, Tuareg in Niger rebelled after the government failed to fund promised Tuareg relocation projects. Conflict spread across the Sahel into Mali, as Tuareg separatist groups demanded the creation of an all-Tuareg Saharan Republic. Although fighting subsided after peace pacts in the mid-

1990s, many wonder how long the Tuareg's customary nomadic ways can survive. Already, economic necessity has made many Tuareg permanent fixtures in cities such as OUAGADOUGOU, NIAMEY, and BAMAKO, where they make a living selling leather goods to tourists.

See also Ethnicity and Identity in Africa: An Interpretation; Islam in Africa; Languages, African: An Overview; Nationalism in Africa; Trans-Saharan and Red Sea Slave Trade.

Elizabeth Heath

Tubby, King

1941–1989

Skilled sound engineer who pioneered dub reggae in Jamaica.

Born Osbourne Ruddock in KINGSTON, JAMAICA, King Tubby gained prominence in 1968 for playing his instrumental mixes accompanied by the crowd-pleasing "talk-over" deejaying of U-Roy (Ewart Beckford). The duo was known as Tubby's Hi-Fi and became highly popular in the impoverished Watertown section of Kingston where Tubby lived. U-Roy's verbal wordplay provided a perfect compliment to Tubby's increasingly experimental song versions. Using homemade and modified studio equipment, Tubby started dropping in vocal snippets, adding ghostly layers of echo and reverberation, soloing various instruments, inserting sudden silences, and employing unusual equalization and other studio effects. Crowds loved the soulful roots REGGAE mutated by technical wizardry and avant-garde mixing approaches. Following Tubby's lead, many musicians and engineers began dubbing.

By 1972 DUB fever had arrived. Fierce competition between sound systems kept creative pressures high, although King Tubby remained on top. In 1976 police attempted to shut down a dance at Tubby's Hi-Fi by shooting and axing his speakers on claims that his music attracted a hostile crowd. Dub's largest buying audience was the urban poor, and middle- and upper-class Jamaicans sought to suppress the form for being "rough" and "uncouth."

King Tubby turned to training studio apprentices in the 1980s as dub's popularity waned. Tubby's ideas and techniques have influenced a new generation of electronic musicians who value dub's aggressive reinvention and studio science. Dozens of dub albums feature King Tubby's mixing skills, and contemporary interest has fueled a steady stream of rereleases, such as the superlative *Glen Brown and King Tubby: Termination Dub and King Tubby and Soul Syndicate: Freedom Sounds in Dub.*

See also Jamaica; Music, Caribbean.

Jace Clayton

Tubman, Harriet Ross

1820?–1913

American abolitionist who escaped from slavery and returned repeatedly to the South to lead other slaves to freedom.

Harriet Ross Tubman was born on Maryland's Eastern Shore, one of eleven children of Harriet Greene and Benjamin Ross, both slaves. As a child, she was called Araminta but later defiantly took her mother's first name. (Slaves were often forbidden to form such public attachments.) At a young age, Tubman worked in her owner's house as well as in other households to which she was rented. As a teenager, she worked in the fields, gaining strength and endurance. Still in her teens, she shielded a slave who was fleeing his owner. The owner hurled a two-pound weight at the runaway that missed and struck Tubman on the head, nearly killing her. For the rest of her life, she was prone to sudden sleeping spells, dizziness, and headaches, and bore a deep gash.

In 1844 she married John Tubman, a free black man. Shortly after their marriage, she hired a lawyer to trace her mother's history as a slave. The lawyer discovered records showing that her mother had been briefly free because an earlier owner had died without making provision for her. Apparently, nobody told Harriet Greene that she was free, and a short while later she was returned to slavery. This discovery haunted Tubman. When Tubman's owner died in 1849, Tubman feared that she and members of her family would be sold to the horrible conditions of the Deep South. Resolved to escape, she tried to persuade her husband to join her, but he refused. She fled without him, traveling at night and hiding by day until she came to Pennsylvania, a free state.

Tubman went to PHILADELPHIA, PENNSYLVANIA, where she cleaned and cooked for a living, saving her earnings for a return trip to the South to bring out other members of her family. In 1850 she made her first covert trip to BALTIMORE, MARYLAND, where she rescued her enslaved sister and two children. Tubman soon became allied with black leader WILLIAM STILL of Philadelphia, white Quaker Thomas Garrett of Wilmington, Delaware, and other activists of the UNDERGROUND RAILROAD. The Underground Railroad was a loose network of abolitionists who arranged for fugitive slaves to travel safely from South to North, and Tubman became its most successful conductor. In an estimated nineteen trips to the South from 1850 to 1860, she guided more than 300 men, women, and children to freedom, including her own entire family. In 1857 she made perhaps her most remarkable journey, returning to the North with her aging parents.

In her work, Tubman carried a gun, not to fend off enemies, but to goad fugitives who grew fainthearted or weary and wanted to return. "Live North, or die here," she is said to have told them. She also used drugs to quiet crying babies and employed several disguises. It is believed that all of the slaves in Tubman's care made it safely to the North, despite large bounties offered for her and her charges' capture. After Congress passed the Fugitive Slave Act of 1850, which required Northern states to return escaped slaves, Tubman settled runaways in CANADA, in what is now Ontario. She lived intermittently in Canada, settling with her parents in Auburn, New York, in the late 1850s.

As Tubman's reputation grew (she was known among blacks and Northern whites as "Moses"), she gained the support and friendship of the day's leading progressives, including writer Ralph Waldo Emerson, abolitionist SOJOURNER TRUTH, and reformer Susan B. Anthony. Another supporter, William Seward, a New York senator and the United States secretary of state, sold Tubman the land for her Auburn home on generous terms. Among abolitionists, Tubman most admired JOHN BROWN, with whom she helped plan the raid on Harpers Ferry in 1859. She failed to join Brown in the raid only because of illness, and she grieved deeply at his hanging. In 1860, she undertook her most public rescue when she led a crowd in Troy, New York, to free a fugitive slave who was being returned to the South.

During the CIVIL WAR (1861–1865), Northern officials asked Tubman to help the Union Army. She traveled to South Carolina, where she served as liaison between the army and newly freed blacks, training the latter in self-sufficiency. Tubman also nursed wounded soldiers, organized and trained scouts, and helped lead a raid against Confederate troops. Although she received commendation from officers, she received no pay. After the war, Tubman returned to Auburn to care for her parents. Though poor and illiterate herself, she devoted her time to raising money for the education of former slaves, gathering clothes for poor children, and helping former slaves who were too old for manual labor. Eventually, she converted her house to a home for the old and poor. (With the help of Auburn's AFRICAN METHODIST EPISCOPAL ZION CHURCH, the Harriet Tubman Home for Aged and Indigent Colored People was formally opened in 1908.)

In 1869 Tubman married a former slave and Union Army veteran, Nelson Davis. Also in 1869 Tubman's friend Sarah Bradford published a brief biography of her, some of the proceeds of which supported Tubman and her causes. Prominent friends tried for two decades to persuade the government to give Tubman a pension for her wartime services. Failing this, they succeeded in 1890 in gaining her a small veteran's pension as the widow of Davis, who had since died. Tubman spent many of her later years working on behalf of women's suffrage.

See also Abolitionism in the United States; Fugitive Slave Laws; Slavery in the United States.

Tubman, William Vacanarat Shadrach

1895–1971

President of Liberia from 1944 to 1971, often called the maker of modern Liberia.

Born in Harper, of American-Liberian descent, William Vacanarat Shadrach Tubman was trained as a preacher and lawyer. Having served as a county attorney and trial judge, he was elected to the Liberian Senate (1923), where he remained (though not uninterruptedly) until 1937; he then became associate justice of the Liberian Supreme Court. The candidate of the ruling True Whig party, he was elected president in 1943 and assumed office in 1944. During his twenty-seven years as president, he made some attempts to bring African men into government and give them, as well as women, a legal status equal to that of the Americo-Liberian elite. To improve the living standard in LIBERIA, he followed an open-door economic policy, which opened the country to extensive foreign investment, while externally acting as a U.S. ally and moderate. Tubman sponsored the 1961 conference of African heads of state to promote continental cooperation. He was also an outspoken opponent of white rule in AFRICA.

Tugen

Ethnic group of Kenya; also known as Kamasya.

The Tugen primarily inhabit Rift Valley Province in west-central KENYA. They speak a Nilo-Saharan language and are one of the KALENJIN peoples. Over 200,000 people consider themselves Tugen.

See also Ethnicity and Identity in Africa: An Interpretation; Languages, African: An Overview.

Tukulor

Fulani-speaking ethnic group of Senegal, Mali, Guinea, and Mauritania.

The Tukulor are a FULANI-speaking ethnic group who, traditionally, are sedentary agricultural farmers of the Futa Toro region in SENEGAL. Historically, they have a special commitment to Islam: the partly Tukulor ruling classes of the kingdom of Tekrur converted to Islam in the eleventh century, and the Tukulor claim with pride to be the first black Africans to embrace Islam.

Despite their conversion, Tukulor traditional religious beliefs in spirits, witches, and ghosts remain powerful. There are five castes in traditional Tukulor society. In descending order by status, they are the Torobe, or aristocratic Islamic scholars and leaders; the Rimbe, or farmers, traders, and administrators who also act as warriors; the Nyenbe, or craftsworkers; the Gallunkobe, meaning freedpeople or descendants of slaves; and the Matyube, or slaves.

In the nineteenth century many Tukulor, inspired by the dynamic religious leader UMAR TAL joined the purist Islamic Sufi order, the Tijaniyah. Umar mobilized his mostly Tukulor followers in a *jihad* (Islamic holy war) in 1854 against the BAM-

BARA states of Ségu and Kaarta. After conquering these states, Umar founded the vast Tukulor empire in 1864, centered at Ségu and encompassing most of present-day MALI. The Bambara of Ségu never completely surrendered to Tukulor rule; Tukulor power was weak and confined mostly to the towns and major villages. Umar died in 1864, leaving his empire to his sons. Mustafa ruled from 1864 to 1870, when Ahmadu took over, but under the reign of both sons, the empire slowly disintegrated, as local leaders rebelled against the ruling dynasty. Invading French colonial troops forced Ahmadu to flee, and in 1891 the empire fell to the French.

Because the Torobe control disproportionate amounts of land, and because the lower castes own very little, during the twentieth century many lower caste Tukulor have given up agriculture for wage labor in the cities. There are nearly one million Tukulor spread across West Africa.

See also African Religions: An Interpretation; Ethnicity and Identity in Africa: An Interpretation; Guinea; Languages, African: An Overview; Mauritania; Sufism.

Leyla Keough

Tulsa Riot of 1921

White riot that devastated some forty city blocks in the mostly black Greenwood district of Tulsa, Oklahoma.

The growth of the oil industry had made Tulsa, Oklahoma, a rich town by 1921. Its predominantly black section, Greenwood, achieved a level of wealth that earned it a reputation as the "Negro Wall Street of America." African Americans accounted for about 12 percent of the city's overall population. Whites reacted to the success of African Americans with violence and formed "whipping parties" that randomly assaulted blacks on a daily basis. Several LYNCHINGS had also taken place in the vicinity of Tulsa, a major KU KLUX KLAN center, and blacks armed themselves for protection. These racial tensions culminated in the riot of 1921.

In 1921 a nineteen-year-old black man named Dick Rowland took a break from his downtown job as a shoe shiner to use the restroom at the top of a nearby building. Sarah Page, a seventeen-year-old white girl who was operating the elevator there, claimed that Rowland assaulted her. Rowland was arrested the following day and incarcerated at the local courthouse.

Before the incident had been investigated, the *Tulsa Tribune* reported (on May 31) that Rowland, who was identified only by his color, "attacked [Page], scratching her hands and face, and tearing her clothes off." That evening, a crowd of whites gathered outside the courthouse.

The sheriff tried unsuccessfully to disperse the crowd, which by 10:30 P.M. had grown to nearly 2,000 people. A group of around sixty armed black men, who previously had been turned away, returned to the courthouse to help the sheriff defend Rowland. When one of the white men tried to disarm one of the blacks, a shot was fired, and the two groups opened fire. Vastly outnumbered, the blacks retreated to Greenwood. Whites who did not have arms seized them from hardware stores and pawnshops and headed for the Frisco Railroad tracks, the boundary line that separated the black and white communities. On June 1, at around 1:00 A.M., warfare resumed.

After several drive-by shootings, whites invaded the Greenwood district in force around 6:00 A.M. and began to burn houses and businesses. They shot at the fleeing blacks, sometimes throwing their bodies back into the flames. Blacks were largely outnumbered and, during the rioting, police worked continuously to disarm them. By the time the National Guard arrived at 9:15 a.m., the gunfire had diminished and the troops helped the police round up and place African Americans in holding areas, which were manned by armed guards. Approximately 6,000 blacks—half of Tulsa's African American population—were reportedly incarcerated during the riot.

By late morning, the violence had ceased and the Red Cross had arrived to provide medical treatment to the injured blacks. In the week that followed, the Red Cross treated 531 people and operated on another 163. They also erected 350 tents for African Americans whose homes had been destroyed and continued to administer aid through the late fall of 1921. Records kept by the Red Cross estimate that 1,115 houses and businesses belonging to blacks had been burned, and that another 314 had been looted. The records further indicate that 715 families left Tulsa, some of whom returned after the riot; and that 300 people died—only a small percentage of these were white. Historical sources disagree about these statistics.

In the midst of Red Cross relief efforts, Tulsa's white authorities announced to the nation that they would assume the responsibility of rebuilding Greenwood, and that additional external assistance would not be accepted. The white community, however, abandoned the reconstruction project and tried unsuccessfully to prevent African Americans from rebuilding on their own land. The city's white officials delayed their reconstruction efforts, causing around 1,000 black Tulsans to spend the winter of 1921 to 1922 in tents.

In the end, blacks were blamed for inciting the riot by showing up at the courthouse with firearms. No white Tulsans were arrested or jailed. Sarah Page refused to prosecute Dick Rowland. Follow-up investigation found that Rowland had bumped into the girl as he was getting off the elevator, and all charges were dropped. Little discussion of the riot occurred before its seventy-fifth anniversary on June 1, 1996, when, at a ceremony in Tulsa, African American survivors of the riot addressed the public. Until that time, both whites and blacks in Tulsa had avoided serious discussion of the riot.

See also Race Riots in the United States.

Bibliography

Ellsworth, Scott. *Death in A Promised Land: The Tulsa Race Riot of 1921.* Louisiana State University Press, 1982.

Aaron Myers

Tumbuka

**Ethnic group of southern Africa; also known as
Batumbuka, Matumbuka, and Tumbukwa.**

The Tumbuka primarily inhabit northern MALAWI and northeastern ZAMBIA. They speak a Bantu language related to that of
the TONGA. More than two million people consider themselves
Tumbuka.

See also Bantu: Dispersion and Settlement; Ethnicity and
Identity in Africa: An Interpretation; Languages, African: An
Overview.

Tunisia

**Country on the Mediterranean coast of North Africa,
bordered by Algeria to the west and south and Libya to
the east.**

Tunisia has often been described as an oasis in the desert. The
metaphor refers both to the country's natural beauty, which attracts thousands of tourists, and to its political and social climate. Tunisia has promoted itself as a secular, progressive oasis in North Africa, a haven from the troubles of the rest of the
Arab world. Indeed, the country has been on the vanguard of
Western-inspired reform since the nineteenth century. Yet, with
growing populist support within the nation for an Islamic party,
it is worth noting that Tunisia has never really been isolated
from its North African neighbors—neighbors with whom it
shares the religion of ISLAM, and the legacy of Phoenician, Roman, Arab, and European conquest.

Ancient Tunisia

The BERBER people have maintained a continual presence since
the earliest time in the region that is now Tunisia. They were
joined, in the first millennium B.C.E., by traders from the Phoenician Empire who established centers along the Mediterranean
coast. During the seventh century B.C.E., the city of CARTHAGE
developed as an important maritime trade metropolis in an empire that stretched from North Africa to the Iberian Peninsula,
Sardinia, and Sicily. The city's diverse population reached about
a half million, including a number of Jews, who first brought
monotheism to the region.

During the reign of the Phoenicians, many of the formerly
pastoral Berber people began to cultivate the plains around
Carthage, transforming them into rich farmlands. The leaders
of the Roman Empire saw the advantage of acquiring the fertile region, and beginning in the third century B.C.E. they
launched the Punic Wars, finally overcoming the Phoenicians
in northern Africa in 146 B.C.E. The victors tore down the conquered city of Carthage, but maintained the region's agriculture to produce wheat, wool, and olive oil for the empire. Once
rebuilt, Carthage became a center for Christian scholarship and
the home of Berber philosopher St. AUGUSTINE. Some of the

Berber inhabitants converted to Christianity, for the most part
joining the Donatist sect.

In general, the Berbers resented Roman rule, for the empire
had appropriated much of the best land. In the fifth century
C.E., disgruntled Berbers assisted the Germanic Vandals as they
took Carthage, by then the third most important city of the Roman Empire. A century later, the Byzantine army under Emperor Justinian attempted to reestablish Roman rule, but was
mostly limited to coastal areas by active Berber resistance. The
Byzantines were finally defeated by a Bedouin raiding party
from Egypt in the seventh century.

Islamic Conquest and Rule

When the Arabs swept into North Africa during the seventh
century, they founded the city of KAIROUAN, south of present-
day TUNIS, as the cultural center and holy city of a land known
to the Arabs as Ifriqiya, or Africa. For centuries, the region was
part of an Islamic empire, the Maghreb, stretching across much
of North Africa.

Although Islam spread through the region with relative ease,
the original Arab conquerors in Ifriqiya faced a series of Berber
revolts. One of the great resistance leaders was the KAHINA, a
Berber queen who led her army against the Arabs, checking
their advancement in Ifriqiya for more than ten years. In 800
C.E., Ibrahim ibn Aghlab consolidated rule in the province,
founding the Aghlabid Dynasty that over the next century profited from the trade that passed from the trans-Saharan route to
the Mediterranean. In 909 C.E., the Fatimids, with the assistance of Berber forces, overthrew this dynasty and took control of Ifriqiya. Basing their empire to the east, they relegated
the region to vassal state and left it in the care of the Berber
ally Buluggin ibn Ziri. When his descendants revolted a century later, the Fatimids mobilized Arab Bedouins against them.
Yet as the Zirids fell in the twelfth century, it was not the Fatimids who took power, but the al-Muwahhid kingdom of the
west.

During the thirteenth century the Hafsid monarchy, Berber
descendants of the al-Muwahhid Dynasty, rose to power. They
shifted the capital from the interior to coastal Tunis, near the
ruins of Carthage, signifying an increased emphasis on maritime trade in a region that would soon after become known
as Tunisia. In 1534, as the powerful Ottoman Empire cast its
shadow over the region, the Hafsids entered into an alliance
with the Spanish Hapsburgs.

The Spanish were defeated in 1574 by the Ottoman Empire,
assisted by a population that resented Christian rule. Junior Ottoman officers settled the area, mixing in with the Berber inhabitants. During the seventeenth and eighteenth centuries, the
region was controlled by local governors, deys (later beys),
nominally subject to the Ottoman Empire, but in fact operating semi-independently. Like all previous regimes, the deys, including the Muradid and Husaynid dynasties, emphasized trade
and enriched the region through the production and export of
olive oil. These dynasties also profited from piracy and protection money extracted from nations trading in the Mediterranean.

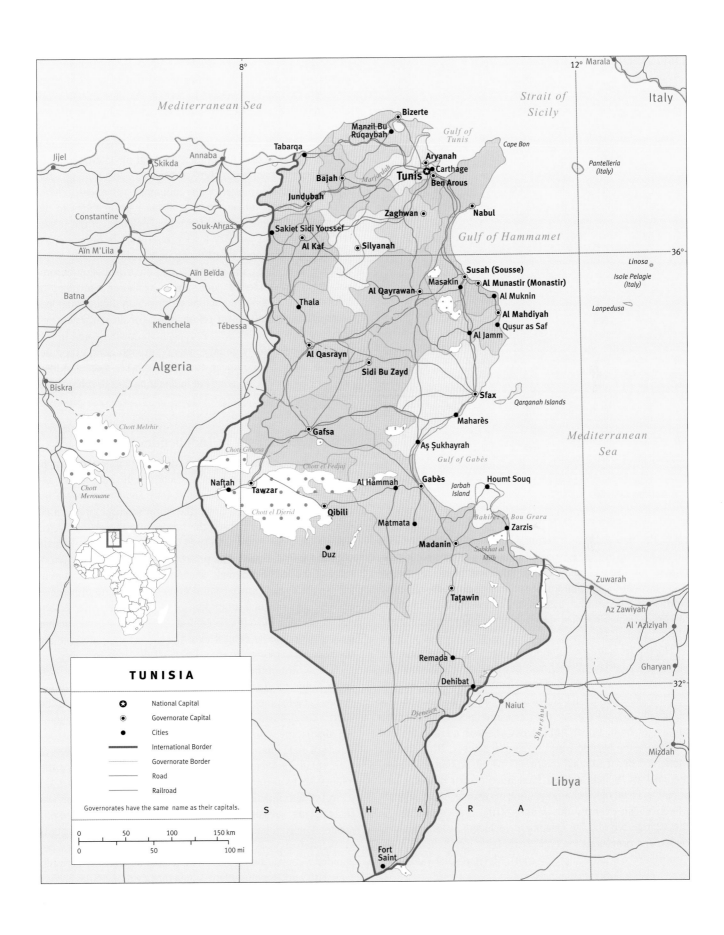

Mediterranean Sea

Strait of
Sicily

Italy

Marala

Jijel

Skikda

Annaba

Tabarqa

Manzil Bu
Ruqaybah

Bizerte

Gulf of
Tunis

Cape Bon

Pantelleria
(Italy)

Constantine

Souk-Ahras

Bajah

Jundubah

Sakiet Sidi Youssef

Al Kaf

Aryanah

Carthage

Tunis

Ben Arous

Marjardah

Zaghwan

Nabul

Gulf of Hammamet

36°

Aïn M'Lila

Silyanah

Linosa

Isole Pelagie
(Italy)

Aïn Beïda

Susah (Sousse)

Masakin

Al Munastir (Monastir)

Batna

Al Qayrawan

Al Muknin

Lanpedusa

Khenchela

Thala

Al Mahdiyah

Quşur as Saf

Tébessa

Al Jamm

Biskra

Al Qasrayn

Sidi Bu Zayd

Algeria

Sfax

Qarqanah Islands

Maharès

Mediterranean
Sea

Chott Melrhir

Gafsa

Aş Şukhayrah

Gulf of Gabès

Naftah

Al Hammah

Gabès

Houmt Souq

Chott Ghursa

Chott el Fedjaj

Jarbah
Island

Chott
Merouane

Tawzar

Qibili

Matmata

Zarzis

Bahiret el Bou Grara

Chott el Djerid

Sabkhat al
Milh

Duz

Madanin

Zuwarah

Taţawin

Az Zawiyah

Al 'Aziziyah

Remada

Gharyan

Dehibat

32°

TUNISIA

National Capital

Governorate Capital

Cities

International Border

Governorate Border

Road

Railroad

Governorates have the same name as their capitals.

Naiut

Djeneien

Shurshuf

Libya

Mizdah

0   50   100   150 km

0   50   100 mi

S   A   H   A   R   A

Fort
Saint

8°

12°

France reinforced its African defenses in Tunisia at the start of World War II. *Bettman/Corbis*

In the mid-eighteenth century, a series of plagues swept through North Africa, killing Tunisians by the thousands. This population loss, combined with a simultaneous prolonged drought, sent the agricultural economy into crisis. By the 1830s North Africa was further destabilized by the imperial ambitions of FRANCE, which had just seized ALGERIA, and the death throes of the Ottoman Empire.

Hoping to maintain autonomy in the face of European imperialism, Tunisian ruler Ahmad Bey set out to strengthen the Tunisian state through modernization. He modeled his government after European bureaucracies, conscripted peasants for his greatly expanded army and navy, and imposed heavy taxes to pay for both. Under Ahmad Bey, Tunisia became the first country in the Islamic world to abolish slavery. His successor Mohamed Bey continued reform efforts, instituting the Fundamental Pact, which allowed foreigners to own property, and adopting a civil rights charter. During his regime, MAMLUK leader Khayr ad-Din oversaw the writing of the first constitution in the Islamic world. The document included a declaration of rights, and provisions for a legislative body called the Supreme Council and a secular supreme court. Khayr ad-Din was elected leader of the Supreme Council.

Some Tunisians opposed the reforms because they saw them as representative of excessive European influence, and pushed for changes more compatible with Islamic law and culture. Many others opposed the high taxes. Provincial leaders and tribal chiefs saw the national constitution as a threat to their autonomy. Although Ahmad Bey hoped that loans from European banks would help build a new nation, the Tunisian economy stagnated as it fell deeper into debt. The situation was exacerbated by erratic spending and massive embezzlement by Prime Minister Mustafa Khaznader. While civil unrest mounted, Tunisia declared bankruptcy in 1869, and an international financial commission consisting of France, GREAT BRITAIN, and ITALY was formed to oversee the monarchy's finances.

In 1873 Khayr ad-Din, then Tunisian representative to the international financial commission, was elected prime minister. In a last effort to delay foreign intervention, he attempted to boost the economy by restoring guild control in artisan industries, investing more in education, and eradicating corruption from the ranks of government, including the allies of Mustafa Khaznader. Although he worked with the international commission, his efforts to reform the agricultural system led him into direct conflict with European landowners, and his attempt to secure the national economy through grain export set him up against a European-controlled market system. Khayr ad-Din was unable to avoid the impending catastrophe of foreign intervention.

From Colonialism to Independence

Enemies from within the Tunisian court who supported Mustafa Khaznader plotted with European consuls to oust Khayr ad-Din. The French, who vied against Italy and Great Britain for control in the region, occupied the country on the pretext that some Tunisians had crossed the border into French-controlled Algeria. In 1881 France declared a protectorate over Tunisia with the Bardo Treaty. The protectorate maintained the structures of the old government, such as the monarchical figure of the bey, but gave France control of the finances and the French resident general final arbitration of all decisions. After crushing an uprising in southern Tunisia, the French signed another treaty tightening its control over the protectorate, and paving the way for settler colonies.

By the turn of the century, French settlers had appropriated some of the most fertile farmland—much of it devoted to export vegetable production—and began phosphate mining in the south. Yet compared to the European population in neighboring Algeria, the settlers exercised relatively minor influence over Tunisian religious and cultural life. This was in part due to their small numbers, which never exceeded 7 percent of the total population throughout the period of French control.

In the late nineteenth century, reformist social movements such as the Western-educated Young Tunisians lobbied for greater Tunisian participation in government and better access to Western-style education. In 1920 the Destour Party demanded a constitutional government ensuring equality between Tunisians and French settlers. When the bey took up the party's cause two years later, the French used the threat of military force to shut down the movement.

Tunisia (At a Glance)

OFFICIAL NAME: Tunisian Republic

AREA: 163,610 sq km (63,170 sq mi)

LOCATION: Northern Africa, bordering the Mediterranean Sea, Algeria, and Libya

CAPITAL: Tunis (population 690,940); 2001 estimate

OTHER MAJOR CITIES: Safaqis (Sfax) (population 263,840), Al-Arianah (205,940), Susah (Sousse) (149,420); 2001 estimates

POPULATION: 9,924,742 (2003 estimate)

POPULATION DENSITY: 60.7 persons per sq km (about 157 persons per sq mi); about 75 percent of the population live in the coastal region

POPULATION BELOW AGE 15: 27 percent (male 1,388,839; female 1,297,313); 2003 estimate

POPULATION GROWTH RATE: 1.1 percent (2003 estimate)

LIFE EXPECTANCY AT BIRTH: Total population: 74.4 years (male 72.77 years; female 76.15 yea); 2003 estimate

INFANT MORTALITY RATE: 26.91 deaths per 1,000 live births (2003 estimate)

LITERACY RATE (AGE 15 AND OVER WHO CAN READ AND WRITE): Total population: 74.2 percent (male 84 percent; female 64.4 percent); 2003 estimate

EDUCATION: Education in Tunisia is free, and virtually all eligible children attend primary school. In the early 2000s, Tunisia sepnt about 20 percent of its GDP on education.

LANGUAGES: Arabic is the official language of Tunisia, but French is used widely, particularly by the educated.

ETHNIC GROUPS: Arab-Berber 98 percent, European 1 percent, Jewish 1 percent

RELIGIONS: Muslim 98 percent, Christian 1 percent, Jewish 1 percent

CLIMATE: A mild Mediterranean climate prevails in the north of Tunisia, with temperatures averaging 8.9° C (48° F) in January and 25.6° C (78° F) in July; the northern regions have a rainy season that lasts from October to May, with an average annual rainfall of 610 mm (about 24 in). Toward the south the climate becomes progressively hotter and drier, with an annual rainfall of about 200 mm (about 8 in) in the Sahara.

LAND, PLANTS, AND ANIMALS: In the north low-lying spurs of the Maritime Atlas Mountains traverse the country, interspersed with fertile valleys and plains. The country's only major river, the Majardah, crosses the region from west to east, emptying into the Gulf of Tunis. To the south a plateau descends gradually to a chain of low-lying salt lakes, known as *shatts*, or *chotts*. On the south the shatts adjoin the Sahara, which constitutes about 40 percent of Tunisia's land area. The regions of the north are characterized by flourishing vineyards and by dense forests of cork oak, pine, and juniper trees. In the extreme south date palms flourish in oases. Among the wildlife are hyena, wild boar, jackal, gazelle, and hare, as well as several varieties of poisonous snakes, including cobras and horned vipers.

NATURAL RESOURCES: Petroleum, phosphates, iron ore, lead, zinc, and salt

CURRENCY: The Tunisian dinar

GROSS DOMESTIC PRODUCT (GDP): $67.13 billion (2002 estimate)

GDP PER CAPITA: $6,800 (2002 estimate)

GDP REAL GROWTH RATE: 4.8 percent (2002 estimate)

PRIMARY ECONOMIC ACTIVITIES: The Tunisian economy is dominated by agriculture and mining. Tourism is also important, and manufacturing is expanding.

PRIMARY CROPS: Wheat, barley, tomatoes, vegetables, melons, grapes, oranges, olives, and dates; sheep, goats, cattle, camels, horses, and poultry; sardines, pilchards, tuna, and whitefish

INDUSTRIES: Petroleum, mining, tourism, textiles, footwear, food, and beverages

PRIMARY EXPORTS: Hydrocarbons, agricultural products, phosphates, chemicals, textiles, mechanical goods

PRIMARY IMPORTS: Industrial goods and equipment, hydrocarbons, food, and consumer goods

PRIMARY TRADE PARTNERS: European Union countries, Middle East, Algeria, India, United States, Japan, and Switzerland

GOVERNMENT: According to the constitution of 1959 Tunisia is a free, independent, and sovereign republic. National executive power in Tunisia is exercised by the president, currently Zine El Abidine Ben Ali, who appoints a council of ministers headed by a prime minister, currently Mohamed Ghannouchi. Legislative power in Tunisia is vested in the unicameral National Assembly, with 182 members popularly elected to five-year terms. The National Assembly is currently dominated by the Constitutional Democratic Rally Party (RCD; formerly the Destour Socialist Party). Tunisia is divided into twenty-four governorates, each headed by a governor who is appointed by the president.

In 1934 HABIB BOURGUIBA formed the Neo-Destour Party, an organization that became extraordinarily successful at mobilizing populist support for NATIONALISM. By 1937 the party had 28,000 activists and 49,000 supporters working out of 400 village branches. The Neo-Destour led the way for future decolonizing struggles through acts of civil disobedience, including a general strike in solidarity with nationalist movements in other North African countries. In 1938 the Neo-Destour Party

Tunisian woman spins wool for rugs. *Inge Yspeert/CORBIS*

was outlawed and Bourguiba and other leaders were arrested and deported to France. Four years later, when the Germans occupied both France and Tunisia, Bourguiba was released. Despite his refusal to support the Axis powers, he was allowed to return to Tunis, where he took a leading role in the nationalist struggle emerging in German-occupied Tunisia.

After the war, the French returned to power and arrested the bey for collaborating with the Nazis. Bourguiba fled and began an international tour campaigning for Tunisian independence. Following a brief period of liberalism, during which time Bourguiba returned to Tunisia, the nationalist movement gathered militant momentum, and revolutionaries based in the mountains waged a two-year guerrilla campaign. France gradually capitulated, first with the promise for internal autonomy, and later full sovereignty. During this time, many French citizens fled the country.

Post-Independence Tunisia

In 1956 Tunisia became an independent constitutional monarchy headed by the last Husainid bey with Bourguiba as president of the National Assembly (renamed the Chamber of Deputies in 1981). The next year, the bey was deposed and Bourguiba was elected president of a new republic. During the first years of the new republic, the war for independence in neighboring Algeria strained relations between Tunisia and its former colonial power. France accused Tunisia of siding with Algerian pro-nationalist forces, and in 1958 bombed the Tunisian village of Saqiyat Sidi Yusuf. A UNITED NATIONS–

mandated cease-fire eventually eased military tension, but France subsequently withdrew all financial aid. In turn, Tunisia forged alliances with other Arab countries, especially Saudi Arabia, but maintained its Western orientation.

The 1960s and 1970s were a dynamic period, as the nation followed a path of moderate SOCIALISM. Campaigns for social justice, women's rights, and education transformed the small country into one of the most literate and progressive in Africa. Bourguiba limited military spending, and allocated most of the national budget to education, agriculture, and health.

Yet popular opinion of Bourguiba and his policies was mixed, and many saw the legal and social reforms as an affront to traditional Islamic law and custom. He put formerly religious schools under secular control, abolished Islamic courts, and even advised workers to break the religious Ramadan fast in order to increase productivity—a suggestion that generated considerable public outrage. Some dissidents also noted that Bourguiba used extreme measure to consolidate his own power and that his tolerance for political opposition faded over the years. After driving his opponents from the Socialist Destour Party, the only legal political party, Bourguiba was named president for life in 1975, at the age of seventy-two.

The country remained in economic flux during this time. Bourguiba's early emphasis on state intervention gave way to economic liberalization. As the prices of consumer goods rose sharply while wages remained constant, workers organized mass strikes in 1978. Popular discontent combined with growing support for Islamic parties generated fears on the part of the administration of a fate similar to that of the rise of ISLAMIC FUNDAMENTALISM in Algeria. Bourguiba authorized mass arrests of union-based leftists and Islamic fundamentalists.

In 1987 Prime Minister Zine el-Abidine Ben Ali deposed Bourguiba, declaring him mentally unfit. The new president continued efforts to halt the rise of Islam, outlawing the main Islamic party, Al Nahda, in 1991, and arresting or exiling its leaders. Under Ben Ali, some 8,000 students and activists have been arrested, and human rights observers have accused the government of using detention and torture to quash dissent. Ben Ali has won re-election in each election since—1989, 1994, and 1999—and some outside observers question whether Tunisia's electoral process is completely free and fair. Nevertheless, in a May 2002 referendum, over 99 percent of voters agreed to changes in the constitution proposed by Ben Ali, and the voter turnout was an overwhelming 95 percent. One major constitutional change eliminates presidential term limits, allowing Ben Ali to run for a fourth term in 2004.

Since he has been president, Ben Ali has spearheaded social and economic modernization reforms such as the provision of electricity, running water, and health facilities to impoverished parts of the country. Under his leadership, Tunisia has developed into one of the most modern and prosperous countries in Africa. A greater proportion of its citizens (70 percent) are middle class than in any other African or Arab nation, it has the highest level of literacy and lowest level of poverty in Africa, and it spends more per person on education than any nation on earth.

Tunisian women enjoy a greater legal and social status than in most Arab countries. Women were granted full legal equality shortly after independence, and the practice of polygamy (taking more than one wife) was outlawed at that time. Parents are required to educate their daughters, and in the early twenty-first century over half of all Tunisian university students were female. However, some have accused Ben Ali of using reforms to undermine popular support for the Islamic movement—women, for example, have been encouraged to take more public roles, but then warned not to observe Islamic tradition by wearing headscarves. The conflicts are familiar ones for Tunisia, a nation that for more than a century has negotiated a path between Western-inspired reform and the religious and cultural legacy of Islam.

See also Colonial Rule; North Africa, Roman Rule of; North Africa and the Greco-Roman World; Slavery in Africa.

Marian Aguiar

Tunis, Tunisia

Capital of the North African country of Tunisia.

With a population of 690,940 (2001 estimate), the city of Tunis is now the most important political, commercial, and industrial center in Tunisia. This was not always the case, however. Although some historians claim that the ancient city was founded by Phoenicians as early as the ninth century B.C.E., for centuries Tunis was overshadowed by other Tunisian cities.

Tunis grew up along the shore of Lake Tunis, about ten miles from the metropolis of Carthage. When the Romans waged war on the Phoenicians during the second century, they made Tunis their base for their attack on Carthage. Victorious, the Romans destroyed both cities in 146 B.C.E.

Although the Romans rebuilt Tunis, the city remained obscured by the importance of Carthage, which by this time was a Christian center. When the Arabs arrived in North Africa in the seventh century, they valued Tunis as a strategic location able to withstand potential naval attacks. Arab leader Hassan ibn Numan also used Tunis as a base for his land-based military campaigns in the region the Arabs called Ifriqiya, including the struggle against the Berber resistance leader the Kahina. Most of the subsequent Arab dynasties ruled from the city of Kairouan, but Tunis also attracted immigrants from the Arab world. An urban elite of government officials, merchants, and scholars flocked to Tunis, including a sizeable population of Jews.

When the Berber Hafsids came to power in the thirteenth century, they revived Tunis as a royal city as well as a market town for handling goods passing along the trans-Sahara trade route to the Mediterranean Sea. Accumulating wealth through trade and piracy, the Hafsids built schools, mosques, and fortresses. During the sixteenth century, control of Tunis passed back and forth between the competing powers of Spain and the ultimately victorious Ottoman Empire. Ottoman direct rule was

short-lived, however: in 1591, a group of officers in the Ottoman military staged a coup and set up an independent monarchy. The subsequent rulers of Tunis, known as beys, continued maritime raiding until 1816, when the British ended the practice by bombarding the city. In the nineteenth century, European investors financed railways, a telegraph system, and other projects in Tunis. Europeans also settled in the city and along the lake, especially after Tunisia became a French protectorate in 1881.

In 1956, Tunis became the capital of independent Tunisia. Internationally, the city gained prominence when the Arab League moved its headquarters there in 1979, and then the Palestinian Liberation Organization (PLO), along with several thousand PLO leaders and their families, relocated there in 1982. Today, the city is home to about one-fifth of the country's total population. Tunisians have migrated to the city for its schools, hospitals, and employment opportunities. Industrial plants in Tunis produce chemicals, especially superphosphates, processed foods, and textiles, and a shipping channel carries exports of olives, olive oil, carpets, fruit, and iron ore to the Mediterranean Sea. Overall, Tunis produces about one-half of the national industrial output. Amid the new city, vestiges of the past remain—including the ruins of a Roman aqueduct, Roman baths, and the eighth-century Mosque of the Olive Tree—making Tunis an increasingly popular tourist destination. One of the city's newest attractions is a government-owned theme park, including amusement rides, that opened in 2002.

See also Jewish Communities in North Africa; North Africa and the Greco-Roman World; North Africa, Roman Rule of.

Bibliography
Perkins, Kenneth J. *Historical Dictionary of Tunisia.* 2nd ed. Scarecrow Press, 1997.

Marian Aguiar

Tunjur

Ethnic group of eastern Chad and western Sudan; also known as Tungur.

Although the Tunjur have dwindled in number to a population of around 10,000, they once ruled over a powerful kingdom, Darfur. The excavated palaces and citadels of the Tunjur dot the region today.

The origins of the Tunjur are unclear. Some scholarly sources maintain that they are an indigenous Nilotic group, and not of Arabic origin. Tunjur oral history, in contrast, traces their ancestry to Arabs from Tunisia. During the thirteenth century they apparently peacefully replaced the Daju, a neighboring ethnic group, as rulers of a large kingdom centered around the cities of Uri and Ayn Farah in northern Darfur. The kingdom stretched from Darfur in present-day Sudan to Wadai (Ouaddai) in present-day Chad. During the sixteenth century the Tunjur were themselves overthrown at Darfur by the Keira, a chiefly clan claiming Arab origin, who later merged with the region's predominant ethnic group, the FUR. The Tunjur remained in power, however, at Wadai. In the early seventeenth century, the MABA expelled the Tunjur from Wadai and installed an Islamic government. Many Tunjur subsequently migrated west to settle in the city of Mao in the Kanem kingdom. The rise of the Bornu kingdom frustrated the Tunjurs' renewed attempts at empire building.

Today most Tunjur, who are devout Sunni Muslims, continue to live in Darfur Province, Sudan, and in the Kanem and Wadai prefectures of Chad. Small numbers of Tunjur also live in NIGERIA. The Tunjur language is now extinct; most Tunjur speak Fur, Arabic, or Beri. Most cultivate cereal crops, such as MILLET and sorghum, and dates. Some Tunjur also grow fruits and vegetables in irrigated gardens, while others keep cattle, sheep, and goats.

See also Ethnicity and Identity in Africa: An Interpretation; Islam in Africa; Languages, African: An Overview.

Bibliography

Nachtigal, G. *Sahara and Sudan: Wadai and Darfur.* C. Hurst and Co., 1971.

O'Fahey, R. S., and J. L. Spaulding. *Kingdoms of the Sudan.* Methuen and Co., 1974.

Weekes, R. V., ed. *Muslim Peoples: A World Ethnographic Survey.* Aldwych Press, 1984.

Ari Nave

Tupur

Ethnic group of West Africa; also known as Toupouri, Tuburi, and Tupuri.

The Tupur primarily inhabit northern CAMEROON, southwestern CHAD, and northeastern NIGERIA. They speak an Afro-Asiatic language in the Chadic group. Over 400,000 people consider themselves Tupur.

See also Ethnicity and Identity in Africa: An Interpretation; Languages, African: An Overview.

Turkana

Ethnic group of Kenya.

The Turkana inhabit the arid region west of LAKE TURKANA in northwestern KENYA and regions in neighboring parts of northeastern UGANDA. They speak an Eastern Nilotic language. Scholars remain uncertain about the group's origin, but Turkana legend is more colorful: It claims that the people moved to their present homeland by following a lost ox. It is likely that they moved to their present location at least 200 years ago from Uganda, where they separated from the Jie and the KARIMOJON,

A Turkana woman carries a gourd of water on her head in Lokichar, in northern Nigeria. *David Keith Jones/Images of Africa Photobank*

who still live there. The Turkana descended the Dodoth escarpment into the Lake Turkana area.

The Turkana have historically been a pastoral society, raising cattle, CAMELS, sheep, goats, and donkeys, which provide the majority of their livelihood. The traditional diet of the people comprises meat, milk, butter, ghee, yogurt, and blood—all provided by their herds. In addition, their herds supply bones, skins, and horns for tools and clothing, and serve as bride wealth. To supplement their diet, the Turkana engage in small-scale cultivation (MILLET and vegetables), fishing, hunting, and gathering.

Traditionally, the Turkana establish no permanent settlements, and, because they live in areas that regularly receive less than fifteen inches of rain per year, they migrate seasonally with their herds in search of water and pasturage. The Turkana, therefore, establish temporary homesteads, including cattle pens and huts constructed of tree branches and palm fronds, in a thorn-fenced enclosure called a *kraal*. A traditional Turkana "camp" contains three or four such enclosures grouped loosely around a common amenity, such as a watering hole.

The basic social unit among the Turkana is an elementary family: a husband, a wife or wives, and their unmarried children. Though traditional Turkana society is based on clans—cattle are given an identifying clan brand—and based loosely on age sets, they do not strictly observe these social conventions. Age-sets have historically functioned only as a method of organizing raiding parties.

Though they number only about 300,000, many Turkana have clung to their traditional way of life in the face of mounting pressures. The British struggled to impose colonial authority in their territory long after establishing their rule in other parts of Kenya. Even as late as 1918, the British military was still trying to subdue the Turkana in a campaign that, while damaging to the people and their herds, did not bring an end to the group's independence. Since the 1950s, the Turkana population has tripled. In addition, many Turkana have become agriculturists cultivating marginal lands that were historically used for pasture, straining the remaining resources. These changes, combined with a series of droughts and cattle-raiding by rival nomadic groups from Uganda, ETHIOPIA, and the SUDAN, have devastated Turkana herds, and made the Turkana dependent on food aid from relief organizations. In addition, Kenya's former president, DANIEL ARAP MOI, gave oil-drilling concessions in the region to a close associate, Nicholas Biwott. This has exacerbated problems based on the Turkana's land shortage. Many observers predict that these factors will ultimately undermine the Turkana's way of life.

See also Ethnicity and Identity in Africa: An Interpretation; Languages, African: An Overview; Pastoralism.

Robert Fay

Turkana, Lake

One of the lakes of the Great Rift Valley, where Kenyan fossil hunter Richard Leakey discovered important hominid fossils; formerly called Lake Rudolf.

Commonly called the Jade Sea because of its color, Lake Turkana is located in the volcanic rock desert of northwestern KENYA; its northern tip lies in ETHIOPIA. The shallow, narrow lake is about 250 kilometers (160 miles) long and covers an area of 7,100 square kilometers (2,700 square miles). It is fed by the Omo River, from the north, but has no outlet.

Lake Turkana is most famous as the site where RICHARD LEAKEY unearthed fossils that transformed scientific understanding of human evolution. But the lake is also home to the pastoral TURKANA people, who keep cattle, CAMELS, goats, and sheep. The Turkana practice transhumance, moving their herds away from the lake during the dry season to areas of better pastures, and returning to the lake during the rainy season. Lake Turkana also provides refuge for the largest crocodile population in the world. Poachers ignore these crocodiles because the lake's alkaline water renders their hides worthless; consequently, many of them grow extremely large. In addition, Lake Turkana supports large numbers of fish, including Nile perch, tigerfish, bichir, and TILAPIA.

See also Rift Valleys.

Bibliography

Pern, Stephen. *Another Land, Another Sea: Walking Round Lake Rudolph.* Gollancz, 1979.

Robert Fay

Turks and Caicos Islands

Two groups of islands in the North Atlantic Ocean, southeast of the Bahamas.

In *The History of Mary Prince, A West Indian Slave* (1831), the first female SLAVE NARRATIVE from the Americas, MARY PRINCE writes of her experience in the salt mines off Grand Turk Island—where slaves were forced to stand in the water and rake salt from the ocean beds, from four in the morning until nightfall every day:

> We . . . worked through the heat of the day; the sun flaming upon our hands like fire, and raising salt blisters in those parts which were not completely covered. Our feet and legs, from standing in the salt water for so many hours, soon became full of dreadful boils, which eat down in some cases to the very bone, afflicting the sufferers with great torment . . . Oh that Turk's Island was a horrible place! The people in England, I am sure, have never found out what is carried on there. Cruel, horrible place!

The sad irony was that the horrible conditions under which Prince labored were enforced by English slaveholders, and their Spanish and French counterparts, for thousands of slaves in the Turks and Caicos Islands throughout the sixteenth and seventeenth centuries. The lucrative salt trade was the mainstay of these islands for several hundred years, and the cost to workers in the salt mines was tremendous.

The Turks and Caicos Islands' indigenous inhabitants were probably Taíno Indians. They were gradually replaced by Lucayan Arawak Indians around 500 C.E., and the Arawaks lived there peacefully for almost 900 years. The islands were changed forever with their "discovery" by European colonists at the turn of the sixteenth century. There is still discussion over who first sighted the islands; some scholars believe it was Ponce de Leon in 1512, while others claim the Turks were actually the site of Christopher Columbus's first landing in the New World in 1492. It is clear, however, that during the next 150 years the Spanish returned to the islands just long enough to capture the Lucayans who lived there and sell them into slavery in other Spanish holdings in the Caribbean. The name *Caicos* is one of the Lucayans' lasting legacies, since it comes from their word *caya hico,* or "string of islands." The name *Turks* refers to an indigenous cactus that the colonists thought resembled a Turkish fez.

In 1678 English settlers from BERMUDA began mining the salt flats in the Turks and Caicos Islands, bringing African slaves

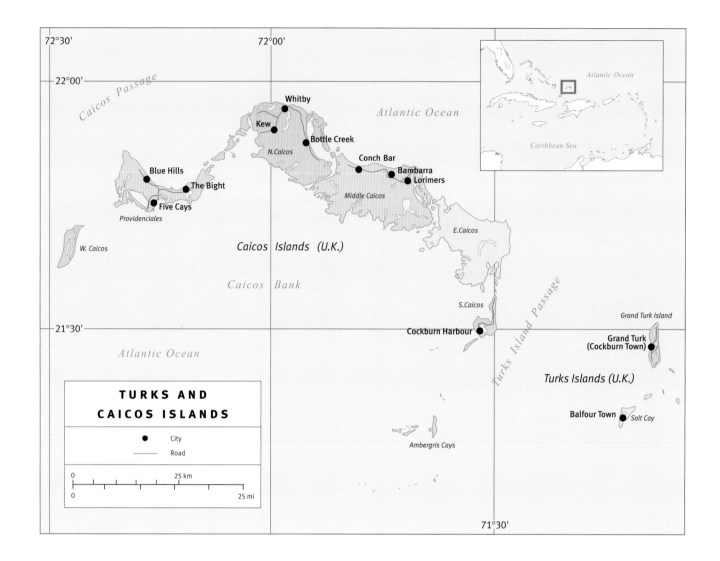

with them to do the miserable work. Salt immediately proved extremely profitable, and soon the British, Spanish, and French were fighting over the right to control the islands. Each group primarily used black slaves to carry out the mining. Cotton and sisal plantations were also established in the islands, but when the soil proved too thin to support them for very long, the focus returned to the salt flats.

By 1776 the Turks and Caicos Islands were officially declared part of the British Bahamian colony. The scene Mary Prince describes is from the beginning of the nineteenth century, when British rule had been firmly established. In 1834 slaves in the Turks and Caicos Islands finally became free when slavery was abolished in all British territories. But life in the islands remained dependent on the salt industry, and was very difficult for workers for decades to come.

As with many other territories in the Caribbean, the black majority in the Turks and Caicos Islands was prevented from holding any real political power until well into the twentieth century. The British themselves seemed unsure about how the Turks and Caicos Islands should be administered. From 1799 to 1848, they were governed as part of the Bahamas; from 1848 to 1873, they were granted their own internal government, con-

trolled by the island's white elite; and from 1873 to 1959, they were considered a dependency of JAMAICA

Throughout this period the population in the islands remained relatively small and scattered, which influenced the British decision to administer them together with larger territories. By 1959 the push for more self-government was growing throughout the Caribbean. That year, when Jamaica was granted its own governor for the first time, the governor of Jamaica also became governor of the Turks and Caicos Islands. But when Jamaica won full independence three years later, the Turks and Caicos Islands were declared a separate British dependency. In 1969 the constitution was changed so that the governor, who was nominated by the British monarch, shared power with a state council, whose members were largely elected.

In 1976 the constitution was changed once more to establish ministerial government, giving the position of chief minister to the leader of the legislature's ruling party. The People's Democratic Movement party won the 1976 elections, and supported independence for the Turks and Caicos Islands. They promised to push for independence if they were reelected in 1980, essentially making the 1980 elections a referendum on

Turks and Caicos Islands (At a Glance)

OFFICIAL NAME: Turks and Caicos Islands

AREA: 430 sq km (166 sq mi)

LOCATION: Two groups of islands in the North Atlantic Ocean southeast of the Bahamas and north of Haiti

CAPITAL: Grand Turk (population 4,500; 2000 estimate)

POPULATION: 19,350 (2004 estimate)

POPULATION DENSITY: 39.5 persons per sq km (102.7 per sq mi)

POPULATION BELOW AGE 15: 32.5 percent (male 3,202; female 3,094; 2003 estimate)

POPULATION GROWTH RATE: 3.14 percent (2003 estimate)

TOTAL FERTILITY RATE: 3.15 children born per woman (2003 estimate)

LIFE EXPECTANCY AT BIRTH: Total population: 74 years (male 71.82 years; female 76.3 years; 2003 estimate)

INFANT MORTALITY RATE: 16.87 deaths per 1,000 live births (2003 estimate)

LITERACY RATE (AGE 15 AND OVER WHO HAS EVER ATTENDED SCHOOL): Total population: 98 percent (male 99 percent; female 98 percent; 1970 estimate)

EDUCATION: Education is free and compulsory for children between the ages of five and fifteen.

LANGUAGES: English is the official language of the Turks and Caicos Islands.

ETHNIC GROUPS: 90 percent black, 10 percent mixed-race, European, or North American

RELIGIONS: 40 percent of the inhabitants of the Turks and Caicos Islands are Baptist, 16 percent are Methodist, 18 percent are Anglican, 12 percent are Church of God, and 14 percent are other religions

CLIMATE: Tropical savanna, with winter temperature ranges of 75° to 80° F (24° to 27° C) and summer ranges of 85° to 90° F (29° to 32° C). Grand Turk sees an average yearly rainfall of about 29 inches (736 millimetres); there is a shortage of drinking water. Hurricanes strike about once every decade during the May through November hurricane season.

LAND, PLANTS, AND ANIMALS: The coralline limestone Turks and Caicos islands are low-lying, with caverns, caves, and sea cliffs. There is little soil suitable for agriculture. Vegetation on these, the driest of the Bahamas islands, includes scrub, mangroves, pines, and cacti. Wildlife includes iguanas, flamingos, and migratory birds, but mostly insects (particularly mosquitos and butterflies).

NATURAL RESOURCES: Spiny lobster and conch

CURRENCY: United States dollar (USD)

GROSS DOMESTIC PRODUCT (GDP): $231 million (2002 estimate)

GDP PER CAPITA: $9,600 (2002 estimate)

GDP REAL GROWTH RATE: 4.9 percent (2002 estimate)

PRIMARY ECONOMIC ACTIVITIES: Government, agriculture and fishing, tourism, financial and other services

PRIMARY CROPS: Corn, beans, cassava (tapioca), citrus fruits, and fish

INDUSTRIES: Tourism and offshore financial services

PRIMARY EXPORTS: Lobster, dried and fresh conch, and conch shells

PRIMARY IMPORTS: Food and beverages, tobacco, clothing, manufactures, and construction materials

PRIMARY TRADE PARTNERS: United States and United Kingdom

GOVERNMENT: The Turks and Caicos islands are an overseas territory of the United Kingdom. The chief of state is Queen Elizabeth II, represented by Governor Jim Poston (since December 2002; appointed by the monarch). The head of government is Chief Minister Derek H. Taylor (since January 1995; the leader of the majority party is appointed chief minister by the governor following legislative elections). The legislative branch is the nineteen-member unicameral Legislative Council (thirteen members are popularly elected to serve four-year terms). The judicial branch is the Supreme Court.

Shelle Sumners

independence. However, they subsequently lost their reelection campaign.

Many Turks and Caicos Islands voters remain hesitant about independence for their tiny country. For much of the twentieth century, there was a serious push by many islanders to have their country annexed to Canada; in the mid-1970s, the question was considered in the Canadian Parliament. Canada ultimately declined because of fears of racial tensions between black islanders and the white Canadian majority, but in the mid-1980s 90 percent of Turks and Caicos residents continued

to support association with Canada. In 1985 a major corruption scandal hit the islands—the chief minister, the minister of commerce and development, and another member of the Legislative Council were all arrested in the United States for drug trafficking. This did little to instill confidence in the Turks and Caicos Islands' own government.

But in the 1990s, economic conditions were slowly improving, and helping to stabilize the country. It was not until the 1960s that the salt industry, formerly the mainstay of the economy, finally collapsed, after international competition had proved too much for the islands' unprofitable production techniques. Like many other Caribbean countries, the Turks and Caicos Islands then turned to tourism. Many Turks and Caicos Islanders have left the island seeking higher education or employment. But as tourism develops, poor immigrants from neighboring islands have begun coming to the Turks and Caicos Islands in search of jobs. Offshore banking has also brought new jobs to the islands. As a result of these developments, the population has fluctuated several times over the last few decades as the ratio of immigrants to emigrants continues to shift. These changes are still in progress, and they will shape the course of the Turks and Caicos Islands for the next century.

Lisa Clayton Robinson

Turner, Big Joe

1911–1985

African American singer, one of the most distinctive blues performers and a major influence on early rock music.

Joseph Vernon Turner was born in KANSAS CITY, MISSOURI. As a child he sang in church and performed for tips on the streets of his hometown. In the mid-1920s, though still just a boy, he began singing in clubs and was soon working regularly. At one such club he alternated between bartending and singing with the house band, which included BOOGIE-WOOGIE pianist Pete Johnson. In December 1938 Turner and Johnson traveled to NEW YORK CITY for music critic and concert producer John Hammond's "Spirituals to Swing" concert at Carnegie Hall. Together they gave a stunning performance of "It's All Right, Baby" (also called "Roll 'em Pete"). A few days later Turner, accompanied by pianists Johnson, Albert Ammons, and MEADE "LUX" LEWIS, began an extended engagement at Café Society on 52nd Street. In the early 1940s Turner moved to the LOS ANGELES, CALIFORNIA, area to sing in the musical *Jump for Joy,* which was produced by bandleader DUKE ELLINGTON.

In 1951 Turner began a long association with Atlantic Records. During those years his versions of "Shake, Rattle, and Roll" (1954), "Corrina Corrina" (1956), and other songs became well known in the RHYTHM AND BLUES (R&B) world. However, the songs became much more famous when rerecorded by rock-and-roll singers, such as Bill Haley. Late in Turner's life obesity and other health problems forced him to limit his performing activities. In 1970 he appeared in the film short *L.A. All-Stars,* and he later revisited Kansas City to take part in the film *The Last of the Blue Devils* (1979).

Turner and fellow Midwesterner JIMMY RUSHING were perhaps the two finest BLUES singers of the 1930s and 1940s. Both men had powerful tenor voices with which they easily projected their songs, and they became known as blues shouters. But while Rushing sang popular songs as well as blues, Turner concentrated almost entirely on blues numbers throughout his career. In later years his diction became increasingly slurred. As music critic Whitney Balliett wrote in *American Singers*

(1988), Turner would "push his words together, lopping off the consonants and flattening the vowels." His vocal range and tone quality never changed, and his impeccable sense of time and blues melody never diminished. Turner was inducted posthumously into the Rock and Roll Hall of Fame in 1987.

See also Film, Blacks in American; Music, African American.

Turner, Charles H(enry)

1867–1923

African American biologist and educator.

Charles Henry Turner was born in CINCINNATI, OHIO, the son of Thomas Turner, a church custodian, and Adeline Campbell, a nurse. Although neither parent had attended college, Thomas Turner would eventually earn a reputation as "a well-read man, a keen thinker, and a master of debate [who] surrounded himself with several hundred choice books." Both parents, but especially the father, imparted a love of learning to young Charles. After graduating valedictorian of his high school class in Cincinnati, he proceeded to the University of Cincinnati, where he earned a B.S. in 1891 and an M.S. in 1892. His goal was to teach science and ultimately to head a technological or agricultural school for African Americans. As an undergraduate he came under the influence of Clarence Luther Herrick, a professor of biology at Cincinnati and pioneer in the field of psychobiology. When Herrick established the *Journal of Comparative Neurology* in 1891, Turner became a regular contributor; he published eight research articles and at least six abstracts in the journal between 1891 and 1901. Text and illustrations from his undergraduate thesis, "Morphology of the Avian Brain," appeared in the inaugural volume.

Turner's first teaching appointments were at the Governor Street School in Evansville, Indiana (1888–1889), and for a brief period subsequently (1889) as a substitute in the Cincinnati public schools. In 1891 he was appointed to an assistantship in the biological laboratory at the University of Cincinnati, a position he held for two years. Anxious, as he put it, to "get to work among my own people," he wrote to BOOKER T. WASHINGTON in April 1893 requesting notification of any openings at black colleges. Later that year he became professor of biology and head of the department of science and agriculture at the all-black Clark University in ATLANTA, GEORGIA. His tenure at Clark (1893–1905) was followed by posts at other black schools: principal of College Hill High School, Cleveland, Tennessee (1906); professor of biology and chemistry at Haines Normal and Industrial Institute, Augusta, Georgia (1907–1908); and instructor in biology at Sumner High School, St. Louis, Missouri (1908–1923). Sumner, founded in 1875, was highly regarded for the caliber of its faculty, which at one time had included EDWARD A. BOUCHET, the first African American to receive a Ph.D. (in physics from Yale, 1876).

In 1907 Turner earned his Ph.D. in zoology (magna cum laude) at the University of Chicago. At Chicago he worked under the eminent zoologists Charles Otis Whitman, Charles Manning Child, and Frank Rattray Lillie. He was one of the earliest black Americans to earn a doctorate in the biological sciences (Alfred O. Coffin had earned one at Illinois Wesleyan University in 1889). Turner's doctoral thesis, a study of the "homing" mechanism in ants, marked a watershed in his scientific research. Earlier, his work had followed classic morphological lines—that is, examination of an organism's form and structure by means of microscopic observation in the laboratory. Following his time at Chicago, his work became more behavioral, focusing on animals in the field, in their natural habitat. His goal was to continue developing insights into elusive problems of neurology and comparative psychology—problems first introduced to him by Herrick at Cincinnati.

While teaching in St. Louis, Turner established himself as an authority on insect behavior. He was the first to fully describe a unique movement—a pattern of gyration—that certain species of ant go through when returning to their nests. This movement came to be widely known, in the scientific literature, as "Turner's circling." Turner also showed that ant movement is influenced by landmarks and light, that bees respond to color and pattern as well as odor, that wasps and burrowing bees may memorize landmarks adjacent to their nests, that ant lions lie motionless for prolonged periods out of an involuntary response to external stimuli ("terror paralysis") rather than as a self-concealment or camouflage reflex, that certain insects can hear and distinguish pitch, and that cockroaches learn by trial and error (but forget quickly). The innovative experimental techniques and ingenious devices that Turner developed to carry out his work were admired and often emulated by other scientists. His reputation for accuracy and thoroughness resulted in several invitations to contribute annual literature reviews on insect behavior, vertebrate and invertebrate behavior, tropisms, and other topics to *Psychological Bulletin* and *Journal of Animal Behavior*. In all, he published over fifty scientific articles (with at least three others appearing posthumously). His work appeared in major journals, such as *Science, American Naturalist,* and *Biological Bulletin.*

Turner's research was carried out with his own resources and in his spare time. The focus of his professional life was teaching. At Sumner he inspired in his students a curiosity about the natural world that outlasted their high-school years. Also active in black civic organizations, Turner served as a director of the Colored Branch, St. Louis YMCA. He wrote occasional papers on racial issues for the *Southwestern Christian Advocate* and other publications. One article, "Will the Education of the Negro Solve the Race Problem?" (1902), supported W. E. B. Du Bois's contention (in opposition to Booker T. Washington) that college or university education—not industrial training—was the best way to stimulate prosperity for blacks and to promote interracial harmony. Drawing on his work as a biologist, Turner compared human and animal "societies." He theorized, for example, that "animals are prejudiced against animals unlike themselves, and the more unlike they are the greater the prejudice," but that with humans "dissimilarity of minds is a more potent factor in causing prejudice than un-

likeness of physiognomy." He advanced this theory in support of his argument for equal educational opportunity, irrespective of race.

Turner was a member of the Entomological Society of America, the Academy of Science of Illinois, and the Academy of Science of St. Louis. He held elective office in the latter organization, serving terms as secretary of the entomology section and as council member. He was twice married, first (in 1888) to Leontine Troy of Cincinnati (she died in 1894) and later to Lillian Porter of Augusta, Georgia. Following his death in CHICAGO, a school for the physically handicapped—the Charles H. Turner School in St. Louis—was built in his memory.

Bibliography

A few Turner letters survive in the Herrick papers (part of the Neurology Collections), Department of Special Collections, Kenneth Spencer Research Library, University of Kansas.

Haines, D. E. "The Contributors to Volume 1 (1891) of *The Journal of Comparative Neurology*: C. L. Herrick, C. H. Turner, H. R. Pemberton, B. G. Wilder, F. W. Langdon, C. J. Herrick, C. von Kupffer, O. S. Strong, T. B. Stowell." *Journal of Comparative Neurology* 314 (1991): 9–23.

Hayden, Robert C. "Charles Henry Turner." In *Seven Black American Scientists*, 68–91. 1970.

Transactions of the Academy of Sciences of St. Louis 24 (December 1923), a special memorial issue in Turner's honor.

From *American National Biography.* John A. Garraty and Mark C. Carnes, eds. Oxford University Press, 1999. Reprinted by permission of the American Council of Learned Societies.

Kenneth R. Manning

Turner, Henry McNeal

1834–1915

African Methodist Episcopal Church leader, Reconstruction-era Georgia politician, outspoken defender of African American rights, prominent leader of back-to-Africa movements, and supporter of the American Colonization Society.

Henry McNeal Turner was, along with FREDERICK DOUGLASS and the Reverend HENRY HIGHLAND GARNET, one of the preeminent African American leaders of the late nineteenth century. Turner was born free to a teenaged mother, Sarah Turner, in Newberry Courthouse, South Carolina. His maternal grandmother, Hannah Greer—who voiced great pride in her African heritage—had a powerful influence on young Henry. From an early age, he envisioned becoming a leader of his people. While he was a teenager, Turner experienced a powerful religious conversion during a Methodist camp meeting at Sharon Camp Ground and soon decided to pursue a career in the ministry. In 1853 the nineteen-year-old Turner became a traveling evangelist for the METHODIST EPISCOPAL CHURCH-South.

In 1858 Turner joined the AFRICAN METHODIST EPISCOPAL CHURCH (AME) and during the next five years served as a minister to three different congregations in BALTIMORE, MARYLAND, and WASHINGTON, D.C. In 1863, when the Union Army began accepting African American enlistments, Turner raised the first black regiment of the CIVIL WAR and was commissioned as its chaplain. Following the war, he traveled to Georgia and, after serving briefly as an agent of the Freedmen's Bureau, became responsible for all of Georgia's AME missions.

Turner's energetic efforts led to a rapid expansion of AME membership throughout the state. In 1876 he was made manager of the church's publishing department. In taking up this new challenge, he declared, "[A] race that cannot produce its own literature hardly amounts to a cypher." In 1880 he was elevated to bishop, one of the first southern-born bishops in the history of the denomination.

Between 1867 and 1871, however, Turner devoted most of his prodigious energy to politics. In 1867 he helped organize the REPUBLICAN PARTY in Georgia and was elected as a delegate to the state constitutional convention. In the following year, he won a seat in the state legislature, but in 1869 all twenty-three black legislators were illegally unseated by their white Democratic and Republican colleagues. Turner then served briefly as postmaster in Macon, Georgia, and in 1870 he was again elected to the state legislature.

During the immediate postwar years Turner's political outlook was quite conservative. When he arrived in Georgia, for example, he opposed the distribution of land to former slaves and instead encouraged freed blacks to welcome their newly won "freedom of labor." While serving as a state legislator, he supported a petition of clemency for Jefferson Davis, former leader of the Confederate rebellion, and opposed the forced sale of plantations for nonpayment of taxes. He was, however, an active supporter of public education, which had been virtually nonexistent in Georgia and most of the South prior to RECONSTRUCTION.

But as Turner encountered the pervasive and vitriolic antiblack hostility of many white southerners, he became more politically militant. In particular, he revised his earlier sanguine assessment of the opportunities available to his people. He was a staunch defender of the Civil Rights Act of 1875 and harshly condemned the U.S. Supreme Court for an 1882 decision that largely vitiated that legislation.

During the 1870s Turner grew disenchanted with the prospects for African Americans in the United States. In 1871 he argued for black migration out of the South and suggested HAITI as a possible destination. Three years later he proposed that the federal government reserve New Mexico Territory for African American settlement. From the early 1870s he also advocated immigration to AFRICA. He saw a twofold purpose in this move to Africa: African Americans would be able to win credit for their accomplishments, and they would fulfill God's purpose by Christianizing the Africans.

Throughout his life, Turner remained passionately devoted to the interests of African Americans, but his black national-

ism also at times led him into suspect alliances with antiblack whites. In 1876, for example, he became vice president of the white-dominated AMERICAN COLONIZATION SOCIETY, which many blacks regarded as a racist organization. In speeches, pamphlets, and conferences, Turner pressed his point that emigration offered African Americans their best opportunity to prosper and advance. He also argued that the federal government should underwrite the enterprise in partial reparation for slavery.

During the 1890s Turner made four trips to Africa, visiting LIBERIA, SIERRA LEONE, British SOUTH AFRICA, and the TRANSVAAL. Yet he never limited himself to a single issue, including colonization. During the 1890s he vehemently opposed America's imperialist ventures in Hawaii, CUBA, and the Philippines. In 1892 he became editor of the AME magazine *Voice of Missions* and, in the years that followed, published articles on African American history, civil rights issues, racial discrimination, and other topics.

During the 1890s more African Americans were the victims of LYNCHING than at any other time in American history. In the *Voice of Missions* for March 1897, Turner advised every black man to acquire firearms and "to keep them loaded and prepared for immediate use." Should their homes be "invaded by bloody lynchers or any mob day or night," Turner proclaimed, they should "blow the fiendish wretches into a thousand giblets."

Turner's outspoken stand against lynching was the subject of widespread discussion, noted his biographer Stephen Ward Angell, and it extended as far away as South Africa. Yet during the early twentieth century Turner once again made a conservative shift, siding with the conciliatory BOOKER T. WASHINGTON rather than the more militant W. E. B. DU BOIS. Turner died of a stroke while attending an AME gathering in Windsor, CANADA; he was eighty-one years old.

See also Antilynching Movement; Clergy in Politics; Military, Blacks in the American.

James Sellman

Turner, Lorenzo Dow

1895–1972

American linguist and ethnologist who identified and analyzed African survivals in African American language.

Lorenzo Dow Turner received a bachelor's degree from HOWARD UNIVERSITY in 1914, a master's degree from Harvard University in 1917, and a doctoral degree from the University of Chicago in 1926. He taught English at several black colleges, and initially became interested in linguistics after hearing the black GULLAH dialect.

In 1931, Turner became the first African American member of the Linguistics Society. His research on Gullah, Creole, and the Niger-Kordofanian language family established connections between African languages and African American dialects, and helped rebut the common Western belief that African culture had not influenced the New World.

See also Languages, African: An Overview.

Bibliography

Turner, Lorenzo Dow. *Africanisms in the Gullah Dialect.* University of Chicago Press, 1949. Reprint, University of Michigan, 1974.

Lisa Clayton Robinson

Turner, Nat

1800–1831

American slave who led the largest and most significant slave revolt in United States history.

Nat Turner was born on Benjamin Turner's plantation in Southampton County, Virginia, five days before the execution of African American revolutionary Gabriel Prosser, who planned a slave revolt in RICHMOND, VIRGINIA. Turner's father, a Benjamin Turner slave whose name is unknown, successfully escaped and is believed to have spent his life with other escaped slaves in the Great Dismal Swamp, which lies in southern Virginia and in North Carolina.

Turner's mother, a slave named Nancy who had been kidnapped from Africa in 1793, believed that her son was destined for great things in his life, and she instilled a sense of this in him. As a boy, Turner learned to read and write, adding weight to his mother's convictions. Turner also accepted CHRISTIANITY in his youth, became a preacher, and identified religion with freedom. He claimed to receive religious visions throughout his life.

Turner sought his own freedom, running away in 1821 after he became the property of Benjamin Turner's son, Samuel. Nat Turner escaped when Samuel Turner hired a harsh overseer, and he remained free for approximately one month. During that time he experienced a vision indicating that he would lead a slave rebellion, and he returned to the plantation to await his signal to begin his campaign.

From 1825 to 1830, Turner was a popular preacher to African American congregations throughout Southampton County. His sermons focused on conflict and liberation and gained him many followers, some of whom believed he was a prophet. Traveling from church to church allowed Turner to gather the knowledge he needed to organize his revolt, such as road locations and hiding places.

In February 1831, Turner, who was now a slave in the home of Joseph Travis, believed that an eclipse of the sun signaled that the time had come for him to launch his rebellion. He recruited four other slaves, and they developed several plans before accepting one and deciding to begin on the symbolic date of July 4. However, Turner became ill and the uprising was delayed. On August 13, Turner interpreted a bluish-green sky as

a positive sign. The group, now consisting of Turner and seven other slaves, agreed to strike after midnight on August 22. The revolt began at the Travis home, where the rebels killed everyone in the household. Turner intended to move from house to house killing whites regardless of age and sex. He hoped that the show of force would intimidate neighboring whites and encourage other slaves to join the rebellion. After they had obtained a foothold, they agreed that the wholesale slaughter would cease.

Turner's destination was Jerusalem, Virginia, the Southampton County seat and home of an arsenal that would allow the insurgents to arm themselves adequately. As the band moved from house to house, more slaves joined the rebellion until it eventually totaled sixty or seventy. As the group got bigger, the rebels were weakened because they became less organized and they lost the element of surprise that had worked so effectively. A militia met the insurrectionists on the afternoon of August 22 but retreated soon after to reorganize.

When the slave army stopped at James Parker's farm for fresh recruits and supplies, the militia, which had regrouped, struck again. Turner's army was dispersed, and although Turner attempted to rally his troops, white reinforcements arrived and began a brutal counterattack in which they killed over 100 blacks. Turner survived and fled, eluding his captors until October 30. He was quickly tried, sentenced to death, and hanged in Jerusalem, Virginia, on November 11, 1831. While awaiting execution, he told his story to his court-appointed attorney, Thomas Gray. The result was an extraordinary account of his life and of the rebellion, which Gray published as *Nat Turner's Confessions*.

Turner's rebellion lasted almost three days, killed fifty-seven white people, and resulted in the executions of over 100 African American rebels. Some call this rebellion the "First War," the AMERICAN CIVIL WAR (1861–1865) being the second. Turner's rebellion was significant in that it was more violent than any other slave uprising and reshaped the debate over SLAVERY IN THE UNITED STATES in ways that led to the Civil War a generation later. The uprising intensified both the antislavery movement, and the corresponding proslavery forces. It reinforced the notion held by some abolitionists that slaves would be willing to fight if outside forces organized and armed them. Proslavery forces began to endorse reducing the number of free blacks through colonization. Turner's rebellion also disproved the myth of the contented slave and proved that African Americans would die to end slavery.

See also Abolitionism in the United States; Slave Rebellions in the United States.

Bibliography

Aptheker, Herbert. *Nat Turner's Slave Rebellion.* Humanities Press, 1966.

Oates, Stephen B. *The Fires of Jubilee: Nat Turner's Fierce Rebellion.* Harper &Row, 1975.

Robert Fay

Turner, Tina

1939–

American pop singer and actress, who made one of the biggest comebacks in recording history.

Tina Turner was born Anna Mae Bullock in Brownsville, Tennessee. As a child she sang and danced with a local trombonist named Bootsie Whitelaw. After her parents separated in 1950, she lived with her maternal grandmother. Six years later, Bullock moved to St. Louis, Missouri, to live with her mother and older sister. That same year, she met guitarist Ike Turner after spontaneously performing a song with his group, the Kings of Rhythm, in an East St. Louis nightclub. Bullock joined the group in 1957 and changed her name to Tina in 1960, at which time the Kings of Rhythm became the Ike and Tina Turner Revue. Ike Turner and Tina married in 1962, and toured throughout the United States and Europe. Their biggest hit, "Proud Mary," won a Grammy in 1971. Driven away by Ike's emotional and physical abuse, Tina left the group in 1976.

After finalizing her divorce in 1978, Turner embarked on a solo career in Europe with the help of David Bowie, Mick Jagger, and Rod Stewart. She secured a recording contract with Capitol Records in 1983 and released the successful single "Let's Stay Together," originally recorded by AL GREEN in 1971. Turner's 1984 album *Private Dancer,* which featured the hit single "What's Love Got to Do With It," won three Grammy Awards and sold over twenty-five million copies worldwide. Each of Turner's next two albums, *Break Every Rule* (1986) and *Tina Live in Europe* (1988), received a Grammy. As an actress she played leading roles in *Tommy* (1975) and *Mad Max: Beyond Thunderdome* (1985). She was the subject of the film *What's Love Got to Do with It* (1993). Turner was inducted into the Rock and Roll Hall of Fame in January 1991. A few months after releasing *Twenty Four Seven* (1999), Turner announced her retirement from touring. She performed the final concert of her farewell tour in December 2000. In 2003 she recorded "Look Through My Eyes Great Spirits" for the movie *Brother Bear,* her first new song in four years.

See also Film, Blacks in American; Music, African American.

Aaron Myers

Turu

Ethnic group of Tanzania; also known as Nyatura and Rimi.

The Turu primarily inhabit central TANZANIA. They speak a Bantu language. Over 700,000 people consider themselves Turu.

See also Bantu: Dispersion and Settlement; Ethnicity and Identity in Africa: An Interpretation; Languages, African: An Overview.

Tuskegee Airmen

Segregated Army Air Corps units in World War II that broke barriers in the U.S. military and fought successfully as fighter pilots in Europe.

Africans Americans fought in every American war in racially segregated units, and with the generally unrealized expectation that patriotism and courage would demonstrate their right to first-class citizenship at home. As planes and flying developed following World War I, blacks pressured for admission to the air force, but a 1925 study commissioned by the Army War College claimed scientific proof that Negroes were innately unable to operate aircraft because of their limited cranial capacity. Not until April 3, 1939, as EUROPE prepared for war, did Congress pass Public Law Eighteen that called for a major expansion of American air forces. The bill provided for the establishment of training programs for Negroes, but for support services only, at several black colleges.

One program was authorized to train black pilots. The 66th Air Force Flying School was to be established at Tuskegee, Alabama, site of Tuskegee Institute, partly because the weather permitted year-round training, partly because the South was already heavily segregated. Under considerable pressure from the NATIONAL ASSOCIATION FOR THE ADVANCEMENT OF COLORED PEOPLE (NAACP) and the black press, the War Department authorized the creation of an all-black flying unit, the 99th Pursuit Squadron, later called the 99th Fighter Squadron. African Americans wanted to be eligible for the regular air force, but most white civilians and military personnel did not want them in the service at all. The compromise was a segregated unit.

Nearly 500 black soldiers, all male, entered the Tuskegee program, which was run by white officers. Since those in charge both expected and wanted African Americans to fail, the black trainees were expelled for the slightest reason, resulting in a high drop-out rate from the program. The first class preparing to be pilots began their training on August 25, 1941. The class consisted of thirteen men, five of whom graduated in June 1942. The class included BENJAMIN O. DAVIS, JR., who later rose to become the country's first black three-star general. Because the officers at Tuskegee considered the African American pilots unfit for combat and thus insisted on prolonging their practice time, the Tuskegee pilots emerged from the program especially well trained. The men who survived the rigorous training programs were an elite group, largely college educated, and highly motivated.

Eventually, nearly 1,000 men won their wings as trained pilots, and another 1,000 graduated from the program with various support skills. When finally allowed to fight, some 450 pilots flew combat missions. The segregated black 332nd Fighter Group was formed which comprised four fighter squadrons, the 99th, the 100th, 301st, and 302nd. Assigned largely to ITALY, their record was impressive. Their fighter planes escorted bombers on their way to Europe and in 1,578 missions and 15,552 sorties, never lost a bomber. They destroyed or damaged 409 enemy planes. In Trieste harbor they actually sank a

German destroyer, the first time a ship of that size and offensive capability had ever been sunk simply by machine gun fire. By war's end, the Fighter Group had lost sixty-six men, and been awarded 100 Distinguished Flying Crosses.

On September 5, 1946, the government disbanded the fighter units and closed the Tuskegee base. The outstanding success and courage of the Tuskegee Airmen was a contributory factor in President Harry S. Truman's signing Executive Order 9981 in 1948. The order officially ended racial segregation in the U.S. armed forces, which went on to become a model of racial integration. In addition to their extraordinary war record and their role in the integration of the U.S. military, many graduates of the Tuskegee program went on to become leaders in other fields: COLEMAN YOUNG, mayor of DETROIT; ALBERT MURRAY, literary and music scholar; Roscoe Brown, president of Bronx Community College; and PERCY SUTTON, president of Manhattan Borough.

See also Desegregation in the United States; Military, Blacks in the American; Segregation in the United States; Tuskegee University; World War II and African Americans.

Tuskegee Civic Association

African American group dedicated to civil rights, voter education, and community welfare in Alabama.

Formed in 1941, the Tuskegee Civic Association grew out of a group of men who had been meeting since 1910 as The Men's Meeting and, later, The Tuskegee Men's Club. Its members worked on several fronts to improve the lives of African Americans in Tuskegee, Alabama, and its surrounding area, Macon County.

Under its first president, Charles G. Gomillion, a sociology professor at Tuskegee Institute, the association published a voters' handbook and held a "school for voters" on the Tuskegee campus to educate local African Americans. With help from the NATIONAL ASSOCIATION FOR THE ADVANCEMENT OF COLORED PEOPLE (NAACP), the association approached the U.S. Department of Justice for help in enforcing blacks' legal rights, which were denied by local voter registration boards. Their efforts met with success, as the number of black registered voters in Macon County swelled from under 100 in 1941 to more than 7,000 in 1967.

The association also fought for school desegregation. In 1962 it initiated a lawsuit, *Lee v. Macon County,* that demanded the integration of the local school system, which had stubbornly resisted implementing the U.S. Supreme Court's call for desegregation as put forth in *BROWN V. BOARD OF EDUCATION* (1954). Despite violent white resistance, which included cross burnings and a KU KLUX KLAN rally, a federal district court sided with the Tuskegeeans in 1966.

Perhaps the organization's most important achievement was defeating a 1957 statutory redrawing of Tuskegee's city limits—a classic case of gerrymandering that effectively disenfranchised the area's growing black vote. In *Gomillion v. Light-* *foot,* the U.S. Supreme Court ruled that such redistricting had violated the FIFTEENTH AMENDMENT rights of Tuskegee's African Americans.

Following a period of deactivation in the 1970s, the Tuskegee Civic Association re-formed in the 1980s, led by its first woman president, Claudine Penson. Currently presided over by the Rev. L. M. Randolph, the organization continues its efforts in voter registration and education, school reform, and community relations.

See also Desegregation in the United States; Tuskegee University.

Bibliography

Guzman, Jessie P. *Crusade for Civic Democracy: The Story of the Tuskegee Civic Association, 1941–1970.* Vantage Press, 1985.

Kate Tuttle

Tuskegee Institute

See also Tuskegee University; Washington, Booker Taliaferro.

Tuskegee Syphilis Experiment

Widely condemned study of the natural course of syphilis, in which United States public health officials withheld treatment from 600 African American males, two-thirds of whom were infected with syphilis.

The Tuskegee Study, commonly known as the Tuskegee syphilis experiment, conducted by the United States Public Health Service (PHS) and the Tuskegee Institute, began in 1932 and was originally planned to last one year. Its founders intended to document the degenerative effects of syphilis, with the ultimate goal of appropriating state funding to treat Southern rural blacks. The study involved 399 syphilitic black males, all in the final stage of the disease, and a control group of 201 noninfected black males. PHS officials based the investigation in and around Tuskegee, in Macon County, Alabama, where severe poverty and insufficient medical care contributed to the highest incidence of syphilis in the South. Most PHS doctors ascribed high syphilis rates among blacks to sexual promiscuity and ignorance. They never considered that African Americans were systematically denied medical services, nor the overt moral and racial implications that overshadowed the experiment from the beginning.

In order to secure participants, PHS officials offered a series of incentives: free medical treatment for minor illnesses, occasional hot meals, travel to and from the study site, and burial stipends paid to the person's family if the subject died. For men whose daily existence was harsh, such inducements were attractive, especially since the burial fee often represented their only life insurance. Not once did PHS doctors inform participants of their real diagnosis, nor of the true purpose of the study or the dangers to which it exposed them. The sick men were led to believe they were being treated for rheumatism, stomach disorders, or "bad blood," an umbrella phrase used by rural blacks to describe a range of maladies, including syphilis. They were subjected to an array of tests and medical examinations over the years, while the syphilis was deliberately left untreated.

When the use of penicillin as an antibiotic for syphilis became widespread in the 1940s, Tuskegee participants did not receive it. Indeed, PHS officials threatened to cut off the benefits of those who attempted to be treated elsewhere and advised local black doctors not to see them. By 1969 approximately 100 men had died from untreated syphilis, while numerous others suffered painful disease-related complications. Many unknowingly spread syphilis, which is highly contagious, to their wives and children.

Interaction between the researchers and their black subjects was facilitated by a black nurse and Tuskegee resident, Eunice Rivers. Fully aware of what the study involved, she kept track of the men and often chauffeured them back and forth between their homes and the experiment site. The men trusted her because she was African American and understood the men's cultural background. In the book *Bad Blood: The Tuskegee Experiment* (1993), author James H. Jones points out, the men came to see themselves as "members of a social club and burial society called 'Miss River's Lodge.'"

The study was never a secret. Between 1932 and 1972, PHS officials published numerous scientific papers on the experiment in leading U.S. medical journals and gave presentations at medical conventions. At the same time, the civil rights movement was changing white society's perceptions of blacks, culminating in significantly improved ethical standards regarding the medical treatment of nonwhite patients. It was only when a PHS worker informed the Associated Press of the study that the U.S. Department of Health, Education, and Welfare (HEW) abruptly ended it in 1972. Some leading white doctors continued to defend the study publicly. What Jones refers to as the nineteenth-century legacy of "racial medicine," in which black study participants were seen as subjects to be experimented on, rather than as human beings, remained strong in many public health circles.

Compensation to victims of the Tuskegee experiment has come slowly. After the study became widely publicized in 1972, HEW and leading U.S. newspapers decried the study as "ethically unjustified." Commentators condemned the fact that public health officials had failed to obtain formal consent from the men and had denied them penicillin. An out-of-court settlement guaranteed treatment and modest cash payments for the survivors and families of the deceased, while Congress enacted laws to protect people who participated in medical experiments. It was not until May 1997, however, that the government fully acknowledged its role in the Tuskegee experiment. In a public apology, President Bill Clinton admitted that the study was "racist" and "profoundly, morally wrong," and that "what the

United States government did was shameful." He also announced government plans to found a memorial to the study's legacy: the Center for Bioethics in Research and Health Care. Yet the Tuskegee experiment cultivated a mistrust of the public medical establishment among many African Americans, and little has been done since 1972 to remedy the problem of high syphilis rates among rural Southern blacks.

See also Disease, Medicine, and Health; Tuskegee University.

Bibliography
Jones, James H. *Bad Blood: The Tuskegee Syphilis Experiment.* Rev. ed. Free Press, 1993.

Roanne Edwards

Tuskegee University

Historically black college in Tuskegee, Alabama, organized by Booker T. Washington to emphasize industrial education.

Tuskegee's roots lie in the post-Reconstruction era in the South, when African Americans' opportunities for higher education were still severely limited. Tuskegee University was technically chartered by the Alabama state legislature to repay black voters for their support. However, its early history is almost synonymous with the name of its first administrator, nineteenth-century African American leader Booker T. Washington.

In February 1881 the Alabama legislature voted to set aside $2,000 each year to fund a state and normal school for blacks in Tuskegee. The trustees asked officials at several other black institutions to recommend someone to head the new school. Although they were implicitly asking for white candidates, Hampton Institute's president Samuel Chapman Armstrong suggested his black protégé, Booker T. Washington. The trustees agreed to hire Washington as principal. Washington arrived in Tuskegee on June 24, 1881, and opened the Normal School for colored teachers at Tuskegee in a shack adjacent to the black Methodist church on July 4. The first thirty students ranged in age from sixteen to forty, and most were teachers hoping to further their own education.

Washington's most significant contribution was his strong belief in industrial education and training as the key to success for African Americans. Students were required to learn a trade and perform manual labor at the school, including making and laying the bricks for the buildings that became the first campus. Tuskegee's charter had mandated that tuition would be free for students who committed to teaching in Alabama public schools. The students' labor helped with financial costs, and Washington solicited much of the remaining funding from northern white philanthropists.

Tuskegee was incorporated as a private institution in 1892, and its name was changed to the Tuskegee Normal and Industrial Institute that year. Social conventions would have prohibited white instructors from serving under a black prin-

Students at Tuskegee Institute listen to a history lecture in 1902. In 1986, five years after its centennial, the school renamed itself Tuskegee University.
CORBIS

cipal, so Tuskegee became the first institution of higher learning with a black faculty. In 1896 the school hired GEORGE WASHINGTON CARVER, whose groundbreaking agricultural research received international recognition. Washington became nationally accepted as a black leader during the 1890s because many whites appreciated his accommodationist approach to race relations, and Tuskegee gained wide recognition and substantial funding.

The original industrial training approach gradually changed after Washington's death in 1915. Tuskegee awarded its first baccalaureate degree in 1925 and began its first college curriculum in 1927 and nurses' training. In 1937 its name was changed to Tuskegee Institute. During World War II (1939–1945) the Army Air Corps established an airfield at Tuskegee that trained more than 900 black pilots, known as the TUSKEGEE AIRMEN. Graduate programs in veterinary medicine, nursing, business, architecture, agriculture and home economics, education, and arts and sciences were eventually

added. In the 1960s and 1970s Tuskegee became the first black college to be designated a Registered National Historic Landmark and a National Historic Site.

By the school's centennial in 1981, Tuskegee's campus included 150 buildings on 2,000 hectares (5,000 acres), and its endowment was approximately twenty-two million dollars. Five years later, the school changed its name to Tuskegee University. Today, approximately 2,500 undergraduates are enrolled at Tuskegee, and there are an additional 350 graduate students. The school offers seventy different degrees and has an especially strong engineering program.

Notable Tuskegee graduates include writer RALPH ELLISON, who portrays a fictionalized version of the school and its founder in his novel *Invisible Man* (1952); Arthur W. Mitchell, the first black Democratic congressman; and actor/comedian Keenan Ivory Wayans. Tuskegee's 30,000 living alumni are professionals in communities across the country and throughout the world.

See also Colleges and Universities, Historically Black, in the United States.

Bibliography

Butler, Addie Louise Joyner. *The Distinctive Black College: Talladega, Tuskegee and Morehouse.* Scarecrow Press, 1977.

Lisa Clayton Robinson

Tutu, Desmond Mpilo

1931–

Archbishop of the Anglican Church in South Africa, winner of the 1984 Nobel Peace Prize, and head of the Truth and Reconciliation Commission.

An outspoken critic of SOUTH AFRICA's APARTHEID system, Desmond Tutu became one of his country's most prominent symbols of resistance and hope, along with NELSON MANDELA. Born in Klerksdorp, South Africa, Tutu was raised in the TRANSVAAL region. The son of a schoolteacher father, he walked miles each day to overcrowded and under-equipped schools. The family was better off than most, however, and Tutu has described his childhood as happy. An attack of tuberculosis at age fourteen kept Tutu out of school for nearly two years. While recuperating, he met Father Trevor Huddleston, a white Anglican priest known for his opposition to apartheid. Under Huddleston's influence, Tutu first became interested in the church, an interest that complemented his plans to become a teacher. In 1954 he graduated from Bantu Normal College outside PRETORIA, and was certified as a teacher. Tutu cut short his teaching career after the apartheid government created an inferior education system for blacks in the 1950s.

With a family to support—Tutu had married Leah Nomalizo Shenxane in 1955—he entered seminary at Saint Peter's College in Rosettenville. In 1960 he graduated summa cum laude. He credited the Community of the Resurrection, the order than ran St. Peter's, with his view that religious study "is authenticated and expressed in our dealings with our neighbor." It was a lesson he would take to his first posts as parish priest in two government-created townships. Tutu became known as a man of the people, treating his flock with warmth, humor, and love; he later wrote that "a good shepherd knows his sheep by name."

Advanced theological study at the University of London took Tutu away from South Africa in 1962, a time of increasing antiapartheid activism. While Tutu was then still relatively apolitical, it is clear that his time in England impressed upon him the depth of the injustices he and his countrymen faced at home. Along with his wife, Leah, and their four children, Tutu returned to South Africa in 1968, and became a lecturer at his alma mater, St. Peter's College, which had recently become part of the Federal Theological Seminary. He witnessed the violent reprisals against black student protesters at the nearby University of Fort Hare, which at the time was the center of the Black Consciousness Movement led by STEPHEN BIKO.

Tutu spent another two years as a university lecturer in LESOTHO, then returned with his family to England, where he became associate director of the Theological Educational Fund in London. His role as a leader in the antiapartheid struggle began in 1975, when he was elected to the position of Dean of JOHANNESBURG. Refusing to occupy the Dean's residence, Tutu instead settled in the sprawling black township of SOWETO, where a year later police massacred black schoolchildren who were protesting peacefully.

From 1976 to 1978 Tutu served as bishop of Lesotho. During this time Steve Biko died in police custody, and Tutu gave the eulogy. He compared the martyred leader to Jesus Christ, and prayed for black South Africans to find "a place in the sun in our own beloved country." In 1978 he returned to his own country to stay. For seven years he served as the general secretary of the South African Council of Churches, an organization known for its outspoken opposition to apartheid. The whole country was now Tutu's parish. At home, he worked tirelessly to free the country's many political prisoners; abroad, he called on the international community to use diplomatic and economic sanctions to pressure the apartheid regime.

In 1984 Tutu won the Nobel Peace Prize, and shortly thereafter he was named Bishop of Johannesburg. Two years later Tutu became Archbishop of CAPE TOWN, where he continued to speak out against apartheid from a Christian perspective. He once said, "if Christ returned to South Africa today he would almost certainly be detained under the present security laws, because of his concern for the poor, the hungry and the oppressed." In the decade after Tutu's appointment, he saw most of his goals achieved; Nelson Mandela was released from prison in 1990 and in 1994 won the presidency in the country's first-ever democratic vote. Upon his retirement in 1996 Tutu became chairman of the TRUTH AND RECONCILIATION COMMISSION, the body charged with investigating crimes committed during the apartheid era. He then presided over the testimony from hundreds of perpetrators and victims—a duty which at times severely tested his skills as a peacemaker. In October 2003 Tutu accepted a position as visiting professor in post-conflict studies at King's College London.

See also Antiapartheid Movement; Black Consciousness in Africa.

Bibliography

Du Boulay, Shirley. *Tutu: Voice of the Voiceless.* Hodder and Stoughton, 1989.
Tutu, Desmond. *Hope and Suffering.* Skotaville Publishers, 1983.

Kate Tuttle

Tutuola, Amos

1920–1997

Nigerian novelist known for his use of Yoruba folktales.

The son of a YORUBA COCOA farmer, Amos Tutuola built his literary career retelling and expanding the stories he heard as a child, listening to elders in the evenings. His ten books, all drawing on Yoruba folklore, have since become classics of African literature.

Tutuola, whose family struggled financially, entered the Salvation Army School in ABEOKUTA, NIGERIA, at the age of ten, his tuition paid by an uncle. Two years later, financial need led Tutuola to seek work as houseboy for F. O. Mornu, a local civil servant. In 1934 Tutuola, by then a promising student, moved to LAGOS with his employer and enrolled in Lagos High School. But Tutuola suffered hunger and abuse while living in Lagos with Mornu, and he returned to Abeokuta in 1936. His father's death in 1939 effectively ended his formal education.

After a failed attempt at farming, Tutuola learned blacksmithing, and plied his trade in the British Royal Air Force. Upon his discharge in 1945 he attempted to launch his own business, but this failed too. In 1946, while working as a messenger in Lagos, Tutuola wrote his first novel, *The Palm-Wine Drinkard and His Dead Palm-Wine Tapster in the Deads' Town*, in just two days. After three months of intensive revision—a creative pattern he would repeat in subsequent books—Tutuola sought a publisher. Finally in 1952 the London firm Faber & Faber published the novel. It was one of the first Nigerian works of fiction to reach an international audience.

Reviews in EUROPE and America were enthusiastic; some in the Nigerian literary community, however, criticized the book for its use of traditional folklore and Yoruba-influenced English. Tutuola's popularity among Western readers—*The Palm-Wine Drinkard* was translated into eleven languages—led some educated Nigerians to suggest that his work merely confirmed the exotic image of AFRICA held by non-Africans. Tutuola's second book, *My Life in the Bush of Ghosts*, which was published in 1954, also blended myth, magic, and coming-of-age themes, and also received international acclaim.

Tutuola, married since 1947, went to work for the Nigerian Broadcasting Company in 1956, and was transferred from Lagos to IBADAN the following year. Although the notably shy and quiet Tutuola was never a part of the then-thriving Nigerian literary scene—in fact, his friends were mostly illiterate tradesmen—he continued to write, and helped adapt his first two books for the stage in 1958. Praise from critics abroad dwindled, however; reviewers saw as "deliberately childish" what they had found "pleasingly childlike" a few years earlier. Some Nigerian critics charged that Tutuola imitated too heavily an earlier Yoruban writer, D. O. Fagunwa. Yet Tutuola credited the Christian novel *Pilgrims Progress* as well as Greek mythology as influences, and Gerald Moore, writing in the literary magazine *BLACK ORPHEUS*, identified universal storytelling patterns in Tutuola's work. Later books such as *The Witch-Herbalist of the Remote Town* (1981) confirmed the critical reappraisal of Tutuola as Africa's premiere storyteller.

See also Theater, African.

Twa

Mostly forest-dwelling people, sharing an ethnic identity with, and commonly referred to as, pygmies who live in Burundi, Rwanda, and eastern parts of the Democratic Republic of the Congo.

The seminomadic Twa were the first inhabitants of present-day BURUNDI and RWANDA, though their exact origins are debated. Archaeological evidence places Twa hunter-gatherers in the area beginning around 70,000 B.C.E., but some ethnographers contend that they migrated to the region from West Africa around 5,000 years ago. Some ethnographic evidence supports the argument that the Twa are closely related to the Ituri forest people of Central Africa, while still other evidence suggests that the Twa entered the region from the northeast.

When the HUTU AND TUTSI migrated into the region in the eleventh and mid-sixteenth centuries, respectively, they believed that the short-statured Twa, as the region's original inhabitants, held spiritual and magical powers. As the Twa were gradually incorporated into Hutu and Tutsi society, they lost their own language and became dependents of the Tutsi royal court, particularly the king, whom they served as storytellers, dancers, musicians, spies, executioners, and guardians of the royal court's sacred fire. The king gave the Twa cattle, and they legitimized his rule through their purported spiritual powers. But because of their physical characteristics and their eating of mutton, a taboo food, the Hutu and Tutsi considered them impure, and they were socially segregated. German and Belgian COLONIAL RULE further marginalized the Twa by destroying the monarchy on which they depended, and by favoring the Tutsi in colonial education and employment. Except for pottery-making, neither the forest-dwelling Twa nor the "court" Twa acquired skills applicable to a cash economy.

Today there are approximately 25,000 and 60,000 Twa in Rwanda and Burundi, respectively, comprising less than 1 percent of the total national populations. Largely neglected by development programs and hurt by ongoing strife in both countries, they make their livelihood as day laborers, potters, basket-makers, and trackers for the military and wildlife safaris.

See also Ethnicity and Identity in Africa: An Interpretation; Languages, African: An Overview; Pygmy.

Eric Young

Twilight, Alexander Lucius

1795–1857

Educator, probably the first African American college graduate.

Alexander Lucius Twilight, born to a free black family in Vermont, graduated from Middlebury College in 1823, making him, so far as is known, the first African American to receive a degree from an American college. He was licensed to preach by the Presbyterian Church and served several Congregational churches.

Twilight became principal of the Orleans County Grammar School in Brownington, Vermont, and in 1836 built a massive three-story granite building, Athenian Hall, which became Brownington Academy. In the 1836–1837 term, Twilight served in the Vermont state legislature, the first African American to do so.

See also Clergy in Politics; Free Blacks in the United States.

Richard Newman

2 Live Crew

See Campbell, Luther.

Tyson, Cicely

1933–

African American stage, motion-picture, and television actor, known for portraying strong female characters.

Born in NEW YORK CITY, Cicely Tyson was educated at New York University and at the Actors Studio. After working as a successful fashion model, Tyson acted in HARLEM and in off-Broadway productions in New York in the late 1950s. She had a small role in the motion picture *Odds Against Tomorrow* (1959) and later became widely known as a regular cast member on the critically praised television drama series *East Side, West Side* (1963–1964). After appearing in supporting parts in films, such as *A Man Called Adam* (1966), *The Comedians* (1967), and *The Heart Is a Lonely Hunter* (1968), she costarred in *Sounder* (1972), about a black American sharecropper family in the 1930s. Tyson received a 1972 Academy Award nomination for best actress for her performance in *Sounder*. She is best known for her role in the television movie *The Autobiography of Miss Jane Pittman* (1974), for which she received an Emmy for best actress, and for her work in the television miniseries *Roots* (1977), which was adapted from the book of the same title by American author ALEX HALEY. Her other films include *The River Niger* (1976), *A Hero Ain't Nothin' but a Sandwich* (1978), and *Fried Green Tomatoes* (1991). In 1994 she returned to television drama as a costar in the series *Equal Justice*. She followed with appearances in several television movies, including *Riot* (1997), *Ms. Scrooge* (1997), *A Lesson Before Dying* (1999), and *The Rosa Parks Story* (2002). Tyson returned to the big screen in *Because of Winn-Dixie* (2004). After more than five decades, Tyson's acting career is still going strong.

See also Acting and Actors; Film, Blacks in American; Television and African Americans.

Tyson, Mike

1966–

African American heavyweight boxing champion known as "Iron Mike" who encountered problems in and out of the ring.

Mike Tyson grew up in a single-parent home in the Brownsville section of Brooklyn, New York. Throughout his youth Tyson was frequently involved in minor criminal offenses. At age thirteen, Tyson was sent to a juvenile detention center called the Tyron School, in Johnstown, New York. There Tyson met the legendary trainer Cus D'Amato and discovered the sport of BOXING. D'Amato recognized Tyson's potential and became the young boy's mentor, acting as both Tyson's coach and legal guardian.

Tyson turned professional in 1985 after winning the 1984 Golden Gloves amateur heavyweight championship. Known as "Iron Mike," Tyson enjoyed several years of major victories, amassing both titles and wealth. His personal life was less successful as his brief marriage to actress Robin Givens ended in 1988 with allegations of domestic abuse. Following a 1990 unanticipated championship loss to challenger Buster Douglas, Tyson's career declined. In 1991 he was charged with rape, leading to conviction and a three-year jail sentence.

After his release from prison, Tyson returned to the ring in 1995 and regained two heavyweight title belts the following year. He lost these titles, however, after EVANDER HOLYFIELD beat him in 1996. In a rematch against Holyfield the following year, Tyson was disqualified after biting his opponent's ear, actually severing a piece of it. Fined and suspended from boxing, Tyson was forced to reevaluate his career and personal choices. He was imprisoned again in 1999, this time for assaulting two motorists after a traffic accident and for violating parole. He was released after serving three and a half months. After winning several bouts, Tyson received another shot at the heavyweight title in 2002, but was knocked out by Lennox Lewis. Tyson has since returned to the ring seeking to reestablish himself as a viable contender. In the summer of 2003, after years of financial difficulties, Mike Tyson filed for bankruptcy.

See also Sports and African Americans.

Bibliography

Berger, Phil. *Blood Season: Tyson and the World of Boxing.* Morrow, 1989.
Heller, Peter. *Bad Intentions: The Mike Tyson Story.* New American Library, 1989.

Tyus, Wyomia

1945–

American track and field athlete who won the 100-meter dash at both the 1964 and 1968 Olympic Games.

Born in Griffin, Georgia, Wyomia Tyus attended Tennessee State University. In 1964 she won the 100-meter dash at the United States outdoor national track championships. She was not expected to win the event at the 1964 Olympic Games in Tokyo because her teammate Edith McGuire had dominated the event over the previous few years. Tyus did win, however, setting a world record of 11.2 seconds in a preliminary race. She was also a member of the second-place 4 × 100-meter relay team.

At the United States outdoor national championships, Tyus won the 100-yard dash in 1965 and 1966 and the 220-yard dash in 1966. In addition, at the U.S. indoor championships she won the 60-yard dash three consecutive years (1965–1967). In 1967 she won the 200-meter dash at the Pan American Games in Winnipeg, Manitoba, Canada.

At the 1968 Olympic Games in Mexico City, Tyus repeated her title in the 100-meter race, setting a new world record of 11.08 seconds. She thereby became the first woman to win the event twice at the Games. She also earned her third Olympic gold medal by anchoring (running the last leg for) the winning 4 × 100-meter relay team. She retired from amateur track competition after the 1968 Olympic Games. In 1974, with tennis player Billie Jean King, swimmer Donna de Varona, diver Micki King, and speed skater and cyclist Sheila Young, Tyus helped found the Women's Sports Foundation, an organization to enhance women's sports experiences. She was inducted into the National Track & Field Hall of Fame in 1980 and into the U.S. Olympic Hall of Fame in 1985. Tyus currently lives in Los Angeles, California, where she has taught and commentated for televised track events. She has also worked with the U.S. Olympic Committee and the UCLA Black Studies Center.

See also Olympics, African Americans and the; Sports and African Americans; Track and Field in the United States.

U

Ubangi River

Major branch of the Congo River that separates the Central African Republic and the Democratic Republic of the Congo.

The Ubangi River stretches 2,300 kilometers (approximately 1,400 miles) from the headwaters of its main tributary, the Uélé River, to the CONGO RIVER. From the confluence of the Uélé and Mbomou (or Bomu) rivers, the Ubangi first flows west, then bends south at BANGUI. On average, the Ubangi discharges 4,280 cubic meters of water per second (cm/s) into the Congo, but in the rainy season—from May to December—the flow can rise to 14,000 cm/s. In its upper reaches, the river descends through a series of dramatic rapids. However, once it enters the Congo basin above Bangui, the Ubangi becomes navigable and flows past sandy shoals and dense equatorial forests. The river takes its name from the trading people, the Bubangui, who inhabit its banks.

For thousands of years, the great river and its tributaries have provided abundant fish (an important food source) and a vital transportation route for the people of the region, who include the earliest known inhabitants, the Aka. During the eighteenth century, the river carried thousands of captives to the Atlantic for shipment to the Americas in the TRANSATLANTIC SLAVE TRADE. The Russian explorer Wilhelm Junker determined the course of the Ubangi in 1882–1883, and French colonialists traveled up the river a decade later to conquer much of Central Africa. Today the Ubangi provides a major transportation route for the CENTRAL AFRICAN REPUBLIC. It links the capital, Bangui, to BRAZZAVILLE, from which a railroad provides access to the ocean. The Ubangi basin contains a wide array of animal life and includes the world's largest gorilla and chimpanzee reserve.

See also Transatlantic Slave Trade.

Eric Young

Uganda

Equatorial East African country, bordered on the north by Sudan, on the east by Kenya, on the south by Tanzania and Rwanda, and on the west by the Democratic Republic of Congo.

Uganda has widely varied landscapes, including low inland swamps, sprawling forests, high plains, and mountains towering more than 4,000 meters (13,000 feet) high. Uganda's population is also extraordinarily diverse. Nilotic and central Sudanic speakers originally made their homes in the low savannas of the north, and BANTU speakers settled the fertile rolling hills in the south. Although the British, who colonized the region in the late 1800s, used ethnicity and religion to divide the people of Uganda, competition between the country's strong indigenous kingdoms preceded colonial rule. The political, economic, and social significance of ethnic identities has changed over time, but ethnic antagonisms remain a formidable obstacle to the development of a national identity and a unified political culture in contemporary Uganda.

Early History

Uganda lies at the heart of the Great Lakes region of East Africa, the fertile, often humid region near LAKE VICTORIA and the other major lakes of Central Africa. During the first millennium B.C.E., Bantu-speaking peoples migrated to the region from the east, displacing the existing populations of foragers, possibly KHOISAN speakers. Archaeological evidence indicates that the Bantu-speaking immigrants used sophisticated furnaces for iron smelting as early as the fourth century B.C.E. They also practiced shifting cultivation, a form of agriculture that requires regular clearing of forests to plant crops. As the Bantu-speaking populations moved east into the savanna zones of the Great Lakes region, they encountered pastoralists (herders) who spoke languages from the Nilo-Saharan family. From these populations

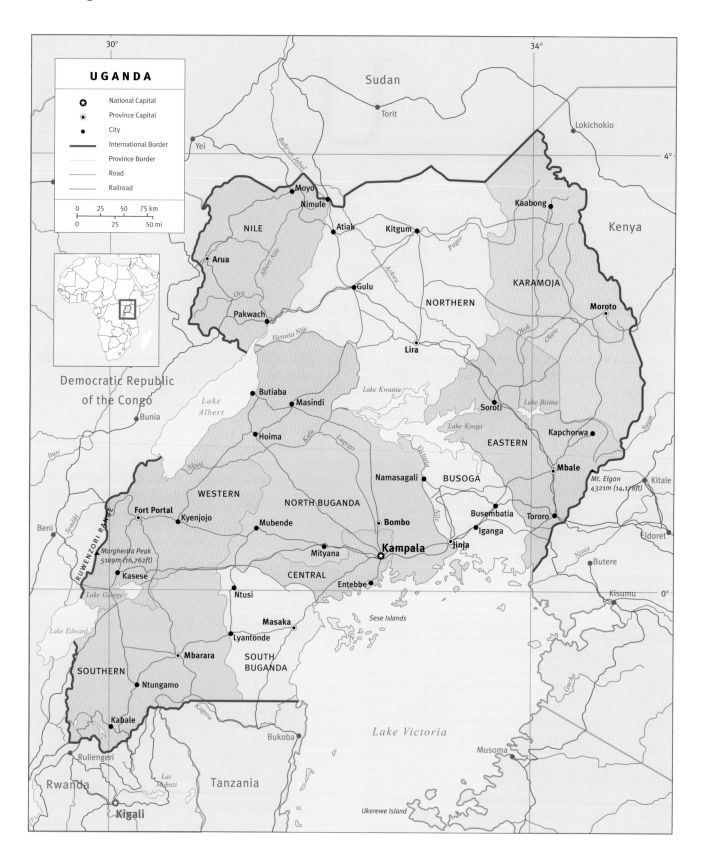

the early Bantu learned how to cultivate new crops, primarily arid-climate grains such as sorghum and MILLET.

The Bantu-speaking immigrants settled primarily in the lower half of present-day Uganda, while the Nilo-Saharan speakers continued to dominate the arid northern regions that were more suitable to PASTORALISM. Over generations, increasingly centralized political systems evolved, giving rise to a number of kingdoms during the first half of the second millennium

Made homeless by the threat of violence from rebel groups, this family lives in a displaced persons camp in northern Uganda. *CORBIS/Liba Taylor*

C.E. Some scholars attribute the rise of kingdoms to the shift to banana cultivation. Bananas are an extremely high-yield crop, so cultivating them reduced the labor required for day-to-day subsistence and made it possible for some people to build large fortunes based on the new agricultural surpluses, while others remained poor. Other scholars trace the rise of centralized political units to the development of patron-client relationships between sedentary Bantu-speaking agriculturalists and more nomadic Nilotic-speaking pastoralists. According to this theory, pastoralists offered protection in exchange for having the agriculturalists tend their cattle.

The first kingdom, Bunyoro-Kitara, developed after pastoralists known as the Tembuzi began establishing cattle-clientship over the region's agriculturists around 1200 C.E. Over the next several centuries, a series of royal dynasties controlled the kingdom of Bunyoro-Kitara. The kingdom's borders expanded when pastoral Binto rulers in the sixteenth century established control over numerous smaller agricultural polities, including Buganda, Ankole, and Toro. These, in turn, developed into full-fledged kingdoms when Bunyoro-Kitara began to collapse in the nineteenth century.

Kingdom of Buganda

Buganda played a central role in the history of modern-day Uganda. Its rulers traded IVORY and slaves for cloth and firearms brought by merchants from EGYPT and ZANZIBAR. The trade transformed Buganda into a wealthy and well-armed kingdom by the time European EXPLORERS such as JOHN HANNING SPEKE and HENRY MORTON STANLEY passed through the region in the mid-nineteenth century, searching for the source of the NILE RIVER. The explorers described the grand, efficiently run court of Kabaka (King) MUTESA I on the northern shores of Lake Victoria. The explorers' accounts raised the interest of missionary societies in Europe, and these groups later established several missions in the region.

British authorities also began to see great strategic advantage in occupying an area from where it might be possible to control the headwaters of the Nile, which was discovered to originate mainly in Lake Victoria. When GREAT BRITAIN took control of Egypt in 1882, its determination to control Buganda grew. Both Britain and GERMANY claimed possession of Buganda until the signing of the Anglo-German Agreement of 1890. In this agreement Germany ceded control over the area of present-day Uganda (which includes Buganda) in exchange for British concessions elsewhere in East Africa.

At the end of 1890 the king of Buganda signed a treaty with agents of the British East Africa Company. In the treaty the company agreed to protect the kingdom, and the king agreed to refrain from entering into trade agreements with any other country and to permit missionaries to work in the area. Using Buganda as a base, Britain began to take control of surrounding kingdoms and ethnic groups through both diplomacy and force. On June 18, 1894, the British government asserted control over Buganda and nearby kingdoms as the Uganda Protectorate, creating a political entity where none had previously existed. Although in this sense Uganda was a colonial creation, Buganda and some other kingdoms of the Great Lakes region were themselves products of precolonial military conquest and diplomatic alliance. The history of conquest and domination in the region meant that many societies were ethnically diverse and economically stratified long before the advent of European colonialism.

Colonial Rule

The British used the kingdom of Buganda as a means of controlling other parts of the Uganda Protectorate. In the 1890s

Uganda (At a Glance)

OFFICIAL NAME: Republic of Uganda

AREA: 236,040 sq km (91,135 sq mi)

LOCATION: Eastern Africa, borders Kenya, Rwanda, Sudan, Tanzania, Democratic Republic of the Congo

CAPITAL: Kampala (population 1,208, 544); 2002 estimate

OTHER MAJOR CITIES: Gulu (population 113,114), Lira (89,871), and Jinga (86,520); 2002 estimates

POPULATION: 25,632,794 (2003 estimate)

POPULATION DENSITY: 108.6 persons per sq km (about 281.2 persons per sq mi)

POPULATION BELOW AGE 15: 50.8 percent (male 6,528,724; female 6,486.736); 2003 estimate

POPULATION GROWTH RATE: 2.96 percent (2003 estimate)

TOTAL FERTILITY RATE: 6.72 children born per woman (2003 estimate)

LIFE EXPECTANCY AT BIRTH: Total population: 44.88 years (male 43.42 years; female 46.38 years); 2003 estimate

INFANT MORTALITY RATE: 87.9 deaths per 1,000 live births (2003 estimate)

LITERACY RATE (AGE 15 AND OVER WHO CAN READ AND WRITE): Total population: 69.9 percent (male 79.5 percent; female 60.4 percent); 2003 estimate

EDUCATION: The British educational system has been influential in Uganda, and missionary schools have played an important role in educating the people. In the late 1980s about 2.6 million pupils attended some 7,900 primary schools in Uganda, and some 240,000 students were enrolled in more than 900 secondary, technical, and teacher-training schools. Makerere University in Kampala has historically been one of the top universities in sub-Saharan Africa.

LANGUAGES: English, the official language, and Swahili, the language of commerce, are both widely spoken. About two-thirds of the people also speak one of several Bantu or Nilotic languages.

ETHNIC GROUPS: About two-thirds of the people are included in the Ganda, Soga, Nyoro, Nkole, and Toro ethnic groups. The Acholi, Lango, and Karimojon ethnic groups predominate in the north.

RELIGIONS: About 66 percent of Uganda's inhabitants are Christian; approximately 16 percent are Muslim; others follow traditional religions.

CLIMATE: Uganda's climate is mild and equable, mainly because of relatively high altitude. Temperature ranges from about 16° to 29°C (60° to 85°F). The average annual rainfall varies from some 760 mm (30 in) in the northeast to about 1,520 mm (60 in) near Lake Victoria.

LAND, PLANTS, AND ANIMALS: The area of Uganda includes Lake George and Lake Kyoga; parts of Lake Victoria, Lake Edward, and Lake Albert; and the Nile River from its outlet at Lake Victoria to Nimule on the Sudan frontier. The landscape is varied, with elevated plains, vast forests, low swamps, arid depressions, and snowcapped peaks, the highest of which is Margherita Peak (5,109 m/ 16,762 ft) in the Ruwenzori Range. Much of the south is forested, and most of the north is covered with savanna. Plant life includes mvuli tree and elephant grass of the Uganda plateau to the dry thorn scrub, acacia, and euphorbia of the southwest. Animals include chimpanzees, antelope (including the eland and hartebeest), elephants, rhinoceroses, lions, and leopard.

NATURAL RESOURCES: Soil, gold, copper, tin, tungsten, and hydroelectricity potential

CURRENCY: Ugandan shilling (USh)

GROSS DOMESTIC PRODUCT (GDP): $30.49 billion (2002 estimate)

GDP PER CAPITA: $1,200 (2002 estimate)

GDP REAL GROWTH RATE: 5.5 percent (2002 estimate)

PRIMARY ECONOMIC ACTIVITIES: Agriculture, industry, and services

PRIMARY EXPORTS: Coffee, cotton, tea, gold, fowers, fish and fish products

PRIMARY IMPORTS: Petroleum products, machinery, textiles, metals, transportation equipment, medical supplies, and food

PRIMARY TRADING PARTNERS: United States, European Union, and Kenya

GOVERNMENT: Uganda is a republic with a modified parliamentary system. The 1995 constitution officially prohibited political parties until the year 2000, but allowed for nonparty presidential and legislative elections in 1996. Lieut. Gen. Yoweri Museveni, in power since a coup in 1985, won that presidential election by a wide margin. He is both chief of state and head of government; his appointed prime minister is Apollo Nsibambi. The unicameral legilature, known as the National Assembly, includes 303 members, of whom 214 are directly elected by popular vote. All but eight of the remaining seats are allocated to special interest groups including women, the army, youth, the disabled, and labor. The next elections for both president and the assembly are scheduled for 2006.

Kabaka Mwanga, the king of the BAGANDA (the people of Buganda), sought to limit British influence. He deftly managed alliances with competing Catholic, Muslim, and Protestant groups in an effort to fend off the colonizers. When the British persuaded Baganda Christians to join them in expanding British control of the region, Kabaka Mwanga took refuge in the Bunyoro kingdom to the north. Bunyoro was a center of anticolonial resistance in the region, but ultimately the British and their Baganda allies managed to seize large parts of Bunyoro. In 1900 the British rewarded the Baganda Christians with the Uganda

Ugandan copper miner takes a break. Rich in copper and other minerals, Uganda's natural resources appealed to colonial nations, such as Great Britain and Germany. *CORBIS/Hulton-Deutsch Collection*

Agreement, which formally recognized the Baganda expansion into Bunyoro and granted the Buganda kingdom increased autonomy.

The British concessions came with a price. Under the agreement, the Baganda kabaka was subject to British authority, although the kabaka retained broad discretion over internal policies. Through this manipulation of indigenous leaders, Uganda, like Nigeria, became an example of the British policy of indirect rule in Africa. The British further undermined the kabaka's own power by dividing the lands of Uganda among about 4,000 local leaders. Through a strategy of divide-and-rule, the British installed Baganda leaders as local administrators and tax collectors throughout the protectorate, even in areas dominated by other ethnic groups. Resentment toward Baganda dominance sparked a number of early-twentieth-century rebellions by the Bunyoro and other groups, but the British manipulated tensions between these groups and were able to suppress the rebellions relatively quickly. These conflicts persisted for decades and stalled the development of nationalist politics. An especially divisive issue dating to British rule was the Bunyoro's repeated demand for the return of their "lost countries"—land the British reallocated to Baganda collaborators.

In Uganda, British colonial authorities pursued an African agriculture policy, in which Africans grew the bulk of the commercial crops. By contrast, in neighboring KENYA, British authorities encouraged white settlers to establish huge agricultural plantations that relied heavily on coerced African labor. From the British perspective, Uganda's comparatively rigid social and political organization made it much easier to organize the profitable cultivation of cash crops and to tax those profits.

Yields of cotton and coffee, the main export crops, were much higher in the more fertile south. Consequently, the long-standing cultural differences between the north and the Baganda-dominated south were increasingly reinforced by economic and political stratification. Buganda, already home to KAMPALA, the largest town in the colony, grew wealthy from agriculture and trade. Baganda chiefs, many of them owners of large cotton estates, were able to provide high-quality education for their children, leading to the rise of a literate elite. In the 1950s a group of educated Baganda created the Young Baganda Association, hoping to replace older Baganda leaders who held important positions in the colonial government.

Anticolonial Agitation

During the 1950s youth associations such as the Young Baganda Association proliferated, along with more overtly nationalist political parties. Most of the groups were organized along ethnic lines. Even the Uganda National Congress (UNC), which formed in 1952 as a countrywide Ugandan political party, attracted primarily Baganda members. Britain had granted independence to India in 1947, and pressure for independence from colonial powers swept through Africa during the 1950s. Ghana's independence in 1957 seemed to confirm that independence for African colonies was inevitable. Partly as a result of these trends, by the end of the 1950s many Ugandan political organizations were jockeying themselves into position to take power upon independence.

The UNC split in 1959. MILTON OBOTE, a leader who had joined the colonial legislative council in 1958, broke away from the UNC with a group that eventually formed the Uganda People's Congress (UPC). In opposition to the UPC was the Democratic Party (DP). The DP was formed by Roman Catholic Baganda who were intent on preventing the Protestant Baganda king, Kabaka Freddie (Frederick Mutesa), from dominating postcolonial Uganda. The DP's concerns were based on the fact that the British had recently granted the kabaka real political power. In particular, leaders of the DP were wary of the kabaka's power to appoint and fire chiefs, a right he gained by pledging to put aside demands for complete Bugandan sovereignty. Despite this significant concession of power by the British, the kabaka's supporters, who called themselves the King's Friends, called for a boycott of the preindependence elections in 1961. Consequently, most Baganda did not vote, and the ethnically and geographically diverse Democratic Party won a majority of seats in the national assembly.

Independence

Uganda was granted independence on October 9, 1962. In subsequent elections, Obote's UPC allied with the Baganda sepa-

Idi Amin declared himself president for life when he overthrew Uganda's civilian government in 1971. His rule, characterized by corruption and brutality, ended in 1979 when Tanzanian troops joined with Ugandan rebels to force the dictator into exile. *CORBIS/Reuters NewMedia Inc.*

ratist party, Kabaka Yekka (KY) ("The King Only"). The UPC-KY alliance won and Obote became prime minister, while Kabaka Freddie became president. The following year Uganda became a federal republic of four semiautonomous regions: Ankole, Buganda, Bunyoro, and Toro. Shortly afterward relations between Obote and Kabaka Freddie began to deteriorate because Obote moved to eliminate Buganda's special status and to return the "lost countries" to the Bunyoro. Obote also sought to bolster his political power by expanding the military and using the expansion as a source of patronage. Obote endeavored to build a close relationship with the military by relying on IDI AMIN, one of a small number of African officers in the Ugandan military at independence.

In 1966 Obote and Amin faced an official investigation into allegations that they had smuggled gold and ivory out of the DEMOCRATIC REPUBLIC OF THE CONGO. Faced with the potential demise of his government, Obote quickly moved to centralize his authority and to eliminate his opposition. In addition to arresting five ministers, he declared himself head of state, and then ordered Amin to attack the kabaka's palace. He next suspended the constitution, replacing it with a new charter that radically reduced regional autonomy, dissolved the Buganda monarchy, and created an executive presidency, which Obote then claimed for himself.

Obote, an advocate of African SOCIALISM, further consolidated his power by nationalizing businesses. He relied on Amin and the Ugandan army to maintain order. Meanwhile, however, Amin's loyalty was becoming increasingly suspect, and Obote sought to curb the general's power. Obote survived an assassination attempt in 1969, but Amin seized power in 1971 while Obote was out of the country. Obote lived in exile in TANZANIA until Amin himself was overthrown several years later.

Amin's Reign of Terror

Ugandans initially welcomed Amin as a change from Obote's authoritarianism. However, the brutality, corruption, and volatility of the Amin regime quickly won international infamy. Amin is best known for ordering the military to assassinate his political opponents. These killings spread fear and chaos throughout the country, leading Amin to order even more executions in an effort to control the growing turmoil. Eventually the dead numbered in the hundreds of thousands.

Amin gained a reputation for quirky and impulsive decision-making. In 1972 he ordered the expulsion of all of Uganda's Asian merchants—about 50,000 people. Amin then took the expropriated farms and businesses and gave them to army officers loyal to his regime. Many of the enterprises failed, dealing a serious blow to Uganda's already weak economy. Amin was also known for his collaboration with the Palestine Liberation Organization in the hijacking of an Air France plane in 1976. In response, Israel dispatched a group of commandos to the airport at the southern Uganda city of Entebbe, where the hijacked aircraft sat. The Israeli commandos eventually rescued most of the hostages, humiliating Amin and his military.

In October 1978, perhaps in an effort to deflect attention away from Uganda's political and economic problems, Amin sent troops across the Kagera River into northern Tanzania. The Tanzanian army counterattacked and found Amin's forces weak and unable to mount an effective defense. Soon afterward Tanzanian troops allied with exiled Ugandan opposition forces to invade Uganda, and the combined force drove Amin from power in 1979. Amin fled to LIBYA and later to Saudi Arabia.

A coalition of civilian and military groups organized an interim government to restore order, but the fragile consensus soon broke down. After two brief transitional governments, Paulo Muwanga, an ally of former president Obote, seized control of the government. When national elections were held in December 1980 under a new constitution, Obote's Uganda People's Congress won. Obote again became president, despite claims by his opponents that the vote had been heavily rigged.

Continued Stagnation and Warfare under Obote

Initially Obote made some headway in rebuilding the economy and government institutions, both devastated by the Amin years. But formidable guerrilla forces soon began a war against the Obote regime. The most significant challenge came from the National Resistance Army (NRA) led by YOWERI MUSEVENI, a former Obote ally who charged that Obote and the UPC had stolen the 1980 elections. Obote responded through a brutal campaign to suppress the NRA and deprive it of civilian support. The Ugandan army focused on a small part of Buganda known as the Luwero Triangle, where the NRA had substantial support. Eventually, about 200,000 people died in the conflict, and a similar number became refugees.

As Obote became increasingly preoccupied with winning the war against the NRA, Uganda's economic reconstruction floundered. Austerity measures mandated by a World Bank development program failed, and Ugandans struggled to cope with skyrocketing inflation and shortages of staple goods. Obote was further distracted by violent conflicts between ACHOLI and LANGO members of the military. Acholi soldiers led by General Tito Okello ousted Obote in July 1985 after Obote appointed a Lango to a top army post. In January 1986 Okello was in turn pushed from power by Museveni's NRA.

Recovery Begins under Museveni

After his swearing in as president, Museveni began a ten-point program to ensure basic human rights, cultivate a sense of national unity, and redress the past abuses of Amin and Obote. Believing that a return to multiparty politics would invite the reemergence of ethnic and religious conflicts, Museveni banned all political parties. All candidates were required to run under the umbrella of the National Resistance Movement (NRM), the political party affiliated with Museveni's NRA. Although he postponed elections for several years, Museveni created an effective system of resistance councils to govern at the national, regional, and village levels. Museveni also abandoned the socialist principles that he had earlier embraced and cooperated with World Bank and other international financial institutions. Museveni thus won much praise and support from abroad, despite the fact that his government imposed restrictions on political opposition and was ruthless in dealing with rebel groups.

After single-party national elections in February 1989, Museveni's government announced it would extend its term until 1995 to provide adequate time to develop a new constitution, ensure free elections, and develop the country's social services. He took several steps to reconcile long-term grievances, including the reinstating of the traditional monarchies in Buganda and elsewhere, though only for ceremonial purposes. Museveni also invited Uganda's expelled Asians to return and reclaim assets that had been confiscated from them, and he radically reduced the size of the army.

Despite these measures, small rebel groups cropped up in several parts of the country. Most notably, in the late 1980s the government brutally defeated the forces of the HOLY SPIRIT MOVEMENT, a rebel group led by an Acholi priestess who claimed she could protect her followers with magic. The Holy Spirit Movement was soon revived as the Lord's Resistance Army, which suffered severe losses by the mid-1990s and began forcibly recruiting children to serve as soldiers. The group was still actively opposing the Museveni government in the early twenty-first century.

Museveni, most recently reelected in 1996, remains a firm advocate of what he calls a no-party electoral system, in which all potential candidates must be members of the NRM. Museveni argues that Western-style multiparty systems cannot be easily transferred to the African context. He argues that multiparty democracy might further divide the country along ethnic lines. Instead, Uganda's constitution allows candidates to campaign as individuals. In a referendum held in March 2000, widely criticized for irregularities, some 70 percent of voters agreed to keep the no-party system. Meanwhile, Museveni's regime has had success in rebuilding the economy—one of the fastest growing in Africa in the mid-1990s—and restoring relative domestic peace and stability. For example, inflation decreased from 240 percent in 1987 to less than 5 percent by 2001. These accomplishments have boosted his standing among foreign donors and investors, as well as among Africans. Indeed, Uganda is becoming an increasingly influential player in the regional politics of East and Central Africa.

Uganda supported LAURENT-DÉSIRÉ KABILA in his successful 1997 campaign to oust President MOBUTU SESE SEKO of Zaire (since renamed the Democratic Republic of the Congo, or DRC). In 1998, however, Uganda's government became frustrated that Kabila had been unable to stop Ugandan rebels from using the DRC as a safe haven. In mid-1998 Ugandan troops intervened in support of a TUTSI-led rebellion against Kabila's regime. This intervention threatened to engulf Uganda in a broader Central African war when forces from ANGOLA, ZIMBABWE, and NAMIBIA intervened in support of Kabila. The Sudanese government moved to cooperate with Kabila's alliance against Uganda because Uganda supported the People's Liberation Army led by JOHN GARANG DE MABIOR in southern SUDAN. These military entanglements darken the prospects that Uganda will maintain peace and economic growth despite looming problems such as ethnic strife, chronic rural poverty, and the spread of ACQUIRED IMMUNODEFICIENCY SYNDROME (AIDS), which had infected over a million Ugandans by 2003.

See also Christianity: Missionaries in Europe; Colonial Rule; Ethnicity and Identity in Africa: An Interpretation.

Ari Nave

Umar Tal

1797–1864

Muslim cleric and founder of the Tukulor empire of present-day Mali; also known as Umar ibn Siid Tal and al-Hajj Umar.

Umar Tal's religious movement popularized the Tijaniya Sufi order and influenced religious reformers throughout nineteenth-century West Africa. He was born in Halwar, in what is now SENEGAL. The son of a prominent TUKULOR cleric, Umar was influenced by the teachings of the Tijaniya brotherhood at an early age. In 1826 he made a pilgrimage to Mecca and on his return home visited several West African Islamic states, including the SOKOTO CALIPHATE in northern Nigeria, then ruled by MUHAMMAD BELLO. He moved to the FOUTA DJALLON region after Bello's death in 1837.

For the next decade, Umar divided his time between religious and commercial pursuits. Having already accumulated considerable wealth abroad, he acquired firearms by selling non-Muslim captives to the French. He also gained renown as a religious scholar. Umar's greater ambition, however, was to convert the non-Muslim BAMBARA and MANDINKA, and to unite the peoples of the region into one empire—not unlike the Sokoto Caliphate—based on the tenets of Tijaniya Sufism. In 1852 Umar mobilized his followers and launched the first of several jihads (holy wars) in the Senegal and NIGER RIVER valleys.

Umar's early campaigns easily conquered some of the smaller city-states and kingdoms, which he united under the rule of his sons. In the late 1850s, however, he met opposition from the French, who viewed the cleric's growing empire as a threat to French trade and future colonization. After a series of clashes Umar and the French signed a treaty in 1860. Ultimately, Umar was defeated by the Bambara kingdom of Ségou, once the kingdom allied with other rival forces from TOMBOUCTOU. Umar died in a fire that was set by his enemies. After Umar's death, his empire quickly disintegrated; most of the territory between the Senegal and Niger rivers was later colonized by the French.

See also Islam in Africa; Mali; Sufism.

Bibliography

Robinson, D. *The Holy War of Umal Tal: The Western Sudan in the Mid-Nineteenth Century.* Oxford University Press, 1985.

Willis, J. R. *Studies in West African Islamic History: The Cultivators of Islam.* Frank Cass, 1979.

Elizabeth Heath

Umbanda

Religion practiced by millions of Brazilians that combines elements of African religious traditions with Catholicism and European Spiritism.

Umbanda is the most widely practiced African-based religion in BRAZIL, with an estimated twenty million followers. Unlike CANDOMBLÉ, whose fame is linked to the efforts of its leaders to reproduce faithfully the rituals and practices of its West African forebears, Umbanda represents a tendency toward eclecticism. In Umbanda, diverse African traditions have blended with one another, with Catholicism, and with Spiritism, a form of Spiritualism known in Brazil as *Espiritismo* or *Kardecismo*.

Umbanda's rituals trace their roots to religions practiced by African slaves that were overlain by other religious influences encountered in the Brazilian environment. The popularity of those rituals—like the popularity of the religion itself—has moved far beyond the Afro-Brazilian population from which it derives. Modern followers of Umbanda are racially and ethnically diverse, ranging from Afro-Brazilian to Portuguese, Spanish, Italian, German, Lebanese, and Japanese. They come from every economic level, from the wealthy elite to the poorest res-

idents of shantytowns. Umbanda's membership has come to reflect the diversity of Brazil's population, and it is often viewed as a "Brazilian" rather than an "African" religion. Characteristically, many, though not all, practitioners also consider themselves Catholics. While some adherents emphasize Umbanda's Spiritist dimensions, others defend its African identity and practices. Before examining how its "Brazilianization" has come about, and the dynamics of its internal differences, it is useful to lay out the central features of Umbanda ritual and its pantheon of deities and spirits.

Umbanda Rituals

Umbanda shares with other Afro-Brazilian religions and Spiritism the belief that a wide variety of deities and spirits may intervene in the daily lives of humans to help or to harm them. Through Umbanda rituals, its followers pay homage to these entities, seek their protection, and solicit their help in resolving individual illnesses and personal problems. Umbanda is understood as a pragmatic and instrumental problem-solving religion.

At public ceremonies held each week in thousands of Umbanda churches (known as *centros* or *terreiros*), initiates and members of the congregation gather to celebrate Umbanda deities and spirits. Worshipers praise the deities with hymns, dancing, drumming, and hand clapping and call them to descend from the spirit world. They ask the spirits to take over or "possess" the bodies of trained initiates and, acting through them, to conduct healing rituals and give advice. Members of the congregation then have individual consultations with the spirit counselors, receive ritual cleansings, and may discuss their problems. People confide in the spirits about their health, employment, finances, and family and romantic problems. The spirits may recommend further ritual treatments, give practical advice, or inform clients that they can recover only through undergoing initiation into Umbanda. This is a particularly common diagnosis when clients experience spontaneous spirit possession while watching the ceremony or during their consultation, and it is the most common route through which clients become initiated into ritual roles. New initiates undergo stages of initiation as well as training sessions in mastering spirit possession. But this process is less time consuming and less costly than in Candomblé, and new initiates may rise rapidly within the ritual hierarchy. Within a few years they may gain sufficient knowledge, prestige, and authority to found their own centro.

Umbanda Deities and Spirits

The most powerful spiritual personages of Umbanda are African deities known by the Yoruban term ORISHA (the same deities found in Candomblé). Each orisha is syncretized, or strongly identified with a particular Catholic saint or member of the Holy Family, and is often represented in its Catholic form on Umbanda altars. Thus Ogun—Yoruban god of ironworking and of war—is identified with Saint George, and his representation

A typical Umbanda altar combines Catholic images, purifying water, and representations of Indian and African deities and spirits. *Peter Kloehn*

on Umbanda altars is often in the form of a Catholic statue of Saint George slaying the dragon. The orishas' histories are recounted in the Yoruba origin myth, and each has a distinctive personality and is identified with certain colors, foods, and with certain healing herbs.

While the orishas are often petitioned for aid, the major spiritual entities in Umbanda are the *caboclos* (spirits of Brazilian Indians) and *pretos velhos* ("old blacks," or spirits of Africans enslaved in Brazil). Disincarnated spirits of women and men who once lived on earth, they are less powerful than the orixás but more central because they conduct the healing activities in Umbanda ceremonies. Caboclo spirits are proud forest dwellers and warriors and can be male or female. The caboclo spirits each have individual names and hymns that detail their exploits, and they can often be identified in the ceremonies by their feather headdresses and large cigars. Pretos velhos are elderly, humble, and wise; they bear tales of enslavement. They are addressed familiarly as Father (Pai) or Aunt (Tia), and hobble about on canes puffing on their pipes. Both of these categories of spirits are considered expert in providing healing and advice.

Various other spiritual personages also appear on their appointed days in the centros. These include child spirits called Cosme and Damião, the twins, who cause great commotion as they crawl about the floor demanding pacifiers and candy; cowboy spirits, a branch of the caboclos whose hymns recount their

exploits in the northeastern backlands, or *sertão*; gypsy spirits; and *exús*. Exús are complicated and controversial figures in Umbanda. They are properly African orixás, messengers to the other orixás and trickster figures, doing good or evil according to whim and payment. However, under the influence of Catholicism and Spiritism, exús have become syncretized with the Christian Devil and associated with evil and ignorance. Exú and his female counterpart, Pomba Gira, a prostitute, are depicted in Umbanda as devils, with red bodies, and often scantily dressed.

In fact, the place of Exú in the pantheon is a good diagnostic and provides a point of departure for discussing internal differences within Umbanda. More Spiritist forms of Umbanda consider the exús to be amoral and minimize their role, while emphasizing Spiritist and Christian doctrine. These groups conduct very restrained ceremonies that feature initiates in white uniforms, while often eliminating dancing and drumming. More Afro-Brazilian forms give Exú, and the orishas in general, a more important ritual role and the ceremonies are far livelier, with drumming and dancing and initiates dressed in brightly colored outfits. Healing often occurs outside of the public ceremonies. Another African ritual element emphasized more in this form of Umbanda is the sacrifice of animals to the deities.

Roots of Umbanda

To appreciate fully the vitality of African religions and culture in Brazil, one must understand the nature of slavery in Brazil. From the beginning of the slave period in 1530 through the end of the trade in the 1850s, Brazilian slave owners continued to rely on slaves imported from Africa, rather than on a native-born slave labor force. This phenomenon resulted in continuing infusions of African cultures into Brazil over a period of more than 300 years. When Brazil abolished slavery in 1888, many of the newly freed slaves were still African born.

In the coastal province of BAHIA, the intensity of trade with West Africa resulted in a great numerical predominance of Yoruban and Dahomean slaves, which is reflected in the dominance of these traditions in Bahian Candomblé. By contrast, the slaves imported to RIO DE JANEIRO were of much more diverse origins. This diversity was compounded by the southward migration of many northern slaves and free blacks to Rio during the nineteenth century. By the 1920s the resultant blending of African religious traditions loosely referred to as "Macumba" showed some similarities to the Umbanda rituals described above and clearly formed a basis for the development of Umbanda.

The brutal incorporation of slaves into the economic and political system of the colony led to the forced destruction of many aspects of African culture, but religious practices were not as closely controlled. Some scholars have argued that the Catholic brotherhoods that exercised social control over urban slave populations actually contributed to the preservation of African religious practices. These brotherhoods were a major source of Afro-Catholic syncretism, as slaves worshiped African

This Umbanda altar (photographed in Brazil in 1988) celebrates Father Joaquim and Mother Congo, preto velho spirits. The former slaves who have become preto velhos are now important Umbanda healers. A background mural depicts Brazilian slave scenes. *Peter Kloehn*

deities in the guise of Catholic saints. As the brotherhoods declined in the nineteenth century, Afro-Brazilian religious practices emerged in Rio as in many urban areas of Brazil. Although they were declared illegal and frequently persecuted by the police, the clandestine practices continued, as Afro-Brazilians refused to give up this major part of their heritage. Rio was also the center of Spiritism, which originated in FRANCE in the mid-nineteenth century and quickly became popular among affluent Brazilians. Spiritists summoned disincarnated spirits, practiced healing, and through their charitable activities spread their practices to the popular classes.

Founding of Umbanda

In the 1920s a group of middle-class Spiritists in Rio de Janeiro came together to create a "new" religion called Umbanda. At the time, Brazil was involved in a period of intense nationalism, its leaders defining a national identity and struggling to unify the country and control its rapidly expanding urban lower classes. Influenced by European racist ideas, Brazil's leaders worried about how the country's large African-descended population could become a part of this modernity, and how its African cultural practices could be symbolically redefined as Brazilian. For many members of the dominant classes, including Umbanda's founders, Afro-Brazilian religions became, and have remained, a key element in this redefinition.

The founders of Umbanda drew upon existing Afro-Brazilian practices but sought to reorganize and transform them, to present a form of Umbanda whitened and purified from many of its African practices. They emphasized how its pantheon of Catholic saints, Brazilian Indian spirits, orixás, and pretos velhos provided a symbolic expression of Brazil's unique blend of Portuguese, Native Brazilian, and African peoples and

cultures, following the theme developed in Giberto Freyre's famous work *The Masters and the Slaves*. In short, the leaders' reorganization of Umbanda represented an effort by members of the dominant classes to appropriate and transform Afro-Brazilian religious culture into national Brazilian culture. Many of the older, more African-oriented centros recognized the racism and the appropriation implicit in this form of Umbanda, and ignored or resisted it. Within Umbanda's history and practice, efforts to appropriate the African religious heritage and resistance to this appropriation are each linked to particular forms of ritual and practice in Umbanda centros.

Given this history, it would be easy to imagine that divisions within Umbanda today would break down along class and racial lines, with more affluent white adherents preferring more Spiritist rituals, and the less empowered—especially Afro-Brazilians—identifying far more closely with the more African type of Umbanda. But although such identifications do occur, the overall situation is far more complicated. First, although continuing racial discrimination has greatly limited social mobility for Afro-Brazilians, most of whom remain among the poor, racial identities and solidarities in Brazil are not as clearly drawn as in the United States. Thus, there are few exclusively Afro-Brazilian constituencies that might form around Afro-Brazilian religions, though certainly there is a middle-class-based white constituency for the more Spiritist type of Umbanda. Moreover, some scholars argue that the Afro-Brazilian religious heritage itself has been so successfully appropriated into Brazilian national culture that it may have lost its power to symbolize a distinct Afro-Brazilian identity. Finally, the advantages of legitimacy, protection from police persecution, possible political favors, and Umbanda's influence in electoral politics have influenced many of the older, more Afro-Brazilian terreiros to join new Umbanda organizations and reshape their rituals in accord with the new mode of practice. Thus, it is very hard to draw clear linkages between particular forms of ritual practice and particular sectors of the population.

Nevertheless, recent research suggests that many new forms of opposition are developing to the "whitening" and blending of Afro-Brazilian religions represented in Umbanda. Some centros are turning to more African forms of ritual, and others rejecting the term *Umbanda* in favor of the older term *Macumba*. Even within those centros that continue to practice Umbanda in the form described here, the preto velho spirits appear in recent years to have become far more ambivalent figures than the humble spirits of the past. It has been suggested that these spirits serve as cultural heroes for many people of African descent. The accounts of their lives that the pretos velhos now tell to their followers give more emphasis to their acts of resistance to slavery, while some now claim they were never enslaved and served in African revolutionary movements. Umbanda, then, like other Afro-Brazilian religions, is always changing, responsive to the changing ways in which Brazilians relate to and identify with Brazil's African heritage. Its continuing vitality is also reflected in its spread to ARGENTINA, URUGUAY, and the United States.

See also Afro-Brazilian Culture; Catholic Church in Latin America and the Caribbean; Freyre, Gilberto; Race and Class in Brazil: An Interpretation; Religions, African; Yoruba (religion).

Bibliography

Bastide, Roger. *The African Religions of Brazil.* Translated by Helen Sebba. Johns Hopkins University Press, 1978.

Brown, Diana DeG. *Umbanda: Religion and Politics in Urban Brazil.* Columbia University Press, 1994.

Ortiz, Renato. "Ogum and the Umbandista Religion." In *Africa's Ogun: Old World and New.* Edited by Santra Barnes. Indiana University Press, 1989.

Diana Brown

Umm Kulthum

1904?–1975

Egyptian singer and one of the most popular Arab performers of the twentieth century.

Umm Kulthum was born in a small Egyptian village in the NILE RIVER Delta. Her father, al-Shaykh Ibrahim al-Sayyid al-Baltaji, an imam at the local mosque, earned extra money by singing religious songs at weddings and other ceremonies. Her mother, Fatmah al-Maliji, was a homemaker. At about five years old, she began attending the local Qur'an (Koran) school. Her father, noticing the unusual strength of the young girl's voice, taught her to sing. She began accompanying her father at the festivities and before long was the featured performer. Her reputation grew as she and her father toured the Nile Delta region as singers for the next ten years.

In around 1923, the family moved to CAIRO to enter the commercial music business. Although her powerful voice attracted favorable publicity, Umm Kulthum was not yet a technically polished singer. She spent the next five years studying with various musicians and expanding her repertory, and also began working with professional accompanists instead of her family. By 1928 Umm Kulthum was one of the leading singers in Cairo. Her recordings, along with monthly performances on Egyptian national radio beginning in 1934, boosted her popularity. She also starred in six musical films, beginning in 1935.

Umm Kulthum's increasing skill as a musician led her to take control of her career. She made both musical and professional decisions herself, produced her concerts, and negotiated contracts. In the 1940s, she joined the Listening Committee, which screened songs for airplay, and thereby extended her influence over the music industry. She also became the president of the Musician's Union.

A staunch supporter of the Egyptian Revolution that brought GAMAL ABDEL NASSER to power, Umm Kulthum recorded several patriotic songs and became an outspoken supporter of Egyptian culture. Over time, she became a close friend of President Nasser. During the 1950s, she advocated government support of Arab culture and musicians. After Egypt's humiliating defeat in the 1967 Six Day War with Israel, Umm Kulthum gave a series of concerts throughout the Arab world, the proceeds of which (over $2.3 million) she donated to the rearmament of Egypt's armed forces.

Umm Kulthum's failing health ended her career in the early 1970s, and she died of heart failure associated with kidney disease in 1975. Millions of Egyptians thronged the Cairo streets to join in her funeral procession, taking turns carrying the body of the "voice of Egypt" while reputedly chanting, "Good-bye! Good-bye our beloved songstress!" In her lengthy career, Umm Kulthum recorded more than 300 songs, including "Raqq al-Habib" (1944) and "al-Atial" (1966). In the late 1990s, she remained famous for her powerful voice, masterful interpretations of songs, and encouragement of traditional Arab music. More than twenty years after her death, her recordings still sold more than 300,000 copies annually.

See also Music, North African; Singer-Songwriters.

Kate Tuttle

Uncle Tom's Cabin

Best-selling but controversial 1852 American novel that increased worldwide sentiment against slavery.

When Harriet Beecher Stowe's antislavery novel *Uncle Tom's Cabin* was published, it was an immediate best seller, and became the most sensational and popular book of the nineteenth century. French writer George Sand described the international phenomenon: "This book is in all hands and in all journals. It has, and will have, editions in every form; people devour it, they cover it with tears." Since then, the novel has been criti-

A theater poster advertises a stage version of Harriet Beecher Stowe's antislavery novel, which was first published in 1852. *CORBIS/Bettmann*

cized for its stereotypical depictions of black characters, as well as its sentimentalism and moralism. But as problematic as some of the book's language and descriptions are, in the 1850s, *Uncle Tom's Cabin* evoked international sympathy for African American slaves.

Harriet Beecher Stowe was born in Connecticut in 1811, the daughter of Lyman Beecher, a prominent Congregational minister. The Beechers, who were white, had never owned slaves, but in 1832 they moved to CINCINNATI, OHIO, just across the Ohio River from slaveholding Kentucky. There, Stowe taught at a school for former slave children and was able to see at firsthand race riots, terrified runaway slaves, bounty hunters, and suffering freedpersons. Upon returning to New England in 1850, she decided to write a book about her insights, one of the only forms of protest available to her: "My heart was bursting with the anguish excited by the cruelty and injustice our nation was showing to the slave, and praying God to let me do a little and cause my cry for them to be heard."

Uncle Tom's Cabin's strong religious overtones appealed to its largely Christian, white, nineteenth-century audience. Its plot follows the story of Uncle Tom, a pious and faithful slave, as he is sold to several owners. His last owner beats him to death, but even as the Christ-like Uncle Tom is dying, he prays that his master will repent and be saved. A favorite character among

readers was Little Eva, a white child who treats her slaves with angelic love and kindness, and dies surrounded by weeping servants. Stowe complements these melodramatic deathbed scenes with equally dramatic descriptions of beatings, sexual abuse, and family separations, all of which added to the novel's powerful effect on its readers.

Uncle Tom's Cabin has had its critics. The first were Southern slaveholders, who argued that the book was horribly exaggerated fiction; ownership of the book was made illegal in the South. In response, Stowe published in 1853 *A Key to Uncle Tom's Cabin*, a collection of SLAVE NARRATIVES, newspaper clippings, and other facts that verified the details in her novel. In more recent years, many readers have criticized the condescending racist descriptions of the appearance, speech, and behavior of many of the book's black characters, and the excessive pietism of Uncle Tom.

Uncle Tom's Cabin was so widely read that its characters helped spread common stereotypes of African Americans. These included lazy, carefree Sam, an example of the "happy darky"; Eliza, Cassy, and Emmeline, beautiful light-skinned women who are the products and victims of sexual abuse and stereotypes of the tragic mulatto; and several affectionate, dark-skinned women house servants who are examples of the mammy (including a character named Mammy, the cook at the St. Clare plantation).

The name Uncle Tom has itself become a stereotype for an African American who is too eager to please whites. Soon after the book was published, traveling "Tom shows" became popular throughout the United States. These were essentially minstrel shows loosely based on *Uncle Tom's Cabin*, and their grossly exaggerated caricatures further perpetuated some of the stereotypes that Stowe used.

These negative associations now sometimes overshadow Stowe's original intentions, as well as the historical impact of *Uncle Tom's Cabin* as a vital antislavery tool. At the time of its publication, though, its impact was without question. Some have claimed that it so affected British readers that it kept GREAT BRITAIN from joining the American CIVIL WAR (1861–1865) on the side of the Confederacy. When President ABRAHAM LINCOLN met Stowe in 1862, he reportedly called her "the little woman who wrote the book that started this great war!" The cry that Stowe had hoped to sound about African Americans was indeed heard, and while *Uncle Tom's Cabin* did perpetuate cultural stereotypes of African Americans, it also turned the tide of public opinion against slavery in the United States.

See also Minstrelsy; Racial Stereotypes; Slavery in the United States.

Bibliography

Hedrick, Joan D. *Harriet Beecher Stowe: A Life.* Oxford University Press, 1994.

Reynolds, Moira Davidson. *Uncle Tom's Cabin and Mid-Nineteenth Century United States: Pen and Conscience.* McFarland, 1985.

Lisa Clayton Robinson

Descendents of fugitive slaves in this Underground Railroad village are returning to their roots and the key to their success—education—to raise funds to restore the historic 139-year school, shown here with the class of 1909/1910. Both black and white children attended the "colored" school, one of the few to offer a classical curriculum in North America, a century before desegregation. *Photo courtesy of Buxton Historic Site and Museum REUTERS*

Underground Railroad

Secret network devoted to helping runaway slaves in the Southern United States escape to freedom in the Northern states and Canada.

Beginning in the early nineteenth century and continuing up to the American CIVIL WAR, the Underground Railroad, or so-called freedom train, was the greatest hope of freedom for African Americans fleeing slavery in the South. This extensive network of people, places, and modes of transportation helped lead thousands of RUNAWAY SLAVES to freedom. Many slaves made the journey with the help of guides, who were often FREE BLACKS committed to the cause of abolition. White abolitionists also made significant contributions, but the freedom train was a powerful political statement made by African Americans who chose to "vote for freedom with their feet."

Freedom was always on the minds of African American slaves; it was a destiny that became idealized in many African American SPIRITUALS such as the following:

Well I don't know how and I don't know when,
But we're gonna be free one day.
That the freedom train's comin' round the bend
And we're gonna be free one day.
But it's comin' sure and its comin' fast
That we're gonna be free one day.
We're gonna step on board and be free at last!

The "freedom train" came infrequently and was often not on time. But when it did arrive, it was big enough and strong enough to carry the souls of the weary and to lighten the burdens of the downtrodden. The freedom train even brought hope and inspiration to those who could not physically make it on board. For years slaveholders mistakenly attributed the imagery

UNDERGROUND RAILROAD

Free States and Territories
Slave States
Decision Left to Territory
Escape Routes

300 km
300 mi

Atlantic Ocean

Gulf of Mexico

Canada

Mexico

MAINE
St. John
St. John River
Bangor
Portland
Montpelier
N.H.
VT.
MASS.
Boston
CONN.
R.I.
New Haven
New York
NEW JERSEY
Albany
Montreal
Kingston
Rochester
NEW YORK
Lake Ontario
Erie
Collingwood
Lake Erie
PENNSYLVANIA
Philadelphia
Baltimore
Md.
Washington, D.C.
DELAWARE
Cumberland
Harpers Ferry
Norfolk/Portsmouth
VIRGINIA
Greensboro
New Bern
Wilmington
NORTH CAROLINA
Charleston
SOUTH CAROLINA
Cleveland
Marietta
Columbus
OHIO
Ironton
Ripley
Sandusky
Toledo
Detroit
Port Huron
Lake Huron
Lake Michigan
Lake Superior
MICHIGAN
WISCONSIN
Milwaukee
Chicago
ILLINOIS
Springfield
Quincy
Chester
Cairo
INDIANA
Indianapolis
Jeffersonville
Leavenworth
Evansville
KENTUCKY
Berea
Gallatin
TENNESSEE
Memphis
Mississippi
ARKANSAS
MISSOURI
Joplin
Mound City
IOWA
Des Moines
Davenport
Percival
MINNESOTA
NORTH DAKOTA
SOUTH DAKOTA
NEBRASKA
KANSAS
COLORADO
WYOMING
MONTANA
Missouri
Natchez
Bunkie
LOUISIANA
MISSISSIPPI
ALABAMA
GEORGIA
Savannah
Jacksonville
St. Augustine
FLORIDA
OKLAHOMA
TEXAS
NEW MEXICO
Rio Grande

75°
90°
105°
45°
30°

of the freedom train in Negro spirituals to fanciful illusions in the minds of slaves about dying and going to heaven. It is now generally known, as the slaveholders learned, that the freedom train was real and powerful.

Historians have traditionally underestimated and understated the role of blacks, and overestimated the role of sympathetic whites, in the Underground Railroad. White abolitionists did provide safe houses, money, boats, and other material resources that were sometimes vital to successful escapes. But free blacks often risked much more—their own freedom and lives—in order to travel south to help lead others to safety. Among the more prominent "conductors" of the freedom train was HARRIET TUBMAN. A former slave who had escaped to the North, Tubman traveled to the South an estimated nineteen times and guided more than 300 slaves to freedom. She epitomized the success and daring of the freedom train. Through her stories and those of others, there exists a rich legacy detailing the network that is said to have helped over 1,000 slaves each year to free themselves from bondage.

Few details of the Underground Railroad are known because of the extreme secrecy required in its operation, but there are reports of its existence as early as 1837. The exact number of slaves who were freed by the railroad is also not known because, in the interests of security, the conductors of the railroad could not keep records. Although this number was never high enough to threaten the institution of slavery itself, the l egends and metaphor of the freedom train proved much more ominous to slaveholders. Tales that were often repeated throughout the nation included, for example, the story of HENRY "BOX" BROWN, a black man who packed himself in a wooden crate and shipped himself to freedom in Philadelphia. Another popular story concerned WILLIAM AND ELLEN CRAFT, a married couple whose escape was based on their disguise—she as a "Spanish gentleman" and he as her black slave. The accounts of runaway slaves instilled fear in the hearts of Southern slaveowners, and inspired Northern abolitionists to form larger and stronger antislavery organizations.

As the Underground Railroad gained notoriety, it became even more secret. A virtually undetected escape route ran from Texas to MEXICO, but almost no information exists about how it functioned or how many African Americans quietly blended into the Mexican populace. It became difficult to distinguish between fact and fiction in accounts of the escapes. However, researchers have been able to uncover many details, especially from the accounts of free blacks who wrote memoirs or autobiographies. Free blacks such as WILLIAM STILL, DAVID RUGGLES, WILLIAM WELLS BROWN, FREDERICK DOUGLASS, and HENRY HIGHLAND GARNET joined Tubman in the struggle for self-emancipation. Most worked in silence and sometimes even in disguise.

Runaway slaves waded through swamps, concealed themselves in the hulls of ships, hid on the backs of carriages, and navigated circuitous routes by using the North Star at night— always with the understanding that they might be caught or betrayed at any time. Many were pursued by professional slave catchers (some with dogs), who all had the authority to detain and hold itinerant African Americans south of the Mason-Dixon Line. The Southern press was full of advertisements for escaped slaves. These descriptions constitute one of the few sources of accurate personal details about individuals in the slave community. The advertisements, in the slaveholders' own words, often mentioned maimed limbs and scars from whipping—vivid descriptions that Northern abolitionists used verbatim in their condemnation of slavery.

On the way to freedom, slaves and their guides often found it difficult to obtain food, clothing, and shelter. Free blacks in cities such as PHILADELPHIA and BOSTON formed "vigilance committees" to meet these and other needs. The committees cared for runaways after they arrived on free soil, hid them to prevent their recapture, and aided them on their way to Canada. The Philadelphia Association for the Moral and Mental Improvement of the People of Color was one of the most prominent black vigilance committees.

With the aid of black vigilance committees the Underground Railroad continued to guide slaves to freedom up until the time of the Civil War itself, when thousands of slaves freed themselves by leaving the plantations and escaping behind Union Army lines. For those who still labored as slaves at the beginning of the Civil War, the legend of the Underground Railroad held out hope. In the words of another Negro spiritual:

I know my Lord is a man of war;
He fought my battle at Hell's dark door.
Satan thought he had me fast;
I broke his chain and got free at last.

See also Abolitionism in the United States; Slavery in the United States.

Alonford James Robinson

UNESCO Race Relations Project

Series of research projects on race relations in Brazil from 1951 to 1952, sponsored by the United Nations Educational, Scientific, and Cultural Organization (UNESCO), aimed at revealing the country's experience in race relations, which at the time was deemed unique and successful.

After World War II, one of UNESCO's major missions was to understand the conflict and its most perverse consequence, the Holocaust. With the persistence of racism in the United States and SOUTH AFRICA, the emergence of the Cold War, and the process of decolonization in Africa and Asia, the issue of race continued to attract attention. UNESCO stimulated the development of scientific knowledge about racism, looking at motivations, consequences, and possible ways of overcoming it.

In the late 1940s, two events highlighted the agency's efforts against racial intolerance. First, at a meeting of experts from the social and natural sciences, participants discussed the scientific standing of the concept of race. The resulting "Statement on Race," published in May 1950 at UNESCO's Fifth General Conference in Florence, was the first document published with the support of a supranational agency that denied any deterministic association between physical characteristics, social behaviors, and moral attributes, beliefs that were still in fashion during the 1930s and 1940s. Second, at the same conference, BRAZIL was selected as the object of a comprehensive investigation of the economic, social, political, cultural, and psychological aspects that influenced, or did not, the emergence of cooperative relations between races and ethnic groups. In choosing Brazil, the purpose was to focus on potentially positive experiences and thus offer the world a new political consciousness based on the possibility of harmony between the races.

Since the nineteenth century, travelers to Brazil from EUROPE and the United States recorded with surprise the apparently peaceful coexistence of races and ethnic groups. This image of a "racial paradise," in contrast with the persistently turbulent North American experience, also connected with the fears of Brazilian elites. Especially after the belated abolition of slavery and adoption of a republican form of government, Brazil's elites saw the large proportion of blacks in the population, and the frequency of MISCEGENATION, as obstacles to the country's progress toward modernity. However, during the first decades of the twentieth century, particularly between the 1920s and 1940s, this view began to change. Due to Brazil's economic, social, and political transformations, and because of the importance given by intellectual circles to the precise identification of the country's national identity, the pessimistic view about the contributions of the founding races was preempted by a positive perspective. In this view, Brazil's racial mix was seen as an indicator of tolerance and harmony, and as a positive and unique feature of the country's national identity. The controversial belief in Brazilian racial democracy was elaborated in the most sophisticated analysis by Brazilian sociologist GILBERTO FREYRE. The belief became one of the major ideological components of Brazilian nationalism, and was substantial enough to gain an international audience.

It was in the wake of Nazi genocide that Brazil's seemingly harmonious racial and ethnic relations gained increased notoriety, attracting UNESCO's attention. In 1949, the Brazilian anthropologist Arthur Ramos, a specialist in Afro-Brazilian cults, became the head of UNESCO's Department of Social Sciences. He proceeded to draw the outlines of a research project to be developed in Brazil. His concerns merged with those of several social scientists involved in research about Brazilian issues and who were aware that certain demands—such as industrialization and the struggle against illiteracy—had been included in the agenda of the international agency on account of pressures generated specifically by underdeveloped countries. It was the combination of this belief in the positive nature of Brazilian sociability and of the idea that certain sectors of the population—such as blacks—needed to be incorporated into modernity that gave origin to the UNESCO project.

Research for the project was conducted during the early 1950s in both the traditional North and Northeast and in the more modernized Southeast. Social scientists from Brazil, FRANCE, and the United States, such as FLORESTAN FERNANDES, Roger Bastide, and Charles Wagley, participated in the project. The UNESCO project findings showed not only an enormous social distance between whites and blacks but also little social mobility among nonwhites. In the North and Northeast, racial prejudice was deemed to be subtle but nonetheless existent. Research in southeastern areas looked at racial relations in Brazil's major development centers, RIO DE JANEIRO and São Paulo, where economic and social changes were intense. Here blacks and mulattoes had to deal, during the last years of slavery, with large numbers of European immigrants, and racial tensions were deemed more visible. Although findings differed from one region to another, there was a consensus about the higher congeniality in the relations between blacks and whites in Brazil, as compared to the United States and South Africa. The project also found that racial classification in Brazil combined phenotypic definitions with nonbiological attributes such as class, status, and education. Thus a complex system of racial classification was revealed.

Research under UNESCO's auspices in the 1950s brought, first, a reinforcement of the Brazilian sociological tradition of investigating relations between whites and blacks, which had gained earlier prominence in the 1930s with the writings of Gilberto Freyre and Donald Pierson. Second, social sciences in Brazil, which were then being institutionalized, expanded their scope and have since systematically studied the issue of race relations. The project produced a vast documentation about the existence of prejudice and discrimination against Brazilian blacks. Focusing on these issues, the UNESCO projects prompted new questions about Brazil and helped identify difficulties, deadlocks, and conflicts in a society in the process of urbanization and industrialization. However, the recognition that there was a "Brazilian style of racism" did not preclude the participating social scientists from noticing, nonetheless, the existence of a set of social relations that could contribute to an authentic racial democracy in Brazil.

See also Decolonization in Africa: An Interpretation; Race and Class in Brazil: An Interpretation.

Bibliography

Skidmore, Thomas E. *Black into White: Race and Nationality in Brazilian Thought*. Duke University Press, 1993 .

Wagley, Charles, ed. *Race and Class in Rural Brazil*. UNESCO, 1952.

Marcos Maio

United Nations in Africa

United Nations (UN) agencies and programs, which have been involved in decolonization, peacekeeping, famine relief, human rights, and economic development in Africa.

AFRICA has been the site of some of the United Nations' greatest achievements as well as its biggest failures. The UN played an important role in assuring many African colonies' peaceful transition to independence, and has since mobilized successful international campaigns for children's health and the eradication of diseases. UN-sponsored diplomacy has helped resolve a number of long-running conflicts, especially in southern Africa. However, long-term solutions to chronic poverty, social inequality, and political instability in Africa have eluded the UN, and the questionable effectiveness of UN peacekeeping troops in SOMALIA and RWANDA provoked widespread criticism, both in Africa and abroad.

When the UN was created in 1945, only ETHIOPIA, LIBERIA, and SOUTH AFRICA were independent nations in Africa. But for Europe's colonial powers, the costs of maintaining COLONIAL RULE were growing unsustainably high, due in part to burgeoning nationalist movements throughout much of Africa. Decolonization was thus one of the UN's first concerns in Africa, and the transition to independence was a principal concern during the early postwar period. In accordance with one of the four guiding UN principles—the development of friendly international relations based on equality and self-determination—the UN General Assembly created a special committee to oversee conditions in colonial territories in 1947. The committee gathered information on the territories and supported their right to self-determination.

In addition, after World War II, the UN took over from the League of Nations trusteeships of six former German and Italian colonies in Africa, among them TANGANYIKA (now TANZANIA) and TOGO. Like most French, British, and Belgian colonies in Africa, these trusteeships were all independent by the early 1960s. White minority rule persisted in much of southern Africa, however. In 1965 the UN imposed sanctions on SOUTHERN RHODESIA, but only after a long liberation war did IAN SMITH's regime step down, leading to independence for the renamed ZIMBABWE in 1980.

The UN also supported independence for Portuguese-ruled ANGOLA and MOZAMBIQUE and opposed South Africa's occupation of SOUTH-WEST AFRICA, now NAMIBIA. There, a UN program to lead Namibia to independence was established in 1968. After years of resistance, South Africa agreed to relinquish Namibia provided that Cuban troops left nearby Angola. The UN-supervised elections took place in 1989, and full Namibian independence was declared the following year. Finally, the UN General Assembly repeatedly condemned APARTHEID in South Africa itself. When apartheid was finally dismantled in the early 1990s, UN monitors observed the 1994 elections that swept to victory NELSON MANDELA, South Africa's first black president.

Soon after the first wave of African decolonization in the early 1960s, UN diplomacy on the continent turned to conflict resolution and peacekeeping. The results have been mixed. The 1960–1964 UN operation in the REPUBLIC OF THE CONGO became the first of many such endeavors. UN troops, mostly African, were called to the Republic of the Congo after a secession attempt by Katanga Province led to intervention by Belgian troops, purportedly to protect Belgian citizens. Dag Hammarskjöld, then UN secretary-general, died in a plane crash en route to the Republic of the Congo. The UN troops left after the rebels surrendered, but ongoing civil conflict led to a coup in 1965 by MOBUTU SESE SEKO, whose dictatorship contributed to political instability in Central Africa for decades.

UN peacekeeping troops and observers have since served in many African countries. As of 2003 the UN was involved in seven ongoing peacekeeping missions in Africa (SIERRA LEONE, WESTERN SAHARA, Liberia, CÔTE D'IVOIRE, DEMOCRATIC REPUBLIC OF THE CONGO, and ETHIOPIA/ERITREA). Two of its most controversial interventions occurred in the early 1990s. In Somalia, the UN's Operation Restore Hope, from 1993 to 1995, was intended to secure the distribution of famine relief aid under conditions of civil war. The operation was widely criticized for strengthening the hand of SOMALI warlords in the capital of MOGADISHU, and for causing the deaths of eighty-three UN soldiers. Media images of the bodies of dead American soldiers being dragged through the streets provoked outrage in the United States. In the wake of the 1994 genocide in Rwanda, many both in Rwanda and abroad blamed the UN peacekeeping force in the country for failing to prevent it. The UN has since defended its role, attributing the force's inaction to opposition from the United States.

The Rwandan genocide and other civil conflicts made refugee crises one of the UN's chief concerns in Africa in the 1990s. In 1995 the UN high commissioner for refugees (UNHCR) estimated that some 4.5 million refugees from thirty African countries were in need of assistance.

The UN has been extensively involved in food security in Africa. The Food and Agriculture Organization (FAO) runs many programs to improve agriculture and nutrition. For example, a program was introduced in Zimbabwe in 1996 to reduce pesticide use through the introduction of natural predators, crop rotation, and disease-resistant plant varieties; and a 1993 erosion control plan in BURUNDI encouraged tree, shrub, and grass planting. The United Nations Development Program (UNDP) also devotes about 25 percent of its aid to food-related projects in Africa. Yet warfare and drought, among other factors, have led to repeated regional food shortages since the 1960s, including famines in the SAHEL and the Horn of Africa in the 1970s and mid-1980s and in SUDAN in the late 1990s. By the 1970s, the FAO was heavily involved in distributing food aid, including emergency relief aid, through its World Food Program (WFP). The proportion of FAO resources devoted to disaster relief rather than long-term food security rose even higher in the early 1990s, but the organization is also engaged in crop research and development projects and in programs to improve food distribution systems in African countries.

Since the early 1980s, the UN's International Bank for Reconstruction and Development, commonly known as the World Bank, has engaged most countries in Africa in multiyear programs to reduce high national debts and promote economic growth. Known as structural adjustment programs (SAPs), they tie multilateral loans to economic reforms, such as price and currency deregulation and the privatization of state-run enterprises. The World Bank also provides funds for many development projects in Africa as well as technical assistance and project evaluation. In the 1990s the World Bank became Africa's largest source of loan funds.

Another major player in the African arena is the UN's World Health Organization (WHO). WHO's most outstanding achievement may have been the eradication of smallpox. Starting in 1958, WHO mounted a massive international vaccination campaign. The last smallpox case was reported in 1977, and in 1980 the disease was declared eradicated worldwide. WHO also made great progress against ONCHOCERCIASIS (or river blindness), a debilitating disease that had made large regions of Sahelian West Africa uninhabitable. WHO's Onchocerciasis Control Programme, begun in 1974, had eliminated the disease from West Africa by 2002. In 1996 WHO launched a similar program to combat onchocerciasis in Central and East Africa. WHO also hopes to eradicate both poliomyelitis and iodine deficiency disorders by the year 2005. WHO's Global Programme on acquired immunodeficiency syndrome (AIDS) was launched in 1985. With some twenty-nine million Sub-Saharan Africans infected with human immunodeficiency virus (HIV)/AIDS—about 70 percent of the world's total number of cases—AIDS prevention and treatment have become major WHO priorities. The agency is also involved in stopping the spread of other diseases, especially MALARIA, the world's number-one infectious disease in fatalities.

Other UN entities active in Africa include the United Nations Children's Fund (UNICEF); the United Nations Educational, Scientific and Cultural Organization (UNESCO); and the United Nations Environment Programme (UNEP). Both the present UN secretary-general, KOFI ANNAN of GHANA, and his predecessor, the Egyptian BOUTROS BOUTROS-GHALI, are African, indicating the increasing presence of Africans in high-ranking UN positions and helping to focus UN priorities on Africa and other Third World regions. Secretary-General Annan has urged member nations to devote more attention to the needs of the poor and to pay their UN dues (many countries are far behind in payments) so that the organization can more effectively address Africa's problems and conflicts.

See also Acquired Immunodeficiency Syndrome in Africa: An Interpretation; Decolonization in Africa: An Interpretation; Diseases, Infectious, in Africa; Economic Development in Africa; Human Rights in Africa; Hunger and Famine; Nationalism in Africa; Structural Adjustment in Africa.

David P. Johnson, Jr.

United Negro College Fund

An American organization founded on April 25, 1944, to provide financial support to students at historically black colleges and universities.

At its inception, the United Negro College Fund (UNCF) was a consortium of twenty-seven institutions with 14,000 students. Today there are thirty-nine member colleges, and the UNCF

has financially helped more than 300,000 African Americans to graduate. The current president is WILLIAM GRAY III, a Baptist minister from PHILADELPHIA who is a former congressperson. The UNCF headquarters are in Fairfax, Virginia, and there are twenty regional offices.

With the motto "A mind is a terrible thing to waste," the UNCF's programs help provide low-cost quality education for deserving students and include premedical summer enrichment seminars, international exchange, and technical assistance to faculty and administration at historically black colleges and universities. Many alumni of historically black schools who received UNCF support have gone on to become leaders in the legal and medical fields, academia, politics, and government.

In 1998 the Lilly Endowment, one of the country's largest foundations, gave the UNCF a gift of $42 million. According to the UNCF, the grant contributed to the fund's capital projects by providing money for new construction, building renovation, laboratory equipment, and information technology upgrades. This is in addition to need-based as well as merit scholarships, and faculty support via endowed chairs and curriculum development.

In 2000 Microsoft, AT&T, and IBM formed a partnership with UNCF to support its Technology Enhancement Capital Campaign (TECC). Microsoft helped launch the campaign with a $50 million software donation. The TECC has strengthened the technology capabilities of UNCF's member institutions and enhanced the educational experiences of their students.

See also Educational Organizations in the United States.

College Enrollments, 1972–2002 (Figures in thousands)

Year	Total Male	Total Female	Black Males	Black Females
1972	3,982	3,010	287	253
1975	4,393	3,715	294	372
1978	4,445	4,502	305	390
1981	4,724	5,245	325	424
1984	4,725	5,185	367	419
1987	4,878	5,426	377	445
1990	5,030	6,077	426	457
1993	5,442	6,517	387	511
1996	5,533	6,772	422	561
1999	5,554	6,492	501	644
2002	5,929	7,497	475	751

Source: 2002, U.S. Census Bureau. Current Population Survey, Table A-5 "The Population 14 to 24 Years Old by High School Graduate Status, College Enrollment, Attainment, Sex, Race, and Hispanic Origin: October 1967 to 2002" and Table A-7 "College Enrollment of Students 14 Years Old and Over, by Type of College, Attendance Status, Age, and Gender: October 1970 to 2002."

Admissions to Four-Year Colleges and Universities

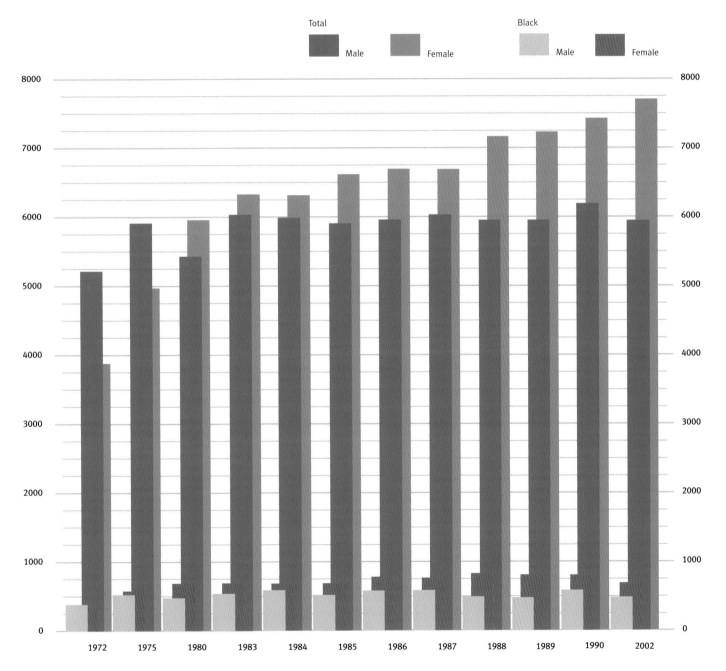

Source: *Encyclopedia of African-American Culture and History* (1996): "College Enrollment, 1972–1991" (Table 6.12); *Statistical Abstracts*, 1993 and *Source*: 2002, U.S. Census Bureau. Current Population Survey, Table A-5 "The Population 14 to 24 years Old by High School Graduate Status, College Enrollment, Attainment, Sex, Race, and Hispanic Origin: October 1967 to 2000" and Table A-7 "College Enrollment of Students 14 years Old and Over, by Type of College, Attendance Status, Age, and Gender: October 1970 to 2002".

Historically Black Colleges and Universities

State	City	Institution	Founding Date	State	City	Institution	Founding Date
Alabama	Birmingham	Miles College	1905	Georgia (cont.)	Atlanta	Turner Theological Seminary	1894
	Huntsville	Oakwood College	1896		Augusta	Paine College	1882
	Montgomery	Alabama State University	1866		Fort Valley	Fort Valley State College	1895
	Normal	Alabama A&M University	1875		Savannah	Savannah State College	1890
	Talladega	Talladega College	1867	Kentucky	Berea	Berea College	1855
	Tuscaloosa	Stillman College	1876		Frankfort	Kentucky State University	1886
	Tuskegee	Tuskegee University	1881	Louisiana	Baton Rouge	Southern University and A&M College, Baton Rouge	1880
Arkansas	Little Rock	Arkansas Baptist College	1884				
	Little Rock	Philander-Smith College	1877		Grambling	Grambling State University	1901
	Pine Bluff	University of Arkansas at Pine Bluff	1873		New Orleans	Dillard University	1869
					New Orleans	Southern University at New Orleans	1956
Delaware	Dover	Delaware State University	1891		New Orleans	Xavier University of Louisiana	1915
District of Columbia	Washington	Howard University	1867		Shreveport	Southern University at Shreveport	1964
	Washington	University of the District of Columbia	1851	Maryland	Baltimore	Coppin State College	1900
Florida	Daytona Beach	Bethune-Cookman College	1904		Baltimore	Morgan State University	1867
	Jacksonville	Edward Waters College	1866		Bowie	Bowie State College	1865
	Miami	Florida Memorial College	1879		Princess Anne	University of Maryland, Eastern Shore	1886
	Tallahassee	Florida A&M University	1887	Mississippi	Holly Springs	Rust College	1866
Georgia	Albany	Albany State College	1903		Itta Bena	Mississippi Valley State University	1946
	Atlanta	Atlanta University	1865		Jackson	Jackson State University	1877
	Atlanta	Charles H. Mason Theological Seminary	1970		Lorman	Alcorn State University	1871
	Atlanta	Clark College	1869		Tougaloo	Tougaloo College	1869
	Atlanta	Gammon Theological Seminary	1883		Tuscaloosa	Stillman College	1876
	Atlanta	Johnson C. Smith Theological Seminary	1867	Missouri	Jefferson City	Lincoln University	1866
	Atlanta	Morehouse College	1867		St. Louis	Harris-Stowe State University	1857
	Atlanta	Morehouse School of Medicine	1974	North Carolina	Charlotte	Johnson C. Smith University	1867
	Atlanta	Morehouse School of Religion	1867		Concord	Barber-Scotia College	1867
	Atlanta	Morris Brown College	1881		Durham	North Carolina Central University	1909
	Atlanta	Phillips School of Theology	1945				
	Atlanta	Spelman College	1881				

(continued)

Historically Black Colleges and Universities (*Continued*)

State	City	Institution	Founding Date	State	City	Institution	Founding Date
North Carolina (*cont.*)	Elizabeth City	Elizabeth City State University	1891	Tennessee	Jackson	Lane College	1882
					Knoxville	Knoxville College	1863
	Fayetteville	Fayetteville State Univesity	1867		Memphis	LeMoyne-Owen College	1862
	Greensboro	Bennett College	1873		Nashville	Fisk University	1866
	Greensboro	North Carolina A&T State University	1891		Nashville	Meharry Medical College	1876
	Raleigh	Shaw University	1865		Nashville	Tennessee State University	1912
	Raleigh	Saint Augustine's College	1867	Texas	Austin	Huston-Tillotson College	1875
	Salisbury	Livingstone College	1879		Hawkins	Jarvis Christian College	1912
	Winston-Salem	Winston-Salem State University	1892		Houston	Texas Southern University	1927
Ohio	Wilberforce	Central State University	1887		Marshall	Wiley College	1873
	Wilberforce	Wilberforce University	1856		Prairie View	Prairie View A&M University	1876
Oklahoma	Langston	Langston University	1897		Tyler	Texas College	1894
Pennsylvania	Cheyney	Cheyney University	1837		Waco	Paul Quinn College	1872
	Lincoln	Lincoln University	1853	Virginia	Hampton	Hampton University	1868
South Carolina	Columbia	Allen University	1870		Lawrenceville	Saint Paul's College	1883
	Columbia	Benedict College	1870		Norfolk	Norfolk State University	1935
	Denmark	Vorhees College	1897		Petersburg	Virginia State University	1882
	Orangeburg	Claflin College	1869		Richmond	Virginia Union University	1865
	Orangeburg	South Carolina State University	1872	West Virginia	Bluefield	Bluefield State College	1895
	Sumter	Morris College	1908		Institute	West Virginia State College	1891

Source: *Encyclopedia of African-American Culture and History* (1996): "Historically Black Colleges and Universities" (Table 6.13).

United States Economy and African Americans

African Americans and issues of work, business, finance, and economic science.

For information on
Work and the relations of African Americans to the workplace: *See* Business and African Americans; Development of Technology, African Americans and the; Labor Unions in the United States; Sharecropping; Work, African Americans and the Changing Nature of, in the Post–World War II Era: An Interpretation.

Successful African American businesspeople: *See* Antoine, Caeser Carpentier; Binga, Jesse; Boyd, Henry Allen; Bush, George Washington; Church, Robert Reed, Sr.; Clark, Alexander G.; Cook, John Francis, Jr.; Downing, George Thomas; Flora, William; Forten, James, Sr.; Lewis, Reginald F.; Llewellyn, James Bruce; Merrick, John; Muhammad, Elijah; Smith, Stephen; Thomas, James P.; Walker, Madame C.J.; Walker, Maggie Lena; Winfrey, Oprah Gail; Wormley, James.

Economic analysts: *See* Brimmer, Andrew F.; Wilson, William Julius.

Government economic programs: *See* Affirmative Action; American Electoral Politics, Blacks in; National Welfare Rights Organization; New Deal; Works Progress Administration.

United States House of Representatives, African Americans in

See Congress, African Americans in.

United States Judiciary, Blacks in the

The nominee for the newly created position on the United States Court of Appeals for the Third Circuit approached confirmation hearings with impressive credentials. He was a graduate of Amherst College (Phi Beta Kappa and magna cum laude) and Harvard Law School (J.D., S.J.D.; law review editor) as well as a member of the faculty, and later dean, of Howard University School of Law. He served as assistant solicitor in the U.S. Department of the Interior, civilian aide to the secretary of war in World War II, and was a personal adviser to President Harry S. Truman. He was a former governor and U.S. District Court judge. The nominee in question was WILLIAM HENRY HASTIE, the first African American appointed to the federal bench. His nomination was roundly endorsed by the attorney general and the American Bar Association. Moreover, the sitting judges on the Third Circuit—his colleagues by virtue of his recess appointment to the new judgeship—actively lobbied their U.S. senators on his behalf. Yet his unprecedented appointment was engulfed in often vicious political controversy—at one point even degenerating to the branding of Hastie by some as a Communist, which in the climate of the times was a deadly accusation. Between his nomination and eventual confirmation ten months later, hearings were postponed, a special subcommittee was impaneled to consider his nomination, and the political nerves of those both on and off the bench were rubbed raw.

Federal judges are important not only because they decide conflicts (cases) between individuals and groups in society, but also because they interpret the Constitution. In the process they determine how broad statements like "equal protection under the laws" in the FOURTEENTH AMENDMENT apply to specific situations such as the legality of segregation or affirmative action. Federal judges are nominated by the president and must be confirmed by the U.S. Senate. They "hold their Offices during good Behavior," which means they serve for life unless removed from office (a truly extraordinary event). Consequently, the mark that presidents place on the courts with their appointments is evident for years or even decades after they leave office. For example, twenty-three years after Lyndon Johnson left the White House, THURGOOD MARSHALL was still on the U. S. Supreme Court.

At the dawn of the twenty-first century, some are proclaiming the start of an almost revolutionary diversification of the federal courts. This process was spearheaded by the efforts of President Bill Clinton, who promised to use his appointment power to create a bench that "looks like America." Indeed almost 20 percent of President Clinton's appointments went to African Americans, which raised substantially the overall percentage to 10.1 by the end of his presidency. (African Americans comprise 12.7% of the population generally, by comparison.) Nevertheless, the preponderance of these appointments was to certain states or regions: African Americans have never been represented in the district courts of nineteen states and one circuit.

That percentage was unchanged at the close of the 107th Congress in 2002. Moreover, the general trend toward diversification is diluted because the bulk of appointments have been to the district courts, rather than to the more prestigious and powerful appeals courts where the current percentage of sitting African American judges is 8.8 percent.

Research on federal judicial selection indicates that minority appointments are likely to come from areas where there are higher concentrations of African American voters and economic power, often in the form of business ownership. The African American community in those areas is a force to be recognized and reckoned with, which leads to representation on the bench. Given the structure of the judicial selection process, however, the president is the key player, and the degree to which diversification is achieved is, in large measure, a product of how important that goal is to a president.

The First Inroads: 1937–1976

The federal judiciary—by nature of a shared institutional appointment process—is inextricably bound to the president and Congress, which in turn interact with the larger society. Genuine progress is rarely made until all the elements in this complex mix are prepared to support change. This principle is demonstrated in the chain of events that started with the Supreme Court's decision in BROWN V. BOARD OF EDUCATION in 1954, which among other things set the stage for congressional approval of the Civil Rights Act of 1964 and the VOTING RIGHTS ACT OF 1965. These two acts were, in turn, enforced vigorously by President Johnson's attorney general, Ramsey Clark.

No African American was appointed to the federal judiciary until 1937. Even after that, the first two—William Hastie and his successor, Herman Moore—were named as district judges to the Virgin Islands. Unlike judicial appointments from states, territorial appointments are set for a fixed term rather than for life. Additionally, even though territorial appointees must be confirmed by the Senate, they do not serve an area that is represented by a senator. Accordingly, they elude the "not in my backyard" mentality of elected politicians serving in a pervasively racist political climate. Hastie's appointment, in other words, was part of no grand effort to diversify the judiciary. Prior to his nomination he served with distinction as the Interior Department's assistant solicitor in charge of the Virgin Islands; he was subsequently the governor of this territory. Interior Secretary Harold Ickes recommended him to President Roosevelt when a vacancy occurred on the Virgin Islands court.

For his time, Roosevelt's successor, Harry Truman, was progressive with regard to issues of race; he ordered the desegregation of the armed forces and an end to discrimination in the civil service. Although he commissioned only three African American judges, two of the three are of special significance. Irvin Mollison was the first African American lifetime appointee, albeit to the Customs Court, which has a specialized rather than general jurisdiction. William Hastie reemerged as another first—this time as the first African American appointed to the prestigious U. S. Circuit Court of Appeals, where he served with distinction until his retirement in 1971.

The election of Dwight Eisenhower in 1952 stalled the process of bench diversification. Eisenhower's opposition to racial justice in general and to the decision in *Brown v. Board of Education* in particular are well documented. Both are illustrated in his judicial appointees: in his eight years as president Eisenhower allowed only 1 of his 173 appointments to go to an African American candidate—Walter Gordon, who was posted to the Virgin Islands.

To some, John F. Kennedy symbolized a commitment to racial justice, and his election in 1960 heralded to many a new dawn in securing minority appointments to the federal courts. The fact remains, however, that throughout his abbreviated presidency Kennedy was very cautious not to antagonize powerful Southerners in the Congress. While it is impossible to know what might have transpired had he served two full terms, Kennedy's timidity in this regard is reflected in his judicial appointments: only 3 percent (4 of 128) went to African Americans. Judge Spottswood Robinson's appointment to the District of Columbia notwithstanding, all of Kennedy's African American appointments were to federal courts in Northern states.

Judicial diversity was fundamentally advanced under Lyndon Johnson. Johnson, for one thing, appointed more than twice as many African Americans (nine) as did his predecessor. Further, in 1966 he nominated Constance Baker Motley, the first female African American jurist, to the Southern District of New York. He followed that appointment in 1967 with the stunning announcement that Thurgood Marshall was his choice for a seat on the U.S. Supreme Court.

Judge Motley was born in New Haven, Connecticut, in 1921 and graduated from New York University and Columbia Law School. Prior to her appointment to the bench she was an attorney for the NATIONAL ASSOCIATION FOR THE ADVANCEMENT OF COLORED PEOPLE (NAACP) Legal Defense Fund, a New York state senator, and borough president of Manhattan. She retired in 1986. Justice Marshall was born in Baltimore, Maryland, in 1908 and graduated from Lincoln University and Howard University Law School. He was solicitor general of the United States (the government's chief lawyer) and prior to his elevation to the Supreme Court he served on the Second Circuit Court of Appeals. He received national prominence when, as director of the NAACP LEGAL DEFENSE FUND he argued *Brown v. Board of Education* before the high court. He retired from the bench in 1991.

Richard Nixon, in his 1968 presidential campaign, complained often and vehemently about the liberal decisions made by the Supreme Court in the 1950s and 1960s and pledged that he would appoint only "strict constructionists" to the federal bench. Then and again in his reelection effort in 1972 he pursued a "Southern strategy" designed to attract voters from the nation's southland who otherwise might be inclined to vote for segregationist George Wallace. Once Nixon was elected the consequences for the federal bench were predictable. Nixon and his caretaker successor, Gerald Ford, appointed only ten African Americans to the federal bench, and six of those were Republicans; none were appointed to either the more prestigious circuit courts or the Supreme Court. In one case WHITNEY YOUNG, executive director of the National Urban League, lobbied the president to replace the retired William Hastie with Clarence Ferguson. The latter was a life-long Republican, former dean of Howard University Law School, and professor at Rutgers Law School. Despite Young's plea that Hastie's replacement was a matter of grave concern to the black community, Ferguson was rejected as being too liberal, and Hastie's seat went to a white male.

Jimmy Carter: 1977–1980

Carter was the first president elected from the Deep South in over a century, and he brought to the Oval Office a personal commitment to racial progress. African Americans were a crucial element of his electoral coalition, especially in the Southern states that ended up providing his margin of victory. During the 1976 campaign he pledged to appoint judges on the basis of merit rather than traditional political considerations, and once in office he worked with Congress to establish merit selection commissions in the states and circuits. Throughout its term, the Carter administration promoted racial and gender diversity. Compared to those of his predecessors, Carter's results in this regard were stunning. Thirty-eight (14 percent) of his appointments went to African Americans. In contrast to that of other presidents, Carter's appointment rate for African Americans was higher in the circuit courts than in the district courts (he made no appointments to the Supreme Court). Carter made the first African American judicial appointment to a Deep South state—Robert Collins to the Eastern District of Louisiana. Moreover, by the time he left office, he had made the first African American appointments to fourteen states, including eleven Southern and border states, as well as the first such appointment on three circuits. So, in just four years, Carter made considerable strides in diversifying the bench in two respects—numerically and geographically.

Republican Reversal: 1981–1992

Ronald Reagan entered office armed with a conservative political agenda and an avowed hostility to affirmative action. The consequences for racial diversification of the federal bench followed suit: only 7 of Reagan's 369 appointees (1.9 percent) were African American. Only one African American was placed on the circuit courts, and none went to the Supreme Court. Perhaps the only saving grace of Reagan's appointments was that they completed the task—spearheaded by Carter—of integrating the Deep South bench by assigning African American district judges to Virginia and Mississippi.

As Reagan's administration wore on, the level of criticism by the Democrat-controlled Senate rose over the president's apparent inattention to racial and gender diversity on the federal courts. George H. W. Bush experienced pressure from the same criticism when he entered office. Additionally, postelection analyses revealed that Bush faced a gender gap with female voters (a considerably lower percentage of his supporters were women), and minority voters held the balance of power in several states that would be critical to his reelection efforts. Accordingly, Bush was more attentive to appointing women and Latinos than African Americans, but he improved on Reagan's record by awarding 13 of his 187 appointments to African Americans. Bush also appreciated that minority candidates could be nominated without conceding political or legal agendas contrary to his own: only 2 of Bush's 13 appointees were Democrats. Indeed, Justice CLARENCE THOMAS was appointed to the Supreme Court in 1991, and he is now one of the staunchest conservatives on the high court.

Justice Thomas was born in Savannah, Georgia, and was educated at Holy Cross College and Yale Law School. He was assistant attorney general for the State of Missouri, legislative assistant to Senator John Danforth (MO), assistant secretary for civil rights in the U.S. Department of Education, and chair of the Equal Employment Opportunity Commission. Prior to Thomas's elevation to the Supreme Court, President Bush appointed him to the U.S. Court of Appeals for the District of Columbia Circuit in 1990.

A Bench That Looks Like America: 1993–

Bill Clinton entered office without wanting to recast the ideological profile of the federal judiciary; he did not base his selection of appointees on litmus tests on issues such as abortion, as had the Reagan administration. While Clinton did have perhaps the most ambitious domestic policy agenda in a generation, he sought to implement it in ways other than a judicial selection strategy. Reluctant to have heated confirmation battles jeopardize his policy aspirations in other areas, he consistently nominated moderate candidates with sound credentials. Nevertheless, during his campaign and once in office Clinton was unambiguous in his intention to broaden representation both in the executive branch and on the federal courts. He made good on his promise by appointing the largest percentage of African Americans in history (19.6); these were by and large moderates to be sure.

Since George W. Bush assumed the presidency, in 2001, the pace of diversification has ebbed somewhat, but in no way receded to the levels of the Reagan/George H. Bush years. Apparently African Americans have attained some measure of "institutionalized representation" in the federal judiciary. The point is illustrated by comparing the case of William Hastie—who as the first African American appointee had a drawn out and torturous confirmation process—with Allyson Duncan, a recent appointee to the U.S. courts of appeals. Judge Duncan

is an African American woman (also a Republican), who was nominated by George W. Bush on April 28, 2003, for a seat on the Fourth Circuit—which has the largest concentration of African American citizens. Judge Duncan sailed through the selection process and was confirmed on July 17, 2003, less than three months after her nomination, quite an extraordinary event in the fractious confirmation politics of recent years, and perhaps a harbinger that, at least in federal judicial appointments, race may no longer trump qualifications.

Bibliography

Barrow, Deborah J., Gary Zuk, and Gerard S. Gryski. *The Federal Judiciary and Institutional Change.* University of Michigan Press, 1996.

Goldman, Sheldon. *Picking Federal Judges.* Yale University Press, 1997.

Goldman, Sheldon, Elliot Slotnick, Gerard Gryski, and Gary Zuk. "Clinton's Judges: Summing Up the Legacy." *Judicature* 84 (March–April 2001): 228–254.

Goldman, Sheldon, Elliot Slotnick, Gerard Gryski, Gary Zuk, and Sara Schiavoni. "W. Bush Remaking the Judiciary: Like Father Like Son?" *Judicature* 86 (May–June 2003): 282–309.

Gryski, Gerard S., Gary Zuk, and Deborah J. Barrow. "A Bench That Looks Like America? Representation of African Americans and Latinos on the Federal Courts." *Journal of Politics* 56 (November 1994): 1076–1086.

Gerard Gryski
Gary Zuk

United States Senate, African Americans in the

See Congress, African Americans in.

Universal Negro Improvement Association

International organization advocating African repatriation, self-government, and economic autonomy, that thrived during the 1920s under the leadership of founder Marcus Garvey.

Founded in KINGSTON, JAMAICA, in 1914 by black nationalist MARCUS GARVEY, the Universal Negro Improvement Association (UNIA) is widely recognized as the largest international organization in the history of people of African descent. Its full name, the Universal Negro Improvement Association and Conservation and African Communities (Imperial) League, reflects its dual purpose: to promote black social mobility through racial uplift and economic prosperity, and to aid black repatriation and the creation of an autonomous black state in Africa.

The UNIA first emerged as a charitable organization. Garvey envisioned an organization modeled after Masonic and

Greek-letter societies that would provide Jamaican blacks with the kind of industrial education offered in the United States by Tuskegee Institute (now Tuskegee University). Yet Garvey was unable to find sufficient support for the UNIA in Jamaica. Attributing this disinterest to a lack of a racial consciousness among black Jamaicans, Garvey moved the UNIA to Harlem, New York, in 1918.

Adopting a strident black nationalist posture in response to the antiblack violence of the Red Summer of 1919, the UNIA provided a vehicle for the political aspirations of the New Negro. The organization flourished, aided by the brisk sale of shares in the Black Star Line, a shipping company intended to forge economic ties between the United States and Africa and to support repatriation. The UNIA saw itself as Africa's government in exile, replete with a national flag and uniformed officers spectacularly displayed at its conventions and parades, and with Garvey as its provisional president. The association's journal, the *Negro World,* was cited as an instrument of anticolonial insurrection and banned in several African countries. By the early 1920s the UNIA slogan, "One God, One Aim, One Destiny," had become the rallying cry for an estimated one million members distributed among thousands of local branches throughout the African diaspora.

The UNIA declined as quickly as it ascended. In 1925, in the wake of the collapse of the Black Star Line, the organization was thrown into disarray when Garvey was imprisoned on charges of mail fraud. The charges were in fact orchestrated by integrationist African Americans. After Garvey's release and deportation to Jamaica, the UNIA was splintered by competing claims to its leadership. Garvey tried to resurrect the UNIA in Jamaica in 1929, but the stock market crash that year depleted the organization's resources. In 1935 Garvey tried again to launch the organization, this time in London, England, but lost support when he openly criticized the policies of the Ethiopian emperor Haile Selassie I during the Italo-Ethiopian War. Although membership had dwindled by the time of Garvey's death in London in 1940, a number of UNIA branches have tenaciously survived until the present day, preserving the legacy of the most powerful movement of black self-determination in the twentieth century.

See also Black Nationalism in the United States; Nationalist Movements and Blacks in Latin America and the Caribbean.

Bibliography

Hill, Robert A. *The Marcus Garvey and Universal Negro Improvement Association Papers.* University of California Press, 1983–1991.

Martin, Tony. *Race First: The Ideological and Organizational Struggles of Marcus Garvey and the Universal Negro Improvement Association.* Africa World Press, 1988.

Smith-Irvin, Jeannette. *Footsoldiers of the Universal Negro Improvement Association: Their Own Words.* Africa World Press, 1988.

Peter Hudson

Upper Senegal and Niger

Former name of Mali.

See also Mali.

Upper Volta

Former name of Burkina Faso.

See also Burkina Faso.

Uprisings and Rebellions

Armed struggles against the oppressive institutions of slavery, colonialism, and apartheid.

For information on:

Uprisings and rebellions in Latin America: *See* Berbice Slave Rebellion; Maroonage in the Americas; Muslim Uprisings in Bahia, Brazil; Rethinking Palmares: Slave Rebellions in Colonial Brazil: An Interpretation; Role of Slaves in Abolition and Emancipation in Latin America and the Caribbean; Slave Rebellions in Latin America and the Caribbean; Zumbi.

Specific rebellions and black rebel leaders in the Caribbean: *See* Bussa's Rebellion; Cacos; Conspiración de la Escalera; Cudjoe; Dessalines, Jean-Jacques; Haitian Revolution; Maceo y Grajales, Antonio; Makandal; Morant Bay Rebellion; Nanny; Péralte, Charlemagne Masséna; Sharpe, Samuel; Toussaint Louverture, François Dominique;

Uprisings and rebellions in the United States: *See* Amistad Mutiny; Christiana Revolt of 1852; Cinque, Joseph; Creole Affair; Denmark Vesey Conspiracy; Gabriel Prosser Conspiracy; New York Slave Conspiracy of 1741; New York Slave Rebellion of 1712; Slave Rebellions in the United States; Stono Rebellion; Turner, Nat.

Resistance and revolts in Africa: *See* Antiapartheid Movement; Maji-Maji Revolt; Mau Mau Rebellion; Sharpeville, South Africa.

Urbanism and Urbanization in Africa

Process of urban population growth and expansion in Africa, occurring especially rapidly since 1945.

Historically only a small proportion of Africa's population has lived in cities, yet cities have long played an important role as centers of empire, long-distance trade, and scholarship, particularly in West and North Africa. Colonization in the late eighteenth and early nineteenth century stimulated the growth of cities important to the European powers that controlled Africa, but significant urbanization did not occur until after World War II. The expansion of cities during the late twentieth cen-

20 Largest Cities in Africa

City	Population in Thousands	Country
Lagos	8682.2	Nigeria
Cairo	8113.6	Egypt
Kinshasa	6789.9	Democratic Republic of Congo
Alexandria	3977.3	Egypt
Casablanca	3741.2	Morocco
Abidjan	3548.4	Ivory Coast
Kano	3412.9	Nigeria
Ibadan	3201.5	Nigeria
Cape Town	2984.1	South Africa
Addis Ababa	2763.5	Ethiopia
al-Jizah	2655.2	Egypt
Dakar	2613.7	Senegal
Dar es Salaam	2538.1	Tanzania
Durban	2531.3	South Africa
Nairobi	2504.4	Kenya
Luanda	2405.6	Angola
Khartoum	2211.5	Sudan
Harare	1976.4	Zimbabwe
Johannesburg	1975.5	South Africa
Conakry	1851.8	Guinea

Source: www.world-gazetteer.com

tury, however, has produced a variety of urban problems with which many African countries are struggling to cope.

Precolonial Urbanization

North Africa has the longest recorded history of urban dwelling. One of the earliest cities in this region was CARTHAGE, a port on the coast of modern-day TUNISIA founded by the Phoenicians around 800 B.C.E. At its peak in the fourth century B.C.E., Carthage served as the center of a vast empire that stretched from LIBYA and Sicily to the Balearic Islands in the western Mediterranean Sea. Carthage was purported to be the wealthiest city in the ancient Mediterranean world; historians believe that it may have had as many as half a million inhabitants. Another old North African city is CAIRO, the capital of modern EGYPT. Cairo was founded in 969 C.E. but is located only twenty-five kilometers (fifteen miles) from the site of the capital of ancient Egypt, Memphis, which was established in the fourth millennium B.C.E. Cairo reached the peak of its prosperity in the thirteenth century, under the rule of the Mamluks. In addition

to its role in regional and long-distance trade, the city also housed one of the world's most famous institutions of Islamic scholarship, al-Azhar University. Although devastated by the bubonic plague in 1348, Cairo remained a political capital under Turkish and then British rule, and has since become one of the continent's largest cities.

West Africa also has a long history of urbanization. DJENNÉ-JENO, located about three kilometers (two miles) from contemporary DJENNÉ in MALI, is the earliest known city in this region, dating back to at least the second century B.C.E. Between 700 and 900 C.E., the town had a population of at least 10,000. Other early cities in the West African savanna included KOUMBI SALEH (the capital of ancient GHANA), TOMBOUCTOU (Timbuktu), and KANO in northern NIGERIA, all of which served as important markets for caravan traders traveling between North Africa and coastal West Africa. Early explorers remarked on the gold and other wealth apparent in these savanna cities, but many of their inhabitants were ordinary farmers. At their peak, both Kano and Tombouctou also had sizable populations of scholars, who came from parts of North and West Africa to study ISLAM.

In coastal West Africa, the YORUBA peoples of southwestern Nigeria have lived in towns since around the eighth century C.E. Ife is the oldest Yoruba town, and is the spiritual capital of the YORUBA RELIGION. As in the savanna cities, many residents of Yoruba towns farmed in the surrounding countryside. Living in dense settlements gave them regular opportunities to trade their goods and provided protection from enemy invasions (a consideration that became particularly important in the nineteenth century).

In East Africa, precolonial urbanization was concentrated along the coastline, where vessels from the Arabian Peninsula began landing by around 600 C.E. The coastal region between southern SOMALIA and northern MOZAMBIQUE became the birthplace of the town-centered SWAHILI culture, which attracted traders and other settlers from the Arabian Peninsula and from the East African interior. Some of the largest precolonial cities along the SWAHILI COAST—such as Somalia's capital MOGADISHU, MOMBASA in KENYA, and ZANZIBAR in TANZANIA—are still important ports, while others, such as LAMU in Kenya and Kilwa in Tanzania, have lost much of their former commercial and political clout.

Trade was a clearly a driving force in precolonial urbanization. The fortunes of a particular city might rise and fall as traders of important commodities such as gold, ivory, and slaves shifted their routes to avoid raiders or to take advantage of new supplies. The populations and activity levels of precolonial cities also shifted seasonally, because many residents moved to rural areas during the cultivating season.

Colonial-Era Urbanization

With European colonization, new cities were established and many existing ones were transformed. The colonial powers built some of their administrative capitals in preexisting cities, such as LAGOS in Nigeria, Mogadishu in Somalia, and OUAGADOUGOU

Cape Town, located on the site of the first European settlement in southern Africa, is the legislative capital and largest city in South Africa. *David Keith Jones/Images of Africa Photobank*

in Upper Volta (now Burkina Faso). Other colonial capitals were built in locations chosen for their port access, such as Dakar in Senegal, or for their temperate climate, such as Nairobi in Kenya. In colonies with sizable populations of European settlers, such as Kenya and Rhodesia (now Zimbabwe), the newly built cities became settler enclaves, with strict laws limiting which Africans could live in them and where.

Other colonial-era cities grew up around mining operations. In the Belgian Congo (present-day Democratic Republic of the Congo), for example, Elisabethville (present-day Lubumbashi) was built up after copper and diamonds were discovered nearby. In South Africa the discovery of gold deposits in the Witswatersrand hills in 1886 attracted huge numbers of both African and European migrants. Within ten years, the mining camp of Johannesburg had become a city with a population exceeding 100,000. This rate of growth was exceptional; most cities, whether or not they existed before the colonial era, grew relatively slowly during the late nineteenth and early twentieth centuries.

Following World War II, rates of urbanization increased dramatically throughout much of Africa. Several factors contributed to the urban boom. First, some of the colonial governments that had previously limited African migration to ur-

ban areas now loosened these restrictions. Second, expanding civil-service bureaucracies and new industries increased opportunities for urban employment. Third, many people migrated to the cities seeking not only jobs but also access to education and other social services. Finally, natural population growth, which was on the rise, coupled with falling mortality rates, aided urban expansion.

Urbanization in Contemporary Africa

Today, Africa is still the least urbanized continent in the world. According to United Nations figures for 1994, only 34 percent of Africa's population lives in urban areas, compared to the world average of 44.8 percent. The actual percentages, however, vary significantly between regions. The most urbanized regions are southern Africa (48 percent) and North Africa (46 percent), followed by West Africa (36 percent) and Central Africa (33 percent). East Africa is the least urbanized part of the continent, at 21 percent. The percentage of population living in cities also varies dramatically between countries. In Libya, for example, almost 86 percent of the population is urban-based, while less than 10 percent of the population of Burundi and Rwanda lives in cities.

At the same time, Africa's urban population growth rates are among the highest in the world—4.3 percent annually, compared to the world average of 2.5 percent. These rates also vary between regions and countries: cities in East Africa and West Africa are growing most rapidly (at average rates of 5.4 and 5.2 percent per annum, respectively), followed by Central Africa (4.5 percent), North Africa (3.2 percent), and southern Africa (3.1 percent). Burkina Faso's urban growth rate averaged 11.2 percent between 1990 and 1995 (a figure reflecting the fact that its cities were small to begin with), while MAURITIUS had only a 1.2 percent urban growth rate during the same period.

Since DECOLONIZATION, much of the urban growth in Africa has been concentrated in national capitals, due in large part to the concentration of employment opportunities, government services, and schools in those cities. Among the few exceptions are those political capitals that have been established relatively recently, and invariably have much smaller populations and economies than the capitals established during the colonial era. Since 1983 YAMOUSSOUKRO has been the capital of CÔTE D'IVOIRE, for example, but with a population of only 120,000 (1990 estimate) it hardly compares to the former capital, ABIDJAN (1988 population 1.9 million), which is still home to most of the country's industries, many of its schools, and its most important port.

Similarly, Nigeria's political capital was moved from Lagos to the more centrally located ABUJA in 1991. However, with 339,100 people (1995 estimate), the new capital is considered small and sleepy compared to Lagos, which by the late 1990s was sub-Saharan Africa's largest city, with an estimated population in 1995 of 1.5 million. According to growth rate trends, this number is projected to reach 26 million by 2030—and if the projections are accurate, it will then be one of the world's largest cities. The population of Africa's largest city, Cairo, had reached 6.8 million by 1998. It is estimated that 6.9 percent of the African population—almost 39 million people—will live in one of these two cities by the year 2015. Other mega-cities in Africa include Nairobi, KINSHASA, and Johannesburg.

Since the 1970s, many organizations and scholars have viewed Africa's high rates of urban growth as indicative of "overurbanization" and failed DEVELOPMENT policies. Well into the 1980s, African governments (as well as the international agencies that supported them financially) were accused of "urban bias," meaning that their budgetary priorities and monetary policies were blamed for the impoverishment of the countryside and the resulting rural exodus. It is certainly true that politicians in the 1960s and 1970s were especially sensitive to the demands of their urban constituents, and some leaders, such as FÉLIX-HOUPHOUËT BOIGNY of Côte d'Ivoire, spent lavishly on projects to turn their capitals into "showcase" cities. But the relationship between "urban-biased" government policies and rural economic conditions is not a simple one, primarily because many urban dwellers in contemporary Africa, as in the past, maintain ties to the countryside. One urban wage earner may support a dozen people in his or her home village.

Cities also offer noneconomic attractions, of course. For women especially, urban life in Africa can offer freedom from the restrictive social norms of village life. Women living in cities have better access to education than their rural counterparts, and with the exception of the relatively few urban communities that enforce Islamic norms of female seclusion, even women with little or no education can make a living—occasionally a fortune—in marketplace trading. In cities such as LOMÉ and ACCRA in West Africa, market women have traditionally been a powerful political as well as economic force. In addition, African women in cities tend to have more control over marriage and family planning decisions than they would in rural areas.

Urban Problems

In the 1990s, alarm about the proliferation of mega-cities in Africa has been mixed with the realization, expressed in forums such as the 1996 United Nations Habitat II conference in Istanbul, that urbanization is not only inevitable but in some ways advantageous. Cities everywhere have historically served as centers of creativity and innovation; they are also places where, in principle, it is easier and cheaper for governments to provide services such as clean water, electricity, and medical care. Greater population density, in other words, allows for economies of scale.

In reality, neither urban economies nor urban public services in Africa have been able to keep up with the demands of rapidly growing populations. Especially after economic crisis hit many African countries in the early 1980s, public investment in urban services declined significantly. The Nairobi City Commission's per capita expenditures on water and sewerage, for example, declined from nearly $28 in 1981 to $2.47 in 1987. As a result, the infrastructures in many cities are inadequate and poorly maintained, and urban unemployment and underemployment rates are high.

Housing, for example, is a serious problem in most African cities. Public housing estates are too expensive for many urban dwellers, and city center rents tend to be high. Although the absence of high-rise apartment buildings in most African cities (with the exception of larger cities in North Africa and South Africa) means that urban population densities are not very high compared to those in Asia and Latin America, single-story dwellings are often extremely crowded. In Lagos and Johannesburg, for example, it is common for five or six people to share a single room.

The lack of affordable "legal" housing has given rise to the development of "spontaneous" or squatter settlements (called *bidonvilles* in Francophone countries) on the outskirts of many African cities. Whether this kind of settlement is legal depends on a municipality's property laws. Squatter shelters are often built from insubstantial materials such as cardboard or corrugated iron, though over time their owners may build more solid dwellings. Although the governments of some cities, such as Nairobi and HARARE, have in the past periodically bulldozed squatter settlements, since the 1980s it has become more common for municipalities to tolerate or even encourage "self-help" housing.

The provision of services such as clean water, sewerage, waste disposal, and electricity is often nonexistent in settlements on urban peripheries, and such services tend to be poorly maintained even in city centers. Piped water to individual houses is a rarity in the poorer neighborhoods of many cities, so many residents rely on wells, public taps (which are often turned on only a few hours each day), or purchased water. Consequently, poor city dwellers routinely pay more for water than their wealthy counterparts. Even treated, piped water supplies in many cities are of dubious quality, due to old and leaky pipes. Combined with inadequate sanitation services, the poor quality of urban water supplies contributes to the spread of cholera and other waterborne DISEASES.

Finally, the growth of Africa's urban populations is outpacing the growth of urban labor markets, leading to high rates of unemployment and underemployment. This is not a new problem—the International Labor Organization began to express concern about urban unemployment in Africa in the 1970s—but it has been exacerbated by the economic crisis and subsequent World Bank–designed STRUCTURAL ADJUSTMENT programs (SAPs) most African countries have undergone since the early 1980s. Among other things, structural adjustment has required African governments to cut back on their own personnel and to downsize and privatize state-run industries. The bulk of the lost jobs have been urban-based.

It is nearly impossible to provide accurate estimates of urban unemployment rates in Africa, because in many cities most working-age people earn at least part of their livelihood from employment in the so-called informal sector. This term describes a wide range of economic activities that are relatively unregulated by the state, though they are not necessarily illegal. Common informal-sector activities in African cities include the vending of street foods and other consumer goods, small-scale crafts industries, and a multitude of services ranging from message delivery to bicycle repair to open-air haircutting.

Informal-sector enterprises often depend on family labor and operate on shoestring budgets, and many are relatively short-lived. The numbers of people attempting to earn money by selling goods on the streets of cities such as Lagos and Dakar are so large that it is difficult for individual vendors to break even, much less to make a profit. On the other hand, the informal sector provides low-cost goods and services to a large proportion of the urban population (not just the poor), and income earned in this sector helps support many families—many of them female-headed—who might otherwise be destitute. This is one reason that African governments and institutions such as the World Bank, which in the past viewed the informal sector as evidence of economic backwardness, now encourage certain kinds of informal-sector enterprises through training and credit programs. The hope is that such support will help informal-sector enterprises grow and thus generate more jobs. Clearly, easing the problem of unemployment in African cities will also require the sustained growth of Africa's national economies.

See also Ancient African Civilizations; Colonial Rule; Egypt, Ancient Kingdom of; Ghana, Early Kingdom of.

Elizabeth Heath

Urban Life, African American

See Atlanta, Georgia; Baltimore, Maryland; Birmingham, Alabama; Boston, Massachusetts; Charleston, South Carolina; Chicago, Illinois; Cincinnati, Ohio; Detroit, Michigan; Durham, North Carolina; Harlem, New York; Houston, Texas; Kansas City, Missouri; Los Angeles, California; Louisville, Kentucky; Memphis, Tennessee; New Orleans, Louisiana; New York, New York; Newark, New Jersey; Philadelphia, Pennsylvania; Pittsburgh, Pennsylvania; San Francisco and Oakland, California; Seattle, Washington; and Washington, D.C.

Urbano Gilbert, Gregorio

1899–1970

Afro-Dominican guerrilla fighter who resisted the United States occupation of the Dominican Republic in 1916 and left one of the few written testimonies of the events.

Beginning in 1906, the United States administrated and controlled the Dominican Republic's customs department and undertook the adjustment of the Dominican government's foreign debt. Increasing debts, internal disorder, and international pressures prompted President Woodrow Wilson of the United States to order the deployment and intervention of the U.S. Navy in the DOMINICAN REPUBLIC. The troops arrived on November 29, 1916, and remained in control of the country until 1924.

The U.S. Marines invaded the Dominican Republic, easily occupying the town of San Pedro de Macorís to the passive acceptance of its inhabitants. However, Gregorio Urbano decided to confront the marines on his own with only the support of his .32-caliber revolver. In self-defense, he killed U.S. Marine Corps Colonel C. H. Button and then fled to join the nationalist guerrillas and their anti-imperialist struggle. After being tracked down and captured by the Dominican Army, he went to trial and was sentenced to death. However, in 1922 he was pardoned. When Urbano Gilbert came out of prison, he tried to join Haitian forces struggling against the U.S. occupation of that neighboring country (1915–1934), but his attempt was not successful.

He went into exile to CURAÇAO and CUBA where he worked as a sugarcane cutter. Urbano Gilbert came back to the Dominican Republic in 1927, where he rallied in favor of the Puerto Rican independence along with PEDRO ALBIZU CAMPOS. In 1928 he went to NICARAGUA and joined Augusto César Sandino's *Ejercito Libertador* in their struggle against U.S. imperialism. He then went back to the Dominican Republic in

1929, a year before Rafael Leónidas Trujillo's dictatorship of more than thirty years began. He worked as street-seller while he studied in what is now the Autonomous University and completed his doctorate in philosophy in 1956.

Urbano Gilbert wrote one of the few historical testimonies about the 1916 invasion—published after his death in 1975—under the title *Mi lucha contra el invasor yanqui de 1916* (My Struggle against the Yankee Invader). It includes his personal experiences with the guerrilla leaders who fought against the United States. He also wrote another testimonial narrative entitled *Junto a Sandino* (Beside Sandino; 1979), about his years with the Nicaraguan rebels and his struggle against imperialism. While in his sixties, Urbano also joined the Dominican military forces that faced the second U.S. invasion in April 1965. He died in poverty five years later. In his writings, Gregorio Urbano Gilbert left his testimony of struggle against imperialism and for popular causes, and his experiences with Dominican guerrilla fighters, about whom there is limited information.

See also Cacos; Trujillo, Rafael Leónidas.

Mayda Grano de Oro

Uruguay

Republic of southeastern South America bordered on the northeast and north by Brazil, on the west by Argentina, and on the east by the Atlantic Ocean.

Uruguay has long enjoyed a reputation as the "Switzerland of the Americas," due in part to its small size, its dominant population of European descent, and a perception that it is a country free of racial tensions or other conflicts. The true racial history of Uruguay is much more complicated than this image suggests. Blacks constitute a tiny minority of present-day Uruguayans (about 6 percent of the population), but this was not always the case; in fact, throughout Uruguay's history, blacks played an integral role in the nation's development. Afro-Uruguayans today are the inheritors of this legacy, though in standard histories they are sometimes reviled and more often than not forgotten.

Political History

Before Spaniards arrived in the area now known as Uruguay, a number of seminomadic indigenous groups inhabited the region. The largest of these groups were the Charrúa and the Chaná, who survived principally by hunting and fishing. In 1516 the Spanish explorer Juan Díaz de Solís sailed into the Río de la Plata (the estuary that separates western Uruguay from eastern ARGENTINA) and established a small, short-lived settlement on the riverbank. Before the year was out, the Charrúa killed Díaz and his party. The region was of little interest to Spanish colonizers, as it seemed of minimal economic value. The first permanent Spanish settlement would not be established in Uruguay until 1624, when a small party encamped at the Río Negro at Soriano.

This area came to be known as the Banda Oriental (Eastern Bank), and from the late seventeenth through much of the eighteenth century, it was a zone of contention between Spanish colonists and Portuguese colonists from BRAZIL. In 1680 the Portuguese founded Colônia do Sacramento on the bank of the Río de la Plata, opposite Buenos Aires. The Spanish made little effort to displace this settlement until the 1720s, when they constructed the fortified city of San Felipe de Montevideo, from which they launched attacks on the Portuguese. The Portuguese finally ceded in 1777, and the region came under the administrative control of the viceroyalty of La Plata.

In the second decade of the nineteenth century, Uruguayans fought successfully for their independence but the country was occupied by and finally annexed to Brazil in 1821. An insurgent group known as the Immortal Thirty-Three, led by Juan Antonio Lavalleja and aided by Argentina, fought the occupation. A treaty signed in 1828, with British mediation, established Uruguay as an independent buffer zone between Argentina and the Brazilian Empire, and a provisional assembly was established. On July 18, 1830, the assembly ratified a constitution that officially founded the República Oriental del Uruguay (Eastern Republic of Uruguay).

During most of the nineteenth century, the new republic was plagued by fighting between two contending political factions, comprising supporters of the nation's first two presidents: Fructuoso Rivera (served 1830–1834 and 1838–1842) and Manuel Oribe (1835–1838). The factions were named for the colors adopted by each: the Colorado Party (red), supporting Rivera, and the Blanco Party (white), for Oribe. Both survive today as the dominant political parties. Between 1865 and 1870, Uruguay allied itself with Brazil and Argentina against PARAGUAY in the War of the Triple Alliance. The Colorado Party became dominant during the course of the century; after 1865 the Blanco Party would remain out of power until 1958.

Uruguay in the twentieth century gained a reputation as a progressive, democratic republic. President José Batlle Ordóñez (1903–1907; 1911–1915) initiated a period of social reforms that included concessions to labor as well as provisions for social security. Democratic rule was disrupted by a period of authoritarian rule in the 1930s and by a repressive military government between 1973 and 1984. Uruguay's transition to democracy since 1984 has been regarded as one of the most successful in Latin America, as the traditional Blanco and Colorado parties reemerged in what appears to be a remarkably stable regime.

Africans in Colonial Uruguay

Spaniards brought Africans to the region as early as 1534. These *ladinos* (slaves who had been Hispanicized in SPAIN rather than being brought directly from Africa) took part in early explorations of the Río de la Plata. Nearly all of them, however, eventually settled with their masters in what is now Argentina.

The Uruguayan slave trade was born from a quirk of conquest and geography. By the end of the sixteenth century Spain had extended its slave-capture and -trading operations to the

Uruguay (At a Glance)

OFFICIAL NAME: Oriental Republic of Uruguay

FORMER NAME: Banda Oriental, Cisplatine Province

AREA: 176,220 sq km (68,039 sq mi)

LOCATION: Southern South America between Argentina and Brazil, bordered by the South Atlantic Ocean

CAPITAL: Montevideo (population 1,329,000; 2002 estimate)

POPULATION: 3,415,000 (2004 estimate)

POPULATION DENSITY: 20 persons per sq km (51 per sq mi)

POPULATION BELOW AGE 15: 24.3 percent (male 425,642; female 404,987; 2003 estimate)

POPULATION GROWTH RATE: 0.79 percent (2003 estimate)

TOTAL FERTILITY RATE: 2.35 children born per woman (2003 estimate)

LIFE EXPECTANCY AT BIRTH: Total population: 75.87 years (male 72.54 years; female 79.38 years; 2003 estimate)

INFANT MORTALITY RATE: 13.8 deaths per 1,000 live births (2003 estimate)

LITERACY RATE (AGE 15 AND OVER WHO CAN READ AND WRITE): Total population: 98 percent (male 97.6 percent; female 98.4 percent; 2003 estimate)

EDUCATION: Education is free and compulsory for ages six to eleven, and technical school and university are also free. Higher education is offered at the University of the Republic in Montevideo and the Catholic University of Uruguay, and other schools.

LANGUAGES: Spanish, Portunol, or Brazilero (Portuguese-Spanish mix spoken on the Brazilian frontier)

ETHNIC GROUPS: 88 percent white, 8 percent mestizo, 4 percent black, and very few Amerindians

RELIGIONS: 66 percent of Uruguayans are Roman Catholic, 2 percent are Protestant, 1 percent are Jewish, and 31 percent have other or no religion affiliation

CLIMATE: Generally temperate, with an average winter temperature of 50°F (10°C) and an average summer temperature of 72°F (22°C) at Montevideo. The autumn months of March and April see the heaviest rainfall, though rain is more frequent in winter. Summer thunderstorms are common, as well.

LAND, PLANTS, AND ANIMALS: Uruguay is a land of hills, low plateaus, valleys, plains, and ridges. The highest elevation is in the southeast at Mount Catedral, which rises to 1,685 feet (514 meters). The coast is lined with sand dunes and tidal lakes. Uruguay has two navigable rivers, the Uruguay River and the Río de la Plata. Most of the land is prairie or pasture, with little forest. Existing trees and plants include pine, poplar, willow, carob, aloe, mimosa, and rosemary. Animals include foxes, wildcats, deer, armadillos, owls, partridges, and hummingbirds. Venomous snakes and spiders are common in some areas. National parks and reserves are maintained to preserve wildlife populations.

NATURAL RESOURCES: Arable land, hydropower, minor minerals, and fisheries

CURRENCY: Uruguayan peso (UYU)

GROSS DOMESTIC PRODUCT (GDP): $26.82 billion (2002 estimate)

GDP PER CAPITA: $7,900 (2002 estimate)

GDP REAL GROWTH RATE: −10.8 percent (2002 estimate)

PRIMARY ECONOMIC ACTIVITIES: Agriculture, industry, and services

PRIMARY CROPS: Rice, wheat, corn, barley, livestock, and fish

INDUSTRIES: Food processing, electrical machinery, transportation equipment, petroleum products, textiles, chemicals, and beverages

PRIMARY EXPORTS: Meat, rice, leather products, wool, vehicles, and dairy products

PRIMARY IMPORTS: Machinery, chemicals, road vehicles, and crude petroleum

PRIMARY TRADE PARTNERS: Brazil, Argentina, United States, Germany, Italy, and Venezuela

GOVERNMENT: Uruguay is a constitutional republic. The chief of state and head of government is President Jorge Batlle Ibanez (since March 2000; popularly elected for a five-year term). The legislative branch is the bicameral General Assembly, consisting of the thirty-member Chamber of Senators and the ninety-nine-member Chamber of Representatives (members of both bodies are popularly elected to serve five-year terms). The judicial branch is headed by the Supreme Court, whose judges are nominated by the president and elected by the General Assembly to serve ten-year terms.

Shelle Sumners

ANGOLA region of southern Africa. As with the slave trade in northern Africa, captives were shipped by sea to bustling colonies such as MEXICO and the Audiencia de CARTAGENA (in present-day COLOMBIA), all in the northern half of the Americas. The sea voyage from Angola, however, was even more brutal than from northern Africa, and many more slaves died en route. Spanish slave traders realized by the end of the six-

teenth century that if slaves were transported across a shorter sea route—say, to the Río de la Plata—and then transferred overland to distant points, fewer of them would die. As a result, Buenos Aires (in what would later become Argentina) soon became a major point of disembarkation for slaves from southern Africa. By the end of the seventeenth century the Spaniards had discovered that Montevideo, 200 kilometers (120 miles) east of Buenos Aires on the Río de la Plata, had a remarkable natural harbor. In 1724 they began a settlement there, and in no time the bulk of the slave trade had moved from Buenos Aires to Montevideo—the future capital of Uruguay.

From the earliest days, the Spanish government tried to exercise strict control over the arrival of slaves in the Río de la Plata region, mostly in order to tax the lucrative trade. Only a few authorized traders were allowed to bring slaves to a region. However, as in other parts of Spanish America, slave traders in the Río de la Plata often succeeded in smuggling contraband slaves past officials. In *La trata de negroa en Río de la Plata durante el siglo XVIII* (1958), historian Elena Fanny Scheüss de Studer calculates that only 288 of nearly 13,000 slaves who came to the Río de la Plata region between 1606 and 1655 arrived legally. She estimates that between 1680 and 1806—an era of mostly tighter Spanish control—perhaps 50 percent of all arrivals from Africa were still smuggled into Río de la Plata. In addition to these contrabands, it appears likely that many slaves were shipped to Montevideo from RIO DE JANEIRO in Portuguese Brazil—in violation of both Spanish and Portuguese law.

Beginning in 1740, Spain bowed to the reality of its ineffectual control of the slave trade and allowed any colonist with the means to buy a *licencia* (license) to purchase as many Africans as he wanted from any slave trader of any nation not warring against Spain. The licencias were costly, so only a few could afford them; nonetheless, the introduction of licencias opened the door to a much larger legal slave trade. Colonial records show that in one brief period—from 1780 to 1783—seventeen licencias were granted in the Río de la Plata region, allowing the importation of 3,400 blacks to Montevideo and Buenos Aires. From 1783 to 1792, ten more licencias allowed the importation of 4,600 more slaves. Most of these slaves were, presumably, shipped to distant points, like PERU and New Granada (present-day Colombia, ECUADOR, VENEZUELA, and PANAMA), since by 1803 Montevideo had only 899 slaves.

During roughly the same era—in 1776—Spain recognized the increasing importance of the Río de la Plata region by establishing the viceroyalty of La Plata, which included what is today Uruguay, Argentina, BOLIVIA, and Paraguay. The viceregal seat of La Plata was in Buenos Aires. Two decades later, Spain acknowledged that even its efforts under the licencia system to control the slave trade were futile; in 1795 the viceroyalty of La Plata abandoned the system altogether. Any Spanish citizen was allowed to buy slaves from any source not at war with Spain.

Slave Labor, Life, and Rebellion

The conditions under which slaves labored in Uruguay are "difficult to analyze," according to historian Leslie Rout in *The African Experience in Spanish America*. Aside, perhaps, from domestic service, slaves did not dominate any industry or occupation in Uruguay; moreover, the plantations or mines that were the province of slaves in much of the rest of Spanish America were virtually nonexistent in Uruguay. Montevideo, a commercial port and practically the only settlement of importance in Uruguay, was indisputably the home of most Uruguayan slaves. Female slaves dominated the domestic industries of cooking, cleaning, laundering, and child-rearing, while male slaves worked as manual laborers on docks and in the ranching operations around Montevideo.

The burden of Africans in Uruguay was worsened by the sharp distinctions that Spanish colonists drew between dark-skinned and light-skinned blacks. The latter were in all things favored (if only slightly) and the former disparaged. In May 1760 the *cabildo* (council) of Montevideo passed a series of acts governing *pardos* (mulattoes, usually lighter skinned) and *morenos* ("full-blood" blacks, usually darker skinned). Under the acts, pardos were allowed to become certain types of tradesmen, including tailors and cobblers, while morenos were forbidden to do anything but physical and domestic labor.

Such racial distinctions persisted despite a few efforts by the Spanish government to diminish them. In 1795, for example, the Spanish Crown allowed blacks to buy writs of *gracias al sacar,* meaning literally "thanks for the exclusion." The writs were a royal dispensation that freed a person from certain caste restrictions. However, in the viceroyalty of La Plata, writs were rarely issued, and only those issued to very light-skinned blacks were honored. Darker-skinned blacks who bought them often found them unredeemable. Because of these and similar caste barriers, intermarriage of blacks and whites in La Plata was quite rare; however, as in the rest of Spanish America, the prohibition against white men taking female slaves as concubines was less strict.

Avenues to freedom that were open to slaves in other parts of the Spanish Empire were relatively less accessible to Afro-Uruguayans. In *Negro uruguayo hasta abolición* (The Uruguayan Black until Abolition; 1965), historian Paulo de Carvalho Neto holds that, with the exception of some illegitimate mulatto children with white fathers, the only way for blacks to escape slavery was through death. Historian Carlos Rama agrees, for the most part, adding that a very few slaves were freed as a result of being treated with extreme cruelty, and a few more were allowed to buy their freedom.

Rebellion, then, was one of the very small number of paths to freedom, but even this method was less successful in Uruguay than elsewhere. In 1803, twenty black men, most but not all slaves, gathered in secret to devise a plot for fleeing Montevideo, and soon thereafter fled with their wives and children. After several days of travel they established a settlement on a small island in the River Yi, some 200 kilometers (120 miles) north of Montevideo. Their freedom, however, was short-lived; a militia from the town of Villa de la Concepción de Minas attacked them soon after they had settled. In the skirmish that followed, all of the blacks were either captured and reenslaved or killed in the fighting.

War against Spain and Emancipation

The first hint of change in the life of the Uruguayan slave came during the wars of liberation against Spain in the second decade of the seventeenth century. Afro-Uruguayans quickly learned that they could better their social standing by serving in the rebel armies. The rebels, for their part, were not typically possessed of a liberal attitude toward blacks; they were simply desperate enough for troops to enlist anyone who could fight. At first this meant allowing free blacks to fight; later it meant giving guns to slaves.

José Artigas, who would later be considered the father of Uruguay, put together the most formidable army of blacks and mulattoes—most of them freedpeople but many of them slaves—to serve alongside white rebels. In 1812 the Sixth Regiment, composed almost entirely of blacks, gained enduring fame through its part in a daring bayonet charge at El Cerrito. Another battalion, Los Libertos Orientales ("The Freedmen of the East"), fought almost continuously between 1816 and 1820.

Although their fighting earned blacks a measure of respect, the limitations of caste did not fall away. Indeed, black soldiers were usually assigned to the most dangerous fighting yet received the worst food and equipment. Their lot had changed little enough that when a Brazilian force took advantage of the wars against Spain and invaded Uruguay in 1817, more than a hundred of Artigas's black troops switched sides for the flimsy promise that "someday" Brazil would make them free. Many blacks nonetheless remained loyal to the rebel forces, and as the target of rebel attacks shifted from Spanish to Brazilian troops, blacks continued to play a crucial role.

Brazil completed its conquest and annexation of Uruguay by 1821, under the name Cisplatine Province. A small group of insurgents, known as the Immortal Thirty-Three, reasserted the independence of Uruguay in 1825. Little acknowledged among modern Uruguayans is that a handful of the Immortal Thirty-Three were black. Black rebels are not completely forgotten, however. Colonel Lorenzo Barcala, an Argentinian known as "the black caballero," played a major role from 1825 to 1828 in the eviction of the Brazilians from Uruguay. Manuel Antonio Ledesma ("Ansina") is known as the aide who faithfully accompanied Artigas to his death in Paraguay. Barcala and Ansina were among the few blacks, however, to attain high-ranking positions.

On September 7, 1825, the rebel forces established a congress at which they passed a free-womb law: anyone born to a slave from that date forward was born free. They then opened the ranks of their army to blacks and mulattoes—both free and slave. In May 1829 another provisional legislature, established after the 1828 peace agreement recognizing Uruguayan independence, freed all slaves who fought in the struggle for liberation.

In 1830 the legislature ratified the republic's first constitution, which included several positive changes for slaves. It reaffirmed the acts of the earlier congresses, asserting that all newborn children of slaves were born free. The overseas slave trade was banned, and any slave whose master had fled to Brazil during or after the fighting was declared free. Still, the old caste distinctions remained. Former slaves found it extremely difficult to find work or decent housing, and many slaves who had fought in the war were denied their freedom because they had no proof of their enlistment.

In 1832 a group of slaves and freedpeople prepared for revolt behind an Afro-Uruguayan named Santa Colombo, who had been a military aide to President Fructuoso Rivera. The government uncovered the plot in May 1832, sentenced the freedpeople to death or long jail terms, and sentenced slaves to 200 lashes. Because several of the plotters had fought against Spain and Brazil in the liberation, many Uruguayans pleaded for leniency on behalf of the prisoners. Eventually the death sentences were commuted.

The constitution's promises to end the slave trade notwithstanding, between 1829 and 1841 some 4,000 slaves were brought illegally from Brazil to Uruguay. President Rivera apparently abetted much of the illegal trade. In 1837 a law was passed declaring that all blacks thenceforth brought into the country would be free (with some exceptions, such as runaway slaves from other countries, who were to be returned). The law also established a system of *patronato*, which effectively extended the period of servitude by placing blacks under the "tutelage" of their masters for a determined period of time.

Abolition in Uruguay was given impetus by the conflicts in the country and the need for soldiers. Fighting between Blanco and Colorado factions flared following Rivera's 1838 coup against President Manuel Oribe. In 1841, in response to threats from Argentine-supported Blanco rebels, Rivera freed his many slaves and drafted them into the army. The following year, his successor, Joaquín Suárez, abolished slavery throughout the country and drafted all former male slaves into the army. In the hope of winning compliance from slave owners, Suárez promised compensation for the freed slaves, but most slave owners flouted the law and many sold their slaves in neighboring Brazil.

In 1843 Suárez's troops were backed into Montevideo. The rebels, led by deposed president Oribe, laid siege to the city until 1851, when a signed truce declared that there were no victors or vanquished. Like the besieged, the attacking army also relied heavily on black forces. In October 1846, the third year of the siege, Oribe too declared slavery in Uruguay abolished. Following the truce, a law passed in 1853 abolished the patronato system, freeing all blacks in the country.

In addition to prompting some Uruguayan slave owners to sell their slaves in Brazil, abolition produced a substantial immigration of escaped Brazilian slaves to Uruguay. Given the extent of this migration, the 1851 peace agreement, in which Brazilian intervention was decisive, included an agreement to return escaped slaves to Brazil, but this provision was largely ignored.

Beyond Emancipation

Despite abolition, many former slaves had no choice but to continue working for their former masters, and slave-like conditions and racial discrimination persisted. In 1860, for example, the Montevideo police force prohibited blacks from being hired as night watchmen. In 1878 a furor erupted when supporters of civil rights tried to gain admittance for blacks to public schools alongside whites.

Afro-Uruguayans, however, were also confronted with a flood of white immigrant labor that reduced their economic opportunities. In 1842, nearly 20 percent of Montevideo's residents were black. After emancipation, Uruguay faced two problems that could be addressed with one solution: it needed a larger labor base to fuel its economic growth, and it "needed" to preserve its white character. Hence between 1850 and 1930 more than a million Europeans, almost all of them white, immigrated to Uruguay. A few blacks also found their way to Uruguay during the early part of this period, but in 1886 the Uruguayan government made clear its preference for white immigrants: people of African origin were barred from settling in Uruguay. A study conducted by Uruguay's National Statistics Institute in 1996–1997 found that approximately 4 percent of Uruguayans self-identify as black.

In the context of the new European competition for jobs in Uruguay, the stigma of being black persisted. Afro-Uruguayans were clustered in low-paying positions and typically lived in the slums of Montevideo well into the twentieth century. In May 1956 the magazine *Marcha* studied nearly 15,000 barbers, hotel porters, bus drivers, conductors, guards, and store clerks; only eleven of them were black or mulatto, indicating that Afro-Uruguayans had not achieved even the faintest hold on the middle class. *Marcha* also reported that from 1900 to 1956, the National University of Uruguay graduated just two lawyers and one doctor of African heritage. In a separate study in the same year, 700 white Uruguayan students were asked whether they would marry a black; 77 percent said no. When asked whether they would invite a black person to a birthday party, 62 percent said no.

Under such conditions, Afro-Uruguayans created political and cultural organizations of their own. In the early twentieth century, they formed groups for socializing and other kinds of support, such as the Black Race Cultural Association and the Colonia Sport and Social Club, both headquartered in Montevideo. In 1917 the magazine *Nuestra raza* (Our Race) began reporting on issues of concern among the black community. Before going out of business in 1948, *Nuestra raza* helped introduce Afro-Uruguayans to the music of Julián García Rondeau, the art of Ramón Preya, and the poetry of its editor, PILAR BARRIOS. Barrios was also the secretary of the Black Autochthonous Party. Organized in 1937 and comprising mainly black intellectuals, many connected with *Nuestra raza*, it took a stand for social justice while seeking to appeal broadly to all Afro-Uruguayans. Nonetheless, after its poor showing in the 1938 elections, its activities weakened, and it finally disbanded in 1944.

After World War II the Uruguayan government extended free education to all classes, allowing all blacks for the first time to enter school with whites. Black culture, however, was not studied, a fact that recent historians have attributed to the broader ideal of WHITENING the country, which emphasizes its European influences while erasing its African ones. Most Afro-

Uruguayan ethnic societies disappeared; the few that existed in the 1990s were generally weak and often dependent on overseas donations. In its 1996–1997 study, the National Statistics Institute found that the average income of blacks was about 65 percent that of whites. Historian Alejandrina da Luz wrote in 1995, "Thus 'invisibility' became official policy. As they grow up, young Afro-Uruguayans today will find that their nation's history records only one black person: the loyal soldier Ansina. There are no black writers in Uruguayan literature; only in the United States are there black musicians; and in painting, black people appear only on canvas. Dozens of Afro-Uruguayan writers, dramatists, painters, musicians, and so on, seem to have faded away."

In recent years, however, CANDOMBE, an African-inspired music form created by slaves during the colonial period, has become the most popular music among Uruguayans of all races. Candombe grew in popularity as the music of resistance to the military dictatorship of the 1970s and 1980s, but many white Uruguayans at the time perceived it as the music of the poor black community. By the early twenty-first century, however, white, blacks, and mixed-race Uruguayans have embraced candombe and some see it as a potential vehicle for bridging Uruguay's racial divide. Still, in a country with no full-time black representatives in Congress, and few in other positions in government or academia, Afro-Uruguayans still face an uphill struggle against racism and discrimination.

See also Colonial Latin America and the Caribbean; Mining in Latin America and the Caribbean; Political Movements in Latin America and the Caribbean; Political Parties and Black Social Movements in Latin America and the Caribbean; Transatlantic Slave Trade.

Usuman dan Fodio

1754–1817

Muslim religious leader and founder of the Sokoto Caliphate in what is now northern Nigeria.

A FULANI born in the HAUSA state of Gobir, Usuman dan Fodio studied the Qu'ran (Koran) with his father, an eminent Islamic scholar, then moved from place to place to study with other religious scholars. When he was twenty-five, he began teaching and preaching, and from this time his reputation as a holy man grew. He taught ISLAM in Gobir, and he was probably engaged as tutor to the future sultan Yunfa because of his learned reputation.

Usuman criticized the Hausa ruling elite for their heavy taxation and other practices that he claimed violated Islamic law. His call for Islamic reform (and tax reduction) earned him a wide following in the 1780s and 1790s, when he became a political threat to Gobir sultan Nafata. When Yunfa assumed power as sultan in 1802, the repression of Usuman's followers worsened. Following the example of the prophet Muhammad,

Usuman went on a *hijrah* (spiritual migration), was elected *imam* (leader) of the reformist Muslims, and launched the *jihad* (holy war) that would bring down the Hausa royalty.

In the conquered areas, Usuman set up emirates whose leaders acknowledged his religious sovereignty, and in October 1808 the Gobir capital, Alkalawa, fell. In former Gobir, Usuman established a new capital, Sokoto, from which he ruled virtually all of Hausaland. After 1812 Usuman withdrew into private life, writing many works on the proper conduct of the pious Islamic community. After his death in 1817, his son MUHAMMAD BELLO succeeded him as the ruler of the SOKOTO CALIPHATE, then the largest state in Africa south of the SAHARA.

See also Hausa States; Nigeria.

V

Vai

Ethnic group of West Africa; also known as Vei and Vey.

The Vai primarily inhabit LIBERIA and SIERRA LEONE. They speak a MANDE language and are related to the MENDE people. Approximately 200,000 people consider themselves Vai.

See also Ethnicity and Identity in Africa: An Interpretation; Languages, African: An Overview.

Valdés, Gabriel de la Concepción ("Plácido")

1809–1844

Cuban poet, journalist, patriot, and martyr best known for his protest poems and his alleged involvement in the Conspiración de las Escalera.

Gabriel de la Concepción Valdés, more generally known by his pseudonym "Plácido," was born in MATANZAS to a white mother, the Spanish dancer Concepción Vásquez, and a black father, Diego Ferrer Matoso. Plácido was abandoned as an infant, left at an orphanage on April 6, 1809; a note found with him was inscribed with the name "Gabriel de la Concepción." He was given the last name Valdés, and the phrase "al parecer, blanco" ("appears white") was inscribed on his baptism certificate. In his *Biografías Americanas* (1906), Enrique Piñeyro laments the fact that Plácido's remorseful father retrieved him soon after abandoning him; if he had not reclaimed his son, Plácido would have "lost any trace of his previous servile condition." As it was, Piñeyro says, his father's retrieval of him "condemned the poor thing to a perpetual inferior situation, to an irredeemable fortune." Even free blacks in 1840s CUBA enjoyed little economic and social mobility; however, Plácido's paternal grandmother taught him to read and write.

At the age of fourteen, Plácido began working as a cashier in a publishing house. The pay was meager, and the few books and periodicals the business managed to publish were strictly regulated by colonial censorship. Plácido abandoned the press to become a *peinetero* apprentice, crafting women's haircombs from tortoiseshell. Known for his improvisational skills as a poet, in 1837 he started contributing a daily poem to the newspaper *La Aurora de Matanzas*. His "poetry of occasion"—laudatory poems commissioned for distinguished members of society—supplemented his income.

In 1838 Plácido published *Poesías,* followed in 1842 by a collection of *letrillas* and *epigramas* entitled *El Veguero.* In that same year, a promotion at *La Aurora* enabled him to dedicate his professional efforts to literary pursuits and his personal ones to married life with a new wife. The "nearly white" poet clearly established his political and ethnic affiliations when he married a woman "de pura sangre africana" (of pure African blood). Many Spanish epic poems compared Spain's empire to that of Rome. In this vein, poems like "Death of Caesar," or the following verses from "Juramento"—which challenged imperial rule and which many Cubans knew by heart—set the stage for Plácido's impending demise: "to be an eternal enemy of the tyrant . . . / and to die at the hands of an executioner / if necessary to break the yoke" (Ser enemigo eterno del tirano . . . / Y morir a las manos de un verdugo / Si es necesario por romper el yugo.)

In 1844 Plácido was executed by colonial troops, accused of participating in a plot to organize a slave revolt in the state of Matanzas and ultimately to win independence for Cuba. Many blacks, slaves and free alike, were brought in for questioning, tortured, and executed. The purge nearly wiped out the leaders of Cuba's free black population, and in the aftermath of the CONSPIRACIÓN DE LA ESCALERA, prominent mulattoes like journalists Rafael Serra y Montalvo ("the Cuban BOOKER T. WASHINGTON"), politician and activist JUAN GUALBERTO GÓMEZ, and ANTONIO MACEO Y GRAJALES, a general in the independence forces, would continue to be the focus of white fears of blacks. Plácido himself was tried partly on the basis of his verse. Three of his most famous poems, "Adiós a mi lira" (Goodbye to My Lyre), "Despedida a mi madre" (Farewell to My Mother), and "Plegaria a Dios" (Prayer to God), are said to have been written in prison only a few days before his death.

Though Plácido's fame increased after his death, he was renowned during his lifetime. His work has received a varied reception. One Spanish critic compared him to Luis de Góngora y Argote, a pillar of seventeenth-century baroque poetry. Some honor Plácido simply for the heroic circumstances of his death; others deem his verse "inferior," citing a lack of education. Most critics remark on his versatility both in style and form. His themes ranged from love to religion to liberty, and his styles included the didactic, elegiac, patriotic, improvised, and satiric. Nor did he limit his choice of form; he composed ballads, letrillas, redondillas, octavas, and décimas in the "popular" styles and "learned" verse in odes and sonnets. Some critics, like Richard Jackson, argue that Plácido should be celebrated both as a poet and a national hero.

See also Poetry, Caribbean; Racism in Latin America and the Caribbean; Slave Rebellions in Latin America and the Caribbean.

Joy Elizondo

Valdés, Jesús (Chucho)

1941–

Cuban Afro-Latin jazz pianist and one of the foremost musicians in Cuba; founder of Irakere, Cuba's most significant jazz orchestra.

Born in Quivican, CUBA, Jesús "Chucho" Valdés is the son of the Cuban pianist and bandleader Bebo Valdés, who was for many years musical director at HAVANA's famed Tropicana nightclub. In 1960, when his father defected from Cuba following FIDEL CASTRO's revolution, Chucho Valdés remained behind. Because of the embargo that the United States imposed on Cuba in 1960, Valdés remained virtually unknown to the American JAZZ public for many years. But during the 1990s, he found opportunities to perform and record in the United States, and has begun to reach a wider American audience, despite the continued political intransigence between the United States and Cuba.

Valdés began playing piano at age three, and by the time he was sixteen was leading his own group. He was particularly inspired by American jazz trumpeter DIZZY GILLESPIE, the co-creator—along with alto saxophonist CHARLIE PARKER—of BEBOP. During the 1940s and 1950s, Gillespie also participated in some of the formative experiments in Afro-Cuban jazz, including his recording of Chico O'Farrill's arrangement of "Manteca" (1947). Following the U.S. embargo on Cuba, Valdés and other Cuban jazz players were effectively cut off from the musical developments taking place in the United States, except via Willis Conover's "Music U.S.A." program on Voice of America. Valdés went on to study at the Havana Conservatory, and in 1967 founded the *Orquestra Cubana de Música Moderna* (OCMM).

Around 1972 Valdés and several other prominent Cuban jazz musicians left OCMM and formed a new group that ultimately took the name IRAKERE, the YORUBA word for forest or woods. Valdés served both as the group's leader and as its principal composer and arranger. Irakere played an infectious Afro-Cuban jazz-rock that, in part, reflected the musical influence of trumpeter MILES DAVIS, who was instrumental in popularizing the use of rock-style rhythms and electric instruments in

jazz. Irakere gained a wide following in Cuba and in the many other parts of the world where the band toured. Because of lingering Cold War hostilities, however, it has had few opportunities to play in the United States.

During the 1970s, word of Valdés and his superb ensemble gradually reached the United States, particularly through the reports of the few American jazz musicians who performed in Cuba. When Dizzy Gillespie and his quintet first appeared in Cuba in 1977, they played a memorable concert with Irakere, and Gillespie befriended two of Irakere's founding members: trumpeter ARTURO SANDOVAL and saxophonist PAQUITO D'RIVERA. Sandoval and D'Rivera subsequently left Cuba and commenced successful jazz careers in the United States, including stints during the 1980s with Gillespie's United Nation Orchestra. Valdés, however, by again choosing to stay in Cuba, remained unknown to the wider American jazz public.

In the 1990s, however, Valdés found new opportunities to bring together the two nations as well as the African American and Cuban musical heritages. In 1992 he became president of the Havana Jazz Festival, where he has presented a number of prominent jazz musicians, including trumpeter Roy Hargrove and saxophonist David Sanchez. In 1996 Valdés joined Crisol, a Cuban American big band under the leadership of Hargrove, which on a number of occasions brought him to NEW YORK CITY. On one of those visits, he played for several nights at Bradley's, the New York nightclub. More recently, Valdés signed a recording contract with EMI Canada—as *New York Times* music critic Ben Ratliff observed, to do so "with the company's American office would constitute trading with the enemy."

Early in 1998 Valdés played two well-received solo concerts at New York City's Lincoln Center for the Performing Arts, as part of an extended program celebrating Cuban music. Ratliff vividly depicted Valdés's playing in one of those concerts, particularly emphasizing his rhythmic artistry:

> [H]e opened with big, sonorous chords, then attenuated his playing into a waltz rhythm, then dived into swirling atonality. In serpentine legato runs, he never missed a note; dozens of tiny dots whizzed by each second, steely and well-defined. . . . One of Mr. Valdés's best conceits was to bring wild abstractions into *montuno* sections: as the right hand pumped out a two-three clavé, the left hand sketched a torrid storm that hewed to no rhythmic cycle.

In his Lincoln Center debut, Valdés not only performed such jazz standards as "Yesterdays" and "Autumn Leaves," but also "La Comparsa," written by Cuban classical composer ERNESTO LECUONA.

During his years as director of Irakere, Valdés often found himself playing electric keyboards rather than the piano. But recently he has cut back his involvement in that group—turning over its leadership to his son Chuchito—in order to concentrate on his piano playing. Valdés, who continues to record and tour, released the album *New Conceptions* in 2003.

See also Jazz, Afro-Latin; Music, Afro-Cuban; Music, Classical, in Latin America and the Caribbean.

James Sellman

Valdés, José Manuel

1767–1843?

Afro-Peruvian doctor, poet, professor, philosopher, and member of parliament.

The child of a washerwoman and a musician, José Manuel Valdés was born in Lima, Peru's capital city, when nearly half its population was black. Though his parents could not afford to educate him, his godparents and mother's employers stepped in, seeing to his early education at a prominent religious school. He would later become the first black writer to publish in PERU, both as a doctor and as a poet, as early as 1791.

After completing school, Valdés yearned to become a priest, but during the colonial period blacks were denied access to the priesthood by the CATHOLIC CHURCH, and he turned instead to medicine. He could have prospered as a *romancista*, a type of medical practitioner that required little training and was restricted to "external remedies." In 1788 he took the more challenging route and pursued the title of *latinista* surgeon, for which he studied anatomy and surgical techniques. As a latinista surgeon he was allowed to perform emergency surgeries and administer purgatives.

As his finances continued to improve, he threw himself wholeheartedly into his work, importing the latest surgical instruments and books on surgery from Europe while learning French, English, and Italian. The fruits of his labor appeared in a published dissertation on methods for curing dysentery. During these years, another hypothesis of his, namely that uterine cancer is not contagious, was sharply criticized by some of his contemporaries, but was proven correct not long after by European researchers.

The 1790s witnessed the heyday of French philosophers and encyclopedists, spreading liberalism and expounding on the universality of political rights, yet Valdés, a free black, was denied access to the priesthood, the military, and the university. It took a *dispensa,* an official permission from King Carlos VI, to "pardon" his color and allow him to attend the University of Lima in 1807. Later on, he was issued a similar document from the pope granting him access to the priesthood, but the Cabildo Metropolitano, upset by his petition, discouraged him from following through. As a practicing physician, he became well known in Europe for his medical theories; and as a university professor in Lima, he continued to publish medical papers. In 1815, before Peru achieved independence from SPAIN, he was welcomed into the Royal Academy of Medicine in Madrid.

His literary career developed later in life. Valdés is one of a handful of well-known early republican writers of African descent, such as CANDELARIO OBESO (1849–1884) in COLOMBIA. Valdés wrote mainly mystical poetry, in addition to a biogra-

phy of FRAY MARTÍN DE PORRES (1579–1639), the black Peruvian saint canonized by the Roman Catholic Church. Valdés also wrote *Poesías espirituales* (1818; Spiritual Poetry) and *Salterio Peruano* (1833), a poetic translation of the Psalms. Not all of his work was strictly religious in nature. He contributed articles to *El Mercurio Peruano,* a progressive and republican newspaper, and composed odes to independence-era generals José de San Martín ("Oda a San Martín") and SIMÓN BOLÍVAR ("Lima libre y pacificada"), well known for their pro-abolition stance.

With the advent of the Peruvian Republic, Valdés was elected to Congress to represent Lima in 1831. He became a member of the illustrious Patriotic Society and was appointed Médico de Cámara del Gobierno, a position similar to United States surgeon general. He received an important Peruvian award, the Order of the Sun of Peru, before attaining a succession of important medical and university titles, among them director of Lima's Medical College of Independence.

See also Latin America and the Caribbean, Blacks in; Literature, Black, in Spanish America.

Joy Elizondo

Valdés, Merceditas

1928–1996

Afro-Cuban singer, interpreter, and arranger of religious and secular Afro-Caribbean music, and a well-known practitioner of the traditional Yoruba religion Santería.

Mercedes Valdés, or Merceditas, as she was widely known, was born in HAVANA, CUBA. She began her distinguished artistic career in the 1940s, studying at Havana's Supreme Art Institute under José Alonso. As a student, she received awards for several works, including "Babalú," "La Negra merece," and "El chureo." During the late 1940s Valdés began to display her interpretive talents over the airwaves on Radio Cadena Suaritas. These appearances established the young artist's position as one of Cuba's most prominent interpreters of traditional Yoruban religious music. In the late 1950s Valdés's SANTERÍA recordings for the Panart label helped to secure her importance in the Afro-Cuban movement.

Throughout her career Valdés gained the recognition of Cuba's most acclaimed musicologists and critics, including the anthropologist FERNANDO ORTIZ and the musicologist Argeliers León. In addition, she performed with many notable Cuban artists such as the composer ERNESTO LECUONA, the *tres* player and maestro ARSENIO RODRÍGUEZ, the great *sonero* singer BENY MORÉ, the percussionist MONGO SANTAMARÍA, and the jazz pianist Charlie Palmieri. In 1995 Valdés performed as a member of the Cuban All Stars, and her recordings have been featured on several Cuban compilations, including *Messidor's Finest* and *Cuba: I Am Time* (1997).

By the time of her death in 1996 Merceditas Valdés had succeeded in bringing Afro-Cuban culture to the world through her acclaimed live appearances and recordings. She also proved her versatility, performing dancehall BOLERO, RUMBA, and sonu music alongside traditional Santería music. Valdés consistently received the highest recognition for her work, including a national recognition medal from the Cuban Cultural Ministry. Musicologist Angeliers León aptly characterized Merceditas Valdés's importance to Cuban culture, and the preservation of Yoruban tradition: "Merceditas Valdés is one of the best exponents of the Yoruban language and its rites, transmitting them through their ancestors and contributing towards a greater knowledge of this African heritage."

See also Music, Afro-Caribbean Religious; Music, Afro-Cuban Secular; Yoruba (religion).

Bibliography

Cuba. I Am Time: Cuban Invocations. Blue Jackel Entertainment Inc. BJAC 5010–2, 1997.

Moore, Robin. *Nationalizing Blackness: Afrocubanismo and Artistic Revolution in Havana, 1920–1940.* University of Pittsburgh Press, 1997.

Tumi Cuba Classics. Vol. 2. Tumi CD050, 1995.

Gordon Root

Valentim, Rubem

1922–1991

Contemporary Brazilian sculptor and painter whose work uses geometric symbols associated with *orixás,* Afro-Brazilian deities.

Rubem Valentim was born in Salvador, BAHIA. Although he studied dentistry in college, he could not resist the appeal of fine arts. For more than four decades Valentim was one of Brazil's most celebrated painters and sculptors. Even after his death in 1991, Valentim's work was widely exhibited across Latin America.

See also Art in Latin America and the Caribbean.

Valiente, Juan

?–1553

Slave who fought with Spanish colonial armies in Central America and the Southern Cone, and who is thought to be the first black to have been given a land grant, or *encomienda.*

See also Chile.

Vallenato

Accordion music from Colombia's Caribbean coastal region that, since the 1970s, has become the best-selling Colombian musical style in the country.

The origins of this syncretic music lie in a pan-Latin American tradition of versification that included *romances* (ballads), *coplas* and *trovas* (rhyming verses), *décimas* (ten-line stanzas), *cantos* (songs), and different forms of oral poetry, sung unaccompanied or perhaps with a guitar. European influences were important, but many singers were of African descent. For Colombia's Caribbean coastal region, African influence is evident in twentieth-century work songs and some funerary songs, as well as in the *bailes cantados* ("sung dances"), the dancing to drums and singing that forms a parallel tradition. In the late nineteenth century, accordions and harmonicas imported from Germany began to appear in the region and were used in this corpus of songs. Although probably something of a rarity in this genre, they were also used in other local styles played by traditional lineups of African and indigenous drums, flutes, maracas, and so on, and by wind bands. The accordion has usually been described as being in the hands of the troubadour or wandering minstrel, perhaps accompanied by a small hand drum (now known as a *caja*) and a scraper (*guacharaca*).

Accordion music from this region began to be labeled *vallenato* in about the 1940s, shortly after the appearance of the type of accordion that produced the distinctive sound of the genre. The term *vallenato* means "born in the valley" and usually refers to Valledupar, a town in the eastern part of the region, and its surrounding areas. In the early 1900s, the term was used locally to refer not to music but to local lower-class people. However, similar sorts of accordion music could be found all over the Colombian Caribbean coastal region at the time. The Valledupar zone was important for the number of important accordionists who came from there, including Chico Bolaños, Pacho Rada, Emiliano Zuleta, ALEJANDRO DURÁN, and Leandro Díaz. The locality was also constructed as the primary birthplace of this music when local elites (including songwriters Rafael Escalona, Tobías Enrique Pumarejo, Freddy Molina, and Gustavo Gutiérrez) began to write songs for the accordion and claim the music as a tradition special to their area. This development occurred at a time when the area itself was becoming increasingly integrated into the rapidly modernizing nation-state. At this time, too, accordionists were making early recordings in Colombia's fledgling record industry, based in nearby Cartagena and Barranquilla, and were performing on the new radio stations. Claims by the local elite about the unique character of their region were reinforced in the 1960s with political campaigns—which used vallenato music—for a new *departamento* (administrative province) status for the region. In 1968 an annual vallenato festival was established that insisted on "traditional" three-piece lineups consisting of an accordion, drum, and scraper.

Accordion music was seen as very plebeian for most of the twentieth century. Vallenato subgenres (particularly *paseo,* MERENGUE, and *son*) became popular nationwide in the 1940s and 1950s, but the tunes were played on the guitar by, for example, Guillermo Buitrago. Accordion vallenato started to become popular nationally in the 1970s, but it was still associated with the lower classes, even as the lineups became larger, more professional, more standardized musically. Vallenato also grew less parochial in lyrical content, emphasizing generally the romantic themes that gave it, for some listeners, an air of "schmaltz." By the 1980s, it had become Colombia's best-selling single national genre, with stars such as Diomedes Díaz, Julio Oñate, and *El Binomio de Oro*. In the 1990s, vallenato of the 1950s and 1960s gained a new popularity and status as a national symbol, after the broadcast of a television dramatization of the life of songwriter Rafael Escalona and albums of "modernized" versions of the music by singer Carlos Vives. These albums broke sales records, appealed to middle-class youth (who generally disparaged vallenato), and also sold well abroad.

See also Colombia; Music, Afro-Caribbean Secular.

Peter Wade

Valley of the Kings

Area west of the Nile River that contains the tombs of many ancient Egyptian pharaohs.

During the Old and Middle Kingdoms of ancient EGYPT (2575–1640 B.C.E.), the pharaohs commissioned pyramid tombs and temples in anticipation of their journeys to the afterlife. They filled these tombs with the goods considered necessary for the next life, including jewels, precious metals, food, tools, furniture, and even royal servants and pets. These riches lured grave robbers, who stripped most of the known tombs virtually bare. Beginning with Amenhotep I (1525–1504 B.C.E.), however, the pharaohs located their burial complexes on the west bank of the NILE, across the river from THEBES, in a valley hidden by cliffs and a narrow entrance. Amenhotep I had his temple and tomb built into the side of the limestone cliffs in the valley, with deep corridors stretching as far as 100 meters (325 feet) below the earth. Traditionally, work on a pharaoh's tomb began the day he ascended the throne and ended the day he died.

More than sixty such tombs have been rediscovered since the eighteenth century. Over time, desert sand had covered the entrances to most of the tombs, and their locations had been forgotten. In 1799, however, army engineers accompanying France's emperor Napoleon I rediscovered several of them, and Europeans proceeded to excavate the tombs and remove their precious contents to museums in their home countries. Perhaps the most extraordinary discovery was of the tomb of the boy king Tutankhamen, found in 1922. Located on the valley floor, it was robbed twice but escaped large-scale looting because the construction of a later tomb covered its entrance with sand and rubble. Although it is by far the smallest tomb in the valley, archaeologists recovered more than 5,000 artifacts from the tomb, many of which now reside in the Cairo Museum. During the 1980s archaeologists discovered a tomb that they believe contains fifty-two sons of Ramses II (1290–124 B.C.E.). Scientists have been excavating this tomb ever since. In late 1997 they commissioned the DNA testing of four mummies to determine if they were in fact Ramses' offspring. The Valley of the Kings is also the final resting-place for one of the few women who ever ruled Egypt, Hatshepsut, who reigned from 1473 to 1458 B.C.E.

Archaeologists worry that these ancient monuments, which have faced centuries of humidity, pollution, and flash floods, are deteriorating. Some say that it is only a matter of time before they are lost forever. In addition, thieves and vandals have been plundering the monuments for thousands of years. Yet the walls of these tombs still contain elaborate bas-relief artwork that provides information and insight into the beliefs and practices of one of the world's oldest and greatest civilizations. As a result, Egyptologists have declared the valley the richest archaeological site in the world. Archaeologists are currently developing preservation plans, creating detailed topographic maps of the tombs they have already discovered, and outlining possibilities for further excavations.

The Valley of the Kings is among Egypt's greatest tourist attractions, and has been for millennia, as graffiti from ancient Greek and Roman visitors testify. The continuing fascination with ancient Egypt lures as many as 3,000 visitors per day to the valley sites and generates more than $3 billion nationwide each year. In November 1997, fundamentalist Muslim rebels attacked tourists visiting the Hatshepsut Temple in the Valley of the Kings, killing fifty-eight visitors. The attack devastated the TOURISM industry, on which Egypt depends economically. Despite the government's heightened security measures, the attack left many foreigners unwilling to travel to Egypt, especially to vulnerable areas such as the Valley of the Kings.

See also Egypt, Ancient Kingdom of.

Robert Fay

Van der Post, Sir Laurens Jan

1906–1996

South African writer, best known for his books on travel and anthropology and for the striking imagery and minute observation of his work.

Born in Philippolis, Jan van der Post was raised on a working ranch and educated at Grey College in Bloemfontein, SOUTH AFRICA. In 1925, with two other South African writers, Roy Campbell and William Plomer, he helped start the magazine *Voorslag*, which was strongly opposed to the South African APARTHEID government. Due to his involvement with the periodical, van der Post was forced to leave South Africa and so traveled to Japan, where he wrote his first novel, *In a Province* (1934), an early indictment of South African racism. Van der Post served with the British Army during WORLD WAR II and spent three years (1943–1946) in a Japanese prisoner-of-war camp. He based his books *The Seed and the Sower* (1963; filmed as *Merry Christmas Mr. Lawrence* in 1983), *The Night of the New Moon* (1970), and *Portrait of Japan* (1968) on these experiences.

Van der Post's early exposure to Sᴀɴ myths led to a lifelong fascination with this ethnic group of the Kᴀʟᴀʜᴀʀɪ Dᴇsᴇʀᴛ of northern South Africa. In his writings van der Post has idealized the San's traditional way of life as an intuitively spiritual state of perfect harmony with the natural environment. His works on San culture, *The Lost World of the Kalahari* (1958), *The Heart of the Hunter* (1961), *A Mantis Carol* (1975), and *Testament to the Bushman* (with Jane Taylor, 1984), are probably his best-known books. Other books by van der Post include *Venture to the Interior* (1952), *Flamingo Feather* (1955), *Jung and the Story of Our Time* (1976), *Yet Being Someone Other* (1982), *A Walk with a White Bushman* (with Jean-Marc Pottiez, 1986), *About Blady* (1991), and *Feather Fall: An Anthology* (edited by Jean-Marc Pottiez, 1994). Van der Post was knighted by the British government in 1981.

See also Literature and Popular Resistance in South Africa in the 1960s.

VanDerZee, James Augustus

1886–1983

African American photographer.

James Augustus VanDerZee was born in Lenox, Massachusetts, the son of Susan Elizabeth Brister and John VanDerZee, who had served as maid and butler, respectively, in Ulysses S. Grant's home in Nᴇᴡ Yᴏʀᴋ Cɪᴛʏ in the early 1880s. After the Grants lost their fortune in 1884, the VanDerZees moved to Lenox to be near relatives. VanDerZee's father then worked as an Eᴘɪsᴄᴏᴘᴀʟ Cʜᴜʀᴄʜ sexton. VanDerZee (whose surname is sometimes spelled as two or three words rather than one) attended the public schools of Lenox. At the age of twelve he won a simple box camera by selling twenty packets of sachet powder, so he began to experiment with photography as a hobby.

In 1906 VanDerZee moved to Hᴀʀʟᴇᴍ with his brother Walter to join their father, who was already working there. In 1907, while working as a waiter, he met and married Kate L. Brown. Shortly thereafter, the couple moved to Phoebus, Virginia, where VanDerZee worked as a waiter and took some notable photographs of people in the city and in nearby Hampton at the Whittier (preparatory) School. After the birth of their first child, the couple returned to New York, where VanDerZee pursued his love of music. There, he formed the Harlem Orchestra and played the violin and piano. During the next eight years VanDerZee frequently visited his hometown, where he photographed family and friends in soft-focus with diffused light. In 1910 his son Emile was born, but he passed away the following year. VanDerZee and his wife separated in 1912.

VanDerZee's musical career languished as radios, photographs, and jukeboxes became popular, so in 1915 he began work as a darkroom technician in the Gertz Department Store in Nᴇᴡᴀʀᴋ, Nᴇᴡ Jᴇʀsᴇʏ. In 1916 he opened his own studio, Guaranty Photo, on 135th Street in New York, one of Harlem's busiest thoroughfares. His photographic window displays and his use of creative poses for both his black and white clients ensured his success as a portrait photographer. In the 1920s VanDerZee began photographing funerals of Harlem's famous residents, using an eight-by-ten-inch camera. Some of these were memorial allegories that featured superimposed family members of the deceased with biblical figures in multiple-image photographs. In addition, VanDerZee was the official photographer for Mᴀʀᴄᴜs Gᴀʀᴠᴇʏ and the Uɴɪᴛᴇᴅ Nᴇɢʀᴏ Iᴍᴘʀᴏᴠᴇᴍᴇɴᴛ Assᴏᴄɪᴀᴛɪᴏɴ (UNIA), and he documented the organization's conventions, rallies, parades, and families.

In 1932 VanDerZee opened a larger shop, GGG Studio, at 272 Lenox Avenue, with his second wife, Gaynella Greenlee Katz, as his partner. They had married in 1916. Together they specialized in photographing church groups and social organizations. VanDerZee went beyond mere documentation; he employed skillfully painted backdrops and artificial fireplaces, libraries, and genre scenes, hand-tinted and retouched negatives for beautification and dramatization, and creatively synthesized design elements and composition. He recalled, "Well, it seems as though I had a personal interest in the pictures . . . sometimes they seemed to be more valuable to me than they did to the people I was photographing because I put my heart and soul in to them. I was never satisfied with things the way they looked" (Willis-Braithwaite, "James VanDerZee," p. 160).

VanDerZee took photographs both in the studio and on location in Harlem. His diverse subjects included Elks, Masons, and other fraternities, athletic teams, and family gatherings, especially women and children, often posed in their best clothing and finest jewelry. Oval or circular formats frame these works. Among his better-known sitters were the first African Americans in the Army of Fʀᴀɴᴄᴇ to receive the Croix de Guerre; singers Mᴀᴍɪᴇ Sᴍɪᴛʜ, Hᴀᴢᴇʟ Sᴄᴏᴛᴛ, and Fʟᴏʀᴇɴᴄᴇ Mɪʟʟs; poet Cᴏᴜɴᴛéᴇ Cᴜʟʟᴇɴ; heavyweight boxing champions Jᴀᴄᴋ Jᴏʜɴsᴏɴ, Jᴏᴇ Lᴏᴜɪs, and Hᴀʀʀʏ Wɪʟʟs; religious leaders Aᴅᴀᴍ Cʟᴀʏᴛᴏɴ Pᴏᴡᴇʟʟ, Aᴅᴀᴍ Cʟᴀʏᴛᴏɴ Pᴏᴡᴇʟʟ, Jʀ., Father Divine, and Daddy Grace (Cʜᴀʀʟᴇs Eᴍᴍᴀɴᴜᴇʟ Gʀᴀᴄᴇ); and heiress and patron A'Lelia Walker. VanDerZee also produced and sold sensual, melancholy nude studies as artistic work.

In 1943 VanDerZee purchased the building he had been renting on Lenox Avenue; however, his business began to decline in the late 1940s as inexpensive cameras became popular. He supplemented occasional commissions with a mail-order retouching service, but severe financial problems led to the loss of his house and studio in 1969. Fortunately, curator Reginald McGhee at the Metropolitan Museum of Art met the photographer in the 1960s and preserved his archives. That institution featured four decades of VanDerZee's work in the exhibition *Harlem on My Mind* in 1969, and the exhibition caused a resurgence of interest in the photographer's career. McGhee helped found the James VanDerZee Institute, which showed his work throughout the world. Three monographs on VanDerZee's work were published in the 1970s, and he was appointed a fellow of the International Society of Magazine Photographers. After his wife died in 1976, VanDerZee spoke at many conferences and gave numerous interviews. In 1978 he published, in conjunction with poet Owen Dodson and artist Camille Billops, *The Harlem Book of the Dead,* a book of poems and photographs of African-American funeral rites, ceremonies, and mourning customs in Harlem, and he became the first recipient of the New York Archdiocese Pierre Toussaint Award. The same year he married Donna Mussendon, who was sixty years his junior.

With his third wife's encouragement, in 1980 VanDerZee began to photograph again. Celebrities such as BILL COSBY, LOU RAWLS, MILES DAVIS, CICELY TYSON, MUHAMMAD ALI, and EUBIE BLAKE had their portraits done with many of the same props VanDerZee had used in the 1920s and 1930s. He made his last portrait for art historian Regenia Perry in February 1983. His work continues to be exhibited internationally.

Bibliography

VanDerZee's photographs are in many public and private collections, including those of the Metropolitan Museum of Art, the Lunn Gallery in Washington, D.C., the Schomburg Center for Research in Black Culture and History, the National Museum of American Art, the New York Public Library, Regenia Perry, and the Studio Museum in Harlem. VanDerZee's papers are in the collection of Donna Mussendon VanDerZee and the Schomburg Center for Research in Black Culture and History, New York Public Library.

De Cock, Liliane, and Reginald McGhee. *James VanDerZee.* 1973.
Haskins, Jim James. *VanDerZee: The Picture Takin' Man.* 1991.
McGhee, Reginald. *The World of James VanDerZee: A Visual Record of Black Americans.* 1969.
Obituary, *New York Times,* May 16, 1983.
Willis-Braithwaite, Deborah. *VanDerZee, Photographer, 1886–1983.* 1993.
———. "James Van Der Zee." *Harlem Renaissance: Art of Black America.* 1987.

From *American National Biography.* John A. Garraty and Mark C. Carnes, eds. Oxford University Press, 1999. Reprinted by permission of the American Council of Learned Societies.

Theresa Leininger-Miller

Vann, Robert Lee

1879–1940

African American newspaper publisher, lawyer, civil rights leader, and government official.

Robert Lee Vann was born on August 27, 1879, in Ahoskie, North Carolina to former slaves who eked out a living by operating a general store. As a youth, Vann enjoyed playing with boys of prominent white families in nearby Harrellsville. After graduating as valedictorian of Baptist-run Waters Training School in Winton, North Carolina, he enrolled at Wayland Academy in RICHMOND, VIRGINIA in 1901. While at Wayland,

Vann was influenced by John T. Mitchell, editor of the *Richmond Planet,* who opposed the disenfranchisement of blacks and the virulent segregation laws known as JIM CROW.

In 1903, with the aid of a $100 Charles Avery scholarship, Vann entered Western University of Pennsylvania in PITTSBURGH as a sophomore. There he gained a reputation as an orator and debater, and served for two years as a regular contributor to the school newspaper. In his senior year he was the paper's editor-in-chief, the first African American to achieve that position. Vann graduated as class poet in 1906, received his law degree in June 1909, and passed the bar examination in December of that year. Two months later, he married Jessie E. Matthews.

Working for the Newspaper

To supplement his income, Vann served as counsel for the PITTSBURGH COURIER, a newspaper organized by a small group of blacks in 1910. In the fall he became editor, treasurer, and legal counsel, positions that he held until his death in 1940. With Ira Lewis as business manager, Vann developed the *Courier* into one of the leading black newspapers of his era. Its crusades against segregation and discrimination, and for fuller recognition of blacks in the white press, increased the paper's circulation. Also increasing its circulation was the MIGRATION of many blacks from the South during WORLD WAR I (1914–1918) to the rapidly growing city of Pittsburgh.

The decade of the 1920s laid the foundation for the *Courier's* leadership among black newspapers in the 1930s. From 1925 to 1929 Vann devoted most of his time to the paper, which published columns by satirist GEORGE SCHUYLER, historian JOEL A. ROGERS, and novelist WALTER WHITE. The *Courier* joined the Associated Negro Press in 1925 and used the services of promising reporter Louis Lautier, the syndicate's Washington correspondent. Cartoons, as well as photographs of beauty queens and socialites, suggested by business manager Ira Lewis, attracted many readers.

Vann was a crusading editor, taking forceful, although often inconsistent stances on a variety of issues. For example, he first opposed then later supported a boycott against Kaufmann's, the oldest department store in Pittsburgh. In 1917 he condemned the members of a black battalion of the United States Army who rioted in response to white harassment and were eventually court-martialed. He later demanded not only commutation of their sentences but a full pardon for the rioters. In 1925 Vann supported attempts by A. PHILIP RANDOLPH to gain recognition of the BROTHERHOOD OF SLEEPING CAR PORTERS, the first successful African American trade union. Three years later he demanded Randolph's resignation as the trade union leader, asserting that his socialist past impeded his achieving an agreement with the Pullman Company.

Vann was frequently on the wrong side of public opinion on many of these issues. In 1924, for example, he futilely advocated enforcement of the second section of the FOURTEENTH AMENDMENT, which guaranteed that if male citizens—including blacks—are denied the right to vote, their representation in

Congress would be reduced proportionately. In the early 1930s his vigorous denunciation of the AMOS 'N ANDY radio program was weakened by some black leaders' enjoyment of this lampooning of black life. The *Courier* also alienated many readers by insisting that participation by the "Communist-led" International Labor Defense jeopardized efforts to save from execution the nine black males accused of rape in the SCOTTSBORO CASE of the early 1930s.

Despite the checkered record of its editorial page, the *Courier's* circulation continued to increase. By 1926 it reached 55,000 readers and the numbers grew so rapidly that by 1929 Vann had to purchase a larger plant. Circulation reached a quarter of a million by 1938, in part due to Vann's editorial support of several popular issues. Among these were his enthusiastic backing for ETHIOPIA after the 1935 Italian invasion of that nation, his support of African American boxer JOE LOUIS, and the paper's reporting of the 1936 Olympic Games that featured extensive coverage of the four gold medals won by JESSE OWENS as well as Adolf Hitler's contempt for blacks.

The gathering storm of WORLD WAR II (1939–1945) prompted Vann to fight vigorously in the *Courier* for better treatment of blacks in the armed services. He protested against the demeaning duties assigned to blacks in the four regular army regiments, the small number of black officers, and the widespread publicity given to the alleged failure of black combat officers in WORLD WAR I. He assigned Percival L. Prattis, then city editor of the *Courier* and a veteran of World War I, to publicize these protests. Vann engaged the cooperation of attorneys CHARLES H. HOUSTON and Louis R. Mehlinger (both veterans of World War I), as well as Lautier, to advocate a separate black division. Vann and Prattis further supported the Committee on Participation of Negroes in the National Defense Program. This publicity, continued after Vann's death, helped the *Courier* maintain a leading position among black newspapers.

The financial success of the *Courier* was due in large measure to Vann's editorship and Ira Lewis's business management. However, Vann was less successful in his own business enterprises. His monthly magazine *The Competitor: The National Magazine,* founded in January 1920, failed after eighteen months. His law practice, like that of most other black lawyers of his era, was confined largely to unremunerative criminal cases. He did make a notable contribution in 1921 by advancing the relatively novel argument that pretrial newspaper accounts prejudiced a murder trial for which he sought commutation of the death sentence. Although he lost the case, extensive coverage in the *Courier* substantially increased sales. Vann also lost additional sums in other business enterprises before and during the GREAT DEPRESSION.

Political Career

In addition to his work at the *Courier,* Vann also entered into local and national politics. In 1918 he used his influence among black voters in Pittsburgh to win appointment as fourth assistant city solicitor. This was the highest position held by an African American in the municipal government. His whole-hearted support of black participation in World War I probably accounts for the fact that he escaped government scrutiny and criticism, unlike black activists such as A. Philip Randolph, CHANDLER OWEN, W. E. B. DU BOIS, and ROBERT S. ABBOTT. In 1921 Vann failed to secure reappointment as assistant solicitor and later ran unsuccessfully for judge of the Allegheny Court of Common Pleas.

Although a Republican, Vann grew disenchanted with the policies of U.S. presidents Warren G. Harding, Calvin Coolidge, and Herbert Hoover. In 1932 he supported Democrat Franklin D. Roosevelt in his bid for the presidency, and Roosevelt rewarded him with the position of special assistant to the U.S. attorney general. However, the attorney general assigned him to insignificant duties, and Vann perceived earlier than some members of the so-called BLACK CABINET (an organization of black community leaders helping to shape New Deal programs) and some historians the limited achievements of the New Deal for blacks. Instead, he devoted more time to supporting Democrats in Pennsylvania, where in 1935 he helped obtain the enactment of a state equal rights law he had first sponsored as early as 1918. Vann resigned from the Department of Justice as of January 1936. In 1940 he returned to his Republican roots, supporting Wendell Willkie for president. However, in January of that year Vann underwent surgery for abdominal cancer. He died on October 24, less than two weeks before the election.

Vann's Legacy

Along with T. THOMAS FORTUNE, WILLIAM MONROE TROTTER, Robert S. Abbott, CARL MURPHY, ROSCOE DUNJEE, and P. B. YOUNG SR., Vann was among the foremost black newspaper editors of the first half of the twentieth century. Like them, he used his paper as a vehicle generally to support the advancement of worthwhile causes. He contributed in no small measure to changing despondency among African Americans at the turn of the century into the hopes that preceded rising black expectations in the mid-twentieth century.

After Vann's death a bronze plaque was placed on the wall in the entranceway of the *Pittsburgh Courier:* "In Loving Memory of Robert L. Vann: Publisher, Lawyer, Statesman, Brilliant Editor, Loyal Friend, Fearless Champion of Rights. Erected by His Admiring Employees Who Profited Greatly by His Precepts and Example." Public schools were named for him in Ahoskie and in the Hill District of Pittsburgh. Virginia Union University and the University of Pittsburgh established scholarships in his name, funded from bequests Vann left to the schools. At Virginia Union, the Robert L. Vann Memorial Tower was erected. In a testament to his influence on American life, on October 10, 1943 the Liberty Ship *Robert L. Vann* was launched in Portland, Maine, taking its place alongside two other vessels named after prominent African Americans, the *Booker T. Washington* and the *George Washington Carver.* A detailed treatment of Vann can be found in Andrew Buni's biography, *Robert L. Vann of the* Pittsburgh Courier: *Politics and Black Journalism* (1974).

From *Dictionary of American Negro Biography* by Rayford W. Logan and Michael R. Winston, editors. Copyright ©1982 by Rayford W. Logan and Michael R. Winston. Reprinted by permission of W. W. Norton & Company, Inc.

See also Press, Black, in the United States.

Rayford W. Logan

Van Peebles, Melvin

1932–

African American author, filmmaker, and playwright, perhaps best known for his groundbreaking 1971 independent film, *Sweet Sweetback's Baadasssss Song.*

Melvin Van Peebles has traded stocks on the floor of the American Stock Exchange, published several novels, and directed, produced, composed, and starred in American films and plays. He is an innovative and successful entrepreneur who has worked for more than four decades to offer new, and sometimes controversial, images of African Americans.

Van Peebles was born in 1932 on the South Side of CHICAGO, but spent most of his adolescent years with his father, a tailor in Phoenix, Illinois. After graduating from high school in 1949 and from Ohio Wesleyan University in 1953, Van Peebles served as a flight navigator for three and a half years in the U.S. Air Force. After the military he spent brief periods in Mexico and San Francisco (where he married) before moving to Europe. He studied at the Dutch National Theatre in the Netherlands, then moved to FRANCE in the early 1960s. During nearly a decade in Paris, Van Peebles wrote and published several novels in French, including *La Permission*, which he filmed under the title of *The Story of the Three Day Pass*, which concerns a black U.S. serviceman. The film won critical acclaim, and helped Van Peebles earn a studio contract with Columbia Pictures.

Van Peebles returned to the United States, and in 1969 directed *Watermelon Man*, a comedy about a racist white insurance salesman who wakes up one day to find that he has become black. Van Peebles took the proceeds from the film and made *Sweet Sweetback's Baadasssss Song* (1971), one of the most successful and controversial independent films of the era. *Sweetback* pushed the limits of cinematic décor, combining sex and violence in its depiction of a black sex worker who witnesses the murder of a young black revolutionary by two white police officers. It was one of the first "BLAXPLOITATION" FILMS of the 1970s and its success opened doors for African American directors, camera operators, designers, and editors.

In the early 1970s, Van Peebles staged two plays on Broadway, a musical, *Ain't Supposed to Die a Natural Death*, and *Don't Play Us Cheap*, based on his novel *Don't Play Us Cheap: A Harlem Party*. Later in the decade he wrote scripts for two television productions, "Just an Old Sweet Song" and "Sophisticated Gents." Van Peebles turned his attention to business in the early 1980s and became an options trader on the floor of the American Stock Exchange. Drawing on his success, he published two books on the Options Market. Since then he

has written a novel and appeared in his son Mario Van Peebles's 1993 movie *Posse,* an all-black Western.

Now in his seventies, Van Peebles remains busy. His recent film appearances include *Time of Her Time* (1999), *Smut* (1999), and *The Hebrew Hammer* (2003). In 2002 he directed and wrote the songs for a musical review, *Melvin Van Peebles et ses Potes* (and his Pals), performed in Paris, France. His son Mario portrayed him in the film *Gettin' the Man's Foot Outta Your Asssss!* (2004). The movie, which is also directed by his son, covers Van Peebles's pioneering work in motion pictures in the 1970s.

See also Film, Blacks in American; Literature, African American.

Alonford James Robinson

Van Riebeeck, Jan

1619–1677

Founder and first Dutch commander of the European settlement at the Cape of Good Hope, on the site of present-day Cape Town, South Africa.

The Dutch East India Company commissioned Jan Van Riebeeck to establish a rest and resupply station at the Cape for Dutch ships en route to the East Indies. After landing at Table Bay on April 6, 1652, with about 100 men, he built a fort and hospital on the site. He also established farms in the area around the bay.

Unsuccessful at securing the labor of the indigenous KHOIKHOI and SAN peoples, he advocated the importation of slaves to work the farms well before slavery was established in the colony. Van Riebeeck tackled the problem in 1657 by releasing men from their company employment to farm as free burghers, while still maintaining the interests of the company. This practice created the class of independent farmers who became known as Afrikaners, or Boers. The station was not meant to be expanded beyond the area of the bay, and Van Riebeeck's instructions were to keep the Cape establishment as confined and small as possible. Despite this, he actively encouraged exploration in the interior, ultimately leading to colonial expansion. In 1659, he waged a year-long war on the Khoikhoi. In 1662 Riebeeck was transferred to Malacca, after repeated requests to be moved. By then the Cape settlement was well established.

See also Afrikaner; Cape Town, South Africa; Explorers in Africa, 1500 to 1800; Netherlands, The.

Varick, James

1750–1827

Founder of the African Methodist Episcopal Zion Church.

Born in Orange County, New York, James Varick was a widely influential free black in NEW YORK CITY at the turn of the nineteenth century. Although both his parents had Dutch Reformed Church connections, he joined the white John Street Methodist Church, but he and other blacks withdrew to create the first African American congregation in New York. A shoemaker by trade, he also taught school; participated in black Masonic, mutual aid, and anticolonization societies; petitioned for the right to vote; and was one of the founders of FREEDOM'S JOURNAL, the first black American newspaper.

The congregation Varick established grew into a denomination, the AFRICAN METHODIST EPISCOPAL ZION CHURCH (AME Zion), and on July 30, 1822, Varick was elected its first bishop. The denomination, like the AFRICAN METHODIST EPISCOPAL CHURCH founded by RICHARD ALLEN, kept Methodist theology, polity, and worship, but in a black organization under black control. Largely middle class in makeup, the AME Zion Church has been a major institution in African American history. Varick's ashes are preserved in Mother Zion AMEZ Church on 137th Street in HARLEM.

See also Black Church, The.

Bibliography

Walls, William J. *The African Methodist Episcopal Zion Church: Reality of the Black Church.* A.M.E. Zion Publishing House, 1974.

Richard Newman

Vasconcelos, José

1722?–1760?

Afro-Mexican poet famous for his wit and humor of whom very little information is known, and whose improvised verses were published under the title *El negrito poeta mexicano y sus populares versos* (The Little Black Mexican Poet and His Popular Verses).

See also Literature, Black, in Spanish America.

Vasconcelos, Naná

1944–

Afro-Brazilian percussionist and master of the traditional Brazilian *berimbau*.

Naná Vasconcelos, born Juvenal de Hollanda Vasconcelos, is one of the most significant and influential percussionists of the last forty years. At the age of twelve, he began playing percussion—bongos and maracas—in the band led by his guitarist father. Later he took up drums and played in a bossa nova band. He is a master of the odd-numbered rhythms, such as 5/4 and 7/4, that are common in northeastern BRAZIL. In the mid-1960s Vasconcelos joined the band of Afro-Brazilian singer MILTON NASCIMENTO and moved to RIO DE JANEIRO. There he learned to play the BERIMBAU, a traditional Afro-Brazilian per-

cussion instrument shaped like an archer's bow with an attached gourd resonator. The berimbau produces a distinctive buzzing tone when the instrument's single wire string is struck with a thin wooden stick. Its tonal quality can be altered depending on the position of the gourd resonator, and its pitch depends on whether the musician places a coin against the wire.

In 1971 Vasconcelos joined the band of Argentine tenor saxophonist Gato Barbieri and toured ARGENTINA, the United States, and Europe. After the end of the tour, he stayed in Paris for two years, performing and working with handicapped children. In Europe he played with American avant-garde JAZZ trumpeter Don Cherry and with Brazilian jazz musician Egberto Gismonti. Together with Cherry and Collin Walcott, Vasconcelos formed Codona, an influential trio that combined the musical traditions of several continents. In 1976 Vasconcelos moved to NEW YORK CITY, where, as a multitalented percussionist, he was soon in demand.

Vasconcelos has recorded with such diverse musicians as BLUES legend B. B. KING, jazz pianist Keith Jarrett, fusion guitarist Pat Matheny, and the rock group Talking Heads. He has played with a wide variety of Brazilian musicians, including guitarist and political activist Caetano Veloso, pianist and singer Ivan Lins, and vocalist Marisa Monte. In addition, Vasconcelos has released several albums under his own name, among them *Bush Dance* (1986) and *Storytelling* (1995), both featuring his unique and complex multi-instrumental sound. In 2000 he composed the musical score for the movie *Meia Noite* and released the album *If You Look Far Enough* with Ralph Towner and Arlid Anderson.

See also Jazz, Afro-Brazilian.

James Sellman

Vashon, George Boyer

1824–1878

African American educator.

George Boyer Vashon was born in Carlisle, Pennsylvania, the son of John B. Vashon, a freeborn African American master barber, and Anne Smith. In 1829 the family moved to PITTSBURGH, PENNSYLVANIA, where John Vashon headed a number of self-help efforts in the African American community, including the establishment of a school for black children. Young George Vashon attended this school and, later, public schools in the city. In 1838 he and his classmates established the earliest Juvenile Anti-Slavery Society west of the Alleghenies. Two years later Vashon enrolled at Oberlin College in Ohio, which was one of a few colleges in the United States that then admitted black students. As a college student he gave orations and participated in the literary society. During the winter term of 1843 he taught school at Chillicothe, Ohio, instructing JOHN MERCER LANGSTON, who in later years became the first African American congressman from Virginia. Returning to college, Vashon graduated with a bachelor's degree in 1844, the first black graduate of Oberlin.

After graduation Vashon returned to Pittsburgh, where he worked as a law clerk under Judge Walter Forward and contributed to MARTIN R. DELANY's African American newspaper, the *Mystery*. In 1847 Vashon completed his law studies and applied for admission to the Pennsylvania bar, but his application was rejected on racial grounds. Dejected, he made plans to emigrate to HAITI. While en route there, however, he stopped in NEW YORK CITY, where in January 1848 he gained admittance to the bar. It is believed that he was the first black admitted to legal practice in New York state. He then refocused his attention on Haiti, sailing there in February 1848. He became the Haitian correspondent for FREDERICK DOUGLASS's newspaper, the *North Star*. Finding the political situation in Haiti in turmoil, Vashon turned his attention to teaching at academies in PORT-AU-PRINCE and at Collège Faustin, the major Haitian educational institution.

Vashon returned to the United States in 1850. Finding his admittance to the bar blocked again in Pennsylvania, he moved to Syracuse, New York, and entered private law practice. There he participated in antislavery actions and the Liberty party. In 1853 he joined Frederick Douglass, his own father, and others in calling for a "Colored National Convention," which was held in Rochester in July of that year. He also penned and published an epic poem, "Vincent Ogé," that same year. In 1854 Vashon joined the faculty at New York Central College, at McGrawville, as professor of mathematics and belles-lettres. Three years later financial difficulties at the college forced him to resign and return to Pittsburgh, where he became principal teacher in a black public school. While there, in 1859 he married Susan Paul Smith, an assistant teacher in the school; they had seven children.

In late 1863 Vashon became president of Avery College in Allegheny City, Pennsylvania, serving in that capacity until 1867. He remained active in the black convention movement. In 1865 he attended the National Equal Rights League meeting in Cleveland, Ohio, and was elected its corresponding secretary. That same year he was involved with the Pennsylvania Equal Rights League Convention as a speaker and corresponding secretary.

Vashon again sought admission to the Pennsylvania bar in 1867. However, the bar's delay in deciding the matter forced him to apply for several government posts in WASHINGTON, D.C., in late 1867. He was appointed an assistant in the Solicitor's Office of the Freedmen's Bureau, where he served as counsel for freedmen appearing before magistrate's courts. Concurrently, he was placed in charge of the night school at HOWARD UNIVERSITY, becoming that institution's first black faculty member, but lack of tuition fees forced the closing of the night school the following year. Vashon went on to work in a variety of positions with the Interior and Treasury departments until the fall of 1873. He simultaneously worked as a teacher examiner for the black schools in the District of Columbia and served on the boards of trustees for various black schools in the district. He contributed essays, poems, and translations to the national black weekly newspaper, *New Era*. He participated in the 1869 National Convention of Colored Men, held in the District of Columbia. In September 1873 Vashon became professor of mathematics at Alcorn University (later Alcorn State University) in Lorman, Mississippi, a position he retained until his death there of yellow fever.

Vashon's contributions as an early African American educator are significant through his teaching at several institutions of higher education and his administration of secondary and post-secondary institutions. Equally important was his participation in the black convention movement as a writer, speaker, and officer from the 1840s until his death. His substantial literary output, essays, poems, and position papers published in the black press, emphasized the general themes of moral improvement, education, and self-help.

Bibliography

Vashon's correspondence, including his extant academic records, is in the Oberlin College Archives. Other poems and essays that he published include "A Life Day" (1864) and "Ode on the Proclamation of the Fifteenth Amendment" (1870).

Dyson, Walter. *Howard University . . . A History 1867–1940*. 1941.

Foner, Philip S., and George E. Walker. *Proceedings of the Black State Conventions 1840–1865*. Vol. 1. 1979.

——. *Proceedings of the Black National and State Conventions 1865–1900*. Vol. 1. 1986.

Hanchett, Catherine M. "George Boyer Vashon, 1824–1878: Black Educator, Poet, Fighter for Equal Rights." *Western Pennsylvania Historical Magazine* 68 (1985): 205–219, 333–349.

Sherman, Joan R. *Invisible Poets*. 1974.

Smith, Clay. *Emancipation: The Making of the Black Lawyer*. 1994.

From *American National Biography*. John A. Garraty and Mark C. Carnes, eds. Oxford University Press, 1999. Reprinted by permission of the American Council of Learned Societies.

Frank R. Levstik

Vaughan, Sarah

1924–1990

American jazz singer and pianist, lauded for her pitch and range, whose singing style was informed by the harmony and improvisation of jazz horn sections.

Sarah Vaughan was born in NEWARK, NEW JERSEY. Her parents, both of whom were musicians, cultivated and nurtured her early interest in music. She began taking piano lessons at age seven and organ lessons at eight. By the age of twelve, she was playing the organ for the Mount Zion Baptist Church and singing in its choir. She later attended Arts High School in Newark.

In 1942 Vaughan entered and won an amateur-night contest for which she sang "Body and Soul." Her award was ten dollars and a week of performances at the APOLLO THEATER, an engagement which led to her being hired as a vocalist and second pianist in the big band led by EARL "FATHA" HINES. In 1944, she joined singer BILLY ECKSTINE and his band. She recorded the hit "Lover Man" (1945) with CHARLIE PARKER and DIZZY GILLESPIE, also members of Eckstine's ensemble, before launching her solo career in 1946 at the New York Cafe Society. In 1949, she landed a five-year recording contract with Columbia Records. Vaughan sustained her success as a singer through the early 1980s, recording on numerous labels, performing with a variety of JAZZ artists, and touring several countries.

Nicknamed "Sassy" and the "Divine One," Vaughan repeatedly was voted the top female vocalist by *Down Beat* and *Metronome* jazz magazines between 1947 and 1952. Her 1982 album *Gershwin Live!* won a Grammy Award, and in 1989 she received the Grammy Lifetime Achievement Award. Vaughan was inducted into the Jazz Hall of Fame in 1990.

See also Music, African American.

Aaron Myers

Vee Jay Records

Influential and successful African American–owned record company before the Motown era.

Vee Jay Records was founded in CHICAGO in 1952 and soon became America's most successful black-owned record company. Vee Jay recorded GOSPEL MUSIC, JAZZ, BLUES, RHYTHM AND BLUES, and early SOUL, but it was unique in concentrating on vocal harmony groups. Like many small record companies, Vee Jay was a family affair, involving Vivian Carter Bracken, her husband James Bracken, and her brother Calvin Carter. Vivian was a disc jockey in Gary, Indiana, where she and James owned a record store. Carter suggested the name Vee Jay, based on the first initials of his sister's and his brother-in-law's first names.

Vee Jay's first vocal group was the Spaniels, featuring the cool lead of James "Pookie" Hudson, who had a major hit with "Goodnight Sweetheart Goodnight" (1954). Other important Vee Jay vocal group hits included the El Dorados's "At My Front" (1955); the Dells's "Oh What a Nite" (1957); a memorable "For Your Precious Love" (1958) by the original Impressions, featuring Jerry Butler and CURTIS MAYFIELD. Perhaps the best-known Vee Jay hit was "Duke of Earl" by the Dukays, credited solely to the group's lead singer, Gene Chandler.

Within two years of releasing its first Spaniels single, Vee Jay owned a building on Chicago's Michigan Avenue directly across from the offices of Chess Records, which was a major producer of music for the African American market, featuring such best-selling artists as MUDDY WATERS, CHUCK BERRY, and the Moonglows. Besides vocal groups, Vee Jay recorded a number of other significant talents in the late 1950s and early 1960s, including bluesmen JOHN LEE HOOKER and Jimmy Reed, solo vo-

calists Jerry Butler, Dee Clark, and Betty Everett, and gospel singers such as the STAPLE SINGERS and ALEX BRADFORD. The company also recorded jazz, including tenor saxophonist Wardell Gray's last recording session, in 1955.

During the early 1960s Vee Jay stood on a par not only with Berry Gordy's fast-growing MOTOWN RECORDS, but also with the independents that focused on the audience for African American R&B and soul music: Chess, Atlantic, and STAX RECORDS. But rapid expansion, sloppy finances, and internal bickering forced the company to declare bankruptcy in 1965.

See also Music, African American.

James Sellman

Vega, Ana Lydia

1946–

Writer, feminist critic, and professor of French and Caribbean at the University of Puerto Rico at Rio Piedras, who regards Afro–Puerto Rican themes and popular language as central to her intellectual production.

Notable among the works of Ana Lydia Vega are *Vírgenes y mártires* (1981), the author's first book, which was coauthored with Carmen Lugo Filipp; *Encancaranublado y otros cuentos de naufragio* (1982), which won Vega the 1982 Casa de Las Americas Prize; *La gran fiesta* (1986), a screenplay that was made into a movie; *Pasión de historia y otras historias de pasión* (1987); and *Falsas crónicas del sur* (1991). Various Vega stories and a novella were translated into English by Andrew Hurley and appeared under the title *True and False Romances* (1994). Vega has received numerous awards for her work, including the PEN (International Association of Poets, Playwrights, Editors, Essayists, and Novelists) Club of PUERTO RICO National Literature Prize on several occasions, the prestigious Casa de Las Americas Prize of CUBA (1982), the Juan Rulfo International Short Story Prize (1984), the Premio Casa del Autor Puertorriqueño (1985), and the Guggenheim Fellowship for Literary Creation (1989).

Vega's profound knowledge of Spanish and African oral tradition has been an important influence on her writing. The author wrote her 1978 doctoral thesis on HAITI's King Christophe in Antillean theater and in black theater in the United States, and her narratives often include tales and thematic elements from African folklore. Vega received early exposure to oral tradition through her father, who was an expert in DÉCIMAS, an oral form of poetic improvisation typical of Black troubadours. She has a superb ear for popular language that allows her to skillfully use various types of verbal play such as jokes, puns, and riddles to underscore her biting humor. Vega's writing is also characterized by an alternation between formal and vernacular speech, an incisive examination of machismo in Caribbean societies, and vivid depictions of socially motivated violence. All of this serves her well and contributes to the powerful, distinctive quality of her writing. Vega has gained a wide following and her works engender much discussion in a variety of publications.

See also Literature, Black, in Spanish America; Literature, French-Language, in the Caribbean; Theater in the Caribbean.

Martha Davis

Venda

Ethnic group of southern Africa; also known as Bavenda.

The Venda primarily inhabit northeastern SOUTH AFRICA (TRANSVAAL) and southern ZIMBABWE. They speak a BANTU language related to both SOTHO and SHONA. Approximately 700,000 people consider themselves Venda.

See also Ethnicity and Identity in Africa: An Interpretation; Languages, African: An Overview.

Venezuela

South American country bordered on the east by Guyana, on the south by Brazil, on the west and southwest by Colombia, and on the north by the Caribbean Sea and the North Atlantic Ocean.

For more than a century, Venezuelans have used the phrase *café con leche* (Spanish for "coffee with milk") to describe themselves as a people of predominantly mixed-race descent. Europeans, Africans, and to a lesser extent, Native Americans played a part in Venezuelans' racial heritage. Some 75 percent of Venezuelans are of partial African descent, referred to locally as *pardos* or mestizos.

Official Venezuelan histories pay scant attention to the origins of the populace. Slavery, emancipation, and *mestizaje* (racial mixing) are treated as part of the country's distant colonial past. Thus, Venezuelan schoolchildren learn to take pride in their nation's multiracial and multicultural society but discover nothing about the blacks who contributed to that social mix. Rather, students spend a great deal of time studying the exploits of South America's independence leader SIMÓN BOLÍVAR and the illustrious, mostly white Creole (American-born) founders of the independent republic of Venezuela in 1821. At all levels, Venezuelan historians have largely avoided topics beyond the country's independence struggle, and only a handful of scholars—such as folklorist Juan Pablo Sojo, historian Ramón Díaz Sánchez, and anthropologist Miguel Acosta Saignes—make any reference to race and race relations in modern Venezuela.

Spanish Conquest and Slave Labor

When Spaniards first explored the coast of present-day Venezuela in 1498, the population of the area comprised a variety of indigenous cultures, with many different ethnic groups and hundreds of linguistic groups. Their lives varied considerably by region. Some lived in small shaman-led communities in isolated regions of southern Venezuela, surviving by means of slash-and-burn agriculture and food-gathering methods of subsistence. Others lived as hunter-gatherers and fishers in the Orinoco River delta or along the lowland coastal plains. Meanwhile, the inhabitants of the western Andes mountain ranges and river valleys and of the central coastal regions had developed sedentary agricultural communities.

The territory of present-day Venezuela, which the Spanish began to settle in the 1520s, did not have the potential to become one of the major centers of the Spanish Empire. Its indigenous peoples were scattered and therefore not easily exploitable, and it lacked large gold deposits for MINING. For that reason, small enclaves of Spanish settlers established a diversified agricultural and pastoral economy. They produced a variety of crops, including cacao, wheat, indigo, tobacco, and cotton. While some of these commodities went to markets in other Spanish territories in the region, the bulk of agricultural production met local needs.

For the better part of the first century of Spanish occupation, Native Americans provided most of the labor force under personal service *encomienda* obligations (The encomienda was a system of colonial rule that required forced labor from indigenous populations). The labor force therefore consisted primarily of indigenous workers. By 1530 a small group of African slaves had been imported to work as miners, carpenters, cooks, farmers, and cattle hands at the copper mines of Buria, near the northwestern city of Barquisimeto, joining indigenous workers in these tasks. At about the same time, a small group of Africans replaced Native Americans as divers for pearls around the islands of Cubagua and Margarita, located off the coast.

During the first half of the seventeenth century, Caracas emerged as the most prosperous and populous region in present-day Venezuela. By 1650 a small group of Caracas-based *encomenderos* (encomienda grantees) began to realize substantial profits from selling cacao to the Mexican market. At first the encomenderos took advantage of lax governmental controls by having indigenous laborers gather cacao from wild trees. With the onset of a booming cacao trade and the development of new cacao plantations, however, the encomenderos needed a larger workforce. The indigenous peoples did not conform to the disciplined regimen of the plantations. Furthermore, many of them fled the area rather than serve the Spanish. Thus, the wealthier planters began to acquire African slaves to do their work. Africans not only provided the needed labor but also brought their own agricultural technology to the arduous tasks of clearing land, digging irrigation ditches, planting shade crops to protect the cacao seedlings, and caring for the trees as they matured. The importation of African slaves into the province of Caracas during the seventeenth century far exceeded previous use of African slave labor in Venezuela. By the end of the century, slaves constituted the majority of all rural laborers in the colony and made up a substantial part of the domestic servant class in the city of Caracas.

The increasing number of black slaves had a profound demographic impact on Venezuela. By the end of the 1600s the population of the central coastal sections of Caracas was transformed, with blacks, *zambos,* and *pardos* (both terms for persons of partial African descent) forming a racially mixed majority. Most indigenous peoples had fled the region, and few whites lived outside the urban centers. Black enclaves cropped up in the coastal region of Barlovento, the eastern shore of Lake Maracaibo, and numerous coastal hamlets from the city of Coro in the northwest to Carúpano in the northeast. By 1800 people with at least partial African ancestry accounted for nearly 75 percent of the population of Venezuela.

Slave Resistance and Rebellions

African slaves and their black Creole (American-born) descendents at times successfully escaped their bondage in what was itself a form of rebellion. By the mid-sixteenth century fugitive slaves, called *cimarrones* (maroons), had established their own communities, locally known as *cumbes,* in remote areas. In 1552 one cimarrón leader, a Creole slave named Miguel, gathered together some 800 blacks, mulattoes, and zambos to build a series of fortified refuges near Barquisimeto. Calling himself King Miguel, he led his followers in attacks against Spanish settlements. They stole cattle, took white hostages for ransom, and fought as a guerrilla band against Spanish forces. In 1555 Spanish forces defeated King Miguel at Barquisimeto. By then, Miguel had augmented his forces with indigenous recruits whom the Spanish, in turn, used to hunt down Miguel's followers.

During the 1560s slaves from the mines at Buria fled and established a cumbe west of Caracas. After almost forty years of efforts to subdue these cimarrones, Spanish authorities offered a general amnesty for all fugitive slaves in the province. In 1601 the Spanish crown recognized the founding of the town of Nirgua, where the black fugitives could live under their own control as long as they pledged their allegiance to the monarch

of SPAIN and promised to support campaigns against renegade Native Americans in the region.

The most serious racial conflict of the first half of the eighteenth century occurred in the cacao-growing region of the Yaracuy Valley, northwest of Caracas. In 1731 ANDRÉS LÓPEZ DEL ROSARIO, a zambo known as Andresote, led a band of rebels, composed mainly of blacks, zambos, and Native Americans, against the colonial government. Their rebellion was in response to the government's decision to enforce the royal monopoly on the exportation of cacao, because the enforced monopoly threatened the rebels' illicit trade with the Dutch colony of CURAÇAO. After the rebels successfully ambushed a colonial military envoy in January of 1732 and some of the pardo soldiers joined Andresote, the royal governor and white planters grew fearful that the uprising was inciting other blacks, both free and slave, to rebel. They decided to take drastic measures and put together an army of 1,500 men that finally scattered Andresote's army. After a year of skirmishes, several of the rebels were captured and condemned to death, while others were imprisoned for life.

Following the outbreak of the HAITIAN REVOLUTION in 1791, a series of abortive slave uprisings occurred in Venezuela. In early May 1795 a free zambo tenant farmer named JOSÉ LEONARDO CHIRINOS led a three-day revolt of slaves, free blacks, pardos, zambos, and Native Americans near Coro. But Chirinos abandoned his followers after they killed the owner of his wife and children. Without leadership, the movement succumbed quickly to militia forces. Minor revolts that occurred in 1796, 1798, and 1799 in Coro and Maracaibo kept alive the fear of racial warfare in Venezuela, but none of the revolts seriously threatened white supremacy in the colony.

Slaves, Free Blacks, and the Economy

By 1800 the colony, then known as the Audiencia of Caracas, had a thriving agricultural and pastoral economy. No one crop

Roughnecks work on an oil rig in the middle of Lake Maracaibo in western Venezuela. Several oil companies operate on the lake. *Steve Starr/CORBIS*

Venezuela (At a Glance)

OFFICIAL NAME: Bolivarian Republic of Venezuela

AREA: 912,050 sq km (352,144 sq mi)

LOCATION: Northern South America between Colombia and Guyana, bordered by the Caribbean Sea and the Atlantic Ocean

CAPITAL: Caracas (population 3,177,000; 2002 estimate)

OTHER MAJOR CITIES: Maracaibo (population 1,901,000), Valencia (population 1,893,000) (2004 estimates)

POPULATION: 25,699,000 (2004 estimate)

POPULATION DENSITY: 29 persons per sq km (75 per sq mi)

POPULATION BELOW AGE 15: 31 percent (male 3,944,749; female 3,700,799; 2003 estimate)

POPULATION GROWTH RATE: 1.48 percent (2003 estimate)

TOTAL FERTILITY RATE: 2.36 children born per woman (2003 estimate)

LIFE EXPECTANCY AT BIRTH: Total population: 73.81 years (male 70.78 years; female 77.07 years; 2003 estimate)

INFANT MORTALITY RATE: 23.79 deaths per 1,000 live births (2003 estimate)

LITERACY RATE (AGE 15 AND OVER WHO CAN READ AND WRITE): Total population: 93.4 percent (male 93.8 percent; female 93.1 percent; 2003 estimate)

EDUCATION: Primary education in Venezuela is free and compulsory for ages six to fifteen. Two years of free secondary education is also offered, but not required. Half the adults in Venezuela have no secondary education. Wealthy families usually send their children to private schools. Caracas has several universities, among them the National Open University and the Central University of Venezuela.

LANGUAGES: Spanish is the official language of Venezuela. Many indigenous dialects are also spoken.

ETHNIC GROUPS: Spanish, Italian, Portuguese, Arab, German, African, and indigenous people

RELIGIONS: The population is 96 percent Roman Catholic, 2 percent Protestant, and 2 percent other religions.

CLIMATE: Tropical, with temperature and precipitation variations depending on elevation. The average temperature in most of Venezuela is above 75°F (24°C). The rainy season is May to October, the dry season December through March, with regional variations. The northeastern coast is rainy during the summer, and the northwestern coast is drier, with less than 20 inches (500 mm) of rainfall in certain areas. The southern interior receives enough rain to support agriculture as well as tropical savanna and rainforest.

LAND, PLANTS, AND ANIMALS: Venezuela can be divided into three general regions based on elevation: the lowland plains, the mountains, and the forested uplands. The lowland coastal plains are in northern Venezuela. This area also includes the Caribbean Leeward islands and several peninsulas. Two parallel ranges of Andes mountains comprise the Coastal Range and the Interior Range, between which are located the major cities: Caracas, Valencia, and Maracay. An upland zone lies between the mountains in the northwest, where Venezuela's only desert is located. The lightly populated Llanos region of tropical rainforests and savannas follows the course of the Orinoco River in central Venezuela. The southernmost two-fifths of the country comprise the Guiana Highlands, a little-explored upland area of ancient hills and valleys. Angel Falls, the highest waterfall in the world, is found in the southeastern portion of this region. Venezuela's vegetation varies with region and elevation from tropical to evergreen or semi-deciduous. There are grasslands, mangrove swamps, fern forests, and alpine shrubs. Wildlife includes seven species of cat, among them jaguars, pumas, and ocelots. There are also bears, deer, wild dogs, skunks, and several types of monkeys. Reptiles include alligators, lizards, and turtles, and many species of snake. Birds such as cranes, herons, and storks live in the coastal swamps.

NATURAL RESOURCES: Petroleum, natural gas, iron ore, gold, bauxite, other minerals, hydropower, and diamonds

CURRENCY: bolivar (VEB)

GROSS DOMESTIC PRODUCT (GDP): $131.7 billion (2002 estimate)

GDP PER CAPITA: $5,400 (2002 estimate)

GDP REAL GROWTH RATE: −8.9 percent (2002 estimate)

PRIMARY ECONOMIC ACTIVITIES: Services, industry, and agriculture

PRIMARY CROPS: Corn, sorghum, sugarcane, rice, bananas, vegetables, coffee, beef, pork, milk, eggs, and fish

INDUSTRIES: Petroleum, iron ore mining, construction materials, food processing, textiles, steel, aluminum, and motor vehicle assembly

PRIMARY EXPORTS: Petroleum, bauxite and aluminum, steel, chemicals, agricultural products, and basic manufactures

PRIMARY IMPORTS: Raw materials, machinery and equipment, transport equipment, and construction materials

PRIMARY TRADE PARTNERS: United States, Netherlands Antilles, Canada, Colombia, Brazil, and Mexico

GOVERNMENT: Venezuela is a federal republic. The chief of state and head of government is President Hugo Chavez Frias (since February 1999), elected by popular vote for a six-year term. The legislative branch is the 165-member unicameral National Assembly, whose members are elected by popular vote to five-year terms. The judicial branch is the Supreme Tribunal of Justice, whose magistrates are elected to single twelve-year terms by the National Assembly.

Shelle Sumners

or labor system prevailed. Wealthy landholders adopted a wide range of land tenure and labor arrangements to produce a variety of cash crops. Cacao still led as an export crop, but indigo, coffee, SUGAR, and tobacco combined with livestock to form a diversified economy. Slave gangs worked on some of the large cacao estates and on sugar plantations, but many of the former used a mixed labor system of day laborers and slaves. Slaves represented no more than 13 percent of the population. For this reason, tobacco and indigo planters depended almost entirely on paid laborers rather than on slaves. Landowners who switched to growing coffee in the early nineteenth century used slaves if they could, but most had to hire workers to meet their production demands. As for livestock, most of which went to domestic markets, the owners of ranches on the *llanos* (plains) relied mostly on free frontiersmen, or *llaneros*.

The majority of Venezuela's free blacks lived as tenants, squatters, or owners on small plots (*conucos*), where they produced foodstuffs, such as corn, beans, rice, cassava, and plantains, for local consumption. These conucos enabled free blacks to shape their relationship with the *hacendado* (large landholding) class. The farmers remained relatively independent of the hacendados and determined their work patterns for themselves because they met their basic needs on their conucos. Although they remained poor, they enjoyed a degree of freedom from forced labor not found in most parts of the Spanish Empire. Racial and cultural fusion took place rapidly throughout Venezuela, especially among the impoverished common classes. From the beginning, white and pardo day laborers, black slaves, and indigenous personal attendants worked side by side, mixing not only their cultures but also their bloodlines.

By the end of the colonial era, a white Creole planter elite and their allies among Spanish bureaucrats and wealthy merchants controlled the economic and governmental institutions. Another white group, composed of poorer mainland Spaniards and people from the Canary Islands, made up a class of small-plot planters, farmers, renters, artisans, day laborers, and muleteers (mule drivers). Some of these resided in rural districts, others in urban centers. Below the identifiably European groups, people of mixed race held more menial positions. A few owned land, and some worked as artisans, shopkeepers, and farmers. But the majority never rose above making their living by vending fruits, vegetables, and other foodstuffs in the towns. In the rural areas they served as laborers or eked out an existence as subsistence farmers. Free blacks performed similar tasks, although many along the coast lived as fishers or worked as stevedores at the ports.

Blacks in the Struggles for Independence

The real threat to white supremacy came from pardos (mulattoes), not from free blacks and slaves. During the protracted and bloody struggles for independence, which lasted from 1810 to 1822, Venezuelans of mixed race held the balance of power. When it suited their needs, they supported Spanish royalists against the pro-independence leader SIMÓN BOLÍVAR and the Creole aristocrats. In 1813 Bolívar suffered defeat because the Spanish royalist José Tomás Boves led slaves and mixed-race llanero troops, who shouted "Death to the whites" (meaning the white CREOLES, who were the owners of the land and traditional supporters of slavery) as they defeated the Creoles.

On his return to Venezuela in 1816, Bolívar—who had banned blacks from enlisting with his troops in 1813—made a special appeal to attract pardos, blacks, and slaves to join his forces, offering the latter freedom in return for their participation in his armies. This was in response to Boves's success in recruiting larger armies, which threatened to finish Bolívar. Consequently, a small group of slaves joined free llanero horsemen under Bolívar's general José Antonio Páez. Their slogan was now "Death to the *godos*" (referring to Spanish-born people in the Americas).

The inclusion of pardos and black troops in the independence movement shattered the old colonial social order. To some of these soldiers and officers, it represented a hope for reforming the social order and subverting their political marginalization. Involvement in Bolívar's military organization gave many pardos opportunities to rise as officers in the new republican army. When several Afro-Venezuelan officers gained what white officers considered too much power within the rebel army, they were accused of attempting to incite a race war and executed. The execution of General Manuel Piar, a mulatto, in October 1817 is the most noted example. Still, slaves discovered a sense of power as the contending armies wooed their support and, although most slaves were not convinced of the value of these struggles for independence, the army did provide refuge for runaway slaves. Others simply fled the war zones, and in so doing, contributed to the collapse of plantation discipline.

Abolition of Slavery

Following Venezuela's independence, secured in 1821, free blacks and slaves lived much as they had during the late colonial period. Most free blacks worked at menial tasks. A few became military chieftains (*caudillos*), bureaucrats, landowners, artisans, or shopkeepers. Some 13,000 remained enslaved, and slavery continued to fester as a dying institution until it was abolished in 1854. A free-womb law was first passed by the National Constituent Congress of Cúcuta in 1821. The Congress, which met near the border of Colombia and Venezuela, integrated these two republics with PANAMA and ECUADOR in the Republic of Gran Colombia and issued its formal constitution.

When Venezuela seceded from Gran Colombia in 1830, the free-birth law was incorporated into the Venezuelan constitution of 1830, guaranteeing the gradual abolition of slavery. Under this law, slaves born after July 21, 1821, would become freedpeople (*manumisos*) upon reaching the age of eighteen. Manumission commissions were established to enforce this legislation and to collect taxes that were to pay for the manumission (formal release) of slaves born before July 21, 1821. In 1830 the law was changed to move the age of liberation to twenty-one. Slave owners again warded off the date of eman-

cipation in 1840 by forcing manumisos to remain enslaved as "apprentices" until the age of twenty-five.

Two developments brought about abolition. First, the shift from the cultivation of cacao to the cultivation of coffee eroded the economic base of slavery. Growing cacao depended heavily on slave labor, and after independence the productivity of the industry declined steeply. Coffee, however, did not depend on slavery and enjoyed favorable prices in the international markets. Second, slaves were escaping in increasing numbers, many joining the factions that participated in the various conflicts that plagued the country during the first half of the century. During the late 1840s, a civil struggle between Venezuela's two main political parties, Conservatives and Liberals, led the latter to openly recruit slaves for its armed forces. Once the Liberals assumed power in 1848, the Conservatives followed the same strategy. They promised blacks and pardos complete abolition of slavery and further incited them to rebel against a government that, Conservatives alleged, intended to return free blacks to slavery. Faced with the disintegration of slavery because of the economic crisis, slave flight, and the possibility of slave rebellions, President José Gregorio Monagas of the Liberal Party averted political disaster by announcing the end of

slavery on March 24, 1854. By this time, slaves constituted an insignificant portion of the workforce.

Black Life after Emancipation

Emancipation did not end factional fighting. In 1858 a coalition of moderate Liberals and Conservatives overthrew the increasingly authoritarian regime of Monagas. The peace established by the new government soon gave way to warfare, as demagogues calling themselves Federalists stirred up racial and class feelings by rebelling against the moderates in power. Federalists opposed the centralized government because they believed it represented the interests of an oligarchy of rich landowners, bankers, and merchants. Representing the debtor class, they identified whites as their enemies. Nonetheless, blacks and people of color fought on either side during the so-called Federal Wars (1858–1863), and white elites led both factions. It was not a race war, per se, and most blacks ended up fighting in the conflict as unwilling conscripts, victims of forced recruitment by regional bosses.

After slavery collapsed, planters feared that the flight of their former slaves would exacerbate an existing labor shortage.

Thus, during the 1850s they pressed for vagrancy and work codes that enabled them to coerce unemployed laborers to work. But such codes proved unenforceable for lack of rural police officers, and workers moved from one employer to another without punishment.

Most former slaves, uneducated and underskilled, had few employment options. Freed slaves moved horizontally on the social scale from bondage to peonage. Many ended up as soldiers or bandits, but the majority either stayed on the estates as day laborers or moved to coastal areas, where they found work as stevedores and sailors or fished for a living. In the larger cities they worked as domestic servants, street cleaners, garbage collectors, door attendants, or porters, or they ended up as street vendors of ice, bread, water, or pots and pans.

Women had fewer opportunities for improvement. Many remained on the large estate plantations or shared the misery of their husbands eking out existences as seasonal rural workers, tenant farmers, or *conuqueros* (owners of small land plots). Women also replaced men on the large farms as the latter were conscripted into armies. In the cities women worked as domestics or vendors of sweets and *arepas* (cornbread). The less fortunate turned to prostitution to survive.

Despite these conditions, several blacks attained some measure of prominence in the period after the Federal Wars. José Victorio Guerra served as minister of development and as a diplomat under General Antonio Guzmán Blanco, whose military regime prevailed from 1870 until 1888. Educator Alberto Gonzalez helped to initiate the first pedagogic congress held in Venezuela during the early 1870s. Marcelino Rojas, a political orator, and physician-publicist Gabriel Muñoz Tebar, who wrote for the biweekly newspaper *El Monitor Industrial* (The Industrial Monitor), played active roles in intellectual and political circles.

A few blacks met with considerable success through careers in the military, including José Félix Mora and Cecilio Padrón. In 1892 General Mora was appointed governor of the northwest state of Carabobo under the mulatto president Joaquín Crespo (1892–1898). Mora surrounded himself with capable advisers and met with enthusiastic support during his term in office. Another black ally of Crespo, Natividad Soloranzo, known as Zambo y Medio, held power in the state of Guarico before his death fighting against the followers of Guzmán Blanco in 1881. But most blacks and zambos in the military were not as fortunate. Many died forgotten on battlefields or eked out wretched lives as underpaid and malnourished foot soldiers, unless they deserted.

Race in the Era of Popular Politics

Racism in Venezuela was especially apparent from the 1890s to the 1930s. During that period white elites openly subscribed to white supremacist theories, such as British philosopher Herbert Spencer's version of social Darwinism (EUGENICS). They called for the regeneration of the Venezuelan "race" by WHITENING the population. This they hoped to accomplish by overwhelming the nation's black population with European immigrants. Using Venezuelan historian and writer José Gil Fortoul's definition of race as a social or cultural phenomenon, they believed they could incorporate nonwhites, through mestizaje, into a predominantly white race within a few generations. During this period, Venezuela's elites equated whiteness with what they called "civilization," or a modern European culture. In any number of ways they discriminated against blacks, whom they satirized in cartoons, magazine articles and advertisements, theater, and fiction. Nowhere did positive images of blacks appear to offset the widely held notion of black inferiority and backwardness.

On July 20, 1891, a new immigration law prohibited the entry of nonwhites into Venezuela. Despite strict measures to ban nonwhite immigration, the nation's economy depended on black laborers from the Antilles (island chains of the WEST INDIES) during the first three decades of the twentieth century. Owing to demand for workers, between 6,000 and 11,000 Antillean blacks arrived annually to work at the docks, and still more worked seasonally on the private estates of the elites. Their numbers remained high at the gold fields of Ciudad Guayana, in the Orinoco River region of eastern Venezuela. Most of the domestic servants in Caracas arrived from MARTINIQUE, CURAÇAO (NETHERLANDS ANTILLES), TRINIDAD, and other Caribbean islands, including CUBA. In addition, petroleum companies took advantage of loopholes in the immigration and colonization code of 1918 to bring in large numbers of Antilleans to work at the oil fields, ostensibly due to the scarcity of qualified Venezuelan laborers. By 1935 petroleum had replaced coffee as Venezuela's chief export.

Venezuelan elites especially believed that blacks and pardos could not govern themselves. For that reason, and to retain their elitist positions, they supported brutal dictatorships such as that led by General Juan Vicente Gómez from 1908 to 1935. Not until the 1940s did any political movement incorporate nonwhites into its leadership. The advent of the social democratic party Acción Democrática (AD; Democratic Action) and its rise to power in 1945 gave Venezuela's blacks and mixed-race pardos a short-lived political success. That year, when three Caracas hotels refused to provide a room to North American baritone singer Todd Duncan, the Acción Democrática faction passed a strong antidiscrimination law. In 1948 a military coup overthrew the government of pardo Romulo Gallegos Freire and led to the dictatorship of General Marcos Pérez Jiménez (1948–1952 as part of a junta; 1952–1958 as sole ruler), who reasserted white supremacy. The government once again banned the immigration of nonwhites and did not enforce the antidiscrimination law.

Since 1958 Venezuelans have enjoyed an era of democracy that has enabled men and women of all colors to access political power, at both local and national levels. Through the 1980s, blacks held high positions as members of Acción Democrática or as candidates of several splinter parties. The best known include educator Luis Prieto Figueroa, who was a presidential candidate in three elections (1968, 1973, and 1978), and Aristúbolo Isturiz, who served as mayor of the Federal District of Caracas from 1992 to 1995. In December 1998 former colonel

Hugo Rafael Chávez Frías, who is of partial African descent, was elected president of Venezuela on his own party platform.

Opportunities have also opened up in other areas. Blacks have comprised an increasing number of students at the once exclusively white Universidad Central de Venezuela, the nation's largest and most prestigious university, located in Caracas. Blacks also have become a noticeable part of Venezuela's officer corps, although they are still a distinct minority in the military.

From the time of slavery, blacks in Venezuela have become absorbed into the dominant European culture. One reason for this is no single African ethnic group predominated to hold blacks together and to provide them with a cohesive culture of their own. Some traces of an African heritage are evident in language and religion, albeit in fragmentary form. Venezuelan Spanish, spoken by all blacks, uses some African words. Some religious cults, such as that of Maria Lionza, are a syncretic blend of African, indigenous, and European beliefs. The national dance, the *joropo*, retains the polyrhythmic beat of African music.

Throughout the twentieth century, succeeding generations of Venezuelan elites have made a widely accepted myth of racial equality the official racial doctrine of Venezuela. According to this belief, termed "racial democracy" by some scholars, no forms of racial prejudice or discrimination exist in Venezuela. Although this myth persists to the present among the elites, the nation's black population knows better. They fully realize that they have lived in the shadow of their slave past, and that in subtle and insidious ways they have lived as victims of racial discrimination and prejudice.

Since 1990 several black movements have challenged the myth of racial democracy and have begun to protest openly the racism that exists in Venezuela. To raise consciousness among Venezuelans, Jesus "Chucho" Garcia founded the Fundación Afro-America (Afro-American Foundation), which coordinates efforts to publicize the plight of impoverished blacks. In the predominantly black Barlovento region, east of Caracas, Modesto Luiz, mayor of San José de Barlovento, created an organization of black mayors who meet regularly to press for reforms aimed at removing the obstacles that hold back their black constituents. Other black leaders include Ligia Montañez, who has studied black identity and socioeconomic status; Reina Arratia, who works on black culture; and Geronimo Sánchez, founder of an Afrocentric school for black children. As a result of their efforts, all of the political parties in Venezuela have inserted the discussion of Afro-Venezuelans as part of their platforms. Moreover, open discussions of race and racism are beginning to appear more frequently on the nation's television stations.

Although he is only part black, even President Chavez has openly denounced the Venezuelan attitude toward race, stating:" There's an incredible racism in the society. They call me the monkey or the black; they can't stand that someone like me was elected president." Some observers praise Chavez for championing the cause of black Venezuelans; others worry that his populist rhetoric against the white elite risks inflaming class war. In addition, black Venezuelans have not seen much improvement in their economic situation, Chavez's rhetoric notwithstanding. However, it seems clear that most of the nation's poor black population is behind Chavez. During an aborted coup against the government in 2002, black Venezuelans stood firmly in support of their president.

See also African Linguistic influences in Latin American and the Caribbean; Agriculture, African, in the Americas: An Interpretation; Colonial Latin America and the Caribbean; Complexities of Ethnic and Racial Terminology in Latin America and the Caribbean; Maroonage in the Americas; Myth of Racial Democracy in Latin America and the Caribbean; Racism in Latin America and the Caribbean; Role of Slaves in Abolition and Emancipation in Latin America and the Caribbean Slave Rebellions; Slavery in Latin America and the Caribbean; Transculturation, Mestizaje, and the Cosmic Race: An Interpretation; Venezuelan Religion, African Elements in.

Venezuelan Religion, African Elements in

Because slaves first arrived in VENEZUELA before 1800 and were immediately converted, at least superficially, to Catholicism, African religious elements in Venezuela have survived only in fragmentary form in popular rituals for saints and in a few beliefs and practices. African elements in Venezuelan folk-Catholic practices are found in rural regions with a predominant black population, such as the Barlovento, the central coast, the southern coast of Lake Maracaibo, and some areas of Yaracuy, Lara, and Carabobo. African elements in the folk Catholicism of these areas are incorporated into the festivals held for particular saints by local brotherhoods. In Carabobo, Yaracuy, Miranda, and Aragua, for example, Saint John is the patron of black peasants and fishermen. On the eve of his feast, *erum* dances are held, while old women sing sirenas for the saint, similar to African praise songs. Early the next morning, Saint John's icon is bathed in the river and is then carried from house to house, where drummers, singers, and dancers are offered food and drinks. The participants use special homemade drums for the ceremony, which are used only during rituals. The faithful thank the saint for having answered their prayers. A similar ceremony is held in Lara in honor of Saint Anthony: celebrants engage in ritual stick fights during a procession with his statue—a custom also widely seen in West Africa.

In the region of Zulia, San Benito of Palermo is the patron of black peasants. His feast is celebrated with drum dances and processions held between Christmas and January 6th in different black villages. The rhythms and drumbeats used in this ceremony have kept their original African flavor. In recent years, many traditional customs have disappeared, and the dances for the patron saints, once considered a solemn obligation, are now becoming tourist attractions.

Another Venezuelan festival that exhibits African elements is called "devil dances," held on the annual Catholic festival of Corpus Christi Day in eight or nine different villages with predominantly black inhabitants. The most traditional dances take place in the isolated village of Chuao, in Aragua, where the male-only fraternity of *Diablos* (or devils) is responsible for the celebration, while the dances in honor of Saint John are organized by a female-dominated group. The "devils" wear colorful gowns and masks made of papier-mâché, which are reminiscent of masks used in similar rituals and masked dances in Central Africa. During these dances, which are considered a solemn obligation, the gender dichotomy also exists: one man wears a female mask, representing the "wife of the devil." It is important to note that the "devils" are not evil. On the contrary, the dancers dressed as devils visit the homes of the fraternity members in order to chase evil away. The dancers can also be compared to the *egunguns* in Benin and Nigeria, who represent the departed ancestors, visiting their living kin in order to bring good luck and chase evil away. Although in San Francisco de Yare the annual "devil dances" are watched by thousands of tourists, the members of the fraternity have preserved their original solemn ritual.

Some African elements are also found in the funeral rites in the Yaracuy and Barlovento regions. During the nightly wake held in the home of the departed, the women wail for the deceased while the men play cards. Mourners place a glass of water next to the coffin, as it is believed that the soul of the dead is still present and may be thirsty. They also place some personal objects, such as a comb, a toothbrush, and a cap, into the coffin for the spirit's journey to the other world. Afterwards they take the coffin out of the house through a hole made in the wall that is carefully covered up again so that the spirit cannot find its way back. After praying for nine nights in front of an improvised altar in the house of the departed, the people smash a table upon which flowers, candles, and photos of the dead have been placed. They make noise to indicate to the dead soul that the ritual is over and that it may now depart in peace and not disturb the living. On the night before All Souls' Day, celebrated annually on November 2, black peasants visit the graves of their departed relatives and sometimes spend the whole night in the cemetery. They leave food and libations there for the dead.

In addition to rituals and festivals that historically developed in Venezuela, other Afro-Latin religions are increasingly popular. During the past forty years, for example, Santería has been introduced to Venezuela by Cubans and Venezuelans who have traveled to Miami and Puerto Rico. The majority of converts to this religion belong to the middle class, because initiation ceremonies are expensive. However, Venezuelans of all classes consult *babalawos*, or priests of the Santería religion, to help solve personal problems.

Santería beliefs and practices have also been introduced into the native cult of Maria Lionza, which has its roots in both Amerindian beliefs and the teachings of Allan Kardec, a European spiritist. In this cult, spirits of different origin are summoned to take possession of mediums in trance, and the spirits can then be consulted by the faithful. This cult is utilitarian in nature: the spirits prescribe cleansing rituals to get rid of evil influences and give advice on how to heal illnesses.

Until about thirty years ago most spiritual entities consulted in the cult of Maria Lionza were spirits of nature or of departed persons of importance, such as Amerindian chiefs who fought the Spanish conquerors, or Simón Bolívar, the hero of Latin American independence. In recent years, the *Siete Potencias Africanas*—the seven most important orishas of the Cuban-Yoruba pantheon—are consulted through the mediums. Animal sacrifices are offered to them, drums are used to call the spirits, and colors have a symbolic value, just as in Santería. Venezuelan cultists often ignore the true African origin of these entities, although today they speak about the "African court," to which, incidentally, the Viking spirits also belong, although they are depicted as bearded white savages. Recently, Venezuelan folk healers have begun to mention specific countries in their divination practices, and they may invoke the African spirits to help them in their spiritual work.

In addition to Santería, the Brazilian religion of Umbanda was introduced to Venezuela in the late twentieth century by a white Uruguayan *pai de santo,* or priest. He presides over a center, frequented by members of the middle class, where Afro-Brazilian *caboclo* and *preto velho* spirits manifest themselves in initiated mediums who are consulted by adherents.

Overall, the globalization of Afro-American religion, and the influence of religions such as Santería and Umbanda in Venezuela, stem from media coverage, the expansion of esoteric literature, and frequent reunions of cultists and esoterics. The prospects for historically Venezuelan religions, though, are quite different. While the cult of Maria Lionza is subject to a re-Africanization process, in which spirits are increasingly identified as being of African origin, traditional folk religiosity is vanishing as the population of Venezuela is becoming more urbanized.

See also Orisha; Religions, African, in Latin America and the Caribbean.

Angelina Pollak-Eltz

Ventura, Johnny

1940–

Afro-Dominican politician and merengue musician who incorporates the issues of race, politics, and social change in his music.

Johnny Ventura, affectionately called *El Caballo* (The Horse), has been praised as one of the few artists to successfully blend politics and music. His achievements are facilitated by a strong sense of national identity and a connection with the masses. Ventura made merengue the country's main musical form and a symbol of national identity accessible to all social classes. Unlike most other politicians, Ventura expresses pride in his African heritage within a society that emphasizes its Spanish and indigenous ancestry. Ventura has used music not only to provide entertainment but also as a medium through which meaningful issues like Dominican identity and concepts of race can be expressed.

Johnny Ventura began his musical career under his birth name, Juan de Dios Ventura Soriano. After winning a 1956 radio station singing competition that drew attention to his powerful, smoky voice, the singer changed his name to the stylish Johnny Ventura for artistic as well as political reasons. Ventura's singing career took off soon after his debut. He was well received by Dominican society because his lyrics criticized the country's political system and its denial of an African heritage. Ventura entered the music scene at a time when Dominicans were eager for a new beginning after experiencing the oppressive rule of dictator RAFAEL TRUJILLO.

Between 1930 and 1961 the Trujillo government chose merengue to symbolize national culture and identity. The music was used as a political tool, and its lyrics praised the dictator. Only upon Trujillo's death in 1961 was merengue able to regain the vitality it once had and develop through foreign musical influences forbidden by the Trujillo government. Johnny Ventura led others in revolutionizing merengue, changing the musical instruments merengue artists used and incorporating elements inspired by SALSA and rock music. These changes resulted in Ventura's first hit—"La Agarradera" (The Handle)—which gained both national and international notice.

In 1964 the young artist formed a band called Johnny Ventura y su Combo-Show and became a model for other *merengueros* (merengue performers). Breaking traditional form, the band's music was livelier and less inhibited than previous forms of merengue. Johnny Ventura y su Combo-Show—the top merengue band of the 1960s—traveled throughout the DoMINICAN REPUBLIC, taking merengue out of the ballrooms of the elite and performing it for the rest of society.

Inspired by Elvis Presley and JAMES BROWN, to whom he was later compared, Johnny Ventura choreographed dance moves for his band. The artist also created a flashy wardrobe and provocative stage presence for himself. Although Ventura's music and style were influenced by foreign cultures, his political views remained grounded in Dominican thought. During the civil war of 1965 he allied himself with the nationalist party, which once again used merengue as a political tool to promote patriotism and assert Dominican national identity against the invading United States forces.

As a social activist Ventura joined with friends and colleagues to create El Club de Los Monos (The Monkeys' Club), a group whose objective was to eliminate the concept of black racial inferiority in Dominican society. According to Ventura, the group wanted to "demonstrate the brilliance of men and women of our [black] race . . . strengthening the idea of a reencounter with [Afro-Dominican] cultural values." Appropriating *monos,* a derogatory name for blacks, the club gathered celebrities from various professions to demonstrate the contributions Afro-Dominicans made to their nation. Ventura's overall purpose in establishing the club reflected his personal goal

of promoting awareness among a people who often disavow their African heritage.

Johnny Ventura's involvement in politics was not limited to his musical lyrics and social activism. His energy and drive carried over into a political career as a congressman, deputy mayor, and finally mayor of SANTO DOMINGO, the nation's capital. This accomplishment in May of 1998 followed the release of Ventura's autobiography, entitled *Un poco de mí* (A Little of Me). His term as mayor ended in 2002. The following year he released the album *Sin Desperdicio.* Ventura's contributions to music and politics in the Dominican Republic continue to gain him international notice, yet little information is available on Johnny Ventura outside of his island nation.

See also Merengue: Music, Race, and Nation in the Dominican Republic.

Rob Garrison

Veracruz, Mexico

City and port located in the Mexican state of Veracruz, on the shores of the Gulf of Mexico.

Situated in an important oil-producing region, Veracruz is MEXICO's principal seaport, as well as a prominent commercial, agricultural, and industrial center. One of the city's main points of interest is the enormous castle of San Juan de Ulúa, built on the Gallega reef in the mouth of the harbor. The fort was built by the Spanish in 1528 to defend the port and continued to protect the last Spanish possession in Mexico until 1825; also noteworthy is the Plaza de la Constitución (Constitution Square), the most important square in the city since colonial times. An institute of technology and several other educational and cultural institutions surround the plaza.

The modern city of Veracruz was first settled by Hernán Cortés in 1519, although he soon abandoned the site; the city was definitively founded in 1600. It was captured by United States forces in 1847, during the MEXICAN WAR. The French occupied Veracruz in the 1870s, while U.S. troops returned for a brief period in 1914 under the command of Admiral Fletcher. The U.S. occupation of Veracruz was devised to block the unloading in Tampico of arms and material destined for the government of Victoriano Huerta; steps taken by the new president Venustiano Carranza resulted in Veracruz being liberated by the end of that same year.

In 1996 the facilities of the port of Veracruz were privatized. The ensuing competition has greatly improved the port's efficiency. Recent modernization programs have increased the port's handling capacity. Nearly half of Mexico's total grain imports now come through Veracruz. In 2003 the city's population was 549,500.

See also Colonial Latin America and the Caribbean.

Verger, Pierre Fatumbi

1902–1996

French ethnographer and photographer.

The holder of a Ph.D. degree in African Studies from the University of Paris, Pierre Verger traveled through various countries between 1932 and 1945 as a as a professional photographer and researcher for the *Musée Ethnographique du Trocadéro* (Ethnographic Museum of Trocadéro; today the *Musée de l'Homme*). He eventually settled in the city of SALVADOR in the Brazilian province of BAHIA in 1946, where he explored in depth the black culture of Africa and BRAZIL, writing several books on the subject. Verger's pioneering work traced strong links between the religion and culture of DAHOMEY (now BENIN) and Brazil. In 1952, while in Dahomey, he was initiated into the YORUBA RELIGION, given the name Fatumbi, and made a *babalawo*, or priest, of the IFA divination system.

Some of Verger's publications include *Fiestas y danzas en el Cuzco y en los Andes* (Celebrations and Dances in Cuzco and the Andes, 1945), *Retratos da Bahia* (Images of Bahia, 1980), and *50 Años de fotographía* (Fifty Years of Photography, 1982). His last publication, *Ewé, o uso das plantas na sociedade iorubá* (Ewé, The Use of Plants in Yoruban Society, 1995) compiled the results of many years of documenting the medicinal and religious use of plants in Yoruba society. Since 1989, the *Fundação Pierre Verger* (Pierre Verger Foundation) has conserved 62,000 photographic negatives, his vast library, and his personal archives, and it has promoted the diffusion of his anthropological and photographic contributions.

Verwoerd, Hendrik Frensch

1901–1966

Prime minister of South Africa and one of the original engineers and promoters of the policy of apartheid.

Born in Amsterdam, THE NETHERLANDS, Hendrik Verwoerd was a professor of sociology and editor of an Afrikaans nationalist newspaper in SOUTH AFRICA before he was appointed senator in 1948. Rising to cabinet posts, he was made minister of native affairs in 1950 and was responsible for engineering much of the Nationalist Party's social and political policy of APARTHEID, legalizing racial segregation and discrimination. Verwoerd was elected to the House of Assembly in 1958 and became prime minister shortly afterward. In 1959 he initiated the Bantustans policy for resettling South Africa's blacks into eight reservations. In 1961 he withdrew the country from the Commonwealth of Nations after criticism over South Africa's racial policies. Verwoerd was assassinated in CAPE TOWN in 1966.

See also Afrikaner.

Viana, Alfredo da Rocha, Jr.

See Pixinguinha.

Victoria Falls

Largest waterfall in the world, located in south Central Africa.

Called *Mosi-oa-Tunya* ("the smoke that thunders") by the Makololo people, Victoria Falls is located on the ZAMBEZI RIVER, on the border between ZIMBABWE and ZAMBIA. The river, more than 1.6 kilometer (one mile) wide at that point, plunges 110 meters (360 feet) down basalt gorges, producing a vast mist (or "smoke") that is visible from more than forty-five kilometers (about twenty-five miles) away. Scottish missionary and explorer DAVID LIVINGSTONE, who in 1855 became the first European to visit the falls, named them after Queen Victoria and believed that the falls were created by a cataclysmic event and not by erosion. In addition to the falls themselves, Livingstone chanced upon the Makololo, who dominated the area at that time. Since the 1905 completion of a railroad bridge spanning the gorge below the falls, Victoria Falls has become a popular tourist destination, providing both the Zimbabwean and Zambian governments with much-needed TOURISM revenue. The falls are now part of the 2,340-hectare (5,782-acre) Victoria Falls National Park, which offers canoeing, kayaking, whitewater rafting away from the falls, and wildlife safaris.

Robert Fay

Victoria, Lake

Also called Lake Nyanza, the world's second-largest freshwater lake and primary source of the Nile River.

Lake Victoria is located in East Africa, where it is bordered by UGANDA, KENYA, and TANZANIA. Occupying an area of 69,490 square kilometers (26,830 square miles), it lies 1,130 meters (3,720 feet) above sea level. The lake is 337 kilometers (209 miles) long and in places stretches about 240 kilometers (about 150 miles) wide. It is drained by the NILE RIVER and its chief affluent is the Kagera River.

An estimated thirty million people in the Lake Region of East Africa, one of the most densely populated parts of the continent, depend on Lake Victoria for their livelihood. Fishing and boatbuilding are the most significant economic activities. In addition, the Owen Falls Dam at Jinja, Uganda, where the Victoria Nile flows out of the lake, produces the hydroelectricity that fuels the surrounding industries and urban areas.

In recent years, however, the ecological deterioration of Lake Victoria has begun to undermine the economic as well as physical health of local communities. For years the lake has been polluted by raw sewage, industrial waste, and agricultural chemicals. The more recent and perhaps the most serious dangers, however, are the depletion of native fish stocks by over-fishing, the introduction of the predacious Nile perch (scientists believe that only four main species of the 300 species of fish formerly registered in the lake remain), and the proliferation of the water hyacinth. Although the Nile perch is profitable for commercial fisheries, which sell its meat, hide, and bladder, it feeds on cichlids, shallow-water fish that provide both a revenue and protein source for the traditional fishing communities. These communities cannot fish for Nile perch because they have neither the boats nor the equipment necessary to catch the large (up to six feet long and 200 pounds), deep-water species.

Another threat to Lake Victoria's ecosystem is the water hyacinth, a floating weed native to the Amazon region of South America. First brought to AFRICA and introduced into the Nile River in the late nineteenth century, the water hyacinth has spread throughout the continent, reaching Lake Victoria in 1989. The plants grow in thick mats that begin at the shore and spread toward the lake center, inhibiting navigation. The density of this vegetation slows down fishing trips and makes some parts of the lake completely inaccessible to ordinary boats. Local communities have lost access to the livelihood and sustenance once provided by fishing in these areas, resulting in widespread malnutrition. In some cases, the weed has prevented villagers from obtaining lake water for domestic use. In addition, water hyacinth provide a habitat for snails that cause bilharzia or schistosomiasis. It also blocks sunlight, reduces the amount of oxygen in the water, and alters its chemical composition, all changes with possibly detrimental consequences for the lake's remaining plants and animals.

In 1992, the governments of Kenya, Tanzania, and Uganda created the Lake Victoria Organization, aimed at restoring the ecosystem. One of its projects is to rebuild the cichlid population by breeding forty new species in aquariums, and educating local people about the benefits of fish farming. In addition, several scientific groups are experimenting with possible solutions to the water hyacinth problem, the most promising of which is biological pest control through the introduction of a hyacinth-eating species of beetle.

These recent efforts have not yet reversed the threat to Lake Victoria. Scientists predict that pollution may soon render the lake incapable of supporting life. Tanzania alone adds two million liters of industrial waste and untreated sewage to the lake each day. Fishermen leave 100 tons of human waste in the lake on a daily basis.

Despite the lake's dire state, it is still a contested resource. In December 2003 Kenya declared it will no longer honor a 1929 treaty with Egypt, and has demanded greater use of Lake Victoria and Nile River waters.

See also Tilapia.

Bibliography

Ayot, H. Okello. *Historical Texts of the Lake Region of East Africa.* Kenya Literature Bureau, 1977.

Robert Fay

Victoria, Seychelles

Capital of the Indian Ocean island nation of Seychelles.

Victoria, the capital of SEYCHELLES, is located on the northeastern edge of its largest island, Mahé. Approximately one-quarter of the country's total population of 82,800 live in Victoria. The city's natural protective harbor induced many early explorers, including French explorer Lazare Picault in 1744, to anchor there. It was near this harbor in 1756 that Captain Corneille Nicolas Morphy placed a stone proclaiming the island a possession of the French crown. The site, originally named *L'Establissement du Roi,* seemed the logical place to begin settlement when the French formally colonized the island in 1772. FRANCE controlled Seychelles only until 1810, when, under the Treaty of Paris, the British formally took possession.

In 1841 the town's name was changed to Victoria, in honor of Britain's Queen Victoria. To celebrate the country's transition to a Crown Colony, a replica of the Vauxhall Bridge clock tower was erected in the capital in 1903. During the twentieth century, Victoria has become the island's commercial as well as political capital. The international airport—built on the outskirts of the city in 1971 by the British, in return for possession of several small atolls as part of the British Indian Ocean Territory—enabled the country to build a tourist industry that now dominates the economy. Ferries to neighboring islands leave from Victoria's harbor, as do boats carrying Seychelles's major export crops, including coconut copra and cinnamon bark. Victoria's physical size and population have grown in recent decades, as landslides and land reclamation programs have extended the land area of the city into what was once part of the port. Population 23,200 (2004 estimate).

Ari Nave

Vieira, João Bernardo

1939–

President of Guinea-Bissau from 1980 to 1999.

João Bernardo Vieira was born in BISSAU and trained first as an electrician and later as a military commander. He joined the socialist, revolutionary African Party for the Independence of GUINEA and CAPE VERDE (PAIGC) in 1960, studying under founder Amílcar Cabral at the PAIGC school in CONAKRY, GUINEA. After serving as a regional military commander and political commissioner (1961–1964) and receiving military training in China, he was given military command of the southern front of the war of independence in 1964 and later of the entire war theater in 1970, while also serving as a ranking member of the council of war (1965–1967; 1971–1973). A member of the PAIGC political bureau, the party's policy-making body, since 1964, Vieira was named deputy secretary-general of the party in 1973. Following independence in 1974, he was elected president of the National People's Assembly, remaining in his position as commander of the armed forces and serving as the minister for the armed forces as well. He was appointed prime minister by President Luís de Almeida Cabral, a Cape Verdean, in August 1978.

By the late 1970s the PAIGC's goal of uniting Guinea-Bissau and Cape Verde became unlikely. Capitalizing on growing resentment among mainland Guineans against the predominance of Cape Verdean *mestiços* (of indigenous and European descent) within the PAIGC leadership, Vieira overthrew Cabral in November 1980. Dissolving the National Assembly, Vieira installed the National Revolutionary Council, staffed entirely by mainland Guinean military officers. Having initially criticized the former regime for its betrayal of the socialist revolution, Vieira, attempting to attract foreign investment and International Monetary Fund (IMF) and World Bank support, soon began encouraging private enterprise and limiting government control of trade. After surviving a series of coup attempts, and consolidating his power through constitutional revisions, Vieira reinstated the National Assembly and began, in 1990, the transition toward a multiparty state. In July 1994 multiparty elections, PAIGC retained a majority in the National People's Assembly and Vieira was narrowly reelected. An army rebellion erupted in 1998 after Vieira dismissed the army chief of staff, General Ansumane Mane. In 1999 Mane's rebel forces overthrew the president. Vieira has since remained in exile in Portugal.

See also African Socialism; Political Movements in Africa.

Vietnam War

War that divided Americans and had profound social and political consequences for African Americans.

The United States government had opposed the Communist insurgency in Vietnam since the early 1950s, but few Americans, black or white, knew of the conflict prior to the commitment of U.S. ground troops in 1965. On August 7, 1964, Congress passed the Tonkin Gulf Resolution, granting President Johnson broad discretion in Southeast Asia. By December 1965 there were nearly 200,000 American troops in Vietnam.

For the first time in its history, America entered a war with racially integrated armed forces. Black soldiers quickly proved their bravery: two of the war's earliest Congressional Medal of Honor recipients, Private Milton Olive and medic Lawrence Joel, were African Americans. Yet compared to the sweeping changes brought about by the Civil Rights Movement, the Vietnam War seemed distant and insignificant. A black reporter for the *New York Times* noted that for the first time in American history, "national Negro figures are not urging black youths to take up arms [in order to] . . . improve the lot of the black man in the United States."

Despite the military's overall success with racial integration, there were still striking imbalances in the Vietnam era. During 1965–1967, the black casualty rate of 20 percent was roughly twice that of whites. In 1969–1970 the army reduced the imbalance by assigning more blacks to support roles, but African Americans realized that for years their young men had borne the brunt of the dying. However, discrimination began long before combat, with predominantly white local draft boards that preferred to conscript young black men. During 1967, 64 percent of eligible blacks were drafted, compared with only 31 percent of whites. Blacks—who were less likely to meet the higher educational requirements of the navy and air force—overwhelmingly entered the army. They were also underrepresented in the officer corps. In 1968 blacks made up nearly 10 percent of total American military personnel, but only 2 percent of all officers.

The Vietnam War affected not only black soldiers in battle but also African Americans at home. For example, as military expenditures escalated, Congress forced Johnson to curtail his domestic War on Poverty. The war also helped split the civil rights coalition. White liberals once active in civil rights became preoccupied with the war, and white student activists, part of the civil rights struggle since the 1961 Freedom Rides, were overwhelmingly drawn to antiwar protests. Moderate black leaders in the Civil Rights Movement such as Martin Luther King, Jr., Bayard Rustin, and Whitney Young were at first reluctant to speak out against the war. The earliest protests came from radicals such as Malcolm X, who in 1964 linked the war to racial discrimination at home. In January 1966 the leadership of the Student Nonviolent Coordinating Committee (SNCC) condemned the draft. A year later, heavyweight boxing champion Muhammad Ali refused to be drafted. Ali insisted that he would not "murder and kill and burn other people simply to help continue the domination of the white slave masters over the dark people of the world." That same year, King finally denounced the war. Speaking on April 4, 1967, at New York City's Riverside Church, he lamented that "the Great Society has been shot down on the battlefields of Vietnam." The war revolutionized King's thinking, helping him place the Civil Rights Movement in a world context.

Over time, black opinion turned steadily against the war. A 1971 Gallup poll found a higher level of dissatisfaction with the war among blacks (83 percent) than among whites (67 percent). Yet Vietnam remained a place of much interracial cooperation. Combat troops realized that they had to count on one another regardless of race. In 1968, however, the morale of American troops collapsed due to the Communist Tet Offensive, and racial hostilities sharpened considerably following King's assassination.

The war so divided the nation that Johnson declined to run for re-election in 1968. His successor, Richard Nixon, implemented a program of "Vietnamization," in which South Vietnamese troops were expected to take over the brunt of the fighting. After peaking at 540,000 during 1969, U.S. troop levels began to decline, and the last units came home in the spring of 1973. The war ended two years later with the fall of South Vietnam.

See also Military, Blacks in the American.

James Sellman

Vieyra, Paulin

1925–1987

Senegalese filmmaker, film critic, and film historian, who was the first African graduate of l'Institut des Hautes Études Cinématographiques and the director of the first film by a black African.

One of the founding figures in African filmmaking, Paulin Vieyra was responsible for dismantling barriers blocking the birth of film in Africa. Not only famous for these achievements, Vieyra was also influential as a film critic and film historian and did much to promote African cinema abroad.

Vieyra was born in Porto Novo, BENIN, where he spent his early childhood. His father, a high-ranking civil servant in the French colonial administration, sent him to school in FRANCE at the age of ten. An excellent student, Vieyra was admitted to the University of Paris. When a bout of tuberculosis sent him into the hospital, Vieyra met film school students there who encouraged him to enroll in film school. He was admitted to l'Institut des Hautes Études Cinématographiques in Paris and in 1955 became the first African to graduate from the school.

After graduation, Vieyra organized the film group LE GROUPE AFRICAIN DU CINÉMA and attempted to film a movie in SENEGAL. Forbidden by the French government to film in that part of Africa, the group filmed another movie in Paris called *Afrique sur scène*. Released in 1955, this was the first film produced by an African director.

After *Afrique sur scène*, Vieyra made only a handful of fictional movies. He instead served in a variety of ministerial positions, including head of the Senegalese Film Bureau. While working in these positions, he produced newsreels as well as several historical documentaries. Subjects of these documentaries include Africans in colonial Europe, the decolonization of Francophone Africa, and the state trips of Senegal president LÉOPOLD SÉDAR SENGHOR to Europe and the Americas. The documentaries are considered remarkable for their sophistication and artistry.

Vieyra's historical writing deserves at least as much attention as his films. He made important contributions to the study of African film through his biographies of African film directors and his documentation of various film organization meetings. He spoke on African film during extensive lecture tours of AFRICA, EUROPE, the United States, and the former Soviet Union, and in classes he taught at the University of Dakar. All these activities have helped build an international market for African films. Many film critics consider Vieyra's educational work just as valuable as his earlier accomplishments as a filmmaker.

See also Cinema, African.

Elizabeth Heath

Villa, Ignacio

See Bola de Nieve.

Villa-Lobos, Heitor

1887–1959

Brazilian composer of the twentieth century.

Heitor Villa-Lobos was born March 5, 1887, in RIO DE JANEIRO and was primarily self-trained. In 1912 he accompanied a scientific expedition to the interior of BRAZIL to study the music of Native American tribes, later an important influence on his own music. Villa-Lobos also came in contact with contemporary French music while studying in Paris from 1922 to 1930 on a fellowship from the Brazilian government. After 1931 he was director of musical education in the public schools of Rio de Janeiro. In this position he revolutionized public musical education throughout Brazil. He also supervised the systematic accumulation of a large collection of African and indigenous Brazilian folk and popular music, which served to focus nationwide attention on this rich source of musical material. He conducted orchestras in Brazil, the United States, and EUROPE.

A prolific composer, Villa-Lobos wrote about 2,000 works, employing almost every existing form of musical composition. In his works he did not generally use actual Brazilian folk tunes but rather wrote original melodies in a Brazilian folk style, developing them in his own manner. From a popular Brazilian dance, he developed the *chôros* ("serenade"), expanding its form from the guitar solo of his first *chôros* to the large orchestral and choral ensembles of his later ones. Also famous are his *Bachianas brasileiras* (1930–1945), nine suites, varied in their instrumentation, in which the musical idiom of Johann Sebastian Bach is ingeniously blended with the powerful rhythms and melodic styles of the African-derived folk music of northeastern Brazil. Villa-Lobos's other works include operas, ballets, symphonies, concertos, chamber music, piano pieces, and songs. He died in Rio de Janeiro on November 17, 1959.

See also Music, Classical, in Latin America and the Caribbean.

Vincent, Sténio J.

1874–1959

President of Haiti.

Sténio Vincent was a member of Haiti's mulatto (of African and European descent) elite, who came to the presidency during the United States occupation of the country from 1915 to 1934. In 1934 he persuaded President Franklin D. Roosevelt to withdraw U.S. troops from the island. In 1935 Vincent's tenure in office was extended by five years. Vincent was widely regarded as being anti-black, and he created a presidential guard to counterbalance the army left behind by the United States, which was dominated by black officers.

See also Haiti.

Viper

Common name for snakes in a family of venomous snakes.

Vipers are distributed throughout most temperate and tropical regions of the world, except Australia. They occur from lowlands to elevations of more than 4,500 meters (14,800 feet), from deserts to rain forests, and even in arctic regions. Vipers are characterized by a pair of long, hollow fangs, usually with reserve fangs beside them, in the front of the upper jaw. The fangs fold back against the palate when not in use and quickly swing forward to strike, injecting deadly venom that kills prey and also serves as a defense. The viper generally has a broad, triangular head, and the eyes have vertical pupils. Most vipers give birth to living young from eggs hatched inside the mother's body. Vipers are usually divided into two groups: the true vipers—including certain adders and asps, the horned and Gaboon vipers of Africa, and the Indian viper—and the pit vipers, which have a distinctive heat-sensitive pit between the eye and nostril, and which include the rattlesnakes, copperhead, and cottonmouth.

Scientific classification: Vipers make up the family Viperidae. The true vipers are classified in the subfamily Viperinae; the horned viper is classified as *Bitis nasicornis,* the Gaboon viper as *Bitis gabonica,* and the Indian viper as *Echis carinatus.* The pit vipers are classified in the family Crotalidae, which contains the rattlesnakes, placed in the genera *Crotalus* and *Sistrurus:* the copperhead, *Agkistrodon contortrix:* and the cottonmouth, *Agkistrodon piscivorus.*

See also Animals in Africa.

Virgen de la Caridad

Religious icon in Cuba since the early 1600s and the patron saint of the island since 1916; also known as La Virgen Mulata and Our Lady of Charity.

The Virgen de la Caridad is the focus of near-universal devotion and petition by practitioners of Catholicism and Afro-Cuban faiths in Cuba. Many devotees display her image in small household shrines. Her national shrine in the eastern town of Cobre is the destination of many pilgrimages, which become especially frequent in early September on the annual feast day held in her honor. The shrine dates from the early 1600s, when the first vision of the Virgen de la Caridad was reported. During the colonial period in the Americas, people often erected shrines to commemorate the finding of relics or images of Catholic saints, especially localized versions of the Virgin Mary. This practice, introduced in the early 1500s by the earliest colonists and missionaries in the Americas, was in the tradition of early Christian practices in Europe.

According to legend, the first apparition of the Virgen de la Caridad occurred in 1606 in the Bay of Nipe, on Cuba's southeastern coast. Three men had come there to collect salt, but their small boat was foundering in a storm. The men—two brothers of indigenous descent, Juan and Rodrigo de Hoyos, and a young black slave, Juan Moreno—saw her wooden image floating in the water, and they reported that the figure was a mulatta (woman of mixed African and European descent) dressed in yellow. She carried a cross in her right hand and the baby Jesus in her left, and a tablet affixed to her identified her as the Virgen de la Caridad.

Devotion to the Virgen de la Caridad first developed among slaves of Kongo origin (from west central Africa). The slaves worked in the mountainous copper mines near the town of Cobre, in the eastern province of Santiago de Cuba. Catholic officials, who sought to Christianize the slaves of Cuba, encouraged the slaves' devotion to her, as she was seen as a local manifestation of the Virgin Mary. Many miracles were attributed to the Virgen de la Caridad's intercession, and her popular cult began to spread to other parts of the island. The indigenous Taíno people identified her with their supreme goddess of fertility, Abatey. Blacks in western Cuba who practiced the Yoruba-derived religion of Santería began identifying her with their orisha (deity) Oshún, a goddess associated with rivers and ideals of feminine beauty. In the eastern province of Oriente, blacks of largely Kongo heritage who practiced Regla de Palo, another African-derived religion, sometimes identified her with Mama Chola, the mother of water. This syncretism of religions, which was less pronounced in Regla de Palo than in Santería, was part of a widespread phenomenon that occurred throughout the colonies during the early years of slavery. Catholicism was the predominant European religion in most of the slave-holding colonies, and slaves were expected to convert to the religions of their masters. For the slaves, it was only natural to view the Catholic saints as manifestations of their orishas and worship them in this guise.

In 1916 a group of distinguished black Cuban veterans of the Spanish-American War (1895–1898) petitioned Pope Benedict XV to designate the Virgen de la Caridad as Cuba's patron saint. The pope granted the request, perhaps unaware of her non-Catholic associations. After the triumph of the Marxist revolution in Cuba in 1959, Cubans who fled to the United States established a pilgrimage church to the Virgen de la Caridad in Miami, Florida. Although the iconography of the Virgen always portrays her as a mulatta, depictions of her original apparition scene often show her with a lighter skin color and replace the indigenous brothers with whites. Some scholars interpret the iconography and legends of the Virgen de la Caridad as an allegory of race in Cuba: The different races, working together in a precarious boat, find their saving grace in the racially mixed Virgen.

See also Catholic Church in Latin America and the Caribbean; Religions, African, in Latin America and the Caribbean.

Virgin Islands

Group of over one hundred Caribbean islands located between the Caribbean Sea and the Atlantic Ocean, east of Puerto Rico.

When Christopher Columbus first sighted this archipelago of islands in November 1493, he named them *Las Once Mil Virgenes* (The Eleven Thousand Virgins) both to commemorate the legend of Saint Ursula and her 11,000 martyred virgins, and to exaggerate the magnitude of his find to his patron, Queen Isabella of Spain. In reality, the total number of Virgin Islands is much closer to 110 than 11,000. Many of them are small and uninhabited, and to outsiders the Virgin Islands are often synonymous with the five large islands that have become immensely popular tourist destinations: Saint Croix, Saint John, and Saint Thomas on the United States side, and Tortola and Virgin Gorda on the British. The fact that the islands are split into United States and British territories is the end result of the region's complex history of slavery, colonization, and resistance—the story that lies behind its modern resorts and restaurants.

Early History and Colonial Rule

The first inhabitants of the Virgin Islands were probably the Ciboney Amerindians, who appear to have migrated from South America to what is now Saint Thomas in approximately 300 B.C.E. Within 500 years they were replaced by the Arawaks, who were mainly farmers, and who eventually spread out to Tortola and several other Virgin Islands. Beginning at the end of the fourteenth century, the Arawaks were overtaken by the more aggressive Caribs, who named Saint Croix "Ay Ay" and established themselves on many other islands as well. But it was Columbus's intrusion that would have the most lasting effects.

Columbus and his crew were the first Europeans to "discover" the Caribbean Islands, and in their journeys they nominally claimed each island they saw for the Spanish flag. Because the Virgin Islands were smaller than many of the other Caribbean islands and were not as rich in minerals and other natural resources, the Spanish chose not to settle them, and the islands were largely ignored during the first century of Caribbean colonization. By the 1600s, however, the European craze for expansion in the region hit them in earnest.

The struggle for domination inevitably resulted in some conflicts. Saint Croix was shared by the English and Dutch, then held solely by the English, overtaken by the Spanish, then the French, then given to the Knights of Malta, and returned to the French before it was sold to the Danish West India and Guinea Company in 1733. Saint Thomas was occupied by the Danish,

attacked by the Dutch, and captured and then abandoned by the English before being reclaimed by Denmark in 1671. Tortola was settled by Dutch buccaneers before being attacked and captured by the English in 1665. It was not until the beginning of the eighteenth century that the Virgin Islands had reached a more or less stable political configuration, with the islands grouped into Danish and English holdings. By then it was clear just what was at stake for each of these colonial powers: the Virgin Islands were developing into flourishing slave economies.

Once it was discovered that the islands' soil would support both cotton and SUGAR, settlers were eager to cultivate these crops. The white population at the time was an unpredictable assortment that included Quaker religious dissenters, then-infamous buccaneers, and ex-convicts who were sent to the WEST INDIES as part of their jail sentences. It was clear that these white settlers would not provide all of the labor the new plantations would require. In 1673 the first consignment of 103 African slaves, probably taken from homes in GUINEA, landed in Saint Thomas. By 1715 the island had 160 plantations and 3,042 slaves.

Similarly drastic gains were made across the region by the mid-1700s, and in response to the new demand, Charlotte Amalie in Saint Thomas became one of the world's largest slave markets in the eighteenth century. In both sets of islands, working conditions were arduous, the clothing and food given in compensation was minimal, and punishments were strict. As one historian said, "It is difficult to characterize any slave system as more repressive than that of the Virgin Islands."

A drought in 1725–1726 resulted in a scarcity of food, and many planters chose simply to let their slaves starve to death. In all cases, slaves were left with virtually no avenues of formal redress. In the British islands, a slave who resisted a white owner could have his nose split, or a limb cut off, and "as many number of stripes" as the master chose to inflict. In the Danish islands a slave who struck a white person or even threatened to strike one "should be pinched and hung"—or, if the person chose to pardon him, "should lose his right hand." Death by various means of torture was permitted for a wide range of crimes, and especially for being suspected of any plans to run away. But it was little surprise that many slaves still took the opportunity to escape when they could, and also little surprise that slaves in the Virgin Islands led two of the most dramatic revolts in the Caribbean.

The first was the Saint John revolt in 1733. In the months leading up to the protest, a drought, two hurricanes, and an insect plague had made the slaves' already desperate situation intolerable. The passage of a new brutally restrictive slave code in September 1733 proved to be the last straw. The leaders of the revolt were allegedly African-born slaves who had been royalty in their West African homelands, and after they captured Saint John's only fort, they gave the signal for an island-wide uprising. At that time, Saint John had 1,087 slaves to 208 whites, and the slaves were able to control the island for six months.

It was not until August 1734 that the last rebels finally surrendered; although they had been promised a free pardon, they were instead publicly executed by torture. Many other rebels had committed suicide rather than be recaptured. While their daring effort ultimately ended in tragedy, it provided a powerful signal of their uncompromising commitment to freedom. In 1790 British slaves led an uprising on Tortola after a rumor spread that England had granted them their freedom and their masters were holding it back. However, the rumors had some basis in reality, because by

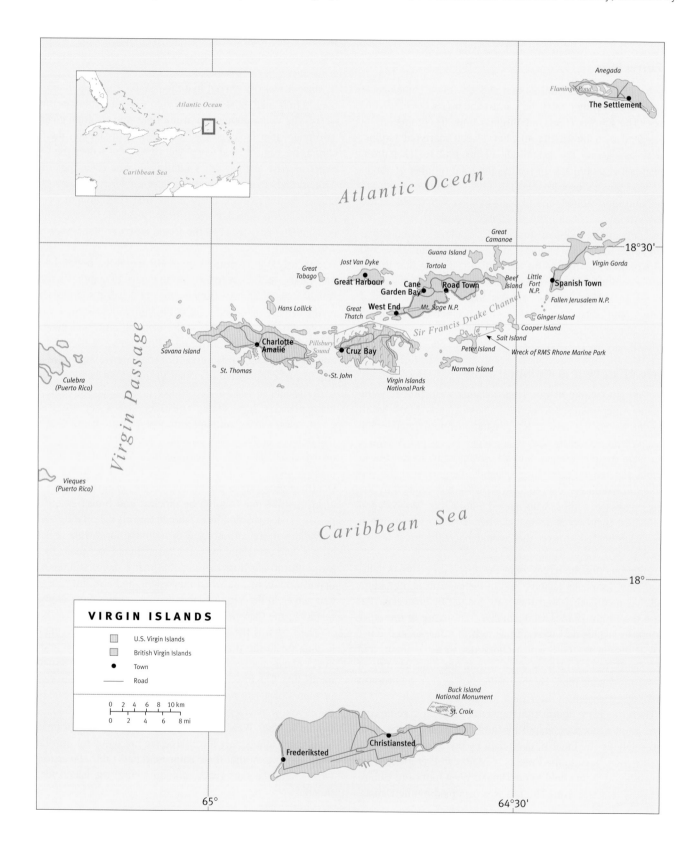

Virgin Islands (At a Glance)

OFFICIAL NAME: United States Virgin Islands/British Virgin Islands

FORMER NAME: Danish West Indies

AREA: 352 sq km (171 sq mi)/153 sq km (59 sq mi)

LOCATION: Group of islands east of Puerto Rico, between the Caribbean Sea and the Atlantic Ocean; the main inhabited islands are Saint Croix, Saint Thomas, and Saint John (U.S. territories), and Tortola, Anegaga, Virgin Gorda, and Jost Van Dyke (all British possessions)

CAPITAL: Charlotte Amalie (population 12,500)/Road Town (population 9,400; 2004 estimates)

POPULATION: 124,778/21,730 (2003 estimates)

POPULATION DENSITY: 358 persons per sq km (931.2 per sq mi)

POPULATION BELOW AGE 15: 26 percent (male 16,685; female 15,794)/21.0 percent (male 2,401; female 2,358; 2003 estimates)

POPULATION GROWTH RATE: 1.02 percent/2.1 percent (2003 estimates)

TOTAL FERTILITY RATE: 2.22 children born per woman/1.72 children born per woman (2003 estimates)

LIFE EXPECTANCY AT BIRTH: Total population: 78.59 years (male 74.73 years; female 82.68 years)/76.06 years (male 75.07; female 77.1 years; 2003 estimates)

INFANT MORTALITY RATE: 9 deaths per 1,000 live births/18.8 per 1,000 live births (2003 estimates)

EDUCATION: Education is free and compulsory in the U.S. Virgin Islands, although many students attend private schools. Students attend branches of the University of the Virgin Islands on St. Croix and St. Thomas. Nearly 98 percent of British Virgin Islanders are literate.

LANGUAGES: English is the official language of both the U.S. and British Virgin Islands; Spanish and Creole are also spoken in the U.S. Virgin Islands.

ETHNIC GROUPS: 78 percent black, 10 percent white, and 12 percent other ethnicities/83 percent black, 17 percent white, Indian, Asian, and mixed.

RELIGIONS: The population of the U.S. Virgin Islands is 42 percent Baptist, 34 percent Roman Catholic, 17 percent Episcopalian, and 7 percent other religions. The population of the British Virgin Islands is 86 percent Protestant, 10 percent Roman Catholic, 2 percent other, 2 percent none.

CLIMATE: Tropical, cool, and pleasant, with low humidity and an average temperature of 78° F (26° C). February to July is the dry season, and September to December is the rainy season, with rare hurricanes occurring between August and November. Water is scarce, and most buildings have individual water catchments.

LAND, PLANTS, AND ANIMALS: Three of the fifty or so U.S. Virgin Islands are the most significant: St. Croix, St. Thomas, and St. John. St. Croix is about forty miles south of the other islands and is the largest. The capital, Charlotte Amalie, is on St. Thomas. St. John is the smallest of the three main islands, with Virgin Islands National Park covering about three-quarters of its area. The islands offer a variety of landscapes, from beaches and coral reefs to jungle regions and mountainous areas. Some of the smaller islands are completely uninhabited. Tropical vegetation includes royal poinciana trees, mangoes, coconut palms, breadfruit, and wild orchids. The lowlands support cactus, grass, and sugarcane. There are many varieties of birds. Offshore and coastal marine life includes kingfish, sailfish, marlin, and tarpon.

NATURAL RESOURCES: Sun, sand, sea, and surf

CURRENCY: United States dollar (USD) for both U.S. and British Virgin Islands

GROSS DOMESTIC PRODUCT (GDP): $2.4 billion (2001 estimate)

GDP PER CAPITA: $19,000 (2001 estimate)

GDP REAL GROWTH RATE: 2 percent (2001 estimate)

PRIMARY ECONOMIC ACTIVITIES: Services, light industry, agriculture, tourism

PRIMARY CROPS: Fruit, vegetables, sorghum, and livestock

INDUSTRIES: Tourism, petroleum refining, watch assembly, rum distilling, construction, pharmaceuticals, textiles, and electronics

PRIMARY EXPORTS: Refined petroleum products

PRIMARY IMPORTS: Crude oil, foodstuffs, consumer goods, and building materials

PRIMARY TRADE PARTNERS: United States and Puerto Rico

GOVERNMENT: The U.S. Virgin Islands is a territory of the United States. The chief of state is President George W. Bush (since January 2001). The head of government is Governor Dr. Charles Wesley Turnbull (since January 1999; popularly elected for a four-year term). The legislative branch is the fifteen-member unicameral Senate (members elected by popular vote to two-year terms). The judicial branch includes the U.S. District Court of the Virgin Islands (under Third Circuit jurisdiction) and the Territorial Court (judges appointed to ten-year terms by the governor).

Since 1952 Queen Elizabeth II has been the head of state for the British Virgin Islands, which is a hereditary monarchy, represented by Governor Tom Macan (since 2002). The governor is appointed by the monarch. Following legislative elections, the leader of the majority party or the leader of the majority coalition is appointed by the governor to serve as chief minister. Orlando Smith has been the chief minister since June 2003. The unicameral Legislative Council consists of the thirteen members elected by direct popular vote to serve four-year terms. The Eastern Caribbean Supreme Court consists of the High Court of Justice and Court of Appeal; Magistrate's Court; Juvenile Court; Court of Summary Jurisdiction.

Shelle Sumners

the end of the eighteenth century Britain was already calling for abolition.

Abolition and Its Aftermath

Several planters on the British islands had already begun manumitting groups of slaves, leading to a growing class of free blacks, and the numbers grew even larger after GREAT BRITAIN abolished the slave trade in 1807. From that time on, illegal cargoes of slaves found on British ships were seized and "liberated"; but instead of being returned to their African homes, they were brought to the West Indies and set free there. Not surprisingly, as the number of free blacks in the islands increased, blacks who remained enslaved grew even more convinced of their own right to be free. British Virgin Islands slave insurrections flared up in 1823, 1827, 1830, and 1831. Full emancipation of all English slaves was finally established on August 1, 1834.

The APPRENTICESHIP period that followed emancipation mandated that all slaves remain with their former owners for another four years, and so essentially extended slavery until 1838. But black British Virgin Islanders were still relieved, above all, to be finally free. In the Danish West Indies, although the slave trade had been abolished in 1792, slavery itself remained legal until 1848. That year, on July 3, Moses Gottlieb, also known as Buddhoe, led fellow Saint Croix slaves in another dramatic uprising—arguably among the most successful in history.

In this action, slaves sacked the houses of the police assistant, the town bailiff, and a wealthy merchant and then took over the fort, threatening to burn the entire town if they were not emancipated within the hour. Most of the whites had already taken refuge on ships docked in the harbor. Sensing just how serious the threat was, within the hour the governor general read the Proclamation of Emancipation, which declared that "all unfree in the Danish West India Islands are from today free." So these Saint Croix slaves became one of the few groups of enslaved people to succeed in liberating themselves.

Across the Caribbean, however, true economic and social freedom came slowly for black Virgin Islanders. In the Danish West Indies the 1849 Labor Act made working conditions for newly emancipated blacks nearly as restrictive as they had been under slavery. In the British West Indies the 1867 reversion to an appointed governing council—and the abolition of free elections—ensured that the colonies would be governed by their white minorities. In both sets of colonies, prevailing social traditions continued to enforce racism and racial separation, on the theory that free blacks were still different from and inferior to free whites. In the Virgin Islands and across the Caribbean, the abolition of slavery also led to a decline in economic productivity—and in a tight economy, it was the black workers who suffered most.

It was this economic decline that first led Denmark to contemplate selling its colonies to the United States in 1866. After talks that extended over the next fifty years, the transfer became a reality on March 31, 1917. The twentieth century had already brought some small improvements to the Virgin Islands, as both the Danish and British governments had begun establishing schools and banks, and in 1915 events in Saint Croix marked the beginning of changes that eventually spread throughout the Caribbean. That year, D. Hamilton Jackson formed the first labor union in the West Indies. Within decades, the labor movement became the basis not only for a dramatic improvement in working conditions across the region but also for the push for increased self-government. In islands across the Caribbean, the black workers who joined labor unions eventually became the black politicians and voters who won independence from their colonial powers.

Virgin Islanders were no different in their desire for greater political authority, and over time legislative changes ensured that the majorities would indeed rule in the islands. Full electoral government came to the British islands in 1967, and the U.S. islands in 1970. But both groups of islands chose not to push for full independence, undoubtedly because of the strong economic benefits that the islands received from the United States and Britain. This was especially true in the case of the U.S. islands, and in 1958 the British islands had even declined to join the West Indies Federation established by the rest of the British Caribbean because of their own wish to keep their strong economic ties to the U.S. islands. In 2003 Great Britain announced that it would be willing to grant independence to all of its Caribbean colonies, but the Virgin Islands again expressed no interest in becoming an independent nation.

Virgin Islands Today

The economies of each of the Virgin Islands also changed dramatically with the advent of the tourist industry. Today, the Virgin Islands have some of the highest standards of living in the Caribbean, and the U.S. islands in particular have become a haven for other West Indian immigrants. This prosperity comes largely from the islands' continuing status as dependent territories. But much of it is also directly linked to their popularity as tourist destinations, particularly among American and British tourists. For the islands' black majorities, this has meant jobs in every sector of the tourist industry, from service to construction.

Virgin Islanders today enjoy citizenship status in their respective countries but retain the Afro-Caribbean cultural heritage of their island homes. A 1995 hurricane caused significant damage in the islands, but by 1998 the tourist industry had already begun its comeback. The Virgin Islands entered the twenty-first century as one the Caribbean's most successful regions, and this relative prosperity was a welcome change and reward for Virgin Islanders.

See also Colonial Latin America and the Caribbean; Colonial Rule; Punishment of Slaves in Colonial Latin America and the Caribbean; Slave Rebellions in Latin America and the Caribbean; Slavery in Latin America and the Caribbean; Transatlantic Slave Trade.

Lisa Clayton Robinson

Vodery, Will (Henry Bennett)

1884–1951

African American composer and arranger.

Will Vodery was a native of PHILADELPHIA, PENNSYLVANIA. His father, Will Vodery, was an instructor of Greek at Pennsylvania's LINCOLN UNIVERSITY. Young Will, who is said to have inherited his talent from his mother, played piano for his Sunday school when he was nine years old. Four years later, he was his church's organist, in the interim having composed his first song, "My Country, I Love Thee" (1903). Upon graduation from Philadelphia's Central High School in 1902, Vodery entered the Hugh A. Clark University in Pennsylvania to study music. There, working with the German-trained Louis Koemmennich, he began the serious study of the rudiments of his profession. Two years later he was in NEW YORK CITY embarking on a professional career. His first job was making arrangements for the M. Whitmark & Sons musical *A Trip to Africa* (1904). Vodery had been introduced to Whitmark by comedian BERT WILLIAMS, who had become aware of Vodery's ability during his frequent stays at the Philadelphia boarding house run by the Vodery family.

In 1905, Vodery worked as custodian of the Theodore Thomas Chicago Symphony Orchestra. When not discharging his duties, he studied symphony under concert manager Frederick Stock. Returning to New York in 1907, he wrote the title song for *The Oyster Man* (1907), starring ERNEST HOGAN. He also arranged the music for *Bandana Land* (1908), by Williams and his partner GEORGE WALKER and traveled abroad as music director with the production. More songwriting, and the management of a stock company in WASHINGTON, D.C., brought Vodery into partnership with J. Lubrie Hill, another excellent black showman of the Williams and Walker company.

The partners worked together on Hill's hit show *My Friend from Dixie* (1911), which was seen in New York by celebrated impresario Florenz Ziegfeld. Impressed, Ziegfeld bought the finale and incorporated it into his *Follies*. Vodery also wrote the music for *Dr. Beans from Boston* (1910), starring comedian S. H. DUDLEY, a show that featured one of the most popular hit songs of the day, "At the Ball, That's All" (1912). Further musical work with the vaudeville show featuring Ada Overton and Walker again drew Ziegfeld's attention to Vodery. This time Ziegfeld hired composer-arranger Vodery to do a complete show in 1915 in which Williams was featured. One of Vodery's songs written especially for Williams, "Darktown Poker Club" (1914), was popularized by singer-comedian Phil Harris.

When the United States entered WORLD WAR I in 1917, Vodery received a commission of lieutenant and bandmaster of the 807th Infantry Band. Perhaps the only black in the French school for bandmasters at Fort Beteu, France, he graduated after the war with highest honors and returned to New York. Back with Ziegfeld and in the milieu of Broadway, Vodery prepared the music for such popular postwar shows as *Show Boat* (1927). It was in New York that Vodery introduced young George Gershwin to Clifford Goldmark, who became Gershwin's teacher. Vodery was the first to bring a black band to a Broadway nightclub. In 1921 he not only introduced the band to the Plantation Club but also brought in a black chorus line.

Vodery's subsequent work with *Show Boat* and *Shuffle Along* (1921) brought him in close touch during the 1920s with performers such as FLORENCE MILLS, JOSEPHINE BAKER, EUBIE BLAKE, NOBLE SISSLE, Flournoy Miller, AUBREY LYLES, and ETHEL WATERS. Later editions of *Kid Boots* (1923) starring Eddie Cantor and *Show Boat* starring PAUL ROBESON used Vodery's music. Hollywood beckoned to Vodery in 1929. There he supervised the music for Fox Films and provided direction for several studio orchestras.

An often-overlooked Vodery contribution to the development of JAZZ was his work with bandmaster and orchestra leader James Reese Europe. Together the two pioneered in consolidating the sweet music of the reed instruments with the hot music of the brasses. Unhappily, Vodery, in being loosely labeled an arranger, along with other similarly trained and motivated black musicians of the 1920s, was denied the rank of the creative composer that he actually was. Vodery could not have worked for twenty-three years for the Ziegfeld Productions, as well as productions of the British producer Charles Cochran, had he not possessed exceptional skills.

A victim for many years of diabetes and kidney trouble, Vodery died in New York at age sixty-seven and was buried with full military honors. For an account of Vodery's early life, see Bart Kennett's *Colored Actors' Union Theatrical Guide* (1920), John Jacob Niles's *Singing Soldiers* (1926), and James Weldon Johnson's *Black Manhattan* (1930). Later biographical details are in Loften Mitchell's *Black Drama: The Story of the American Negro in the Theater* (1967) and Eileen Southern's work *The Music of Black Americans, A History* (1971).

From *Dictionary of American Negro Biography* by Rayford W. Logan and Michael R. Winston, editors. Copyright © 1982 by Rayford W. Logan and Michael R. Winston. Reprinted by permission of W. W. Norton & Company, Inc.

See also Music, African American; Musical Theater in the United States.

Elton C. Fax

Vodou

Religion originally developed and practiced by slaves and freed blacks in Haiti; since the 1987 Constitution it has been recognized as the country's national religion.

The slave trade displaced millions of Africans from their native lands. Uprooted from their societies, the Africans brought with them their family values, beliefs, traditions, and religious practices. Although HAITI's culture derives from three sources—African, Amerindian, and European—Haiti emerged as a nation whose African contributions form its principal cultural traits. The *Vodou* religion must be interpreted within this framework.

Origins of the Religion

The slaves from over a hundred different ethnic groups who came to Haiti lacked a common language. They were able to unite only through their recreated African religion, Vodou. The colonial powers systematically intermixed Africans so that any recollection of language, lineage, and ties to the motherland, known as *Ginen*, the term for the mythical African homeland, would be permanently lost. Colonialists imposed European values and Roman Catholicism upon the slave population. In an attempt to stop the practice of Vodou, slave gatherings were forbidden. Thus slaves were forced to worship their African deities secretly and to hide their allegiance to their ancestral religion. These interdictions, repressive measures, and the clandestine nature of Vodou ceremonies led to the revalorization of the very African cultural values that Europeans tried to suppress.

This regrouping around a common past and ideal has consistently played a role in Haitian political life and has fueled a number of mass movements, culminating in the war for independence, and much later in the 1986 overthrow of the Duvalier dictatorship. A turning point in this saga was the 1791 Bois Caiman Vodou ritual and political congress, orchestrated by BOUKMAN, which led to a general slave uprising and became a war of national liberation. Vodou's close ties to its African origins are also a result of Haiti's isolation from the rest of the world following its 1804 successful slave revolution.

The history of persecution of Vodou practitioners continued with the 1896, 1913, and 1941 antisuperstition campaigns, which destroyed shrines and led to the massacre of hundreds of people who admitted their adherence to Vodou. The period of the American occupation (1915–1934) as well as the post-Duvalier era were also times of severe persecution of Vodouists. Roman Catholicism, headed exclusively by Westerners until the 1960s, had the political and financial support of the state and remained the country's sole official religion until the Constitution of 1987 recognized freedom of religion.

Meaning and Significance

Popular labeling of Vodou as "witchcraft" and "magic" has been a historical tradition perpetuated in Hollywood films and supermarket tabloids, which sustain these same popular myths. *Vodou*, the preferred term to designate the Haitian religion, is of Dahomean origin and derives from the FON word for "God" or "Spirit." Other accurate spellings include *Vodun, Vodoun*, or the French *Vaudou*, but never *voodoo*, the sensationalist and derogatory Western creation. Vodou is a comprehensive system of knowledge that has nothing to do with simplistic and erroneous images such as sticking pins into dolls, putting a hex on an adversary, or turning innocents into zombies. It is an organized form of communal support that provides meaning to the human experience in relation to the natural and supernatural forces of the universe.

Despite media portrayals, Vodou shares many elements with other religions. Like members of other persuasions, Vodouists believe in creating harmony, in keeping a balance, in cultivating virtues and positive values. With its reverence for the ancestors, Vodou is the cement that binds family and community life in Haiti.

Vodou is essentially a monotheistic religion, which recognizes a single and supreme spiritual entity or God, known as Mawu-Lisa among the Fon, OLORUN among the YORUBA, and

The Adoration of the Vodou God (1949) is an oil on masonite painting by Rigaud Benoit, considered to be Haiti's most famous painter. Vodou practitioners are shown here honoring their god with gifts. *Christie's Images*

Bondye or Gran Met in Haiti. The Haitian religion originated from the fusion of rituals of a range of African ethnic groups—in particular, the Fon, Yoruba, IGBO, HAUSA, EWE, and KONGO. Scholars have called African culture "additive," in the sense that it often adapted foreign elements into its structure. Following the same pattern, Vodou absorbed many aspects of Catholicism into its ritual. Vodouists use Roman Catholic prayers and hymns at the beginning of ceremonies and use the Gregorian calendar to mark the celebrations of the *lwas*, the spirit intermediaries between humans and God, who have been linked to the iconography and stories about Roman Catholic saints. For the *servitors* of the spirits, as Vodouists typically refer to themselves, there is no conflict between Vodou and Roman Catholicism. This SYNCRETISM is the subject of debates among scholars: some hold that Roman Catholic practices were actually absorbed into Vodou; others contend that the Haitians never accepted the European elements and instead simply used the saints and Christian rituals as a cover to continue their own practices. Whichever interpretation one accepts, syncretism remains a basic part of Haitian Vodou.

In addition to its visible cultural and ritual dimensions, expressed through the arts, especially in Haitian music and dance, Vodou's teaching and belief system includes social, economic, political, and practical components. Today, for example, Vodou's teachings are concerned with what can be done to overcome the limiting social conditions in Haiti, a country that has been strenuously challenged from within and outside its borders. For example, questions that Vodou addresses include: what to do in case of illness in a country that counts only one physician for 23,000 people, and what to do before embarking upon major undertakings, such as marriage, business transactions, or traveling abroad. Vodou gives its adherents positive means to address these issues and support in times of challenging economic moments and difficult political transitions.

Most Vodou ceremonies conform to one of two major rites. The Rada rite retained from the Old Kingdom of Dahomey (present-day NIGERIA, BENIN, and TOGO) is generally agreed to be most faithful to West African tradition. The Petwo rite is a newer development that arose out of the crucible of the New World plantation system and encompasses elements of the KONGO culture as well as the practices of many other groups from Central Africa to ANGOLA in the southwest. The Rada rite is Vodou's most elaborate rite and includes the great communal spirits or lwa, such as Atibon Legba, Marasa Dosou Dosa, Danbala and Ayida Wedo, Azaka Mede, Ogou Feray, Agwe Tawoyo, Ezili Freda Daome, Lasirenn and Labalenn, and Gede Nimbo. It is generally assumed, by Vodou practitioners and researchers alike, that the Rada Lwa are *dous*, or sweet. These *fle Ginen*, or true spirits of Africa, are the first lwas to be saluted in ceremonies. Many maintain that the Petwo lwa are *anme*, or bitter. Associated with fire, they are said to be *lwa cho*, or hot lwa, engaging in forceful behavior. The Petwo rite includes major lwa such as Met Kalfou, Simbi Andezo, Ezili Danto, and Bawon Samdi. Some of the lwa exist *andezo*, or in two cosmic substances, and are served in both Rada and Petwo rituals. Contrary to popular conception, the line between Rada and

Members of a Rara band participate in a Vodou parade in Haiti. *Dolores Yonker/Hutchinson*

Petwo is not as rigid as it appears: much of what is described as Rada goes for Petwo.

Possession, an important dimension of Vodou worship, is among the least understood aspects of the religion. Through possession, both the lwa and the community are affirmed. The participants (in particular, the priests and priestesses, the *houngans* and *manbos*, and the other initiates, the *ounsis*) transcend their materiality by becoming spirits, and the spirits renew their vigor by dancing and feasting with the *chwal*, or horses, for it is said that during possession the lwa rides a person like a cavalier rides a horse. Equally as important, possession is a time when the lwa communicate in a tangible way with the people, who during such times receive answers to pressing questions.

Future of Vodou

Though Vodou continues to be seen in an ambivalent manner, increasingly people have been practicing it more openly in Haiti and abroad. Scholars, patriots, and grassroots organizers continue a crusade for greater respect for Haiti's ancestral religion. Reputable artists, scholars, and writers are affirming their involvement with Vodou. In the past ten years, with the advent of the "root culture" movement driven by the progressive wing of culturalists, Vodou-inspired musical groups such as BOUKMAN EKSPERYANS, Boukan Ginen, RAM, and the Fugees, and organizations such as Zantray, Bode Nasyonal, and New Rada Community have emerged. The touring Sacred Arts of Haitian Vodou exhibition constitutes one more effort in a series of activities aiming at fostering better understanding of Vodou. A 1997 conference held at the University of California, Santa Barbara, where Haitian scholars and Vodou practitioners met to discuss the role of Vodou in the development of Haiti, led to the creation of the Congress of Santa Barbara, an international scholarly association for the study of Haitian Vodou. However, no single person or organization has the final word on Vodou.

Today, Vodou continues to increase in popularity, especially among Americans. The NEW ORLEANS grave of Marie Laveau, the "Vodou queen" who died in 1881, is currently one of the most visited gravesites in the United States. A growing number of whites are embracing Vodou, which remains a complex but decentralized system of universal knowledge, cultural practices, and communal support.

See also Catholic Church in Latin America and the Caribbean; Dahomey; Duvalier, Jean-Claude; Haitian Revolution; Magic, Sorcery, and Witchcraft in the Americas: An Interpretation; Slave Rebellions in Latin America and the Caribbean; Transatlantic Slave Trade.

Gerdes Fleurant
Claudine Michel

Volta, Lake

Reservoir on the Volta River in central Ghana, formed by the Akosombo Dam.

With a length of about 400 kilometers (about 250 miles) and an area of 8,482 square kilometers (3,275 square miles), Lake Volta is one of the largest artificially created lakes in the world. It is also a classic example of the ambitious but often poorly designed development projects implemented throughout Africa during the early years of independence. The dam and lake are part of the Volta River Project, a development plan undertaken by the government of GHANA, with financial support from the World Bank, the United States, and GREAT BRITAIN. Construction of the dam began in 1961, and water began to fill Lake Volta in 1964. The lake submerged nearly 740 villages and displaced about 80,000 people.

About 70,000 people were moved into forty-two newly constructed settlements that were to have small concrete houses, schools, wells, and mechanized agriculture. Most of the settlements, however, had major problems. For example, many lacked housing for large families, as well as adequate farmland and water to raise crops and livestock. Although the resettlement agency provided settlers with machinery and land, the machinery was not repaired when broken. Also, cases of water-related DISEASES such as schistosomiasis, onchocerciasis, and

malaria increased as much as 85 percent near the reservoir, not only because of the proximity of the lake but also because of the poor sewer systems in the villages. The increase in illness was compounded by the lack of adequate medical facilities and the failure of the resettlement agency to educate settlers about ways to prevent the diseases. Not surprisingly, within four years the majority of settlers had migrated elsewhere.

Construction of the Akosombo Dam and creation of Lake Volta were intended to encourage the establishment of new industries, stimulate agricultural development, provide opportunities for fishing, and increase water transportation between Ghana's northern savanna and the coast. The hydroelectric power generated by the dam was supposed to provide a reliable energy source for large industrial activities, and water from the lake was targeted for irrigation projects. The dam and reservoir have contributed less than anticipated, however, to Ghana's industrial growth and other developments. During the early 1980s and early 1990s, very low water levels caused by drought greatly reduced the generation of hydroelectric power by Akosombo Dam, disrupting both industrial production and energy exports to TOGO and BENIN. Agriculture in the resettlement area remains marginal and irrigation small-scale. The lake has, in fact, hindered travel and trade between northeastern and southern Ghana, since attempts to develop water transportation have had few results. Fishing has been more successful, although less than 10 percent of Ghana's fish consumption comes from Lake Volta.

The Volta Lake Research Project, established in 1968, has conducted research on the resettlement experience and on ways to enhance the development potential of the region. Although research has identified problems and suggested ways to improve the productivity of the lake and Akosombo Dam, economic recessions have prevented the government from implementing action. As a result, the Lake Volta project remains a lesson for future development projects rather than an example.

See also Development; Lakes in Africa.

Bibliography

Hart, David. *The Volta River Project: A Case Study in Politics and Technology.* Edinburgh Press, 1980.

Elizabeth Heath

Vorster, Balthazar Johannes

1915–1983

Prime minister and president of South Africa.

Born in Jamestown, the son of an AFRIKANER sheep farmer, Balthazar Vorster was trained as a lawyer. A founder of an anti-British extremist group opposed to participation in WORLD WAR II, he was interned by the South African government from 1942 to 1944. He subsequently entered politics, but did not gain a parliamentary seat until 1953. Having previously held a minor government post, Vorster was made minister of justice in 1961, when his mentor, Prime Minister HENDRICK VERWOERD, needed to restore order in the aftermath of the SHARPEVILLE shootings (1960). Vorster did not fail; he imposed drastic detention and security measures on black dissidents. As prime minister after Verwoerd's assassination, Vorster further tightened security and continued the APARTHEID policy, but also attempted to open a dialogue with black African states. He relinquished the prime minister's office for that of president in 1978 as a result of a government scandal and cover-up; ultimately, the same affair forced him into retirement the following year.

See also South Africa.

Voting Districts and Minority Representation in the United States

Relationship between the drawing of electoral districts and the political representation of African Americans and other minority groups.

The year 1872 marked the first reapportionment of districts in the United States Congress after male African Americans won the right to vote everywhere in the country. At this time, white North Carolina Democrats packed blacks into a strangely shaped, predominantly black congressional district with a much higher population than the average district. The move was a racially discriminatory and partisan effort to minimize the influence of black Republican voters. Neither this nor any of the myriad of other anti-black manipulations of voting districts in the nineteenth century were challenged in court.

In 1992, 120 years later, an interracial Democratic coalition in North Carolina found itself under pressure from the U.S. Department of Justice to improve black voting power in congressional elections. The Democrats drew a district map designed to enhance the chances of black voters to elect candidates of their choice while still preserving the seats of other Democratic members of Congress. This time white voters sued. A conservative Republican majority on the U.S. Supreme Court ruled that district lines were unconstitutional if they appeared to track racial population concentrations too closely. Ironically, the Court based its decision on the Fourteenth Amendment, which was enacted to protect the rights of blacks. Manipulating electoral district boundaries to take in minority neighborhoods, the 5-4 Supreme Court majority asserted, was a violation of "traditional districting principles."

Congressional and Minority Opportunity Districts

The districts of the U.S. HOUSE OF REPRESENTATIVES, like those of the state legislatures, are determined by population measurements and by legislative decisions. After the nationwide census at the beginning of every decade, each state is apportioned a number of House seats based on its population. At that point, state legislatures determine the actual borders of the districts within their state. Often those districts are drawn so as to maximize the number of U.S. representatives for the dominant party in the state legislature.

This process of gaining political advantages through redistricting is known as *gerrymandering,* a term that has been particularly applied when such advantages are gained by drawing districts with irregular or elongated boundaries in order to arrange population groups most favorably. At times, these district lines have also been drawn with attention to racial groupings, either to dilute the electoral power of minorities by spreading minority voters across a number of districts or to increase minority voting power by concentrating those voters within districts in which they compose a majority. This process of redistricting has traditionally been in the hands of state legislatures. That changed after the Supreme Court's "one person, one vote" decision in *Reynolds v. Sims* (1964), which required equality of population among a state's districts, and after the VOTING RIGHTS ACT OF 1965 outlawed districting that diluted minority voting power. In recent decades, federal courts and the U.S. Department of Justice have overseen, and often overturned, the districting plans of individual states.

When a nonwhite group (or groups) in the United States makes up a majority of the voters within a particular district, they make up what has often been called a "majority-minority" district. Because of racially polarized voting, and because lower-class voters have tended to have lower rates of registration and turnout for elections, African Americans have historically required district-wide majorities, sometimes substantial majorities, to elect candidates of their choice, black candidates in particular. There have been exceptions to this strict equation between the electability of blacks and their majority status as voters in the district. In the idealistic aftermath of the CIVIL WAR (1861–1865), a scattering of blacks were elected in the North by overwhelmingly white constituencies. More recently, high-profile black politicians who could raise substantial campaign funds could sometimes successfully appeal to enough whites or Latinos to gain election even in districts where blacks were a minority. Therefore, many scholars now prefer to call districts where African American or Latino voters have a good chance to elect candidates of their choice, of whatever ethnic group, as "minority opportunity" districts, rather than "majority-minority" districts. However, it has been quite unusual for black candidates to be elected without a black majority in their district.

Reconstruction and Black Disfranchisement

In 1870 the states ratified the FIFTEENTH AMENDMENT, which guaranteed the right to vote to all male citizens regardless of race. In the 1872 elections, at the height of RECONSTRUCTION in the South, the newly enfranchised freedmen elected more than 300 black candidates to the U.S. Congress and to state legislatures. Nearly all the black representatives belonged to the REPUBLICAN PARTY and were from districts where blacks were a majority. When white Democrats used force and fraud to defeat the Republican Reconstruction state governments, one of their first legal actions after regaining power was always to gerrymander black voters so that their votes would determine a minimum of seats, often drawing extremely irregular boundaries to do so. These statutory means were just one way that the political power of blacks and their white Republican and Populist allies was reduced. Other devices used to curtail and dilute the African American vote included poll taxes, registration laws, secret ballot acts (which operated as literacy tests for the largely illiterate ex-slaves), and at-large elections (in which representatives were elected across entire cities or counties rather than in smaller districts that might have black majorities). With the political and racial opposition weakened, Democrats could insert more permanent literacy and property qualifications for voting into state constitutions and engage in such massive administrative discrimination as to effectively disfranchise many poor whites and the vast majority of blacks. Thus, vote dilution, including widespread racial gerrymandering, was a key step along the road to black disfranchisement and white Democratic supremacy in the late nineteenth and early twentieth centuries. White Southerners referred to this process as REDEMPTION, and it led to the JIM CROW system of racial segregation.

As African Americans moved north and west, where they could vote much more freely than in the South, they successfully sought political offices. Such victories were almost always won as a result of constituencies that concentrated the black vote, usually forming the majority in a district. These black officeholders used their power to lead efforts to end discrimination in public accommodations, schools, housing, jobs, and nationally, in voting.

Civil Rights Era

In their efforts to make the Fifteenth Amendment a reality in the South nearly a century after the amendment was enacted, civil rights advocates passed the national Civil Rights Acts of 1957 and 1960, which created some judicial oversight over voting in the South. They also filed suit against particularly egregious apportionment practices. For example, the TUSKEGEE CIVIC ASSOCIATION successfully appealed a notorious racial gerrymander in Tuskegee, Alabama, in which city limits were redrawn to move black residential areas outside the city's borders. These rather timid measures failed to produce quick results and Southern campaigns for voting rights met with massive and often violent resistance. In response, the administration of President Lyndon B. Johnson passed the Voting Rights Act of 1965, which was aimed at suspending literacy tests and other laws prone to bias. Section 5 of the act gave the U.S. attorney general the duty of approving any changes in voting laws in states and counties where discrimination was thought to be particularly severe. The purpose of Section 5 was to prevent such "covered jurisdictions" from substituting new discriminatory laws or practices for those banned by the Voting Rights Act. In the 1969 case of *Allen v. Board of Elections,* the U.S. Supreme Court

ruled that Section 5 applied to changes in electoral structures, such as at-large elections and redistricting, as well as to limits on voter registration.

The Supreme Court's "one person, one vote" decisions such as *Reynolds v. Sims* earlier in the 1960s mandated that nearly any redistricting could be challenged in court. When boundaries were redrawn, however, black and Latino areas throughout the country were often split so that those voters, whose allegiance by that time was largely with the DEMOCRATIC PARTY, could help elect more white Democrats. However, the number of districts in which blacks or Latinos constituted a majority was kept to a minimum. In 1966, for instance, the Mississippi legislature responded to increased black voting participation by splitting a black-majority area along the Mississippi River and diluting it into three majority-white districts. But the conjunction of increased minority voting and political assertiveness on the one hand, and heightened judicial scrutiny of reapportionment on the other, pressured Congress and the courts to ensure that minority rights were adequately protected in the redistricting process, as well as in the voting booth.

Before and After *Shaw v. Reno*

The Supreme Court limited judicial oversight over racial redistricting in the *Mobile v. Bolden* decision in 1980, which stated that intent to racially discriminate must be proven in order for districts to be overturned. Over the objections of President Ronald Reagan, overwhelming majorities of both houses of Congress responded by passing far-reaching amendments to the Voting Rights Act in 1982 that placed an emphasis on the results of redistricting, rather than on its intent. In doing so, Congress ensured that redistricting in the 1990s would differ from the experiences in earlier, more discriminatory decades. In its major interpretation of the 1982 amendments—the 1986 case of *Thornburg v. Gingles*—a majority of the Supreme Court, led by liberals William Brennan and THURGOOD MARSHALL, backed the vigorous application of the Voting Rights Act to redistricting.

Pressured by the amended law and favorable judicial decisions, legislators in the 1990s substantially increased the number of minority opportunity districts. As a result, in 1992 five Southern states elected African American members of Congress for the first time in the twentieth century, and the number of blacks in Congress grew more than after any redistricting since the 1870s. In order to preserve the seats of white incumbents while increasing the chances for blacks and Latinos, however, many districts of every ethnic composition were given peculiar shapes.

Led by Reagan appointee Sandra Day O'Connor, a 5-4 majority of the Supreme Court signaled its displeasure at these results in the 1993 case of *Shaw v. Reno,* which overturned the 1992 redistricting in North Carolina. Since the 1970s, minorities who challenged a law or practice as racially discriminatory under the Fourteenth Amendment had to show not only that the law had a discriminatory purpose, but also that it had an adverse effect on them. O'Connor waived this proof of effect for whites in districting cases by characterizing the Fourteenth

Amendment as banning discrimination *between* persons, not just discrimination *against* some of them. Appropriating the language of the CIVIL RIGHTS MOVEMENT, O'Connor termed the two congressional districts in which blacks held a slim majority as "segregated," based on "stereotypes," and likely to lead to "APARTHEID." Black legislators from such districts, she predicted, would ignore their white constituents. After deriding the shape of the twelfth district, which followed Interstate 85 from Charlotte to Durham, North Carolina, O'Connor endorsed an earlier Republican-proposed district that was longer and much more difficult to traverse.

Although the Court seemed to draw back from the *Shaw* decision in two 1994 cases interpreting the Voting Rights Act, the same five-person majority dramatically extended *Shaw* in the 1995 Georgia case of *Miller v. Johnson*. In his majority opinion, another Reagan appointee, Justice Anthony Kennedy, ruled that the shape of a district should be only one consideration in the larger inquiry into whether race was the "predominant factor" in drawing a district. Even districts in which minority voters could strongly influence the outcome of an election might be ruled illegal. Only an intent to follow "traditional districting principles," such as compactness, the preservation of county or municipal boundaries, and the recognition of nonracial "communities of interest," in the majority's view, satisfied the Fourteenth Amendment's promise of equal protection to all citizens. Districts securely controlled by whites, however, did not have to satisfy such exacting standards.

A series of other, less important opinions by the same five-person majority in racial gerrymandering cases from 1993 to 1997 emphasized the Court's return to the "traditional districting principle" of diluting African American and Latino political power and disadvantaging the political party with which minorities primarily identified. When huge numbers of blacks and Latinos were openly packed into districts in Ohio and California in a way that benefited Republicans, those districts were considered constitutionally acceptable by the *Shaw* majority. A desire to remedy a century of discrimination in boundary setting, however, was considered insufficient to justify race-conscious redistricting that helped Democrats in North Carolina. Overwhelmingly white Republican districts in Texas could have extremely jagged edges, but minority opportunity districts in the same state had to be as compact as possible. Section 5 of the Voting Rights Act became a ceiling on minority political power, instead of a floor, when Justice O'Connor interpreted it to mean that the percentage of a minority group in a minority opportunity district could not be increased. The Court's ruling also said that to win a Section 5 case, minorities had to show not only that a legal change made them worse off, but also that it was intended to do so. And in a 1999 case, *Department of Commerce v. U.S. House of Representatives*, the *Shaw* justices halted Democratic efforts to use scientific sampling to reduce the undercount of minorities in the 2000 census. The decision will almost certainly reduce the influence of minorities in future redistricting and elections.

See also Congress, African Americans in.

Bibliography

Grofman, Bernard, Lisa Handley, and Richard G. Niemi. *Minority Representation and the Quest for Voting Equality.* Cambridge University Press, 1992.

Kousser, J. Morgan. *Colorblind Injustice: Minority Voting Rights and the Undoing of the Second Reconstruction.* University of North Carolina Press, 1999.

Whitby, Kenny J. *The Color of Representation: Congressional Behavior and Black Interests.* University of Michigan Press, 1997.

Voting Rights Act of 1965

Legislation that charged the federal government with helping disenfranchised African Americans in the South regain the right to vote.

In the century following RECONSTRUCTION, African Americans in the South faced overwhelming obstacles to voting. Despite the Fifteenth and Nineteenth Amendments to the Constitution of the United States, which had enfranchised black men and women, southern voter registration boards used poll taxes, literacy tests, and other bureaucratic impediments to deny African Americans their legal rights. Southern blacks also risked harassment, intimidation, economic reprisals, and physical violence when they tried to register or vote. As a result, African Americans had little, if any, political power, either locally or nationally. In Mississippi, for instance, only 5 percent of eligible blacks were registered to vote in 1960.

The Voting Rights Act of 1965, meant to reverse this disenfranchisement, grew out of both public protest and private political negotiation. Starting in 1961, the SOUTHERN CHRISTIAN LEADERSHIP CONFERENCE (SCLC), led by MARTIN LUTHER KING JR., staged nonviolent demonstrations in Albany, Georgia, and BIRMINGHAM, ALABAMA. King and the SCLC hoped to attract national media attention and pressure the U.S. government to protect African Americans' constitutional rights. The strategy worked. Newspaper photos and television broadcasts of Birmingham's notoriously racist police commissioner, Eugene "Bull" Connor, and his men violently attacking the SCLC's peaceful protesters with water hoses, police dogs, and nightsticks awakened the consciences of white Americans.

The site of the next campaign was Selma, Alabama. In the first three months of 1965, the SCLC led local residents and visiting volunteers in a series of marches demanding an equal right to vote. As in Birmingham, they met with violence and imprisonment. King himself wrote a letter from the Selma jail, published in the *New York Times*, in which he said, "there are more Negroes in jail with me than there are on the voting rolls" in Selma. In the worst attack yet, on Sunday, March 7, a group of Alabama state troopers, local sheriff's officers, and unofficial possemen used tear gas and clubs against 600 peaceful marchers. By now, as King had predicted, the nation was watching.

President Lyndon B. Johnson, who had succeeded to the presidency after the 1963 assassination of John F. Kennedy,

Black Voter Registration in the South 1940–2000

Estimated percentage of voting-age blacks registered

State	1940	1947	1952	1960	1962	1964	1968	1976	1980	1982	1984	1996	2000
Alabama	0.4	1.2	5.0	13.7	13.4	23.0	56.7	58.4	55.8	69.7	74.0	69.2	72.0
Arkansas	1.5	17.3	27.0	37.3	34.0	49.3	67.5	94.0	57.2	63.9	67.2	65.8	60.0
Florida	5.7	15.4	33.0	38.9	36.8	63.8	62.1	61.1	58.3	59.7	63.4	53.1	52.7
Georgia	3.0	18.8	23.0	29.3	26.7	44.0	56.1	74.8	48.6	50.4	57.9	64.6	66.3
Louisiana	0.5	2.6	25.0	30.9	27.8	32.0	59.3	63.0	60.7	61.1	65.7	71.9	73.5
Mississippi	0.4	0.9	4.0	5.2	5.3	6.7	54.4	60.7	62.3	64.2	77.1	67.4	73.7
North Carolina	7.1	15.2	18.0	38.1	35.8	46.8	55.3	54.8	51.3	50.9	65.4	65.5	62.9
South Carolina	0.8	13.0	20.0	15.6	22.9	38.7	50.8	56.5	53.7	53.9	58.5	64.3	68.6
Tennessee	6.5	25.8	27.0	58.9	49.8	69.4	72.8	66.4	64.0	66.1	69.9	65.7	64.9
Texas	5.6	18.5	31.0	34.9	37.3	57.7	83.1	65.0	56.0	49.5	71.5	63.2	69.5
Virginia	4.1	13.2	16.0	22.8	24.0	45.7	58.4	54.7	53.2	49.5	62.3	64.0	58.0
Average	3.0	12.0	20.0	29.1	29.4	43.1	62.0	63.1	55.8	56.5	66.2	64.1	65.0

Source: 2000, U.S. Census Bureau. Current Population Survey, Documents P20-504 and P20-542.

Southern African American Voters, Potential and Eligible, 1980–2000

	Population (in millions)		% Registered				% Voted			
			Presidential Election Years		Congressional Election Years		Presidential Election Years		Congressional Election Years	
	Total	Black	Total	Black	Total	Black	Total	Black	Total	Black
1980	227.2	26.8	64.8	59.3	—	—	55.6	48.2	—	—
1982	231.7	27.5	—	—	61.7	56.9	—	—	41.8	38.3
1984	235.8	28.2	66.9	65.6	—	—	56.8	53.2	—	—
1986	240.1	28.9	—	—	63.0	64.6	—	—	43.0	42.5
1988	244.5	29.7	65.6	63.3	—	—	54.5	48.0	—	—
1990	249.6	30.6	—	—	61.3	59.0	—	—	42.4	39.8
1992	256.5	31.7	67.2	64.7	—	—	59.0	54.3	—	—
1994	263.1	32.7	—	—	61.1	58.8	—	—	40.9	34.6
1996	269.4	33.5	65.9	64.7	—	—	52.2	50.0	—	—
1998	275.8	34.4	—	—	62.7	61.5	—	—	38.6	38.9
2000	282.2	35.5	64.5	65.2	—	—	53.2	58.9	—	—

Source: 2000, U.S. Census Bureau. Mini Historical Statistics, No. HS-2 "Population Characteristics: 1900 to 2000" and Historical Time Series Tables, Table A-1 "Reported Voting and Registration by Race, Hispanic Origin, Sex and Age Groups: November 1964 to 2000."

made civil rights one of his administration's top priorities. Johnson used his formidable political skills to pass the Twenty-Fourth Amendment, which outlawed poll taxes, in 1964. A week after "Bloody Sunday" in Selma, Johnson gave a televised speech before Congress in which he not only denounced the assault but said it was "wrong—deadly wrong" that African Americans were being denied their constitutional rights. Johnson went on to dramatically quote the movement's motto, "we shall overcome."

Two days later, the president sent the Voting Rights bill to Congress. The resolution, signed into law on August 6, 1965, empowered the federal government to oversee voter registration and elections in counties that had used tests to determine voter eligibility or where registration or turnout had been less than 50 percent in the 1964 presidential election. It also banned discriminatory literacy tests and expanded voting rights for Americans who do not speak English.

The law's effects were wide and powerful. By 1968, nearly 60 percent of eligible African Americans were registered to vote in Mississippi, and other southern states showed similar improvement. Between 1965 and 1990, the number of black state legislators and members of Congress rose from two to 160. Despite finally reclaiming their constitutional voting rights, however, many African Americans in the South and elsewhere saw little progress on other fronts. They still faced illegal job discrimination, substandard schools, and unequal health care. Following its major victories—the Civil Rights Act of 1964 and the Voting Rights Act of 1965—the liberal, integrationist CIVIL RIGHTS MOVEMENT began to be eclipsed by the more radical Black Power Movement.

The Voting Rights Act was extended in 1970, 1975, and 1982, the last time despite vigorous resistance from the Reagan administration. Fearing a largely Democratic black vote, the REPUBLICAN PARTY adopted various means to minimize it, including at-large elections and districts redrawn to dilute black representation. They also attacked as racial gerrymandering the new "majority-minority" congressional districts drawn by the U.S. Justice Department. In *Miller v. Johnson* (1995) the Supreme Court agreed, limiting the use of racial factors in deciding district lines. Some prominent African Americans, such as Harvard University law professor Lani Guinier, argued that minority votes would be more effective in a system of proportional representation.

Despite these setbacks and debates, the Voting Rights Act had an enormous impact. It reenfranchised black southerners, helping put 9,101 African Americans in elected offices at the local, state, and national levels by 2001. A large number of these officeholders were in the South. Mississippi alone accounted for 892 of the black-held offices that year.

See also Black Power in the United States; Congress, African Americans in; Democratic Party; Fifteenth Amendment.

Bibliography

Garrow, David J. *Protest at Selma: Martin Luther King, Jr., and the Voting Rights Act of 1965.* Yale University Press, 1978.

Kate Tuttle

Vulture

Common name for two groups of carrion-eating birds, one of which is indigenous to Africa.

There are two distinct families of vultures: American vultures and Eurasian and African vultures. The latter group probably descended from eaglelike birds. American vultures, although superficially similar to large birds of prey, are probably more closely related to storks, with which they share some anatomical and behavioral features. American vultures also differ from the Eurasian group in that they have longitudinal, perforated nostrils without a partition and lack a voice, due to the absence of a vocal organ called a syrinx.

All vultures are large birds with a naked head and hooked bill. They feed almost entirely on carrion, occasionally attacking newborn or wounded living animals. Most hunt by sight, soaring and watching for other vultures descending to feed. There are seven separate species of African vultures, and within the mixed-species flocks seen at lion kills in Africa, there is a definite hierarchy. Smaller species, such as the Egyptian vulture, must wait until the more powerful species, such as Rüpell's griffon, are finished.

One of the largest extant flying birds is the Andean condor, with a wingspread of up to 3.2 meters (10.5 feet). The familiar turkey vulture is found from South America north to southern Canada. It shares much of this range (north to Pennsylvania) with the American black vulture, whose naked head is black rather than red. The largest North American vulture is the California condor.

Scientific classification: The Eurasian and African vultures belong to the family Accipitridae. The Egyptian vulture is classified as *Neophron percnopterus* and Rüpell's griffon as *Gyps rueppelli*. Vultures belong to the order Falconiformes. The American vultures make up the family Cathartidae. The Andean condor is classified as *Vultur gryphus*, the turkey vulture as *Cathartes aura*, the American black vulture as *Coragyps atratus*, and the California condor as *Gymnogyps californianus*.

W

Wala

Ethnic group of West Africa; also known as Oule, Walba, Walo, and Wilé.

The Wala primarily inhabit northwestern GHANA and neighboring BURKINA FASO. They speak a Niger-Congo language related to MOSSI. Over 100,000 people consider themselves Wala.

See also Ethnicity and Identity in Africa: An Interpretation; Languages, African: An Overview.

Walatta Petros, Saint

1594–1643

One of the few women saints of the Ethiopian Orthodox Church.

Saint Walatta Petros was born into an aristocratic Ethiopian family and married Makea Krestos, who was a prominent person during the reign of Emperor Susenyos. Walatta Petros, however, rejected her wealth and status, wishing instead to pursue a religious life in the ETHIOPIAN ORTHODOX CHURCH. Her devotion to the Orthodox Church increased during the reign of Susenyos, who had converted to Catholicism and sought to make it the state religion in ETHIOPIA. Susenyos sparked a bitter struggle between the adherents of the Ethiopian church and those of Catholicism.

Makea Krestos had prohibited Walatta Petros from retiring to an Ethiopian convent. However, during a rebellion in 1617, both Susenyos's son-in-law and the Archbishop of Ethiopia died. Their deaths allowed Walatta Petros to withdraw from her marriage and commit herself to religious life. She, her close associate Eheta Krestos, and other followers established themselves at Waldebba, a famous site for Ethiopian hermits.

Walatta Petros's anti-Catholic activities soon drew the ire of Susenyos, who summoned her to court. After the Catholic archbishop tried repeatedly and unsuccessfully to convert Walatta Petros to Catholicism, Susenyos exiled her to Jabal in the far west of Ethiopia. Although she continued to suffer persecution, she still actively opposed Catholicism and promoted the Orthodox faith.

Susenyos's abdication in 1632 meant the restoration of the Ethiopian Orthodox Church and led to Walatta Petros's release. Walatta Petros spent the remaining twelve years of her life traveling, teaching, and founding religious communities. She died a revered and respected champion of the Ethiopian Orthodox Church, and was buried on the holy island of Remna near the southeast shore of Lake Tana.

See also Christianity, African: An Overview.

Robert Fay

Walcott, Derek Alton

1930–

Poet, playwright, and Nobel laureate who developed a distinctly Caribbean literary style rooted in a mastery of classical European tradition.

Derek Alton Walcott, winner of the 1992 Nobel Prize for literature, is widely regarded as one of the most important writers to emerge from the English-speaking Caribbean. While other Caribbean writers have responded to what Patricia Ismond has called the West Indian "crisis of historylessness," brought about by the devastating effects of slavery and colonialism, by searching for roots, Walcott celebrates the possibilities of the "newness" of the region. The figure of Robinson Crusoe recurs in his poetry and plays, exemplifying both the predicament of Caribbean isolation and the potential that isolation offers to West Indians for creating a vocabulary uniquely suited to the complexity and richness of their world.

For Walcott, the artistic legacy of classical Western civilization is integral to this creative process. At an early age, he "fell madly in love with English." Born in Castries, SAINT LUCIA, he became familiar with the Western canon through his colonial education in Saint Lucia and the influence of his mother, a schoolteacher who staged productions of Shakespeare. "In the manner of Joyce and Yeats," wrote critic Stephen Breslow soon after Walcott was awarded the Nobel Prize, "Walcott has merged a profound, rhapsodic reverie upon his remote birthplace—its people, its landscape, and its history—with the central, classical tradition of Western civilization."

Many postcolonial critics have charged, however, that Walcott is out of touch with the very West Indians who are his subject matter. His embrace of Europe, combined with his disavowal of the Africanist aesthetic advocated by black nationalists in the 1960s and 1970s, has led to accusations of elitism. Walcott's writing is often unfavorably compared with that of fellow West Indian author EDWARD KAMAU BRATHWAITE, whose work is deemed more populist. Walcott dismisses this criticism as reactionary and bristles at the suggestion that art should be subservient to politics.

Walcott believes in the universal potential of art and its ability to transcend the particularities of local political issues. These beliefs manifest in a cosmopolitanism that moves beyond a simple valorization of the European canon. He admires the work of German dramatist and composer Bertolt Brecht, whose interest in Oriental theater introduced Walcott to Asian cultural traditions. Japanese film director Kurosawa Akira's *Rashomon* (1950) helped inspire the development of Walcott's Obie Award-winning masterpiece, *Dream on Monkey Mountain* (1967).

Nonetheless, Walcott makes extensive use of Caribbean vernaculars. The dialogue in *The Sea at Dauphin* (1954), for example, uses the Creole spoken by Saint Lucia's fishers. These fishers are also the subject of his celebrated epic poem, *Omeros* (1990). *Drums and Colour* (1958), the retelling of Caribbean history that was commissioned for the opening of the inaugural Federal Parliament of the WEST INDIES, has the energy and flavor of Carnival. Masquerade, mime, and CALYPSO were incorporated into the play, and revelers danced and sang during intermissions, creating the atmosphere of West Indian bacchanal. Additionally, during his seventeen-year relationship with the Trinidad Theatre Workshop, which he founded in 1959, Walcott combined regional art, music, language, and dance to create almost ritualistic performances. Walcott describes the cultural synthesis within his work as a "mulatto" aesthetic that reflects the Caribbean's "illegitimate, rootless, mongrelized" nature in a tradition that is unequivocally Caribbean.

Walcott currently teaches creative writing at Boston University each fall and spends the rest of the year in St. Lucia, where he is a professor of Education at St. Mary's College. In October 2003, the HARLEM School of the Arts presented his Obie award-winning play, *Dream on Monkey Mountain* (1967).

See also Carnivals in Latin America and the Caribbean; Creoles; Literature, English-Language, in the Caribbean; Poetry, Caribbean; Theater in the Caribbean.

Bibliography

Hamner, D. Robert, ed. *Critical Perspectives on Derek Walcott*. Three Continents Press, 1993.

Olaniyan, Tejumola. *Scars of Conquest/Masks of Resistance: The Invention of Cultural Identities in African, African-American, and Caribbean Drama*. Oxford University Press, 1995.

Peter Hudson

Walcott, Jersey Joe

1914–1994

American boxer and former heavyweight champion of the world.

Jersey Joe Walcott was born Arnold Raymond Cream in Merchantville, New Jersey. His parents were immigrants from BARBADOS. When he was fourteen his father died, and Arnold started working at a soup factory and at odd jobs to support himself and his eleven siblings. In 1930 he launched his professional BOXING career as a lightweight and took as his nickname the name of the well-known Barbadian welterweight champion Joe Walcott. Walcott's earnings in the lightweight and light-heavyweight classes was not enough to cover the family's living expenses, so from the mid-1930s to the mid-1940s he spent the majority of his time working and boxed only intermittently.

Walcott returned to boxing in 1945, and over the course of the next two years won eleven of fourteen bouts, seven by knockout. JOE LOUIS first defeated Walcott in a 1947 title bout and again in 1948 before Louis retired in 1949. Walcott lost two more title bouts to Ezzard Charles, one in 1949 and another in 1951. On June 15, 1952, in their third match, Walcott knocked Charles out in the seventh round. At age thirty-seven, he became the oldest man up to that point to win a heavyweight championship. He lost his heavyweight title to Rocky Marciano on September 23, 1952. Walcott attempted to reclaim the championship the following year, but he was knocked out in the first round and retired. He went on to serve as a Camden County (New Jersey) sheriff, athletic commissioner (New Jersey state), and then as a coordinator of youth programs. He died in Camden, New Jersey, in 1994.

See also Sports and African Americans.

Aaron Myers

Walker, Aaron ("T-Bone")

1910–1975

American blues guitarist, pioneer of the electric guitar, and a key figure in the creation of modern blues.

Aaron Thibeaux Walker was born in Linden, Texas. As a boy growing up in Dallas, Walker befriended blues legend BLIND LEMON JEFFERSON, holding his tin can and collecting his tips. In return, Jefferson taught him the basics of BLUES. In 1929 Walker recorded "Wichita Falls Blues" and "Trinity River Blues" under the name Oak Cliff T-Bone. The nickname "T-Bone" is a corruption of "Thibeaux." In the 1930s, in LOS ANGELES, CALIFORNIA Walker introduced an early form of the electric guitar into his music. His innovative rhythmic playing influenced almost every major blues and rock 'n roll guitarist after him, including B.B. KING, JIMI HENDRIX, and Otis Rush. Walker said that

"You've got to feel the blues to make them right . . . It's played from the heart and if the person listening, understands and is in the right mood, why, man, I've seen them bust out and cry like a baby." His signature songs include "T-Bone Shuffle" and "Call It Stormy Monday," which many consider to be the best blues song of all time.

Walker was also a first rate singer and master showman, often playing the guitar behind his back or between his legs. His career continued until the 1970s, when he suffered a stroke. Walker died of bronchial pneumonia in 1975.

See also Music, African American.

Walker, Aida Overton

1880–1914

Singer, dancer, actress, and choreographer who is regarded as the leading African American female performing artist at the turn of the twentieth century.

Aida Overton began her career as a teenage chorus member of "Black Patti's Troubadours." While performing in *Senegambian Carnival* (1899) she met GEORGE WALKER, and the two were married on June 22, 1899. After the marriage, Aida Walker worked as a choreographer for Williams and Walker, her husband's vaudevillian comedy duo. By presenting RAGTIME musicals with all black casts, Williams and Walker helped bring authentic black songs and dances to a form of entertainment that had been dominated by demeaning minstrel shows. Walker played the female lead in *The Policy Players* (1899), *Sons of Ham* (1900), *In Dahomey* (1902), *In Abyssinia* (1906), and *Bandanna Land* (1908). A command performance at Buckingham Palace in 1903 transformed Walker into an international star.

In 1908, George Walker became ill and could not continue in the run of *Bandanna Land*. Wearing her husband's male costumes, Aida Walker performed both his role and her own. After her husband's death in 1911, Walker's own career went into decline, although she was celebrated for her part in the spectacular *Salome* at Oscar Hammerstein's Victoria Theater in NEW YORK CITY. This was the last major performance of her career before her own death in 1914.

As one of the first international black stars, Aida Walker brought versatility to her performances and authenticity to ragtime songs and CAKEWALK dances. Her dancing and singing ability has been compared to and sometimes applauded over that of her successors FLORENCE MILLS and JOSEPHINE BAKER.

See also Minstrelsy; Musical Theater in the United States.

Bibliography

Fletcher, Tom. *One-Hundred Years of the Negro in Show Business*. Da Capo Press, 1984.

Aaron Myers

Walker, Alice

1944–

American writer, essayist, and poet, and Pulitzer Prize-winning author of *The Color Purple*.

In a passage from her 1983 essay collection *In Search of Our Mothers' Gardens: Womanist Prose*, Alice Walker reflects that "one thing I try to have in my life and in my fiction is an awareness of and openness to mystery, which, to me, is deeper than any politics, race, or geographical location." Born in Eatonton, Georgia, Walker was the youngest of eight children of share-cropping parents Wille Lee Walker and Minnie Tallulah (Grant) Walker. Her childhood was colored by an accident at age eight: she lost sight in one eye when an older brother shot her with a BB gun. Socially outcast as a result of her disfigured appearance, Walker became absorbed in books and began to write poetry while young.

Walker has said that while she was in high school, her mother gave her three important gifts: a sewing machine, which gave her the independence to make her own clothes; a suitcase, which gave her permission to leave home and travel; and a typewriter, which gave her permission to write. Walker graduated from high school as class valedictorian, and from 1961 to 1963 attended SPELMAN COLLEGE in ATLANTA on a scholarship. But when the "puritanical atmosphere" at Spelman became oppressive, Walker transferred to Sarah Lawrence College, where she completed a B.A. degree in 1965.

Walker then spent time in Georgia and Mississippi, where she registered voters, and in NEW YORK CITY, where she worked at the Welfare Department. She also married white human rights lawyer and activist Mel Leventhal in 1967, and in 1969 gave birth to their daughter, Rebecca. She was divorced in 1977. But through all this activity, Walker continued to write.

Walker published her first novel, *The Third Life of Grange Copeland*, in 1970 at age twenty-six. Two years later she published *In Love and Trouble*, a short story collection, and the poetry collection *Revolutionary Petunias and Other Poems*. In 1976 she published her second novel, *Meridian*. By this point, Walker was well established among the rising generation of black women writers. Her work is often praised for its portrayals of individuals and individual relationships, but it is also known for its depictions of the ways in which individuals can rely on their collective culture and cultural heritage to sustain them.

As Walker continued publishing her essays and poetry, she developed a second career as an educator. She has taught black studies and creative writing at Jackson State College, Tougaloo College, Wellesley College, and the University of Massachusetts at Boston; has served as a distinguished writer in African American studies at the University of California at Berkeley; and was named the Fannie Hurst Professor of Literature at Brandeis University. In 1983, however, she became internationally known as a writer with the publication of her third novel, *The Color Purple*.

The Color Purple portrays Celie, a rural black woman in an abusive marriage, as she struggles to find her self-worth. Told entirely in the form of letters—Celie's simple letters to God, her letters to her lost sister Nettie, and Nettie's letters to Celie—the powerful narrative won the 1983 Pulitzer Prize and established Walker as a major American novelist. In 1985 *The Color Purple* was made into a popular movie that was both praised for its portrayal of African American heroines and condemned as well for its portrayal of African American men. Walker reflected on the complicated issues surrounding the film's production in her essay collection *The Same River Twice: Honoring the Difficult* (1996).

One year after *The Color Purple* Walker published *In Search of Our Mothers' Gardens,* an influential essay collection that introduced the new term WOMANISM as a way of defining black women's feminism. In 1984 she cofounded Wild Tree Press in Novarro, California. In the following years, Walker's publications included the novels *The Temple of My Familiar* (1989) and *Possessing the Secret of Joy* (1992), another essay collection, several volumes of poetry, and a children's book. Her recent works include *A Poem Traveled Down My Arm: Poems and Drawings* (2003) and *Now Is the Time to Open Your Heart* (2004).

Walker's numerous honors and awards include a National Endowment for the Arts grant and fellowship, a Radcliffe Institute fellowship, an honorary Ph.D. from Russell Sage College, a National Book Award Nomination, a Guggenheim Award, and an O'Henry Award. She is highly in demand as a lecturer, and is not only a writer but also an outspoken liberal political activist. Walker's *Anything We Love Can Be Saved: A Writer's Activism* was published in 1997.

See also Literature, African American; Poetry, Black, in English; Women Writers, Black, in the United States.

Walker, David

1785?–1830

African American abolitionist, civil rights activist, and advocate of African independence, best known for the fiery pamphlet he wrote in 1829.

During the antebellum years, David Walker was prominent among a generation of politically outspoken free blacks that included FREDERICK DOUGLASS, MARTIN ROBISON DELANY, and the Reverend HENRY HIGHLAND GARNET. Walker, according to historian Sterling Stuckey, deserves recognition as "the father of black nationalist theory in America." His most lasting achievement was his 1829 pamphlet, *David Walker's Appeal . . . to the Colored Citizens of the World,* in which he called on African American slaves to revolt against their masters to gain their freedom.

The son of a white mother and a slave father, Walker was born free in Wilmington, North Carolina, taking the status of his mother as stipulated by North Carolina law. Little is known of his life before he moved to BOSTON in the late 1820s. In particular, it is not known how he learned to read and write. The antebellum South made scant provision for educating African Americans, whether slave or free. Yet before moving to the North, Walker had acquired an education that included a familiarity with Thomas Jefferson's *Notes on the State of Virginia* (1785). He also had ample opportunity to observe the evils of slavery firsthand.

In Boston, Walker started a used clothing business and quickly gained recognition in the local black community. Walker was evidently a natural leader. He was physically impressive: his wife Eliza described him as "prepossessing, being six feet in height, slender and well-proportioned. His hair was loose, and his complexion was dark." Walker played an active role in the Massachusetts General Colored Association, established in 1826, and was an agent for the first African American newspaper, FREEDOM'S JOURNAL (1827–1829).

In an 1828 address to the Massachusetts General Colored Association, Walker exhorted free blacks to improve their lot through mutual aid and self-help organizations. He roundly condemned the passivity of those who acquiesced in racial injustice. In September of the following year, Walker published his *Appeal*, which further extended his argument for black activism and solidarity. Rejecting Jefferson's contention in *Notes on the State of Virginia* that blacks were inherently inferior, Walker called upon African Americans to acquire copies of the book, in order to study and refute it. "[L]et no one of us suppose," he wrote, "that the refutations which have been written by our white friends are enough—they are *whites*—we are *blacks*." Besides advocating the violent overthrow of slavery and the formation of black civil rights and self-help organizations, the *Appeal* called for racial equality in the United States and independence for the peoples of Africa. As Stuckey observed, Walker was "the precursor of a long line of advocates of African freedom, extending all the way to PAUL ROBESON and MALCOLM X in our time."

To distribute his pamphlet, Walker relied on the mails and on seamen traveling to southern ports. Alarmed southern leaders responded by passing stricter laws against such "seditious" literature and against teaching free blacks to read or write. The Georgia state legislature went so far as to place a price on Walker's head: $10,000, if he were delivered alive, or $1,000, if dead. Walker encountered sharp criticism in the North as well, including from such white abolitionists as WILLIAM LLOYD GARRISON and Benjamin Lundy. In 1830, nine months after publishing his *Appeal*, Walker died under mysterious circumstances. Rumor held that he had been poisoned, but the charge was never verified. The complete text of *Walker's Appeal* appears in the Library of Black America.

See also Abolitionism in the United States; Black Nationalism in the United States.

James Sellman

Walker, Edward (Edwin) G(arrison)

1831?–1901

African American businessman, lawyer, legislator, and politician.

The only child of Eliza and DAVID WALKER, Edward Walker was born in BOSTON after his father's death. His mother, known as Miss Eliza, was probably a fugitive slave. His father was the author of the supposedly subversive *David Walker's Appeal . . . to the Colored Citizens of the World,* published in Boston in 1829. Walker's exact birth date is uncertain. An obituary, which called him Edwin, listed the date as September 28, 1835. However, since the father is said to have died in 1830, Edward must have been born in either 1830 or 1831.

Walker attended public schools in Boston and earned his living as a leather worker and owner of his own shop with as many as fifteen workers. The heritage of his father and the Boston abolition atmosphere led Walker to aid in the release of the slave Shadrach from capture in 1851. Among others in the party were well-known Boston abolitionists LEWIS HAYDEN and ROBERT MORRIS. Such an episode may have been the key to the fact that Walker later acquired a copy of *Blackstone's Commentaries* and while in the leather business began to read law. He devoured other law books, and he studied law in the offices of John Q. A. Griffin and Charles A. Tweed in Charlestown, a part of Boston. In May 1861, after easily passing his law examination, he became probably the third African American to be admitted to the Suffolk bar. A tall, dark man of imposing figure, he had strong argumentative skills and fine oratorical ability. Since his practice thrived, he gave up his leather business.

It was an easy step from law practice to politics, at first as a Republican. In 1866 Walker ran for a seat in the Massachusetts General Court legislature. When Democrats and the Republicans split in his electoral district, Walker surprisingly won a seat for a one-year term from Ward 3, despite the fact that there were only three black voters in the ward. Since the polls in Ward 3 closed a few hours earlier than did those in Ward 6, where Charles L. Mitchell was elected, Walker was probably the first black man elected to a state legislature in the United States. An independent thinker, Walker opposed the Republicans and was not nominated in 1867. He then became a Democrat and was said to have brought more blacks in Massachusetts into the DEMOCRATIC PARTY than any other black politician.

Meanwhile, his growing law practice made him one of the prominent lawyers in Boston. Many of Walker's clients were Irish, and he kept pictures of Irish resistance leaders in his office and was the only black member of their secret order. He saw in the Irish a lesson on how to rise in America through politics. Robert Morris and Walker were among the best-known and most successful black lawyers who served Irish clients.

Walker was a staunch follower and a defender of Massachusetts Congressman Benjamin F. Butler, both as a Republican and a Democrat. Walker took to the stump every time Butler ran for governor. In 1883, when Governor Butler nominated Walker for a judgeship, the Republicans in control of the approval machinery rejected Walker three times. The position went instead to George L. Ruffin, the first black graduate of the Harvard Law School and a loyal Republican. Walker remained bitter about this for the rest of his life. In 1885 and 1886 he and civil rights leader GEORGE T. DOWNING of Rhode Island helped start the black political independence movement in New England. In the 1890s Walker served as president of the Colored National League and in 1896 was proposed for president of the United States on a black party ticket. Walker died on January 13, 1901, a well-honored pioneer of Boston black attorneys.

From *Dictionary of American Negro Biography* by Rayford W. Logan and Michael R. Winston, editors. Copyright © 1982 by Rayford W. Logan and Michael R. Winston. Reprinted by permission of W. W. Norton & Company, Inc.

See also Abolitionism in the United States; Law and Legal Cases.

Clarence G. Contee Sr.

Walker, George

1873–1911

African American comedian, dancer, singer, actor, producer, and promoter.

Born in Lawrence, Kansas, George Walker left home at an early age to join a traveling medicine-man show that took him to California. On the road, Walker rattled bones, shook tambourines, mugged, and grinned to win laughs and applause. By the time he arrived in San Francisco, he disliked the traveling show and searched for theater work.

On a city sidewalk in San Francisco, the sprightly twenty-year-old entertainer, down on his luck, met another man who was in search of a partner for a new comedy routine. Neither knew anything about the other, yet they decided to cast their lots together, casually exchanging names. Without further fanfare, George Walker and BERT WILLIAMS embarked on one of the most successful and celebrated stage careers in the annals of American theatrical history, a partnership that endured for sixteen years. In recent years more attention has been paid to Bert Williams than to George Walker. But Walker was a remarkable figure in his own right. Williams tended to be withdrawn and melancholic. Walker, however, was all razzle-dazzle, a back-slapping extrovert, and it was his fiercely ambitious drive that helped get their act on the road.

They called themselves Walker and Williams at first, then they flipped a coin and changed the billing. In the beginning, their act failed; in the tough, frenetic honky-tonks and grease joints of San Francisco, they were ignored. On a tour through the South, they were booed and jeered. In 1895 they had their first big CHICAGO, ILLINOIS, engagement with John Isham's Octoroons, one of the first black companies that attempted to transcend the rigidity of minstrel-man humor and give its performers a chance to discover new forms of self-expression. Williams and Walker "bombed" their first week and were promptly fired.

After this string of setbacks, the two reworked some of their old material and changed roles, with Williams becoming the comic and Walker something of a flamboyant straight man. They billed themselves as Two Real Coons, so that audiences, accustomed to the old-style white minstrel performers who went in blackface and cruelly parodied and burlesqued the antics of blacks, might know they were seeing a new kind of genuine black humor. The billing change worked, and the two had their first bona fide success.

Shortly afterward, they made their New York debut in 1896 in *The Gold Bug*. The show failed, but a few months later the team was booked into Koster and Bial's Music Hall, then the city's most important vaudeville house. Shrewdly, the pair ended their act on a spectacular note. Dressed to kill, and ready for action with two lush "coppertone" beauties by their side, they threw themselves into an exuberant, uninhibited, high-stepping rendition of a dance long popular in the black community, the CAKEWALK. Audiences had never seen it done quite that way before, and soon the cakewalk as performed by Williams and Walker became the ultimate city sensation. White socialites were taking it up, and Williams and Walker, who had been booked into the music hall for one trial week, stayed on for forty weeks and became the rage of a craze-hungry nation.

In 1898 the two took over important roles in a musical by composer WILL MARION COOK and poet PAUL LAURENCE DUNBAR called *Clorindy, or The Origin of the Cake Walk*. The following year they appeared in *A Lucky Coon*, and in 1900, *The Policy Players*. By then, the two men had developed their own company of stock performers and situations. Eventually, with shows such as *Sons of Ham* in 1900, *In Dahomey* in 1902, and *In Abyssinia* and *Bandana Land*, both in 1908, they further extended black theater. *In Dahomey* emerged as a historic event, the first black show to open downtown in the heart of Manhattan's theater district, at the prestigious New York Theater. Onstage, too, another historic event took place. No longer were audiences seeing simply a skillful rehash of minstrel or medicine-man-show antics. Nor was there the crude disjointedness of typical vaudeville fare. Instead there was MUSICAL THEATER, with a fully developed plot and carefully defined characters, as well as music, comedy, and dance, all incorporated to flow with the mood of the script. American musical comedy was in its brilliant infancy, and two black performers with the first important all-black company had helped father it.

The comedy of Williams and Walker may appear to have been merely that of the city slicker in heated contest with the country bumpkin. Yet beneath the surface, something else was at work: the theme of survival. On one hand, the plots of *Sons of Ham* and *In Dahomey* reveal the black man—usually played by Walker—compelled to live by his wits and ingenuity. Walker

was always the wise guy who couldn't be told anything because he already knew it all. He was the flashy, outrageously extravagant dresser, the loudmouth dude at odds with the civilized world, the system, the almighty self-righteous Establishment itself. He was the black man of ambition forced into being a sharpster because, at heart, as the black audience surely knew, there was no other outlet for a black man so strongly aggressive and energetic. The plays never spelled out America's racism, but they didn't have to because the audience filled in the gaps in the scripts.

Yet curiously—and perhaps as an outgrowth of the Edwardian age of which it was a part—the comedy of Williams and Walker also had as its winners the simple ordinary black folks. The plot outlines maintain that virtue triumphs and deceit fails. However, black virtue was different from white virtue. The black winners were never simply innocents lent a helping hand by a kind fate. Generally they were realists dramatically aware of life's shady adversities. They used their mother wit to outslick the slicker. Many of the howling, hooting, hollering routines of Williams and Walker, in which absurdity was piled upon absurdity, looked dated later. Quite frankly, the humor was of the "coon" variety, where watermelon-stealing and chicken-eating caricatures of blacks were perpetuated by blacks themselves. Their work, wild and untempered, apparently struck a nerve and delighted white audiences, but also pleased black ones, too.

Generally, the planning, staging, and promoting were left to Walker. In the later productions, he vehemently sought to incorporate an African theme, although that theme was never fully thought out. He also fought with white producers reluctant to back a full-scale black extravaganza. For *In Dahomey* he got a budget of $15,000, an almost unheard-of amount then. Later, the show made four times that amount. Afterward, his ambition growing, Walker pushed for a $30,000 budget for *In Abyssinia*. He envisioned an elaborate, "totally African" production with live tigers and giraffes, a mountain pass with a real waterfall, and a cast of 125 performers. He was turned down repeatedly. During negotiations, Williams was ready to give in to the producers' cutbacks, but Walker tirelessly muscled his way ahead. In the end he had to settle for some compromises, including mere live camels instead of the tigers and giraffes. More importantly, though, he got his waterfall—and his $30,000 budget. The show was a hit.

Onstage, Walker was an expert dancer and a charismatic singing comedian who popularized the song "Bon Bon Buddy" in 1908. Offstage his life was a further exercise in showmanship and a celebration of his own stardom. In 1899 he married talented showgirl Aida Overton, but the marriage did little to change his private life. An inveterate clotheshorse given to the latest fads, he was said to have spent more time at his tailor's than at home. He continued frequenting the bars, cafés, and nightspots where he was surrounded by adoring fans. His love affairs were reportedly numerous.

Walker's last stage appearance before a lingering and painful death from syphilis in 1911 was in *Bandana Land*. After that, the company fell apart. Unfortunately, no one, not even Bert

Williams, who was to go on to a spectacular career alone, seemed possessed with the stamina and administrative industriousness to keep such a big troupe going.

The comedy of the two, as well as the kind of showmanship and promotion Walker was so fond of, had an incalculable influence on American entertainment. The team's distinct brand of comedy was the precursor of Broadway shows such as *Shuffle Along* in 1921, *The Chocolate Dandies* in 1924, *Don't Play Us Cheap* in 1970, and later *The Wiz* and *Bubblin' Brown Sugar*, both in 1975. That brand of comedy was the forerunner of movies such as *Stormy Weather* in 1936, *Cabin in the Sky* in 1943, *Let's Do It Again* in 1953, and *Uptown Saturday Night* in 1974. Walker's career is described in Donald Bogle's *Toms, Coons, Mulattoes, Mammies and Bucks, An Interpretive History of Blacks in Films* (1973). There are also valuable comments in James Weldon Johnson's *Black Manhattan* (1940).

From *Dictionary of American Negro Biography* by Rayford W. Logan and Michael R. Winston, editors. Copyright © 1982 by Rayford W. Logan and Michael R. Winston. Reprinted by permission of W. W. Norton & Company, Inc.

See also Minstrelsy; Walker, Aida Overton.

Donald Bogle

Walker, James Edward

1874–1918

African American teacher, school administrator, and army officer.

James Walker was born in Albermarle County, Virginia, one of two children of former slaves Peter and Lucy Ella Walker. About 1881 the family moved to WASHINGTON, D.C. , where James's father obtained employment. This enabled James to attend the Preparatory High School for Colored Youth (renamed the M Street High School in 1891). Completing the requirements at M Street in 1893, he graduated a year later from Miner Normal School and began teaching in Division Thirteen of the Washington public school system. As teacher, principal of the Syphax and Banneker schools, and supervising principal of the division, Walker spent twenty-four years in the public schools. In 1906 he married Beatrice Louise Johnson, who had attended the same schools and also taught at the Banneker School.

Walker is best known for his service in the army. Originally enlisted as a noncommissioned staff officer, he was commissioned a first lieutenant on May 1, 1896, in the First Separate Battalion, District of Columbia National Guards, and assigned the duties of adjutant. He was promoted to captain in 1909. Three years layer he succeeded Major ARTHUR BROOKS as major and commanding officer of the battalion. Walker was in command when the battalion was mustered into federal service in 1916 and sent to guard waterworks near Naco, Arizona, during the Mexican Border Campaign. He also served as an intelligence officer. After engaging in several field exercises, the battalion returned to Fort Myer, Virginia, and was mustered out of service on October 23, 1916.

When the United States entered WORLD WAR I in 1917, U.S. president Woodrow Wilson and Secretary of War Newton D. Baker reactivated the First Separate to guard government facilities and structures in and around Washington. In the summer and fall of 1917, the First Separate also guarded railroads and bridges east of Harpers Ferry, West Virginia. On January 1, 1918, the First Separate became the first battalion of the 372nd Infantry Regiment organized at Camp Stuart, Newport News, Virginia. The regiment was on the high seas when it learned that Walker had died at Fort Bayard, New Mexico, of tuberculosis on April 4, 1918. He was buried in Arlington National Cemetery.

Like Major Arthur Brooks, Walker inspired many young men to seek a military career. A notable example was Arthur C. Newman, who had married Walker's sister-in-law. Newman served as a captain in World War I and later commanded the First Separate Battalion. Among the many posthumous tributes accorded to Walker, American Legion Post 26 was named in his honor. In 1938 the Board of Education renamed the Benjamin Banneker Elementary School, located at Third and K Streets NW, the James E. Walker School "because of his educational and patriotic contributions to his community and nation." A new school, Walker-Jones, at First and K Streets NW, also perpetuates his memory.

From *Dictionary of American Negro Biography* by Rayford W. Logan and Michael R. Winston, editors. Copyright © 1982 by Rayford W. Logan and Michael R. Winston. Reprinted by permission of W. W. Norton & Company, Inc.

See also Military, Blacks in the American.

Charles Johnson Jr.

Walker, Kara

1969–

American artist who questions stereotypical images of race and identity through the use of a nineteenth-century method of portraiture.

Born in Stockton, California, Kara Walker studied at the Atlanta College of Art, where she received a BFA degree. She continued her studies at the Rhode Island School of Design in Providence, where in 1994 she received an MFA degree. Walker works primarily in figurative, cutout silhouettes, a cheap, rapid method of portraiture popular in the nineteenth century. Her work features figures, black and white, engaged in a variety of activities of a sexual or violent nature. Framing these images in the "theater" of the CIVIL WAR, she creates narratives of the disturbing sides of themes such as romance, and the pleasurable or powerful sides of themes such as war, genocide, and shame. "The nigger wench," she said of a recurring caricature in her work, "is the body that I sort of inhabited accidentally . . . that somebody else placed over me at some point." In exposing stereotypical images of the past in an ironic and playful way Walker deals with issues of race and identity in a controversial manner that confounds traditional dichotomies of black and white, male and female, dominant and submissive, young and old, and North and South.

Walker's work has been exhibited throughout the U.S. and Europe in both group and solo exhibitions. In 1997, she had a solo exhibition at both the San Francisco Museum of Modern Art and the Renaissance Society in CHICAGO. She has participated in several group shows, including *New Histories* at the Institute of Contemporary Art in BOSTON (1996), *La Belle et la Bête* at the Musée d'Art Moderne de la Ville de Paris (1995), and the Whitney Museum of American Art Biennial (1997). In 1997, she was named a recipient of a prestigious "genius grant" from the MacArthur Foundation. Walker was the U.S. representative to the 2002 São Paolo Bienal in BRAZIL. She currently resides in NEW YORK CITY, where she teaches in the MFA program at Columbia University.

See also Art, African American; Artists, African American; Race: An Interpretation; Racial Stereotypes.

Bibliography

Gangitano, Lia, and Steven Nelson, eds. *New Histories*. Institute of Contemporary Art, 1996.

Walker, Maggie Lena

1867–1934

American businesswoman, clubwoman, newspaper founder, lecturer, feminist, and first African American female bank president.

For Maggie Lena Walker, who rose from humble beginnings to become the first black woman bank president, the future of the race was dependent upon the education and advancement of black women. In her words, she was "not born with a silver spoon in mouth: but, instead, with a clothes basket almost upon my head." Former slaves, Walker's mother, Elizabeth (Draper), was a cook's helper and her father, William Mitchell, was the family butler in the Van Lew mansion in RICHMOND, VIRGINIA. After her father was found floating in the James River, apparently murdered, Maggie Walker assumed multiple responsibilities as delivery person and babysitter while she kept up with her studies, church attendance, and public service.

Educated in segregated public schools in Richmond, Walker finished at the head of her class in 1883. After graduation, she taught for three years at the Lancaster school while she took classes in accounting and business management. In 1886, she married Arstead Walker, an active member of her church, with whom she had two children, Russell and Melvin DeWitt. She then turned from teaching to community organizing.

In ten years, Walker ascended the ranks of the Independent Order of St. Luke, a mutual benefit society she had served since her teens, moving from executive secretary to grand secretary-treasurer, a position she held for thirty-five years. In 1903, she founded the St. Luke Penny Savings Bank, which became the St. Luke Bank and Trust Company. During the GREAT DEPRESSION, the institution absorbed other black banks to become the Consolidated Bank and Trust Company, with Walker as the board chair. Today, the Company is the oldest continually black-owned and black-run bank in the nation.

See also Business and African Americans; Mutual Benefit Societies.

Walker, Margaret

1915–1998

Poet, novelist, university teacher, and the first African American woman to win a prestigious literary prize.

Born in BIRMINGHAM, ALABAMA, Margaret Walker began writing poems at age eleven. Poet LANGSTON HUGHES read her POETRY when she was sixteen and persuaded her parents to take her out of the South so she could "develop into a writer." She matriculated at Northwestern University, where she was influenced by writer W. E. B. DU BOIS and graduated in 1935. Walker left CHICAGO in 1939 to enter the creative writing program at the University of Iowa. There she published in 1942 a collection of poems, *For My People,* which won the prestigious Yale Younger Poets award. The book's poems, like her work as a whole, display a pride in her African American heritage and interweave autobiographical elements with larger themes of black history. She also wrote an historical novel, *Jubilee,* not completed until 1966, which was based on the life of her grandmother, who lived during the CIVIL WAR (1861–1865). It is one of the first modern novels about slavery told from an African American perspective.

Walker published over ten books, including poems, essays, and short stories. Among these are her *Ballad of the Free* (1966), *Prophets for a New Day* (1970), and *October Journey* (1973). In the 1960s she received her Ph.D. from Iowa and began teaching creative writing at Jackson State College in Mississippi, where she retired in 1979. The books she published since then include a biography of African American novelist RICHARD WRIGHT, a volume of poetry that includes old and new works, and her first essay collection.

See also Literature, African American.

Walker, Sarah ("Madame C. J.")

1867–1919

American entrepreneur who developed special hair care products and techniques for black women.

Sarah Walker was born in Delta, Louisiana, to indigent former slaves Owen and Minerva Breedlove. She grew up in poverty on the Burney plantation in Delta, working in the cotton fields from sunrise to sunset. Uneducated in her youth, she learned as an adult to read and write. At fourteen, she married Moses McWilliams who was reportedly killed by a white lynch mob two years after their daughter A'Lelia's birth in 1885.

Walker worked as a domestic until she took several risks as an entrepreneur in black woman's hair care products. To meet the needs of women who did not have running water, supplies, or equipment, Walker created a hot comb with specially spaced teeth to soften or straighten black hair, as well as her Wonderful Hair Grower for women who had experienced hair loss through improper care. Business differences ended her marriage to C. J. Walker, a newspaperman whose advertising and mail order knowledge contributed to the business.

Walker was the first woman to sell products via mail order, to organize a nationwide membership of door-to-door agents, The Madame C. J. Walker Hair Culturists Union of America, as well as to open her own beauty school, the Walker College of Hair Culture. She and her daughter A'Lelia established a chain of beauty parlors throughout the U.S., the Caribbean, and South America. By 1914, company earnings grossed over a million dollars.

In addition to her substantial contributions to black women's education, Walker owned a house in HARLEM, dubbed the "Dark Tower," and Villa Lewaro, a neo-Palladian-style, thirty-four-room mansion designed by Vetner Woodson Tandy, the first registered black architect. Walker's homes were frequented by HARLEM RENAISSANCE notables after her death in 1919, when her daughter took over the business. Walker's empire, in keeping with her wishes, has since been exclusively managed only by her female descendants. In 1976, Villa Lewaro was listed on the National Register of Historic Places.

See also Business and African Americans; Hair and Beauty Culture.

Walker, Wyatt Tee

1929–

American minister and chief strategist for the Southern Christian Leadership Conference during the Civil Rights Movement.

Born in Brockton, Massachusetts, Wyatt Tee Walker left a ministerial post in Petersburg, Virginia, in 1960 to become executive director of the SOUTHERN CHRISTIAN LEADERSHIP CONFERENCE (SCLC). He proved an excellent tactician, authoring protest strategies that included the BIRMINGHAM campaign of April 1963. Walker left the SCLC in 1964, settled in NEW YORK CITY, and continued to work for social justice. An expert on GOSPEL MUSIC, he wrote *Somebody's Calling my Name: Black Sacred Music and Social Change* (1979). He has been the pastor of Canaan Baptist Church of Christ in HARLEM since 1967.

See also Civil Rights Movement.

Robert Fay

Wallace, Christopher

See Notorious B.I.G. ("Biggie Smalls").

Wallace, Sippie

1898–1986

American blues singer famous for her spirited, hard-edged singing.

Born Beulah Belle Thomas, one of thirteen children, Sippie Wallace was first exposed to music through her father's Shiloh Baptist Church. As a child she received the nickname "Sippie" either because of her habit of sipping or a lisp. After singing for several years in Texas and NEW ORLEANS, Wallace moved with her brothers in 1923 to CHICAGO where she quickly became a BLUES star with songs like "Up the Country Blues" and "Shorty George." Her singing was a combination of the Chicago blues tradition and her Texas-style blues background, which had a rougher singing style and often racier lyrics. Other well-known songs she recorded include "Special Delivery Blues" (1926), "I'm a Mighty Tight Woman," (1920) and, with LOUIS ARMSTRONG, "Dead Drunk Blues" (1927).

Wallace moved to DETROIT in 1929, and her reputation as a recording star began to wane. Until the 1970s she was the organist at the Leland Baptist Church in Detroit. Longtime friend and blues singer VICTORIA SPIVEY persuaded her in 1966 to come out of retirement. Although she suffered a stroke in 1970, she continued her new recording career. Musician Bonnie Raitt, whom Wallace heavily influenced, helped sign her to a contract with Atlantic Records in 1982. Her 1983 album *Sippie*, featuring Raitt on guitar, won the W. C. HANDY Award for the best blues album of the year.

See also Music, African American.

Waller, John Louis

1853–1907

African American politician and foreign service officer.

John Louis Waller was born in New Madrid County, Missouri, the son of Anthony Waller and Maria (maiden name unknown), household slaves of Marcus S. Sherwood. Early in the CIVIL WAR, Union troops relocated Waller's family to Inka, Iowa, where his father was able to acquire a small farm. However, they lived in such poverty that his father hired John out to a local farmer at the age of twelve to help support the family. To John's good fortune, his employer encouraged literacy and allowed him to begin formal education in a rural schoolhouse in 1863. With the aid of citizens in nearby Toledo, Iowa, he was then able to gain admission to the local high school in 1867, graduating around 1870. At about this time he began to support himself by working as a barber, a trade he was also to pursue intermittently in later years when necessary. He married Amelia Lewis (date unknown); they divorced in 1876. He enrolled at Cornell College in Mount Vernon, Iowa, in 1871 but had to abandon his studies again to help his family. In 1874 Waller began legal studies through the encouragement of Judge N. M. Hubbard of Cedar Rapids, who gave him free access to his personal library. In 1877 Waller was admitted to the Iowa bar and in 1878 to the Kansas bar, among the first of his race in both instances.

Seeking to assume leadership of the blacks who were then migrating to Kansas from the South in what was called the great exodus of 1879 to 1892, Waller spent the next decade in Leavenworth, Lawrence, Topeka, and Kansas City, Kansas. He practiced law when the rare clients for a black lawyer appeared, became active in politics, and published two newspapers that promoted the cause of civil rights for blacks and furthered colonization schemes for frontier areas in Kansas, Oklahoma, Nebraska, and other western states. In 1879 Waller married Susan T. D. Bray, a widow with two children; they had four more children. In 1882 he and his wife began publishing a weekly newspaper, the *Western Recorder*, which lasted almost three years. His second newspaper venture was the *American Citizen*, launched in 1888 in Topeka with his cousin Anthony Morton and his brother L. J. Waller, who was managing editor.

Aware of the access to privilege that the REPUBLICAN PARTY afforded selected blacks in this era, by 1880 Waller became a member of the Douglas County Republican central committee and of the Kansas state central committee. In 1883 he was elected to the Lawrence Board of Education. In the late 1880s he became a noted orator and a leading Republican campaigner, helping to ensure that the black vote, numbering some 10,000 at the time, would remain behind Republican candidates. As additional rewards, he was elected assistant sergeant at arms in the state house of representatives in 1887, was chosen as a Republican elector for Kansas in 1888, and was chosen as deputy county attorney in Topeka, Kansas, in 1889. However, his unsuccessful bid for election as state auditor at the Republican convention in 1890 convinced him that his prospects for further political advancement in the state were doubtful. He sold his interest in the *American Citizen* and concentrated his ambitions abroad.

At the time of his application to President Benjamin Harrison (1833–1901) for a Foreign Service consular post in 1889, Waller was supported by all the state's leading Republican organizations, the governor, and the Republican congressmen. Despite this, he failed to obtain one of the more prestigious posts. He was appointed instead as consul to Tamatave, MADAGASCAR, where he served from February 1891 to January 1894. Remaining there afterward, he became embroiled in a bizarre international incident that resulted in his suffering eleven months of solitary confinement in a French prison. The French government, which was in the process of seizing control of Madagascar from 1894 to 1896, charged Waller through its military court of violating French postal regulations and transmitting military intelligence to the Malagasy through one of his letters to his wife that detailed the conduct of the French forces

as they took the island. His trial resulted in a sentence of twenty years of solitary confinement, for which he was transported to FRANCE.

The underlying purpose of France's action against Waller appears to have been to establish a basis for refusing to recognize a large land concession he had gained through close ties he had established with the reigning Malagasy government during his service. Waller had planned to exploit the 225 square miles he claimed, worth millions in rubber, mahogany, teak, and agricultural products, by leasing it out to establish an African American colony. The French invasion, however, discouraged potential investors. Among the attorneys who worked for Waller's release was the famous black educator and diplomat JOHN M. LANGSTON. Waller's release came only after resolutions from both houses of the U.S. Congress and vigorous activity on the part of the State Department. A condition of Waller's release from prison was that the U.S. government would not pursue his claims for any type of redress. His subsequent private appeals to the French government proved fruitless.

Returning to Kansas, Waller resumed his law practice and involvement in politics and also served as editor in chief of the *American Citizen* in 1896 and 1897. Responding to the SPANISH-AMERICAN WAR, in 1898 he helped organize Company C of the Twenty-third Kansas Volunteer Infantry Regiment, of which he was elected captain. He commanded it through its training and service in CUBA in 1898. After receiving an honorable discharge in 1899 in the United States, he returned to Cuba briefly to investigate its potential for his resettlement ideas. In July 1899 he published a letter through the Associated Press calling for emigration of three million blacks from the southern United States to Cuba, PUERTO RICO, and the Philippines. For this purpose he proposed that Congress appropriate $20 million to be repaid through duties on exports once the emigrants were settled and productive. Later the same year he announced formation of the Afro-American Cuban Emigration Society. Waller viewed emigration as the best solution to the racial problem in the United States and the best access to economic prosperity for African Americans. Without emigration of part of the black population to alleviate white fears of being overwhelmed, he wrote, blacks would either be annihilated as the American Indians had or become amalgamated with whites, which he believed unfeasible. After all of his emigration projects failed, the repeated frustration of his own ambitions, and the lack of recognition of the contribution of black troops in the Spanish-American War, Waller became disillusioned with the Republican party and supported the DEMOCRAT William Jennings Bryan in 1900. Waller died of pneumonia in Mamaroneck, New York.

A fair assessment of Waller's career should fall somewhere between the extremes that appeared in the press at the height of his notoriety in 1896. The *New York Times*, in a lengthy editorial of February 22 roundly criticizing the appointment of black politicians to consular posts, concluded that Waller was a good illustration that "of American negroes, the better class are not seeking or accepting offices." In contrast, noting earlier praise of his journalism in the *London Times* and *London*

Daily Telegraph, his own *American Citizen* in its June 26 issue called him "the greatest living Afro-American." What Waller's manifold career best demonstrates is the breadth of the scope of activities attempted by enterprising black intellectuals of his day and the strictures racism placed on their achievements.

Bibliography

A collection of documents concerning Waller is included in U.S. State Department, Foreign Relations of the United States 1895, pt. 1, pp. 251–396, and in "Case of John Waller," House Document No. 225, 94th Congress, 1st session, 1895–1896, series no. 3425.

Woods, Randall Bennett. *A Black Odyssey: John Lewis Waller and the Promise of American Life, 1878–1900.* 1981.

From *American National Biography.* John A. Garraty and Mark C. Carnes, eds. Oxford University Press, 1999. Reprinted by permission of the American Council of Learned Societies.

Allison Blakely

Waller, Odell

1917?–1942

American sharecropper whose conviction on murder charges symbolized the struggle to desegregate juries in the South.

In July 1940 Odell Waller, an uneducated sharecropper, shot and killed his white landlord, Oscar Davis, in a dispute over the shares Davis owed to him. Waller claimed self-defense, but the all-white jury found him guilty of first-degree murder and sentenced him to death. Waller's defense attorneys argued that Waller did not receive a fair trial because sharecroppers did not pay the poll tax and were thus excluded from jury service. Although several civil rights organizations appealed Waller's conviction for more than two years, he was executed July 2, 1942.

See also Law and Legal Cases.

Bibliography

Sherman, Richard B. *The Case of Odell Waller and Virginia Justice, 1940–1942.* University of Tennessee Press, 1992.

Robert Fay

Waller, Thomas Wright ("Fats")

1904–1943

American jazz pianist, vocalist, organist, and composer whose combination of musical sophistication and lyrical humor made him one of the most popular entertainers of his day.

Fats Waller, born Thomas Wright Waller, was born and raised in NEW YORK CITY where his father was a Baptist minister. As a boy, he charmed his classmates with animated facial gestures while playing piano at school talent shows. During his teenage years, he played the organ at various HARLEM theaters to accompany silent films. In 1920, the year he left home, he married Edith Hatchett. They divorced three years later, and in 1926, Waller married Anita Rutherford.

Having learned the fundamentals of piano in his childhood, Waller later studied stride piano under Russell Brooks and James P. Johnson. In the 1920s, Waller played at Harlem rent parties and nightclubs and composed music for shows and revues. He collaborated with songwriter Andy Razaf to produce some of his best-known numbers: "Honeysuckle Rose" (1928), "(What Did I Do to Be So) Black and Blue" (1929), and "Ain't Misbehavin'" (1929). During the 1930s, Waller toured the United States and Europe with his own band, appeared on radio broadcasts and in Hollywood films, and recorded hundreds of songs on the Victor label.

On April 27, 1928, Waller became the first JAZZ soloist to perform at Carnegie Hall. He is also credited with being the first musician to record jazz music on a pipe organ. *Ain't Misbehavin',* a tribute to Fats Waller, was voted best Broadway musical in 1978.

See also Music, African American; Singer-Songwriters.

Aaron Myers

Wall of Respect, The

Street mural on the South Side of Chicago, Illinois, depicting numerous black heroes; considered the founding work of the black mural movement.

In 1967, at the beginning of the BLACK POWER MOVEMENT, painter William Walker assembled a group of some twenty African American artists to execute a mural celebrating prominent figures in black history. Most of these artists were members of a Chicago-based organization called the Visual Arts Workshop of OBAC (Organization of Black American Culture). Together, these artists planned the mural's design and raised the money needed to finance the project. They decided to paint the mural on the side of a two-story, boarded-up tenement building at the intersection of 43rd Street and Langley Avenue. Once a thriving part of the city, this predominantly black area of CHICAGO had deteriorated into a slum. The mural itself is a patchwork of famous black Americans, including MUHAMMAD ALI, GWENDOLYN ELIZABETH BROOKS, and CHARLIE PARKER.

The artists' objective in painting the *Wall of Respect* was to lift the local black community's morale through highly visible, dignified images of famous black Americans. The response was overwhelmingly positive. People arrived from miles around to view the mural, and the publicity it generated led to the construction of a human resources center in the impoverished neighborhood. Furthermore, the *Wall of Respect* sparked a national black mural movement in which inner-city African American artists began to embellish their neighborhoods with positive black imagery. This movement was ideologically linked to the contemporary Black Power Movement in that it sought to challenge the white-supremacist social order, and aesthetically linked to the mural traditions of post-revolutionary Mexico and Depression-era America in that its artists portrayed historical figures in a social realist vein.

Shortly after completing the *Wall of Respect,* the artists who comprised the Visual Arts Workshop of OBAC broke up. Many of the artists went on to found AfriCOBRA (African Commune of Bad Relevant Artists) in 1968. Although a fire destroyed the *Wall of Respect* in 1971, AfriCOBRA has continued to produce public works of art meant to liberate and uplift the black community.

See also Black Power in the United States; Chicago, Illinois.

Aaron Myers

Walls, Josiah T(homas)

1842–1905

African American congressman during Reconstruction.

Josiah Thomas Walls was born near Winchester, Virginia. His parents' names are unknown and Walls's public statements regarding his parents' status during slavery are contradictory. Quite possibly he was born the slave of Dr. John Walls, a Winchester physician, but his dark skin casts doubt on the premise that Dr. Walls was also his father.

In 1861 Josiah Walls was kidnapped by Confederate artillerymen and put to work as a servant. He was freed by Union troops during the battle of Yorktown in May 1862 and sent to Harrisburg, Pennsylvania, where he attended school for a year, his only known formal education. In July 1863 he enlisted in the Third Infantry Regiment, U.S. Colored Troops (USCT), and took part in that unit's siege of Batteries Wagner and Gregg near CHARLESTON, SOUTH CAROLINA. After their fall, his unit was stationed in northern Florida. In June 1864 Walls was transferred to the Thirty-fifth Regiment, USCT, in Picolata, Florida, where he served as a first sergeant and instructor of artillery.

When Walls left the army in October 1865, he settled in nearby Alachua County, finding work first as a lumberer and later as a teacher at the Freedmen's Bureau School in Archer. In 1868 he bought an eighty-acre farm in Newnansville. In 1873 Walls embarked on three business ventures. He bought at a low price a former cotton plantation of almost 1,200 acres that had been confiscated from a Confederate general, on which he began raising oranges and tomatoes; he was admitted to the Florida bar (legal training was not a prerequisite for admission in this frontier state) and, with two other black lawyers, opened a law firm in Gainesville; and he purchased the Gainesville *New Era.* In his first editorial, Walls promised to promote "every legitimate and judicious effort to develop the resources of the

county" and that the "wants and needs of the people of color will receive special attention."

Walls's political career began in 1867, when he attended the state REPUBLICAN convention as a delegate. In 1868 he served as delegate to the state constitutional convention and was elected to the lower house of the Florida legislature. The next year he was one of five freedmen elected to the 24-member state senate. In 1870 he was elected to the state's lone seat in the U.S. House of Representatives in spite of the removal of voting restrictions from most whites and the intimidation tactics employed by white terrorists to keep blacks from the polls. His white Conservative party opponent contested the results of this election and eventually was declared the winner by a slender margin, but not before Walls had served in the House for almost two years. In 1872 Walls was renominated and returned to WASHINGTON, and during the 1873 recess he served as mayor of Gainesville. He was reelected to Congress in 1874 and served for over a year before the results of this election also were overturned in April 1876. Denied his party's nomination that year by Republicans eager to gain support from white voters, Walls successfully ran for state senator, a position he held until his retirement from public life in 1879. He then returned to his farm in Alachua County, which by now included more than 1,500 acres and a sawmill. He attempted two political comebacks—first in 1884 when he ran for Congress as an independent and then in 1890 when he ran for state senator—but was decisively defeated both times. Despite these defeats, he continued to play a major part in state and local politics through his activities on the Alachua County Commission and School Board as well as important posts on county and state GOP executive committees. He also served as a brigadier general in the Florida militia.

Walls was one of only fourteen blacks to serve in the House during RECONSTRUCTION. He was not a gifted orator and usually read his speeches from a prepared text. He made up for his lack of eloquence by working ceaselessly for the interests of his constituents. He introduced bills to fund the construction of a railroad from the Georgia border to Key West and to improve Florida's rivers and harbors. He also sponsored acts to build customhouses, courthouses, and post offices and to create seven new postal routes in Florida; to protect the state's infant fruit industry from foreign imports in the tariff of 1872; and to secure a land grant for a state agricultural college.

Walls spoke out persuasively in favor of a national education fund financed by the sale of federal public lands to augment state-supported public education, because he believed that "education is the panacea for all our social evils, injustices, and oppressions." By improving public education in the South, Walls hoped to provide black children with the means of advancement while providing poor white children with opportunities to overcome nascent racial prejudice. He was particularly criticized by some of his supporters when he introduced a bill to lift the FOURTEENTH AMENDMENT's restrictions on former prominent Florida Confederates (despite that the bill was a quid pro quo rider to a civil rights bill) and again when he appointed to the Naval Academy the son of an ex-governor who was outspokenly opposed to black participation in politics and government. These moves, however, were consistent with his decision to "secure equal civil and political rights to all" and should not be interpreted as an attempt by Walls to curry white favor. He incurred the wrath of many white Republicans when at a southern black convention in 1871 he called on the GOP to nominate JOHN MERCER LANGSTON, the black orator and political leader, for vice president in 1872.

Walls was married twice. In 1864, while stationed at Picolata, he married Helen Fergueson, with whom he had his only child. When Helen Walls died in 1885, he married her cousin Ella Angeline Gass. After a frost ruined his crops in 1895, Walls moved to Tallahassee, where he became director of the farm at Florida Normal College, a position he held until his death there.

Walls was a political pragmatist who believed that whites and blacks must share power, and he worked for this ideal on the national, state, and local levels. Much of his political success can be attributed to the conciliatory stance he took toward white involvement in Reconstruction government, while at the same time quietly insisting on a major role in that government for blacks.

Bibliography

Klingman, Peter D. Josiah. *Walls: Florida's Black Congressman of Reconstruction.* 1976.

Richardson, Joe M. *The Negro in the Reconstruction of Florida, 1865–1877.* 1965.

From *American National Biography.* John A. Garraty and Mark C. Carnes, eds. Oxford University Press, 1999. Reprinted by permission of the American Council of Learned Societies.

Charles W. Carey, Jr.

Walrond, Eric Derwent

1898–1966

Writer hailed in the 1920s as one of the most promising young novelists of the Harlem Renaissance.

Eric Walrond was born in British Guyana but was taken by his mother to the Panama Canal Zone to search for his father, who had abandoned them. Though unsuccessful in their search, they settled there in 1910. After writing as a reporter for the *Panama Star* for two years, Walrond emigrated to NEW YORK in 1918. He attended the College of the City of New York, and became an associate editor of MARCUS MOZIAH GARVEY's *The Negro World.* He eventually broke with Garvey, critical of his "fondness for pageantry," and become one of his leading African American critics. After leaving Garvey, he became business manager for the magazine OPPORTUNITY.

While with *Opportunity,* Walrond published his only book, *Tropic Death* (1926). It did not sell well, but was acclaimed by such critics as W. E. B. Du BOIS and LANGSTON HUGHES. *Tropic Death* is a collection of ten stories which take place in BARBA-DOS, the Canal Zone, and British Guiana. The work was praised for its impressionistic depiction of the physical suffering and racism African Americans encounter in the imperial setting of the tropics. It vividly recreates the day-to-day reality of African Americans in part by incorporating native dialects into its prose.

Walrond received a Guggenheim Fellowship in 1928 and became a Zona Gale scholar at the University of Wisconsin. Later that year he moved to Europe where he eventually reconciled with and wrote for Garvey. Though his work garnered much attention during the HARLEM RENAISSANCE, Walrond's literary output diminished in the 1930s and stopped altogether in 1940.

See also Guyana; Panama.

Walters, Alexander

1858–1917

African Methodist Episcopal Zion Church leader and early-twentieth-century civil rights advocate.

Alexander Walters was born into a slave family, the sixth of eight children. Displaying academic promise, he was awarded a scholarship by the AFRICAN METHODIST EPISCOPAL ZION CHURCH (AMEZ) to attend private school in 1868. Receiving his license to preach in 1877, he began his pastoral duties in Indianapolis, Indiana. He went on to serve as pastor in Louisville, San Francisco, Portland, Oregon, Chattanooga and Knoxville, Tennessee. After taking a church in NEW YORK, NEW YORK, he continued as a minister until he was consecrated in 1892 as bishop at the Seventh District of the African Methodist Episcopal Zion Church.

Walters's contribution to civil rights activism began in 1898, when he and T. Thomas Fortune, the editor of the *New York Age,* founded the National Afro-American Council. As president of this council, Walters focused on several issues at the heart of current politics: battling the *PLESSY V. FERGUSON* "separate but equal" Supreme Court ruling of 1896, opposing Bishop HENRY McNEAL TURNER's call for blacks to return to Africa, and challenging BOOKER TALIAFERRO WASHINGTON's ideas of accommodation to segregation and discrimination. A conflict in 1902 with Fortune over Washington's views resulted in Walters's removal as president of the council.

In 1908, Walters joined activist W. E. B. Du BOIS's NIAGARA MOVEMENT, from which he helped organize the founding conference of the NATIONAL ASSOCIATION FOR THE ADVANCEMENT OF COLORED PEOPLE (NAACP). He became vice president of this organization in 1911. With Walters's leadership of AMEZ churches and education programs in West Africa, he felt compelled to encourage the American government to increase economic support in Africa. In 1915, President Woodrow Wilson offered Walters a post as minister to LIBERIA, which he declined in order to continue organizing AMEZ Church education programs in the United States and internationally. Walters maintained this involvement in AMEZ Church affairs until his death in 1917.

Walvis Bay, Namibia

Important port of Namibia.

In the mid-fifteenth century, when Europeans first entered what is today known as Walvis Bay, they found it teeming with a variety of fish and whales. It is very likely that at this time KHOIKHOI and Topnaar Nama peoples were already living in the area. During the next 300 years, the bounty of Walvis Bay—which means "Bay of Whales" in Afrikaans—attracted hundreds of whalers. In 1793 the Dutch claimed sovereignty over the region, but lost it two years later to the British. Throughout the nineteenth century, European missionaries, fishermen, and traders landed at the bay, and the latter group eventually established an overland route from it to the settlement of WINDHOEK.

In 1878 Britain made the first permanent claim of sovereignty over Walvis Bay, a claim transferred to the Cape government of South Africa six years later. SOUTH AFRICA held on to the bay even between 1884 and 1915, when GERMANY controlled the surrounding territory of SOUTH-WEST AFRICA. In the 1940s, after the bay's whales were hunted to extinction, the fishing industry switched to pilchard and mackerel, and South Africa invested in improved port facilities. As South-West Africa moved toward independence, ownership of the strategically as well as economically important bay became a contested issue, which South Africa temporarily resolved by formal annexation in 1977. NAMIBIA finally won control of Walvis Bay in 1994, four years after independence, and has since invested extensively in it, creating a major free port to attract international investment and use. The Namibian government also financed construction of a desalinization plant in the bay to provide water for the local residents. Today Walvis Bay's fish industry continues to thrive and its salt fields produce 400,000 tons of high quality salt each year. As Namibia's largest commercial port, Walvis Bay handles about 2.5 million tons of cargo annually.

See also Fisheries, African.

Eric Young

Wanga

Ethnic group of East Africa.

The Wanga primarily inhabit western KENYA and southeastern UGANDA just north of LAKE VICTORIA. They speak a Bantu language and are one of the LUHYA peoples. Approximately 100,000 people consider themselves Wanga.

See also Bantu: Dispersion and Settlement.

War Between the States

See Civil War, American.

Ward, Samuel Ringgold

1817–c. 1866

African American abolitionist and newspaper editor.

Samuel Ringgold Ward was born on the eastern shore of Maryland, the son of William Ward and Anne (maiden name unknown), slaves. In 1820 Ward and his parents escaped to Greenwich, New Jersey, and, six years later, settled in NEW YORK CITY. There Ward attended the AFRICAN FREE SCHOOL, sponsored by the New York Manumission Society. He then clerked for two years in the law offices of DAVID RUGGLES and Thomas L. Jennings, African American reformers. Ward later recalled in his autobiography that he was "initiated . . . into the antislavery fraternity" after being wrongly imprisoned in 1834 on the charge of inciting a riot at Chatham Street Chapel, where African Americans were conducting an antislavery meeting.

Ward moved to NEWARK, NEW JERSEY, in 1835 and taught school there until 1839. In 1838 he married Emily E. Reynolds of New York City; they had four children. The family moved in 1839 to Poughkeepsie, New York, where Ward taught at the Colored Lancastrian School. Licensed to preach by the New York Congregational Association in 1839, he held two pastorates in upstate New York, one an all-white congregation in the village of South Butler, Wayne County (1841–1843), and one in Cortland Village (1846–1851). He was apparently well received, for he said of the South Butler congregation, "The mere accident of the colour of the preacher was to them a matter of small consideration."

Ward was an eloquent orator and staunch advocate of African American rights. He made his debut as a lecturer in 1839 as an agent of the New York State Anti-Slavery Society. The AMERICAN ANTI-SLAVERY SOCIETY hired him as a traveling lecturer in 1840. A man of imposing physical presence, over six feet tall and weighing more than 200 pounds, Ward made an excellent platform speaker. He condemned northern antiblack prejudice as well as southern slavery and developed an antislavery theology based on his interpretation of the life and mission of Jesus. Advertisements hailed Ward as "the Black Daniel Webster," and the *New York Tribune* called him "the ablest and most eloquent black man alive."

After the split within WILLIAM LLOYD GARRISON's American Anti-Slavery Society in 1840, Ward joined the newly formed American and Foreign Anti-Slavery Society, believing that slavery must be attacked with political weapons as well as with moral suasion. He became a lecturer for the Liberty party in upstate New York around 1841 and was appointed a vice president of the American Missionary Association. The right of African Americans to vote became one of his most persistent themes. He also lectured on land reform and temperance. Unlike prominent black abolitionist FREDERICK DOUGLASS, Ward endorsed the Liberty party position that the U.S. Constitution could be used to argue the abolitionist case. In 1848 he participated in the founding of the Free Soil party, much to the displeasure of some of his former allies in the Liberty party who believed that the Free Soil movement yoked political antislavery with forces hostile to the complete emancipation of African Americans from slavery in the South and racism in the North.

In addition to his powerful antislavery oratory, Ward contributed to reform efforts by writing for and editing several newspapers. He wrote editorials for the *True American* in Cortland for a short period, purchasing it in 1847. The paper was merged with Stephen A. Myer's *Albany Northern Star and Freeman's Advocate* in 1849 and renamed the *Impartial Citizen*. Beginning publication in Syracuse as a semimonthly sheet on February 14, 1849, Ward's paper was converted into a weekly organ of the Liberty party that June. It ceased publication in Syracuse on 19 June 1850 but resumed the next month in BOSTON. Ward struggled to keep the paper afloat until October 1851, when he declared bankruptcy.

While in Boston, Ward delivered an impassioned denunciation of the FUGITIVE SLAVE Act of 1850 in a speech at Faneuil Hall. He put his own freedom at risk in 1851 by participating with other members of the Syracuse Vigilance Committee in the rescue of William "Jerry" McHenry from federal officers acting under the Fugitive Slave Act. To avoid arrest and prosecution for his part in the rescue, Ward took his family to the Buxton settlement in Canada West (now Ontario). During the next two years, he promoted international support of the American abolitionist movement as an antislavery agent in CANADA, and in 1853 he founded the *Provincial Freeman* as a voice of the Canadian African American community. That winter Ward went on a six-week, 565-mile tour of southwestern Canada West, later reporting, "Our tour satisfied us abundantly that the colored people of Canada are progressing more rapidly than our people in the States—that the liberty enjoyed here makes different men of those once crushed and dispirited in the land of chains."

The Anti-Slavery Society of Canada sent Ward to the British Isles in 1853 to solicit financial support for fugitive slave communities in Canada. His two and a half years in GREAT BRITAIN were successful ones; he was well received by British audiences at his lectures against slavery and in behalf of the free produce movement. Ward published his autobiographical narrative, *Autobiography of a Fugitive Negro: His Anti-Slavery Labours in the United States, Canada and England*, in 1855.

Possibly because of defaulting on a loan, Ward and his family sailed for JAMAICA in the WEST INDIES in 1855. He served a small BAPTIST congregation in KINGSTON until 1860 and was involved in local politics. In 1860 he began farming fifty acres of land in St. George Parish, which had been given to him while he was in England. In 1866 he wrote *Reflections on the Gordon Rebellion*, an examination of Jamaica's revolutionary leader, GEORGE WILLIAM GORDON.

Ward died in Jamaica, poverty-stricken and far from central New York, where he had first established himself as a compelling and courageous opponent of slavery. FREDERICK DOUGLASS wrote of Ward: "As an orator and thinker he was vastly superior, I thought, to any of us, and being perfectly black and of unmixed African descent, the splendors of his intellect went directly to the glory of race. In depth of thought, fluency of speech, readiness of wit, logical exactness, and general intelligence, Samuel R. Ward has left no successor among the colored men amongst us, and it was a sad day for our cause when he was laid low in the soil of a foreign country."

Bibliography

Ward's letters and speeches can be found in the microfilm collection, C. Peter Ripley, ed., *The Black Abolitionist Papers (1981–1983)*, some of which are published in Ripley, et al., *The Black Abolitionist Papers, 1830–1865* (5 vols., 1985–1992).

Burke, Ronald K. "The Anti-Slavery Activities of Samuel Ringgold Ward in New York State." *Afro-Americans in New York Life and History* 2 (1978): 17–28.

From *American National Biography*. John A. Garraty and Mark C. Carnes, eds. Oxford University Press, 1999. Reprinted by permission of the American Council of Learned Societies.

Milton C. Sernett

Warfare in Africa before Independence

Armed conflicts in Africa prior to European decolonization.

The nature, scale, and causes of warfare in Africa have varied greatly both over time and across the continent. In general, conflicts between decentralized polities were the smallest and simplest, while wars between centralized polities were larger, more complex, and much more destructive.

The oldest form of conflict in Africa occurred in and between societies without centralized states, such as the DINKA, NUER, MAASAI, and SAN. The chiefs and elders of nomadic bands and agricultural communities used kinship ties to mobilize small militias in disputes that typically centered on claims over land and livestock, or alleged crimes. Due in part to cultural norms and in part to the limited capacity of the weapons—usually modified hunting or agricultural implements—relatively few people died in these conflicts. Even when bands created loose federations against common opponents, military campaigns were short and rarely resulted in one group taking control of another.

Since at least the sixteenth century, however, centralized polities, from chiefdoms to kingdoms to states, engaged in more extensive and often more destructive military campaigns. Rulers either mobilized large numbers of men from a certain age group or kept standing armies, sometimes comprised partly of slaves. Troops could number in the hundreds or thousands. Depending on the objectives and resources of the warring parties, military campaigns might last months or even years; traveling armies often pillaged the countryside to feed themselves.

Such militaries were rationally organized and possessed new forms of transportation and increasingly sophisticated weapons.

Many North African and Sahelian kingdoms, for example, deployed cavalry troops, as did the SONGHAI. In SOUTH AFRICA, Dingiswayo and SHAKA of the ZULU created a new military organization based on age groupings with innovative tactics and short thrusting spears rather than long throwing spears. By the seventeenth century many African armies had firearms bought from the Europeans, and in the mid-1800s Ethiopians deployed locally forged cannons.

These wars were fought to gain control of people and territory. Captives taken during warfare were often kept or sold as slaves, especially between the sixteenth and nineteenth centuries, when the TRANSATLANTIC SLAVE TRADE and INDIAN OCEAN SLAVE TRADE generated high demand. Wars of conquest also created subject peoples, whose tributes of crops, livestock, or labor provided a source of revenue for expansionist states. By gaining control over territory, kingdoms and states were able to dominate trade routes; secure access to pasture, farmland, and water sources; and control access to gold, iron, and salt mines. In many societies warfare was also culturally important as a rite of passage for young males. Although most soldiers were male, in a few societies women were renowned fighters and leaders. In the kingdom of Dahomey, for example, women served in the AMAZON forces, and in ANGOLA Queen NZINGA led her troops into battle.

Many of Africa's largest precolonial wars were fought in the name of spreading or purifying Islam. For example, in the early nineteenth century the FULANI cleric USUMAN DAN FODIO waged a series of jihads, or holy wars, against the HAUSA STATES of northern NIGERIA, eventually creating the powerful SOKOTO CALIPHATE. In some cases, the holy wars were waged against European colonizers. In the late 1800s Abdallahi ibn Muhammad, considered the Mahdi, or Messiah, waged a jihad in which he defeated the Anglo-Egyptian forces at KHARTOUM, SUDAN in 1885.

Both small societies and large states resisted imperialist incursions from Europe. For small societies, these wars of resistance proved costly, as their forces were easily overpowered by wealthier and better-armed foreign armies. Peoples with centralized states, such as the Bunyoro, HERERO, MANDINKA, Nandi, NDEBELE, TUKULOR, and Zulu, were more successful in resisting European incursions, due to their higher level of organizational and technical sophistication. In the long run, however, Europeans, with powerful Maxim guns and repeating rifles, crushed most African resistance by the 1920s. It was only in the late 1950s that resistance to COLONIAL RULE flared into open war in ALGERIA, Angola, CAMEROON, GUINEA-BISSAU, KENYA, MOZAMBIQUE, and ZIMBABWE. These wars killed thousands of Africans, but ultimately succeeded in their goal of independence.

See also Dahomey, Early Kingdom of; Ethiopia; Gold Trade; Iron in Africa; Islam in Africa; Rites of Passage and Transition; Salt Trade.

Bibliography

Copson, Raymond. *Africa's Wars and Prospects for Peace.* M. E. Sharpe, 1994.

Zartman, William. *Ripe for Resolution: Conflict and Intervention in Africa.* Oxford University Press, 1989.

Eric Young

Warfare in Africa since Independence

Open conflict between parties, nations, or states in Africa since European decolonization.

Since most of AFRICA gained independence in the 1960s, numerous conflicts have erupted into open warfare. Most of these wars have been internal, effecting no changes in international borders. Yet many have nonetheless had disastrous consequences, displacing communities, exacerbating poverty, and killing hundreds of thousands.

Although warfare has existed in Africa for centuries, the scale and deadliness of armed conflicts has increased dramatically in the past several decades. The exact toll is difficult to measure, however, given the indirect casualties caused by famine, disease, and displacement. Major conventional wars fought with heavy weapons have occurred in ANGOLA (1974–1995), EGYPT (1956, 1967), ERITREA (1962–1991), ETHIOPIA (1985–1991), Ethiopia-SOMALIA (1977–1978), NIGERIA (1967–1970), SUDAN (1955–1972 and 1983–2002), UGANDA (1979–1982), the WESTERN SAHARA (1974–1982), and Ethiopia-Eritrea (1998–2000). In addition, guerrilla wars have been fought in BURUNDI (1972 and 1993-present), LIBERIA (1989–2003), REPUBLIC OF THE CONGO (1997–2003), CÔTE D'IVOIRE (2002–2003), MOZAMBIQUE (1980–1992), RWANDA (1994), SIERRA LEONE (1993–2003), Somalia (1991-present), and ZAIRE, now the DEMOCRATIC REPUBLIC OF THE CONGO (1960–1964, 1977–1978, and 1997–2003).

Modern wars in Africa fall into roughly three categories. The first type is a product of postcolonial state formation, which in many African countries has failed to forge a common identity or value system. Struggles to write a young nation's political rules and gain access to state power and resources have driven some rebel groups to attempt government takeovers, while others have fought for regional autonomy or even independent statehood. An example of the latter was the secession attempt by eastern Nigeria in 1967, which led to the Biafran war.

In Angola and Mozambique, the rebel groups NATIONAL UNION FOR THE TOTAL INDEPENDENCE OF ANGOLA (UNITA) and MOZAMBICAN NATIONAL RESISTANCE (RENAMO) justified their wars against communist-leaning central governments on ideological grounds. In the long-running civil war in Sudan, religious and other cultural differences fuel southern Christians' struggle for autonomy from the Islamic government in KHARTOUM. In Burundi, Liberia, and Rwanda, governments and rebel leaders alike have used ethnic identity to mobilize forces against each other. Many observers have noted that ethnic nationalism has become an increasingly common source of conflict in the post-Cold War era, while ideology has become relatively less important.

The second type of postcolonial war in Africa arises from competition between states for regional influence and resources. Libyan forces, for example, fought CHAD, Sudan, and TUNISIA in an effort to access natural gas deposits and expand LIBYA's influence in the MAGHREB. SOUTH AFRICA fought wars and supported insurgents in Angola, Mozambique, and NAMIBIA from the mid-1970s to the late 1980s. More recently, Angola has sent its own troops into neighboring countries; one of its chief priorities is to assure control over trade in Angolan diamonds. Nigeria and Uganda have also intervened militarily in regional conflicts. Non-African governments concerned with preserving political influence or access to valuable resources have at times exacerbated internal and cross-border conflicts by supporting one side or the other. Although former colonial powers such as Belgium and FRANCE have historically been particularly active on this front, nations ranging from CUBA to China to the United States have also intervened in African territorial conflicts.

The third type of modern African war concerns disputed international borders, most of which were drawn by European colonial powers with little heed to preexisting territorial claims. Some of these conflicts are also over resources—for example, CAMEROON and Nigeria have fought intermittently for years over a border defining which country has access to valuable petroleum reserves on the Bakassi peninsula. Violent border disputes have also taken place between ALGERIA and MOROCCO, Ethiopia and Somalia, Ethiopia and Eritrea, Chad and Libya, BURKINA FASO and MALI, MAURITANIA and SENEGAL, and Morocco and the Western Sahara. Yet internal pressures and the doctrine of the ORGANIZATION OF AFRICAN UNITY (now the African Union) on the inviolability of colonial boundaries have almost always prevented the redrawing of borders, with the exception of the border created between Ethiopia and the new nation of Eritrea in 1993.

The overthrow of the Ethiopian government that coincided with Eritrea's secession was just one of several successes for rebel forces since the end of the Cold War, when the withdrawal of superpower support left many regimes vulnerable. Since 1990 insurgent militaries have also brought down the governments of Chad, the Republic of the Congo, Liberia, Rwanda, Sierra Leone, Somalia, and Zaire, now the Democratic Republic of the Congo. This has led to the rise of a new breed of African leaders who came to power through warfare and are willing to use military might to influence regional affairs.

Despite some regional and international diplomatic successes in ending conflicts in Africa, wars continue to create huge refugee populations throughout the continent, and to contribute to the spread of disease. Infrastructure destruction and prolific military spending have also drained the budgets of already impoverished governments. International players, increasingly reluctant to become involved, have recently called for the creation of more aggressive inter-African peacekeeping methods and forces, but these plans remain in their infancy.

See also Cold War and Africa; Decolonization in Africa: An Interpretation; Diseases, Infectious, in Africa; Ethnicity and Identity in Africa: An Interpretation; Ethnicity in Burundi: An Interpretation; Ethnicity in Rwanda: An Interpretation; Hunger and Famine; Islam in Africa; Nationalism in Africa.

Eric Young

Waring, Laura Wheeler

1887–1948

African American educator and portrait painter.

Born in Hartford, Connecticut, the fourth of six children of Robert Foster and Mary (Freeman) Wheeler, Laura Wheeler Waring had the advantages of an upper-class upbringing and excellent public schools. Her father, the minister of the Talcott Street Congregational Church, received his diploma from the Theology Department of HOWARD UNIVERSITY in 1877. After graduation from Hartford High School, Laura Waring studied for six years, from 1906 to 1912, at one of America's finest art schools, the Pennsylvania Academy of the Fine Arts. In 1914 a William Emlen Cresson Memorial Travel Scholarship enabled her to study briefly in several European cities. She established the art and music departments at Cheyney Training School for Teachers, near PHILADELPHIA, PENNSYLVANIA, directing them for more than thirty years. In 1924 she made a second trip abroad, this time accompanied by teacher, editor, and novelist JESSIE REDMON FAUSET. After her return, Waring exhibited her paintings in some of the most noted art galleries. She was in charge of black art during the Sesquicentennial Exposition in Philadelphia in 1926 and director of black exhibits in the Texas Centennial Exposition in 1937. She married Walter E. Waring, a professor at LINCOLN UNIVERSITY, Pennsylvania.

Laura Wheeler Waring had the advantages of training unusual for American artists of her era. On her first trip abroad in 1914 she spent much time in the Louvre Museum in Paris and studied the works of several masters, particularly the landscapes of Claude Monet. During her second trip, in 1924, she studied at the Académie de la Grande Chaumière, Paris, where she was influenced especially by Boutet de Monvel and Eugène Delecluse. Her visits to France; London, England; Dublin, Ireland; Rome, Italy; and North Africa provided subjects for some of her paintings, such as *Houses at Semuré, France* (1924). A versatile artist, she shared in the mural painting for the Pennsylvania Building during the Sesquicentennial Exposition in 1926. Her landscapes of Chester and Delaware counties in Pennsylvania gained wide acclaim.

Waring was best known, however, for her portraits. Some of these are documentary, especially those of writer JAMES WELDON JOHNSON, intellectual and activist W. E. B. Du BOIS, John Haynes Holmes, activist Mary White Ovington, and educator LESLIE PINCKNEY HILL. It is understandable that she has been accused of being primarily a painter of upper-class blacks and whites; few others could afford the cost of having their portraits painted by a famous artist. Yet some of her paintings, such as that of Anne Washington Derry, for which Waring received the second Harmon Award in 1927, do not fall into this category. Of special sociological significance was a canvas, *Mother and Daughter* (1927), that portrayed a mixed-race mother and daughter. Other paintings that were well known at the time are *The Co-Ed* and *The Musician*.

Waring's work was exhibited in the Pennsylvania Academy of the Fine Arts, the Philadelphia Museum of Art, the Corcoran Gallery in WASHINGTON, D.C., the Brooklyn Museum in New York, and many others. During her third trip abroad, she exhibited at a one-woman show in the Galerie du Luxembourg, Boulevard Saint-Germain, Paris.

Waring died after a long illness at her home, 756 N. 43rd Street, Philadelphia, on February 3, 1948. Private funeral services were held on February 7, and she was buried in Eden Cemetery. She was survived by her husband, a sister, and two brothers. In May and June 1949 she was honored by an exhibit of her works in the Howard University Gallery of Art.

There is an obituary, probably written by CARTER G. WOODSON, in the *Journal of Negro History* (July 1948, pp. 385–6). Another obituary is in the *Philadelphia Tribune* (February 7, 1948, pp. 1, 2). A longer biographical sketch and evaluation is "Laura Wheeler Waring," by Milton M. James, in the *Negro History Bulletin* (March 1956, pp. 126–8), with reproductions of portraits of her husband and an oil painting of Anne Washington Derry. *In Memoriam, Laura Wheeler Waring, 1887–1948. An Exhibition of Paintings, May and June, 1949. Washington, D.C. Howard University Gallery of Art* (1949) is in the Moorland-Spingarn Research Center, Howard University.

From *Dictionary of American Negro Biography* by Rayford W. Logan and Michael R. Winston, editors. Copyright © 1982 by Rayford W. Logan and Michael R. Winston. Reprinted by permission of W. W. Norton & Company, Inc.

Rayford W. Logan

War of 1812

War fought between the United States and Great Britain from June 18, 1812 to December 24, 1814.

Although black soldiers fought in the War of 1812, their numbers were small, and to a large extent those who took part did so despite government policy. The Militia Act of 1792 restricted militia service to "free and able-bodied white citizen[s]," and the U.S. Army and Marine Corps did not permit African Americans to enlist. Although free blacks and slaves did fill support roles as laborers and teamsters in army camps, the Navy was the only service that officially admitted blacks in a fighting capacity.

There were, however, exceptions to the exclusion of blacks from the nation's land forces. As the war continued, a number of states organized black militias. Louisiana enrolled a volunteer militia unit of free black landowners, known as the Battalion of Free Men of Color, which had a white commander and three black lieutenants. And after the British burning of WASHINGTON, D.C., in 1814, New York recruited approximately

2,000 slaves and free blacks in two regiments, promising slaves their freedom at the war's end.

Even the regular Army recruited some black soldiers late in the war. In PHILADELPHIA, the 26th U.S. Infantry Regiment accepted 247 African American enlistees. None of these recruits appears to have seen active service. They were discharged in 1815 with the note, "unfit to associate with . . . American soldiers." Nevertheless black troops did serve in the war's two most important battles, the Battle of Lake Erie (September 10, 1813) and the Battle of New Orleans (January 8, 1815). Ironically, black veterans of the latter were excluded from subsequent parades commemorating that victory.

See also Free Blacks in the United States.

James Sellman

Warthog

Wild pig that has two pairs of tusks and two pairs of wartlike protuberances on its long, wide head.

Warthogs have stocky bodies with thin legs and long, tufted tails. They are widespread on the plains and open woodlands of Africa, and their diet includes grass, berries, bark, roots, and carrion. They are normally diurnal, spending the night in burrows, but in places with heavy human activity warthogs may become nocturnal. One or two females with young form small groups, which a male may join briefly during mating season. Young males form bachelor groups, but older males are solitary. Male offspring separate from their mothers after a maximum of fifteen months. Female offspring may stay in the mother's herd for their entire lives. Offspring, regardless of gender, are driven off when new offspring are born. The older offspring sometimes return to the mother later. The warthog's tusks are sharp weapons used against predators, such as LIONS. Fights with other warthogs are mostly pushing matches, the tusks seldom used.

Scientific classification: The warthog belongs to the family Suidae, of the order Artiodactyla. It is classified as *Phacochoerus aethiopicus*.

Warwick, Dionne

1940–

African American popular and soul singer, one of the top non-Motown artists to emerge from the 1960s.

Born Marie Dionne Warwick in East Orange, New Jersey, she got her start singing in a Methodist church. In 1960 she met songwriters Burt Bacharach and Hal David, who asked her to start making demonstration records with them, and in 1962 the threesome was offered a contract with Scepter Records.

Bacharach and David wrote songs for Warwick that highlighted her diction and mellow alto voice. She remained with Scepter until 1971 and had numerous hits, including the number-one hit "Anyone Who Had a Heart" (1964). In the mid-1970s her career faltered amid family troubles and the breakup of Bacharach and David. In 1979 she again achieved popularity with the number-five hit "I'll Never Love This Way Again." Other hits after her comeback include "Deja Vu" (1979) and "That's What Friends Are For" (1986).

Warwick has given her money and talent to support hunger relief and research into acquired immunodeficiency syndrome (AIDS). In 1986 she was named Entertainer of the Year by the National Association for the Advancement of Colored People (NAACP) at the Image Awards. Warwick continues to record new music and to perform live around the world.

See also Music, African American; Soul Music.

Washington, Booker Taliaferro

1856–1915

Prominent African American who founded the Tuskegee Institute in Alabama and urged blacks to accommodate to life in the white South and concentrate on economic self-advancement.

Washington was born Booker Taliaferro, a slave, in rural Virginia on April 5, 1856. His mother, Jane, was the plantation's cook; his father was a white man whose identity he never knew. Washington worked as a servant in the plantation house until he was liberated by Union troops near the end of the American Civil War (1861–1865). After the war, his family moved to Malden, West Virginia, where they joined Washington Ferguson, also a former slave, whom Jane had married during the war.

Booker T. Washington established Tuskegee Institute in 1881 and shaped it as a school that emphasized industrial education. Tuskegee was the first black institution of higher learning to have a black faculty. *Photo by Elmer Chickering; National Portrait Gallery, Smithsonian Institution/Art Resource*

Discipline and Efficiency

To help support the family, Washington worked first in a salt furnace, then in a coal mine, and later as a houseboy in the home of General Lewis Ruffner, who owned the mines. In Ruffner's home he came under the influence of Viola Ruffner, the general's wife, who taught him a respect for cleanliness, efficiency, and order. During this time, and despite opposition from his stepfather, Booker attended a school for blacks while continuing to work. At school, he gave himself the last name Washington for reasons still debated by historians.

In 1872 Washington left Malden, traveling on foot to Virginia's Hampton Normal and Agricultural Institute (now Hampton University), which had opened only a few years earlier as a school for blacks. Its white principal, General Samuel Chapman Armstrong, was the son of missionaries to Hawaii and a commander of black Union troops during the war. The South's freed blacks, Armstrong believed, needed a practical, work-based education that would also teach character and morality. Hampton offered not only agricultural and mechanical classes but also training in cleanliness, efficiency, and discipline.

Washington arrived at the school ragged and penniless. He was given work as a janitor, which paid for his room and board, and Armstrong secured a white benefactor to pay his tuition. Washington was a diligent student, adopting Armstrong's credo so thoroughly that many historians have concluded that the rest of Washington's public life was a manifestation of Armstrong's philosophy.

Graduating with honors in 1875, Washington returned to West Virginia to teach. In 1878 he attended Wayland Seminary in Washington, D.C., a school that offered decidedly conventional training in the liberal arts. At Wayland, the black students knew little of manual labor, and moreover, seemed uninterested in returning to the South to help rural blacks. Washington's experience at Wayland further convinced him of the rightness of Armstrong's methods. After a year, Washington returned to Hampton, this time as a member of the faculty. His relationship with Armstrong grew closer, and in 1881, when the state of Alabama asked Armstrong to nominate a white principal to head a new school for blacks, he suggested Washington instead.

Establishing Tuskegee

The new school, known as the Tuskegee Institute (now TUSKEGEE UNIVERSITY) and located in Macon County, Alabama, had been apportioned $2,000 by the state legislature for salaries, but nothing for land or buildings. Washington began classes with a handful of students in a shanty owned by a black church. Intending Tuskegee to be a replica of Hampton, he established a vocational curriculum for both boys and girls that included courses in carpentry, printing, tinsmithing, and shoemaking. Girls also took classes in cooking and sewing, and boys learned crop and dairy farming.

Manners, hygiene, and character also received heavy emphasis, and each day was rigidly structured by a schedule that included daily chapel. The earliest students were set to work building a kiln, then making bricks, and finally erecting buildings. The school sold additional bricks to earn income to pay part of its expenses. Washington secured additional funds from philanthropists, mostly white and mostly Northerners, to whom Armstrong had introduced him.

Much of Washington's work took place beyond the school's walls. He placated the hostile whites of Tuskegee with assurances that he was counseling his students to set aside political activism in favor of economic gains. He also assured skeptical legislators that his students would not flee the South when they completed their education but would instead remain productive contributors to the rural economy. These messages resonated with whites not just in the South but also among Tuskegee's benefactors in the North.

Steel magnate Andrew Carnegie, who became the most generous donor to Tuskegee during Washington's lifetime, said Washington was "one of the most wonderful men . . . who has ever lived." Blacks also praised the man who built a successful school from virtually nothing in the Deep South. By 1890, Tuskegee had trained 500 African Americans a year on a mere 500 acres of land.

These triumphs, however, were underscored by incidents of tragedy in Washington's personal life. His first wife, Fanny Smith Washington, a graduate of Hampton, died from a fall in 1884, after just two years of marriage. His second wife, OLIVIA AMERICA DAVIDSON, also a graduate of Hampton and in chronically poor health, died in 1889. Washington's third wife, MARGARET MURRAY WASHINGTON, was a graduate of FISK UNIVERSITY and, like Olivia Washington, held the title of principal of Tuskegee. Margaret Washington helped her husband for the rest of his life and also led regional and national federations of black women.

National Prominence

Although Tuskegee earned him a measure of popularity, Washington did not become a national leader until he spoke at the Cotton States and International Exposition (also known as the Atlanta Exposition) in 1895. In the years preceding the exposition, relations between the races had steadily deteriorated. The South had codified its discriminatory JIM CROW laws, and violence, especially LYNCHING, was common. In early 1895 FREDERICK DOUGLASS, the acknowledged leader of blacks in the North

and the South, died, and no clear successor had emerged. Washington was the only black speaker chosen to address the mixed-race crowd that September in Atlanta.

He urged southern blacks to "cast down your bucket where you are," that is, to remain in the South and to accept discrimination as unchangeable for the time being. "In all things that are purely social," he said, "we can be as separate as the fingers, yet one as the hand in all things essential to mutual progress." Blacks should first commit themselves to economic improvement, Washington stated; once they had achieved that, he assured his listeners, improvement in civil rights would follow.

The speech, which critics called the Atlanta Compromise, won nearly unanimous acclaim from both blacks and whites. Even the black intellectual W. E. B. DU BOIS, who later broke sharply with Washington's accommodating position, praised Washington's message at the time. Donations from white Americans flowed in larger amounts to Tuskegee, and soon white journalists, politicians, and philanthropists sought Washington's word on all things racial.

In 1898 President William McKinley visited Tuskegee, offering praise that further elevated Washington's stature. Although in public Washington disdained politics, in private he assiduously cultivated his own power. He secretly owned stock in several black newspapers, which he influenced to provide favorable reports about him and Tuskegee. Other black newspapers he quietly cajoled, persuaded, and occasionally coerced into giving him positive coverage. At his heavily attended lectures around the country, he endeared himself to whites by telling stories about "darkies," blacks who fit racist stereotypes, and portraying them as lovable, gullible, and shiftless. These stories alienated black intellectuals.

In 1901 Washington published his ghostwritten autobiography, *Up from Slavery*. Told simply but movingly, it is a classic American tale of success through hard work. It became a bestseller and was translated into several languages. Theodore Roosevelt, who had become president that same year, invited Washington to lunch at the White House, prompting a flurry of angry editorials in the white South but further increasing Washington's power and appeal elsewhere. Roosevelt (as did President William Howard Taft after him) sought Washington's advice on racial and Southern issues.

In short time, Washington became a dispenser of REPUBLICAN PARTY patronage throughout the South and parts of the North. Blacks soon learned that Washington's endorsement was essential for a political appointment, or for that matter, for funding by white philanthropic groups, who readily deferred to Washington's opinions. Washington, in turn, used his wealth and influence to finance court cases and other activities that challenged Jim Crow laws. He also provided the main impetus for founding the National Negro Business League, which served to promote his Tuskegee philosophy throughout the country.

Stung by Criticism

In 1903 Du Bois published *The Souls of Black Folk*. In one of its essays, "Of Mr. Booker T. Washington and Others," he criticized Washington for failing to realize that economic power could not be had without political power, because political power was needed to protect economic gains. Moreover, Du Bois believed that Washington's disparagement of liberal arts education would rob the race of well-trained leaders.

Du Bois insisted that in a time of increasing segregation and discrimination, blacks must struggle for their civil rights rather than accommodate inequality. Washington, then at the peak of his power, was stung by Du Bois's criticisms, and "Of Mr. Booker T. Washington and Others" paved the way for more open criticism of Washington over the next several years.

The greatest threat to Washington's conservatism and influence came in 1909 with the founding of the NATIONAL ASSOCIATION FOR THE ADVANCEMENT OF COLORED PEOPLE (NAACP). The NAACP, which sought to address the neglected civil rights of blacks, was a direct challenge to Washington, as was its predecessor, Du Bois's NIAGARA MOVEMENT. Washington tried to stifle the group at first; failing that, he sought a rapprochement. That failed as well as increasing numbers of blacks gravitated to the NAACP and Washington's base of power weakened.

The election in 1913 of Democrat Woodrow Wilson to the presidency dealt Washington another blow, as his duties as dispenser of Republican patronage ended. Washington nonetheless remained prominent until his death on November 14, 1915. At that time, the Tuskegee Institute had a faculty of 200, an enrollment of around 2,000, and an endowment of $2 million.

Bibliography

Meier, August. *Negro Thought in America: Racial Ideologies in the Age of Accommodation, 1880–1915.* University of Michigan Press, 1963.

This turn-of-the-century street scene shows the east front of the United States Capitol. *Getty Images*

Washington, D.C.

Capital of the United States and the only major city whose citizens—the majority of whom are black—lack the authority to govern fully their own affairs.

Established in 1790 under the direction of President George Washington and named in his honor, Washington, D.C., was created to meet the constitutional mandate for the establishment of a federal district. (Washington originally intended the city's name to be "District of Columbia" in honor of Christopher Columbus.) Established as a unique entity, separate from states, Washington, D.C., ironically has been hampered by its nether position, both in terms of race and voting rights. Located between Maryland, a state in the Union, and Virginia, which joined the Confederacy during the AMERICAN CIVIL WAR (1861–1865), Washington has struggled throughout much of its existence to be a city for both the nation and local residents.

In 1800 the city's population of 14,103 persons comprised 10,066 whites, 783 free blacks, and 3,244 slaves. Designed principally by the French architect Pierre L'Enfant, the survey for the city was completed in part by the self-taught African American scientist and mathematician BENJAMIN BANNEKER. Planned as a grid with four quadrants, Washington is about 175.5 sq

km (68 sq mi) in size and includes both the Potomac and Anacostia rivers.

During its first fifty years, Washington became a center for both abolitionist activity as well as the establishment of businesses and institutions led by free blacks, including the several schools organized by and for African American women (the most notable being the Miner Normal School, which later evolved into the University of the District of Columbia). Due in part to the federal government's growing uneasiness with the slave trade, this activity increased the city's attractiveness to free blacks, who began to migrate there in significant numbers after 1820. The increase in the number of free blacks coming to the nation's capital, however, led to unease among the leaders of the city. The District's city council and other local city councils responded by passing laws that attempted to restrict blacks' movement and activities, including preaching and business ownership. Tensions erupted in the Washington Navy Yard and Georgetown during 1835 and 1836 when whites rioted against abolitionists and free blacks.

During the CIVIL WAR, Congress moved to redress these problems by abolishing slavery in the capital in 1862, one year before the EMANCIPATION PROCLAMATION. More than 3,000 black residents of the District volunteered in the Union Army, and the city itself became an important stop for runaway slaves. The war also encouraged the formation of several black charitable organizations, including the Contraband Relief Organization and Freedman's Hospital. During RECONSTRUCTION, the effort to rebuild the South and bring the full rights of citizenship to the former slaves after the Civil War, many notable African Americans settled in Washington, D.C., including FREDERICK DOUGLASS, ALEXANDER CRUMMELL, and Senator BLANCHE KELSO BRUCE of

POPULATION OF THE DISTRICT OF COLUMBIA 1800-1990

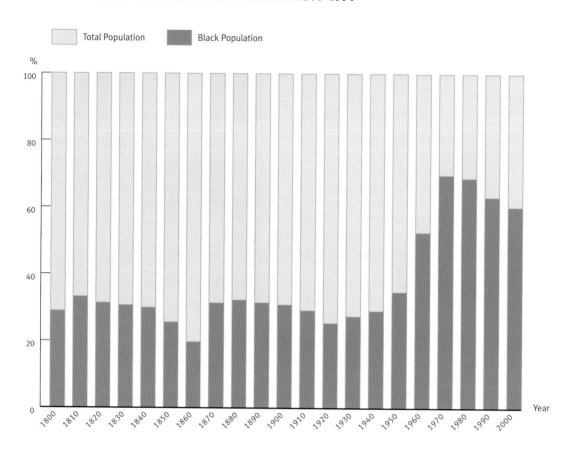

Population of the District of Columbia 1800–2000

Year	Total Population	Black Population	% Black
1800	14,093	4,027	28.57
1810	24,023	7,944	33.07
1820	33,039	10,425	31.55
1830	39,834	12,271	30.81
1840	43,712	13,055	29.87
1850	51,687	13,746	26.59
1860	75,080	14,316	19.07
1870	131,700	43,404	32.96
1880	177,624	59,596	33.55
1890	230,392	75,572	32.80
1900	278,718	86,702	13.11
1910	331,069	94,446	28.53
1920	437,571	109,966	25.13
1930	486,869	132,068	27.13
1940	663,091	187,226	28.24
1950	802,178	280,803	35.01
1960	763,956	411,737	53.90
1970	756,510	537,712	71.08
1980	638,333	448,370	70.24
1990	606,900	399,604	65.84
2000	572,059	343,235	60.0

Source: U.S. Census Bureau

Mississippi. By 1880 more than 175,000 people lived in Washington, of whom one-third were African Americans.

Although home rule had been a part of the city's political charter since its beginning, suffrage for black voters was repeatedly denied by popular election in the city from 1856 until 1864. It was only after the Civil War that voting rights were conferred on black males by virtue of an act of Congress (the Sumner Civil Rights Amendment). Shortly thereafter, in 1868, the first black mayor of Washington, Sayles Jenks Bowen, was elected. Defeated two years later by antisuffrage forces, Bowen and other members of Washington's new black political establishment suffered a grievous defeat in 1874 when Congress established a three-person commission for the city that was appointed by the president. As a result, political control of the city remained exclusively white until 1961.

From Reconstruction until WORLD WAR I (1914–1918), black life in Washington advanced most importantly with the establishment of learning organizations such as the AMERICAN NEGRO ACADEMY, established by Crummell, and the Association for the Study of Negro Life and History (later the ASSOCIATION FOR THE STUDY OF AFRO-AMERICAN LIFE AND HISTORY), founded by CARTER GODWIN WOODSON; fraternities and sororities such as Omega Psi Phi and Alpha Kappa Alpha; and the founding of HOWARD UNIVERSITY in 1867. Newspapers such as the *Washington Bee* and *Washington Afro-American* also contributed to the city's black life. In addition, Washington D.C. continued to attract a large number of black migrants from the South; by 1910 nearly 100,000 African Americans lived in the city, with poor blacks often living in hastily constructed alleys and elite members of the African American community living in neighborhoods such as LeDroit Park.

Despite the distinct class differences that appeared within the black community in Washington, D.C., the continued growth of the black population in the city remained a tense issue for its white leaders and their followers. Two days of riots in 1919 confirmed the impression that racial tensions were a persistent part of the city's character. The riots were fueled by newspaper accounts of alleged crimes against white women by black men. In a city populated with soldiers returning from World War I, whites attacked black citizens in many downtown locations, and black citizens retaliated with attacks in white neighborhoods. Four people died as a result of the riot, including two African Americans, and federal troops were called in to restore an uneasy calm.

With the establishment of the New Deal in 1932, and the rise of Howard University as a center for some of the leading black activists and writers of the day—including CHARLES HAMILTON HOUSTON, RALPH JOHNSON BUNCHE, and EDWARD FRANKLIN FRAZIER—organized protests within the District's black community became more common. The New Negro Alliance, whose members included Houston, ROBERT CLIFTON WEAVER, and MARY McLEOD BETHUNE successfully led protests against employment discrimination. Organized black protest in Washington achieved national recognition when the accomplished opera singer MARIAN ANDERSON was denied use of Constitution Hall by the Daughters of the American Revolution in 1939, and instead sang at the Lincoln Memorial before an audience of 75,000 people. (Ironically, the dedication of the Lincoln Memorial itself in 1922 occurred under segregated conditions.) Despite these successes, primary control of Washington remained firmly in the hands of the three-member commission appointed by Congress, and inevitably in the hands of individual Congress members, some of whom—such as Senator Theodore Bilbo and Congressman Ross Collins, both Mississippi Democrats—were avowed racists.

While congressional oversight of District matters continued, organized efforts to remove JIM CROW laws, coupled with strong migration to the city, meant that the District's black population grew significantly after WORLD WAR II (1939–1945). By 1960 the black population of Washington, D.C., exceeded 411,000 and represented more than half of the city's citizens. In 1961 ratification of the Twenty-third Amendment to the Constitution occurred, giving residents of Washington, D.C., the right to vote in presidential elections for the first time. The growth of the CIVIL RIGHTS MOVEMENT in the 1950s and 1960s and the use of Washington as a site for protests by other activist movements brought additional political reforms to the District, including the appointment of African Americans to the newly established office of mayor and the three-member commission. Political reform was hastened by the riots of 1968, which occurred shortly after the assassination of MARTIN LUTHER KING, JR. Reaction to

Mayor Anthony Williams addressed Washington Center interns after the terrorist attacks of September 11, 2001. *Getty Images*

King's assassination began peacefully when BLACK POWER advocate STOKELY CARMICHAEL asked downtown businesses to close their doors out of respect for the slain civil rights leader. The reaction grew violent as large crowds gathered and reacted to the news of King's death. For three days, rioting and looting occurred at a cost of some twelve lives, 7,600 arrests, and $27 million in property damage before federal troops were able to restore order.

The 1968 riots, despite their economic devastation, sped the reestablishment of home rule in the city. In 1974, for the first time in nearly 100 years, all citizens of Washington, D.C., were permitted to elect a city council and a mayor. The previously appointed mayor, Walter Washington, was elected mayor in 1974. MARION SHEPILOV BARRY, JR., a former leader of the STUDENT NONVIOLENT COORDINATING COMMITTEE (SNCC) who moved to Washington after working in Mississippi, was elected to the post in 1978 to serve the first of three consecutive terms as mayor. A populist leader whose first-term coalition of poor blacks and white downtown real estate developers would undergo substantial changes in subsequent years, Barry was initially an effective leader who revitalized downtown and energized long-neglected citizens with his pledges of inclusion. However, Barry's own struggles with drug use, coupled with his desire to expand the city bureaucracy significantly, severely limited his effectiveness as a mayor. In the 1991 election the voters chose newcomer Sharon Pratt Kelly to succeed Barry.

The first black woman elected mayor of a major city, Kelly instituted reform efforts that failed, largely as a result of her inexperience, leaving the city with mounting financial deficits and increasingly frustrated citizens. When Barry was returned to the office of mayor in 1994, the Congress and President Bill

Clinton established the D.C. Financial Responsibility and Management Assistance Authority (known commonly as the control board), a congressionally appointed body with the power to manage most of the fiscal and administrative affairs of the District until its fiscal condition was stabilized. The control board struggled to convince the city's residents that meaningful reform was possible without a self-representative governing body, but it gained some financial and administrative successes. In 1998, despite the control board's contentious history, District voters easily elected Anthony Williams, who had been the city's chief financial officer under the control board, as their new mayor, after Barry declined to seek reelection. Williams, reelected in 2002, cited his administration's progress in reducing crime rates and improving city services.

See also Emancipation Proclamation and the Thirteenth Amendment.

Peter Glenshaw

Washington, Denzel

1954–

Academy Award–winning African American actor.

Denzel Washington grew up in the middle-class family of a Pentecostal minister and a beauty shop owner. Washington won a small role in the 1977 television motion picture *Wilma,* about Olympic track star WILMA RUDOLPH, before he graduated from Fordham University in 1977 with a bachelor of arts degree in journalism. After graduating, Washington pursued acting professionally, studying drama at the American Conservatory in SAN FRANCISCO, CALIFORNIA.

Washington first achieved recognition for his stage performances. His portrayal of activist MALCOLM X in *Chickens Coming Home to Roost* and of Private Peterson in the Obie award-winning *A Soldier's Play* won Washington critical acclaim for carefully chosen roles that resisted Hollywood's stereotypical options for blacks. Washington's stage performances led to a role in the popular television drama *St. Elsewhere* in which he played dedicated Dr. Philip Chandler, from 1982 to 1988. In 1984 Washington began a successful transition from television to film when critics praised his reprisal of the Private Peterson role in *A Soldier's Story,* the screen adaptation of *A Soldier's Play.*

By the end of the 1980s Washington had become one of Hollywood's most critically and commercially successful actors. He has received three Academy Award nominations, twice for best supporting actor (*Cry Freedom,* 1987; *Glory,* 1990, for which he won), and once for best actor as Malcolm X in SPIKE LEE's film of the same name. In addition to his collaborations with Lee (*Mo' Better Blues* in 1990 and *Malcolm X* in1992), Washington has worked with some of film's most respected directors, including Jonathan Demme (*Philadelphia,* 1993) and Kenneth Brannagh (*Much Ado About Nothing,* 1993). He solidified his leading-man status with a role opposite WHITNEY HOUSTON in *The Preacher's Wife* (1996), a remake of a Cary Grant film.

Washington continued his string of critically acclaimed performances with his work in *He Got Game* (1998), another Spike Lee film; *The Hurricane* (1999), based on the life of imprisoned boxer Rubin "Hurricane" Carter; and *Remember the Titans* (2000), about a tough high school football coach who leads his racially mixed team to the state title. But it was for his role as a corrupt, dangerous police officer in the film *Training Day* (2001) that Washington earned an Oscar for best actor. It was the first such honor for an African American actor since Sidney Poitier won the award for *Lilies of the Field* (1963). Washington followed his Oscar performance with roles in *John Q* (2002) and *The Manchurian Candidate* (2004). He made his directorial debut with *Antwone Fisher* (2002). Washington remains one of Hollywood's top leading men.

See also Actors and Acting; Film, Blacks in American; Television and African Americans.

Bibliography

Brode, Douglas. *Denzel Washington: His Films and Career.* Birch Lane Press, 1996.

Robert Fay

Washington, Dinah

1924–1963

African American singer and pianist whose performances included rhythm and blues, gospel, and pop music; also known for her efforts to promote other musicians.

Dinah Washington was born Ruth Lee Jones in Tuscaloosa, Alabama. Her parents, Alice Williams and Ollie Jones, moved the family to CHICAGO, ILLINOIS in 1928, where Ruth and her three siblings attended the city's public schools, including Wendell Phillips High School.

Taught piano by her mother, Ruth sang and played solos at St. Luke's Baptist Church while still in elementary school, and gave gospel recitals with her mother at various black churches. At the age of fifteen, she won an amateur contest at Chicago's Regal Theater with her rendition of "I Can't Face the Music." She then began to sing without her mother's knowledge at local nightclubs.

In 1940, Washington was discovered by gospel singer SALLIE MARTIN, who hired her as an accompanist and singer for The Sallie Martin Colored Ladies Quartet. She performed for two years with Martin's ensemble. It was with Martin's group that she took her professional name, before being hired by bandleader LIONEL LEO HAMPTON in 1943.

Washington's career as a soloist was boosted in 1946 when she secured a sixteen-year recording contract with Mercury Records. During this time, she toured extensively and had forty-five songs on *Billboard* magazine's RHYTHM-AND-BLUES charts. Her biggest hit was "Baby, You've Got What It Takes" (1960).

Nicknamed the Queen of the Blues, Dinah Washington died of an accidental overdose of sleeping pills.

See also Blues; Gospel Music.

Aaron Myers

Washington, Fredi

1903–1994

American actor who worked for equal opportunity for African American performers.

Fredi Washington's most famous acting role typified her Hollywood experience. In *Imitation of Life* (1934), she played a woman who passes for white. Although she won critical acclaim, she was typecast after that as the light-skinned "tragic mulatto." Her performance was so convincing that many African American journalists believed that she carried racial self-hatred. In fact, however, Washington was positive about her heritage and worked on behalf of African American performers by cofounding the Negro Actors Guild in 1937 and serving as its first executive secretary. In 1975, she was inducted into the Black Filmmakers Hall of Fame.

See also Film, Blacks in American; Passing in the United States.

Bibliography

Rule, Sheila. "Fredi Washington, 90, Actress; Broke Ground for Black Artists." *New York Times,* Jun. 30, 1994.

Robert Fay

Washington, George

1817–1905

African American frontiersman and Oregon Trail pioneer.

George Washington was born near Winchester in Frederick County, Virginia, the son of a mixed-race African American slave father named Washington and a white mother whose name is unrecorded. The nature of his parentage violated social conventions; his father was immediately sold, never to be involved in his life again, and his mother allowed baby George to be adopted by James C. Cochran and his wife, a white family. At age four George moved west with the Cochrans, settling first near Delaware City, Ohio; when he was nine, the family moved farther west, eventually to Bloomington on the Missouri frontier. As a black youth in the slave state of Missouri, Washington was denied a formal education, but he taught himself the rudiments of reading, writing, and mathematics. He also acquired the skills in woodcraft and marksmanship for which he would later become renowned.

By 1841 Washington and a partner had established a sawmill near St. Joseph, Missouri, but again he had to confront racial discrimination when a white customer purchased lumber on credit but refused to pay when the note came due. Washington sued and won a judgment, but before he could collect, the customer countersued and had Washington arrested for violating the requirements of Missouri's Free Negro Codes. Under this law all free blacks in Missouri were required to register and to receive a special license from local authorities before they could engage in business or use the court system. Washington had not been properly registered before entering business or filing his suit.

Several factors had probably allowed Washington to initially circumvent the law's provisions. The area where he lived was on the remote Missouri frontier, where the systems and mechanisms of civil administration were not yet well established. In addition, being part of a white family had shielded him from the full impact of local racial conventions. The countersuit forced Washington to face the full implications of the law. Conviction could have meant enslavement. Fortunately, however, both Washington and his adoptive father were respected and well liked by their neighbors, lending them political influence in the state legislature. A special bill, rushed through the legislature in January 1843, retroactively granted Washington all rights accorded to properly registered and licensed blacks under the 1835 law, removing the legal grounds for his prosecution under the countersuit.

Missouri's harsh anti-black laws continued to compromise Washington's aspirations. After the destruction of his mill in a flood, he relocated to Schuyler County, Missouri, and endeavored to start a distillery. Before production could begin, the legislature passed a bill prohibiting any person of color from manufacturing, handling, or selling alcohol, forcing Washington to abandon his plans.

By 1848, exasperated by such race-based limitations in Missouri, Washington moved to Illinois in search of better treatment, but Illinois, fearing the immigration of fugitive slaves, was also passing prohibitive legislation. On his arrival in Quincy, Illinois, Washington learned of a recently adopted law that compelled immigrating blacks to post a $6,000 bond to guarantee good behavior and demonstrate financial self-sufficiency. He returned to Missouri determined to move to the Oregon Territory to escape the stifling racism of the Midwest. When he informed his parents, they decided to go, too. Without their cooperation, Washington, as a black, would have been unable to acquire land in the Oregon Territory.

Their party left for Oregon on March 15, 1850, arriving 117 days later in Oregon City. By 1852 Washington had staked a claim at the fork of the Skookumchuck and Chehalis rivers in present-day Washington state. Frontier racial politics continued to haunt him. In 1849 the Oregon Territorial Legislature had adopted the Black Exclusion Law, which made Washington's immigration illegal. The Homestead Act of Oregon, adopted by Congress in 1850, had barred blacks from the homesteading process. Washington avoided exclusion by settling north of the Columbia River, in an area that in 1853 separated from the Oregon Territory and became the new territory of Washington, placing him outside the jurisdiction of the Oregon exclusion law. He was still, however, prohibited by law from the right to homestead. When later white immigrants attempted to claim Washington's land, they were foiled only when he sold his land and buildings to his white father James Cochran, who legally claimed the homestead before the interlopers could file on it. After completing the required four years of occupation to gain clear title, Cochran sold the claim back to Washington, legally securing his son's possession.

Washington prospered as a frontier farmer. In 1869 he married Mary Jane Cooness, a widow of black and Jewish descent who had a young son.

By 1872 the Northern Pacific Railroad pushed its line across Washington's farm. On January 8, 1875, foreseeing economic development in the area, Washington registered at the county seat in Chehalis a town plat he called Centerville; In 1883 he changed the name to Centralia. The area and town continued to grow, and Washington prospered; by 1893 his personal wealth was estimated at $150,000. He donated to the town plots for churches, parks, and public buildings, establishing a reputation for generosity among his neighbors.

Mary Jane Washington died in 1889. The following year Washington married Charity E. Brown, a widow with three children. On December 15, 1891, they had a son; shortly afterward they divorced, and the son was raised by Washington.

The depression of 1893 hit the area hard. Washington endeared himself to many of his neighbors by his generosity to the needy, buying and distributing large amounts of food. He lent money to many at no interest. The town survived, and eventually prosperity returned when the depression receded. Some white newcomers, however, resented the success and prominence of the black town founder. In 1898 Washington was mysteriously poisoned, but survived. The responsible party was never discovered.

Friends, however, greatly outnumbered enemies. When Washington died from injuries in a buggy accident, all businesses closed so the residents could attend the funeral. Washington encountered and overcame the difficulties of frontier life, exacerbated by virulent racial prejudice. Most black Americans in this era, held as slaves, had no chance to participate in the western movement. Washington is an example of the success achieved by some who did, most of whose names and stories have been lost to history.

Bibliography

The best sources on Washington are local newspaper accounts and clippings held in the Centralia Public Library, Centralia, Wash. Herndon Smith, ed., *Centralia, the First Fifty Years 1845–1900* (n.d.), compiled from local accounts by students at Centralia High School, contains a chapter by Dorothy Riggs with useful information on Washington.

Anderson, Martha. *Black Pioneers of the Northwest 1800–1918.* 1980.

Freedman, Ralph. *This Side of Oregon.* 1983.

Katz, William Loren. *The Black West.* 1973.

McLagan, Elizabeth. *A Peculiar Paradise: A History of Blacks in Oregon, 1778–1940.* 1980.

Savage, W. Sherman. "George Washington of Centralia Washington." *Negro History Bulletin* 27 (1963): 27–30.

———. *Blacks in the West.* 1976.

From *American National Biography.* John A. Garraty and Mark C. Carnes, eds. Oxford University Press, 1999. Reprinted by permission of the American Council of Learned Societies.

Darrell M. Milner

Washington, Harold

1922–1987

American politician; first African American mayor of Chicago, Illinois.

Harold Washington was born in CHICAGO, ILLINOIS, to Bertha and Roy Lee Washington, who separated when he was young, and he was raised by his father. After dropping out of high school during his junior year, Washington earned a high school equivalency degree in the Army, after he was drafted during WORLD WAR II. He graduated from Roosevelt University in 1949 with a degree in political science followed by a degree in law from Northwestern University in 1952.

Washington began his political career when he succeeded his deceased father in 1953 as a DEMOCRATIC PARTY precinct captain. After positions as a city attorney (1954–1958) and a state labor arbitrator (1960–1964), he served in the Illinois House of Representatives (1965–1976). He then advanced to seats in the Illinois State Senate (1976–1980) and the United States House of Representatives (1980–1983). Washington was instrumental in the 1982 effort to extend the VOTING RIGHTS ACT OF 1965.

In 1977, Washington made an unsuccessful bid to become the mayor of Chicago. In 1983, he again entered the mayoral race and defeated Jane Byrne and Richard M. Daley in the primaries. He edged out Republican Bernard Epton in the general election on April 12, 1983 to become the city's first African American mayor.

Washington increased racial diversity in city administration, assuring equal opportunities for women and minorities seeking employment, and ended city patronage. He had difficulty implementing his initiatives since the majority of the fifty City Council seats were held by his political opponents. But 1986, after a Federal court called for new elections in certain wards that were deemed racially biased, Washington achieved more legislative success. He unexpectedly died of a heart attack shortly after his reelection in 1987, ending hope for a popular, progressive, multiracial city government.

Bibliography

Kleppner, Paul. *Chicago Divided: The Making of a Black Mayor.* Northern Illinois University Press, 1985.

Rivlin, Gary. *Fire on the Prairie: Chicago's Harold Washington and the Politics of Race.* H. Holt, 1993.

Aaron Myers

Washington, James Melvin

1948–1997

American historian and minister whose work on African American religious experience has changed the shape of American church history.

James M. Washington was born April 24, 1948, in Knoxville, Tennessee, the son of Annie and James W. Washington. He was ordained in 1967 by his home church, Mount Olive Baptist, for the pastorate of the Riverview Missionary Baptist Church. He earned degrees from the University of Tennessee, Harvard Divinity School, and Yale University, where he received a doctorate in 1979.

Washington taught at Union Theological Seminary in NEW YORK, NEW YORK from 1975 until his death, being promoted to full professor in 1986. He was the author of *Frustrated Fellowship: The Black Baptist Quest for Social Power* (1986), *A Testament of Hope: The Essential Writings of Martin Luther King Jr.* (1986), and *Conversations with God: Two Centuries of Prayers by African Americans* (1994). He held dual membership at Concord Baptist Church in Brooklyn, and the Riverside Church in Manhattan where he served as chair of the Church Council.

Washington's scholarly work had three major emphases: the development of African American spirituality, the Christian response to human existence, and the modes of human accommodation and resistance to oppressive social structures. American church history began to be reconsidered and rewritten in light of Washington's investigation of the African American religious experience. He died in New York from hypertension and a massive stroke on May 3, 1997, survived by his wife Patricia and their daughter Ayanna Washington.

Bibliography

Washington, James M. *Conversations with God: Two Centuries of Prayers by African Americans.* HarperCollins Publishers, 1994.

Richard Newman

Washington, John Edwin

1880–1964

African American dentist, teacher, and collector of Lincoln memorabilia.

Born in Annapolis, Maryland, on February 2, 1880, John Edwin Washington received his education in WASHINGTON, D.C., where he lived with his grandmother, Caroline Washington, in her boarding house on E Street, just around the corner from the old Ford Theater. He graduated from Miner Normal School in 1900. Working his way through HOWARD UNIVERSITY, he earned a bachelor of pedagogy degree in 1901 and a doctor of dental surgery degree in 1904. In July 1904 he received his license to practice dentistry in the District of Columbia.

For the next fifty years Washington successfully combined the two careers for which he had prepared himself. He taught in the Washington public schools and conducted a part-time practice of dentistry. In 1924 he received a B.A. degree with a major in art from Howard University. He was a teaching principal in the elementary schools for twenty-five years and a teacher of commercial art and civics in the secondary schools for twenty-six years. During those years he also organized and coached teams in track and basketball in the Public School Athletic League. He organized the South Atlantic Athletic Association and became the first athletic coach of Cardozo High School. He was one of the organizers of the Tri-State and Inter-State dental associations. These organizations were forerunners of the National Dental Association, which twice honored him for his contribution to organized dentistry and his devotion to his profession. After 1905 he served in every office of the Robert T. Freeman Dental Society. In 1908 he married pharmacist Virginia Ross, of Washington, D.C.

Washington's interest in ABRAHAM LINCOLN began when he was a child. His grandmother had taught him reverence for the martyred president, and the humble, elderly African Americans who frequented her home talked of Lincoln as a "messenger of God." His grandmother's Lincoln scrapbook was the start of his own collection. For years he acquired Lincoln memorabilia and doggedly pursued little-known facts about him. He interviewed elderly African Americans across the country, asking them what they recalled about Lincoln. He sought out former White House servants, messengers, and personal aides and talked to them or to their children, uncovering an intimate side of Lincoln's life that was unknown to historians. In 1942 these reminiscences were published, with an introduction by biographer Carl Sandburg. *They Knew Lincoln* (1942) was the culmination of thirty-five years of patient collecting, interviewing, and recording.

In 1947 Washington was awarded a Library of Congress citation for his Lincolniana collection. In 1959 he was designated an honorary member of the Lincoln Sesquicentennial Commission for his "unusual devotion and enduring contribution to the recollection of Abraham Lincoln and to the principles for which he stood."

Washington died on December 6, 1964, of pneumonia at the age of eighty-four in St. Elizabeth's Geriatric Division, Washington, D.C. He was buried in Lincoln Cemetery, Washington, D.C.

Sources of information consist of materials in the Moorland-Spingarn Research Center, including Washington's book, clippings about his career, obituaries, a typescript of a radio interview, and a résumé prepared in 1952 at his direction. Information was also supplied by his niece, Catherine Gray Hurley, Washington, D.C.

From *Dictionary of American Negro Biography* by Rayford W. Logan and Michael R. Winston, editors. Copyright © 1982 by Rayford W. Logan and Michael R. Winston. Reprinted by permission of W. W. Norton & Company, Inc.

Charlotte S. Price

Washington, Margaret Murray

1861–1925

American educator and president of the National Association of Colored Women.

Margaret Murray Washington was born in Macon, Mississippi. After graduating in 1889 from Fisk University's Preparatory School in Nashville, Tennessee, she joined the faculty at Tuskegee Institute (later Tuskegee University), becoming dean of the women's department in 1890. In 1891 she married Tuskegee's founder and president, Booker Taliaferro Washington.

In addition to teaching and helping Washington administer Tuskegee, she participated in women's clubs, becoming the president of the National Association of Colored Women in 1914. She was also involved in the temperance movement and coordinated self-improvement programs for women in the Tuskegee area. After Washington's death in 1915, she continued to work at Tuskegee.

Robert Fay

Waters, Ethel

1896–1977

American singer and actress who brought black urban blues into the mainstream.

Ethel Waters was born in Chester, Pennsylvania, to twelve-year-old Louise Anderson, who had been raped by a white man, John Waters. Although she was raised by her maternal grandmother, Ethel took her father's surname. Reared in poverty, she left school at the age of thirteen in order to support herself through domestic housework.

Waters performed for the first time at the age of five in a children's church program. She was called Baby Star and later, performing on the black vaudeville circuit, became known as Sweet Mama Stringbean. After moving to New York, New York in 1919, at the start of the Harlem Renaissance, Waters recorded songs for Black Swan Records and then Colombia Records while playing in revues and performing on the white vaudeville circuit during the 1920s. Two of her more popular songs were "Dinah" (1925) and "Stormy Weather" (1933). By refining the lyrics and the performance, Waters introduced urban blues to a white audience. Her stylistic alterations created a niche for the black nightclub singers who gained popularity from the 1930s through the 1950s.

In 1927, Waters's career as an actress began with the musical *Africana*. She played singing roles in other Broadway productions: *Blackbirds* (1930), *Rhapsody in Black* (1931), *As Thousands Cheer* (1933), *At Home Abroad* (1936), and *Cabin in the Sky* (1940). Waters played more dramatic roles in *Mamba's Daughters* (1939) and *The Member of the Wedding* (1950). Appearing in nine films between 1929 and 1959, she received an Academy Award nomination as Best Supporting

Actress in *Pinky* (1949). Through these roles, Waters transformed the image of the older black woman from that of the servile "Mammy" to the self-sufficient Earth Mother. She toured with evangelist Billy Graham from 1957 to 1976. Waters is the author of two autobiographies: *His Eye Is on the Sparrow* (1951) and *To Me It's Wonderful* (1972).

Bibliography
Knaack, Twila. *Ethel Waters: I Touched a Sparrow.* Word Books, 1978.

Aaron Myers

Waters, Maxine Moore

1938–

Democratic member of the United States House of Representatives from California.

Maxine Moore Waters gained national recognition during the Los Angeles riots of 1992, when she emerged as one of the black community's principal voices in Congress. She assailed the long-term neglect of America's inner cities, an issue that had propelled her political career from its beginning.

The fifth of thirteen children born to Remus and Velma Lee Carr Moore, Waters grew up in a housing project in St. Louis, Missouri. Inspired by a fifth-grade math teacher who took a special interest in her, Waters set high expectations for herself and assumed leadership roles in school. In the late 1960s, she became a spokesperson for the Los Angeles-based Head Start program, where she taught after working as a factory worker and telephone operator. Meanwhile, Waters attended California State University, majoring in sociology, and brought up her two children with her husband Edward Waters, a factory worker.

In 1973 Waters was appointed chief deputy to city council member David Cunningham, and she later campaigned for United States Senator Alan Cranston and Los Angeles mayor Tom Bradley. She launched her own political career in 1976, when she was elected to the California State Assembly. During her fourteen-year tenure as an assemblyperson, her legislative successes were numerous and diverse, ranging from a law that curbed California's business investment in South Africa to a training program for child abuse prevention. She prioritized women's rights and helped to found the National Political Congress of Black Women in 1984. In 1990 Waters was elected to the United States Congress as a representative from the Twenty-ninth Congressional District, where she advocated for minorities and urban renewal. (After redistricting in 1992, the Twenty-ninth District was renumbered the Thirty-fifth District.) In 1993 she introduced and won passage of a bill that provided $50 million for an innovative training program for disadvantaged youth nationwide. In 1997 she became the third woman to chair the Congressional Black Caucus. Waters has served as Chief Deputy Whip of the Democratic Party since 1999, and in 2002 she was named co-chair of the influential

House Democratic Steering Committee. Waters was reelected to her Congressional seat in 2002, receiving over three-quarters of the votes cast.

See also United States House of Representatives, African-Americans in.

Bibliography
Collier, Aldore. "Maxine Waters: Telling It Like It Is in L.A." *Ebony*, Oct. 1992.

Mills, Kay. "Maxine Waters: 'I don't pretend to be nice no matter what . . .'." *The Progressive*, Dec. 1993.

Roanne Edwards

Waters, Muddy

1915–1983

African American musician, a pioneer of postwar electric blues.

Muddy Waters's long life in music essentially encompasses the story of the BLUES in the twentieth century. Born McKinley Morganfield in Rolling Fork, Mississippi, he grew up in the Mississippi Delta, immersed in the rural blues tradition. He was particularly fond of SON HOUSE and ROBERT LEROY JOHNSON. Waters got his nickname from his hobby of fishing in a nearby creek. He was also musically active, first playing harmonica and then guitar in small bands around the Delta and, briefly, in St. Louis, Missouri.

In 1941 and 1942 the traveling folklorist, Alan Lomax, recorded Waters, revealing a talented but still imitative singer. In 1943 Waters moved to CHICAGO, ILLINOIS, and got a job in a paper mill. A year later, he bought his first electric guitar, and the impact on his music was profound. This new musical technology effectively complemented his powerful voice, and he was soon popular as a singer at house parties and clubs on the South Side. He also began recording in 1946, although none of these songs were hits, and he remained a local phenomenon.

In 1948 Waters signed with CHESS RECORDS and released his first single, "Rollin' Stone," from which the British rock band, the Rolling Stones, took its name in the 1960s. It was a hit, and many more followed, including "I Can't Be Satisfied" and "I Feel Like Going Home." These recordings from the late 1940s, with their primitive electric sound and Waters's barely controlled musical and vocal energy, helped form the foundation of modern rock music.

Waters continued his pioneering work through the 1950s, enlarging his band to include piano, and working with talent such as Otis Spann, Little Walter, WILLIE DIXON, and Buddy Guy. Waters helped define an exciting new urban blues sound associated with Chicago music in the 1950s, reminiscent of the Delta blues, yet different from it. This mix appealed strongly to the large population of blacks who had relocated from Mississippi to Chicago. Songs from this period include "I'm Your Hoochie Coochie Man," "I Just Want to Make Love to You,"

and "Mannish Boy." Though his records did little on the pop charts, he was consistently near the top of the RHYTHM-AND-BLUES charts.

Waters failed to achieve mainstream success in the United States and was largely unknown to white Americans. He did influence later musicians, however—particularly the rising generation of English rock and rollers in the 1960s who had attended Waters's performances when he toured England in 1958, the first of many successful visits. Waters was honored late in his career with several Grammy Awards and an appearance in The Band's film, *The Last Waltz* (1978).

Bibliography
Palmer, Robert. *Deep Blues.* Viking Press, 1981.

Watt, Melvin

1945–

African American lawyer, politician, and member of the United States House of Representatives from North Carolina.

Melvin Watt was born in Steele Creek, North Carolina. He received a bachelor's degree from the University of North Carolina at Chapel Hill in 1967 and a law degree from Yale University in 1970. He pursued a career as a civil rights attorney in Charlotte, North Carolina, between 1971 and 1992. Watt served one term in the North Carolina Senate from 1985 to 1987. In 1992 he ran successfully for a seat in the United States House of Representatives representing North Carolina's Twelfth Congressional District. The district was created in 1992 as one of two North Carolina minority districts mandated by the United States Justice Department. However, in June 1996 the U.S. Supreme Court declared the district illegally drawn. Although the North Carolina Legislature reshaped the district in 1997, Watt was still easily reelected the following year and has been returned to office in subsequent elections. *Congressional Quarterly* magazine named him one of the fifty most effective members of Congress in 1999. Watt serves as a member of the CONGRESSIONAL BLACK CAUCUS, the House Financial Services Committee, and the House Judiciary Committee.

See also United States House of Representatives, African Americans in.

Wattleton, Faye

1943–

Former president of the Planned Parenthood Federation of America (PPFA), largely responsible for the group's advocacy of abortion rights.

Alyce Faye Wattleton was born in St. Louis, Missouri, the only child of Ozie Walton, a seamstress and minister, and George Wattleton, a factory worker. She graduated from high school at the age of sixteen and attended Ohio State University, from which she received a degree in nursing in 1964. She later entered Columbia University to pursue a master's degree in maternal and infant care. At Columbia—during a time when almost all abortions were illegal—her patients included many girls and women who had attempted to abort their pregnancies, often with catastrophic results. Wattleton soon became active in Planned Parenthood. In the late 1960s, she headed a local chapter in Dayton, Ohio, dramatically expanding its services to women and children as well as its donor base. In 1978, she was named president of the PPFA.

At the time, Planned Parenthood was known mainly for its several hundred clinics offering such services as birth control, prenatal care, and abortions. Although most types of abortions became legal after the Supreme Court confirmed their constitutionality in the 1973 case *Roe v. Wade*, abortion opponents were fighting back. In 1977 the congressional Hyde Amendment restricted federal funding for abortions, and in the 1980 presidential campaign, candidate Ronald Reagan promised to support the so-called pro-life cause.

Wattleton used her position in Planned Parenthood to advocate reproductive rights. Along with other abortion-rights groups, she fought to secure federal funding for birth control and prenatal programs; to forbid states from restricting abortions; and to legalize the sale in the United States of RU-486, the French-made pill that induces abortions. Wattleton and her allies suffered a number of setbacks, including the Supreme Court's 1989 decision in *Webster v. Reproductive Health Services* to allow states to restrict abortions. Wattleton used such defeats to further mobilize activists and donors. In 1992, Wattleton resigned from Planned Parenthood to host a talk show based in CHICAGO.

Wattleton has received awards from many national organizations, including the American Public Health Association, the CONGRESSIONAL BLACK CAUCUS, and the American Nurses Association. In 1993 she was elected to the National Women's Hall of Fame, and in 1997 the National Mother's Day Committee honored her as its Outstanding Mother. Wattleton has also been presented with twelve honorary doctoral degrees. She is currently president of the Center for Gender Equality, a nonprofit research and educational institution dedicated to removing obstacles to full equality for women, and she is also a widely sought-after speaker and guest lecturer.

Watts, André

1946–

African American concert pianist and the first black American instrumental superstar.

Since his rise to prominence in 1963, André Watts has been one of the world's leading classical pianists. At the age of sixteen, he became the first black instrumental soloist in more than sixty years to perform with the New York Philharmonic Orchestra, under conductor Leonard Bernstein. Within a decade

he was renowned worldwide for his technical brilliance, poetic style, and fiery temperament. According to music critic Elyse Mach, "Watts is to a concert stage as lightning is to thunder. Explosive. More than any other pianist, his performances are reminiscent of what a Liszt concert must have been like: mesmerizing, theatrical, charged with energy."

Watts ascribes his career success largely to luck and what he calls "a combination of those funny, indefinable qualities that are in a person at birth." He also cites his mother as a critical influence: "I wouldn't be a pianist today if my mother hadn't made me practice." He was born in a United States Army camp in Nuremberg, Germany, the only child of Herman Watts, an African American career soldier, and Maria Alexandra Gusmits, a Hungarian who had been displaced in Germany following WORLD WAR II. When he was four he began playing a miniature violin and at the age of seven studied piano with his mother, an accomplished pianist. In 1954 his family moved to PHILADELPHIA, PENNSYLVANIA, where he received a private school education and studied at the Philadelphia Academy of Music.

Watts first performed publicly at the age of nine, playing the Haydn Concerto in D Major in a children's concert sponsored by the Philadelphia Orchestra. Several performances with other orchestras followed, and at the age of sixteen he won an audition to perform in a nationally televised Young People's Concert with the New York Philharmonic, playing Liszt's Piano Concerto No. 1. His performance stunned audiences and music critics alike.

In late January 1963, a few weeks after the Liszt performance, Leonard Bernstein, who predicted "gianthood" for the young pianist, invited Watts to substitute as a soloist for ailing pianist Glenn Gould. Bernstein proved instrumental in Watts's success: his second New York Philharmonic performance won him a ten-minute standing ovation and invitations to perform with the world's major orchestras, which were generally closed to black instrumentalists without the backing of an eminent conductor or music manager. Spared the ordeals of competitive life, he focused on his artistry and academic education.

In 1969 Watts enrolled at Baltimore's Peabody Conservatory of Music, where he studied with pianist Leon Fleisher and, in 1972, received his Artist's Diploma. That same year, he became the youngest person ever to receive an honorary doctorate from Yale University. Meanwhile, his international career flourished. In 1966 he made his European debut with the London Symphony Orchestra and also performed his first solo recital in New York. He recorded extensively and continued to tour throughout Europe, Asia, and the United States. During the late 1960s and 1970s he was often chosen to perform at important political occasions: he became the first American pianist to play in the People's Republic of China, as a soloist with the Philadelphia Orchestra. In 1973 he toured Russia.

Although the quality of Watts's playing has not been consistent throughout his career, his recent recordings and concerts have reaffirmed his musical brilliance. In 1995 he recorded Tchaikovsky's Piano Concerto No. 1 and Saint-Saëns's Piano Concerto No. 2 with the Atlanta Symphony—his first concerto recording in more than ten years. "His playing is technically superb, fluent and melodious," wrote music critic Alexander Morin. "A concert always is an incredible exposition of one's daring and insides," said Watts of his own playing. "If you're not willing to do that . . . then there's a limit to what you can offer the people."

Watts has been artist-in-residence at the University of Maryland since 2000. He regularly appears at major summer music festivals, and continues to tour and perform with some of the world's leading symphony orchestras.

Roanne Edwards

Watts, J(ulius) C(aesar)

1957–

Republican member of the United States House of Representatives from Oklahoma.

J. C. Watts was born in Eufaula, Oklahoma, where his father was the town's first African American police officer. Watts himself made history in Eufaula, helping to integrate the local elementary school and becoming the first black quarterback on the Eufaula High School football team. He attended the University of Oklahoma, where he earned statewide recognition playing quarterback for the school's football team and leading them to two consecutive Orange Bowl victories. Watts graduated in 1981 with a Bachelor of Arts degree in journalism, after which he enjoyed a successful career in the Canadian Football League. After retiring from football in 1986, he returned to Oklahoma to pursue business interests.

Watts says his fascination with politics was sparked when he was a journalism student covering political events. In his initial foray into politics, he was elected to a seat on the Oklahoma Corporation Commission, a state entity charged with regulating the oil and natural gas utilities. This position led him to seek the seat for Oklahoma's Fourth Congressional District in 1994, which he won after a close runoff in the Republican primary. Watts was reelected in 1996, capturing fifty-eight percent of the vote in a district that was traditionally Democratic and more than eighty percent white. He was returned to office in subsequent elections.

Watts, who is also an ordained Baptist minister, is a charismatic speaker. His party featured him prominently at the Republican National Convention in 1996 and selected him to offer its response to President Bill Clinton's State of the Union address in January 1997. By the time he was elected chair of the Republican Conference in November 1998, Watts had solidified his position as a rising star in the REPUBLICAN PARTY. The only African American Republican in the U.S. HOUSE OF REPRESENTATIVES—and the only black representative who did not belong to the CONGRESSIONAL BLACK CAUCUS—Watts heartily endorsed much of his party's conservative platform, including calls for individual responsibility, a strong national defense, welfare reform, and tax cuts.

Watts did not stand for reelection to Congress in 2002, and decided to serve as chairman of J. C. Watts Companies, a business and lobbying firm with offices in WASHINGTON, D.C. and Norman, Oklahoma. He remained active in Republican Party politics and in 2003 was named chairman of GOPAC, the leading organization for education and training of Republican candidates and activists.

See also United States House of Representatives, African Americans in.

Watts Riot of 1965

First major racially-charged rebellion of the 1960s, an event that foreshadowed the widespread urban violence of the latter half of the decade.

With the arrest of a twenty-one-year-old African American on August 11, 1965, the South Central neighborhood of Watts in LOS ANGELES, CALIFORNIA erupted into violence. A Los Angeles police officer flagged down motorist Marquette Frye, whom he suspected of being intoxicated. When a crowd of onlookers began to taunt the policeman, a second officer was called in. According to eyewitness accounts, the second officer struck crowd members with his baton, and news of the act of police brutal-

Residents in the Watts neighborhood of Los Angeles make their way through rubble in the aftermath of the 1965 riots. *Getty Images*

**MAJOR RACIAL RIOTS
1931–1999**

There were "civil disturbances" in more than 40 cities in each of the summers of 1966 and 1977 and in 125 cities after the assassination of Rev. Martin Luther King Jr., on April 4, 1968.

0   300 km
0   300 mi

Harlem, New York City
1935, 1943,
1964, 1968

1967 Newark

Washington,
D.C.

1968 Md.

Miami
1980

Cleveland
1966, 1968

1943, 1967 Detroit

1966
Nashville Tennessee

1963 Birmingham

Chicago 1968

1965, 1992 Los Angeles

ity soon spread throughout the neighborhood. The incident, combined with escalating racial tensions, overcrowding in the neighborhood, and a summer heat wave, sparked violence on a massive scale. Despite attempts the following day aimed at quelling antipolice sentiment, residents began looting and burning local stores. In the rioting, which lasted five days, more than thirty-four people died, at least 1,000 were wounded, and an estimated $200 million in property was destroyed. An estimated 35,000 African Americans took part in the riot, which required 16,000 National Guardsmen, county deputies, and city police to put down.

Although city officials initially blamed outside agitators for the insurrection, subsequent studies showed that the majority of participants had lived in Watts all their lives. These studies also found that the protesters' anger was directed primarily at white shopkeepers in the neighborhood and at members of the all-white Los Angeles police force. The rioters left black churches, libraries, businesses, and private homes virtually untouched.

The Watts Riot was the first major lesson for the American public on the tinderbox volatility of segregated inner-city neighborhoods. The riot provided a sobering preview of the violent urban uprisings of the late 1960s and helped define several hardcore political camps: militant blacks applauded the spectacle of rage; moderates lamented the riot's senselessness and self-destructiveness; and conservative whites viewed the uprising as a symptom of the aggressive pace of civil rights legislation.

The Watts Riot changed California's political landscape and damaged a number of political careers, including that of Governor Edmund G. "Pat" Brown. The liberal Brown lost his office to challenger Ronald Reagan, in part because Reagan was able to pin the blame for the riot on the incumbent.

Eric Bennett

WDIA

Powerful radio station in Memphis, Tennessee, known as "The Mother Station for the Negroes," which in 1948 became the first to target an African American audience.

WDIA, the first black-format radio station in the United States, sought an African American audience through black disc jockeys (DJs) playing mostly RHYTHM-AND-BLUES (R&B) music. Its success led other urban radio stations to take a similar approach, providing airplay for African American musicians and jobs for black DJs. WDIA also played a role in laying the foundations for white rock and roll. It and similar stations attracted many young white listeners. As southern white teenagers discovered the exciting sound of R&B, they began purchasing R&B records and attending R&B concerts. And some began playing music shaped by black R&B, including young Elvis Presley.

WDIA's success reflected the transforming effect of the GREAT MIGRATION, a massive shift of the southern black population from rural to urban. While many blacks moved to urban areas in the North and West, others headed for southern cities such as MEMPHIS, TENNESSEE. WDIA sought to tap this new market. When white businessmen Robert Ferguson and John Pepper purchased the station in 1947, it had a tiny 250-watt transmitter and was restricted to daytime broadcasting. Ferguson and Pepper initially broadcast classical music, but, finding few listeners, they vastly increased the station's power and targeted a black audience. WDIA adopted the slogan "50,000 Watts of Goodwill," and later, "The Black Spot on Your Radio Dial—50,000 Watts of Black Power" but was commonly known as "The Mother Station for the Negroes."

WDIA's success was due in considerable measure to Nat D. Williams, hired in 1948 as a DJ and, in effect, the station's program director. However, WDIA and similar white-owned radio stations regarded African Americans strictly as employees, not partners or managers, and Williams never had a formal role in station management. WDIA did hire many black DJs, including two who found fame as musicians, Rufus Thomas and RILEY B. KING. Thomas began at WDIA in 1950 and had a number of hits in the 1950s and 1960s. King worked for the station from 1948 to 1952. "They put me on . . . for about ten minutes every day," he later told Stanley Booth. "They didn't pay me . . . but I could advertise where I was going to play." The station dubbed him "Blues Boy from Beale Street," and the nickname, shortened to B. B., stuck.

WDIA continues to broadcast from Memphis today.

See also Radio and African Americans.

James Sellman

Weah, George

1966–

Liberian international soccer player.

In the 1990s George Weah emerged as one of the best SOCCER players in the world and the unofficial leader of the approximately 350 Africans who play soccer in Europe. After a difficult childhood in MONROVIA, where he was born, Weah became a devout Muslim and a talented athlete, then using his African name, Oppong. Weah began his career playing for teams in Monrovia and YAOUNDÉ, CAMEROON. A striker, the six-foot-tall Weah was known for his ball control and ferocious shooting.

In 1988 Weah moved to Europe, where he played for AS Monaco (1987–1992), Paris St. Germain (1992–1995), and AC Milan (1995–2000), a team which he led to Italian league championships in 1996 and 1999. In 1995 soccer's international governing body, Federation Internationale de Football Association (FIFA), named Weah the top player of the year, the first time the award had gone to an African. In 1998 he was named African player of the century. Weah left Milan in 2000 to play for Chelsea in England's Premiere League, and he later spent a short time with clubs in Manchester, England and Marseilles, France before retiring from competitive play. In 2002 he returned to play for AC Milan in a series of exhibition matches in the United States.

Weah is usually soft-spoken, but he was a vocal critic of groups that were fighting in Liberia's civil war. Afterward, his relatives were attacked and his house and property were destroyed. In 1996 Weah spent over $50,000 of his own money to help finance Liberia's ultimately unsuccessful bid to play in the 1998 World Cup, an act that won him the FIFA Fair Play Award. Since retiring from soccer, Weah has served as ambassador for the SOS Children's Village in Enneralde, SOUTH AFRICA as well as a sports representative for the United Nations Children's Fund (UNICEF).

See also Athletes, African, Abroad.

Kate Tuttle

Weaverbird

General name for birds of a passerine family found mainly in Africa, with five species inhabiting Asia.

The weaverbird's name reflects the structure of its nests, woven of grasses and other plant materials. Many species are colonial, building dozens of nests in a single tree; many pairs of the sociable weaver of southern Africa nest in a single huge, cooperatively built structure with separate entrances. Males of the representative genus are mostly patterned in black and yellow, while females are inconspicuous, sparrowlike birds, colored in buff and brown. Among the bishops, which are popular cage birds, the males are black with touches of bright red, orange, or yellow, but again, females are sparrowlike. In several species of weaverbirds, the males molt into a femalelike "eclipse" plumage after the breeding season.

The red-billed quelea, of the dry savannas of sub-Saharan Africa, is one of the greatest agricultural pests on that continent. About 13 centimeters (about 5 inches) long, it is a sparrowlike bird with a bright pink bill. Breeding males have a black face and a pink wash on the head and underparts; "eclipse" males and females lack the black face and pink wash. Great clouds of hundreds of thousands of these birds descend on grain fields, often completely wiping out a crop.

Scientific classification: Weaverbirds make up the family Ploceidae of the order Passeriformes. They are sometimes placed in the family Passeridae. The representative genus is *Ploceus*. The sociable weaver is classified as *Philetairus socius*. Bishops make up the genus *Euplectes*. The red-billed quelea is classified as *Quelea quelea*.

Weaver, Robert Clifton

1907–1997

First African American United States Cabinet member, secretary of housing and urban development from 1966 to 1968.

Robert Clifton Weaver with President Lyndon Johnson after being sworn in as secretary of HUD. *CORBIS*

Born in WASHINGTON, D.C., the son of Mortimer and Florence Weaver, Robert Clifton Weaver grew up attending segregated schools. After graduating from high school, he attended Harvard University, where his older brother, Mortimer, was pursuing graduate studies in English. Weaver was refused dormitory accommodations because he was black, so he lived off campus with his brother. Robert Weaver graduated cum laude with a degree in economics in 1929, the same year Mortimer died unexpectedly. Weaver remained at Harvard, earning an M.A. in 1931 and a Ph.D. in economics in 1934.

Weaver began his government career in 1933 when Secretary of the Interior Harold Ickes hired him as a race-relations adviser in the housing division. By 1937 he had become special assistant to the administrator of the U.S. Housing Authority, a post he held until 1940. As a high-ranking African American in President Franklin D. Roosevelt's administration, Weaver was a member of the BLACK CABINET, an informal network of African Americans who worked to end racial discrimination in the federal government and the programs it administered.

In 1944, after serving on the National Defense Advisory Committee, the Manpower Commission, and the War Production Board, Weaver was appointed the director of the Mayor's Committee on Race Relations in CHICAGO, ILLINOIS, and then director of the American Council on Race Relations. During this time he published two critical studies of discrimination in the United States, *Negro Labor: A National Problem* (1946), and *The Negro Ghetto* (1948).

In 1955 Weaver became the first African American to hold a state cabinet-level position when New York governor Averell Harriman named him state rent commissioner. Weaver held this post until 1960, when President John F. Kennedy named him director of the U.S. Housing and Home Finance Agency, making him the highest-ranking African American in government.

Kennedy intended to establish a cabinet-level agency to address urban affairs and make Weaver its head. But Southern members of Congress who opposed an African American cabinet member in general and Weaver's strong support of integrated housing in particular blocked Kennedy's plan. The agency, the Department of Housing and Urban Development (HUD), was not established until President Lyndon B. Johnson was elected in 1965. In 1966, with Johnson better able to exercise power in the Congress, Weaver became the first HUD secretary and the first African American cabinet member.

Weaver effectively administered HUD, but his more ambitious and imaginative plans, such as Demonstration Cities and the Metropolitan Development Act, were unsupported because the federal government gave precedence to the Vietnam War (1959–1975) and because of conservative reaction to ghetto rioting from 1965 to 1968. In 1969 Weaver ended his career in government and became president of City College of New York (CCNY)'s Baruch College. In 1971 he became distinguished professor of urban affairs at CCNY's Hunter College, and he became professor emeritus in 1978.

Weaver's public service extended beyond his careers in government and education. He chaired the board of directors of the NATIONAL ASSOCIATION FOR THE ADVANCEMENT OF COLORED PEOPLE (NAACP) in 1960 and was president of the National Committee against Discrimination in Housing from 1973 to 1987. In addition, Weaver received the Spingarn Medal in 1962, the New York City Urban League's Frederick Douglass Award in 1977, the Schomburg Collection Award in 1978, and the Equal Opportunity Day Award from the National Urban League in 1987.

Robert Fay

Webb, Chick

1909?–1939

African American bandleader, one of the greatest big-band drummers of the swing era.

William Henry Webb was born in Baltimore, Maryland. He bought his first drum set around 1919, with money he earned as a newsboy. He then worked as a street musician and in some local bands in BALTIMORE. In the mid-1920s he moved to NEW YORK CITY and began leading small groups in clubs and ballrooms. His first band, called the Jungle Band, made its first recording in 1929 for Brunswick Records. For the next few years Webb worked at popular clubs such as the Roseland and Savoy ballrooms and the COTTON CLUB. By the early 1930s his band of eleven or twelve musicians was appearing regularly at the SAVOY BALLROOM, then the most famous dancehall in HARLEM, NEW YORK.

In 1934 Webb hired JAZZ vocalist ELLA FITZGERALD, who was still a teenager, to sing with the band. Two years later saxophonist and singer Louis Jordan joined the group. The band's fame increased, due largely to recordings and radio broadcasts featuring Fitzgerald and Jordan. Sadly, during his years of greatest professional success Webb suffered increasingly from tuberculosis, which particularly affected his spine. Though sometimes forced to take time off from his performing schedule, he continued to play whenever he could, including one last performance just days before his final hospitalization. After his death the band continued to perform for three more years, billed initially as Ella Fitzgerald and the Famous Chick Webb Orchestra, then as Ella Fitzgerald and Her Famous Orchestra.

Webb conquered serious obstacles to achieve his place in music. Injured in a fall during childhood, he had a curved spine and was barely four feet tall. Consequently, he had to use special attachments to play his drum set. He had little formal education and did not read music. As a self-taught drummer he relied on his natural musicianship and quick memory to master his band's library of arrangements. Webb's ability to energize his big band with supportive ensemble playing and inventive solo breaks is readily apparent on such excellent recordings as "Don't Be That Way" (1934), "Go Harlem" (1936), and "Liza" (1938). In a legendary "Battle of the Bands" at the Savoy, Webb's band outdid the Benny Goodman Orchestra, featuring drummer Gene Krupa. According to Krupa, Webb "cut me to ribbons." In the late 1930s, however, Webb's band's fame rested primarily on a series of less substantial popular hits that featured Fitzgerald. Most of them, except for her signature hit "A-Tisket A-Tasket" (1938), subsequently slipped into obscurity.

Shortly after Webb's death, a group of his close friends and fellow musicians held a benefit concert to raise funds for a children's recreation center in East Baltimore. The Chick Webb Recreation Center was completed and dedicated in 1947 and continues to serve disadvantaged youth in Baltimore.

Webb, Frank J.

1828–1894?

American author who wrote about interracial marriage and passing.

Little is known about Frank Webb's life. Raised in PHILADELPHIA, PENNSYLVANIA, he lived in England, FRANCE, and KINGSTON, JAMAICA. Webb returned to the United States in 1870, publishing two novelettes that year, "Two Wolves and a Lamb" and "Marvin Hayle." Following this he moved to Galveston, Texas, where he edited a radical newspaper before running a school until his death. His one novel, *The Garies and Their Friends*, published in 1857, was the second of only four African American novels published before the AMERICAN CIVIL WAR. The first novel about free African Americans in the North, Webb's book explored interracial marriage and passing.

See also Passing in the United States.

Robert Fay

W. E. B. Du Bois: An Interpretation

W. E. B. Du Bois is the towering black scholar of the twentieth century. The scope of his interests, the depth of his insights, and the sheer majesty of his prolific writings bespeak a level of genius unequaled among modern black intellectuals. Yet, like all of us, Du Bois was a child of his age. He was shaped by the prevailing presuppositions and prejudices of modern Euro-American civilization. And despite his lifelong struggle—marked by great courage and sacrifice—against white supremacy and for the advancement of Africans around the world, he was, in style and substance, a proud black man of letters primarily influenced by 19th-century Euro-American traditions.

For those of us interested in the relation of white supremacy to modernity (African slavery in the New World and European imperial domination of most of the rest of the world) or the consequences of the construct of "race" during the Age of Europe (1492–1945), the scholarly and literary works of Du Bois are indispensable. For those of us obsessed with alleviating black social misery, the political texts of Du Bois are insightful and inspiring. In this sense, Du Bois is the brook of fire through which we all must pass in order to gain access to the intellectual and political weaponry needed to sustain the radical democratic tradition in our time.

Yet even this great titan of black emancipation falls short of the mark. This is not to deny the remarkable subtlety of his mind or the undeniable sincerity of his heart. The grand example of Du Bois remains problematic principally owing to his inadequate interpretation of the human condition and his inability to immerse himself fully in the rich cultural currents of black everyday life. His famous notion of the TALENTED TENTH reveals this philosophic inadequacy and personal inability.

In an 1897 article, W. E. B. Du Bois wrote, "One feels his two-ness—an American; a Negro; two souls, two thoughts, two unreconciled strivings; two warring ideals in one dark body, whose dogged strength alone keeps it from being torn asunder." *CORBIS*

What does it mean to claim that Du Bois put forward an inadequate interpretation of the human condition or that he failed to immerse himself fully in the cultural depths of black everyday life? Are these simply rhetorical claims devoid of content—too abstract to yield conclusions and too general to evaluate? Are some interpretations of the human condition and cultural ways of life really better than others? If so, why? These crucial questions sit at the center of my critique of Du Bois because they take us to the heart of black life in the profoundly decadent American civilization at the end of the twentieth century—a ghastly century whose levels of barbarity, bestiality, and brutality are unparalleled in human history.

My assessment of Du Bois primarily concerns his response to the problem of evil—to undeserved harm, unjustified suf-

fering, and unmerited pain. Does his evolving worldview, social analysis, and moral vision enable us to understand and endure this "first century of world wars" (Muriel Rukeyser's apt phrase) in which nearly 200 million fellow human beings have been murdered in the name of some pernicious ideology? Does his work contain the necessary intellectual and existential resources enabling us to confront the indescribable agony and unnamable anguish likely to be unleashed in the twenty-first century—the first century involving a systemic gangsterization of everyday life, shot through with revitalized tribalisms—under the aegis of an uncontested, fast-paced global capitalism? As with any great figure, to grapple with Du Bois is to wrestle with who we are, why we are what we are, and what we are to do about it.

Du Bois was first and foremost a black New England Victorian seduced by the Enlightenment ethos and enchanted with the American Dream. His interpretation of the human condition—that is, in part, his idea of who he was and could be—was based on his experiences and, most important, on his understanding of those experiences through the medium of an Enlightenment worldview that promoted Victorian strategies in order to realize an American optimism; throughout this essay, I shall probe these three basic foundations of his perspective. Like many of the brilliant and ambitious young men of his time, he breathed the intoxicating fumes of "advanced" intellectual and political culture. Yet in the face of entrenched evil and demonic power, Du Bois often found himself either shipwrecked in the depths of his soul or barely afloat with less and less wind in his existential sails.

My fundamental problem with Du Bois is his inadequate grasp of the tragicomic sense of life—refusal candidly to confront the sheer absurdity of the human condition. This tragicomic sense—tragicomic rather than simply "tragic," because even ultimate purpose and objective order are called into question—propels us toward suicide or madness unless we are buffered by ritual, cushioned by community, or sustained by art. Du Bois's inability to immerse himself in black everyday life precluded his access to the distinctive black tragicomic sense and black encounter with the absurd. He certainly saw, analyzed, and empathized with black sadness, sorrow, and suffering. But he didn't feel it in his bones deeply enough, nor was he intellectually open enough to position himself alongside the sorrowful, suffering, yet striving ordinary black folk. Instead, his own personal and intellectual distance lifted him above them even as he addressed their plight in his progressive writings. Du Bois was never alienated by black people—he lived in black communities where he received great respect and admiration. But there seemed to be something in him that alienated ordinary black people. In short, he was reluctant to learn fundamental lessons about life—and about himself—from them. Such lessons would have required that he—at least momentarily—believe that they were or might be as wise, insightful, and "advanced" as he; and this he could not do.

Du Bois's Enlightenment worldview—his first foundation—prohibited this kind of understanding. Instead, he adopted a mild elitism that underestimated the capacity of everyday people to "know" about life. In "The Talented Tenth," he claims, "knowledge of life and its wider meaning, has been the point of the Negro's deepest ignorance." In his classic book *The Souls of Black Folk*, there are eighteen references to "black, backward, and ungraceful" folk, including a statement of his intent "to scatter civilization among a people whose ignorance was not simply of letters, but of life itself."

My aim is not to romanticize those whom Sly Stone calls "everyday people" or to cast them as the sole source of wisdom. The myths of the noble savage and the wise commoner are simply the flip sides of the Enlightenment attempts to degrade and devalue everyday people. Yet Du Bois—owing to his Puritan New England origins and Enlightenment values—found it difficult not to view common black folk as some degraded

"other" or "alien" no matter how hard he resisted. His honest response to a church service in the backwoods of Tennessee at a "Southern Negro Revival" bears this out.

> A sort of suppressed terror hung in the air and seemed to seize us—a pythian madness, a demoniac possession, that lent terrible reality to song and word. The black and massive form of the preacher swayed and quivered as the words crowded to his lips and flew at us in singular eloquence. The people moaned and fluttered, and then the gaunt-cheeked brown woman beside me suddenly leaped straight into the air and shrieked like a lost soul, while round about came wail and groan and outcry, and a scene of human passion such as I had never conceived before. Those who have not thus witnessed the frenzy of a Negro revival in the untouched backwoods of the South can but dimly realize the religious feeling of the slave; as described, such scenes appear grotesque and funny, but as seen they are awful.

Du Bois's intriguing description reminds one of an anthropologist visiting some strange and exotic people whose rituals suggest not only the sublime but also the satanic. The "awfulness" of this black church service, similar to that of my own black Baptist tradition, signifies for him both dread and fear, anxiety and disgust. In short, a black ritualistic explosion of energy frightened this black rationalist. It did so not simply because the folk seem so coarse and uncouth, but also because they are out of control, overpowered by something bigger than themselves. This clearly posed a threat to him.

Like a good Enlightenment philosophe, Du Bois pits autonomy against authority, self-mastery against tradition. Autonomy and self-mastery connote self-consciousness and self-criticism; authority and tradition suggest blind deference and subordination. Self-consciousness and self-criticism yield cosmopolitanism and highbrow culture. Authority and tradition reinforce provincialism and lowbrow culture. The educated and chattering class—the Talented Tenth—are the agents of sophistication and mastery, while the uneducated and moaning class—the backward masses—remain locked in tradition; the basic role of the Talented Tenth is to civilize and refine, uplift and elevate the benighted masses.

For Du Bois, education was the key. Ignorance was the major obstacle—black ignorance and white ignorance. If the black masses were educated—in order to acquire skills and culture—black America would thrive. If white elites and masses were enlightened, they would not hate and fear black folk. Hence America—black and white—could be true to its democratic ideals.

> The Negro Problem was in my mind a matter of systematic investigation and intelligent understanding. The world was thinking wrong about race, because it did not know. The ultimate evil was stupidity. The cure for it was knowledge based on scientific investigation.

This Enlightenment naiveté, not only in regard to white supremacy but also with respect to any form of personal and in-

stitutional evil, was momentarily shaken by a particular case
involving that most peculiar American institution—LYNCHING.

> At the very time when my studies were most success-
> ful, there cut across this plan which I had as a scien-
> tist, a red ray which could not be ignored. I remember
> when it first, as it were, startled me to my feet: a poor
> Negro in central Georgia, Sam Hose, had killed his land-
> lord's wife. I wrote out a careful and reasoned state-
> ment concerning the evident facts and started down to
> the Atlanta Constitution office . . . I did not get there.
> On the way news met me: Sam Hose had been lynched,
> and they said that his knuckles were on exhibition at a
> grocery store farther down on Mitchell Street, along
> which I was walking. I turned back to the university. I
> began to turn aside from my work . . .
>
>   Two considerations thereafter broke in upon my
> work and eventually disrupted it: first, one could not
> be a calm, cool, and detached scientist while Negroes
> were lynched, murdered and starved; and secondly,
> there was no such definite demand for scientific work
> of the sort that I was doing . . .

Then, in the very next month, Du Bois lost his eighteen-month-
old son, Burghardt, to diphtheria. If ever Du Bois was forced
to confront the tragedy of life and the absurdity of existence,
it was in the aftermath of this loss, which he describes in his
most moving piece of writing, "Of the Passing of the First-
Born," in *The Souls of Black Folk*. In this powerful elegiac essay, Du Bois not only mourns his son but speaks directly to
death itself—as Prometheus to Zeus or Jesus to his Heavenly
Father.

> But hearken, O Death! Is not this my life hard enough,
> is not that dull land that stretches its sneering web about
> me cold enough,—is not all the world beyond these four
> little walls pitiless enough, but that thou must needs
> enter here,—thou, O Death? About my head the thun-
> dering storm beat like a heartless voice, and the crazy
> forest pulsed with the curses of the weak; but what
> cared I, within my home beside my wife and baby boy?
> Wast thou so jealous of one little coign of happiness
> that thou must needs enter there,—thou, O Death?

This existential gall to go face-to-face and toe-to-toe with death
in order to muster some hope against hope is echoed in his
most tragic characterization of the black sojourn in white supremacist America.

> Within the Veil was he born, said I; and there within
> shall he live,—a Negro and a Negro's son. Holding in
> that little head—ah, bitterly!—the unbowed pride of a
> hunted race, clinging with that tiny dimpled hand—ah,
> wearily!—to a hope not hopeless but unhopeful, and
> seeing with those bright wondering eyes that peer into
> my soul a land whose freedom is to us a mockery and
> whose liberty a lie.

What is most revealing in this most poignant of moments is
Du Bois's refusal to linger with the sheer tragedy of his son's

death (a natural, not a social, evil)—without casting his son as
an emblem of the race or a symbol of a black deliverance to
come. Despite the deep sadness in this beautiful piece of writing, Du Bois sidesteps Dostoyevsky's challenge to wrestle in a
sustained way with the irrevocable fact of an innocent child's
death. Du Bois's rationalism prevents him from wading in such
frightening existential waters. Instead, Du Bois rushes to glib
theodicy, weak allegory, and superficial symbolism. In other
words, his Enlightenment worldview falters in the face of
death—the deaths of Sam Hose and Burghardt. The deep despair that lurks around the corner is held at arm's length by
rational attempts to boost his flagging spirit.

Du Bois's principal intellectual response to the limits of his
Enlightenment worldview was to incorporate certain insights
of Marx and Freud. Yet Marx's powerful critique of the unequal
relations of power between capitalists and the proletariat in the
workplace and Freud's penetrating attempt to exercise rational
control over the irrational forces at work in self and society
only deepened Du Bois's commitment to the Enlightenment
ethos. And though particular features of this ethos are essential to any kind of intellectual integrity and democratic vision—
features such as self-criticism and self-development, suspicion
of illegitimate authority and suffocating tradition—the Enlightenment worldview held by Du Bois is ultimately inadequate,
and, in many ways, antiquated, for our time. The tragic plight
and absurd predicament of Africans here and abroad requires
a more profound interpretation of the human condition—one
that goes far beyond the false dichotomies of expert knowledge
versus mass ignorance, individual autonomy versus dogmatic
authority, and self-mastery versus intolerant tradition. Our
tragicomic times require more democratic concepts of knowledge and leadership which highlight human fallibility and
mutual accountability; notions of individuality and contested
authority which stress dynamic traditions; and ideals of self-
realization within participatory communities.

The second fundamental pillar of Du Bois's intellectual project is his Victorian strategies—namely, the ways in which his
Enlightenment worldview can be translated into action. They
rest upon three basic assumptions. First, that the self-appointed
agents of Enlightenment constitute a sacrificial cultural elite engaged in service on behalf of the impulsive and irrational
masses. Second, that this service consists of shaping and mold-
ing the values and viewpoints of the masses by managing educational and political bureaucracies (e.g., schools and political parties). Third, that the effective management of these
bureaucracies by the educated few for the benefit of the pathetic many promotes material and spiritual progress. These assumptions form the terrain on which the Talented Tenth are
to operate.

In fact, Du Bois's notion of the Talented Tenth is a descendant of those cultural and political elites conceived by the
major Victorian critics during the heyday of the British Empire
in its industrial phase. S. T. Coleridge's secular clerisy, Thomas
Carlyle's strong heroes, and Matthew Arnold's disinterested
aliens all shun the superficial vulgarity of materialism and the
cheap thrills of hedonism in order to preserve and promote
highbrow culture and to civilize and contain the lowbrow

masses. The resounding first and last sentences of Du Bois's essay "The Talented Tenth" not only echo the "truths" of Victorian social criticism, they also bestow upon the educated few a salvific role. "The Negro race, like all races, is going to be saved by its exceptional men." This bold statement is descriptive, prescriptive, and predictive. It assumes that the exceptional men of other races have saved their "race" (Gladstone in Britain, Menelik in Ethiopia, Bismarck in Germany, Napoleon in France, Peter in Russia?). Here Du Bois claims that exceptional black men ought to save their "race" and asserts that if any "race"—especially black people—is to be saved, exceptional men will do it. The patriarchal sensibilities speak for themselves.

Like a good Victorian critic, Du Bois argues on rational grounds for the legitimacy of his cultural elite. They are worthy of leadership because they are educated and trained, refined and civilized, disciplined and determined. Most important, they have "honesty of heart" and "Purity of motive." Contrast Matthew Arnold's disinterested aliens, "who are mainly led, not by their class spirit, but by a general humane spirit, by the love of human perfection," in *Culture and Anarchy* (1869) with Du Bois's Talented Tenth.

> The men of culture are the true apostles of equality. The great men of culture are those who have had a passion for diffusing, for making prevail, for carrying from one end of society to the other, the best knowledge, the best ideas of their time, who have laboured to divest knowledge of all that was harsh, uncouth, difficult, abstract, professional, exclusive; to humanize it, to make it efficient outside the clique of the cultivated and learned, yet still remaining the best knowledge and thought of the time, and a true source, therefore, of sweetness and light.

> Who are today guiding the work of the Negro people? The "exceptions" of course . . . A saving remnant continually survives and persists, continually aspires, continually shows itself in thrift and ability and character . . .

> Can the masses of the Negro people be in any possible way more quickly raised than by the effort and example of this aristocracy of talent and character? Was there ever a nation on God's fair earth civilized from the bottom upward? Never; it is, ever was and ever will be from the top downward that culture filters. The Talented Tenth rises and pulls all that are worth the saving up to their vantage ground. This is the history of human progress; and the two historic mistakes which have hindered that progress were the thinking first that no more could ever rise save the few already risen; or second, that it would better the unrisen to pull the risen down.

Just as Arnold seeks to carve out discursive space and a political mission for the educated elite in the British Empire somewhere between the arrogance and complacency of the aristocracy and the vulgarity and anarchy of the working classes, Du Bois wants to create a new vocabulary and social vocation for

the black educated elite in America somewhere between the hatred and scorn of the white supremacist majority and the crudity and illiteracy of the black agrarian masses. Yet his gallant efforts suffer from intellectual defects and historical misconceptions.

Let us begin with the latter. Is it true that in 1903 the educated elite were guiding the work of the Negro people? Yes and no. Certainly the most visible national black leaders tended to be educated black men, such as the ubiquitous BOOKER T. WASHINGTON and, of course, Du Bois himself. Yet the two most effective political forms of organizing and mobilizing among black people were the black women's club movement led by IDA B. WELLS and the migration movement guided by BENJAMIN "PAP" SINGLETON, A. A. BRADLEY, and RICHARD H. CAIN. Both movements were based in black civil society—that is, black civic associations like churches, lodges, fraternal orders, and sororities. Their fundamental goals were neither civil rights nor social equality but rather respect and dignity, land and self-determination. How astonishing—and limiting—that Du Bois fails to mention and analyze these movements that will result in the great MARY MCLEOD BETHUNE's educational crusade and the inimitable MARCUS GARVEY's "Back to Africa" movement in a decade or so!

Regarding the intellectual defects of Du Bois's noble endeavor: first, he assumes that highbrow culture is inherently humanizing, and that exposure to and immersion in great works produce good people. Yet we have little reason to believe that people who delight in the works of geniuses like Mozart and Beethoven or Goethe and Wordsworth are any more or less humane than those who dance in the barnyards to the banjo plucking of nameless rural folk in Tennessee. Certainly those fervent white supremacists who worship the Greek and Roman classics and revel in the plays of the incomparable Shakespeare weaken his case. Second, Du Bois holds that the educated elite can more easily transcend their individual and class interests and more readily act on behalf of the common good than the uneducated masses. But is this so? Are they not just as prone to corruption and graft, envy and jealousy, self-destructive passion and ruthless ambition as everyone else? Were not Carlyle's great heroes, Cromwell and Napoleon, tyrants? Was it not Arnold's disinterested aliens who promoted and implemented the inhumane policies of the imperial British bureaucracies in India and Africa? Was not Du Bois himself both villain and victim in petty political games as well as in the all-too-familiar social exclusions of the educated elite?

Du Bois wisely acknowledges this problem in his 1948 revision of "The Talented Tenth":

> When I came out of college into the world of work, I realized that it was quite possible that my plan of training a talented tenth might put in control and power, a group of selfish, self-indulgent, well-to-do men, whose basic interest in solving the Negro Problem was personal; personal freedom and unhampered enjoyment and use of the world, without any real care, or certainly no arousing care, as to what became of the mass of American Negroes, or of the mass of any people.

My Talented Tenth, I could see, might result in a sort of interracial free-for-all, with the devil taking the hindmost and the foremost taking anything they could lay hands on.

He then notes the influence of Marx on his thinking and adds that the Talented Tenth must not only be talented but have "expert knowledge" of modern economics, be willing to sacrifice and plan effectively to institute socialist measures. Yet there is still no emphatic call for accountability from below, nor any grappling with the evil that lurks in the hearts of all of us. He recognizes human selfishness as a problem without putting forward adequate philosophical responses to it or institutional mechanisms to alleviate it. In the end, he throws up his hands and gives us a grand either/or option. "But we must have honest men or we die. We must have unselfish, far-seeing leadership or we fail."

Victorian social criticism contains elements indispensable to future critical thought about freedom and democracy in the twenty-first century. Most important, it elevates the role of public intellectuals who put forward overarching visions and broad analyses based on a keen sense of history and a subtle grasp of the way the world is going in the present. The rich tradition of Victorian critics—Thomas Carlyle, John Ruskin, Matthew Arnold, John Morley, William Morris, and, in our own century, L. T. Hobhouse, J. A. Hobson, C. E. G. Masterman, R. H. Tawney, Raymond Williams, E. P. Thompson, and others—stands shoulders above the parochial professionalism of much of the academy today. In our era, scholarship is often divorced from public engagement, and shoddy journalism often settles for the sensational and superficial aspects of prevailing crises. As the distinguished European man of letters George Steiner notes in regard to the academy,

> Specialization has reached moronic vehemence. Learned lives are expended on reiterative minutiae. Academic rewards go to the narrow scholiast, to the blinkered. Men and women in the learned professions proclaim themselves experts on one author, in one brief historical period, in one aesthetic medium. They look with contempt (and dank worry) on the "Generalist." . . . It may be that cows have fields. The geography of consciousness should be that of unfenced errance, Montaigne's comely word.

Yet the Victorian strategies of Du Bois require not piecemeal revision but wholesale reconstruction. A fuller understanding of the human condition should lead us far beyond any notions of free-floating elites, suspicious of the tainted masses—elites who worship at the altar of highbrow culture while ignoring the barbarity and bestiality in their own ranks. The fundamental role of the public intellectual—distinct from, yet building on, the indispensable work of academics, experts, analysts, and pundits—is to create and sustain high-quality public discourse addressing urgent public problems which enlightens and energizes fellow citizens, prompting them to take public action. This role requires a deep commitment to the life of the mind—a perennial attempt to clear our minds of cant (to use Samuel Johnson's famous formulation)—which serves to shape the public destiny of a people. Intellectual and political leadership is neither elitist nor populist; rather it is democratic, in that each of us stands in public space, without humiliation, to put forward our best visions and views for the sake of the public interest. And these arguments are presented in an atmosphere of mutual respect and civic trust.

The last pillar of Du Bois's project is his American optimism. Like most intellectuals of the New World, he was preoccupied with progress. And given his genuine commitment to black advancement, this preoccupation is understandable. Yet, writing as he was in the early stages of the consolidation of the American Empire (some 8 million people of color had been incorporated after the SPANISH-AMERICAN WAR), when the United States itself was undergoing geographical and economic expansion and millions of "new" Americans were being admitted from eastern Europe, Du Bois tended to assume that United States expansionism was a sign of probable American progress. In this sense, in his early and middle years, he was not only a progressivist but also a kind of American exceptionalist. It must be said, to be sure, that unlike most American exceptionalists of his day, he considered the color line the major litmus test for the country. Yet he remained optimistic about a multiracial democratic America.

Du Bois never fully grasped the deeply pessimistic view of American democracy behind the Garvey movement. In fact, he never fully understood or appreciated the strong—though not central—black nationalist strain in the Black Freedom Movement. As much as he hated white supremacy in America, he could never bring himself to identify intimately with the harsh words of the great performing artist JOSEPHINE BAKER, who noted in response to the EAST ST. LOUIS RIOT of July 1917 that left over 200 black people dead and over 6,000 homeless, "The very idea of America makes me shake and tremble and gives me nightmares." Baker lived most of her life in exile in FRANCE. Even when Du Bois left for Africa in 1961—as a member of a moribund Communist Party—his attitude toward America was not that of an ELIJAH MUHAMMAD or a MALCOLM X. He was still, in a significant sense, disappointed with America, and there is no disappointment without some dream deferred. Elijah Muhammad and Malcolm X were not disappointed with America. As bona fide black nationalists, they had no expectations of a white supremacist civilization; they adhered neither to American optimism nor to exceptionalism.

BLACK NATIONALISM is a complex tradition of thought and action, a tradition best expressed in the numerous insightful texts of black public intellectuals like MAULANA KARENGA, AMIRI BARAKA, Haki R. Madhubuti, Marimba Ani, and MOLEFI ASANTE. Black nationalists usually call upon black people to close ranks, to distrust most whites (since the reliable whites are few and relatively powerless in the face of white supremacy), and to promote forms of black self-love, self-defense, and self-determination. It views white supremacy as the definitive systemic constraint on black cultural, political, and economic development. More pointedly, black nationalists claim that

American democracy is a modern form of tyranny on the part of the white majority over the black minority. For them, black sanity and freedom require that America not serve as the major framework in which to understand the future of black people. Instead, American civilization—like all civilizations—rises and falls, ebbs and flows. And owing to its deep-seated racism, this society does not warrant black allegiance or loyalty. White supremacy dictates the limits of the operation of American democracy—with black folk the indispensable sacrificial lamb vital to its sustenance. Hence black subordination constitutes the necessary condition for the flourishing of American democracy, the tragic prerequisite for America itself. This is, in part, what RICHARD WRIGHT meant when he noted, "The Negro is America's metaphor."

The most courageous and consistent of twentiethth-century black nationalists—Marcus Garvey and Elijah Muhammad—adamantly rejected any form of American optimism or exceptionalism. Du Bois feared that if they were right, he would be left in a state of paralyzing despair. A kind of despair that results not only when all credible options for black freedom in America are closed, but also when the very framework needed to understand and cope with that despair is shattered. The black nationalist challenge to Du Bois cuts much deeper than the rational and political possibilities for change—it resides at the visceral and existential levels of what to do about "what is" or when "what ought to be done" seems undoable. This frightening sense of foreboding pervades much of black America today—a sense that fans and fuels black nationalism.

Du Bois's American optimism screened him from this dark night of the soul. His American exceptionalism guarded him from that gray twilight between "nothing to be done" and "I can't go on like this"—a Beckett-like dilemma in which the wait and search for Godot, or for freedom, seem endless. This militant despair about the black condition is expressed in that most arresting of black nationalist speeches by the Reverend HENRY HIGHLAND GARNET in 1843:

> If we must bleed, let it come all at once—rather die freemen than live to be slaves. It is impossible like the children of Israel, to make a grand Exodus from the land of bondage. The pharaoh's on both sides of the blood-red waters!

Du Bois's response to such despair is to say "we surely must do something"—for such rebellion is suicidal and the notion of a separate black nation quixotic. So, he seems to say, let us continue to wait and search for Godot in America—even if it seems, with our luck, that all we get is "Pozzo" (new forms of disrespect, disregard, degradation, and defamation). American optimism couched within the ideals of the American experiment contains crucial components for any desirable form of black self-determination or modern nationhood: precious standards of constitutional democracy, the rule of law, individual liberties, and the dignity of common folk. Yet American optimism—in the ugly face of American white supremacist practices—warrants, if not outright rejection, at least vast attenuation. The twenty-first century will almost certainly not be a time in which American exceptionalism will flower in the world or American optimism will flourish among people of African descent.

If there are any historical parallels between black Americans during the 21st century and other peoples in earlier times, two candidates loom large: Tolstoy's Russia and Kafka's Prague—soul-starved Russians a generation after the emancipation of the serfs in 1861 and anxiety-ridden Central European Jews a generation before the European Holocaust in the 1940s. Indeed, my major intellectual disappointment with the great Du Bois lies in the fact that there are hardly any traces in his work of any serious grappling with the profound thinkers and spiritual wrestlers in the modern West from these two groups—major figures obsessed with the problem of evil in their time.

We see in Du Bois no engagement with Leo Tolstoy, Fyodor Dostoyevsky, Ivan Turgenev, Alexander Herzen, Lev Shestov, Anton Chekhov, or Franz Kafka, Max Brod, Kurt Tucholsky, Hermann Broch, Hugo Bergmann, or Karl Kraus. These omissions are glaring because the towering figures in both groups were struggling with political and existential issues similar to those facing black people in America. For example, the Russian situation involved the humanity of degraded impoverished peasants, the fragile stability of an identity-seeking empire, and the alienation of superfluous intellectuals; the Central European Jewish circumstance, the humanity of devalued middle-class Jews, the imminent collapse of a decadent empire, and the militant despair of self-hating intellectuals. The intellectual response on the part of the Russian authors was what Hegel would call "world-historical"—they wrote many of the world's greatest novels, short stories, essays, and plays. The writers I cite put forward profound interpretations of the human condition which rejected any Enlightenment worldview, Victorian strategy, or worldly optimism. And although the Central European Jewish authors are often overlooked by contemporary intellectuals—owing to a tendency to focus on Western Europe—their intellectual response was monumental. They composed many of this century's most probing and penetrating novels, short stories, autobiographies, and letters.

Both Russian and Central European Jewish writers share deep elective affinities that underlie their distinctive voices: the "wind of the wing of madness" (to use Baudelaire's phrase) beats incessantly on their souls. The fear of impending social doom and dread of inevitable death haunt them, and they search for a precious individuality in the face of a terror-ridden society and a seductive (yet doubtful) nationalist option. In short, fruitful comparisons may be made between the Russian sense of the tragic and the Central European Jewish sense of the absurd and the black intellectual response to the African American predicament. Tolstoy's *War and Peace* (1869), *The Death of Ivan Ilych* (1886), and "How Much Land Does a Man Need?" (1886), Chekhov's *The Three Sisters* (1901)—the greatest novel, short story, brief tale, and play in modern Europe—and Kafka's "The Judgment" (1913), "The Metamorphosis" (1915), "In the Penal Colony" (1919), and "The Burrow"(1923)—some of the grandest fictive portraits of twentieth-century Europe—constitute the highest moments and most ominous murmurings in Europe before it entered the ugly and fiery inferno of totalitarianism. Similarly, the intellectual response of highbrow black artists—most of whom are musicians and often of plebeian origins—probe the depths of a black sense of the tragic and absurd which yields a subversive joy and sublime melancholia unknown to most in the New World. The form and content of Louis Armstrong's "West End Blues," Duke Ellington's "Mood Indigo," John Coltrane's "Alabama," and Sarah Vaughan's "Send in the Clowns" are a few of the peaks of the black cultural iceberg—towering examples of soul-making and spiritual wrestling which crystallize the most powerful interpretations of the human condition in black life. This is why the best of the black musical tradition in the twentieth century is the most profound and poignant body of artistic works in our time.

Like their Russian and Central European Jewish counterparts, the black artists grapple with madness and melancholia, doom and death, terror and horror, individuality and identity. Unlike them, the black artists do so against the background of an African heritage that puts a premium on voice and body, sound and silence, and the foreground is occupied by an American tradition that highlights mobility and novelty, individuality and democracy. The explosive products of this multilayered cultural hybridity—with its new diasporic notions of time and space, place and face—take us far beyond Du Bois's enlightened optimism. Instead, the profound black cultural efforts to express the truth of modern tragic existence and build on the ruins of modern absurd experiences at the core of American culture take us to the end of that dreadful century. These black artistic endeavors prefigure and pose the most fundamental and formidable challenges to a twilight civilization—an American Empire adrift on turbulent seas in a dark fog. William Faulkner, Mark Twain, Thomas Pynchon, and, above all, the incomparable Herman Melville—the only great Euro-American novelists to be spoken of in the same breath as Tolstoy and Kafka, Armstrong and Coltrane—grasp crucial aspects of this black condition. Just as Richard Wright, Ralph Ellison, James Baldwin, and, preeminently, Toni Morrison guide us through the tragedies and absurdities within the Veil (or behind the color curtain) to disclose on the page what is best revealed in black song, speech, sermon, bodily performance, and the eloquence of black silence. Yet despite his shortcomings, the great Du Bois remains the springboard for any examination of black strivings in American civilization.

On Black Strivings

Black strivings are the creative and complex products of the terrifying African encounter with the absurd in America—and the absurd as America. Like any other group of human beings, black people forged ways of life and ways of struggle under circumstances not of their own choosing. They constructed structures of meaning and structures of feeling in the face of the fundamental facts of human existence—death, dread, despair, disease, and disappointment. Yet the specificity of black culture—namely, those features that distinguish black culture

from other cultures—lies in both the African and American character of black people's attempts to sustain their mental sanity and spiritual health, social life and political struggle in the midst of a slaveholding, white supremacist civilization that viewed itself as the most enlightened, free, tolerant, and democratic experiment in human history.

Any serious examination of black culture should begin with what W E. B. Du Bois dubbed, in Faustian terms, the "spiritual strivings" of black people—the dogged determination to survive and subsist, the tenacious will to persevere, persist, and maybe even prevail. These "strivings" occur within the whirlwind of white supremacy—that is, as responses to the vicious attacks on black beauty, black intelligence, black moral character, black capability, and black possibility. To put it bluntly, every major institution in American society—churches, universities, courts, academies of science, governments, economies, newspapers, magazines, television, film, and others—attempted to exclude black people from the human family in the name of white supremacist ideology. This unrelenting assault on black humanity produced the fundamental condition of black culture—that of black invisibility and namelessness.

This basic predicament exists on at least four levels—existential, social, political, and economic. The existential level is the most relevant here because it has to do with what it means to be a person and live a life under the horrifying realities of racist assault. To be a black human being under circumstances in which one's humanity is questioned is not only to face a difficult challenge but also to exercise a demanding discipline.

The sheer absurdity of being a black human being whose black body is viewed as an abomination, whose black thoughts and ideas are perceived as debased, and whose black pain and grief are rendered invisible on the human and moral scale is the New World context in which black culture emerged. Black people are first and foremost an African people, in that the cultural baggage they brought with them to the New World was grounded in their earlier responses to African conditions. Yet the rich African traditions—including the kinetic orality, passionate physicality, improvisational intellectuality, and combative spirituality—would undergo creative transformation when brought into contact with European languages and rituals in the context of the New World. For example, there would be no jazz without New World Africans with European languages and instruments.

On the crucial existential level relating to black invisibility and namelessness, the first difficult challenge and demanding discipline is to ward off madness and discredit suicide as a desirable option. A central preoccupation of black culture is that of confronting candidly the ontological wounds, psychic scars, and existential bruises of black people while fending off insanity and self-annihilation. Black culture consists of black modes of being-in-the-world obsessed with black sadness and sorrow, black agony and anguish, black heartache and heartbreak without fully succumbing to the numbing effects of such misery—to never allow such misery to have the last word. This is why the "ur-text" of black culture is neither a word nor a book, not an architectural monument or a legal brief. Instead, it is a guttural cry and a wrenching moan—a cry not so much for help as for home, a moan less out of complaint than for recognition. The most profound black cultural products—John Coltrane's saxophone solos, JAMES CLEVELAND's gut gospels, BILLIE HOLIDAY's vocal leaps, Rev. GARDNER TAYLOR's rhapsodic sermons, James Baldwin's poignant essays, ALVIN AILEY's graceful dances, Toni Morrison's dissonant novels—transform and transfigure in artistic form this cry and moan. The deep black meaning of this cry and moan goes back to the indescribable cries of Africans on the slave ships during the cruel transatlantic voyages to America and the indecipherable moans of enslaved Afro-Americans on Wednesday nights or Sunday mornings near god-forsaken creeks or on wooden benches at prayer meetings in makeshift black churches. This fragile existential arsenal—rooted in silent tears and weary lament—supports black endurance against madness and suicide. The primal black cries and moans lay bare the profoundly tragicomic character of black life. Ironically, they also embody the life-preserving content of black styles—creative ways of fashioning power and strength through the body and language that yield black joy and ecstasy.

Du Bois captures one such primal scene of black culture at the beginning of *The Souls of Black Folk* (1903), in chapter one, "Of Our Spiritual Strivings." He starts with thirteen lines from the poem "The Crying of Water" by Arthur Symons, the English symbolist critic and decadent poet who went mad a few years after writing the poem. The hearts of human beings in a heartless slave trade cry out like the sea: "All life long crying without avail, / As the water all night long is crying to me."

This metaphorical association of black hearts, black people, and black culture with water (the sea or a river) runs deep in black artistic expression—as in LANGSTON HUGHES's recurring refrain "My soul has grown deep like the rivers" in "The Negro Speaks of Rivers." Black striving resides primarily in movement and motion, resilience and resistance against the paralysis of madness and the stillness of death. As it is for Jim in Mark Twain's *The Adventures of Huckleberry Finn* (1885), the river—a road that moves—is the means by which black people can flee from a menacing racist society. Du Bois continues with the musical bars of the Negro SPIRITUAL "Nobody Knows the Trouble I've Seen." This spiritual is known not simply for its plaintive melody but also for its inexplicable lyrical reversal.

Nobody knows the trouble I've seen
Nobody knows but Jesus
Nobody knows the trouble I've seen
Glory hallelujah!

This exemplary shift from a mournful brooding to a joyful praising is the product of courageous efforts to look life's abyss in the face and keep "keepin' on." This struggle is sustained primarily by the integrity of style, song, and spirituality in a beloved community (e.g., Jesus' proclamation of the Kingdom). It is rather like Ishmael's tragicomic "free and easy sort of genial, desperado philosophy" in *Moby Dick,* but it is intensified by the fiery art of ARETHA FRANKLIN's majestic shouts for joy.

The first of Du Bois's own words in the text completes the primal scene of black culture:

Between me and the other world there is ever an unasked question: unasked by some through feelings of delicacy; by others through the difficulty of rightly framing it. All, nevertheless, flutter round it. They approach me in a half-hesitant sort of way, eye me curiously or compassionately, and then, instead of saying directly, How does it feel to be a problem? they say, I know an excellent colored man in my town; or, I fought at Mechanicsville; or, Do not these Southern outrages make our blood boil? At these I smile, or am interested, or reduce the boiling to a simmer, as the occasion may require. To the real question, How does it feel to be a problem? I answer seldom a word.

And yet, being a problem is a strange experience,—peculiar even for one who has never been anything else, save perhaps in babyhood . . .

This seminal passage spells out the basic components of black invisibility and namelessness: black people as a problem-people rather than people with problems; black people as abstractions and objects rather than individuals and persons; black and white worlds divided by a thick wall (or a "Veil") that requires role-playing and mask-wearing rather than genuine humane interaction; black rage, anger, and fury concealed in order to assuage white fear and anxiety; and black people rootless and homeless on a perennial journey to discover who they are in a society content to see blacks remain the permanent underdog.

To view black people as a problem-people is to view them as an undifferentiated blob, a homogeneous bloc, or a monolithic conglomerate. Each black person is interchangeable, indistinguishable, or substitutable since all black people are believed to have the same views and values, sentiments and sensibilities. Hence one set of negative stereotypes holds for all of them, no matter how high certain blacks may ascend in the white world (e.g., "savages in a suit or suite"). And the mere presence of black bodies in a white context generates white unease and discomfort, even among whites of goodwill.

This problematizing of black humanity deprives black people of individuality, diversity, and heterogeneity. It reduces black folk to abstractions and objects born of white fantasies and insecurities—as exotic or transgressive entities, as hypersexual or criminal animals. The celebrated opening passage of Ralph Ellison's classic novel *Invisible Man* (1952) highlights this reduction.

I am an invisible man. No, I am not a spook like those who haunted Edgar Allan Poe; nor am I one of your Hollywood-movie ectoplasms. I am a man of substance, of flesh and bone, fiber and liquids—and I might even be said to possess a mind. I am invisible, understand, simply because people refuse to see me. Like the bodiless heads you see sometimes in circus sideshows, it is as though I have been surrounded by mirrors of hard, distorting glass. When they approach me they see only my surroundings, themselves, or figments of their imagination—indeed, everything and anything except me.

This distorted perception—the failure to see the humanity and individuality of black people—has its source in the historic "Veil" (slavery, JIM CROW, and segregation) that separates the black and white worlds. Ironically, this refusal to see a people whose epidermis is most visible exists alongside a need to keep tight surveillance over these people. This Veil not only precludes honest communication between blacks and whites; it also forces blacks to live in two worlds in order to survive. Whites need not understand or live in the black world in order to thrive. But blacks must grapple with the painful "double-consciousness" that may result in "an almost morbid sense of personality and a moral hesitancy which is fatal to self-confidence." Du Bois notes,

> The worlds within and without the Veil of Color are changing, and changing rapidly, but not at the same rate, not in the same way; and this must produce a peculiar wrenching of the soul, a peculiar sense of doubt and bewilderment. Such a double life, with double thoughts, double duties, and double social classes, must give rise to double words and double ideals, and tempt the mind to pretence or to revolt, to hypocrisy or to radicalism.

Echoing PAUL LAURENCE DUNBAR'S famous poem "We Wear the Mask," Du Bois proclaims that "the price of culture is a Lie." Why? Because black people will not succeed in American society if they are fully and freely themselves. Instead, they must "endure petty insults with a smile, shut [their] eyes to wrong." They must not be too frank and outspoken and must never fail to flatter and be pleasant in order to lessen white unease and discomfort. Needless to say, this is not the raw stuff for healthy relations between black and white people.

Yet this suppression of black rage—the reducing "the boiling to a simmer"—backfires in the end. It reinforces a black obsession with the psychic scars, ontological wounds, and existential bruises that tend to reduce the tragic to the pathetic. Instead of exercising agency or engaging in action against the odds, one may wallow in self-pity, acknowledging the sheer absurdity of it all. After playing the role and wearing the mask in the white world, one may accept the white world's view of one's self. As Du Bois writes,

> It is a peculiar sensation, this double-consciousness, this sense of always looking at one's self through the eyes of others, of measuring one's soul by the tape of a world that looks on in amused contempt and pity.

Toni Morrison explores this dilemma of black culture through her moving portrayal of the character of Sweet Home in her profound novel *Beloved* (1987), similar to JEAN TOOMER'S Karintha and Fern in his marvelous and magical text *Cane* (1923).

> For the sadness was at her center, the desolated center where the self that was no self made its home.

This theme of black rootlessness and homelessness is inseparable from black namelessness. When James Baldwin writes about these issues in *Nobody Knows My Name* (1961) and *No Name in the Street* (1972), he is trying to explore effective ways to resist the white supremacist imposition of subordinate roles, stations, and identities on blacks. He is attempting to devise some set of existential strategies against the overwhelming onslaught of white dehumanization, devaluation, and degradation. The search for black space (home), black place (roots), and black face (name) is a flight from the visceral effects of white supremacy. Toni Morrison characterizes these efforts as products of a process of "dirtying you."

> That anybody white could take your whole self for anything that came to mind. Not just work, kill, or maim you, but dirty you. Dirty you so bad you couldn't like yourself anymore. Dirty you so bad you forgot who you were and couldn't think it Up.

Toni Morrison's monumental novel holds a privileged place in black culture and modernity precisely because she takes this dilemma to its logical conclusion—that black flight from white supremacy (a chamber of horrors for black people) may lead to the murder of those loved ones who are candidates for the "dirtying" process. The black mother, Sethe, kills her daughter, Beloved, because she loved her so, "to out-hurt the hurter," as an act of resistance against the "dirtying" process.

> And though she and others lived through and got over it, she could never let it happen to her own. The best thing she was, was her children. Whites might dirty her all right, but not her best thing, her beautiful, magical best thing—the part of her that was clean. No undreamable dreams about whether the headless, feetless torso hanging in the tree with a sign on it was her husband or Paul A; whether the bubbling-hot girls in the colored-school fire set by patriots included her daughter; whether a gang of whites invaded her daughter's private parts, soiled her daughter's thighs and threw her daughter out of the wagon. She might have to work the slaughterhouse yard, but not her daughter.
>
> And no one, nobody on this earth, would list her daughter's characteristics on the animal side of the paper. No. Oh no . . . Sethe had refused—and refused still.
>
> . . . [W]hat she had done was right because it came from true love.

Is death the only black space (home), place (roots), and face (name) safe from a pervasive white supremacy? Toni Morrison's Sethe echoes Du Bois's own voice upon the painful passing of his first-born. For Sethe, as for Tolstoy's Ivan, Chekhov's Bishop Pyotr, Kafka's Josephine, Hawthorne's Goodman Brown, Hardy's Jude, Bilchner's Woyzeck, Drelser's Hurstwood, and Shakespeare's Lear, death is the great liberator from suffering and evil.

> But Love sat beside his cradle, and in his ear Wisdom waited to speak. Perhaps now he knows the All-love,

and needs not to be wise. Sleep, then, child,—sleep till
I sleep and waken to a baby voice and the ceaseless
patter of little feet—above the Veil.

The most effective and enduring black responses to invisibility
and namelessness are those forms of individual and collective
black resistance predicated on a deep and abiding black love.
These responses take the shape of prophetic thought and action: bold, fearless, courageous attempts to tell the truth about
and bear witness to black suffering and to keep faith with a vision of black redemption. Like the "ur-texts" of the guttural cry
and wrenching moan—enacted in Charlie Parker's bebop
sound, DINAH WASHINGTON's cool voice, RICHARD PRYOR's comic
performances, and James Brown's inimitable funk—the
prophetic utterance that focuses on black suffering and sustains
a hope-against-hope for black freedom constitutes the heights
of black culture. The spiritual depths (the how and what) of
MARTIN LUTHER KING's visionary orations, NAT KING COLE's silky
soul, AUGUST WILSON's probing plays, Martin Puryear's unique
sculpture, Harold and Fayard Nicholas's existential acrobatics,
JACOB LAWRENCE's powerful paintings, MARVIN GAYE's risky
falsettos, FANNIE LOU HAMER's fighting songs, and, above all,
John Coltrane's "A Love Supreme" exemplify such heights. Two
of the greatest moments in black literature also enact such high-
quality performances. First, James Baldwin's great self-
descriptive visionary passage in *Go Tell It on the Mountain*
(1953):

Yes, their parts were all cut off, they were dishonored,
their very names were nothing more than dust blown
disdainfully across the field of time—to fall where, to
blossom where, bringing forth what fruit hereafter,
where?—their very names were not their own. Behind
them was the darkness, nothing but the darkness, and
all around them destruction, and before them nothing
but the fire—a bastard people, far from God, singing
and crying in the wilderness! Yet, most strangely, and
from deeps not before discovered, his faith looked up;
before the wickedness that he saw, the wickedness from
which he fled, he yet beheld, like a flaming standard in
the middle of the air, that power of redemption to which
he must, till death, bear witness; which, though it crush
him utterly, he could not deny; though none among the
living might ever behold it, he had beheld it, and must
keep the faith.

For Baldwin, the seemingly impossible flight from white supremacy takes the form of a Chekhovian effort to endure lov-
ingly and compassionately, guided by a vision of freedom and
empowered by a tradition of black love and faith. To be a bastard people—wrenched from Africa and in, but never fully of,
America—is to be a people of highly limited options, if any at
all. To bear witness is to make and remake, invent and reinvent oneself as a person and people by keeping faith with the
best of such earlier efforts, yet also to acknowledge that the
very new selves and peoples to emerge will never fully find a
space, place, or face in American society—or Africa. This peren-

nial process of self-making and self-inventing is propelled by a
self-loving and self-trusting made possible by overcoming a colonized mind, body, and soul.

This is precisely what Toni Morrison describes in the great
litany of black love in Baby Suggs's prayer and sermon of laughter, dance, tears, and silence in "a wide-open place cut deep
in the woods nobody knew for what at the end of a path known
only to deer and whoever cleared the land in the first place."
On those hot Saturday afternoons, Baby Suggs "offered up to
them her great big heart."

She told them that the only grace they could have was
the grace they could imagine. That if they could not see
it, they would not have it. "Here," she said, "in this
here place, we flesh; flesh that weeps, laughs; flesh that
dances on bare feet in grass. Love it. Love it hard. Yonder they do not love your flesh. They despise it. They
don't love your eyes; they'd just as soon pick em out.
No more do they love the skin on your back. Yonder
they flay it. And O my people they do not love your
hands. Those they only use, tie, bind, chop off and leave
empty. Love your hands! Love them. Raise them up and
kiss them. Touch others with them, pat them together,
stroke them on your face 'cause they don't love that either. You got to love it, you! And no, they ain't in love
with your mouth. Yonder, out there, they will see it broken and break it again. What you say out of it they will
not heed. What you scream from it they do not hear.
What you put into it to nourish your body they will
snatch away and give you leavins instead. No, they
don't love your mouth. You got to love it. This is flesh
I'm talking about here. Flesh that needs to be loved.
Feet that need to rest and to dance; backs that need
support; shoulders that need arms, strong arms I'm
telling you. And O my people, out yonder, hear me,
they do not love your neck unnoosed and straight. So
love your neck; put a hand on it, grace it, stroke it and
hold it up. And all your inside parts that they'd just as
soon slop for hogs, you got to love them. The dark, dark
liver—love it, love it, and the beat and beating heart,
love that too. More than eyes or feet. More than lungs
that have yet to draw free air. More than your life-
holding womb and your life-giving private parts, hear
me now, love your heart. For this is the prize." Saying
no more, she stood up then and danced with her twisted
hip the rest of what her heart had to say while the others opened their mouths and gave her the music. Long
notes held until the four-part harmony was perfect
enough for their deeply loved flesh.

In this powerful passage, Toni Morrison depicts in a concrete
and graphic way the enactment and expression of black love,
black joy, black community, and black faith that bears witness
to black suffering and keeps alive a vision of black hope. Black
bonds of affection, black networks of support, black ties of empathy, and black harmonies of spiritual camaraderie provide

the grounds for the fragile existential weaponry with which to combat black invisibility and namelessness.

Yet these forceful strategies in black culture still have not successfully come to terms with the problem. The black collective quest for a name that designates black people in the United States continues—from colored, Negro, black, Afro-American, Abyssinian, Ethiopian, Nubian, Bilalian, American African, American, African to African American. The black individual quest for names goes on, with unique new ones for children—for example, Signithia, Tarsell, Jewayne—designed to set them apart from all others for the purpose of accenting their individuality and offsetting their invisibility. And most important, black rage proliferates—sometimes unabated.

Of all the hidden injuries of blackness in American civilization, black rage is the most deadly, the most lethal. Although black culture is in no way reducible to or identical with black rage, it is inseparable from black rage. Du Bois's renowned eulogy for ALEXANDER CRUMMELL, the greatest nineteenth-century black intellectual, is one of the most penetrating analyses of black rage. Du Bois begins his treatment with a virtually generic description of black childhoods—a description that would hold for ARTHUS ASHE or ICE CUBE, KATHLEEN BATTLE or QUEEN LATIFAH.

> This is the history of a human heart,—the tale of a black boy who many long years ago began to struggle with life that he might know the world and know himself. Three temptations he met on those dark dunes that lay gray and dismal before the wonder-eyes of the child: the Temptation of Hate, that stood out against the red dawn; the Temptation of Despair, that darkened noonday; and the Temptation of Doubt, that ever steals along with twilight. Above all, you must hear of the vales he crossed,—the Valley of Humiliation and the Valley of the Shadow of Death.

Black self-hatred and hatred of others parallels that of all human beings, who must gain some sense of themselves and the world. But the tremendous weight of white supremacy makes this human struggle for mature black selfhood even more difficult. As black children come to view themselves more and more as the degraded other, the temptation of hate grows, "gliding stealthily into [their] laughter, fading into [their] play, and seizing [their] dreams by day and night with rough, rude turbulence. So [they ask] of sky and sun and flower the never-answered Why? and love, as [they grow], neither the world nor the world's rough ways."

The two major choices in black culture (or any culture) facing those who succumb to the temptation of hate are a self-hatred that leads to self-destruction or a hatred of others—degraded others—that leads to vengeance of some sort. These options often represent two sides of the same coin. The case of Bigger Thomas, portrayed by Richard Wright in his great novel *Native Son* (1940), is exemplary in this regard.

> Bigger's face was metallically black in the strong sunlight. There was in his eyes a pensive, brooding amuse-

ment, as of a man who had been long confronted and tantalized by a riddle whose answer seemed always just on the verge of escaping him, but prodding him irresistibly on to seek its solution. The silence irked Bigger; he was anxious to do something to evade looking so squarely at this problem.

The riddle Bigger seeks an answer to is the riddle of his black existence in America—and he evades it in part because the pain, fear, silence, and hatred cut so deep. Like the "huge black rat" which appears at the beginning of the novel, Bigger reacts to his circumstances instinctually. Yet his instinct to survive is intertwined with his cognitive perception that white supremacy is out to get him. To make himself and invent himself as a black person in America is to strike out against white supremacy—out of pain, fear, silence, and hatred. The result is psychic terror and physical violence—committed against black Bessie and white Mary.

> Bigger rose and went to the window. His hands caught the cold steel bars in a hard grip. He knew as he stood there that he could never tell why he had killed. It was not that he did not really want to tell, but the telling of it would have involved an explanation of his entire life. The actual killing of Mary and Bessie was not what concerned him most; it was knowing and feeling that he could never make anybody know what had driven him to it. His crimes were known, but what he had felt before he committed them would never be known. He would have gladly admitted his guilt if he had thought that in doing so he could have also given in the same breath a sense of the deep, choking hate that had been his life, a hate that he had not wanted to have, but could not help having. How could he do that? The impulsion to try to tell was as deep as had been the urge to kill.

The temptation to hate is a double-edged sword. Bigger's own self-hatred not only leads him to hate other blacks but also to deny the humanity of whites. Yet he can overcome this self-hatred only when he views himself as a self-determining agent who is willing to take responsibility for his actions and acknowledge his connection with others. Although Wright has often been criticized for casting Bigger as a pitiful victim, subhuman monster, and isolated individualist—as in James Baldwin's "Everybody's Protest Novel" and "Many Thousands Gone" in *Notes of a Native Son* (1955)—Wright presents brief moments in which Bigger sees the need for transcending his victim status and rapacious individualism. When his family visits him in jail, Bigger responds to their tears and anger.

> Bigger wanted to comfort them in the presence of the white folks, but did not know how. Desperately, he cast about for something to say. Hate and shame boiled in him against the people behind his back; he tried to think of words that would defy them, words that would let them know that he had a world and life of his own in spite of them.

Wright does not disclose the internal dynamics of this black world of Bigger's own, but Bigger does acknowledge that he is part of this world. For example, his actions had dire consequences for his sister, Vera.

> "Bigger," his mother sobbed, trying to talk through her tears. "Bigger, honey, she won't go to school no more. She says the other girls look at her and make her 'shamed . . ."
>
> He had lived and acted on the assumption that he was alone, and now he saw that he had not been. What he had done made others suffer. No matter how much he would long for them to forget him, they would not be able to. His family was a part of him, not only in blood, but in spirit. He sat on the cot and his mother knelt at his feet. Her face was lifted to his; her eyes were empty, eyes that looked upward when the last hope of earth had failed.

Yet even this family connection fails to undercut the layers of hate Bigger feels for himself and them. It is only when Bigger receives unconditional support and affirmation across racial lines that his self-hatred and hatred of others subsides—for a moment, from white Jan, the boyfriend of the slain Mary.

> He looked at Jan and saw a white face, but an honest face. This white man believed in him, and the moment he felt that belief he felt guilty again; but in a different sense now. Suddenly, this white man had come up to him, flung aside the curtain and walked into the room of his life. Jan had spoken a declaration of friendship that would make other white men hate him: a particle of white rock had detached itself from that looming mountain of white hate and had rolled down the slope, stopping still at his feet. The word had become flesh. For the first time in his life a white man became a human being to him; and the reality of Jan's humanity came in a stab of remorse: he had killed what this man loved and had hurt him. He saw Jan as though someone had performed an operation upon his eyes, or as though someone had snatched a deforming mask from Jan's face.

In both instances, Bigger lurches slightly beyond the temptation of hate when he perceives himself as an agent and subject accountable for the consequences of his actions—such as the victimization of his own black sister and a white person. Yet the depths of his self-hatred—his deep-seated colonized mind—permit only a glimpse of self-transformation when the friendship of a white fellow victim is offered to him.

Similar to Bigger Thomas, Alexander Crummell was inspired by a white significant other—Beriah Green. This sort of sympathetic connection makes the temptation of hate grow "fainter and less sinister. It did not wholly fade away, but diffused itself and lingered thick at the edges." Through both Bigger Thomas and Alexander Crummell we see the tremendous pull of the white world and the tragic need for white recognition and affirmation among so many black people.

The temptation of despair is the second element of black rage in Du Bois's analysis. This temptation looms large when black folk conclude that "the way of the world is closed to me." This conclusion yields two options—nihilism and hedonism. Again, two sides of the same coin. This sense of feeling imprisoned, bound, constrained, and circumscribed is a dominant motif in black cultural expressions. Again, Wright captures this predicament well with Bigger Thomas.

> "Goddammit!"
> "What's the matter?"
> "They don't let us do nothing."
> "Who?"
> "The white folks."
> "You talk like you just now finding that out," Gus said.
> "Naw. But I just can't get used to it," Bigger said. "I swear to God I can't. I know I oughtn't think about it, but I can't help it. Every time I think about it I feel like somebody's poking a red-hot iron down my throat. Goddammit, look! We live here and they live there. We black and they white. They got things and we ain't. They do things and we can't. It's just like living in jail. Half the time I feel like I'm on the outside of the world peeping in through a knot-hole in the fence.

The temptation of despair is predicated on a world with no room for black space, place, or face. It feeds on a black futurelessness and black hopelessness—a situation in which visions and dreams of possibility have dried up like raisins in the sun. This nihilism leads to lives of drift, lives in which any pleasure, especially instant gratification, is the primary means of feeling alive. Anger and aggression usually surface in such lives. Bigger says, "I hurt folks 'cause I felt I had to; that's all. They was crowding me too close; they wouldn't give me no room . . . I thought they was hard and I acted hard . . . I'll be feeling and thinking that they didn't see me and I didn't see them."

The major black cultural response to the temptation of despair has been the black Christian tradition dominated by music in song, prayer, and sermon. The unique role of this tradition is often noted. Du Bois writes "that the Negro church antedates the Negro home, leads to an explanation of much that is paradoxical in this communistic institution and in the morals of its members. But especially it leads us to regard this institution as peculiarly the expression of the inner ethical life of a people in a sense seldom true elsewhere."

Even Bigger Thomas—the most cynical and secular of rebels in the black literary tradition—is captivated by the power of black church music, the major caressing artistic flow in the black *Sittlichkeit* (ethical life).

> The singing from the church vibrated through him, suffusing him with a mood of sensitive sorrow. He tried not to listen, but it seeped into his feelings, whispering of another way of life and death . . . The singing filled his ears; it was complete, self-contained, and it mocked

his fear and loneliness, his deep yearning for a sense of wholeness. Its fullness contrasted so sharply with his hunger, its richness with his emptiness, that he recoiled from it while answering it.

The BLACK CHURCH tradition—along with the rich musical tradition it spawned—generates a sense of movement, motion, and momentum that keeps despair at bay. As with any collective project or performance that puts a premium on change, transformation, conversion, and future possibility, the temptation of despair is not eliminated but attenuated. In this sense, the black church tradition has made ritual art and communal bonds out of black invisibility and namelessness. Ralph Ellison updates and secularizes this endeavor when he writes,

> Perhaps I like Louis Armstrong because he's made poetry out of being invisible. I think it must be because he's unaware that he is invisible. And my own grasp of invisibility aids me to understand his music . . . Invisibility, let me explain, gives one a slightly different sense of time, you're never quite on the beat. Sometimes you're ahead and sometimes behind. Instead of the swift and imperceptible flowing of time, you are aware of its nodes, those points where time stands still or from which it leaps ahead. And you slip into the breaks and look around. That's what you hear vaguely in Louis' music.

The temptation of doubt is the most persistent of the three temptations. White supremacy drums deeply into the hearts, minds, and souls of black people, causing them to expect little of one another and themselves. This black insecurity and self-doubt produces a debilitating black jealousy in the face of black "success"—a black jealousy that often takes the form of what ELDRIDGE CLEAVER called "nigger rituals"—namely, a vicious trashing of black "success" or a black "battle royal" for white spectators. Understandably, under conditions of invisibility and namelessness, most of those blacks with "visibility" and a "name" in the white world are often the object of black scorn and contempt. Such sad, self-fulfilling prophecies of black cowardice make the temptation of doubt especially seductive—one which fans and fuels the flames of black rage. Du Bois states,

> Of all the three temptations, this one struck the deepest. Hate? He had outgrown so childish a thing. Despair? He had steeled his right arm against it, and fought it with the vigor of determination. But to doubt the worth of his life-work,—to doubt the destiny and capability of the race his soul loved because it was his; to find listless squalor instead of eager endeavor; to hear his own lips whispering, "They do not care; they cannot know; they are dumb driven cattle,—why cast your pearls before swine?"—this, this seemed more than man could bear; and he closed the door, and sank upon the steps of the chancel, and cast his robe upon the floor and writhed.

The two principal options for action after one yields to the temptation of doubt in black culture are authoritarian subordination of the "ignorant" masses or individual escape from these masses into the white mainstream. These two options are not two sides of the same coin—though they often flow from a common source: an elitist vision that shuns democratic accountability. And although this elitist vision—that of the Exceptional Negro or Talented Tenth who is "better than those other blacks"—is found more readily among the black educated and middle class, some of the black working poor and very poor subscribe to it, too. Even Bigger Thomas.

> As he rode, looking at the black people on the sidewalks, he felt that one way to end fear and shame was to make all those black people act together, rule them, tell them what to do, and make them do it. . . . But he felt that such would never happen to him and his black people, and he hated them and wanted to wave his hand and blot them out. Yet, he still hoped, vaguely. Of late he had liked to hear tell of men who could rule others, for in actions such as these he felt that there was a way to escape from this tight morass of fear and shame that sapped at the base of his life. He liked to hear of how Japan was conquering China; of how Hitler was running Jews to the ground; of how Mussolini was invading Spain. He was not concerned with whether these acts were right or wrong; they simply appealed to him as possible avenues of escape. He felt that some day there would be a black man who would whip the black people into a tight band and together they would act and end fear and shame. He never thought of this in precise mental images; he felt it; he would feel it for a while and then forget. But hope was always waiting somewhere deep down in him.

This hope for black unity and action was based on a profound doubt concerning the ability of black people to think for themselves and act on principles they had examined, scrutinized, and deliberately chosen. Ironically, this same elitist logic is at work among those who uncritically enter the white mainstream and accuse black people of lacking discipline and determination. Alexander Crummell overcame the difficult challenge of self-doubt and the doubt of other black folk by moving to Africa and later returning to America to fight for and "among his own, the low, the grasping, and the wicked, and with that unbending righteousness which is the sword of the just."

In the end, for Du Bois, Alexander Crummell triumphed over hate, despair, and doubt owing to "that full power within, that mighty inspiration" within the Veil. He was able to direct his black rage through moral channels sustained primarily by black bonds of affection, black networks of support, and black ties of empathy. Yet few today know his name and work, principally due to the thick Veil of color then and now:

> His name today, in this broad land, means little, and comes to fifty million ears laden with no incense of memory or emulation. And herein lies the tragedy of

the age: not that men are poor,—all men know something of poverty; not that men are wicked,—who is good? not that men are ignorant,—what is Truth? Nay, but that men know so little of men.

For Du Bois, "the problem of the twentieth century is the problem of the color-line" largely because of the relative lack of communication across the Veil of color. For Du Bois, the vicious legacy of white supremacy contributes to the arrested development of democracy. And since communication is the lifeblood of a democracy—the very measure of the vitality of its public life—we either come to terms with race and hang together, or ignore it and hang separately. This is why every examination of black strivings is an important part of understanding the prevailing crisis in American society.

Twilight Civilization in Our Time

At the beginning of the twenty-first century the crisis of race in America is still raging. The problem of black invisibility and namelessness, however, remains marginal to the dominant accounts of our past and present and is relatively absent from our pictures of the future. In this age of globalization, with its impressive scientific and technological innovations in information, communication, and applied biology, a focus on the lingering effects of racism seems outdated and antiquated. The global cultural bazaar of entertainment and enjoyment, the global shopping mall of advertising and marketing, the global workplace of blue-collar and white-collar employment, and the global financial network of computerized transactions and megacorporate mergers appear to render any talk about race irrelevant.

Yet with the collapse of the Soviet Empire, the end of the Cold War, and the rise of Japan, corrupt and top-heavy nation-states are being eclipsed by imperial corporations as public life deteriorates owing to class polarization, racial balkanization, and especially a predatory market culture. With the vast erosion of civic networks that nurture and care for citizens—such as families, neighborhoods, and schools—and with what might be called the gangsterization of everyday life, characterized by the escalating fear of violent attack, vicious assault, or cruel insult, we are witnessing a pervasive cultural decay in American civilization. Even public discourse has degenerated into petty name-calling and finger-pointing—with little room for mutual respect and empathetic exchange. Increasing suicides and homicides, alcoholism and drug addiction, distrust and disloyalty, cold-heartedness and mean-spiritedness, isolation and loneliness, cheap sexual thrills and cowardly patriarchal violence are still other symptoms of this decay. Yet race—in the coded language of welfare reform, immigration policy, criminal punishment, affirmative action, and suburban privatization—remains a central signifier in the political debate.

As in late nineteenth-century Russia and early twentieth-century Central Europe, the ruling political right hides and conceals the privilege and wealth of the few (the 1 percent who own 48 percent of the net financial wealth, the top 10 percent who own 86 percent, the top 20 percent who have 94 percent!) and pits the downwardly mobile middlers against the downtrodden poor. This age-old strategy of scapegoating the most vulnerable, frightening the most insecure, and supporting the most comfortable constitutes a kind of iron law signaling the decline of modern civilizations, as in Tolstoy's Russia and Kafka's Central Europe: chaotic and inchoate rebellion from below, withdrawal and retreat from public life from above, and a desperate search for authoritarian law and order, at any cost, from the middle. In America, this suggests not so much a European style of fascism but rather a homespun brand of authoritarian democracy—the systemic stigmatizing, regulating, and policing of the degraded others—women, gays, lesbians, Latinos, Jews, Asians, Indians, and especially black people. As Sinclair Lewis warned over a half-century ago, fascism, American-style, can happen here.

Welfare reform means, on the ground, poor people (disproportionately black) with no means of support. Criminal punishment means hundreds of thousands of black men in crowded prisons—many in there forever. And suburban privatization means black urban poor citizens locked into decrepit public schools, dilapidated housing, inadequate health care, and unavailable child care. Furthermore, the lowest priorities on the global corporate agenda of the political right—the low quantity of jobs with a living wage and the low quality of life for children—have the greatest consequences for the survival of any civilization. Instead, we have generational layers of unemployed and underemployed people (often uncounted in our national statistics) and increasing numbers of hedonistic and nihilistic young people (of all classes, races, genders, and regions) with little interest in public life and with little sense of moral purpose.

This is the classic portrait of a twilight civilization whose dangerous rumblings—now intermittent in much of America but rampant in most of black urban America—will more than likely explode in the twenty-first century if we stay on the present conservative course. In such a bleak scenario—given the dominant tendencies of our day—Du Bois's heralded Talented Tenth will by and large procure a stronger foothold in the well-paid professional managerial sectors of the global economy and more and more will become intoxicated with the felicities of a parvenu bourgeois existence. The heroic few will attempt to tell unpleasant truths about our plight and bear prophetic witness to our predicament as well as try to organize and mobilize (and be organized and mobilized by) the economically devastated, culturally degraded, and politically marginalized black working poor and very poor. Since a multiracial alliance of progressive meddlers, liberal slices of the corporate elite, and subversive energy from below is the only vehicle by which some form of radical democratic accountability can redistribute resources and wealth and restructure the economy and government so that all benefit, the significant secondary efforts of the black Talented Tenth alone in the twenty-first century will be woefully inadequate and thoroughly frustrating. Yet even progressive social change—though desirable and necessary—may not turn back the deeper and deadly processes of cultural decay in twenty-first-century America.

As this Talented Tenth comes to be viewed more and more with disdain and disgust by the black working poor and very poor, not only class envy but class hatred in black America will escalate—in the midst of a more isolated and insulated black America. This will deepen the identity crisis of the black Talented Tenth—a crisis of survivor's guilt and cultural root-lessness. As the glass ceilings (limited promotions) and golden cuffs (big position and good pay with little or no power) remain in place for most, though not all, blacks in corporate America, we will see anguish and hedonism in-tensify among much of the Talented Tenth. The conservative wing of black elites will climb on the bandwagon of the po-litical right—some for sincere reasons, most for opportunis-tic ones—as the black working poor and very poor try to cope with the realities of death, disease, and destruction. The pro-gressive wing of the black elite will split into a vociferous (primarily male-led) black nationalist camp that opts for self-help at the lower and middle levels of the entrepreneurial sectors of the global economy and a visionary (dispropor-tionately woman-led) radical democratic camp that works as-siduously to keep alive a hope—maybe the last hope—for a twilight civilization that once saw itself as the "last best hope of earth."

After ninety-five years of the most courageous and unflag-ging devotion to black freedom witnessed in the twentieth cen-tury, W. E. B. Du Bois not only left America for Africa but con-cluded, "I just cannot take any more of this country's treatment. We leave for Ghana October 5th and I set no date for return . . . Chin up, and fight on, but realize that American Negroes can't win."

In the end, Du Bois's Enlightenment worldview, Victorian strategies, and American optimism failed him. He left America in militant despair—the very despair he had avoided earlier—and mistakenly hoped for the rise of a strong postcolonial and united Africa. Echoing Tolstoy's claim that "it's intolerable to live in Russia . . . I've decided to emigrate to England forever" (though he never followed through) and Kafka's dream to leave Prague and live in Palestine (though he died before he could do so), Du Bois concluded that black strivings in a twilight civilization were unbearable for him yet still imperative for others—even if he could not envision black freedom in Amer-ica as realizable.

For those of us who stand on his broad shoulders, let us begin where he ended—with his militant despair; let us look candidly at the tragicomic and absurd character of black life in America in the spirit of John Coltrane and Toni Morrison; let us continue to strive with genuine compassion, personal in-tegrity, and human decency to fight for radical democracy in the face of the frightening abyss—or terrifying inferno—of the twenty-first century, clinging to "a hope not hopeless but unhopeful."

See also Communist Party, African Americans and the; Black Nationalism in the United States; Nicholas Brothers.

Cornel West

Webster, Ben

1909–1973

African American tenor saxophonist renowned for his highly idiosyncratic, warm, and moving tone.

Benjamin Francis Webster was born in Kansas City, Missouri. After beginning his musical life as a violinist, Webster took piano lessons from his neighbor, the famed JAZZ, BLUES, and BOOGIE-WOOGIE pianist Pete Johnson. He worked as a cinema and jazz pianist in Amarillo, Texas, before taking up the sax-ophone in his early twenties.

He quickly began playing with several name bands, in-cluding those of LESTER YOUNG and his family, BENNIE MOTEN, and Andy Kirk. After moving to NEW YORK in 1934, he worked with several more well-known big-band leaders, including BENNY CARTER, CAB CALLOWAY, FLETCHER HENDERSON, JR., and again Andy Kirk. Under the influence of Carter and JOHNNY HODGES, both saxophonists, Webster began to develop his dis-tinctive style: at one moment exceptionally smooth and lush, at another gruff and honking, but always masterfully composed, evocative, and full of sentiment.

Webster's style came into its maturity when he worked briefly with the famed orchestra of DUKE ELLINGTON in 1935 and 1936, becoming the band's first featured tenor saxophonist from 1940 to 1943. Along with Paul Gonsalves, he was the most im-portant tenor saxophonist in the history of the Ellington band. Webster left to work with various leaders, including bass player John Kirby and CBS music director Raymond Scott, while also running his own bands. He returned to the Ellington organi-zation in 1948 and 1949 before a stint with the star-studded touring group Jazz at the Philharmonic. He spent much of the 1950s on the West Coast to be near his mother and sister.

Throughout this period, Webster was much in demand for recordings. Some of his finest were with singers BILLIE HOLIDAY, CARMEN MCRAE, and ELLA FITZGERALD. Also ranking very highly are his own albums as a leader during the 1950s with musi-cians such as Benny Carter, trumpeter HARRY "SWEETS" EDISON, and pianist OSCAR EMMANUEL PETERSON. During the last decade of his life, he lived and worked in Copenhagen, Denmark, ap-pearing and recording with many American and local players. For Webster it was a period of occasional personal disarray, but his musical output remained superb.

Wedderburn, Robert

1762–1835

Jamaican abolitionist in Great Britain noted for his evocative speeches as a Methodist preacher and Spencean radical.

Despite his lack of formal education, Robert Wedderburn pos-sessed a flair for inciting political action with fiery speeches and eccentric burlesque. He is best known as a follower of the underground millenarian and land-reform advocate Thomas

Spence. In Spencean radicalism, Wedderburn found a way to express the disaffection he had experienced throughout his life.

Wedderburn was born in KINGSTON, JAMAICA. His father, a plantation owner, sold his mother while she was still pregnant because of her "troublemaking," and he later rejected Robert's pleas for financial assistance. Wedderburn was reared by his maternal grandmother, "Talkee Amy." A noted preacher, she instilled in Wedderburn a predilection for proselytizing. He joined the navy at seventeen and arrived in England in 1778. Like many black sailors, he was refused his wages by the British government. Although he found work as a tailor, his trade skills were devalued by mechanization. Poor and disaffected, he turned to religion, and became a licensed Unitarian preacher in 1786; in the 1790s he became a fervent Methodist. His sermons often involved foolish antics, which gained him a reputation as a "holy fool" but also drew large crowds.

After several years of association with fringe revolutionaries, Wedderburn joined the Spenceans. With them, he opposed the judicial system, criticized the established clergy, and advocated self-armament and universal suffrage. As unofficial leader of the Spenceans in 1817, Wedderburn published the journal *Axe Laid to the Root*. In this publication, by demanding land rights for all people, he linked the English working-class movement to the fight for the abolition of plantation slavery and the equal redistribution of land among all of the population—black and white. He encouraged slaves to strike and use guerrilla tactics in order to change their conditions, warning planters that some day, "they will slay man, woman, and child, and not spare the virgin, whose interest is connected with slavery." As a result of his views, in 1820 he was imprisoned for blasphemy for over a year. He served a sentence again in 1831—two years' hard labor—for running a brothel.

Wedderburn died in 1835, proud of the manner in which he had led his life. As he asserted, "I thank my God, that through a long life of hardship and adversity I have ever been free both in mind and body: and I have always raised my voice on behalf of my enslaved countrymen."

See also Great Britain.

Leyla Keough

Weems, Carrie Mae

1953–

American photographer, folklorist, and self-proclaimed "image-maker" whose provocative images depict gender and racial stereotypes.

Born in Portland, Oregon, Carrie Mae Weems grew up in a working-class family. After studying at California Institute of Arts she earned a Master of Fine Arts degree in photography from the University of California, San Diego in 1984. A self-proclaimed "image-maker," Weems deals with issues of history, gender, and class by combining photographic images and narrative text. Often achingly personal, Weems's images ex-

plore issues of bigotry, self-presentation, and relationships by incorporating African American folklore and bigoted or stereotypical narratives into her work. Her early work dealt with issues of family and class and quite often featured Weems and members of her own family. Portraits such as *Honey Coloured Boy, Chocolate Coloured Man, Golden Yella Girl* and *Blue Black Boy*—taken with a Polaroid camera and then hand tinted—illustrate both real and unreal varieties of "black" skin, calling into question the category "black" itself.

Weems' *Sea Islands Series* focuses on aspects of African American folklore and history from the Sea Islands area of Georgia. Her *Untitled (Kitchen Table Series)* features a sequence of posed photographs exploring relationships between black men and women. In her photographs of degrading and stereotypical bric-a-brac, and her portraits and self-portraits exploring stereotypes of black people, Weems uses cultural symbols such as watermelons, fried chicken, jump rope, rhymes, folklore, and proverbs to interrogate existing stereotypes.

Weems has received numerous grants and awards and has been published extensively. Her first retrospective was held in 1993 at The National Museum of Women in the Arts in Washington, D.C., and featured her works from 1978 to 1992. She has participated in group exhibitions around the country including the 1991 Biennial at the Whitney Museum of American Art in New York. Her recent work includes the Hampton Project (2000), a multimedia exhibition combining large fabric hangings, original and historical photographs and reproductions, and audio recordings. Originally scheduled to open at Hampton University, the exhibition became a source of controversy when the university cancelled its run due to objections about Weems' interpretation of Hampton's history and ideals.

See also Photography, African American.

Bibliography

Kirsh, Andrea, and Susan Fisher Sterling. *Carrie Mae Weems (exhibition catalogue)*. National Museum of Women in the Arts, 1993.

Wells, Willie

1906–1989

African American star of the Negro Baseball Leagues who was posthumously elected to the Baseball Hall of Fame.

Born in Austin, Texas, Willie Wells grew up playing baseball in the sandlots of San Antonio. In 1924, at the age of sixteen, he signed to play with the St. Louis Stars of the Negro National League (NNL). A gifted fielder at shortstop, Wells worked hard to develop his hitting and won batting titles in the 1929 and 1930 seasons. A fierce competitor (fans nicknamed him "El Diablo" when he played in Mexico), Wells led the Stars to NNL championships in 1928, 1930, and 1931.

The NNL folded after the 1931 season, and Wells signed with the Chicago American Giants. The Giants won the 1932 championship as part of the Negro Southern League, and the 1933 championship as part of a revamped NNL. In 1936 Wells joined the Newark Eagles of the NNL, where he was part of what was called the "million dollar infield." He spent the late 1930s starring in the Latin American leagues in Cuba and Mexico. In 1942 he became Newark's player-manager, batted .361, was chosen for Cum Posey's All-American Dream Team, and was considered one of the top five players in baseball.

Wells retired in 1949 with a career batting average of .334 in the NEGRO LEAGUES (.392 in exhibition games against major leaguers) and played in eight All-Star games. He later managed the Winnipeg Buffaloes in Canada and the Birmingham Black Barons in the United States. In 1997 he was posthumously voted into the Baseball Hall of Fame.

See also Baseball in the United States.

Robert Fay

Wells-Barnett, Ida Bell

1862–1931

African American journalist; advocate of civil rights, women's rights, and economic rights; and antilynching crusader.

Ida B. Wells-Barnett, the first of Jim and Elizabeth Wells's eight children, was born six months before the EMANCIPATION PROCLAMATION went into effect. She attended Shaw University (now Rust College) in her hometown of Holly Springs, Mississippi, until she was forced to drop out because her parents died of yellow fever in 1878. Following their deaths, Wells-Barnett supported herself and her siblings by working as a schoolteacher in rural Mississippi and Tennessee. She took summer courses at FISK UNIVERSITY and continued to teach through 1891. She was fired from her teaching job for writing an editorial that accused the MEMPHIS, TENNESSEE, school board of providing inadequate resources to segregated black schools.

In May of 1884 Wells-Barnett filed suit against a railroad company after she was forced off of a train for refusing to sit in the JIM CROW car designated for blacks. She was awarded $500 by a circuit court, but the decision was overruled by the Tennessee Supreme Court in 1887, a rejection that ultimately strengthened her resolve to devote her life to upholding justice.

Wells-Barnett embarked on a career in journalism when she was elected editor of the *Evening Star* and then the *Living Way,* weekly church newspapers in Memphis. She became the editor of *Free Speech,* also in Memphis, in 1889. Her articles, written under the alias "Iola," were direct and confrontational. Two editorials she wrote in 1892, in response to the persecution and eventual LYNCHING of three black businessmen, were particularly controversial. The first, published on March 9, encouraged blacks to leave Memphis for Oklahoma and to boycott

Portrait of Ida B. Wells-Barnett, journalist and civil rights activist. *Oscar B. Willis, Chicago, IL.*

segregated transportation. The second, which appeared on May 21, suggested that white women often willingly initiated interracial relationships. Whites who were angered by her work responded by wrecking the offices and press of *Free Speech.*

Wells-Barnett took refuge in the North, reporting in the black newspapers the *New York Age* and the *Chicago Conservator* on the violence and injustices being perpetrated against African Americans. Through a lecture tour of England, Scotland, and Wales in 1893 and 1894, Wells-Barnett inspired international organizations to pressure America to end segregation and lynching. In 1895 she published an analysis of lynching entitled *A Red Record: Tabulated Statistics and Alleged Causes of Lynching in the United States,* which argued that the impetus behind lynching was economic.

Marrying Ferdinand Barnett, a lawyer and editor from CHICAGO, ILLINOIS, in 1895, Wells-Barnett put her writing on hold to focus on her family of four children, but she remained politically active. She helped to found the NATIONAL ASSOCIATION OF COLORED WOMEN in 1896, the Negro Fellowship League and the NATIONAL ASSOCIATION FOR THE ADVANCEMENT FOR COLORED PEOPLE (NAACP) in 1910, and the Alpha Suffrage Club in 1913. In 1916 she became involved with MARCUS MOZIAH GARVEY's UNIVERSAL NEGRO IMPROVEMENT ASSOCIATION.

During the last fifteen years of her life, Wells-Barnett wrote extensively on the race riots in East St. Louis, Illinois (1917), Chicago (1919), and Arkansas (1922). She continued to promote civil rights and justice for African Americans. A low-income housing project in Chicago was named in her honor in 1941, and in 1990 the United States Postal Service issued an Ida B. Wells-Barnett stamp.

Aaron Myers

Wesley, Charles Harris

1891–1987

American historian, educator, and minister who was an early proponent of African American studies.

Charles Harris Wesley attended public schools in his hometown of Louisville, Kentucky and then went on to receive a B.A. from FISK UNIVERSITY in 1911, an M.A. in economics from Yale University in 1913, and a Ph.D. from Harvard University in 1925. Wesley's doctorate in history was the third awarded by Harvard to an African American. Wesley served on the HOWARD UNIVERSITY faculty from 1913 to 1942. In 1916, Wesley began a long association with CARTER GODWIN WOODSON'S AS-SOCIATION FOR THE STUDY OF NEGRO LIFE AND HISTORY, serving as president from 1950 to 1965, and as executive director until 1972. In 1942, Wesley became president of WILBERFORCE UNI-VERSITY in Ohio, a school supported by the AFRICAN METHODIST EPISCOPAL CHURCH. As president until 1965, Wesley improved the faculty, founded new programs (such as African Studies), and integrated the student body. Wesley served as director of the Afro-American Historical and Cultural Museum in Philadelphia from its opening in 1974 to 1976.

In addition to his work as an educator, Wesley was AME Church minister and elder from 1914 to 1937. Awarded a Guggenheim Fellowship in 1930, Wesley went to England to study slave emancipation in the British Empire. From 1931 to 1946, he was president of Alpha Phi Alpha, a black fraternity about which he wrote *The History of Alpha Phi Alpha* (1953). Wesley also wrote many other articles and books on African American history, leaders and organizations, including *Negro Labor in the United States, 1850–1925* (1927), *Collapse of the Confederacy* (1937), and his last book, *The History of the National Association of Colored Women's Clubs: A Legacy of Service* (1984).

Wesley, Dorothy Burnett Porter

1905–1995

Librarian and bibliographer responsible for building Howard University's Moorland-Spingarn Research Center into one of the world's largest collections of material by and about people of African descent.

Historian and author of several hundred articles and books, Dorothy Porter Wesley is best known for her work as a librarian. At the age of twenty-five, she was the first to consolidate HOWARD UNIVERSITY's materials by and about African Americans toward building the renowned Moorland-Spingarn Research Center; the rest of her life was spent organizing and making accessible the major archive of black history and culture.

Dorothy Burnett was born in Warrenton, Virginia, and educated in New Jersey, WASHINGTON D.C., and later at Howard University. She married JAMES AMOS PORTER, the painter and historian, in 1929, and in 1932, she became the first African American woman to receive a master's degree in library sciences from Columbia University. She returned to Howard to serve as curator of the collection, a position she held until 1973; following her retirement and the death of her first husband, Porter married Charles H. Wesley, the historian, in 1979.

In her career as curator, Wesley contributed to the library's collection in the capacity of scholar, writing articles about topics ranging from Afro-Brazilian poet Caldas Barbosa to the abolitionist movement. More important, though, Wesley produced valuable bibliographies about people of African descent, such as *The Negro in the United States: A Selected Bibliography* (1967) and *Afro-Braziliana: A Working Bibliography* (1978). Her scholarship and her development of the MOORLAND-SPINGARN RESEARCH COLLECTION opened the door to a new wave of African American scholarship. She earned several honorary degrees, including doctorates of humane letters from Syracuse University and Radcliffe College.

West, Cornel

1953–

African American philosopher, theologian, and activist.

Cornel West was born in Oklahoma, a place once envisioned as a homeland for Native Americans displaced by European colonization, and for African Americans acting on the freedom promised by emancipation. The grandson of a Baptist minister, he was reared in the Baptist Church, and the church has remained a significant presence in his life since. Even as a child, West was articulate, outspoken, and politically engaged. In elementary school he convinced a group of his classmates to stop saluting the flag to protest the second-class citizenship afforded to African Americans.

West encountered the activities of the BLACK PANTHER PARTY while living in Sacramento, California. The Panthers informed his early thinking about democratic socialism and acquainted him with an internationalist vision for black enfranchisement. He was also inspired by the teachings of MARTIN LUTHER KING JR. and MALCOLM X, as well as by the music of JOHN COLTRANE and JAMES BROWN. By the time he won a scholarship to Harvard University in 1970, West was already well on his way to becoming an activist-scholar. "Owing to my family, church, and the black social movements of the 1960s," he recalled, "I arrived at Harvard unashamed of my African, Christian, and militant decolonized outlooks." While in Cambridge, he worked with the Black Panther Party, volunteering at their children's breakfast program.

West thrived at Harvard, consuming the work of the black intellectual tradition, including that of W. E. B. DU BOIS and ST. CLAIRE DRAKE, as well as European philosophers such as Max Weber, Karl Marx, and Friedrich Nietzsche. At the core of West's developing self as a scholar lay the belief in integrating a religious faith with both a political engagement and an intellectually rigorous course of study. "For me there was always a vital spiritual dimension to politics," West has explained. "Issues of death, disease, and despair have always been the fundamental issues of being human, and you didn't get too much talk about these issues in political circles."

After three years at Harvard, West graduated magna cum laude in 1973 and chose to pursue graduate studies in philosophy at Princeton. In 1977 he began teaching at Union Theological Seminary in New York. His doctoral dissertation, completed in 1980, was later revised and republished as the *Ethical Dimensions of Marxist Thought* (1991).

A center of liberation theology and black theological education, Union was an ideal place for West's commitment to what he calls a prophetic criticism: "a self-critical and self-corrective enterprise of human 'sense-making' for the preserving and expanding of human empathy and compassion." It is through this philosophic and spiritual enterprise that West understands the experience of race in America, a point made clear by *Prophesy Deliverance! An Afro-American Revolutionary Christianity,* published in 1982.

In 1984 West left Union for Yale Divinity School, where he was granted a full professorship in religion and philosophy. He returned to Union in 1987, but shortly after was recruited to direct Princeton University's program in African American studies. In 1988 he joined Princeton as professor of religion and, working with a community of scholars that included novelist TONI MORRISON, he helped revitalize the African American studies program.

Other universities were also eager to have West join their faculty. When HENRY LOUIS GATES, JR., took leadership of Harvard University's Department of African American Studies in 1991, he immediately began to strategize how to lure to Harvard the man he called "the preeminent African American intellectual of our generation." Excited by the possibilities of a group of scholars working across disciplines in the field of African American studies, West joined Harvard in 1993. In 1998 he was appointed to a prestigious university professorship at Harvard, becoming the first Alphonse Fletcher Jr. University Professor. In 2002, however, West decided to leave Harvard to return to Princeton, where he is the Class of 1943 University Professor of Religion.

West's scholarly writing pursues philosophical inquiry into the realm of the political, exploring the existential dimension within the moral, spiritual, and political space. Moreover, he traces this relationship in the work of his philosophic forbears. In *The American Evasion of Philosophy* (1989), West explores the history of American pragmatism, reading the American philosophic tradition, from Ralph Waldo Emerson to Richard Rorty, as an ongoing cultural commentary that responds to American society itself. In *Keeping Faith: Philosophy and Race in America* (1993), he continues to engage with philosophy, spiritual tradition, and history.

A mesmerizing speaker, West draws upon an African American tradition of rhetoric and improvisational public speaking. He has collected some of his many talks and essays in a four-volume work, *Beyond Eurocentrism and Multiculturalism* (1993). After publishing several books and articles addressed primarily to an academic audience, West turned to a broader readership with *Race Matters* (1993). His most well-known work, *Race Matters* reads like a sermon and unflinchingly confronts one of the most sensitive issues at the heart of American society: race. Yet West does not offer a specific program in this book. Rather, as he explained in an interview with Jervis Anderson, "I'm just trying to establish a framework within which we can come together for dialogue, and open-ended conversation within which other constructive voices might emerge."

Indeed, West has consistently placed a heavy emphasis on the conversational form as intellectual inquiry. The issues he takes up—sexism, anti-Semitism, homophobia, affirmative action—are timely ones for both black people and the community at large. In 1991 West engaged in a lively conversation on issues of race and gender with the feminist scholar BELL HOOKS in *breaking bread: insurgent black intellectual life* (1991). He has also taken a particular interest in black-Jewish relations, publishing in 1995 a conversation with Jewish intellectual Michel Lerner titled *Jews and Blacks: Let the Healing Begin.* West has also participated in several discussions on the relationship between African Americans and Hispanics, including a conversation with scholar Jorge Klor de Alva and author Earl Shorris in "Our Next Race Question," published in *Harper's Magazine* in 1996. He and Gates co-published *The Future of the Race* in 1996, and in 1998 West coauthored a book on parenting and family policy with Sylvia Ann Hewlett. His recent works include *Making It on Broken Promises: African American Male Scholars Confront the Culture of Higher Education* (2002) and *Heart of Darkness: The Underside of the City on the Hill* (2004).

See also Black Theology in the United States.

Marian Aguiar

West, Dorothy

1907–1998

African American author and journalist who participated in the Harlem Renaissance and wrote numerous short stories over a long literary career.

The only child of Rachel Pease Benson and Isaac Christopher West, Dorothy West began her education in BOSTON, MASSACHUSETTS, at the age of two under the tutelage of Bessie Trotter, sister of WILLIAM MONROE TROTTER, the militant editor of the

Boston Guardian. After attending Farragut and Martin Schools, she went to Girls' Latin School, from which she graduated in 1923. West continued her education at Boston University and the Columbia University School of Journalism.

She began writing stories at the age of seven, and at the age of fourteen published her first short story, "Promise and Fulfillment," in the *Boston Post*. In 1926 West, then living in NEW YORK among the luminaries of the HARLEM RENAISSANCE, shared second place honors with ZORA NEALE HURSTON in a national writing competition organized by *OPPORTUNITY*, the magazine of the NATIONAL URBAN LEAGUE. Her interest in the arts was not only literary, and in 1927, she traveled to London as a cast member of the play *Porgy*. In the early 1930s she went to the Union of Soviet Socialist Republics to participate in the film *BLACK AND WHITE*, where she stayed for a year after the project was abandoned.

Returning to New York, West founded two short-lived literary journals: *Challenge* in 1934 (six issues) and *New Challenge* in 1937 (one issue). After working as a welfare investigator for a year and a half, West found employment with the FEDERAL WRITERS' PROJECT of the government's WORKS PROGRESS ADMINISTRATION through the early 1940s. She moved to Martha's Vineyard in Massachusetts in 1945 and wrote regularly for the *Vineyard Gazette*. She published the novels *The Living Is Easy* (1948) and *The Wedding* (1995), as well as more than sixty short stories. In 1997 television producer OPRAH GAIL WINFREY made *The Wedding* into a popular television miniseries.

Aaron Myers

Western Cape

Province in southwestern South Africa, bounded by the Atlantic Ocean on the west, the Indian Ocean on the south, and by Northern Cape and Eastern Cape provinces on the north and east.

Created in 1994 from part of Cape Province, one of the four former provinces of SOUTH AFRICA, Western Cape covers about 129,370 sq km (about 49,950 sq mi). Western Cape can be divided into three climatic zones. The western region, around CAPE TOWN, has dry summers and rainy winters (from May to August); the average annual rainfall in Cape Town totals 510 mm (20 in). The southern section of the province, along the Indian Ocean, receives some rain throughout the year; the average annual rainfall at Mossel Bay (Mosselbaai), a town in the southern region, totals 380 mm (15 in). The third climatic zone is the interior of Western Cape, which contains the Great Karroo, a large, flat, sparsely vegetated plateau that is dry most of the year. Overlooking Cape Town is the magnificent backdrop of Table Mountain (1,086 m/3,563 ft). A chain of mountain ranges, including the Outeniekwaberge, Hexrivierberge, Cederberg, and Tsitsikammaberge ranges, separates the coastal areas from the interior. Average temperatures in Western Cape range from 16° to 32° C (60° to 90° F) in the summer and from 7° to 18° C (44° to 64° F) in the winter.

The population of Western Cape was estimated at 4.3 million in 2003. People of mixed racial descent make up the majority of the population. Afrikaans, English, and XHOSA are the three primary languages spoken in the province. Most residents are Christians, but the province has a large Muslim community, including many Indians. Founded in 1652, Cape Town is the province's capital and largest city, as well as the legislative capital of South Africa. Other important towns include Beaufort West, George, Oudtshoorn, Saldanha Bay, Stellenbosch, and Worcester. Important cultural and historical sites in the province include Groot Constantia, home of Simon van der Stel, one of the Dutch governors of the Cape Colony (later Cape Province); Groote Schuur, located in Cape Town, the official residence of South Africa's president and formerly the home of CECIL RHODES, who was prime minister of the Cape Colony from 1890 until 1896; the Castle, a Dutch colonial administrative center begun in 1665 and the oldest building in Cape Town; Genadendal, the first mission station established in South Africa; and ROBBEN ISLAND, the site of a notorious prison that housed South Africa's most famous antiapartheid political prisoners. Western Province has three universities: the University of Cape Town (founded as South African College in 1829; established as a university in 1918), the University of Stellenbosch (1918), and the University of the Western Cape (1960).

Textiles, fishing, and printing and publishing rank as Western Cape's most important industries, and tourism has recently become a significant part of the economy. The province is also an important farming region, producing wheat and fruits such as apples, grapes, peaches, and oranges. Wine is produced in Western Cape as well. The Karroo has many sheep ranches and is noted for its wool production. Ostrich farms around Oudtshoorn make the area a famous source of ostrich feathers. The waters off the Atlantic coast provide a rich fishing ground.

The government of Western Cape consists of a premier, an executive council of ministers, and a legislature. The provincial assembly and premier are elected for five-year terms, or until the next national election. Political parties are awarded assembly seats based on the percentage of votes each party receives in the province during the national elections. The assembly elects a premier, who then appoints the members of the executive council.

See also Antiapartheid Movement; Indian Communities in Africa; Tourism in Africa.

Western Pioneers

African Americans who left the South after Reconstruction for a new life in the West.

The last half of the nineteenth century in America saw a large westward migration, both black and white. Though the story of white pioneers has been memorialized in film and fiction, that of African American pioneers is less often told. As the historian William L. Katz points out, the black population of the mountain states alone—Montana, Idaho, Wyoming, Colorado,

New Mexico, Arizona, Utah, and Nevada—increased thirteen-fold between 1870 and 1910. Other states, like Kansas, Iowa, and Nebraska, had a steady influx of African Americans starting before the AMERICAN CIVIL WAR.

After emancipation and the promises of RECONSTRUCTION, many Southern freedpeople found themselves locked into bleak social and economic conditions. SHARECROPPING, in which white landowners took large percentages of black farmers' crops as rent, kept most former slaves impoverished. Nightriders from groups like the KU KLUX KLAN and White League used violence—and sometimes murder—to discourage black political activism. Despite slavery's end, the region's ingrained racist traditions continued to make it inhospitable to African Americans who yearned for equality and freedom, and many decided to leave the South. Some Southern blacks planned migrations to LIBERIA, while several thousand EXODUSTERS moved to Kansas in 1879.

Many African American pioneers took advantage of the Homestead Act (1862), which provided the opportunity to own farmland in the West. Others worked on the expanding railroad system, either as Pullman porters or maintenance men. Some black Westerners founded their own businesses and even their own newspapers. Yet the white racism that had driven them out of the South continued to dog the pioneers, creating obstacles in housing, employment, and education. The West was no promised land. But it did, according to historian W. Sherman Savage, "offer blacks relatively more freedom, and those who went there had a better chance than those who remained at home."

Kate Tuttle

Western Sahara

Former Spanish province bordering Morocco to the north, Mauritania to the south, the Atlantic Ocean to the west, and Algeria to the east.

Western Sahara is a former Spanish colony. Today it is the site of a conflict between the POLISARIO FRONT (a political and military organization of the SAHRAWI people) and the kingdom of MOROCCO. The Polisario Front wants independence for Western Sahara, while Morocco wants to annex the province, which it claims on the basis of historical events. Although the area's environment is largely desert, vast phosphate deposits make it economically attractive.

Early History

The area now known as Western Sahara has been populated for thousands of years. What is now the desolate SAHARA was once a plentifully watered grassland with a great deal of wildlife. During prehistoric times it supported a small population of hunters and gatherers. The transformation from grass-land to desert, beginning around 2500 B.C.E., drove this population south into what is now sub-Saharan Africa. BERBER people from the Mediterranean coastal region eventually moved into the area. They were nomadic pastoralists who could manage to exist in the austere environment. Around the first century C.E., the introduction of the CAMEL from the Middle East, a beast of burden that excels in the harsh conditions of the Sahara, improved Berber living standards and increased their military capacity.

The Berber peoples of the western Sahara region have faced many challenges for control of the area. The first major challenge came in 1039 C.E., with the invasion of ALMORAVIDS, who were for the most part Moroccan and who followed a militant Islamic leadership. By 1110 the Almoravids had subdued the western Sahara, as well as parts of present-day ALGERIA, MAURITANIA, Morocco, and SPAIN. After the Almoravids came the Bani Hassan (or Maqil) Arabs, who arrived during the fifteenth century and eventually dominated the resident Berbers. The leadership of the modern Polisario Front claims descent from the Bani Hassan.

The European powers of Spain and PORTUGAL also made brief attempts during the fifteenth century to establish fortified trading posts on the coast, but they were vulnerable to raids, either from European rivals or from the indigenous nomads. By 1476 the Spanish had established only one post of note, which they abandoned by 1496. Following the Spanish withdrawal, the Moroccan sultans attempted to subdue the area in a series of raids from the mid-seventeenth century until the early 1880s. Although the Moroccans failed to achieve firm control over the vast and sparsely populated region, they did establish lasting ties with some of the local peoples, such as the Tekna.

Colonization

In 1884 Spain declared the coastal areas of Western Sahara, including the settlements of Boujdour and Dakhla, a protectorate. Spanish colonization of the area was minimal. At first, the Spanish settled only at Dakhla, which they renamed Villa Cisneros. The Spanish had to contend with not only the French, who occupied Morocco and Mauritania, but also the Sahrawi leader Shaikh Ma al-Ainin, who fiercely resisted European occupation until his defeat in 1910 at the hands of the French. Still, the Sahrawi tribes of the interior proved hard to subdue. The Spanish did not gain full control of Western Sahara until 1934. The colony was reorganized as Spanish Sahara in 1958.

In 1957 the newly independent nation of Morocco claimed Western Sahara as its own. Spain was forced to repel a series of Moroccan military incursions. In 1960 Mauritania achieved independence and it, too, claimed a share of Spanish Sahara. The colony of Spanish Sahara lacked profitable resources, and the Spanish saw it as a financial drain. Thus, the Spanish government was unwilling to invest in its possession, and the Spanish presence remained minimal. The indigenous Sahrawi people of the interior continued their centuries-long tradition of nomadic existence. In 1963 scientists discovered vast reserves

Western Sahara (At a Glance)

OFFICIAL NAME: Western Sahara

FORMER NAME: Spanish Sahara

AREA: 267,000 sq km (about 103,000 sq mi)

LOCATION: North Africa, on the Atlantic Ocean; borders Morocco, Algeria, and Mauritania

CAPITAL: None (under de facto control of Morocco)

OTHER MAJOR CITIES: El Aaiún and Ad Dakhla (Villa Cisneros) (population data unavailable)

POPULATION: 261,794 (2003 estimate)

POPULATION DENSITY: Data unavailable

POPULATION BELOW AGE 15: Data unavailable

POPULATION GROWTH RATE: 2.4 percent (1998 estimate)

TOTAL FERTILITY RATE: 6.75 children born per woman (1998 estimate)

LIFE EXPECTANCY AT BIRTH: Total population: 48.41 years (male 47.32 years; female 49.83 years; 1998 estimate)

INFANT MORTALITY RATE: 139.74 deaths per 1000 live births (1998 estimate)

LITERACY RATE (AGE 15 AND OVER WHO CAN READ AND WRITE): Data unavailable

EDUCATION: Data unavailable

LANGUAGES: Hassaniya Arabic and Moroccan Arabic

ETHNIC GROUPS: Arab and Berber

RELIGION: Muslim

CLIMATE: Hot, minimal rainfall inland, moist winds offshore; harmattan haze predominates inland, fog along the shore

LAND, PLANTS, AND ANIMALS: Almost entirely desert, interrupted by occasional rocky or sandy areas, with low mountains in the south and northeast. Vegetation is sparse, but occasional rainfall permits some nomadic animal husbandry (of sheep, goats, and camels).

NATURAL RESOURCES: Phosphates and iron ore

CURRENCY: The Moroccan dirham

GROSS DOMESTIC PRODUCT (GDP): Data unavailable

GDP PER CAPITA: Data unavailable

GDP REAL GROWTH RATE: Data unavailable

PRIMARY ECONOMIC ACTIVITIES: Pastoral nomadism, fishing, oasis gardening, and phosphate mining

PRIMARY CROPS: Various fruits and vegetables; camels, sheep, and goats

INDUSTRIES: Animal husbandry and subsistence farming are practiced by half the labor force.

PRIMARY EXPORT: Phosphates

PRIMARY IMPORTS: Fuel for fishing fleets, and foodstuffs

PRIMARY TRADE PARTNERS: Morocco claims and administers Western Sahara, so trade partners are included in overall Moroccan accounts.

GOVERNMENT: Territory administratively controlled by Morocco. The territory's legal status and sovereignty have not been resolved. Both Morocco and the Popular Front for the Liberation of the Saguia el-Hamra and Rio de Oro (Polisario Front) have contested the territory. In February 1976 the Polisario declared a government-in-exile of the Sahrawi Arab Democratic Republic (SADR), and thousands of Sahrawis were displaced by political turmoil and relocated to a settlement in southwest Algeria. In April 1976 Morocco and Mauritania divided the territory between the two countries. Polisario guerrillas forced Mauritania to surrender its claims in 1979; Morocco has had administrative control since then. The Polisario's government-in-exile became a member of the Organization of African Unity in 1984. United Nations forces have been monitoring the territory since a 1991 cease-fire on guerrilla activities. In late 1997 Polisario and Moroccan representatives tentatively agreed to allow a referendum on Western Sahara self-determination to be held sometime in 1998. The referendum was postponed repeatedly due to disagreements over voter eligibility.

Barbara Worley

of phosphates in the northern part of the colony, and Spanish interest in the area revived. Spanish mining activities began in the late 1960s.

In the mid-1960s, however, the United Nations (UN) general assembly, after appeals from Sahrawi representatives, passed a resolution calling for Spain's withdrawal from the colony. Muhammad Sidi Ibrahim Bassiri led Sahrawi anti-Spanish protests in 1970 in the capital of Al-Ayun. The Spanish responded brutally. Spanish troops crushed the demonstrations and captured Bassiri, who died in prison under suspicious circumstances. Spanish repression, however, fostered increased Sahrawi nationalism.

In 1973 a group of Sahrawis formed the Polisario Front (whose full name in Spanish is Frente Popular para la Liberación de Saguia el-Hamra y Río de Oro) and began armed guerrilla activities against the Spanish. These attacks persuaded Spanish leader General Francisco Franco to offer limited Sahrawi autonomy, in the form of a handpicked council, the *Djemaa*, composed mainly of "acceptable" Sahrawi who held political views sympathetic to Spain. Polisario demanded Sahrawi self-determination and continued its guerrilla war. In August 1974 Spain agreed to a referendum on self-determination.

Sahrawi calls for self-determination met with stiff resistance from the governments of Morocco and Mauritania, which continued to claim the territory. Both governments requested that the International Court of Justice at the Hague rule on their historical claims to Western Sahara. The court ruled in October 1975 that the two countries had no claim to Western Sahara and that the Sahrawi had a right to self-determination.

The ruling proved moot; by 1975 Spain, whose leader Franco was seriously ill, had become unwilling to risk any conflict over Western Sahara. Moroccan troops were poised at the border of the territory, and if Spain had attempted to hold a referendum, there was a risk that Morocco might launch attacks on Spain itself. Spain agreed, as did Morocco and Mauritania, to partition the territory without a referendum, with the northern two-thirds going to Morocco and the southern one-third to Mauritania. Spain withdrew from Western Sahara on February 26, 1976; Moroccan and Mauritanian forces surged across the border and occupied the area.

Unresolved Conflict

Within twenty-four hours of Spain's withdrawal, Polisario declared independence as the Sahrawi Arab Democratic Republic (SADR) and vowed to continue the fight. It began to evacuate as many Sahrawis as possible from Western Sahara and to relocate them across the border in Algeria, its most significant patron. Algeria, alarmed at perceived Moroccan expansionism, supplied weapons to the guerrillas and provided Polisario forces and Western Saharan refugees with a safe haven in its southwestern Tindouf region.

After the evacuation, Polisario went on the offensive. At first the group focused on the weaker Mauritanian army, and attacked Mauritanian targets in Western Sahara as well as in Mauritania. With their superior knowledge of the desert, Polisario forces penetrated the Mauritanian border and attacked deep inside the country. In June 1976 Polisario forces attacked the Mauritanian capital, NOUAKCHOTT, and fired artillery shells at the presidential palace before hastily retreating. The conflict drove Mauritania's government into bankruptcy and wrecked the country's economy, turning Mauritanian public opinion against President MOKTAR OULD DADDAH. A small band of Mauritanian military officers led an almost bloodless coup d'état against Daddah in 1979, and agreed to an armistice with Polisario and a quick pullout from its Western Saharan holdings.

Shortly after the Mauritanian withdrawal, Moroccan forces began to occupy the remaining one-third of Western Sahara. Polisario, however, inflicted heavy losses on Morocco. Morocco managed to hold the territory only at great expense. Its military presence of 100,000 troops consumed up to half the national budget. But the military campaign brought political benefit to Morocco's King Hassan: it defused political opposition by uniting Moroccans behind a patriotic cause while keeping the military occupied, well-supplied, and disinclined to stage a coup.

The ORGANIZATION OF AFRICAN UNITY (OAU), whose members were divided on the issue of supporting Morocco or Polisario, attempted to broker a peace deal in the early 1980s. In 1982 the OAU officially recognized SADR as the rightful government of Western Sahara and admitted it to the organization. As a result, Morocco later withdrew from the organization, and the OAU abandoned attempts to mediate the dispute. Diplomatic activity halted almost completely between 1984 and 1986.

The military conflict moved toward a stalemate as Morocco consolidated its control over the territory. During the mid-1980s Polisario resumed its attacks, receiving continued support from Algeria. Moroccans, however, built an earthen wall that was armed with mines and motion detectors to defend the major economic and population centers of Western Sahara. This wall severely limited Polisario's military options. Any attempt to breach the barrier would now cost dearly in resources and casualties, although Polisario could still drain Moroccan resources by attacking the wall itself and the soldiers who defended it.

UN secretary general Javier Pérez de Cuéllar began indirect negotiations. By 1991 negotiators tentatively agreed to a cease-fire agreement and a plan for a referendum on independence. Both Morocco and Polisario agreed to yield to UN forces, which would mediate the agreement's main sticking point: who would be eligible to vote. For years, Morocco had been settling Western Sahara with Moroccan citizens. Meanwhile, many Sahrawi who had been living in Western Sahara under the Spanish had fled to refugee camps outside the territory. Polisario argued that only those people (and their descendants) who had been in Western Sahara at the time of the final Spanish census in 1974 should vote, while Morocco favored allowing any person living there at the time of the referendum to vote.

By the mid-1990s both parties desired a peaceful agreement. Morocco had come under pressure from international lenders to cut its military budget, while Algerian support for Polisario had diminished. The UN suggested a compromise solution to determine voter eligibility, to which Polisario finally agreed in 1997. The arduous process of registering and authenticating eligible voters began again.

A referendum to determine whether Western Sahara would become independent or integrate with Morocco was scheduled for late 1998, but has been repeatedly postponed. In 2003 U.S. Secretary of State James Baker brought to the UN an updated plan for Western Sahara's self-determination; though secretary general KOFI ANNAN urged acceptance of the plan, Morocco rejected it. The referendum on final status has been postponed repeatedly. Those who have benefited from phosphate earnings and Moroccan government spending may choose to cast their lot with Morocco, while those who have faced Moroccan repression, as well as the many Sahrawis who have spent decades in Polisario's refugee camps, will almost certainly side with Polisario.

See also Pastoralism; United Nations in Africa.

Bibliography

Mercer, John. *Spanish Sahara.* Allen & Unwin, 1976.

Thompson, Virginia McLean. *The Western Saharans: Background to Conflict.* Barnes & Noble Books, 1980.

Robert Fay

West Indies

Archipelago in the northern part of the Western Hemisphere, separating the Caribbean Sea from the Atlantic Ocean.

Called the "Indies" by Christopher Columbus, the West Indies (as distinguished from the East Indies archipelago) consists of three main island chains that extend in a roughly crescent shape from the eastern tip of the Yucatán Peninsula in MEXICO and southeastern Florida in the United States to the Venezuelan coast of South America. THE BAHAMAS, in the north, form a southeasterly line. The Greater Antilles, comprising the islands of CUBA, HISPANIOLA, JAMAICA, and PUERTO RICO, lie in the center. To the southeast, arching southward from Puerto Rico and then westward along the Venezuelan coast, are the Lesser Antilles, comprising the Leeward Islands and Windward Islands. BARBADOS, TRINIDAD AND TOBAGO, and the NETHERLANDS ANTILLES are often considered part of this third chain. The land area of the West Indies totals about 235,700 sq km (about 91,000 sq mi), and the total population is around 34 million.

Most of the islands of the West Indies are mountainous, projecting remnants of submerged ranges related to Central and South American mountain systems. Elevations of about 2,100 to 2,400 m (about 7,000 to 8,000 ft) are common in the Greater Antilles; the highest point (3,175 m/10,417 ft) is Pico Duarte in the Cordillera Central of the DOMINICAN REPUBLIC. The inner chain of the Lesser Antilles, part of a submerged volcanic ridge, consists mainly of volcanic cones, a number of which are still active. The outer chain is composed largely of coral and uplifted limestone. Elevations in the Lesser Antilles rarely exceed 1,500 m (5,000 ft). The southernmost part of the archipelago, from Trinidad to ARUBA, is geologically related to South American rock and mountain formations. The Bahamas and northern central Cuba, relatively flat limestone and coral formations, are geologically related to formations in Florida and the Yucatán Peninsula. Several deep ocean trenches lie close offshore and parallel to the islands of the Greater and Lesser Antilles, marking unstable crustal zones in which earthquakes may occur.

Climate

Except for part of the Bahamas chain, all the West Indies islands lie within the Tropic Zone, but temperate climatic conditions exist in many mountainous regions, and weather conditions at lower elevations are modified by such oceanic influences as the trade winds. Two seasons are distinguishable: a relatively dry season, from November through May; and a wet season, from June through October. Hurricanes, formed in the Atlantic, may occur between July and October, destroying much life and property when they sweep onshore.

Political Divisions

Politically, the West Indies comprises thirteen independent nations and a number of colonial dependencies, territories, and

possessions. The Republic of Cuba, consisting of the island of Cuba and several off-lying islands, is the largest West Indies nation. HAITI and the Dominican Republic, two other independent nations, occupy Hispaniola, the second largest of the archipelago. Jamaica, Barbados, the Bahamas, Trinidad and Tobago, DOMINICA, GRENADA, SAINT KITTS AND NEVIS, SAINT LUCIA, SAINT VINCENT AND THE GRENADINES, and ANTIGUA AND BARBUDA are the other sovereign nations.

Sovereignty over nearly all the other West Indies islands is distributed among the United States, FRANCE, the NETHERLANDS, and GREAT BRITAIN. Puerto Rico, fourth largest island of the archipelago, is a commonwealth of the United States; and several of the VIRGIN ISLANDS are United States territories. The French West Indies includes MARTINIQUE, GUADELOUPE, and a number of small island dependencies of Guadeloupe. The Dutch possessions consist of Curaçao, Bonaire, Aruba, and smaller Lesser Antilles islands. VENEZUELA holds about seventy Lesser Antilles islands. Dependencies of Great Britain are the CAYMAN ISLANDS, TURKS AND CAICOS ISLANDS, and some of the Virgin Islands.

Weston, Randolph (Randy)

1926–

African American jazz pianist and composer known for combining elements from jazz and African music in his performances and compositions.

Born in Brooklyn, New York, Randy Weston studied classical piano as a youth and also heard much JAZZ, CALYPSO, and GOSPEL MUSIC in his community. In the 1940s he studied informally with THELONIOUS MONK, the jazz pianist and composer known as one of the originators of BEBOP, a modern jazz style. After a tour of duty in the United States Army, Weston ran a restaurant in Brooklyn from 1947 to 1949. In 1949 he began playing professionally for several bandleaders, including drummer ART BLAKEY, saxophonist and singer Eddie "Cleanhead" Vinson, trumpeter Kenny Dorham, and saxophonist Cecil Payne.

By the mid-1950s Weston was leading his own groups almost exclusively, and he began incorporating African elements into his compositions. In 1961 and 1963 he performed in LAGOS, NIGERIA. In 1967 he visited a number of West African countries on a tour that was sponsored by the United States Department of State. Weston took up residence in MOROCCO, and in 1969 opened his African Rhythms Club in TANGIER, MOROCCO. He moved to Paris, FRANCE, in 1973 and then back to Morocco a decade later. Weston continues to perform around the world.

Weston developed a powerful playing style rooted in bebop and also encompassing musical elements drawn from SWING (a jazz-based dance music) and post-bebop (an updated version of bebop begun in the 1970s). He performed and recorded in a variety of contexts, ranging from piano soloist on several albums, such as the critically acclaimed *Blues to Africa* (1974), to bandleader on others, such as *The Spirits of Our Ancestors* (1991). His longtime collaborator Melba Liston served as the arranger on many of his albums, including *Little Niles* (1958),

Tanjah (1973), and *Volcano Blues* (1993). Beginning in the 1960s, his son Azzedin, a jazz percussionist, played conga drums on several albums.

The majority of Weston's recordings since the mid-1950s have been of his own compositions. Many of his compositions are suggestive of Africa. *Uhuru Africa* (1960) explored African links with jazz and used lyrics by LANGSTON HUGHES. However, his most famous compositions—the jazz standards "Hi-Fly" and "Little Niles" (Azzedin's childhood name)—are straightforward bebop pieces. In 1998 Weston recorded *Khepera,* which combined American jazz traditions and African rhythms in an exploration of African links with China. His interest in traditional African music is also apparent in *Spirit! The Power of Music* (2003), a collaboration between Weston's group African Rhythms and the Gnawa Master Musicians of Morocco.

See also Music, African; Music, African American

Wharton, Clifton Reginald, Sr.

1899–1990

American lawyer and ambassador who was the first African American to enter the foreign service and the first African American diplomat to head a United States delegation to a European country.

Clifton Reginald Wharton, Sr., a native of BALTIMORE, MARYLAND, was raised in BOSTON, MASSACHUSETTS, where he graduated from English High School and in 1920 received a law degree from Boston University. He received an advanced law degree from the same institution after practicing law in Boston from 1920 to 1923. After this, he left Boston and worked in WASHINGTON, D.C., as an examiner in the Veteran's Bureau and as a law clerk in the State Department. In Washington, Wharton embarked on his career in international diplomacy. He served as a diplomat in LIBERIA (1925–1929), SPAIN (1930–1941), and MADAGASCAR (1942–1945). Following these assignments, he was consul general at the U.S. Embassy in PORTUGAL from 1949 to 1950.

Wharton practiced diplomacy under both Democratic and Republican administrations. In 1953, he became the consul general in FRANCE. Five years later, President Dwight D. Eisenhower reappointed him as U.S. Minister to Romania, and in 1961 President John F. Kennedy appointed him U.S. Ambassador to Norway. Wharton retired from the foreign service in 1964, one year after having received an honorary doctorate of law degree from Boston University.

Aaron Myers

Wheatley, Phillis

1753?–1784

Poet who is considered by many to be the founder of African American literature.

This portrait of Phillis Wheatley, attributed to the African American artist Scipio Moorhead, appears on the frontispiece of her first volume of poetry, which was published in 1773. *CORBIS/Bettmann*

Some view our sable race with scornful eye,
"Their colour is a diabolic dye."
Remember, *Christians, Negroes,* black as *Cain,*
May be refined, and join the angelic train.

So ends Phillis Wheatley's poem "On Being Brought From Africa to America" (1773). The poem is remarkable not only for the honest way it speaks about color prejudice among white Christians—never a polite subject, and certainly not one in 1773—but also for the singular achievements of the author. Wheatley wrote the original version of this poem in 1768, at age fourteen, seven years after she came to America as an African slave. At the time of its publication, she was just nineteen years old yet already an internationally celebrated poet whose admirers included George Washington and Benjamin Franklin. She was the first African American, and the second American woman, to publish a book.

Wheatley was born in West Africa, probably in 1753. In 1761 she was stolen from her parents and transported on a slave ship to BOSTON, MASSACHUSETTS. There she was sold to John and Susanna Wheatley. They purchased her to be a domestic servant, but when Susanna realized that Phillis had a talent for learning, she allowed her daughter Mary to tutor Phillis in Latin, English, and the Bible. Wheatley soon began composing her own poetry, and her first published poem appeared in the *Newport Mercury* newspaper on December 21, 1767.

Over the next five years, several more of Wheatley's poems were published in local papers. In October 1770 she wrote an elegy for English evangelical minister George Whitefield that was so popular that it was also reprinted in England, bringing her international recognition. But when Wheatley tried in 1772 to publish her first volume of poetry, publishers still felt they needed to guarantee to skeptical readers that a black slave could have written the poems she claimed were hers. She underwent an oral examination by eighteen of "the most respectable Characters in Boston," including the governor of Massachusetts, to prove that she was indeed literate and articulate enough to have written the poems. Although Wheatley passed the exam, she still could not secure a Boston publisher.

She found an ally across the Atlantic in Selina, countess of Huntingdon, an evangelical Englishwoman with ties to Whitefield who had read her poetry and who arranged for her book to be published in London. In 1773 *Poems on Various Subjects, Religious and Moral* appeared. The frontispiece of the original edition, requested by the countess, makes the author's identity—and ability—very clear: under the caption "Phillis Wheatley, Negro Servant to Mr. John Wheatley of Boston," there is an engraving of the young black woman at her desk, with a piece of paper in front of her, a book at one hand, and a pen in the other. The image is thought to be the work of SCIPIO MOORHEAD, a young African American slave artist.

Wheatley traveled to England to oversee the book's publication, but the trip served other purposes as well. She met many British dignitaries and intellectuals, who celebrated her literary ability, and American diplomat Benjamin Franklin came to call on her in London. Shortly after her trip, her owners decided to free her—according to Wheatley, "at the desire of my friends in England." The trip brought Wheatley fame as an author, and pressure from English abolitionists led to her freedom.

Wheatley's poetic subjects were often the people and places that made news around her. She wrote numerous elegies for friends and acquaintances and also several popular poems supporting the colonists in the AMERICAN REVOLUTION, even though John and Susanna Wheatley were Tories. A poem she wrote in October 1775 in honor of George Washington so impressed the general that he invited her to visit with him at his military headquarters in Cambridge, Massachusetts. Washington was himself a slaveholder, but some scholars have speculated that his conversation with Wheatley may have influenced his later discomfort with slavery.

Some readers have criticized Wheatley because her subject matter is not more distinctly African American, and especially because some of her poetry appears to condone slavery. For example, in "To the University of Cambridge, in New-England," Wheatley refers to Africa as "the land of errors, and *Egyptian* gloom," and goes on to say that it was God's "gracious hand" that "brought [her] in safety from those dark abodes." But while this poem does reflect Wheatley's evangelical Christianity (she believed that the hidden blessing in her capture was that it allowed her to be exposed to the Bible and to be saved), it does not capture the complexities of Wheatley's feelings about her enslavement, or her identification with other African Americans.

In other poems, Wheatley does affirm that her separation from her home was indeed traumatic. For example, in "To the Right Honourable William Legge, Earl of Dartmouth," Wheatley explains that she empathizes with the American colonists because of her own experience with oppression:

When seeming cruel Fate
Me snatched from Afric's fancied happy seat,
. . . Ah! What bitter pangs molest,
What sorrows laboured in the parent's breast?

Wheatley's letters, recently recovered, also clearly show that she was aware of racial prejudice and injustice, and that she identified with other people of African descent. Recent scholars agree with Wheatley's implication that her poems supporting the American colonists are part of a larger discourse on freedom from tyranny, a discourse that was inextricably linked to the question of slavery—but that she chose to express in terms that her immediate audience would receive best.

In 1778 Wheatley married a free black Bostonian, John Peters. The next year, she circulated a proposal for a new collection of poetry, indicating she had written dozens of new poems since 1773. But in a country now at war, the interest that had attended the publication of her first book had waned. Wheatley could not find a publisher and retreated from the public eye. Her short marriage was unhappy, and marred by the deaths of her first two children in their infancy. On December 5, 1784, Wheatley died in childbirth along with her third child.

At the time of her death, Wheatley was living in poverty and obscurity on the outskirts of Boston, but the memory of the famed "Ethiopian muse" was strong enough that her obituary was printed in the Boston papers. Since the early nineteenth century, African American writers have continually acknowledged their debt to her accomplishments. Wheatley is celebrated as the founder of the African American literary tradition, and contemporary readers continue to learn more about the complexities she brought to that role.

Bibliography

Robinson, William H. *Phillis Wheatley and her Writings.* Garland, 1984.
Wheatley, Phillis. *The Collected Works of Phillis Wheatley.* Edited by John Shields. Oxford University Press, 1988.

Lisa Clayton Robinson

Whipper, Ionia R(ollin)

1872–1953

African American moral reformer and founder of the first black home for unwed mothers in Washington, D.C.

Ionia Whipper was born in Beaufort, South Carolina, the daughter of William J. and Frances A. Rollin Whipper. Her paternal grandfather, WILLIAM WHIPPER, was a prominent moral reformer and conductor on the UNDERGROUND RAILROAD, helping fugitive slaves escape to safety in the North. Her father was a delegate to the 1868 South Carolina Constitutional Convention, a municipal judge, and a member of the 1895 state constitutional convention. In 1889 he had published a pamphlet portraying the attempt of Democrats to win by fraud in the 1888 election in Beaufort County. Her mother and aunts were noted activists in Charleston, South Carolina.

After coming to WASHINGTON, D.C., at an early age, Whipper graduated from the HOWARD UNIVERSITY College of Medicine in 1903, where she specialized in obstetrics. With a heritage steeped in social reform, she would later dedicate her life to helping others. Frances Whipper died before her daughter could complete her studies. As a result, Ionia Whipper was forced to borrow money to complete her education and to teach in order to pay her debts before establishing a private practice. In 1911 she began a career of medical service to the Washington community that lasted more than forty years.

Whipper was greatly concerned about the plight of the unwed mothers, whose babies she delivered at FREEDMEN'S HOSPITAL. Many of these women were social outcasts who had no place to go during and after their pregnancy, and Whipper cared for many of them in her own home. In 1931 she organized the Lend-A-Hand Club to raise funds to build a permanent home for unwed mothers. In the meantime, Whipper organized the Tuesday Evening Club for maladjusted girls, supervising the club for many years.

By 1941 the efforts of the Lend-A-Hand Club resulted in the founding of the Ionia R. Whipper Home for Unwed Mothers, which remained the only such institution for blacks in Washington until similar facilities for whites were desegregated in the 1960s. Attempts to obtain financial help from the local United Fund organization were unsuccessful. The home was sustained by the fundraising efforts of various black groups in the Washington area. During the early years at the home, Whipper assumed many roles, including social worker, instructor, mother confessor, and physician. The budget was so low that she could not afford to employ special personnel. According to the Saint Luke's Episcopal Church obituary notice after Whipper's death, "Her aim was to rehabilitate the unwed mothers upon whom society had placed a great stigma."

Whipper died after a long illness in Harlem Hospital, New York City, on April 23, 1953. Her funeral was held on April 27 at St. Martin's Protestant Episcopal Church, 122nd Street and Lenox Avenue; interment was in Fresh Pond Crematorium. She was survived by her brother, Leigh Whipper, a well-known stage and screen actor, and a niece, Leighla Whipper Ford, both of New York City.

Ironically, the following month, the East Capitol Street home was closed to make way for public housing. Although the board of directors purchased a building shortly afterward, they had to raise funds for renovation. In the meantime, the homes for white unwed mothers refused to admit blacks, even on a temporary basis. The new home finally opened in the summer of 1955. The void created by the closing of the original home was filled by the efforts of Washington's black community. The name of the new home was changed to the Ionia Whipper Rehabilitation Home for Unwed Mothers.

Source material about Ionia R. Whipper is difficult to find, since it is widely scattered in newspaper articles and manuscript collections. A set of news clippings is located in the vertical file on the Whipper Home at the Martin Luther King Memorial Library in Washington, D.C. The Leigh R. Whipper Papers in the Moorland-Spingarn Research Center at Howard University contain biographical data about the Whipper family, including the Saint Luke's Church obituary notice. For Whipper's newspaper obituaries, see the *Washington Evening Star,* April 24, 1953, p. A14 and the *New York Times,* April 25, 1953, p. 15.

From *Dictionary of American Negro Biography* by Rayford W. Logan and Michael R. Winston, editors. Copyright © 1982 by Rayford W. Logan and Michael R. Winston. Reprinted by permission of W. W. Norton & Company, Inc.

Rosalyn Terborg-Penn

Whipper, William

1804–1876

American moral reformer and businessman.

Little is known about William Whipper's early life. By 1830, he had moved to PHILADELPHIA, PENNSYLVANIA where he worked as a clothes cleaner and grocery manager.

In the 1820s and 1830s Whipper worked as a moral reformer in literary circles. He delivered an "Address Before the Colored Reading Society of Philadelphia" in 1828, and in 1833 he was one of the nine founders of the Philadelphia Library of Colored Persons. In 1834, he spoke about the centrality of moral reform to racial uplift before the Colored Temperance Society of |Philadelphia. At the 1835 annual National Negro Convention (NNC), an event he had attended every year since 1830, Whipper led the movement to create the short-lived American Moral Reform Society (AMRS) and went on to serve as the editor of its journal, the *National Reformer.* He drafted the constitutions of both the NNC and AMRS.

In the mid-1830s, Whipper forged a partnership with local lumber merchant Stephen Smith to form a business that served the Philadelphia and Columbia communities. In 1835, Whipper moved to Columbia, Pennsylvania, where his house became one of the stops on the UNDERGROUND RAILROAD. Although the AMRS collapsed in 1841, Whipper remained politically active, attending the NNC in 1848, 1853, and 1855. He purchased property in Dresden, Canada (1853) and New Brunswick, New Jersey (1868) before returning to Philadelphia.

Aaron Myers

Whipple, Prince

?–1797

Slave, Revolutionary War veteran, abolitionist, and jack-of-all-trades.

Prince Whipple was born in "Amabou, Africa," probably Anomabu, GHANA, formerly the Gold Coast. The names of his parents are unknown, but mid-nineteenth-century oral tradition suggests that he was born free and maintains that he was sent abroad with a brother (or cousin) Cuff (or Cuffee), but parental plans went awry and the youths were sold into slavery in North America. A collective document Whipple signed with twenty others in 1779 describes their shared experience as being "torn by the cruel hand of violence" from their mothers' "aching bosom," and "seized, imprisoned and transported" to the United States and deprived of "the nurturing care of [their] bereaved parent" (New Hampshire *Gazette,* July 15, 1780).

Prince was acquired by William Whipple, and Cuff by William's brother Joseph Whipple, white merchants in Portsmouth, New Hampshire. William Whipple's household also included Windsor Moffatt and other slaves. There are several possible reasons for the confusion about whether Prince and Cuff were brothers or cousins: linguistic translation difficulties, uncertain community memory after their deaths, and white indifference to such distinctions in a marginalized race.

Likewise, Prince Whipple maintained that his given name reflected his actual status in Africa, although the numerous enslaved black men named Prince suggests that white owners frequently gave the name in sentimentality or mockery. If Prince's name records his African status, it represents a rare case of resistance to white renaming, a practice that stripped away African identity and dissociated the enslaved from both the dominant society and their own humanity. However, the persistence of Cuff's African name in a town where only a few other African names persisted lends some credence to this interpretation of Prince's name.

Nineteenth-century tradition spins an elaborate tale of Prince's participation in the American Revolution, fragments of which may be verified, disproved, or called into doubt. No documentation substantiates that Prince accompanied William Whipple, a colonel in the First New Hampshire Regiment, on early revolutionary campaigns or to the Continental Congress in Philadelphia in 1776.

Documentation also argues against a tradition that Prince was with George Washington at the crossing of the Delaware River in December 1776. On that date, William Whipple was attending Congress, first in Philadelphia and then in Baltimore. If Prince had been with him, it seems unlikely that William would have sent the enslaved Prince unaccompanied 130 miles to a war zone in which the enemy promised manumission in exchange for defection. The pervasive story about Prince's crossing the Delaware first appears in William C. Nell's *Colored Patriots of the Revolution* (1855), written at the height of the abolitionist movement. It is unclear whether Nell recorded an undocumented but accurate account circulating among Prince's heirs or a confused family tale, or whether he symbolically attached to one individual the forgotten reality of black participation in both the Revolution and Washington's crossing. Heroic paintings of this event by the nineteenth-century artists Thomas Sully (1819) and Emmanuel Leutze (1851) do indeed include a black man, illustrative of the lingering memory of black participation. New England traditions place other black men in Washington's boat, for example Prince Estabrook of Lexington (later of Ashby), Massachusetts.

Prince Whipple did, however, participate in the Revolution. He accompanied William Whipple, by then a brigadier general, on the military campaigns to Saratoga, New York, in 1777 and Rhode Island in 1778. Prince was attuned to revolutionary philosophy. In 1779 he and Windsor Moffatt were among twenty enslaved men who signed a petition to the New Hampshire legislature for the abolition of slavery in the state. All the signatories were held as slaves in prominent and politically active white patriot families, and thus had ample opportunity to overhear, contemplate, and reinterpret revolutionary rhetoric. The petition was tabled, however, and slavery was not formally abolished in New Hampshire until 1857.

After the Revolution, Prince gained his freedom in gradual, if unclear, stages. On Prince's marriage day, February 22, 1781, William Whipple prepared a special document that allowed Prince the rights of a freeman. The actual status conveyed by this document is obscure, as Prince was not formally manumitted until three years later, on February 26, 1784. The document may have been in response to a request from his bride's clergyman owner, who may have wished to legitimize the marriage according to his religious standards. Prince's bride, twenty-one-year-old Dinah Chase of New Castle and Hampton, New Hampshire, was manumitted by her owner on her wedding day.

In freedom, the black Whipples faced the daunting task of making a living in a context of social and economic marginalization. In his widow's obituary, Prince was remembered as "the Caleb Quotem of the old fashioned semi-monthly assemblies, and at all large weddings and dinners, balls and evening parties. Nothing could go on right without Prince." That is, he served as master of ceremonies at the Assembly House balls for white socialites. (Caleb Quotem was an eccentric, voluble character in *The Review, or The Wags of Windsor* [1801], by the English playwright George Colman.) On various occasions, these balls included other black people as caterers and musicians, and it is likely that Prince's role was to bring together this supportive talent. He was "a large, well proportioned, and fine looking man, and of gentlemanly manners and deportment" (*Portsmouth Journal of Literature and Politics,* February 22, 1846). William Whipple died one year after Prince's manumission, and his widow carved out a house lot in the back corner of the pleasure garden behind the Whipple mansion and loaned it to the former slaves. Prince and Dinah, along with Cuff, who had been manumitted in 1784, and his wife Rebecca Daverson (married on August 24, 1786) moved an old house to the lot, where they and their children lived for forty years.

Their home life was crowded. In addition to the adults and first child who occupied the house when the 1790 census was taken, others were soon born, including Prince's daughters, Esther and Elizabeth. In addition, Dinah operated the Ladies Charitable African School for black children, probably in their house, as well as working for the North Church.

Prince died in Portsmouth in 1797, Cuff in 1816. Dinah's obituary in 1846 described Prince's earlier death as "much regretted both by the white and colored inhabitants of the town; by the latter of whom he was always regarded as their prince." This reminiscence notwithstanding, Prince was not an officer of the Negro Court that held annual coronations in eighteenth-century Portsmouth. However, his signature on the abolition petition alongside those of Portsmouth's black king, viceroy, sheriff, and deputy confirms Prince's active participation in the local black community.

Prince was not buried in Portsmouth's segregated Negro Burial Ground, suggesting that it may have been closed by the 1790s. Following local tradition for black people, his grave in North Burial Ground was marked with two rough stones. Its location was later identified by a grandson, John Smith, and a more impressive stone installed. Today it is marked as that of a Revolutionary War veteran. Prince's age at death is unknown, but he was almost certainly a decade or more older than the age (forty-six) sometimes supposed.

Prince Whipple's life characterizes white Portsmouth's preference for the importation of enslaved children rather than adults, and also exemplifies his generation's participation in and advocacy for a coherent black community. The loaned residence, extended family, and his heirs' continuation in Portsmouth throughout much of the nineteenth century diverge from a local pattern of frequent changes of residence and of filial out-migration. Prince's participation in the Revolution while enslaved, even if elaborated in folk memory, verifies the black role in that conflict, and illustrates the revival of memory during the abolitionist debate.

Bibliography

Kaplan, Sidney. *The Black Presence in the Era of the American Revolution 1770–1800* (1973).

Melish, Joanne Pope. *Disowning Slavery: Gradual Emancipation and "Race" in New England, 1780–1860* (1998).

Nell, William C. *The Colored Patriots of the American Revolution* (1855).

Piersen, William D. *Black Yankees: The Development of an Afro-American Subculture in Eighteenth-Century New England* (1988).

Sammons, Mark J., and Valerie Cunningham. *Black Portsmouth* (2003).

Mark J. Sammons

White Abolitionists in Brazil

Brazilians of European descent who, beginning in the 1870s, worked to abolish slavery in that nation.

Slaves in BRAZIL had persistently fought against their own enslavement as well as slavery itself, most notably by revolting and forming escaped slave communities known as *quilombos*. Nevertheless, the movement to abolish slavery in Brazil is gen-erally associated with the activities of a group of mainly white abolitionists during the nine years leading up to emancipation in 1888. That year, Brazil became the last country in the New World to abolish slavery. Brazil's overwhelming economic dependence on agriculture and mining, and thus on slavery, meant that the abolitionist movement came late to Brazil in comparison with other Latin American countries and the United States. Furthermore, until the last few years before abolition, the antislavery movement was limited in terms of its participants and the reforms it was able to realize.

Some of Brazil's leading abolitionists, such as LUÍS GONZAGA PINTO DA GAMA, JOSÉ CARLOS DO PATROCÍNIO, and ANDRÉ REBOUÇAS were Afro-Brazilians. As a group, however, they cannot be characterized as easily as the movement's white advocates, the most prominent of whom included JOAQUIM NABUCO, RUI BARBOSA, and ANTÔNIO DE CASTRO ALVES. Although they were not a homogeneous group, white abolitionists in Brazil shared similar backgrounds and views about slaves, and sought similar reforms. In general, this group opposed slavery not out of empathy with the slaves, but because they felt that the reliance upon slave labor and the preponderance of slaves in Brazil had a negative impact on the country's society and culture.

Although a few women, such as Luciana de Abreu and Maria Firmina dos Reis, contributed to the abolitionist cause, most white abolitionists in Brazil were male and members of the elite class. They typically grew up on slaveholding plantations in the northeast and attended Brazilian academies or European institutions of higher learning, where they first joined or formed abolitionist societies and adopted more critical views of slavery. The liberal ideals of the French Enlightenment and the success of the abolition movement in the United States also fueled their antislavery efforts. White abolitionists usually pursued their fight in the political sphere and/or through the press. They almost always affiliated themselves with the Republican Party and considered themselves liberals, if not radicals. White abolitionists generally sought legal means of abolition, though toward the end of the 1880s many sanctioned more radical activities, such as helping slaves escape.

An important shared characteristic of many whites involved in the abolition movement was a northeastern background. In the late eighteenth century the once-thriving SUGAR industry of the northeast declined, resulting in a demographic shift in the slave population to the southern provinces of RIO DE JANEIRO, São Paulo, and MINAS GERAIS, where the coffee industry was expanding. Thus, by the 1880s whites from the northeast could more easily challenge slavery because they did not have the economic stake in preserving it that planters in the south had.

White abolitionists in Brazil often shared with slaveholders negative views about slaves. Like many Brazilians, they saw slaves as domestic enemies, irrational beasts without morals. Nabuco, for example, contended that slaves did not have the mental capacity to advocate their own freedom. Unlike abolitionists of African descent, he discouraged their involvement in the abolition movement. White abolitionists also excluded free and enslaved blacks from the antislavery struggle because they feared setting off a large-scale, violent revolt.

Because there was little communication or interaction between white abolitionists and black slaves, white abolitionists lacked empathy toward slaves and their plight. At the same time, white abolitionists tended to regard slaveholders as humane and capable of being persuaded by reason. They praised Brazilian slaveholders for their supposedly mild treatment of slaves and for their desire to switch to free labor.

White abolitionists appealed primarily to the economic sensibilities of the elite, arguing that Brazil's lack of industrial progress resulted from slavery, and that the only way to advance agriculture and industry was to abolish slavery and encourage European immigration. The presence of European immigrants, it was believed, would purify the Brazilian population, offsetting the allegedly corrupt influence of the slaves. Nabuco, for example, stated that through MISCEGENATION, "the vices of the African blood ended up making their way into the general circulation of the country." Thus, white abolitionists were often more concerned with slavery's detrimental impact on the white population than with the suffering of slaves.

Both white and black abolitionists pursued abolition through emancipation funds. In order to raise money to liberate slaves, they organized conferences in city theaters that featured musical and dramatic performances in addition to speeches by the abolitionists. White abolitionists often contended that slaveholders deserved financial compensation for the loss of their slaves. In addition, they generally advocated that slaves should be freed gradually, after a period of compulsory service to be determined by the owner.

Nevertheless, by the late 1880s the small and elite abolitionist movement quickly gained popular support. When, under strong British pressure, Brazil in effect ended the international slave trade in 1850, it seemed that the end of slavery was inevitable: Brazil's slave population had never domestically reproduced itself, and plantations relied upon importation to renew their slave labor force. With a slave population that invariably grew older, slavery's days were numbered. This, combined with the declining sugar economy in the northeast, stimulated a late popular abolition movement. In the years immediately before abolition, antislavery movements in several states purchased the freedom of slaves, or convinced slaveholders to manumit their servants. In 1884 Ceará became the first state to declare itself completely emancipated.

During and after abolition, few white antislavery proponents concerned themselves with facilitating the slaves' transition to citizenship. They expected ex-slaves and their offspring to integrate into society and, with increased European immigration, eventually disappear. Nevertheless, Nabuco called for expanding the education of former slaves. The most common postemancipation reform, pursued by white and black abolitionists alike, was land reform, which sought to break up large agricultural estates and distribute them to the emancipated population.

Because the aim of Brazil's abolition movement was to replace slavery with a free-labor system rather than to transform ex-slaves into citizens, some historians have labeled it a white revolution. Having educational and political opportunities denied to black abolitionists, white elites were more likely to direct antislavery organizations. Yet numerous Afro-Brazilian freedom fighters, including generations of anonymous slaves—the most enduring opponents of slavery—were instrumental in realizing abolition. Still, abolition in Brazil was not a simple matter of black or white, enslaved or elite. As scholar Robert Conrad points out, Brazilians from every ethnicity, class, and profession eventually became involved in abolitionism.

See also Slave Rebellions in Latin America and the Caribbean.

Aaron Myers

White, Charles

1918–1979

American artist specializing in black and white graphic work whose oeuvre celebrates the courage and dignity of historic black leaders and common African Americans.

Charles White was born in CHICAGO, ILLINOIS to unmarried parents, Ethel Gary and Charles White, Sr., who separated when he was three years old. He was raised by his mother in Chicago. After winning a national pencil sketch contest in 1937, White attended the Art Institute of Chicago for a year, then worked as an artist in the WORKS PROGRESS ADMINISTRATION during the late 1930s. In 1941, White traveled through the South on a Rosenwald Fellowship. The following year, he moved to NEW YORK, NEW YORK and studied at the Art Students League.

In 1944, while serving in the Army, White was diagnosed with tuberculosis and was hospitalized for three years. In 1947, he had his first one-man show at the ACA Gallery in New York City, after which he went to Mexico, where he worked for nearly a year at the printmaking workshop Taller de Graphica. During this time, White divorced his wife, the sculptor ELIZABETH CATLETT, whom he had married in 1941. He married Frances Barrett in 1950 and honeymooned with her in Europe. The couple moved in the mid-1950s to Los Angeles, where White became a teacher at the Otis Art Institute in 1965. White also served as a distinguished professor at HOWARD UNIVERSITY's School of Art before his death in 1979.

Among White's better-known works are the mural *Contribution of the Negro to American Democracy* (1943), executed at HAMPTON INSTITUTE in Virginia, and his series of works based on Civil War posters announcing slave auctions or awards for runaway slaves. One of White's most prestigious honors came in 1972 when he became the second African American to be elected a member of the National Academy of Design since the 1927 election of HENRY OSSAWA TANNER. President Jimmy Carter honored White posthumously at the twenty-second annual meeting of the National Conference of Artists.

Aaron Myers

White, Clarence Cameron

1880?–1960

African American concert violinist and composer.

Clarence Cameron White was born in Clarksville, Tennessee, the son of James William White, a medical doctor, and Caroline Virginia Scott, an educator. His parents were originally "free Negroes" from Fayetteville, North Carolina, who migrated before the CIVIL WAR to Oberlin, Ohio, and then to Tennessee. Soon after the death of his father, White went to live with his grandmother and his grandfather John H. Scott, a harness maker and former abolitionist. White received his early education in Oberlin and Chattanooga. In about 1890 his mother married Dr. W. H. Connor, a medical examiner for the U.S. Government Pension Office, and the family moved to WASHINGTON, D.C., where White attended public schools. When he was eleven White began studying the violin with the celebrated violinist Will Marion Cook, and at age fourteen he took lessons with Joseph Douglass, a HOWARD UNIVERSITY professor and the grandson of FREDERICK DOUGLASS.

White worked as a bellhop in Cleveland, Ohio, to earn his tuition to Oberlin Conservatory, where he was admitted in 1896. He left in 1901, apparently without receiving a degree (evidence indicates that he returned to the conservatory in 1923 and again left for reasons unrelated to scholarship). White accepted a job teaching in a PITTSBURGH school immediately following his departure from Oberlin in 1901; however, all salaries at the school were suspended after a month's time, and he was forced to return to Washington.

Shortly thereafter, White decided to move to BOSTON for further study. On the way, he briefly visited New Haven, Connecticut, and was enticed by a scholarship advertisement from Hartford College. Drawing on his thorough musical background and demonstrating commendable virtuosity, he won a scholarship for a year's study with Franz Micki, head of the violin department. The close proximity of New Haven to NEW YORK allowed White to perform at various concerts, one of which was held at the Manhattan Casino before an audience of 4,000. It was at that point that he felt that his concert career had been launched, "for my engagements came rapidly and I played in practically all the large cities east of Denver." After leaving New Haven in 1902, Boston became his headquarters.

In 1903 White was appointed director of the string department at the Washington, D.C., Conservatory of Music. He taught there and in the District of Columbia public schools for the next five years. Also in 1903 White traveled to England, where he met Anglo-African composer SAMUEL COLERIDGE-TAYLOR. Deciding to stay for a summer, White studied orchestration with HUBERT HARRISON, the conductor at the Coronet Theater. When he ran low on money, White returned to the United States and resumed his teaching duties. In late 1904 or early 1905 he married Beatrice Louise Warrick, a pianist; they had two children.

With support from concert singer-composer E. Azalia Hackley, who was studying and teaching in Europe, and several other benefactors such as Henry O. Tanner, White was able to travel to London in 1908, accompanied by his family, to resume musical study. During his two years there, he studied violin with the famous Russian violinist Michael Zacharewitsch, studied composition with Coleridge-Taylor, and performed as one of the first violinists in Coleridge-Taylor's String Players Club.

Around 1910, White returned to the United States with his family and once again settled in Boston, where he established a teaching studio, gave many concerts, continued composing, and performed in concert tours (including one to Oberlin in 1911). He also conducted the Victoria Concert Orchestra, a multiracial group of fifty-three musicians, in a series of successful concerts over seven years. White was appointed director of the West Virginia Collegiate Institute (now West Virginia State College) in 1924. His duties included teaching violin and conducting the Young Men's Glee Club, which made eight recordings and several radio broadcasts. Also performing frequently, he held the position until 1930, at which time he was awarded the Rosenwald Foundation fellowship for two years of European study. He studied violin with Raoul Laparra in Paris and completed an opera and a string quartet.

On his return to the United States in 1932, White succeeded R. NATHANIEL DETT as music director at Hampton Institute in Hampton, Virginia. This appointment, he wrote, afforded him the "most excellent opportunities for development, especially in the field of Negro Music and in my individual work." At Hampton, he taught, performed, and conducted the choir until 1935, at which time he secured the directorship of music at the National Recreation Association in New York City, where he organized community music groups. In 1943, following the death of his first wife, White married Pura Belpré. He died in New York.

White was hailed by the New York *Amsterdam News* as "the most finished violinist his race has produced in America." He also attained distinction as a composer of neoromantic works that ranged from operatic and symphonic pieces to Negro spirituals. White had compositions published by Carl Fischer, the Boston Music Company, Theodore Presser, John Church, C. C. Birchard, Gamble Hinged, and Sam Fox. His output consists of pieces for violin, voice (some of which were performed by Marian Anderson and Roland Hayes), piano, orchestra, band, organ, chorus, and other vocal ensembles. His opera, *Ouanga* (1932), with a libretto by John Matheus, is based on the life of the Haitian slave insurrectionist JEAN-JACQUES DESSALINES. The work, which was premiered by the H. T. Burleigh Music Association of South Bend, Indiana, in 1949, was awarded the David Bispham Memorial Medal, and notable performances were presented by the Dra-Mu Opera Company at the Philadelphia Academy in 1950 and by the National Negro Opera Company at the Metropolitan Opera House in 1956. His *Elegy* for orchestra won the 1953–1954 Benjamin Award for Tranquil Music, and excerpts of his *Bandanna Sketches* (1918) for violin were played by Fritz Kreisler and Zacharewitsch. Violinist Jascha Heifetz recorded his *Levee Dance* (1927), and leading symphony orchestras performed his *Pantomime,* his *Suite of Folk Tunes,* and arrangements of *Bandanna Sketches.* Other works include studies for violin technique, a string quartet, a violin concerto, *Five Songs* (1949), *Forty Negro Spirituals* (1927), and *Negro Rhapsody* for orchestra.

White also excelled as a conductor. Newspaper accounts note his "masterly touch" with the Hampton Institute Choir and his success with other ensembles in West Virginia, Boston, and Washington. In addition, he authored several articles for such publications as *Etude, Musical Observer,* and *Modern Quarterly,* mainly on the subject of "Negro Music" but also about Joseph White, the internationally renowned nineteenth-century Afro-Cuban violinist and court musician for the emperor of Brazil who had served as a model inspiration for White. White overcame many difficulties during the depression era to realize his goals of becoming a virtuoso, conductor, composer, and educator. He also succeeded in his aim "to show the Negro's contribution to American art."

Bibliography

White's papers and music are in the New York Schomburg Library, the Oberlin Conservatory, the Howard University Moorland-Spingarn Room, and the Azalia Hackley Room in the Detroit Library.

Cuney-Hare, Maud. *Negro Musicians and Their Music.* 1936; repr. 1974.

Edwards, Vernon, and Michael Mark. "In Retrospect: Clarence Cameron White." *Black Perspective in Music* 9, no. 1 (Spring 1981).

"In Retrospect: Letters of Clarence Cameron White in the Collections of the Music Division of the Library of Congress," edited by Wayne Shirley. *Black Perspective in Music* 10, no. 2 (Fall 1982).

Obituary, *New York Times,* July 2, 1960.

Obituary, *Washington Post,* July 3, 1960.

Roach, Hildred. *Black American Music: Past and Present.* 1992.

Southern, Eileen. *Biographical Dictionary of Afro-American and African Musicians.* 1982.

From *American National Biography.* John A. Garraty and Mark C. Carnes, eds. Oxford University Press, 1999. Reprinted by permission of the American Council of Learned Societies.

Hildred Roach

White, George H(enry)

1852–1918

African American lawyer and member of Congress.

George Henry White was born in Bladen County, North Carolina, the son of Mary (maiden name unknown) and Wiley F. White. With one grandmother Irish and the other half American Indian, White jocularly described himself as no more than "mostly Negro." Like most black boys in the antebellum South, he had little opportunity for education. A biographical sketch in the *New York Tribune* on 2 January 1898 put it, in graphic understatement, "His early studies were much interrupted because of the necessity he was under to do manual labor on farms and in the forests, and it was not until he was seventeen years old that his serious education was actually begun." After attending a combination of local schools, public and private, and saving up $1,000 from farm work and cask making, White enrolled at HOWARD UNIVERSITY.

White graduated in 1877 and returned to North Carolina. He settled in the old coastal town of New Bern, where he quickly became active in local affairs. At various times he was principal of three black schools, including the state normal school, and read enough law with Judge William J. Clark to earn his law license. In 1880 he won a seat in the state house of representatives as a REPUBLICAN. After an initial defeat in 1882, he was elected to the state senate and served in the legislature of 1885. In 1886, a few weeks before his thirty-fourth birthday, he won a four-year term as district solicitor for the Second Judicial District, defeating the black incumbent and a white DEMOCRAT. Reelected to this position in 1890, he was, according to the *New York Freeman,* the only Negro prosecutor in the country. White prosecuted superior court cases in a six-county area, and his ability was so marked that even his political opponents occasionally praised him. Some whites resented his "presumption" and his demand to be "mistered" like other attorneys, rather than be addressed by an unadorned last name, as was customary with educated African Americans.

In 1894 White moved his home from New Bern to Tarboro so he could seek the Republican nomination in the Second Congressional District, a gerrymandered district that had elected three black congressmen since 1874. The district convention "broke up in a row," however, with both White and his brother-in-law, HENRY P. CHEATHAM, claiming to be the regular nominee. After arbitration by the Republican National Committee, White withdrew from the race, but Cheatham was defeated in the general election, thanks partly to Republican disunity. In 1896, after another tumultuous convention, White won the Republican nomination for Congress and defeated the Democratic incumbent and a Populist nominee. Despite a statewide white supremacy campaign in 1898, he was elected to a second term.

As the only black member of Congress, White believed he spoke for all the nation's black people, not just the voters of the Second District, and he was prepared to reply spiritedly to racist pronouncements by southern congressional colleagues. "How long must we keep quiet," he asked, "constantly sitting down and seeing our rights one by one taken away?" He introduced the first federal antilynching bill and denounced disfranchisement and vote fraud. He also used the patronage power of his office to secure government jobs for his constituents, including some twenty black postmasters.

White supremacy zealots gave Congressman White special prominence during their struggle to defeat the Republican-Populist "fusion" in 1898 and the subsequent movement to disfranchise North Carolina blacks. Under the editorship of Josephus Daniels, the *Raleigh News and Observer* pilloried White as a belligerent man eager "to invite the issue" of white against black. An incident at a Tarboro circus, in which White refused to surrender his seat to a white man, became an "outrage" to many Democratic journalists anxious to demonstrate the dangers of "Negro domination." In 1900, after White denied from the floor of the House that rape was the primary cause of LYNCHING, noting as well that white men were guilty of abusing black women, Daniels fired off an editorial broadside, describing the "nigger Congressman" as "venomous, forward," and "appealing to the worst passions of his own race."

In fact, the prosperous, middle-aged black lawyer was not a fiery militant. Though some historians have portrayed White as "impetuous" or "vindictive," he was in fact a fairly conventional Republican politician, supportive of tariffs and imperialism and suspicious of civil service reform. On racial matters, he advocated caution and strict respect for the law among both black and white. In the climate of the turn of the century, however, he was considered radical merely for demanding, as he said in one speech, "all the privileges of an American citizen."

After the passage in 1900 of the state constitutional amendment disfranchising most black voters, White decided to leave his native state. "I cannot live in North Carolina and be a man and be treated as a man," he told a northern interviewer. In a widely noticed valedictory address during his final session of Congress, he offered the Negro's "temporary farewell to the American Congress," adding the prediction that "Phoenix-like he will rise up some day and come again."

Unsuccessful in seeking an appointive office, White practiced law, first in the District of Columbia, then in PHILADELPHIA. He continued to support efforts to secure CIVIL RIGHTS for African Americans, including lawsuits and organized protests through organizations such as the NATIONAL ASSOCIATION FOR THE ADVANCEMENT OF COLORED PEOPLE (NAACP). An investor and visionary, he helped establish an all-black community called Whitesboro in the Cape May region of New Jersey.

White married twice, first to Fannie B. Randolph, and after Fannie's death to Cora Lina Cherry, daughter of Henry C. Cherry, a former legislator from Edgecombe County. White had one child with his first wife and three children with his second. He was an active layman in the Presbyterian church and a leader among the Colored Masons. He died in Philadelphia.

Bibliography

No collection of White's papers exists. A few manuscripts in his handwriting are preserved in the N.C. legislative papers and court documents of the Second Judicial District, available at the North Carolina Department of Archives and History in Raleigh, and scattered letters. White's personality is revealed in his congressional speeches and in his testimony before the Industrial Commission, *Report of the Industrial Commission,* vol. 10, 1901.

Anderson, Eric. *Race and Politics in North Carolina, 1872–1901: The Black Second.* 1981.

Christopher, Maurine. *America's Black Congressmen.* 1971.

Justesen, Benjamin R. *George Henry White: An Even Chance in the Race of Life.* 2001.

From *American National Biography.* John A. Garraty and Mark C. Carnes, eds. Oxford University Press, 1999. Reprinted by permission of the American Council of Learned Societies.

Eric Anderson

White, José

1836–1918

Afro-Cuban violinist and professor of classical music, author of the famous "La bella Cubana" (The Beautiful Cuban Maid), a nationalistic composition popular during the nineteenth-century Cuban struggles for independence.

José White was born and grew up in MATANZAS, CUBA, an important city east of HAVANA and a major center of African culture, where he began studying violin, first with his father and later with another Afro-Cuban violinist, J. M. Roman. During this period White developed an impressive reputation as a virtuoso performer and made the acquaintance of the North American romantic composer Louis Gottschalk. Gottschalk was so impressed by White's talent that he offered to accompany him in a concert, which took place in Matanzas on March 21, 1855.

A year later, at age nineteen, White moved to Paris, where he studied classical composition with the famous French violinist Jean Delphin Alard at the Paris Conservatory. By this time, he could play eighteen other instruments in addition to the violin. While studying at the conservatory, White met Italian opera composer Rossini, whose salon attracted such distinguished musicians as Liszt and Chopin. Soon after, Rossini organized several private concerts featuring the Cuban violinist. French composers Charles Gounod, Daniel Auber, and Charles Ambriose began writing music for White.

In 1864, after the death of Alard, White was offered his teaching position at the Paris Conservatory. He later served briefly as the director of the Rio Conservatory in BRAZIL. Mounting political tensions, however, soon prompted him to leave his post and return to FRANCE.

Though he was principally known as a performer, White also made a name for himself as a composer. Many of his works still survive today, including a concerto, a string quartet, a collection of studies for violin, and several nationalistic pieces such as "Marcha cubana," and perhaps his most famous composition, the habanera (a Cuban dance in slow duple time) "La Bella Cubana." Indeed, because of such overtly patriotic pieces he was forced to flee the wrath of Spanish authorities, as CUBA would not gain its independence until 1898.

By the time of his death in 1918 José White had given concerts throughout Europe and Latin America. In addition, he had performed with orchestras in the United States during a time when few North American blacks were afforded such an opportunity.

See also Music, Classical, in Latin America and the Caribbean.

Gordon Root

Whitening

Term used to describe both the process and the concept of genetic mixing of races; called *blanqueamiento* in Spanish and *branqueamento* in Portuguese.

As a process, whitening it is simply one value-laden way of referring to the combining of gene pools that human populations have always experienced. This process has carried many labels, some of them now of dubious respectability, such as "interbreeding" and MISCEGENATION. The value implied in the term itself suggests the alleged superiority of the "white" component. The emergence of the term in the nineteenth century makes it a late addition to the popular interpretation of reproductive mixture among humans. It is based on the concept of race, a term with at least two meanings in the history of the Americas.

When the Portuguese and Spanish first colonized the continent, the Iberians were using race (*raça* or *raza*) to distinguish between Iberian Christians and Iberian non-Christians, such as the Jews and the Moors. In case of dispute over an individual's racial status, church and secular authorities often demanded church records and/or genealogical evidence of the individual's descent from forbears of the proper religion. This meaning of race was transferred to both Spanish and Portuguese America. The Inquisition was the most infamous institution charged with enforcing this system of racial classification. The second meaning of race, which became rooted in social practice, defined race by physical appearance and especially by what twentieth-century scientists would call a racial phenotype. The stimulus for development of this new concept was the growing number of African slaves arriving in the Americas, especially throughout the Caribbean, in the early sixteenth century.

In BRAZIL, for example, the sexual contact between Portuguese and Africans produced the new physical phenotype of the mulatto. Since the nonwhite population—that is, black and mulatto—outnumbered the white population from the early seventeenth to the late nineteenth century, some of the mixed-race contingent were likely to rise socially because there was no consistent color line established in colonial Brazil. Instead, a de facto threefold racial stratification emerged: white (European), mulatto, and black, with notoriously blurred lines between the first and second and the second and third.

Within this hierarchy, whiteness had the highest social and therefore political value. The predominance of this white ideal penetrated the entire society, including nonwhites. This helps to explain how an explicitly racist society managed to maintain (and still maintains) a surprising degree of legitimacy. The lesson for the nonwhite population was to strive to become whiter, whether by producing whiter offspring (by their choice of mate) or by behaving white. Thus the entire society could look to the redemption of the nonwhite, even if on a distant timetable. This rationale was much reinforced by the widespread acceptance after about 1870 in Latin America of "scientific racist" doctrine, which employed a scientific discourse to ascribe variable qualities and capabilities to different races, seen as superior and inferior.

Between 1880 and 1930 the Brazilian government (controlled by whites) sponsored massive European immigration to accelerate the whitening of the population as well as to create a new workforce. During this time, whiteness was explicitly proclaimed, even by nonwhite intellectuals, as having the highest moral and aesthetic value. Brazilian scientists lectured abroad proclaiming that their society would be entirely white in less than a century. This pattern of stratification and elevation of whiteness appeared in other Latin American countries, such as CUBA and the DOMINICAN REPUBLIC, where there had been a heavy influx of African slaves.

The discussion of whitening has been made more difficult for its advocates by the inconsistency of census definitions in countries such as Brazil and Cuba. In Brazil, scholars have detected a clear tendency for mulattos to reclassify themselves as white in successive censuses. This renders suspect any attempt to analyze trends in the racial composition of populations. VENEZUELA has solved this problem by eliminating race and color from the census. This has not, of course, eliminated the discussion of race in Venezuela. Rather it has made it possible for the elite to claim that Venezuela is already a "white" society. In Cuba, the government under FIDEL CASTRO long delayed the inclusion of race in its censuses, while at the same time claiming that the revolution had eradicated racial discrimination. The Brazilian military government eliminated race from the 1970 census in an effort to undercut discussions of race relations in that country. After vigorous protest by demographers and by the nonwhite community, race was restored in the Brazilian censuses of 1980 and 1990. "Blackness" has sometimes emerged as a counterpart to white hegemony, but primarily in cultural form through music, dance, and religion. Its greatest influence is undoubtedly in the WEST INDIES, in such expressions as REGGAE. But nowhere, except HAITI, has it seriously challenged the concept of white superiority inherent in the doctrine of whitening.

The concept of whitening is still alive in present-day multiethnic Latin America. It can be found in folklore, popular humor, and popular culture. At the same time, it has lost all intellectual respectability in the wake of the death (since the 1940s) of scientific racism. Whitening is now a kind of contraband idea surviving in popular thought but long since repudiated by scientific inquiry.

See also Eugenics; Race in Latin America.

Thomas E. Skidmore

White, Walter Francis

1893–1955

African American civil rights leader and influential author of the Harlem Renaissance.

Walter White grew up in a racially mixed neighborhood and, as a light-skinned, blue-eyed man, was able to pass for white. He credited a 1906 race riot in ATLANTA, during which he defended his family's home from fire, as the incident that ignited his race consciousness as a black man. From that point on, he chose to live as an African American fighting for political and social justice.

After graduating from Atlanta University in 1916, White began a career in activism with the Atlanta branch of the NATIONAL ASSOCIATION FOR THE ADVANCEMENT OF COLORED PEOPLE (NAACP). In 1918 he moved to NEW YORK to serve as assistant to NAACP executive secretary JAMES WELDON JOHNSON. He was an invaluable researcher for the NAACP's work in the ANTI-LYNCHING MOVEMENT; passing for white, he investigated lynchings and other racially-motivated crimes without hindrance. White's reports for the NAACP were fodder for his fiction; his two novels, *The Fire in the Flint* (1924) and *Flight* (1926), both concern the responses of educated blacks, or "New Negroes," to racial injustice. Although the novels sometimes sacrifice plot and characterization to political message, they earned White a Guggenheim Fellowship in 1926. White used money from the fellowship for support while writing a seminal investigation of lynching, *Rope and Faggot: A Biography of Judge Lynch* (1929).

As executive secretary of the NAACP from 1931 to 1955, White worked with A(SA) PHILIP RANDOLPH to secure the establishment of the FAIR EMPLOYMENT PRACTICES COMMITTEE in 1941; his efforts also helped produce the executive orders banning discrimination in war-related industries that same year and in the entire United States military in 1948. A delegate with W. E. B. DU BOIS and MARY MCLEOD BETHUNE to the founding of the United Nations in 1945, White also became involved with seeking justice for the African diaspora. One of White's most lasting achievements as NAACP executive secretary was the recruitment of CHARLES HAMILTON HOUSTON to serve as the NAACP's first fulltime chief counsel. Under Houston's leadership and fueled by White's tireless fund-raising efforts, the NAACP undertook a series of legal challenges to segregation, culminating in 1954's historic *BROWN V. BOARD OF EDUCATION* decision, which toppled segregated education in the United States.

See also Lynching; Military, Blacks in the American; Passing in the United States.

Whitfield, James Monroe

1822–1871

African American poet, abolitionist, and emigrationist.

James Monroe Whitfield was born in Exeter, New Hampshire, the son of parents whose names are unknown. Little else is known of his family except that he had a sister, a wife, two sons, and a daughter.

A celebrated poet, Whitfield published two volumes of poetry, *Poems* in 1846 and *America, and Other Poems* in 1853, the latter launching his career as an abolitionist and emigrationist. Richard Barksdale and Keneth Kinnamon point out Lord Byron's influence on his poetry's "brooding melancholy and latent anger" but see his strong abolitionist protest as more important. His poem "America" voiced the paradox of America as he saw it: "a boasted land of liberty" and "a land of blood and crime." One of the most forceful writers and speakers for the abolitionist cause, Whitfield was seen by *Frederick Douglass* as unjustly "buried in the precincts of a barber's shop" by the "malignant arrangements of society," and MARTIN DELANY appraised his potential to be the equal of John Greenleaf Whittier and Edgar Allan Poe (Miller, p. 138). Jane R. Sherman (p. 176) praises Whitfield as "outstanding [among nineteenth-century black poets] for his metrical smoothness and breadth of classical imagery" and his poetry as among the most robust and convincing of the time . . . describ[ing] the crippling of a creative soul by race prejudice."

Whitfield's life exemplifies the ambivalence of African Americans toward the emigration and abolitionist/CIVIL RIGHTS movements of the nineteenth century as well as the frustrations of talented African Americans barred from the pursuits of higher education and creativity. On one hand he signed the 1853 Rochester Colored National Convention's "Address to the People of the United States" that called for whites to allow blacks full access to what Whitfield accepted as his "native land" in his poem "America" and that simultaneously accepted segregation. On the other hand, a few months later, he signed Delany's 1853 call for the National Emigration Convention and, in letters to the *Frederick Douglass Paper,* advocated emigration and the establishment of a black nation. As late as 1862 he, along with almost 240 blacks, petitioned Congress for funds to "promote the emigration of free colored resident natives of the United States to Africa or to the tropical regions of America" (Miller, p. 265).

Whitfield, along with James T. Holly and Martin Delany, became one of the most prominent supporters of nationalist emigration during the 1850s. Whitfield's letter to the *Frederick Douglass Paper* began the extended debate over the Rochester convention proposals and Delany's call for emigration. His exchanges with William J. Watkins, Douglass's associate editor, and subsequent letters from the public anticipated the death knell for a viable emigration movement. Whitfield argued the connection between blacks' acceptance of their separate position in U.S. society, from which they would advocate their right to full participation, and emigration, from which they could form a separate black nationality to both elevate the race and free the slaves. He saw his embracing of emigration as a logical extension of the Rochester convention and the National Council it had established, and he advocated the emigration of a few blacks to form a nationality where they "can help strike an effective blow against the common foe" (Sherman, p. 174) should efforts for equality in the United States fail. By raising the nationality issue, Whitfield and Delany drew negative responses from Canadian and U.S. blacks, who saw themselves as part of a nation already, and Douglass saw to it that his paper used its unprecedented influence to discredit the emigration movement. Nonetheless, Whitfield served as one of the five notable delegates to Delany's 1854 National Emigration Convention in Cleveland. That convention's constitution of the National Board of Commissioners was ridiculed by antiemigrationists (who were by far the majority) as an impracticable and foolish plan of political neophytes. The national black community met the plan with either indifference or ambivalence, except in CINCINNATI, where leaders sought unsuccessfully to rally black support for emigration in opposition to white supporters of slavery and colonization. White colonizationists advocated removal of all blacks from the United States. Black emigrationists, on the other hand, advocated voluntary emigration and sought to maintain family and political ties with those remaining in the United States to advance the uplift of the race.

Although Whitfield and significant other nationalist-emigrationists did not attend the 1858 Chatham (CANADA) convention, with its broadened platform and more inclusive title, the Association for the Promotion of the Interests of the Colored People of Canada and the United States, that followed the Cleveland convention, he remained active in the emigration movement until 1858. He signed a prospectus (published in the *Provincial Freeman,* 6 Dec. 1856) for a quarterly to publicize the nationalist-emigrationist cause, the *Afric-American Repository.* Whitfield edited the *Repository* for a year, publishing the first issue in July 1858.

Whitfield then moved to SAN FRANCISCO and may have traveled to "tropical regions." Settling in California in 1862, he worked as a barber, briefly moving to Portland, Oregon, then to the towns of Placerville and Centerville in Idaho, before returning to establish a "hairdressing shop" in San Francisco. On New Year's Day on the fourth anniversary of the EMANCIPATION PROCLAMATION, Whitfield published *A Poem,* a history of the founding of America and of slavery and its effects. Whitfield dedicated this poem to PHILIP A. BELL, the editor of the *Elevator,* a San Francisco publication in which Whitfield published poems and letters from 1867 to 1870.

Whitfield, a Masonic grand master of California, died in San Francisco of heart disease. He ranks among the leading articulate and prescient nationalist-emigrationists who, sadly foreseeing the intractability of American racism, embraced America's highest ideals and argued vociferously against racism while simultaneously struggling to realize the dream of establishing a black nation to free the slave and uplift the race worldwide.

Bibliography

Whitfield's *America* may be found in the Buffalo and Erie County Historical Society, Howard University's Moorland and Spingarn Collection, and the New York Public Library's Schomburg Collection. The Bancroft Library, University of California, holds a copy of *A Poem* in Ezra Rothschild Johnson, *Emancipation Oration . . . and Poem . . .*

Barksdale, Richard, and Keneth Kinnamon. *Black Writers of America: A Comprehensive Anthology.* 1972.

Brown, Sterling. *Negro Poetry and Drama.* 1969.

Loggins, Vernon. *The Negro Author: His Development in America.* 1931.

Miller, Floyd J. *The Search for a Black Nationality: Black Emigration and Colonization, 1787–1863.* 1975.

Robinson, William H. *Early Black American Poets.* 1969.

Sherman, Jane R. "James Monroe Whitfield, Poet and Emigrationist: A Voice of Protest and Despair." *Journal of Negro History* (April 1972): 169–176.

From *American National Biography.* John A. Garraty and Mark C. Carnes, eds. Oxford University Press, 1999. Reprinted by permission of the American Council of Learned Societies.

Johnnella E. Butler

Whittaker, Johnson Chesnutt

1858–1931

African American military cadet and educator.

Johnson Chesnutt Whittaker was born one of a set of twins, on the plantation of James Chesnutt, Sr., near Camden, South Carolina, the son of James Whitaker, a freedman, and Maria J. (maiden name unknown), a slave. His twin brother died from an accident at the age of thirteen.

Johnson Whittaker (he added the second t sometime later in life) spent his early years in slavery, his mother at times serving as personal slave to Maria Boykin Chesnutt, the author of *A Diary from Dixie* (1905). His father had purchased his own freedom, but at the birth of the twins he refused responsibility for them and an older son because he insisted that never before had twins been born in his family.

With the coming of emancipation, Whittaker and his mother, both very light-skinned, took up residence in Camden, where she worked as a domestic and Johnson attended a freedman's school. After five years he began receiving special tutoring from a local black minister while he worked as a bricklayer's assistant. In 1874 he entered the University of South Carolina, briefly integrated during RECONSTRUCTION, in Columbia. He did so well during his two years there that one of his teachers, RICHARD GREENER, Harvard's first black graduate, suggested him as a candidate for appointment to West Point. He entered the military academy in 1876 on the nomination of a local white REPUBLICAN congressman, S. L. Hoze.

The man destined to become the military academy's first black graduate, HENRY O. FLIPPER, was in his final year when Whittaker arrived. The two men shared a room because no white cadet would room with either of them. Flipper passed along his nonviolence philosophy, which Whittaker, who was deeply religious, accepted enthusiastically. Throughout his time at West Point, he responded to insults and total social ostracism with patience. He refused to allow any provocation to take his mind off his ultimate goal—graduation. When a white cadet struck him, for example, Whittaker did not fight back but reported the offender to academy authorities. As a result, West Point cadets labeled him a coward.

On April 6, 1880, as Whittaker slept alone in a two-man room, three masked men entered, dragged him out of his bed, lashed his legs to the bed's side, and tied his arms in front of him. They slashed his ear lobes, gouged his hair, and made him look into a mirror that they then smashed against his forehead. He later recalled hearing one say, "Let us mark him as we mark hogs down South." After they had completed their vicious work, the attackers warned Whittaker not to make any noise. "Cry out, or speak of this affair, and you are a dead man," they said, and also told him he should leave the academy.

The next morning, when Whittaker was absent from reveille, another cadet was sent to his room and discovered him unconscious, surrounded by large blotches of blood. West Point authorities quickly decided that he had mutilated himself to avoid final examinations two months later.

General John M. Schofield, the military academy superintendent, established a court of inquiry to begin meeting on April 9. The board took more than 3,000 pages of testimony, some of it casting grave doubts on the West Point position. Nonetheless, it found Whittaker guilty of mutilating himself. Hoping to clear his name, Whittaker demanded a court-martial. A panel that began hearings on February 3, 1881, recorded 9,000 pages of testimony. After taking his June 1880 oral examinations, Whittaker was placed on leave. Meanwhile, O. O. Howard, the one-time head of the Freedman's Bureau, replaced Schofield as West Point superintendent.

Like the court of inquiry, the court-martial was a national cause célèbre. Three presidents (Rutherford B. Hayes, James A. Garfield, and Chester A. Arthur), army commanding general William T. Sherman, and the nation's major newspapers all followed these judicial proceedings closely. Former South Carolina governor, Daniel Chamberlain, and leading army lawyer, Asa Bird Gardiner, were on opposite sides in the four-month trial. Once again Whittaker was found guilty; his race continued to be the major determinant in the military court decision.

On December 1, 1881 the army's judge advocate general, D. G. Swaim, found irregularities and prejudice in the proceedings and overturned the decision. Benjamin Brewster, the attorney general, agreed on March 17, 1882, and five days later President Arthur officially threw out the guilty verdict. Whittaker was exonerated. That same day, however, Secretary of War Robert T. Lincoln, the Great Emancipator's son, issued an army special order discharging Whittaker from the military academy for failing an oral examination in June 1880. Whittaker was innocent of wrongdoing, but he was separated from the academy anyway.

Whittaker tried for several years to fight the dismissal, even going on a brief national speaking tour to drum up support. "With God as my guide," he said in his first speech, "duty as my watchword, I can, I must, I will win a place in life!" Unsuccessful in his efforts to reverse the dismissal, he moved back to South Carolina, where he became a teacher in CHARLESTON and Sumter, a member of the South Carolina bar in 1885, and a lawyer and school principal in Sumter. In 1890 he married Page Harrison, the daughter of a white Sumter city employee and his black wife. They had two sons, one of whom became a college president.

In 1900 Whittaker became secretary of the college and principal of the academy at the Colored Normal, Industrial, Agricultural, and Mechanical College of South Carolina (now South Carolina State University) in Orangeburg. In 1908, because of a son's asthma, the family moved from Orangeburg to Oklahoma City, where they had to contend with nightly gunfire when they moved into a white neighborhood. Whittaker became a teacher at all-black Douglass High School and in the early 1920s became the school's principal. One of his students was the novelist RALPH ELLISON.

In 1925, at the age of sixty-seven, Whittaker returned to the black college in Orangeburg, South Carolina, again as principal of the academy. He maintained his post until his death there, a revered teacher but unknown outside of his community. It was not until the publication of a book about him and a made-for-television motion picture that Whittaker received the lieutenant's bars denied him in the 1880s. On 24 July 1995 in a White House ceremony, President Bill Clinton presented to Whittaker's descendants a posthumous commission.

Bibliography

No collection of Johnson C. Whittaker papers exists. The records of his court of inquiry and his court-martial are preserved in the Records of the Judge Advocate General (Army), RG 153, National Archives. A made-for-television motion picture and a video about his court-martial are both titled *Assault at West Point* (1994).

Marszalek, John F. *Assault at West Point: The Court Martial of Johnson Whittaker.* 1994.
——. "A Black Cadet at West Point." *American Heritage* 12 (August 1971): 30–37, 104–106.
New York Times, July 25, 1995.

From *American National Biography.* John A. Garraty and Mark C. Carnes, eds. Oxford University Press, 1999. Reprinted by permission of the American Council of Learned Societies.

John F. Marszalek

Whittaker, Miller F(ulton)

1892–1949

African American architect and college president.

The son of Johnson Chesnutt and Page (Harrison) Whittaker, Miller Fulton Whittaker grew up in Sumter and Orangeburg, South Carolina, and Oklahoma City, Oklahoma. He attended the Colored Normal Industrial, Agricultural, and Mechanical

College of South Carolina (now South Carolina State University). In 1913 he received a B.S. degree in architecture from Kansas State College (later Kansas State University). In 1928 he received an M.S. degree in architecture from the same institution. He also studied at Harvard University in Massachusetts and Cornell University in New York.

Whittaker joined the faculty of South Carolina Agricultural and Mechanical College in 1913 as a member of both the Drawing and Physics Departments. From 1925 to 1932 he held the position of dean of the Mechanical Arts Department. He became a registered architect in South Carolina in 1918 and in Georgia in 1928. He superintended the design and construction of all the college buildings erected while he was a faculty member. It is believed that during his lifetime he was the only black architect in South Carolina. During WORLD WAR I (1914–1918) Whittaker joined the United States Army and served as a second lieutenant with the 368th Infantry for one year in FRANCE, where he studied at the Army School at Langres.

After the death of the college's president Robert Shaw Wilkinson in 1932, Whittaker became president of South Carolina Agricultural and Mechanical College. His appointment at the age of thirty-nine prompted THE CRISIS in August 1932 to write that he "had attracted wide attention, brought visitors from over the world to examine, study and appreciate the campus buildings which he had designed."

Whittaker was the third president of the college. Thomas E. Miller and Robert Shaw Wilkinson had preceded him. During Whittaker's seventeen-year tenure, the college's existence continued to be a difficult one, but it progressed physically and academically. Eight new buildings were added and an additional thirty-hectare (seventy-five-acre) farm was purchased. The college's financial position was strengthened, the student body was enlarged, the existing vocational curriculum was improved, and new programs, notably a Law Department, were added. Whittaker maintained close ties throughout the state and nation by speaking engagements, personal acquaintance, and membership in educational organizations. He was president of the Conference of Land Grant Colleges from 1936 to 1937. Several times he was head of the State Association of College Presidents, Deans, and Registrars. In 1933 he was chosen one of the seven outstanding presidents of land grant colleges and was awarded a summer scholarship to Cornell University. He was listed in *Who's Who in America*.

Whittaker died of congestive heart failure at the relatively young age of fifty-six. His funeral was attended by leading educators and state officials, including Governor J. Strom Thurmond and Representative Hugo S. Simms, Jr. BENJAMIN E. MAYS, then president of MOREHOUSE COLLEGE in ATLANTA, GEORGIA, delivered the eulogy. Burial was at Orangeburg Cemetery. In 1969 South Carolina State College honored his memory by naming its new library the Miller F. Whittaker Library. He was survived by his niece Cecil Whittaker Boykin (later McFadden) and his nephew Peter Whittaker.

Whittaker perhaps best expressed his philosophy when he addressed the 1937 graduating class: "I have an ideal for this College. It is this: That each student shall give evidence of high moral character and personal worth, serious intellectual effort, an understanding of his obligations to society. Things of the spirit, the common virtues of courtesy, honesty, integrity, and tolerance are just as important as the training of the intellect. To this end we would have this College put an indelible stamp of culture and refinement on its students."

Whittaker is mentioned in the brief history of his college, Nelson C. Nix's *South Carolina State College, A History* (1937). He is also briefly mentioned in his father's biography: John F. Marszalek's *Court-Martial: A Black Man in America* (1972). A eulogy is K. W. Green's "Miller Fulton Whittaker" (*Negro Educational Review* 1, April 1950).

From *Dictionary of American Negro Biography* by Rayford W. Logan and Michael R. Winston, editors. Copyright © 1982 by Rayford W. Logan and Michael R. Winston. Reprinted by permission of W. W. Norton & Company, Inc.

See also Architects and Architecture; World War I and African Americans.

John F. Marszalek

Widekum

Ethnic group of Cameroon.

The Widekum primarily inhabit the North-West Province of CAMEROON. Others live in eastern NIGERIA. They speak a Niger-Congo language and are closely related to the BAMILÉKÉ people. Over 200,000 people consider themselves Widekum.

See also Ethnicity and Identity in Africa: An Interpretation; Languages, African: An Overview.

Wideman, John Edgar

1941–

African American author and scholar hailed as one of the most gifted writers of his generation.

According to the title of one of John Edgar Wideman's collections of short stories, "all stories are true." Guided by that principle, Wideman has spent his career as a scholar and author in pursuit of a more truthful history or chronicle of his own experience and that of other African Americans.

John Edgar Wideman was born in Washington, D.C., the oldest of five children born to Edgar and Betty French Wideman. He spent the first ten years of his life in Homewood, the predominantly black middle-class section of PITTSBURGH, PENNSYLVANIA. Homewood had been founded by Wideman's great-great-great grandmother (escaped slave Sybela Owens), with help from her former owner's son Charles Bell, whom she later married. It is also the setting for Wideman's most acclaimed series of books, *The Homewood Trilogy* (1981–1983). The Wideman family moved from Homewood to Shadyside, an upper-middle-class, white neighborhood, where John attended high school. A basketball star, class president, and valedictorian, he went to the University of Pennsylvania on a Benjamin Franklin Scholarship in 1959. There he majored in English and was a celebrated scholar-athlete. Named to the Big Five Basketball Hall of Fame and inducted into Phi Beta Kappa when he graduated in 1963, Wideman was the second African American (after ALAIN LOCKE) to receive a Rhodes Scholarship to Oxford University. Wideman took a degree in eighteenth-century literature from Oxford in 1966.

The famed Iowa Writers' Workshop welcomed Wideman as a Kent Fellow in 1966 and 1967. There he wrote his first novel, *A Glance Away* (1967). This and his second novel, *Hurry Home* (1970), received critical accolades for their experimental language, form, and style. Although the novels focus on black characters, both black and white critics found them more akin to works by great American or European modernists such as James Joyce, T. S. Eliot, and William Faulkner than to a black literary tradition.

While teaching at the University of Pennsylvania in the early 1970s, Wideman had a transformative experience when his black students asked him to teach a course on African American literature. At first he gave them what he called "the jive reply that it wasn't [his] field," but he eventually accepted the challenge and re-educated himself. The discovery of an alternative literary tradition spurred Wideman to establish and direct the University of Pennsylvania's first African American Studies department from 1971 to 1973. After writing a more "black" novel, *The Lynchers,* in 1973, Wideman took a break from writing fiction and left Pennsylvania for a teaching position at the University of Wyoming, which he held until 1986.

In 1981 the first two installments of Wideman's *Homewood Trilogy, Hiding Place* and *Damballah,* were published. These two books mark the maturation of Wideman's aesthetic philosophy. Deeply concerned with the importance of memory, history, and the interweaving of multiple cultural and historical traditions, the *Homewood* books explore Wideman's own African American roots. The third book in the trilogy, *Sent for You Yesterday* (1983), won the 1984 PEN/Faulkner Award for fiction.

Wideman's next book, *Brothers and Keepers* (1984), continued this autobiographical impulse. In a series of essays about his brother Robbie, who was serving a life sentence for murder, the book explores the very different lives of the two men. *Brothers and Keepers* was nominated for the 1985 National Book Award. In 1986 Wideman's son Jacob, then eighteen, was convicted of murdering a camping companion and was also sentenced to life in prison. After this personal tragedy, Wideman returned to the East Coast and accepted a full professorship at the University of Massachusetts at Amherst. (Wideman has two other children: a daughter, Jamila, who followed her father's athletic footsteps as a player for the Los Angeles Sparks women's professional basketball team; and a son, Danny, who is also a published writer.)

Wideman's literary reputation was secured with the publication of *Fever* (1989), a novel about the yellow fever epidemic in nineteenth-century PHILADELPHIA, PENNSYLVANIA; *Philadelphia*

Fire (1990), a novel about the incidents surrounding the black radical group MOVE (for which he won a PEN/Faulkner Award in 1991); the acclaimed memoir *Fatheralong: A Meditation on Fathers and Sons* (1994); and the novels *Cattle Killing* (1996) and *Two Cities* (1998). In *Hoop Roots* (2001), Wideman explored the connections between basketball and jazz, as well as the sport's ties to black history and culture in the United States. He followed this with a travel memoir, *Island,* in 2003. Among his many awards and honors, Wideman received a MacArthur Foundation "genius grant" in 1993, and was appointed a Distinguished Professor by the University of Massachusetts in 2001.

See also Literature, African American.

Wilberforce University

Predominantly black university located near Dayton, Ohio; one of the first black institutions of higher learning established in the United States.

Wilberforce University's stated goals for its students include helping them "to think logically and act creatively in all areas of human experience, to develop social awareness and a sense of responsibility to self and others, [and] to acquire an acquaintance with the various areas of human knowledge." Wilberforce was founded as Ohio African University, by the METHODIST EPISCOPAL CHURCH in 1843. Within a few years the college changed its name to honor eighteenth-century British abolitionist William Wilberforce.

The school's first students were former slaves and freeborn blacks; the college offered its first post-secondary instruction in 1856, and its first baccalaureate degree in 1857. In 1863 the AFRICAN METHODIST EPISCOPAL CHURCH (AME) bought the property, and merged it with the AME Union Seminary, which had been established in Columbus, Ohio. AME Bishop DANIEL ALEXANDER PAYNE took over the combined institution, making him the first black college president in the United States.

Prominent members of Wilberforce's faculty have included Women's Club Movement leader HALLIE QUINN BROWN, who graduated from Wilberforce in 1873 and returned twenty years later to teach English and elocution; intellectual W. E. B. DU BOIS, who taught there from 1894 to 1896; and historian CHARLES H. WESLEY, who served as president from 1942 to 1947. Four-year degree programs were first offered in 1922, and in 1947 the university's normal and industrial department became a separate institution, now named Central State University. A mandatory cooperative education program instituted in 1964, which places students in career-oriented work assignments, remains one of Wilberforce University's strongest features. Today, Wilberforce offers bachelor of arts and science degrees in twenty areas of concentration to approximately 1,200 enrolled students.

See also Colleges and Universities, Historically Black, in the United States.

Lisa Clayton Robinson

Wilder, Lawrence Douglas

1931–

First African American to be elected governor in the United States.

L. Douglas Wilder has served his home state of Virginia as state senator, lieutenant governor, and governor. A native of RICHMOND, VIRGINIA and the son of an insurance agent and a domestic worker, Wilder has made a career of conciliating tensions between the races.

Douglas Wilder was educated at the historically black Virginia Union University and graduated from HOWARD UNIVERSITY Law School in WASHINGTON, D.C., in 1959. He was always aware of the political possibilities of his own success. He received the Bronze Star for bravery in the KOREAN WAR, and he used his recognition to fight successfully for the promotion of passed-over African American military commanders. His law practice made him a millionaire, and he parlayed his money and influence into a campaign for state senator in 1969. Wilder's success as a Democrat in a largely white, Republican state flows from his position as a "healer" of racial strife, his moderate views on social policy, his fiscal conservatism, and his ability to remake himself to suit the national political climate.

In the Virginia state legislature, from 1969 to 1985, Wilder worked tirelessly to end discrimination in the areas of employment and housing opportunities. In 1985 he ran successfully for lieutenant governor, and four years later he became governor of Virginia. Wilder was the first African American to be elected governor in the United States. (Before Wilder, only one other black person had served as governor. P. B. S. Pinchback became governor of Louisiana briefly in 1872 after the sitting governor was impeached.)

Wilder's record as governor was mixed. Some claim that too much of Virginia's economic success came at the expense of social programs; others cite Wilder's flip-flopping on issues, such as capital punishment, as evidence of his pandering to conservative white voters. Nevertheless, Wilder was still a political hot ticket in 1991, when he made an unsuccessful bid for the Democratic nomination for president. Although he withdrew from the race, he emerged as a major spokesperson for the Democratic Party at the national level when he delivered the nominating speech for Vice President Al Gore at the Democratic National Convention. Wilder's gubernatorial term ended in 1994. He currently teaches politics at Virginia Commonwealth University and is actively pursuing the establishment of a slavery museum, an idea he first proposed in 1993.

Wildlife Management in Africa

Policies and practices aimed at protecting Africa's wild animal species without adversely affecting the welfare of its human population.

AFRICA is the world's second largest continent, with a total land area of more than nineteen million square kilometers (about 11.8 million square miles). It is home to more mammal species than any other land region in the world. But these animals share the continent with approximately 800 million people—whose numbers are increasing at a rate of about 2.8 percent annually—as well as with growing populations of domestic livestock. While humans and wildlife have long coexisted in Africa, unprecedented human population growth over the past century has brought with it an increase in wild habitat destruction and certain forms of hunting. These trends have already driven many animal species to extinction and left many others threatened. But they have also given rise to a wide range of national, regional, and local wildlife management programs, and to ongoing debates about the best means of preserving Africa's biodiversity while meeting human needs.

Early Conservationism in Africa

Wildlife management, as the term is currently understood, began in Africa in 1900, when European colonial administrators met at the Convention for the Preservation of Animals, Birds, and Fish in Africa. Their wildlife management plans were intended to ensure the continued survival of animals that they considered either useful or harmless to people. Elephants and RHINOCEROSES were highly valued, for example, for their tusks and horns. These and other big-game species, such as ZEBRAS, LIONS, and HIPPOPOTAMUSes, were also considered prize trophy animals by wealthy European and American safari hunters. To ensure conservation of these species, the convention limited elephant and rhino hunting, and prohibited the hunting of infant and adolescent elephants as well as adult female elephants with calves. A few species defined as "harmless," that is, those that did little or no damage to human beings or their property—including GORILLAS, CHIMPANZEES, pygmy hippopotamuses, white-bearded wildebeests (a subspecies of the blue wildebeest), GIRAFFES, and mountain zebras—were also fully protected. Some of these species, especially the primates, were also considered of scientific interest. Lions, LEOPARDS, HYENAS, and wild dogs, which attacked domestic animals, were defined as vermin and therefore considered open game.

Approaches to wildlife management shifted in the 1920s with the widespread introduction of national parks to Africa. National parks were modeled on those in the United States, such as Yellowstone National Park, which were themselves modeled on hunting parks in medieval Britain. At a time of rapid industrialization and urbanization in the United States, national parks were seen to preserve "unspoiled" scenic areas for tourists. Colonial governments adopted this model for Africa, but their priority was not so much scenery as wildlife. It was to be preserved, observed, and studied, but in a way that would not threaten humans or their property. Thus a central tenet of wildlife management that developed during this period was to *contain* animals in a "wild" but bordered setting. The land set aside for parks, however, was often already inhabited by people, many of whom had long depended on both the land and the wild animals for survival.

In both colonial and independent Africa, the creation of national parks often resulted in the eviction of farming communities and nomadic herders from their traditional lands. During the 1950s the British colonial government evicted the MAASAI people from Serengeti National Park. As recently as 1988 in TANZANIA more than 5,000 pastoral people were relocated to create parkland. Inside park borders, activities such as cutting timber, gathering wild foods, hunting, grazing, and watering domestic livestock are generally officially prohibited. In practice, the prohibitions have proven difficult to enforce. People in local communities who have historically depended on access to the parklands' natural resources for subsistence often sorely resent the restrictions. Poaching is a particularly serious concern to wildlife managers, but it is believed that at least some of the poachers—especially those who target rare species like the black rhino—are not local people killing for meat but rather "professionals" hired by smugglers of rhino horn and other animal products banned from international trade. The governments of KENYA and ZIMBABWE have responded to the poaching problem by authorizing park rangers to shoot suspected poachers on sight.

Changing Views on Wildlife Management

For a number of reasons, wildlife management experts in recent years have begun to look beyond the standard strategies of creating national parks and banning hunting to ensure wildlife conservation. One reason is the difficulty that authorities have controlling poaching. In addition, groups who have been threatened with eviction from their traditional lands have become increasingly vocal in defense of their property rights. Tanzanian Maasai, for example, organized the group Korongoro Integrated Peoples Oriented to Conservation (the acronym KIPOC means "we shall recover" in Maasai) in the early 1990s to lobby for the rights of "indigenous minority peoples." At the same time, however, international conservation groups such as the World Wildlife Fund continue to call for stronger measures to protect certain African wildlife species.

These international groups have launched letter-writing and fund-raising campaigns that have made African wildlife conservation an issue of global concern. Yet their stance on certain issues has not always won support in Africa. In the past, they have been criticized for ignoring regional variations in wildlife populations and their significance to people, and in some cases for ignoring the counsel of wildlife biologists. These conflicts were especially apparent in the debate leading up to the 1989 global ban on ivory trading, agreed to by the 130 member-nations of the Convention on International Trade in Endangered Species of Wild Fauna and Flora (CITES). American and European conservation and animal rights groups led the call for the ban and based their arguments on the endangered status of elephant populations in East Africa. In fact, the elephant populations had declined drastically just in the years since independence: in Kenya, for example, poachers had re-

duced the elephant population from 167,000 in 1973 to a mere 19,000 by 1989. In southern Africa, on the other hand, elephants had become so numerous that they were regularly damaging not only farmers' crops but also wild vegetation. Some parks in this region cull their elephant populations simply to prevent them from eating all their food supply. Not surprisingly, governments in southern African countries such as BOTSWANA, SOUTH AFRICA, and Zimbabwe, along with many wildlife biologists, all opposed the proposed universal IVORY TRADE ban, which would deprive the countries of millions of dollars of revenue. Nevertheless, the ban was initiated because of the pressure that conservationist groups put on CITES member-nations.

It took eight years before the southern African nations convinced other CITES members to agree to a partial lifting of the ivory trade ban. The agreement that passed in June 1997 permitted Botswana, NAMIBIA, and Zimbabwe to sell their excess ivory stocks to Japan. Animal rights groups, such as the United States Humane Society (USHS), which are also against culling, opposed the agreement. Instead, they promote contraception and park expansion to handle wildlife population growth: in 1996, for example, the USHS gave South Africa's Kruger National Park five million dollars to fund both research on hormonal birth control for elephants and additional land purchases.

Recent Approaches to Wildlife Management

Despite the controversies surrounding certain species, wildlife managers have agreed on a few basic strategies needed for effective conservation. Many experts endorsed the notion of reserves that will be able to provide for the largest number of species with the largest range. In areas where large amounts of land cannot be set aside, several small reserves can be linked to one another to allow migration. The need for such links became clear in the 1990s in Botswana where, although the country had reserved approximately 40 percent of its total land area for wildlife habitat, the wildebeest population fell by 94 percent between 1979 and 1994, and the hartebeest population by 83 percent. Scientists discovered that farm fencing had cut off these animals' migratory routes, and huge numbers had died of thirst or hunger.

Managers must also attempt to keep the genetic diversity alive with the species. Inbreeding can be dangerous. Only a 10 percent increase in inbreeding can lower reproductive performance by 10 to 25 percent, which could explain much of the CHEETAH's declining numbers. Scientists have determined that cheetahs are heavily inbred. If species numbers drop too low, then captive breeding in zoos or special reserves can help restore genetic diversity. Animals born in captivity, however, then have to be reintroduced into the wild, which raises another set of risks.

Another principle of contemporary wildlife management is to minimize the harm wildlife can inflict on nearby human settlements. One approach is to set aside buffer zones between game reserves and farmland, so wildlife straying off a reserve are less likely to trample crops or attack domestic livestock. The idea of the buffer zone assumes that park authorities are responsible for patrolling the park boundaries, and that once animals cross the buffer zone into human habitat, people should be able to kill them in self-defense.

Perhaps the most difficult task facing wildlife managers is to make wildlife conservation worthwhile for local people. One well-known example of an attempt to make conservation profitable for village communities is Zimbabwe's Communal Areas Management Programme for Indigenous Resources (CAMP-FIRE). Initiated in the mid-1980s, this program seeks to promote economic development in the long-impoverished communal lands (roughly 42 percent of Zimbabwe's total land area) through the sustainable use of natural resources—including elephants. Zimbabwean farmers have traditionally had an adversarial relationship with elephants, because the animals do so much damage to their fields. A single animal can easily eat or trample a family's entire food crop. To make conservation more attractive to farming communities, the Zimbabwean government gave them a voice in determining how many elephants could be hunted each year within their own districts, and then planned to turn over to these communities a portion of the profits generated by hunting tours.

The benefits to local communities from controlled elephant hunting are significant. The mostly foreign hunters who come to shoot elephant and other game in Zimbabwe pay as much as $12,000 for one trophy, in addition to a daily hunting fee of $1,000. In 1993, twelve districts with a total population of 400,000 earned more than $1.5 million through trophy fees. Some of this money has gone into village projects such as schools and granaries, but some has also gone into building fences to protect crops from elephants. The revenue has also helped discourage poaching and encouraged communities actively to promote wildlife survival in their districts.

Another approach to reconciling the needs of people and wildlife is the creation of luxury resorts that provide protected space for animals as wells as abundant employment and entrepreneurial opportunities for local communities. This approach is controversial but increasingly popular with cash-poor African governments. Plans for tourist parks and game reserves that include golf courses and casinos as well as guided tours through areas containing wildlife have been proposed. Developers anticipate that once animal populations sufficiently grow, controlled hunting can be introduced as a way to cull herds and attract high-end big-game hunters. Yet these plans do not please everyone since they could displace many small farming and fishing communities. Those in favor of these parks argue that employment opportunities, ranging from game trackers to construction workers to domestic jobs in the hotels, would mitigate the hardship.

Other reserves in Namibia and Botswana offer basically the same kinds of luxury wildlife tourism, but with one important modification. The parks' developers attempted to win the acceptance of nearby communities by building clinics and schools and by employing as many local people as possible. They offered jobs not only for cooks and chambermaids but also in

ironworking and construction. In addition, some of these parks encouraged local farmers to grow produce that could be purchased and used by their hotel restaurants and catering facilities.

Tourism alone offers no definitive solution to the challenges of preserving wildlife and its habitat, and in any case it is only feasible in countries that boast the big-game species and scenic landscapes that attract visitors from overseas. Moreover, foreign tourist companies still receive the "lion's share" of the profits generated from "safari" tourism in the game-rich countries of East and southern Africa. Still, wildlife management strategies in Africa are now more sensitive than they once were to the needs of both animals and people.

See also African Elephant; African Hunting Dog; Animals in Africa; Hunting in Africa; Safari Hunting; Tourism in Africa.

Robert Fay

Wilkerson, Doxey Alphonso

1905–1993

American educator and Communist Party spokesperson on the "Negro question" during the 1940s and 1950s.

In 1944, Doxey Alphonso Wilkerson published an essay in the anthology *What the Negro Wants,* drawing parallels between the struggle for African American civil rights and the Allied struggle in WORLD WAR II. In addition to teaching at HOWARD UNIVERSITY, in WASHINGTON, D.C., and Yeshiva University in New York, Wilkerson worked to further the African American struggle through his work with the Communist Party, which resulted in repeated investigations by the U.S. House Un-American Activities Committee. He resigned from the party in 1957, and was active in the CIVIL RIGHTS MOVEMENT through the 1960s. He continued civil rights and educational work until retiring in 1984.

Robert Fay

Wilkins, Roy Ottoway

1901–1981

American journalist, civil rights leader, director of the National Association for the Advancement of Colored People.

Before Roy Ottoway Wilkins was born, his father had been forced to flee St. Louis to avoid being lynched for refusing to follow a white man's order to get out of the road. Wilkins was reared in St. Paul, Minnesota, where he attended racially integrated schools. He became urgently aware of racial matters at the age of eighteen, when three Minnesotan black men were lynched by a mob of 5,000 whites. Upon enrolling in the University of Minnesota, Wilkins became active in the NATIONAL ASSOCIATION FOR THE ADVANCEMENT OF COLORED PEOPLE (NAACP), as well as on the campus newspaper, both activities he would pursue in KANSAS CITY following graduation. Wilkins worked for the *Kansas City Call,* an African American newspaper until 1931, when he became assistant executive secretary for the NAACP, a position he held while editing the organization newspaper THE CRISIS until 1949.

In 1955, Wilkins was appointed to serve as the NAACP's Executive Director, the organization's highest administrative post. He steered the NAACP through the CIVIL RIGHTS MOVEMENT's most turbulent era, and with MARTIN LUTHER KING JR., helped to organize the MARCH ON WASHINGTON in 1963. Throughout his career, Wilkins upheld the principle of nonviolent, legal forms of redress, which tended to alienate him from more radical black groups. Wilkins's struggles for equality and civil rights brought him many awards, and earned him the nickname "Mr. Civil Rights."

See also Press, Black, in the United States.

Willemstad, Netherlands Antilles

Capital of Netherlands Antilles, West Indies, on the Caribbean Sea, southern Curaçao.

Willemstad is a free port and has excellent harbor facilities. The principal industry is the refining and transshipment of petroleum, chiefly from VENEZUELA. The tourist trade is also important. Among the points of interest are Fort Amsterdam, the governor's palace, the town hall, Wilhelmina Park, an eighteenth-century Protestant church, and the Jewish cemetery (dating from 1650).

The city was settled by the Spanish in 1527 and taken by the Dutch in 1634. During the seventeenth and eighteenth centuries, it was a center of the slave trade. Its later importance dates from 1916, when a petroleum refinery was established here. In 2003 Willemstad had a population of 60,100.

See also Colonial Latin America and the Caribbean; Curaçao; Netherlands Antilles; Transatlantic Slave Trade.

Williams, Bert

1874?–1922

Actor and comedian of the vaudeville team of Williams and Walker, who elevated racial caricature to an art form.

Bert Williams's exact date and place of birth in the Caribbean is unknown. It is known that he moved to Riverside, California in 1885 with his parents, Fred and Julia Williams. After high school, he lived in San Francisco where he entertained audiences in restaurants and saloons before touring with a small minstrel company.

In 1893 Williams met GEORGE WALKER. They developed an act that soon brought them national recognition as they com-

bined Negro comedy with RAGTIME music and CAKEWALK dancing. Williams played the unkempt, fumbling "darky" while Walker was the dapper, smooth-stepping "dandy." Williams's hit songs included "I'm a Jonah Man" and "Nobody." Before Walker fell ill and retired in 1909, they performed several of their ragtime musicals on Broadway: *Son of Ham* (1900), *In Dahomey* (1902), *Abyssinia* (1906), and *Bandanna Land* (1908). *In Dahomey* was performed for the British royal family on the lawn of Buckingham palace. They also recorded a number of skits for the Victor Company.

Williams continued to perform, becoming in 1910 the first African American to appear in the Ziegfeld Follies, the leading variety extravaganza of the time. After leaving the Follies in 1919, Williams performed his own shows until his death in 1922 during a run of *Under the Bamboo Tree.* Wearing blackface and using a "darky" dialect, Williams played a racially stereotyped caricature throughout his entire career. Williams's friends reported that, despite his stage success, the discrimination and rejection he faced in everyday life drove him to deep depression.

See also Dance, African American; Minstrelsy; Musical Theater in the United States; Racial Stereotypes.

Aaron Myers

Williams, Billy Dee

1937–

American actor known for his suave character in stage productions, movies, and television shows.

Billy Dee Williams was born William December to a Texan father and a West Indian mother in HARLEM, NEW YORK. His parents juggled several jobs while his maternal grandmother helped raise Williams and his twin sister, Loretta. With aspirations of becoming a painter, Williams attended New York's High School of Music and Art and the National Academy of Fine Arts and Design. While pursuing his art studies, Williams learned about the Stanislavsky method of natural acting through his acquaintance with SIDNEY POITIER and Paul Mann at the Actors Workshop in Harlem. Williams initially viewed acting as a way to earn money for art supplies, but by the early 1960s had begun to devote all of his energy to acting.

Williams first appeared on stage at the age of seven in the musical *The Firebrand of Florence* (1945). His first screen appearance was in *The Last Angry Man* (1959). *A Taste of Honey* (1960), which won the New York Drama Critic's 1961 award for best foreign play, featured him in one of his earliest stage performances. After the failure of two marriages, first to Audrey Sellers and then to Marlene Clark, Williams fell into a depression in 1964.

He made a triumphant return to acting in 1970 with his Emmy nominated portrayal of Chicago Bears football player Gale Sayers in *Brian's Song.* William's success earned him a seven-year film contract with Motown's Berry Gordy, and he co-starred with DIANA ROSS in *Lady Sings the Blues* (1972) and *Mahogany* (1975). In the 1980s, he was featured in the movies *The Empire Strikes Back* (1980) and *Return of the Jedi* (1983), as well as in the television programs *Dynasty* and *Star Trek*. In 1984, Williams was inducted into the Black Filmmaker's Hall of Fame, and in 1985, he was awarded a star on the Hollywood Walk of Fame. Williams continues to make frequent appearances in both television and movie roles. Some of his recent work includes *The Ladies Man* (2000), *Undercover Brother* (2002), and *Constellation* (2003).

See also Cinema, African Americans in; Motown; Television, African Americans in.

Aaron Myers

Williams, Daniel Hale

1856–1931

American surgeon who performed the first successful open-heart surgery.

The son of a barber, Daniel Hale Williams lived on his own after the age of twelve. As a youth, he worked as a shoemaker, a roustabout on a lake steamer, and a barber. Moving with his sister to Wisconsin he met Henry Palmer, a prominent physician, the surgeon general of Wisconsin for ten years. Williams was apprenticed by Palmer, who became his mentor and helped pay his tuition at the Chicago Medical School.

Graduating with an M.D. in 1883, Williams opened a medical practice on the South Side of CHICAGO, ILLINOIS. An adept doctor, he served as an attending physician at the Protestant Orphan Asylum and as a surgeon at the South Side Dispensary. Williams also worked as a clinical instructor at the Chicago Medical College and as a physician with the City Railway Company. He was appointed in 1889 to the Illinois Board of Health, where he served for four years, helping to enforce medical standards in handling infectious diseases.

Williams accomplished this in a time and place where African Americans were not permitted hospital staff positions or allowed the use of equipment at area hospitals. African American women were also barred from the nurses' training programs at these hospitals. In response to these circumstances, Williams founded Provident Hospital in 1891. It was the first black-owned hospital and boasted an interracial staff and a nurses' training school. In 1894, Williams was named the Chief Surgeon at FREEDMEN'S HOSPITAL in WASHINGTON, D.C. This hospital was funded by the federal government and affiliated with HOWARD UNIVERSITY's medical school, although when Williams arrived it was in need of reorganization and leadership.

Reorganizing the hospital into departments, reestablishing a nurses' training school, and developing an internship program, Williams brought new life to the hospital. He returned to Chicago in 1898 to rejoin Provident Hospital and reopen his private practice. Widely published in prominent medical journals, in 1913 he was appointed associate attending surgeon at Chicago's St. Luke's Hospital. He was also the only black charter member of the American College of Surgeons. In 1924, Williams retired to Michigan and died there seven years later.

The feat for which Williams is most known was the successful surgery he performed on James Cornish in 1893. Cornish, a street tough, had been stabbed in the chest. After the external wounds were sewn up, Cornish's condition continued to deteriorate. Concluding that Cornish was bleeding internally, Williams decided to open his chest cavity and try to stop the bleeding. Finding the knife had slashed an artery and tissue around the heart, Williams used catgut thread to sew up these internal wounds. The operation was a success and Cornish lived another twenty years, making Williams the first physician to perform successful open-heart surgery.

See also Doctors, African American; Hospitals, Black.

Williams, Edward Christopher

1871–1929

African American librarian, teacher, and writer.

Edward Christopher Williams was born in Cleveland, Ohio, the only son of Daniel P. Williams, an African American, and Mary (Kilkary) Williams of Tipperary, Ireland. He was educated in the public schools of Cleveland. In 1892 he received his B.A. degree from Cleveland's Adelbert College of Western Reserve University (now Case Western Reserve University). There he was elected to Phi Beta Kappa and was valedictorian of his class. From 1892 to 1894 Williams was first assistant librarian of Adelbert College, and from 1894 to 1898, the librarian of the Hatch Library of Western Reserve. From 1898 to 1899 he was university librarian of Western Reserve. A brilliant and stimulating teacher, he taught library courses in bibliography, reference work, public documents, and book selection. Williams was granted a leave of absence from Western Reserve from 1899 to 1900 to study at the New York State Library School in Albany, where he completed the two-year course in one year. Returning to Western Reserve, he was admired by his students for his scholarship in history, literature, and language. They spoke of him as an excellent teacher who "vitalized books by connecting them with human interests and needs," as an individual who had a "keen sense of the picturesque and the humorous" and "from whom one always caught some fire of inspiration." While at Western Reserve, Williams was secretary of the Ohio Library Association and chairman of its college section. He lectured each year at the Ohio Institute of Library Workers held at the annual meeting of the Ohio Library Association.

In 1909 Williams left Cleveland and became principal of the M Street High School (in 1916 named Dunbar High School) in WASHINGTON, D.C., a position he held until June 1916. A continued interest in library training and organization led him to accept the position of librarian of HOWARD UNIVERSITY in 1916, where during the next several years he developed library training courses, expanded library resources, and increased the staff. In 1921 he was appointed head of the Romance Languages Department, teaching courses in Italian, French, and German. In addition to his teaching and library duties at Howard, Williams engaged in many aspects of campus life, serving on committees, working as associate faculty editor of the *Howard University Record,* to which he contributed many articles, and actively supporting dramatics. Along with his university duties he addressed civic, literary, and professional groups, serving on the staff of the 135th Street branch of the New York Public Library during his summer vacations.

Had Williams lived longer, he might have become a creative writer of note. The Howard University Players performed his unpublished classical dramas *The Exile, The Sheriff's Children,* and *The Chasm.* His series on Washington black society, "Letters of Davy Carr, A True Story of Colored Vanity Fair," was published in 1925 and 1926 in *The Messenger* magazine. Williams published poems and short stories anonymously and under the pseudonym of Bertuccio Dantino.

While on leave from Howard University in December 1929, Williams became ill in NEW YORK CITY where he was attending the School of Library Service at Columbia University working toward a Ph.D. degree. He died on December 24 in FREEDMEN'S HOSPITAL, Washington, D.C., leaving a wife Ethel Chesnutt Williams, who was a daughter of author CHARLES WADDELL CHESNUTT; a son Charles; and a granddaughter Patricia Ann Williams. The funeral of Edward Williams, who had lived during most of his Washington years at 912 Westminster Street NW, was held on December 27 in Andrew Rankin Memorial Chapel, Howard University, with President MORDECAI W. JOHNSON officiating. His body was interred at Lincoln Cemetery, Suitland, Maryland.

Additional information on Williams can be found in the following: Dorothy B. Porter's "Edward Christopher Williams" (*Phylon* 8, no. 4, 1947), E. L. Josey's "Edward Christopher Williams, Librarian's Librarian" (*Negro History Bulletin* 33, no. 3, March 1970), and Russell H. Davis's *Memorable Negroes in Cleveland's Past* (1969). Obituaries appeared in the *Washington Evening Star* (December 26, 1929, p. 7) and *Washington Tribune* (December 27, 1929, p. 1).

From *Dictionary of American Negro Biography* by Rayford W. Logan and Michael R. Winston, editors. Copyright © 1982 by Rayford W. Logan and Michael R. Winston. Reprinted by permission of W. W. Norton & Company, Inc.

See also Literature, African American.

Dorothy B. Porter

Williams, Eric

1911–1981

Distinguished Afro-Caribbean historian and politician who helped found Trinidad's People's National Movement (PNM) party and held several different high-ranking political offices, including prime minister.

Eric Williams was born in PORT-OF-SPAIN, Trinidad, the eldest of twelve children in a family of modest means. His education was funded by a series of competitive scholarships awarded to those who excelled academically. He attended Queen's Royal College, a preparatory school for boys, and in 1931 won a scholarship to study at a British university. At Oxford University, Williams earned a bachelor's degree and in 1938 a doctorate in history. His dissertation, "Economic Aspects of the Abolition of the West Indies Slave Trade," would later be published as *Capitalism and Slavery.*

In 1939 Williams moved to the United States to establish an academic career teaching social sciences at HOWARD UNIVERSITY. Rising through the academic ranks, he was offered a tenured position in 1946.

Williams returned to Trinidad in 1948 and worked as deputy chairman of the Caribbean Research Council of the Caribbean Commission. The commission was designed to encourage the United States and Britain to cooperate in the Caribbean. Williams was defiantly unwilling to adhere to the Commission's strict requirement of absolute neutrality in political affairs, and his contract was not renewed in 1955.

Shortly after, Williams declared his intention to remain in Trinidad. It is unclear to what extent this decision was influenced by a dispassionate assessment of the limited career prospects available to a colonial abroad. Williams soon began to deliver a series of public lectures in forums throughout the island, but most often in Port-of-Spain's Woodford Square. The lectures addressed a number of issues, ranging from the need for constitutional and economic reform to race relations in the Caribbean.

The enthusiastic public response to the lectures coupled with the emergence, under Williams's influence, of a group of political strategists intent on both shaping and promulgating a nationalist, political vision led to the founding in January 1956 of a new political party, the People's National Movement (PNM). The multiracial PNM championed a political agenda that mirrored the concerns of its target constituency, the rapidly emerging middle class.

By virtue of his international reputation and experience, Williams was the most authoritative figure in the development of the new party. He proved to be a shrewd political entrepreneur and an inspiring public speaker. Under Williams's leadership the PNM championed colonial nationalism and economic decolonization; the need for territorial integrity; the expansion of the voting franchise; educational and curricular reform, with a heightened emphasis on Caribbean history; and the necessity of Caribbean economic integration.

In Trinidad's 1956 general election, the PNM won a majority of seats. Williams was elected representative to the legislative council for his district of South Port-of-Spain. The trajectory of his political career, with its increasingly sophisticated administrative responsibilities—chief minister from 1956 to 1959, premier from 1959 to 1962, and prime minister from 1962 until his death in office on March 29, 1981—paralleled the country's eventual transformation from a British colony into an independent republic.

See also Independence Movements in the British Caribbean; Trinidad and Tobago.

Lorraine Anastasia Lezama

Williams, Fannie Barrier

1855–1944

African American lecturer and clubwoman.

Fannie Barrier Williams was born in Brockport, New York, the daughter of Anthony J. Barrier and Harriet Prince, free persons of color. She graduated from the State Normal School at Brockport in 1870 and attended the New England Conservatory of Music in Boston and the School of Fine Arts in Washington, D.C. She then taught in southern schools and in Washington, D.C., for a short time. In 1887 Barrier retired from teaching to marry S. Laing Williams, a prominent attorney in Chicago. The couple had no children.

Williams became known for her club work and lecturing. Though many of her early lectures and written works supported the militant, egalitarian protest ideology of Frederick Douglass, she later became a staunch supporter of Booker T. Washington's accommodationist views, including his emphasis on industrial education and practical training. She encouraged employers to hire qualified black women for clerical positions and sought other job opportunities for blacks. She did not, however, reject the value of education beyond that of industrial training.

Williams's prominence arose from her efforts to have blacks officially represented on the Board of Control of the Columbian Exposition in 1893. She was able to persuade the board to include black affairs in the exhibits planned for the celebration. At the exposition, Williams delivered an address, "The Intellectual Progress of Colored Women in the U.S. since the Emancipation Proclamation," to an enthusiastic, integrated audience of the World's Congress of Representative Women. In this address, Williams dismissed the charges of sexual immorality among black women with the claim that continued harassment by white men was the source of the problem. She stated that after emancipation black women were quick and eager to "taste the blessedness of intelligent womanhood," and she urged white women who were concerned about morality to find ways to help black women.

In 1895 Williams was a state representative at the National Colored Women's Congress, which was convened by the Negro Department of the Cotton States and International Exposition in Atlanta, Georgia. In the same year, following an initial rejection, she became the first black woman admitted to the Woman's Club of Chicago. She was also the first black woman to be appointed to the Chicago Library Board, on which she served from 1924 to 1926.

Active in many community and civic organizations, she was a director of the Frederick Douglass Center, Chicago's first interracial organization, and a member of the Abraham Lincoln Center. She also worked with the Phillis Wheatley Home Association. She was a founding member of the National League of Colored Women in 1893 and served as president of the Woman's Council, which hosted the 1899 meeting of its successor, the National Association of Colored Women. She wrote a column about women's activities for T. Thomas Fortune's *New York Age* and the *Chicago Record-Herald*.

Williams's political activism, which began with the 1893 Columbian Exposition in Chicago, continued with the black women's club movement. She often spoke on the need for black women to emancipate their minds and spirits. In the speech "Club Movement among Colored Women of America," she stated that "the struggle of an enlightened conscience against the whole brood of miseries [is] born out of the stress and pain of a hated past." Williams advocated feminist thinking through her efforts in the club movement. She noted that black women had reached an age in which they were moving beyond the patriarchal notion of women doing what men felt they ought to do. "In our day and in this country, a woman's sphere is just as large as she can make it." Williams's activism focused on the social condition of the entire race, which distinguished the black women's club movement from that of white women. She strongly supported education of black women in order to move them out of domestic work, where sexual harassment was so prevalent. She also advocated voting rights and equal employment opportunities.

Williams sought to combat and defy Jim Crow laws in whatever manner she could. She once used her light complexion and knowledge of French to ride in the white-only section of a southern train. She wrote in "A Northern Negro's Autobiography" (1904) that "[I] quieted my conscious by recalling that there was a strain of French blood in my ancestry, and too that their barbarous laws did not allow a lady to be both comfortable and honest."

Williams worked closely with Dr. Daniel Hale Williams in establishing the Provident Hospital in 1891. It housed the first training school for black nurses in Chicago, which she helped organize, and which was distinctive for its biracial staff of doctors. After her husband's death in 1921, Williams withdrew from many of her activities. She died in Brockport.

Bibliography

Gibson, J. W., and W. H. Crogman, eds. *Progress of a Race.* 1903.

Lerner, Gerda. *The Black Woman in White America: A Documentary History.* 1972.

McBrady, J. E., ed. *A New Negro for a New Century.* 1900.

Meier, August. *Negro Thought in America, 1880–1915: Racial Ideologies in the Age of Booker T. Washington.* 1963.

Sewall, May Wright, ed. *World's Congress of Representative Women.* 1894.

Williams, Fannie Barrier. "A Northern Negro's Autobiography." In the *Independent,* July 14, 1904.

From *American National Biography*. John A. Garraty and Mark C. Carnes, eds. Oxford University Press, 1999. Reprinted by permission of the American Council of Learned Societies.

Mamie E. Locke

Williams, Franklin Hall

1917–1990

American lawyer, head of the African division of the Peace Corps, and United States Ambassador to Ghana.

After graduating from the New York public school system, Franklin Williams acquired a bachelor's degree from LINCOLN UNIVERSITY and a law degree from Fordham Law School. Following service in WORLD WAR II, he worked as an assistant to THURGOOD MARSHALL, then assistant counsel to the NATIONAL ASSOCIATION FOR THE ADVANCEMENT OF COLORED PEOPLE (NAACP), until 1950. Williams served as West Coast director of the NAACP until 1959.

After conducting voter registration dinners that helped elect John F. Kennedy president, Williams was selected to head the African branch of the newly created Peace Corps. Part of his job entailed traveling throughout Africa with Peace Corps director Sargent Shriver to plan the organization's future. His experiences in a wide range of foreign nations primed him for a diplomatic post. In 1964, President Lyndon B. Johnson appointed Williams to serve on a delegation to the Economic and Social Council in Geneva, and one year later, named him United States ambassador to GHANA, a position he held until 1968.

Williams returned to the United States to serve as director of Columbia University's Urban Center, and then became president of the Phelps-Stokes Fund, which provides financial support for the education of Africans and African Americans. Hall also served on the Council on Foreign Relations from 1975 to 1983.

Williams, George Washington

1849–1891

Scholar and minister, he is considered the first major American historian of African descent.

George Washington Williams left school at fourteen and lied about his age in order to enlist in the Union Army during the CIVIL WAR. He later enlisted in the Mexican Army, where he quickly rose to the rank of Lieutenant Colonel, and then joined the United States Cavalry in 1867 where he served in the Indian campaigns.

In 1868 he enrolled at Newton Theological Seminary, in Cambridge, Massachusetts. Graduating in 1874, he became the school's first African American alumnus. Immediately upon graduation, Williams was ordained as pastor of Twelfth Baptist Church in BOSTON. Fascinated with the church, he wrote an eighty-page study of its history. He left, however, after one

year, and in WASHINGTON, D.C. started an unsuccessful academic journal about African Americans. Williams became pastor of Union Baptist Church in CINCINNATI, OHIO, where he became a regular contributor to the *Cincinnati Commercial* under the pen name "Aristides." He also passed the bar exam to practice law in Ohio (and he would later in Boston), and in 1879 he became the first African American elected to the Ohio legislature.

At this time Williams also began to make his mark as an historian. He was a staunch supporter of the view, current at that time, that history was an objective science, and he was determined to apply this approach to African American history. In Ohio he began researching for his comprehensive two-volume *History of the Negro Race in America, 1619–1880* (1882), which was the first-full length study of African American history by a person of African descent. He dedicated himself to African American history because of his opinion that African Americans had "been the most vexatious problem in North America from the time of its discovery down to the present day . . . [and writing] such a history would give the world more correct ideas of the Colored people, and incite the latter to greater effort in the struggle of citizenship and manhood." Williams also later wrote a *History of Negro Troops in the War of Rebellion* (1887), which argued that African Americans were among the most gallant soldiers in the Civil War.

Williams's scholarship brought him renown as an African American historian and advocate. In 1885 he was appointed Minister to HAITI by President Chester A. Arthur. However, the presidency was assumed by Grover Cleveland, who refused to give Williams his post.

Williams became frustrated with Washington politics and turned his attention to international affairs, particularly the colonization and exploitation of AFRICA. He attended a major antislavery conference in Brussels in 1889. Belgium then sent him to the Congo to study conditions there. The country's abysmal poverty so distressed him that, along with his official report, he wrote for wider circulation, *An Open Letter to His Serene Majesty, Leopold II, King of Belgium*. This was the first public critique of King Leopold for his savage oppression of the Congo. After his survey Williams traveled widely throughout Africa, and apparently contracted a disease that killed him soon upon his return to England.

See also Congo, Belgian; Historians, African American; Leopold II; Military, Blacks in the American.

Williams, John Alfred

1925–

American writer and educator whose works explore racial and social injustices from an African American perspective.

John Alfred Williams grew up in Syracuse, New York, where he returned after Navy service in WORLD WAR II to finish high school and graduate from Syracuse University with a degree in English and journalism in 1950. Williams's writing career developed in the late 1950s and early 1960s, when he began serving as a correspondent for numerous magazines, including JET, EBONY, Newsweek, and Holiday. His first novel, The Angry Ones, was published in 1960. It has been followed by over twenty other novels and nonfiction works (including a book on the comedian RICHARD PRYOR entitled If I Stop I'll Die: The Comedy and Tragedy of Richard Pryor), as well as numerous articles, essays, anthologies, and a play.

Williams's writings examine African American personal and communal struggles. His tone ranges from the romantic to the brutally apocalyptic. Williams's uncompromising calls for social justice and stylistic innovations have strongly influenced the African American literary tradition and contemporary African American aesthetics. His major work, The Man Who Cried I Am (1967), fictionalized the events surrounding the retraction of the 1962 Prix de Rome Award by the Academy of American Arts and Letters for his novel Night Song, presumably because of academy members' disapproval of Williams's engagement to a white woman. Other works, such as !Click Song! (1982) and The Berhama Account (1987) deal with love's healing power in the midst of adversity.

Williams has taught at various colleges and universities, including Rutgers University in Newark, New Jersey, as Paul Robeson Distinguished Professor of English. He retired from teaching in 1994. Williams has received various awards, including the Before Columbus Foundation's American Book Award in 1983, and the John A. Williams Archive was founded at the University of Rochester in New York in 1987. More recently, his poetry volume Safari West (1998) won the American Book Award. Williams currently lives in Teaneck, New Jersey.

See also Literature, African American.

Bibliography

Cash, Earl A. John A. Williams: The Evolution of a Black Writer. Third Press, 1975.

Marc Mazique

Williams, Lacey Kirk

1871–1940?

American minister and denomination leader.

Lacey Kirk Williams was converted and baptized in 1884 at the Thankful Baptist Church, which his parents helped found in Brazos Bottom, Texas. From the start of his career as a Baptist minister he was involved in the government of the Baptist church. In 1916 Williams was named pastor of CHICAGO's 4,000 member Olivet Church. During his pastorship the church's membership increased to 12,000 and the church became a positive force in the life of Chicago's black community providing it numerous social services. He achieved national prominence

as president of the General Baptist Convention of Illinois (1917–1922), as president of the National Baptist Convention (1922–1940), and as vice president of the Baptist World Alliance (1928–1940). He was killed in a plane crash in 1940.

See also Baptists.

Williams, Mary Lou

1910–1981

American pianist, composer, arranger, and educator; considered by many to be the most significant female instrumentalist in jazz history for her contributions to the development of both the Kansas City swing style of the 1930s and bebop style of the early 1940s.

Born Mary Elfrieda Scruggs in ATLANTA, GEORGIA, Mary Lou Williams began playing piano professionally at age six in PITTSBURGH, PENNSYLVANIA. Her early influences included EARL HINES, JELLY ROLL MORTON, and Lovie Austin. As an adolescent, Williams performed in the Theater Owners Booking Association (TOBA) black vaudeville circuit alongside such figures as FATS WALLER, DUKE ELLINGTON, and WILLIE "THE LION" SMITH. In 1926, she married John Williams, a saxophonist and band leader.

Williams began arranging in 1929 after she joined the Andy Kirk Band, first based in Oklahoma City and later in KANSAS CITY, composing BLUES-based works which influenced the de-

Pianist and arranger Mary Lou Williams was the most influential woman instrumentalist in the history of jazz, influencing Kansas City swing and bebop. *CORBIS/Bettmann*

velopment of 1930s SWING. During the 1930s, she performed and arranged for LOUIS ARMSTRONG, CAB CALLOWAY, Ellington, and others. Williams moved to NEW YORK in 1942, and joined Duke Ellington's band as principal arranger and pianist, composing such notable works as "Trumpet No End" (1942). In the 1940s, she mentored and jammed with many of the young beboppers, including THELONIUS MONK, BUD POWELL, CHARLIE PARKER, and DIZZY GILLESPIE. Her famous *Zodiac Suite*, written in 1945, was adapted and performed by the New York Philharmonic in Carnegie Hall the following year.

In the 1950s Williams converted to Catholicism and concentrated on prayer and charitable activities. In 1957 she resumed performing and began composing religious pieces, and also formed Mary Records, the first record company established by a woman. Her major religious work, *Mary Lou's Mass* (1969), was commissioned by the Vatican and adapted for ballet by ALVIN AILEY two years later. Williams went on to receive two Guggenheim Fellowships, and numerous honorary doctorates. She taught courses on JAZZ at a number of colleges and universities, including Duke University, where she died in 1981.

See also Bebop; Music, African American.

Marc Mazique

Williams, Oswald

See Ossie, Count.

Williams, Peter, Jr.

1780–1840

American minister, abolitionist, and church founder.

Peter Williams Jr. was raised in the Methodist church under the tutelage of the white minister Thomas Lyell. In 1818, with the blessing of the white congregation of Lyell's John Street METHODIST EPISCOPAL CHURCH, he organized a separate black congregation. St. Philip's African Church was consecrated in HARLEM on July 3, 1819, and in 1826, Williams was ordained, making him the first black Episcopalian priest. An ardent abolitionist, he helped found *FREEDOM'S JOURNAL* in 1827, a black-owned newspaper that demanded an end to slavery and the inception of racial equality. For two years he served as a manager of the AMERICAN ANTI-SLAVERY SOCIETY. Rumors that he had performed an interracial marriage ended his public career, but he continued to be active in his church until his death in 1840.

See also Abolitionism in the United States.

Williams, Peter, Sr.

1749–1823

American church founder of the African Methodist Episcopal Zion denomination.

Born a slave in the NEW YORK CITY area, Peter Williams, Sr., joined a Methodist church and became sexton in 1778. When his master, a Loyalist, returned to England in 1783, the church's trustees bought Williams. Williams firmly believed in equality and was upset when black members of the church were required to sit in segregated pews at the rear of the sanctuary. In 1795, Williams led a group of black members in founding their own church, which was chartered six years later as the AFRICAN METHODIST EPISCOPAL ZION CHURCH. It was the mother church for the denomination of the same name and it was the first black church in New York.

Williams, Robert Franklin

1925–1996

Civil rights activist and prominent advocate of black self-defense and revolutionary nationalism.

Robert Franklin Williams grew up in a tradition of resistance to white supremacy. His grandfather, born a slave, had been a REPUBLICAN PARTY activist during RECONSTRUCTION after the Civil War, when former slaves sought to establish themselves as equal citizens but found their efforts dashed by white terrorists. His grandfather edited a newspaper called *The People's Voice*. His grandmother, who lived through these struggles, was a daily presence in his life as he grew to manhood. She told young Williams stories of the crusading editor's political exploits and gave him his grandfather's gun before she died.

World War II transformed Williams's life; he moved to DETROIT to work in the defense industries, fought white mobs in the DETROIT RIOT OF 1943, and marched for freedom in a segregated U.S. Army. Military training "instilled in us what a virtue it was to fight for democracy," he said, "but most of all they taught us to use arms."

When he returned to Monroe in 1955 Williams served as president of the Monroe chapter of the NATIONAL ASSOCIATION FOR THE ADVANCEMENT OF COLORED PEOPLE (NAACP). Confronted by KU KLUX KLAN terrorism, Williams organized the local chapter into a black militia that repelled armed Klan attacks. In 1959, after an all-white jury acquitted a white man charged with attempted rape of a pregnant black woman, Williams called for blacks "to meet violence with violence," by which he meant "the right of armed self-defense against attack." The NAACP suspended Williams for his remarks in a struggle over the meaning of nonviolence for the African American freedom struggle. The following year, Williams debated prominent pacifists, including MARTIN LUTHER KING JR., the leading spokesperson of the black freedom struggle.

In 1961 followers of King came to Monroe, many of them intent on proving that nonviolence could work. Armed racial conflict broke out, forcing Williams to flee to CUBA under federal indictment on trumped-up kidnapping charges. From HAVANA, Williams broadcast "Radio Free Dixie," which spread his gospel of "armed self-reliance." He also published his newsletter *The Crusader*, whose readership was about 40,000. His 1962 book *Negroes with Guns* was a decisive influence on the BLACK PANTHER PARTY for Self-Defense, founded in Oakland, California, in 1966, and on a generation of increasingly defiant black activists.

Moving to North Vietnam and then China in 1966, Williams wrote antiwar propaganda aimed at African American soldiers fighting in Vietnam and called for revolution in the United States. In China Williams moved in the upper circles of the Chinese government. The REVOLUTIONARY ACTION MOVEMENT and the REPUBLIC OF NEW AFRICA, two important revolutionary black nationalist groups in the United States, both chose him as their president-in-exile. In 1969, as the U.S. government moved to open diplomatic relations with China, Williams traded his knowledge of China for safe passage home and a post at the University of Michigan's Center for Chinese Studies. Just before he died in 1996, Williams completed his autobiography, *While God Lay Sleeping.* Above the desk where he wrote hung the ancient rifle his grandmother had given him.

Robert Williams was typical of the generation of black southerners who launched the African American freedom movement. His evolution from local NAACP leader to international revolutionary underlines both the growing radicalism of the movement and its origins in traditions of militant African American self-assertion.

See also Black Nationalism in the United States; Military, Blacks in the American; World War II and African Americans.

Timothy Tyson

Williams, Sherley

1944–1999

American poet, novelist, and scholar who emphasized the importance of history and folklore in shaping black identity.

In an introduction to her first novel, *Dessa Rose,* Sherley Anne Williams wrote, "Afro-Americans, having survived by word of mouth—and made of that process a high art—remain at the mercy of literature and writing; often, these have betrayed us." Williams's awareness of skewed histories shaped her own writing. Her consistent ability to tell black stories truthfully through poetry and fiction brought her prominence among twentieth-century black American writers.

Born in Bakersfield, California, Williams was raised in low-income housing projects in Fresno. She earned a bachelor's degree in English at California State University. After a lengthy absence from school, she received a master's degree from Brown University. Williams subsequently returned to California to join the faculty of the University of California, San Diego, in 1975.

Although Williams began writing in 1967, it was not until the publication of *Give Birth to Brightness: A Thematic Study in Neo-Black Literature* in 1972 that her theories about the value of black folklore in shaping racial identity were fully articulated. These principles took artistic form when her book, *The Peacock Poems,* was published in 1975, to critical and popular acclaim, ultimately winning a nomination for the National Book Award in poetry. Among her other writings were *Some One Sweet Angel Chile* (1982) and *Dessa Rose* (1986), which was named a notable book by the *New York Times.* In 1992 Williams published her first children's book, *Working Cotton,* which describes her childhood experiences picking fruit and cotton with her parents. Her last published work was another children's book, *Girls Together* (1999), about the friendship between five girls growing up in the projects.

See also Literature, African American; Poetry, African American.

Williams, Smokey Joe

1886–1951

Baseball player and manager.

Smokey Joe Williams was born Joseph Williams in Seguin, Texas, the son of an unknown African American father and Lettie Williams, a Native American. He attended school in San Antonio, but it is not known how many years he completed. As a young boy Joe was given a baseball, which he carried with him everywhere and which he even slept with under his pillow. He pitched in the sandlots around Seguin until 1905, when he began playing professionally with the San Antonio Black Broncos. Williams quickly became the ace of the pitching staff and in the following seasons posted records of 28-4, 15-9, 20-8, 20-2, and 32-8, all with San Antonio except 1906, when he played with Austin. In the autumn of 1909 he signed to play with the Trilbys of Los Angeles, California, marking the first of many years that he played baseball in both summer and winter.

In 1910 Williams was recruited by Chicago Giants' owner Frank Leland, who wrote, "If you have ever witnessed the speed of a pebble in a storm you have not even seen the speed possessed by this wonderful Texan Giant" (Riley, 856). The Giants were the only black team in the semiprofessional Chicago League that season and then played during the 1910–1911 winter in California, where Williams compiled a 4–1 record with 78 strikeouts in 60 innings. After another season with the Giants, Williams made his first visit to Cuba, where he tied for the most wins, with a 10-7 record for the 1911–1912 Cuban Winter League champion Havana Reds. In the spring of 1912 Williams toured with the Chicago American Giants on the West Coast and defeated every Pacific Coast League team except Portland, finishing the tour with a 9–1 record.

After the 1912 tour Williams joined the New York Lincoln Giants for $105 a month; he remained with the franchise through 1923. At this point of his career he was called "Cyclone," but later in his career he would become better known as "Smokey Joe." With the Lincoln Giants, Joe joined another hard-throwing right-hander, "Cannonball" Dick Redding, and the duo pitched the Lincolns to the Eastern Championship in 1912. After the close of the 1912 regular season, Williams shut out John McGraw's National League champion New York Giants 6-0 on four hits while fanning nine. A week later he tossed another four-hit shutout, defeating Hal Chase's All-Stars, a team comprised mostly of New York Yankees. Williams was at his best against white major leaguers and compiled a lifetime 20-7 record against them. When the weather turned cold, the Lincoln Giants toured Cuba, where Williams split a pair of games with Cuban ace José Mendez. After the tour ended, Williams stayed on the island and had a 9-5 record to lead the Fe team to the 1913 Cuban Winter League championship.

After returning to the United States for the 1913 summer season, Williams jumped to the Mohawk Giants of Schenectady, New York, but the Lincoln Giants quickly paid him five hundred dollars to return, and he pitched the team to their finest season, capping the year with six victories in the championship series against RUBE FOSTER's Chicago American Giants. When the triumphant Lincoln Giants returned to New York, a large crowd was on hand at Olympic Park to welcome them home. In the fall Williams resumed his postseason performances against major leaguers. He struck out sixteen in a two-hit 9-1 win over Mike Donlin's All-Stars, fanned nine in defeating Hall-of-Famer Grover Cleveland Alexander and the Philadelphia Phillies 9-2, whiffed twelve in a 1-0 loss to Earl Mack's All-Stars, avenged that loss when he fanned fourteen to take a 7-3 win over the same team, and hurled a three-hit 2-1 victory over a white all-star team that featured Chief Bender, the Philadelphia Athletics ace pitcher.

In 1914 Williams joined the Chicago American Giants during their preseason spring barnstorming tour through the Northwest and pitched a no-hitter against Portland. Back with the Lincoln Giants for the regular season, he compiled a record of 41-3 against all levels of opposition. In the fall Williams again faced major league opposition, defeating the Philadelphia Phillies 10-4, and then fanning a dozen as he battled Hall-of-Famer Rube Marquard and the New York Giants to a 1-1 draw that was ended by darkness.

Williams suffered two injuries in 1915, a broken arm and a broken wrist, and missed much of the season, but was back in action by the fall exhibition games against major leaguers. He struck out nine in a 3-0 shutout over a combination of players from the Federal League's Buffalo and Brooklyn franchises, and fanned ten in pitching a three-hit 1-0 shutout over the National League champion Philadelphia Phillies. In the winter of 1915–1916 Williams pitched for the Chicago American Giants in California, making his last appearance on the West Coast. Later that winter he also made his final appearance in Cuba, when he joined the struggling San Francisco franchise for the second half of the season. He finished with a lifetime 22-15 record in the Cuban Winter League.

In 1917 Hilldale, a team based in the Philadelphia suburb of that name, scheduled a postseason series against major leaguers and recruited Williams to pitch. Williams rose to the occasion and defeated Connie Mack's Philadelphia Athletics 6-2, beating Athletics' ace Joe Bush, and then whiffed ten in a ten-inning 5-4 win over Rube Marquard and Chief Meyers's All-Leaguers. Joe also fanned twenty and tossed a no-hitter against John McGraw's National League champion New York Giants but lost the game 1-0 on an error. According to oral accounts, in this game Giants' star Ross Youngs gave him the nickname "Smokey Joe."

As manager of the Lincoln Giants, Williams took his team to Palm Beach, Florida, in the winter of 1917–1918 to represent the Breakers Hotel in the Florida Hotel League, where they opposed Rube Foster's Royal Poinciana team. In one memorable match-up, Williams struck out nine and tossed a two-hitter to out-duel his old rival Dick Redding, 1-0. Williams continued playing and managing in the winter Florida Hotel League for several years, including a stint as manager of the Royal Poinciana team in 1926.

There was no dominant team in the East in 1918, but when Williams pitched, the Lincoln Giants were the best team. He defeated rival Brooklyn Royal Giants' ace lefthander John Donaldson 1-0 and 3-2 on successive weekends, and in the fall he continued his pitching prowess against major leaguers and fashioned an 8-0 shutout over Marquard and his All-Nationals team. On opening day 1919 the largest crowd to ever attend a game in Harlem watched Williams hurl a no-hit 1-0 masterpiece over Redding and the Brooklyn Royal Giants.

In 1922 Williams married Beatrice Johnson, a Broadway showgirl, and they had one daughter. In the spring of 1924 he became a victim of the Lincoln Giants' youth movement and was released. He joined the Brooklyn Royal Giants and, although he was their top pitcher, was released after the season. Williams then joined the Homestead Grays in 1925 and remained with the franchise through 1932. During his years with the Grays, the nickname "Smokey Joe" was used almost exclusively, and he developed a mystique about his age, encouraging people to think that he was older than he was, that the press kept alive.

In 1929 owner CUM POSEY entered the Grays in the American Negro League, and Williams, appointed captain, compiled a 12-7 record. The league folded after its only year of existence, and in the absence of an eastern league, the Grays returned to independent play. In 1930 Williams and Chet Brewer hooked up in a historic pitching duel under the Kansas City Monarchs' portable lighting system, with Joe fanning twenty-seven batters in the twelve-inning game while allowing only one hit in a 1-0 victory. At the end of the season the Grays defeated Williams's old team, the New York Lincoln Giants, in a play-off for the Eastern championship. In 1931 the Grays fielded one of the greatest teams in the history of the Negro Leagues. As an aging veteran, Williams paired with the youthful JOSH GIBSON to form an exceptional battery.

Following his retirement from baseball, Williams worked as a bartender in Harlem. In 1950 he was honored with a special day at the Polo Grounds in ceremonies before a game between the New York Cubans and Indianapolis Clowns. Less than a year later, in 1951, he died of a brain hemorrhage in New York City. In a 1952 poll conducted by the *Pittsburgh Courier,* Smokey Joe was chosen the greatest pitcher in the history of black baseball, winning over SATCHEL PAIGE by one vote. In 1999 he was elected to the National Baseball Hall of Fame in Cooperstown, New York.

Bibliography

Holway, John. *Black Ball Stars: Negro League Pioneers* (1988).

Peterson, Robert. *Only the Ball Was White* (1970).

Riley, James A. *The Biographical Encyclopedia of the Negro Baseball Leagues* (1994).

James A. Riley

Williams, Spencer, Jr.

1893–1969

American television and movie director, actor, and writer, best known for his role on the *Amos 'n' Andy* television show.

Born in Vidalia, Louisiana, Spencer Williams Jr. attended the University of Minnesota, dropping out to join the Army. Returning South after his 1923 discharge, he got his start in movies by writing for a series of short black films based on stories by Octavus Roy Cohen. These films were made by an affiliate of Paramount Pictures, and Williams soon moved to an office on Paramount's lot in Hollywood.

A talented actor, he appeared in some of the first African American talking movies of the 1920s, including *The Lady Fare, Oft in the Silly Night,* and *Music Has Charms.* His work as a producer included silent films such as *Hot Biscuits* (1929) and the earliest black Westerns, *Bronze Buckaroo* (1938) and *Harlem Rides the Range* (1939). Films that Williams wrote, directed, and starred in range from the comedy *Juke Joint* (1947) to the allegorical *The Blood of Jesus* (1941).

In 1951 Williams accepted the role for which he is most famous, Andy Brown on the television version of AMOS 'N' ANDY. The show used exaggeration and stereotypes as a comic motif, but, airing in a changing and turbulent political climate, it was denounced by the NATIONAL ASSOCIATION FOR THE ADVANCEMENT OF COLORED PEOPLE. Suffering from lack of support, the show lasted three years. After its cancellation Williams supported himself on a veteran's pension and social security, until his death from a kidney disorder in 1969.

See also Film, Blacks in American; Television and African Americans.

Williams, Vanessa L.

1963–

African American singer and actress and the first black woman to be crowned Miss America.

Vanessa Williams has enjoyed a successful and diverse career as a singer and actress. Since the release of her debut album

in 1988, she has produced several albums and won lead roles in stage and motion picture productions, including the critically acclaimed movie *Soul Food* in 1997.

Williams was born in Tarrytown, New York, and grew up in predominantly white Millwood. Encouraged by her parents, both music teachers, she learned to play the piano, French horn, and violin, and pursued intensive dance training. While in high school she starred in plays and musicals, and received numerous scholastic and theatrical awards.

Aspiring to become a stage actress, in 1981 she enrolled at Syracuse University as a musical theater major. Prompted by a talent scout, she entered and won the Miss Syracuse beauty pageant, a victory that propelled her to the 1983 Miss America pageant, where she made history as the first black woman ever to be crowned Miss America. While some black leaders attributed Williams's victory to her light skin and middle-class background, others compared her breakthrough to that of JACKIE ROBINSON, who in 1947 became the first black since the 1890s to play major league baseball.

In July 1984 Williams again made history—this time as the first woman forced to resign her Miss America title—after *Penthouse* magazine published explicit photos of her taken when she was nineteen. For many observers, Williams's predicament revealed the tension between the pageant's moral code and its business of judging scantily dressed women. Prominent feminists, such as Gloria Steinem and Susan Brownmiller, rallied to her defense, as did black leaders JESSE JACKSON and BENJAMIN HOOKS.

Although Williams lost her crown and a $900,000 advertising contract with the Gillette Company, the setback only steeled her resolve. In 1987 she launched a singing career with Mercury Records. Her debut album, *The Right Stuff,* released in 1988, received three Grammy Award nominations and the Best New Female Artist Award from the NATIONAL ASSOCIATION FOR THE ADVANCEMENT OF COLORED PEOPLE (NAACP). Her second album, *The Comfort Zone* (1991), which featured hit singles "Save the Best for Last" and "Work to Do," sold more than two million copies. In 1994 Williams won rave reviews for her lead role in the Broadway musical *Kiss of the Spider Woman,* and she performed the song "Colors of the Wind" on the Academy Award–winning soundtrack to the Disney film *Pocahontas.* She later performed in the Broadway revival of the Steven Sondheim musical *Into the Woods* (2002).

Williams has appeared in numerous television shows and Hollywood films, including the 1996 action film *Eraser* with Arnold Schwarzenegger and the 2000 remake of *Shaft.* She also appears in several television commercials, including a popular series of advertisements for Radio Shack featuring former football star Howie Long and actor Ving Rhames. Williams, who is married to professional basketball player Rick Fox, has four daughters.

See also Cinema, African Americans in; Music, African American.

Roanne Edwards

Williamson, Johnny Lee ("Sonny Boy")

1914–1948

American musician, revered for transforming the blues harmonica from a novelty instrument to an integral component of Chicago-style blues.

Johnny Lee Williamson was born in Jackson, Tennessee. He taught himself to play the harmonica as a child. In his teens he left home and traveled, hobo-style, throughout the South with mandolin player Yank Rachel and guitarist Sleepy John Estes. He moved to CHICAGO in 1937 and quickly became one of the city's most popular bluesmen, recording such hits as "Good Morning Little School Girl" and "Sugar Man Blues."

Williamson's imaginative style and stunning virtuosity brought the harmonica to the forefront of BLUES and have influenced virtually every major blues harmonicist after him. Williamson pioneered numerous playing techniques which are now considered standard. Among them are manipulating the sound of the harmonica by cupping the hands; and "crossed key" playing, where one tunes the harmonica a fourth below the key of the song. This allows the musician to play in the right key by inhaling rather than exhaling, affording him a greater ability to "bend" the notes.

Williamson was known for his distinctive "mumbling" singing style. One sign of his renown, is that harmonicist Aleck "Rice" Miller began recording under the name Sonny Boy Williamson, and came to be known as Sonny Boy #2.

Williamson was murdered on the steps of his home at the height of his popularity. In 1980 he was inducted into the Blues Foundation's Hall of Fame.

See also Music, African American.

Wills, Harry

1889–1958

African American boxer.

Harry Wills was born in NEW ORLEANS, LOUISIANA. He was known as the Brown Panther and began his BOXING career in 1911. Discrimination forced him to fight in PANAMA and CUBA for several years. He returned to the United States in 1920 and won the "colored" heavyweight title. Boxing promoter George Lewis "Tex" Richard then booked Wills to fight the white heavyweight champion Jack Dempsey in 1922. Richard later squelched the deal, claiming pressure from politicians, thus depriving the highly qualified Wills of a shot at the title. Wills retired in 1932 with an official record of ninety-four wins and eight losses. He died in NEW YORK CITY in 1958.

See also Sports and African Americans.

Wilmington Riot of 1898

White-supremacist campaign of violence and murder directed at black political officials in Wilmington, North Carolina.

In 1898, Wilmington, with a population of approximately 20,000, was the major city in the eastern region of North Carolina. It was one of the most integrated cities of the South, with blacks and whites living in each of the five wards. African Americans constituted a majority of the city's residents and successfully competed with whites for jobs. A significant number of blacks were successful businessmen and professionals, and many also held important municipal positions such as police chief, deputy sheriff, and federal collector of customs. Wilmington was part of the second Congressional District, often called the "Black Second" on account of its large number of black political officials.

Part of what had allowed black Republicans to assume important political posts was their alliance with Populists. These two parties controlled the local government until 1898 and, to ensure black representation, had passed a resolution in 1897 to appoint African Americans to five of the ten alderman positions. Blacks were approaching a level of political and social equality that many whites found unacceptable. As a result, white Democrats, determined to oust the black officials from office, began campaigning well before the 1898 election. They claimed that the presence of blacks in the local government "emboldens bad Negroes to display their evil, impudent, and mean natures." White Democrats misrepresented black speakers by exaggerating their arguments and threatened to kill them if they did not withdraw from the election. Wilmington's white leaders issued a "Declaration of White Independence" calling for the expulsion of black politicians and businessmen and organized a "secret nine" committee to facilitate this task.

As part of their attack on black Republicans, white Democrats printed and distributed 300,000 copies of an article that had been written by Alex Manly, editor of the *Wilmington Record,* who was of mixed African descent, in August of 1898. It read, "Our experience among poor white people in the country teaches us that the women of that race are not any more particular in the matter of clandestine meetings with colored men, than are the white men with the colored women." This assertion against white womanhood fueled anger within the white community and emboldened them to vote black officials out of office. As a result, the white Democrats swept the 1898 elections.

On the morning of November 10, the day after the election, a group of approximately 500 men who had been summoned by the white Democrats armed themselves with firearms, formed a mob, and marched into Brooklyn, a predominantly black section of town. They burned down the office of Alex Manly, who had reportedly left town eleven days earlier, and local Africans Americans began to fear that the mob would turn on them next. Upon receiving news of what had happened, African American officials resigned and many black employees at the local cotton compress left work to find and defend their families. The mob disbanded and headed home in small groups.

One of these groups of white men encountered a group of armed black men at the intersection of Fourth and Harnett Streets and advised them to return to their homes. The group of blacks crossed the street and refused to move any further. A shot was fired and one of the white mob, William Mayo, was injured. The two groups opened fire at each other and a running shootout ensued. Whites quickly received notice of the incident and flooded Wilmington's black neighborhoods where they indiscriminately shot at blacks. Whites not participating in the riot sought refuge in churches and schools while blacks fled to the forest to save their lives.

The governor sent in the state militia to aid whites in disarming the blacks, who were regarded by both as the antagonists. Up-to-the-minute telegraph coverage was wired across the country. By 3:00 p.m., gunfire ceased. It is estimated that seven to thirty blacks were killed. The few remaining blacks who ventured into the open to return home were stopped and searched by white soldiers and pedestrians. In the days following the riot, there was an exodus of large numbers of blacks and a small part of the white community out of Wilmington. The white Democrats quickly disenfranchised the remaining black community by instituting literacy tests at the polls. By the turn of the century, the town had a white majority.

See also Democratic Party; Race Riots in the United States; Republican Party.

Aaron Myers

Wilson, August

1945–

American playwright and poet, two-time winner of the Pulitzer Prize for drama.

August Wilson was born Frederick August Kittel in a poor, mixed-race neighborhood of PITTSBURGH, PENNSYLVANIA known as the Hill. His father, a white German baker, was rarely around; his mother did cleaning jobs and received welfare payments to support her six children. When Wilson was a young teenager, his mother remarried and the family moved to a mostly white neighborhood. Wilson's encounters with racism in his new home were more direct, including a pivotal incident in which a teacher wrongly accused him of plagiarizing a paper.

In 1960 Wilson dropped out of school but continued his education in the libraries of Pittsburgh, where he read black writers such as RICHARD WRIGHT and RALPH ELLISON. He received another sort of education in the barbershops, cafés, and on the street corners that were frequented by a wide range of blacks. In 1965 Wilson began to write poetry. He was heavily influenced by the lyricism of Welsh poet Dylan Thomas and, later, by the BLACK NATIONALISM of African American poet and playwright AMIRI BARAKA. Baraka and other activists of the late 1960s argued that blacks, especially black artists, needed to be more race-conscious. Wilson agreed and spent many of the following years bringing life to black history and culture.

In 1968, with little previous experience in the theater, Wilson and a friend founded the Black Horizon Theatre Company in his old neighborhood, the Hill. The company featured minor plays by and about blacks. Around this time, he also discovered and immersed himself in the BLUES. The genre's pained, harmonic realism inspired many of his later plays. In a culminating act of symbolism, he rejected the name of his white father and took his mother's maiden name, Wilson, in recognition of her black heritage.

Wilson still saw himself as a poet, but in the early 1970s he began writing plays. In 1977 he wrote *Black Bart and the Sacred Hills,* a musical satire about an outlaw of the Old West, which was produced four years later in St. Paul, Minnesota. He finished two more plays (one of which, *Jitney,* was produced regionally) before Lloyd Richards, dean of the Yale Drama School, noticed his play *Ma Rainey's Black Bottom* in 1982.

Set in Chicago, Illinois, in the 1920s, *Ma Rainey* presents a fictional day in the real life of blues legend GERTRUDE "MA" RAINEY. Using realistic dialogue, the play depicts black musicians being exploited by white record companies and directing their rage at other blacks instead of their white oppressors. Richards produced the play first at the Yale Repertory Theatre, then on Broadway, establishing a pattern that he and Wilson, working collaboratively, used for Wilson's future plays. Although a few reviewers criticized *Ma Rainey* for overemphasizing politics, others praised it for presenting a poignant account of the effects of racism.

Shortly after writing *Ma Rainey,* Wilson wrote *Fences,* which focuses on the frustrations and responsibilities of a former baseball player in the NEGRO LEAGUES, now a garbage man, who was barred from playing in the major leagues. *Fences* won the 1987 Pulitzer Prize for drama, strengthening Wilson's reputation for deft presentation of the consequences of racism. His next play, *Joe Turner's Come and Gone* (1986), further distinguished Wilson by debuting on Broadway while *Fences* was still running there. Set in a Pittsburgh boardinghouse in 1911, *Joe Turner* chronicles the life of a black freedman who came north to find his wife, who fled while he was enslaved. Mystical and metaphorical, the play explores assimilation by African Americans into American society and is at once bitter and optimistic.

The Piano Lesson, immensely popular with both critics and audiences, followed in 1987. Set in 1936, its main characters are descendants of a slave family whose father and grandmother were traded for a piano. The grieving grandfather carved likenesses of his wife and son in the piano, which is now in the family's possession. The family is divided between those who want to sell the piano to buy the land where their ancestors were slaves and those who revere the piano as an heirloom. *The Piano Lesson* won both a Pulitzer Prize and a Tony Award for best play.

In 1990 Wilson wrote *Two Trains Running,* a portrayal of friendships and conflicts during the sweeping changes of the late 1960s. In 1995 he wrote *Seven Guitars,* a portrayal of re-

After more than two decades as a playwright, August Wilson made his acting debut in 2003 performing his autobiographical monologue "How I Learned What I Learned." *Associated Press*

lationships among a group of musicians set in Pittsburgh in 1948. Wilson declared that he would write a drama about black American life in each decade of the twentieth century. The eighth work in the series was *King Hedley II* (1999), about the difficulties faced by a former convict returning to society during the 1980s. *Gem of the Ocean* (2003) tells the story of a Hill District resident who, convinced he has committed a mortal sin, seeks spiritual cleansing from Aunt Ester, a local icon celebrating her 287th birthday. In addition to plays, Wilson has also published two books about African American theater, *The Ground on Which I Stand: Dramatic Contexts* (2001) and *Cultivating the Ground on Which We Stand* (2003).

See also Literature, African American; Poetry, Black, in English.

Wilson, Carlos Guillermo

1941–

Afro-Panamanian novelist, poet, and scholar best known for his portrayals of West Indians in Panama.

"Cubena," the pen name of Carlos Guilllermo Wilson, is a Hispanicized version of *Kwabena*, which means "Tuesday" in the Asante culture of Ghana. Wilson lived through an era marked by profound changes and racial awareness for thousands of West Indian laborers employed in the excavation, construction, and administration of the Panama Canal.

Wilson's grandparents migrated to Panama from the West Indies for the construction of the waterway. Adopted and raised by James Duglin from Barbados and Lena MacZeno from Jamaica, he was born and spent his childhood and most of his adolescence in Panama City, where he had extensive contact with West Indians and developed an intimate understanding of their culture. His poetry, short stories, and novels reflect his knowledge of West Indians and their descendants in Panama.

In 1959 Wilson relocated to the United States and lived in Mississippi. In 1964 he moved to Los Angeles, California, where he received his first master's degree from UCLA in 1970, and a doctoral degree in Latin American literature from the same institution in 1975. He also holds a master's in urban education (1982) and a master's in counseling (1983) from Loyola Marymount University in Los Angeles. He has been a professor of Spanish at San Diego State University, California, since 1992.

Wilson launched a literary career in 1977 with a collection of twelve short stories, *Cuentos del negro Cubena*. The stories emphasize the day-to-day life and experiences of discrimination and hardship that blacks endured in Panama. In 1977 he also published a volume of poems, *Pensamiento del negro Cubena: Pensamiento afro-panameño*, which explores such subjects as slavery, love, racial consciousness, and sociopolitical protest. Both books have been translated to English.

Wilson's novels include *Chombo* (1981), which examines the lives of West Indians and their descendants during and after the construction of the Panama Canal, and *Los nietos de Felicidad Dolores* (1991), which is rooted in the experiences of people of African descent in the Americas from slavery to the 1990s. *Los mosquitos de orixá Changó*, which contains short fiction and poems, was published in 2000.

In addition to his literary work, Wilson has contributed numerous critical articles to scholarly journals. He is a founder of the *Afro-Hispanic Review* and a contributing editor to the *Publication of the Afro-Latin/America Research Association* (PALARA). His own work has been the subject of many critical studies. He has received several honors, including an Excellence in Literature award from the African American Caribbean Culture Arts Commission in 1994, and induction as a Grand Caballero of the National Order of Vasco Nunez de Balboa by the Republic of Panama in 2002.

LaVerne M. Seales-Soley

Wilson, Cassandra

1955–

African American jazz vocalist and songwriter, acclaimed for her smoky contralto and musical versatility.

Hailed by *Time* magazine as "the most accomplished jazz vocalist of her generation," Cassandra Wilson has enjoyed a success and visibility usually reserved for pop singers. Her singing is eclectic and innovative: she performs both original and standard songs, drawing upon many musical influences, including JAZZ, BLUES, folk, HIP-HOP, FUNK, and rock. According to music critic Gene Santoro, "she is the direct descendent of BILLIE HOLIDAY and DINAH WASHINGTON, with their bluesy pop tunes and wicked jazz feel for the unexpected twist, and can rivet audiences with her languid, curling voice while lighting a room with simmering sexual energy."

Wilson grew up in Jackson, Mississippi, where her mother was an elementary school teacher and her father was a jazz bassist. Her father nurtured her passion for music, and as a child she studied classical piano and taught herself to play the acoustic guitar. Her mother and grandmother were her role models: while Wilson admired her mother's strength of character, she found inspiration in her grandmother's religiosity and powerful, uninhibited singing in church. "I come from a long line of women who, against all odds, did what they wanted to do," she told *Ms.* magazine in 1997.

After graduating with a degree in communications from Jackson State University, Wilson worked at a NEW ORLEANS television station. She also performed as a singer in local nightclubs. Set on a musical career, in 1982 she moved to NEW YORK CITY. There she met avant-garde saxophonist Steve Coleman, who introduced her to M-BASE, a Brooklyn-based collective of musicians who fused rock, hip-hop, funk, and jazz. Wilson became the group's main vocalist, and in collaboration with Coleman and M-BASE musician Jean-Paul Bourelly, she recorded her first album, *Point of View* (1985), on the German label JMT. Subsequent albums won her comparisons to jazz vocalist BETTY CARTER, and in 1989 her *Blue Skies* became the top-selling jazz album of the year.

In 1993 Wilson took a new direction when she signed with Blue Note Records, one of the world's greatest jazz labels. "Once a daredevil of the avant-garde, Wilson is drawing on the very fundamentals of black-music expression, which is in itself a classic avant-garde gesture," said *New York* magazine writer Chris Norris. Collaborating with producer Craig Street, Wilson recorded the widely acclaimed top-selling album *Blue Light 'Til Dawn*, which featured fresh renditions of vintage blues and folk songs as well as songs written by Wilson.

Wilson's album *New Moon Daughter* (1996), for which she won a Grammy Award for best vocal jazz performance, was praised by the *New York Times* as one of the best albums of the decade. Covering songs from such disparate artists as U2, the Monkees, Hoagy Carmichael, and SON HOUSE, the album appealed to a wide audience, from jazz aficionados to mainstream listeners, and propelled Wilson into the limelight as the jazz diva of the 1990s. She has since recorded *Rendezvous* (1997), with jazz pianist Jacky Terrasson, and is the featured vocalist on *Blood on the Fields* (1997), an epic oratorio about SLAVERY IN THE UNITED STATES, composed by WYNTON MARSALIS.

In 1999 Wilson continued to further her range with the release of *Traveling For Miles*, an album honoring MILES DAVIS. Wilson, who also produced the album, included five Davis tunes for which she wrote lyrics. In 2001 the singer returned to Mississippi to record *Belly of the Sun*, which included songs by Bob Dylan, Robbie Robertson, James Taylor, B. B. KING, and ROBERT JOHNSON in addition to several of Wilson's own compositions. *Glamoured* (2003) offered several Wilson originals as well as covers of songs by Willie Nelson, Sting, Dylan, MUDDY WATERS, and ABBEY LINCOLN.

Acknowledging criticism about her eclectic influences, Wilson has said: "It's still jazz. . . . I often ask people 'What do you think Charlie Parker would sound like if he was playing today? What would DUKE ELLINGTON be creating? And Miles?' . . . People often associate the blues with sadness, but it's beyond sadness: It's what you do with the sadness. It's the higher part of humanity that's able to look at the sadness and shape it in such a way that it's a giving force, to transmute it or transfigure it into something that's loving and compassionate."

Roanne Edwards

Wilson, Eric Arthur ("Dooley")

1894–1953

American jazz drummer popular in America and Europe, who also achieved renown as an actor.

Born in Tyler, Texas, Eric Arthur Wilson began playing bit parts in vaudeville while in his early teens. In 1910 he moved to NEW YORK to work as a musician, where he helped popularize RAGTIME. He formed a JAZZ quintet, the Red Devils, with whom he toured EUROPE from 1919 to 1934. Upon his return to the United States, Wilson worked on Broadway and in Hollywood, most notably as the pianist Sam in the motion picture *Casablanca* (1942). He also appeared in the all-black musicals *Night in New Orleans* (1942) and *Stormy Weather* (1943).

See also Film, Blacks in American; Music, African American.

Wilson, Fred

1954–

American sculptor, mixed media and installation artist.

Born in NEW YORK CITY to parents of mixed descent, Fred Wilson received a bachelor of fine arts degree from the State University of New York at Purchase in 1976. He then worked as an administrator in various New York City museums, including the Metropolitan Museum of Art and the Museum of Natural History. Between 1978 and 1980 he worked as an artist in East HARLEM, NEW YORK and was funded by the Comprehensive Employment Training Act (CETA).

Wilson began an association with the Just Above MidTown Gallery in 1981, a space known for its congeniality to African American artists. In 1987 Wilson was the director of the Longwood Art Gallery of the Bronx Council of the Arts, where he curated the show *Rooms with a View: The Struggle Between Culture and Content and the Context of Art.* The show employed three spaces in the gallery. One was appointed like a "turn of the century salon" museum space, another like a contemporary gallery, and a third like an ethnographic museum. The exhibition questioned issues of institutional space and history, challenging viewers to radically interrogate their conception of a museum and museums' relationship to African Americans.

In 1992 Wilson created the award-winning installation, "Mining the Museum," sponsored by the Museum for the Contemporary Arts in Baltimore. The installation used artifacts found at the Maryland Historical Society to explore the ways in which the Historical Society defined itself and Maryland's history by excluding the experience of African Americans in the state. Wilson juxtaposed seemingly unrelated objects to reinforce his point. For example, in a vitrine displaying nineteenth-century silver work from the state of Maryland, he included a set of slave shackles crafted at the same time.

Wilson's recent work has involved installations featuring racially stereotypical bric-a-brac, such as "Aunt Jemima" dolls, that raise questions about stereotypes and racial prejudice. In installations such as "Speaking in Tongues: A Look at the Language of Display" (1998) he subverted the differences in how museums display and label European and American art compared to art from Africa, Oceania, and Native America, using terms such as "fetish figures" to identify Western artifacts. In "Aftermath" (2003) his subject is war and its influence on art and material culture. "According to Wilson," wrote associate curator Alla Efimova of the Berkeley Art Museum and Pacific Film Archive, "the installation is intended to look like a ruin site or archaeological dig; it also evokes visions of a battlefield, and, certainly, Ground Zero."

Wilson has had solo exhibitions at the Indianapolis Museum of Art, the Seattle Art Museum, the Museum for Contemporary Art in Baltimore, and the Museum of Contemporary Art in Chicago, as well as a major retrospective, "Fred Wilson: Objects and Installations, 1979–2000." In 1994 Wilson represented the United Sates in the Fourth International Cairo Biennial in Egypt. He has also participated in numerous group shows across the country and around the world, including the 1996 show New Histories at the Insititute for Contemporary Art in BOSTON. In addition to the numerous awards and grants he has received in recognition of his work, Wilson has lectured at universities and art colleges across the United States.

See also Art, African American.

Wilson, Harriet E. Adams

1828?–1870?

Author of *Our Nig,* which is considered to be the first novel published by an African American woman, and the first to be published by an African American, in the United States.

Little is known about the life of Harriet E. Adams Wilson. The 1850 federal census lists a twenty-two-year-old "Black" woman named Harriet Adams living with the Samuel Boyles family in the town of Milford, New Hampshire, which suggests that she was born around 1828. In 1851, she married Thomas Wilson, a free man who passed as a fugitive slave from Virginia so he could lecture on the horrors of slavery. Shortly after the birth of their son, George Mason Wilson in May or June 1852, Thomas Wilson abandoned them. Harriet Wilson, who was unable to work because of the physical and emotional abuse inflicted by her employers, lost custody of her son. She began writing to earn enough money to reclaim him. He died five and one-half months after the book's Boston publication in 1859. Neither the dates nor the location of Wilson's death is known.

Our Nig; or, Sketches from the Life of a Free Black, in a Two-Story White House, North. Showing That Slavery's Shadows Fall Even There, is a largely autobiographical novel that explicitly compares the racist conditions suffered by a black indentured servant to slavery in the South. Using the slave narrative as a model, Wilson indicts northern treatment of blacks. Possibly because of its controversial stand, the book was published at the author's own expense and sold poorly.

Told mostly through the eyes of a young girl, the novel's protagonist, Alfrado, is a mulatto who is abandoned by her white mother after her black father dies. Left with a white family, she is severely mistreated by the mother and one of the daughters. Although the men of the family are absentmindedly fond of her, they are unable to protect her from the hunger, beatings, and scolding that she constantly endures. Misfortune continues into Alfrado's adulthood when the husband who she thought would save her, leaves her and her young child. Broken in body but not in spirit, the novel ends with Alfrado's expression of her contempt for a society that allowed her virtual slavery.

See also Literature, African American; Slave Narratives; Women Writers, Black, in the United States.

Robert Fay

Wilson, William Julius

1935–

One of the most influential sociologists in the twentieth century.

As a sociologist, William Julius Wilson has had an impact as wide outside the academy as within. His work has shaped the international discourse on the relationships among race, poverty, and the economy in the United States in the post-World War II era.

Wilson was born in Derry Township, Pennsylvania. He attended WILBERFORCE UNIVERSITY in Ohio, where he received his B.A. in 1958. After earning an M.A. from Bowling Green University in 1961 he was recruited to the doctoral program in sociology at Washington State University by a department chair who had committed himself to training minority sociologists. Wilson has commented that he was the beneficiary of AFFIRMATIVE ACTION before the concept was invented. He received his Ph.D. in 1966.

Wilson published *Power, Racism and Privilege: Race Relations in Theoretical and Sociohistorical Perspective* (1973) while he was a faculty member at the University of Massachusetts. Five years later he won national recognition with the publication of *The Declining Significance of Race: Blacks and Changing America Institutions* (1978) while he was a member of the faculty at the University of Chicago, where he served from 1972 until 1996. The book called attention to factors related to social class—such as lack of education—in the continuing struggle of impoverished African Americans after overt racial prejudice, though still clearly important, had eased somewhat for those with salable middle-class skills. Misread by many of his colleagues, who thought he was suggesting that racism had disappeared from U.S. society, Wilson was censured in 1978 by the Black Caucus of the American Sociological Association.

The Declining Significance of Race exhibited several characteristics that mark Wilson's subsequent scholarship. First, it underscored the importance of economic and macrostructural forces in understanding the position of African Americans. Second, it showed how the economy harmed low-income whites as well as blacks, as both competed for scarce resources. Wilson elaborated this argument in subsequent books in which he underscored the importance of deindustrialization, the movement of manufacturing industries out of U.S. cities—indeed out of the country—in reducing opportunities for the uneducated and unskilled. He argued for "race neutral" policies, which sought to overcome backlash and garner political support for programs that would primarily help African Americans.

In *The Truly Disadvantaged* (1987) Wilson described the plight of poor African Americans and the consequences of social isolation they faced when blacks with greater opportunities moved out of the inner city. That book also introduced and explicated the concept of "underclass" to the educated public. *When Work Disappears: The World of the New Urban Poor* (1996) carried these themes further. Exploring the noneconomic

as well as the economic costs of deindustrialization, Wilson pointed the way to policy initiatives that could help all of the disadvantaged. In these works, Wilson opened the possibility of discourse on controversial matters that had been essentially silenced since the 1960s, when liberal intellectuals objected to the findings of the Moynihan Report (1965), which associated black poverty with female-headed households. Sometimes incorrectly characterized as a conservative, Wilson is actually a social democrat who favors government involvement in the economy through industrial policy, enforcement of antidiscrimination legislation, and affirmative action.

Wilson has received many honors and awards. He was chairman of the sociology department at the University of Chicago from 1984 to 1987, president of the American Sociological Association in 1989, and a MacArthur Foundation "genius award" prize fellow. He is the recipient of twenty-seven honorary degrees. Wilson has been a policy adviser to both President Bill Clinton and Vice President Al Gore, and in 1999 Clinton awarded him a National Medal of Science. In 1996 Wilson joined Harvard University as a professor of social policy at the John F. Kennedy School of Government. He was appointed Lewis P. and Linda L. Geyser University Professor in 1998. He continues to conduct research on welfare reform in the United States.

Richard Taub

Windhoek, Namibia

Capital of Namibia.

Windhoek, with a population of 216,000 (2002 estimate), is by far the largest town in NAMIBIA, as well as being the capital and meeting point of Namibia's major road and rail networks. Situated between several mountain ranges in the center of the country, it was founded in 1840 by the NAMA leader Jonker Afrikander, who initially named it Winterhoek, after a South African region where he once had a farm. Only later did it become known as Windhoek, which means "windy corner."

The HERERO people likely inhabited the area for some time, attracted to the nearby natural hot springs. The arrival of Afrikander and other Nama settlers occurred during a time of increasing conflict between the two groups, as the Herero moved south in search of better pastures and the Nama, led by Afrikander, pushed them back north. The Nama settled in the valley and in 1842 the German Rhenish Mission Society established a mission. But the wars between the Nama and Herero continued until 1885, when GERMANY intervened. Five years later the Germans built a fort at the abandoned mission site. They also built churches, schools, seven hotels, three breweries, and several "castles" overlooking the main street, Kaiserstrasse. Although the completion of a railway in 1904 linked Windhoek to the coast, ongoing Herero and Nama rebellions discouraged many Germans from settling there.

In 1915 South Africa took control of the city and five years later set up a municipal government. Thereafter, the population increased rapidly, from 716 in 1920 to 10,000 in 1949, and to 36,000 in 1959. White residents, numbering around 20,000, lived in exclusive suburbs, while approximately 16,000 black and Coloured (of mixed racial descent) residents lived in the shantytown suburb called the Old Location, and worked as menial laborers and domestic servants. In 1959 Namibia's nationalist struggle began in the streets of Windhoek, when Africans protested their forced removal from the Old Location to a desolate new suburb known as Katutura, or "the place where no one lives."

Just prior to independence in 1990, Windhoek experienced another great building boom, as job-seeking Namibians as well as foreign embassies, companies, and nongovernmental agencies all moved to the city. Today there is a mixture of old German and modern architecture in the city center, which houses most of the white population. Light manufacturing, mainly food and wool processing, is located in the suburbs.

See also Colonial Rule; Nationalism in Africa.

Eric Young

Winfrey, Oprah Gail

1954–

African American talk show host, Academy Award–nominated actor and producer, whose syndicated television show, *The Oprah Winfrey Show*, is possibly the most popular talk show ever.

Oprah Winfrey was born on a farm in Kosciusko, Mississippi. Her paternal grandmother raised her until she was six years old, when she moved to Milwaukee, Wisconsin, to live with her mother, Vernita Lee. Though Winfrey did well in school, she was allegedly sexually abused by male relatives and became increasingly troubled as a teenager. Her mother, a maid who was busy raising two other children, eventually sent Winfrey to live with her disciplinarian father, a barber and businessman in Nashville, Tennessee. Winfrey flowered under Vernon Winfrey's strict supervision, excelling academically and as a public speaker. At sixteen, she won a partial scholarship to Tennessee State University in a public speaking contest sponsored by the Elks Club.

As a freshman at Tennessee State University, Winfrey worked briefly as a radio newscaster before victories in two local beauty pageants helped land her a news anchor position at WTVF-TV in Nashville, which made her the city's first African American woman news anchor. In 1976, only a few months away from earning her bachelor's degree at Tennessee State University, Winfrey accepted a job as a reporter and evening news co-anchor at WJZ-TV in Baltimore, Maryland. She did not succeed in that position, but the station management realized that Winfrey, who had no formal journalistic training, was better suited to cohosting WJZ's morning talk show, *People Are Talking*. Winfrey helped turn the show into a ratings success with her personable interviewing style and charismatic presence.

After eight years as the cohost of *People Are Talking*, Winfrey was offered a job as the host of *A.M. Chicago*, a Chicago, Illinois, talk show that aired opposite Phil Donahue's popular morning show and lagged behind it in the ratings. In one month Winfrey's ratings equaled Donahue's, and in three surpassed them. Donahue acknowledged Winfrey's ratings supremacy by moving his show to New York in 1985. In 1985 *A.M. Chicago* was renamed *The Oprah Winfrey Show*, and it was syndicated in 1986. It eventually became the highest-rated talk show in television history. By 1997, approximately 15 to 20 million viewers watched it daily in the United States, and it was seen in over 132 countries. The show has received twenty-five Emmy Awards, six of them for best host. In 1996 *Time* magazine named Winfrey one of the twenty-five most influential people in the world.

Also a talented actor, Winfrey earned Golden Globe and Academy Award nominations in 1985 for her portrayal of Sofia in the film *The Color Purple*, based on Alice Walker's book of the same title. In 1986 Winfrey founded HARPO Productions, becoming only the third woman to own her own television and film studios. Based in Chicago, HARPO (Oprah spelled backwards) owns and produces *The Oprah Winfrey Show* as well as dramatic miniseries, such as *The Women of Brewster Place* (1988), based on the book by GLORIA NAYLOR, and *The Wedding* (1998), based on the book by DOROTHY WEST. In addition to supporting African American literature through her television films, Winfrey has brought new readers to writers such as TONI MORRISON through her on-air book club. Indeed, her influence on literacy has been so positive that she was honored in 1999 with a Fiftieth Anniversary Medal from the National Book Foundation and an honorary National Book Award, and in 2002 with an award from the Association of American Publishers.

Among her many other awards are a Lifetime Achievement Award from the Academy of Television Arts and Sciences (1998), a Bob Hope Humanitarian Award (2002), and induction into the National Women's Hall of Fame and *Broadcasting and Cable* magazine's Hall of Fame.

A political activist as well as an entertainer, Winfrey testified before the United States Senate Judiciary Committee, describing the sexual abuse she suffered as a child. She worked for the passage of the National Child Protection Act in 1991, which provides for the establishment of a nationwide database of convicted child abusers. In December 1993 President Bill Clinton signed "Oprah's Bill" into law. Her many philanthropic ventures include donations of time and money to efforts to protect children and to the establishment of educational scholarships.

See also Television and African Americans.

Robert Fay

Wings Over Jordan

African American choir and radio program popular in the 1930s and 1940s for its performances of traditional black choral music.

The choir Wings Over Jordan debuted in 1937 in Cleveland, Ohio, on a radio show called "The National Negro Hour." The group was formed by the Reverend Glenn T. Settle of the Gethsemane Church. Airing every Sunday morning on Cleveland's WGAR station, the choir swiftly gained popularity and, in 1939, attracted a national audience when Wings Over Jordan—now a national radio program—was broadcast weekly on Sunday mornings on the CBS national radio network.

During the next fifteen years, Wings Over Jordan gained fame throughout the United States and abroad. Under the direction of various conductors, including Thomas King, the choir toured nationally and recorded on major labels. In 1945, it toured with the United Services Organization throughout Europe, performing powerfully rendered spirituals and gospel songs for military personnel during World War II.

Wings Over Jordan paved the way for other black college choirs to appear on radio, and by 1950 the ABC network hosted a regular Sunday morning program called "Negro College Choirs." After concluding its own radio program in 1949, Wings Over Jordan continued to perform publicly until 1965.

See also Music, African American; Radio and African Americans; Spirituals, African American.

Bibliography

Southern, Eileen. *The Music of Black Americans.* 3rd ed. W. W. Norton & Company, 1997.

Roanne Edwards

Wobé

Ethnic group of West Africa; also known as Ouobe and Wé.

The Wobé primarily inhabit western Côte d'Ivoire. Others live in northeastern Liberia. They speak a Niger-Congo language in the Kru group and are closely related to the Guéré people. Approximately 180,000 people consider themselves Wobé.

See also Ethnicity and Identity in Africa: An Interpretation; Languages, African: An Overview.

Wolfe, George Costello

1954–

African American director and playwright.

George C. Wolfe was born and raised in the racially segregated city of Frankfort, Kentucky, in the 1950s. There he attended a private primary school where his mother was principal. During his high school years, he developed an interest in the theater. He attended college in Frankfort at the historically black Kentucky State University, and then at Pomona College in Claremont, California, where he majored in theater arts. Wolfe received his bachelor's degree in 1976. He moved to New York City in 1979, where he earned a master's degree in dramatic writing and musical theater from New York University in 1983.

Wolfe began his career as a playwright in New York City. Although one of his first works, the musical *Paradise!* (1985), was panned by critics, Wolfe soon achieved success. The next production of his work, 1986's *The Colored Museum*, won him critical acclaim. *The Colored Museum* was a satirical look at African American stereotypes, poking fun at everything from hairstyles to *A Raisin in the Sun*, a play by Lorraine Hansberry about a poor black family living in a ghetto.

Wolfe did not restrict himself to comedy. In 1992 he wrote and directed the theatrical hit, *Jelly's Last Jam*, a musical about Jazz pianist and composer Ferdinand Joseph ("Jelly Roll") Morton that dealt with themes of self-hatred and misogyny. In 1990 Wolfe directed *Spunk: Three Tales,* his well-received theatrical adaptation of three stories by author and folklorist Zora Neale Hurston.

Wolfe is considered one of the stage's finest directors. He directed the two-part Tony Kushner play *Angels in America,* and in 1994 won a Tony Award for his direction of Part One. In addition, Wolfe directed two one-woman shows by actor Anna Deveare Smith: *Fires in the Mirror* (1991), about a racial incident in the Crown Heights section of Brooklyn, New York, and *Twilight: Los Angeles 1992,* about the aftermath of the Rodney King incident in which riots broke out after a jury failed to convict Los Angeles police of brutality against King, an African American, despite a videotape of the beating. Wolfe also cowrote and directed one of the most popular musicals of the 1990s, *Bring in 'Da Noise, Bring in 'Da Funk,* for which he earned a 1996 Tony Award for directing.

In 1993 Wolfe accepted the position of producer of the New York Shakespeare Festival and Joseph Papp Public Theater, an important venue for experimental theater, emphasizing quality rather than box-office receipts. Wolfe succeeded Jo-Anne Akalaitis, whose tenure as producer was troubled by financial problems. Wolfe turned the organization around financially, increasing the theater's endowment to approximately $40 million by the late 1990s. He also revitalized the Public Theater artistically. Nevertheless, critics claimed that Wolfe used the Public Theater as a method for underwriting his own productions. They pointed to *Bring in 'Da Noise, Bring in 'Da Funk,* which went from the Public Theater to Broadway. Wolfe's many supporters countered that he was continuing Papp's legacy of bringing more support to multicultural theater.

Though he experienced health problems in 1997 Wolfe continued his artistic output. In 1998 he received a kidney transplant, for which his brother served as donor. That same year Wolfe directed a revival of the 1944 Leonard Bernstein musical *On the Town.* In 2000 Wolfe coauthored and directed *The Wild Party,* a musical based on writer Joseph Moncure March's 1920s poem about New York City in the jazz age. In 2003 he directed the musical *Radiant Baby,* based on the life of pop artist Keith Haring.

See also Los Angeles Riot of 1992.

Wolof

Ethnic group of Senegal, Gambia, and Mauritania.

The Wolof, numbering approximately four million people, are the largest ethnic group in SENEGAL and form a minority in THE GAMBIA and in MAURITANIA. The Wolof language is part of the Atlantic subgroup of the Niger-Congo family of languages. Though the Senegalese scholar Cheikh Anta Diop argues that the Wolof language bears a strong resemblance to ancient Egyptian and that the Wolof are descendants of the ancient Egyptians, oral traditions and linguistic evidence suggest that the people known as Wolof originated in the SENEGAL RIVER Valley area and gradually moved south into their present territory. The ancestors of the Wolof were dominated by the kingdoms of Ghana and MALI until the fourteenth century, when the Djolof kingdom asserted its independence.

It was in Djolof that the Wolof developed their characteristic social structure, focused on a small nobility, a large free peasant caste, and smaller artisan castes, including griots, metal workers, and leatherworkers. Slaves were also a part of Wolof society. Caste determined one's occupation and limited one's choice of spouse. Marriage between castes was strictly forbidden. Oral traditions include some mention of women rulers, and maternal descent was of comparable importance to the patrilineage (or extended family based on paternal descent). During this period Wolof farmers eked out a difficult living from growing MILLET and sorghum in the drought-ridden but fertile soils of present-day central and north-central Senegal. They also participated in the commercial networks that fed into the trans-Saharan trade. When European traders expanded their regional presence in the sixteenth century, Wolof traded gum arabic, ivory, gold, and slaves for a variety of European goods.

By the sixteenth century, five predominantly Wolof kingdoms had emerged, though they paid tribute to the Djolof state. These included Walo, Cayor, Baol, Sine, and Saloum. As the TRANSATLANTIC SLAVE TRADE became increasingly important in the seventeenth century, the balance of power in the region shifted from the interior states, like Djolof, toward coastal ones like Baol, Cayor, Sine, and Saloum. Their close proximity to French trading posts at GORÉE ISLAND and Saint-Louis gave the newer coastal kingdoms privileged access to French trade goods, especially gunpowder, muskets, and iron. Some Wolof women at Saint-Louis and Gorée, known as *signare*, married French traders and used their family connections to develop trade routes into the various Wolof states. With easy access to new strategic weapons, the coastal states freed themselves from Djolof dominance. It was during this period that the *tyeddo*, or warrior caste, became central to Wolof political life. ISLAM became the dominant religious tradition among the Wolof during this period, as well.

In the mid-nineteenth century, the French expanded their control into the interior of Senegal and conquered the Wolof kingdoms. Lat Dior, the ruler of Cayor, was the leader of Wolof resistance. His conversion to Islam and alliance with the Islamic leader, Ma Ba Diakhou, failed to prevent French expansion. As the French expanded their control, they encouraged the production of peanuts as a cash crop, and many Wolof migrated into eastern Senegal, where soils were more favorable for peanut production. Members of the Wolof elite, discredited by the colonial conquest, joined an Islamic brotherhood called the Mourides, which was led by an Islamic Sufi mystic named Amadou Bamba. Bamba's rapid success won him the enmity of the French, and he was exiled first to GABON and then to Mauritania. When he was allowed to return to Senegal, he encouraged people to work as a way to honor God. Leaders of this new religious movement became active in the production of peanuts, and encouraged peasants to grow the new cash crop as a way of honoring Allah and supporting the Mouride order. By the 1920s the Mourides dominated Senegalese peanut production and were sending colonies of settlers eastward to plant peanut fields on land that was previously occupied by FULANI herders. Other Wolof became active in the Senegalese division of the French army, the Tirailleurs Sénégalais, which played an important role in the conquest of FRENCH WEST AFRICA and Equatorial Africa. Still others took advantage of their close proximity to the major French ports for all of West Africa, DAKAR, and Saint-Louis, to receive a French education and enter the civil service.

Because of their close proximity to the French colonial centers of power, the Wolof became the most integrated into the French colonial system. As migrant laborers from other ethnic groups went to work in the cities and along the railroad lines, Wolof became the Senegalese lingua franca, facilitating communication among groups speaking different languages, and Wolof culture became the region's dominant culture. Wolof dominance of Senegal's economy and culture has increased since independence. Most Senegalese speak Wolof, though most cannot speak the official language of the country, which is French. Wolof music, food, clothing styles, and social styles have become the norm in postcolonial Senegal. The Wolof are the most urbanized Senegalese people and they dominate the country's cities, including Saint-Louis and Dakar. They are also a major presence in the capital of The Gambia, BANJUL. While the Wolof have dominated Senegalese social life, this power has not translated directly into the political arena. Senegal's first two presidents belonged to the SERER ethnic group. The Wolof, nonetheless, have exercised considerable political influence, particularly through the leaders of the Mouride Islamic brotherhood and from major power bases in the former kingdoms of Sine and Saloum. More than any other Senegalese group, the Wolof have developed a significant written literature in their own language, including several newspapers and political magazines. In recent years Wolof traders have become active in European and North American cities.

See also Egypt, Early Kingdom of; Ethnicity and Identity in Africa: An Interpretation; Ghana, Early Kingdom of; Gold Trade; Islam in Africa; Ivory Trade; Languages, African: An Overview; Sufism.

Robert Baum

Womanism

Term to encompass the variety of ways that African American women support each other and relate to the world.

The term *womanism* was coined by the African American writer ALICE WALKER in her 1983 book *In Search of Our Mothers' Gardens*. Walker defined a *womanist* as a black feminist who continues the legacy of "outrageous, audacious, courageous, and willful, responsible, in charge, serious" African American women—women who are agents for social change for the wholeness and liberation of black people, and, by extension, the rest of humanity. A womanist can be a lesbian, a heterosexual, or a bisexual woman. She celebrates and affirms African American women's culture and physical beauty. She loves herself.

Although the words *religion* or CHRISTIANITY do not appear in Walker's definition, the word *womanism* has religious as well as secular usage. Because Walker emphasizes African American women's love for the spiritual, black Christian women have used the womanist concept to articulate their participation in, and witness to, divine power and presence in the world. Womanist Christian thought and practices began to flourish in the mid-1980s as a way to challenge racist, sexist, and white feminists' religious discourse and practice, all of which ignored the black experience in church and society.

The secular use of the word *womanist* identifies a culturally specific form of women-centered politics and theory. It finds the term *feminist* inappropriate because of its identification with a predominantly white movement, and because "feminist" has often been used to label a woman as a lesbian, regardless of her actual sexual orientation. Because of this, some women have challenged the term *womanist* as homophobic.

See also Feminism in the United States.

Irene Monroe

Women and the Black Baptist Church

Significant role of women in black Baptist congregations in the late nineteenth and early twentieth centuries.

> Black women (and women whose grandmothers were black) are . . . the main pillars of those social settlements which we call churches; and they have with small doubt raised three-fourths of our church property.

Although W. E. B. DU BOIS refers to no specific denomination with these words, he aptly describes women in the black BAPTIST church. Today, as well as in 1918, women represent a preponderance of its membership, its financial strength, and its missionary force. Indeed, these three characteristics form the basis for understanding how black Baptist women, in the face of racial and gender discrimination, contributed to the advancement of the BLACK CHURCH and the black community during the nineteenth and early twentieth centuries.

Large Membership Segment

Baptist women constitute the largest group of black Christians in America. It is the very presence of women that explains the magnitude of the black Baptist church. Census data for the early twentieth century reveal that the black Baptist church formed a microcosm of the black population in America and included men and women from all social classes and geographic regions. In 1906 black Baptists made up 61.4 percent of all black churchgoers. With a membership of 2,261,607, the black Baptist church had more than four times the members of the second largest denominational body, the AFRICAN METHODIST EPISCOPAL CHURCH (AME), with its 494,777 members. By 1916 black Baptists constituted not only the largest black religious group but the third largest of all religious groups, black or white, in America; trailing only the Roman Catholic and the METHODIST EPISCOPAL CHURCHES, black Baptists numbered 2,938,579 that year. In 1936 black Baptists continued to constitute the third largest denomination regardless of race. Equally important, census data consistently have shown that black women make up more than 60 percent of black Baptist membership. From a numerical standpoint, then, the high proportion of female members underscores their vital presence in empowering the Baptist church.

Women's contributions to the church did not begin in the twentieth century but, rather, took root in the efforts of black Baptists to establish congregations independent of white control during the late eighteenth and early nineteenth centuries. Although little is recorded about the black women who participated in this early freedom movement, women certainly were members and financial supporters of those churches founded from the 1750s to 1810 in such places as Mecklenberg, Virginia; Savannah, Georgia; BOSTON, MASSACHUSETTS; and NEW YORK CITY. Mechal Sobel's 1988 study of African-Baptist CHRISTIANITY during the era of slavery notes instances of women being deaconesses, members of separate women's committees, delegates to associational meetings of both men and women, and active participants in revivals. Yet the autonomous polity of each Baptist church precluded a consistent participation by women. Ample evidence exists to indicate that there were gender proscriptions: women were categorically denied the right to preach; they were excluded from the business meetings of most black Baptist churches; and, in many instances, women could not sit beside male members during worship, organize into separate women's societies, or even pray publicly.

The black Baptist church grew tremendously in the years following the CIVIL WAR. With the abolition of slavery, black Baptist women and men expressed their newly won freedom by abandoning the white-controlled churches in which they had been forced to worship. Coming together in black-controlled churches, black Baptist women found a spiritual haven for individual communion with God and a public space for schooling, recreation, and organizational meetings. Indeed,

The Missionary Training Department of Spelman Seminary prepared graduates to provide moral instruction to black communities. The class of 1893, shown here, included such notable women as Emma De Lamotta, (front row, center), who was born a slave in 1836 and went on to lead the department until her death in 1903. *Courtesy Spelman College Archives, Atlanta, Georgia*

women, much more than men, attended church not only for Sunday worship but for a variety of activities that took place throughout the week. For many poor black women who worked in domestic service, SHARECROPPING, and other forms of menial employment, the church offered the only form of social and organizational life outside the family. In choirs, deaconess boards, and missionary societies, women with little income found personal dignity, developed leadership and organizational skills, and forged programs for their people's advancement. At the level of the individual church as well as at the level of the regional association of churches, commonly called conventions, the black Baptist church conflated its private, eschatological witness and its public, political stand, thus becoming a catalyst for the transmission of both spiritual and secular ideas to a broad spectrum of black people.

Convention Movement and the Role of Women

By means of statewide and other regional conventions, black Baptist churches allied their efforts, embarking on programs of racial self-help and self-determination. The ministerial-led movement to unite black Baptists into conventions was unique, for, unlike the structured network and hierarchy of other denominations, it emerged only because otherwise independent black Baptist churches voluntarily and freely worked together as race-conscious collectives. Beginning at the local and state

levels, the convention movement grew in momentum between the 1860s and 1890s and culminated with the formation of the National Baptist Convention (NBC) in 1895. However, the restricted participation of women in the ministerial-led conventions led Baptist women to form their own separate local and state organizations in the 1880s and 1890s and, in 1900, a national auxiliary of the NBC, which by 1903 boasted one million members.

State and national women's conventions offered greater opportunity for effective religious proselytism at home and abroad as well as an arena in which women freely discussed and implemented strategies for racial and gender empowerment. The minutes of black Baptist women's state conventions attest to the extensive and sacrificial efforts of overwhelmingly low-income women to meet the spiritual, social, and economic needs of black people, efforts that would have been impossible without their capacity to raise funds. These efforts included visiting homes and reading the Bible, donating clothes and food to the needy, counseling prisoners, caring for the sick, training women in household and parental responsibilities, establishing and supporting orphanages and old folks' homes, crusading for temperance, establishing day nurseries and kindergartens, publishing newspapers, instituting vocational training programs, and establishing and/or financing educational institutions.

At a time when Southern states had no public facilities at the high school or college level for black students, late-nine-

Students at the National Training School for Women and Girls were encouraged to regard cooking as a "profession." *Smithsonian Institution, Washington, D.C.*

teenth- and early-twentieth-century women's state conventions worked fervently for the higher education of black men and women. For this reason, black Baptist women's conventions often carried the title "educational" as part and parcel of their missionary identity, for example, the Baptist Women's Educational Convention of Kentucky, the Women's Baptist Educational and Missionary Convention of South Carolina, and the Woman's Baptist Missionary and Educational Association of Virginia. Unquestionably, the black church was the most important institution in the black community, and it was largely through the organized fund-raising of churchwomen that this claim came to be actualized. In the racist climate of segregation, disfranchisement, and LYNCHING, women's missionary and financial efforts were decisive factors in the black Baptist church's ability to rally the impoverished masses for the staggering task of building and sustaining self-help institutions.

Women's conventions, notwithstanding their auxiliary relationship to the ministerial-dominated conventions, generated their own distinct dynamism and assertiveness. Women's conventions controlled their own budgets and determined the allocation of funds, and they explicitly denied male participation in any role other than as honorary members. Black women found enormous satisfaction in accomplishing the goals of their conventions and in developing their own individual skills and abilities. In 1888, the president of the Kentucky Baptist group told a predominantly male Baptist audience that the women had learned to delegate authority, to raise points of order, and to transact business as well as men. In 1904, the president of Arkansas Baptist women credited her state association with building the self-confidence of ordinary women regarding their skills and abilities. She explicitly mentioned women's financial

contributions and informed black Baptist ministers: "From a financial standpoint we are prepared to prove that we have given thousands that you would not have, had it not been for the untiring and loyal women in the State." Emboldened by the successes of their separate conventions, black women also were cognizant of their crucial role in building the denomination as a whole.

Gender Proscriptions

The founding and growth of black Baptist women's societies during the 1880s and 1890s did not occur without gender conflict, however. Ironically, the black Baptist convention movement that united men and women in the struggle against racial inequality betrayed a masculine bias in its institutional structures and discourses. Tensions arose when male ministers expected women to be silent helpmates. Yet the rising prominence of black churchwomen and their growing demand for a separate organizational voice during the last two decades of the nineteenth century reflected a heightened gender consciousness on the part of women who were no longer content to operate merely within the boundaries of individual churches or silently within ministerial-led state conventions.

Throughout the 1880s and 1890s, black Baptist women challenged gender proscriptions that thwarted the full utilization of their talents. The debate over women's rights in Arkansas typified that in other states. Ministers argued that separate organizations under the control of women would elicit a desire to rule the men. Some Arkansas ministers contended that women's financial contributions would cease to be under the men's control, whereas others demanded that male officers preside over women's societies—if they were permitted to form. The women of Arkansas responded by stressing their critical importance as a missionary force, insisting that they could better accomplish the work of religiously training the world by uniting as a separate organization. The women claimed their right to be an independent voice in the church on the assumption that they were equally responsible, in proportion to their abilities, as men.

Finding Support in the Scriptures

Outstanding leaders such as Virginia W. Broughton of Tennessee and Mary V. Cook of Kentucky turned to the Bible to defend women's rights in the church and the larger society. Broughton, a schoolteacher and zealous missionary, published *Women's Work, as Gleaned from the Women of the Bible* (1904) in order to disclose biblical precedents for gender equality. Her feminist interpretation of the Bible shaped her understanding of women's roles in her own day, and the book summed up the ideas that had marked her public lectures, correspondence, and house-to-house visitations since the 1880s. Broughton led the women of her state in forming Bible bands for the study and interpretation of the Scriptures, and her gender consciousness united black Baptist women in other states as well, emboldening them to develop their own societies. Traveling throughout the urban and rural areas of Tennessee, Broughton was instrumental in organizing a statewide association of black Baptist women. She advocated training schools for mothers in order to better the home life of black people, and she ardently promoted higher education for women.

Mary Cook of Kentucky also appropriated biblical images to prove that God used women in every capacity. During the late 1880s, Cook, a professor at the black Baptist-owned State University at Louisville (later renamed Simmons University), was the most prominent woman in the ministerial-led convention movement that ultimately led to the founding of the NBC. She urged women to spread their influence in every cause, place, and institution. In newspaper articles and speeches she emphasized woman's suffrage as well as full equality for women in employment, education, social reform, and church work. In a speech given in 1887, Cook praised female teachers, journalists, linguists, and physicians, and she insisted that women must "come from all the professions, from the humble Christian to the expounder of His work; from the obedient citizen to the ruler of the land." Both Cook and Broughton noted male resistance to the formation of women's societies; for example, they claimed that ministers and laymen had locked the doors of their churches, refusing to accommodate women's societies. In her autobiography, *Twenty Years as a Missionary* (1907), Broughton even recalled potentially fatal confrontations and physical threats made against women.

Emerging National Identity

Although the black Baptist convention movement had served the critical role of uniting women and men in the struggle for racial self-determination, it had simultaneously created a separate, gender-based community that reflected and supported women's equality.

In 1900, at the annual meeting of the NBC held in Richmond, Virginia, Nannie Burroughs delivered a speech entitled "How the Sisters Are Hindered from Helping," based on the biblical text, "Ye entered not in yourselves, and them that were entering in ye hindered" (Luke 11:52). Burroughs expressed the discontent and burning zeal of black Baptist women to work unrestricted as a missionary force for the betterment of society. Burroughs's eloquence triumphed. In response to the motion of the influential NBC officer Lewis G. Jordan, and a second from Charles H. Parrish, the male-led convention approved the establishment of the Women's Convention (WC), Auxiliary to the NBC. It is interesting to note that Burroughs worked as Jordan's secretary at the time, and Parrish was married to the aforementioned Mary V. Cook of Kentucky.

By the close of the Richmond meeting, the women had elected the following officers: S. Willie Layten of Philadelphia, president; Sylvia C. J. Bryant of Atlanta, vice president at large; Nannie H. Burroughs of Washington, D.C., corresponding secretary; Virginia Broughton of Nashville, recording secretary; and Susie C. Foster of Montgomery, Alabama, treasurer. The minutes for 1900 listed twenty-six state vice presidents, including one each from Indian Territory, Oklahoma Territory, and Washington, D.C. The women described their mission as coming to the rescue of the world, and they adopted the motto "The World for Christ. Women Arise. He Calleth for Thee." The formation of the WC signaled not only a national identity for black Baptist women but also a black women's congress, so to speak, where women as delegates from local churches, district associations, and state conventions assembled annually as a national body to discuss and debate issues of common concern, disseminate information to broader female constituencies, and implement nationally supported programs.

In her first open letter to the black Baptist women of America, S. Willie Layten urged all existing societies to affiliate with the WC, to work closely with the state vice presidents, and to welcome the formation of new societies where none existed at the state and local level. Layten had a long familiarity with the organized work of black Baptists. Her youth was spent in Memphis, where she acquired her early education and probably her first knowledge of women's missionary activities. After living in California during the late 1880s and early 1890s, Layten moved to Philadelphia in 1894 and became active in religious work and secular social reform. During the first decade of the twentieth century, Layten was a member of the National Association of Colored Women (NACW) and was a leader in the National Urban League and the Association for the Protection of Colored Women.

Baptist Women as Missionaries

By the second decade of the twentieth century, WC programs reflected the influence of both Progressive-era reform and black urbanization. The changing circumstances of employment, housing, and social problems related to the massive migration of black people from the rural South to the urban North prompted the WC to adopt new methods of mission work. The Baptist women's national organization played an important mediating role in connecting local church and state activities throughout the nation with more sophisticated and changing reform trends. Their organizational networks at the state and national level facilitated a wide dissemination of ideas and expertise for utilization at the local level. Officers of the WC alluded to the educational role of their annual meetings when they referred to them as "institutes" and "schools of methods" for local communities. Through the convention, a national network of communication and cooperation identified women with a particular expertise, collected data, and introduced new methods. The annual meetings of the WC featured papers delivered by physicians, social workers, and civic-improvement activists. Convinced that society and not merely the individual soul was at stake, women in the black Baptist church involved themselves in the practical work of social salvation—establishing settlement houses, holding forums to discuss industrial problems and public health, creating social service commissions, and working to improve the conditions in city slums. Support for foreign missions constituted another important aspect of the work of the convention. In 1901, the WC contributed money to support SPELMAN COLLEGE graduate Emma Delaney, who worked as a missionary to Chiradzulu in BRITISH CENTRAL AFRICA (now MALAWI). In 1902, the women supplied funds to build a brick mission house for her. Through their support of Delaney, the women learned of the harsh consequences of European colonialism on African people. In a visit to America in 1905, Delaney spoke of the need for black Americans to redeem AFRICA from COLONIAL RULE. In her speech before the WC's annual meeting, she poignantly described the suffering of African people "who were compelled to secure rubber for the Belgium Government at any cost, even the loss of their limbs, if the required quantity of rubber was not brought." During the early decades of the twentieth century, the WC shipped boxes of food and clothing to missionaries in foreign fields, underwrote the educational expenses of African students in the United States, contributed to mission stations in various parts of Africa, and built a hospital in LIBERIA.

The role of black Baptist women as a force for missions also entailed the effort to rid American society of the sins of racial and gender discrimination. In this regard, the WC went on record against segregation, LYNCHING, injustice in the courts, the inequitable division of school funds, and barriers to voting rights and equal employment. It supported the civil rights agenda of the NATIONAL ASSOCIATION FOR THE ADVANCEMENT OF COLORED PEOPLE (NAACP) and invited representatives from that organization to appear at the Baptist women's annual meetings. In 1914, the WC joined forces with the NAACP in a national campaign to end negative stereotyping of black people in literature, film, textbooks, newspapers, and on the stage. According to their minutes, they also advocated boycotts and written protests to publishers and others who used racial slurs.

Thus the WC afforded black women an arena in which to transcend narrow social and intellectual confines and become exposed to new places, personalities, and ideas that negated both racist and sexist stereotypes and limitations. At the very time when BOOKER T. WASHINGTON refused to use his influence to criticize the black disfranchisement in the South, the leadership of the WC loudly called for suffrage for black women and men. In 1909, these Baptist women specified that their political input in state legislatures and the federal government would help improve the living and working conditions of black people in general and black women in particular.

Understanding the historic role of black Baptist women ultimately must evoke recognition of the multivalent character of the black church itself. The church was not the exclusive voice of a male ministry but the inclusive voice of men and women in dialogue. As the majority of church members, the mainstay of financial support, and the missionary impetus for social change, black Baptist women were never silent. In the struggle to come into their own voice, they empowered their church, their community, and, not least of all, themselves.

See also Christianity: Missionaries in Africa; Migration, Black, in the United States; Racial Stereotypes.

Evelyn Brooks Higginbotham

Women Artists, African: An Interpretation

Overview of the achievements of recent women painters and sculptors in Africa.

Art and life are inseparable in AFRICA. So I discovered in my journeys there from 1986 to 1998, meeting and interviewing artists both in the cities and the villages. For African women, the passion for artistic creation is evident in times of peace and war, under favorable conditions and under the most difficult and dangerous conditions imaginable. Women's utilitarian and decorative art forms include pottery, basket making, leather and beadwork, *bokolanfini*, batik, and mud wall painting. However, in recent years, as more women gain access to modern art training, they are modifying traditional art forms or adopting modern media and making significant contributions to the development of African aesthetics from a feminist perspective.

Historians have long overlooked the contributions of women artists. It is important to transcend stereotypes in order to understand the changing roles of women artists—and women generally—in African society today. While women in the past may not have created stone carvings or acrylic paintings on canvas, some are doing so today.

Contemporary African women painters use media ranging from mud pigments to oil and acrylics, while women sculptors are working in the ancient traditions of mud and bronze construction as well as in the modern schools of cement and stone carving.

Whether they are self-taught or formally trained at a university or workshop, most women artists' figurative expressions explore old and new themes related to women's experiences. These include *biological* themes, related to women's experiences in childbirth and raising and nurturing children; *economic* themes, related to women's work in agriculture, craft production, marketing, teaching, and other professions; *cultural* themes, in which women are represented as healers, goddesses, revered elders ensuring cultural continuity, or even health workers; and *political* themes, focusing on women's active roles resisting oppression and participating as war combatants in liberation struggles.

Many of the African women artists working in modern media are young, and as their work matures and they gain recognition, they pave the way for the next generation. African women artists do experience some of the same obstacles in achieving mainstream recognition as their counterparts do in the West. Their creative innovations need to be better supported, documented, and celebrated nationally and internationally. The following overview of women sculptors and painters from various parts of the continent illustrates African women's artistic achievements and their active involvement in processes of social change.

Sculpture

Princess Elizabeth Olowu was born in 1945 in NIGERIA. Her father, Oba Akenzua II, was an enlightened member of the BENIN royal family, and when she expressed the desire to learn the ancient technique of bronze casting (traditionally a male profession), her father gave his permission. Olowu completed her education at the University of Benin, and is now a professor of sculpture there.

An energetic mother of eight, Olowu creates life-size, expressionistic sculptures, frequently inspired by personal experiences. *Zero Hour* is an impressive life-size cement sculpture about the moment of birth, when a woman's existence hovers between life and death. In contrast, *Acada,* or Bookworm, portraying a young girl deeply engrossed in a book, offers a new role model that encourages women's education. Olowu has also created monumental sculptures on themes of the Biafran War and a life-size portrait of her father.

In ZIMBABWE, the carving of monumental stone sculptures representing the half-human, half-animal forms of SHONA spirits began approximately thirty-five years ago. The catalyst was Frank McEwen, the English art critic and the first director of the National Art Gallery in Salisbury (now HARARE). In the 1960s, McEwen initiated a workshop at the gallery and invited Africans "to come and make art." They began with drawing and painting but soon turned to sculpture. They used simple hand tools to carve the soapstone and the harder serpentine stone, both of which were abundantly available, and finished their pieces with emery paper and wax polish.

In those early years, Shona sculptures were considered grotesque by the Rhodesian English colonial establishment. However, in 1970, at the first major overseas exhibit held at Musée d'Art Moderne in Paris, every sculpture sold on the first day.

The war against COLONIAL RULE was by then well under way in RHODESIA, and it continued until the country gained independence in 1980 and Rhodesia became Zimbabwe. Although Shona women participated actively in the liberation struggle, they did not join the growing numbers of men who practiced Shona stone carving. Recently, however, women who formerly assisted their fathers, husbands, or other family members in polishing their stone forms, have begun to pick up the hammer and chisel to do their own carvings. Some have benefited from attending National Art Gallery workshops. Approximately 800 sculptors are currently working in Zimbabwe, but fewer than twenty are women. However, their achievements are remarkable, as exemplified by the work of Agnes Nyanhongo and Alice Sani.

Born in 1960, Agnes Nyanhongo is now considered by Roy Guthrie, the director of Harare's Chapungu Park (a sculpture park), to be "one of the most prominent and successful of the 'second generation' of Zimbabwe's sculptors." Nyanhongo began her sculpting career working for her father and other relatives. Her decision to become a sculptor herself was encouraged at a National Art Gallery workshop. She studied there for three years and later married fellow sculptor Joseph Munemo.

Nyanhongo's roles as a wife and mother of three children have provided many of her aesthetic themes, such as *Sisters, Mother and Child,* and *Thinking Man.* Her residency at Chapungu Park, where she is one of twelve sculptors, has also been a stimulus to her work, as she benefits from an impressive permanent collection of Shona sculpture, access to large, high-quality stones, interaction with other sculptors, and the critical support of a formal gallery system for exhibits and sales.

Alice Sani was born in 1948 in MOZAMBIQUE, but since the late 1980s she has been living and working in the Tengenenge Village in Zimbabwe, a community of over 200 sculptors located approximately 150 kilometers (ninety-three miles) outside Harare. Tengenenge was founded by Zimbabwean farmer Tom Blomefield, and its resident sculptors come from countries throughout southern Africa.

Sani's sculptural themes reflect not only motherhood and personal relationships but also experiences of war and hunger, represented in works such as *Mother and Child, One-Eyed Man from Mozambique,* and *Hungry Woman.* She also carves smaller pieces, influenced by nature.

Painting

Inji Efflatoun was born in CAIRO, EGYPT, in 1924 into a traditional Muslim family. She began studying art with a private tutor who encouraged the development of Efflatoun's expressionistic images, which drew on themes of social injustice, male oppression, and the struggle against British colonial rule. In the early 1950s, Efflatoun helped to form the Women's Committee for Popular Resistance. In 1959 she and twenty-five other upper-class Egyptian women, all political activists, were incarcerated without a formal sentencing or trial.

During Efflatoun's four and a half years of confinement, she managed to bribe the guards so that she could receive art supplies and paint. The works she then created were a powerful documentation of women prisoners and prison conditions, as in *Portrait of a Young Prostitute*, *Dormitory of Political Prisoners*, and *Behind the Bars*. After her release in 1964, Efflatoun continued to paint political themes, such as *Homage to Angela* (Davis) and *Bride of the South*, which depicted a woman carrying a rifle. However, her expressionistic brush strokes now exposed the white canvas, creating a sense of space and sunlight.

Pama Sinatoa was born in approximately 1945 near Mopti, a major port along the NIGER RIVER in MALI. She learned drawing at school, which she attended for seven years. She later married a cloth merchant and moved to DJENNÉ, an ancient Islamic city. There she learned from the local women traditional *bokolanfini* painting, a popular technique for applying geometric patterns to strips of cotton cloth stitched together for skirts, pants, shirts, and baby carriers.

Eventually Sinatoa began to create wall paintings, drawing her own scenes from Malian history and traditions. She also enjoyed creating large panoramic paintings of Djenné, or of boats on the Niger River. In addition, Sinatoa paints images depicting women's creative activities at the Djenné Women's Collective, where she exhibits and sells her work.

Grace Chigumira first learned to paint in 1991 at a workshop held at the Weya Women's Training Center in Zimbabwe. German artist Ilse Noy initiated the workshop, and, with funding from the German Volunteer Service, also helped establish the Cold Comfort Farm Weaving Collective, located near Harare. In workshops at Weya and other rural areas, Noy and the women participants experimented with various art media in order to develop marketable products. The women—many of them subsistence farmers—hoped to increase their cash income, but Noy encouraged them to take on innovative projects, expressing experiences important in their own lives.

Chigumira begins each painting by drawing freehand on plywood all the basic shapes of her personal story. She carefully fills them in with acrylic colors she pre-mixes before outlining each object in black and adding textures and details. Many of her paintings depict scenes of Weya daily life, such as *Getting Water from the Well*, *UNICEF at Weya*, and *Family Planning*, all of which portray the activities of health workers.

Theresa Musoke was born in 1945 in UGANDA. Her father, a chief, sent her to a Catholic boarding school where she first learned to draw and paint and where her talent gained recognition. Her professional career was launched in 1965 when she became the first black woman artist to receive a show in NAIROBI, KENYA.

Musoke continued her art education at Uganda's Makerere University before receiving scholarships to study for advanced degrees in London and at the University of Pennsylvania from 1969 to 1973. When she returned to Africa she made Kenya her home. She has since taught art there from the elementary to university level. Musoke's mixed-media images on canvas are based on a variety of themes, ranging from animal life to marketplace scenes to social issues. One series of paintings, for example, focuses on preventing teenage pregnancy.

Women Artist-Fighters

During ERITREA's thirty-year war for independence from ETHIOPIA, a Culture Unit was formed in the war zone in the early 1980s by the Eritrean People's Liberation Front (EPLF). Twenty-five combatants were trained as artists, including five women (altogether, more than a third of Eritrea's troops were women). Since the end of the war in 1991, two of these women artists, Elsa Jacob and Terhas Iyassu, have continued to paint. Their art offers a unique feminist perspective of war and reflects their hopes and aspirations during this time of peace.

During the war, the "artist-fighters" exhibited their work, when possible, in Eritrea's rural villages, to educate and promote solidarity. Drawings and paintings were also exhibited in Europe and the United States to raise financial support for the EPLF. Since the end of the war, publicly displayed poster reproductions of the artist-fighters' paintings have been used to commemorate national holidays and to honor women's participation in the liberation struggle. Other posters depict scenes of postwar reconstruction of roads and houses, and the building of new health centers and schools.

Elsa Jacob, born in the Eritrean town of Keren, had just completed the tenth grade when she made the decision to join the EPLF in 1977. After six months of military training she was sent to the Araq base, where the art section of the Culture Unit was organizing to use art as "a weapon to help in the struggle for liberation." Once the trainees learned basic art skills, they began producing illustrations for military manuals, showing the maintenance and repair of equipment such as rifles, tanks, and trucks. The manuals required careful illustrations because many of the fighters were illiterate and spoke different languages.

Jacob fought in a number of major battles; she took advantage of periods of calm to paint scenes from her personal experiences as well as portraits of the nomadic people of the Sahel and Barka provinces where she was stationed. One powerful watercolor, *Woman Hero*, depicts a woman combatant in the midst of battle. Possibly a self-portrait, the painting portrays a warrior holding a grenade in one hand and a Kalishnikov rifle in the other as she stands over the body of a slain enemy soldier. This painting was later reproduced as a poster and widely displayed throughout Eritrea.

Since the end of the war and the birth of her children, Jacob has painted family portraits as well as a series of symbolic pen-and-ink drawings on traditional themes, such as *Coffee Ceremony* and *The Bride*. Jacob is on the faculty of the newly formed Asmara School of Art, with the goal of training elementary and secondary art teachers. As a member of the Eritrean Fine Arts Association, she has participated in the association's mural painting projects. The murals now cover many walls of ASMARA, the capital, with historic scenes of the liberation struggle as well as new visions of peace.

Terhas Iyassu was born in 1960 in Asmara, and became a "child-informant" for the EPLF when she was only fourteen.

Two years later she was relocated to the SAHEL, where she met and trained with Elsa Jacob. She recalls that the art studio at the Araq base was, like many EPLF facilities, built underground in order to avoid Ethiopian bombings. Some of Iyassu's sketches from the wartime period depict hardship, such as *Famine* and *Woman Carrying Her Child for Resettlement*. She also painted portraits of soldiers and desert nomads. When Eritrean troops liberated the coastal city of MASSAWA in 1990, Iyassu was there with her sketchpad. Since Eritrean independence she has lived in Asmara with her two daughters (both born during the war); she continues to paint portraits and desert scenes.

See also Art and Architecture, African; Artists, African; Benin, Early Kingdom of.

Betty La Duke

Women, Black, in Brazil: An Interpretation

Challenges facing black women in Brazil.

BRAZIL's illusory "racial democracy" has mistakenly transformed us in the eyes of the world into a country with no racial prejudice. But it exists. It is reflected in statistics of unemployment and underemployment, in low salaries, and in sexual and racial discrimination.

To be a black woman in Brazil is to occupy many spaces in the media, but none that would affirm our dignity or our citizenship. To be a black woman in my country is to be the mother of children murdered by death squads or children forced at young ages to work on the streets in order to eat. To be a black woman is to be the victim of many forms of violence: sexual violence, racial violence, and police violence. To be a black woman is to live stories of discrimination and exploitation. It means being stereotyped as a *mulatta* sex symbol or as a passive slave. A history of struggle is thus denied. Recapturing citizenship and dignity, however, is accomplished in the day-to-day forms of resistance against marginalization; in fighting poverty and racism; in raising one's head to move forward; and in raising one's consciousness. Racism is a form of violence against women's rights that undermines the exercise of citizenship. Its manifestations include the aesthetic devaluation of blacks and unequal access to work, education, health care, and other social rights.

Brazil's social pyramid puts men of European descent at the top. Women of European descent occupy the second rung. Beneath them are Afro-Brazilian men. And at the fourth and bottom level of Brazil's socioeconomic ladder are women of African descent. Of every 100 working Afro-Brazilians, thirty-three earn the minimum wage (in U.S. dollars, about $103 per month), and only two reach the privileged income level of U.S. $1,000 per month.

The social and economic policies adopted by the country intensify Afro-Brazilian women's marginalization. With insuffi-

cient professional qualifications, most are forced into marginal jobs. It should be emphasized that we are speaking of no minority but of almost half of the female population, given that approximately 44 percent of Brazilians are descendants of Africans. The marked inequities faced by this group are many; those governing access to work and education are among the more apparent.

In the job market Afro-Brazilians are largely distributed into three occupational categories: the agricultural sector; construction and public works; and the service sector. About 70 percent of the Afro-Brazilian work force is concentrated in these sectors. This figure clearly reflects the location of blacks in the country's occupational structure: a concentration in activities receiving the lowest wages and corresponding to the lowest levels of schooling.

Afro-Brazilian women find even fewer opportunities in the labor market. The economic and social advancement of black women is slower than that of black men or white women. On average, white male heads of families earn more than twice the income of black women; white female heads of families also earn considerably more. Black women face discrimination on three counts: race, gender, and, generally, class.

According to a survey conducted by the survey agency Instituto Brasileiro de Geografia e Estatística (IBGE), 62.7 percent of black women and 58.2 percent of "brown" women (*pardas*) earn at or below the minimum wage, as compared to 34 percent of white women. The lower the salary for a given occupation, the greater the presence of black women; the higher the salary, the more diminished is our presence. Sixty-nine percent of black women work in the agrarian or the service sector, many as domestic servants. Even those attaining higher levels of education will face discrimination barring them from jobs and giving preference to white women. Often they are forced to accept jobs for which they are overqualified. Only 2 percent of black women attain a professional-managerial status, and these earn 48 percent of what white women earn in the same position.

Statistics in the area of education paint a similar scenario. Most Brazilians attain, at best, an elementary school education. Here again, the picture is bleaker among Afro-Brazilians, 71 percent of whom have reached a level at or below elementary school, as compared to 64 percent of "browns" and 57 percent of whites. Only 14 percent of Afro-Brazilians complete five to eleven years of schooling, compared to 25 percent of whites and 41 percent of Asians. The number of black women attending universities is negligible in statistical terms. The direct consequence of this is their concentration in low-wage jobs. It should also be noted that even at the same level of schooling, black women earn less than black men.

From these disturbing figures, a number of conclusions can be drawn. First, the Afro-Brazilian woman's role in production is at a disadvantage relative to white men and women, Asian men and women, and black men. She is located at the base of the social hierarchy and penalized in her chances of social mobility. Second, the disparities generating these distortions will infuse black women's struggle with a specific character, molded by the economic and political forces that shape their lives.

Third, measures of education and income indicate that white women are more advantaged than black men, a point that underscores the greater weight ascribed to race over gender in Brazil. At the same time, the distance separating Afro-Brazilian men and women represents the product of both machismo and sexism, which continue to infuse our society's selection mechanisms and which are given further impulse by ideologies of WHITENING and of social mobility.

Finally, the economic models pursued by our government in the last decades have widened regional disparities. In this context, they have themselves had discriminatory implications, particularly with regard to Afro-Brazilians. With illicit enrichment, institutionalized corruption, the excessive speculation of finance capital, and the privileging of certain sectors of the economy, modernization in Brazil has implanted a society in which the consumption of wealth coexists with subsistence strategies of survival, magnifying the profound differences separating individuals and groups.

My own work in the National Congress aims at a universal social justice, seeking to reverse the negative conditions faced by Afro-Brazilians in general and Afro-Brazilian women in particular. We believe that racial and sexual equality, together with democratic forms of association, are the necessary conditions for attaining social peace. This, for us, also means suppressing police violence against Afro-Brazilians; ending unemployment, which reaches such tragic proportions in the black population; and guaranteeing an equitable participation in the goods produced by society. However, we are aware that we have a long road to travel before tearing down the walls of discrimination, racial prejudice, and sexism which exist in Brazil.

See also Afro-Brazilian Culture; Human Rights in Latin America and the Caribbean; Image of the Mulatta in Latin America and the Caribbean; Myth of Racial Democracy in Latin America and the Caribbean.

Benedita da Silva

Women, Black, in Colonial Hispanic Caribbean

Black women who, along with the Spanish expansionists, moved to Cuba, the Dominican Republic, and Puerto Rico during the colonial era.

Black slaves and freedpeople were common in Spanish and Portuguese urban centers like Seville, Lisbon, and Valencia. Female slaves performed mostly domestic duties in these cities. The ownership of domestic slaves was a status symbol for residents of the Spanish peninsula. Thus, as Spanish fortune seekers moved into the newly occupied islands in the Caribbean, some of them brought along their domestic slaves.

The historical record has ignored the presence of slave and free black women in the early stages of Spanish colonial expansion in HISPANIOLA, PUERTO RICO, and CUBA; nevertheless, these women were participants in the early difficulties experienced in the new colonies. Many women were employed as domestics or worked in food-related artisan trades. Still, black women were considered a problematic influence in the islands, and many were victims of the accusations and punishments of the Inquisition. A sexually unbalanced population, in which men outnumbered women, also made black women the target of physical abuse and rape. This situation, alongside marriage and concubinage, made for the spread of *mestizaje*, or interracial mixing between Africans, Spanish, and Taíno people in the island colonies.

Female slaves were coveted not only for their labor, but also for their reproductive potential. It was the mother who passed down the slave status in the Hispanic Caribbean. Planters wanted female slaves in order to multiply their slave holdings and avoid purchasing "new" slaves from AFRICA. This strategy intensified during the nineteenth century when British pressure to eradicate the slave trade made the direct importation of Africans more expensive and cumbersome. The masters' wishes aside, the slave populations in the Hispanic Caribbean did not reproduce sufficiently to meet the demand for slaves, which required the continuous importation of bonded people from Africa.

Although Spanish law made it clear that marriages among slaves ought to be respected, planters made it very difficult for slave families to exist. Notwithstanding, slaves formed families that withstood the difficulties of physical separation. Also, black women challenged traditional Spanish religious marital practices by living in common-law marriages. This practice angered Spanish Catholic Church and colonial officials and was persecuted at various times throughout the colonial period and in the nineteenth century. The tendency of black women and other women of color to live in common-law marriages reflected not only distinct cultural practices, but also the skewed sexual demographics in the colonies and the high fees charged by the clergy to provide the sacrament of marriage. In addition, the institutional presence of the Roman Catholic Church was traditionally weak in rural areas and plantations.

During the seventeenth and eighteenth centuries, slavery was a feeble institution in the Hispanic Caribbean in contrast to the plantation societies in other Caribbean islands such as BARBADOS, JAMAICA, and Saint Kitts. The Hispanic Caribbean colonies received many runaway slaves from the British and French colonies during these two centuries. Slaves who left a non-Spanish colony became free after one year in the Hispanic Caribbean. The only condition for their freedom was converting to Catholicism and going through catechism. As a result, a small but ever-increasing class of free blacks—*libertos*, as they were called in Spanish—emerged in the Hispanic Caribbean. These black freedpeople proved to be a problematic group for Spanish officials once SUGAR-based plantation societies returned to Cuba and Puerto Rico starting in the second half of the eighteenth century.

Black women played an important role in the urban economies of the Hispanic Caribbean during the eighteenth and nineteenth centuries. Many black women roamed the city streets selling foodstuffs door-to-door. Others sold their goods near the marketplaces or had small shops. Other black women operated small food-selling shacks, like the *mondonguerías*, where tripe stew was sold to the lower classes within the city. Most of the domestics, slave or free, were black women. They labored alongside other women of color as laundresses, cooks, maids, wet nurses, midwives, and servants. Many black women served as domestics not only to middle- and upper-class families but also to the governmental, military, and religious bureaucracies housed in cities like HAVANA and SAN JUAN. Some female slaves performed such services for other people for a fee, and shared a percentage of the fee with their masters. This practice seems to have been widespread in the cities of Havana, San Juan, and SANTO DOMINGO and seems to have been among the strategies used by planters to supplement their income in times of economic difficulty. Life in urban areas also provided female slaves with more personal freedom compared to those working on plantations. Another area of economic activity for black women was artisan trades such as cigar making. Although the actual job of rolling and finishing cigars was done by men, many black women worked in small tobacco shops classifying, stemming, and stacking tobacco leaves.

The access that female slaves had to additional earnings through domestic work, charging fees for their services, or street selling allowed them to secure the funds to pay for their freedom or that of other family members. One special feature of urban life for black women in the Hispanic Caribbean was the high rate of manumission. Outright manumission, or gradual self-purchase (known as *coartación*), was much more common in urban areas than on rural plantations. Female slaves were manumitted, or purchased their freedom, more often than male slaves.

Plantation life was as difficult for female slaves as it was for male slaves. Black women were involved in the arduous agricultural tasks associated with sugarcane cultivation, including field clearing, planting, weeding, and cane cutting. Only from the industrial side of sugar producing—working in the boiling and curing houses, where the sugarcane was crushed and its juice turned into crystals—were female slaves usually excluded. Other black women worked as domestics in the master's family quarters. This strenuous work included tending the plantation's gardens, preparing and cooking meals, repairing, washing, and ironing clothes, supervising children, cleaning, nursing the ill and aged, and tending to the personal requests of the master and his family.

The advent of plantations in the Hispanic Caribbean changed the ideological, legal, and economic perception of black women in the region. As racial purity and separation became more important, churches began to keep different books dividing baptisms, marriages, and deaths by race. Where Cuba and Puerto Rico had provided a haven for runaway British, Danish, and French slaves in the seventeenth and eighteenth centuries, punitive laws were passed by the Spanish government limiting and policing the entry of non-Spanish freedpeople after slavery was abolished in other Caribbean colonies. Colonial officials feared the potential rebellious and agitating influence of blacks coming from colonies where slavery had ended. The ghost of the Haitian slave rebellion also haunted the minds of Hispanic Caribbean planters and of Spanish colonial and military authorities.

Black women were always active in the struggles to eradicate slavery in the Hispanic Caribbean. Either through quotidian resistance or by involving themselves in larger uprisings, black women attempted to undermine slavery. In Cuba, for example, the slave Fermina was sentenced to death by a war council for her participation and leadership in an 1843 revolt. Many black domestics were accused of attempting to poison their masters or employers. Female slaves often went to court to defend their rights, be it a violation of a *coartación* agreement or of the promise of manumission upon the death of the master. Black women joined bands of *cimarrones* (maroons), the term used for slaves who had escaped to the countryside to avoid the indignities of plantation bondage.

Few black women of the colonial period have had their contributions recognized by historians of the Hispanic Caribbean. A notable exception is Mariana Grajales, mother of the famous Cuban nineteenth-century pro-independence leader ANTONIO MACEO. Grajales, the mother of thirteen children (nine of them died in the independence wars against SPAIN), has been canonized as a secular symbol of protest and rebellion against colonialism in Cuba. She ran a hospital for wounded rebels during the TEN YEARS' WAR (1868–1878), the first major war fought by Cubans for independence from Spain. Grajales also became famous for compelling one of her younger sons to go into the battlefield upon seeing her son Antonio arrive at the hospital seriously wounded. Grajales was exiled from Cuba at the end of the war and lived in KINGSTON, JAMAICA, until her death at age eighty-five in 1893.

See also Catholic Church in Latin America and the Caribbean; Colonial Latin America and the Caribbean; Haitian Revolution; Maroonage in the Americas; Slave Rebellions in Latin America and the Caribbean; Slavery in Latin America and the Caribbean.

Felix V. Matos Rodriguez

Women's Organizations, Early African American

Mutual relief associations, benevolent societies, literary societies, and antislavery organizations formed by African American women in the first half of the nineteenth century.

"Visited Mrs. Jones with the Committee and gave her 50 cts worth of groceries. She had been confined 10 days."

This 1821 note—recording the delivery of provisions to a shut-in neighbor—documents one of the basic functions of many of the earliest African American women's organizations. Throughout the nineteenth century, the reality of life for many black families, even those who were not slaves, included constant economic pressure. Because women and children were especially vulnerable to poverty, women quickly realized that they needed to be at the forefront of efforts to create mutual aid and benevolent societies to help support neighbors in need. The first black women's mutual aid society, the Female Benevolent Society of Saint Thomas, was founded in PHILADELPHIA, PENNSYLVANIA, in 1793.

Similar societies quickly sprang up elsewhere in Philadelphia as well as in Newport, Rhode Island, and Salem, Massachusetts, and soon they existed in towns and cities across the Northeast. In some, members contributed regular dues that were pooled together when an individual member had an emergency; in others, members simply worked together to give help wherever it was needed. Both models made use of their members' commitment to serving their communities—as the Salem Colored Female Religious and Moral Society stated in 1818, "to be charitably watchful over each other."

Black women also began organizing to share their talents for other causes: says one scholar, "'mutual relief' became 'mutual improvement.'" Literary societies, such as the Female Literary Association and Minerva Literary Association in Philadelphia and the Colored Ladies' Literary Society in New York, gave women the chance to express their recommendations for racial uplift as they wrote essays and poetry to be discussed. For example, activist SARAH MAPPS DOUGLASS, who cofounded the Philadelphia Female Society in 1831, argued in her essay "Family Worship" that moral and scholarly instruction would allow blacks to fill their place in American society: "Yes, religion and education would raise us to an equality with the fairest in our land."

These literary societies also gave black women a rare chance to express their political views, which helped galvanize the antislavery movement. Many women included condemnations of slavery in the writings they shared at literary meetings. In 1832 African American women in Salem, Massachusetts, founded the first Female Anti-Slavery Society. Similar organizations quickly followed, and from then on women such as Douglass, the Forten sisters, and FRANCES ELLEN WATKINS HARPER were active in both literary and antislavery societies.

As the century drew to a close, these societies and associations were joined by similar clubs in the South and West. Even after slavery ended, black women's organizations were still needed to provide social services in their communities and to continue fighting for black women's economic and political rights. Eventually, these societies became the foundation of the national BLACK WOMEN'S CLUB MOVEMENT, which continues today as a major source of assistance in the African American community.

See also Abolitionism in the United States; Mutual Benefit Societies.

Lisa Clayton Robinson

Women Writers, Black, in Brazil

Literature written by women of African descent in Brazil.

Despite a literary history that extends back to the eighteenth century and a veritable explosion of productivity since the 1980s, the literary tradition of black Brazilian women has been marginalized. From its beginning black Brazilian women's literature transgressed boundaries, challenged authority, and subverted institutional power.

The writing of Rosa Maria Egipcíaca da Vera Cruz (1725–1767) was the cause of her trial persecution by the Portuguese Inquisition. At the age of six she was kidnapped, enslaved, and brought to RIO DE JANEIRO. When she was fourteen, she was sold and brought to the state of MINAS GERAIS, where she suffered public beatings and exorcism after claiming she had mystical visions. She became a nun, and learned to read and write. Her organizational acumen led her to establish a shelter for women in Rio de Janeiro. Her autobiographical writing, *A Sagrada Teologia do Amor de Deus, Luz Brilhante das Almas Peregrinas* (1752, The Sacred Theology of God's Love, Bright Light of the Pilgrim Souls), a text of more than 200 pages, described her religious experiences and mystic visions. The book caused such a furor that she was seized, taken to PORTUGAL, and tried for false religious claims and heresy. According to her biographer, the Brazilian historian Luiz Mott, a portrait of Rosa Maria Egipcíaca da Vera Cruz hung in the shelter she established that pictured her with a pen in hand. This image of an influential black woman who dared to write at a time and place that denied literacy to slaves and women must have been a powerful, subversive message for other black women.

A century later, Maria Fermina dos Reis (1825–1917), from Maranhão, became the first Brazilian woman novelist. Her book *Ursula* was ahead of its time as BRAZIL's first abolitionist novel. It was published in 1859 (second edition, 1975), long before the actual abolition of slavery in 1888.

Auta de Souza (1876–1901), from Rio Grande do Norte, wrote romantic poetry. She came from a prosperous family, was well educated, and wrote in both Portuguese and French. Her volume *O Horto* (The Garden, 1901) does not have themes dealing with race or racial heritage.

CAROLINA MARIA DE JESUS (1914–1977) wrote about life in the *FAVELAS* (squatter settlements) of São Paulo in her autobiographical work *Quarto do despejo* (Child of the Dark) in 1960. The book caused a sensation in Brazil and was later published in twenty countries and translated into thirteen languages. Her other books were *Casa de Alvenaria* (1961; I'm Going to Have a Little House, 1997), *Pedaços de fome* (Pieces of Hunger, 1963), *Proverbios* (Proverbs, 1969), and *Diario de Bitita*, published posthumously in 1986 (Bitita's Diary, 1998). Carolina Maria de Jesus revealed the hypocrisy of society and she anticipated the themes such as racial identity, reclaiming the black female body, and quality of life that would gain popularity with subsequent black women writers. Black women writers of the post-dictatorship generation regard Carolina Maria de Jesus as their literary forerunner.

The retreat of the military dictatorship in Brazil in 1978, the emergence of the MOVIMENTO NEGRO UNIFICADO, a political Black Consciousness Movement, and increased freedom of expression ended more than forty years of repression and prohibitions against an authentic discussion of race and ethnic heritage. Consequently a generation of Afro-Brazilian writers gradually emerged, providing a variety of black voices including those of black women to depict aspects of African-Brazilian life. When Brazilian feminists emerged in the 1980s addressing matters such as equal pay for equal work, reproductive rights, and access to higher education, their ranks were dominated by middle-class white women who did not represent the concerns of black women. Black women formed their own organizations to discuss the problems that affected their quality of life such as illiteracy, hunger, substandard housing, health care, and lack of modern conveniences such as electricity and sewerage. Literary works by black women paralleled the themes of those of the African-Brazilian women's organizations.

The most frequent site of publication for black women has been *Cadernos Negros* (Black Notebooks), a refereed anthology produced by the literary organization QUILOMBHOJE, established to provide publication opportunities for black authors who were marginalized by the commercial and academic presses. *Cadernos Negros* publishes poems and short stories in alternate years. Because of the lack of receptivity in academic and commercial presses to literature dealing with racial questions, only a handful of women have published extended genres such as the novel.

In 1988, after years of discussion about the role of black women writers, a group of thirty women writers contributed their poetry to a publication project, under the leadership of poet Miriam Alves. It was designed to commemorate the one hundredth anniversary of the abolition of slavery in 1888 by presenting a comprehensive collection of writing by black Brazilian women for the first time. The project was to be funded by the government, but for some reason funding became unavailable and the project was postponed. Later, segments of the work were published in the United States as a bilingual anthology, *Finally Us: Contemporary Black Brazilian Women Writers* (1995).

Women in Brazilian literature traditionally have been presented as either spiritual or carnal. This division, according to Roberto Reis, has tended to follow racial lines. Stereotypes of the docile mammy and the lascivious mulatto woman have existed for centuries in Brazilian literature and would go unchallenged if it were not for the writing of black Brazilian women writers like Miriam Alves, who called for a broadening of perspectives by "writing our vision of the world." The author Esmeralda Ribeiro, stating that black women writers are the best equipped to remedy the lack of authentic images of black women in Brazilian literature, suggested that women writers have a responsibility to create an array of credible images by "telling our stories and experiences." Such literature can be used as a tool for intervention in the political process. The author Sônia Fátima da Conceição maintained that the three af-flictions of Afro-Brazilian communities—poverty, illiteracy, and racism—can be addressed by using literature as a strategy for survival. She further suggested that the aesthetics of such work should have a basis in the Afro-Brazilian artistic and oral literary tradition.

The desire to reflect a positive identity resulted in an expanded, dynamic portrayal of black women and the pressures that affect them. Conceição Evaristo replaced the docile mammy with the assertive, unrelenting mother who cultivates influence because of her many abilities: "I rape the eardrums of the world/I foresee/ . . . I the female matrix/I, the motive power/I-woman shelter of the seed/continual motion/of the world." Lourdes Teodoro asked for opportunity in life: "I ask only for a road/that doesn't have unripe fruit/or illusions/or an end." Alzira Rufino expressed the sense of peril and hardship felt by many women when she declared, "I am the knot on wood/Something that the blade insists on."

The quality of life, poverty, and conditions in the favelas appear frequently in black women's writing. In *"Navega coração"* ("Sail Heart") by Andrea Cristina Rio Branco, the words wind across the page like a favela ascending the hillside. The poem ends with the words "If I live on the hillside, if I die reaching . . . ," a play on words in Portuguese in which the words "I live, I die," and the hillside are pronounced similarly so that they are almost interchangeable. The device suggests that living and dying are the same in the favela. Lourdes Teodoro writes of a life that consists of subsisting, in *"Litania"* ("Litany") a poem that reiterates "We just hold on." Terezinha Malaquias writes of "human cadavers that roll through the gutters of life."

The reconstitution of identity required writing about the psychological effects of discrimination. In much of her prose and poetry, Geni Mariano Guimarães describes how rejection of the Eurocentric standard of beauty and the struggle to affirm one's physical characteristics such as hair, color, and body build facilitates a process of self-affirmation for black women. In *A cor de ternura*, (The Color of Tenderness), her award-winning book, she chronicles the life of a black family. Guimarães states that one of the merits of the book is the theme of the stages of racial prejudice. Her early volumes of poetry *Terceiro Filho* (Third Son, 1979) and *Da flor o afeto, da pedra o protesto* (Of the Flower the Affection, Of the Stone the Protest, 1981) were written before she began to address the theme of racial identity. In 1995 she published *Balé das emoções* (Ballet of Emotions).

The omission of black women from the historical record is an oversight that Miriam Alves seeks to correct with her poetry. She writes a type of epic poetry that deals with the important events of the black community. "Mahin, amanhã" ("Mahin, Tomorrow") tells of the role of Luiza Mahín, the woman who was a leader of the Great Revolt of the Males of 1835, the last great slave rebellion in SALVADOR, BAHIA. It provides a portrayal of a heroic, assertive, black woman whose word alone unites the various enslaved African ethnic groups and mobilizes them to strike a blow for freedom. This image is in contrast to the popular belief that black Brazilians are passive and nonconfrontational. *"Passo a praça"* ("Passageway to the Plaza") describes the Plaza of Paissandu in São Paulo, where slaves constructed a church in 1711. The poem reminds the reader that the church has been a site of political resistance and the quest for justice across the centuries. It alludes to the maintenance of African religious tradition and the continuity of African social organization despite the imposition of the Portuguese regime. Her poem *"Vudu"* recalls the Law of the Free Womb, a deceitful law that caused further disorganization of the black family because it encouraged slave mothers to abandon their babies so that the babies could be granted freedom. The law began the cycle of abandonment that persists to the present day. In *"Noticiario"* ("News Report") Alves writes of intolerable contemporary living conditions that have continued from the time of slavery, linking the quality of life in the slave shacks to life in the shacks of today's favelas.

Alves also writes poetry with a highly personal tone that speaks of the effects of oppression on the individual. With the publication of *Momentos de busca* (Moments of Search) in 1983, Alves conveyed her personal vision of a world that oppressed her yet failed to bridle her creative imagination. *Estrelas no dedo* (Stars on the Finger) in 1985 describes her dreams deferred, disillusionment, unfulfilled ambitions, and potential waiting to unfold. The anthropologist and literary critic Abelardo Rodrigues wrote that Alves's poetry shows how the "unresolved crisis of the forced labor and sexual violence of slavery continues to affect the descendants of slaves today."

When Esmeralda Ribeiro called for the expansion of the portrayal of black women, she remembered the women of previous generations who made sacrifices so that their daughters could make educational and professional progress and showed her gratitude by portraying them respectfully in her work. She invents authentic characters by writing about her observations of the African-Brazilian people whom she knows. The grandmother is a key figure in her works because Ribeiro says that the grandmother's role in the family as a caregiver for the children is essential for the economic advancement of many African-Brazilian families. Ribeiro subverts the image of the tragic, sexually exploited mulatto woman in her short story *"Keep a Secret."* Rather than dying of love, the protagonist turns the table on her unfaithful white lover and seeks revenge. The story is a black feminist revision of a novel, *Clara dos Anjos* (1948) by Afonso Henriques de Lima Barreto (1881–1922). At the end of the story, Ribeiro slyly indicates the power of authorship when the revengeful character tells the ghost of Lima Barreto that she, the wronged mulatto woman, wrote a better ending than he did, and that we all have the choice to write our own stories. Ribeiro examines the nature of the family in her stories using prose loaded with irony and humor. She believes that Brazilian literature has failed to include representations of black families, often depicting black characters as isolated and merely ornaments in a white world. She concentrates on showing the roles that each member plays in sustaining the family in an adverse world.

This is particularly clear in *Malungos e milongas* (1988), a novella describing the disputes among four siblings. It is an allegory about the struggle among blacks since the time of slavery that results when some are given favor and access while others are denied a viable role.

The portrayal of the lascivious mulatto in the past is a cause of sensitivity for black women and for this reason, there are few portrayals by women of romantic love. An exception is the poetry of Ruth Souza, who affirms her love for the black man. Nevertheless, the romantic love that she writes about is reserved, discreet, and understated.

Sônia Fátima da Conceição's straightforward prose fiction treats complicated social issues. Her novel *Sonhos, marcos e raízes* (Dreams, Marks, and Roots, 1992) examines the Movimento Negro Unificado (Black Unified Movement), one of Brazil's most influential contemporary social movements. Conceição, who is a social worker in the state orphanage in São Paulo, provides insight into the struggles of black women and abandoned children in her short stories. As a result of her professional experience and training as a social scientist she describes numerous true-to-life situations such as the struggles of the working poor, intergenerational poverty, domestic violence, substance abuse, and the living conditions in the favelas. Conceição's black female characters often represent the 85 percent of black Brazilian women who have less than a fourth-grade education and are functionally illiterate. In one of her short stories she shows that for this segment of the population, middle-class feminism is a joke. The remedy for many of the problems that she analyzes is education and literacy. Conceição's poetry shows her compassion and concern. She touches on the sensitive topics of reproductive health, teen motherhood, and child abuse. In "If Only I Could" she laments that because of the loss of knowledge of the healing arts traditionally passed from mother to daughter in African societies she is unable to cure illnesses that cause the high mortality rates among poor Brazilian children. In *"Beija Flor Show"* ("Hummingbird's Show") she deplores the commercialization of African religious values and the degradation of women in *mulata* shows for tourist consumption. The constant theme throughout her work is the need for a return to African family values so that the African-Brazilian community can survive.

Black women writers in Brazil for over 200 years have kept a tradition of using the pen to empower themselves. They have spoken of the unspeakable in order to bring about change. They have seized the word in order to lay claim to themselves and their future. They have inscribed themselves as an irrefutable part of history that would otherwise exclude them.

See also Afro-Brazilian Culture; Black Consciousness in Brazil; Image of the Mulatta in Latin America and the Caribbean; Literature, Black, in Brazil; Slavery in Latin America and the Caribbean.

Carolyn Richardson Durham

Women Writers, Black, in Spanish America

Women of African descent whose contributions to modern literature articulate perspectives specific to black women in the Spanish-speaking countries of Latin America and the Caribbean.

Black women in Spanish America have been telling their story for hundreds of years, since the time of slavery. They have always been involved in the creation and formation of an oral tradition, preserving their personal and cultural history through the oral communication of stories, songs, and poems. Yet spanning the centuries, there were no personal SLAVE NARRATIVES, no testimonial accounts, and no documented histories that gave firsthand accounts of the lives and experiences of black women in the Spanish-speaking countries of Latin America and the Caribbean. Instead, they were depicted in many male-authored poems and novels of the nineteenth and early twentieth centuries as mother, wet nurse, lover, and domestic servant. Most often, these male writers described only the sexual and physical attributes of the black woman. Beyond these literary images, she had neither voice nor life of her own.

Only within the last century have black women in Spanish America begun to tell their stories in published form. Rebelling against centuries of silence, women such as VIRGINIA BRINDIS DE SALAS, AÍDA CARTAGENA PORTALATÍN, Luz Argentina Chiriboga, Eulalia Bernard Little, NANCY MOREJÓN, Shirley Campbell Barr, and Cristina Rodríguez Cabral bring to the public a more realistic representation of the black woman's experience and culture. They represent the collective memory of their ancestors. They craft in their own voice the world around them. They speak of race, love, motherhood, sexuality, marginality, self-empowerment, class, oppression, national identity, and the struggle to exist in a white, male-dominated society.

Paving the Way

Virginia Brindis de Salas, who published during the 1940s, was the pioneer of black women writers in Spanish America. She also was a pioneer in Uruguay's early black literary tradition, along with poet PILAR BARRIOS. Although she died in 1958, she is highly regarded as the preeminent female black poet of URUGUAY and is to this day considered one of the most radical of all Afro-Uruguayan writers. After Barrios, she was the second black Uruguayan writer whose work appeared in book form. She published two volumes of poetry: *Pregón de Marimorena* (The Call of Mary Morena) in 1945 and *Cien cárceles de amor* (One Hundred Prisons of Love) in 1949. In *Pregón de Marimorena*, Brindis de Salas shapes the extraordinary victories, large and small, of a poor black woman who walks the streets selling newspapers. In the book, she captures the musicality of the *pregón*, the rhythmic and melodic cry of the black street vendor. Brindis de Salas molds this oral tradition into poetic form. The social and cultural hardships of being black, fe-

male, and poor in Uruguay in the 1940s are evoked in *Pregón*. Similarly, the poems in her only other published work, *Cien cárceles de amor*, serve as universal testimonies to the daily obstacles, the racism, the social inequities, and the oppression experienced by the black Uruguayan community.

Aída Cartagena Portalatín was another early black woman writer in Spanish America. She, too, confronted the issue of race in her country, the DOMINICAN REPUBLIC. Cartagena Portalatín's published writings—poems, essays, novels, and short stories—span a period of forty years, from the 1940s to the 1980s. While much of her early work reflects on inner life, the end of the dictatorship of RAFAEL TRUJILLO in 1961 marked a turning point in her work. In her poetry of the 1960s, she asserts her racial identity and speaks out against theories of racial purity and social dominance in the Dominican Republic. Her racial discourse is straightforward, not bound by the limits of traditional literary forms. Her use of nonconventional forms exemplifies her literary and political approach to force Dominicans to examine the racial reality and attitudes of the country. In addition to writing, Cartagena Portalatín taught art history and directed serial literary publications. Selections of her works were translated into English in the bilingual anthology *Del desconsuelo al compromiso* (*From Desolation to Compromise*), published in 1988 and edited by Dominican literary critic Daisy Cocco de Filippis.

Next Generation

The forceful poetry of Eulalia Bernard Little explores social and racial relations in COSTA RICA. Bernard is one of Costa Rica's few published black writers. She produced her first collection of poems, *Negritud* (Négritude), as a recording in 1976. She later published two volumes of poetry: *Ritmoheroe* (Rhythmic Hero) in 1982, and a bilingual anthology titled *My Black King* in 1991. She also authored the essay "Nuestro ensayo sobre la existencia y libertad política" (Our Essay on Existence and Political Freedom) edited by the Ministry of Culture in 1981. Bernard's poetry demands to be heard. She does not shy away from sensitive subjects such as racial stereotyping, and she openly attacks the notion of self-hate resulting from these negative stereotypes. Born in Limón, Costa Rica, of Jamaican parents, Bernard brings to her work a personal interest in the SYNCRETISM of the cultures of JAMAICA and Limón. Like other black women writers in Spanish America, she resists the traditional forms of poetry and language, and she does so by writing in the distinctive Creole language of blacks in Limón. In this alone, she challenges the claim of white cultural dominance that has prevailed since colonial times. Bernard exalts the legacy of black Costa Ricans and encourages them to look to their own culture for strength and pride. She is also noted for establishing the first program on black studies at the prominent University of Costa Rica, in San José.

The issues of sexual and racial exploitation are topics in the work of Afro-Ecuadorian writer Luz Argentina Chiriboga. Her distinctly feminist work is centered on the black female protagonist, within the cultural and historical framework of people of African descent in ECUADOR. Together with Cuban Excilia Saldaña (whose work has not been published in English and rarely circulates outside of CUBA), Chiriboga is one of the first black writers in Spanish America to celebrate the sexuality and eroticism of the black woman. Chiriboga, who was born in ESMERALDAS in 1940, authored three novels that were published in the 1990s: *Bajo la piel de los tambores* (1991; *Drums Under My Skin*, 1996); *Jonatas y Manuela* (1994); and *En la noche del viernes* (1997; Friday Night). *Drums Under My Skin* is the first work by an Afro-Ecuadorian female writer to be published in English. It is a narrative that subverts, or overturns, the conventional constructs of gender, class, and race in Latin American society. Chiriboga has also published *Contraportada del deseo* (1992; The Other Side of Desire), a volume of poetry.

Probably the best-known black woman writer in all of Spanish America is Nancy Morejón of Cuba. Writing since the age of nine, she has published numerous collections of poetry, including: *Mutismos* (1962; Silences); *Amor, ciudad atribuida* (1964; Love, Attributed City); *Richard trajo su flauta* (1967; Richard Brought His Flute); *Parajes de una época* (1979; Places of an Era); *Octubre imprescindible* (1982; Essential October); *Cuaderno de Grenada* (1984; Grenada's Notebook); *Piedra pulida* (1986; On Polished Stone); *Fundacion de la imagen* (1988; Image's Foundation); and *Paisaje celebre* (1993; Famous Landscape). Morejón's work and reputation have reached beyond the shores of Cuba, gaining international recognition. Her poetry has been translated into several languages, and many of her poems are included in poetry anthologies, including the English-translated poetry selections *Where the Island Sleeps Like a Wing* (1985) and *Ours the Earth* (1990). Her poems speak of Cuba and her love for her country, at times reflecting a consciousness of her role as a black woman and writer in Cuba's revolutionary politics. Morejón writes in a private way, using words for her own self-enlightenment and personal growth. She writes about family, her African ancestry, social class, economic deprivation, and the barriers that face her country, such as international isolation as a result of the U.S.-led embargo. Morejón is most noted for her poem "Mujer negra" (Black Woman), which first appeared in *Parajes de una época*, and in which she chronicles the historical development of the black Cuban woman.

In the New Era

Black women writers in Spanish America who were born in the 1950s and 1960s bring a new perspective of the black experience to the reading public. Most importantly, they document the reality of blacks in Spanish America, using their medium as a potent reminder that many ills continue to plague the black community.

In Uruguay, for example, black women began to raise their voices in the 1980s, emulating Brindis de Salas and the many women who wrote for the black journal NUESTRA RAZA (Our Race), published from 1933 to 1958. This new generation is redefining the black literary history of Uruguay, which has been broken and sporadic. One example of this literary renaissance

is Cristina Rodriguez Cabral, the granddaughter of Elemo Cabral, who was one of the editors of *Nuestra Raza*. Cabral's work provides a glimpse into the current realities of the black Uruguayan community. She molds in her own form the social context that illustrates the racial discrimination, social inequities, and oppression she experiences. Her work can be seen as a continuation of *Nuestra Raza*'s mission to fight for racial, social, and economic justice.

Cabral's work first appeared in 1988 in Uruguay's newest black periodical, *Mundo Afro* (Black World). With the debut of her poetry and her participation in many poetry readings in both Uruguay and BRAZIL, Cabral was hailed as one of the most talented black writers of the Southern Cone (the southernmost region of SOUTH AMERICA that includes Uruguay, CHILE, and ARGENTINA). Her work has since appeared in Uruguay's first anthology of black poetry, *Antologia de poetas negros* (1990), edited by Alberto Britos. One year later, Cabral's work was introduced to the reading public in the United States in the article "New Voices of Afro-Uruguay," published in the *Afro-Hispanic Review*. Cabral's books of poetry include *Pajaros sueltos* (1987; Free Birds), *Entre giros y mutaciones* (1988; Between Twists and Turns), *De par en par* (1989; Wide Open), *Cuento y canto de par en par* (1990; At the Same Time I Sing and Tell a Story), *La del espejo y yo* (1990; The One in the Mirror and Me), *Desde mi trenchera* (1993; Down in the Trenches), and *Memoria y resistencia* (1998; Memory and Resistance). Her literary contributions also include three essays, "La literatura como forma de resistencia" (1988; Literature as a Form of Resistance); "Cien años de abolición" (1988; One Hundred Years of Abolition); and "La literatura Afro-Uruguaya" (1993; Afro-Uruguayan Literature).

The literary renaissance also is exemplified by the work of Costa Rican writer Shirley Campbell Barr. She published her first book of poetry, *Naciendo* (I Rise), in 1988 and her second, *Rotundamente negra* (Totally a Black Woman), in 1994. In this second volume, Campbell affirms her identity as a black Costa Rican. She rejects all notions of white domination by proclaiming that she is a proud black woman. Her poetic task is to be understood as a young black Costa Rican mother. Interwoven with themes of motherhood, Campbell's poems speak of her courage and triumphs. She rejects the recurrent images of black Costa Ricans as lazy, illiterate, and in poverty. Her main message is to the children of her country. Because they are indoctrinated early by negative stereotypes and racial distinctions, she communicates to them a proud people, full of role models, love, hope, and inspiration. Overall, as a writer-activist, Campbell calls for an enlightened and responsible black Costa Rican citizenry. According to literary critic Carlos Manuel Moreno, Barr's poetic voice reflects the vision of American civil rights leader and clergyman MARTIN LUTHER KING, JR., and the militancy of American political activist and author ANGELA DAVIS.

In addition to the above-mentioned authors, other notable black female writers are Puerto Rican Mayra Santos; Cubans Marta Rojas, Excilia Saldaña, and Balbina Herrera; Colombians Yvonne América Truque and Edelma Zapata; and Uruguayans

Beatriz Santos and Marta Gularte. Their works are not widely distributed outside their countries, and even in their own countries their texts are often difficult to find. For this reason, a younger generation of North American and Latin American literary critics and cultural historians are in the process of bringing their work to a wider audience through anthologies and translations.

Conclusion

Although these writers are separated by geographical boundaries, they tell a communal story that speaks of the black female experience. They articulate the thoughts, feelings, and ideas of black women who have been rejected, suppressed, and ignored in Spanish American society. Their works represent an attempt to regain their voice. Their purpose as writers is to reaffirm their identity, lessen the burdens of inferiority, educate those unfamiliar with their culture, and instill pride in their own people.

Despite the presence of these authors, there continues to be a paucity of literature by black women in Spanish America. Black women are underrepresented in all aspects of literary productions, primarily due to economic barriers in publishing. The fact that their voice continues to be unheard serves as a reminder that race and gender continue to function as two of the most powerful shapers of black female experience. With the triple burden of being black, female, and economically disadvantaged, they remain the poorest of the poor and the least educated.

From the Caribbean to the Southern Cone, black female writers remain optimistic about the question of race and gender. They are hopeful and inspire a vision of hope in others. Their contributions incite change as well as increase and enrich the literary landscape of Spanish America. In sum, black female writers and their works amplify the historical understanding of the female experience in the Americas.

See also Image of the Mulatta in Latin America and the Caribbean; Literature, Black, in Spanish America; Poetry, Caribbean; Press, Black, in Latin America and the Caribbean; Race in Latin America; Racial Stereotypes; Slavery in Latin America and the Caribbean.

Women Writers, Black, in the United States

African American women who have written poetry, fiction, and drama.

In his introduction to the Schomburg series of books by nineteenth-century black women, scholar HENRY LOUIS GATES, JR. points out that when PHILLIS WHEATLEY published her 1773 collection of poetry, she "launched two traditions at once—the black American literary tradition *and* the black woman's literary tradition." He continues,

That the progenitor of the black literary tradition was a woman means, in the most strictly literal sense, that all subsequent black writers have evolved in a matrilineal line of descent, and that each, consciously or unconsciously, has extended and revised a canon whose foundation was the poetry of a black woman.

Black women writers have pioneered in several literary genres throughout the last three centuries. They have also been among the most beloved and celebrated American authors for a wide range of readers—black and white, male and female. Writers such as ZORA NEALE HURSTON, TONI MORRISON, ALICE WALKER, and TERRY MCMILLAN often represent "black literature" to contemporary audiences. Morrison, the recipient of the 1993 Nobel Prize in literature—and the first African American to receive that literary honor—is internationally recognized as one of the most significant living American writers.

Academic courses exclusively devoted to black women writers have become common. Within the black literary tradition, women writers are often celebrated for their gift of conveying the fullness of the African American experience. As essayist and activist ANNA JULIA COOPER said in her 1892 book, *A Voice from the South from a Black Woman of the South*, "Only the Black Woman can say 'when and where I enter, in the quiet, undisputed dignity of my womanhood, without violence and without suing or special patronage, then and there the whole *Negro race enters with me*'."

The first milestone in African American literature was reached in 1746 by Lucy Terry. Terry's poem "Bars Fight," which commemorated several residents of her Massachusetts town who had been killed during a clash with NATIVE AMERICANS, is the first known piece of literature by an African American. Three decades later, Phillis Wheatley's *Poems on Miscellaneous Subjects* (1773) became the first book to be published by an African American writer. Wheatley remained the only African American woman to publish a book of creative literature through the first half of the nineteenth century, although black women continued to write, and in genres other than poetry. ANN PLATO wrote a collection of essays and poetry, CHARLOTTE FORTEN GRIMKÉ kept a diary, MARIA STEWART collected her speeches, JARENA LEE wrote a spiritual autobiography, and HARRIET JACOBS wrote an autobiographical SLAVE NARRATIVE.

Two new milestones came in 1859, when HARRIET WILSON published *Our Nig*, the first known novel written by an African American, and FRANCES ELLEN WATKINS HARPER published "The Two Offers," the first short story by an African American. Harper, who had already published her first volume of poetry, became the most prominent nineteenth-century black female writer, publishing several more collections and editions of poetry and short stories, three serialized short novels, and the landmark novel *Iola Leroy* (1892). Other black women novelists of the 1880s and 1890s included Katherine Chapman Tillman, Amelia E. Johnson, and Emma Dunham Kelly-Hawkins. So many black women became known for their literary ability and political activism in the 1890s alone that the decade is called the "Women's Era" in African American literary history.

Popular turn-of-the-century women writers included novelist PAULINE E. HOPKINS and poet ALICE DUNBAR-NELSON. In 1916 *Rachel*, a play by ANGELINA WELD GRIMKÉ, became the first staged play by an African American. Grimké's poetry was also widely anthologized during the HARLEM RENAISSANCE, the movement of black writers and artists centered in NEW YORK CITY during the 1920s. This movement also included novelists NELLA LARSEN and JESSIE FAUSET, poet GEORGIA DOUGLAS JOHNSON, and Zora Neale Hurston, who was a folklorist and essayist, as well as a novelist. Hurston, in particular, has become one of the most beloved and widely read African American writers, now best known for her novel *Their Eyes Were Watching God* (1937).

The 1940s and 1950s saw the publication of the novels *The Street* (1946) by ANN PETRY, *The Living is Easy* (1948) by DOROTHY WEST, and *Maud Martha* (1953) by GWENDOLYN BROOKS. Brooks had already become the first African American to win a Pulitzer Prize for the poetry collection *Annie Allen* (1949). LORRAINE HANSBERRY published her award-winning play *A Raisin in the Sun* in 1955. In the 1960s PAULE MARSHALL and ROSA GUY wrote novels that reflected their West Indian heritage; MARGARET WALKER published her historical novel *Jubilee;* and poets NIKKI GIOVANNI and SONIA SANCHEZ were among the voices of the BLACK ARTS MOVEMENT. But the second "Women's Era" in black literary history—one that continues in the twenty-first century—began with a series of significant publications in 1970.

That year Toni Morrison and Alice Walker published their first novels, and MAYA ANGELOU published her first autobiography. These three writers have since established themselves as key figures in African American and American literary history. Morrison, a novelist and essayist, has written several important novels, including *The Bluest Eye* and *Beloved*, which won the Pulitzer Prize in 1988. Walker has written novels, poetry, essays, autobiography, and children's books, and is best known for her 1982 Pulitzer Prize–winning novel *The Color Purple*, which Steven Spielberg made into an Oscar-nominated film. Angelou is widely acclaimed for her poetry, autobiographical works, and essays. She was selected to compose and read a poem—"On the Pulse of Morning"—for the inauguration of President Bill Clinton in 1993.

The emergence of these and other women writers, such as poets AUDRE LORDE and MARI EVANS and novelists GAYL JONES and TONI CADE BAMBARA, coincided with the rise of the women's movement, when audiences became especially receptive to female authors. An interest in black women writers, in particular, developed at this time. Novelists GLORIA NAYLOR and Terry McMillan, as well as American poet laureate RITA DOVE are among the many other women writers who achieved critical and commercial success during the 1980s and 1990s.

Each of these writers ensures that this women's era will continue. With their powerful, eloquent voices, contemporary black women extend a literary tradition that has been handed down for more than 200 years. In the process, they continue to create new milestones and open new doors, still proving that "when and where they enter," they carry with them the fullness of African American experience.

Bibliography

Christian, Barbara. *Black Women Novelists: The Development of a Tradition, 1892–1976.* Greenwood Press, 1980.

Evans, Mari. *Black Women Writers (1950–1980): A Critical Evaluation.* Anchor Press/Doubleday, 1984.

Foster, Frances Smith. *Written By Herself: Literary Production by African American Women, 1746–1892.* Indiana University Press, 1993.

Shockley, Ann Allen. *Afro-American Women Writers, 1746–1933: An Anthology and Critical Guide.* G. K. Hall, 1988.

Lisa Clayton Robinson

Women Writers, English and French Caribbean

Caribbean women's writing went almost unnoticed until the late 1970s, due in part to the domination of the literary scene by male writers such as GEORGE LAMMING, EDWARD BRATHWAITE, and DEREK WALCOTT. These writers were regarded as the spokespeople for the region. Women writers, however, have gained considerable momentum and visibility since that time, especially with the First International Conference sponsored by Wellesley College in 1988, which brought together more than fifty Caribbean women writers, and the subsequent publication of *Caribbean Women Writers*, edited by Selwyn Cudjoe (1990). Other publications had also helped to pave the way—a special issue of *Savacou* (1977) on "Caribbean Woman," published by the Caribbean Artists Movement, and *Lionheart Gal* (1986), a collection of the life stories of the women who formed the SISTREN COLLECTIVE, a Jamaican theater group that performs plays based on the lives of working-class women. Similarly, the founding of CAFRA (Caribbean Association Feminist Research and Action) and the publication of Ramabai Espinet's poetry anthology *Creation Fire* (1990) contributed to the visibility of women writers and women's issues.

Rapidly becoming a well-established literary tradition, women writers of the English- and French-speaking Caribbean share a common history that draws on the traumatic experience of COLONIAL RULE and slavery and the subsequent struggles for independence, decolonization, and migration. Caribbean women writers are subject to what the critic Deborah King has termed "multiple jeopardy"—the intertwining of gender, race, class, and sexuality factors that define and restrict women's lives. Thus they raise their voices against the multilayered oppression arising from the combination of these factors by offering an alternative—a countering discourse that challenges and subverts both Western and male configurations of female identities—and effectively resists them by means of appropiation and indigenization of that dominant culture and canon. The works of Caribbean women writers account for their specificities and their differences, while simultaneously creating a collective female space in which the exploration of key notions of self, gender, community, female bonding, and homeland allows for a radically new and female-centered perspective. It is precisely their diversity of voices, cultures, experiences and languages that ensures the vitality that is so enriching and engaging in their texts, while celebrating the production of unique works of art.

Women Writing in English

Despite the popularity of contemporary women writers, their contribution to the development of Caribbean literature remained virtually unknown until Selwyn Cudjoe's introduction to *Caribbean Women Writers*, in which he traced it back to slave narratives, such as *The History of Mary Prince, A West Indian Slave, Related by Herself* (1831). Mary Prince's story, probably the first female slave account of the region, depicts in great detail the cruelty of slavery and the particularly degrading treatment of slave women. Another nineteenth-century work, Mary Seacole's *Wonderful Adventures of Mrs. Seacole in Many Lands* (1857), strikes a different chord, recounting events in the author's adventurous life. Seacole, a highly educated black Jamaican woman, takes an unconventional path travelling extensively, practicing medicine, and setting up her own business. Even as she defines herself as "an unprotected female," Seacole asserts her independence and her pride in her blackness, establishing new venues for twentieth-century definitions of Caribbean womanhood.

The first significant work of the twentieth century was JEAN RHYS's *Voyage in the Dark* (1934), a different version of Caribbean female subjectivity, addressed from the point of view of a white CREOLE woman from DOMINICA attempting to come to terms with her lost heritage. Set after World War I, Anna Morgan's journey back to the Caribbean of her childhood memories entails a reconnection to her past, which she tries to achieve by means of sexual encounters that progressively become more dehumanizing and self-alienating. Anna finally dies from complications after an abortion, having failed to complete her passage back to a notion of self-centered self. Contradictory forces eroding a healthy sense of self are also at the core of Rhy's next novel, *Wide Sargasso Sea* (1966), in which the author examines the consciousness of another white Creole woman, Antoinette Cosway, and the ways in which she tries to make sense of the changing world surrounding her. Antoinette is rejected by both her mother and her husband—her mother prefers Antoinette's brother and her husband is suspicious of Antoinette's dark complexion. At the end of this bleak story, Antoinette burns down the house in which she is kept prisoner in a way that recalls the burning of her family's estate by their former slaves. The fire, reminiscent of Charlotte Bronte's *Jane Eyre*, is significant because, like other Caribbean writers, Rhys was using the literature of the colonial period to make an important statement.

Another white Dominican woman writer who contributed to female-centered literature is Phyllis Allfrey. Her novel *The Orchid House* (1953) is a meditation on the mutable realities of white women's lives after decolonization and especially their

endurance, as seen through the eyes of Lally, the black female narrator. Two poets are also essential in the development of a distinct female tradition in the Caribbean. They are Una Marson, who actively engaged in the struggle against racism and sexism, and Louise Bennett, both Jamaican-born. Of Marson's three volumes of poetry, *The Moth and the Stars* (1937) emerges as her most racially conscious book. In it she questions the Western conception of beauty and its internalization by black people. Bennett, whose first volume of poetry, *Dialect Verse*, was published in 1942, reflects the feelings of Jamaican people by making use of dialect and popular oral forms. She also integrated these forms in her development of a dramatic form known as "speech theater."

A well-known author whose work appeared in the 1960s is PAULE MARSHALL, born in New York to Barbadian parents. Her first three novels, *Brown Girl, Brownstones* (1959), *The Chosen Place, the Timeless People* (1969), and *Praisesong for the Widow* (1983), form a trilogy that deals with a search for self in a community straddling two worlds—everyday life in the United States and a strong cultural and spiritual bond to a Caribbean heritage. In her third novel, especially, Marshall traces the journey that Avey Johnson, an upper-class black widow, needs to undertake in order to rediscover and reclaim her past, her true self, and her intimate connection to her community—leaving the stagnant and materialistic United States for Africa, the homeland, by way of the Caribbean. In this sense, Marshall inaugurates the investigation of a widening of the concept of community that encompasses all people of the African diaspora as symbolized by the "nation dance" that closes the novel, in which Africans, African Americans, and Afro-Caribbeans join hands and celebrate the unity in their multiplicity. She has also written four novellas, collected under the title *Clap Hands and Sing* (1961), linking different black communities: Barbados, Brooklyn, British Guiana, and Brazil; a collection of short stories, *Reena and Other Stories* (1982); and her most recent novel *Daughters* (1991).

Other women writers whose work came to light in the 1960s include Clara Rosa de Lima, ROSA GUY, and Sylvia Winter. De Lima's novel *Tomorrow Will Always Come* (1965), set in Brazil, dissects the corruptive political situation of the country and the role of women, who are sexually and socially exploited as part of the political process. Her next novel, *Not Bad, Just a Little Mad* (1975), focuses on upper-class Trinidad society but also fails to provide a credible picture of black women. Trinidadian Rosa Guy published her novel *Bird at My Window* in 1966. In it she examines the crippling effects of racism on both African Americans and Caribbean immigrants in the United States through the disastrous relationship between Wade, the protagonist, and his mother, whose pervading influence suffocates her son and leads him to murder in his attempt to break away from her. *Hills of Hebron* (1966) by Sylvia Winter completes the picture of this first period offering an idealistic community in Jamaica, founded to overcome the oppression of colonial rule, but which does not succeed due to misguided guidance. As Selwyn Cudjoe argues, these works heralded a new day, one in which Caribbean people showed that they were ready to repossess themselves and claim their actual voices.

In a way, Winter's novel issues a call for a kind of creative writing that finds its response in the explosion of new female voices that addressed gender issues in a more direct and deliberate manner from 1970 onward. Critics agree that the Trinidadian Merle Hodge's *Crick Crack Monkey* (1970) ushered in this new era by relying on oral forms for guidelines of the narrative that involves the growing process of Tee, the young protagonist, and her need to choose between the black Creole culture personified by her grandmother Tantie and the metropolitan values upheld by Aunt Beatrice. At the end of the novel, Tee is unable to resolve the conflicting tensions and decides to leave for London, having internalized Beatrice's colonial values. Despite the pessimistic ending, Hodge's novel tackles key questions that will be further developed by subsequent women writers. Her last contribution after almost three decades is the children's novel *For the Love of Laetitia* (1995), in which the protagonist wins a scholarship to attend a city school, but rejects it by refusing to stay in this hostile environment and returns to her nurturing village community.

The 1980s saw an unprecedented rise of female voices emerge and gain access to a wide audience. Leading the trend was Jamaican ERNA BRODBER with her novel *Jane and Louisa Will Soon Come Home* (1980). Like Hodge, Brodber presents Nellie, an adolescent girl with clashing models: Aunt Becca, who lost herself in order to become the wife of a respected schoolteacher, and Aunt Alice, a liberated modern woman. By understanding her "kumbla," or the different survival strategies that black women have traditionally resorted to, Nellie is able to effect her journey back to self and community, reconciling herself with her Caribbean heritage and the opposing forces that have caused her identity crisis. Brodber has written two other novels: *Myal* (1988) and her most recent novel *Louisiana* (1994).

A young girl and her maturing process are the basic concerns of *At the Bottom of the River* (1984) by Jamaica Kincaid, born in Antigua. Kincaid combines dream visions and metaphor in ten surreal prose poems to investigate the complex and highly ambivalent relationship between a powerful maternal figure and her frightened, but delighted, daughter. A similar theme runs through Kincaid's second novel, *Annie John* (1985), set in Antigua, in which the conflictive relationship with her mother leads Annie to feel caught between two sides, two allegiances—her mother's proper and ladylike colonial imitation style, personified by her friend Gwen, and her other friend (Red Girl), who represents the most rebellious aspect of her personality. Helped through her identity crisis by her maternal grandmother, Annie needs to separate from her mother and thus she leaves for England to recover psychic balance. Largely autobiographical, as Kincaid herself admits, *Annie John* was followed by *Lucy* (1990), in which the protagonist goes to New York to work as an au pair, but despite the geographical distance, is still unable to resolve the relationship with her mother. The sequel, *The Autobiography of My Mother* (1996) obliterates the conflict by opening with the mother's death in the first lines

of the novel, but the protagonist does not fare any better—victimized by her father and later marrying an English doctor, while madly in love with a married black man. In 2000, Jamaica Kincaid published *A Small Place*, an appeal to tourists to look beyond the natural beauty of Antigua to reach an understanding of how COLONIAL RULE affected the lives of ordinary Antiguans.

MICHELLE CLIFF, a white Jamaican writer, deals with identity, gender, and heritage issues in her first work *Claiming an Identity They Taught Me to Despise* (1980). Cliff's book opens by tracing the passage from Caribbean childhood to American adulthood of a hybrid Creole trying to come to terms with her mixed ancestry and her cultural and class legacy. Love for her homeland is filtered through her desire to account for the multiple facets of her personality and the inevitable contradictions that continually arise. The same concerns surface in her collected essays *The Land of Look Behind* (1985) and in her poetry. Other important works by Cliff include *Abeng* (1984) and *No Telephone to Heaven* (1987).

The "coming of age" characterizes ZEE EDGELL's novel *Beka Lamb* (1982), in which Belize's independence, and the birth of the new nation, is directly related to Beka's emerging female consciousness. Beka's middle-class father's authoritative and colonial attitude leads her to a crisis that her grandmother's healing, based on popular beliefs, counteracts. Beka learns that through reclaiming her personal autonomy and her female community, she will ensure her survival. Edgell's trilogy gives voice to Belizean people and is completed with two other novels that focus on different social classes and their contribution to Belizean independence. The upper-class protagonist of *In Times like These* (1991) decides to return to Belize from England and the working-class mestizo narrator of *The Festival of San Joaquin* (1997), based on a real incident, deals with the arrest of a woman for the murder of her common-law husband. Two other writers who have contributed to the analysis and depiction of Caribbean female identity are AUDRE LORDE (born in Carriacou) and Merle Collins (from Grenada). *Zami: A New Spelling of My Name* (1984) by Lorde also takes up the question of definition of self within two strongly opposed cultures and value systems: Caribbean and American. This autobiographical work is considered groundbreaking because it is the first statement of outspoken lesbianism. Lorde is also well known for her poetry, including *From a Land Where Other People Live* (1973), *The Black Unicorn* (1978), and *Undersong: Chosen Poems Old and New* (1992). But probably her most influential book is the collection of essays entitled *Sister Outsider: Essays and Speeches* (1984) where she fully articulates her theory of difference, explicitly claiming her multiple identities as "black, lesbian, feminist, mother, lover, poet."

Poet Merle Collins lived in Grenada until 1983, and her first poems, *Because Dawn Breaks* (1985), are dedicated to Grenadian people. *Angel* (1987), her first novel, is also concerned with Grenadians, in this case three generations of politically active women, Angel representing the third generation who participates in the 1983 American invasion as a black "angel" subverting conventional Western mythology. Other notable women writers include Beryl Gilroy from Guyana (*Frangipani House*, 1985); Dionne Brand, a Toronto-based Trinidadian, also recounts the American invasion of Grenada in her poems *Chronicles of a Hostile Sun* (1984) and in her novel *Another Place, Not Here* (1996); Marlene Nourbese Philip, (*Looking for Livingstone*, 1991 and *The Fat Black Woman's Poems*), works to revise stereotypes of black femininity.

Edwidge Danticat stands out among the new voices in a growing literary field. At age fourteen Danticat published her first writing in English, including the newspaper article about her immigration to the United States that inspired her first novel, *Breath, Eyes, Memory* (1994). Other new voices, include Olive Senior, Opal Adissa Palmer, Joan Riley, Christine Craig, Velma Pollard, Vernella Fuller, Pauline Melville, Andrea Levy, Amryl Johnson, and Alecia McKenzie.

French-Speaking Women Writers

Within the Caribbean female discourse, French-speaking women writers have often been neglected, as they were in the groundbreaking conference at Wellesley College in 1988. The great majority of the writers attending the conference came from the English-speaking islands. This imbalance was corrected during the Third International Caribbean Women Writers Conference, which was held in Curaçao in 1992. The proclaimed purpose, using Lorde's phrase, was "to attend the silences." For this reason, it paid more attention to other literatures, especially to the Francophone Caribbean writers. These writers share many concerns with the Anglophone women writers—a common history of slavery and colonialism, and their aftermath. But the particular focus of French-speaking women writers is what the critic Marie-Denise Shelton summarizes as "the problem of feminine exclusion and dispossession." In other words, Francophone women writers seem to be interested in the interstices of the so-called "female experience" from the vantage point of women who feel enclosed in their environment and are unable to come to terms with it, and by extension, themselves. Thus they fall prey to the alienating consequences of a deep and unsolvable identity crisis, complicated by the need to write in two languages—French and Creole.

Like their Anglophone counterparts, Francophone male writers also enjoyed primacy, until the 1950s when the first seeds of contemporary women's literary tradition were planted. Among the first Francophone female writers to gain recognition were MAYOTTE CAPÉCIA and MARIE CHAUVET, both of whom who seemed to adopt conventional tragic mulatto paradigms in their characterizations. In her first novel, actually her autobiography, *Je suis martiniquaise* (1948), Capécia depicts the adverse conditions that surrounded her life, making her regard her blackness as a curse, and like a tragic mulatto figure, she voices her wish of being liberated by a miraculous whitening of her skin or by marrying a white man. Writing at the same time, Marie Chauvet explores in *Fille d'Haiti* (1954) the difficult life of her protagonist, Lotus, who feels endangered by both her inner struggle to define herself and the outer situation of social and political violence of the

country. Socially, she is nowhere, because her mother is an elite prostitute, precluding Lotus's acceptance by either the upper or lower class. Racially speaking, she is even more in-between, since she is a mulatto with no definitive racial allegiances. Personally, she is an unstable character who shows her hatred toward men by seducing and later discarding them. All of which implies a self-hatred the character is not able to sustain, so she turns to madness as a means of liberation. Madness also awaits Claire, the protagonist of her second novel, *Amour* (1960). Unable to marry, Claire feels socially unfit and demonstrates her rebellion against the norm by going mad, too. Chauvet draws a highly critical picture of the Haitian elite of the time and their priviledged status enforced by a class structure based on color.

Writing in the 1960s, Michèle Lacrosil centers her two novels *Sapotille et le serin d'Argile* (1960) and *Cajou* (1961) on female alienation and the crippling effects of a hierarchical color system, according to which her black women feel ugly and want to remain invisible to a society that continuously despises and excludes them. Sapotille, a Guadeloupean woman, keeps a journal on her journey to France, in which she records her desire to become invisible because of all the racial prejudice and a consequent internalization of a sense of inferiority she has endured throughout her life. Cajou takes Sapotille's despair to the extreme—suicide—to break free from the constraints that her black skin imposes on her. Also writing during this period, Nadine Marglorie follows Chauvet's lead in criticizing life in Haiti in her two novels *Le mal de vivre* (1968) and *Le sexe mystique* (1975).

Many more writers gained recognition and wider audiences in the 1970s, among them Thérèse Colimon for the two novels she published in 1973: *Fils de misère* and *Le chant des Sirènes*. In the former, Colimon explores the life of the working-class people through Lamercie, the protagonist, who tries to challenge the system and raise herself from poverty, but is ultimately unable to do so. In the latter, a collection of short stories, the focus shifts to Haitian migration which, Colimon demonstrates, is bound to fail because dreams do not come true. Liliane Devieux also explores the inherent contradictions of migration and the accompanying risks in her novel *L'amour oui, la mort non* (1976).

The real blossoming of women writers from the Francophone Caribbean came in the late 1970s and 1980s. MARYSE CONDÉ, SIMONE SCHWARTZ-BART, and Myriam Warner-Vieyra continued to analyze the so-called "female condition" in their specific Caribbean context. Born in Guadeloupe, Condé in her first novel (*Heremakhonon*, 1976) portrays Veronica, the quintessence of the bewildered self who, not belonging to any particular world, feels forlorn everywhere she goes. The same could be applied to her second novel *Une saison à Rihata* (1982), in which Marie-Hélène feels a complete stranger in Africa, even though she is married to an African. In her last novel, *La vie scélèrate* (1987) Condé tries to broaden her horizons by reconstructing the history of a Guadeloupean family over several generations in the Caribbean, in the United States, and in Panama. Also from Guadeloupe, Schwartz-Bart's prose differs from the previous writers in that she affirms the potentiality of life and identity in the female characters she portrays. Télumée, the heroine of *Pluie et vent sur Télumée miracle* (1972), refuses to accept the oppression she is subjected to, taking strength instead from her intimate contact with her island culture. Similar to the characters of some Anglophone writers, such as Paule Marshall, Schwartz-Bart's protagonist is self-assured because she does not feel estranged from her roots or from her own body. In her second novel, *Ti-Jean l'Horizon* (1979), Schwartz-Bart prefers to recount the heroic tale of Ti-Jean, who initiates an epic quest to recover the sun that has been swallowed by a beast.

Myriam Warner-Vieyra returns to a depiction of the tragic puzzled female self. Her characters are immersed in a chaotic and meaningless life that frequently leads to madness. The heroine of *Le Quimboiseur l'avait dit* (1982) is sent to a French psychiatric asylum after being abused by her mother and her lover. For the protagonist of *Juletane* (1982), the only way out of her disintegrating state is madness, discovering on her arrival in Africa that her husband has other wives. Becoming "the mad one" in the community, Juletane can sustain at least some kind of self-worth in the face of deterioration and isolation.

Other writers, such as Jacqueline Manicom, Françoise Ega, Gisèle Pineau, or Jan Dominique, are deeply engaged in articulating the Caribbean self with respect to gender and community, sharing many concerns with their predecessors, but also offering new and fresh perspectives from which to explore women's literature in the twenty-first century.

Mar Gallego

Women Writers in French-Speaking Africa

Contributions of Francophone African women writers since the 1970s.

The beginning of the Francophone novel in AFRICA (works written by French-writing African authors) is usually associated with the late 1950s to the early 1960s, when African countries gained their independence from FRANCE. The first female voices, however, did not emerge until the early 1970s.

Until then, African women appeared either as peripheral, misrepresented, or nonexistent under men's pens. OUSMANE SEMBÈNE and MONGO BETI did grant prominent roles to female characters, giving them a certain complexity. But for the most part, African women were literally and literarily silenced in public. There was thus a definite need for women to speak out.

Still, the 1970s saw only a handful of titles, mostly from SENEGAL: Nafissatou Diallo's *De tilène au plateau: Une enfance dakaroise* (1975) (A Dakar Childhood, 1982); Aoua Keita's *Femme d'Afrique: La vie d'Aoua Keita racontée par elle-même* (1975) (Woman of Africa: The Life of Aoua Keita as Told by Herself); *Le revenant* (1976) (The Ghost); *La grève des bàttu* (1979) (*The Beggars' Strike*, 1982) by Aminata Sow Fall; and

Mariama Bà's *Une si longue lettre* (1979) (*So Long a Letter*, 1981). With the exceptions of Aminata Sow Fall and the Malian Aoua Keita, whose narratives carry more overt sociopolitical overtones and reflect women's interest in the construction of a nation, the other writers emphasize the notion of intimate voices and personal testimony, often adopting the autobiographical form, or first-person narrative. Typically, these earlier works depict a female protagonist in the process of speaking out, not out of an artistic impulse but because she must vent her frustration, suffering, and loneliness. Usually set in a middle-class urban environment, she is described as trapped in a deteriorating marital relationship, unable to develop professionally, and burdened by the demands of family and in-laws. The narrator's daily experience in her triple role as daughter, wife, and mother characterizes her oppression. The early goal of these pioneer women writers was to portray African women from within, correcting the stereotypical metaphors in male writing of women merely as symbols of mother Africa or the postcolonial state.

MARIAMA BÀ's *Une si longue lettre* (1980) constitutes a landmark in the Francophone literary production. Awarded the Japanese Noma Prize in 1980, the novel catapulted Bà and the other women novelists into the limelight. For the first time, Francophone African women writers were becoming visible on the literary stage. The novel addresses most of the issues approached in Francophone female writing in the early 1980s: marital difficulties within a polygamous family, tensions between modernity and tradition, the search for personal happiness. Other aspects of women's experience that were explored during that period were questions of mandatory motherhood and barrenness. Works such as Ken Bugul's *Le baobab fou* (1983) (The Abandoned Baobab, 1991) dealt with women's sense of hybridity and estrangement in a changing environment, particularly after a Western education in EUROPE.

Using the personal has gradually enabled Francophone women writers in Africa to touch on larger issues. No African woman's history can be written without taking the community into consideration: each and all of a woman's key moments (from birth to childhood to puberty to womanhood to marriage to motherhood to death) are defined by the society she lives in. Writers went from unveiling themselves to disclosing family life to a more public role as social critics.

Initially, literary critics, mostly male, saw the choice of the autobiography as a sign of lack of mastery of literary techniques. In the mid-1980s, with the birth of a body of feminist African criticism, critics began to acknowledge that autobiographical emphasis was a chosen form, for such a narrative style enabled the authors to create an empathic tie with the reader. Still, unlike the African male writer, whose words are often seen as representing both self and his country, the female writer was not yet seen as synonymous with her society.

From the mid-1980s on, a second generation of female voices has appeared, showing a more aggressive and overtly rebellious tone. While well-established authors like Aminata Sow Fall have continued to examine sociopolitical issues in their countries, rising writers are gaining new recognition: for example, WEREWERE LIKING, Calixthe Beyala (who published eight novels in about ten years), Evelyne Mpoudi Ngolle, and Philomène Bassek, all from CAMEROON; the Ivorians Véronique Tadjo and Tanella Boni; and the Gabonese Angèle Rawiri.

Systematic oppression is at the core of these new narratives. Female characters are often from the margins of society, such as the foreign spouse, the prostitute, or the madwoman. The works explore areas hitherto branded as culturally trivial or taboo, such as mother-daughter relationships, the female body, pain and desire, and the search for new sexual ethics. Fusing the genres of poetry, oral forms, legends, and myths, these writers renew the quality of writing, creating polyphonic narratives. A number of them are in fact poets and playwrights as well as novelists.

Using their female characters' position of marginality, these writers have been able to address openly a number of sociopolitical aspects facing postcolonial Africa. As part of a process of catharsis, they paint the violence and horror that Africans have experienced. Unlike their male counterparts, whose novels often strike the reader as sharply accusatory, these works show a visionary quality and an attempt to search for alternative solutions for a healthier Africa. For example, Calixthe Beyala's early works try to delineate a program for women that would remedy today's hardships. These works suggest a fundamental rethinking of African societies, from the meaning of womanhood and motherhood, to the corruption of governments, to the relationships that form the basis of societies. The work of Werewere Liking, such as *Elle sera de Jaspe et de corail: Journal d'une mysovire* (1983) (She Will Be of Jasper and Coral: Diary of a Manhater) and Tadjo's *Le royaume aveugle* (1990) (The Kingdom of the Blind) best represent this kind of comprehensive rethinking of life and society. Throughout these very diverse and personal voices, a common notion recurs: one cannot expect to change a society until one changes one's own expectations and dreams of success. Thus they reexamine basic philosophical concepts: philosophy and religion (Liking), education, traditions, and government (Sow Fall), history (Boni), and love (Liking and Tadjo). Today, many of the works considered African literature are written from abroad. Writers such as Calixthe Beyala, who resides in France, give a different voice to African literature.

This second generation of female writers has created a new form of political novel, moving away from a certain status quo in postcolonial African societies to offer a promising vision. Far from constituting a minor literature, Francophone African women writers have created a voice that is central to the Francophone African novel. Accessing areas of language and themes that were until recently regarded as men's prerogative, in particular politics, they have gained equal authority and contributed to reshape the canon.

See also Contemporary African Writers in France; Feminism in Africa: An Interpretation; Francophone Writing; Literature, French-Language, in Africa.

Odile Cazenave

Women Writers of the Caribbean

Women born into Caribbean families and known for their contributions to literature in poetry and prose. Some of these writers left the Caribbean, others remained or returned; but for all, their Caribbean heritage is a significant element in their writing.

For information on
Writers in French: *See* Chauvet, Marie; Schwartz-Bart, Simone.
Writers in English: *See* Cliff, Michelle; Guy, Rosa Cuthbert; Kincaid, Jamaica; Marson, Una M.; Philip, Marlene Nourbese; Rhys, Jean.
Writers in Spanish: *See* Morejón, Nancy; Vega, Ana Lydia.
African American writers of Caribbean heritage: *See* Marshall, Paule.

Wonder, Stevie

1950–

African American singer, songwriter, and musician.

Stevie Wonder was born Steveland Morris in Saginaw, Michigan. Wonder is one of the most prolific and inventive artists in American popular music and RHYTHM AND BLUES. Blind since birth, Wonder was first introduced to music as a young child and quickly developed musical skills beyond his years. At age twelve he was discovered by Ronnie White of THE MIRACLES and won an audition at the MOTOWN Record Company in Detroit, Michigan. When Motown's founder, Berry Gordy, witnessed the young boy's startling talents, he dubbed him "Little Stevie Wonder." Wonder was quickly adopted into the Motown "family" at Hitsville Studios. He charmed everyone with his prodigious musical range and lively sense of humor. Although he played the drums, piano, and organ, Wonder's first number-one hit, "Fingertips, Part 2" (1963), featured his exceptional skill on the harmonica, which became a trademark of his early career. More hits followed, including "Workout Stevie, Workout" (1963), "Hey Harmonica Man" (1964), and "Uptight (Everything's Alright)" (1966).

In 1966 Wonder recorded a cover version of Bob Dylan's antiwar song, "Blowin' in the Wind." Wonder's interpretation of the song became an anthem of the struggling CIVIL RIGHTS MOVEMENT and foreshadowed his future involvement in political causes. Always an independent spirit, Wonder sought more creative control over his music as he grew into adulthood. He began producing his own albums in 1970 and, in 1971, renegotiated his Motown contract to receive complete artistic control over his recordings.

The new artistic freedom resulted in one of the most productive phases of Wonder's career, which included hits such as "My Cherie Amour" (1969), "Signed, Sealed, Delivered I'm Yours" (1970), "Superstition" (1972), and "You Are the Sunshine of My Life" (1973). A musical visionary, Wonder combined poetic lyrics with experimental electronic music that he developed through his mastery of the synthesizer. He also took the idea of a "concept" album—an album based on a central theme—to new heights. Albums including *Talking Book* (1972), *Innervisions* (1973), *Fulfillingness' First Finale* (1974), and *Songs in the Key of Life* (1976) reflected Wonder's spiritual style and won him more Grammy Awards than any other Motown artist has received.

Wonder's music and life have always engaged with social issues and political causes. Songs such as "Living for the City" (1973) offered commentary on urban poverty, and one of his later hits, "Happy Birthday" (1980), was instrumental in the campaign to recognize the birthday of MARTIN LUTHER KING, JR., as a national holiday. Wonder also performed in the United States for Africa's "We are the World" fund-raising song for hunger relief and was a leader in the ANTIAPARTHEID MOVEMENT in the United States. Wonder's recent work includes the soundtrack for Spike Lee's film *Jungle Fever* (1991) and the album *Conversation Peace* (1995). Wonder has received many awards in recognition of his musical achievements. He was inducted into the Songwriter's Hall of Fame in 1982 and the Rock and Roll Hall of Fame in 1989, and in 1996, at the age of forty-six, Wonder received the Grammy's Lifetime Achievement Award. In 1999 he received a Kennedy Center for the Performing Arts Award, and in 2002 received the Sammy Khan Lifetime Achievement Award from the Songwriters Hall of Fame. In 2003 the tribute album *Conception: An Interpretation of Stevie Wonder's Songs* was released, which included covers of several Wonder hits by such diverse singers as Eric Clapton, John Mellencamp, Mary J. Blige, and India.arie.

Bibliography

Bianco, David. *Heat Wave: The Motown Fact Book.* Popular Press, 1988.

Swenson, John. *Stevie Wonder.* Harper and Row, 1986.

Robert Fay

Woodbey, George Washington

1854–1937

American Baptist minister, who was the first African American man to join the Socialist Party of America.

George Washington Woodbey was born a slave in Johnson County, Tennessee. He was ordained a Baptist minister in Emporia, Kansas, in 1874 and soon became the pastor of the African Church in Omaha, Nebraska. During his tenure as pastor, Woodbey became active in politics and joined both the REPUBLICAN PARTY and the Prohibition Party. In 1896 he ran for lieutenant governor on the Nebraska Prohibition ticket but was unsuccessful. Later that year, after reading Edward Bellamy's *Looking Backward 2000–1887* and upon hearing a speech by the socialist labor leader Eugene V. Debs, Woodbey embraced the tenets of SOCIALISM. He resigned his pastorship and dedicated the rest of his life to the socialist movement.

Woodbey joined the Socialist Party of America in 1902 and moved to San Diego, California. In San Diego he lectured widely and often appeared as a soapbox orator around town on behalf of the socialist movement. He soon became known as The Great Negro Socialist Orator. In addition, Woodbey served as minister of the Mount Zion Baptist Church in San Diego and used his pulpit to convert members of his African American congregation to socialism. In 1904 he published "What to Do and How to Do It or Socialism vs. Capitalism" and "The Bible and Socialism," two booklets intended to illustrate the compatibility of socialism and CHRISTIANITY.

Woodbey's writings, like his lectures, were highly valued by members of the Socialist Party, not only because they clearly enunciated the socialist position but also because they were widely read by the African American community. Woodbey was elected to the state executive board of the California state Socialist Party and served as the only African American delegate to the 1904 and 1908 Socialist Party conventions. Despite the lack of black representation in the Socialist Party, Woodbey never questioned the organization's position on race. Instead, Woodbey supported the socialist contention that racial inequality, like class stratification, was the direct result of the capitalist system. He argued that racial equality could only be attained through the institution of a socialist system: "And then the men of all races will share in the results of production according to their services in the process of production. This is Socialism and the only solution to the race problem."

After the 1908 convention, Woodbey embarked on a speaking tour of northern cities to promote the Socialist Party in African American communities. He published a booklet entitled "Why the Negro Should Vote the Socialist Ticket." From 1921 to 1927 he served as editor of the *New Idea*, a black socialist newspaper in San Diego.

See also Baptists; Clergy in Politics.

Elizabeth Heath

Woodruff, Hale Aspacio

1900–1980

American painter and teacher who was best known for *The Amistad Murals.*

Hale Aspacio Woodruff was born in Cairo, Illinois. He attended public schools in Nashville, Tennessee, where he was raised by his mother. In 1920, he moved to Indianapolis to study art at the John Herron Art Institute, supporting himself with part-time work as a political cartoonist. He developed an interest in African art during this period, which influenced his later work. In 1926 Woodruff won a Harmon Foundation Award to study at the Académie Moderne de la Grande Chaumière in Paris from 1927 to 1931.

Woodruff returned to the United States in 1931, and founded the art department at Atlanta University, where he helped to develop a cohesive national African American arts community.

In addition to teaching, Woodruff brought exhibitions to Atlanta University that featured a wide range of past and present African American artists who were often excluded from mainstream art exhibitions. To further promote African American art and artists, Woodruff organized the Atlanta University Annuals in 1942, a national juried exhibition that continued until 1970. Woodruff used the Annuals to promote the interests of his students, including Frederick Flemister, Eugene Grigsby, Wilmer Jennings, and Hayward Oubré, and independent artists such as CHARLES ALSTON, LOIS MAILOU JONES, ELIZABETH CATLETT, and William H. Johnson.

A gifted artist as well as teacher, Woodruff achieved his greatest fame with the *Amistad Murals*, painted for Talladega College's Slavery Library. The work reflects the influence of Mexican muralist Diego Rivera, with whom Woodruff studied briefly in 1934, and depict moments of "the Amistad Incident," the 1839 mutiny by kidnapped Africans aboard a slave ship against their captors. The first panel, *The Mutiny Aboard the Amistad, 1839*, shows the violent struggle that occurred when the enslaved Africans sought to capture the ship. The second panel, *The Amistad Slaves on Trial at New Haven, Connecticut, 1840*, depicts a scene from the trial, as a white sailor who survived the attack accuses the African Cinqué of leading the mutiny. The third panel, *The Return to Africa, 1842*, portrays the mutineers after winning their court case and returning home.

Woodruff moved to NEW YORK in 1946 and began teaching at New York University (NYU). During this period he abandoned figurative painting, and his style shifted to an abstract expressionist style. He adopted abstract expressionism's spontaneity but also included design components of the African art he became interested in as a student, including ASANTE goldweights, DOGON masks, and YORUBA SHANGO implements. Woodruff also continued to support other African American artists. In 1963 Woodruff cofounded Spiral, a group whose members sought to represent the CIVIL RIGHTS MOVEMENT in the visual arts. Woodruff was awarded a Great Teacher Award by NYU in 1966, and in 1968, he became professor emeritus at NYU. In April 1980, shortly before his death, he was one of ten African American artists honored by President Jimmy Carter at a White House reception for the National Conference of Artists.

See also Art and Architecture, African; Amistad Mutiny; Artists, African American.

Robert Fay

Woods, Granville T.

1856–1910

African American mechanical and electrical engineer and inventor.

Granville Woods was born in Columbus, Ohio. Nothing is known of Woods's parents except that they may have been named Tailer and Martha Woods. The effects of racism in Columbus, shortly before and during the Civil War, were somewhat blunted by the economic influence of a sizable African American population, which included artisans and property holders, and by growing sympathy among whites for abolitionism. A few years before Woods's birth, the city had established a system of segregated schools for black children, which provided him an education until he was ten years old.

Like almost all American engineers during the nineteenth century, Woods obtained his technical training largely through self-study and on-the-job experience, rather than from formal schooling. Sometime after 1866 he began apprenticing as a blacksmith and machinist, probably in CINCINNATI, where several decades earlier German immigrants had established a flourishing machine tool industry. Machinists considered themselves members of an elite profession, and by and large they selected only the most promising and ambitious candidates for apprenticeships. Success depended on a vivid spatial imagination, mathematical adroitness, and draftsmanship. Indeed, Woods's letters patent displayed abundant evidence of all these talents, most apparently the latter. His drawings were consistently rendered with the flair of a first-rate draftsman—presumably Woods himself.

Most of Woods's inventions were electromechanical devices and systems related to railroad technology. His interest in these fields grew out of an eclectic early experience with railroads and from dogged self-study. In November 1872 Woods moved east and was soon hired as an engineer on the St. Louis and Iron Mountain Railroad in Missouri. Given his training and youth, he likely operated lathes and drillpresses in a machine shop. During his employment with Iron Mountain, he began studying electricity—at least three years before Thomas Edison patented his revolutionary lighting system. Because very few American universities provided such training, Woods had to learn about electricity from technical books and periodicals. He left the Iron Mountain Railroad in early 1876, and then spent two years studying at Stern's Institute of Technology. In February 1878 he signed on to the British steamer *Ironsides* as chief engineer. Two years later he returned east, where he handled locomotives for the Southern Railway, whose line ran near Danville, Kentucky.

Sometime after 1880 Woods began his career as an inventor in Cincinnati, probably only to sell one or two ideas. He chose a propitious historical moment and region. Cincinnati was home to a larger and more cohesive and prosperous African American community than the one in Columbus, and southwestern Ohio boasted some of the best machine shops in the nation. With few corporations willing to invest in their own research laboratories, independent inventors like Woods filled a niche by feeding the burgeoning appetite of those corporations for technological innovation. From the outset he made money. His first patent, filed on June 18, 1883, was a replacement for Alexander Graham Bell's crude telephone transmitter (i.e., mouthpiece). His second invention followed almost immediately, an improved steam-boiler furnace. Significantly, he sold the transmitter to two local investors for a modest fee. This success sharply contrasted with the typical experience of a patentee during the period, when ownership of almost all inventions remained forever in the hands of their profitless inventors.

Woods lived in Cincinnati for most of the 1880s, applying for some seventeen patents while residing there. Around 1886 he founded the Woods Electric Company. One newspaper reported Woods's intention to capitalize his new firm at one million dollars and to sell shares for fifty dollars, which suggests that he planned a large-scale factory, but if so the proposal fell through and the firm functioned only as a temporary assignee (i.e., the legal owner) for ten of his patents. The company last appears in the historical record in April 1890, as assignee for Woods's last Ohio patent.

By August 1891 Woods had relocated to the New York City area. Earlier, he had traveled extensively among large northeastern cities, probably as an engineering consultant, so he likely moved to be nearer to his work. He lived out the remaining seventeen years of his life in New York, maintaining the vigorous pace he had established in Ohio. The U.S. Patent Office issued him twenty-eight letters patent for his New York inventions, seven of which listed a brother, Lyates, as co-inventor. Incredibly, he found assignees for all but five.

As an engineer, Woods was no revolutionary, and his inventions characteristically tackled problems associated with established technological systems. He focused primarily on inventing communications, power distribution, and control devices for electric trains, a cutting-edge technology that large cities such as New York, Boston, Philadelphia, and Washington, D.C., were increasingly adopting. In 1884 he filed a patent application for "Telegraphony," a combination telegraph and telephone system that he sold to American Bell Telephone. His "Induction Telegraph System" enabled moving railroad cars to exchange telegraph messages, which proved crucial for preventing collisions. Today his most recognizably famous idea is the "third rail," a high-current electrical conductor laid inside the two ordinary rails that guide the wheels of an electric-powered train. The Woods invention with the widest-ranging importance, though, was a method of regulating the rotational velocity of electric motors. Formerly, motors were slowed by diverting part of their electrical current to resistive elements that transformed the excess power to dangerous waste heat. Woods devised a dramatically safer tapped-inductive system that wasted far less energy. The speed of virtually every alternating-current electric motor today is controlled by a similar method.

Regrettably, no historian has thoroughly assessed the true technological and commercial significance of all Woods's inventions. For that matter, no one has accurately determined their number, although one reliable authority on black inventors in 1917 credited him with "upwards of fifty different inventions." The fact that Woods sold the rights to well over half of his patents to corporations, many of which included future electrical giants like Westinghouse, General Electric, and American Bell, and one for a reported $10,000, however, indicates that he was not only a prolific inventor

but also a commercially successful entrepreneur and respected engineer.

Woods died in New York City of a cerebral hemorrhage, some five years after applying for his last known patent in October 1904, and perhaps in poverty. He left a distinguished but ambiguous legacy. On one hand, he merits a place in the top tier of independent electrical inventors of the late nineteenth and early twentieth centuries. On the other hand, his position with respect to African American history must remain unfixed. Americans have admired the "Black Edison" for well over a century, but even contemporary African American writers rarely mentioned public statements on his part, except for matters of patent litigation, or when he lectured to Cincinnati audiences "on the various laws and theories that pertain to electricity and magnetism" (*Cleveland Gazette*, August 7, 1886). Doubtless, white journalists, who almost entirely ignored him, deserved blame for much of the mystery surrounding Woods. But to the extent that he chose his reticence, he resembled engineers in general, who, thanks to the increasing influence of capitalism during the nineteenth century, began to adopt a hands-off approach to political and social questions, rather than risk their clients and employers. In any case, his exceptional success as an independent inventor depended on an ability to negotiate a career in an increasingly discriminatory society, and it is difficult to see how a more outspoken individual could have survived professionally in such an environment.

Bibliography

Brodie, James Michael. *Created Equal: The Lives and Ideas of Black American Innovators* (1993).

Haber, Louis. *Black Pioneers of Science and Invention* (1970).

James, Portia P. *The Real McCoy: African-American Invention and Innovation, 1619–1930* (1989).

Jenkins, Edward S. *To Fathom More: African American Scientists and Inventors* (1996).

Gary L. Frost

Woods, Tiger

1975–

The first African and Asian American, and the youngest golfer, to win a major golf tournament.

Eldrick "Tiger" Woods was born in Cypress, California, and showed interest in his father's golf clubs while he was still only a toddler. Earl Woods began teaching the game to his son, and young Tiger displayed extraordinary natural talent, making two holes-in-one by the age of six. Young Tiger Woods dominated amateur GOLF, setting records when he won an unprecedented three straight U.S. Junior Amateur titles (1991–1993) and three U.S. Amateur crowns (1994–1996). He attended Stanford University in Stanford, California, where he won the 1996 National Collegiate Athletic Association (NCAA) title. Woods then decided to turn professional, knowing he possessed a complete and polished game with the power to routinely hit 300-yard drives and the touch necessary for a solid "short game" (shots from within sixty yards of the hole, including putting). Experts particularly lauded his competitive desire and mental composure, for which Woods credited his father, a former Green Beret in the VIETNAM WAR.

Woods won two of the first seven pro tournaments he entered. In April 1997 Woods won The Masters, golf's most prestigious tournament, shooting a record-setting 270 and winning by the largest margin in Masters history, twelve strokes. He also set a handful of unofficial records, including the first African American and Asian American (his mother, Kutilda Punsawad Woods, is a native of Thailand) to win a major golf tournament, as well as being the youngest Masters winner at age twenty-one. Woods ended 1997 with four tournament wins and nine top-ten finishes overall.

After tinkering with his swing through much of 1998, Woods won his second major tournament, the PGA Championship, in 1999. In 2000 he won nine tournaments, including three straight major titles: the U.S. Open, the British Open, and the PGA Championship. He followed this with a victory in the 2001 Masters, becoming the first golfer to hold all four major professional titles at the same time. He repeated as Masters champion in 2002, becoming just the third player to win that tournament in back-to-back years and the seventh to win it three times. In 2003 he won his seventh World Golf Championship, making him the top player on the tour for an unprecedented fifth consecutive year. Woods was named PGA Player of the Year in 1997, 1999, and 2002, and was named Associated Press Male Athlete of the Year in 1997 and Sportsman of the Year in 2001.

Woods has also had a great impact on the social aspects of golf. When Woods won the Masters for the first time, many credited him with breaking racial barriers that had kept minorities out of golf's top echelons in the past. Woods himself cited golfers who paved the way for him, such as ROBERT LEE ELDER, the first African American to play in the Masters, and Ted Rhodes, the first African American to play in the U.S. Open. In addition to winning the respect and admiration of his colleagues on the tour, Woods has increased golf's popularity among African Americans and other minorities—a development he has further enhanced through the Tiger Woods Foundation, which offers golf clinics to youths in underserved areas.

Robert Fay

Woodson, Carter Godwin

1875–1950

African American historian and educator who pioneered the research and dissemination of African American history; initiator of Black History Month.

One of nine children, Carter Godwin Woodson was born in New Canton, Virginia, and grew up on his family's farm in rural Virginia. His mother, a former slave who had secretly

learned to read and write as a child, and two of his uncles, who had received training at Freedmen's Bureau schools, tutored him and cultivated his interest in learning. In 1892 Woodson moved to Huntington, West Virginia, where he worked in coal mines.

At age twenty, Woodson enrolled at Frederick Douglass High School, the only all-black school in the area. He completed the four-year curriculum in two years while working to pay his tuition. Following graduation he obtained a teaching position in Winona, West Virginia. But in 1901 Woodson returned to his former high school to teach and later to serve as principal. Meanwhile, he intermittently attended Berea College, an integrated school established by abolitionists in Kentucky, from which he graduated in 1903.

Woodson was then hired by the United States War Department to teach English to Spanish-speaking students in the Philippines. While abroad, he studied Spanish and other romance languages through University of Chicago correspondence courses. Returning to the United States after traveling in EUROPE, he matriculated at the University of Chicago in 1907 and received both a B.A. degree and a M.A. degree in European history in 1908. Woodson then entered the doctoral program in history at Harvard University, and the next year he initiated a ten-year teaching career at Dunbar High School in WASHINGTON, D.C. He received a Ph.D. in 1912, making him the second African American to earn a Harvard doctoratal degree.

In 1915 Woodson established the Association for the Study of Negro Life and History (ASNLH, later the ASSOCIATION FOR THE STUDY OF AFRO-AMERICAN LIFE AND HISTORY). The organization's aim was to encourage, publish, and raise funds to support research and writing about the black experience. As an extension of the ASNLH, Woodson founded THE JOURNAL OF NEGRO HISTORY (1916), the Associated Publishers (1921), and the *Negro History Bulletin* (1937). *The Journal of Negro History* was intended for the general reader. The Associated Publishers generated revenue to "make possible the publication and circulation of valuable books on colored people not acceptable to most publishers." The *Negro History Bulletin* provided lessons in African American history to elementary and secondary teachers.

Woodson had continual difficulty securing funds for the ASNLH. He solicited numerous foundations without much success. Although he could have alleviated the ASNLH's financial problems by affiliating it with a university, he rejected this solution in order to maintain his own independence and control over the organization. Money came from Woodson's own meager teaching salary, the income generated by his numerous publications, and the contributions of the African American community.

One of Woodson's enduring achievements is his initiation of BLACK HISTORY MONTH. In 1926 he launched NEGRO HISTORY WEEK, a commemoration of black achievement held the second week of February, which marks the birthdays of FREDERICK DOUGLASS and ABRAHAM LINCOLN. To encourage African Americans to celebrate Negro History Week, Woodson distributed kits containing pictures of and stories about notable African Americans. Negro History Week was changed to Black History Month in the 1960s.

Woodson was prodigious, authoring or coauthoring nineteen books on various aspects of African American history. He was one of the first scholars to consider slavery from the slaves' perspective, to compare SLAVERY IN THE UNITED STATES with slavery in Latin America, and to note the African cultural influences in New World slave culture.

His mission was to dispel the racist myths about African Americans and their past as promulgated by the historical writings of white scholars. He asserted, "If a race has no history, if it has no worthwhile tradition, it becomes a negligible factor in the thought of the world, and it stands in danger of being exterminated."

Perhaps more than any other person, Woodson helped African American history develop into a widely recognized and respected academic discipline. In regards to the humanitarian efforts of African Americans, Woodson firmly believed that "the achievements of the Negro properly set forth will crown him as a factor in early human progress and a maker of modern civilization."

See also Historians, African American.

Aaron Myers

Work, African Americans and the Changing Nature of

Recent economic trends that have impacted the African American workforce.

Despite African Americans' strong focus on racial discrimination in employment, their economic fate is inextricably connected with the structure and functioning of the modern economy, including the global economy. Racial bias continues to be an important factor that aggravates black employment problems. Nonetheless, to overemphasize the racial factor would obscure the nonracial economic forces that have sharply increased joblessness and declining real wages among many African Americans in the last several decades. As the late black economist Vivian Henderson (1975) argued several years ago, racism put blacks in their economic place and stepped aside to watch changes in modern economy disrupt that place.

In the following sections of this essay, I underline the importance of understanding race-neutral economic forces that impact heavily on the African American community, forces that represent changes in the new economy.

Demand for Labor

A "twist" in the demand for different types of labor has occurred in recent years. Today's close interaction between technology and international competition has eroded the basic institutions of the mass production system. In the past several decades almost all of the improvements in productivity have been associated with technology and human capital, thereby drastically reducing the importance of physical capital and natural resources. At the same time that changes in technology are producing new jobs, they are making many others obsolete.

The workplace has been revolutionized by technological changes that range from the development of robotics to information highways. While educated workers are benefiting from the pace of technological change, involving the increased use of computer-based technologies and microcomputers, more routine workers face the growing threat of job displacement in certain industries. In the new global economy, highly educated and thoroughly trained men and women are in demand. This may be seen most dramatically in the sharp differences in employment experiences among men. Unlike men with lower education, college-educated men are working more, not less.

The shift in demand has been especially devastating for those low-skilled workers whose incorporation into the mainstream economy has been marginal or recent. Even before the economic restructuring of the nation's economy, low-skilled African Americans were at the far end of the employment queue. Their economic situation has been further weakened because they tend to reside in communities that not only have higher jobless rates and lower employment growth but that also lack access to areas of higher employment and employment growth as well.

Of the changes in the economy that have adversely affected low-skilled African American workers, perhaps the most significant have been those in the manufacturing sector. One study revealed that in the 1970s "up to half of the huge employment declines for less-educated blacks might be explained by industrial shifts away from manufacturing toward other sectors." The manufacturing losses in some northern cities have been staggering. In the twenty-year period from 1967 to 1987, PHILADELPHIA lost 64 percent of its manufacturing jobs; CHICAGO lost 60 percent; NEW YORK CITY, 58 percent; DETROIT, 51 percent. In absolute numbers, these percentages represent the loss of 160,000 jobs in Philadelphia, 326,000 in Chicago, 520,000—over half a million—in New York, and 108,000 in Detroit.

Another study examined the effects of economic restructuring in the 1980s by highlighting the changes in both the variety and the quality (which was measured in terms of earnings, benefits, union protection, and involuntary part-time employment) of blue-collar employment in general. The authors found that both the relative earnings and employment rates among unskilled black workers were lower. Two reasons were given: traditional jobs that provide a living wage (high-wage blue-collar cluster, of which roughly 50 percent were manufacturing jobs) declined, as did the quality of secondary jobs on which they increasingly had to rely. The result was lower relative earnings for the remaining workers in the labor market. As employment prospects worsened, rising proportions of low-skilled black workers dropped out of the legitimate labor market.

Industrial restructuring has had serious consequences for African Americans across the nation. John Kasarda states, "As

Household Income Growth 1960–2002

	1960	1970	1980	1990	2002
Total (in current dollars)					
All Families	5,620	9,867	21,023	35,353	53,106
Married-couple families	5,688	10,169	23,141	39,895	61,433
Female householder, no spouse	2,983	4,797	10,408	16,932	28,590
Black					
All Families	3,233	6,516	12,674	21,423	33,525
Married-couple families	N/A	7,816	18,593	33,784	52,246
Female householder, no spouse	N/A	3,576	7,425	12,125	21,189

Source: U.S. Census Bureau.

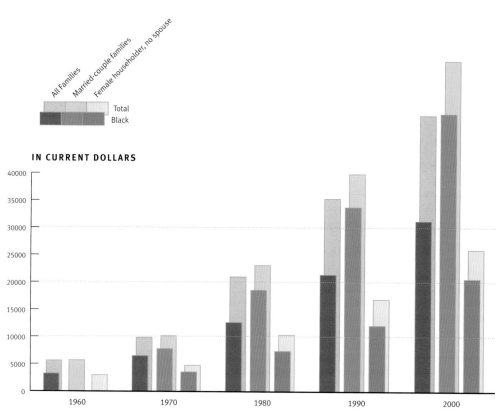

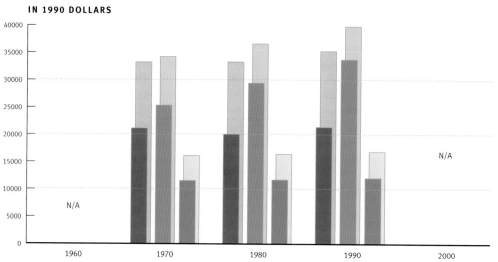

late as the 1968–1970 period, more than 70 percent of all blacks working in metropolitan areas held blue-collar jobs at the same time that more than 50 percent of all metropolitan workers held white-collar jobs. Moreover, of the large numbers of urban blacks classified as blue-collar workers during the late 1960s, more than half were employed in goods-producing industries."

The number of employed black males ages twenty to twenty-nine working in manufacturing industries fell dramatically between 1973 and 1987 (from three of every eight to one in five). Meanwhile, the share of employed young black men in the retail trade and service jobs rose sharply during that period (from 17 to almost 27 percent and from 10 to nearly 21 percent, respectively). And this shift in opportunities was not without economic consequences: in 1987 the average annual earnings of twenty to twenty-nine-year-old males who held jobs in the retail trade and service sectors were 25 to 30 percent less than those of males employed in manufacturing.

The structural shifts in the distribution of industrial job opportunities are not the only reason for the declining earnings among young black male workers. There have also been important changes in the patterns of occupational staffing within firms and industries, including those in manufacturing. These changes have primarily benefited those with more formal education. Substantial numbers of new professional, technical, and managerial positions have been created. However, such jobs require at least some years of postsecondary education. According to a study by Andrew Sum and Neal Fogg, young high school dropouts and even high school graduates "have faced a dwindling supply of career jobs offering the real earnings opportunities available to them in the 1960s and early 1970s."

Most of the new jobs for workers with limited training and education are in the service sector and are disproportionately held by women. This is even more true for those who work in social services, which include the industries of health, education, and welfare. Within central cities the number of jobs for less-educated workers has declined precipitously. However, many workers stayed afloat thanks to jobs in the expanding social service sector, especially black women with less than a high school degree. Among all women workers, the proportion employed in social services climbed between 1979 and 1993 (from 28 to 33 percent). The health and education industries absorbed nearly all of this increase. Of the 54 million female workers in 1993, almost one-third were employed in social service industries. Social services tend to feature a more highly educated work force. Only 20 percent of all female workers with less than a high school degree were employed in social services in 1993. (The figure for comparable males is even less. Only 4 percent of employed less-educated men held social service jobs in 1993.) Nonetheless, the proportion of less-educated female workers in social services is up notably from 1989.

Indeed, despite the relatively higher educational level of social service workers, 37 percent of employed less-educated black women in central cities worked in social services in 1993, largely in jobs in hospitals, elementary schools, nursing care, and child care. In central cities in the largest metropolitan ar-

eas, the fraction of low-educated African American female workers in social services sharply increased from 30.5 percent in 1979 to 40.5 percent in 1993. Given the overall decline of jobs for less-educated central-city workers, the opportunity for employment in the social service industries prevented many inner-city workers from joining the growing ranks of the jobless. Less-educated black female workers depend heavily on social service employment. Even a small number of less-educated black males were able to find jobs in social services. Although only 4 percent of less-educated employed males worked in social services in 1993, 12 percent of less-educated employed black men in the central cities of large metropolitan areas held social service jobs.

Computers Change the Demand for Labor

The computer revolution is a major reason for the shift in demand for skilled workers. Whereas only one-fourth of workers directly used a computer on their jobs in 1983 in the United States, by 1993 that figure had risen to almost half the workforce. According to the economist Alan Krueger, "the expansion of computer use can account for one-third to two-thirds of the increase in the payoff to education between 1984 and 1993 [in the United States]." Two reasons are cited: first, even after a number of background factors, such as experience and education, are controlled, those who use computers at work tend to be paid more than those who do not; second, the industries with the greatest shift in employment toward more highly skilled workers are those in which computer technology is more intensively used. The share of workers with college degrees increased most sharply in the industries with the most rapid expansion of computer use.

Early studies of the diffusion of computer technology revealed a strong positive relationship between computer ownership and income and education. And although systematic research is lacking, it is clear that in jobless ghetto areas and depressed rural areas, computerization and telecommunications are severely underrepresented.

A recent study revealed that the problems of lack of access to key resources attributed to race and class may be even more clear-cut with respect to access to and use of the Internet than in other areas. Whereas 73 percent of white students had access to home computers, only 32 percent of black students did. However, African Americans with income above $40,000 were as likely as comparable whites to own home computers. Thus, it is bad enough if you are a low-income family, it is even worse if you are a low-income black family. And since this study was based on a nationwide telephone survey, as opposed to face-to-face in-home interviews, it probably understates the actual use and access to computers among disadvantaged segments of the populations, many of whom do not have telephones.

This study not only reveals how class intersects with race at the lower income levels, it also shows that the disparity in computer access according to income is greater among blacks than among whites. The study found a sharp divide in the use of the computer network according to race among households below the median income of $40,000. However, home computer ownership among African Americans with incomes over $40,000 is roughly equal to that of comparable whites. Moreover, these higher-income African Americans were even more likely than their white counterparts to have access to the Internet at work. Nonetheless, since the proportion of higher-income blacks (that is, those with incomes above $40,000) is considerably lower than the proportion of higher-income whites, the problem of computer access for blacks as a group is more serious. The telephone survey revealed that whereas 44.3 percent of whites owned a home computer, only 29 percent of blacks did.

Rising demands for computer workers has compensated for declining demands for workers in other sectors of the economy. Because an overwhelming majority of all new jobs will require the use of computers, the have-not population, especially the minority have-nots, will be in danger of becoming permanent economic proletarians. Let's consider this problem in central-city areas.

Effects on Black City Residents

As urban economies have transformed from goods processing to information processing, black central-city residents with no education beyond high school have become increasingly displaced. Indeed, with the transition from manufacturing to services, cognitive and interpersonal skills have become prerequisites even for many low-paying jobs.

Surveying 3,000 employers in ATLANTA, BOSTON, and LOS ANGELES, the economist Harry Holzer of Michigan State University found that only 5 to 10 percent of the jobs in central-city areas for workers who are *non-college graduates* require very few work credentials or cognitive skills. This means that most inner-city workers today not only need to have the basic skills of reading, writing, and performing arithmetic calculations but also need to know how to operate a computer as well.

Moreover, the growing suburbanization of jobs, particularly manufacturing and services, has isolated inner-city minorities from many job opportunities. Most ghetto residents cannot afford an automobile and therefore have to rely on public transit systems, which makes the connection between inner-city neighborhoods and suburban job locations difficult and time-consuming.

However, increasing the skills of inner-city workers is not the only problem. Many central-city job applicants are physically isolated from places of employment and socially isolated from the informal job networks that have become a major source of job placement. Unlike the markets in previous years, labor markets today are mainly regional. A disproportionate number of metropolitan jobs are in the suburbs. Many inner-city residents lack information or knowledge about suburban job opportunities and/or have difficulty commuting to them. In the segregated inner-city ghettos the breakdown of the informal job information network aggravates the problems of job spatial mismatch.

Effects of Changes in the Global Economy

The shift in demand for skilled versus low-skilled workers can also be related to changes in the global economy. Two developments facilitated the growth in global economic activity: (1) advances in information and communications technologies, which significantly lowered transportation and communications costs and thereby encouraged companies to shift work to low-wage areas; and (2) the expansion of free trade, which reduced the price of imports and raised the output of export industries.

Whereas the increased output of export industries aids skilled workers, simply because skilled workers are heavily represented in export industries, increasing imports that compete with labor-intensive industries (for example, apparel, textile, toy, footwear, and some manufacturing industries) hurt unskilled labor. According to economic theory, the expansion of trade with countries that have a large proportion of relatively unskilled labor will not only increase competition with unskilled workers in the United States and result in downward pressure on their wages but lower the price of goods produced by unskilled labor in the United States as well. Because of the concentration of low-skilled black workers in vulnerable labor-intensive industries (e.g., 40 percent of the workforce in the apparel industry is African American), developments in international trade may further exacerbate their labor market experiences.

Conclusion

The preceding analysis shows that many of the economic woes in the African American community (job displacement—including changes in the variety and quality of jobs—declining real wages, unemployment, and non-labor-force participation) can be traced to fundamental shifts in the demand for labor in the global economy. While the more educated and highly trained African Americans, like their counterparts among other ethnic groups, have benefited from the shifts in labor demand, those with lesser skills have suffered.

The sharp decline in the relative demand for low-skilled labor has had a more adverse effect on blacks than on whites in the United States because a substantially larger proportion of African Americans are unskilled. Although the number of skilled blacks (including managers, professionals, and technicians) has increased since the mid-1990s, the proportion of those who are unskilled remains large, because the black population, burdened by cumulative experiences of racial restrictions, was overwhelmingly unskilled just several decades ago.

Although racial discrimination and segregation exacerbate the labor-market problems of the low-skilled African Americans—that is, render them more severe—we should not lose sight of the fact that they derive from and are driven by fundamental changes in the new global economy.

Nonetheless, there is a tendency among policymakers, scholars, and black leaders alike to separate the economic problems in the black community from the national and international trends affecting American families and neighborhoods. If the economic problems of the African American community are defined solely in racial terms, they can be isolated and viewed as only requiring race-based solutions. Vivian Henderson warned the nation against this short-sighted vision: "The economic future of blacks in the United States is bound up with that of the rest of the nation. Politics designed in the future to cope with the problems of the poor and victimized will also yield benefits to blacks. In contrast, any efforts to treat blacks separately from the rest of the nation are likely to lead to frustration, heightened racial animosities, and a waste of the country's resources and the precious resources of black people."

See also Discrimination in Employment in the United States; Segregation in the United States.

William Julius Wilson

Work, Monroe Nathan

1866–1945

African American sociologist.

Monroe Nathan Work was born in rural Iredell County, North Carolina, the son of Alexander Work and Eliza Hobbs, former slaves and farmers. His family migrated to Cairo, Illinois, in 1866 and in 1876 to Kansas, where they homesteaded, and Work remained to help on the farm until he was twenty-three. He then started secondary school and by 1903 had received his master of arts degree in sociology from the University of Chicago. That year he accepted a teaching job at Georgia State Industrial College in Savannah.

Living in the Deep South for the first time, Work became concerned about the plight of African Americans, who constituted a majority of Savannah's population. In 1905 he answered a call from W. E. B. Du Bois to attend the conference that established the NIAGARA MOVEMENT, a militant black rights group that opposed BOOKER T. WASHINGTON's accommodationist approach to black advancement. While continuing to participate in the Niagara Movement, Work founded the Savannah Men's Sunday Club. It combined the functions of a lyceum, lobbying group, and civic club, engaging in such activities as petitioning the city government, opening a reading room, organizing youth activities, and conducting a health education campaign among lower-class African Americans. Quickly accepted into the city's black elite, he married Florence E. Henderson in 1904. Their marriage lasted until his death, but no children survived infancy.

In 1908 Work was offered a position at Washington's TUSKEGEE INSTITUTE in Macon County, Alabama. As an ally of Du Bois, Work found it difficult to accept the position, but he did. By 1908 he had begun to doubt the efficacy of protest. A streetcar boycott had not halted legalized segregation in Savannah and the Niagara Movement had failed to expand. Work had begun to see another way to use his talents on behalf of

black advancement. He was not a dynamic speaker or a natural leader, but a quiet scholar and researcher. He believed that prejudice was rooted in ignorance, and this suggested reliance on education rather than protest. In a 1932 interview, Work declared that while still a student, "I dedicated my life to the gathering of information, the compiling of exact knowledge concerning the Negro." Disillusioned about the power of protest, Work believed that the resources and audience available at Tuskegee would allow him to make his skills useful: "It was the center of things relating to the Negro," he noted.

Although Washington had hired Work primarily as a record keeper and researcher for his own articles and speeches, Work used every opportunity to expand the functions of his Department of Records and Research. In 1908 he began compiling a day-to-day record of the African American experience. His sources included newspaper clippings, pamphlets, reports, and replies to his own letters of inquiry. All were organized by category and date, providing the data for the *Negro Yearbook* and the Tuskegee Lynching Report, both of which began in 1912. Each year he distributed the Tuskegee Lynching Report to southern newspapers and leaders to publicize the extent and injustice of lynch law. Under his editorship, nine editions of the *Negro Yearbook* provided information on discrimination and black progress to educators, researchers, and newspaper editorialists. In 1928 Work supplied another valuable research tool with the publication of *A Bibliography of the Negro in Africa and America*. It was the first extensive, classified bibliography of its kind.

Work did not spend all his time compiling data for others; he was also a teacher, department head, crusader, and researcher. He published over seventy articles and pamphlets. His research usually highlighted either the achievements of Africans and African Americans or the obstacles to black progress. Earlier than most black scholars, Work wrote in a positive manner about African history and culture. In a 1916 article for the *Journal of Negro History*, he declared that "Negroes should not despise the rock from which they were hewn." Work also investigated African American folktales and their African roots. Even before the HARLEM RENAISSANCE, Work celebrated the distinctiveness of African American culture. His meticulous scholarship was widely recognized in the academic community. In 1900 he became the first African American to publish an article in the *American Journal of Sociology;* the article dealt with black crime in CHICAGO and pointed to the lack of social services for African Americans. In 1929 he presented a paper at the American Historical Association meeting.

Although Work eschewed protest when he left the Niagara Movement and went to Tuskegee, he remained a quiet crusader for change. Early in his career Work developed a special interest in black health issues. In Savannah he started health education programs through the churches. He encouraged Booker T. Washington to establish National Negro Health Week in 1914. Work organized the week for seventeen years before it was taken over by the United States Public Health Service. He was also deeply concerned with the problem of LYNCHING, and he became active in a southern-based movement to eradicate the evil. Work's estrangement from Du Bois made cooperation with the NATIONAL ASSOCIATION FOR THE ADVANCEMENT OF COLORED PEOPLE'S (NAACP) antilynching campaign difficult, but Work found allies in the Atlanta-based Commission on Interracial Cooperation and the Association of Southern Women for the Prevention of Lynching. The latter groups sought to change the South through education, while the NAACP sought change through legislation. Through his contacts in the antilynching campaign, Work became actively involved in numerous interracial groups in the South.

Monroe Work overestimated the power of education to eliminate prejudice, but his numerous articles and his quiet, dignified presence in biracial professional organizations and reform groups undoubtedly helped to dispel some of the southern white stereotypes of African Americans. He accepted the constraints required to work in the Deep South in order to use his abilities to change it. After his death, in Tuskegee, two of his protégés established the Tuskegee Civic Association, which brought majority rule and desegregation to Macon County. Monroe Work was one of the lesser-known figures who tilled the soil from which the CIVIL RIGHTS MOVEMENT sprouted in the 1950s and 1960s.

Bibliography

A small collection of Work's personal papers is kept in the Tuskegee University Archives in Alabama, and a 1932 interview by Lewis A. Jones and other biographical materials can be found among the Jessie P. Guzman papers also at Tuskeegee.

McMurry, Linda O. *Recorder of the Black Experience: A Biography of Monroe Nathan Work*. 1985.

From *American National Biography*. John A. Garraty and Mark C. Carnes, eds. Oxford University Press, 1999. Reprinted by permission of the American Council of Learned Societies.

Linda O. McMurry

Works Progress Administration

Program implemented during the Great Depression, as part of President Franklin D. Roosevelt's New Deal, which provided jobs for many unemployed African Americans.

During the 1930s, as the United States struggled through the GREAT DEPRESSION, millions of people were left unemployed or underemployed. The Works Progress Administration (WPA)—established in 1935 and four years later renamed the Work Projects Administration—was a massive program to provide jobs for the unemployed. It was part of President Roosevelt's NEW DEAL, a set of initiatives designed to revive the American economy. In March of 1936, a year after its creation, the WPA had 3.6 million people on its rolls.

Between 1935 and the program's demise in 1943, the WPA constructed more than 650,000 miles of streets and highways.

It built or worked on more than 850 airports, 8,000 parks, 120,000 bridges, and 125,000 public buildings. African Americans, who accounted for less than 10 percent of the American population, particularly benefited from the WPA, making up 15 to 20 percent of its 8.5 million employees. Moreover, in 1935 Roosevelt signed an executive order forbidding discrimination in WPA projects, one of his strongest actions in support of equality for African Americans and other minorities.

Although mainly employing people to perform manual labor, the WPA also established a variety of educational and arts projects. ELLA BAKER, later instrumental in founding the STUDENT NONVIOLENT COORDINATING COMMITTEE (SNCC), taught literacy and consumer education classes—and learned about grassroots political organizing—under the auspices of the WPA. Similarly, future lawyer and civil rights activist PAULI MURRAY worked in the New York City public schools with the WPA's Remedial Reading Project as well as in the WPA Workers' Education Project. For Baker, Murray, and others, experience in the WPA played a role in their subsequent activism in the CIVIL RIGHTS MOVEMENT.

The WPA supported the arts and sponsored cultural activities through the FEDERAL WRITERS' PROJECT (FWP), the WPA Dance Theater, the Federal Music Project, and the Federal Theater Project. The Federal Theater Project, which Congress abolished in 1939, supported touring theatrical companies and circuses that brought inexpensive entertainment, including an all-black production of Shakespeare's *Macbeth*, to towns and cities across the country.

The Federal Writers' Project employed such noted black writers as RALPH ELLISON, CLAUDE MCKAY, RICHARD WRIGHT, ZORA NEALE HURSTON, and ARNA BONTEMPS. Among its various activities, the FWP undertook a large-scale oral history project to interview former African American slaves and collect narratives of their experiences under slavery. In most states, the interviewers were white, but Virginia's FWP was notable for its extensive use of black interviewers.

In response to an apparent economic recovery in 1936, Roosevelt and Congress made sharp cuts in the WPA budget. The cutbacks resulted in many workers—including many African Americans—being dismissed from WPA projects and helped trigger an economic downturn between 1937 and 1939, known as the "Roosevelt Recession." WPA policies were the subject of controversy, as seen in such topical BLUES as Casey Bill Weldon's "WPA Blues" (1936) and Porter Grainger's "Pink Slip Blues," recorded by singer Ida Cox in 1939. But the main opponents of the WPA were Republicans and white southern Democrats, who constituted a conservative anti-New Deal coalition that in 1943 succeeded in abolishing the agency.

James Sellman

World Economy and Africa

See Globalization and Africa: An Interpretation.

World Music, World Beat, and the Re-Africanization of Latin American Popular Music

The term *world music* has long been used by ethnomusicologists and folklorists for everything that was not Western art music—that is, ethnic music, folk music, and non-Western classical music. Typically recorded in situ by scholars, records were released by museums or other cultural institutions in austere record jackets with extensive liner notes, and were clearly considered to be serious educational documents for specialists rather than entertainment for mass audiences. This pattern of musical dissemination changed dramatically in the wake of immigration from so-called Third World countries to cities such as London, Paris, and New York. During the 1960s, recordings (mostly imported) of a variety of non-Western musics, both traditional and contemporary popular, began to circulate within immigrant communities with little if any mediation by scholars. However, as immigrant musicians—especially those whose music was intended for dancing—began taking advantage of the sophisticated recording and broadcast technologies available in northern metropoles, their potential for appealing to audiences beyond their own ethnic communities was greatly increased.

In the early 1980s a handful of entrepreneurs from the United States and Europe who recognized the commercial possibilities of these non-Western musics began establishing small, independent record labels specifically designed to market to general U.S. and European audiences. Since the musics didn't fit into existing marketing categories, the term *world music* was appropriated from ethnomusicology.

This "new" category of world music quickly differentiated itself from its highly specialized scholarly antecedent by the nature of its production and dissemination: an extensive, interlocking commercial infrastructure comprised of specialty record companies, retail and mail order outlets, radio shows, dance clubs, magazines, music festivals and the like, all dedicated to promoting exotic sounds from developing countries to consumers in the industrialized world, who on the whole were urban, affluent, well educated—and in Europe and the United States—mostly white. Some of the musics promoted via this new infrastructure were the sort of traditional and folk-oriented music that had formerly been categorized by music specialists as world music, but others were technologically sophisticated, stylistically hybridized, and commercially oriented products that fell well beyond the traditional purview of ethnomusicologists.

The marketing term *world beat*, which emerged about the same time as *world music*, referred to a subset of world music that included commercially oriented dance musics. Since the single most important element of dance music is rhythm, it is no accident that most of the musics initially categorized as world beat originated in areas where percussion has been most consistently and successfully cultivated over time—in Africa and its diaspora. Indeed, even a partial listing of musics marketed as world beat confirms the importance of Africa and the diaspora: JUJU from NIGERIA, soukous from Congo-Brazzaville/Congo-Kinshasa/Senegal, CHIMURENGA from ZIMBABWE, ZOUK from MARTINIQUE and GUADALOUPE, SOCA from TRINIDAD AND TOBAGO, voudou-jazz and MISIK RAISIN from HAITI, and SAMBA from BRAZIL.

Taking advantage of these new musical sources as well as of the growing demand for non-Western popular music, rock musicians such as Paul Simon, Peter Gabriel, and David Byrne began creating pop cross-fertilizations between First and Third World styles—especially those from the diaspora. As interest in Third World popular music grew, styles from places as disparate as Yemen, Pakistan, and Australia began to be marketed as world beat as well. The ever increasing range of styles and nationalities falling under the world beat umbrella challenged scholars trying to define it; as Goodwin and Gore wrote: "World Beat might be identified as Western pop stars appropriating non-Western sounds, as third world musicians using Western rock and pop, or as the Western consumption of non-Western folk music." Even such a comprehensive definition, however, did not account for the multilateral stylistic exchanges that began taking place between Third World regions themselves.

In order to assist fans to negotiate the potentially confusing array of new musical offerings, guides and directories to world music began to appear, each arbitrarily dividing up the world into geostylistic regions (e.g., "The Nile and the Gulf" or "The Middle East and the Indian Subcontinent") to facilitate consumer sampling and selecting. As the number of new or previously "unknown" musical genres and styles from around the world has burgeoned, it has become increasingly difficult to distinguish between world music and world beat, and indeed, the terms are often used interchangeably; the above-mentioned guides, for example, do not distinguish between the two.

While most world beat musics originated in Third World contexts, they were far from the pristine traditional folk musics that had been studied by ethnomusicologists as world music; on the contrary, they were highly hybridized products of cross-fertilization between Third World aesthetics and First World technologies and styles—primarily rock. World beat entrepreneurs, however, tried to distinguish themselves from their pop music counterparts by employing the discourses of education and cultural exchange in order to market their products. For example, detailed liner notes accompanied recordings, mail order catalogues were extensively annotated, and world music magazines and radio programming provided consumers with in-depth information on the origins and cultural contexts of the diverse musical styles. A handful of scholars specializing in non-Western popular musics collaborated with world beat record companies, assisting with content selection as well as preparation of liner notes, while others began writing for industry-related magazines such as *Beat*. Such scholarly participation clearly lent credibility and authority to industry efforts to mark their products as genuine and to avoid the taint of crass commercialism.

As world beat became a more visible feature of the international popular musical landscape in the late 1980s and early 1990s, popular music scholars began to analyze its economic and cultural implications. Most analyses focused on the inequalities characterizing the bilateral relationships between north and south and accused the industry of exploiting Third World cultural resources. Others were concerned about the potentially disastrous consequences of homogenization and westernization upon folk cultures being swept up in and transformed by what has been called global culture flows. The most trenchant critics also charged the world music industry with racism, for ignoring the harsh realities of economic and political subordination experienced by Third World peoples of color, and instead constructing images of cultural authenticity in order to satisfy the desires of northern whites safely to consume exotic otherness. Musicologist Paul Gilroy, for example, denounced the world music industry for using festive images of diasporan people and culture to suggest that the essence of diasporan musics is a good time rather than endorsing its implicit ideological consciousness.

While these concerns are certainly justified, the cultural repercussions of world beat have not been entirely negative. More optimistic observers, for example, have suggested that the powerful forces of cultural and economic hegemony are being resisted by culturally and technologically savvy Third World musicians who are taking control of the production of their own music, revitalizing local musical traditions by modernizing them. Furthermore, the international popular musical landscape, so long dominated by U.S. and European pop and rock, has unquestionably been diversified and enriched by the increased circulation of musics from multiple locations around the globe.

The Spanish Caribbean region serves as a useful case study for examining the impact of world music—world beat in particular—on a particular locality. Prior to the emergence of the world music phenomenon, musical exchanges within the Spanish Caribbean seldom extended beyond linguistic boundaries; for example, Colombian musicians would borrow from Cuban, Puerto Rican, or Dominican music—but not from Haitian or Jamaican music, and certainly not from contemporary African music. Indeed, the Spanish Caribbean was not a propitious region in which the sort of musics under the world beat umbrella would take root: in spite of a racially mixed population, the region had historically ignored or downplayed its African heritage in favor of a more Iberocentric identity, and (with the exception of CUBA) there was little interest, by either the music industry or government cultural agencies, in promoting distictively Afro-Caribbean expressive culture. In the wake of the world beat-stimulated circulation of diasporan dance musics, however, local Afro-Caribbean genres were revitalized and revalidated, and cross-fertilizations with musical styles from non-Hispanic regions of the diaspora became more frequent, thereby significantly "re-Africanizing" the region's popular music landscape.

The city of CARTAGENA DE INDIAS, located on Colombia's Caribbean north coast, has the distinction of being the vanguard of this "re-Africanization" process, thanks to the successful local development of mechanisms for importing and circulating recordings of diasporan dance musics originating outside the Spanish Caribbean. These musics were first introduced to Cartagena via locally constructed mobile sound systems called *picós*—resembling but not identical to Jamaican sound systems—which provided music for dance parties attended by the city's predominantly black and poor populace, excluded by poverty and racism from other recreational venues such as discotheques and clubs. Initially these sound systems relied on records of Spanish Caribbean dance music (primarily SALSA), but by the mid-1970s—even before the northern emergence of world beat in the 1980s—recordings of various diasporan popular musics had been taken to Cartagena by merchant marine sailors, who had purchased them in immigrant music shops in U.S. or European port cities, and given or sold them to picó owners, who included them in an evening's repertoire as novelties. While stylistically unfamiliar and sung in unintelligible languages, these highly danceable musics—especially West African soukous—eventually became extremely popular among black Cartagena dancers, who began referring to them generically as *música africana* (whether they originated in Africa or other Afro-Caribbean countries) because the people knew—from record jacket photographs—that the musicians were black. Since neither the Colombian music industry nor the international record companies doing business in Colombia was interested in promoting such musics, picó owners turned the local unavailability of recordings into an opportunity, constructing a complex and highly effective system of acquiring and disseminating these musics built upon the concept of "exclusivity," wherein they could profit by attracting fans to their dances because they possessed a scarce but highly desirable product—diasporan dance musics.

Cartagena's middle classes, on the other hand, never attended picó parties, which were considered disreputable, so they were not exposed to non-Spanish Caribbean dance musics until the early 1980s, when a major multicultural popular music festival was established by two Cartagena-based entrepreneurs who had noticed the development of world beat in the north and astutely recognized its economic potential within Colombia. With backing from prestigious private and public institutions and the media, the *Festival de Música del Caribe* was a high-profile event scheduled during Easter week, when Cartagena is inundated with middle- and upper-class tourists from throughout the country as well as neighboring countries such as VENEZUELA, to maximize exposure. Unlike other pan-Caribbean festivals focusing on folk traditions (e.g., Cuba's now defunct Carifesta) or popular music festivals featuring only one genre of music (e.g., Reggae Sunsplash) and sung in one language (e.g., Trinidadian Carnival), Cartagena's festival was explicitly designed to feature the range and diversity of contemporary popular musics from throughout the region. In this regard, the festival was identical to the sort of world music festivals (e.g., World of Music, Arts, and Dance [WOMAD] festivals) that were simultaneously emerging in the north—except for the important distinction that it was locally organized and financed. Year after year, major performers of French Caribbean zouk, English Caribbean *soca* and REGGAE, Haitian *compas* and vodou-jazz were invited to Cartagena, where they alternated with Spanish Caribbean dance bands playing long-popular genres such as Cuban SON, Dominican MERENGUE, Puerto Rican PLENA, and, of course, salsa; beginning in 1986, popular West African soukous bands such as Loketo were invited to perform as well. The back-to-back appearance of these diverse Afro-Caribbean and African popular musics dramatically highlighted the region's shared diasporan roots.

In the early 1990s, stimulated by the festival's success, Colombian music industry entrepreneurs began releasing compilation recordings of popular diasporan musics (much of it unlicensed) targeted at mainstream Colombian audiences, for whom the music was identified as *terapia* (therapy), a marketing term intended to suggest the music's feel-good quality. Additionally, world beat recordings released by U.S. and European labels began to be imported into Colombia. In a region that has long looked upon the United States and Europe as models of cultural progressiveness, these recordings, especially those associated with rock superstars such as Paul Simon and David Byrne, gave a further stamp of approval to diasporan musics.

By the late 1980s, the circulation of non-Spanish Caribbean—mostly diasporan—dance musics within Colombia had begun to influence local musical production in a variety of ways. A handful of Colombian musicians were experimenting with non-Colombian genres such as soca and soukous, and also modernizing older, often African-derived Colombian genres such as CUMBIA and *porro* that had been swept aside by the salsa craze in the early 1970s. An example is the Cartagena-born musician Joe Arroyo, who began his career as a salsa singer in the 1970s, but who, in the 1980s, began producing the sort of African and Afro-Caribbean-influenced music that in the north would have been classified as world beat. (He called his zouk- and soca-influenced songs *caribeños,* and his soukous-influenced salsas *joesons.*) But more importantly, he resuscitated the traditional coastal cumbia by reintroducing the hot, syncopated rhythms that had been eliminated in the late 1960s, when rhythmically simpler variants of cumbia appeared, specially tailored for export to Mexico, Central America, and the Andean region. Subsequently, other Colombian musicians began experimenting with traditional coastal genres as well; examples would be Carlos Vives's tremendously successful reinterpretations of the VAL-LENTO and Moises Angulo's more rock-influenced versions of the porro. In Colombia, then, world beat expanded rather than decreased the musical horizon, by revalidating the country's own African-derived musical heritage, introducing others from the non-Spanish Caribbean and Africa, and reclaiming all of them as sources for musical experimentation. These changes directly challenge assertions that the hegemonic northern-based culture industry always controls the flow of products, profits, and meaning, and that folk cultures are inevitably destroyed by the introduction of mass-mediated musics.

While other Spanish Caribbean countries have not been as directly and extensively involved with diasporan musics as coastal Colombia, musical cross-fertilizations clearly stimulated by world beat began emerging elsewhere in the region as well. In the 1980s, the most influential non-Spanish Caribbean music in the region (other than rock) was *reggae en español,* inspired by Jamaican reggae and its successor DANCEHALL. PANAMA—which, not coincidentally, has a significant black population of Jamaican origin—has produced the most successful Spanish reggae musicians, Nando Boom and El General, but reggae and dancehall have become extremely popular in other countries as well, especially Puerto Rico. By the early 1990s, the degree of cross-fertilization among the various Caribbean linguistic/cultural areas as well as with Africa increased even further. For example, the *punta,* a combination of Dominican merengue and West Indian soca, originated simultaneously in Spanish-speaking Honduras and its English-speaking neighbor, BELIZE. In Cuba, groups such as Sintesis combined traditional Afro-Cuban music with rock, while others, such as Mezcla, introduced stylistic elements from contemporary Afropop as well as from French and English Caribbean popular styles. The Dominican Republic's most prestigious merengue musician, Juan Luis Guerra, released a Grammy-winning recording in 1991 (*Bachata Rosa*) that included a Spanish-language, merengue version of "Dede Priscilla," a hit song from the CENTRAL AFRICAN REPUBLIC; his subsequent recording (*Fogaraté*) also included a soukous-inflected merengue called "Mangos Bajitos," with Congolese Diblo Dibala performing on guitar. Even Miami's pop-oriented Gloria Estefan, on her aptly titled recording *Abriendo Puertas* ("Opening Doors"), mixed salsa, merengue, cumbia, and vallenato with Afro-Latin genres such as Colombian *currulao* and *chandé* and Venezuelan *tamborito.* This new eagerness on the part of Spanish Caribbean musicians to experiment with traditional Afro-Latin genres and to incorporate non-Spanish Caribbean resources surely reflects an interest in gaining access to world beat consumers, but above all it speaks to the increased legitimacy of African-derived music within a region that had long rejected cultural expressions too visibly invoking its African heritage.

This new interest in diasporan musical resources spread to the rest of Spanish Latin America as well as Brazil; an example would be SUSANA BACA's efforts to recover, reinterpret, and disseminate Afro-Peruvian traditions. Brazilian musicians in BAHIA have drawn heavily on Jamaican and other diasporan influences in developing AXÉ and other musical hybrids. Interestingly, much of the experimentation has been done by musicians whose primary identification was with rock; for example, ARGENTINA's Fabulosos Cadillacs and Venezuela's Desorden Público, who have produced Spanish-language hybrids of reggae, SKA (reggae's stylistic predecessor), and RAP. Other rock bands, such as MEXICO's Cafe Tacuba, have taken an even more experimental approach, making unlikely combinations of rock with traditional national styles as well as with other Latin American and diasporan sources.

This is not to say that world beat-influenced musics have swept aside long-popular Spanish Caribbean genres such as salsa, merengue, and cumbia; on the contrary, these styles are alive and well not only throughout the Spanish Caribbean and Latin America but also among U.S. Latinos. Even salsa, merengue, and cumbia, however, have been transformed by a new generation of young musicians eager to reinvent these traditions by hybridizing them with other diasporan sources; for example, a recent recording by the New York-based Dominican merengue band Fulanito includes a *meren-rap* version of a classic 1950s-era Colombian cumbia; another cut is a lively cross-fertilization of accordion-based merengue *típico* and rap. In sum, world beat has stimulated new forms of local musical production and encouraged transnational and transcultural musical exchanges, both of which have served to re-Africanize the region's popular music landscape. Clearly, world beat can be more than just a marketing category for certain cultural artifacts (recordings); it can indicate participation in an ongoing process in which Latin Americans are rediscovering and revalidating the African sources underpinning so many of the region's diverse musical traditions.

See also Axé Music; Diaspora and Displacement.

Deborah Pacini Hernandez

World War I and African Americans

European conflict that involved the overseas service of around 200,000 African American soldiers.

For most African Americans, the United States' entry into World War I in the spring of 1917 held the promise that patriotic service could improve their opportunities and treatment in postwar America. W. E. B. Du Bois, the nation's principal African American leader, called on fellow blacks to "close our ranks shoulder to shoulder with our white fellow citizens." Unstinting patriotism, he wrote, would result in "the right to vote and the right to work and the right to live without insult."

Before they could fight the Germans in Europe, however, blacks had to face the opposition from many white Americans. Sen. James K. Vardaman (D-Mississippi) condemned any mobilization plan that would result in "arrogant, strutting representatives of black soldiery in every community." Black leaders had to overcome considerable resistance, especially from southern Democrats, to their insistence that African Americans be included in any wartime draft. Ultimately, their efforts were successful, and 367,710 African Americans were drafted during the war. By this time, however, blacks had come to expect little in the way of recognition for their service in any branch of the armed forces. Few African Americans served in the U.S. Navy and none in the Marine Corps. The army was strictly segregated, maintaining four black units, the 24th and 25th Infantry and the 9th and 10th Cavalry Regiments—all under the command of white officers.

When posted in the western and southern United States, African American soldiers faced harsh treatment, intimidation, and Lynching—yet no white citizen was ever punished for engaging in such assaults. On the other hand, in the 1906

Brownsville Affair, 167 black enlisted men were discharged without honor after a Texas shooting incident in which the men quite likely had no part. President Theodore Roosevelt ordered the discharges despite the regiment's recent and courageous service in Cuba and the Philippines during the Spanish-American War of 1898.

As the nation mobilized for war, African American leaders faced great difficulties in furthering the opportunities for blacks within the armed services. In light of the service academies' longstanding hostility to black cadets, the National Association for the Advancement of Colored People (NAACP) pressed for the establishment of a training school for black officers. NAACP efforts resulted in the establishment of a Colored Officers' Training Camp (COTC) at Fort Dodge in Des Moines, Iowa. During the war, Fort Dodge trained and commissioned 639 African American officers. Although symbolically important, the existence of these black officers did little to alter the great racial imbalance: African Americans comprised 13 percent of active-duty military manpower during the war, but only seven-tenths of 1 percent of the officers.

Black aspirations were dealt a further setback when members of the 3rd Battalion of the 24th Infantry took part in the Houston Mutiny of August 23, 1917—the first race riots in American history in which more whites than blacks died. The violence left sixteen whites and four black soldiers dead. After hasty courts-martial, nineteen more African American soldiers were executed for their part in the mutiny, and numerous others received lengthy jail sentences. Lieutenant Colonel (Retired) Michael Lee Lanning, author of *The African-American Soldier*, concluded that a key factor in the riot was, ironically, the previous transfer of twenty-five of the battalion's most senior sergeants to Des Moines to attend COTC, leaving only one experienced company first sergeant and seriously undermining battalion discipline. In the years to come, this incident effectively undermined any proposal to increase the role of black troops.

African Americans did find greater opportunities once the nation entered the war, which had been ongoing in Europe since August 1914. Many Southern blacks moved to the North to take industrial jobs created by the wartime economy. Their numbers added to what would later be known as the Great Migration, a population movement that created or greatly augmented black communities in many northern cities. In addition, 200,000 black soldiers were deployed to Europe, some serving with the American Expeditionary Force and others detailed to the French Army. But the vast majority of these troops were relegated to Services of Supplies (SOS) units and labor battalions. The War Department did not order its four black regiments to Europe, evidently in response to the Brownsville Affair and the Houston Mutiny. Rather than taking part in World War I, the army's most experienced soldiers remained at their posts along the Mexican border.

Instead the army organized two new black combat divisions, the Ninety-second and Ninety-third Divisions, through which some 40,000 soldiers saw combat in Europe. But Gen. John J. "Black Jack" Pershing, the supreme commander of the American Expeditionary Force (AEF), evidently had misgivings about using African American combat troops. When the Ninety-third arrived in FRANCE, General Pershing turned the unit over to the French army.

Both the Ninety-third Division and the French inadvertently benefited from white Americans' unwillingness to serve alongside blacks. The 369th Regiment of the Ninety-third Division included Lieutenant James Reese Europe, the black society musician from NEW YORK CITY who organized the regimental band. Lieutenant Europe was the first black officer to lead troops into combat in World War I, and he and his band introduced the French to AFRICAN AMERICAN MUSIC, preparing the way for a lasting French fascination with JAZZ.

With the French, the Ninety-third experienced far greater acceptance and more equal treatment than that provided by the U.S. Army. The unit served heroically throughout the remainder of the war, suffering a casualty rate of 35 percent. The 369th Infantry Regiment spent more than six months on the front lines—longer than any other American unit—during which it neither surrendered an inch of Allied territory nor lost a single soldier through capture. In the 369th alone, 171 officers and men received either Croix de Guerre or Legions of Merit from the French government.

During the war, no black soldier received the Congressional Medal of Honor, America's highest award for military heroism. In 1991, however, President George Bush presented relatives of Corporal Freddie Stowers with what he termed a "long overdue" Medal of Honor in recognition of Stowers's heroism on September 28, 1918, while serving in France with the 371st Infantry Regiment, Ninety-third Infantry Division. Stowers rallied his company after it encountered withering machine-gun and mortar fire that exacted 50 percent casualties and killed or wounded all of the company's more senior officers. After capturing a German machine-gun position in the first trench, Stowers was leading his men against a second trench line when he was mortally wounded by machine-gun fire. Even after being hit, he continued to crawl forward, and when he could crawl no farther, he continued to shout encouragement to his men. Inspired by Stowers's heroism, the company overran the remaining German positions.

Yet despite their record of wartime service, black soldiers faced a hostile and often violent reception on their return from France. The KU KLUX KLAN, reborn in 1915, spread for the first time into the North as well as throughout the South. Between 1914 and 1920, a total of 382 African Americans were lynched—in some cases, the victims were recently discharged soldiers still wearing their uniforms. A city official in NEW ORLEANS reportedly told a group of returning World War I veterans, "You niggers were wondering how you are going to be treated after the war. Well, I'll tell you, you are going to be treated exactly like you were before the war; this is a white man's country, and we expect to rule it."

There were serious race riots during and after the war, especially in northern cities that had growing black populations—the 1917 riot in East St. Louis, Illinois, for example. In the Red Summer of 1919, riots broke out in more than two dozen cities.

Of these, the deadliest by far was the CHICAGO RIOT OF 1919, which resulted in the deaths of twenty-three African Americans and fifteen whites, with a total of 520 whites and blacks injured. This wave of violence effectively quashed black hopes for social advance until President Franklin D. Roosevelt's NEW DEAL and, especially, WORLD WAR II. Yet the war and its aftermath had profound consequences for black culture, setting the stage for the Black Nationalism of MARCUS GARVEY and the UNIVERSAL NEGRO IMPROVEMENT ASSOCIATION and leading to the emergence of the self-assured and politically militant New Negro, the CHICAGO jazz and BLUES scene, and the HARLEM RENAISSANCE.

See also Black Nationalism in the United States; Brownsville, Texas, Affair; East St. Louis Riot of 1917; Race Riots in the United States; Spanish-American War, African Americans in the.

James Sellman

World War II and African Americans

Most destructive military conflict in Europe, but one that gave America renewed prosperity and established its postwar dominance in world affairs; for African Americans the war provided new economic opportunities, accelerated the black migration from the South to Northern urban areas, and prepared the way for the Civil Rights Movement.

World War II had a transforming effect on African Americans. Despite white reluctance and hostility, the black community took pride in its contributions to the war effort at home and overseas. African Americans served in every branch of the military and in every theater of conflict. The war provided new opportunities on the home front and vastly increased the movement of blacks out of the South. It also encouraged civil rights activism, as African Americans broadened their efforts to secure full citizenship rights.

During the war, the NATIONAL ASSOCIATION FOR THE ADVANCEMENT OF COLORED PEOPLE (NAACP), along with the black press and other organizations, mounted a "DOUBLE-V CAMPAIGN" intended to achieve victory over fascism abroad and over racism at home. The war contributed to a complex process of change that would transform the whole of African American life. In confronting the nation with a grave crisis, it swept away much of the rationale for segregation.

Adolf Hitler's racist doctrines—and, to a lesser extent, the chauvinism of his Japanese and Italian allies—came to the attention of African Americans long before fighting actually broke out. During the 1930s international sports provided an important surrogate to war, and blacks exulted in boxer JOE LOUIS's victories over Italian Primo Carnera and German Max Schmeling, and in the gold medals won by sprinter JESSE OWENS and other black athletes at the 1936 Munich Olympic Games. Nazi racism forced some Americans to consider the blemishes on their own democratic principles, above all, America's subordination of blacks and other racial minorities.

American Mobilization

War broke out in EUROPE after Hitler invaded Poland in September 1939, and the United States began to mobilize for war. But the nation was still struggling through the GREAT DEPRESSION, and Americans were little concerned with events in Europe and Asia. They welcomed the defense buildup mainly because it provided much-needed jobs. Indeed, World War II—far more than President Franklin D. Roosevelt's NEW DEAL economic programs—was responsible for ending the decade-long depression and returning the nation to full prosperity.

But there were few opportunities for African Americans in the booming defense industry. In 1941 black labor leader and civil rights activist A. PHILIP RANDOLPH took a dramatic step in protesting blacks' exclusion. He began organizing a massive march on Washington, and President Roosevelt, who was eager to head off the protest, signed EXECUTIVE ORDER 8802, banning racial discrimination in defense industry and federal government hiring. Executive Order 8802 also established the FAIR EMPLOYMENT PRACTICES COMMITTEE to implement and oversee the new policy.

Randolph's victory would be the first of many during the war years. The NAACP launched its Double-V campaign in the belief that the war offered an opportunity to "persuade, embarrass, compel, and shame our government and our nation into a more enlightened attitude toward a tenth of its people." The wartime years indeed yielded a great number of firsts, advancements, and breakthroughs.

Blacks on the Home Front

On the home front, African Americans faced difficulties and great opportunities. The war spurred a renewal of black migration to the North, which had been slowed by the Great Depression. The resulting population movement did not subside for some thirty years. Between the 1940s and late 1960s about 4.5 million blacks would leave the South for the urban North and West. Upon arrival, they faced severe housing shortages and overt hostility from white residents.

There was considerable wartime friction between whites and blacks. In 1943, with the nation in the second year of war, the racial hostilities erupted into violence. During the summer of that year there were more than 250 racial conflicts in forty-seven American cities, including Mobile, Alabama, and HARLEM. The worst race riot of the war took place in DETROIT, when a controversy over the employment of blacks escalated into thirty hours of violence that left twenty-five blacks and nine whites dead. The federal government did little to address the causes of such confrontations or to prevent their recurrence.

In the aftermath of that violent summer, black poet LANGSTON HUGHES posed trenchant questions for American society:

Looky here, America What you done done—Let things drift Until the riots come—Yet you say we're fightin For democracy. Then why don't democracy Include me? I ask you this question Cause I want to know How long I got to fight BOTH HITLER—AND JIM CROW?

Blacks rankled at other forms of racial segregation. For example, during the war, the Red Cross segregated the blood in its blood banks, as if there were any real difference between "white" blood and "black" blood.

Yet the war also had undeniably positive effects. The wartime migration northward had major political and economic consequences. Escaping the poll taxes and literacy tests of the South, southern migrants found themselves able to vote freely, in many cases, for the first time in their lives. In many northern cities, black voters came to be a significant factor in electoral politics. Migration from the South also brought a large number of African Americans into industrial manufacturing. More than half a million blacks, including many former southerners, joined Congress of Industrial Organizations (CIO) unions such as the United Automobile Workers or the United Steelworkers. The war thus helped establish a relatively prosperous black working class.

Serving in a Segregated Military

The war also commenced a process of change that in 1948 would begin the formal integration of the American armed services. But initially, as in past American wars, African Americans encountered resistance from the white majority. Throughout the war, it was American policy "not to intermingle colored and white enlisted personnel in the same regimental organizations." Moreover, the army's mobilization plan on the eve of World War II would have allowed African Americans to contribute only 6 percent of total army manpower, considerably less than their proportion in the overall population.

In 1940 President Roosevelt promoted Colonel BENJAMIN O. DAVIS, SR., to brigadier general, making him America's first black general. Roosevelt also committed the nation to establishing combatant and noncombatant black units in each branch of the armed forces. But the military command resisted giving African American soldiers combat assignments. The U.S. Navy remained the most obdurate on racial issues. Secretary of the Navy Frank Knox and senior naval officers resisted assigning African American sailors to any but the most menial shipboard duties, as servants to officers, in construction battalions, or as messmen or stewards in ships' galleys.

For example, in the heat of the Japanese attack on Pearl Harbor, DORIE MILLER manned a machine gun and shot down two, and possibly four, enemy aircraft. Miller was a messman, like virtually every other African American in the U.S. Navy, and was ineligible for military training. Moreover, he was ignored for months following the battle. Only after concerted protests in the African American press did he receive a Navy Cross and an invitation to speak to the 1942 graduating class at the Great Lakes Naval Training Center. Miller was then assigned to the aircraft carrier USS *Liscome Bay*; but a year later, when a Japanese submarine sank the ship, the black hero of Pearl Harbor died as a messman.

In 1942 the U.S. Marine Corps admitted African Americans for the first time in its 144-year history, taking George Thompson, a former dogcatcher in Nashville, Tennessee, as its first recruit. But the navy did not commission its first group of black officers, known as the "Golden Thirteen," until March 17, 1944. Three days later, it commissioned the USS *Mason*, an antisubmarine ship that was the first navy vessel manned by black sailors. Although it sailed under the command of white officers, the *Mason* at least provided African Americans with an official opportunity for naval combat. But the navy would not desegregate its shore facilities until after the end of the KOREAN WAR (1950–1953). Understandably, during World War II, African Americans accounted for just 5 percent of the total navy manpower.

Blacks in the U.S. Army

The U.S. Army was more forthcoming; yet African Americans never accounted for more than 8.7 percent of army manpower, and only 15 percent of that number received combat assignments. In 1941 the army activated its first black tank unit, the 758th Tank Battalion, and established a segregated Army Air Force pilot-training facility in Tuskegee, Alabama. The NAACP opposed the idea of segregated training but believed that the decision was a step in the right direction. On the other hand, the black National Airmen's Association condemned the plan, insisting that they would rather be "excluded than segregated."

In 1942 the U.S. Army Air Force commissioned its first black pilots, part of the all-black Ninety-ninth Pursuit Squadron—the famed TUSKEGEE AIRMEN—that Colonel BENJAMIN O. DAVIS JR., son of General Davis, would command. By 1944 there were 145,242 blacks in the air force, but only one in ninety was an officer; for white personnel, the proportion was one in six.

Most blacks in the army served in support roles. In 1942 the army accepted the first black women for the Women Auxiliary Army Corps (WAAC), later simplified to the Women's Army Corps (WAC). Black men also found themselves treated as wartime auxiliaries, as in the famed Red Ball Express, an overwhelmingly black unit that drove supplies by truck to advancing American forces following the D-Day invasion and performed yeoman service during the Battle of the Bulge late in 1944.

Red Ball Express drivers were not combat troops, but their jobs involved great danger. One driver recalled that they drove "with those slits . . . at night [which dimmed the headlights to minimize the danger of attack by enemy aircraft], loaded with high-octane gas and all kinds of ammunition and explosives [at speeds of] 30 to 40 miles an hour no matter what the weather."

Challenges to Jim Crow

White Americans were wholly unprepared for black servicemen's militant protests against racial segregation. The protest-ers were in many cases northern blacks unable to abide the JIM CROW policies enforced on U.S. military bases, which were often located in the South. U.S. Air Force historian Alan M. Osur concluded that the story of black airmen in World War II is "a history of attacks on discrimination and segregation."

The army, which had the largest number of black servicemen, first experienced problems in 1941. In 1942 there were protests within the other military branches. The disturbances peaked in 1943 but continued through the final two years of the war. In 1944, for example, sixteen black officers entered a whites-only restaurant in Fairfax, South Carolina. After being refused service, they shouted "Go to hell" and "Heil, Hitler!" Such protests were by no means restricted to the South. In 1943 four black soldiers damaged a California restaurant after being refused service. In addition, whites instigated race riots on a number of military bases, and white civilians repeatedly assaulted individual black servicemen.

During the war the U.S. Army itself took its first tentative steps against Jim Crow. In 1941 it began integrating its officers' candidate schools. In 1944 the War Department prohibited discrimination in transportation and recreational facilities on all army bases. On a Texas military base not long after this directive was issued, Lieutenant JACKIE ROBINSON—soon to become the first African American to integrate the whites-only world of major league baseball—refused to go to the back of a bus, resulting in his court-martial and vindication.

Robinson's refusal to abide southern Jim Crow practices was by no means an isolated example. Indeed, in the postwar years, the pride and confidence of African American military veterans and their unwillingness to endure further discrimination would help provide the impetus for the CIVIL RIGHTS MOVEMENT.

On December 26, 1944, during the worst days of the Battle of the Bulge, the army issued a directive requesting African American volunteers for racially integrated combat units, a request that marked the beginning of the end for the Jim Crow army. The army found many volunteers among its black cooks, engineers, quartermaster personnel, and truckers. Black veteran Chester Jones recalled, "Those blacks who did volunteer did a creditable job, which shows all they ever needed was an honest-to-goodness chance."

Conclusion

In the postwar years, no branch of the American military welcomed the prospect of integration. The persistent delaying tactics of the various service heads outraged African Americans, whose pressure in 1948 moved President Harry S. Truman to sign Executive Order 9981, ordering the integration of America's armed forces and establishing the President's Committee on Equality of Treatment and Opportunity in the Armed Services.

In civilian life, African Americans were no less committed to achieving full social and political equality. Membership in the NAACP burgeoned from 50,000 in 1940 to 450,000 six years later. In 1942 JAMES FARMER and other civil rights activists founded the CONGRESS OF RACIAL EQUALITY (CORE). CORE advocated the Gandhian approach of nonviolent direct action and staged sit-ins at theaters and restaurants in several northern cities, presaging the SIT-IN movement begun in 1960 in Greensboro, North Carolina. Thus, in a number of vital respects, World War II prepared the way for the civil rights struggles of the 1950s and 1960s.

See also American Federation of Labor and Congress of Industrial Organizations; Detroit Riot of 1943; March on Washington, 1941; Migration, Black, in the United States; Military, Blacks in the American; Segregation in the United States.

James Sellman

Wormley, James

1819–1884

African American hotelkeeper.

James Wormley was born in WASHINGTON, D.C., the son of Pere Leigh Wormley and Mary (maiden name unknown). Both his parents were free people of color before their 1814 arrival in Washington, where his father became proprietor of a livery stable on Pennsylvania Avenue between Fourteenth and Fifteenth streets, near the famous Willard Hotel. Wormley's early life is obscure, but it is certain that he went to work at a young age as a hack driver for his father, whose business was thriving by the 1820s. Eventually Wormley bought a horse and carriage of his own and began to work independently. Wormley's exposure to the city's fine hotels and high society through his clientele, which inevitably included many prominent public figures, might perhaps have influenced his later vocation.

In 1841 Wormley married Anna Thompson; they had four children. In 1849 he left his home to join the multitude of prospectors who traveled to California during the gold rush. Shortly before or after this, he was engaged as a steward aboard the elegant riverboats that plied the Mississippi. Eventually Wormley returned to Washington, where he worked as a steward at the fashionable Metropolitan Club. On the eve of the CIVIL WAR, he opened a catering business at 314 I Street (near Fifteenth Street), next-door to a candy store run by his wife. By the mid-1860s he had expanded his business to include a restaurant at the same address. Wormley's restaurant attracted members of Washington's political elite, particularly the Radical REPUBLICANS. The patronage of such men as Senator Charles Sumner (after whom Wormley named one of his sons) and Henry Wilson (later vice president under Ulysses S. Grant) ensured the establishment's success.

The next step in Wormley's career entailed a brief absence from Washington and his family. In 1868 REVERDY JOHNSON, recently appointed ambassador to GREAT BRITAIN, persuaded Wormley to accompany him to London as his personal steward. One of Wormley's tasks was the preparation of such exotic American dishes as diamondback terrapin (a turtle caught in Chesapeake Bay and the Potomac River), which

Johnson was persuaded would do much to "warm up" the reserved British worthies he was required to entertain at embassy functions.

When Wormley returned to Washington, he lost no time in capitalizing on the enhanced reputation he had gained as a connoisseur of fine dining. Representative Samuel Hooper of Massachusetts agreed to buy a five-story building on the southwest corner of H and Fifteenth streets and rent it to Wormley when Wormley was unable to finance the purchase himself. In 1871 Wormley opened the hotel that soon made him famous.

Wormley's Hotel, which included as an annex the building that housed his old restaurant on the other side of the block, could accommodate 150 guests in the sleeping apartments of its upper four stories. The halls and corridors were wide, and the rooms were spacious and elegantly furnished. The dining rooms, on the ground floor, acquired a reputation for attentive service and an elaborate menu, and the bar in the basement, where patrons also found a first-class barbershop, was known for its outstanding selection of wines and liquors. The hotel boasted the latest innovations of the day, including elevators, telephones, and electric bells for room service. The parlors on the upper floors were also beautifully appointed. One of them, known as the Sumner Parlor, was decorated with furnishings from the house of Wormley's old friend Sumner, which Wormley purchased from the estate after Sumner's death. In 1876 the room rate at Wormley's was a competitive five dollars a day.

With Lafayette Square, the White House, and the Departments of the Navy and the Treasury all near at hand, Wormley's Hotel was ideally located to serve the congressmen, diplomats, and other politicians who already knew Wormley as a restaurateur. Among his long-term residents were Vice President Schuyler Colfax, Assistant Secretary of State John Hay, and Senator Roscoe Conkling of New York. The hotel was equally popular with foreign dignitaries. The German legation resided there during the 1880s, as did at various times members of the French and Chilean diplomatic corps. Wormley's also housed delegates to the Pan-American Congress in 1889–1890.

Wormley's acquired a small but significant place in American history in the aftermath of the disputed presidential election of 1876. A conference held at the hotel in February 1877 among representatives of Republican candidate Rutherford B. Hayes and a group of southerners led by Major E. A. Burke yielded the "Wormley Agreement," which became in turn the basis for the "Compromise of 1877." In effect, the southerners acquiesced to Hayes's accession to the presidency in return for the withdrawal of the northern states' military support for the remaining RECONSTRUCTION governments in the South. Wormley played no part in and likely had no awareness of these negotiations, whose outcome signaled the North's final abandonment of southern blacks to the ravages of southern reaction. It is no small irony, nonetheless, that the hotel in which these dealings took place was owned by one of the capital's most prominent African American citizens at a time when the city was noted for the enterprise and brilliance of its black citizenry.

Wormley's hotel and catering business continued to prosper until his death in BOSTON. In an obituary, the *Washington Star* called him "one of the most remarkable colored men in the country" (18 Oct. 1884). The well-known black minister FRANCIS GRIMKÉ remarked that Wormley "demanded respect from others and respected himself." A public school on Prospect Avenue between Thirty-third and Thirty-fourth streets, built in the year of Wormley's death and named in his honor, remained in service until the 1950s.

Bibliography

Major, Gerri. *Black Society.* 1976.

Obituary, (Washington, D.C.) *Evening Star*, October 18, 1884.

Obituary, *Washington Post*, October 18, 1884.

Turner, Geneva C. "For Whom Is Your School Named?" *Negro History Bulletin* 23, no. 8 (May 1960): 185.

Waynes, Charles E. "James E. Wormley of the Wormley Hotel Agreement." *Centennial Review* 19 (Winter 1975): 397–401.

Woodson, Carter G. "The Wormley Family." *Negro History Bulletin* 11, no. 4 (January 1948): 75–84.

From *American National Biography.* John A. Garraty and Mark C. Carnes, eds. Oxford University Press, 1999. Reprinted by permission of the American Council of Learned Societies.

John Ingham

Wright, Jonathan Jasper

1840–1885

African American politician and jurist.

Jonathan Jasper Wright was born in Luzerne County, Pennsylvania. Little is known of his parents except that his father was a farmer and that the family moved to Susquehanna County, Pennsylvania, during Wright's childhood. Wright attended Lancasterian University in Ithaca, New York, and later studied law at the offices of Bently, Fith, and Bently in Montrose, Pennsylvania. He also taught school and read law in the office of Judge O. Collins of Wilkes-Barre, Pennsylvania. Wright attended the 1864 national black convention in Syracuse, New York, which opposed slavery, supported universal manhood suffrage, and endorsed equality before the law.

At the end of the CIVIL WAR in April 1865, the American Missionary Association sent Wright to Beaufort, South Carolina, where he taught adult freedmen and soldiers of the 128th U.S. Colored Troops. In November 1865 he served as a delegate to the Colored Peoples' Convention in CHARLESTON. Disappointed that the state's recent all-white, all-male constitutional convention relegated the black population to second-class status through a series of measures known as the black code, the forty-five delegates to the Charleston convention supported the enfranchisement of black men and the abolition of the black code and appealed for "even handed justice." Seven years later,

in a speech assessing black political progress, Wright denounced the code as an attempt to keep blacks virtually enslaved by depriving "the colored people of all and every opportunity of being elevated an iota above their former condition. They were left totally at the mercy of the white man."

In 1866 Wright returned to Pennsylvania, where he became the first black admitted to the state bar. A few months later he was back in Beaufort as a legal adviser for the Freedmen's Bureau, representing the interests of former slaves and offering legal advice to the bureau's commanding officer in South Carolina, General Robert K. Scott. Though some bureau agents were accused of cooperating closely with white planters and ignoring the needs of the freedmen, Wright insisted that he would not do the bidding of white men. "Had I been contented to settle down, and been what the masses of white persons desired me to be (a boot-blacker, a barber, or a hotel waiter) I would have been heard of less."

When Congress authorized the reorganization of the southern states and adopted universal manhood suffrage in the 1867 Reconstruction Acts, Wright promptly joined in organizing the REPUBLICAN PARTY and speaking on its behalf. At a rally in July 1867, he urged the party to nominate a black man for U.S. vice president in 1868. He resigned from the Freedmen's Bureau in 1868 and was elected to represent Beaufort at the state constitutional convention.

Wright played a prominent part in the convention, serving as one of two black vice presidents (of five total vice presidents) and as a member of the Judiciary Committee. He persuaded the convention to support the legislative election of judges to fixed terms rather than to permit gubernatorial appointment of judges for life. Wright was also deeply concerned about education. Like most of the convention's delegates (black and white), he showed little interest in integrated public schools, claiming that he did "not believe the colored children will want to go to the white schools, or vice versa."

Wright was involved in a major controversy when he supported the adoption of a $1 poll tax, the proceeds of which would be devoted to education. Wright and Francis L. Cardozo believed the tax was necessary to finance the establishment of public schools, while other black delegates led by ROBERT BROWN ELLIOTT feared the failure to pay the tax would disfranchise large numbers of black voters. The tax was not included in the constitution.

In 1868 Wright, Elliott, and WILLIAM WHIPPER were the first three black men admitted to the South Carolina bar. Shortly thereafter Wright was elected to the South Carolina Senate, representing Beaufort County. In 1869, while traveling through Virginia, Wright was removed from a first-class, all-white coach on the Richmond and Danville Railroad. He subsequently won a $1,200 lawsuit against the railroad.

On February 1, 1870 the general assembly elected Wright to the state supreme court to fill the unexpired term of Solomon L. Hoge, who had been elected to Congress. The following December Wright was elected to a full six-year term. Wright's elevation to the court was part of a larger effort by South Carolina black leaders to secure the election of more black men to major political offices. In 1870 black men were elected lieutenant governor, treasurer, Speaker of the house, and to three seats in Congress.

Wright's seven-year tenure on the three-member court was largely uneventful. Only his most biased critics considered him less than competent and effective. Wright participated in 425 cases; he wrote eighty-seven opinions and dissented on just one occasion. Wright's judicial career ended in controversy in 1877 during the prolonged dispute involving the results of the 1876 gubernatorial election, when Democratic candidate Wade Hampton (1818–1902) and Republican incumbent Daniel Chamberlain each claimed victory. In a supreme court case testing Hampton's authority as governor, Wright and Associate Justice A. J. Willard upheld a pardon issued by Hampton. (Chief Justice Franklin Moses, Sr. was ill.) Two days later Wright attempted to reverse his decision as well as the order releasing the prisoner.

The revocation of the order was not accepted, and rumors circulated that black Republicans bribed Wright or had gotten him drunk to compel him to change his position. Counter rumors contended that black Republican legislator Thomas E. Miller was offered a bribe by Democrats to testify that Wright was drunk. Other reports claimed that Wright was threatened by one party or the other. A month later Hampton's claim to executive authority was supported by Republican president Rutherford B. Hayes, and the Republican party lost political control of South Carolina. Though a special legislative committee under Democratic control recommended the impeachment of Wright for misconduct for allegedly accepting a bribe to uphold Hampton's pardon, no formal charges were presented. Wright resigned from the court on August 6, 1877.

Wright resumed his career as a lawyer. He supported Hampton's reelection in 1878, and in 1879 he moved to Charleston and opened a law practice on Queen Street. In 1881 the Board of Trustees of Claflin University in Orangeburg, South Carolina, authorized Wright to teach law courses for the university. He offered the courses in Charleston on behalf of Claflin until his death. Wright never married. He died of tuberculosis in Charleston.

Wright was one of the vanguard of black men who rose to political power in the 1860s and 1870s and is noteworthy as the only black state supreme court justice in the nineteenth century. Moderate in his political views and restrained in his legal decisions, he nevertheless persistently sought expanded political influence for African Americans while defending the rights they so recently had gained. His life and career illustrate both the possibilities and the limitations that black men encountered in the post–Civil War era.

Bibliography

A number of Wright's letters are contained in the American Missionary Association collection at Tulane University. His supreme court opinions can be found in Reports of Cases Heard and Determined in the Supreme Court of South Carolina, vols. 2–9 (1872–1879).

Holt, Thomas. *Black over White: Negro Political Leadership in South Carolina during Reconstruction*. 1977.
Oldenfield J. R. "A High and Honorable Calling: Black Lawyers in South Carolina, 1868–1915." *Journal of American Studies* 23 (1989): 395–406.
Rogers, George C., Jr. *Generations of Lawyers: A History of the South Carolina Bar*. 1992.
Tindall, George B. *South Carolina Negroes, 1877–1900*. 1952.
Williamson, Joel. *After Slavery: The Negro in South Carolina during Reconstruction, 1861–1877*. 1965.
Woody, Robert H. "Jonathan Jasper Wright, Associate Justice of the Supreme Court of South Carolina, 1870–1877." *Journal of Negro History* 18 (April 1933): 114–131.

From *American National Biography*. John A. Garraty and Mark C. Carnes, eds. Oxford University Press, 1999. Reprinted by permission of the American Council of Learned Societies.

William C. Hine

Wright, Louis Tompkins

1891–1952

African American surgeon, hospital administrator, and civil rights leader.

Louis Tompkins Wright was born in La Grange, Georgia, the son of Ceah Ketcham Wright, a physician and clergyman, and Lula Tompkins. After his father's death in 1895, his mother married William Fletcher Penn, a physician who was the first African American to graduate from Yale University Medical School. Raised and educated in ATLANTA, Wright received his elementary, secondary, and college education at Clark University in Atlanta, graduating in 1911 as valedictorian of his class. His stepfather was one of the guiding influences that led to his choice of medicine as a career.

Wright graduated from Harvard Medical School, cum laude and fourth in his class, in 1915. While in medical school he exhibited his willingness to take a strong stand against racial injustice when he successfully opposed a hospital policy that would have barred him (but not his white classmates) from the practicum in delivering babies (obstetrics) at Boston-Lying-In Hospital. Despite an early record of publications, because of restrictions based on race, Wright completed an internship during 1915–1916 at FREEDMEN'S HOSPITAL, the teaching hospital at the HOWARD UNIVERSITY School of Medicine in WASHINGTON, D.C., one of only three black hospitals with approved internship programs at that time.

While he was an intern at Freedmen's Wright rejected a claim in the medical literature that the Schick test for diptheria could not be used on African Americans because of their heavy skin pigmentation. A study he conducted proved the validity of the usefulness of this test on dark-skinned people and was the basis of his second published paper, "The Schick Test, with Especial Reference to the Negro" (*Journal of Infectious Diseases* 21 [1917]: 265–68). Wright returned to Atlanta in July 1916 to practice medicine. In Atlanta he launched his CIVIL RIGHTS career as a founding member of the Atlanta branch of the NATIONAL ASSOCIATION FOR THE ADVANCEMENT OF COLORED PEOPLE (NAACP), serving as its first treasurer (1916–1917).

With the onset of WORLD WAR I, Wright applied for a military commission and became a first lieutenant in the U.S. Army Medical Corps. A month before going overseas in June 1918, he married Corrine M. Cooke in NEW YORK CITY. They would have two daughters, both of whom would become physicians: Jane Cooke Wright and Barbara Penn Wright.

While Wright was in FRANCE his unit was gassed with phosgene, causing him permanent lung damage. Because his injury (for which he received a Purple Heart) imposed physical limitations, he served out the rest of the war in charge of the surgical wards at three field hospitals. As a medical officer he introduced the intradermal method for smallpox vaccination, which was officially adopted by the U.S. Army.

In 1919, when Wright settled in HARLEM to start a general medical practice, Harlem Hospital, a municipal facility with a 90 percent black patient population, had no African American doctors or nurses on staff. With an assignment effective 1 January 1920 as a clinical assistant (the lowest rank) in the Out-Patient Department, he became the first African American to be appointed to the staff of a New York City hospital. His steadfast and successful efforts during the 1920s working with hospital administrators and with city officials led gradually to appointments for other African Americans as interns and attending physicians. His push for greater opportunities for African American professionals at Harlem Hospital culminated in a reorganization mandated in 1930 by William Schroeder, commissioner of the Department of Hospitals for the City of New York. The result was the first genuine effort to racially integrate the entire medical staff of a major U.S. hospital. By then Wright had risen to the position of visiting surgeon, and in October 1934 he became the second African American to be admitted to the American College of Surgeons (established in 1913). In 1938 he was appointed to a one-year term as the hospital's director of surgery. In 1929 he had achieved yet another breakthrough, as the first African American to be appointed as a police surgeon through the city's competitive civil service examination. He retained the position until his death.

In 1935 Wright was elected chairman of the national board of directors of the NAACP, a position he held until 1952. As a civil rights leader he opposed the establishment of hospitals exclusively for black people, and in the 1940s he argued for national health care insurance; he also challenged discriminatory policies and practices of the powerful American Medical Association. In a published open letter (dated 28 Jan. 1931) in response to an offer from the Julius Rosenwald Fund to build a hospital for blacks in New York City, Wright wrote: "A segregated hospital makes the white person feel superior and the black person feel inferior. It sets the black person apart from all other citizens as being a different kind of citizen and a different kind of medical student and physician, which you know and we know is not the case. What the Negro physician needs is equal opportunity for training and practice—no more, no less."

Treating common injuries in the surgical wards of Harlem Hospital led Wright to develop, in 1936, a device for handling fractured and dislocated neck vertebrae. In addition to this neck brace, he also designed a special metal plate to treat certain fractures of the femur. He became an expert on bone injuries and in 1937 was asked to write the chapter on head injuries for Charles Scudder's monumental textbook *The Treatment of Fractures* (1938), this being the first contribution by an African American to a major authoritative medical text.

Wright became ill with tuberculosis in 1939 and for nearly three years was confined to Biggs Memorial Hospital in Ithaca, New York. In 1939, while hospitalized, he was elected a diplomate of the American Board of Surgery. The year before, *Life* magazine had recognized him as the "most eminent Negro doctor" in the United States. In 1940 he was awarded the NAACP's prestigious Spingarn Medal for his achievements and contributions to American medicine.

In 1942, after returning to Harlem Hospital, Wright was appointed director of surgery, a position he held until his death. In 1945 he established a certified four-year residency program in surgery, a first for a black hospital. In 1948 he led a team of resident doctors in the first clinical trials of the antibiotic aureomycin with human beings. This pioneering testing at Harlem Hospital and subsequently at other hospitals paved the way for the approval of this drug and eventually other antibiotics by the U.S. Food and Drug Administration. In 1948 he established and became director of the Harlem Hospital Cancer Research Foundation, funded by the U.S. Public Health Service. Perhaps his crowning achievement was his election, that year, as president of the hospital's medical board.

Over the course of his long career at Harlem Hospital, Wright welded together into a harmonious whole the various white and black groups within the hospital. He recognized and confronted directly the problems faced by other ethnic professionals, particularly Jewish and Italian-American physicians, so that shortly before his death, at the dedication of the hospital's Louis T. Wright Library, he said, "Harlem Hospital represents to my mind the finest example of democracy at work in the field of medicine."

Wright died in New York City. His presence at Harlem Hospital and on the national civil rights scene, and his voice and actions in public and private health forums and debates, had significant consequences for American medicine in three areas: it led to a rapport between black and white doctors that generated scientific and clinical research yielding important contributions in several areas of medicine; it dispensed with myths regarding black physicians that excluded them from any hospital staff on grounds other than those related to individual competence and character; and it led to the admittance of qualified physicians who were African American into local and national medical and scientific societies.

Bibliography

Wright published eighty-nine scientific articles in leading medical journals: thirty-five on antibiotics, fourteen in the field of cancer, six on bone trauma, and others on various surgical procedures on the colon and the repair of gunshot wounds.

Cobb, William Montague. "Louis Tompkins Wright, 1891–1952." *Journal of the National Medical Association* 45 (March 1953): 130–148.

de L'Maynard, Aubre. *Surgeons to the Poor: The Harlem Hospital Story.* 1978.

Obituary, *New York Times*, October 9, 1952.

From *American National Biography*. John A. Garraty and Mark C. Carnes, eds. Oxford University Press, 1999. Reprinted by permission of the American Council of Learned Societies.

Robert C. Hayden

Wright, Richard

1908–1960

African American novelist, among the first to show the destructive effects of white racism on both blacks and whites.

Richard Wright was born in rural Roxie, Mississippi, near Natchez, where white hostility was pervasive. His mother was a former schoolteacher. His father, a farmer who drank heavily, abandoned the family in 1914. In the absence of her husband, Wright's mother took a series of low-wage, unskilled jobs to support her two boys. Moving from town to town, they settled in MEMPHIS, TENNESSEE, then in rural Arkansas, often going hungry. After his mother suffered a debilitating stroke, Wright returned to Mississippi in the care of his stern, religious grandmother, who disapproved of his literary inclinations. The experience left Wright eager to leave the area and disdainful of religion.

Upon completing the ninth grade, Wright went north, first to Memphis, then to CHICAGO, ILLINOIS. He discovered and read H. L. Mencken, whose journalism inspired Wright's later writing, as well as Fyodor Dostoyevsky, Sinclair Lewis, Sherwood Anderson, and Theodore Dreiser. In Chicago in the late 1920s and early 1930s he held odd jobs, eventually settling in the United States post office, which was nicknamed "the University" for its high density of radical intellectuals.

Wright attended meetings of the John Reed Club, an organization of leftist writers, and soon became active in the Communist Party. Encouraged by party members, Wright published poetry, short stories, and articles in Communist newspapers and other left-wing journals. He later said that he had hoped his writings would bridge the gap between party leaders and common people. Beginning in 1935, he wrote travel guides for several years for the Depression-era FEDERAL WRITERS' PROJECT, first in Chicago, then in HARLEM in NEW YORK CITY. He also produced fiction—a collection of forceful short stories about racial

oppression and a humorous novel about working-class blacks in Chicago. Some of these stories were published in leftist periodicals; the novel was published in 1963, after his death, as *Lawd Today*.

Wright's debut in mainstream publishing came in 1938 with the publication of *Uncle Tom's Children*, a collection of cruel novellas based on his Southern childhood. The book was widely read, and its accounts of the pernicious effects of racism moved and impressed reviewers. Still, Wright was disappointed. He had intended readers to see and feel the devastation of racism on all of society, not just on African Americans.

His next novel, *Native Son* (1940), was merciless. In the story, Bigger Thomas, a young black man hardened by racism and ignorance, accidentally kills a white woman and is condemned to death. Bigger's Communist lawyer argues that guilt belongs to a society that would not accept him and drove him to brutality. Bigger, however, has tasted his first freedom in the act of murder: for once in his alienated life, he has brought about an event to which others must respond. Editors toned down the original manuscript (the restored original version was published only in 1992), but *Native Son* was still the most militant protest novel about American race relations of its time. It became a huge bestseller, a Book-of-the-Month Club selection, and was dramatized on Broadway in a production by Orson Welles. Many reviewers marveled that Wright could make Bigger Thomas an unsympathetic character yet nonetheless force white readers to see their own guilt in Bigger's crime. Other reviewers, while appreciative of the novel's power, criticized Wright for presenting a stereotype and a victim in Bigger Thomas.

In 1944 Wright wrote an essay for *The Atlantic Monthly* titled "I Tried to Be a Communist" in which he expressed his long disenchantment with the dogma of the Communist Party as well as its refusal to speak and act on black civil rights. Shortly thereafter he published *Black Boy* (1945), the autobiography of his youth in the South. Like his previous works, *Black Boy* was unrelenting in its depiction of the scarring effects of racism and poverty. A few critics complained that it gave a one-sided picture of the South, but most heralded it as searing and precise, even a masterpiece.

In the late 1940s Wright traveled to FRANCE at the invitation of American expatriate writer Gertrude Stein. He was warmly received in Paris, where he met many of the country's leading intellectuals, including Jean-Paul Sartre and Simone de Beauvoir. Feeling the tensions of racism on his return to New York and annoyed at being acclaimed only as a great *black* writer, he moved to France with his second wife—he had been briefly married at the beginning of the 1940s—and young daughter.

In France, Wright was deeply influenced by existentialism, a philosophy emphasizing the isolation of the individual in a hostile or indifferent universe. He wrote three more novels, none of which were well received in America. Some critics thought Wright overintellectualized the question of race, some perceived the books as out of touch with recent developments in American race relations, and others were upset with him for leaving the United States. Wright also wrote extensively about colonialism in AFRICA. In his last years, he became an international spokesman for PAN-AFRICANISM. He died in Paris.

Among Wright's other works are the novels *The Outsider* (1953), *Savage Holiday* (1954), and *The Long Dream* (1958); a collection of stories, *Eight Men* (1961); nonfiction works *Black Power* (1954), *The Color Curtain* (1956), *Pagan Spain* (1957), and *White Man, Listen!* (1957); and an expanded autobiography, *American Hunger* (1977).

See also Literature, African American.

Bibliography

Fabre, Michel. *The Unfinished Quest of Richard Wright.* Translated by Isabel Barzun. Morrow, 1973.

Gates, Henry Louis, Jr., and K. A. Appiah, eds. *Richard Wright: Critical Perspectives Past and Present, 1993.* Amistad, 1993.

Wright, Theodore Sedgwick

1797–1847

African American Presbyterian minister and reformer.

Theodore Sedgwick Wright was born in New Jersey and brought up in Schenectady, New York, the son of R. P. G. Wright, an early opponent of the AMERICAN COLONIZATION SOCIETY's program of returning American blacks to AFRICA. (His mother's name is unknown.) He was named after a distinguished Massachusetts jurist, Theodore Sedgwick (1746–1813), whose defense of a slave woman against her master's claim of ownership had effectively abolished slavery in that state.

Wright received a good education in spite of rejection by a number of colleges to which he applied. After several years at NEW YORK's AFRICAN FREE SCHOOL he was admitted into Princeton Theological Seminary in 1825 at the age of twenty-eight. Well-treated there by both fellow students and faculty, he graduated in 1828, thus becoming the first American of his race to complete a theological seminary program. That same year Wright was chosen to be pastor of New York City's First Colored Presbyterian Church, which had been founded some years earlier by pioneer black journalist SAMUEL CORNISH. Wright devoted the remaining two decades of his life to building this church into a large (more than 400 members) and socially concerned black congregation.

Angered by the oppression of his race, Wright became a social activist on many fronts. He and Cornish were charter members of the largely white AMERICAN ANTI-SLAVERY SOCIETY, founded in 1833. They served for several years with white radicals Arthur and Lewis Tappan on the society's executive committee. Both of them withdrew from the Presbytery of New York because of its opposition to censuring southern Presbyterian slave owners and joined the abolition-inclined Third Presbytery. When the New York Vigilance Committee was founded in 1835 to combat the kidnapping of free blacks off the streets of Manhattan into slavery, and to help fugitive slaves, Wright

became its first chairman. In 1839, when the American Anti-Slavery Society's founder and chief staff member, WILLIAM LLOYD GARRISON, denounced political activity as a means of reform, Wright withdrew from the AASS. He had become a strong supporter of the most extensive African American political effort to date: the New York State campaign to recover full voting rights for black males by securing signatures on petitions to the state legislature and by lobbying individual legislators.

Wright's blend of spiritual fervor, clarity of thought, anger over racial discrimination, and political activism helped to influence young black pastors such as Charles Ray, HENRY HIGHLAND GARNET, and Amos Beman, who later became leaders of the drives for re-enfranchisement in New York State and Connecticut. Wright's speeches to gatherings of mostly white abolitionists denounced slavery, the American Colonization Society, and prejudice against free blacks and commanded their rapt attention.

Bitter personal experience lay behind Wright's denunciation of prejudice. During an alumni gathering at Princeton, he had been publicly humiliated by being called "nigger" and kicked several times by a Princeton alumnus. Several years later, in excoriating discriminatory treatment of black passengers on shipboard, Wright cited three cases of black people whose deaths had resulted from the exposure forced on them when, refused cabins, they had had to stay on deck through a cold and stormy night. One of those casualties had been his young wife, whom he probably married in 1828 and who had died in 1829, a few months after such exposure on a boat from Brunswick, New Jersey, to New York City and again on her passage up the Hudson to Schenectady. Wright had suffered in less dramatic ways, too, by being made to feel like a pariah at presbytery meetings when white clergy entered the pew where he was sitting at prayer, saw that he was black, and hastily withdrew looking for another pew.

For Wright the exclusion of blacks from equal education was, next to slavery, American society's greatest crime against his race. "They keep us down," he agonized, "drive us out of their schools, mob and break down our schools and then point at us in scorn as an inferior race of men. 'Can't learn anything.' Why don't they let us try?" (1836). Wright was a central figure in the founding of the Phoenix Society, a many-faceted educational enterprise for blacks in New York City. Begun in 1833, the society aimed to provide basic schooling for children and assistance to young men toward apprenticeships and long-term employment as "mechanics." That same year Wright, Cornish, and black EPISCOPAL priest PETER WILLIAMS, JR., opened a private high school for black males; they established one for women three years later. But by 1838 both schools had to close for lack of funds.

In May 1837 Wright married Adeline T. Turpin of New Rochelle, New York. There is no record of children borne by either of his wives. Wright died in New York City. His death at age fifty was said to have been hastened by overwork and by undue exposure to the elements in covering a huge parish on foot—blacks risked humiliation and physical injury if they tried to board the "horse cars." Thousands attended his funeral or joined in an extended funeral march through the streets of lower Manhattan. William Lloyd Garrison, setting aside earlier bitter disagreement with Wright over political action, published a lengthy and generally laudatory obituary in his weekly, *The Liberator*.

Bibliography

Wright's published works include *A Pastoral Letter Addressed to the Colored Presbyterian Church, in the City of New York, June 20th, 1832*. 1832.

Cornish, Samuel E. *The Colonization Scheme Considered, in Its Rejection by the Colored People—in Its Tendency to Uphold Caste—in Its Unfitness for Christianizing and Civilizing the Aborigines of Africa, . . .* 1840.

Gross, Bella. "Life and Times of Theodore S. Wright, 1797–1847." *Negro History Bulletin* 3 (1939–1940): 133–138, 144.

Ray, Charles B., and James McCune Smith. *An Address to the Three Thousand Colored Citizens of New York Who Are the Owners of One Hundred and Twenty Thousand Acres of Land in the State of New York, Given to Them by Gerrit Smith, Esq. . . .* 1846.

Swift, David E. *Black Prophets of Justice: Activist Clergy before the Civil War*. 1989.

"The Progress of the Anti-slavery Cause" and "Prejudice against the Colored Man" (September 1837), reprinted in *Negro Orators and Orations*, 86–95, edited by Carter Woodson. 1925.

From *American National Biography*. John A. Garraty and Mark C. Carnes, eds. Oxford University Press, 1999. Reprinted by permission of the American Council of Learned Societies.

David E. Swift

Writing, History of, in Africa

Africa's contribution to the art and science of writing has gone largely unacknowledged or underappreciated in the annals of history. The common myth and prejudice against Africa as an historically illiterate continent ignores the many long, rich, and diverse traditions of writing which have existed on the continent from ancient times to the present. Indeed, the earliest extant evidence of phonetic writing anywhere in the world is to be found on the African continent, birthplace of the Egyptian system.

Cradle of Writing

Hieroglyphs emerged in the fourth millennium B.C., their origin attributed by early Egyptian scribes to a god, Toth. The phonetic nature of the hieroglyphic script was likely achieved via the *rebus principle*, in which a symbol associated with a word (logogram), for example ☼/ "sun," was applied to a lexically unrelated word or constituent of a word which sounds

the same (homophone), such as "son." Following the hieroglyphic script were two adapted cursive scripts called Heratic and Demotic. The successive stages and development of the Egyptian system of writing spanned nearly 4,000 years.

Despite the fact that the Egyptian system is one of the longest literary traditions ever to exist, the ability to read hieroglyphs—and therefore know the story of ancient Egypt—was lost for almost 1,400 years. In 1799, however, Napoleon Bonaparte's army discovered a large basalt slab near Rosetta in the Nile Delta. This slab, famously known today as the Rosetta Stone, enabled decipherment as it was inscribed in three scripts which provided a key: hieroglyphic, Demotic, and Greek. Despite the fact that the British seized the Rosetta Stone from the French in 1802 (the Rosetta Stone remains a central attraction in the British Museum today), it was a Frenchman, Jean-François Champollion, who achieved the first significant decipherment of hieroglyphs from a copy of the stone.

Historians have traditionally asserted that the world's earliest phonetic script tradition was cuneiform, born at the end of the fourth millennium B.C. in Mesopotamia. Here Sumerians incised pictographs for commodities and numerals into clay tablets. It was believed that around 3100 B.C. the idea of writing diffused south to ancient EGYPT. Over the course of the last twenty years, however, research in Egypt has uncovered the world's earliest extant specimens of writing some 500 miles south of the Nile Delta. In 1988, archaeologists involved in the excavation of a palace tomb, at Umm el-Qa'ab cemetery at Abydos, discovered 150 small labels written in hieroglyphs and carved into ivory or bone. These and other finds have been dated to about 3300 B.C.—the earliest extant evidence for phonetic writing anywhere in the world. Recent estimates for the emergence of writing in Egypt have been dated as early as 3500 B.C.

Early Scripts from Africa

The Egyptian system of writing inspired many of our modern scripts, such as Hebrew and Arabic, and indirectly scripts such as Greek, Roman, and Cyrillic. Not surprisingly, many of these subsequent scripts—which evolved outside of Africa—later returned to Africa. The earliest was the Phoenician consonantal alphabet, which arrived in Africa with the establishment of the colony of Carthage on the coast of modern Tunisia. By the ninth century B.C., the alphabet took on a distinctly African flavor known as Punic and spread throughout northern Africa as well as to Spain, Italy, and France. This script, in turn, inspired the script known as Neo-Punic, which emerged following the fall of Carthage. Although Punic did not survive in Africa beyond the second century A.D., it inspired a handful of scripts for writing the BERBER languages of North and Saharan Africa (some of which have not been entirely deciphered), the most legendary being the Tifinagh script. This consonantal alphabet has survived in Africa for over 2,000 years, used by the TUAREG people for writing the Tamasheq language, largely in the form of inscriptions on rocks from ALGERIA and MOROCCO and through the Sahara to MALI and NIGER.

Two other important scripts to arrive in Africa were the Aramaic and Sabaic (also Sabaean) alphabets, both as early as the sixth century B.C. Aramaic, derived from Phoenician, arrived in Egypt with Persian occupation. Outside of Africa, the Aramaic alphabet inspired the creation of the Hebrew square alphabet, which would be employed by North African Jews. Some of the oldest extant documents in Africa are written in Hebrew. The Sabaic alphabet, originating from the Arabian Peninsula, was carried by settlers to ancient ETHIOPIA (or Abyssinia, in the region of present-day ERITREA). Here it would be transformed by Christian Ethiopians into an Ethiopian (or Ethiopic) syllabary in the fourth century A.D. The Ethiopian script was used to write the language Ge'ez (from the South Arabic for "emigrant"). After the death of Ge'ez as a spoken language in the fifteenth century—and after its continued use as a liturgical language of the ETHIOPIAN ORTHODOX CHURCH—the script was adapted to write Amharic and other Ethiopian languages. The Ethiopian syllabary, along with the Tifinagh consonantal alphabet noted earlier, are the two longest surviving script innovations born in Africa—both remaining in continuous usage for about 2,000 years.

The Greek alphabet arrived in Egypt with the founding of Alexandria in 322 B.C. and, along with traces of influence from the Egyptian Demotic script (the last stone inscription A.D. 452), inspired the creation of the Coptic alphabet, which emerged in the second century A.D. for writing Egyptian and Christian literature. Coptic fell into gradual disuse beginning about A.D. 800, a result of the penetration into the region of Islam and the Arabic script. By the fourteenth century, Coptic survived solely as a liturgical language of the Egyptian Coptic Church. The influence of the Coptic alphabet, however, extended south to northern SUDAN, where it inspired the creation of the Nubian alphabet of Christian NUBIA. This script was used beginning in the eighth century A.D., but fell into decline when Nubia was besieged in the thirteenth century by the Muslim Mamluks.

Prior to the emergence of the Nubian alphabet, another script emerged in Sudan. This was the Meroïtic script of the Nile Valley, used for only a short time, from about 180 B.C. to the fourth century A.D., until Meroë fell to AKSUM. Like the Egyptian system that inspired it, the Meroïtic script had both hieroglyphic and cursive styles.

Arabic and Roman Scripts

From a contemporary perspective, two of the most important scripts to diffuse throughout Africa were the Arabic and Roman alphabets. The Arabic alphabet (a consonantal alphabet), originated in the fifth century, and arrived in Africa—first in Egypt—with the arrival of Islam in the first part of the seventh century. The script spread throughout North Africa via trade and proselytization, and diffused through the Sahara Desert and to the West and East African coasts. The earliest Arabic script inscription in West Africa has been dated to 1013–1014, the earliest for East Africa 1104–1105. The Arabic script has a number of variants and calligraphy styles associated with it, including Kūfīc (book), Naskhī (cursive), and Maghribī (West-

ern Islamic). Variant forms of the Arabic script, in many environments referred to as Ajami (from Ar., "non-Arabic"), have been used for centuries for writing African languages. There exists a substantial amount of literature employing Ajami for transcribing African languages such as Swahili, Hausa, Fula, and many related Manding languages.

The Roman script arrived first in Africa when the Romans conquered Carthage in the second century B.C. The spread of Islam and the Arabic script led to the decline of the alphabet by the eleventh century. The Roman script, however, reemerged in western Africa with Portuguese arrivals via the coast in the fifteenth century. Through contacts with these Portuguese and subsequently other Europeans along coastal regions of Africa, Africans gained literacy skills that they applied not only to European languages and variant pidgin forms of those spoken languages, but to their own languages as well. For many Africans who had previously not been in contact with literate traditions, the idea of writing had an enormous impact on them and inspired them to learn foreign scripts and to experiment with creating new scripts of their own.

There exist a number of examples of prominent Africans—kings, sultans, chiefs, and other leaders—who through the course of history have attempted to invent original scripts for their languages. One such example was King AGAJA of DAHOMEY who, in 1724, inspired by the literacy skills of an Englishman who he had made his slave, is alleged to have experimented at inventing his own script. There is no evidence to suggest that Agaja's script ever gained any currency among his people, but other scripts successfully emerged in the two centuries after Agaja, many of which have been sustained to this day. Most famous of these is the VAI syllabary of LIBERIA.

African Invented Scripts

"It has fallen to my lot to make a discovery of such importance to the civilization of Africa, that I am anxious my own profession should bear the honour it may deserve. The discovery consists of a written language of the Phonetic order."

Thus began the dramatic January 1849 report of the "discovery" of the Vai script by Lieutenant Frederick E. Forbes, Commander of the British naval squadron engaged in an anti-slave trade patrol along the western coast of Africa. While landed at Cape Mount, in the Vai country of what is present-day Liberia, his curiosity was aroused by characters written on the house of a Liberian settler. He learned about the phonetic/syllabic nature of the Vai script and subsequently conducted a short study of the language and script while anchored in the waters off Cape Mount. After receiving confirmation of the novelty of his information from such authorities as President Joseph J. Roberts of Liberia and the Reverend Edward Jones, Principal of the Fourah Bay Institution in Freetown, Forbes communicated his news to EUROPE.

The Vai syllabary is the earliest known phonetic script tradition to emerge and sustain itself in sub-Saharan Africa. The script was devised in 1832 or 1833 in Dsondu/Jondu, in Cape Mount, Liberia. The primary individual associated with its creation was Momolu Duwalu Bukele, who was assisted by five friends. Bukele maintained that he received his inspiration to invent the script in a dream in which he was met by a tall venerable looking white man who taught him to write syllabic Vai characters in the sand. Apart from being the earliest phonetic script born in sub-Saharan Africa, the Vai script has the distinction of being the script that has the longest record of continuous usage. The script remains popular among the Vai today, used by about 20 percent of Vai men for purposes of record keeping, correspondence, translations from the Qur'an and Bible, public announcements, and for the creation of original texts. The script remains an important expression of Vai identity. In its modern form, the syllabary contains up to 212 characters and is written from left to right.

Momolu Duwalu Bukele is regarded by many as the "inventor" of the Vai script. Those Vai men who assisted him in devising characters might also be regarded as inventors. The enterprise of inventing the script and creating a novel set of characters to fill it out, and then introducing it to the Vai community at large, must be attributed to Bukele and his associates. But the general history of inventions unmistakably demonstrates that both an invention itself and its historical "take-up" depend on appropriate historical circumstances. In the early nineteenth century the Vai were under cultural pressure from several different directions, and by the 1820s were in contact with four literate groups: European traders with their accounts, Islamic teachers with their Qur'an, Christian missionaries with their Bible, and literate Liberian colonists. The last two elements were the most recent arrivals and their combined influence was probably the reason why the decisive moment for the construction and social success of a Vai script occurred when it did. Thus, the emergence of the Vai script illustrates a balance between "independent invention" and "stimulus diffusion."

In recent years compelling evidence has emerged suggesting that the organizational design for the Vai syllabary was not suggested by either the Roman alphabet or the Arabic consonantal alphabet, but rather another syllabary: the Cherokee syllabary of North America (invented ca. 1821). The decade of the invention of the Vai syllabary was marked by American missionary experimentation in Liberia with the Cherokee syllabary as a model for writing Liberian languages. It may also be important that one of the leading men in Vai country at the time of the invention of the Vai script was a Cherokee. This man, Austin Curtis, had emigrated to Liberia after the spread of the Cherokee syllabary and settled in Vai country four years before the invention of the Vai syllabary. It is perhaps not a coincidence that the famous inscription on a house at Cape Mount noticed by British naval officer Lieutenant F.E. Forbes, which led to international attention for the Vai script, was written on the house of Austin Curtis, a Cherokee.

In the immediate vicinity of the Vai, four subsequent script traditions emerged in the first part of the twentieth century among neighboring peoples: the MENDE, KPELLE, LOMA, and BASSA. The stimulus for these scripts was the Vai script.

The Mende syllabary, which script practitioners call Kikakui (after its first three characters), was devised in southern SIERRA LEONE around 1917 by Mohamed Turay, a celebrated Islamic scholar from Maka, Barri chiefdom (close to the Liberian border). A second stage in the development of the script probably occurred under the direction of Kisimi Kamara, an important Chiefdom Speaker (*Ndolo Lavale*) from Barri chiefdom, also the key figure involved in propagating the script. Turay was Kamara's great maternal uncle, his Qur'anic teacher, and later his father-in-law. Turay and Kamara were Mende, but with strong KONYAKA (Manding) roots. While Turay and Kamara filled out the script with a novel set of characters, many of which were based on an indigenous corpus of Mende graphic imagery, the Vai influence is instantly recognizable in the syllabic organization of Kikakui. The script contains roughly 195 characters and is written from right to left. It is still employed today for purposes of correspondence, record keeping, creating court documents, and in the writing of Islamic and Christian texts.

Two other syllabaries were devised in the Liberia-Sierra Leone region in the first part of the twentieth century. The Kpelle and Loma are, like the Vai and Mende, related Mande peoples and both operate syllabaries similar to Vai—providing strong internal evidence that the Vai script provided the syllabic blueprint for their writing systems. The Kpelle syllabary, with eighty-eight characters and written from left to right, was invented in the early 1930s by Chief Gbili of Sanoyea, Liberia. It continues to be used today by a small number of script literates for correspondence and record keeping. The Loma syllabary, which contains at least 185 characters and is written from left to right, was created in the late 1930s by Wido Zobo of Boneketa, Liberia, who was assisted in his task by an associate named Moriba. The Loma script continues to be used in Liberia and Guinea—where the language and script are called Toma—for record keeping and correspondence.

The final script of the Liberia-Sierra Leone region devised in the first part of the twentieth century occurred among the Bassa. The Bassa are not a Mande people and their script differs from the others in that it is an alphabet. The Bassa alphabet, called Vah by script practitioners, was invented by Thomas N. Lewis, a Bassa man who arrived in the United States about 1892 and studied at Lincoln and Syracuse Universities. Lewis first thought to create a script for Bassa while working in Plainfield, New Jersey, around 1895. He perfected his system several years later, had print types designed, and printed Christian religious texts in the script. He returned to Liberia in 1907 and his script was earnestly taken up by many Bassa. The Bassa script is written from left to right and contains thirty characters and five tonal diacritics. Although he designed an alphabet for Bassa, Lewis was probably stimulated to design a script for Bassa by the Vai script. He had been educated in Vai country, at the Episcopal Mission School at Cape Mount, and it was likely that here he was inspired to create an original script for Bassa, having been exposed to the Vai script at an early age.

The two final scripts discussed here are the Bamum and Bagam scripts, both syllabaries, which emerged in the early twentieth century in the Cameroon Grassfield, over 2,000 miles away from Cape Mount, Liberia (Vai country). The standard history of the Bamum script relates that Sultan Ibrahim Njoya created a pictographic script for writing Bamum as early as 1896. After a series of developments, the script was transformed into a syllabary as late as 1903. In its most widely employed form, known as A-ka-u-ku (after its first four characters) it contained about eighty syllabic characters and the direction of writing was from left to right. Certain accounts of the origin of the script stress a dream episode which inspired Sultan Njoya, other explanations point to Njoya's admiration for literate traditions of Muslim Hausa and Fulani with whom the Bamum were in contact. Printed accounts of the origin of the Bamum script have tended to undervalue the central role played in the invention by one of Sultan Njoya's chief notables, Nji Mama. Today the Bamum script continues to be used, albeit largely for ceremonial purposes and as an expression of Bamum cultural identity and pride, with very few script practitioners still living.

Also in the Grassfield, a syllabary emerged among the Bagam people around 1910. The script, which contained some seventy characters, and was written from left to right, fell into disuse by the 1950s. During its short period of use it was used for creating records such as farming calendars. The Bagam oral tradition contends that the Bagam king, Pufong, and his royal retainer, Nde Temfong, independently dreamed the same dream in which they were called to create a script for the Bagam. While the Bagam people stress the independent nature of their script, the chronologies of the inventions of the Bamum and Bagam scripts, along with the fact that both scripts are organized as syllabaries, strongly suggests an influence flowing from Bamum to Bagam.

The area of the Cameroon Grassfield is over 2,000 miles away from Vailand, situated in Cape Mount, Liberia. The allegedly independent invention of a syllabary among the Bamum has long proved an enigma for scholars. Around the turn of the century, the Bamum were in contact with two literate traditions, the Roman alphabet and the Arabic consonantal alphabet. While contact with such literate traditions might explain the desire for writing, neither served as a model for the Bamum syllabary. Not surprisingly, mounting evidence is pointing to influence from the Vai, who at the end of the nineteenth century traveled in great numbers to Cameroon where they were employed in the Grassfield by the Germans as carriers, soldiers, envoys, and negotiators. Indeed, Vai influence in the Grassfield was so important that German treaties were translated into Vai. Not surprisingly, the period around the turn of the century might be regarded as the heyday of Vai script literacy—a period in which Vai traveling to Cameroon certainly carried their syllabic Vai script with them.

Other Scripts, Orthographies, and Graphic Systems

This entry has attempted to provide a brief introduction to the history of scripts in Africa. Two scripts which were not discussed here, but would have fit into the theme of the discussion, are the N'ko Alphabet (1949) and the Wolof Alphabet (1961). On the other hand, it has been impossible to deal here with the many scripts invented in Africa in the twentieth century (especially second half) which were never (or not yet) adopted by society. For such scripts, there is no evidence available to confirm their past or current usage apart from that of their inventors. The scripts include: Aladura Holy Alphabet (1927), Oberi-Okaime Alphabet (ca. 1930), Bamana Syllabary (1930s), Bete Syllabary (1956), Oromo Syllabo-Alphabet (1956), Fula Alphabet of Oumar Dembélé (from ca. 1958), Fula Alphabet of Adama Ba (from ca. 1963), Kru Alphabet (1972), Nwagu Aneke Igbo Syllabary (ca. early 1960s), Aka Umuagbara Igbo Logo-Syllabary (1993), and Esan Oracle Rainbow Syllabary (ca. 1996). In this essay I featured only a single modern African script (Bagam) that gained some currency before falling into extinction—Bagam was included because it is connected to the relevant Bamum script discussion. The Osmaniya Alphabet (1922) and Somali Alphabet (1933) were left off because these scripts are no longer actively employed.

Likewise, it has not been possible to deal here with orthographic scripts introduced in Africa, most of which were based in part on the Roman script. Such scripts include (among many candidates) the Bassa Syllabary (1836), the Yoruba Alphabet (1846), and the Africa Alphabet (also "Westermann script") introduced by the International Institute for African Languages and Cultures in 1927. Finally, the entry was meant to deal specifically with phonetic script traditions as opposed to nonphonetic systems of graphic symbolism that record and communicate information. These systems include the likes of rock art, Nsibidi symbols, Akan symbols, Bogolanfini symbols, Rhonko symbols, Poro symbols, Cenda symbols, Dogon Cosmograms, Kongo Cosmograms, among many other possible examples.

Bibliography

Andrews, Carol. *The Rosetta Stone*. British Museum Publications, 1981.

Dalby, David. "A Survey of the Indigenous Scripts of Liberia and Sierra Leone: Vai, Mende, Loma, Kpelle and Bassa." *African Language Studies* VIII (pp. 1–51), 1967.

Dugast, I., and M. D. W. Jeffreys. *L'Écriture des Bamum*. Institut Français d'Afrique Noire, 1950.

Forbes, F. E. "Despatch Communicating the Discovery of a Native Written Character at Bohmar, on the Western Coast of Africa, near Liberia, accompanied by a Vocabulary of the Vahie or Vei Tongue. Communicated by the Admiralty. Received April 23 1849." *Journal of the Royal Geographical Society of London* 20, 1851.

Gregersen, Edgar A. *Language in Africa: An Introductory Survey*. Gordon and Breach, 1977.

Harms, Robert. *The Diligent: A Voyage Through the Worlds of the Slave Trade*. Basic Books, 2002.

Scribner, Sylvia, and Michael Cole. *The Psychology of Literacy*. Harvard University Press, 1981.

Tuchscherer, Konrad. *Black Scribes: A History of Africa and the Written Word*. Forthcoming.

——. "The Baptist and the Bassa Syllabary: William Crocker's Liberia Experiment in the 1830s." *American Baptist Quarterly* 12/2 (pp. 212–220), 2003.

——. "The Lost Script of the Bagam." *African Affairs* 98 (pp. 55–77), 1999.

——. "African Script and Scripture: the History of the Kikakui (Mende) Writing System for Bible Translations," *African Languages and Cultures* 8 (pp. 169–188), 1995.

——, and P. E. H. Hair. "Cherokee and West Africa: Examining the Origins of the Vai Script." *History in Africa* 29 (pp. 427–486), 2002.

Konrad Tuchscherer

Wu-Tang Clan

An avant-garde rap collective whose musical innovation and business acumen made them one of the most influential groups of the past decade.

When the Wu-Tang Clan released its debut album—*Enter the Wu-Tang (36 Chambers)* (1993)—the RAP world had to confront eight new MCs at once: RZA, Genius/GZA, Ol' Dirty Bastard, Method Man, U-God, Raekwon, Ghostface Killah, and Rebel INS (a.k.a. Inspectah Deck). Although The Genius had released a pre-Wu-Tang solo album and the RZA (formerly Prince Rakeem) had released two pre-Wu-Tang singles, *Enter the Wu-Tang* was completely unexpected: a rap record that owed nothing to the slow, heavy production style of rap's then-regnant superstar, Dr. Dre, formerly of NWA. The Wu-Tang Clan layered Kung-Fu mythology (hence the name) over RZA's involved beats, delivering boasts of street violence in impossibly complex narratives. Hardcore rap classics like "Protect Ya Neck" and "Clan in da Front" balanced the album's successful single, "C.R.E.A.M."—a reminder that "Cash Rules Everything Around Me."

The Wu-Tang Clan's revolutionary record contract permitted its individual members to sign solo deals with other record labels. And following the success of *Enter the Wu-Tang*, the Clan members released a dizzying series of solo albums, including Method Man's commercially successful ode to marijuana, *Tical* (1994); Raekwon's labyrinthine gangster narratives, *Only Built for Cuban Linx* (1995); Ol' Dirty Bastard's bizarre Rabelaisian ramblings, *Return to the 36 Chambers (The Dirty Version)* (1995); the tongue-in-cheek horror stories of RZA's side project, The Gravediggaz (*Six Feet Deep*, 1994); and

many other affiliated records, all yoked together by endless intra-Clan guest appearances and by the weird, icily organic soundscapes created by RZA. The Wu-Tang Clan capitalized on their collaborative and solo success with Wu-Wear, a profitable line of hip-hop clothes advertised in a radio-friendly single called "Wu-Wear: The Garment Renaissance."

In 1997, the highly-anticipated *Wu-Tang Forever* continued the group's remarkable run of critical and commercial success. The album hawked everything from Wu-Wear to phone lines to Internet access, alongside the group's increasingly cryptic lyrics ("Grow like a fetus / With no hands and feet to complete us") and RZA's experimental beats. Though the group has not toured together since 1997, Wu-Tang Clan did record two more albums, *The W* (2000) and *Wu Tang Iron Flag* (2001).

See also Music, African American.

Andrew Du Bois

Wynn, Albert R.

1951–

Democratic member of the United States House of Representatives from Maryland, and the first black candidate elected to the House from the suburbs of Washington, D.C.

Albert Russell Wynn was born in PHILADELPHIA, PENNSYLVANIA, and received a bachelor's degree from the University of Pittsburgh in 1973. After graduate studies in political science at HOWARD UNIVERSITY (1973–1974), he received a law degree at Georgetown University in 1977. Wynn was executive director of the Consumer Protection Commission in Prince George's County, Maryland, from 1977 to 1981, and then became a practicing attorney.

Wynn served in the Maryland House of Delegates for five years from 1982 to 1987, and then served five years in the Maryland Senate from 1987 to 1992. He was known as a staunch Democrat and a friend of labor unions. In 1992 Wynn ran in a tightly contested Democratic primary for a U.S. House seat from Maryland's Fourth Congressional District, where, in the wake of redistricting, blacks had become the majority of voters. He won 75 percent of the vote in the 1992 general election, and was elected to a sixth consecutive term in 2002. He is a member of the CONGRESSIONAL BLACK CAUCUS.

X–Z

Xangô

Orisha, or Yoruba deity, of lightning and masculine virility.

Known as Xangô in BRAZIL, the ORISHA is called Changó or Shangó in CUBA and the United States, and Shango in Trinidad. Xangô wears red and carries a double-headed ax, the symbol of justice, which he represents.

See also Candomblé; Orishas; Religions, African, in Latin America and the Caribbean; Santería.

Xhosa

Ethnic group of South Africa.

The Xhosa are one of several peoples belonging to the broader NGUNI linguistic group. They number about eight million, the majority of whom live in South Africa's Cape Province and belong to one of three subgroups—the Xesibe, Gcaleka, and Rharhabe. Although a number of other groups in this region speak Xhosa, such as the Thembu, Mfengu, and Mpondo, they have historically maintained a distinct identity from the Xhosa.

Like other Nguni groups, the Xhosa are descendants of Bantu speakers who migrated into southeastern Africa from East Africa around 200 C.E. and established village communities based on grain farming and PASTORALISM. According to oral tradition, the Xhosa nation was founded by a king named Cirha. Cirha was later accused of stinginess and overthrown by his younger brother, Tshawe. Tshawe founded the royal amaXhosa Dynasty to which all Xhosa chiefs trace their ancestry.

For most of their history, the Xhosa people have been governed by loosely connected autonomous chiefdoms. Xhosa custom required the sons of a chief to leave their fathers' homes and found new settlements. As the Xhosa dispersed, they moved into land occupied by KHOISAN-speaking pastoralists. Over time the Xhosa incorporated KHOIKHOI communities and adopted aspects of their language and religion; today, nearly one-sixth of the Xhosa language consists of Khoi "clicks."

During the late eighteenth century, AFRIKANER settlers (also known as Boers) began encroaching on Xhosa grazing land,

setting off a series of nine wars—the Frontier Wars—which lasted from 1779 to 1878. The first conflict was prompted by Boer attempts to settle the lush Zuurfeld region, which Xhosa herders used as a summer pasture. Although the Xhosa initially fought off the Boers, they suffered serious losses in battles with the British, who took control of the Cape in 1806. Continual warfare, livestock losses, and social upheaval gradually weakened the Xhosa. In 1856 thousands of Xhosa followed the prophecy of a young girl named Nongquwuse and killed over 400,000 of their own cattle, resulting in severe famine. By the 1870s the Xhosa had lost much of their land to white settlers.

During the late nineteenth and early twentieth centuries many Xhosa migrated in search of wage work in SOUTH AFRICA's gold and diamond mines. They also converted to CHRISTIANITY in large numbers, although they retained many traditional Xhosa spiritual practices. After the NATIONAL PARTY government began imposing APARTHEID policies in the early 1950s, the Xhosa as well as other Xhosa-speaking groups were forcibly relocated onto Bantustans—TRANSKEI and CISKEI. In this period large numbers of black South Africans, including many Xhosa, became staunch supporters of the AFRICAN NATIONAL CONGRESS (ANC). One of the ANC's most prominent Xhosa members, NELSON MANDELA, later became South Africa's first black president, but his appeal transcended ethnic lines. Today, most rural Xhosa depend on a combination of farming and remittances from migrant laborers. The Xhosa also account for a large number of South Africa's urban professionals and craftspeople.

See also Bantu Migrations in Sub-Saharan Africa; Ethnicity and Identity in Africa: An Interpretation; Languages, African: An Overview.

Elizabeth Heath

Xuma, Alfred Bitini

1890–1962

South African black nationalist and president general of the African National Congress from 1940 to 1949.

Alfred Bitini Xuma came from a poor but aristocratic XHOSA family in TRANSKEI, a former bantustan, or black homeland (now part of EASTERN CAPE province), in SOUTH AFRICA, and received his early education at Clarkebury Mission. He saved money to travel to the United States where he put himself through high school and then studied agriculture at the Tuskegee Normal and Industrial Institute (now TUSKEGEE UNIVERSITY, Alabama) for blacks. Xuma obtained a bachelor of science degree in 1920 and then graduated from medical school at Northwestern University in CHICAGO in 1926. He went on to gain further medical qualifications at Edinburgh University in Scotland before returning to South Africa to establish his own successful private practice in JOHANNESBURG. Xuma became involved in politics and served on the Board of the South African Institute of Race Relations. In 1940 he was elected president general of the AFRICAN NATIONAL CONGRESS (ANC). He revised and modernized its constitution and worked closely with the South African Indian Congress, staging protests and strikes calling for improvements in the rights of nonwhites.

The more radical members of the ANC, however, became increasingly dissatisfied with Xuma, who was seen as too conservative. In 1944 several younger members, including NELSON MANDELA, WALTER SISULU, and OLIVER TAMBO, formed a Youth League within the ANC that pushed for more militant action. Reluctantly, Xuma agreed to endorse it. In 1945 he further distanced himself from the radicals when he announced his belief in the goodwill of the Afrikaner prime minister Jan Smuts. In 1946 Xuma went to NEW YORK CITY to present to the United Nations the first petition of the Hereros of South-West Africa (modern NAMIBIA) demanding South Africa's withdrawal from their country. By 1949, after a year of NATIONAL PARTY rule under Daniel François Malan, Xuma said "South Africa has chosen the road that leads to national suicide and racial clashes." Although he was aware of the direction in which the country was heading, he did not, according to his critics, take the necessary radical actions. At a dramatic ANC conference at the end of 1949, the party split between the older, more conservative members and the young radicals led by the Youth League. Xuma lost the presidency of the ANC to J. S. Moroka, the candidate of the young radicals.

Yacob, Zara

1599–1692

Ethiopian philosopher and theologian, who developed a rational inquiry of faith during the same time period that French philosopher and mathematician René Descartes formulated his similar critique.

The little information known about Zara Yacob's life is derived from the autobiographical nature of his philosophical treatise, which he wrote in the mid-seventeenth century. Yacob was born in 1599 (or 1592 in the Julian calendar) near AKSUM, the ancient capital and center of religious learning in present-day ETHIOPIA. He followed a traditional training within the ETHIOPIAN ORTHODOX CHURCH, a Christian church. Yacob studied music,

qene (poetry or hymns), and especially the biblical Psalms of King David.

After studying the scriptures for ten years, Yacob taught for four years in Aksum. Living as a monk, he acquainted himself with the teachings of the Roman Catholic Church, which had been introduced to Ethiopia by Portuguese Jesuit missionaries beginning in the middle of the sixteenth century. During this period the competition between the Catholic and the Ethiopian church was fierce, and many people linked adherence to the Orthodox Church with the very existence of an Ethiopian nation. According to Yacob's autobiography, he questioned many of the biblical interpretations of both the Roman Catholic and the Ethiopian branches of CHRISTIANITY, but he kept his doubts secret.

After the Ethiopian emperor Susenyos declared his allegiance to Catholicism in 1626, persecution of Orthodox practitioners and monks began. Falsely denounced to the emperor by a priest, Yacob fled Aksum. He wandered for several days, praying to God for direction. Ultimately, Yacob discovered an uninhabited cave, where he lived for two years, praying and meditating. During this time he developed his rational analysis of the Bible and Christianity. After the death of Susenyos, the persecution subsided and Yacob left his cave. He lived the remainder of his life in Enfranz (a town in what is now northwest Ethiopia) with a wealthy man named Habtu, whose sons Yacob taught in exchange for room and board. Yacob married Habtu's maidservant, Hirut, and he declared in his treatise that she was his "equal in marriage." The couple had nine children. At the insistence of Habtu's son Walda Heywat (known as Metku), Yacob finally wrote his treatise at the age of sixty-eight. In it he set forth the ideas about reason and faith that he had developed during his stay in the cave many years earlier. Through his autobiographical treatise, Yacob became the first self-conscious founder of a philosophical tradition in Ethiopia. Previously, autobiography had been confined to literary traditions outside of AFRICA. In much of Africa, ideas and philosophies were typically the product of an oral tradition and did not come from an individual "author." Yacob's treatise is also a masterful example of self-presentation and ideological narrative. Responding to the clashing forces of Christianity, he attempted through his independent study of scripture to correlate personal faith with saving Ethiopia from foreign rule.

Yacob's philosophical method could be described as a logical subjection of faith—any faith—to a critical examination by intelligence or natural reason. This examination takes the form of honest searching or uncovering. (In the language of the treatise, Ge'ez, his method is referred to as Hasasa or Hatata, from a root meaning "to question bit by bit.") The idea that reason itself is incomplete without God's guidance is central to his thesis. However, another primary tenet is that reasonable human beings must subject their faith to critical self-examination before they believe.

Yacob maintained that faith in God comes after profound reasoning. All human perceptions, imaginations, judgments, and apprehensions should undergo critical examination. Yacob believed that truth is clearly revealed to those who seek it "with the pure intelligence set by the creator in the heart of each man." Thus, for him, faith was not an irrational form of giving oneself to an unknown external power called God.

According to Yacob, God does not order irrational behavior such as "Eat this, do not eat that; today eat, tomorrow do not eat; do not eat meat today, eat it tomorrow." He saw such pronouncements as unreasonable laws created by human beings—laws behind which God could not possibly stand. Furthermore, he believed that these rules could not have emanated from human intelligence, because God does not subject the human body to such traumatic deprivations.

Yacob instructs that all humans are equal in the eyes of God. This equality is expressed by the belief that God created all humans with intelligence and that all humans are destined to die. Furthermore, all humans, given their intelligence, can understand God's doctrines through revelation. These revelations constitute moments of truth. False faith is manifestly "nontruth" and cannot be revealed to those destined to experience truth. Truth occurs only when all people agree on a given matter or value. According to Yacob, it is possible for all to agree on truth, but it is not possible for all to agree on falsity.

Yacob maintained that the love of others is a singularly true and compelling value on which all humans can agree. However, hate in any form cannot be elevated to a value without serious resistance coming from human reason. The belief in hate as a value is an example of a false faith that cannot pass the test of reason guided by God's doctrine. To hold such a value would be a failure of human intelligence. According to Yacob, this failure is caused not by God's refusal to reveal a majestic truth that commands love, but rather by humans' notorious weakness, which prevents them from loving deeply and unconditionally. Yacob believed that God gives reason to everyone, hoping it will be used to search for truth and to avoid falsehood. Human nature, however, is too sluggish and weak to withstand the challenge of temptation.

According to Yacob, human beings are exceptional beings because—should they exercise their willpower to its fullest capacity—they can distinguish truth from falsehood and will unfailingly choose truth. However, he also believed that human nature on its own is not adequate to enable such will and choice. Under their own direction humans cannot distinguish between truth and falsehood. God's direction, demonstrated in humans by the possession of intelligence, is the power that enables individuals to judge and choose correctly. Unaided by the reason God has instilled in them, humans are easily lured by the trappings of falsehood, wealth, status, and power.

Yacob believed that the fundamental obligation of humans is toward God. That is the first wisdom, the beginning of all knowledge. God created humans and endowed them with superior intelligence, with the hope that humans would use that endowment for the service of knowing God. As Yacob stated in his treatise, "God created us intelligent so that we may meditate on his greatness, praise him and pray to him in order to obtain the needs of our body and soul." It is reason, God's gift to us, that commands absolutely to love others as we love ourselves.

Zara Yacob's critical examinations of religious teachings represented a significant departure from previous modes of thinking, which emphasized adherence to religious dogma. Reexamined in the twentieth century by Canadian scholar Claude Sumner, Yacob's work was recognized as the foundation of modern Ethiopian philosophy.

See also Christianity: Missionaries in Africa.

Yaka

Ethnic group of west central Africa.

The Yaka primarily inhabit southern Bandundu Province of southwestern DEMOCRATIC REPUBLIC OF THE CONGO and neighboring northeastern ANGOLA. They speak a Bantu language and are related to the KONGO people. Approximately 300,000 people consider themselves Yaka.

See also Bantu: Dispersion and Settlement; Ethnicity and Identity in Africa: An Interpretation; Languages, African: An Overview.

Yalunka

Ethnic group of West Africa; also known as Dialonke, Djalonke, Dyalonké, Jalonké, Jalonca, and Jalunka.

The Yalunka primarily inhabit northeastern SIERRA LEONE and central GUINEA. Other Yalunka also live in eastern GUINEA-BISSAU. They speak a MANDE language and are closely related to the SOSO people. Approximately 300,000 people consider themselves Yalunka.

See also Ethnicity and Identity in Africa: An Interpretation; Languages, African: An Overview.

Yamoussoukro, Côte d'Ivoire

The capital of Côte d'Ivoire and birthplace of former president Félix Houphouët-Boigny.

Located 249 km (155 mi) inland from the former capital of ABIDJAN, Yamoussoukro became the official capital of CÔTE D'IVOIRE in 1983. Little is known about the early history of Yamoussoukro, except that it was originally a village inhabited by the BAULE ethnic group, who still account for the majority of the town's population. The town received little attention until FÉLIX HOUPHOUËT-BOIGNY became president of the newly independent nation in 1960. During his thirty-year rule, Houphouët-Boigny directed vast amounts of federal funds to his hometown, encouraging developers to mold it into his vision of an "African Versailles." As a result, Yamoussoukro, with a population of only 120,000 (1990 estimate), is full of amenities considered luxuries in most of the Côte d'Ivoire—vast parks, well-maintained multilane highways, reliable utilities, and a regional airport.

Yamoussoukro's most extravagant constructions followed the National Assembly's decision to move the national capital there in 1983, to honor Houphouët-Boigny. One of these is a huge, marble presidential palace surrounded by a lake of crocodiles, the totem animals of Houphouët-Boigny's family. The daily feeding of live chickens to the crocodiles has since become one of the town's few tourist attractions. The other extravaganza is Our Lady of Peace of Yamoussoukro Basilica. Estimated to have cost between 150 and 800 million dollars, at least some of which came from government coffers, it is the world's largest church, surpassing even St. Peter's Basilica in Rome. Although the pope once visited the basilica, most Ivoirian Catholics live nowhere near Yamoussoukro and thus do not attend services there.

The decision to move the capital to Yamoussoukro has been widely criticized as a waste of money, given that Abidjan remains the country's economic and cultural center, and that Yamoussoukro's remote location holds little appeal to foreign diplomats or businesspeople. One group to benefit from this move was Houphouët-Boigny's own family, who at the time of the decision owned vast tracts of land in the town and surrounding region.

Elizabeth Heath

Yams

Edible tuberous root, belonging to any of several hundred species of the genus Dioscorea, that has long been a staple of African agriculture.

Many species of yam are indigenous to AFRICA. Although yams occurred naturally in many regions, people began to domesticate the tubers roughly 3,500 to 4,500 years ago in a region known as the "yam zone," where the forest and savanna zones meet in West Africa. Indonesian immigrants to MADAGASCAR probably brought yams from Southeast Asia around 2,000 years ago. The Portuguese also carried tropical American species of yams to West Africa by the end of the sixteenth century. Today approximately 90 percent of all African-grown yams continue to be cultivated within the yam zone, where the tuber has special cultural significance.

Over the millennia, people recognized and protected naturally occurring yams and gradually began to cultivate them. The plants were probably among the earliest and easiest to be domesticated, as yams can regenerate once the tuber is removed, if the vine and roots are not damaged. Domestication of yams permitted the spread of agriculture in Africa's forest zones, which are not suited to grain cultivation. Today some species of African yam have become completely domesticated, having lost the ability to flower and reproduce in the wild.

Over time a yam cultural complex evolved, principally among proto-Kwa speakers, including ancestors of the AKAN

and the YORUBA. Yam cultivation requires that the plant be protected from consumption during certain stages in its growth cycle. This requirement prompted social sanctions to prevent individuals from constantly fulfilling their short-term desire to consume the crop. Some scholars suggest that yam cultivation created population pressures that played a role in the spread of Bantu speakers across Central, East, and Southern Africa.

Yams are particularly suited to the tropics; the crop can be stored in a humid environment for long periods. Although they are rich in carbohydrates, yams are poor in fats, proteins, and many vital minerals. Consequently, a diet based on yams needs to include other foods, such as palm oil and fish or meat.

See also Bantu: Dispersion and Settlement; Food in Africa.

Ari Nave

Yanga

Leader of a group of runaway slaves in early seventeenth-century; also known as Ñaga or Ñanga.

Beginning in the 1560s the lowlands and foothills around the port of VERACRUZ on MEXICO's Caribbean coast teemed with slave revolts and sporadic attacks on settlements by maroons, or escaped slaves. It is likely but not certain that Yanga participated in or even led many of these attacks. The inaccessible jungle-covered mountains lying inland from Veracruz favored the maroons, who established small settlements there called *palenques*. From the palenques, the maroons stepped up their attacks on nearby plantations and towns, destroying property and freeing slaves.

Local officials were sent out from time to time to destroy the palenques, but the maroons had situated them in such rugged locations that they were not easily overcome, and often the communities could not even be found. Reports indicate that by 1606 the maroons had made travel between Veracruz and Mexico City unsafe and costly—a troublesome development, since Veracruz was the main port of entry for goods and people to Mexico. That year, the viceroy of New Spain (as colonial Mexico was called at that time) sent a force from Mexico City to quell the maroons, but this force also failed to overcome the fugitives.

In 1609 the viceroy sent another force under the command of Captain Pedro Gonzalo de Herrera. A Jesuit who accompanied Herrera and his 350 troops recorded one of the first detailed accounts of Yanga, told to the Jesuit by a Spaniard whom Yanga had captured and released. "This Yanga was a Negro of the Bron nation," he related, "of whom it is said that if they had not captured him, he would have been king in his own land. . . . He had been the first maroon to flee his master and for thirty years had gone free in the mountains, and he has united others who held him as chief, who are called Yanguicos." The "Bron nation" was probably a reference to the Brong, or ABRON, an AKAN group from what is today the African nation of GHANA. Yanga's village was said to have sixty dwellings, eighty men, more than twenty women (both African and Indian), and several children. The Yanguicos apparently moved their village often, but not so often that they could not cultivate cotton, sweet potato, sugarcane, chile, corn, squash, and other crops. They also maintained a small herd of cattle.

Yanga divided his people into farmers and warriors. The farmers stayed near the village, while the warriors roamed the jungle scouting for advancing Spaniards and raiding the countryside. Yanga apparently delegated most military matters to an Angolan commander, while he himself oversaw the affairs of civil government.

In late February 1609, Herrera's troops surprised Yanga's forces while they were raiding a Spanish settlement. The maroons fled and warned the palenque of the approaching Spaniards. Two days later Herrera arrived to find the village deserted. He pursued the fleeing villagers, caught up with them, and waged a bloody battle in the jungle. Both sides suffered heavy casualties, prompting a cease-fire by Herrera, who sought to negotiate a truce. Yanga and his followers used the opportunity to flee further into the jungle, eluding Herrera's troops.

Although it is not known exactly how it came about, some time later Herrera and Yanga agreed to terms for a truce. Herrera sought a pledge from Yanga that his people would no longer raid Spanish settlements or help slaves escape from their masters. Yanga agreed, stipulating several demands: (1) all of the Yanguicos who had fled before September 1608 were to be granted their freedom (those who had fled thereafter would be returned to their masters); (2) the palenque was to be chartered as a free town, of which Yanga would be governor; and (3) Spaniards could visit the town only on market days. The viceroy in Mexico City, deciding it would be less costly to accommodate Yanga than to fight him, agreed to the terms, with one further stipulation: Yanga and his followers would help New Spain capture escaped slaves, a service for which they would be paid. After Yanga agreed, he and his people settled in the new town of San Lorenzo de los Negros, a short distance from their destroyed palenque. Yanga's followers became the only blacks in colonial Mexico to secure their freedom through rebellion and to have that freedom guaranteed by law.

See also Maroonage in the Americas; Slave Rebellions in Latin America and the Caribbean.

Yao

Ethnic group numbering approximately two million people living in Malawi, Tanzania, and Mozambique.

The Yao migrated from northeastern MOZAMBIQUE to MALAWI in the mid-nineteenth century, when Alolo and Makwangala people began to infringe upon Yao lands. There the Yao became middlemen between the slave and ivory suppliers and the Arab traders from the coast. A large percentage of Yao adopted ISLAM as a consequence of their close association with Arab and Swahili traders. While the Yao sold many slaves to Arab caravans, they also integrated many of the slaves into their own communities in order to increase the size, power, and prestige of their particular villages. Yao men were permitted to marry slave women. Unlike children born to Yao women who remained within their mother's lineage, children from unions between Yao men and slave women remained tied to the man, increasing the size of his lineage and the number of his allies. Thus by acquiring slaves, villages could grow in size and military strength. European efforts to abolish slavery in the late nineteenth century, therefore, met with strong resistance from the Yao men.

The Yao have historically lived in settlements of seventy-five to 100 people. Clusters of Yao villages, each with a headman, are grouped under the political authority of a hereditary chief. Among the chief's responsibilities is the resolution of disputes, with the help of assemblies of village elders and headmen. The matrilineal Yao are also matrilocal: men, upon marriage, move to the village of their wives. When girls are about five years of age, they move in with their maternal grandmothers; boys move to communal dwellings.

Most Yao have historically practiced swidden (or "slash-and-burn") agriculture, whereby fields are cleared of vegetation through burning, and the ash is worked into the soil as a natural fertilizer. Maize and sorghum are among their staple foods. Since the colonial era the Yao have also produced tobacco as a cash crop. Fishing is an important economic activity among other Yao who live along rivers and lakes.

See also Ethnicity and Identity in Africa: An Interpretation; Islam in Africa; Ivory Trade; Slavery in Africa; Swahili People.

Ari Nave

Yaoundé, Cameroon

Capital of Cameroon.

In 1888 German explorer and scientist Georg Zenker founded the settlement of Yaoundé in the hilly Ewondo region between the Nyong and Sanaga rivers. Although dense forests separated it from the coast, in 1909 Yaoundé was made the capital of German Kamerun. After a brief Belgian occupation, Yaoundé became the capital of French Cameroun and, later, independent CAMEROON. During the colonial period, road and rail projects established links to the port city of Douala, as well as to the northern regions of Cameroon.

Yaoundé's population has grown rapidly, from 100,000 at independence in 1960 to 1.4 million in 2004. Its population is diverse; especially after the 1972 centralization of government functions, it has come to include many FULANI and BAMILÉKÉ employed in the large civil service. The cost of living is high, and many public services are not able to meet demand. Perennially under construction, the city has seen many of its historic buildings replaced by modern architecture.

After Douala, Yaoundé is Cameroon's second largest city. Although not highly industrialized, Yaoundé does have a cigarette factory, a plywood-manufacturing plant, a quarry, and a sugar refinery. It is also home to the national university, established in 1962, and several research centers, and serves as the center of a rich agricultural region.

Eric Young

Yerby, Frank Garvin

1916–1991

African American novelist.

Frank Garvin Yerby was born in Augusta, Georgia, where he attended Paine College, graduating in 1937 with a degree in English. He earned a master's degree from FISK UNIVERSITY in 1938, and pursued further graduate study at the University of Chicago, in Illinois. Before becoming a full-time writer, Yerby taught at Florida Agricultural and Mechanical College (now University) in Tallahassee, Florida, from 1939 to 1940. From 1940 to 1941 he taught at Southern University and Agricultural and Mechanical College in Baton Rouge, Louisiana. After teaching for a year at the University of Chicago, he moved to DETROIT, MICHIGAN, where he worked in a Ford Motor Company plant from 1942 to 1944. In 1945 Yerby worked for Ranger Aircraft in Jamaica, New York. He began writing full time shortly thereafter.

Yerby was remarkably successful with his first novel, *Foxes of the Harrow* (1946). The story of a white family on a southern plantation, the novel sold more than two million copies, was translated into twelve languages, and in 1947 was made into a movie of the same name starring Maureen O'Hara and Rex Harrison. Yerby continued to publish novels at the rate of one per year, including *The Vixens* (1947), *The Golden Hawk* (1948), *A Woman Called Fancy* (1951), and *The Saracen Blade* (1952). His novels were mainly historical fiction, often set in the United States South around the time of the Civil War (1861–1865). Other settings for his novels include the Crusades of the eleventh to thirteenth centuries and the French Revolution at the end of the eighteenth century. The novel many consider his best, *The Dahomean* (1971), is the story of a prominent African who is sold into slavery by his own people.

Yerby's popular success came at the expense of critical acclaim, however. His first published fiction, the short story "Health Card," deals with racial injustice and won the O. Henry Memorial Award in 1944. He published five additional short pieces during the 1940s, each of which deals with conditions facing African Americans. Yerby later claimed that writing alienated readers when its focus was on complex and troubling social issues, such as race. He likened such writing to "shouting one's head off in Mammoth Cave." His popular novels, however, earned him the title "king of the pulpsters" from one critic, and some African Americans criticized him for turning his back on the race and its problems.

In 1955, to escape racism in the United States, Yerby moved to Madrid, SPAIN, where he lived for the rest of his life. By the time of his death in 1991, he had published thirty-three novels that had sold more than 55 million copies worldwide.

See also Dahomey, Early Kingdom of; Literature, African American.

Yombe

Ethnic group of west central Africa; also known as the Mayombe.

The Yombe primarily inhabit the southwestern highlands of the REPUBLIC OF THE CONGO. Others live in neighboring western DEMOCRATIC REPUBLIC OF THE CONGO and northwestern ANGOLA, particularly the Cabinda region. They speak a Bantu language and are closely related to the KONGO people. Approximately one million people consider themselves Yombe.

See also Bantu: Dispersion and Settlement; Ethnicity and Identity in Africa: An Interpretation; Languages, African: An Overview.

Yorke and Talbot Opinion

Eighteenth-century legal opinion that established the precedent that African slaves did not become free after entering Great Britain.

In the early eighteenth century, West Indian plantation owners traveling with their slaves were alarmed by persistent rumors that in England their slaves could become legally freed through escape or baptism. Indeed, slaves traveling to England with their owners often tried to run away, seeking freedom in that reputedly free land. But the Yorke and Talbot Opinion of 1729 provided slaveholders with a legal justification for holding slaves while in England, as well as a means of forcing their escaped slaves back into slavery.

The legal status of escaped slaves in England had been wavering for decades. More often than not, English courts ruled in favor of slaveholders, at least in part because West Indian plantation slavery brought great wealth to the British Empire. Nevertheless, the notion that a slave became free the moment he or she stepped foot on English soil had been upheld in several legal cases, as well as by comments made at the HOLT DECISION of 1706.

Tired of the uncertainty they faced bringing slaves into GREAT BRITAIN, in London in 1729 several West Indian planters and merchants—an influential group because of the profit they brought to the empire—approached Attorney General Philip Yorke and Solicitor General Charles Talbot for a legal opinion. After consideration, Yorke and Talbot stated that a slave brought by his or her master from the WEST INDIES to England did not become free on English soil, and could be forcibly returned to West Indian slavery. In addition, they asserted that baptism did not confer freedom. This declaration, which became known as the Yorke and Talbot Opinion, was welcomed by the English merchants on both sides of the Atlantic who profited from the fruits of plantation slavery; these people publicized the opinion widely.

Although the Yorke and Talbot Opinion was neither a formal legal decision nor a set of comments made in court, it reflected the most popular interpretation of English common law and was generally accepted as the "law of the land." To buttress the opinion, when Yorke became Lord Chancellor Hardwick he spelled out his view on the bench in the 1749 case of *Pearne v. Lisle,* declaring that blacks were property and that a runaway slave could be recovered legally. The Yorke and Talbot Opinion stood undisputed until the abolitionist GRANVILLE SHARP contested the issue in his legal battles of the late 1760s and early 1770s. It was finally overruled in the JAMES SOMERSET CASE of 1772.

See also Slavery in Latin America and the Caribbean.

Leyla Keough

Yoruba

Group of peoples sharing the Yoruba language and a range of cultural traditions, concentrated in Nigeria but forming smaller communities in Benin and Togo.

Today more than twenty million people speak some dialect of Yoruba, which belongs to the Kwa group of the Niger-Congo languages. Most Yoruba speakers live in southwestern NIGERIA. They form a majority in LAGOS, Africa's most populous city.

Yoruba speakers are traditionally among the most urbanized African people. For centuries before British colonization, most Yoruba speakers inhabited a complex urbanized society organized around powerful city-states. These densely populated cities centered on the residence of the king, or *oba.* The basic social units were patrilineages in which inheritance, descent, and political position pass through the male line. Though they lived in cities, traditionally most Yoruba men farmed crops such as YAMS, maize, plantains, peanuts, MILLET, and beans in the surrounding countryside. Many men also engaged in crafts such as blacksmithing, manufacturing textiles, and woodworking. Traditionally, Yoruba women specialized in marketing and trade, and could gain considerable independence, status, and wealth through their commercial activity. While many Yoruba speakers continue to farm and trade today, they generally also grow and sell cash crops such as COCOA. Meanwhile, the millions of Yoruba in modern cities such as Lagos pursue a diverse array of manufacturing and service occupations.

Originally HAUSA speakers used the name Yoruba for the people of the Oyo kingdom. Europeans appropriated the term to refer to all speakers of the Yoruba language. Yoruba speakers identify themselves as members of several different groups, including the IFE, Isa, and Ketu. Some of these Yoruba-speaking groups identify with the larger community of Yoruba speakers. Others, such as the Sabe, Idaisa, and Ketu consider themselves separate ethnic groups and do not feel a sense of community with other Yoruba speakers, though they share Yoruba origin myths. All of these groups, however, share a similar material culture, mythology, and artistic tradition.

Art historians consider thirteenth- and fourteenth-century Yoruba bronzes and terra-cotta sculptures among Africa's greatest artistic achievements. Yoruba oral histories, folklore, and proverbs have also won international acclaim. Traditional Yoruba religious beliefs recognize a supreme god presiding over a complex pantheon of hundreds of lesser gods. Over the past several centuries ISLAM and CHRISTIANITY have spread to Yorubaland. Many Yoruba take a pluralistic approach to religion that integrates traditional religious elements with Christian and Muslim beliefs, as in the Aladura spiritualist movement.

According to folklore, the Yoruba originated from the mythical Olorun, God of the Sky, whose son, Oduduwa, founded the ancient holy city of Ile-Ife around the eighth century C.E. Linguistic and archaeological evidence suggest that, in fact, speakers of a distinct Yoruba language emerged near the Niger-Benue confluence some three to four thousand years ago. From there they migrated west to Yorubaland between the eighth and eleventh centuries. Strategically located on the fertile borderland between the savanna and the forest zones, Ile-Ife was the center of a powerful kingdom by the eleventh century, one of the earliest in Africa south of the SAHEL. Its rulers taxed both food surpluses and trade. While the institution of kingship probably predates the emergence of Ile-Ife, the holy city became the preeminent Yoruba spiritual and cultural center.

In time, other Yoruba cities rose to prominence. Oyo probably originated in the eleventh century and became a substantial city by the fourteenth century. Other Yoruba city-states emerged around the same time. During the fifteenth and sixteenth centuries, the nearby non-Yoruba kingdom of BENIN conquered parts of eastern and southern Yorubaland.

Oyo, however, became a powerful military state by the seventeenth century. The rulers of Oyo acquired horses by selling slaves to Europeans and reselling the manufactured goods to Hausa traders. The Oyo cavalry invaded neighboring Yoruba and non-Yoruba kingdoms alike, including Dahomey. By the late eighteenth century, however, Oyo, suffering from internal rivalries, began to disintegrate. During the early nineteenth century Dahomey won its independence in a war that further weakened Oyo. During the 1830s Muslim FULANI from the SOKOTO CALIPHATE conquered northern regions of Oyo and cut off its access to trade with the Hausa. By 1840 the Oyo kingdom had completely collapsed.

Wars among Yoruba groups and city-states raged for much of the rest of the nineteenth century. The protracted warfare left many Yoruba vulnerable to enslavement. Large numbers were sold to traders who brought them to LATIN AMERICA. To this day, Yoruba culture remains influential in BRAZIL and CUBA, where SANTERÍA religious practice carries on Yoruba traditions.

Aiming to repress the slave trade, encourage the production of raw materials, and open markets for British manufactures,

GREAT BRITAIN sought a foothold in the region. In 1851 the British navy seized Lagos, allegedly to shut down the slave market there. In 1888 most of Yorubaland became a protectorate of Great Britain. The colonial administration imposed peace among warring groups after 1892 in an effort to promote its commercial interests. Under the British policy known as indirect rule, Yoruba kings lost their sovereignty but retained a role in local government.

As the capital of British Nigeria, Lagos, dominated by Yoruba, became the center of Nigerian political and economic life. Colonial authorities introduced cocoa as a cash crop in Yorubaland and developed a modern infrastructure of railroads, highways, and schools in the region. As a result large numbers of Yoruba earned substantial cash incomes, became literate in English, and gained positions in the colonial civil service. By the time of independence, Yoruba speakers occupied a dominant position in Nigeria's economy and government. Since independence, however, the more numerous northern Hausa have dominated the elected and military governments that have ruled Nigeria, and the relatively prosperous Yoruba have tended to remain political outsiders, often subject to repression.

See also Dahomey, Early Kingdom of; Ethnicity and Identity in Africa: An Interpretation; Islam in Africa; Languages, African: An Overview; Oyo, Early Kingdom of; Religions, African.

Bibliography

Eades, Jeremy Seymour. *The Yoruba Today.* Cambridge University Press, 1980.

Falola, Toyin, ed. *Yoruba Historiography.* African Studies Program, University of Wisconsin-Madison, 1991.

Smith, Robert Sydney. *Kingdoms of the Yoruba.* University of Wisconsin Press, 1988.

Olatunji, Olatunde O., ed. *The Yoruba History, Culture and Language.* Ibadan University Press, 1996.

Ari Nave

Yoruba Religion

System of beliefs, among the Yoruba people, that strive to answer the basic questions of existence.

For information on

Traditional Yoruba beliefs: *See* African Religions: An Interpretation; Ifa; Orishas; Xangô.

Effects of commercial trade between West Africa and Brazil on the Yoruba religion: *See* Afro-Atlantic Culture: On the Live Dialogue Between Africa and the Americas; Candomblé.

Yoruba religion in Cuba: *See* Santería; Zapata Olivella, Manuel.

Religious pluralism among the Yoruba in Africa: *See* Yoruba.

Youlou, Fulbert

1917–1972

Catholic priest, nationalist leader, and president of the Republic of the Congo.

The son of a Lari merchant, Fulbert Youlou, whose surname means "Heaven" in Lari, was born in Madibou, Moyen-Congo (now the REPUBLIC OF THE CONGO). He was baptized at age nine and entered the seminary three years later. While attending mission schools in GABON and CAMEROON, he befriended BARTHÉLEMY BOGANDA, the future president-emperor of the CENTRAL AFRICAN REPUBLIC. Youlou later taught in mission schools in what was then French Moyen-Congo, and was ordained in 1946. When Youlou began campaigning for public office, however, he was defrocked. Ignoring the censure, he insisted on wearing his ecclesiastical robes. He also claimed the mantle of Andre Matsou, the dead leader of an anti-French, quasi-religious Lari self-help organization. In 1956 Youlou was elected mayor of BRAZZAVILLE, and founded the Lari-dominated Democratic Union for the Defense of African Interests (UDDIA), a party supporting close ties with FRANCE. A year later he was elected vice president of the government council, and in 1960 he became president of the newly independent Republic of the Congo.

Fulbert Youlou's rule was short-lived. A political conservative, he sought close ties with France and its former colonies, and attempted to create a single-party state. But he faced ongoing pressure from labor unions, and after three days of labor unrest in 1963, Youlou resigned. After a two-year imprisonment, supporters aided his escape, first to Zaire (present-day DEMOCRATIC REPUBLIC OF THE CONGO), then EUROPE, where he finally settled in SPAIN. In 1972 he died in exile.

Bibliography

Bontet, Remy. *Les "Trois glorieuses," ou La chute de Foulbert Youlou.* Editions Chaka, 1990.

Gauze, Rene. *The Politics of Congo-Brazzaville.* Hoover Institution Press, 1973.

Eric Young

Young, Andrew

1932–

African American civil rights activist and politician, and the first black United States ambassador to the United Nations.

Born and raised in an affluent African American family in NEW ORLEANS, LOUISIANA, Andrew Young had opportunities as a child that were available to few blacks in the South, including an exceptional education. He attended HOWARD UNIVERSITY and Hartford Theological Seminary. Ordained a Congregational minister in 1955, he soon after accepted a pastorate in Thomasville, Georgia. This experience made him keenly aware of the poverty African Americans suffered in the rural South and inspired his work as a civil rights activist.

In 1959 Young moved to NEW YORK to become assistant director of the National Council of Churches and to raise financial support for activities related to the CIVIL RIGHTS MOVEMENT in the South. He returned to Georgia two years later and joined the SOUTHERN CHRISTIAN LEADERSHIP CONFERENCE (SCLC). His energetic work as funding coordinator and administrator of the SCLC Citizenship Education Programs soon won him the admiration of MARTIN LUTHER KING, JR. They became close associates, and Young helped King organize SCLC marches in the South.

Young became executive director of the SCLC in 1964 and executive vice president in 1967. After King's death, Young helped guide the SCLC to work for social and economic improvement for African Americans. He retired from these positions in 1970 but remained on the board of directors until 1972.

In 1972 Young became the first African American to be elected to the U.S. House of Representatives from Georgia since the post–Civil War RECONSTRUCTION period, roughly a century earlier. While a Representative, Young helped presidential candidate Jimmy Carter obtain crucial support from members of the African American community who had questioned Carter's commitment to civil rights.

Young resigned from the House of Representatives in 1977 when Carter appointed him U.S. ambassador to the United Nations (UN). As ambassador, Young improved communications between the United States and African nations. He was instrumental in focusing U.S. foreign policy on sub-Saharan Africa and in bringing the attention of the United States to APARTHEID conditions in SOUTH AFRICA. Young resigned from the position in 1979 after he was criticized for his contacts with the Palestine Liberation Organization (PLO).

In 1982 Young was elected mayor of ATLANTA, GEORGIA, an office he held until 1989. In 1990 he made an unsuccessful bid in the Georgia gubernatorial race and retired from politics. In 1994 he published his memoir *A Way Out of No Way* and returned to public life to co-chair the Atlanta Committee for the 1996 Summer Olympic Games. He has also written *An Easy Burden*.

In 2000 Young served as president of the National Council of Churches, and he was later named to the National Security Study Group by the U.S. Secretary of Defense. He is chairperson of the global consulting group Good Works International, and is a professor at Georgia State University, where the Andrew Young School of Policy Studies was named in his honor in 1999. Among his numerous awards are the Presidential Medal of Freedom, the French Legion d'Honneur, and more than forty-five honorary degrees.

See also United Nations in Africa.

Elizabeth Heath

Young, Charles

1864–1922

African American army officer.

Charles Young was born in Mayslick, Kentucky, the son of Gabriel Young and Armintie Bruen, former slaves. When he was nine years old, Young's family moved north to Ripley, Ohio. Young graduated from WILBERFORCE UNIVERSITY, a black college in Xenia, Ohio, and then embarked on a career as a public school teacher. Inspired by Ohio native JOHN H. ALEXANDER, the second African American to graduate from West Point, Young sought and won his state's nomination to the military academy in 1884. He graduated from West Point in 1889, despite an atmosphere of racial prejudice and the hostility of his fellow cadets.

On leaving West Point, Young was assigned as second lieutenant with the Tenth Cavalry. He was transferred to the Ninth Cavalry in 1889 and in 1894 was assigned to Wilberforce University as a professor of military science and tactics. This was one of a very small number of assignments available to black officers. While at Wilberforce, Young taught French, German, and mathematics and helped to run the University's drama group. His record at Wilberforce so impressed the president of nearby all-white Antioch College that Young was asked to teach a course in military training there. Young remained intellectually active throughout his career and displayed artistic talent in a number of areas. In addition to a collection of poetry and a monograph entitled "Military Morale of Nations and Races" (1912), Young wrote a play about the leader of the Haitian slave revolt, TOUSSAINT L'OUVERTURE. As a musician he wrote numerous compositions and played the piano, harp, ukelele, and cornet. While in the Philippines he would add a proficiency in Spanish to the two languages he learned in college, German and French.

Young's primary calling, however, was in the military, and he devoted the bulk of his energy to climbing the ranks of the officer corps. Following the death of John H. Alexander in 1894, Young became the highest-ranking black officer in the U.S. Army. He would own this distinction and the racial burden that accompanied it until his death. By the time the SPANISH-AMERICAN WAR broke out in 1898, he had been promoted to first lieutenant. As the only black commissioned officer in the army, he was assigned to command and oversee the training of the Ninth Ohio Battalion, a black volunteer unit. While Young's regular regiment, the Ninth Cavalry, saw action in CUBA, the Ninth Ohio Battalion never left the United States. In 1901 Young was promoted to captain, and for the following year he saw service with the Ninth Cavalry in quelling the Philippine insurrection. Young questioned the pervading view in the army that black troops could succeed only under the command of white officers, when he wrote in 1912 that the experience of the SPANISH-AMERICAN WAR and the Philippine Insurrection demonstrated clearly the ability of black officers to command their own men.

Young's race, however, continued to undermine his military assignments. Between 1904 and 1907 he served in HAITI as U.S. military attaché, a post for which the *Army and Navy Journal* believed black officers were best suited because they could deal better with the local population than their white counterparts. Also in 1904 he married Ada Mills of Xenia, Ohio; they would have two children. While in Haiti, Young surveyed the military preparedness and the terrain of the island nation. According to the U.S. ambassador to Haiti, Young took great personal risk in his endeavors, traveling deep into previously uncharted territory. By the time he left the country, Young had completed a map of Haiti and written a monograph entitled "Handbook of Creole as Spoken in Haiti." His work would later prove invaluable to the U.S. Marines during their occupation of the Caribbean republic. In 1912 Young was promoted to the rank of major, and in the same year he was once again assigned as a military attaché, this time to the African Republic of LIBERIA. Young's assignment, as part of the 1912 loan agreement between the William Howard Taft administration and the Liberian government, was to oversee the training and reorganization of the country's defense forces, the Liberian Frontier Force. Although he saw himself as an adviser, leaving the day-to-day command to three African American officers he appointed to assist him, Young was occasionally called on to command troops. In one incident, he led a force deep into the Liberian interior to rescue fellow American, Captain Arthur A. Browne. Browne and an attachment of Liberian troops were trapped by a group of native Africans, who were rebelling against the Americo-Liberian government, the descendants of freed American slaves who had founded the country and who monopolized power by excluding the African population from any form of political participation. Young's expedition succeeded in rescuing Browne, and during his tour of duty the Liberian Frontier Force succeeded in quelling numerous native rebellions. Young believed that Liberia was "a heritage" for all black people; so, it is ironic that his successful performance of duty there helped to perpetuate an oligarchy that for many years to come would remain ethnically exclusive.

Upon his return to the United States in 1915, Young was awarded the Spingarn Medal by the NATIONAL ASSOCIATION FOR THE ADVANCEMENT OF COLORED PEOPLE (NAACP) in recognition of his work in AFRICA. Young's success in the hostile racial environment of the early twentieth century made him a natural role model for the African American community. In 1916 he reunited with the Tenth Cavalry to take part in General John Joseph Pershing's Punitive Expedition to MEXICO, where he distinguished himself by leading the rescue of a unit of the Thirteenth Cavalry at Parral. During his tour of duty in Mexico he was promoted to lieutenant colonel. The racial question, however, was to bring a premature end to Young's career in the regular army. Fearing that U.S. entry in WORLD WAR I in 1917 would result in Young's being given command of the Tenth Cavalry, the white officers in the regiment protested the prospect of serving under a black officer. Their protests were taken up by a number of U.S. senators, causing the War Department to force Young into early retirement, ostensibly for

medical reasons. Young sought to demonstrate his health by riding his horse from his home in Ohio to WASHINGTON, D.C., but to no avail. He was retired in 1917 at the rank of colonel, the highest rank ever achieved to that date by an African American officer. Although Young was recalled to train troops in the last days of the war, the actions of the War Department in 1917 cost him the prospect of promotion to brigadier general. Young returned to Liberia as U.S. military attaché in 1919, and while visiting LAGOS, NIGERIA, he contracted Bright's disease and died. His body was returned to the United States, and he was buried with full military honors at Arlington National Cemetery.

Young is a figure of historical significance, not just because of what he achieved but because of the manner and circumstance in which he achieved it. One generation removed from slavery, Young demonstrated tremendous courage in entering and graduating from the white-dominated world of the U.S. Military Academy. Young's determination to succeed despite the racial barriers that were placed in his path was tempered by his restraint in the face of racial hostility. His career is more remarkable for the fact that he rose to the rank of colonel during a period when prejudice against African Americans was worse than at any time since the CIVIL WAR. Although Young's determination to succeed was often resented by the black troops under his command, his achievements won him the respect of the African American community at large. He remains a significant figure in the history of African American people and their struggle against racism in the United States.

Bibliography

Although there is no collection of Young's papers, the records of the U.S. War Department for this period and the records of the U.S. State Department for Liberia and Haiti contain numerous materials by and pertaining to him.

Fletcher, Marvin. *The Black Soldier and Officer in the United States Army. 1891–1917.* 1972.
Gatewood, Willard B., Jr. *"Smoked Yankees" and the Struggle for Empire; Letters from Negro Soldiers, 1898–1901.* 1971.
Nalty, Bernard C. *Strength for the Fight: A History of Black Americans in the Military.* 1986.

From *American National Biography.* John A. Garraty and Mark C. Carnes, eds. Oxford University Press, 1999. Reprinted by permission of the American Council of Learned Societies.

David P. Kilroy

Young, Coleman Alexander

1919–1997

Five-term mayor of Detroit, Michigan, former auto worker, member of the Tuskegee Airmen, and founder of the National Negro Labor Council.

Coleman Alexander Young, DETROIT's first black mayor, presided for nearly twenty years over America's eighth-largest city—and one of its most troubled. By 1973, when Young first ran for mayor, the auto industry that had been Detroit's economic base was in serious decline. Most whites fled to the nearby suburbs, leaving the city with a population that was approximately 70 percent African American. Poverty sent the crime rate soaring, and the city's infrastructure fell into a state of decay. Young, a state senator at the time, received 92 percent of the black vote when he defeated police chief John Nicholls in the mayoral election.

During his twenty years in office, Young launched a series of revitalization projects, including a new rail system and General Motors automobile plant as well as construction of the Joe Louis Arena and multi-use Renaissance Center on Detroit's waterfront. He worked to integrate the police department, which he had dubbed "an army of occupation" during his first campaign. In addition, Young dramatically increased city contracts with minority-owned businesses, winning lasting popularity among the city's working-class African Americans. Despite his often abrasive style, which drew criticism from many white suburbanites and the local media, he was elected to an unprecedented five terms, stepping down in 1993 at the age of seventy-five. Young died of respiratory failure in Detroit four years later.

See also National Negro Labor Council; Tuskegee Airmen.

Kate Tuttle

Young, Lester Willis ("Prez")

1909–1959

African American tenor saxophonist whose distinctive approach and tone inspired many musicians during the 1940s and 1950s.

Singer BILLIE HOLIDAY gave Lester Willis Young his nickname Prez, short for president, during the 1930s: it was an era of dukes, counts, and kings of swing, and she insisted that Young should hold the highest office in the land. Today he is most widely heard through his musical collaborations with Holiday. During and after the SWING era, he and COLEMAN HAWKINS offered the major alternative approaches to the tenor saxophone in JAZZ.

As an improviser, Hawkins relied upon arpeggios built over the harmonies of each chord in a song. Young's improvisations were linear—melodies stretched across the chord sequence. Hawkins aggressively pushed the beat; Young's playing was gentle, and consistently behind the beat. Hawkins's tone was full, even harsh; Young's was light.

Born in Woodville, Mississippi, Young came from a musical family that moved during his childhood from Mississippi to NEW ORLEANS to Minneapolis. He learned several instruments and played in the successful Young family band. In 1927, while playing with another group, he took up the tenor saxophone. Eventually, he settled in KANSAS CITY, then a booming jazz center. He joined Bennie Moten's band in 1933, then left for NEW YORK CITY to fill the saxophone chair, recently vacated by Cole-

man Hawkins, in FLETCHER HENDERSON's band. The Henderson band, accustomed to Hawkins's style, ridiculed Young, and he soon returned to Kansas City. But while he was in New York City, a chance encounter in a HARLEM jam session introduced him to Billie Holiday, with whom he would collaborate in a classic series of recordings in the late 1930s and early 1940s.

Young influenced few saxophonists during the 1930s. However, the musician that he had the greatest impact on—alto saxophonist CHARLIE PARKER—became the key jazz soloist to arise between LOUIS ARMSTRONG in the 1920s and JOHN COLTRANE in the 1960s. Parker, a creator of bop during the 1940s, extended Young's style and made it his own. Parker's early recordings reveal his deep debt to Young.

Young rejoined the COUNT BASIE band in 1935, and in 1936 he made his recording debut with a quintet drawn from that band. Producer John Hammond later recalled it as "one of the only perfect sessions I ever had." Musicologist Gunther Schuller depicted Young's solo on "Oh, Lady Be Good" as "quintessential Lester Young: economical and lean . . . and masterful in its control of form." Young remained with Basie between 1935 and 1940, and returned in 1943 for a stint that ended when he was drafted. During the late 1930s, he also recorded regularly with Holiday. His improvised fills and counter melodies behind her vocals define the interplay that is the essence of jazz.

After WORLD WAR II, Young did not fare well, although his musical star was clearly ascendant. A large number of saxophonists—including Wardell Gray, Paul Quinichette (nicknamed the Vice President), and numerous white saxophonists such as Stan Getz and Zoot Sims—modeled their playing on Young's. On the other hand, his recordings suggest his unhappiness, which some attributed to his traumatic military experience, and others to his heavy drinking.

Even in the 1950s, Young occasionally recaptured the fragile beauty of his early playing. In a 1956 series of recordings—including *The Jazz Giants,* and three albums recorded at a nightclub in WASHINGTON, D.C.—Young was in prime form. But when he performed with Holiday in the 1957 television special *The Sound of Jazz,* their performance had an aura of tragic finality. Young and Holiday died in 1959 within four months of each other.

See also Music, African American.

James Sellman

Young, Plummer Bernard

1884?–1962

Editor of the *Norfolk Journal and Guide,* one of the most influential African American newspapers in the United States.

Plummer Bernard Young was the son of Sally and Winfield Young, the founders and publishers of the *True Reformer,* an independent newspaper in Littleton, North Carolina. Having learned the trade from his father, Young served as a printing instructor from 1903 to 1905 at St. Augustine's College in Raleigh, North Carolina. He was simultaneously a student but did not graduate.

Young moved to Norfolk, Virginia, to pursue his career as a journalist and by 1910 had bought *The Lodge Journal and Guide,* the organ of the fraternal Knights of the Gideon. He rechristened his paper the *Norfolk Journal and Guide* and nurtured it over the next several years from a small, irregularly published paper with a circulation of 500 to a large weekly paper with a circulation of more than 30,000. In addition to being one of the largest black newspapers in the country, the *Journal and Guide* was the largest weekly newspaper in the South.

Young, a moderate by nature, refused to indulge in the sensationalist reporting then favored among many other newspapers. Instead, the *Journal and Guide* gained a reputation for quiet, well-researched articles and solid, constructive editorials. Young's views that blacks could do much to help themselves were similar to those of BOOKER T. WASHINGTON, although Young was quicker to advocate an end to statutory discrimination than was Washington.

In the 1930s, the *Journal and Guide* supported the NEW DEAL and condemned the high rate of black unemployment and poverty. In 1943, Young was appointed to the President's Commission on Fair Employment Practices, which investigated workplace discrimination. From the end of World War I to the end of World War II, Young was generally considered to be the most powerful African American in Virginia. In his later years, he turned over much of the publishing and editing of the *Journal and Guide* to his two sons.

See also Black Journalism in the United States; Press, Black, in the United States.

Young, Whitney Moore, Jr.

1921–1971

Former executive director of the National Urban League who shaped the organization's policy and lobbied industry to provide employment opportunities for African Americans.

When he was named executive director of the NATIONAL URBAN LEAGUE (NUL) in October 1961, many observers believed Whitney Moore Young, Jr., was not qualified to hold the position. He had served as industrial relations secretary for the St. Paul, Minnesota, branch of the NUL from 1947 to 1949; as executive secretary of the Omaha, Nebraska, branch from 1949 to 1954; and as dean of the Atlanta University School of Social Work from 1954 to 1961. Still, by traditional NUL standards, he was young and inexperienced. As its executive director during the 1960s, however, Whitney Young Jr. guided the organization through one of the most socially and politically tumultuous decades in U.S. history.

The NUL was much less militant than many other organizations involved in the CIVIL RIGHTS MOVEMENT. Since its inception in 1910, it had sought to promote African American participation in the U.S. political system, rather than to change the system itself. In the 1960s, though the NUL did not embrace the direct action of other civil rights organizations—it did not sponsor SIT-INS, protest marches, bus boycotts, or voter registration drives—under Young's leadership it took a more active stance that better aligned it with black political and social thought of the day. The NUL provided support for civil rights activists, including cosponsorship of the MARCH ON WASHINGTON for Jobs and Freedom in 1963.

Young was born in Lincoln Ridge, Kentucky, and grew up on the campus of the Lincoln Institute, a vocational high school for blacks where his father was the principal. The faculty of the institute was integrated, and Young was accustomed to interracial cooperation. He used his considerable social and political skills to become an unofficial adviser to Presidents John F. Kennedy, Lyndon B. Johnson, and Richard Nixon. Johnson drew on some of Young's ideas for his War on Poverty. Young's relationships with white business leaders brought increased employment to blacks and increased funding for the NUL.

Young, who held a master's degree in social work from the University of Minnesota, also called for a "Domestic Marshall Plan" for blacks. In 1968 he introduced the NUL's "New Thrust," a program designed to help eliminate ghettos, and to increase affordable housing, health care, and educational opportunities for the poor. In addition, Young wrote a weekly column, "To Be Equal," for the *New York Amsterdam News*. In 1964 a collection of those columns was published as *To Be Equal.* Young died in 1971 while swimming during a visit to NIGERIA.

See also March on Washington, 1963.

Bibliography

Weiss, Nancy J. *Whitney M. Young, Jr., and the Struggle for Civil Rights.* Princeton University Press, 1989.

Parris, Guichard, and Lester Brooks. *Blacks in the City: A History of the National Urban League.* Little, Brown, 1971.

Robert Fay

Youssou N'Dour

1959?–

Senegalese singer of world beat music, best known for blending traditional Senegalese musical techniques with Cuban and jazz inflections.

Youssou N'Dour was born in DAKAR, SENEGAL. His mother was a *GRIOT* (a traditional Senegalese musician), and she taught him the basics of local music, including *tasso* (a kind of RAP) and *bakou* (a traditional chant).

Youssou began singing with local music and theater groups at age twelve. At fifteen he joined the Senegalese band Super Diamono, touring West Africa in 1975. The following year he began his singing career with the Star Band No. 1, and in 1977 he formed his own band, the Étoile de Dakar, renaming it Super Étoile de Dakar in 1981. Super Étoile de Dakar toured Europe in 1984, playing a modern version of *mbalax* (a traditional rhythm throughout WOLOF-speaking Senegal). The band made its North American debut in 1985.

After recording the songs "Immigrés" and "Nelson Mandela," Youssou gained the attention of British rock singer and songwriter Peter Gabriel. He played on Gabriel's best-selling album *So* (1986), and in 1987 he went on tour with Gabriel in the United States, Japan, and Europe. Youssou also sang on *Graceland* (1986), the highly successful album by American singer and songwriter Paul Simon, and in 1988 he played at the London birthday concert held for South African activist and future president NELSON ROLIHLAHLA MANDELA. In 1989 Youssou toured in support of Amnesty International, a human rights organization.

By the time Youssou recorded *The Lion* (1989), which was sung partly in English and partly in Wolof, his music had become an intricate blend of Western pop instrumentation, including distorted guitars and synthesizers, and traditional Senegalese instruments, such as the *tama* (talking drum). Youssou's 1994 album *Wommat* (Wolof for "The Guide") includes "Seven Seconds," his hit duet with Swedish-born pop singer Neneh Cherry. Among his recent albums are *Birth of a Star* (2001), *Nothing's in Vain* (Coono du réér; 2002) and *Sant Yalla* (2003).

Youssou has served as Goodwill Ambassador to the United Nations and an Ambassador to UNICEF. He was named Best African Artist in 1996 and African Artist of the Century in 1999.

Zafy, Albert

1931–

Former president of Madagascar.

Albert Zafy was born in Antsiranana in northern MADAGASCAR. He traveled to France in 1954 to attend medical school in Montpellier and remained in France until 1971. Upon his return to Madagascar, he joined General Gabriel Ramanantsoa's regime as minister of public health. When Lieutenant Commander DIDIER RATSIRAKA assumed power in 1975, Zafy resigned from his post and took a position at the University of Madagascar. In 1989 he returned to politics and created the National Union of Democrats for Development (UNDD). The following year Zafy became the leader of a coalition of opposition parties, the Comité des Forces Vives (CFV). Never having served under Ratsiraka's Democratic Republic of Madagascar, Zafy was seen as an ideal candidate to spearhead opposition to Ratsiraka.

On July 16, 1991, the CFV unilaterally announced the formation of a new government with Zafy as prime minister. The sixteen-member CFV shadow cabinet began to occupy Ratsiraka's ministries until the president declared a state of emergency, arresting and detaining several key players, including Zafy. After his release, Zafy was wounded during a mass protest march to the presidential palace, when Ratsiraka's forces fired mortar shells at the 400,000 demonstrators.

The event destroyed Ratsiraka's legitimacy and soon after, facing pressure from France and continued CFV strikes, he agreed to relinquish power while remaining the symbolic head of state. In October 1991 Zafy was appointed chairman of a transitional government, marking a return of civilian rule, multiparty elections, and the birth of the Third Republic.

Zafy enjoyed overwhelming support in the 1992–1993 elections, but his administration soon faced an economic quagmire. Handed an economy weakened by years of mismanagement, Zafy was unwilling to impose unpopular austerity measures required as a condition for aid from the International Monetary Fund and World Bank. Instead he turned to private investors to raise funds for economic development, a strategy he termed "parallel financing." The World Bank traced one such source of funds to a money-laundering racket run by drug cartels.

By 1995 the Malagasy faced skyrocketing inflation and crippling international debt. In desperation, the prime minister, Francisque Ravony, dismissed the governor of the central bank and negotiated new, less difficult conditions for assistance. Angered by Ravony's insubordination, Zafy successfully pressured for his resignation.

In 1996 Zafy's own national assembly impeached him on the grounds that he had violated elements of the constitution and had failed to institute democratic reforms, a decision upheld by the high constitutional court. Despite his poor economic track record, Zafy ran again for president in 1997, but lost by a slight margin to Ratsiraka.

Ari Nave

Zaghawa

Ethnic group of north-central Africa.

The Zaghawa primarily inhabit east-central CHAD and western SUDAN. They speak a Nilo-Saharan language and are closely related to the BERI people. About 300,000 people consider themselves Zaghawa.

See also Ethnicity and Identity in Africa: An Interpretation; Languages, African: An Overview.

Zaire

Former name of Democratic Republic of the Congo.

See also Congo, Democratic Republic of the.

Zambezi River

River in southern Africa, fourth longest of the continent.

The Zambezi River is 2,650 kilometers (1,650 miles) long and drains an area of some 1,300,000 square kilometers (some 500,000 square miles). It rises in northwestern ZAMBIA and flows in a double S curve southeast to the Indian Ocean. From its headwaters, about 1,500 meters (about 5,000 feet) above sea level, it flows through eastern ANGOLA, traverses western Zambia, and forms the border of northeastern BOTSWANA; it forms the boundary between Zambia and ZIMBABWE, and flowing through Lake Kariba, created by the hydroelectric Kariba Dam, it crosses central MOZAMBIQUE (where it forms a lake behind the Cabora Bassa Dam) and empties into the Mozambique Channel through many mouths.

In its upper course, totaling about 800 kilometers (about 500 miles), the Zambezi falls only about 180 meters (about 600 feet). About 100 kilometers (about 60 miles) below its confluence with the Kwando River, it forms the great cataract known as VICTORIA FALLS (Mosi-Oa-Tunya), and for the next 72 kilometers (45 miles) it rushes through a narrow gorge 122 meters (400 feet) deep. It then enters its middle course and flows through hilly country for about 1,300 kilometers (about 800 miles) to Quebrabasa Rapids, the last great natural barrier to navigation, in Mozambique. In its lower course, it flows through a broad valley to the sea. Besides the Kwando River, the chief tributaries of the upper river are the Kabompo and the Lung-webungu. The Zambezi receives no important tributaries in its middle course; the chief affluent of the lower river is the Shire.

Despite such barriers as cataracts, rapids, and sandbars, the Zambezi is navigable for long distances. The navigable reaches of the river and its tributaries total about 740 kilometers (about 460 miles). The Scottish missionary DAVID LIVINGSTONE was the first European to explore the Zambezi.

Zambia

Landlocked country in Central Africa that borders Angola, Democratic Republic of the Congo, Tanzania, Malawi, Mozambique, Zimbabwe, Botswana, and Namibia.

An unbalanced economy, the legacy of COLONIAL RULE, has stunted Zambia's economic and political development. For years, foreign firms shipped mineral wealth from the region that is today Zambia. In an era of declining world market prices, however, Zambia's continued reliance on mining, particularly copper, thwarted the ambitions of nationalist leaders to harness the country's mineral wealth for the good of its people. Poor soils aggravated Zambia's economic stagnation by impeding successful cash crop production and agricultural self-sufficiency. Rural villagers fleeing the impoverished countryside contributed to an unusually high rate of urbanization. However, as earnings from copper exports declined since the 1970s, and as international donors forced Zambia's government to introduce painful austerity measures, the nation's city dwellers experienced hardship as well. Popular unrest and urban rioting compelled Zambia's nationalist leader, KENNETH

KAUNDA, to abandon authoritarian rule in 1991 and to accept multiparty elections that resulted in his defeat. Ironically, the country's first freely elected government, led by FREDERICK CHILUBA, faced allegations of corruption and took questionable steps to exclude opponents, including Kaunda, from power.

Early Zambian Societies

Traces of human occupation date back over a million years in Zambia, as in other parts of East and Central Africa. Human remains dating from 30,000 to 100,000 years ago have been uncovered at KABWE. Early rock art in Zambia shows animals, people, and objects dwarfed by abstract designs. Difficult to date, this art may be as much as 6,000 years old. Anthropologists believe that the region's earliest inhabitants—hunters and gatherers—may have been the ancestors of present-day KHOISAN speakers or PYGMY populations.

Bantu-speaking settlers displaced or absorbed this early population beginning around the fourth century C.E. Contemporary Khoisan speakers in the southwest may be the descendants of foragers who chose to move to more marginal lands rather than lose their way of life to the Bantu expansion. The Bantu speakers brought a new way of life to the region, including ironworking, domestication of sheep and goats, and cultivation of cereal grains. Of the contemporary ethnic groups of Zambia, at least one group, the TONGA, can trace direct descent through material culture to these early immigrants. From an early date the inhabitants participated in extensive trade networks. By around the seventh century C.E. they were smelting and trading copper for glass beads and seashells from outside the area. From at least the eleventh century, Arab and Indian traders ventured into the region along the ZAMBEZI RIVER to exchange cloth, guns, and Chinese porcelain for products from the interior, such as ivory, gold, and copper ingots, which they then shipped across the Indian Ocean.

By the early 1800s small chiefdoms had been established in much of the northern and eastern regions. Later immigrants, however, including the LUNDA, LUBA, CHEWA, and BEMBA, established centralized chiefdoms that enabled them to overpower these earlier inhabitants. Other groups migrated into the region to flee the ZULU expansion in SOUTH AFRICA during the early nineteenth century. They include the NGONI, who conquered the Chewa of southeastern Zambia, and a Sotho group (the Kololo), who absorbed the Luyama-speakers of the south to form the present-day LOZI people.

Explorer Antonio Fernandes visited the area in 1514; his account of the Zambezi trade sparked PORTUGAL's interest in the region. Portuguese merchants competed with Arab and Swahili traders, and the volume of trade in the region increased. Foreign traders exchanged guns and other exotic products, particularly glass beads and European-manufactured goods, for ivory, precious metals, and slaves. The demand for slaves and the supply of firearms provoked increased warfare and slave raiding, which caused suffering and depopulation in the region well into the nineteenth century. Though the Portuguese established Christian missions

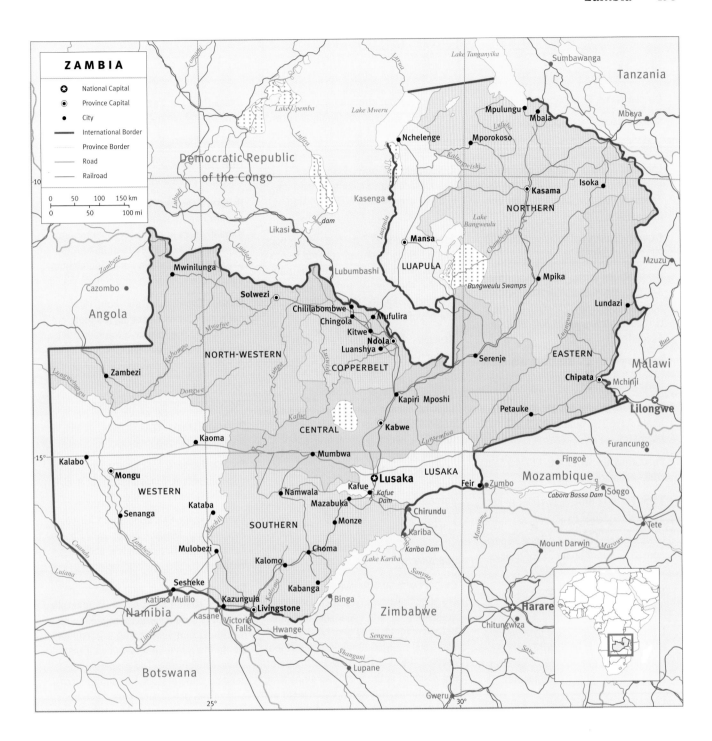

Colonial Rule

In 1851 the missionary DAVID LIVINGSTONE explored the Zambezi River basin and surrounding areas. Other missionaries followed. They succeeded in converting large numbers of people to CHRISTIANITY. Today over half of the population professes Christianity, although many Christians also maintain indigenous beliefs. Livingstone hoped to stimulate the

along the Zambezi during the eighteenth century, they never effectively occupied the region.

export of cotton and metals as an alternative to the slave trade. His *Missionary Travels and Research in South Africa* received wide attention in GREAT BRITAIN, particularly among industrialists and colonialists who sought to open new markets for British industry. There were, however, several obstacles to British political-economic control over the area. Britain's primary rival for influence, the Portuguese, had become entrenched over the centuries. In addition, many of the chiefdoms, including the Bemba, had successfully resisted Portuguese control of important trade routes, and would likely do the same with the British.

Zambia (At a Glance)

OFFICIAL NAME: Republic of Zambia

FORMER NAME: Northern Rhodesia

AREA: 752,610 sq km (290,586 sq mi)

LOCATION: Southern Africa; borders Angola, Democratic Republic of the Congo, Tanzania, Malawi, Mozambique, Zimbabwe, and Namibia

CAPITAL: Lusaka (population 1,265,000; 2003 estimate)

OTHER MAJOR CITIES: Ndola (population 349,300), Kitwe (306,200; 2003 estimates); Kabwe (population 219,000), Chingola (151,000), Mufulira (131,500; 2003 estimates)

POPULATION: 10,307,333 (2003 estimate)

POPULATION DENSITY: Data unavailable

POPULATION BELOW AGE 15: 46.3 percent (male 2,396,313; female 2,378,567; 2003 estimate)

POPULATION GROWTH RATE: 1.52 percent (2003 estimate)

TOTAL FERTILITY RATE: 5.25 children born per woman (2003 estimate)

LIFE EXPECTANCY AT BIRTH: Total population: 35.25 years (male 35.25; female 35.25 years; 2003 estimate)

INFANT MORTALITY RATE: 99.29 deaths per 1000 live births (2003 estimate)

LITERACY RATE (AGE 15 AND OVER WHO CAN READ AND WRITE IN ENGLISH): Total population: 80.6 percent (male 86.8 percent; female 74.8 percent; 2003 estimate)

EDUCATION: School attendance increased substantially after Zambia's independence in 1964. In the early 1990s about 1.5 million pupils were enrolled in primary schools. In the late 1980s about 161,300 pupils were enrolled in secondary schools; vocational and teacher-training schools had 8,000 pupils; and the University of Zambia (founded in 1965), at Lusaka, had about 7,400 students. Through the 1990s, however, the education system seriously deteriorated, with only a marginal increase in primary school attendance (estimated in 2003 at 66 percent of eligible children). Only two-thirds of children who begin first grade complete primary school.

LANGUAGES: The official language is English. More than seventy African languages are spoken, including Bemba, Lozi, Luvale, Tonga, and Nyanja.

ETHNIC GROUPS: 98.7 percent of the population belong to one of seventy Bantu-speaking ethnic groups, including the Bemba, the Nyanja, and the Tonga. Europeans make up less than 2 percent of the population.

RELIGIONS: Christian (50 percent to 75 percent), Muslim and Hindu (24 percent to 49 percent), indigenous beliefs (1 percent)

CLIMATE: Zambia enjoys a pleasant subtropical climate because of its high altitude. The average temperature in Lusaka during July, the coldest month of the year, is 16° C (61° F); the hottest month, January, has an average temperature of 21° C (70° F). Annual rainfall ranges from 750 mm (30 in) in the south to 1300 mm (51 in) in the north. Nearly all of the rain falls between November and April.

LAND, PLANTS, AND ANIMALS: Most of Zambia is high plateau with a flat or gently undulating terrain. Elevations average between about 1,100 and 1,400 m (3,500 and 4,500 ft). Mountains in the northeast reach 2,164 m (7,100 ft). Major rivers are the Zambezi in the west and south and its tributaries, the Kafue in the west and the Luangwa in the east; and the Luapula and Chambeshi in the north. Lake Bangweulu, in the north, is surrounded by a vast swampy region. Lake Kariba is a large reservoir formed by Kariba Dam on the Zambezi River. Animals include elephants, lions, rhinoceroses, and several varieties of antelope..

NATURAL RESOURCES: Copper, cobalt, zinc, lead, coal, emeralds, gold, silver, uranium, and hydropower potential

CURRENCY: The Zambian kwacha

GROSS DOMESTIC PRODUCT (GDP): $8.9 billion (2002 estimate)

GDP PER CAPITA: $890 (2002 estimate)

GDP REAL ANNUAL GROWTH RATE: 4.2 percent (2002 estimate)

PRIMARY ECONOMIC ACTIVITIES: Zambia's copper mining sector accounts for more than 80 percent of the nation's foreign currency intake. More than 85 percent of Zambia's population are employed in agriculture.

PRIMARY CROPS: Corn, sorghum, rice, peanuts, sunflower seeds, tobacco, cotton, sugarcane, cassava (tapioca), livestock, and poultry

INDUSTRIES: Copper mining and processing, construction, foodstuffs, beverages, textiles, chemicals, and fertilizer

PRIMARY EXPORTS: Copper, zinc, cobalt, lead, and tobacco

PRIMARY IMPORTS: Machinery, transportation equipment, foodstuffs, fuels, and manufactures

PRIMARY TRADE PARTNERS: South Africa, Switzerland, Malawi, Zimbabwe, Britain, Tanzania, the United States, and Thailand

GOVERNMENT: Zambia won independence from the United Kingdom on October 24, 1964. It is a constitutional republic and a multiparty democracy with a president elected to a five-year term by direct universal suffrage. The president appoints a cabinet from among the members of the unicameral legislative body, the National Assembly. The 150 members of this body are likewise directly elected for five-year terms. In December 2001 Levy Mwanawasa was elected president; he launched a major anti-corruption campaign in 2002. The dominant political party is the Movement for Multiparty Democracy; others include the National Party and the Zambian Democratic Congress.

Alonford James Robinson, Jr.

Miner hard at work at the Consolidated Copper mine in Zambia. Despite the country's mineral wealth, little of the economic benefit of mining reaches the miners. *Jason Lauré/Woodfin Camp*

With the SCRAMBLE FOR AFRICA occurring among the European powers, the British used chartered companies as a tool to achieve control over particular regions, such as the Zambezi basin, which was believed to be rich in natural resources. CECIL RHODES's British South Africa Company (BSAC) received a mandate in 1889 to take possession of the region, to exploit it economically, and to prevent further Portuguese infiltration into the interior. Agents of Rhodes had already secured the agreement of several chiefs to treaties surrendering mineral rights in exchange for arms. While the Ngoni temporarily resisted British rule, they faced military conquest in 1898. Divisions among other groups limited their ability to resist British domination.

The British gradually extended their control over the region. Deposits of copper were discovered, and in 1902 a zinc and lead mine was opened at Kabwe. By 1909, the BSAC completed a rail line through the region linking the copper mines of Katanga, in the present-day DEMOCRATIC REPUBLIC OF THE CONGO, to the South African coast. In order to force the African population into the colonial economy, the BSAC imposed hut taxes (a kind of poll tax) after 1900. Desperate to acquire the currency needed to pay the tax, tens of thousands of men left their villages to work in mines, including the diamond mines of Southern Rhodesia (present-day ZIMBABWE) to the south, leaving many areas practically devoid of adult males.

After World War I, European settlers came to Northern Rhodesia, as the territory was named in 1911; by 1924 the white population totaled 4,000. These settlers challenged the legitimacy of the BSAC's jurisdiction. Consequently the British government assumed jurisdiction and declared Northern Rhodesia a protectorate in 1924, a status it would retain until independence in 1964. The colonial office instituted a policy of indirect rule through compliant chiefs, or through other collaborators where they could not identify cooperative chiefs.

While the colonial office now controlled the region politically, the BSAC retained mineral rights until 1960. In the 1920s and 1930s, the BSAC opened mines to exploit the vast copper deposits of the north-central region, since then known as the Copperbelt. Mining there attracted working-class immigrants from England who organized unions that excluded Africans. This exacerbated the already tense race relations. The European settlers lobbied for the formation of a single colony, joining Northern Rhodesia with Southern Rhodesia, where the larger white settler population controlled the colonial government. World War II, however, interrupted the formation of a Central African Federation (CAF). In the 1920s and 1930s, conditions only worsened for Africans as large companies, such as the Anglo-American Corporation, formed a cartel controlling an overwhelming majority of mining interests. This effective monopoly hurt both small entrepreneurs and African miners, who faced an entrenched system of segregation, lower pay than European miners, and limits on their ability to organize. Mining companies invested little in urban amenities in order to discourage permanent settlement in the mining belt by African workers, who mostly migrated from other parts of the country. The colony's mineral wealth thus flowed out of the country and brought little benefit to the African population.

In response to the inhumane conditions, the conspicuous color bar, and the privileged position of European colonists, African laborers organized periodic strikes and uprisings beginning in 1935, only to be suppressed by the colonial authorities. Blaming the unrest on "detribalization" rather than unjust conditions, the colonial government argued that urban life and the absence of tribal chiefs caused African insubordination, a view that was consistent with their advocacy of indirect rule. The colonial administration feared the development of African nationalism in Northern Rhodesia. Since the turn of

A tailor sews in his stall at Bamba Market in Lusaka, the capital of Zambia. *CORBIS/Caroline Penn*

the century, the religious group that is now known as Jehovah's Witnesses had gathered increasing support among Africans and become a forum for political resistance. Wary colonial authorities carefully monitored the organization and banned publications and events considered too provocative.

Meanwhile, Africans formed more explicitly political organizations. The Lusaka and Luanshya Welfare Association formed in 1932 to voice African discontent. Likewise the Northern Rhodesia Congress (renamed the Northern Rhodesia African Congress in 1951) emerged in 1937 to lobby against the formation of the CAF. In 1948 the African Mineworkers' Union organized. HARRY MWAANGA NKUMBULA of the Congress led the campaign against the creation of the CAF, but the conservative British government sided with white settlers and established the Federation. This Federation united Southern Rhodesia, Northern Rhodesia, and NYASALAND (present-day MALAWI) in 1953 under a single, white-dominated government, although whites made up less than 2 percent of the population of Northern Rhodesia. African workers continued to strike against the mining companies of the Copperbelt, but remained unable to secure significant concessions. A rise in copper prices brought an economic boom during the mid-1950s, and African workers won limited improvements in their status.

When the boom ended in 1956, however, many Africans were laid off, and resentment over the continued diversion of the country's wealth grew. In 1958, disillusioned young nationalists, including Kenneth Kaunda, split off to form the Zambia African National Congress (ZANC). That year Kaunda, along with Nyasaland nationalist Hastings Banda, attended the All-African Peoples' Conference in ACCRA, GHANA. Shortly after Kaunda's return to Northern Rhodesia, ZANC was banned and Kaunda was imprisoned. Released in 1960, Kaunda was elected to head the newly formed United National Independence Party

(UNIP). The UNIP soon thereafter embarked upon a campaign of civil disobedience and sabotage. The British government recognized that control could only be maintained by force, but they were reluctant to impose rule through violence. They introduced a new constitution, giving Africans the majority of seats in the federation legislature in 1962. The federation was dissolved in 1963. Elections in 1964 resulted in a large legislative majority for UNIP. The newly formed government acquired BSAC's mineral rights for £4 million, half paid by Zambia, half paid by Great Britain.

Independence

On October 24, 1964, the country assumed independence as the Republic of Zambia, with Kaunda as president. Kaunda faced a need for an improved infrastructure and social services to support the African majority, and not only the 43,000 whites who resided predominately in the Copperbelt. The government built numerous schools and mandated significant wage increases for mine workers. Revenues from rising world copper prices financed large infrastructure investments. The government failed, however, to invest in economic diversification, ultimately to the detriment of the country's growth.

In 1965, the white government of Southern Rhodesia (known as Rhodesia until it became Zimbabwe in 1980) unilaterally declared independence. The resulting United Nations sanctions against Rhodesia, including an economic embargo, eliminated one of Zambia's chief outlets to world markets. The Zambian government invested heavily to develop alternative sources of energy (previously imported from the south) and new export routes. China contracted to build a railroad from Zambia to the port of DAR ES SALAAM, TANZANIA, in exchange for trading concessions. The Zambian government also commissioned construction of an oil pipeline and a paved road to Dar es Salaam.

Despite these difficulties, Zambia, unlike other newly independent African countries, initially earned nearly enough foreign exchange through the export of copper in order to pay for necessary development projects. In 1969 the government nationalized both the mines and mining firms to increase government revenues. Zambia required relatively little foreign aid, mostly in the form of low-interest loans from the World Bank and the International Monetary Fund (IMF), until the economy faltered in the mid-1970s. Wage increases among miners in the 1960s eased racial tensions but failed to address the needs of subsistence farmers. Though rich in copper ore, Zambia's poor soils prevented the widespread cultivation of cash crops for export. The weak rural economy exacerbated the migration from rural areas to urban areas. A survey in 1980 estimated that 2 million of Zambia's 5.7 million inhabitants lived in cities. By 2015 it is expected that 45.2 percent of Zambia's total population will live in urban areas.

During the postindependence years, Kaunda steadily consolidated his power. He reshuffled his cabinet to ensure balanced ethnic representation, but he continued to suppress po-

while its export earnings fell when the price of copper collapsed after 1975. Civil war then erupted in Angola and shut down the Benguela railway, one of the few remaining conduits for Zambia's trade. In 1976, Kaunda declared a state of emergency before instituting IMF austerity measures the following year. As the population faced increased hardship, discontent mounted.

Kaunda's increasingly authoritarian government responded to discontent with repression. In 1978 the government introduced constitutional amendments further limiting the ability of opposition groups to voice dissent. Later that year, Rhodesia began to bomb LUSAKA to retaliate for Zambia's role in harboring rebel forces; this further disrupted the Zambian economy and destabilized Kaunda's regime. Following a failed coup attempt in 1980 and strikes and riots in 1981, Kaunda arrested several prominent trade union leaders. Food shortages, riots, and strikes continued into 1985. Invoking emergency powers, Kaunda banned industrial actions against vital services. Kaunda closed the universities in response to student demonstrations in 1986. Further IMF austerity measures, particularly the elimination of the maize subsidy, sparked several riots later that same year. Finally in 1987 Kaunda was forced to abandon the IMF program and restore the subsidies. (IMF STRUCTURAL ADJUSTMENT programs resumed in 1992.) Kaunda became increasingly fearful of being ousted from power and he accused various politicians, businessmen, and soldiers of colluding with South Africa and its allies to orchestrate his overthrow. Accusations, arrests, and deportations followed. Price hikes for maize again instigated riots in 1989 and 1990.

In 1990 Kaunda announced a popular referendum to determine whether multiparty politics should be reintroduced. Proponents of such a move formed the Movement for Multiparty Democracy (MMD). Bowing to the political pressure, Kaunda abandoned his opposition and suggested that the constitution be modified, without holding a referendum, to legalize multiparty politics. The MMD and eleven other opposition parties were recognized when the constitutional amendments were signed into law. International observers were invited to ensure that the 1991 elections were free and fair. The elections resulted in UNIP's defeat and Kaunda's removal from power. FREDERICK CHILUBA, a union activist leading the MMD, assumed office as president.

Despite this relatively peaceful return to multiparty politics, the Zambian government remained authoritarian and corrupt. Chiluba stifled political dissent, preventing the development of democracy. In March 1993 Chiluba declared a state of emergency when documents were allegedly discovered implicating UNIP in a plot to destabilize the government. Several of

Water cascades down Rainbow Falls and Knife Edge at the eastern cataract of Victoria Falls, on the border between Zambia and Zimbabwe. The local name for the falls is *Mosi-oa-Tunya,* which means "the smoke that thunders." *CORBIS/Charles & Josette Lenars*

litical opposition and to detain his rivals. Finally, in 1972 Kaunda declared Zambia a one-party state under the umbrella of the UNIP. Because of Zambia's linguistic and ethnic diversity, Kaunda asserted that multiparty democracy would lead to tribalism and ethnic discord. With no limit on his term in office, and with no real political opposition, Kaunda was guaranteed a prolonged political career. Beginning in 1973 he won elections as the sole candidate every five years through 1988. Kaunda further solidified his control when UNIP took command of Zambia's leading newspaper in 1975.

During the 1970s economic hardships sparked popular discontent. The economy's heavy dependence on copper exports made it vulnerable to fluctuations in market prices. Zambia's import bill climbed when oil prices skyrocketed after 1973,

Kaunda's sons, members of UNIP, were arrested. Kaunda ended a brief retirement and won reelection as president of UNIP with the intention of running against Chiluba in the forthcoming elections. Constitutional amendments adopted in 1996, however, prevented Kaunda from running, introducing a provision that a candidate's parents must be Zambian-born. (Kaunda's parents were Malawian.) Consequently, UNIP and other opposition parties boycotted the elections and embarked on a program of civil disobedience. Amid student riots and widespread popular dissent, Chiluba was reelected, though much of the electorate refrained from voting. The results were immediately challenged. Civil disturbances continued and international monitoring agencies denounced police brutality. Later, Kaunda was shot during a rally; he accused the government of trying to assassinate him. After an aborted coup attempt by drunken soldiers in October 1997, Chiluba's government declared martial law and detained Kaunda, despite little evidence of Kaunda's involvement.

In December 2001 elections, MMD presidential candidate Levy Mwanawasa received more votes than any of the eleven opposition candidates. Mwanawasa therefore succeeded Chiluba as president in January 2002, despite having received only 29 percent of the popular vote. In 2002 Mwanawasa launched an anticorruption campaign and arrested Chiluba and many of his supporters. The government charged the ex-president with embezzling more than $30 million in public funds. Mwanawasa's opponents, meanwhile, pressured parliament in 2003 to consider impeachment proceedings against him.

See also Bantu Migrations in Sub-Saharan Africa; Indian Ocean Slave Trade; Iron in Africa; Minerals and Mining in Africa.

Ari Nave

Zambo

Term used in Spanish America to refer to people of mixed African and Indian descent.

See also Latin America, Blacks and Indians in: An Interpretation.

Zanj Rebellion

Uprising by African slaves in Iraq in the ninth century.

Thousands of African slaves labored in the MIDDLE EAST during the early medieval period. Arab writers called these Bantu-speaking peoples from East Africa the *Zanj*, which means "black." Historians are uncertain about when and how the Zanj first arrived in the Middle East, but both of the powerful Islamic empires that dominated the region during this period, the Umayyad caliphate (661–750) and the Abbasid caliphate (750–1258), were known to have imported Zanj slaves. Muslims most likely acquired them through trade and as tribute from subject states. Although most slaves in medieval Islamic society were domestic servants, the Zanj toiled in harsh con-

ditions on plantations and in the salt mines of lower Iraq's canal region.

Early Rebellions

According to Arab historians, the earliest Zanj uprisings occurred in the late seventh century C.E. In 689–690 small gangs of slaves roamed about pillaging before they were stopped by Umayyad troops. A few years later the Zanj launched a more organized revolt that achieved some success before government forces restored order. Aside from a few other minor insurrections, the Zanj receive little mention in Muslim history until the ninth century.

Africans slaves in Iraq lived in appalling conditions—forcibly packed into work camps by the thousands, separated from their families, given meager rations for food, and left with little hope. Stereotyped by Arabs as criminals with little intelligence, the Zanj worked long grueling hours. As discontent simmered in the large work camps of southern Iraq, political and economic chaos festered in the heart of the Abbasid empire in the ninth century. Turkish military officers had gained control of the royal court, installing and removing caliphs at will. Political instability in the Abbasid capital, Samarra, weakened the caliphate's grip on the provinces. Several provincial leaders broke away from the central government and established new states.

Ali ibn Muhammad was born in a Persian village to Arab parents. As a young man he traveled to Samarra and became a poet in the caliph's court. He later traveled throughout the region attracting many loyal followers who considered him a prophet. Ali eventually settled in Basra, the major city in southern Iraq. After making contact with the oppressed Zanj, and distressed at the treatment he observed, Ali helped to plan an insurrection. Promising freedom and wealth to the 15,000 African slaves in the region, Ali and his followers launched a full-scale revolt in 869. Masses of Zanj slaves joined the movement.

When local troops failed to put down the uprising, Basra residents appealed to the central government for help. Underestimating the extent of the rebellion, the caliph sent insufficient forces to quell the insurrection. Ali ibn Muhammad's growing Zanj army wreaked havoc throughout the region, killing and plundering, and cutting off trade routes to Basra. The Zanj capped a series of victories against Abbasid troops by capturing Basra in the fall of 871.

By 873 the troops of Ali ibn Muhammad, who was now known as the Master of the Zanj, controlled the canal region of southern Iraq. He built a capital in al-Mukhtara and set up an independent government that collected taxes and minted its own coins. Abbasid and Zanj forces continued to clash though the remainder the 870s. The Abbasid government, however, could not devote its full attention to the Zanj movement. Challenges from the Saffarids, and other rival dynasties, diverted the caliph's military resources, enabling the Zanj to continue their military operations virtually unchecked. Ali ibn Muhammad's armies captured several more cities, threatened the Abbasid capital, and disrupted much of the empire's economy.

By 879 the Saffarid threat to the Abbasid caliphate had been reduced. Caliph al-Muwaffaq then raised a 10,000-man army to crush the Zanj. Learning from earlier campaigns, Abbasid commanders equipped their army with boats to maneuver through the canal region more easily. In 880 the caliph raised a second army to join in the campaign against the rebels. The combined Abbasid forces won a succession of victories. Ali withdrew his troops back to al-Mukhtara. The Abbasid army laid siege to the city in 881. Al-Muwaffaq's offer of amnesty to rebel troops resulted in many desertions among the Zanj rebel fighters. Nonetheless, the defenders held off an Abbasid force of approximately 50,000 men for more than two years. In 883 the Abbasids finally captured the city, killing Ali ibn Muhammad and ending the Zanj rebellion. Between 500,000 and 2.5 million people died during the fourteen-year war.

Despite its ultimate fate of the rebellion, the Zanj uprising had a lasting significance. The work camps of southern Iraq were abandoned and the living conditions of slaves in the region improved. The large-scale Abbasid importation of slaves from East Africa was effectively halted. Moreover, those Africans who had defected to the caliph's army were not returned to slavery. A precursor to the slave rebellions in Latin America and the Caribbean centuries later, the Zanj rebellion demonstrated the powerful potential of a captive population that rises up in solidarity.

See also Bantu: Dispersion and Settlement; Slave Rebellions in Latin America and the Caribbean; Uprisings and Rebellions.

Kent Krause

Zanzibar

Island off of the east coast of Africa; it is part of the United Republic of Tanzania.

An island often overshadowed by its larger partner in the United Republic of Tanzania, Zanzibar nevertheless maintains a history and culture different and separate from that of the mainland. Once a key port on the thriving Indian Ocean trade routes, Zanzibar has been shaped by the people who sought to participate in and control these trades. Consequently, Zanzibar's population (estimated at 372,400 in 2003) and culture reflect not only its proximity to the East Africa coast, but the influences of Asians, Arabs, and Europeans. During the colonial era, European powers took advantage of Arab hegemony to assume economic control of this thriving city-state and, in an effort to increase its prosperity, turned Zanzibar into a mono-crop export economy. Since independence Zanzibar, with the aid of its mainland TANZANIA, has tried to overcome this colonial legacy and prepare to compete in the globalized economy.

Precolonial history

Although little is known about the island's early history, it is believed that Zanzibar was first inhabited by fisherpeople who traveled to the island from mainland Africa around 4000 B.C.E.

By 1000 B.C.E., Zanzibar and the islands off the coast of East Africa were familiar to the Phoenicians, Greeks, Romans, and the peoples of EGYPT. As these Mediterranean empires extended their trade routes to the south and east, Zanzibar became one of several major commercial ports along the East African coast. Around the third century, the trade in goods attracted the attention of merchants from southwestern Arabia who also began trading with the island residents, bringing weapons, wine, and wheat to barter for ivory and other luxury goods.

By the eighth century, the Arabs controlled the trade routes that passed through the coastal islands. Their preeminence was further strengthened by the SHIRAZI, a twelfth-century Arab trading empire based on the nearby island of Kilwa Kisiwani. As the Arabs settled among the island's Bantu-speaking residents a new culture developed, characterized by its hybridized SWAHILI LANGUAGE. The Swahili culture soon spread to the coastal regions of mainland Africa, including Tanzania.

Arab control lasted until the late fifteenth century, when the explorers from PORTUGAL arrived via the Indian Ocean. Within eight years of Portuguese explorer VASCO DA GAMA's first visit in 1498, the Portuguese took control of the trade routes and islands and imposed taxes on the residents. In 1729, however, the forces of the Sultan of Oman successfully mobilized popular support and forced the Portuguese off the islands.

Sultan of Zanzibar

Although Zanzibar was now under the authority of the Sultanate of Oman, life there changed little until the accession of SAYYID SA'ID IBN SULTAN in 1791. During the first years of his reign, Sa'id increased Zanzibar's role in the INDIAN OCEAN SLAVE TRADE by hiring traders, such as TIPPU TIP, to bring slaves from the African interior to be sold to American and European merchants at the Zanzibari market. Within twenty years, however, European naval forces were attempting to shut down the Indian Ocean slave trade, and Sa'id was forced to sign agreements that not only forbade him to sell slaves to non-Muslims but to North Africans as well. Seeking to diversify his interests, the sultan built clove plantations and soon turned Zanzibar into the world's leading exporter of cloves. In addition, Sa'id extended his empire to the mainland coast, where he increased his fortune by collecting export duties. By the time Sa'id moved his capital to Zanzibar in 1840, the island's economy had recovered the prosperity it enjoyed at the peak of the slave trade and had reestablished its power over the neighboring coastal towns and nearby islands, facts that did not go unnoticed by European powers.

Colonialism

GREAT BRITAIN forged close relations with Sa'id and his successors Barghash ibn Sa'id and Hamoud bin Muhammad by acting as international advisers and confidantes. In 1890 the British took advantage of this relationship to establish their own protectorate over the coastal islands of Zanzibar and Pemba. They installed an Anglophone sultan to the throne, but exercised their influence over him only rarely, on issues such as the internal slave trade. Otherwise, the sultan and Arabs assumed control of the economy, island government, and schools.

For almost a century Britain supported the sultan's rule and sanctioned the minority Arab population's economic dominance over Zanzibar's African and Asian (mostly Indian) inhabitants. These policies met with little resistance until 1948, when the mainland independence movement inspired African dockworkers and trade unionists to protest British colonialism and Arab domination.

As ethnic divisions deepened, Arabs, Asians, and Africans began to create their own civic and political associations, such as the Zanzibar Nationalist Party, the Afro-Shirazi party, and the Zanzibar and Pemba People's party. The British tried to channel these organizations into a parliamentary government under the sultan, and held elections for a legislative council in 1957. In the first election, the Africans won five of six available seats. The results, which were far from satisfactory to the British, further strained ethnic relations and led to new divisions among the political groups. The British attempted to appease the Arab minority by holding another election for a newly enlarged council, but when this and a third election failed to promote Arab interests, riots erupted throughout the island. Fearful of the spread of violence, the British once again enlarged the council and planned one last election. Although the Afro-Shirazi party won more than 54 percent of the popular vote, the Arab alliance between the Zanzibar Nationalist party and the Zanzibar and Pemba People's party claimed the plurality and took control of the government. Despite obvious inconsistencies, Britain accepted the results and declared Zanzibar independent on December 10, 1963.

Independence

Within a month of independence, violent revolution took hold of the island. The Arab coalition was overthrown and the sultan was forced to flee after riots incited by Ugandan John Okello. Okello, however, lacked the support to create his own government, and was overpowered by the Afro-Shirazi party and the radical party, Umma. They soon formed a coalition government headed by Sheikh Abeid Armani Karume. As the worldwide drop in clove prices began to devastate the vulnerable Zanzibari economy, however, hardship deepened and popular discontent increased. Aware of his increasingly precarious position, Karume appealed to mainland Tanzania for help. After a series of talks and negotiations with mainland president JULIUS KAMBARAGE NYERERE, the two agreed on a union between the two countries, and on April 26, 1964, the United Republic of Tanzania and Zanzibar—later shortened to the United Republic of Tanzania—was formed. Under this new arrangement Zanzibar retained a great deal of economic and internal independence. The Zanzibaris elected their own president, who controlled Zanzibar internal affairs and served in a national government as one of two vice-presidents under the Tanzanian president. In addition, Tanzania gave the much smaller Zanzibar overrepresentation in the National Assembly (fifty of 169 seats) and control over its own judicial system. Despite these concessions, however, some Zanzibaris, such as Karume himself, viewed the union with hostility, and as a mainland plot to take over the island.

Zanzibar under the United Republic of Tanzania

Although Karume had initiated and agreed to the union, he did much to prevent real economic and political unity between the countries and consequently guided Zanzibar on a course separate from the mainland. Dismissing Nyerere's socialist program as ineffectual, Karume attempted to institute hard-line communism in Zanzibar. He nationalized private businesses and deported Asian noncitizens, whom he accused of plotting to take over the economy. He also sought to boost export revenues by building new state-run clove plantations (the profits of which he did not share with mainland Tanzania) with funding from Cuba, China, and the Soviet Union. But persistent economic stagnation combined with unpopular social laws, such as a mandate for interracial marriages between Africans and Arabs, cost Karume public support. In 1972 he was killed by an unknown assassin.

Karume was succeeded by Aboud Jumbe, a moderate who desired closer relations with mainland Tanzania. In 1977 he united Zanzibar's Afro-Shirazi party with the Nyerere's Tanzania African National Union (TANU) and formed the Chama Cha Mapinduzi (Party of the Revolution). This unification proved to be the first step toward a more cohesive political unity in the Republic government and paved the way for Jumbe's successor and CCM member, ALI HASSAN MWINYI, to win the Tanzanian presidential election in 1985. Both Jumbe and Mwinyi presided over a period of relative political stability and economic growth. Faced with volatile clove prices during the 1970s and early 1980s, the Zanzibari government enacted economic reforms to encourage diversification and foreign investment. In addition, Mwinyi promoted the island's nascent tourist industry, helping the industry grow almost 18.5 percent each year between 1982 and 1992. By the end of Mwinyi's term in 1985, it seemed that Zanzibar had overcome the economic stagnation and ethnic and political divisions that had plagued it since the colonial era.

Mwinyi's successor, Idris Abdul Wakil, was elected president and immediately adopted a political style similar to Karume. Intolerant of political opposition and hostile toward the union with the mainland, Wakil neglected the political and economic progress made by Jumbe and Mwinyi. In January 1988 Wakil seized control of the military and dismissed his council and ministers, accusing them of planning a coup d'état. When mainland Tanzania then began investigations into government corruption and deployed soldiers to the island, Wakil claimed it was merely a front to enable Tanzania to take over the island. Such rhetoric, combined with Wakil's blatant disregard for civil liberties, eventually turned public support against him, and in October 1990, under pressure from the Tanzanian government, he resigned from the presidency.

Dr. Salmin Amour won the subsequent election, and during his tenure he has strengthened relations between the island and the mainland. Working closely with Tanzanian presidents Mwinyi and BENJAMIN MKAPA, Amour has tried to attract legitimate foreign investment to the island. In addition, he has instituted reforms to stop the island's notorious money-laundering businesses, tax evasion, and a thriving black market in electronics. Amour has also promoted tourism associated with the island's exotic history. The government has begun to promote spice tours of the island's clove plantations, which now produce nutmeg, ginger, cinnamon, and cardamom as well as cloves. In addition, the government has funded a number of restoration projects. One of the most ambitious projects is the renovation of the capital's Stone Town, the former Arab and European quarters. Once renowned for its Saracenic architecture and beautiful hand-carved teak doors, the quarter was basically abandoned for new buildings in the African section, Ngambo, after independence and most buildings are now unusable. The government has also begun a project to restore part of the Marahubi palace, the former center of the Zanzibari sultanate. Amour hopes that these projects will increase the island's tourism, an industry that he believes will play an integral part in stabilizing the Zanzibar economy in the twenty-first century.

See also Swahili Civilization; Tourism in Africa.

Bibliography

Bennett, Norman. *Arab versus European: Diplomacy and War in Nineteenth-Century East Central Africa.* Africana Publishing Company, 1986.

Clayton, Anthony. *The Zanzibar Revolution and Its Aftermath.* Archon Books, 1981.

Flint, J. E. "Zanzibar 1890–1950." In *History of East Africa.* Edited by Vincent Harlow and E. M. Chilver. Claredon Press, 1965.

Gray, Sir John Milner. *History of Zanzibar from the Middle Ages to 1856.* Oxford University Press, 1962.

Martin, Esmond Bradley. *Zanzibar: Tradition and Revolution.* Hamish Hamilton, 1978.

Otham, Haroub. *Zanzibar's Political History: The Past Haunting the Present?* CDR, 1993.

Elizabeth Heath

Zapata Olivella, Manuel

1920–

Afro-Colombian writer, essayist, physician, anthropologist, diplomat, and leading intellectual and artist of twentieth-century Latin America.

Manuel Zapata Olivella's frequent use of the word "mulatto" (a person of both African and European descent) to describe his background suggests a biological union as much as a cul-

tural mixture. Focusing less on phenotype and more on what the Afro-Cuban poet NICOLÁS GUILLÉN would term *cultural mulatez,* or the mixing of cultures that characterizes the Caribbean, Zapata Olivella explores what unites peoples rather than what separates them. Through his acclaimed works of fiction as well as scholarly studies and public service, Zapata Olivella has significantly advanced the understanding of the contribution of African culture to the world. Together with NANCY MOREJÓN and QUINCE DUNCAN he is one of the twentieth century's most admired Afro-Hispanic writers.

Born in the small town of Lorica on the western Caribbean coast of COLOMBIA to parents of African descent, Zapata Olivella used the area's rich folklore in his first novel, *Tierra mojada* (Wetlands, 1947), to explore the conflicting social relations of the region. The novel recounts in accessible language and a straightforward narrative the struggles between a soon-to-be landless rice-growing community and a large landowner and political boss. Other central characters are the parish priest, with whom the boss works in cahoots, and the local schoolteacher, a communist sympathizer and a civil rights leader who tries to defend the peasant community. Though simplistic in its approach to issues of good and evil and social disparity, *Tierra mojada* contains many of the thematic characteristics of Zapata Olivella's subsequent works: concern for the downtrodden, a sense of history from the viewpoint of the dispossessed, and issues of racial and cultural identity.

Zapata Olivella worked on *Tierra mojada* while traveling through CENTRAL AMERICA to MEXICO and then to the United States. His adventures are delightfully retold in a series of travel narratives. Most noteworthy is *He visto la noche: Las raíces de la furia negra* (I Have Seen the Night: The Roots of Black Fury, 1949), in which the impressionable young man seeks out his African American brothers in the United States in the aftermath of the HARLEM RIOT OF 1943. During his visit to New York City, Zapata Olivella developed a friendship with LANGSTON HUGHES that would last until Hughes's death in 1967.

Zapata Olivella's experiences in the United States helped shape a black worldview that grew sharper with each decade. While several of his later works militantly pursue the theme of blackness, three works in particular stand out: the novel *Chambacú: Corral de negros* (1963; *Chambacú: Black Slum,* 1989); the short story "Un extraño bajo mi piel" ("A Stranger under My Skin," 1967); and the critically acclaimed *Changó, el gran putas* (Shango: The Greatest S.O.B., 1983).

Chambacú: Black Slum, awarded the prestigious Cuban Casa de las Américas literary prize in 1963, highlights the mistreatment of Afro-Colombians in the coastal city of CARTAGENA, COLOMBIA. Set against the backdrop of the Korean War (1950–1953), a war many felt Colombians fought because of U.S. pressure, the novel describes the path of a black community in the small black town of Chambacú. As the war breaks out, the town is surrounded and occupied by the local military forces who try forcefully to recruit soldiers to man the battle lines. The move is resisted by the population, led by Máximo, a local political activist who is captured and tortured by the army. Translated by Jonathan Tittler in 1989, *Chambacú* has been cited as exemplary of Zapata Olivella's aesthetic of protest against the degradation and oppression of Afro-Colombians.

The story "A Stranger under My Skin," published in the collection of short stories *¿Quién dio el fusil a Oswaldo?* (Who Passed the Gun to Oswald?, 1967), is a humorous probe of one black man's self-loathing. A half-black, half-white mulatto, Leroy Elder, the main character in the story, regrets his black side so much that his life is forever altered. Translated by Brenda Frazier and published in the *Afro-Hispanic Review* in 1983, the story takes its cue from the Martinican political philosopher and revolutionary FRANTZ FANON's *White Mask, Black Skin* (1952), and is one of the most powerful psychological explorations of pain and suffering available in fiction.

Changó, el gran putas, first published in 1983, was seen as a significant breakthrough in Spanish American literature. For the first time, black narrators told the story of their own experiences in the Americas from an Afrocentric perspective—providing a sense of the whole of the African diaspora in the Americas. The novel opens with an epic poem that recounts the fall from grace and exile of the ORISHA Changó, a deity in the YORUBA religion of NIGERIA and in Yoruba-derived religious traditions in the African diaspora. As a consequence of his own exile, Changó expels the human race from Africa and condemns them to THE MIDDLE PASSAGE and slavery. Similarly, the novel recounts the struggles for freedom during colonial times, the HAITIAN REVOLUTION, the postcolonial fight for equality, and the civil rights struggles in the United States. Some of the best-known historical figures in black history appear as narrators or literary personae, among them BENKOS BIOHÓ, the sixteenth-century leader of a Colombian maroon community; FRANÇOIS DOMINIQUE TOUSSAINT LOUVERTURE, the Haitian Revolution's military leader; Aleijadinho, the eighteenth-century Brazilian sculptor; and the twentieth-century political thinker MALCOLM X.

In addition to his fiction, Zapata Olivella has been a leading interpreter of racial and cultural *mestizaje* (cultural mixing in Latin America). Unlike the proponents of racial democracy (the belief that racial mixture diluted social tension in Latin America), however, Zapata Olivella views *mestizaje* as the form that oppressed groups have used to resist assimilation and genocide. In his 1990 biography, *¡Levántate mulato!* (Rise Up, Mulatto!, originally in French, 1987), Zapata Olivella writes: "America was blackened by the importation of Africans, not because of their black skin, but because of their resistance, their struggles against slavery, their joining forces with native Americans to fight against the oppressors."

Zapata Olivella also coordinated—in conjunction with ABDIAS DO NASCIMENTO and other black Latin Americans—the first Congress of Black Culture of the Americas, which took place in 1977 in Cali, Colombia. He later served as chargé d'affaires at the Colombian Embassy in PORT-OF SPAIN, TRINIDAD AND TOBAGO. His most recent published work, *La rebelión de los genes: El mestizaje americano en la sociedad futura* (The Revolt of the Genes: *Mestizaje* in the Future of American Societies, 1997), is an extensive essay that presents a historical and political analysis of *mestizaje* and its consequences for an increasingly globalized world.

See also Literature, Black, in Spanish America; Pan-Africanism and Afro-Latin Americans; Racial Mixing in Latin America and the Caribbean.

Yvonne Captain

Zaramo

Ethnic group of Tanzania.

The Zaramo primarily inhabit coastal TANZANIA in and around DAR ES SALAAM. They speak Swahili, a Bantu language. The term *Zaramo* refers both to the Zaramo people (or the Zaramo proper) and to a cluster of related peoples, including the KWERE, the Kaguru, and the Zaramo people themselves. The Zaramo people number around 600,000.

See also Bantu: Dispersion and Settlement; Ethnicity and Identity in Africa: An Interpretation; Languages, African: An Overview; Swahili Language.

Zebra

Striped mammal native to Africa, smaller in size than the related horse and greatly resembling the wild ass in habit and form, having a short mane, large ears, and a tufted tail.

The stripes that distinguish the zebra from other members of the horse family serve as protective coloration in its natural habitat. The chief enemies of the zebra are LIONS and hunters who kill zebras for their flesh and hide. Zebras can be trained to work in harness and are popular animals in zoos and circuses.

Three species and several subspecies are generally recognized, chiefly according to variations in the arrangement of the stripes. The mountain zebra is the smallest species, averaging about 1.2 meters (about 4 feet) high at the shoulders, and has a strong, muscular, and symmetrical body. It is silver-white, striped with black markings that extend to every part of the body except the stomach and the inner part of the thighs. The markings on the head are brown, and the muzzle is a rich bay-tan. The legs are short and wiry. Mountain zebras travel in small herds and inhabit the mountain ranges of SOUTH AFRICA. This species was formerly plentiful but has been decimated by intensive hunting.

Burchell's zebras travel in large herds and inhabit the central and eastern plains; the species is named after the British naturalist William John Burchell. They are pale yellow with broad, black stripes, generally interspersed with fainter markings called shadow stripes. The species has several variations; some have stripes down to the hooves, and the lower legs of others are solid white without any stripes. The Boers refer to all varieties of Burchell's zebra as *quaggas*. The true quaggas, however, were exterminated during the nineteenth century; they were darker in color than the zebra and striped only on the head, neck, and shoulders.

The largest species, Grévy's zebra, is named after the former French president Jules Grévy. It attains a height of about 1.5 meters (about 5 feet) at the shoulders, and its stripes are narrow and numerous. Formerly plentiful and of wide range, this species now inhabits the arid plains of eastern AFRICA and is nearly extinct.

Scientific classification: Zebras belong to the family Equidae. The mountain zebra is classified as *Equus zebra,* Burchell's zebra as *Equus burchelli,* the true quagga as *Equus quagga,* and Grévy's zebra as *Equus grevyi.*

See also Hunting in Africa.

Zebu

Common name for several breeds of domesticated humped cattle common in many parts of Africa.

The zebu is native to southern Asia and is believed to be a descendant of the banteng, the wild ox of Java and Borneo. A large, muscular hump on the back above the shoulders is its most conspicuous characteristic. Most zebus have short horns, pendulous ears, and huge dewlaps (a fold of loose skin hanging under the neck). The animals are used extensively in AFRICA to plow fields and for other heavy work, and are also kept for their milk and flesh.

Because the zebu is highly resistant to heat and tropical diseases, it has been introduced into the United States and SOUTH AMERICA for crossbreeding with native cattle, in order to develop strains with similar qualities.

Scientific classification: The zebu belongs to the family Bovidae. It is classified as *Bos taurus indicus.*

Zeferina

Black female leader of a slave revolt outside of Salvador, Bahia, in 1826.

In the first half of the nineteenth century, the northeastern region of BRAZIL experienced a large number of slave revolts. Historians attribute the high incidence of slave rebellions at this time to the growth of the SUGAR industry, the intensified importation of African slaves, the fact that many of these slaves shared a common language and culture, and the increasing demands made of slave labor, among other factors. These conditions encouraged many slaves to run away and form isolated communities known as *quilombos.* Alone or in cooperation with the free black or enslaved populations, quilombo members planned and carried out rebellions against the slaveholding society. The insurrection led by Zeferina in December 1826 was just one of some twenty revolts that occurred in the northeastern state of BAHIA between 1807 and 1835.

Zeferina was a member of the Urubu (Vulture) quilombo located just outside of Bahia's capital, SALVADOR. With the assistance of other slaves, Zeferina and the Urubu quilombo made plans to invade the city and kill all of its white inhabitants on Christmas Day 1826. On December 16, however, a violent encounter between escaped slaves who were transporting food to the quilombo and a white farming family set the revolt into motion prematurely. In the following days, slave hunters made several unsuccessful attempts to overthrow Urubu; after suffering some casualties, they joined forces with a small group of soldiers from Salvador and the Pirajá district and attacked Urubu again. While many of the slave rebels carried knives and guns, Zeferina armed herself with a bow and arrows. She led a fierce counterattack in which some fifty blacks exchanged gunfire with the soldiers and assaulted them while intermittently yelling, "Death to whites! Long live blacks!" The colonial forces ultimately vanquished the quilombo, killing four blacks and taking ten others as prisoners, including Zeferina. Soldiers extolled her courage and prowess in battle. Upon seeing her, the provincial president Manoel Ignácio da Cunha Menezes called her a "queen." In the end, nearly all of the other captives were returned to their masters, but Zeferina was sentenced to prison and hard labor.

The known personal history of Zeferina begins with the 1826 rebellion she spearheaded and ends with her interrogation and sentencing. As in the case of many slaves, her individual identity is shrouded in ambiguity. Historical documents indicate that after the incident, Zeferina stated that the majority of the Urubu quilombo members were NAGÔS, that is, members of the YORUBA ethnic group originating in the southwest parts of NIGERIA and BENIN. Religious artifacts found in the quilombo living quarters also testify to the Yoruban character of the Urubu quilombo. In particular, the color red found on much of the religious paraphernalia is associated with the African god of thunder and lightning, SHANGO, who is also the ancestral king of the Yoruban kingdom of Oyo.

While women have long occupied an important leadership position as *mães de santos* (priestesses) in the Brazilian religion CANDOMBLÉ, their role as quilombo community leaders during Brazil's long era of slavery has been discussed less often. As members of escaped slave communities, black women were occasionally required to take up arms against colonial forces in defense of their autonomy. In the struggle for freedom, some women died anonymously and others escaped, their valiant efforts unrecorded. Zeferina is a symbol of the spirit with which so many slaves, both men and women, fought to achieve freedom in Brazil.

See also Slave Rebellions in Latin America and the Caribbean.

Aaron Myers

Zenawi, Meles

1955–

Prime minister of Ethiopia.

Meles Zenawi led the Ethiopian People's Revolutionary Democratic Front (EPRDF), which deposed the government of Mengistu Haile Mariam in 1991. After leading Ethiopia's transitional government, Zenawi won election as prime minister in 1995.

Born in Adwa in northern Ethiopia's Tigre Province, Zenawi was educated at the General Wingate School. In 1971 Zenawi began studying medicine at Addis Ababa University. After becoming active in the student political movement, which was agitating against the faltering regime of Emperor Haile Selassie I, he left the university to join the guerrilla fighters in the Ethiopian bush. A committed Marxist, Zenawi at first supported the regime that was headed by Mengistu, which ousted Selassie in 1974.

However, Zenawi opposed Mengistu's use of brutal tactics to hold power. Along with other opponents of the Mengistu regime, Zenawi helped to found the Tigre People's Liberation Front (TPLF), which led a revolt in Tigre. By 1980, in alliance with the Eritrean People's Liberation Front (EPLF), the TPLF had driven out Mengistu's troops and controlled most of the Tigrean countryside. By 1989, with Zenawi in command, the TPLF controlled Tigre and were closing on the Ethiopian capital of Addis Ababa. He helped found the EPRDF in 1989, an umbrella for the TPLF allies outside Tigre, to mobilize national support for what had so far been a regional movement. In early 1991 Zenawi became chairman of the supreme council of the EPRDF. He quickly distanced himself from his Marxist past and promised a more moderate approach that might gain international favor.

In May 1991, EPRDF forces took the capital shortly after Mengistu fled the country. Zenawi became the interim head of state. He quickly agreed to Eritrean independence and worked to develop the Ethiopian economy, which had been ruined after years of warfare and mismanagement under the Mengistu regime. He cut military spending, redistributed land, and fought to end government corruption. Zenawi still faced opposition, however, most notably from the Oromo Liberation Front (OLF), which withdrew from the EPRDF. In addition, some Ethiopians claimed that land distribution unfairly limited land ownership by former supporters of Selassie and Mengistu to one hectare (2.5 acres), while EPRDF supporters could own three hectares. In 1998 Ethiopia and Eritrea became embroiled in a border dispute. Ethiopia claimed that Eritrean forces occupied a part of northwestern Ethiopia. Zenawi responded to international calls for mediation of the dispute by requiring that Eritrea withdraw from the disputed area before Ethiopia would agree to a negotiation. At the end of 2000, Ethiopia and Eritrea signed a peace agreement allowing the International Boundary Commission of the Hague to rule on the dispute; neither side, however, would agree to demilitarize first. In 2002 both sides met in Addis Ababa to discuss humanitarian measures that could facilitate the peace process.

See also Eritrea; Oromo.

Robert Fay

Zenón Cruz, Isabelo

1939–

Afro–Puerto Rican writer and scholar, and professor of literature at the University of Puerto Rico.

Isabelo Zenón Cruz was born in Humacao, Puerto Rico. Influenced by the writings of Martinican political philosopher Frantz Fanon and American political activist Eldridge Cleaver, Zenón Cruz defends the importance of African heritage in the formation of a Puerto Rican identity. His two-volume study, *Narciso descubre su trasero: El Negro en la cultura puertorriqueña* (Narciso Discovers His Behind: The Negro in the Puerto Rican Culture; 1974), questions the often accepted myth of a racial harmony in the definition of a Puerto Rican identity and presents extensive evidence that racism and prejudice have always been part of Afro–Puerto Ricans' reality. The book examines the historical, social, and cultural circumstances that have marginalized Afro–Puerto Ricans.

According to Zenón Cruz, the importance of Afro–Puerto Ricans has always been underestimated. In his extensive and comprehensive discussion about education, politics, language, the arts, religion, sports, and Puerto Rican folklore—to name a few—Zenón Cruz examines commonly accepted ideals and discusses the contributions of outstanding figures in each area. His analysis of this material shows how prejudice is embedded in the way blacks are perceived in Puerto Rico. He also examines how racism is perpetuated in every aspect of the island's social and cultural life, and why it is even perpetuated by Afro–Puerto Ricans.

Zenón Cruz's study also denounces the blind spots of previous scholars, critics, poets, and writers who have ignored Afro–Puerto Rican contributions. His harsh critique addresses the apparent general indifference of the Puerto Rican left to questions of race, especially that of the independence movement. For this reason, his study was received with enthusiasm by some, but it was also dismissed and ignored by others. Nevertheless, in several of the island's newspapers it provoked a debate that had until then been almost nonexistent. Zenón Cruz exposed and addressed the taboos and complexities that permeate notions of race on the island.

In Zenón Cruz's version of the Greek myth, Narcissus discovers his behind rather than his face. This serves as a meaningful image of the ideology and politics concerning race relations in Puerto Rico. It brings to the surface many underlying truths, unveils the underestimation of African heritage and importance in Puerto Rico, confronts and questions official discourses, and plays a key role in the discussions about Afro–Puerto Rican identity.

Zenón Cruz also wrote *El anhelo de la inmortalidad del alma en Unamuno* (The Longing for the Immortality of the Soul in Unamuno; 1961), and his works have been published in newspapers and magazines, including *Guajana, Educación, Llama, Humacao,* and *Ecos Grises.*

Mayda Grano de Oro

Zerma

Ethnic group of West Africa; also known as Djerma, Dyerma, Zabarma, Zaberma, Zabermawa, and Zarma.

The Zerma primarily inhabit northern BURKINA FASO and western NIGER. Others live in northwestern NIGERIA, northern BENIN, GHANA and CÔTE D'IVOIRE. They speak a Nilo-Saharan language and are a subgroup of the SONGHAI people. Approximately four million people consider themselves Zerma.

See also Ethnicity and Identity in Africa: An Interpretation; Languages, African: An Overview.

Zigua

Ethnic group of Tanzania; also known as the Zigula.

The Zigua primarily inhabit interior northeastern TANZANIA. They speak a Bantu language. Approximately 400,000 people consider themselves Zigua.

See also Bantu: Dispersion and Settlement; Ethnicity and Identity in Africa: An Interpretation; Languages, African: An Overview.

Zimbabwe

Country in southern Africa.

The Zimbabwean plateau, bounded in the south by the Limpopo River, in the north by the ZAMBEZI RIVER, and in the east by the Chimanimani mountains and eastern highlands, includes such natural wonders as VICTORIA FALLS and the historic Matopos hills. It is also an area that has experienced three great waves of violence: the first as a result of the ZULU *MFECANE* from SOUTH AFRICA; the second from colonial conquest; and the third during the war for independence. Land, the foundation of Zimbabwe's natural beauty, has been the issue that has most dramatically defined the country's history and politics.

Early History

Remains of *Homo sapiens rhodesiensis* found on the Zimbabwean plateau have been carbon-dated at 100,000 years old. But the first humans to leave behind more extensive records were the KHOIKHOI, hunter-gatherers who produced thousands of rock paintings throughout Zimbabwe, and especially in the Mato-pos hills, between 2,000 and 5,000 years ago. Some time between 200 B.C.E. and 500 C.E., Bantu-speaking agriculturists and herders using iron tools began migrating into the area, forcing the Khoikhoi north. Many of these groups spoke the SHONA language, and by the tenth century, Shona speakers were the most numerous people in the region.

After 1000 B.C.E., centralized states began to develop among the Shona as some groups monopolized the trade with Arabs from the coast of MOZAMBIQUE. In the fourteenth century, competition for trade in gold and ivory resulted in the creation of distinct empires. The first major empire was GREAT ZIMBABWE (1250–1550), followed by the Torwa empire under Khame. At about the same time the Munhumutapa kingdom of the Mutapa, an expansionist trading state, emerged to the northeast. The Munhumutapa kingdom also produced gold, dug from small surface deposits. The last Shona empire was the Changamire, who became known as the Rozvi, a confederation of tribute-paying chieftainships in the southwest. Although the empires and chieftainships differed in style of governance, all Shona groups believed that land was sacred, belonging to all people and held only temporarily by the chief and elders.

In the early 1800s, the violent upheavals known as the mfecane that followed the rise of the warrior-king SHAKA in South Africa pushed new groups into Shona territory, leading to the eventual collapse of the southern Shona empires. The NGUNI under Soshangane attacked the Shona at Manyika in the early 1820s. Two decades later the last emigrant Nguni group, the NDEBELE under Mzilikazi, destroyed the Rozvi state in the southwest. The Ndebele incorporated local Shona inhabitants and established their own kingdom near present-day BULAWAYO, in the area that became known as Matabeleland. The Ndebele kingdom was highly centralized, possessing an effective army led by senior chiefs under the command of the king, first Mzilikazi and later his son Lobengula. Both the Ndebele's gradual expansion and their periodic cattle raids increased tensions over land in Shona territory, or Mashonaland.

Rhodesian Settlers

Until the late 1800s the only Europeans to venture into Matabeleland and Mashonaland were a few missionaries, including DAVID LIVINGSTONE, and explorers. The first settlers came in 1890 when CECIL RHODES sent nearly 200 farmers, artisans, miners, soldiers, doctors, and others—the so-called Pioneer Column—plus more than 300 policemen north from JOHANNESBURG, under the flag of the British South Africa (BSA) company. Rhodes's objective was to find gold, expand British influence, and contain AFRIKANER expansion. But the pioneers found little gold in Mashonaland—the surface deposits had been depleted at least a hundred years earlier. Turning instead to farming and cattle ranching, the settlers fared so poorly for the first several years that they relied on trade with local Africans for foodstuffs. In order to secure better land for themselves, the settlers soon began forcing Africans into tribal reserves.

In Matabeleland land was scarcer than it had been in Mashonaland, and King Lobengula realized that Rhodes and

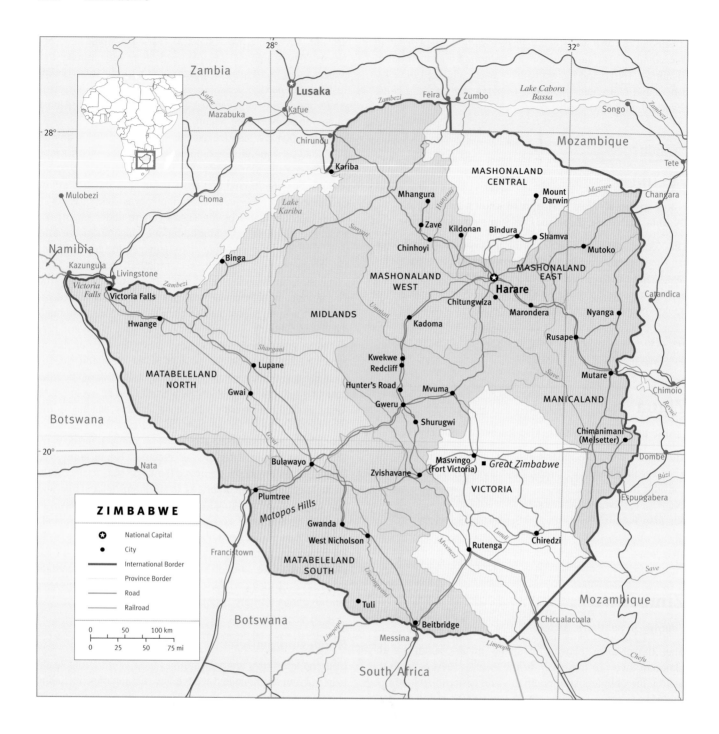

the BSA company wanted to acquire the territory for settlers and prospectors. He turned to the British Crown for protection, but Britain approved of Rhodes's plan and gave a free hand to the BSA. Consequently the BSA, using a cattle dispute as the pretext, invaded Matabeleland and defeated Lobengula in 1893. The imposition of new taxes and tribal reserves led to a rebellion against white rule in 1896–1897. Brutally suppressed, it was the last large-scale rebellion for nearly seventy years.

Offering scant mineral wealth, the Zimbabwean plateau initially attracted few white settlers. Those who did come, mostly from South Africa, sought unfettered access to the best possible land for farming and ranching. Settlers resented the BSA's

intervention in land policies and challenged its supremacy. In 1923 the British held an all-white referendum in Southern Rhodesia, and the settlers voted to become a self-governing rather than company-run territory. This gave white Rhodesians more power to resettle Africans on tribal reserves (later called native reserves) and to impose in-kind taxes of cattle. The settlers also stole cattle outright. The 1930 Land Apportionment Act formally classified land according to race, with over 50 percent of the land European and 30 percent African.

Although Africans bitterly resented the native reserves, other aspects of Rhodesian colonialism also led to the emergence of African nationalism. The few educational opportunities avail-

A woman sifts groundnuts in a village in Zimbabwe. An important ingredient in many African diets, groundnuts are raised primarily for sustenance, not for export. *CORBIS/Hulton-Deutsch Collection*

able to Africans were usually religious or technical in nature. Mission schools taught humility and obedience, and the state school taught manual labor and minor artisan trades. Labor conditions and employment opportunities were also discriminatory. African wages were kept low and trade unions were prohibited in domestic service, mining, and agriculture, the three largest sectors of African employment. Discontent first emerged in the African press, especially in the *Daily News* and the Catholic *Moto,* and among the industrial labor unions that had not been banned. However, nationalist protests were sporadic and the leadership was often fragmented. The African National Congress, or ANC (distinct from the South African counterpart of the same name), founded in 1934, was often the mouthpiece for labor unions and individuals to voice their grievances. But the Rhodesian government, through censorship and the banning of undesirable organizations, firmly suppressed any more militant actions.

In the 1950s Britain gradually began to extricate itself from its colonies throughout Africa. In 1953 politicians in London, PRETORIA, and SALISBURY created the Central African Federation (also known as the Federation of Rhodesia and Nyasaland), uniting Southern and NORTHERN RHODESIA and NYASALAND. Africans initially expressed ambivalence about the federation, but as it became evident that an "indepen-

dent" federation would be more oppressive than British rule, their opposition grew. Under increasing pressure from African nationalists, the federation dissolved in 1963, with Northern Rhodesia and Nyasaland becoming independent ZAMBIA and MALAWI, respectively. The whites of Southern Rhodesia, much more numerous and prosperous than their kin to the north, chose a course of confrontation. Stridently opposed to making concessions to Africans, in 1964 Rhodesian Front party leader IAN DOUGLAS SMITH became prime minister. Smith called a referendum on independence and whites voted overwhelmingly for the Unilateral Declaration of Independence, or UDI. The international community responded with moral condemnation and international sanctions. In independent Rhodesia, although whites numbered less than one-seventeenth of the total population, they held one-third of the land.

Chimurenga II: War for Independence

Given the Rhodesian government's land policies, it is not surprising that the primary reason Africans fought for their independence was for land, the source of their livelihood as well as the sacred home of their ancestors. Traditional chiefs and spirit mediums played a vital role by asking the people to wel-

Zimbabwe (At a Glance)

OFFICIAL NAME: Republic of Zimbabwe

FORMER NAME: Rhodesia

AREA: 390,759 sq km (about 150,873 sq mi)

LOCATION: Southern Africa; borders South Africa, Botswana, Mozambique, and Zambia

CAPITAL: Harare (population 1,919,700; 2003 estimate)

OTHER MAJOR CITIES: Bulawayo (population 965,000), Chitungwiza (411,700), Mutare (189,000), Gweru (154,900), Kadoma (106,000), and Kwekwe (81,000; 2003 estimates)

POPULATION: 12,576,742 (2003 estimate)

POPULATION DENSITY: 30 persons per sq km (about 76 persons per sq mi)

POPULATION BELOW AGE 15: 39.7 percent (male 2,517,608; female 2,471,342; 1998 estimate)

POPULATION GROWTH RATE: 0.83 percent (2003 estimate)

TOTAL FERTILITY RATE: 3.66 children born per woman (2003 estimate)

LIFE EXPECTANCY AT BIRTH: Total population: 39.01 years (male 40.09 years; female 37.89 years; 2003 estimate)

INFANT MORTALITY RATE: 66.47 deaths per 1000 live births (2003 estimate)

LITERACY RATE (AGE 15 AND OVER WHO CAN READ AND WRITE IN ENGLISH): Total population: 90.7 percent (male 94.2 percent; female 87.2 percent; 2003 estimate)

EDUCATION: Primary education in Zimbabwe is free and compulsory between ages seven and fifteen. In the early 1990s approximately 2.4 million students were enrolled annually in primary schools and 657,000 in secondary schools. About 61,600 were enrolled in institutions of higher education, including a number of teachers' colleges and several agricultural and technical schools. From 1995 to 2001, some 80 percent of eligible children attended primary school.

LANGUAGES: English is the official language. The most prevalent Bantu languages are Shona and Sindebele (the language of the Ndebele, sometimes called Ndebele).

ETHNIC GROUPS: The bulk of Zimbabwe's population is formed by two major Bantu-speaking ethnic groups: the Shona, who constitute 80 percent of the total population, and the Ndbele (Matabele), who constitute about 19 percent of the total and are concentrated in the southwestern regions. The country also has small minorities of Europeans, Asians, and persons of mixed race.

RELIGIONS: Half of the population practices various syncretic religions, fusions of traditional African religions and Christianity. Approximately 25 percent are Christian, principally Roman Catholic or Anglican Communion; this number also includes many Protestant sects. About 24 percent practice traditional religions, and about 1 percent are Hindu or Muslim.

CLIMATE: Although Zimbabwe lies in a tropical zone, its climate is moderated by high elevation. The average temperature is 16° C (60° F) in July, and 21° C (70° F) in January. Average rainfall is about 890 mm (35 in) in the High Veld and less than 610 mm (24 in) in most parts of the Middle Veld. The rainy season is from November to March.

LAND, PLANTS, AND ANIMALS: Zimbabwe occupies part of the great plateau of southern Africa. Its most prominent feature is a broad ridge that runs southwest to northeast across the country at elevations of 1,200 to 1,500 m (4,000 to 5,000 ft), the High Veld. On either side of the ridge the land slopes downward, in the north to the Zambezi River and in the south to the Limpopo River. These areas are known as the Middle Veld. Along the eastern border is a mountain range. The land of Zimbabwe is primarily covered with savanna; a particularly lush grass grows during the moist summers. Animals include elephants, hippopotamuses, lions, hyenas, crocodiles, antelope, impalas, giraffes, and baboons.

NATURAL RESOURCES: Mineral resources include coal, chromium ore, asbestos, gold, nickel, copper, iron ore, vanadium, lithium, tin, and platinum group metals.

CURRENCY: The Zimbabwe dollar

GROSS DOMESTIC PRODUCT (GDP): −$26.7 billion (2002 estimate)

GDP PER CAPITA: −$2,100 (2002 estimate)

GDP REAL GROWTH RATE: −13 percent (2002 estimate)

PRIMARY ECONOMIC ACTIVITIES: Until 2000 Zimbabwe's economy depended primarily on agriculture, which employed 70 percent of the labor force and accounted for 40 percent of exports. Mining employed 5 percent of the labor force. A land reform policy implemented in 2000, however, has severely damaged the economy, leading to agricultural shortages, 228 percent inflation in early 2003, and the loss of some 400,000 jobs.

PRIMARY CROPS: Tobacco, corn, cotton, wheat, coffee, sugar cane, and peanuts; cattle, sheep, goats, and pigs

INDUSTRIES: Mining, steel, clothing and footwear, chemicals, food processing, fertilizer, beverage, transportation equipment, and wood products

PRIMARY EXPORTS: Agricultural products (especially tobacco), nickel metal, cotton, manufactures, gold, ferrochrome, and textiles

PRIMARY IMPORTS: Machinery and transportation equipment, other manufactures, chemicals, and fuels

PRIMARY TRADE PARTNERS: South Africa, Democratic Republic of the Congo, European Union (especially United Kingdom, Germany, and Netherlands), China, Japan, Mozambique, and United States

GOVERNMENT: Zimbabwe won independence from the United Kingdom on April 18, 1980. It is a parliamentary democracy. The executive branch has since 1987 been led by President Robert Gabriel Mugabe, whose reelection in 2002 was widely viewed as rigged. He appoints a cabinet, which is in turn responsible to the legislative branch, the 150-member House of Assembly. Of these members, 120 are directly elected by popular vote to serve six-year terms; twelve are chosen by the president; ten are traditional chiefs chosen by their colleagues; and eight are chosen by provincial governors. The dominant political party, that of President Mugabe, is called the Zimbabwe African National Union–Patriotic Front (ZANU–PF).

Lisa Clayton Robinson

Voting during a village meeting. *Gideon Mendel/CORBIS*

come the nationalist soldiers as "sons of the soil" coming to reclaim the land for the people and their ancestors.

Initially peaceful, African nationalism became progressively militant as the Rhodesian government continued to force Africans onto Tribal Trust Lands. After the dissolution of the short-lived National Democratic Party, JOSHUA NKOMO formed the Zimbabwe African People's Union (ZAPU) in 1961. Two years later several leading Shona members of ZAPU broke away, charging that the party was Ndebele-dominated, to form the Zimbabwe African National Union, or ZANU, under the leadership of Ndabaningi Sithole.

In 1964 ZANU and ZAPU began attacking white farms. Lacking popular support and military training, both parties soon recognized that they were no match for the Rhodesian military, and quickly adopted new strategies. ZANU began recruiting militants and politicizing the rural population, using force when necessary. ZAPU, by contrast, concentrated on building a large conventional force in camps in neighboring Zambia and AN-GOLA. It was not until late 1972 that ZANU began launching concerted attacks. The war progressed slowly, as the divided nationalists sought to build popular support for their cause. The Rhodesian military, meanwhile, forced Africans into guarded villages, imposing a *cordon sanitaire* in the north to prevent the insurgents from crossing the border, and increasing white and African conscription into the Rhodesian Security Forces. The Rhodesian government further fragmented the nationalist movements by negotiating with moderate opposition groups. Its position was bolstered by the state-controlled economy, centered on light manufacturing and agriculture, which fared remarkably well despite international sanctions.

The turning point came in 1975 with the independence of Mozambique. This galvanized the opposition groups and provided them with unhindered access to all of eastern Zimbabwe. The Rhodesian government's attempt to negotiate a peaceful compromise, providing for a political system with limited African rights, also failed. In 1977 ZANU and ZAPU reinvigo-

rated their war effort. The number of ZANU insurgents operating in Zimbabwe jumped from approximately 3,000 in 1977 to 10,000 in 1978, and the party, under the new leadership of ROBERT MUGABE, claimed to have liberated one-third of the country. Although both ZANU and ZAPU advocated SOCIALISM as well as national liberation, the former drew support from the Chinese and the latter from the Soviet bloc. ZAPU mounted sustained attacks with large regiments deploying heavy weapons from Eastern bloc countries, while ZANU pursued a classic hit-and-run guerrilla war.

The Rhodesian government responded to the growing strength of the independence forces by creating the pseudo-insurgent group MOZAMBICAN NATIONAL RESISTANCE (RENAMO) as well as the paramilitary Special Auxiliary Forces. But even as these groups pursued insurgents into neighboring states, the Rhodesian military grew weaker and more fragmented, and lost popular support. The Internal Settlement, in which the Rhodesian government convinced three prominent conservative opposition leaders to accept a transition government and limited constitutional reforms in 1978, failed to gain legitimacy among either African Zimbabweans or the international community. ZANU and ZAPU, now briefly joined as the Patriotic Front, boycotted the Internal Settlement and revived the war. By late 1979, at the cost of approximately 25,000 civilian lives—most of them black—the Rhodesian government agreed to negotiations with the Patriotic Front under British auspices.

Independence Politics

On April 18, 1980, Zimbabwe became independent. In elections just prior to independence, Mugabe and ZANU captured fifty-seven of the eighty African seats in parliament, with ZAPU winning twenty seats. Mugabe became prime minister and, in a gesture of reconciliation, made Joshua Nkomo minister of home affairs. At independence, Mugabe asked the country's whites to stay and contribute their wealth and skills to the construction of a prosperous Zimbabwe. Although the transition to independence was peaceful, it did not resolve many of the grievances that had originally sparked the war to overthrow white minority rule. In particular, the inequitable distribution of land remained a source of tension.

Mugabe initially upheld many of the unpopular policies and practices of the Smith regime. His government jailed political opponents, censored the press, and gave extensive powers to the security forces. He also fired Joshua Nkomo after large caches of arms were found on ZAPU-owned farms. This action confirmed what many believed to be the mistreatment of ZAPU soldiers in the Zimbabwean army and the party during the elections, leading ZAPU soldiers and party members to take up arms. In 1982 these dissidents initiated a series of terrorist and criminal attacks in Matabeleland, although their exact goal was unclear and ZAPU officially distanced itself from the dissidents' activities. After six years of a low-intensity war in Matabeleland that resulted in at least 2,000 civilian deaths, ZANU and ZANU agreed to unite under the name ZANU–Patriotic Front, or ZANU–PF. The Zimbabwe National Army (ZNA) also became heavily involved in the war in Mozambique, chiefly to protect the oil pipeline and transportation routes through Mozambique from RENAMO insurgents. As the war drained the Zimbabwean economy and became increasingly unpopular at home, the Zimbabwean government sponsored peace negotiations in the early 1990s, putting pressure on both Mozambique and RENAMO to end the war.

Since independence the Zimbabwean state has progressively become a centralized, de facto one-party regime, as President Mugabe has used patronage and parliamentary legislation to consolidate his own power. He has faced few serious challenges from the fragmented opposition. These are split between various personalities and interests, with parties such as the mainly white and agriculture-based Conservative Alliance of Zimbabwe, the upstart Zimbabwe Unity Movement, and the historic United African National Congress all vying for popular support and represented by discontented politicians.

Mugabe's authoritarianism has been spared domestic and international criticism largely because of his popular appeal, especially in the rural areas, and the prosperous economy. Mugabe has built upon his cult of personality, using visits to communal lands (the previous Tribal Trust Lands) as media events to lash out at white farm owners and triumph government development projects. As a symbolic gesture to promised land reform, in 1982 the government passed a law permitting women to own their own land. But most women in communal land are either not aware of the law or cannot afford to act upon it, and thus most land has remained in the hands of men. The government purchased additional lands, resettling approximately 70,000 families over the years. Despite the underutilization of much of the land, by the late 1980s Zimbabwe had become self-sufficient in grain supplies, and many Zimbabweans saw real improvements in their standard of living. Conditions remained most difficult in the communal lands, which were often arid and barren, especially in the southern regions.

In the early 1990s, widespread drought, combined with economic STRUCTURAL ADJUSTMENT austerity measures, subjected many Zimbabweans to severe hardships. The government's structural adjustment program aimed to reduce government spending, particularly on defense, and to relax controls on prices, imports, and investments. It also led to the privatization of many state-run industries. Zimbabwe's national economy has long been diversified by African standards, being evenly divided between agriculture (tobacco, maize, and cotton), mining (gold, nickel, and asbestos), manufacturing (food-processing and metals), and services. In the late 1990s the government sought to further diversify the agricultural export sector, especially into horticultural products, and build its wildlife tourism industry. It was one of the few African countries where elephants are abundant and it received official clearance to export ivory.

Meanwhile, in 1997 Mugabe announced that he would appropriate more than 4.8 million hectares (more than 12 million acres) of white-owned land and turn it over to landless blacks without compensation, despite the fact that these are the most prosperous farms and employ large numbers of people. Although Mugabe agreed to seek compensation for these landowners from international donors, this did not occur. Indeed, the government tacitly encouraged landless blacks to occupy white farms, and turned a blind eye when violence sometimes ensued. By 2002 twelve white farmers and dozens of black farmers had been killed. That year, Mugabe ordered all remaining white farmers to surrender their property to the government or face jail terms. This order also refused farmers any financial compensation and ordered them instead to make retrenchment payments to their former workers. Although this land reform policy did settle some landless blacks on agricultural land, many had no farming skills and received no training in growing crops. The country faced famine, as well as shortages of other basic commodities. Almost all of the 300,000 blacks who had worked on commercial farms remained jobless, and Mugabe's critics accused him of reserving most of the workable farmland for his family, friends, and close supporters. Foreign investment in Zimbabwe virtually ceased.

Amid growing social unrest, in 1998 Zimbabwe undertook a controversial military intervention to defend the government of the Democratic Republic of the Congo against an armed rebellion. By 2002, when hostilities ended, the war had drained hundreds of millions of dollars from Zimbabwe's already weakened economy. Mugabe, widely denounced in the West, attracted increasing condemnation during the 2002 election, when he jailed opponents and rigged voting to maintain his hold on the presidency. Largely because of the election controversy, the Commonwealth of Nations (a group of fifty-four nations, most of them former British colonies) voted in 2003 to suspend Zimbabwe's membership. In response, Mugabe angrily withdrew from the organization, further isolating himself from potential allies (South Africa, NAMIBIA, Zambia, and Mozambique supported Mugabe at the Commonwealth summit meeting but KENYA and GHANA, in addition to several non-African states, opposed him). By the end of 2003 Zimbabwe's inflation rate had exceeded 500 percent and its unemployment rate exceeded 70 percent. Whether international pressure will succeed in forcing Mugabe to yield power remains uncertain. Meanwhile, once-prosperous Zimbabwe faces continued economic devastation.

See also Decolonization in Africa: An Interpretation; Nationalism in Africa; Structural Adjustment in Africa.

Bibliography

Cheater, A. P. *Idioms of Accumulation: Rural Development and Class Formation among Freeholders in Zimbabwe.* Mambo Press, 1984.

Herbst, Jeffrey. *State Politics in Zimbabwe.* University of California Press, 1990.

Martin, David, and Phyllis Johnson. *The Struggle for Zimbabwe.* Monthly Review Press, 1981.

Eric Young

Zinder, Niger

Second largest city of Niger, was the capital of the precolonial sultanate of Damagaram.

Located 908 kilometers (567 miles) east of NIAMEY, Zinder was once a major center for the lucrative trans-Saharan trade. Overshadowed today by Niamey, Zinder remains an important commercial center, with an estimated population of 209,000.

Zinder was founded in the early sixteenth century. In the early nineteenth century, Suleyman, a KANURI chief, founded the sultanate of Damagaram and made Zinder its capital. Though nominally a vassal of Bornu, he took advantage of the disruptive Bornu-Sokoto wars to expand Damagaram, and he established an alliance with TUAREG peoples, who controlled the important trans-Saharan trade routes to the north. Zinder's trade thrived under the protection of the strong Damagaram army and the Tuareg. In order to consolidate their power, Damagaram traded slaves for firearms. Zinder achieved its greatest prominence during the 1880s, when Damagaram renounced its allegiance to Bornu and challenged the Sokoto empire.

FRANCE claimed Zinder in 1899, and after French campaigns to subdue the Tuareg disrupted the trans-Saharan trade during the 1910s, Zinder's economy began to decline. Although the French made Zinder the capital of the NIGER colony in 1911, they moved the capital to Niamey in 1926. Today Zinder has regained economic vitality as a center for the region that produces Niger's important peanut and cotton crops.

Elizabeth Heath

Zinza

Ethnic group of Tanzania.

The Zinza primarily inhabit northwestern TANZANIA, on the southwestern shores of LAKE VICTORIA. They speak a Bantu language. Approximately 200,000 people consider themselves Zinza.

See also Bantu: Dispersion and Settlement; Ethnicity and Identity in Africa: An Interpretation; Languages, African: An Overview.

Zobel, Joseph

1915–

Martinican writer and critic who portrays the life of the black underclass of Martinique, from whose ranks he comes.

Born in Petit-Bourg, MARTINIQUE, Zobel attended school in FORT-DE-FRANCE. Afterward, he moved to the poverty-stricken southern part of the island. The result of Zobel's time among the peasants of Le Diamant is his first published novel, *Diab'la* (Paris: 1946), a work that underscored the need for land reform by suggesting, not without some temerity, that those who work the land should own it. Although completed in 1942, it was censured by the Vichy government, which occupied Martinique during World War II. A collection of Zobel's stories published just after the war, *Laghia de la mort* (1946), exemplified what could be called Martinican social realism, exposing the brutal existence of plantation workers. In 1946 Zobel moved with his family to France, where he taught school while pursuing studies in literature, drama, and ethnology.

His best-known work, the semiautobiographical coming-of-age story *La Rue cases-nègres* (1950; winner of the Prix des Lecteurs), recounts a young man's transition from the village to the city, from the peasantry to the intellectual class. Zobel's innovative use of Creole dialogue in this novel helped spark the CRÉOLITÉ literary movement that includes PATRICK CHAMOISEAU and RAPHAËL CONFIANT. Like many writers of his generation, Zobel flirted with a return to Africa.

In 1957, he left France for DAKAR, SENEGAL, and in 1962—in a newly independent Senegal under President LÉOPOLD SÉDAR SENGHOR—served as cultural adviser to the nascent Radio Senegal and helped establish and run the Sengalese Cultural Services. Many of the stories in his collection *Et si la mer n'était pas blue* draw from his experiences during this period. Disenchanted with Senghor's NÉGRITUDE-inspired ethnic nationalism, Zobel returned to France, settling in the south, and published a collection of short stories, *Le Soleil partagé* (1964), which promote a model of racial reconciliation based on the values of the peasant class. With the advent of magical realism in the Caribbean, Zobel's brand of Balzacian social commentary fell decidedly out of fashion. The success of the film version of *La Rue cases-nègres* (1983), directed by Euzhan Palcy, has led, however, to a positive reappraisal of his work in recent years. His other novels include *Les Jours immobiles* and *Les Mains pleines d'oiseaux*. He also published a collection of poems, *Poèmes de moi-même*, and *D'Amour et de silence*, a collection of journal entries, poems, and drawings. Zobel, who is also a sculptor and master of Japanese floral design, was awarded the Grand Prix du Livre Insulaire in 2002.

Richard Watts

Zouk

Contemporary popular music of the French- and Creole-speaking Caribbean.

Like American RAP music and Jamaican REGGAE, zouk is the music of the descendants of African slaves in societies previously dominated by whites. The comparison between the genres, though, ends there. Sung in Creole and carried by an up-tempo dance rhythm, zouk is neither didactic nor explicitly political; it is in no way protest music. Rather, as its name implies ("zouk" is a Creole word first employed in MARTINIQUE that means "a party" or "to party"), zouk is a Carnivalesque music that celebrates Caribbean Creole culture, principally by drawing its lyrical themes from Creole folklore. Thanks to the sense of cultural pride (and, it should be noted, the urge to dance) that zouk fosters in its Creole-speaking audience, this festive music has become the most popular genre in the French overseas departments of Martinique and GUADELOUPE as well as in the neighboring islands of DOMINICA, SAINT LUCIA, and HAITI. But zouk's popularity is not confined to the Caribbean sphere. In recent years, zouk performers such as Kassav, Zouk Machine (led by three female vocalists), and Malavoi have developed substantial followings in EUROPE—and, in particular, in FRANCE—as well as in AFRICA.

Although zouk musicians generally steer clear of questions of racial and ethnic origins in their lyrics, they do evoke their African roots in the music. Zouk's rhythm, produced by traditional drums and, more recently, drum machines, has its source in the rhythm of the traditional West African drum or *tam-tam*. This influence can also be felt in zouk's musical predecessors: *gwo ka* (Creole for "large drum"), a traditional Guadeloupean drum music, and BIGUINE, the Martinican music of the 1940s and 1950s that is zouk's clearest musical forebear, both of which integrate elements of African drumming. Kassav, the most successful and influential of zouk bands, used the gwo ka in its earliest recordings, and the traditional rhythms of gwo ka can still be detected in most zouk songs.

But zouk's success can also be attributed to its integration of many contemporary musical styles, including JAZZ, FUNK, SALSA, CALYPSO, cadence-lypso (from Dominica), and compas direct (from Haiti). If there is a controversy surrounding zouk, it centers on this very point. Zouk's detractors maintain that the music has drifted too far from its roots and is no longer representative of Creole culture. This multiplicity of influences is seen by its fans as zouk's strongest point and, paradoxically, that which makes the music distinctly Caribbean. Zouk, like Caribbean culture, is nothing if not the creolization or mixture of American, European, and African cultural practices.

See also Creolization: An Interpretation; Creolized Musical Instruments of the Caribbean; Music, Afro-Caribbean Secular; Salsa Music.

Richard Watts

Zulu

Largest ethnic group in South Africa, numbering approximately eleven million people.

The Zulu are one of many southern African peoples belonging to the broader NGUNI linguistic group. Like other Nguni groups such as the XHOSA, the Zulu speak a Bantu language, and their ancestors are believed to have migrated into southern Africa sometime after the second century C.E. They settled in village communities, cultivated grains such as MILLET, and kept cattle, which became an important symbol of wealth. Also like other Nguni groups, the Zulu developed a distinct language well before they forged a collective identity or a centralized political structure. These did not emerge until the late eighteenth century, when competition for grazing lands and access to sources of ivory, an important trade commodity, fostered conflict among Nguni clans.

At that time only members of one Nguni clan identified themselves as Zulu, which was the name of one of the clan's founding ancestors. But not long after SHAKA became the clan chief in 1815, the Zulu began a campaign of conquest and expansion known as the MFECANE, which led to the incorporation of many other peoples. A brilliant military leader, Shaka soon built an army of more than 40,000 rigorously trained soldiers. Shaka also introduced several important military innovations, such as the short stabbing spear, which gave Zulu troops a distinct advantage over their adversaries. In a period of only ten years, Shaka had built a kingdom—Zululand—that encompassed most of the area now known as Natal Province.

Shaka claimed absolute authority over his kingdom. His hierarchical leadership style was retained by subsequent Zulu rulers and later adopted by Inkatha, a twentieth-century Zulu political organization. In conquered territories, Shaka appointed his own officials; any subjects who refused Shaka's overrule could be killed immediately. In addition, conquered peoples were expected to serve in the Zulu army, herd the king's cattle, and hunt elephants for ivory. Shaka consolidated his authority by conducting frequent cattle raids on neighboring groups, such as the MPONDO. A portion of the cattle was distributed to Shaka's chiefs and army officers to encourage their loyalty.

Despite these tactics, however, Shaka faced internal opposition, and in 1828 he was assassinated by his half-brother DINGANE. But Dingane lacked Shaka's military acumen and fared poorly in battles against the expansionist AFRIKANERS (also known as Boers). Although the Zulu lost land to the Afrikaners during the mid-nineteenth century, they did not fall under

European COLONIAL RULE until 1883, when Zululand was invaded by British troops.

As part of Great Britain's Natal Colony, Zululand was divided into thirteen chiefdoms, and the Zulu king Dinuzulu was exiled. Missionaries encouraged the Zulu to forsake practices of ancestor worship in favor of CHRISTIANITY. Zulu farmers initially profited from strong markets for maize in DURBAN and other rapidly growing cities, but government policies eventually alienated most Zulu farmland. Zulu men were consequently forced to migrate in search of wage labor, typically either in the gold mines or on SUGAR plantations. After the NATIONAL PARTY came to power in SOUTH AFRICA in 1948, its system of APARTHEID assigned all the country's Africans to one of ten ethnic homelands (also known as bantustans). The Zulu homeland was called KwaZulu and ruled by nominally independent "tribal" authorities.

In 1976 MANGOSUTHO GATSHA BUTHELEZI became the chief minister of KwaZulu. He began encouraging Zulu nationalism through the revived Inkatha Ya Ka Zulu, a Zulu cultural organization founded in 1928. A descendant of the nineteenth-century Zulu king Cetshwayo, Buthelezi spoke out against apartheid, but his ethnic separatism and willingness to collaborate with the white-ruled South African government soon put him—and Inkatha's Zulu membership—at odds with anti-apartheid groups such as the AFRICAN NATIONAL CONGRESS (ANC). During the 1980s and early 1990s, the rivalry between the two groups often turned violent. (In 1998 South Africa's TRUTH AND RECONCILIATION COMMISSION issued a report concluding that much of this violence had been directed and organized by the white minority government in an effort to suppress the ANTIAPARTHEID MOVEMENT.)

After Inkatha became an official political party in 1990 (the INKATHA FREEDOM PARTY, or IFP) it joined with far-right Afrikaner organizations to oppose democratic negotiations led by the ANC and the National Party, and Buthelezi pressed for a separate Zulu state. After the election of NELSON MANDELA as president of postapartheid South Africa in 1994, the IFP pulled out of the South African Constitutional Assembly to protest the ANC government. Relations between the two parties remain contentious. In the former Zulu homeland, however, organizations such as the KWAZULU-NATAL Arts and Culture Council are encouraging "nonpartisan" forms of Zulu nationalism.

See also Bantu: Dispersion and Settlement; Christianity: Missionaries in Africa; Ethnicity and Identity in Africa: An Interpretation; Languages, African: An Overview; Nationalism in Africa.

Bibliography

Golan, Daphna. *Inventing Shaka: Using History in the Construction of Zulu Nationalism.* Rienner Publishers, 1994.

Taylor, Stephen. *Shaka's Children: A History of the Zulu People.* Harper Collins, 1994.

Elizabeth Heath

Zumbi

1655?–1695

Legendary leader of Palmares, the seventeenth-century community of runaway slaves in northeastern Brazil.

Zumbi, the most vehement opponent of slavery in colonial BRAZIL, is closely linked with the settlement of Palmares, established by escaped slaves in Brazil's northeastern state of Alagoas. Escaped slaves first settled in this mountainous, forested region sometime between the end of the sixteenth century and the early years of seventeenth century. Because of the abundance of palms, the settlement became known as Palmares. During the Dutch occupation of northeastern Brazil (1630–1654), Palmares received a large number of fugitive slaves and grew into a formidable, populous federation of villages covering a vast area of land from northern Alagoas to southern Pernambuco. Palmares' sophisticated fortifications and well-equipped defense force enabled it to resist repeated military incursions following the expulsion of the Dutch until it was finally conquered in 1694. The story of Zumbi is closely tied to Palmares, the largest and longest lasting quilombo in the history of the colonial Americas.

What little is known about Zumbi's early life is based on the personal records of a seventeenth-century priest named Antônio Melo, which have not been reliably documented. According to these sources, Zumbi was born in Palmares in 1655 and was captured that same year during a Portuguese attack on the quilombo. Zumbi was later placed under the care of Antônio Melo, who baptized him Francisco and taught him Latin, Portuguese, and other subjects. Research on Melo's written records indicate that in 1670, Zumbi ran away to Palmares.

Zumbi then began to appear in firsthand accounts of military missions sent by the Portuguese to destroy Palmares. Reports from a 1675–1676 campaign relate that Zumbi suffered a leg wound and describe him as "a black man of singular bravery, great spirit, and rare constancy." At this time, Zumbi served as the war commander under Ganga Zumba, Zumbi's uncle and the leader of Palmares during the second half of the seventeenth century.

After being wounded in a 1677 attack, Ganga Zumba agreed to a peace treaty with the governor of Pernambuco the following year and, under its terms, relocated part of Palmares to the Cucaú Valley. According to official state documents, at this time Zumbi was part of the rebel faction that opposed the concession to colonial authorities. In 1680 he allegedly poisoned Ganga Zumba and became the new king of Palmares. Zumbi successfully spearheaded the defense of Palmares through 1694, when military units from São Paulo and the Northeast vanquished the quilombo following a series of campaigns that lasted some two years.

Zumbi and a small band of his followers escaped during the final, twenty-two-day battle. He avoided captured for over a year until a member of his group disclosed his whereabouts to colonial forces, which ambushed and killed him on November 20, 1695. Following his death, colonial authorities publicly displayed his head in Pernambuco's capital, Recife. An alternate version of his death recounts that he and some 200 other residents of Palmares jumped off a cliff during the final battle rather than be reenslaved.

Until recently, the memory of Zumbi survived only in the oral histories of Afro-Brazilians. There are records of Zumbi being publicly celebrated by Bahian *afoxés* around the turn of the twentieth century and in an Afro-Brazilian festival in Alagoas in the 1930s. But during the 1970s this black hero began to gain much more recognition. Civil rights activism in the United States prompted a surge of black consciousness throughout Brazil and renewed interest in Afro-Brazilian history. In 1978, the Movimento Negro Unificado (Unified Black Movement) declared November 20 National Black Consciousness Day. On May 13, 1988, the centenary of the abolition of slavery in Brazil, Afro-Brazilians invoked Zumbi during their protests of enduring discrimination and inequalities. In 1995 there were widespread observances of the tercentenary of Zumbi's death, including the first continental congress of blacks in São Paulo (Congreso Continental dos Povos Negros das Américas) and a march in the capital Brasília led by the Movimento Negro Unificado.

Such actions have helped make Zumbi a national hero, and Palmares, a registered historical landmark. To many black Brazilians, Zumbi symbolizes the ongoing Afro-Brazilian struggle for economic and political equality. In the words of Joel Rufino, president of the Palmares Foundation, a commission that organizes the annual celebration of Zumbi, "For us blacks, the example of Zumbi inspires our fight for justice and the right to be full-fledged citizens without fear and shame of our blackness."

See also Afoxés/Blocos Afros; Black Consciousness in Brazil; Colonial Latin America and the Caribbean; Maroonage in the Americas; Palmares: An African State in Brazil.

Aaron Myers

Zydeco

Music of black Creoles in southwest Louisiana whose principal instruments are the accordion and the washboard.

Zydeco music, like the Louisiana cuisine gumbo, is an amalgamation of several cultural influences. It is rooted most strongly in French and African musical traditions, but Native American, German, and Spanish cultures have also informed its development. The history of settlement in Louisiana reveals how these various groups of people came together to forge the hybrid culture that spawned zydeco music.

Around 1700, several thousand Acadians who had been exiled from Nova Scotia by the British formed a French-speaking colony in Louisiana. They became known as Cajuns, a colloquialism for Acadians, and worked primarily as tenant farmers. Very few owned slaves, and they had a mutually influential relationship with the people of African descent, known as Creoles, who had been brought to Louisiana from other North American colonies or from the French- and Spanish-speaking Caribbean. These two ethnic groups, in turn, interacted with Native Americans and European immigrants. The sociocultural exchanges between these different ethnic groups during the late nineteenth century resulted in the emergence of two musical forms in the early twentieth century: zydeco and Cajun.

Zydeco and Cajun are closely related yet distinct musical forms. They have a similar instrumentation, including at least one fiddle, a guitar, and a button accordion backed by a bass and drums. Both zydeco and Cajun are played in such contexts as nightclubs, picnics, and house parties, where people often dance as couples. Historian Barry Jean Ancelet explains that although both zydeco and Cajun are bluesy, improvisational dance music that speak of lost love and hard times, Cajun music is smoother and emphasizes melody while Zydeco tends to be faster and more syncopated. Part of this rhythmic difference stems from the use in zydeco music ensembles of a corrugated sheet of metal worn over the shoulders like a vest that, when played with eating utensils, makes a raspy sound. In addition, even though zydeco and Cajun musicians sing in both French Creole and English, there seems to be a greater prevalence of English lyrics in zydeco music.

The first commercial recordings of zydeco and Cajun music were made during the late 1920s and early 1930s. In 1928 accordion player Joseph Falcon accompanied his wife Cleoma, who sang lead vocals and played the guitar, on the earliest Cajun music recording. The first black Creole to make a record was accordion player Amédé Ardoin, who, after performing with Cajun fiddler Dennis McGee on a 1929 record, recorded his own songs in the early 1930s. In the late 1930s, folklorists John and Alan Lomax made numerous recordings of early zydeco music for the Library of Congress, including the famed "Les haricots sont pas salés." The term *zydeco* is in fact a creolized pronunciation of the first two words of this song's title, which literally translates to "the snap beans ain't salty," but is used colloquially to convey the idea that "times are hard."

Many historians agree that Creoles were first to pick up and master the button accordion, which became a staple of zydeco music. The accordion player widely recognized as the king of zydeco, Clifton Chenier, continued the legacy of Amédé Ardoin. Chenier emerged as a musician in the 1950s and pioneered the use of the piano accordion and brass horns, which replaced the fiddle, in zydeco music. His compositions were influenced by the sounds of Rhythm and Blues, soul, and Blues music popular during the post–World War II period. Some of his better-known songs are "Black Gal" (1965), "Jambalaya" (1975), and "Country Boy Now" (1984) from his Grammy Award–winning album *I'm Here!* Two other major zydeco artists are accordionist Boozoo Chavis and singer Queen Ida.

Though the bayou region of Louisiana continues to be the cradle of zydeco music, it is played along the Gulf Coast from Louisiana to Texas and is gaining national and international recognition.

See also Music, African American; Soul Music.

Bibliography

Gould, Philip. *Cajun Music and Zydeco*. Louisiana State University Press, 1992.

Lichtenstein, Grace. *Musical Gumbo*. W. W. Norton, 1993.

Aaron Myers

Contributors

ROSANNE ADDERLEY, *Tulane University*
MARIAN AGUIAR, *Amherst, Massachusetts*
EMMANUEL AKYEAMPONG, *Harvard University*
SUZANNE ALBULAK, *Cambridge, Massachusetts*
SAMIR AMIN, *Director of the Forum Tiers Monde, Dakar, Senegal*
GEORGE REID ANDREWS, *University of Pittsburgh*
ABDULLAHI AHMED AN-NA'IM, *Emory University*
RACHEL ANTELL, *San Francisco, California*
KWAME ANTHONY APPIAH, *Princeton University*
JOEL ZITO ARAUJO, *Rio de Janeiro, Brazil*
JORGE ARCE, *Boston Conservatory of Music*
ALBERTO ARENAS, *University of California at Berkeley*
PAUL AUSTERLITZ, *Brown University*
KAREN BACKSTEIN, *City University of New York, College of Staten Island*
ANTHONY BADGER, *University of Cambridge*
LAWRIE BALFOUR, *Babson College*
MARYLSE BAPTISTA, *University of Georgia*
ROBERT BAUM, *Iowa State University*
STEPHEN BEHRENDT, *Harvard University*
AMINA BEKKAT, *Blida, Algeria*
PATRICK BELLEGARDE-SMITH, *University of Wisconsin at Milwaukee*
ERIC BENNETT, *Iowa City, Iowa*
STEPHANIE BESWICK, *Ball State University*
SUZANNE PRESTON BLIER, *Harvard University*
JUAN BOTERO, *Former Executive Director, Instituto de Ciencia Politica, Bogotá, Colombia*
KEITH BOYKIN, *Washington, D.C.*
ESPERANZA BRIZVELA-GARCIA, *London, England*
DIANA DEG. BROWN, *Bard College*
EVA STAHL BROWN, *University of Texas at Austin*
BARBARA BROWNING, *New York University*
ERIC BROSCH, *Cambridge, Massachusetts*
BETH ANN BUGGENHAGEN, *University of Rochester*
JOHN BURDICK, *Syracuse University*
ANDREW BURTON, *London, England*
ALIDA CAGIDEMETRIO, *University of Udine, Italy*
CHLOE CAMPBELL, *London, England*
SOPHIA CANTAVE, *Tufts University*
YVONNE CAPTAIN, *George Washington University*
JUDY CARNEY, *University of California at Los Angeles*
VINCENT CARRETTA, *University of Maryland at College Park*
CLAYBORNE CARSON, *Editor, Martin Luther King, Jr., Papers Project, Stanford University*
ODILE CAZENAVE, *University of Tennessee*
ALISTAIR CHISHOLM, *London, England*
JACE CLAYTON, *Cambridge, Massachusetts*

PATRICIA COLLINS, *University of Cincinnati*
NICOLA COONEY, *Harvard University*
BELINDA COOPER, *New School for Social Research*
BRENDA COOPER, *University of Cape Town*
FREDERICK COOPER, *University of Michigan at Ann Arbor*
JUAN GIUSTI CORDERO, *Universidad de Puerto Rico*
THOMAS CRIPPS, *Morgan State University*
SELWYN R. CUDJOE, *Wellesley College*
CARLOS DALMAU, *San Juan, Puerto Rico*
DARIÉN J. DAVIS, *Middlebury College*
JAMES DAVIS, *Howard University*
MARTHA SWEARINGTON DAVIS, *University of California at Santa Barbara*
A. J. DE VOOGT, *Leiden, The Netherlands*
CRISTOBAL DIAZ-AYALA, *Independent Scholar*
RAFAEL DIAZ-DIAZ, *Pontificia Universidad Javeriana, Bogotá, Colombia*
QUINTON DIXIE, *Indiana University*
ANDREW DU BOIS, *Cambridge, Massachusetts*
CHRISTOPHER DUNN, *Tulane University*
ANANI DZIDZIENYO, *Brown University*
GERALD EARLY, *Washington University in St. Louis*
JONATHAN EDWARDS, *Belmont, Massachusetts*
ROANNE EDWARDS, *Arlington, Massachusetts*
JOY ELIZONDO, *Cambridge, Massachusetts*
DAVID ELTIS, *Emory University*
ROBERT FAY, *Medford, Massachusetts*
MARTINE FERNÁNDEZ, *Berkeley, California*
PAUL FINKELMAN, *University of Tulsa Law School*
VICTOR FIGUEROA, *Harvard University*
GERDES FLEURANT, *University of California at Santa Barbara*
JUAN FLORES, *Hunter College and City College of New York Graduate Center*
PAUL FOSTER, *Chicago, Illinois*
BALTASAR FRA-MOLINERO, *Bates College*
GREGORY FREELAND, *California Lutheran University*
SUSANNE FREIDBERG, *Dartmouth College*
NINA FRIEDEMANN, *Pontificia Universidad Javeriana, Bogotá, Colombia*
HEIDI GLAESEL FRONTANI, *Elon University*
FURUKAWA TETSUSHI, *Kyoto University*
ROB GARRISON, *Boston, Massachusetts*
HENRY LOUIS GATES, JR., *Harvard University*
ERIK GELLMANN, *Northwestern University*
JOHN GENNARI, *University of Virginia*
DANIELLE GEORGES, *New York, New York*
PETER GERHARD, *Independent Scholar*
MARK GEVISSER, *Editor of* Defiant Desire: Gay and Lesbian Lives in South Africa
PATRIC V. GIESLER, *Gustavus Adolphus College*
PETER GLENSHAW, *Belmont, Massachusetts*
MATTHEW GOFF, *Chicago, Illinois*

FLORA GONZÁLEZ, *Emerson College*
MAYDA GRANO DE ORO, *San Juan, Puerto Rico*
SUE GRANT LEWIS, *Harvard University*
RODERICK GRIERSON, *Independent Scholar*
BARBARA GROSH, *New York, New York*
GERARD GRYSKI, *Auburn University*
BETTY GUBERT, *Former Head of Reference, Schomburg Center for Research in Black Culture, New York Public Library*
MICHELLE GUERALDI, *San José, Costa Rica*
STUART HALL, *The Open University, London*
MICHAEL HANCHARD, *Northwestern University*
JULIA HARRINGTON, *Banjul, Gambia*
ELIZABETH HEATH, *San Francisco, California*
ANDREW HERMANN, *Former Literary Associate, Denver Center Theatre Company*
EVELYN BROOKS HIGGINBOTHAM, *Harvard University*
JESSICA HOCHMAN, *New York, New York*
CYNTHIA HOEHLER-FATTON, *University of Virginia*
J. C. HOLBROOK, *University of Arizona*
PETER HUDSON, *Toronto, Canada*
MICHELLE HUNTER, *Cambridge, Massachusetts*
ABIOLA IRELE, *Harvard University*
DAVID P. JOHNSON, JR., *Boston, Massachusetts*
BILL JOHNSON-GONZÁLEZ, *Cambridge, Massachusetts*
ANDRÉ JUSTE, *New York, New York*
CHUCK KAPELKE, *Boston, Massachusetts*
KETU KATRAK, *University of California at Irvine*
RAY A. KEA, *University of California at Riverside*
ROBIN KELLEY, *New York University*
R. K. KENT, *University of California at Berkeley*
LEYLA KEOUGH, *Cambridge, Massachusetts*
MUHONJIA KHAMINWA, *Boston, Massachusetts*
DAVID KIM, *Cambridge, Massachusetts*
MARTHA KING, *New York, New York*
FRANKLIN W. KNIGHT, *Johns Hopkins University*
PETER KOLCHIN, *University of Delaware*
CORINNE KRATZ, *Emory University*
KENT M. KRAUSE, *Lincoln, Nebraska*
MODUPE LABODE, *Iowa State University*
PETER LAU, *New Brunswick, New Jersey*
CLAUDIA LEAL, *Bogotá, Colombia*
ANTHONY A. LEE, *West Los Angeles College*
RENÉ LEMARCHAND, *University of Florida*
W. T. LHAMON, JR., *Florida State University*
MARGIT LIANDER, *Belmont, Massachusetts*
DAVID LEVERING LEWIS, *Rutgers University*
MARVÍN LEWIS, *University of Missouri at Columbia*
LORRAINE ANASTASIA LEZAMA, *Boston, Massachusetts*
LEIF LORENTZON, *Stockholm University*
KEVIN MACDONALD, *University of London*
MARCOS CHOR MAIO, *Rio de Janeiro, Brazil*

MAHMOOD MAMDANI, *University of Cape Town*
LAWRENCE MAMIYA, *Vassar College*
PATRICK MANNING, *Northeastern University*
PETER MANUEL, *John Jay College of Criminal Justice*
DELLITA MARTIN-OGUNSOLA, *University of Alabama at Birmingham*
WALDO MARTIN, *University of California at Berkeley*
J. LORAND MATORY, *Harvard University*
FELIX V. MATOS RODRIGUEZ, *Northeastern University*
MARC MAZIQUE, *Seattle, Washington*
JOSÉ MAZZOTTI, *Harvard University*
ELIZABETH MCHENRY, *New York University*
JIM MENDELSOHN, *New York, New York*
GABRIEL MENDES, *Annandale, New York*
CLAUDINE MICHEL, *Wellesley College*
GEORGES MICHEL, *Military Academy of Haiti, Port-au-Prince, Haiti*
GWENDOLYN MIKELL, *Georgetown University*
ZEBULON MILETSKY, *Boston, Massachusetts*
IRENE MONROE, *Harvard Divinity School*
SALLY FALK MOORE, *Harvard University*
JUDITH MORRISON, *Inter-American Foundation at Arlington, Virginia*
GERARDO MOSQUERA, *Independent Scholar*
LUIS MOTT, *Federal University of Bahia, Brazil*
LUPENGA MPHANDE, *Ohio State University*
SALIKOKO S. MUFWENE, *University of Chicago*
EDWARD MULLEN, *University of Missouri at Columbia*
KURT MULLEN, *Seattle, Washington*
STUART MUNRO-HAY, *Independent Scholar*
AARON MYERS, *Cambridge, Massachusetts*
ABDIAS DO NASCIMENTO, *Former Senator, Brazilian National Congress, Brasilia*
ARI NAVE, *New York, New York*
MARCOS NATALÍ, *University of Chicago*
OKEY NDIBE, *Connecticut College*
NICK NESBITT, *Miami University (Ohio)*
RICHARD NEWMAN, *Harvard University*
JENNIFER M. NEWSOM, *Yale University*
M. TRACEY OBER, *Brooklyn, New York*
LILIANA OBREGÓN, *Harvard Law School*
KATHLEEN O'CONNOR, *Cambridge, Massachusetts*
EDDIE ENYEOBI OKAFOR, *University of Nigeria*
TEJUMOLA OLANIYAN, *University of Virginia*
MARK O'MALLEY, *Cambridge, Massachusetts*
YAA POKUA AFRIYIE OPPONG, *London, England*
CARMEN OQUENDO-VILLAR, *Cambridge, Massachusetts*
KENNETH O'REILLY, *University of Alaska at Anchorage*

CARLOS L. ORIHUELA, *University of Alabama at Birmingham*
FRANCISCO ORTEGA, *Harvard University*
JUAN OTERO-GARABIS, *Universidad de Puerto Rico*
DEBORAH PACINI HERNANDEZ, *Brown University*
CARLOS PARRA, *Harvard University*
BEN PENGLASE, *Cambridge, Massachusetts*
PEDRO PÉREZ-SARDUY, *London, England and Havana, Cuba*
JULIO CESAR PINO, *Kent State University*
DONALD POLLOCK, *State University of New York at Buffalo*
ANGELINA POLLAK-ELTZ, *Universidad Catolice A. Bella*
KAREN A. PORTER, *University of Puget Sound*
PAULETTE POUJOL-ORIOL, *Port-au-Prince, Haiti*
RICHARD J. POWELL, *Duke University*
SAM RADITLHALO, *University of Cape Town*
JEAN MUTEBA RAHIER, *Florida International University*
JOÃO JOSÉ REIS, *Federal University of Bahia, Brazil*
CAROLYN RICHARDSON DURHAM, *Texas Christian University*
ALONFORD JAMES ROBINSON, JR., *Washington, D.C.*
LISA CLAYTON ROBINSON, *Washington, D.C.*
SONIA LABRADOR RODRIGUÉS, *University of Texas at Austin*
MICHELE VALERIE RONNICK, *Wayne State University*
GORDON ROOT, *Cambridge, Massachusetts*
ANINYDO ROY, *Colby College*
SARAH RUSSELL, *Cambridge, England*
MARVETA RYAN, *Indiana University (Pennsylvania)*
ALI OSMAN MOHAMMAD SALIH, *University of Khartoum*
LAMINE SANNEH, *Yale University*
JALANE SCHMIDT, *Cambridge, Massachusetts*
CHARLES SCHMITZ, *Sonoma State University*
BROOKE GRUNDFEST SCHOEPF, *Harvard University*
LAVERNE M. SEALES-SOLEY, *Canisius College*
JAMES CLYDE SELLMAN, *University of Massachusetts at Boston*
ELIZABETH SHOSTAK, *Cambridge, Massachusetts*
THOMAS SKIDMORE, *Brown University*
JAMES SMETHURST, *University of North Florida*
PAULETTE SMITH, *Tufts University*
SUZANNE SMITH, *George Mason University*
KEITH SNEDEGAR, *Utah Valley State College*
BARBARA SOLOW, *Associate of the W. E. B. Du Bois Institute for Afro-American Research, Harvard University*

DORIS SOMMER, *Harvard University*
REBECCA STEFOFF, *Portland, Oregon*
THOMAS STEPHENS, *State University of New Jersey*
PHILLIPS STEVENS, JR., *SUNY at Buffalo*
JEAN STUBBS, *London, England and Havana, Cuba*
PATRICIA SULLIVAN, *Harvard University*
SHELLE SUMNERS, *Hightstown, New Jersey*
CAROL SWAIN, *Princeton University*
PHYLLIS TAOUA, *University of Arizona*
KATHERINE TATE, *University of California at Irvine*
RICHARD TAUB, *University of Chicago*
APRIL TAYLOR, *Boston, Massachusetts*
JOHN THORNTON, *Boston University*
ANTONIO D. TILLIS, *Purdue University*
CHRISTOPHER TINÉ, *Cambridge, Massachusetts*
KONRAD TUCHSCHERER, *St. John's University, New York*
RICHARD TURITS, *Princeton University*
KATE TUTTLE, *Cambridge, Massachusetts*
TIMOTHY TYSON, *University of Wisconsin*
CHARLES VAN DOREN, *Former Vice President/Editorial, Encyclopædia Britannica Inc.*
ALEXANDRA VEGA-MERINO, *Harvard University*
JOËLLE VITIELLO, *Macalester College*
PETER WADE, *University of Manchester*
JAMES W. ST. G. WALKER, *University of Waterloo*
PHILLIPE WAMBA, *Cambridge, Massachusetts*
WILLIAM E. WARD, *Harvard University*
SALIM WASHINGTON, *Boston, Massachusetts*
CHRISTOPHER ALAN WATERMAN, *University of California at Los Angeles*
RICHARD WATTS, *Tulane University*
HAROLD WEAVER, *Independent Scholar*
NORMAN WEINSTEIN, *State University of New York at New Paltz*
AMELIA WEIR, *New York, New York*
TIM WEISKEL, *Harvard University*
ALAN WEST, *Northern Illinois University*
CORNEL WEST, *Princeton University*
NORMAN WHITTEN, *University of Illinois at Urbana*
TED WIDMER, *Washington College*
ANDRE WILLIS, *Cambridge, Massachusetts*
DEBORAH WILLIS, *Center for African American History and Culture, Smithsonian Institution*
WILLIAM JULIUS WILSON, *Harvard University*
BARBARA WORLEY, *Cambridge, Massachusetts*
ERIC YOUNG, *Washington, D.C.*
GARY ZUK, *Auburn University*

Topical Outline of Selected Entries

Abolitionism

Abolitionism in the United States
Abolitionist Novels in Cuba
Afro-Colombians: From Maroons to
    Constitutional Reformers
American Anti-Slavery Society
Americo-Liberians
Amistad Mutiny
Anderson, Osborne Perry
Antiabolitionism
Antislavery Movement in Latin America
Baptist War
Berbice Slave Rebellion
Black Seminoles
Brown, Henry "Box"
Brown, John
Bussa's Rebellion
Christiana Revolt of 1852
Colonial Critics of Slavery
Conspiración de la Escalera
Creole Affair
Cudjoe
Cugoano, Ottobah
Cultural and Political Organizations in Latin
    America
Denmark Vesey Conspiracy
Douglass, Frederick
Free Blacks in the United States
Free Womb Laws
Fugitive Slaves
Gabriel Prosser Conspiracy
Ganga-Zumba
Garrison, William Lloyd
Green, Shields
Grimké, Charlotte
Grimké, Francis
Henson, Josiah
Joseph Knight Case
Liberator, The
Manumission Societies
Muslim Uprisings in Bahia, Brazil
Nanny
Nat Turner's Rebellion
New York Manumission Society
New York Slave Conspiracy of 1741
New York Slave Rebellion of 1712
Palenque de San Basilio
Palmares: An African State in Brazil
Patronato
Quakers
Rethinking Palmares: Slave Resistance in
    Colonial Brazil
Role of Slaves in Abolition and
    Emancipation in Latin America and the
    Caribbean
Runaway Slaves in the United States
Sharp, Granville
Slave Rebellions in Latin America and the
    Caribbean

Slave Rebellions in the United States
Sociedad Abolicionista Española
Sociétédes Amisdes Noirs
Society of Friends of the Blacks
Spanish Abolitionist Society
Stono Rebellion
Suriname and French Guiana, Maroon
    Communities in
Tacky
Toussaint Louverture
Truth, Sojourner
Tubman, Harriet
Turner, Nat
Underground Railroad
White Abolitionists in Brazil
Yanga
Zeferina
Zumbi

Animals

Aardvark
Aardwolf
African Elephant
African Hunting Dog
Antelope
Baboon
Bee-Eater
Boomslang Snake
Camel
Cheetah
Chimpanzee
Cobra
Colobus Monkey
Crocodile, Nile
Duiker
Earth Pig
Eland
Fennec
Flamingo
Galago
Gecko
Giraffe
Gnu
Gorilla
Guinea Fowl
Hartebeest
Hippopotamus
Honeyguide
Hornbill
Hyena
Hyrax
Impala
Kola
Kudu
Lemur
Leopard
Lion
Manatee
Mongoose

Ostrich
Rhinoceros
Secretary Bird
Serval
Tilapia
Tsetse Fly
Viper
Vulture
Warthog
Weaverbird
Zebra
Zebu

Daily Life

African Ethnic Groups in Latin America and
    the Caribbean
Afro-Brazilian Culture
Afro-Latin American and Afro-Caribbean
    Identity
Alcohol in Africa
Black Families in Latin America and the
    Caribbean
Blackness in Latin America and the Caribbean
Bush Negroes
Clothing in Africa
Colonial America, Blacks in
Cultural Politics of Blackness in Latin
    America and the Caribbean
Culture, Black, in Colombia
Favelas
Female Circumcision in Africa
Food in Africa
Food in African American Culture
Gauchos
Homosexuality in Africa
Homosexuality in Latin America and the
    Caribbean
Homosexuality in the United States
Hunting in Africa
Image of the Mulatta in Latin America and
    the Caribbean
Latin America, Blacks and Indians in
Latin America and the Caribbean, Blacks in
Marriage, African Customs of
Passing in the United States
Pastoralism
Race in Latin America
Racial Mixing in Latin America and the
    Caribbean
Rites of Passage and Transition
South America, Blacks and Indians in
South America, Blacks in
Syncretism
Tia Ciata
Transculturation, Mestizaje, and the Cosmic
    Race
Women, Black, in Brazil
Women, Black, in Colonial Hispanic
    Caribbean

Religion

Bibliography

ART

BARNETT, ALAN W. *Community Murals: The People's Art* (1984).

BEARDEN, ROMARE, AND HARRY HENDERSON. *A History of African-American Artists from 1792 to the Present* (1993).

BENBERRY, CUESTA. *Always There: The African-American Presence in American Quilts* (1992).

BIEBUYCK, DANIEL P., SUSAN KELLIHER, AND LINDA MCRAE. *African Ethnonyms: Index to Art-Producing Peoples of Africa* (1996).

BLIER, SUZANNE PRESTON. *African Vodun: Art, Psychology, and Power* (1995).

———. *The Royal Arts of Africa: The Majesty of Form* (1998).

BUSH, MARTIN. *The Photographs of Gordon Parks* (1983).

CASTLEMAN, CRAIG. *Getting Up: Subway Graffiti in New York* (1984).

COURTNEY-CLARKE, MARGARET. *Ndebele: The Art of an African Tribe* (1986).

DONOVAN, NANCY, AND JILL LAST. *Ethiopian Costumes* (1980).

DRAKE, SANDRA E. *Wilson Harris and the Modern Tradition: A New Architecture of the World* (1986).

DRISKELL, DAVID. *Hidden Heritage: Afro-American Art, 1800–1950* (1985).

ELLISON, RALPH. *Romare Bearden: Paintings and Projections* (1968).

———. *Shadow and Act* (1964).

FERRIS, WILLIAM, ED. *Afro-American Folk Arts and Crafts* (1983).

FERRIS, WILLIAM, AND BRENDA MCCALLUM, EDS. *Local Color: A Sense of Place in Folk Art* (1982).

FLOMENHAFT, ELEANOR, ED. *Faith Ringgold: A 25-Year Survey* (1990).

FRY, GLADYS-MARIE. *Stitched from the Soul: Slave Quilts from the Ante-Bellum South* (1990).

GOINGS, KENNETH W. *Mammy and Uncle Mose: Black Collectibles and American Stereotyping* (1994).

GRUDIN, EVA UNGAR. *Stitching Memories: African-American Story Quilts* (1990).

HACKETT, ROSALIND. *Art and Religion in Africa* (1996).

HARRINGTON, OLIVER. *Why I Left America and Other Essays* (1993).

HELDMAN, MARILYN E., STUART MUNRO-HAY, AND RODERICK GRIERSON. *African Zion: The Sacred Art of Ethiopia* (1993).

HENDERSON, HARRY, AND GYLBERT GARVIN COKER. *Charles Alston: Artist and Teacher* (1990).

KIRSH, ANDREA, AND SUSAN FISHER STERLING. *Carrie Mae Weems* (1992).

LEWIS, SAMELLA. *African-American Art and Artists* (1990).

———. *The Art of Elizabeth Catlett* (1984).

LEWIS, SAMELLA, AND RICHARD POWELL. *Elizabeth Catlett: Works on Paper, 1944–1992* (1993).

LIVINGSTON, JANE, JOHN BEARDSLEY, AND REGINIA PERRY. *Black Folk Art in America, 1930–1980* (1982).

MARSHALL, RICHARD, ET. AL. *Jean-Michel Basquiat* (1992).

MATTHEWS, MARCIA M. *Henry Ossawa Tanner, American Artist* (1969).

MCDONNELL, PATRICK, KAREN O'CONNELL, AND GEORGIA RILEY DE HAVENON. *Krazy Kat: The Comic Art of George Herriman* (1986).

MOORE, ROBIN. *Nationalizing Blackness: Afrocubanismo and Artistic Revolution in Havana, 1920–40* (1997).

MOSBY, DEWEY E., DARRELL SEWELL, AND RAE ALEXANDER-MINTER. *Henry Ossawa Tanner* (1991).

MOSQUERA, GERARDO, ED. *Beyond the Fantastic: Contemporary Art Criticism from Latin America* (1996).

MOUNTOUSSAMY-ASHE, JEANNE. *View-finders: Black Women Photographers* (1986).

PERRY, REGINA A. *Free Within Ourselves: African-American Artists in the Collection of the National Museum of American Art* (1992).

PICTON, JOHN, AND JOHN MACK. *African Textiles* (1989).

POLAKOFF, CLAIRE. *Into Indigo: African Textiles and Dyeing Techniques* (1980).

PORTER, JAMES AMOS. *Modern Negro Art* (1943).

POUPEYE, VEERLE. *Modern Jamaican Art* (1998).

POWELL, IVOR. *Ndebele: A People and Their Art* (1995).

POWELL, RICHARD J. *Black Art and Culture in the Twentieth Century* (1997).

———. *Homecoming: The Art and Life of William H. Johnson* (1991).

RESWICK, IRMTRAUD. *Traditional Textiles of Tunisia and Related North African Weavings* (1985).

RINGGOLD, FAITH. *We Flew Over the Bridge: The Memoirs of Faith Ringgold* (1995).

RITCHIE, CARSON. *Rock Art of Africa* (1979).

ROBINSON, JONTYLE THERESA, AND WENDY GREENHOUSE. *The Art of Archibald J. Motley, Jr.* (1991).

RODMAN, SELDEN. *Renaissance in Haiti: Popular Painters in the Black Republic* (1948).

SCHWARTZMAN, MYRON. *Romare Bearden: His Life and Art* (1990).

SILL, ROBERT. *David Hammons in the Hood* (1994).

SMITH, ROBERTA. "A Forgotten Black Painter Is Saved from Obscurity." *New York Times* (June 12, 1992): C18

STEIN, JUDITH E., ET AL. *I Tell My Heart: The Art of Horace Pippin* (1993).

SUPER, GEORGE LEE, MICHAEL GARDEN, AND NANCY MARSHALL, EDS. *P. H. Polk: Photographs* (1980).

THOMPSON, ROBERT FERRIS. *Flash of the Spirit: African and Afro-American Art and Philosophy* (1983).

———. *Jean-Michel Basquiat* (1985).

VANSINA, JAN. *Art History in Africa: An Introduction to Method* (1984).

VLACH, JOHN MICHAEL. *The Afro-American Tradition in the Decorative Arts* (1978).

WAHLMAN, MAUDE SOUTHWELL. *Contemporary African Arts* (1974).

———. *Signs and Symbols: African Images in African-American Quilts* (1993).

WHEAT, ELLEN HARKINS. *Jacob Lawrence, American Painter* (1986).

WILLIS-THOMAS, DEBORAH. *Black Photographers, 1840–1940: An Illustrated Bio-Bibliography* (1985).

———. *An Illustrated Bio-Bibliography of Black Photographers, 1940–1988* (1989).

WOOD, PETER H., AND KAREN C. C. DALTON. *Winslow Homer's Images of Blacks: The Civil War and Reconstruction Years* (1988).

CIVIL RIGHTS

ANDERSON, JERVIS. *A. Philip Randolph: A Biographical Portrait* (1973).

———. *Bayard Rustin: Troubles I've Seen: A Biography* (1997).

BRANCH, TAYLOR. *Parting the Waters: America in the King Years, 1954–63* (1988).

BRODERICK, FRANCIS L., AUGUST MEIER, AND ELLIOTT M. RUDWICK. *Black Protest Thought in the Twentieth Century*. 2d ed. (1971).

CAGIN, SETH, AND PHILIP DRAY. *We Are Not Afraid: The Story of Goodman, Schwerner, and Chaney and the Civil Rights Campaign for Mississippi* (1988).

CARSON, CLAYBORNE. *In Struggle: SNCC and the Black Awakening of the 1960s* (1981).

CLARK, SEPTIMA. *Echo in My Soul* (1962).

CLARK, SEPTIMA, WITH CYNTHIA STOKES BROWN. *Ready from Within: Septima Clark and the Civil Rights Movement* (1986).

EVERS, CHARLES, AND GRACE HASKELL, EDS. *Evers* (1971).

FARMER, JAMES. *Lay Bare the Heart: An Autobiography of the Civil Rights Movement* (1985).

GARROW, DAVID J. *Bearing the Cross: Martin Luther King, Jr., and the Southern Christian Leadership Conference* (1986).

———. *Protest at Selma: Martin Luther King, Jr., and the Voting Rights Act of 1965* (1978).

GRANT, JOANNE. *Fundi: The Story of Ella Baker* (1981).

GREENBERG, JACK. *Crusaders in the Courts: How a Dedicated Band of Lawyers Fought for the Civil Rights Revolution* (1994).

GREGORY, DICK, WITH MARK LANE. *Up From Nigger* (1976).

GREGORY, DICK, WITH MARTIN LIPSYTE. *Nigger: An Autobiography* (1964).

HEDGEMAN, ANNA ARNOLD. *The Trumpet Sounds: A Memoir of Negro Leadership* (1964).

HILL, ROBERT A., ED. *The Crusader*. 3 vols. (1987).

———. *The Marcus Garvey and Universal Negro Improvement Association Papers* (1983–1991).

HORNE, GERALD. *Communist Front? The Civil Rights Congress 1946–56* (1988).

HUCKABY, ELIZABETH. *Crisis at Central High School: Little Rock, 1957–58* (1980).

KEPPEL, BEN. *The Work of Democracy: Ralph Bunche, Kenneth B. Clark, Lorraine Hansberry, and the Cultural Politics of Race* (1995).

KING, CORETTA SCOTT. *My Life with Martin Luther King, Jr.* (1969).

KLUGER, RICHARD. *Simple Justice: The History of Brown v. Board of Education and Black America's Struggle for Equality* (1975).

LAMBERT, BRUCE. "Doxey Wilkerson Is Dead at 88: Educator and Advocate for Rights." *New York Times* (June 18, 1993): D16.

MARKMANN, CHARLES LAM. *The Noblest Cry: A History of the American Civil Liberties Union* (1965).

McADAM, DOUG. *Freedom Summer* (1988).

McNEIL, GENNA RAE. *Groundwork: Charles Hamilton Houston and the Struggle for Civil Rights* (1983).

MOORE, JESSE THOMAS. *A Search for Equality: The National Urban League, 1910–1961* (1981).

"NEW VOICE OF THE NAACP." Interview in *Newsweek* 46 (November 22, 1976).

PATTERSON, WILLIAM. *The Man Who Cried Genocide: An Autobiography* (1971).

PERRY, BRUCE. *Malcolm: The Life of a Man Who Changed Black America* (1991).

POWLEDGE, FRED. *Free at Last? The Civil Rights Movement and the People Who Made It* (1991).

ROBINSON, JO ANN GIBSON. *The Montgomery Bus Boycott and the Women Who Started It: The Memoir of Jo Ann Robinson* (1987).

ROGERS, KIM LACY. *Righteous Lives: Narratives of the New Orleans Civil Rights Movement* (1993).

SACK, KEVIN. "A Dynamic Farewell from a Longtime Rights Leader." *New York Times* (July 29, 1997).

SPOFFORD, TIM. *Lynch Street: The May 1970 Slayings at Jackson State College* (1988).

WATSON, DENTON L. *Lion in the Lobby: Clarence Mitchell, Jr.'s Struggle for the Passage of Civil Rights Laws* (1990).

WEISS, NANCY J. *Whitney M. Young, Jr., and the Struggle for Civil Rights* (1989).

WHITMAN, MARK, ED. *Removing a Badge of Slavery: The Record of Brown v. Board of Education* (1993).

WILKINS, ROY. *Standing Fast: The Autobiography of Roy Wilkins* (1982).

YOUNG, ANDREW. *An Easy Burden: The Civil Rights Movement and the Transformation of America* (1996).

———. *A Way Out of No Way: The Spiritual Memoirs of Andrew Young* (1994).

ZINN, HOWARD. *SNCC: The New Abolitionists* (1965).

COUNTRIES AND REGIONS

ADENAIKE, CAROLYN KEYES, AND JAN VANSINA, EDS. *In Pursuit of History: Fieldwork in Africa* (1996).

ALIE, JOE A. D. *A New History of Sierra Leone* (1990).

AZEVEDO, MARIO. *Historical Dictionary of Mozambique* (1991).

BECHKEY, ALLEN. *Adventuring in East Africa* (1990).

BECKLES, HILARY. *A History of Barbados: Amerindian Settlement to Nation-State* (1990).

BOLLAND, O. NIGEL. *A History of Belize: Nation in the Making* (1997).

BOVILL, E. W. *The Niger Implored* (1968).

BOXER, C. R. *The Dutch in Brazil, 1624–1654* (1957).

———. *The Portuguese Seaborne Empire, 1415–1825* (1969).

BROWN, MERVYN. *A History of Madagascar* (1995).

———. *Madagascar Rediscovered: A History from Early Times to Independence* (1978).

BURCKHARDT, TITUS. *Fez, City of Islam* (1992).

FINLAYSON, IAIN. *Tangier: City of the Dream* (1992).

GIDE, ANDRÉ. *Travels in the Congo* (1962).

HALL, RICHARD. *Stanley: An Adventurer Explored* (1974).

JENKINS, MARK. *To Timbuktu* (1997).

KINCAID, JAMAICA. *A Small Place* (1988).

MARCUS, HAROLD G. *A History of Ethiopia* (1994).

MARTIN, ESMOND BRADLEY. *Zanzibar: Tradition and Revolution* (1978).

MIDDLETON, JOHN, ED. *Encyclopedia of Africa South of the Sahara.* 4 vols. (1997).

MINTZ, SIDNEY, AND SALLY PRICE, EDS. *Caribbean Contours* (1985).

MOOREHEAD, ALAN. *The White Nile* (1971).

OFCANSKY, THOMAS, AND RODGER YEAGER. *Historical Dictionary of Tanzania* (1997).

OGOT, BETHWELL A. *Africa and the Caribbean* (1997).

OSSMAN, SUSAN. *Picturing Casablanca: Portraits of Power in a Modern City* (1994).

PARK, THOMAS K. *Historical Dictionary of Morocco* (1996).

PERKINS, KENNETH J. *Historical Dictionary of Tunisia* (1997).

READER, JOHN. *Africa: A Biography of the Continent* (1998).

ROBERTS, ANDREW. *A History of Zambia* (1976).

TINGAY, PAUL, AND DOUG SCOTT. *Handy Guide: Victoria Falls* (1996).

VANSINA, JAN. *Kingdoms of the Savanna* (1966).

WIENER, LEO. *Africa and the Discovery of America.* Vol. I (1920).

CRIMINAL JUSTICE

ABU-JAMAL, MUMIA. *Live from Death Row* (1996).

BELL, MALCOLM. *The Turkey Shoot: Tracking the Attica Cover-Up* (1985).

BLAND, RANDALL W. *Private Pressure on Public Law. The Legal Career of Justice Thurgood Marshall* (1973).

BRUNDAGE, W. FITZHUGH, ED. *Under Sentence of Death: Lynching in the South* (1997).

FREEDBERG, SYDNEY P. *Brother Love: Money, Murder, and a Messiah* (1994).

KENNEDY, RANDALL. *Race, Crime, and the Law* (1997).

MILES, ALEXANDER. *Devil's Island: Colony of the Damned* (1988).

NEWFIELD, JACK. *Only in America: The Life and Crimes of Don King* (1995).

RAPER, ARTHUR F. *The Tragedy of Lynching* (1933).

SHERMAN, RICHARD B. *The Case of Odell Waller and Virginia Justice, 1940–1942* (1992).

TOOBIN, JEFFREY. *The Run of His Life: The People v. O. J. Simpson* (1996).

WELLS-BARNETT, IDA B. *On Lynchings: Southern Horrors; A Red Record; Mob Rule in New Orleans* (1969).

WHITE, WALTER F. *A Man Called White: The Autobiography of Walter White* (1948; reprint ed., 1995).

———. *Rope and Faggot: A Biography of Judge Lynch* (1929).

WICKER, TOM. *A Time to Die* (1975).

ZANGRANDO, ROBERT. *The NAACP Crusade Against Lynching, 1909–1950* (1980).

ECOLOGY AND GEOGRAPHY

ADAMS, W. M., A. S. GOUDIE, AND A. R. ORME. *The Physical Geography of Africa* (1996).

BASH, BARBARA. *Tree of Life: The World of the African Baobab* (1994).

CARD, TIMOTHY M. *Cheetahs of the Serengeti Plains: Group Living in an Asocial Species* (1994).

CUNNINGHAM, CAROL, AND JOEL BERGER. *Horn of Darkness: Rhinos on the Edge* (1997).

GRENARD, STEVE. *Handbook of Alligators and Crocodiles* (1991).

JOHNS, CHRIS. *Valley of Life: Africa's Great Rift* (1991).

KWAMENAH-POH, M., J. TOSH, R. WALLER, AND M. TIDY. *African History in Maps* (1982).

MAIN, MICHAEL. *Kalahari: Life's Variety in Dune and Delta* (1987).

STUART, CHRIS, AND TILDE STUART. *Africa's Vanishing Wildlife* (1996).

———. *Chris and Tilde Stuart's Field Guide to the Mammals of Southern Africa* (1994).

THOMAS, DAVID S. G. *The Kalahari Environment* (1991).

EDUCATION AND INTELLECTUAL LIFE

ADAMS, BARBARA ELEANOR. *John Henrik Clarke: The Early Years* (1992).

APPIAH, KWAME ANTHONY. *In My Father's House: Africa in the Philosophy of Culture* (1992).

BOWMAN, J. WILSON. *America's Black Colleges: The Comprehensive Guide to Historically and Predominantly Black 4-Year Colleges and Universities* (1992).

BUTLER, ADDIE LOUISE JOYNER. *The Distinctive Black College: Talladega, Tuskegee and Morehouse* (1977).

COLLINS, L. M. *One Hundred Years of Fisk University Presidents* (1989).

COPPIN, FANNY JACKSON. *Reminiscences of School Life, and Hints on Teaching* (1913).

DU BOIS, SHIRLEY GRAHAM. *His Day Is Marching On: A Memoir of W. E. B. Du Bois.* (1971).

DU BOIS, W. E. B. *The Souls of Black Folk: Essays and Sketches* (1903).

GLEN, JOHN M. *Highlander: No Ordinary School, 1932–1962* (1988).

GOGGIN, JACQUELINE ANNE. *Carter G. Woodson: A Life in Black History* (1993).

GREENE, LORENZO JOHNSTON. *Selling Black History for Carter G. Woodson* (1996).

GUY-SHEFTALL, BEVERLY, AND JO MOORE STEWART. *Spelman: A Centennial Celebration* (1981).

HARLAN, LOUIS R. *Booker T. Washington: The Making of a Black Leader, 1856–1901* (1972).

HARPER, MICHAEL S., ET AL., EDS. *Chant of Saints: A Gathering of Afro-American Literature, Art, and Scholarship* (1979).

HOOKS, BELL, AND CORNEL WEST. *Breaking Bread: Insurgent Black Intellectual Life* (1991).

HOUSE, ERNEST R. *Jesse Jackson and the Politics of Charisma: The Rise and Fall of the PUSH/Excel Program* (1988).

JOHNSON, DIANE. *Telling Tales: The Pedagogy and Promise of African-American Literature for Youth* (1990).

LEWIS, DAVID LEVERING. *W. E. B. Du Bois: Biography of a Race* (1993).

———. *When Harlem Was in Vogue* (1981).

LOCKE, ALAIN, ED. *The New Negro* (1925).

LOGAN, RAYFORD. *Howard University: The First Hundred Years, 1867–1967* (1969).

MANGIONE, JERRE. *The Dream and the Deal: The Federal Writers' Project, 1935–1945* (1972).

MANLEY, ALBERT E. *A Legacy Continues: The Manley Years at Spelman College, 1953–1976* (1995).

MEIER, AUGUST. *Negro Thought in America, 1880–1915: Racial Ideologies in the Age of Booker T. Washington* (1963).

MEIER, AUGUST, AND ELLIOTT RUDWICK. *Black History and the Historical Profession* (1986).

METCALF, GEORGE R. *Black Profiles* (1968).

MOSS, ALFRED A., JR. *The American Negro Academy: Voice of the Talented Tenth* (1981).

RAMPERSAD, ARNOLD. *The Art and Imagination of W. E. B. Du Bois* (1990).

———. *The Life of Langston Hughes.* 2 vols. (1986–1988).

READ, FLORENCE. *The Story of Spelman College* (1961).

RICH, WILBUR C. *Black Mayors and School Politics: The Failure of Reform in Detroit, Gary, and Newark* (1996).

ROMAINE, SUZANNE. *Bilingualism* (1989).

SAGINI, MASHAK M. *The African and the African-American University: A Historical and Sociological Analysis* (1996).

SINNETTE, ELINOR DES VERNEY. *Arthur Alfonso Schomburg, Black Bibliophile & Collector: A Biography* (1989).

SINNETTE, ELINOR DES VERNEY, W. PAUL COATES, AND THOMAS C. BATTLE, EDS. *Black Bibliophiles and Collectors: Preservers of Black History* (1990).

SMITH, JESSIE CARNEY. *Black Academic Libraries and Research Collections: An Historical Survey* (1977).

———, ED. *Notable Black American Women.* 2 vols. (1992–1996).

SUMMERVILLE, JAMES. *Educating Black Doctors: A History of Meharry Medical College* (1983).

TUSHNET, MARK V. *The NAACP's Strategy Against Segregated Education, 1925–1950* (1987).

URBAN, W. J. *Black Scholar: Horace Mann Bond 1904–1972* (1992).

WESLEY, CHARLES H. *Charles H. Wesley: The Intellectual Tradition of a Black Historian.* Edited by James L. Conyers, Jr. (1997).

WHITING, ALBERT N. *Guardians of the Flame: Historically Black Colleges Yesterday, Today, and Tomorrow* (1991).

ETHNIC GROUPS

ABRAHAMS, R. G. *The Nyamwezi Today: A Tanzanian People in the 1970s* (1981).

BEACH, DAVID. *The Shona and Their Neighbours* (1994).

HOLM, JOHN. *Pidgins and Creoles.* 2 vols. (1988–1989).

KAPLAN, STEVEN. *The Beta Israel (Falasha) in Ethiopia: From Earliest Times to the Twentieth Century* (1992).

KENYATTA, JOMO. *Facing Mount Kenya: The Tribal Life of the Gikuyu* (1938).

MINORITY RIGHTS GROUP, ED. *No Longer Invisible: Afro-Latin Americans Today* (1995).

OLSON, JAMES STUART. *The Peoples of Africa: An Ethnohistorical Dictionary* (1996).

STEPHENS, THOMAS M. *Dictionary of Latin American Racial and Ethnic Terminology* (1989).

TURNBULL, COLIN M. *The Forest People* (1961).

VANSINA, JAN. *The Children of Woot: A History of the Kuba Peoples* (1978).

FILM, RADIO AND TELEVISION

BLY, NELLIE. *Oprah! Up Close and Down Home* (1993).

BOGLE, DONALD. *Blacks in American Films and Television: An Illustrated Encyclopedia* (1988).

———. *Dorothy Dandridge: A Biography* (1997).

———. *Toms, Coons, Mulattoes, Mammies, and Bucks: An Interpretive History of Blacks in American Films.* 3d ed. (1994).

BRODE, DOUGLAS. *Denzel Washington: His Films and Career* (1996).

CHANAN, MICHAEL. *The Cuban Image: Cinema and the Cultural Politics in Cuba* (1985).

CRIPPS, THOMAS. *Making Movies Black: The Hollywood Message Movie from World War II to the Civil Rights Era* (1993).

———. *Slow Fade to Black: The Negro in American Film 1900–1942* (1977).

DASH, JULIE. *Daughters of the Dust: The Making of an African-American Woman's Film* (1992).

DIAWARA, MANTHIA. *African Cinema: Politics and Culture* (1992).

———, ED. *Black American Cinema* (1993).

ELY, MELVIN PATRICK. *The Adventures of Amos 'n' Andy: A Social History of an American Phenomenon* (1991).

GUERRERO, EDWARD. *Framing Blackness: The African-American Image in Film* (1993).

JACKSON, CARLTON. *Hattie: The Life of Hattie McDaniel* (1990).

JOHNSON, RANDAL. *Cinema Novo x 5: Masters of Contemporary Brazilian Film* (1984).

KLOTMAN, PHYLLIS RAUCH, ED. *Screenplays of the African-American Experience* (1991).

MACDONALD, J. FRED. *Blacks and White TV: African-Americans in Television Since 1948.* Rev. ed. (1992).

MAIR, GEORGE. *Oprah Winfrey: The Real Story* (1994).

MARTIN, MICHAEL T., ED. *Cinemas of the Black Diaspora: Diversity, Dependence, and Oppositionality* (1995).

NOBLE, PETER. *The Negro in Films* (1948).

POITIER, SIDNEY. *This Life* (1980).

PRICE, JOE X. *Redd Foxx, B.S. (Before Sanford)* (1979).

STAM, ROBERT. *Tropical Multiculturalism: A Comparative History of Race in Brazilian Cinema and Culture* (1997).

STAM, ROBERT, AND RANDAL JOHNSON. *Brazilian Cinema.* Rev. and exp. ed. (1995).

XAVIER, ISMAIL. *Allegories of Underdevelopment: Aesthetics and Politics in Modern Brazilian Cinema* (1997).

HISTORY

ABAJIAN, JAMES DE T. *Blacks and Their Contributions to the American West* (1974).

BEETH, HOWARD, AND CARY WINTZ. *Black Dixie: Afro-Texan History and Culture in Houston* (1992).

BENNETT, LERONE, JR. *Before the Mayflower* (1962; revised ed., 1987).

BERLIN, IRA. *Slaves without Masters: The Free Negro in the Antebellum South* (1974).

BERTLEY, LEO W. *Canada and Its People of African Descent* (1977).

DEERR, NOEL. *The History of Sugar.* 2 vols. (1949–1950).

DRAKE, ST. CLAIR. *Black Folk Here and There: An Essay in History and Anthropology.* 2 vols. (1987–1990).

DRAKE, ST. CLAIR, AND HORACE R. CAYTON. *Black Metropolis: A Study of Negro Life in a Northern City* (1945).

DUBOFSKY, MELVYN, AND STEPHEN BURWOOD, EDS. *Women and Minorities During the Great Depression* (1990).

DU BOIS, W. E. B. *Black Reconstruction in America* (1935).

EHRET, CHRISTOPHER, AND M. POSNANSKY. *The Archaeological and Linguistic Reconstruction of African History* (1982).

FONER, ERIC. *Reconstruction: America's Unfinished Revolution, 1863–1877* (1988).

FONER, PHILIP. *Antonio Maceo* (1977).

———. *Black Panthers Speak* (1995)

———. *Organized Labor and the Black Worker 1619–1973* (1974).

FONER, PHILIP, AND RONALD LEWIS. *Black Workers: A Documentary History from Colonial Times to the Present* (1989).

FRANKLIN, JOHN HOPE. *The Free Negro in North Carolina, 1790–1863* (1943).

———. *From Slavery to Freedom: A History of Negro Americans* (1988).

———. *Race and History: Selected Essays, 1938–1988* (1989).

FRIEDMAN, LAWRENCE J. *Gregarious Saints: Self and Community in American Abolitionism, 1830–1870* (1982).

FUNARI, PEDRO PAUL A., MARTIN HALL, AND SIAN JONES, EDS. *Historical Archaeology: Back from the Edge* (1999).

GATES, HENRY LOUIS, JR., AND EVELYN BROOKS HIGGINBOTHAM, EDS. *African-American Lives* (2004).

GREENBERG, CHERYL LYNN. *"Or Does It Explode?": Black Harlem in the Great Depression* (1991).

GREENE, LORENZO JOHNSTON, GARY R. KREMER, AND ANTONIO F. HOLLAND. *Missouri's Black Heritage* (1993).

GROSSMAN, JAMES R. *Land of Hope: Chicago, Black Southerners and the Great Migration* (1989).

HAMILTON, HOLMAN. *Prologue to Conflict: The Crisis and Compromise of 1850* (1964).

HAMILTON, KENNETH MARVIN. *Black Towns and Profit: Promotion and Development in the Trans-Applachian West, 1877–1915* (1991).

HARDESTY, VON, AND DOMINICK PISANO. *Black Wings: The American Black in Aviation* (1983).

HAYWOOD, HARRY. *Black Bolshevik: Autobiography of an Afro-American Communist* (1978).

HENSON, MATTHEW A. *A Black Explorer at the North Pole 1866–1955* (1989).

HIGGINBOTHAM, A. LEON. *In the Matter of Color: The Colonial Period* (1978).

———. *Shades of Freedom: Racial Politics and Presumptions of the American Legal Process* (1996).

HILL, DANIEL G. *The Freedom Seekers: Blacks in Early Canada* (1981).

HINE, DARLENE CLARK, ED. *Black Women in America: An Historical Encyclopedia.* 3 vols. 2d ed. (2004).

HOYOS, F. A. *A History from the Amerindians to Independence* (1978).

ISICHEI, ELIZABETH. *A History of African Societies to 1870* (1997).

KAPLAN, SIDNEY, AND EMMA NOGRADY KAPLAN. *The Black Presence in the Era of the American Revolution.* 2d ed. (1989).

KATZMAN, DAVID. *Before the Ghetto: Black Detroit in the Nineteenth Century* (1973).

KATZ, WILLIAM L. *Black People Who Made the Old West* (1992).

———. *The Black West* (1987).

KUSMER, KENNETH. *A Ghetto Takes Shape: Black Cleveland, 1870–1930* (1976).

LEMANN, NICHOLAS. *The Promised Land: The Great Black Migration and How It Changed America* (1991).

LITWACK, LEON F., AND AUGUST MEIER, EDS. *Black Leaders of the Nineteenth Century* (1988).

LOGAN, RAYFORD, AND MICHAEL R. WINSTON. *Dictionary of American Negro Biography* (1982).

LOTZ, RAINER, AND IAN PEGG, EDS. *Under the Imperial Carpet: Essays in Black History, 1780–1950* (1990).

MCELVAINE, ROBERT S. *The Great Depression: America, 1929–1941* (1984).

MINTZ, SIDNEY. *Sweetness and Power* (1985).

MORELL, VIRGINIA. *Ancestral Passions: The Leakey Family and the Quest for Humankind's Beginnings* (1995).

NAISON, MARK. *Communists in Harlem During the Depression* (1983).

NEWBY, I. A. *Black Carolinians: A History of Blacks in South Carolina from 1895 to 1968* (1973).

OSOFSKY, GILBERT. *Harlem: The Making of a Ghetto: Negro New York, 1890–1930* (1971; revised ed., 1996).

PAINTER, NELL IRVIN. *Exodusters: Black Migration to Kansas after Reconstruction* (1986).

———. "Martin R. Delany: Elitism and Black Nationalism." In *Black Leaders of the Nineteenth Century.* Edited by Leon Litwack and August Meier (1988): 148–171.

———. *Sojourner Truth: A Life, a Symbol* (1996).

POTTER, DAVID M. *The Impending Crisis, 1848–1861* (1976).

QUARLES, BENJAMIN. *Black Abolitionists* (1969).

RIVLIN, BENJAMIN, ED. *Ralph Bunche: The Man and His Times* (1990).

ROULHE, NELLIE C. *Work, Play, and Commitment: A History of the First Fifty Years, Jack and Jill of America, Incorporated* (1989).

ROUT, LESLIE B. *The African Experience in Spanish America, 1502 to the Present Day* (1976).

SALZMAN, JACK, DAVID LIONEL SMITH, AND CORNEL WEST, EDS. *Encyclopedia of African-American Culture and History.* 5 vols. (1996).

SANTINO, JACK. *Miles of Smiles, Years of Struggle: Stories of Black Pullman Porters* (1989).

SNOWDEN, FRANK M., JR. *Before Color Prejudice: The Ancient View of Blacks* (1983).

———. *Blacks in Antiquity; Ethiopians in the Greco-Roman Experience* (1970).

STERLING, DOROTHY. *Black Foremothers: Three Lives* (1988).

———. *The Making of an Afro-American: Martin Robison Delany 1812–1885* (1971).

———. *We Are Your Sisters: Black Women in the Nineteenth Century* (1984).

STEVENSON, BRENDA, ED. *The Journals of Charlotte Forten Grimke* (1988).

SWEETMAN, DAVID. *Women Leaders in African History* (1984).

TENENBAUM, BARBARA A., ED. *Encyclopedia of Latin American History and Culture.* 5 vols. (1996).

VAN SERTIMA, IVAN, ED. *African Presence in Early America* (1987).

———, ED. *African Presence in Early Europe* (1985).

———, ED. *Black Women in Antiquity* (1984).

VAN SERTIMA, IVAN, AND RUNOKO RASHIDI, EDS. *African Presence in Early Asia* (1988).

VANSINA, JAN. *Oral Tradition as History* (1985).

VAN TASSEL, DAVID D., AND JOHN J. GRABOWSKI. *Cleveland: A Tradition of Reform* (1986).

———. *The Encyclopedia of Cleveland History* (1987).

WALKER, GEORGE E. *The Afro-American in New York City, 1827–1860* (1993).

WALKER, JAMES W. ST. G. *The Black Loyalists: The Search for a Promised Land in Nova Scotia and Sierra Leone, 1783–1870* (1992).

WEARE, WALTER B. *Black Business in the New South: A Social History of the North Carolina Mutual Life Insurance Company* (1973).

WHEELER, B. GORDON. *Black California: The History of African-Americans in the Golden State* (1993).

WIKRAMANAYAKE, MARINA. *A World in Shadow: The Free Black in Antebellum South Carolina* (1973).

WINCH, JULIE. *Philadelphia's Black Elite: Activism, Accommodation, and the Struggle for Autonomy, 1787–1848* (1988).

WINKS, ROBIN W. *The Blacks in Canada: A History* (1997).

WOODWARD, C. VANN. *Origins of the New South: 1877–1913* (1951).

———. *Reunion and Reaction: The Compromise of 1877 and the End of Reconstruction* (1951; reprint ed. 1991).

———. *The Strange Career of Jim Crow* (1955).

WRIGHT, GILES R. *Afro-Americans in New Jersey: A Short History* (1988).

WRIGHT, RICHARD R., JR. *The Negro in Pennsylvania, A Study in Economic History* (1969).

LITERATURE: AFRICA

ACHEBE, CHINUA. *Hopes and Impediments: Selected Essays* (1988).

COOK, DAVID, AND MICHAEL OKENIMPKE. *Ngugi wa Thiong'o: An Exploration of His Writing.* 2d ed. (1997).

EMECHETA, BUCHI. *Head Above Water* (1986).

NGUGI WA THIONG'O. *Decolonising the Mind: The Politics of Language in African Literature* (1986).

———. *Moving the Centre: The Struggle for Cultural Freedoms* (1993).

NORRIS, H. T. *The Berbers in Arabic Literature* (1982).

SOYINKA WOLE. *The Burden of Memory, the Muse of Forgiveness* (1999).

———. *Myth, Literature, and the African World* (1976).

———. *The Open Sore of a Continent: A Personal Narrative of the Nigerian Crisis* (1996).

LITERATURE: LATIN AMERICA AND THE CARIBBEAN

ARMAS, JOSÉ R. DE, AND CHARLES W. STEELE. *Cuban Consciousness in Literature: 1923–1974* (1978).

ARNOLD, A. JAMES. *Modernism and Negritude: The Poetry and Poetics of Aimé Césaire* (1981).

BARREDA-TÓMAS, PEDRO M. *The Black Protagonist in the Cuban Novel* (1979).

BROOKSHAW, DAVID. *Race and Color in Brazilian Literature* (1986).

CAMPBELL, ELAINE, AND PIERRETTE FRICKEY, EDS. *The Whistling Bird: Women Writers of the Caribbean* (1998).

CUDJOE, SELWYN, ED. *Caribbean Women Writers: Essays from the First International Conference.* (1990).

——. *Resistance and Caribbean Literature* (1980).

DAVIES, CAROL BOYCE, AND ELAINE SAVORY FIDO, EDS. *Out of the Kumbla: Caribbean Women and Literature* (1990).

FERGUSON, MOIRA. *Jamaica Kincaid: Where the Land Meets the Body* (1994).

GLISSANT, EDOUARD. *Caribbean Discourse: Selected Essays.* Translated by J. Michael Dash (1989).

GONZALEZ ECHEVARRIA, ROBERTO. *Myth and Archive: A Theory of Latin American Narrative* (1998).

HAMNER, ROBERT D., ED. *Critical Perspectives on Derek Walcott* (1993).

JACKSON, RICHARD L. *Black Writers in Latin America* (1979).

KING, BRUCE, ED. *West Indian Literature* (1979).

LEWIS, MARVIN A. *Ethnicity and Identity in Contemporary Afro-Venezuelan Literature: A Culturalist Approach* (1992).

LOOS, DOROTHY SCOTT. *The Naturalistic Novel of Brazil* (1963).

LUIS, WILLIAM. *Literary Bondage: Slavery in Cuban Narrative* (1990).

——, ED. *Voices from Under: Black Narrative in Latin America and the Caribbean* (1984).

MENTON, SEYMOUR. *Prose Fiction of the Cuban Revolution* (1975).

MORDECAI, PAMELA, AND BETTY WILSON, EDS. *Her True-True Name* (1989).

PAQUET, SANDRA POUCHET. *The Novels of George Lamming* (1982).

SCHARFMAN, RONNIE L. *"Engagement" and the Language of the Subject in the Poetry of Aimé Césaire* (1987).

SIMMONS, DIANE. *Jamaica Kincaid* (1994).

SOMMER, DORIS. *Foundational Fictions: The National Romances of Latin America* (1991).

TAYLOR, PATRICK. *The Narrative of Liberation: Perspectives on Afro-Caribbean Literature, Popular Culture, and Politics* (1989).

WEBB, BARBARA J. *Myth and History in Caribbean Fiction: Alejo Carpentier, Wilson Harris, and Edouard Glissant* (1992).

WILLIAMS, LORNA V. *The Representation of Slavery in Cuban Fiction.* (1994).

LITERATURE: NORTH AMERICA

ANDREWS, WILLIAM L. *The Literary Career of Charles W. Chesnutt* (1980).

——. *Sisters of the Spirit: Three Black Women's Autobiographies of the Nineteenth Century* (1986).

——. *To Tell a Free Story: The First Century of Afro-American Autobiography, 1760–1865* (1986).

BABB, VALERIE MELISSA. *Ernest Gaines* (1991).

BAILEY, PEARL. *Between You and Me: A Heartfelt Memoir of Learning, Loving, and Living* (1989).

——. *The Raw Pearl* (1968).

BAKER, HOUSTON A., JR. *Blues, Ideology, and Afro-American Literature: A Vernacular Theory* (1980).

BARAKA, AMIRI. *The Autobiography of LeRoi Jones* (1984).

BELL, BERNARD. *The Afro-American Novel and its Tradition* (1987).

BENSTON, KIMBERLY, ED. *Speaking for You: The Vision of Ralph Ellison* (1995).

BISHOP, JACK. *Ralph Ellison* (1988).

BOYER, JAY. *Ishmael Reed* (1993).

BRATHWAITE, EDWARD KAMAU. *Roots* (1993).

BRUCE, DICKSON D., JR. *Black American Writing from the Nadir: The Evolution of a Literary Tradition, 1877–1915* (1989).

BRYANT-JACKSON, PAUL, AND LOIS MORE OVERBECK, EDS. *Intersecting Boundaries: The Theater of Adrienne Kennedy* (1992).

BUSBY, MARK. *Ralph Ellison* (1991).

CALLAGHAN, BARRY, ED. *The Austin Clarke Reader* (1996).

CARBY, HAZEL V. *Reconstructing Womanhood: The Emergence of the Afro-American Woman Novelist* (1987).

CHRISTIAN, BARBARA. *Black Feminist Criticism: Perspectives on Black Women Writers* (1985).

——. *Black Women Novelists: The Development of a Tradition, 1892–1976* (1980).

CLARKE, GEORGE ELLIOTT, ED. *Fire on the Water: An Anthology of Black Nova Scotian Writing.* 2 vols. (1991–1992).

COLEMAN, JAMES W. *Blackness and Modernism: The Literary Career of John Edgar Wideman* (1989).

COOPER, WAYNE F. *Claude McKay: A Rebel Sojourner in the Harlem Renaissance: A Biography* (1987).

CUENEY, ANNE. *Lorraine Hansberry* (1984).

CULLEN, COUNTEE. *My Soul's High Song: The Collected Writings of Countee Cullen, Voice of the Harlem Renaissance.* Edited by Gerald Early (1991).

DAVIS, ARTHUR P. *From the Dark Tower: Afro-American Writers, 1900–1960* (1974).

DUNBAR-NELSON, ALICE. *Give Us This Day: The Diary of Alice Dunbar-Nelson.* Edited by Gloria T. Hull (1984).

DUNDES, ALAN, ED. *Mother Wit from the Laughing Barrel: Readings in the Interpretation of Afro-American Folklore* (1990).

DURIX, JEAN-PIERRE. *Dictionary of Literary Biography* (1992).

EVANS, MARI. *Black Women Writers (1950–1980): A Critical Evaluation* (1984).

FLYNN, JOYCE, AND JOYCE OCCOMY STRICKLIN, EDS. *Frye Street and Environs: The Collected Works of Marita Bonner Occomy* (1987).

FOWLER, VIRGINIA. *Nikki Giovanni* (1992).

GAINES, ERNEST. *Porch Talk with Ernest Gaines: Conversations on the Writer's Craft.* Edited by Marcia Gaudet and Carl Wooton (1990).

GATES, HENRY LOUIS, JR. *Black Literature and Literary Theory* (1984).

——. *Colored People: A Memoir* (1994).

——. *Figures in Black: Words, Signs, and the Racial Self* (1992).

——. *Loose Canons: Notes on the Culture Wars* (1992).

——. *The Signifying Monkey: Towards A Theory of Afro-American Literary Criticism* (1988).

——, ED. *Bearing Witness: Selections from African-American Autobiography in the Twentieth Century* (1991).

——, ED. *The Classic Slave Narratives* (1987).

——, ED. *Collected Black Women's Narratives: The Schomburg Library of Nineteenth-Century Black Women Writers* (1988).

GATES, HENRY LOUIS, JR., AND KWAME ANTHONY APPIAH, EDS. *Richard Wright: Critical Perspectives Past and Present* (1993).

——, EDS. *Gloria Naylor: Critical Perspectives Past and Present* (1993).

GATES, HENRY LOUIS, JR., AND NELLIE Y. MCKAY. *The Norton Anthology of African-American Literature* (1997).

HEDRICK, JOAN. *Harriet Beecher Stowe: A Life* (1994).

HEMENWAY, ROBERT. *Zora Neale Hurston: A Literary Biography* (1980).

HEMPHILL, ESSEX, ED. *Brother to Brother: New Writings by Black Gay Men* (1991).

HODGES, LEROY. *Portrait of an Expatriate: William Gardner Smith, Writer* (1985).

HULL, GLORIA T. *Color, Sex, and Poetry: Three Women Writers of the Harlem Renaissance* (1987).

HURSTON, ZORA NEALE. *I Love Myself When I Am Laughing . . . and Then Again When I Am Looking Mean and Impressive: A Zora Neale Hurston Reader.* Edited by Alice Walker (1979).

——. *Mules and Men* (1935).

JAMES, ADEOLA. *In Their Own Voices: African Women Writers Talk* (1990).

JOHNSON, JAMES WELDON. *Black Manhattan* (1930).

——. *Preface to The Book of American Negro Poetry* (1922).

JULIEN, ISAAC. *Looking for Langston: A Meditation on Langston Hughes (1902–1967) and the Harlem Renaissance, with the Poetry of Essex Hemphill and Bruce Nugent (1906–1987)* (1992).

KENNEDY, ADRIENNE. *People Who Led to My Plays* (1987).

LEEMING, DAVID. *James Baldwin: A Biography* (1994).

MARTIN, JAY, ED. *A Singer in the Dawn: Reinterpretations of Paul Laurence Dunbar* (1975).

MARTIN, REGINALD. *Ishmael Reed and the New Black Aesthetic Critics* (1988).

MCLENDON, JACQUELYN Y. *The Politics of Color in the Fiction of Jessie Fauset and Nella Larsen* (1995).

MURRAY, PAULI. *Dark Testament and Other Poems* (1970).

——. *Proud Shoes: The Story of an American Family* (1956).

——. *Song in a Weary Throat: An American Pilgrimage* (1987).

NADEL, ALAN, ED. *May All of Your Fences Have Gates: Essays on the Drama of August Wilson* (1994).

NORRIS, JERRIE. *Presenting Rosa Guy* (1988).

NOTTEN, ELEONORE VAN. *Wallace Thurman's Harlem Renaissance* (1994).

O'MEALLY, ROBERT G. *The Craft of Ralph Ellison* (1980).

PENKOWER, MONTY NOAM. *The Federal Writers' Project: A Study in Government Patronage of the Arts* (1983).

PETERSON, CARLA. *Doers of the Word: African-American Women Speakers and Writers in the North (1830–1880)* (1995).

PLATO, ANN. *Essays: Including Biographies and Miscellaneous Pieces, in Prose and Poetry* (1841)

RENDER, SYLVIA LYONS. *Charles W. Chesnutt* (1980).

REYNOLDS, MOIRA DAVIDSON. *"Uncle Tom's Cabin" and Mid-Nineteenth Century United States: Pen and Conscience* (1985).

RICHMOND, MERLE. *Bid the Vassal Soar: Interpretative Essays on the Life and Poetry of Phillis Wheatley (ca. 1753–1784) and George Moses Horton (ca. 1797–1883).* (1974).

ROLLOCK, BARBARA. *Black Authors and Illustrators of Children's Books* (1988).

RUFF, SHAWN STEWART. *Go the Way Your Blood Beats: An Anthology of Lesbian and Gay Fiction by African-American Writers* (1996).

SHANNON, SANDRA G. *The Dramatic Vision of August Wilson* (1995).

SHERMAN, JOAN. *Invisible Poets: Afro-Americans of the Nineteenth Century.* 2d ed. (1989).

SHOCKLEY, ANN ALLEN. *Afro-American Women Writers, 1746–1933: An Anthology and Critical Guide* (1988).

SILVERA, MAKEDA, ED. *The Other Woman: Women of Colour in Contemporary Canadian Literature* (1994).

SIMS, RUDINE. *Shadow and Substance: Afro-American Experience in Contemporary Children's Fiction* (1982).

SMITH, BARBARA, ED. *Home Girls: A Black Feminist Anthology* (1983).

SOLLORS, WERNER. *Amiri Baraka/LeRoi Jones: The Quest for a "Populist Modernism"* (1978).

——. *Neither Black nor White, yet Both: Thematic Explorations of Interracial Literature* (1997).

——, ED. *Multilingual America: Transnationalism, Ethnicity, and the Languages of American Literature* (1998).

STOWE, HARRIET BEECHER. *Uncle Tom's Cabin: Authoritative Text. Backgrounds and Contexts* (Norton Critical Edition). (1994).

SYLVANDER, CAROLYN WEDIN. *Jessie Redmon Fauset, Black American Writer* (1981).

TATE, CLAUDIA. *Domestic Allegories of Political Desire: The Black Heroine's Text at the Turn of the Century* (1992).

TILLERY, TYRONE. *Claude McKay: A Black Poet's Struggle for Identity* (1992).

TORRENCE, RIDGELY. *The Story of John Hope* (1948).

WALKER, MELISSA. *Down from the Mountaintop: Black Women's Novels in the Wake of the Civil Rights Movement, 1966–1989* (1991).

WILLIAMSON, JANICE. *Sounding Differences: Conversations with Seventeen Canadian Women Writers* (1993).

WILLIAMS, PONTHEOLLA T. *Robert Flayden: A Critical Analysis of His Poetry* (1987).

WILLIS, SUSAN. *Specifying: Black Women Writing the American Experience* (1987).

WRIGHT, LEE ALFRED. *Identity, Family, and Folklore in African-American Literature* (1995).

MEDICINE AND SCIENCE

ADAIR, GENE. *George Washington Carver* (1989).

BEDINI, SILVIO. *The Life of Benjamin Banneker* (1971–1972).

BUCKLER, HELEN. *Daniel Hale Williams: Negro Surgeon* (1968).

CLASH, M.G. *Benjamin Banneker, Astronomer and Scientist* (1971).

DUMMETT, CLIFTON O., AND LOIS DOYLE DUMMETT. *Afro-Americans in Dentistry: Sequence and Consequence of Events* (1978).

DUSTER, TROY. *Backdoor to Eugenics* (1990).

ELDERS, JOYCELYN. *Joycelyn Elders, M.D.: From Sharecropper's Daughter to Surgeon General of the United States of America* (1997).

ESTES, J. WORTH. *The Medical Skills of Ancient Egypt* (1993).

JONES, JAMES H. *Bad Blood: The Tuskegee Syphilis Experiment* (1993).

KESSLER, JAMES H. *Distinguished African-American Scientists of the Twentieth Century* (1996).

KEVLES, DANIEL. *In the Name of Eugenics: Genetics and the Uses of Human Heredity* (1985).

KREMER, GARY R., ED. *George Washington Carver in His Own Words* (1987).

MORSE, STEPHEN S. *Emerging Viruses* (1993).

NUNN, JOHN E. *Ancient Egyptian Medicine* (1996).

PETERS, WALLACE, AND HERBERT M. GILLES. *Color Atlas of Tropical Medicine and Parasitology* (1995).

SAMMONS, VIVIAN O. *Blacks in Science and Medicine* (1990).

SIMPSON, DAVID IAN H. *Marburg and Ebola Virus Infections: A Guide for Their Diagnosis, Management, and Control* (1977).

STEPAN, NANCY. *The Idea of Race in Science* (1982).

VAN SERTIMA, IVAN. *Blacks in Science: Ancient and Modern* (1991).

WIGG, DAVID. *And Then Forgot to Tell Us Why: A Look at the Campaign Against River Blindness in West Africa* (1993).

WYNES, CHARLES E. *Charles Richard Drew: The Man and the Myth* (1988).

MILITARY

CORNISH, DUDLEY T. *The Sable Arm: Negro Troops in the Union Army, 1861–1865* (1956).

DALFIUME, RICHARD M. *Desegregation of the U.S. Armed Forces: Fighting on Two Fronts, 1939–1953* (1969).

DAVIS, BENJAMIN O., JR. *Benjamin O. Davis, Jr., American: An Autobiography* (1991).

FLETCHER, MARVIN E. *America's First Black General: Benjamin O. Davis, Sr.* (1989).

———. *The Black Soldier and Officer in the United States Army, 1891–1917* (1974).

FONER, PHILIP. *Blacks in the American Revolution* (1976)

———. *The Spanish-Cuban-American War and the Birth of U.S. Imperialism.* Vol. I (1962).

HIRO, DILIP. *Desert Shield to Desert Storm: The Second Gulf War* (1992).

KLEMENT, FRANK L. *The Copperheads of the Middle West* (1972).

LANNING, MICHAEL LEE, LT. COL. (RET.). *The African-American Soldier: From Crispus Attucks to Colin Powell* (1997).

LECKIE, WILLIAM. *The Buffalo Soldiers: A Narrative of the Negro Cavalry in the West* (1967).

McPHERSON, JAMES M. *The Negro's Civil War: How American Negroes Felt and Acted During the War for the Union* (1965).

MORROW, CURTIS. *What's a Commie Ever Done to Black People?: A Korean War Memoir of Fighting in the U.S. Army's Last All Negro Unit* (1997).

NALTY, BERNARD C. *Strength for the Fight: A History of Black Americans in the Military* (1986).

NUGENT, JOHN PEER. *Black Eagle* (1971).

PHELPS, J. ALFRED. *Chappie: America's First Black Four-Star General: The Life and Times of Daniel James, Jr.* (1991).

QUARLES, BENJAMIN. *The Negro in the American Revolution* (1961).

———. *The Negro in the Civil War* (1953).

RISHELL, LYLE. *With A Black Platoon in Combat: A Year in Korea* (1993).

ROLLIN, FRANK A. *Life and Public Services of Martin R. Delany, Subassistant-Commissioner, Bureau Relief of Refugees, Freedmen, and of Abandoned Lands, and Late Major 104th U.S. Colored Troops* (1868).

SCHUBERT, FRANK. *Black Valor: Buffalo Soldiers and the Medal of Honor, 1870–1898* (1997).

TERRY, WALLACE, ED. *Bloods: An Oral History of the Vietnam War, by Black Veterans* (1984).

MUSIC

ALBERTSON, CHRIS. *Bessie* (1972).

AMMONS, KEVIN. *Good Girl, Bad Girl: An Insider's Biography of Whitney Houston* (1996).

ANDERSON, MARIAN. *My Lord, What a Morning: An Autobiography* (1956).

AUSTERLITZ, PAUL. *Merengue: Dominican Music and Dominican Identity* (1997).

AVERILL, GAGE. *A Day for the Hunter, a Day for the Prey* (1997).

BAKER, DAVID. *The Jazz Style of Cannonball Adderley* (1980).

BARKER, DANNY. *A Life in Jazz* (1986).

BARROW, STEVE, AND PETER DALTON. *Reggae: The Rough Guide* (1997).

BASIE, WILLIAM JAMES ("COUNT"), AS TOLD TO ALBERT MURRAY. *Good Morning Blues: The Autobiography of Count Basie* (1985).

BEGO, MARK. *Aretha Franklin* (1989).

BEHAGUE, GERARD H., ED. *Music and Black Ethnicity: The Caribbean and South America* (1994).

BERENDT, JOACHIM. *The Jazz Book: From Ragtime to Fusion and Beyond.* 6th ed. (1992).

BERRY, CHUCK. *Chuck Berry: The Autobiography* (1987).

BIANCO, DAVID. *Heat Wave: The Motown Fact Book* (1988).

BLANCQ, C. C. *Sonny Rollins: The Journey of a Jazzman* (1983).

BLESH, RUDI, AND HARRIET JANIS. *They All Played Ragtime.* 4th ed. (1971).

BOLCOM, WILLIAM, AND ROBERT KIMBALL. *Reminiscing with Sissle and Blake* (1973).

BRITT, STAN. *Dexter Gordon: A Musical Biography* (1989).

BROUGHTON, SIMON, MARK ELLINGHAM, DAVID MUDDYMAN, AND RICHARD TRILLO. *World Music: The Rough Guide* (1994).

BROWN, GEOFF, AND CHRIS CHARLESWORTH. *A Complete Guide to the Music of Prince* (1995).

BROWN, RUTH, WITH ANDREW YULE. *Miss Rhythm: The Autobiography of Ruth Brown, Rhythm & Blues Legend* (1996).

BROWN, SCOTT E. *James P. Johnson: A Case of Mistaken Identity* (1986).

BUCKLEY, GAIL LUMET. *The Hornes: An American Family* (1986).

CALVO OSPINA, HERNANDO. *Salsa! Havana Heat, Bronx Beat.* (1992).

CARNER, GARY, ED. *The Miles Davis Companion: Four Decades of Commentary* (1996).

CARR, IAN. *Miles Davis: A Biography* (1982).

CHAMBERS, JACK. *Milestones.* 2 vols. (1983–1985).

CHARTERS, SAMUEL B. *The Bluesmen.* 2 vols. (1967–1977).

CHILTON, JOHN. *The Song of the Hawk: The Life and Recordings of Coleman Hawkins* (1990).

CLARK, SEBASTIAN. *Jah Music* (1980).

COLLIER, JAMES LINCOLN. *The Making of Jazz: A Comprehensive History* (1978).

COLLINS, R. *New Orleans Jazz: A Revised History: The Development of American Jazz from the Origin to the Big Bands* (1996).

DAVIS, STEPHEN, AND PETER SIMON. *Reggae International* (1983).

DE WILDE, LAURENT. *Monk* (1997).

DIXON, WILLIE. *I Am the Blues: The Willie Dixon Story* (1989).

DUGGY, JOHN. *Prince: An Illustrated Biography* (1995).

ERLEWINE, MICHAEL, ET AL., EDS. *All Music Guide to Jazz: The Experts' Guide to the Best Jazz Recordings* (1996).

FLOYD, SAMUEL, ED. *Black Music in the Harlem Renaissance* (1990).

GABBARD, KRIN, ED. *Representing Jazz* (1995).

GEORGE, NELSON. *Where Did Our Love Go?: The Rise and Fall of the Motown Sound* (1985).

GEORGE, NELSON, ET AL., EDS. *Fresh: Hip Hop Don't Stop* (1985).

GILLESPIE, JOHN BIRKS ("DIZZY"), WITH AL FRASER. *Dizzy To BE, or Not . . . to BOP: The Autobiography of Dizzy Gillespie* (1979).

GOURSE, LESLIE. *Unforgettable: The Life and Mystique of Nat King Cole* (1991).

GROIA, PHILIP. *They All Sang on the Corner: A Second Look at New York City's Rhythm and Blues Vocal Groups* (1983).

GUILBAULT, JOCELYNE, WITH GAGE AVEHILL, EDOUARD BENOIT, AND GREGORY RABESS. *Zouk: World Music in the West Indies* (1993).

GURALNICK, PETER. *Searching for Robert Johnson* (1989).

———. *Sweet Soul Music: Rhythm and Blues and the Southern Dream of Freedom* (1986).

HANDY, WILLIAM C. *Father of the Blues: An Autobiography.* Edited by Arna Bontemps (1941).

HASKINS, JAMES. *Bricktop* (1983).

———. *Mabel Mercer: A Life* (1987).

HASKINS, JAMES, AND N. R. MITGANG. *Mr. Bojangles: The Biography of Bill Robinson* (1988).

HEILBUT, ANTHONY. *The Gospel Sound: Good News and Bad Times* (1971).

HELM, MACKINLEY. *Angel Mo' and Her Son, Roland Hayes* (1942).

HOSIASSON, JOSE. "Kid Ory." *In New Grove Dictionary of Jazz* (1988).

JAMES, MICHAEL. *Ten Modern Jazzmen: An Appraisal of the Recorded Work of Ten Modern Jazzmen* (1960).

JASEN, DAVID A., AND TREBOR TICHENOR. *Rags and Ragtime: A Musical History* (1989).

KENNEY, WILLIAM ROWLAND. *Chicago Jazz: A Cultural History, 1904–1930* (1993).

KING, B. B., WITH DAVID RITZ. *Blues All Around Me: The Autobiography of B. B. King* (1996).

KITT, EARTHA. *Alone with Me* (1976).

———. *Thursday's Child* (1956).

KNAACK, TWILA. *Ethel Waters: I Touched a Sparrow* (1978).

KNIGHT, GLADYS. *Between Each Line of Pain and Glory: My Life Story* (1997).

LEES, GENE. *Oscar Peterson: The Will to Swing* (1988).

LICHTENSTEIN, GRACE, AND LAURA DANKNER. *Musical Gumbo: The Music of New Orleans* (1993).

LOMAX, ALAN. *Mister Jelly Roll: The Fortunes of Jelly Roll Morton, New Orleans Creole and Inventor of Jazz* (1973).

———. *The Land Where the Blues Began* (1993).

LYONS, LEONARD. *The Great Jazz Pianists: Speaking of Their Lives and Music* (1983).

MANUEL, PETER, ED. *Essays on Cuban Music: North American and Cuban Perspectives* (1991).

MANUEL, PETER, WITH KENNETH BILBY AND MICHAEL LARGEY. *Caribbean Currents: Caribbean Music from Rumba to Reggae* (1995).

MARQUIS, DONALD M. *In Search of Buddy Bolden: First Man of Jazz* (1978).

MARSH, J. B. T. *The Story of the Jubilee Singers with Their Songs* (1880; reprint ed., 1971).

MCGOWAN, CHRIS, AND RICARDO PESSANHA. *The Brazilian Sound: Samba, Bossa Nova, and the Popular Music of Brazil* (1991).

MORGAN, THOMAS L., AND WILLIAM BARLOW. *From Cakewalks to Concert Halls: An Illustrated History of African-American Popular Music from 1895–1930* (1992).

MAKEBA, MIRIAM, WITH JAMES HALL. *Makeba: My Story* (1988).

OLIVER, PAUL. *Songsters and Saints: Vocal Traditions on Race Records* (1984).

——, ED. *Black Music in Britain: Essays on the Afro-Asian Contribution to Popular Music* (1990).

OSPINA, HERNANDO CALVO. *Salsa: Havana Beat, Bronx Beat* (1985).

OTIS, JOHNNY. *Upside Your Head!: Rhythm and Blues on Central Avenue* (1993).

OWENS, THOMAS. *Bebop: The Music and Its Players* (1995).

PALMER, RICHARD. *Oscar Peterson* (1984).

PALMER, ROBERT. *Deep Blues* (1981).

PLACKSIN, SALLY. *American Women in Jazz: 1900 to the Present: Their Words, Lives, and Music* (1982).

POTASH, CHRIS, ED. *Reggae, Rasta, Revolution: Jamaican Music from Ska to Dub* (1997).

PRIDE, CHARLEY. *Pride: The Charley Pride Story* (1994).

PRUTER, ROBERT. *Doowop: The Chicago Scene* (1996).

Rap on Rap: Straight Up Talk on Hip Hop Culture. Compiled by Adam Sexton (1995).

REDD, LAWRENCE N. *Rock Is Rhythm and Blues: The Impact of Mass Media* (1974).

RITZ, DAVID. *Divided Soul: The Life of Marvin Gaye* (1985).

ROBERTS, JOHN STORM. *The Latin Tinge: The Impact of Latin American Music on the United States* (1979).

ROBESON, PAUL. *Here I Stand* (1958).

ROBESON, SUSAN. *The Whole World in His Hands: A Pictorial Biography of Paul Robeson* (1981).

RO, RONIN. *Gangsta Merchandizing the Rhymes of Violence* (1996).

ROSE AL. *Eubie Blake* (1979).

ROSE, TRICIA. *Black Noise: Rap Music and Black Culture in Contemporary America* (1994).

RUSSELL, ROSS. *Bird Lives: The High Life and Hard Times of Charlie (Yardbird) Parker* (1973).

——. *Jazz Style in Kansas City and the Southwest* (1971).

SCHULLER, GUNTHER. *Early Jazz: Its Roots and Musical Development* (1968).

——. *The Swing Era: The Development of Jazz, 1930–1945* (1989).

SHAW, ARNOLD. *Honkers and Shouters: The Golden Years of Rhythm and Blues* (1978).

SILVESTER, PETER. *A Left Hand like God: A History of Boogie-Woogie Piano* (1988).

SIMKINS, CUTHBERT O. *Coltrane: A Musical Biography* (1975).

SINGER, BARRY. *Black and Blue: The Life and Lyrics of Andy Razaf* (1992).

SOUTHERN, EILEEN. *The Music of Black Americans: A History* (1983).

SPELLMAN, A. B. *Black Music: Four Lives* (1970).

STEWART-BAXTER, DERRICK. *Ma Rainey and the Classic Blues Singers* (1970).

STILL, JUDITH ANNE. *William Grant Still: A Bio-bibliography* (1996).

STINSON, SULEE JEAN. *The Dawn of Blaxploitation: Sweet Sweetback's Baadasssss Song and its Audience* (1992).

STORY, ROSALYN M. *And So I Sing: African-American Divas of Opera and Concert* (1990).

SWENSON, JOHN. *Stevie Wonder* (1986).

TAYLOR, FRANK. *Alberta Hunter: A Celebration in Blues* (1987).

TOOP, DAVID. *Ocean of Sound: Aether Talk, Ambient Sound, and Imaginary Worlds* (1995).

TURNER, FREDERICK W. *Remembering Song: Encounters with the New Orleans Jazz Tradition*. Exp. ed. (1994).

ULLMAN, MICHAEL. *Jazz Lives: Portraits in Words and Pictures* (1980).

WEINSTEIN, NORMAN. *A Night in Tunisia: Imaginings of Africa in Jazz* (1993).

WHITE, TIMOTHY. *Catch a Fire: The Life of Bob Marley*. Rev. and enl. ed. (1998).

WILSON, MARY, WITH PATRICIA ROMANOWSKI AND AHRGUS JUILLIARD. *Dreamgirl: My Life as a Supreme* (1986).

WOIDEK, CARL. *Charlie Parker: His Music and Life* (1996).

PERFORMING ARTS

ALPERT, HOLLIS. *The Life and Times of Porgy and Bess* (1990).

ASCHENBRENNER, JOYCE. *Katherine Dunham: Reflections on the Social and Political Aspects of Afro-American Dance* (1981).

BECKFORD, RUTH. *Katherine Dunham: A Biography* (1979).

BORDERS, WILLIAM H. *Seven Minutes at the Mike in the Deep South* (1943).

BOSKIN, JOSEPH. *Sambo: The Rise and Demise of an American Jester* (1986).

BROWNING, BARBARA. *Samba: Resistance in Motion* (1995).

COOPER, RALPH, WITH STEVE DOUGHERTY. *Amateur Night at the Apollo: Ralph Cooper Presents Five Decades of Great Entertainment* (1990).

EMERY, LYNNE FAULEY. *Black Dance in the United States from 1619 to 1970* (1980).

FLETCHER, TOM. *One Hundred Years of the Negro in Show Business* (1984).

FOX, TED. *Showtime at the Apollo* (1983).

FRANK, RUSTY E. *Tap! The Greatest Tap Dance Stars and Their Stories, 1900–1955* (1990).

FUNKE, LEWIS. *The Curtain Rises: The Story of Ossie Davis* (1971).

HASKINS, JAMES. *Black Dance in America: A History through Its People* (1990).

LONG, RICHARD. *The Black Tradition in American Dance* (1989).

MALONE, JACQUI. *Steppin' on the Blues: The Visible Rhythms of African-American Dance* (1996).

MAPP, EDWARD. *Directory of Blacks in the Performing Arts* (1990).

MAYNARD, OLGA. *Judith Jamison: Aspects of a Dancer* (1982).

OLANIYAN, TEJUMOLA. *Scars of Conquest/ Masks of Resistance: The Invention of Cultural Identities in African, African-American, and Caribbean Drama* (1995).

PLASTOW, JANE. *Ethiopia: The Creation of a Theater Culture* (1989).

RULE, SHEILA. "Fredi Washington, 90, Actress; Broke Ground for Black Artists." *New York Times* (June 30, 1994): D21.

STEARNS, MARSHALL, AND JEAN STEARNS. *Jazz Dance: The Story of American Vernacular Dance.* Rev. ed. (1979).

THORPE, EDWARD. *Black Dance* (1990).

WALKER, ETHEL PITTS. "The American Negro Theater." In *The Theater of Black Americans.* Edited by Errol Hill (1987).

WATKINS, MEL. *On The Real Side: Laughing, Lying, and Signifying. The Underground Tradition of African-American Humor* (1994).

WILLIAMS, ELSIE A. *The Humor of Jackie Moms Mabley: An African-American Comedic Tradition* (1995).

POLITICAL AND SOCIAL MOVEMENTS

BERNSTEIN, IVER. *The New York City Draft Riots: Their Significance for American Society and Politics in the Age of the Civil War* (1990).

BOYKIN, KEITH. *One More River to Cross: Black and Gay in America* (1996).

BRACEY, JOHN H., JR., ET AL., EDS. *Black Nationalism in America* (1970).

BRISBANE, ROBERT. *Black Activism: Racial Revolution in the U.S., 1954–70* (1974).

BROWN, H. RAP. *Die, Nigger, Die!* (1969).

BUHLE, PAUL. *C. L. R. James: The Artist as Revolutionary* (1988).

CAPECI, DOMINIC J., JR. *The Harlem Riot of 1943* (1977).

FORMAN, JAMES. *The Making of Black Revolutionaries* (1985).

FRANKLIN, JOHN HOPE, AND AUGUST MEIER, EDS. *Black Leaders of the Twentieth Century* (1982).

GEIS, IMMANUEL. *The Pan-African Movement: A History of Pan-Africanism in America, Europe and Africa* (1974).

HALL, JACQUELYN DOWD. *Revolt Against Chivalry: Jessie Daniel Ames and the Women's Campaign Against Lynching* (1979).

HALL, STUART, AND MARTIN JACQUES, EDS. *New Times: The Changing Face of Politics in the 1990s* (1990).

JACQUES-GARVEY, AMY, ED. *Philosophy and Opinions of Marcus Garvey (1923–1925).*

JAMES, C. L. R. *The Black Jacobins: Toussaint L'Ouverture and the San Domingo Revolution* (1963).

———. *A History of Pan-African Revolt* (1969).

KESSELMAN, LOUIS. *The Social Politics of FEPC: A Study in Reform Pressure Movements* (1948).

KRADITOR, AILEEN S. *Means and Ends in American Abolitionism: Garrison and His Critics on Strategy and Tactics, 1834–1850* (1989).

LIPZITZ, GEORGE. *A Life in the Struggle: Ivory Perry and the Culture of Opposition* (1988).

LYNCH, HOLLIS R. *Black American Radicals and the Liberation of Africa: The Council on African Affairs, 1937–1955* (1978).

MOSES, WILSON JEREMIAH. *The Golden Age of Black Nationalism: 1850–1925* (1978).

PIVEN, FRANCES FOX, AND RICHARD A. CLOWARD. *Poor People's Movements: Why They Succeed, How They Fail* (1977).

REDKEY, EDWIN S. *Black Exodus: Black Nationalist and Back-to-Africa Movements, 1890–1910* (1969).

REDMON, COATES. *Come As You Are: The Peace Corps Story* (1986).

RICHARDS, LEONARD L. *Gentleman of Property and Standing: Anti-Abolition Mobs in Jacksonian America* (1970).

VAN DEBURG, WILLIAM L. *New Day in Babylon: The Black Power Movement and American Culture, 1965–1975* (1992).

VENET, WENDY HAMMOND. *Neither Ballots nor Bullets: Women Abolitionists and the Civil War* (1991).

WEST, GUIDA. *The National Welfare Rights Movement: The Social Protest of Poor Women* (1981).

YELLIN, JEAN PAGAN, AND JOHN C. VAN HORNE, EDS. *The Abolitionist Sisterhood: Women's Political Culture in Antebellum America* (1994).

POLITICS AND GOVERNMENT: AFRICA

ALLEN, PHILIP M. *Madagascar: Conflicts of Authority in the Great Island* (1995).

ASCHERSON, NEAL. *The King Incorporated: Leopold II in the Age of Trusts* (1963).

BEYAN, AMOS J. *The American Colonization Society and the Creation of the Liberian State: A Historical Perspective, 1822–1900* (1991).

BOWMAN, LARRY W. *Mauritius: Democracy and Development in the Indian Ocean* (1991).

CHRISTIE, IAIN. *Samora Machel: A Biography* (1989).

CHRISTOPHER, A. J. *The Atlas of Apartheid* (1994).

COHEN, RONALD, GORAN HYDEN, AND WINSTON P. NAGAN, EDS. *Human Rights and Governance in Africa* (1993).

GOUREVITCH, PHILIP. *We Wish to Inform You that Tomorrow We Will Be Killed with Our Families: Stories from Rwanda* (1998).

HALL, MARGARET, AND TOM YOUNG. *Confronting Leviathan: Mozambique Since Independence* (1997).

HOCHSCHILD, ADAM. *King Leopold's Ghost: A Story of Greed, Terror, and Heroism in Colonial Africa* (1998).

IHONVBERE, JULIUS O. *Economic Crisis, Civil Society, and Democratization: The Case of Zambia* (1996).

LEMARCHAND, RENÉ. *Political Awakening in the Belgian Congo* (1964).

LESLIE, WINESOME J. *Zaire: Continuity and Political Change in an Oppressive State* (1993).

JOYCE, PETER. *Anatomy of a Rebel: Smith of Rhodesia: A Biography* (1974).

MUNSLOW, BARRY, ED. *Samora Machel, an African Revolutionary: Selected Speeches and Writings* (1985).

MANDELA, NELSON. *Long Walk to Freedom: The Autobiography of Nelson Mandela* (1994).

———. *The Struggle Is My Life: His Speeches and Writings Brought Together to Mark His 60th Birthday* (1978).

MANNICK, A. R. *Mauritius: The Politics of Change* (1989).

MAZRUI, ALI A. *The Africans: A Triple Heritage* (1986).

MINTER, WILLIAM. *Apartheid's Contras: An Inquiry into the Pools of War in Angola and Mozambique* (1994).

NKOMO, JOSHUA. *Nkomo: The. Story of My Life* (1984).

———. *Zimbabwe Must and Shall Be Totally Free* (1977).

NYERERE, JULIUS K. *The Arusha Declaration: Ten Years After* (1977).

———. *Freedom and Socialism: Uhuru na Ujamaa: A Selection from Writings and Speeches, 1965–1967* (1968).

———. *Ujamaa: Essays on Socialism* (1971).

ORMOND, ROGER. *The Apartheid Handbook: A Guide to South Africa's Everyday Racial Policies* (1985).

QUINN, CHARLOTTE. *Mandingo Kingdoms of the Senegambia: Traditionalism, Islam, and European Expansion* (1972).

RAKE, ALAN. *Who's Who in Africa: Leaders for the 1990s* (1992).

RUEDY, JOHN. *Modern Algeria: The Origins and Development of a Nation* (1992).

SALEM, NORMA. *Habib Bourguiba, Islam and the Creation of Tunisia* (1984).

SCHATZBERG, MICHAEL. *The Dialectics of Oppression in Zaire* (1988).

SMITH, IAN DOUGLAS. *The Great Betrayal: The Memoirs of Ian Douglas Smith* (1997).

THOMAS, ANTONY. *Rhodes* (1996).

VANSINA, JAN. *Paths in the Rainforests: Toward a History of Political Tradition in Equatorial Africa* (1990).

VINES, ALEX. *Renamo: Terrorism in Mozambique* (1991).

WILLIAMS, MICHAEL W. *Pan-Africanism: An Annotated Bibliography* (1992).

YOUNG, CRAWFORD. *Politics in the Congo: Decolonization and Independence* (1965).

POLITICS AND GOVERNMENT: LATIN AMERICA AND THE CARIBBEAN

ABBOTT, ELIZABETH. *Haiti: The Duvaliers and Their Legacy* (1988).

CONGRESS, RICK. *The Afro-Nicaraguans: The Revolution and Autonomy* (1987).

CONNIFF, MICHAEL L., AND THOMAS J. DAVIS. *Africans in the Americas: The History of the Black Diaspora* (1994).

DAVIS, H. P. *Black Democracy: The Story of Haiti* (1967).

FERGUSON, JAMES. *Papa Doc, Baby Doc: Haiti and the Duvaliers* (1987).

GAY, ROBERT. *Popular Organization and Democracy in Rio de Janeiro: A Tale of Two Favelas* (1994).

JEFFREY, HENRY B., AND COLIN BASER. *Guyana: Politics, Economics, and Society: Beyond the Burnham Era* (1986).

LOCKHART, JAMES. *Spanish Peru, 1532–1560: A Social History* (1994).

LUMDSEN, I. *Society and the State in Mexico* (1991).

MORAN, CHARLES. *Black Triumvirate: A Study of L'Ouverture, Dessalines, Christophe: The Men Who Made Haiti* (1957).

PERLMAN, JANICE. *The Myth of Marginality: Urban Poverty and Politics in Rio de Janeiro* (1973).

THOMAS, HUGH. *Cuba: The Pursuit of Freedom* (1971).

VANDERCOOK, JOHN W. *Black Majesty: The Life of Christophe, King of Haiti* (1934).

WILLIAMS, ERIC. *Inward Hunger: The Education of a Prime Minister* (1969).

WORCESTER, KENT. *C. L. R. James and the American Century, 1938–1953* (1980).

POLITICS AND GOVERNMENT: NORTH AMERICA

AGRONSKY, JONATHAN. *Marion Barry: The Politics of Race* (1991).

BERRY, JASON. *Amazing Grace: With Charles Evers in Mississippi* (1973).

BUNI, ANDREW. *The Negro in Virginia Politics, 1902–1965* (1967).

CARMICHAEL, STOKELY, AND CHARLES V. HAMILTON. *Black Power: The Politics of Liberation in America* (1992).

CHISHOLM, SHIRLEY. *Unbought and Unbossed* (1970).

CLAY, WILLIAM L. *Just Permanent Interests: Black Americans in Congress, 1870–1991* (1992).

CUTLER, JOHN HENRY. *Ed Brooke: Biography of a Senator* (1972).

DUFFY, SUSAN. "Shirley Chisholm." In *American Orators of the Twentieth Century.* Edited by Barnard K. Duffy and Halford R. Ryan (1987).

FRADY, MARSHALL. *Jesse: The Life and Pilgrimage of Jesse Jackson* (1996).

GAVINS, RAYMOND. *The Perils and Prospects of Southern Black Leadership: Gordon Blaine Hancock, 1884–1970* (1977).

GOSNELL, HAROLD F. *Negro Politicians: The Rise of Negro Politics in Chicago* (1967).

HAMILTON, CHARLES V. *Adam Clayton Powell, Jr.: The Political Biography of an American Dilemma* (1991).

HASKINS, JAMES. *Pinckney Benton Stewart Pinchback* (1973).

HAYGOOD, WIL. *King of the Cats: The Life and Times of Adam Clayton Powell, Jr.* (1993).

JORDAN, BARBARA, AND SHELBY HEARON. *Barbara Jordan: A Self-Portrait* (1979).

KIRWAN, ALBERT DENNIS. *John J. Crittenden: The Struggle for the Union* (1962).

KLEHR, HARVEY. *The Heyday of American Communism: The Depression Decade* (1984).

KLEPPNER, PAUL. *Chicago Divided: The Making of a Black Mayor* (1985).

KOUSSER, J. MORGAN. *The Shaping of Southern Politics: Suffrage Restriction and the Establishment of the One-Party South, 1880–1910* (1974).

LYNCH, JOHN ROY. *Reminiscences of an Active Life: The Autobiography of John Roy Lynch.* Edited by John Hope Franklin (1970).

NEWTON, HUEY P. *To Die for the People: The Writings of Huey Newton* (1972).

———. *War Against the Panthers: A Study of Repression in America* (1997).

OBADELE, IMARI. *America the Nation State: The Politics of the United States from a State-building Perspective* (1988).

O'REILLY, KENNETH. *Nixon's Piano: Presidents and Racial Politics from Washington to Clinton* (1995).

PAYNE J. GREGORY, AND SCOTT C. RATZAN. *Tom Bradley: The Impossible Dream: A Biography* (1986).

PHELPS, TIMOTHY M., AND HELEN WINTERNITZ. *Capitol Games: The Inside Story of Clarence Thomas and Anita Hill, and a Supreme Court Nomination* (1993).

POWELL, COLIN L. *My American Journey* (1995).

RAGAN, SANDRA L. ET AL., ED. *The Lynching of Language: Gender, Politics, and Power in the Hill-Thomas Hearings* (1996).

ROTH, DAVID. *Sacred Honor: A Biography of Colin Powell* (1993).

SCHEADER, CATHERINE. *Shirley Chisholm: Teacher and Congresswoman* (1990).

URQUHART, BRIAN. *Ralph Bunche: An American Life* (1993).

WARE, GILBERT. *William Hastie: Grace Under Pressure* (1984).

WEINBERG, KENNETH G. *Black Victory: Carl Stokes and the Winning of Cleveland* (1968).

WEISS, NANCY J. *Farewell to the Party of Lincoln: Black Politics in the Age of FDR* (1983).

YANCEY, DWAYNE. *When Hell Froze Over: The Untold Story of Doug Wilder: A Black Politician's Rise to Power in the South* (1988).

PRESS AND PERIODICALS

BLASSINGAME, JOHN W., AND MAE G. HENDERSON, EDS. *Antislavery Newspapers and Periodicals.* 5 vols. (1980).

BULLOCK, PENELOPE L. *The Afro-American Periodical Press, 1838–1909* (1981).

CROUCHETT, LORRAINE J. *Delilah Leontium Beasley: Oakland's Crusading Journalist* (1990).

DAWKINS, WAYNE. *Black Journalists: The NABJ Story* (1993).

HOFFMAN, FREDERICK J., CHARLES ALLEN, AND CAROLYN R. ULRICH. *The Little Magazine: A History and a Bibliography* (1946).

JACOBS, DONALD M. *Antebellum Black Newspapers* (1976).

JOHNSON, ABBY ARTHUR, AND RONALD MABERRY JOHNSON. *Propaganda and Aesthetics: The Literary Politics of African-American Magazines in the Twentieth Century* (1991).

JOYCE, DONALD FRANKLIN. *Black Book Publishers in the United Slates: A Historical Dictionary of the Presses, 1817–1990* (1991).

———. *Gatekeepers of Black Culture: Black-Owned Book Publishing in the United Slates, 1817–1981* (1983).

MCMURRY, LINDA O. *Recorder of the Black Experience: Biography of Monroe Nathan Work* (1985).

ORIARD, MICHAEL. *Reading Football: How the Popular Press Created an American Spectacle* (1993).

SUGGS, HENRY LEWIS. *P. B. Young, Newspaperman: Race, Politics, and Journalism in the New South, 1910–1962* (1988).

WOLSELEY, ROLAND E. *The Black Press, U.S.A.* (1990).

RACE AND RACE RELATIONS

APPIAH, KWAME ANTHONY. *The Ethics of Identity* (2005).

APPIAH, KWAME ANTHONY, AND AMY GUTMANN. *Color Conscious: The Political Morality of Race* (1996).

ANDREWS, GEORGE REID. *Blacks and Whites in Sao Paulo, Brazil, 1888–1988* (1991).

ASANTE, MOLEFI KETE. *The Afrocentric Idea* (1987).

———. *Afrocentricity* (1988).

———. *Kemet, Afrocentricity, and Knowledge* (1990).

BENNETT, NORMAN. *Arab versus European: Diplomacy and War in Nineteenth-Century East Central Africa* (1986).

BLAKELY, ALLISON. *Blacks in the Dutch World: The Evolution of Racial Imagery in a Modern Society* (1993).

———. *Russia and the Negro: Blacks in Russian History and Thought* (1986).

BROUSSARD, ALBERT S. *Black San Francisco: The Struggle for Racial Equality in the West, 1900–1954* (1993).

BROWN, TONY. *Black Lies, White Lies: The Truth According to Tony Brown* (1995).

CAREW, JAN. *Fulcrums of Change: Origins of Racism in the Americas* (1988).

CONNIFF, MICHAEL L. *Black Labor on a White Canal: Panama 1904–1981* (1985).

CORTNER, RICHARD C. *A Mob Intent on Death: The NAACP and the Arkansas Riot Cases* (1988).

COUNTER, S. ALLEN. *North Pole Legacy: Black, White and Eskimo* (1991).

D'ORSO, MICHAEL. *Like Judgement Day: The Ruin and Redemption of a Town Called Rosewood* (1996).

ELLSWORTH, SCOTT. *Death in a Promised Land: The Tulsa Race Riot of 1921* (1982).

FORBES, JACK D. *Africans and Native Americans: The Language of Race and the Evolution of Red-Black Peoples* (1988).

FRAZIER, E. FRANKLIN. *On Race Relations: Selected Writings. Edited by Gilbert Edwards* (1968).

GATES, HENRY LOUIS, JR. *Thirteen Ways of Looking at a Black Man* (1997).

GATES, HENRY LOUIS, JR., AND CORNEL WEST. *The Future of the Race* (1996).

GILROY, PAUL. *There Ain't No Black in the Union Jack: The Cultural Politics of Race and Nation* (1991).

GUZMAN, JESSIE P. *Crusade for Civic Democracy: The Story of the Tuskegee Civic Association, 1941–1970* (1985).

HAIR, WILLIAM IVY. *Carnival of Fury: Robert Charles and the New Orleans Race Riot of 1900* (1976).

HALL, STUART. "Racism and Reaction." *In Five Views on Multi-Racial Britain* (1978).

HARRIS, FRED R., AND ROGER WILKINS, EDS. *Quiet Riots: Race and Poverty in the United States* (1988).

HARRISON, ALFERDTEEN, ED. *Black Exodus: The Great Migration from the American South* (1991).

HAYDEN, TOM. *Rebellion in Newark: Official Violence and Ghetto Response* (1967).

HIRSH, ARNOLD R., AND JOSEPH LOGSDON. *Creole New Orleans: Race and Americanization* (1992).

HOLDREDGE, HELEN. *Mammy Pleasant* (1953).

HUTCHINSON, EARL OFARI. *Betrayed: A History of Presidential Failure to Protect Black Lives* (1996).

———. *Blacks and Reds: Race and Class in Conflict, 1919–1990* (1995).

LANE, ANN J. *The Brownsville Affair: National Crisis and Black Reaction* (1971).

LANE, ROGER. *Roots of Violence in Black Philadelphia, 1860–1900* (1986).

LOVE, SPENCIE. *One Blood: The Death and Resurrection of Charles Drew* (1996).

MALCOLM X, WITH ALEX HALEY. *The Autobiography of Malcolm X* (1964).

MARTIN, TONY. *Race First: The Ideological and Organizational Struggles of Marcus Garvey and the Universal Negro Improvement Association* (1986).

MILLER, FLOYD J. *The Search for a Black Nationality: Black Colonization and Emigration, 1787–1863* (1975).

MOORE, JOSEPH THOMAS. *Pride Against Prejudice: The Biography of Larry Doby* (1988).

MORRISON, TONI. *Playing in the Dark: Whiteness and the Literary Imagination* (1992).

———, ED. *Race-ing Justice, En-gendering Power: Essays on Anita Hill, Clarence Thomas, and the Construction of Social Reality* (1992).

MUNFORD, CLARENCE. *Race and Reparations: A Black Perspective for the Twenty-First Century* (1996).

MYRDAL, GUNNAR. *An American Dilemma: The Negro Problem and Modern Democracy* (1944).

NASCIMENTO, ABDIAS DO. *Africans in Brazil: A Pan-African Perspective* (1992).

———. *Racial Democracy in Brazil, Myth or Reality?: A Dossier of Brazilian Racism.* Translated by Elisa Larkin do Nascimento; foreword by Wole Soyinka (1977).

NASH, GARY B. *Forging Freedom: The Formation of Philadelphia's Black Community, 1720–1840* (1988).

———. *Race and Revolution* (1990).

PATTERSON, ORLANDO. *Freedom in the Making of Western Culture* (1991).

———. *The Ordeal of Integration: Progress and Resentment in America's "Racial" Crisis* (1997).

———. *Rituals of Blood: Consequences of Slavery in Two American Centuries* (1998).

PRATHER, H. LEON. *We Have Taken a City: Wilmington Racial Massacre and Coup of 1898* (1984).

RABINOWITZ, HOWARD N. *Race Relations in the Urban South, 1865–1890* (1996).

RAMOS, ARTHUR. *The Negro in Brazil* (1951).

RIVLIN, GARY. *Fire on the Prairie: Chicago's Harold Washington and the Politics of Race* (1993).

RUDWICK, ELLIOTT M. *Race Riot at East St. Louis, July 2, 1917* (1964).

SHOGAN, ROBERT, AND TOM CRAIG. *The Detroit Race Riot: A Study in Violence* (1964).

SKIDMORE, THOMAS E. *Black into White: Race and Nationality in Brazilian Thought* (1974; revised ed., 1993).

SMITH-IRVIN, JEANNETTE. *Footsoldiers of the Universal Negro Improvement Association: Their Own Words* (1988).

SULLIVAN, PATRICIA. *Days of Hope: Race and Democracy in the New Deal Era* (1996).

THOMAS, BROOK. *Plessy v. Ferguson: A Brief History with Documents* (1997).

TUTTLE, WILLIAM M., JR. *Race Riot: Chicago in the Red Summer of 1919* (1970).

———, ED. *W. E. B. Du Bois* (1973).

ULLMAN, VICTOR. *Martin R. Delany: The Beginnings of Black Nationalism* (1971).

WADE, PETER. *Blackness and Race Mixture: The Dynamics of Racial Identity in Colombia* (1993).

———. *Race and Ethnicity in Latin America* (1997).

WAGLEY, CHARLES, ED. *Race and Class in Rural Brazil.* 2d ed. (1963).

WEAVER, JOHN DOWNING. *The Brownsville Raid* (1970).

———. *The Senator and the Sharecropper's Son: Exoneration of the Brownsville Soldiers* (1997).

WEST, CORNEL. *Beyond Eurocentrism and Multiculturalism* (1993).

———. *Black Theology and Marxist Thought* (1979).

———. *Keeping Faith: Philosophy and Race in America* (1993).

———. *Prophetic Reflections: Notes on Race and Power in America* (1993).

———. *Race Matters* (1993).

WHITFIELD, STEPHEN J. *A Death in the Delta: The Story of Emmett Till* (1988).

WILLIAMSON, JOEL. *After Slavery: The Negro in South Carolina During Reconstruction, 1861–1877* (1965; reprint ed., 1990).

———. *The Crucible of Race: Black-White Relations in the American South Since Emancipation* (1984).

———. *New People: Miscegenation and Mulattoes in the United States* (1980).

WILSON, WILLIAM JULIUS. *The Bridge over the Racial Divide: Rising Inequality and Coalition Politics* (1999).

WOLFENSTEIN, EUGENE VICTOR. *The Victims of Democracy: Malcolm X and the Black Revolution* (1981).

WOOD, JOE, ED. *Malcolm X: In Our Own Image* (1992).

RELIGION

AUSTIN-BROOS, DIANE. *Jamaica Genesis: Religion and the Politics of Moral Orders* (1997).

BAER, HANS A., AND MERRIL SINGER. *African-American Religion in the Twentieth Century: Varieties of Protest and Accommodation* (1992).

BOFF, C., AND L. BOFF. *Introducing Liberation Theology* (1987).

BRAGG, GEORGE FREEMAN. *The History of the Afro-American Group of the Episcopal Church* (1968).

———. *The Story of the First Blacks: Absalom Jones* (1929).

BROWN, DIANA DEGROAT. *Umbanda: Religion and Politics in Urban Brazil* (1994).

CAMPBELL, JAMES T. *Songs of Zion: The African Methodist Episcopal Church in the United States and South Africa* (1995).

CARVALHO, JOSE JORGE DE, AND RITA LAURA SEGATO. *Shango Cult in Recife, Brazil* (1992).

CONE, JAMES H. *Martin and Malcolm and America: A Dream or a Nightmare* (1991).

CONSENTING, DONALD J., ED. *Sacred Arts of Haitian Vodou* (1995).

COX, HARVEY. *Fire from Heaven: The Rise of Pentecostal Spirituality and the Reshaping of Religion in the Twenty-first Century* (1995).

DAVIS, CYPRIAN. *The History of Black Catholics in the United States* (1990).

DEREN, MAYA. *Divine Horsemen: The Living Gods of Haiti* (1953).

DESMANGLES, LESLIE G. *The Faces of the Gods: Vodou and Roman Catholicism in Haiti* (1992).

DORSEY, THOMAS ANDREW. *Say Amen, Somebody* (1983).

DOUGLASS, WILLIAM. *Annals of the First African Church in the United States of America, Now Styled the African Episcopal Church of St. Thomas, Philadelphia* (1862).

FAIRCLOUGH, ADAM. *To Redeem the Soul of America: The Southern Christian Leadership Conference and Martin Luther King, Jr.* (1987).

FOLEY, ALBERT S. *Bishop Healy: Beloved Outcaste* (1954).

FOOTE, JULIA. *A Brand Plucked From the Fire.* In *Spiritual Narratives.* Edited by Henry Louis Gates, Jr. (1988).

FONER, PHILIP, ED. *Black Socialist Preacher: The Teachings of Reverend George Washington Woodbey and His Disciple Reverend George W. Slater, Jr.* (1983).

GEORGE, CAROL V. R. *Segregated Sabbaths: Richard Alien and the Emergence of Independent Black Churches 1760–1840* (1972).

GLAZIER, STEPHEN D. *Marchin' the Pilgrims Home* (1983).

———, ED. *Perspectives on Pentecostalism: Case Studies from the Caribbean and Latin America* (1980).

GONZÁLEZ-WHIPPLER, MIGENE. *The Santeria Experience: A Journey into the Miraculous.* Rev. and exp. ed. (1992).

GRAY, RICHARD. *Black Christians and White Missionaries* (1990).

HAYES, DIANA L. *And Still We Rise: An Introduction to Black Liberation Theology* (1996).

HIGGINBOTHAM, EVELYN BROOKS. *Righteous Discontent: The Women's Movement in the Black Baptist Church, 1880–1920* (1993).

JONES, RALPH H. *Charles Albert Tindley: Prince of Preachers* (1982).

KLOTS, STEVE. *Richard Alien* (1991).

KOSTARELOS, FRANCES. *Feeling the Spirit: Faith and Hope in an Evangelical Black Storefront Church* (1995).

LINCOLN, C. ERIC, AND LAWRENCE MAMIYA. *The Black Church in the African-American Experience* (1990).

MACROBERT, IAIN. *The Black Roots and White Racism of Early Pentecostalism in the U.S.A.* (1988).

MARTIN, MARIE-LOUISE. *Kimbangu: An African Prophet and His Church* (1975).

MATORY, J. LORAND. *Sex and the Empire That Is No More: Gender and the Politics of Metaphor in Oyo Yoruba Religion* (1994).

MCKIVIGAN, JOHN R. *The War against Proslavery Religion: Abolitionism and the Northern Churches, 1830–1865* (1984).

METRAUX, ALFRED. *Voodoo in Haiti* (1959).

MOSES, WILSON JEREMIAH. *Black Messiahs and Uncle Toms: Social and Literary Manipulation of a Religious Myth* (1982).

MUDIMBE, VALENTIN. *The Invention of Africa: Gnosis, Philosophy, and the Order of Knowledge* (1988).

MURPHY, JOSEPH M. *Working the Spirit: Ceremonies of the African Diaspora* (1994).

OCHS, STEPHEN J. *Desegregating the Altar: The Josephites and the Struggle for Black Priests, 1871–1960* (1970).

PARIS, PETER. *Black Religious Leaders: Conflict in Unity* (1991).

PAYNE, DANIEL A. *History of the African Methodist Episcopal Church.* Vol. I (1891; reprint ed., 1968).

RAY, BENJAMIN. *African Religions: Symbol, Ritual, and Community* (1976).

SIMPSON, GEORGE EATON. *Black Religions in the New World* (1978).

THURMAN, HOWARD. *With Head and Heart: The Autobiography of Howard Thurman* (1979).

TOBIAS, CHANNING. "Autobiography." In *Thirteen Americans: Their Spiritual Biographies* (1953).

WALLS, WILLIAM J. *The African Methodist Episcopal Zion Church: Reality of the Black Church* (1974).

WASHINGTON, JAMES M. *Conversations with God* (1994).

WATTS, JILL. *God, Harlem U.S.A: The Father Divine Story* (1992).

WIPPLER, MIGENE GONZÁLEZ. *Santeria: The Religion* (1982).

SLAVERY AND THE SLAVE COMMUNITY

ABRAHAMS, ROGER, AND JOHN SZWED. *After Africa: Extracts from British Travel Accounts and Journals of the Seventeenth, Eighteenth and Nineteenth Centuries Concerning the Slaves, Their Manners, and Customs in the British West Indies* (1983).

ALLAN D. AUSTIN, ED. *African Muslims in Antebellum America: A Source Book* (1984).

ANDREWS, WILLIAM L., AND HENRY LOUIS GATES, JR., EDS. *The Civitas Anthology of African-American Slave Narratives* (1999).

APTHEKER, HERBERT. *American Negro Slave Revolts.* 6th ed. (1993).

———. *Nat Turner's Slave Rebellion* (1966).

BECKLES, HILARY. *Afro-Caribbean Women and Resistance to Slavery in Barbados* (1988).

———. *Black Masculinity in Caribbean Slavery* (1996).

———. *Black Rebellion in Barbados: The Struggle against Slavery, 1627–1838* (1984).

———. *Natural Rebels: A Social History of Enslaved Black Women in Barbados* (1989).

———. *White Servitude and Black Slavery in Barbados, 1627–1715* (1989).

———, ED. *Inside Slavery: Process and Legacy in the Caribbean Experience* (1996).

BIBB, HENRY WALTON. *Narrative of the Life and Adventures of Henry Bibb, an American Slave* (1849).

BLANCHARD, PETER. *Slavery and Abolition in Early Republican Peru* (1992).

BLASSINGAME, JOHN W., ED. *The Frederick Douglass Papers.* 4 vols. (1979–1991).

———. *The Slave Community: Plantation Life in the Antebellum South.* Rev. ed. (1979).

BLIGHT, DAVID W. *Frederick Douglass' Civil War: Keeping Faith in Jubilee* (1989).

BOWSER, FREDERICK P. *The African Slave in Colonial Peru 1524–1650* (1974).

BROWN, HENRY. *Narrative of Henry Box Brown Who Escaped from Slavery Enclosed in a Box Three Feet Long and Two Wide, with Remarks upon the Remedy for Slavery* (1849).

CAMPBELL, STANLEY W. *The Slave Catchers: Enforcement of the Fugitive Slave Law, 1850–1860* (1968).

COHEN, DAVID W., AND JACK P. GREENE. *Neither Slave nor Free: The Freedman of African Descent in the Slaves Societies of the New World* (1972).

CONRAD, ROBERT EDGAR, ED. *Children of God's Fire: A Documentary of Black Slavery.* (1983).

———. *The Destruction of Brazilian Slavery, 1850–1888* (1993).

CRAFT, WILLIAM, AND ELLEN CRAFT. *Running a Thousand Miles for Freedom; or, The Escape of William and Ellen Craft from Slavery* (1860; reprint ed., 1991).

CURTIN, PHILIP D. *The Atlantic Slave Trade: A Census* (1969).

DAVIS, DARIEN J., ED. *Slavery and Beyond: The African Impact on Latin America and the Caribbean.*

DAVIS, DAVID BRION. *The Problem of Slavery in the Age of Revolution, 1770–1823.* 2d ed. (1998).

———. *The Problem of Slavery in Western Culture* (1966).

———. *Slavery and Human Progress* (1984).

DILLON. MERTON L. *Benjamin Lundy and the Struggle for Negro Freedom* (1966).

DRESCHER, SEYMOUR, AND STANLEY L. Engerman, eds. *A Historical Guide to World Slavery* (1998).

EHRLICH, WALTER. *They Have No Rights: Dred Scott's Struggle for Freedom* (1979).

FARRISON, WILLIAM EDWARD. *William Wells Brown: Author and Reformer* (1969).

FEHRENBACHER, DON E. *The Dred Scott Case: Its Significance in American Law and Politics* (1978).

FIELDS, BARBARA JEANNE. *Slavery and Freedom on the Middle Ground: Maryland during the Nineteenth Century* (1985).

FOGEL, ROBERT W. *Without Consent or Contract: The Rise and Fall of American Slavery* (1989).

FREY, SYLVIA. *Water from the Rock: Black Resistance in a Revolutionary Age* (1991).

GASPAR, DAVID BARRY. *Bondmen and Rebels: A Study of Master-Slave Relations in Antigua* (1985).

GENOVESE, EUGENE D. *Roll, Jordan, Roll: The World the Slaves Made* (1974).

GUTMAN, HERBERT G. *The Black Family in Slavery and Freedom, 1750–1925* (1976).

JACOBS, HARRIET. *Incidents in the Life of a Slave Girl, Written by Herself.* Edited by Jean Pagan Yellin (1987).

JONES, HOWARD. *Mutiny on the Amistad: The Saga of a Slave Revolt and Its Impact on American Abolition, Law and Diplomacy* (1987).

JOYNER, CHARLES. *Down by the Riverside: A South Carolina Slave Community* (1989).

KATZ, JONATHAN. *Resistance at Christiana: The Fugitive Slave Rebellion, Christiana, Pennsylvania, September 11, 1851: A Documentary Account* (1974).

KECKLEY, ELIZABETH. *Behind the Scenes; or, Thirty Years a Slave and Four Years in the White House* (1968).

KIPLE, KENNETH F. *The Caribbean Slave: A Biological History* (1984).

KLEIN, HERBERT S. *African Slavery in Latin America and the Caribbean* (1986).

———. *The Middle Passage: Comparative Studies in the Atlantic Slave Trade* (1978).

———. *Slavery in the Americas: A Comparative Study of Virginia and Cuba* (1967).

KNIGHT, FRANKLIN. *The African Dimension in Latin American Societies* (1974).

———. *Slavery and the Transformation of Society in Cuba, 1511–1760: From Settler Society to Slave Society* (1988).

KOLCHIN, PETER. *American Slavery, 1619–1877* (1993).

LAPP, RUDOLPH M. *Blacks in Gold Rush California* (1977).

LOCKE, MARY. *Anti-Slavery in America from the Introduction of African Slaves to the Prohibition of the Slave Trade (1619–1808)* (1901).

LOFTON, JOHN. *Denmark Vesey's Revolt: The Slave Plot That Lit a Fuse to Fort Sumter* (1983).

MATTOSO, KATIA M. DE QUEIROS. *To Be a Slave in Brazil, 1550–1888.* Translated by Arthur Goldhammer (1994).

McFEELY, WILLIAM S. *Frederick Douglass* (1991).

MILLER, RANDALL M., AND JOHN DAVID SMITH, EDS. *Dictionary of Afro-American Slavery.* 2d ed. (1997).

MORGAN, PHILIP D. *Slave Counterpoint: Black Culture in the Eighteenth-Century Chesapeake and Lowcountry* (1998).

NOONAN, JOHN T. *The Antelope: The Ordeal of the Recaptured Africans in the Administrations of James Monroe and John Quincy Adams* (1977).

NORTHRUP, SOLOMON. *Twelve Years a Slave: Narrative of Solomon Northrup, a Citizen of New York, Kidnapped in Washington City in 1841, and Rescued in 1853, from a Cotton Plantation near the Red River, in Louisiana* (1853).

OATES, STEPHEN B. *The Fires of Jubilee: Nat Turner's Fierce Rebellion* (1975).

———. *To Purge This Land with Blood: A Biography of John Brown.* 2d ed. (1984).

PALMER, COLIN. *Slaves of the White God: Blacks in Mexico, 1570–1650* (1976).

PEASE, JANE H., AND WILLIAM H. PEASE. *They Who Would Be Free: Blacks' Search for Freedom, 1830–1861* (1974).

RAWLEY, JAMES A. *The Transatlantic Slave Trade: A History* (1981).

ROBINSON, DONALD. *Slavery in the Structure of American Politics, 1765–1820* (1971).

ROSE, WILLIE LEE, ED. *A Documentary History of Slavery in North America* (1976).

RUSSELL WOOD, A. J. R. *The Black Man in Slavery and Freedom in Colonial Brazil* (1982).

SAUNDERS, A. C. *A Social History of Black Slaves and Freedmen in Portugal (1441–1555)* (1982).

SHARP, WILLIAM FREDERICK. *Slavery on the Spanish Frontier: The Colombian Choco, 1680–1810* (1976).

SOLOW, BARBARA L., ED. *Slavery and the Rise of the Atlantic System* (1991).

STAMPP, KENNETH M. *The Peculiar Institution: Slavery in the Ante-bellum South* (1956).

STILL, WILLIAM. *The Underground Railroad: A Record of Facts, Authentic Narratives, Letters, &c., Narrating the Hardships, Hairbreadth Escapes, and Death Struggles of the Slaves in Their Efforts for Freedom, as Related by Themselves and Others or Witnessed by the Author: Together with Sketches of Some of the Largest Stockholders and Most Liberal Aiders and Advisers of the Road* (1872).

STUCKEY, STERLING. *Slave Culture: Nationalist Theory and the Foundations of Black America* (1987).

TIBBLES, ANTHONY, ED. *Transatlantic Slavery: Against Human Dignity* (1994).

TOPLIN, ROBERT BRENT. *The Abolition of Slavery in Brazil* (1972).

TREXLER, HARRISON. *Slavery in Missouri, 1804–1865* (1914).

TRUTH, SOJOURNER, AND OLIVE GILBERT. *Narrative of Sojourner Truth, a Northern Slave, Emancipated from Bodily Servitude by the State of New York, in 1828* (1850).

TURNER, MARY. *From Chattel Slaves to Wage Slaves: The Dynamics of Labour Bargaining in the Americas* (1995).

———. *Slaves and Missionaries: The Disintegration of Jamaican Slave Society* (1982).

WASHINGTON, BOOKER T. *Up From Slavery* (1901).

WATSON, ALAN. *Slave Law in the Americas* (1989).

WILLIAMS, ERIC. *Capitalism and Slavery* (1944; reprint ed., 1994).

WOOD, PETER H. *Black Majority: Negroes in Colonial South Carolina from 1670 through the Stono Rebellion* (1974).

SOCIAL CONDITIONS

ABU-LUGHOD, JANET L. *Rabat: Urban Apartheid in Morocco* (1980).

BARFIELD, THOMAS J. *The Nomadic Alternative* (1993).

BECKWOURTH, JAMES P. *The Life and Adventures of James P. Beckwourth, Mountaineer, Scout and Pioneer and Chief of the Crow Nation of Indians.* Edited by T. D. Banner (1965).

BLOCH, HERMAN D. *The Circle of Discrimination: An Economic and Social Study of the Black Man in New York* (1969).

BRISTOW, PEGGY, ET AL. *We're Rooted Here and They Can't Pull Us Up: Essays in African Canadian Women's History* (1994).

BROWN, CLAUDE. *Manchild in the Promised Land* (1965).

CAMINHA, ADOLFO. *The Black Man and the Cabin Boy.* Translated by E. Lacey (1982).

CONNOLLY, HAROLD X. *A Ghetto Grows in Brooklyn* (1977).

CURRY, LEONARD P. *The Free Black in Urban America, 1800–1850: The Shadow of the Dream* (1981).

DANIEL, WALTER C. *Afro-American Journals, 1827–1980: A Reference Book* (1982).

DAVIS, CHARLES T., AND HENRY LOUIS GATES, JR., EDS. *The Slave's Narrative* (1985).

DERRICOTTE, TOI. *The Black Notebooks: An Interior Journey* (1997).

DURHAM, PHILIP, AND EVERETT L. JONES. *The Negro Cowboys* (1965).

GATEWOOD, WILLARD B. *Aristocrats of Color: The Black Elite, 1880–1920* (1990).

GIRVAN, NORMAN. *Poverty, Empowerment and Social Development in the Caribbean* (1997).

HENDERSON, ALEXA BENSON. *Atlanta Life Insurance Company: Guardian of Black Economic Dignity* (1990).

LAWRENCE, ELIZABETH A. *Rodeo: An Anthropologist Looks at the Wild and the Tame* (1982).

LEVINE, DONALD N. *Greater Ethiopia: The Evolution of a Multi-Ethnic Society* (1974).

LEVINE, ROBERT M., AND JOSÉ CARLOS SEBE BOM MEIHY. *The Life and Death of Carolina Maria de Jesus* (1995).

LITWACK, LEON F. *Been in the Storm So Long: The Aftermath of Slavery* (1979).

———. *Trouble in Mind: Black Southerners in the Age of Jim Crow* (1998).

MARKOWITZ, GERALD E., AND DAVID ROSNER. *Children, Race, and Power: Kenneth and Mamie Clark's Northside Center* (1996).

OTTLEY, ROI. *The Lonely Warrior: The Life and Time of Robert S. Abbott* (1955).

OTTLEY, ROI AND WILLIAM WEATHERBY, EDS. *The Negro in New York: An Informal Social History* (1967).

PATTERSON, JAMES T. *America's Struggle Against Poverty, 1900–1994* (1994).

PINO, JULIO CESAR. *Family and Favela: The Reproduction of Poverty in Rio de Janeiro* (1997).

RAINWATER, LEE. *Behind Ghetto Walls: Black Families in a Federal Slum* (1970).

REID, IRA DE AUGUSTINE. *The Negro Immigrant: His Background, Characteristics, and Social Adjustment, 1899–1937* (1939).

TARRY, ELLEN. *The Other Toussaint: A Modern Biography of Pierre Toussaint, a Post-Revolutionary Black* (1981).

VESTAL, STANLEY. *Mountain Men* (1937).

WHITTEN, NORMAN. *Black Frontiersmen: A South American Case* (1974).

———, ED. *Cultural Transformations and Ethnicity in Modern Ecuador* (1981).

WILSON, WILLIAM JULIUS. *When Work Disappears: The World of the New Urban Poor* (1996).

SOCIETY AND CULTURE

ABRAHAMS, ROGER D. *Deep Down in the Jungle: Negro Narrative Folklore from the Streets of Philadelphia* (1964).

———. *Singing the Master: The Emergence of African-American Culture in the Plantation South* (1992).

———. *Talking Black* (1976).

ADJAYE, JOSEPH K., AND ADRIANNE R. ANDREWS, EDS. *Language, Rhythm, and Sound: Black Popular Cultures into the Twenty-first Century* (1997).

CASSIDY, FREDERIC G. *Jamaica Talk: Three Hundred Years of the English Language in Jamaica* (1961).

DANCE, DARYL C. *Shuckin' and Jivin': Folklore from Contemporary Black Americans* (1978).

DATES, JANNETTE L., AND WILLIAM BARLOW, EDS. *Split Image: African-Americans in the Mass Media* (1990).

DYNES, WAYNE R., ED. *Encyclopedia of Homosexuality* (1990).

EDELMAN, MARIAN WRIGHT. *The Measure of Our Success: A Letter to My Children and Yours* (1992).

EWERS, TRAUTE. *The Origin of American Black English: Be-Forms in the HOODOO Texts* (1996).

FERGUSON, SHEILA. *Soul Food: Classic Cuisine from the Deep South* (1989).

HARRIS, JESSICA B. *Iron Pots and Wooden Spoons: Africa's Gifts to New World Cooking* (1989).

HOLLOWAY, JOSEPH E., ED. *Africanisms in American Culture* (1990).

HOOKS, BELL, "Black Is a Woman's Color." *In Bearing Witness: Selections from African-American Autobiography in the Twentieth Century*. Edited by Henry Louis Gates, Jr. (1991).

HUGGINS, NATHAN IRVIN. *Harlem Renaissance* (1971).

HUNTER-GAULT, CHARLAYNE. *In My Place* (1992).

KARENGA, MAULANA. *The African-American Holiday of Kwanzaa: A Celebration of Family, Community, and Culture* (1988).

———. *Introduction to Black Studies.* 2d ed. (1993).

KITWANA, BAKARI. *The Rap on Gangsta Rap: Who Run It? Gangsta Rap and Visions of Black Violence* (1994).

LABOV, WILLIAM. *Language in the Inner City: Studies in the Black English Vernacular* (1972).

LEVINE, LAWRENCE W. *Black Culture and Black Consciousness* (1977).

MINNICK-TAYLOR, KATHLEEN, AND CHARLES TAYLOR II. *Kwanzaa: How to Celebrate It in Your Own Home* (1994).

NEWMAN, RICHARD. *Words Like Freedom: Essays on African-American Culture and History* (1996).

———, comp. *Black Access: A Bibliography of Afro-American Bibliographies* (1984).

SECRETAN, THIERRY. *Going into Darkness: Fantastic Coffins from Africa* (1995).

STEVENS, PHILLIPS, JR. "Magic" and "Sorcery and Witchcraft." *In Encyclopedia of Cultural Anthropology*. Edited by Melvin Ember and David Levinson (1996).

WILSON, CHARLES REAGAN, AND WILLIAM FERRIS, EDS. *Encyclopedia of Southern Culture* (1989).

WOODS, SYLVIA. *Sylvia's Soul Food: Recipes from Harlem's World Famous Restaurant* (1992).

SPORTS

ABDUL-JABBAR, KAREEM, WITH MIGNON MCCARTHY. *Kareem* (1990).

ANGELL, ROGER. *The Summer Game* (1972).

ASHE, ARTHUR. *Days of Grace: A Memoir* (1993).

———. *A Hard Road to Glory: A History of the African-American Athlete* (1988).

BERGER, PHIL. *Blood Season: Tyson and the World of Boxing* (1989).

CHAMBERLAIN, WILT. *The View From Above* (1991).

DAVIS, MICHAEL D. *Black American Women in Olympic Track and Field: A Complete Illustrated Reference* (1992).

FLEISCHER, NAT. *Black Dynamite: The Story of the Negro in the Prize Ring from 1782 to 1838* (1938).

FRAZIER, JOE, AND PHIL BERGER. *Smokin' Joe: The Autobiography of a Heavyweight Champion of the World, Smokin' Joe Frazier* (1996).

GALEANO, EDUARDO. *Football in Sun and Shadow* (1998).

GEORGE, NELSON. *Elevating the Game: Black Men and Basketball* (1992).

GIBSON, BOB. *From Ghetto to Glory: The Story of Bob Gibson* (1968).

GONZALEZ ECHEVARRIA, ROBERTO. *The Pride of Havana: The History of Cuban Baseball* (1999).

GREEN, TIM. *The Dark Side of the Game: The Unauthorized NFL Playbook* (1996).

GUTMAN, BILL. *The Harlem Globetrotters* (1977).

HELLER, PETER. *Bad Intentions: The Mike Tyson Story* (1989).

HOLYFIELD, EVANDER, AND BERNARD HOLYFIELD. *Holyfield: The Humble Warrior* (1996).

HURD, MICHAEL. *Black College Football, 1892–1992: One Hundred Years of History, Education, and Pride* (1993).

JACKSON, REGINALD, WITH MIKE LUPICA. *Reggie* (1984).

JOHNSON, CECIL. *Guts: Legendary Black Rodeo Cowboy Bill Pickett* (1994).

KLAPISCH, BOB. *High and Tight: The Rise and Fall of Dwight Gooden and Darryl Strawberry* (1996).

LIBBY, BILL. *Goliath: The Wilt Chamberlain Story* (1977).

LOPES, JOSE SERGIO LEITE. "Successes and Contradictions in 'Multiracial' Brazilian Football." *In Entering the Field: New Perspectives on World Football*. Edited by Gary Armstrong and Richard Giulianotti (1997).

LOVETT, CHARLES C. *Olympic Marathon: A Centennial History of the Games' Most Storied Race* (1997).

MALTBY, MARC S. *The Origins and Early Development of Professional Football* (1997).

MASON, TONY. *Passion of the People? Football in South America* (1995).

MUSICK, PHIL. *Reflections on Roberto* (1994).

NEFT, DAVID S. *The Football Encyclopedia: The Complete History of Professional NFL Football, from 1892 to the Present* (1991).

PETERSON. ROBERT. *Only the Ball Was White: A History of Legendary Black Players and All-black Professional Teams* (1992).

PLOWDEN, MARTHA WARD. *Olympic Black Women* (1996).

PORTER, DAVID L., ED. *Biographical Dictionary of American Sports: Basketball and Other Indoor Sports* (1989).

RAMPERSAD, ARNOLD. *Jackie Robinson: A Biography* (1997).

RIBOWSKY, MARK. *Don't Look Back: Satchel Paige and the Shadows of Baseball* (1994).

RILEY, JAMES A. *The Biographical Encyclopedia of the Negro Baseball Leagues* (1994).

———. *Dandy, Day and the Devil* (1987).

ROBERTS, RANDY. *Papa Jack: Jack Johnson and the Era of White Hopes* (1983).

ROBINSON, JACKIE, WITH ALFRED DUCKETT. *I Never Had It Made* (1972).

ROBINSON, RAY, AND DAVE ANDERSON. *Sugar Ray* (1969).

SAMMONS, JEFFREY T. *Beyond the Ring: The Role of Boxing in American Society* (1988).

SATCHEL, LEROY. *Pitchin' Man: Satchel Paige's Own Story* (1992).

TYGIEL, JULES. *Baseball's Great Experiment: Jackie Robinson and His Legacy* (1983).

Index

basketball and, **1:**390–391

Bass, Charlotta Spears, and, **1:**394

Bates, Daisy Lee Gatson, and, **1:**396, **2:**99

bebop music and, **1:**406

Belafonte, Harold George (Harry), and, **1:**414–415, 183, 345, 708, 752, **2:**645

Bell, Philip Alexander, and, **1:**423–425, **4:**439

Benjamin, Robert Charles O'Hara, **1:**437

Berry, Mary Frances, and, **1:**447–448, **2:**631

Bethune, Mary McLeod, and, **1:**449–450. *See also* Bethune, Mary McLeod

Birmingham, Alabama, and, **1:**468–470, 505, **2:**96, 102–103, **3:**729, **5:**331. *See also* King, Martin Luther, Jr., arrest of

Black Aesthetic and, **1:**474

Black Arts Movement and, **1:**476–479, **2:**105. *See also* Black Arts Movement

Black Cabinet of FDR and, **1:**449, 485–486, **2:**614, **3:**49, **4:**214, 489

Black Church and, **1:**486–490, **2:**92–93

Black Codes in the U.S. and, 493–496

Black Consciousness and, **1:**504–506

Black Manifesto and, **1:**512

Black Nationalism and, **1:**513–515

Black Panther Party, **1:**519–521. *See also* Black Panther Party

Black Power Movement and, **1:**521–523. *See also* Black Power Movement

black theology in, **1:**535–536

black towns and, **1:**236, 514, 536–539, 688

Black Women's Club Movement and, **1:**540

blacks in American electoral politics and, **1:**178–181

Blackwell, Unita, and, **1:**539

Bloody Sunday and, **2:**105

Bond, Julian, and, **1:**575–576, **2:**600, **4:**169

Borders, William Holmes, and, **1:**580

in Boston, Massachusetts, **1:**582

Bowers, Thomas J., and, **1:**598

in Brazil and, **1:**618–619, **2:**795, **3:**17

Brooks, Gwendolyn Elizabeth, **1:**630–631, **2:**41–42, 455, 628, **3:**638, 596–597, **5:**447

Brotherhood of Sleeping Car Porters (BSCP), **1:**633–634. *See also* Brotherhood of Sleeping Car Porters; labor unions

Brown v. Board of Education in. *See Brown v. Board of Education*

Brown, Charlotte Hawkins, and, **1:**635

Brown, Hubert G. (H. Rap), **1:**522, 637, **4:**517

Browne, Hugh M., **1:**649–650, **5:**64

Bruce, John Edward, **1:**654–655

Bullins, Edward (Ed), **1:**476, 478, 662

Bunche, Ralph Johnson, **1:**191, 486, 662–663, **3:**251, **4:**248, **5:**357

Burroughs, Nannie Helen, **1:**676–677, **4:**726, **5:**434

California Proposition 209 and, **1:**37

Calloway, Nathaniel Oglesby, **1:**707–708

Carmichael, Stokely, **1:**96, 476–477, 514, 522, 536, 646, 744–745, **2:**454, 714, **3:**300, **5:**77, 357

Chaney, James Earl, **2:**23–24, **2:**23, 795

Chavis, Benjamin Franklin, Jr., and, **2:**31–32, **4:**23–24, 169

Chicago Freedom Movement and, **2:**41

children's literature and, **2:**50–51

citizenship schools and, **2:**91, 100–101, 116. *See also* Highlander Folk School

Civil Rights Act of 1957 and, **2:**100

Civil Rights Act of 1964 and, **1:**36

Civil Rights Act of 1964 and, **2:**104

Civil Rights Act of 1991 and, **1:**37

Civil Rights Cases of Supreme Court and, **4:**708–709

Civil Rights Congress (CRC), **2:**91–92

Clark, Alexander G., and, **2:**112–113

Clark, Septima Poinsette, and, **2:**29, 91, 116, 629, **3:**204

Cleaver, Eldridge Leroy, and, **1:**96, 478, 520, 662, **2:**124, **4:**144, 218

Cold War era and, **2:**97–98

Coleman, William Thaddeus, Jr., and, **2:**147–148

Congress of Racial Equality. *See* Congress of Racial Equality (CORE)

Cook, George William, **2:**224–225

Council of Federated Organizations. *See* Council of Federated Organizations (COFO)

criminal justice system and African Americans in, **2:**261

Cuba and Castro in, **2:**280

Currin, Green Jacob, and, **2:**296

Davis, Angela Yvonne, **2:**184, 324–325, 330, 630–631, 774

Deacons for Defense and Justice and, **2:**332–333

Dee, Ruby, **1:**183, **2:**330, 351–352

Democratic Party and, **1:**178–181, **2:**92, 360, *See also* Democratic Party

desegregation. *See* integration and desegregation

Detroit Riot of 1967 and, **2:**371

in Detroit, Michigan, **2:**369

Double V campaign and, **2:**97, 434, **4:**16, **5:**468

Downing, George Thomas, and, **2:**439–441

Dunbar-Nelson, Alice, and, **2:**351, 465–466, **5:**447

Dunjee, Roscoe, and, **2:**470–471

Durham Manifesto and, **2:**474–475

in Durham, North Carolina, **2:**476

Dyer Bill, and, **2:**479–480

Eagleson, William Lewis, **2:**481–482

economic development and African American businesspeople in, **1:**689

Edelman, Marian Wright, **2:**498–499, 631

Ellington, Edward Kennedy (Duke), and, **2:**529–530

Episcopal Church and, **2:**541

Equal Employment Opportunity Commission (EEOC) and, **1:**36, 155, **4:**252

Evers, James Charles, **2:**97, 591

Evers, Medgar Wylie, **1:**224, **2:**97, 101–102, 591–592

Evers-Williams, Myrlie, **2:**592

Executive Order 8802, **2:**595, 603, **3:**49, **4:**16, 184, **5:**468

Eyes on the Prize TV series (PBS) about, **2:**600

Fair Employment Practices Committee (FEPC). *See* Fair Employment Practices Committee (FEPC)

Farmer, James, and, **2:**608–609

Farrakhan, Louis Abdul, **2:**609–610. *See also* Farrakhan, Louis Abdul

Fifteenth Amendment and, **2:**92, 639–640, **4:**167, 488, 535, 557, 796, **5:**329–330

films and movies on, **2:**645–646

desegregation. *See* integration and desegregation

desert and semi-desert in Africa, 1:465–466

Desert Storm. *See* Persian Gulf Wars

Desroches, Numa, 3:125

Desruisseux, Marc S., 2:382

Dessalines, Jean-Jacques, 1:425, 592, 603, 2:367–368, 442, 478, 3:118–119, 129, 4:605. *See also* Haiti; Haitian Revolution

detective novels, 2:456–457. *See also* literature, poetry, and literati

Detroit Riot of 1943, 2:371, 4:499

Detroit Riot of 1967, 2:371, 4:499

Detroit, Michigan, 2:368–370, 371, 4:499, 5:490–491

Dett, Robert Nathaniel, 1:727, 2:119–120, 371–372

Deugenio, Rafael, 2:86

Development of Education in Africa (ADEA) in, 2:504

development theater in Africa, 5:148–149

development, 2:373. *See also* economic development

Devers, Gail, 4:282

Devieux, Liliane, 5:450

Devil's Island, 2:723. *See also* French Guiana

Dew, Thomas R., 1:12

Dhlomo, Herbert, 3:609

Dhlomo, R. R. R. (Rolfes), 2:637, 3:609

Di Prima, Diane, 1:364

Dia, Mamadou, 4:720–721

diablitos, 1:3

Diagne, Amadou Mapate, 3:607

Diagne, Blaise, 1:98, 2:382, 703, 4:195, 324, 720. *See also* Senegal

Diago, Roberto, 1:270

Diakhate, Lamine, 3:617

dialect poetry, 1:646, 2:383, 464–465. *See also* Dunbar, Paul Laurence

Diallo, Bakary, 3:608, 618

Diallo, Felix, 4:386

Diallo, Nafissatou, 3:608, 618, 5:451

Diamini culture, 5:110–111

diamond mining, 1:587–588, 4:30

Dias, E.C., 4:385

Dias, Goncalves, 4:668

Dias, Henrique, 1:526, 2:383–384

Dias, José Unberto, 3:621, 4:667

diaspora and displacement, 2:384, 4:195, 695. *See also* Afro-Atlantic cultural dialog; Great Migration literature of, 4:8

Diaz de Solis, Juan, 5:288

Diaz, Al, 1:393

Diaz, Rolando, 2:86–87

Dib, Mohammed, 2:384, 4:386

Dibala, Diblo, 5:465

Dick v. Mississippi, 4:781

Dickerson, Carroll, 3:214

Dickerson, Earl Burris, 2:384–384

Dickerson, Eric, 2:678

Dickinson, Joseph H., 3:303

Dickerson, Ronald, 2:675

Dickerson, Spencer, 5:188

Dida people, 2:385

Diddley, Bo, 1:550, 556, 2:385, 400, 4:574–575

Diegues, Carlos, 1:438, 2:84–88, 385–386, 4:664–667

Dies, Martin, 2:183

difaquan, 3:812

Diggs, Charles C., Jr., 2:214, 369; 3:577

Dightman, Myrtis, 4:599

Digo people, 2:386

Dihigo, Martin, 1:382, 384

Dike, Fatima, 3:610

Dikobe, Modikwe, 3:610

Dill, Augustus Granville, 2:386 children's literature and, 2:48

Dill, Bonnie Thornton, 2:630

Dillard University, 2:153, 3:578

Dillon, Diane, children's literature and, 2:50

Dillon, Leo, children's literature and, 2:50, 52

Dimension Costerna, 1:120

Din, Khayr ad-, 5:238

Dingane, 2:386–386

Dining Car Cooks and Waiters Association, 3:549–550. *See also* Brotherhood of Sleeping Car Porters

Dinka people, 2:387 religious beliefs of, 1:84

Dinkins, David Norham, 1:605, 2:360, 387–388, 3:150

Diogenes, on slavery, 1:302

Diop, Alioune, 2:388, 3:608, 4:197, 722

Diop, Birago, 3:607–608, 617

Diop, Cheikh Anta, 1:112, 114, 195, 276, 558, 2:388–389, 434, 608. *See also* Afrocentricism

Diop, David, 2:703, 3:617, 4:197

Diop, Doudou, 4:385

Diop, Ousmane Soce, 3:608

Diori, Hamani, 2:390, 4:232–233, 522. *See also* Niger

Diouf, Abdou, 2:390, 4:720–721

discrimination. *See* segregation and discrimination

disease. *See* medicine, health care and disease

Disfranchised American, 2:79

Disposable Heroes, 4:520

Disraeli, Benjamin, 2:515

Divine, Father, 2:397–398

Dixieland jazz, 3:359

Dixon, Dean, 2:120

Dixon, George (Little Chocolate), 2:398–399

Dixon, Graciela, 2:399

Dixon, Ivan, 2:642

Dixon, Julian Carey, 2:399

Dixon, Melvin, 2:457

Dixon, Willie, 1:550, 2:399–400, 3:252, 5:363

Diya, Oladipo, 1:2

DJ Jazzy Jeff, 4:518, 520

DJ Kool Herc, 4:518

Djavan, 2:400, 4:663

Djaw organization, 4:386

Djebar, Assia, 2:400–401

Djenne, Mali, 2:401

Djenne-Jeno culture, 1:44, 196–197

Djenne-Jeno, Mali, 2:401–402

Djibouti, 2:402–407, 3:30
  Asal Lake in, 1:274
  astronomy and, 1:281
  colonialism in, 2:403–404
  democracy in, 3:30
  Djibouti city in, capital of, 2:407–408
  early history of, 2:402–403
  economic development in, 2:407
  ethnic unrest in, 2:406–407
  head of state in, present day, 2:345
  independence movements in, 2:343, 404–406
  Islam and, 2:402
  Organization of African Unity (OAU) and, 2:404
  political figures and parties in, 2:406–407, 3:30
  religions of, 2:402
  statistics on, 2:405

Djibouti City, 2:407–408

Djohar, Said Mohamed, 2:189

DNA and genetics, 1:77–80, 2:408–413
  blood typing and, 2:409–410
  historical and anthropological records vs., limitations to, 2:408–409
  human evolution and, 1:77–80
  mitochondrial, 2:411–412
  parental contribution to, 2:411
  polymorphism research and haplotypes in, 2:412–413
  slave trade and, researching genetic history of people, 2:408–409

U